# THE HUMAN RIGHT TO WATER

In a remarkably short space of time, the right to water has emerged from relative obscurity to claim a prominent place in human rights theory and practice. This book explores this rise both descriptively and prescriptively. It analyses the recognition, use and influence of the right to water in international and comparative law, civil society mobilisation and, increasingly, public policy. It also scrutinises the normative implications of the right to water with a focus on challenges and puzzles it creates for law and policymaking. These questions are explored globally and comparatively within different dynamics of the sector – water allocation, water access and urban and rural water reform – and in conjunction with the right to sanitation where relevant. This multi-disciplinary volume reveals the diverse ways in which the right to water has been adopted but also its limitations when faced with political economy, political ecology and traditional legal thought.

**Malcolm Langford** is a professor of public law at the University of Oslo and Co-Director of the Centre on Law and Social Transformation at the University of Bergen and CMI. He has published widely on human rights, international development and constitutionalism and his publications include *Social Rights Jurisprudence* (2008). He has also served as an advisor to a wide range of UN bodies and was the founding coordinator of the COHRE Right to Water Programme (2002–2006).

**Anna F.S. Russell** is a visiting fellow at the Faculty of Law at the University of Oxford. She was formerly a supervising attorney at the Harvard Human Rights Program and the Louwes fellow and lecturer at Oxford. She has a doctorate in law from Oxford and has published widely in the fields of public international law and international development. She is a barrister and solicitor of the Law Society of Upper Canada, and has worked extensively in Latin America, Africa and Eastern Europe.

# The Human Right to Water

## THEORY, PRACTICE AND PROSPECTS


*Edited by*

MALCOLM LANGFORD

University of Oslo

ANNA F.S. RUSSELL

University of Oxford



CAMBRIDGE
UNIVERSITY PRESS

CAMBRIDGE
UNIVERSITY PRESS

University Printing House, Cambridge CB2 8BS, United Kingdom

One Liberty Plaza, 20th Floor, New York, NY 10006, USA

477 Williamstown Road, Port Melbourne, VIC 3207, Australia

314-321, 3rd Floor, Plot 3, Splendor Forum, Jasola District Centre, New Delhi - 110025, India

79 Anson Road, #06-04/06, Singapore 079906

Cambridge University Press is part of the University of Cambridge.

It furthers the University's mission by disseminating knowledge in the pursuit of education, learning and research at the highest international levels of excellence.

www.cambridge.org
Information on this title: www.cambridge.org/9781108722315
10.1017/9780511862601



First published 2017
First paperback edition 2019

*A catalogue record for this publication is available from the British Library*

ISBN 978-1-107-01070-3 Hardback
ISBN 978-1-108-72231-5 Paperback

# Contents


*List of Figures* — *page* ix
*List of Tables* — xi
*List of Contributors* — xiii
*Foreword* — xvii
*Preface* — xix
*List of Abbreviations* — xxi

1 **Introduction: The Right to Water in Context** — 1
*Malcolm Langford and Anna F.S. Russell*

PART I WATER ALLOCATION — 55

2 **Water Allocation, Customary Practice and the Right to Water: Rethinking the Regulatory Model** — 57
*Barbara van Koppen*

3 **Indigenous Peoples and the Sale of Water Rights: The Case of Chile** — 84
*Domingo A. Lovera Parmo*

4 **Water for Food: A Human Rights Perspective** — 119
*Inga T. Winkler*

5 **Tapping Transboundary Waters: Implications of the Right to Water for States Sharing International Watercourses** — 144
*Anna F.S. Russell and Stephen McCaffrey*

6 **Climate Change and the Right to Water** — 174
*Mac Darrow*

PART II ACCESS TO WATER AND SANITATION 223

7 Determining Progress on Access to Water and Sanitation: The Case of South Africa 225
*Jackie Dugard, Malcolm Langford and Edward Anderson*

8 Quantifying the Affordability Standard: A Comparative Approach 276
*Henri Smets*

9 Engendering the Right to Water and Sanitation: Integrating the Experiences of Women and Girls 300
*Anne Hellum*

10 The Human Right to Sanitation 345
*Malcolm Langford, Jamie Bartram and Virginia Roaf*

11 Development Cooperation and Extraterritorial Obligations 396
*Ashfaq Khalfan*

12 The Occupied Palestinian Territory: Challenges to Progressive Realisation 429
*Lara El-Jazairi*

PART III URBAN WATER REFORM 461

13 Privatisation and the Right to Water 463
*Malcolm Langford*

14 Piped Water in Jakarta: A Political, Economic or Social Good? 503
*Nicola Colbran*

15 Privatisation and Regulatory Autonomy: The Right to Water in International Economic Law 531
*Andrew Lang*

16 Bilateral Investment Treaties and Investment Arbitration 582
*Luke Eric Peterson*

PART IV RURAL WATER REFORM 601

17 A Poor Choice? Public Policy, Social Choice and the Right to Water 603
*Robert A. Hope*

18 Socio-Cultural Norms, Human Rights and Access to Water and Sanitation 624
*Nandita Singh*

19 **Reflections on the Right to Water from a Political Ecology Perspective: Tensions in Zimbabwe's Water Governance** 644
*Bill Derman and Emmanuel Manzungu*

20 **The Right to Water in Rural India and Drinking Water Policy Reforms** 677
*Philippe Cullet*

*List of Cases* 695

*Index* 701

# Figures


| | | |
|---|---|---|
| 1.1 | Constitutional recognition: The right to water | *page* 5 |
| 1.2 | Trends in litigation: Cases decided on human rights and water | 5 |
| 1.3 | Rights considered by courts in human rights and water cases | 6 |
| 2.1 | The multiple-use water ladder of service levels and water uses | 62 |
| 7.1 | Affordability and municipal capacity: South Africa | 254 |
| 7.2 | Indigency thresholds: South Africa | 263 |
| 7.3 | Tariffs for second block of water consumption: South Africa | 266 |
| 8.1 | Water expenses as a proportion of income vs. income level (decile): France and Mexico | 279 |
| 8.2 | Distribution of affordability indices in fourteen European countries | 287 |
| 8.3 | Distribution of population by spending on water: England | 289 |
| 8.4 | Distribution of affordability indices in eleven transitional countries | 290 |
| 8.5 | Distribution of affordability indices in Latin America | 291 |
| 12.1 | Groundwater resources in the West Bank and shared with Israel | 436 |
| 12.2 | Total outflows (from wells and springs) in the three Mountain Aquifer basins, shared between the West Bank and Israel during the Oslo period | 439 |
| 17.1 | Attributes shaping user choices for rural water services | 611 |
| 17.2 | Mapping theoretical perspectives across individual rights and consumer choice | 621 |
| 18.1 | Norm triad | 628 |
| 18.2 | The 'interface' of action leading to rights realisation | 634 |
| 18.3 | The rights realisation continuum | 641 |

# Tables


7.1 Access to water and sanitation in South Africa by municipality: 2001 and 2007 *page* 248

7.2 Regression analysis of water and sanitation access in South Africa by municipality 251

7.3 Identifying under-performers in South Africa: 'negative outliers' approach 252

7.4 Identifying under-performers in South Africa: 'across-the-board' approach 253

8.1 Examples of high affordability indices: population using above 5 per cent of disposable income 293

8.2 Unaffordability limits for water or implementation of aid systems' official policy objectives or legal requirements 294

12.1 The Israeli-Palestinian Interim Agreement on the West Bank and the Gaza Strip (Oslo II), Article 40, 1995 438

13.1 Overview of legal mobilisation strategies and outcomes in different countries 488

# Contributors

**Edward Anderson** is a Senior Lecturer at the School of International Development at the University of East Anglia.

**Jamie Bartram** is the Director of the Water Institute at UNC and the Don and Jennifer Holzworth Distinguished Professor in Environmental Sciences and Engineering of the Gillings School of Global Public Health, University of North Carolina at Chapel Hill.

**Nicola Colbran** is the former Legal Advisor in the Indonesia Programme at the Norwegian Centre for Human Rights and is now working in the legal sector in Australia.

**Philippe Cullet** is a Professor of International and Environmental Law at SOAS University of London and a Senior Visiting Fellow at the Centre for Policy Research in Delhi.

**Mac Darrow** is the Representative, Washington DC Liaison Office, of the Office of the United Nations High Commissioner for Human Rights (OHCHR).

**Bill Derman** is a Professor at the Department of International Environment and Development Studies at the Norwegian University of Life Sciences.

**Jackie Dugard** is an Associate Professor at the University of the Witwatersrand, Johannesburg.

**Lara El Jazairi** was formerly the Programme Policy and Communications Coordinator for Oxfam GB in the Occupied Palestinian Territory and Israel.

**Anne Hellum** is a Professor at the Department of Public and International Law and Director of the Institute of Women's Law, University of Oslo.

**Robert A. Hope** is an Associate Professor at the School of Geography and the Environment and Director of the Water Programme at the Smith School of Enterprise and the Environment at the University of Oxford.

**Ashfaq Khalfan** is the Director of the Law and Policy Programme at Amnesty International. He previously was the Economic, Social and Cultural Rights Policy Coordinator with Amnesty International and led the Right to Water Programme at the Centre on Housing Rights and Evictions (COHRE).

**Andrew Lang** is a Professor at the Department of Law at the London School of Economics.

**Malcolm Langford** is a Professor of Public Law at the University of Oslo. He is also a Co-Director at the Centre on Law and Social Transformation, Chr. Michelsen Institute and University of Bergen.

**Emmanuel Manzungu** is a Professor of Water, Environment and Land Management at the University of Zimbabwe.

**Stephen McCaffrey** is a Distinguished Professor of Law at the University of the Pacific, McGeorge School of Law. He was Special Rapporteur for the International Law Commission's Draft Articles on the Law of the Non-Navigational Uses of International Watercourses.

**Domingo A. Lovera Parmo** is an Assistant Professor at Diego Portales University, Chile.

**Luke Eric Peterson** is the Editor of the Investment Arbitration Reporter, and also an Investment Law Project Affiliate at the Institute for International Law and Justice at the New York University School of Law.

**Virginia Roaf** is an Independent Consultant based in Germany and former Adviser to the UN Special Rapporteurs on the Human Rights to Safe Drinking Water and Sanitation.

**Anna F.S. Russell** is a Visiting Fellow at the Faculty of Law at the University of Oxford. She was formerly the Louwes Fellow and Lecturer at the University.

**Nandita Singh** is a Docent in Water Resources Management and engaged in research and teaching in water and environmental management at the Department of Sustainable Development, Environmental Science and Engineering, Royal Institute of Technology (KTH), Stockholm.

**Henri Smets** is a Member of the Water Academy, France.

**Barbara van Koppen** is the Principal Researcher on Poverty, Gender, and Water with the International Water Management Institute (IWMI).

**Inga T. Winkler** is a Lecturer at the Institute for the Study of Human Rights at Columbia University.

# Foreword

As of 2015 there were 663 million people without a basic water supply, according to the official figures from the World Health Organization (WHO) and the United Nations Children's Fund (UNICEF).[1] Even more concerning is that this figure plays down the scale of the global crisis – it does not take into account the quality, affordability or regularity of the water. The number also camouflages deeper inequalities, since there are obvious profound differences between the developed and the developing world, and within countries themselves, whether it be by geography, land tenure, gender or disability. The figures for the related human right to sanitation are even more devastating, with some 2.4 billion people lacking access to improved sanitation.[2] The target date for achieving the previous Millennium Development Goal (MDG) to halve those without access will probably only be met, on current trends, by 2026, yet States recently committed in the Sustainable Development Goals (SDGs) to achieve universal access only four years later in 2030.[3]

The consequences of this lack of access are enormous as this book shows. An estimated 1.6 million people, mostly children under the age of 5, die each year from water-related diseases.[4] Diarrhoea kills more young children than AIDS, malaria and measles combined.[5] The WHO estimates that a 0.3 percent GDP investment in household access to water and sanitation promotes a 1 percent

1 *The Millennium Development Goals Report 2015* (New York: United Nations, 2015), p. 58.
2 Water Aid, *Ignored: Biggest Child Killer. The World is Neglecting Sanitation*, p. 3.
3 See estimation by WHO/UNICEF, JMP, 2012 Update, p. 15. See also House of Commons, International Development Committee - Second Report the 2010 Millennium Development Goals Review Summit, 14 December 2010.
4 *See* www.unmillenniumproject.org/documents/WaterComplete-lowres.pdf.
5 UNICEF/WHO, *Diarrhoea: Why Children Are Still Dying and What Can Be Done* (2009).

GDP increase.[6] Beyond health and economics, this deprivation is also about dignity. Recognising the human rights to water and sanitation means being outraged by the humiliation experienced in the daily struggle to find water by sundown, the eviction notice that comes from unpaid and unaffordable water services bills, or the military checkpoints that may accompany a journey to a water point. And, this experience is not confined to the South. In my tenure as UN Special Rapporteur, I also encountered communities in highly developed countries that lacked sufficient, affordable, safe, acceptable and accessible water.

Sadly, the international community took decades to acknowledge this human rights dimension. In 2002, General Comment No. 15 on the Right to Water of the Committee on Economic, Social and Cultural Rights was the first comprehensive, yet remarkably controversial, recognition. Yet, the times have changed. By 2010, both the human rights to water and sanitation were given explicit recognition by the UN General Assembly and the Human Rights Council.

I was privileged to serve as the inaugural Special Rapporteur from 2008 to 2014 and witness the growing embrace by the broader water and sanitation community of a human rights framework.[7] States' awareness of their legal obligations to realise the human rights to water and sanitation for all is growing. However, if this recognition of these rights is to mean anything, it must mean something for the third of humanity who still do not have adequate access. Obviously, a human rights perspective is not a solution by itself, but these rights should influence and inspire national laws, policies and strategies and broader international commitments, as well as the work of international organisations. And, this imperative is not simply about raising additional resources. Much more can be done with existing funds through better-targeted and more effective interventions aligned with human rights obligations.

This book therefore serves as a timely reminder that there is still much to do. By probing more deeply the theoretical questions connected to the human right to water, examining the implications of the right in multiple policy and sectoral arenas, and investigating the companion right to sanitation, it helps focus our attention on the underlying issues that need to be addressed if we are to move effectively forward.

***Catarina de Alberquerque***
***First UN Special Rapporteur on the Human Right to Water and Sanitation***

[6] G. Hutton and L. Haller, *Evaluation of the Costs and Benefits of Water and Sanitation Improvements at the Global Level, Water, Sanitation and Health, Protection of the Human Environment* (Geneva: World Health Organization, 2004).

[7] See my reports at http://sr-watersanitation.ohchr.org/

# Preface

Since the start of the new millennium, the human right to water has gained a prominent, yet contested, place in global law, policy and practice. This book provides an in-depth examination of the right to water in theory and in practice, through descriptive and normative analyses. In doing so, it aims to contribute to the growing body of research around this right, and enable scholars and practitioners to better understand its role, both positive and negative, in improving access to adequate water.

The book initially emerged from an international conference on the human right to water jointly hosted by the University of Oslo, University of Oxford and the United Nations Development Programme (UNDP). The three institutions organised the conference with support from the Norwegian Ministry of Foreign Affairs, a special thanks to Geir Løkken in this regard; the Louwes Fund at the University of Oxford, established by Evelyn Blanche Louwes in commeration of her husband, Hendrik Jan Louwes; and Swedish Water House. A number of the papers presented at this conference were subsequently transformed into chapters in this volume, and the speakers, panel chairs and participants at the conference deeply enriched the discussions found in this collection. Additional chapters were added as the project progressed.

This book brings together scholars and practitioners from multiple, disciplinary backgrounds. Thus, in preparing the collection, we not only thank the authors for their chapters, and for patiently updating their writings as the volume moved through the editorial and publication process, but we also thank them for sharing expertise in their respective fields and providing unique insights into different approaches to studying the right to water, and often, human rights more generally.

We greatly appreciate the time colleagues put into independently and carefully reviewing various chapters, including Catarina de Albuquerque, Bronwen Morgan, Stephen McCaffrey, Michael Rouse, Mike Edmunds,

Guy Hutton, Peter Newborne, Inga Winkler, Andrew Newsham and Adrian Di Giovanni.

We thank our colleagues who have supported this publication in varying ways, including those at the University of Oslo, Norwegian Centre for Human Rights, particularly Kristin Høgdahl and Siri Skåre; and at the University of Oxford, Faculty of Law, particularly Guy S. Goodwin-Gill, Dapo Akande, Liz Fisher, Vaughan Lowe, Cathryn Costello and Andrew Shacknove, former Oxford Centre for the Environment, particularly Mark New, Rob Hope and Dave Thomas, Oxford Martin School, particularly Ian Goldin, and Christ Church.

In preparing this book we thank Brian Griffey, Sevda Clark, Tara Smith, Cheryl Lorens, Natasha Telson, Inger Aasgaard, Frida Pareus and Nora Bornø at the University of Oslo for their techncial and research assistance, and Michelle Miao, Alvar Closas and Ilana Cohen at the Univerity of Oxford for their research assistance, in relation to various chapters. We also thank colleagues who kindly forwarded background materials for the collection in the course of their own work.

During the completion of this book, Malcolm had the opportunity to be based at the Center for the Study of Law and Society, University of California (Berkeley). Anna also had the opportunity to be based at, and thanks for their support, the Harvard Human Rights Program, particularly Mindy Roseman, Gerald Neuman and Tyler Giannini, as well as the University of Cape Town, Faculty of Law, particularly Jan Glazewski, and the members of the Democratic Governance and Rights Unit. She also thanks Edith Brown Weiss and Laurence Boisson de Chazournes for their related international law guest lectures at Oxford, as well as colleagues at the Harvard Kennedy School, Carr Center for Human Rights Policy, for many discussions about the right.

We express our gratitude to legal, development and water colleagues on various continents who have challenged our understanding of the right to water and generously shared their views with us as to how the right may affect efforts on the ground aimed at trying to achieve the goal of universal access. We thank our families and friends for their insightful perspectives on the subject and for their encouragement and support over the years.

In the production of the book, we are grateful to John Berger at Cambridge University Press for his support for the project since its early beginnings, Joanna Breeze for guiding the book through its various phases towards publication, and Kalaivani Periassamy for managing the copy editing and production of the manuscript.

The image on the cover of the book is the painting 'Water carriers filling buckets' by the South African artist William Bester. This image is used with the permission of, and our thanks to, the artist.

# Abbreviations

| | |
|---|---|
| CCPR | Human Rights Committee of the International Covenant on Civil and Political Rights |
| CEDAW | Convention on the Elimination of All Forms of Discrimination Against Women |
| CESCR | Committee on Economic, Social and Cultural Rights |
| CRC | Convention on the Rights of the Child |
| ECOSOC | United Nations Economic and Social Council |
| ECtHR | European Court of Human Rights |
| EU | European Union |
| FAO | Food and Agricultural Organization of the United Nations |
| GATS | General Agreement on Trade in Services |
| GATT | General Agreement on Tariffs and Trade |
| GDP | Gross Domestic Product |
| GNP | Gross National Product |
| ICCPR | International Covenant on Civil and Political Rights |
| ICESCR | International Covenant on Economic, Social and Cultural Rights |
| ICJ | International Court of Justice |
| ICSID | International Centre for Settlement of Investment Disputes |
| ILO | International Labour Organization |
| IWRM | Integrated Water Resources Management |
| JMP | Joint Monitoring Programme for Water Supply and Sanitation |
| lpcd | litres per capita per day |
| MDG | Millennium Development Goal |
| NGO | Non-governmental Organisation |
| ODA | Official Development Assistance |

| | |
|---|---|
| OECD | Organisation for Economic Co-operation and Development |
| OHCHR | Office of the High Commissioner for Human Rights |
| SDG | Sustainable Development Goal |
| UN | United Nations |
| UNDP | United Nations Development Programme |
| UNFCCC | United Nations Framework Convention on Climate Change |
| UN-HABITAT | United Nations Human Settlements Programme |
| UNICEF | United Nations Children's Fund |
| WHO | World Health Organization |
| WTO | World Trade Organization |
| WWC | World Water Council |

# 1

# Introduction

## *The Right to Water in Context*

MALCOLM LANGFORD* AND ANNA F.S. RUSSELL**

More than a decade has passed since the emergence of a transnational discourse and practice on the right to water. From a right that attracted previously little attention, it became soon the subject of widespread agreement yet furious contestation. From localised debates over tariff prices, access and disconnections to global debates over privatisation, international watercourses and climate change, the right to water has attained an important and sometimes central place in law and political economy. With this backdrop, it is an opportune time to reflect on the theory and practice related to the human right to water and the prospects for the field.

In this volume, an in-depth examination of the right across diverse contexts is sought. The questions explored are of both a descriptive and prescriptive nature. Descriptively, it asks how and to what degree the right to water has emerged in law, policy and practice? As part of this inquiry, the nature of the adoption of a right to water by various actors, and whether it may have catalysed any positive impacts, is of particular interest. Normatively, it asks how the right can be sensibly justified and what are its implications for public policy and practice? These questions are explored within four broader dynamics of the water sector: (1) the allocation of water resources; (2) the accessibility of water and sanitation for personal and domestic uses; (3) the liberalisation of service delivery; and (4) the politics and practice of contemporary rural water sector reform. The book is structured along these lines.

This introductory chapter, first sets out background to the emergence of the human right to water by probing some of the factors that explain the turn to this right. After setting out the book's contents, a number of the key themes

* Professor, Faculty of Law, University of Oslo; Co-Director, Centre on Law and Social Transformation, University of Bergen.

** Visiting Fellow, Public International Law Group, Faculty of Law, University of Oxford.

that the book raises for theory and practice are examined – the legitimacy of the right in philosophy and law, its content and practical feasibility, and the politics of practice. The chapter concludes with a discussion of general prospects for the right.

## 1 THE EMERGENCE OF THE RIGHT TO WATER

In comparison to other rights, references to the human right to water were almost negligible at the turn of the twenty-first century. They could be found only on the periphery of scholarly literature, human rights legal standards and jurisprudence, policy debates and civil society activism. The right was not explicitly included in the 1948 Universal Declaration of Human Rights, nor was it included in the two major international human rights treaties of 1966 dealing with civil and political rights and economic, social and cultural rights.[1] Why such a seemingly basic right was excluded from these foundational standards has been a matter of conjecture. It might be explained by the fact that water scarcity was not as prominent an issue as it is today or that access to the resource was viewed as a necessary component for fulfilling other internationally recognised human rights.[2]

In any case, this position began to slowly shift from the late 1970s. Governments at the United Nations (UN) Water Conference in 1977 pronounced that 'all peoples, whatever their stage of development and their social and economic conditions, have the *right* to have access to drinking water in quantities and of a quality equal to their basic needs'.[3] Moreover, the 1979 Convention on the Elimination of Discrimination Against Women (CEDAW) referred to the right of women living in rural areas to 'enjoy adequate living conditions', particularly in relation to 'sanitation' and 'water supply'.[4] Water was further mentioned in the context of implementing the right to health of children in the 1989 Convention on the Rights of

[1] International Covenant on Civil and Political Rights, 16 December 1966, 999 UNTS 171 (entered into force 23 March 1976); International Covenant on Economic, Social and Cultural Rights; International Covenant on Economic, Social and Cultural Rights, 16 Dec. 1966, 993 UNTS 3, (entered into force 3 Jan. 1976).

[2] P. Gleick, 'The Human Right to Water', *Water Policy*, Vol. 1, No. 5 (1999), pp. 487–503.

[3] UN Conference on Water, Mar Del Plata Action Plan Resolution (1977), preamble [emphasis added].

[4] Article 14(2)(h) states that State parties 'shall take all appropriate measures to eliminate discrimination against women in rural areas . . . and, in particular, shall ensure to such women the right: [t]o enjoy adequate living conditions, particularly in relation to . . . sanitation . . . and water supply . . .' (Convention on the Elimination of All Forms of Discrimination Against Women, adopted Dec. 18, 1979, GA Res. 34/180 (entered into force 3 Sept. 1981)).

the Child (CRC).[5] While there is debate over whether these two treaties necessarily recognise a human right to water,[6] they at least made the connection between water and human rights more patent.

Shortly afterwards came an explicit recognition of the right in the Dublin Statement of 1991.[7] However, the Dublin Statement is better known for its affirmation of water as an economic and environmental good, rather than as a social good or a right. This focus is illustrative in the outcomes of the UN Conference on Environment and Development, held a few months later in Rio de Janeiro. Reference is made to the right in the resulting Agenda 21 programme of action, but only in passing.[8] At the national level, only a number of countries, such as South Africa in 1996, included the right to water in their constitutions,[9] while scattered instances of jurisprudence emerged in a few countries, such as Ireland, Belgium and India.[10] Likewise, the first scholarly exploration of the right to water appeared in 1992,[11] but this was almost a decade after the first major publications on related social rights, such as the

5 Article 24(2) states that 'States Parties shall pursue full implementation of this right and, in particular, shall take appropriate measures: ... (c) to combat disease and malnutrition, including within the framework of primary health care, through, inter alia, the application of readily available technology and through the provision of adequate nutritious foods and clean drinking-water, taking into consideration the dangers and risks of environmental pollution' (Convention on the Rights of the Child, 20 November 1989, 1577 UNTS 3 (entered into force 2 September 1990)).

6 Compare S. Tully, 'A Human Right to Access Water? A Critique of General Comment No. 15', *Netherlands Quarterly of Human Rights*, Vol. 23, No. 1 (2005) pp. 35–63 and A. Hellum and B. Derman, 'Observations on the Intersections of Human Rights and Local Practice: A Livelihood Perspective on Water', *Law, Social Justice and Global Development*, No. 1 (2008).

7 Dublin Statement on Water and Sustainable Development, International Conference on Water and the Environment: Development Issues for the 21st Century, UN Doc. A/CONF.151/PC/112 (1992). Principle 4 states that 'Water has an economic value in all its competing uses and should be recognized as an economic good. Within this principle, it is vital to recognize first the basic right of all human beings to have access to clean water and sanitation at an affordable price.' It was not a formal government declaration, but the statement was endorsed by international experts from a hundred countries. It is also a formal UN document.

8 Agenda 21, Report of the United Nations Conference on Environment and Development 1992. Section 18.47 briefly recounts historical developments in the water sector making reference to the right to water in the Mar del Plata Action Plan.

9 Constitution of South Africa 1996 art 27(1)(b), Constitution of Uganda,1995, XIV(ii).

10 See the judgments of *Ryan* v. AG. [1965] IR 294, at 315 [High Court of Ireland]; *Arrêt n°36/98 du 1 Avril* 1998, Commune de Wemmel, Moniteur Belge, 24/4/98 *Hussain* v. *Union of India*, High Court of Kerala OP 2741/1988 (26 February 1990).

11 S. McCaffrey, 'A Human Right to Water: Domestic and International Implications', *Georgetown International Environmental Law Review*, Vol. 5, No. 1 (1992), pp. 1–24.

right to food, and it triggered little further scholarly reflection.[12] The same pattern was evident in national and transnational civil society activism: water issues were compartmentalised as largely a concern for the development sector or environmental policy, or addressed where relevant in the context of other rights, such as access to housing, education and health.

With the ushering in of the new millennium, the invocation of the right to water has exponentially increased. Its trajectory though the following fifteen years is perhaps best captured by Google. A closed web search in English for the 'human right to water' yielded over 225,000 hits and even higher if sanitation is included.[13] In the calendar year of 2005, the number of new hits was 105, a number which was reached in the first two months of 2010, and the first two weeks of 2015. These figures track or exceed the human right to food.[14]

Constitutionally, recognition of the right to water (and sanitation) has increased considerably. While a significant number of countries place obligations on States to protect natural water resources or develop a national water policy,[15] the key change concerns personal and domestic access: see Figure 1.1. In the period between 1990 and 1999, eight States included a reference to a basic water supply, but only in one instance was it framed as a right. By 2014, twenty-six States constitutionalised access to water, with thirteen recognising it as a self-standing right[16] and another three as a part of other rights or as a directive principle.[17] In some cases, the right to water has been included as part of a broad-ranging reform of domestic bills of rights (e.g. Kenya, Zimbabwe) although in a few cases it was added as part of a constitutional reform focused on water or sanitation (e.g. Uruguay). In addition, eight States have now recognised a free-standing right to sanitation.[18]

[12] See, for example, P. Alston and K. Tomasevski (eds.), *The Right to Food* (The Hague: Martinnus Nijhoff, 1984).

[13] Search conducted 4 February 2016. In Spanish, the figure was 1.66 million.

[14] This includes a double search that includes the 'right to adequate food' and 'human right to food'.

[15] For example, Article 81 of the Portuguese constitution states that 'In the economic and social field the State shall be under a primary duty: . . . (n) To adopt a national water policy that uses, plans and rationally manages water resources.' Article 20 of the Nigerian Constitution states that 'The State shall protect and improve the environment and safeguard the water, air and land, forest and wild life of Nigeria.'

[16] South Africa, Uruguay, Solomon Islands, Nicaragua, the DRC, Maldives, Ecuador, Bolivia, Niger, Kenya, Mexico, Zimbabwe and Fiji.

[17] Dominican Republic, Algeria and Uganda (the latter as a directive principle).

[18] Uruguay, Panama, Colombia, Maldives, Bolivia, Kenya, Mexico and Fiji.

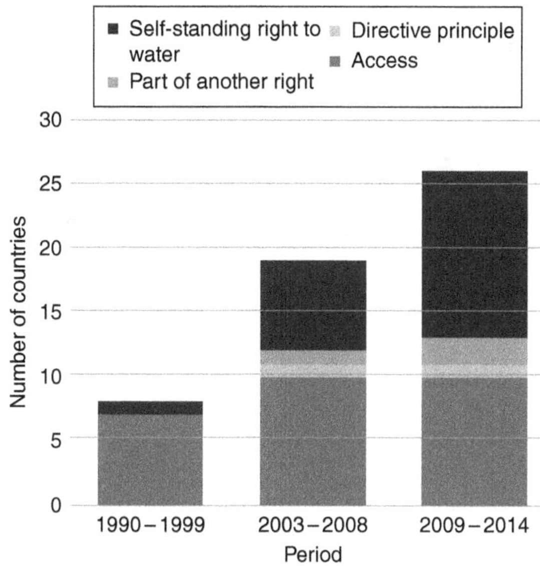


FIGURE 1.1 Constitutional recognition[19]

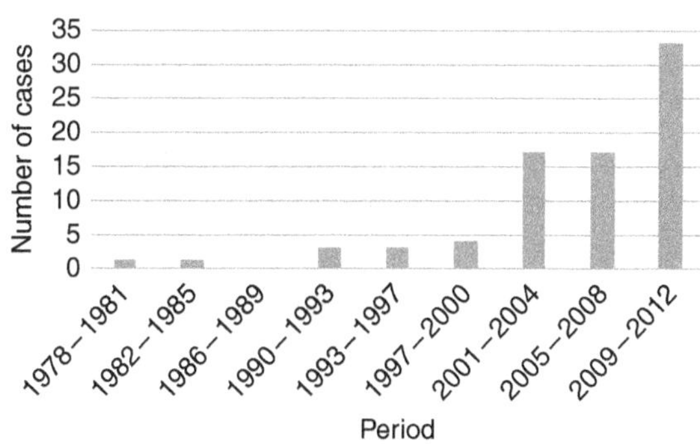


FIGURE 1.2 Trends in litigation: Cases decided

In terms of jurisprudence, there has been a significant upswing in cases addressing water issues through the lens of human rights. Figure 1.2 shows the number of judgments decided in 4-year periods from a collection of cases by WaterLex and WASH United.[20] Of these 79 judgments from 35 countries,

[19] The coding was carried out using constitutional extracts from COHRE, *Legal Resources for the Right to Water and Sanitation: International and National Standards* (Geneva: COHRE, 2008) and the WaterLex Legal Database.

[20] See e.g., *The Human Rights to Water and Sanitation in Courts Worldwide: A Selection of National, Regional and International Case Law* by WaterLex and WASH UNITED (2014). See also examples in COHRE, *Legal Resources for the Right to Water and Sanitation: International*

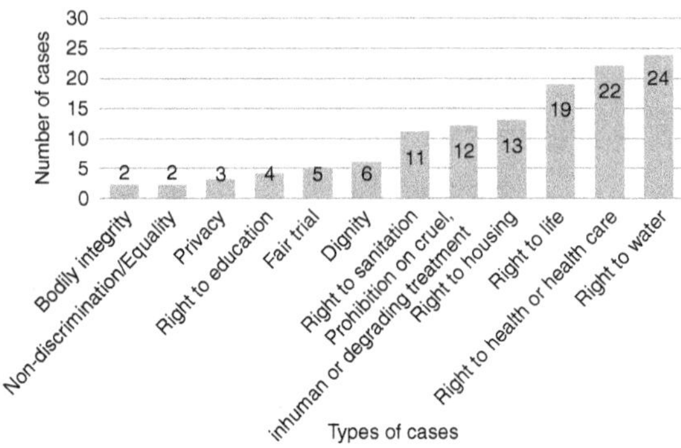


FIGURE 1.3 Rights considered by courts

the vast majority were decided since the start of the new millennium. In terms of success in the selection, 67 per cent of the discrete claims were fully successful and 13 per cent partially successful.[21] However, the list is certainly not comprehensive. For example, the number of cases on the right to water in Costa Rica and Brazil, where legal standing is simplified, exceeds three hundred.

Returning to the sample, as to the right considered by the relevant court, this varied considerably, as depicted in Figure 1.3. Of the discrete claims, twenty-four were considered in relation to the right to water and twelve with the right to sanitation. The rest were considered under various social rights (e.g. health, housing, education), civil rights (e.g. life, cruel and degrading treatment, fair trial, privacy, bodily integrity), and non-discrimination and dignity. The reasons for this appear to be largely of a legal and positivist nature. The right to water was invoked in those countries in which the right was included in the constitution or the International Covenant on Economic Social and Cultural Rights (ICESCR) was incorporated in the constitution. However, in some cases the right was implied from other rights.

Why the dramatic change? Why the growing recognition? The growing appeal of the right to water could be accounted in three principal ways, as set out below. In each instance, particular actors appear to be influential in promoting the idea for either instrumental or intrinsic reasons.

*and National Standards*, pp. 277–315 and M. Langford (ed.), *Social Rights Jurisprudence: Emerging Trends in International and Comparative Law* (New York: Cambridge University Press).

[21] There were ninety-nine discrete claims in the seventy-nine cases. Information was missing on the success of twenty of these claims and these were removed from the calculation.

## 1.1 *Norm Clarification and Legal Diffusion*

The timing of the turn to the right to water correlates with the adoption of the oft-quoted *General Comment No. 15 on the Right to Water* by the UN Committee on Economic, Social and Cultural Rights (CESCR) in 2002.[22] In this document, the Committee responsible for monitoring implementation of the ICESCR stated that the right to water clearly falls within the category of guarantees essential to secure an adequate standard of living, Article 11 of the ICESCR. The Committee also claimed that the right to water is inextricably related to other internationally recognised human rights, such as the right to the highest attainable standard of health in Article 12 of the ICESCR.[23] Although generally considered to be an interpretative instrument, rather than a legally binding document,[24] General Comment No. 15 is often seen as both a building block and key catalyst for subsequent recognition of the right to water by international bodies and States.[25]

A few years later, for instance, the UN Development Programme (UNDP) Human Development Report opened with the statement that 'Water, the stuff of life and a basic human right, is at the heart of a daily crisis faced by countless millions of the world's most vulnerable people – a crisis that

[22] Committee on Economic, Social and Cultural Rights, *General Comment No. 15, The right to water* (Twenty-ninth session, 2002), UN Doc. E/C.12/2002/11 (2003). Note that in 2001 European Governments declared that 'Everyone has the right to a sufficient quantity of water for his or her basic needs' and noted that the right could be derived from international human rights instruments (Committee of Ministers to Member States on the European Charter on Water Resources Recommendation 14 (2001), para. 5). Note also that 2003 was the International Year of Freshwater.

[23] General Comment No. 15 para. 3. The General Comment notes that the right to water is also inextricably related to the right to an adequate standard of housing and adequate food and should be seen in conjunction with other rights such as the right to life and human dignity.

[24] General Comments are designed to assist State parties fulfil their reporting obligations under the ICESCR. By adopting General Comments the Committee on Economic, Social and Cultural Rights (CESCR) endeavours to make the experience it has gained from examining reports available for the benefit of all State parties in order to help them further implement the Covenant (Committee on Economic, Social and Cultural Rights (UNCESCR, *(3rd Session) 'Report of the Committee on Economic, Social and Cultural Rights - Supplement No. 4' (6-24 February 1989) UN Doc E/C.12/1989/5 annex III (Introduction: The Purpose of General Comments)* (1989) paras. 1, 3).

[25] Research indicates that prior to 2002, no State reports to the CESCR explicitly raised the human rights to water and sanitation, and from 2011–2012 about half of the reports did. See B. Mason Meir and Y. Kim, 'Human Rights Accountability through Treaty Bodies: Examining Human Rights Treaty Monitoring for Water and Sanitation', *Duke Journal of Comparative and International Law*, Vol. 26, No. 1 (2016), pp. 139–228, at 195.

threatens life and destroys livelihoods on a devastating scale'.[26] The Report's first recommendation to all States was that they 'make water a human right – and mean it'.[27] This was followed by a statement from the UN High Commissioner for Human Rights encouraging States and other actors to identify good practices in relation to the fulfilment of the right.[28] In 2008, the first special procedures mandate, created by the newly formed UN Human Rights Council, the political body within the UN dealing with human rights, was the establishment of an Independent Expert on Human Rights and Access to Water and Sanitation.[29] In 2010, the UN General Assembly 'declare[d] the right to safe and clean drinking water and sanitation as a human right that is essential for the full enjoyment of life and all human rights'.[30] Later that year, the UN Human Rights Council affirmed the right.[31]

Even if the General Comment can be considered a catalyst, such legal diffusion may simply be isomorphic or mimetic. In other words, the recognition of the right to water may simply be a reflection of a new norm of modernity emulated by all.[32] Such norms may be actively diffused by advocates, consultants, lawyers, judges, corporations or elites[33] but they might lack utility, relevance or strength. The result is that there may be a 'decoupling' of the norm from prevailing policies and one should not expect it to exert significant influence.[34] However, the explanation of the uptake of the right to water extends beyond mere symbolic politics. It has been pushed by actors convinced of its material and discursive values, whether as a

[26] See United Nations Development Programme, *Beyond Scarcity: Power, Power and the Global Water Crisis* (New York: UNDP, 2006) p. 1.

[27] Ibid., p. 8.

[28] OHCHR 'Report of the United Nations High Commissioner for Human Rights on the Scope and Content of the Relevant Human Rights Obligations related to Equitable Access to Safe Drinking Water and Sanitation under International Human Rights Instruments' (16 August 2007) UN Doc A/HRC/6/3.

[29] For information on the work of the Independent Expert, now Special Rapporteur, see www2.ohchr.org/english/issues/water/Iexpert/

[30] UN General Assembly, *The Human Right to Water and Sanitation* (Sixty-fourth session, 2010) UN Doc A/64/L.63/Rev.1, para. 1. There were 122 votes in favour and 41 abstentions, including many developed countries.

[31] UN Human Rights Council, *Human Rights and Access to Safe Drinking Water and Sanitation* (Fifteenth session, 2010) UN Doc. A/HRC/15/L.14 para. 3.

[32] J. W. Meyer, J. Boli, G. M. Thomas and F. O. Ramirez, 'World Society and the Nation-State', *American Journal of Sociology*, Vol. 103, No. 1 (1997), pp. 144–181, 144, 153.

[33] See, e.g., B. Perry, 'Constitutional Johnny Appleseeds: American Consultants and the Drafting of Foreign Constitutions', *Albany Law Review*, Vol. 55, No. (1991–1992), pp. 767–792; A.-M. Slaughter, 'A Typology of Transjudicial Communication', *University of Richmond Law Review*, Vol. 29, No. 1 (1994–5), pp. 99–137.

[34] Meyer, Boli, Thomas and Ramirez, 'World Society and the Nation-State', 144, 153.

framing device and accountability tool, marker in struggles for and against privatisation, or other aspects, which are now discussed.

## 1.2 *Framing Device*

The emergence of the right to water coincides with attempts to foreground water issues in the international political and development agenda. Rights can provide a useful frame for different actors in drawing attention to the sector or their interests.[35] Articulating water concerns in such language can usefully capture two faces of the 'global water crisis' – both environment and poverty.[36] The UN estimates that a quarter of the world currently live in river basins that are 'closed' (water use exceeds minimum recharge levels) and the number of people in water stressed areas is expected to grow from 700 million to 3 billion in 2025.[37] Groundwater reserves continue to rapidly shrink as surface water is exhausted, pollution remains persistent while climate change already appears to be altering rainfall patterns with devastating effect. As regards poverty, estimates of the WHO and UNICEF Joint Monitoring Programme are that 663 million people do not use an improved source of drinking water.[38] Relatedly, diarrhoea is the second leading cause of death amongst children – responsible for the deaths of 760,000 children every year.[39]

However, it is arguable that the interest in the right to water was not primarily driven by the broad paradigms of environment and development. Rather, it is the limitations of these very frameworks to locate and address the underlying causes of the crisis. Those championing human rights often drew attention to the variables of power inequalities, corruption, non-accountability, and discrimination, which they saw as key determinants of whether clean water was accessible in practice for individuals and communities. For example, the surprising

35 On the use of human rights to frame debates and issues, see H. Miller, 'From "Rights-Based" to "Rights-Framed" Approaches: A Social Constructionist View of Human Rights Practice,' in *International Journal of Human Rights*, Vol. 14 (2010), pp. 915–931.

36 See discussion in M. Langford, 'Tragedy or Triumph of the Commons: Human Rights and the World Water Crises', *Human Rights 2006: The Year in Review* (Melbourne: Castan Centre for Human Rights Law, University of Monash, 2007), pp. 9–39. Historically, political inaction and not affording sufficient attention to the sector in the development context may constitute a factor in the 'crisis'.

37 UNDP, *Beyond Scarcity*, pp. 14, 140. The World Bank Water Resources Sector Strategy 2004 is more alarming, concluding that 'an estimated 4 billion people – one half of the world's population will live under conditions of severe water stress in 2025' (p. 5).

38 See WHO/UNICEF *Progress on Sanitation and Drinking Water - 2015 Update and MDG Assessment* (2015) p. 4. See www.wssinfo.org for updated statistics.

39 WHO, *Diarrhoeal Disease*, Fact Sheet No. 330, April 2013.

persistence of a water gap in Europe has been attributed to discrimination on the basis of ethnicity or socio-economic status.[40] And, the failure of projects to improve water access in large informal settlements in Kenya has been attributed to a lack of attention to 'mafia' control and power differentials amongst tenants and landlords.[41]

This explanatory potential of the human rights and broader governance dimension has been partly corroborated by empirical work. For example, in his intra-country regression analysis of Colombia, Krause finds that water governance (including user participation and presence of civil society groups) is highly significant in explaining variance in water outcomes across provinces.[42] Moreover, attention to the different dimensions of the right to water has led to adjusted figures concerning access. In-depth studies by UN-Habitat of informal settlements show that the number of those without adequate water rises considerably if the actual affordability, regularity and potability of water – all key elements of the right to water – are included in the definition.[43]

It is further claimed that approaches based on human rights provide new 'tools'.[44] This ranges from the establishment of legal standards and substantive norms, stronger participatory rights, an emphasis on disaggregation and non-discrimination through to the encouragement of cultures and institutions of accountability. There is also an attempt to shift the focus from technocratic approaches to water resource management to the broader political landscape and the need for a wider range of strategies that address power imbalances, including mobilisation, advocacy, and when appropriate, litigation.

40 Greek Helsinki Monitor et al, *Greece: Continuing Widespread Violation of Roma Housing Rights* (2006) Centre on Housing Rights and Evictions (15 February 2007).

41 Centre on Housing Rights and Evictions, *Listening to the Poor? Housing Rights in Nairobi, Kenya* (Geneva: COHRE, 2006).

42 M. Krause, *The Political Economy of Water and Sanitation* (London: Routledge, 2009).

43 See G. Mboup, 'Existing Indicators in the Water and Sanitation Sector: Indicators for Accessibility, Affordability and Non-Discrimination' in V. Roaf, A. Khalfan and M. Langford (eds.), *Indicators for the Right to Water: Concept Paper* No. 13 (2005). See also J. Bartram, 'Improving on Haves and Have-nots', *Nature* Vol. 452 (20 March 2008), pp. 283–284.

44 See, e.g., R. Offenheiser and S. Holcombe, 'Challenges and Opportunities in Implementing a Rights-Based Approach to Development: an Oxfam America Perspective', *Nonprofit and Voluntary Sector Quarterly*, Vol. 32, No. 2 (2003), pp. 268–301; A. Yamin, 'Defining Questions: Situating Issues of Power in the Formulation of a Right to Health under International Law', *Human Rights Quarterly*, Vol. 18 (1996), pp. 398–438.

## 1.3 *Privatisation*

Another explanatory variable for the rise of the right to water was the controversy over the emergence in the 1990s of policies promoting commodification of water and sanitation services. 'While trade liberalization was perhaps the archetype disagreement on development strategy in the 1980s and 1990s, in the 1990s and 2000s this role ha[d] been taken over by water privatization and the passions it arouses.'[45] While most actors agreed that water utilities' pricing should be adjusted to reflect the 'real' costs of water provision (particularly for commercial use and high volume personal use), more controversial was the strong push by international financial institutions to privatise the management and delivery of water services on the ostensible grounds that it would improve the economic and social performance of water utilities.[46] The result was that close to forty countries experimented with some form of private sector participation although the number of new public-private partnerships awarded has decreased and the global population served by major private operators has not changed significantly.[47] Privatisation reached a peak in 1999 (with thirty partnerships awarded that year) falling to just above ten a year in 2002.[48] This policy shift was not confined to the urban sector.[49] As *Lovera* discusses in his chapter on Chile, commodification of water resources was promoted as a means of optimising allocation.

The human right to water featured strongly in the discourse of the resulting debates and struggles, even if international human rights were normatively neutral on the privatisation of essential services. An array of social movements and non-governmental organisations (NGOs) opposed privatisation on the basis that the potential or actuality of increased prices, slower expansion of access and/or decreased public participation violated the right to water.[50]

45 R. Kanbur, 'Development Disagreements and Water Privatization: Bridging the Divide', *Journal of Poverty Alleviation and International Development*, Vol. 1, No. 1 (2011), pp. 1–20, at 1.

46 G. Pitman, *Bridging Troubled Waters: Assessing the World Bank Water Resource Strategy* (Washington D.C.: World Bank, 2002).

47 P. Marin, *Public-Private Partnerships for Urban Water Utilities: A Review of Experiences in Developing Countries* (Washington D.C.:World Bank, 2009), p. 2; pp. 24, 35.

48 Ibid.

49 See generally, World Bank, *Water Resources Management Strategy*, (Washington D.C.: World Bank, 1993). For a critique, see V. Shiva, *Water Wars: Privatisation, Pollution and Profit* (Cambridge: South End Press, 2002).

50 Some have gone further to argue that privatisation itself is a violation of the right to water on the basis that both water resources *and* water delivery should remain in public or

The wave of constitutional and legislative recognition of the right to water in Latin America over the last decade could be characterised as a response to privatisation. In Uruguay, for example, a referendum in 2004 on the inclusion of the right to water in the constitution, together with a prohibition on privatisation of water services, was successful.[51]

Paradoxically enough, the very vanguard of privatisation, multinational corporations, have equally supported recognition of the right to water. They have argued that private companies may be better placed to work with governments to ensure its realisation.[52] Multinational representatives attended the hearing of the CESCR on its draft General Comment and were visibly active in the campaign for the recognition of a right to sanitation in international law. While corporations and anti-privatisation movements obviously retain different interpretations of both the content of the right and the identity of those responsible for its violation, their collective actions have increased the recognition of the right and partially ensured it becomes the framework in which to situate the ongoing debate. At the same time, the endorsement by corporations of the right to water has confirmed the views of some sceptics, who claim that rights carry a liberal, rather than a transformative, agenda.[53]

## 1.4 *Other Factors*

The global rise of the human right to water cannot be explained by a mere supply-driven processes. This turn to rights was not made in order to produce new legal norms or apply yet another rights template on a social problem. A wide range of actors saw the right to water as a useful political resource in tackling questions of development, environment and privatisation. Other reasons also no doubt exist. Many of the chapters of this book highlight additional factors behind the recognition of the right in a particular setting.

communal hands. For a discussion on this point, see M. Barlow, *Blue Covenant: The Global Water Crisis and the Coming Battle for the Right to Water* (McClelland and Stewart, 2007), pp. 164–175.

[51] See 'Referendum Gives Resounding 'No' to the Privatisation of Water, Inter Press Service News Agency, 1 November 2005. Available at www.ipsnews.net. It was passed with 64 per cent in favour and Article 47 of the Constitution now recognises the right to water and sanitation.

[52] See A. Russell 'Incorporating Rights in Development: Transnational Corporations and the Right to Water', *International Journal of Law in Context*, Vol. 7, No. 1 (2011), pp. 1–30.

[53] See K. Bakker, 'The Commons Versus the Commodity: Alter-globalization, Anti-privatization and the Human Right to Water in the Global South', *Antipode – A Radical Journal of Geography*, Vol. 39, No. 3 (2007), pp. 430–455; See F. Sultana and A. Loftus, 'The Right to Water: Prospects and Possibilities', in Sultana and Loftus, *The Right to Water* , pp. 1–18.

To be sure, this potted history is not intended to over-promote the acceptance of the right to water. There remain challenges by sceptics of different colours. It took many years before the World Water Forum agreed to include the right to water in its declarations – perhaps fuelled by concerns over its legal status or its possible negative message on commodification.[54] More generally, some moral theorists, lawyers and economists remain critical or lukewarm to claims that economic, social and cultural rights generally constitute legitimate human rights,[55] or that the rights contain any determinacy such that can be applied usefully to policy deliberations. Equally, others are less interested in the normative or legal position. They query the instrumental benefits of 'rights talk' in the water sector[56] or its usefulness in political struggles for water justice.[57]

## 2 OVERVIEW OF THE BOOK

This book takes a departure in both the optimism and scepticism surrounding the human right to water. As noted, the aim of the book is two-fold. It critically explores in a descriptive register how the right to water has been recognised and used in law, policy and practice. It also rises to a normative level and examines justifications and implications of the right generally and in specific contexts.

The book emerged from an international and inter-disciplinary conference on the right to water and sanitation hosted by the University of Oslo, University of Oxford and UNDP and further chapters were added as the book progressed. About half of the authors are lawyers by training while half represent the social sciences, including anthropology, economics and geography. Thus, the publication is indicative of a current trend to partly overcome the legal dominance of the study of human rights as the field gradually takes on a more interdisciplinary character.[58] However, current collections tend to be located within one field or discipline[59] and rarely is

[54] See references at footnote 88. [55] See discussion in Section 3.

[56] P. Anand, 'Right to Water and Access to Water: An Assessment', *Journal of International Development*, Vol. 19 (2007), pp. 511–526.

[57] R. D'Souza, 'Liberal Theory, Human Rights and Water-Justice: Back to Square One?', *Law, Social Justice and Global Development*, No. 1 (2008).

[58] See e.g., R. Wilson (ed.), *Human Rights, Culture and Context: Anthropological Perspectives* (London: Pluto Press, 1997); T. Risse, S. Ropp and K. Sikkink, *The Power of Human Rights: International Norms and Domestic Change* (Cambridge: Cambridge University Press, 1999); V. Gauri and D. Brinks (eds.), *Courting Social Justice* (Cambridge: Cambridge University Press, 2008).

[59] For an important study rooted in social science, particularly geography, see F. Sultana and A. Loftus (eds.), *The Right to Water: Politics, Governance and Social Struggle* (London:

traditional legal scholarship in the area of human rights tied with more recent varied strands of social science scholarship. Accordingly, by focusing on one right – the right to water – this edited collection also aims to contribute more broadly to an interdisciplinary approach to the study of human rights.[60] One consequence, however, is that the starting point for the chapters can significantly differ from author to author even if the broader research questions may be shared.

While the book is principally focused on the right to water, about a third of the chapters cover simultaneously sanitation. Even though the rise of a human right to sanitation is more recent, some authors also consider it where relevant. Obviously, the relevance of sanitation varies across the book – salient in certain contexts (e.g. urban services) and less in others (e.g. water allocation in rural areas), so it was left to the authors to discuss it as it pertains to their specific research. It is hoped that the book also opens the door to more sustained research on the important and often neglected subject.

### 2.1 *Water Allocation*

Part I – 'Water Allocation' – explores the right to water and related human rights in the context of water being a limited environmental resource. Unlike many human rights, the finite quantity of the natural resource raises unique questions about allocation, particularly at the domestic level, but also at the transnational and international levels. The challenge for States becomes how to apportion the water within and between their borders in such a way that both the right to water, and related rights, such as food and an adequate standard of living, can be progressively realised, while at the same time recognising both its cultural significance, and its economic value for other uses, such as industry, agriculture and energy.

*Van Koppen* casts a critical eye over contemporary global reforms that involve the conversion of customary law systems, in which water is generally common property, into formal permit systems. These are ostensibly intended to increase the policy space for regulation, including supporting redistribution and small-scale use. However, her research finds that the resulting administratively cumbersome process is inherently discriminatory with the result

Earthscan and Routledge, 2012). An almost exclusively legal approach is taken in E. Reidel and P. Rothen (eds.), *The Human Right to Water* (Berlin: Berliner WissenschaftsVerlag, 2006).

60 On this, see e.g., M. Freeman, *Human Rights: An Interdisciplinary Approach* (Polity Cambridge, 2002).

that many poor, small-scale water users are marginalised even further. Thus, policies seeking to protect the right to water should avoid excessive formalism in this context. The author argues that plural legal systems must be taken into account before any such reforms are instigated and that more creative and simpler mechanisms may be more effective in realising the right.

The following study of Chile by *Domingo Lovera Parmo* takes up one of the most extreme cases where water has been legally commodified in its natural state. The result is that access to water resources for indigenous peoples in particular has been hindered, implicating the right to water and other human rights. Focusing on three specific case studies, the author discusses how indigenous groups have engaged with the international right to water in an attempt to maintain their traditional access to and use of water resources.

*Inga Winkler* takes up the theoretical problematique of the relationship between water allocation, multiple water use and human rights, particularly in rural areas. She firstly asks whether water for producing food for basic human consumption is guaranteed by the right to water or the right to food. She argues for the latter as States have a number of policy options available to them to fulfil the right to food and are not limited to only providing access to water resources for subsistence agriculture. Entering largely unexplored legal territory, she then explores the nature of State obligations to respect, protect and fulfil this aspect of the right to food in the context of constrained water and fiscal resources.

In the latter two chapters, the focus is on the transnational and international levels. *Anna Russell and Stephen McCaffrey* examine the implications of the right to water for States sharing transboundary watercourses. After providing some contextual background to inter-State water disputes and their effects on individual human rights, the chapter discusses potential extraterritorial human rights obligations of States, as well as possible accountability mechanisms for any such violations. The authors conclude by discussing how the right to water may have a more subtle influence in informing current international watercourse law and the operation of joint management institutions or river basin commissions.

A more recent transnational allocative dilemma, the impact of climate change on the distribution of water resources, is addressed by *Mac Darrow*. He argues that the negative impacts of climate change cannot be understood solely within a water sector analysis framework, but that human rights law needs to be studied in connection with its specific interaction with the international climate change regime, including the recent Paris Agreement. Accordingly, he reviews both legal regimes, and analyses legal obligations at issue in the context of climate change harms and the right to water. Taking into account the limited extraterritorial reach of international human rights law, Darrow focuses on national adaptation policies and provides recommendations as to how climate change policies based explicitly on the right to water may strengthen the claims of those vulnerable to the adverse impacts of climate change.

## 2.2 *Access to Water and Sanitation*

Part II – 'Access to Water and Sanitation' – shifts the attention from water allocation and distribution to the relationship between the right to water and accessibility of water and sanitation for domestic uses for individuals. In discussions on the accessibility and the right to water, South Africa is commonly assigned the role of the posterchild.[61] *Jackie Dugard, Malcolm Langford* and *Edward Anderson* begin their chapter by examining the manner in which the right to water has been legalised in South Africa and the harsher realities of access in practice. The chapter pilots quantitative techniques to test which municipalities have exhibited the poorest performance given a range of local capacity indicators. The authors also use qualitative analysis to understand what might be responsible for various faultlines in South African practice. They conclude with an analysis of the effects of invoking legally the right to water – especially in the *Mazibuko* case – in addressing these faultlines.

*Henri Smets* focuses on affordability from a comparative perspective and seeks to inductively quantify the standard by comparing the water bill of households to disposable income. While affordability is often included in various international declarations, including the Sustainable Development Goals (SDGs), countries are not officially measured on performance. Based on a survey of over fifty countries, he finds that in industrial countries, poor households spend on average 2.6 per cent on their income on water, with public authorities often taking measures to keep water bills to less than 3–4 per cent. In transitional and developing countries, expenditure of poor households rises to an average 7.5 per cent of disposable income. While such high numbers are often tolerated, a number of developing States have taken measures to keep water bills to less than 3–5 per cent. Smets concludes by providing a graduated means to measure water affordability, which could be of relevance to not only national and European Union (EU) policy, but current global development goals.

*Malcolm Langford, Jamie Bartram* and *Virginia Roaf* examine the historical neglect of sanitation and its more recent increased recognition as a human

[61] UNDP, *Beyond Scarcity*, p. 63.

right. Noticeably absent from the title of General Comment No. 15, they explore the emerging movement for the right to sanitation. They examine the legal basis for the right, how its individual and collective dimension may fit within a largely individualistic human rights framework, and what it may mean in practice through a series of thematic studies.

*Anne Hellum* takes a point of departure in gender equality and is partly critical of General Comment No. 15 for ignoring water uses for kitchen gardening. She suggests that the right should be better mainstreamed into more general women's and children's rights, such as those outlined in the CEDAW and the CRC. She takes up a number of case studies from Africa that illustrate how contemporary water policies, both local and international, are insufficiently addressing gender dimensions. These include issues of affordability, the rights of girls, access to customary water sources and protection from indirect discrimination.

*Ashfaq Khalfan* moves beyond the vertical paradigm of State obligations to the extraterritorial obligations of States in development cooperation that relate to access to water. He articulates when States may be obliged to refrain from actions that would violate the right in other countries, for example, through the support of projects that exclude the participation of affected peoples. The author also explains when States may have an obligation to protect the rights of people in other countries by influencing actions taken by international organisations, as well as the extent of States' obligations to assist people secure their right through financial and technical cooperation.

*Lara El Jazairi* discusses issues of allocation and access in the case of the Occupied Palestinian Territory. While the extraterritorial human rights duties of an occupying power, such as Israel, are more settled under international law than the case of transboundary waters or climate change, the case of the Occupied Palestinian Territory illustrates the clear challenges of enforcing them in practice. The author considers how Israel's occupation, water policies and practices have impeded the ability of the Palestinian National Authority to realise the right to water and sanitation in terms of securing equitable water allocation, as well as ensuring effective and affordable services for clean water and sanitation. The chapter examines not only the extent of Israel's legal obligations as an occupying power, but also the obligations of the Palestinian authorities.

### 2.3 *Urban Water Reform*

Part III – 'Urban Water Reform' – discusses how since the 1980s, market-based or neo-classical economic principles have increased in importance across the water field, as is clear from chapters in other parts of the book dealing with water allocation regimes[62] or rural water schemes.[63] However, it is the field of urban and peri-urban water services in which a market-based policy has not only been heavily promoted, but reflected in aspects of international law.

*Malcolm Langford* begins by charting the rise and (part) fall of privatisation of urban water services and takes up three specific questions concerning its relation to the right to water. The first is normative: How should the relationship between the right to water and privatisation be understood? The second is empirical: did the shift to privatisation in practice harm or facilitate the realisation of the right? The debate and literature are filled with wildly varying claims over the benefits and costs of privatisation. The third is socio-legal: how did the right to water feature in the local and global movements that resisted privatisation? The author finds it striking that diverse civil society organisations, and many often sceptical to rights, turned, in varying degrees, to rights talk and legal tactics.

*Nicola Colbran* focuses on a particular case of privatisation and traces how water supply in Jakarta, Indonesia has been treated by authorities since the time of Dutch colonialism up until the present and the slow shift of water from a political good to an economic good with minimal focus on its social qualities.[64] The author discusses the concession contracts agreed to at the end of the 1990s for private service delivery of water supply in the city and how this may misalign with the social aspects of water and its recognition as a human right under domestic law. The chapter concludes by examining how the Constitutional Court rejected arguments that the Water Resources Law does not adequately recognise the right to water, as required by the Constitution and, in the alternative, that facilitation of private sector participation was unconstitutional.

In his chapter, *Andrew Lang* traces the rise of calls for liberalisation or privatisation of water services that found its expression in the General Agreement of Trade in Services (GATS) and would lock countries into equal access by multinationals under international trade law. He examines the role that GATS may have on the ability of governments to regulate the water industry in pursuit of various social objectives. After providing an historical account of attempts to develop disciplines under the GATS for the water and sanitation services sector, the author discusses how existing GATS disciplines may be

[62] See Chapters 2 and 3. [63] See Chapters 9, 17, 19 and 20.

[64] It is noted here that piped water is typically seen as a service. In Colbran's chapter, the term 'good' refers to water as a physical good, and she discusses the terminology used in her chapter in more detail.

applied to the sector and how future negotiations may evolve.[65] He notes that this traditional focus on the potentially problematic role of GATS for regulatory autonomy of States has now been partly displaced by three factors. The first is empirical – the enthusiasm for privatisation has since waned and few developing countries have listed their water sectors in the GATS annex as open for automatic private competition. The second is that the World Trade Organisation's adjudicatory bodies have softened their jurisprudence on the ability of States to take trade-restrictive measures on social and environmental grounds. Finally, much of the debate and action has shifted to the international *investment* regime as a result of multinational corporations utilising international arbitration in responses to disputes with developing country governments over the operation of water concessions.

*Luke Peterson* focuses on these investment arbitration cases and the manner in which the right to water has been invoked by States and civil society. He reviews several disputes where foreign investors have claimed that host States have violated the terms of a bilateral investment treaty (BIT) in respect of the operation of specific water utilities. Increasingly, human rights law, including the right to water, has been raised by both State and non-State actors in relation to such disputes in an attempt to justify the actions taken by the host State. The author discusses what lessons can be distilled from the cases to date about the role of human rights law in utilities investment arbitrations.

### 2.4 *Rural Water Reform*

Part IV – 'Rural Water Reform' – provides greater attention to the governance dimension of the right to water in the rural context, with a focus on politics and participation. Particular attention is given to critically analysing contemporary water reform theory and processes from the perspective of the right to water and the potential and limitations of human rights in transforming these political spaces.

*Rob Hope* reviews the various ideological shifts in water policy over the past few decades before focusing on how commonly advocated normative approaches may align with consumer choice in relation to the delivery of rural water supply. He then examines specifically the intersection of the right to water with societal choice, and concludes that while the two approaches may occupy some common theoretical space, the extent to which productive policy

[65] His findings continue to resonate: see K. Connolly, 'Finding Space for Regulatory Autonomy in GATS Article XVII after EC – Seals: Public Services and the "Likeness" of Public and Private Service Providers', Legal Issues of Economic Integration, Vol. 42, No. 1 (2015), pp. 57–84.

engagement and improved coverage will follow likely hinges on the contextual interpretation of the obligation of progressive realisation of the right.

*Nandita Singh* adopts an anthropological approach to the study of the right to water and sanitation in rural India and proposes a framework for understanding micro-level processes for implementing the right. Specifically, Singh looks at the interface of implementing action taken by duty bearers with interpretation of such action by individual rights holders within the context of their socio-cultural norms. The author suggests that both contexts can be understood to consist of distinct 'norm-triads' comprising knowledge, will and systematic conditions – the closer the alignment of the triad, the more likely that the right will be realised in practice.

The following chapters analyse contemporary water reform processes in two Southern countries in the context of both international development cooperation and fast-moving domestic politics. *Bill Derman* and *Emmanuel Manzungu* examine the right to water from a political ecology perspective. Focusing on Zimbabwean water reforms, they highlight the need to combine analyses of power and ecology when looking at conflicts over implementing the right and how multiple layers of actors can shape both national and local water management processes. Water reforms sought to impose a new water management system through the creation of a national water authority with the support of international donors. While new legislation prioritised water as a primary good, the water reform in practice largely focused on development of catchment management and users fees to the neglect of small scale users. For the period since 2000, they analyse how the water reform process in Zimbabwe has been overtaken by domestic factors – an overly centralised system, recession and poor governance – that has led to a devastating decline in water services.

While India is well known for its early jurisprudential recognition of the right to water, *Philippe Cullet*, analyses how reforms are influencing the progressive realisation of the right with a particular focus on participation of rural communities. Although there has been significant investment in enabling access, many rural communities lack access to water of adequate quality and quantity. The author calls for the adoption of legislative measures to realise the right, including giving priority in allocation to personal and domestic uses, and for panchayats to be given effective control over local management decisions.

## 3 KEY THEMES

On the one hand, explicit recognition of a human right to water appears to present no glaring theoretical or normative problems or dilemmas. Water is fundamental to human survival. Moreover, the predominant approach to the right to water in international law and discourse is relatively modest: the right is framed within the constraints of domestic and personal uses of water,[66] rather than productive uses. The latter raise certainly deep questions about feasibility and trade-offs, the sort of dilemmas that have troubled international watercourse law for centuries, if not millennia. In this respect, the absence of reference to water from say the Universal Declaration of Human Rights or the ICESCR seems to be a sleight of hand, an unconscious omission, rather than an exclusion of an intrinsically fundamental interest.[67] In retrospect, a decade or so of debate over the existence or contours of a right to water might seem puzzling, a storm in a teacup.

On the other hand, a closer examination of the debates around the right to water reveals a range of theoretical and conceptual issues that deserve closer inspection. Many of these dilemmas arise throughout the book, in somewhat paradoxical ways. There is minimalist concern that the right lacks sufficient political and environmental relevance on account of its narrow framing. And there is the maximalist worry that the right rides roughshod over difficult questions of prioritisation, economic resource allocation and extraterritoriality. In addition, General Comment No. 15 did not resolve all issues in theory and has faced its own share of critique; while the potential meanings of the right to water only become fully explicable when applied or claimed in a particular context.

In parsing thematic patterns in the book, this section examines associated moral and legal issues, concerns over economic feasibility, and the politics of policy and practice. In doing so, it also seeks to gesture at some of the general concepts associated with the term 'right to water'. However, like any other 'human right', the precise content of the right to water is, obviously and necessarily, the subject of political and legal contestation.

## 3.1 *Legitimacy*

### Justifying a Controversial Right

In political philosophy, the claim that water constitutes a 'human right' may be partly controversial. Along with other economic and social rights, some would consign it to the 'twilight world of utopian aspirations'.[68] However, mounting a moral case for a human right to water does not seem particularly

[66] These are defined as an adequate amount of safe water necessary 'to prevent death from dehydration, to reduce the risk of water-related disease and to provide for consumption, cooking, personal and domestic hygenic requirements'. See General Comment No. 15, para. 2.

[67] P. Gleick, 'The Human Right to Water', *Water Policy*, Vol. 1, No. 5 (1999), pp. 487–503.

[68] M. Cranston, 'Are There Any Human Rights?', *Daedalus*, Vol. 112, No. 4 (1983), pp. 1, 12.

challenging. Even if one begins with a rather classical and Lockean conception of rights,[69] which privileges negative freedoms such as life, liberty and property, it also assumes some pre-existing level of positive or social rights in order to ensure equal power relations in a state of nature.[70] Moreover, Locke himself included health amongst his preferred core rights, of which water is arguably a key element.[71] Indeed, the idea of a right to water could arguably extend back to twelfth- and thirteenth- century discussions, where 'one of the earliest examples offered was the *right* of those in dire need to receive aid from those in surplus'.[72]

Needless to say, there is a range of other philosophical theories that would give equal or more succour to the idea of a right to water. Sen's theory of *capabilities* includes freedom and 'opportunity to pursue our objectives'.[73] In his view, the idea of social rights meshes well with 'understanding the importance of advancing human capabilities'.[74] *Agency*-based accounts that move beyond mere personal autonomy and freedom rights also embrace a minimum provision of key resources. This is because many social rights are not only 'empirical' necessities, including for autonomy and freedom, but are 'logically' necessary since they are intrinsic to agency itself, the exercising of it.[75] *Needs*-based accounts are often invoked to support the right to water, on the 'belief that survival is good is virtually universal'.[76] Pogge takes a similar point of departure in a *justice-oriented* defence of rights. An 'internationally

[69] J. Locke, *Two Treatises of Government* (5th edn, London: Thomas Tegg, 1823). Locke describes a state of 'perfect equality' where 'all the power and jurisdiction is reciprocal, no one having more than another' (Part II, para. 4).

[70] Ibid., para. 7. Locke argues that everyone is 'born to all the same advantages of Nature'. But this assumption is difficult to sustain in a non-ideal world where individuals are born into households of different wealth, opportunity, geography and ethnicity and carry with them different markers of identity that can give rise to prejudice and discrimination. See discussion below on the role of water in Locke's work and the implications discussed by M. Risse, 'The Human Right to Water and Common Ownership of the Earth', *The Journal of Political Philosophy*, Vol. 22, No. 2 (2014), pp. 178–203.

[71] Ibid., para. 6. 'The state of Nature has a law of Nature to govern it, which obliges every one, and reason, which is that law, teaches all mankind who will but consult it, that being all equal and independent, no one ought to harm another in his life, health, liberty or possessions'.

[72] J. Griffin, *On Human Rights* (Oxford: Oxford University Press, 2008), p. 177. Emphasis added.

[73] A. Sen, *The Idea of Justice* (Cambridge, M.A.: Harvard University Press, 2009). Sen has been cautious as to precisely which capabilities are essential, and which capabilities are not rights, but rather primarily 'ethical affirmations' (see, pp. 358, 381). (In regard to capabilties, see also M. Nussbaum, *Creating Capabilities: The Human Development Approach* (Cambridge, M.A.: The Belknap Press of Harvard University Press, 2011).) Ibid., p. 381.

[74] Ibid., p. 381.

[75] J. Griffin, On Human Rights, pp. 180–181.

[76] J. O'Manique, 'Universal and Inalienable Human Rights: A Search for Foundations', *Human Rights Quarterly*, Vol. 12 (1990), pp. 465–485, at 437.

acceptable core criterion of basic justice' would be 'physical integrity, subsistence supplies (of food and *drink*, clothing, shelter, and basic health care), freedom of movement and action, as well as basic education, and economic participation'.[77] According to Pogge, these basic goods should be recognised human rights, but within 'limits' for 'what human beings truly need is secure access to a minimally adequate share of all these goods'.[78] Yet, another and popular approach is rooted in *human dignity*.[79] It is the experience of humiliation, domination, powerlessness and debasement that causes affront, and not simply material need or physical interference. Finally, more *constructivist* and *deliberative* accounts focus on the underlying logic that permeates international human rights law. Beitz, for example, defines human rights as 'requirements whose object is to protect *urgent* individual interests against certain predictable dangers … under typical circumstances of life in a *modern world* order composed of states' to which 'political institutions' must respond.[80]

Few philosophers have focused explicitly on human rights and water. One exception is Risse. He begins with a similar pragmatic approach as Beitz (human rights are universal and urgent moral demands),[81] but grounds universalism in the common ownership of natural water resources. The basic idea is that 'the earth originally belongs to humankind collectively, in the sense that all humans, no matter when and where they are born, must have some sort of symmetrical claim to it'.[82] From this, Risse builds a minimalist claim to common ownership: 'all co-owners ought to have an equal opportunity to satisfy basic needs to the extent that this turns on obtaining collectively owned resources'.[83]

The common thread in all these theories of rights is that they point in the direction of a highly circumscribed right to water: a moderate and non-comparative threshold, namely a minimum or, in most cases, adequate amount of water for each person. The standard controversies raised by many of these theorists around international human rights law would not seem to automatically apply: e.g., doubtful universality and utopian ambition. This is

77 T. Pogge, *World Poverty and Human Rights: Cosmopolitan Responsibilities and Reforms* (2nd edn, Cambridge: Polity Press, 2008), pp. 54, 55. Emphasis added. This is not unfamiliar to the approach of Sen, although Pogge is more interested in actual fulfilment of the rights not opportunities, drawing heavily on Rawl's primary goods (see J. Rawls, *Theory of Justice* (Oxford: Oxford University Press, 1999).

78 Ibid., 55.

79 J. Donnelly, 'Human Dignity and Human Rights', Working Paper, on file with authors.

80 C. Beitz, *The Idea of Human Rights* (Oxford: Oxford University Press, 2009), p. 109. Emphasis added.

81 Risse, 'The Human Rights to Water and Common Ownership of the Earth', p. 191.

82 Ibid., p. 187. 83 Ibid., p. 189.

because the universality of the right is clear (e.g. it is not a claim particular to modernity) and the substance of the claim is not expansive:[84] it is based on reaching a basic threshold, rather than eliminating relative disparities. Instead, the only criteria that would seem to be of direct relevance would be feasibility – the pragmatic concern in moral theory that some States might struggle to meet even this moderate expectation on account of economic and institutional constraints. Thus, it is not surprising that the debate and disagreement seems oriented towards more pragmatic concerns: the *intensity* of the obligation (e.g. immediate versus progressive realisation, the scope of extraterritorial obligations) and *means of implementation* (e.g. affordable water, privatisation, and permissibility of disconnections). Nonetheless, there have been a number of criticisms directed at the minimalist conception of the right, which are taken up below.

The other major debate has been the status of the right to water in *law*, rather than political philosophy. While it was relatively clear that some basic level of water supply was a constituent element of various human rights,[85] it was less clear if it was a self-standing, independent right. The question became particularly salient after the CESCR derived the right to water from the right to adequate standard of living in the ICESCR. Some scholars and States argued that deference should have been given to the State's omission of water in the drafting of the ICESCR.[86] Despite the various international declarations that gave support to the Committee's interpretive position, these critics emphasised the lack of State consensus at a number of international water meetings in the 1990s and early 2000s,[87] and the risk of inflation of human

[84] J. Nickel, 'Rights and Goals: Working Together?' in M. Langford, A. Sumner and A. E. Yamin (eds.), *The MDGs and Human Rights: Past, Present and Future* (Cambridge: Cambridge University Press, 2013), pp. 37–48.

[85] Access to water has been recognised as an element of other rights, such as health, housing and education: See Committee on Economic, Social and Cultural Rights, *General Comment 4, The right to adequate housing*, (Sixth session, 1991), UN Doc. E/1992/23, annex III at 114 (1991); *General Comment 13, The right to education* (Twenty-first session, 1999), UN Doc. E/C.12/1999/10 (1999); *General Comment 14, The right to the highest attainable standard of health* (Twenty-second session, 2000), UN Doc. E/C.12/2000/4 (2000). In addition, and as noted in section 1.1 above, both the CEDAW and the CRC refer to water in the context of other rights.

[86] S. Tully, 'A Human Right to Access Water? A Critique of General Comment No. 15', *Netherlands Quarterly of Human Rights*, Vol. 23 No. 1 (2005), pp. 35–63, M. Dennis and D. Stewart, 'Justiciability of Economic, Social, and Cultural Rights: Should There Be an International Complaints Mechanism to Adjudicate the Rights to Food, Water, Housing, and Health?', *American Journal of International Law*, Vol. 98 (2004), pp. 462–515.

[87] See e.g., Final Declaration, International Conference on Water and Sustainable Development, Paris, 21 March 1998; Ministerial Declaration of The Hague on Water Security

rights by using the right to adequate standard of living to transform a limitless number of goods into human rights. However, the bulk of scholarship has tended to lend support to the Committee's stance.[88] In any case, these debates over the status of the right to water in international law were largely quietened with the resolutions of the General Assembly and Human Rights Council in 2010.[89] This was enhanced by the adoption of the human right to water in many constitutions (see Figure 1.1 above) and policy frameworks.[90] Indeed, a few academics have even gone so far as to claim that the human right to water is now part of international customary law.[91]

Yet, the ease in which prevailing international conceptions of the right to water fit so neatly with many theories of human rights should raise some suspicion. As this book makes clear in some chapters, questions of culture and ambition cannot be entirely removed.

### Cultural Relativism

Paradoxically, the attempt to construct a minimalist version of the right to water raises questions about its cultural sensitivity. In some respects, this

in the 21st Century, The Hague, The Netherlands, 22 March 2000; Ministerial Declaration of the Third World Water Forum, Kyoto, 23 March 2003.

88 See S. Salman and S. McInerney-Lankford, *The Human Right to Water: Legal and Policy Dimensions* (Washington D.C.: World Bank, 2004), A. Cahill, 'The Human Right to Water – A Right of Unique Status: The Legal Status and Normative Content of the Right to Water', *International Journal of Human Rights*, Vol. 9 No. 3 (2005), pp. 389–410, S. McCaffrey, 'The Human Right to Water' in E. Brown Weiss, L. Boisson de Chazournes and N. Bernasconi-Osterwalder (eds.), *Fresh Water and International Economic Law* (Oxford: Oxford University Press, 2005), pp. 93–115, M. Craven, 'Some Thoughts on the Emergent Right to Water' in E. Reidel and P. Rothen (ed.) *The Human Right to Water* (Berlin: Berliner WissenschaftsVerlag, 2006), pp. 35–46; T. Kiefer and C. Brölmann, 'Beyond State Sovereignty: The Human Right to Water', *Non-State Actors and Intl L*, Vol. 5 (2005) p. 183; and M. Langford, 'Ambition that Overleaps Itself? A Response to Stephen Tully's "Critique" of the General Comment on the Right to Water', *Netherlands Quarterly of Human Rights*, Vol. 26, No. 3 (2006), pp. 433–459

89 See Section 1.1. 90 See Handbook on the Human Right to Water.

91 P. Thielbörger, 'Re-Conceptualizing the Human Right to Water: A Pledge for a Hybrid Approach', *Human Rights Law Review*, Vol. 15 (2015), pp. 225–249. Another argument could be that the core of the human right to water is recognised in international customary law: see M. Langford, F. Coomans and F-G. Issa, 'Extraterritorial Duties in International Law', in M. Langford, W. Vandenhole, M. Scheinin and W. Genugten (eds.), *Global Justice, State Duties: The Extraterritorial Scope of Economic, Social, and Cultural Rights in International Law* (Cambridge: Cambridge University Press, 2013), pp. 51–113. McGraw seems to make a similar argument. See G. McGraw, 'Defining and Defending the Right to Water and its Minimum core: Legal Construction and the Role of National Jurisprudence', *Loyala University of Chicago International Law Review*, Vol. 8 (2010–2011), pp. 127–204.

should not be surprising: 'every effort to impose a given set of values on the existing plurality of communities in the name of a common humanity is likely to be met with resistance on the grounds of its very own particularity'.[92] A number of authors such as *Van Koppen* and *Hellum*, are therefore critical of the narrow understanding of domestic uses. In some cultures and rural areas, water for livestock or kitchen gardening is prioritised above some of the household uses. Their studies suggest that further discursive space should be given at the domestic level for recognition of more contextual and enhanced versions of a right to water.[93]

Other scholars warn that a rights conception may not fully incorporate these alternative and community-based visions of water use. In the field of water, it has been claimed that 'individualistic, anthropocentric, state-centric' human rights have blinded organisations from 'thinking about new community economies'.[94] It is not simply a question of re-jigging or contextualising the list of water uses to be recognised as basic in a particular context. Rather, there needs to be a recognition that communal systems of water supply and water-based production may operate on a different logic, which may be both reciprocal and contextual. This challenge is highlighted in particular in chapters by *Van Koppen*, *Hellum*, *Derman* and *Manzungu*, and *Singh*, which discuss how template-like water systems easily falter because they fail to understand local context.[95] At a minimum, there remains a risk that the right to water legitimates dominant frames and forms of water provision, rather than empowers individuals and communities to access water in a manner that is culturally and contextually appropriate. Otherwise, one may pay insufficient attention to localised understandings of development, in what post-developmentalists decry as the 'merciless war against the age-old traditions of communal solidarity'.[96]

[92] J. Bartelson, *Visions of World Community* (Cambridge: Cambrige University Press, 2009), 2. The cultural critique of human rights has a long pedigree. See, e.g., The Executive Board, American Anthropological Association, Statement on Human Rights, American Anthropologist, New Series, Vol. 49, No. 4, Part 1 (1947), pp. 539–543; and more recently, S. Hopgood, *The Endtimes of Human Rights* (Ithaca: Cornell University Press, 2014).

[93] See also P. Parmar, 'Revisiting the Human Right to Water', *Feminist Law Journal*, Vol. 28, No. 1 (2008), pp. 77–96.

[94] K. Bakker, 'The Commons Versus the Commodity', p. 447.

[95] The CESCR does note the importance of ensuring access to water to realise the right to adequate food, as well as means of subsistence, such as subsistence farming and securing the livelihoods of indigenous peoples (see General Comment No. 15, para. 7). And, in the context of rural water supply, common theoretical space may exist, however, between societal choice and the right to water, as discussed later by Hope.

[96] M. Rahnema, 'Introduction' in M. Rahnema and V. Bawtree (eds.), *The Post-Development Reader* (1997), pp. ix–xix, ix–xix.

As to the right to sanitation, questions of culture loom even larger. In the chapter by *Langford, Bartram and Roaf*, the authors note that many of the arguments for a right to sanitation are connected to contemporary and highly modernist understandings of health and the environment. This right may slide less easily into the various moral theories of rights outlined above. However, the dignitarian and utilitarian arguments for the right to sanitation (particularly on the grounds of gender and environmental health) may be sufficient to overcome the concern that this right lacks a sufficient universalist character. It was introduced into the Millennium Development Goals (MDGs) largely on these grounds. Nonetheless, the challenge of implementing this right is illustrated by the low priority it is given in both public discourse and fiscal investment.

### Thicker Claims: Equitable Allocation

Another challenge to the thin conception of the right to water comes from theories of rights based on social relations. Substantive and thicker distributive concerns are often washed out in theories of human rights due to their methodological universalism. The subject is the individual human being. By contrast, in other theories of rights, the subject is social: the individual as a member of polity. In these normative 'citizenship' theories, the point of departure is the relations and interdependence of individuals, whether nationally or globally. This has consequences for how the right to water might be viewed both morally *and* legally.

Citizenship rights approaches are equally diverse as human rights and some are particularly conditional or somewhat specious.[97] The more compelling and relevant theories are grounded in equality of status, egalitarian luck and State legitimation. In Marshall's well-known account, the objective is to achieve an equality of status, though not necessarily equality of outcomes.[98] This means moving beyond 'the right to a modicum of economic welfare' towards a full 'share' in the 'social heritage', such that all individuals could 'live the life of a civilized being'.[99] Equally influential is Rawl's distributive theory of justice (at the domestic level), which is based on egalitarian luck

[97] More limited or specious types might include theories rooted in the patriotic building of national identity; family-like reciprocity; compensatory justice for the undervalued productive contributions; and the self-interest for the privileged in social cooperation. For a critique of each, see C. Fabre, *Social Rights under the Constitution* (Oxford: Oxford University Press, 2000), pp. 57–65.

[98] T. H. Marshall, 'Citizenship and Social Class' in T. H. Marshall (ed.), *Class, Citizenship and Social Development* (Westport: Greenwood Press, 1964), pp. 3–51.

[99] Ibid., p. 72.

(the unfairness of the birth lottery) and State legitimation (citizens should benefit from compliance with authority).[100] From this, Rawls derives not only a constitutional right to a social minimum, but a distribution principle, which constrains inequities in 'primary goods' to those feasible distributions that maximise the rights of the most disadvantaged. At the global level, Caney has invoked egalitarian luck to argue for a global and comparable adequate standard of living.[101]

The shared characteristic in these perspectives is that they pay particular attention to *relative* differences in living standards. Yet, this focus on disparities is only partly captured in standard human rights conceptions. Equality is usually constrained to *formal discrimination* or *substantive inequality*, with reference to various prohibited grounds (e.g., race, religion, political opinion etc.). Substantive equality certainly provides a focus on disparities (in effort and outcomes), but in relation to reaching a certain threshold. Thus, the human right to water is often used as an analytical frame to reveal the inequities concerning a minimum or adequate level of clean water. For example, in one Tanzanian district, researchers found that many of the 358 water points built between 2006 and 2009 were in villages where the national coverage threshold was already met, while a significant number of under-served villages received little or no attention in the programme.[102]

However, citizenship-based approaches highlight *broader disparities*[103] and tend to demand more of the State or society in the level of access to various primary goods. This is because they carry some notion of inter-personal fairness. Indeed, citizenship rights are often invoked to critique the minimalism of human rights.[104] But can this approach be incorporated into

[100] J. Rawls, *A Theory of Justice* (Cambridge M.A.: Colombia University Press, 1971). Note that Rawls does not conflate rights and inequality concerns unlike Marshall.

[101] S. Caney, 'Global Interdependence and Distributive Justice', *Review of International Studies*, Vol. 31, No. 2 (2005), pp. 389–399.

[102] A. Jiménez and A. Pérez-Foguet, 'Building the Role of Local Government Authorities Towards the Achievement of the Human Right to Water in Rural Tanzania', *Natural Resources Forum*, Vol. 34, No. 2 (2010), pp. 93–105, at 96–97.

[103] The clear exception here is gender equality where States are bound to reduce disparities between women and men: see Article 3 of the ICCPR and ICESCR, which explain that State parties are to undertake to ensure the equal right of men and women to the enjoyment of all civil and political rights, and economic, social and cultural rights, respectively.

[104] See, e.g., A. Fischer, 'The Political within the Depoliticised: Poverty Measurement, Implicit Agendas and the MDGs' in M. Langford, A. Sumner and A. E. Yamin (eds.), *The MDGs and Human Rights: Past, Present and Future* (Cambridge: Cambridge University Press, 2013), pp. 119–142; T. Mkandawire, *Targeting and Universalism in Poverty Reduction*, Social Policy and Development Programme Paper No. 23, United Nations Research Institute for Social Development, December 2005.

human rights? It might be possible to fold in some aspect of inter-personal relations. The most promising way forward would be through human dignity. It does take into account social relations.[105] Yet, it is unclear how far the concept of human dignity can be stretched in order to include broader notions of fairness, rather than the narrower inter-personal experiences of shame, humiliation and worthless.[106]

It could be asked though what would a citizenship rights perspective contribute to the right to water and is it recognised in positive law? As to content, there are two possible implications. The first approach is to conceive of a more expansive content for the right to water and include productive uses. This would include water for the production of food and the securing of livelihoods to maintain an adequate standard of living. Given that domestic uses of water account for a tiny fraction of water consumption across the world (5 per cent of total water use in developing countries and 15 per cent in developed countries),[107] such an approach would permit the right to water to speak to the broader water-related challenges of marginalised individuals and groups to foster a more inclusive socio-economic society.

However, such a concept of the right to water is difficult to operationalise in law at a global or even national level. This is because there is extremely wide variance in direct demand for water. Compare, for instance, the needs of farmers with urban dwellers. This suggests that the CESCR was prudent in limiting the *availability* of the water supply to be 'sufficient for personal and domestic uses'.[108] The Committee defends its interpretation on the grounds that it is the only means of making the right coherent at an international (and probably national) level. However, the Committee notes that larger quantities of water may be justified for *other* rights as is conditionally necessary.[109] If water is needed for food production, this should be resolved in connection

[105] S. Liebenberg, 'The Value of Human Dignity in Interpreting Socio-Economic Rights', *South African Journal of Human Rights*, Vol. 21 No. 1 (2005), pp. 1–31.

[106] O. Schachter, 'Human Dignity as a Normative Concept', *American Journal of International Law*, Vol. 77 No. 4 (1983), pp. 848–854.

[107] UNDP Human Development Report, *Beyond Scarcity: Power, Poverty and the Global Water Crisis* (New York: UNDP, 2006), p. 138; M. Falkenmark, 'Meeting Water Requirements of an Expanding World Population', *Philosophical Transactions of the Royal Society of London*, Vol. 352 (1997), pp. 929–936.

[108] General Comment No. 15, para. 2.

[109] 'Water is required for a range of different purposes, besides personal and domestic uses, to realize many of the Covenant rights. For instance, water is necessary to produce food (right to adequate food) and ensure environmental hygiene (right to health). Water is essential for securing livelihoods (right to gain a living by work) and enjoying certain cultural practices (right to take part in cultural life)'. Ibid., para. 6.

with the right to food according to the Committee, and in this book, *Winkler* investigates and defends this interpretation.

The second approach inspired by citizenship rights is to focus on equity. This would highlight inequity within a society in access to water. In this book, the chapters addressing agriculture (*Van Koppen*), occupation (*El Jazairi*) and urban access (*Dugard, Langford and Anderson*) reveal remarkable disparities in availability and access across income, ethnic and geographic stratifiers. In many of these instances, individuals are able to access a basic or even adequate amount of water but other groups have so disproportionately more that the question of equity becomes unavoidable. *Van Koppen* notes that in the Olifants basin, in South Africa, a mere 0.5 per cent of the population (large-scale registered water users) used 95 per cent of the water resources.

Does international human rights law incorporate this perspective? It would be hard to argue that it is included in a non-comparative adequate standard of living unless viewed in a global perspective, as Caney suggests. However, the ICESCR does incorporate aspects of a citizenship rights perspective in the second part of Article 11.1 as well as Article 12. Following the recognition of the right to an adequate standard of living is the right to the *continuous improvement* of living conditions in Article 11; while Article 12 provides for the right to the *highest attainable* standard of health. In its general comments, the CESCR has chosen not to make a literalist interpretation of these two provisions, which is not surprising given that both provisions have been castigated for their excessive maximalism.[110] Instead, the Committee has relied on notions of equity and disparity in giving more subtle meaning to these provisions. In interpreting the right to the continuous improvement of living conditions, it states that 'States parties must give due priority to those social groups living in unfavourable conditions by giving them particular consideration. Policies and legislation should correspondingly not be designed to benefit already advantaged social groups at the expense of others'.[111] Likewise, in its general comment on the right to health, it invokes relative difference as an interpretive technique: 'Equity demands that poorer households should not be disproportionately burdened with health expenses as

[110] M. Cranston, 'Are There Any Human Rights?', *Daedalus*, Vol. 112, No. 4 (1983), pp. 1–17, 13; J. Nickel, *Making Sense of Human Rights* (Malden, Mass: Blackwell Publishing, 2007), 139; J. Griffin, *On Human Rights* (Oxford: Oxford University Press, 2008), 208.

[111] *General Comment 4, The Right to Adequate Housing* (Sixth session, 1991), UN Doc. E/1992/23, annex III at 114 (1991) (CESCR), para. 11.

compared to richer households'.[112] However, the Committee's articulation of this duty as an immediate and core obligation is clearly problematic.

A close examination of General Comment No. 15 reveals that the Committee has travelled partly down this hermeneutic road in relation to the right to water. It interprets the minimum core obligation as requiring a fair institutional arrangement: 'equitable distribution of all available water facilities and services'.[113] The idea that this constitutes a core obligation is rightly controversial, but the idea that there should be narrowing in differences over the basic infrastructure in providing water may arguably be consistent with dignity (think about the indignity of always using an outside tap in a developed economy) if not the right to continuous improvement. Moreover, according to the Committee, the duty to ensure affordable water contains an explicit and similar equity requirement: 'poorer households should not be disproportionately burdened with water expenses as compared to richer households'.[114]

The Committee also focused on the distribution of water resources although here the Committee seems to have a threshold in mind, rather than disparities. In articulating the obligation to protect, the CESCR requires the State to act against private actors to prevent them 'from denying equal access to adequate water; and polluting and inequitably extracting from water resources, including natural sources, wells and other water distribution systems'.[115] And, in articulating the water dimensions of the right to food, its principal emphasis is on equity, as well as non-discrimination in the fostering of basic living standards and the realisation of other rights: 'Attention should be given to ensuring that disadvantaged and marginalized farmers, including women farmers, have equitable access to water and water management systems, including sustainable rain harvesting and irrigation technology'.[116] However, it is difficult to interpret the last statement and it may questionably suggest an overly transformative approach that seeks to tackle deeper structural inequities in access to water supply in agricultural production.

[112] *General Comment 14, The right to the highest attainable standard of health* (Twenty-second session, 2000), UN Doc. E/C.12/2000/4 (2000) (CESCR), para. 12(b).

[113] General Comment No. 15, para. 37(e). (This provision is often criticised.)

[114] Ibid., para. 27. (Certain elements of this paragraph are also often critiqued) Arguably, however, such an approach underpins Smets' quantification of 'affordability' through a cross-country comparison of household water bills to disposable income.

[115] Ibid., para. 23.

[116] Ibid., para. 7.

### 3.2 *Determinacy and Feasibility*

Despite these critiques of the narrowness of the right to water, there remain a number of issues concerning its determinacy and feasibility. It has been claimed that social rights are *indeterminate* since there 'is no universal and non-arbitrary standard for distinguishing need from luxury' and thus it is equally difficult to adduce what a minimum or adequate level of the rights may be.[117] Added to this are worries by some that it can be difficult to identify who is the relevant duty bearer and that social rights lack justiciable qualities. As one critic states: 'We normally regard claims or entitlements that nobody is obligated to respect and honour as null or void, indeed undefined' and that 'abstract rights to goods and services' fall squarely in this category.[118]

Worries about *feasibility* are premised instead on the concern that social rights might demand significant resources. According to sceptics, implementation is enormously complex and carries with it both actual and opportunity costs: 'Enacting entitlements to goods at taxpayer expense has produced exploding costs and a raft of perverse incentives. It is the concept of a right to such goods that gives rise to those and other ill effects'.[119] These concerns can be salient in many discussions over the right to water, particularly in relation to questions as to how access to affordable water might be provided and how quickly implementation of the right might be achieved.

This section examines whether it is possible to discern meaningful and feasible entitlements and obligations in light of international law. It is by no means exhaustive, nor does it provide a comprehensive overview of the debates surrounding the right. Rather the section constitutes a brief overview of key aspects of the right and provides a linkage to many of the discussions in this book.

#### Availability

The 'content' of the right to water in terms of the object of the State's duties has been disaggregated in General Comment No. 15 according to a number of constituent elements: *availability*, *quality* and *accessibility*. Adequacy for

[117] D. Kelley, *A Life of One's Own: Individual Rights and the Welfare State* (Washington, D.C.: Cato Institute, 1998), p. 16.

[118] O. O'Neill, 'The Dark Side of Human Rights', *International Affairs*, Vol. 81 (2005), pp. 427–439, at 430, 428.

[119] D. Kelley, *A Life of One's Own*, p. 12.

'human dignity, life and health' is said by the Committee to require these elements even if these dimensions vary according to context.[120]

The CESCR refrained from indicating a figure for what would constitute available water at the point of consumption. Yet, they acknowledged that some individuals may require more water due to health, climate and work conditions. The only principal guide was a pointer to World Health Organization (WHO) guidelines and the referencing of two expert papers. The first paper by Howard and Bartram ranks different quantitative standards according to the seriousness of health threats. At the extreme, 7.5 litres per capita per day was permissible for some priority uses – consumption (hydration and food preparation) and basic hygiene.[121] A higher amount of 20 litres per person per day would expand the uses, but was considered to result in high health risks. Fifty litres was instead judged as reducing health risks to a low level, while 100 to 200 litres was viewed as optimal access.[122] The second paper by Gleick simply recommends a basic water requirement of 50 litres per person per day.[123] Other water experts, such as Falkenmark, have promoted 100 litres based on global water availability and human needs.[124]

From a feasibility perspective, the main challenge is fiscal and technical. The amount of water needed to fulfil each individual's right to water (whether 7.5, 25, 50 or 100 litres) constitutes such a small portion of domestic water resources meaning that a race to the bottom of water supplies is unlikely to take place as the realisation of the right gradually occurs. In most countries, a higher figure should therefore be achievable, subject to financial resources, although in some water-scarce or climate-stressed countries and water-scarce areas of States, more modest figures may be justifiable.

The more challenging question may be determinacy. The precise figure for the right to water has been the subject of significant contestation at the

[120] General Comment No. 15, paras. 11–12.

[121] G. Howard and J. Bartram 'Domestic Water Quantity, Service Level and Health' (2003) WHO WHO/SDE/WSH/03.02. This was based on estimates of lactating women who engage in moderate physical activity in above-average temperatures. The volume does not account for health and well-being activities outside normal domestic use. The paper also notes that defining a minimum quantity of water for basic needs 'has limited significance as the volume of water used by households depends on accessibility as determined primarily by distance and time, but also including reliability and potentially cost' [Executive Summary].

[122] Note that this figure of 100 litres has been used by some human rights groups such as Amnesty: *Troubled Waters Palestinians Denied Access to Fair Water* (London: Amnesty International, 2009), pp. 4, 86.

[123] This includes drinking water for survival, water for human hygiene, water for sanitation services and modest household needs for preparing food. P. Gleick, 'Basic Water Requirements for Human Activities: Meeting Basic Needs', *Water International*, Vol. 21 (1996), pp. 83–92.

[124] Falkenmark, 'Meeting Water Requirements of an Expanding World Population', pp. 929–936.

national level. The *Mazibuko* case in South Africa, discussed by *Dugard, Langford and Anderson*, concerning the right to water in the constitution is a good example.[125] Residents of Soweto claimed that the national minimum of 25 litres per person per day was too low and, in the alternative, that failure by the City of Johannesburg to increase the amount was unreasonable given its fiscal resources. The Constitutional Court rejected both claims and found 25 litres was not unreasonable. Yet, other jurisdictions reveal rather different results. For example, Argentinean courts have ordered 200 litres a day must be provided directly to residents until piped water systems were extended and environmental pollution halted.[126]

### Quality

As to the quality of water[127] needed to meet the right to water, General Comment No. 15 explains that water for personal and domestic uses must be safe – meaning free from 'micro-organisms, chemical substances and radiological hazards that constitute a threat to a person's health'. Recognising cultural dimensions and possibly customary tests for water quality, the water must also be of acceptable colour, odour and taste.[128] States are then referred to the WHO Guidelines for Drinking-Water Quality, which are now in their fourth edition.[129] The guidelines set out requirements for ensuring drinking water safety, including both procedures and specific guideline values. While unlike the availability or quantity standard of the right to water, which is the subject of significant commentary, this aspect of the right generally remains less contested. In many countries, in practice, however, the right to water has provided both a useful political and judicial platform from which to challenge levels of pollution in particular water sources.[130]

[125] *Mazibuko et al v. City Of Johannesburg et al* Constitutional Court of South Africa (8 October 2009), (Case CCT 39/09); *Mazibuko et al* v. *City of Johannesburg et al* The Supreme Court of Appeal of South Africa Case No. 489/08 (25 March 2009); *Mazibuko et al* v. *City Of Johannesburg et al* High Court of South Africa (Witswatersrand Local Division) (30 April 2008) Case No 06/13885.

[126] *Quevedo Miguel Angel y otros c/Aguas Cordobesas S.A. Amparo*, Cordoba, City, Juez Sustituta de Primera Instancia y 51 Nominación en lo Civil y Comercial de la Ciudad de Córdoba (Civil and Commercial First Instance Court), 8 April 2002. See also R. Picolotti, 'The Right to Safe Drinking Water as a Human Right', *Housing and ESC Rights Quarterly* No. 1 (2005), pp. 1–4.

[127] Falkenmark, 'Meeting Water Requirements of an Expanding World Population', pp. 929–936.

[128] CESCR General Comment No. 15 paragraph 12(b).

[129] *Guidelines for Drinking-Water Quality*, 4th edition (Geneva: WHO, 2011).

[130] See Section 3.3 below.

A number of chapters address the subject of pollution. This includes chapters on transboundary water resources, development cooperation, and country chapters on South Africa, Zimbabwe and India. Moreover, a key cause of contamination is inadequate sanitation, which is addressed in about a third of the chapters. At the same time, Falkenmark has been at pains to point out that quality is a function of both water contamination and availability.[131] All of these aspects are dramatically illustrated in the case of Gaza, taken up in the chapter on the Occupied Palestinian Territory. On one hand, the Palestianian authorities in Gaza have failed to regulate drilling down to the aquifer, which has led to sea-water intrusion and a rise in salinity. On the other hand, over-usage and sewage infiltration of freshwater resources has been driven by Israeli policies that prevented the development of alternative water supplies (such as desalination plants, wastewater treatment for re-use, and bulk water importation) and catalysed the 'near collapse' of wastewater treatment plants.

**Accessibility**

The accessibility standard of the right to water can be broken down into spatial, economic, equality and informational components. The Committee avoided the temptation to require water to be physically accessible within a home or institution, but required that water be within 'safe physical reach' of every household, educational body and workplace. The technologies and services providing such water must be 'culturally appropriate and sensitive to gender, life-cycle and privacy requirements'.[132] Research from WHO, referenced in the General Comment, suggests that if water access points are more than a kilometre away (or 30-minute round trip), then securing 20 litres per person per day is not possible. Basic access is therefore considered to be within the one kilometre (or 30-minute round trip) mark; intermediate access 'on-plot' with a yard tap; and optimal access 'in house' via taps.[133]

Economic accessibility is perhaps the mostly widely misunderstood aspect of the right to water. There is sometimes the mistaken belief that it means the provision of free water. General Comment No. 15 in fact provides that water is to be affordable, including the direct and indirect costs and charges with securing it. Affordability is not defined in any quantitative sense, but is framed

[131] In the transboundary context, see also Chapter 5, as well as S. McCaffrey, *The Law of International Watercourses* (2nd edition, Oxford: Oxford University Press, 2007) for further examples.

[132] CESCR General Comment No. 15, para. 12(c)(i).

[133] G. Howard and J. Bartram, *Domestic Water Quantity, Service Level and Health* (Geneva: WHO, 2003).

by reference to the costs of securing other human rights.[134] In other words, households must not be forced to make trade-offs between basic water and food consumption, schooling for children and basic medical costs.

The importance of affordability had been recognised in a long line of international standards, and high prices of water create unacceptable spending choices for the poor.[135] For example, in 2014, it was alleged that African American residents of Detroit in the United States were forced to make impossible choices between paying their water bill or paying their rent. Two UN independent experts urged that the 'unprecedented scale of shut-offs' were disproportionately affecting the poor and violating their basic human rights.[136]

The question has also taken on a political character due to the privatisation of water services in a range of countries and cities. As *Peterson* analyses in his chapter, Argentinean NGOs and the State itself relied on this dimension of the right to water to defend a post-economic crisis freeze on water price increase in an investment dispute with the company, Suez.[137] Moreover, *Dugard, Langford and Anderson* reveal with statistical analysis that many South African municipalities, with high numbers of poor communities, possessed the resources to provide more affordable water.

Two streams dominate discussion of this standard – the first is focused on defining the parameters for affordability in terms of expenditure on water for personal and domestic uses. At the international level, affordability is often loosely defined as not spending more than about 3 to 5 per cent of disposable household income on water. The chapter by *Smets* in this volume provides an inductive development of standards that results in a more sophisticated approach to measuring affordability in different country contexts.

The measurement of affordability took on certain prominence in the aftermath of the MDGs. The affordability criterion in the Millennium Declaration target was dropped in the subsequent goals without explanation.

[134] CESCR General Comment No. 15, paragraph 12(c)(ii) states 'Water, and water facilities and services, must be affordable for all. The direct and indirect costs and charges associated with securing water must be affordable, and must not compromise or threaten the realization of other Covenant rights'.

[135] COHRE, SDC, AAAS and UN-Habitat, *Manual on the Right to Water and Sanitation* (Geneva: COHRE, 2007); H. Smets, *De l'eau potable à un prix abordable* (Paris: Johanet, 2009).

[136] See UN News Centre 'In Detroit, city-backed water shut-offs "contrary to human rights," say UN Experts', 20 October 2014 online at www.un.org/News.

[137] *Suez, Sociedad General de Aguas de Barcelona S.A., and Vivendi Universal S.A. (Claimants) and The Argentine Republic (Respondent); AWG Group (Claimant) and The Argentine Republic (Respondent)*, ICSID Case No. ARB/03/19, Decision on Liability, 30 July 2010.

It was later argued by one of the architects that this was done because affordability could not be measured.[138] However, this omission seems statistically questionable, if not normatively troublesome. At a regional level, the Organisation for Economic Co-operation and Development (OECD) analysed household water expenditure against income across a range of OECD countries.[139] Hutton undertook a comprehensive global study demonstrating that basic data sets for measuring affordability can be generated.[140] The inclusion of an affordability criterion in Goal 6, Target 6.1 in the 2015 SDGs re-opened the possibility for measurement.[141] However, the susbequent approach to indicator selection has been reductionist and there is no proposed indicator for affordability.[142] *Smets'* work on setting normative thresholds provides one potential way to set targets with the data analysed in the abovementioned studies, but it appears that the effective implementation of water affordability global targeting will remain an outstanding challenge.

The second concern with affordability is how to accomplish this in practice, particularly for poor sections of the population. Methods designed to accomplish this for lower income households may include the adoption of low-cost technologies, cross-subsidisation from other users, or income supplements. In reality, and particularly in informal settlements, the cost of accessing water sometimes consumes a large share of household budgets. Consumption of basic water is highly price inelastic.[143] The poor must purchase water regardless of the expenditure consequences and any national affordability

[138] J. Vandemoortele, 'The MDG Story: Intention Denied', *Development and Change*, Vol. 43, No. 1 (2011), pp. 1–21, at 4.

[139] OECD, *Social Issues in the Provision and Pricing of Water Services* (Paris: OECD, 2003). Fankhauser and Tepic undertook a similar analysis that includes Eastern European countries where they found that poorer households in some countries expended high amounts on water services (see S. Fankhauser and S. Tepic, 'Can Poor Consumers Pay for Energy and Water? An Affordability Analysis for Transition Countries', *Energy Policy*, Vol. 35 (2005), pp. 1038–1049.

[140] G. Hutton, 'Monitoring "Affordability" of Water and Sanitation Services after 2015: Review of Global Indicator Options' (A paper submitted to the UN Office of the High Commissioner for Human Rights, 20 March 2012) .

[141] See Open Working Group of the General Assembly on Sustainable Development Goals (A/68/970) p. 11. Goal 6 is to 'Ensure availability and sustainable management of water and sanitation for all'. Target 6.1 states 'By 2030, achieve universal and equitable access to safe and affordable drinking water for all'.

[142] M. Langford, 'Lost in Transformation? The Politics of the Sustainable Development Goals', *Ethics and International Affairs*, Vol. 30, No. 2 (2016), pp. 167–176.

[143] See Fankhauser and Tepic, 'Can Poor Consumers'; A. Jansen and C. Schulz (2006), Water Demand and the Urban Poor: A Study of the Factors Influencing Water Consumption among Households in Cape Town, South Africa, Working Paper Series in Economics and Management No. 02/06, University of Trømso.

standard.[144] Thus, the use of the term 'having access' to water to cover people who spend a significant proportion of their income on it represents a narrow understanding of the concept.[145]

An issue related to improving the affordability (and availability) of water is the installation and use of prepaid meters as a cost recovery and sustainability mechanism, particularly in high-density, low-income areas. Instead of receiving water on credit and risking running up bills that cannot be paid, consumers purchase water in advance of receiving it. In some localities, consumers may receive an allocated amount of water free, or considerably below cost, and then be required to pay for any additional amount upfront. Often the initial amount provided makes it challenging to meet personal and domestic water needs, particularly for larger households, and consumers are unable to afford to purchase more on credit. The situation obviously worsens with an increased prevalence of disease in such areas (thereby necessitating higher water needs), and often fails to take into account water for emergency uses. However, litigation on the subject has resulted in diverse outcomes. In the United Kingdom, the Court of Queen's Bench held that automatic cut-offs of the water supply upon the exhaustion of credit in a prepaid meter was inconsistent with the statutory requirement of notice before disconnection.[146] In South Africa, the Constitutional Court came to a different result. Not only did it define a cut-off as a 'temporary suspension' rather than a statutory-controlled 'discontinuation', the Court cited the public policy of 'administrative sustainability' to dismiss the practicality of a rights-based procedure: 'It would require the municipality to give advance notice and an opportunity to be heard, possibly several times a month or more to every person who has a pre-paid meter installed.'[147]

The right to water must be realised *without discrimination*. This guarantee is explicitly included in Article 2(2) of the ICESCR and the listed prohibited grounds of discrimination are race, colour, sex, language, religion, political or other opinion, national or social origin, property, birth or other status.[148]

144 For an overview of national and international standards, which are often based on proportion of budget used for water consumption, see M. Krause, *The Political Economy of Water and Sanitation*.

145 P. Anand, *Scarcity, Entitlements, and the Economics of Water in Developing Countries* (Cheltenham: Edward Elgar, 2007), p. 89.

146 *R* v. *Director of Water Services, ex parte Lancashire County Council, Liverpool City Council, Manchester City Council, Oldham Metropolitan Borough Council, Tameside Metropolitan Borough Council and Birmingham City Council* [1999] Env LR 114; [1998] EWHC 213 (QB).

147 *Mazibuko and Others* v. *City of Johannesburg and Others* 2010 (4) SA 1 (CC); 2010 (3) BCLR 239 (CC), paras. 120, 123, 122.

148 The ground of other status has been to interpreted to include age, disability and nationality amongst others: see Committee on Economic, Social and Cultural Rights, *General Comment*

The Committee has interpreted this provision to require that the steps taken must not only not discriminate on their face against an individual or group, but they must be sufficiently oriented towards realising the rights of disadvantaged groups defined by these grounds of discrimination.[149]

The non-discrimination dimension of accessibility requires water to be accessible to all, including the most vulnerable or marginalised sections of the population, in law and in fact, without discrimination on prohibited grounds. States are particularly urged to take steps to remove any existing discrimination and should pay special attention to groups who have historically faced difficulty exercising the right, such as women, children, individuals living in rural areas and informal settlements, indigenous peoples, travelling peoples and refugees and internationally displaced persons.[150]

Many authors in this book take up this dimension of the right to water. *Lovera* provides a historical perspective on discrimination in water rights against indigenous peoples in Chile – reflecting on the cascade of various structural and legal changes that have emasculated effective access to water resources. *Hellum* analyses both direct and indirect forms of discrimination against women and children and argues that specialised UN bodies have largely failed to understand these dynamics in the case of the right to water. It is also important to underscore that issues of discrimination and equality can be prominent in developed States. The discourse of right to water has been mobilised in attempts to improve their access. Examples include indigenous communities in North America, as well as Roma communities in Eastern Europe. The right to seek and receive information concerning water issues can be particularly useful in this regard.

### Obligation of Progressive Realisation

For those unfamiliar with international legal jurisprudence on social economic and rights, an initial perception might be that a human right to water was commensurable with its sister development targets.[151] Target 7.C of the MDGs contained the resolution by States to 'halve, by 2015, the proportion of the population without sustainable access to safe drinking water and basic

No. 20, *Non-Discrimination in Economic, Social and Cultural Rights (art. 2, para. 2)*, (Forty-second session, 2009) UN Doc E/C.12/GC/20 (2009).

[149] General Comment No. 20, ibid. [150] General Comment No. 15, paras. 12(c)(iii), 16

[151] This has even been done by human rights lawyers at times: see P. Alston, 'Ships Passing in the Night: The Current State of the Human Rights and Development Debate Seen Through the Lens of the Millennium Development Goals', *Human Rights Quarterly*, Vol. 27, No. 3 (2005), pp. 755–829.

sanitation'. Some viewed the MDGs as ambitious, whether globally[152] or for particular countries.[153] Thus, the equating of them with the demands of human rights might appear unreasonable.

However, some criticised the MDG targets for their lack of ambition[154] and the water target itself was met in 2010.[155] A more ambitious goal is present in the new Sustainable Development Goals (SDGs). Target 6.1 provides that States will, 'By 2030, achieve universal and equitable access to safe and affordable drinking water for all'.[156] Here, there might be concerns about conflating a political commitment with a human right, particularly for States facing resource constraints, armed conflict or the consequences of climate change. These concerns might be amplified if the right to water was seen to oblige severely resource-constrained States to reach such targets *immediately*. Not only would it impose impossible or politically unrealistic demands, it would provide little utility in guiding policy and budgetary allocations.

Human rights are rarely framed though in absolute terms. Economic, social and cultural rights, in particular, have been nested in a graduated fashion in international law – the right to water is subject to *progressive* realisation. The key international treaty, the ICESCR, provides that States undertake to take steps, individually and through international assistance and co-operation to achieve progressively the full realisation of the rights using the maximum available resources.[157] Recognition of the right to water does not necessarily result in an immediate obligation to ensure that everyone living within a State

[152] M.A. Clemens, C. J. Kenny and T. J. Moss, *The Trouble with the MDGs: Confronting Expectations of Aid and Development Success* 2 (Washington D.C., Center for Global Development, Working Paper 40, 2004).

[153] See J. Vandemoortelle, *MDGs: Misunderstood Targets* (Brasilia: UNDP International Poverty Centre, 2007) and M. Langford, *Human Rights and MDGs in Practice: A Review of Country Strategies and Reporting* (Geneva: UN OHCHR, UNICEF, NCHR, 2008).

[154] See, e.g., T. Pogge, 'The First UN Millennium Development Goal: A Cause for Celebration?'. in A. Føllesdal and T. Pogge, *Real World Justice: Grounds, Principles, Human Rights, and Social Institutions* (Berlin: Springer, 2005), pp. 317–338. For a history of the critiques of the water target, see M. Langford and I. Winkler, 'Muddying the Water? Assessing Target-Based Approaches in Development Cooperation for Water and Sanitation', *Journal of Human Development and Capabilities*, Vol. 15, Nos. 2–3 (2014), pp. 247–260.

[155] WHO/UNICEF Progress on Sanitation and Drinking Water – 2015 Update and MDG Assessment (2015) foreword); See also UNICEF/WHO, *Millennium Development Goal drinking water target met: Sanitation target still lagging far behind*, Joint News Release, 6 March 2012.

[156] *Transforming our World: The 2030 Agenda for Sustainable Development*, A/Res/70/1.

[157] International Covenant on Economic, Social and Cultural Rights Article 2(1): 'Each State Party to the present Covenant undertakes to take steps, individually and through international assistance and co-operation, especially economic and technical, to the maximum of its available resources, with a view to achieving progressively the full realization of the rights

has access to basic water. It is accepted that in many countries full realisation may not be achievable in a short span of time. Thus, it *may* be possible for a significant portion of a State's population to be without access to basic amounts of water and yet no human rights violation may have occurred.[158]

In his chapter, *Hope* takes up this tension between economics and human rights and explores the utilitarian scepticism towards a deontological approach of rights. His approach of social choice veers towards that of authors who claim that it is possible to combine the strengths of each approach, for instance, arguing that human rights provides the normative standards while economics provides the tools for choice-making and trade-offs.[159]

While the terms 'progressive realization' and 'maximum available resources' appear to provide States with considerable flexibility, these standards are circumscribed. The CESCR has interpreted the duty to take steps towards full realisation to mean that States are to move as 'expeditiously and effectively as possible towards that goal'[160] with 'deliberate, concrete and targeted steps'.[161] States are to make use of all appropriate means, including legislative measures, as well as administrative, financial, educational and other social measures.[162] These somewhat nebulous adjectives have been endowed with some concrete substance by the Committee in three ways.

First, States must demonstrate *sufficient progress* over time and the Committee has evinced a strong tendency to expect higher standards from States with greater economic resources.[163] Each State appears before the Committee approximately every five years and attempts were made to institute a more rigorous system of benchmarking, whereby the Committee

recognized in the present Covenant by all appropriate means, including particularly the adoption of legislative measures'.

158 Therefore, it has been argued that determinations as to whether the MDG targets or progress under them are consistent with international human rights obligations can only be made in light of the country context. See M. Langford, 'A Poverty of Rights: Six Ways to Fix the MDGs', *IDS Bulletin*, Vol. 41, No. 1 (2010), pp. 83–91. J. Bartram reaches a similar conclusion on water and sanitation from a developmentist and incrementalist perspective: see, 'Improving on Haves and Have-Nots', *Nature*, Vol. 452 (20 March 2008), pp. 283–284.

159 D. Seymour and J. Pincus, 'Human Rights and Economics: The Conceptual Basis for their Complementarit', *Development Policy Review*, Vol. 26, No. 4 (2008), pp. 387–405.

160 Committee on Economic, Social and Cultural Rights, *General Comment* 3, *The Nature of States Parties' Obligations*, (Fifth session, 1990), UN Doc. E/1991/23, annex III at 86 (1991), para. 9.

161 Ibid., paras 1, 2. General Comment No. 15, para. 17.

162 ICESCR Article 2(1); CESCR General Comment No. 3 para. 7.

163 See analysis of concluding observations in see M. Langford and J. King, 'CESCR: Past, Present and Future', in Langford (ed.), *Social Rights Jurisprudence: Emerging Trends in International and Comparative Law* (Cambridge: Cambridge University Press, 2008), pp. 477–516.

and States are to agree on benchmarks to be met within the next period. In some less developed and conflict-affected States, it is clear that greater time is needed to fully and effectively reach all individuals. Even if corruption, clientism and discrimination were removed, challenges would still remain in ensuring proper information flows in planning and monitoring, addressing sustainability concerns in design, and dealing with rapidly expanding populations.[164]

Second, the failure to meet the *minimum essential level* of the right is said to require strong justification by the State. In legal terms, a government carries the burden of proof to demonstrate that resources are not available from domestic or international sources for reaching this minimum immediately.[165] In situations where resources are severely limited, the State is still to aim for the widest possible enjoyment of the right and ensure that the most vulnerable members of society are protected, through for example, the adoption of relatively low-cost targeted programmes.[166]

Third, *retrogressive measures*, which would entail a general reduction in availability, accessibility or quality of water, similarly require high levels of justification. States carry the burden of proof to demonstrate that such measures were necessary.[167] Indeed, there is evidence that States are not using their maximum available resources towards improving access to water and sanitation. Two authors recalculated the MDG rankings of country progress

[164] Jiménez and Pérez-Foguet, 'Building the Role of Local Government Authorities', pp. 98–102.

[165] More specifically, they state: '[T]he Committee is of the view that a minimum core obligation to ensure the satisfaction of, at the very least, minimum essential levels of each of the rights is incumbent upon every State Party. Thus, for example, a State Party in which any significant number of individuals is deprived of essential foodstuffs, of essential primary health care, of basic shelter and housing, or of the most basic forms of education is, prima facie, failing to discharge its obligations under the Covenant. In order for a State Party to be able to attribute its failure to meet at least its minimum core obligations to a lack of available resources it must demonstrate that every effort has been made to use all resources that are at its disposition in an effort to satisfy, as a matter of priority, those minimum obligations. *General Comment No. 3, The nature of States parties' obligations*, (Fifth session, 1990), UN Doc. E/1991/23, annex III at 86 (1991), para. 10.

[166] CESCR General Comment No. 3, paras. 11, 12. For sceptical views on the utility of this doctrine, see K. Young, 'A Concept in Search of Content', *The Yale Journal of International Law*, Vol. 33 (2008), pp. 113–175. For strong defences of the minimum essential level, see D. Bilchitz, *Poverty and Fundamental Rights: The Justification and Enforcement of Socio-Economic Rights* (Oxford: Oxford University Press, 2007) and for the use of a range of minimum core obligations as the dominant framework, see A. Chapman and S. Russell, (eds.), *Core Obligations: Building a Framework for Economic, Social and Cultural Rights*, (Antwerp/Oxford: Intersentia, 2002).

[167] CESCR General Comment No. 15, para. 19.

by adjusting for a range of resources relevant to the provision of water and sanitation.[168] They found that many low-income countries improve their ranking, while a range of middle-income countries fall significantly.

However, there remains an ongoing debate on the consequences of fiscal investments in social rights.[169] As an example, a former IMF economist found that once the State expands beyond promoting negative rights (such as liberty and property) to more positive welfare rights, economic growth is lower.[170] However, the method is partly questionable. He takes the budget size as a proxy for social rights despite many countries allocating significant portions, and in many cases, the overwhelming share, of their budgets to other issues. This conflation has been avoided in other studies. Comparing 128 States in the 1990s and 2000s, and with arguably a better measure of social rights,[171] two scholars established that there is no simple linear relationship. A minority of States managed to achieve and maintained a virtuous cycle of high growth and high social rights realisation; the bulk of States achieved neither, and a small minority achieved only one of these outcomes.[172] Moreover, as the chapter on sanitation discusses, there is significant evidence of national economic gains from investments in water and sanitation.

[168] E. Anderson and M. Langford, *A Distorted Metric: The MDGs, Human Rights and Maximum Available Resources*, SSRN Working Paper (2013). The resource variables are GDP; ratio of 'disposable national income' (DNI) to GDP; total population (millions); land area (km$^2$); urbanisation (percentage of total population); and the dependency ratio (the share of population aged 15–64 to the sum of the shares aged 0–14 and 65+).

[169] A. McKay and P. Vizard, 'Rights and Economic Growth: Inevitable Conflict or "common ground"?', Rights in Action/ODI, London, 2005.

[170] J.-P. Chauffour, *The Power of Freedom, Uniting Human Rights and Development* (Washington D.C.: CATO Publishing, 2009).

[171] Chauffour, also assumed that the size of the budget corresponds to social rights, which is very problematic. Non-social rights expenditures can be highly significant in some countries (e.g. defence spending).

[172] S. Randolph and P. Guyer, 'Tracking the Historical Evolution of States' Compliance with their Economic and Social Rights Obligations of Result: Insights from the Historical SERF Index', *Nordic Journal of Human Rights*, Vol. 30, No. 3 (2012), pp. 297–323, 319–321. For social rights outcomes they use their Social and Economic Rights Fulfilment Index (SERF Index) data, which adjusts human development outcomes for a State's resources in accordance with the requirement that a State uses its maximum available resources in accordance with Article 2 of the ICESCR. For similar results, see M. Cichon, W. Scholz, A. v. d. Meerendonk, K. Hagemejer, F. Betranou and P. Plamondon, *Financing Social Protection* (Geneva: ILO/ISSA, 2004), and D. Brady, *Structural Theory and Relative Poverty in Rich Western Democracies, 1969–2000*, Luxembourg Income Study, Working Paper Series, Working Paper No. 407 (2005).

### Spectrum of Duties

In addition, this general legal obligation of taking steps has been conceptually sliced according to the nature of the behaviour that is required by States.[173] The first duty in this tripartite vision is the obligation to *respect*, which requires States to abstain from harmful behaviour that interferes directly or indirectly with the rights. The Committee has indicated that it requires, for example, refraining from arbitrarily interfering with traditional water allocation arrangements,[174] unlawfully polluting waters or limiting access to water services as a punitive measure. Various due process elements are built into this obligation elsewhere in General Comment No. 15. For example, disconnection of water must be substantively justified, alternatives must be investigated and legal remedies should be provided.[175]

The second is the obligation to *protect*, which requires States to prevent third parties, such as corporations or other entities, from interfering with individuals' enjoyment of the right to water. Establishing regulatory systems to prevent privately generated pollution or private water utilities compromising access to water is mentioned as an example of the steps required. The Committee made no statement for or against privatisation, but did outline various conditions to be in place prior to its occurrence.[176] The third is the obligation to *fulfil*. This requires States to adopt the necessary measures directed towards the full realisation of the right to water through, for example, adoption of a national water strategy and plan of action and its implementation.[177] The basic principles for national implementation are also set out, including participation in policy making and the establishment of systems of monitoring and accountability.

### Extraterritoriality

What is less clear or perhaps more controversial in international law is the extent of such obligations in an extraterritorial context – where the acts or

[173] Caution needs to be exercised with placing all State obligations within one of the above categories. For sceptical views of the utility of this division see I.E. Koch, 'Dichotomies, Trichotomies or Waves of Duties?', *Human Rights Law Review*, Vol. 5 (2005), pp. 81–103 or warnings about it's overuse see M. Langford and J. King, 'CESCR: Past, Present and Future', in Langford, *Social Rights Jurisprudence*, pp. 477–516, at 484–486.

[174] This is a concern in a number of African countries as Hellum shows in this volume. Moreover, the current UN Special Rapporteur has recently criticised Nigeria for criminalising abstraction of water from natural sources: *Nigeria: When the State Fails to Provide Water, Fetching Water Should Not Be a Criminal Act*, Press Release, 28 February 2017.

[175] CESCR General Comment No. 15, para. 56.

[176] Ibid., para. 24. See further Part III of the book.

[177] General Comment No. 15, paras 20–29.

omissions of a State occur or have effects outside a State's territory.[178] The Committee sets out a number of extraterritorial obligations on the right to water based on the trichotomy of respect, protect and fulfil.[179] The potential application of these duties in the case of transboundary watercourses, climate change, international development cooperation and situations of occupation are taken up in different chapters in this book. With the exception of the latter, these chapters illustrate that not only is the extent of any such extraterritorial obligations not clear, or lacking determinacy in theory, but the feasibility of demonstrating a violation is even more challenging in practice, due to issues of causation, attribution and apportionment, amongst others.

If one returns to the voting record for the 2010 General Assembly Resolution, a number of the forty-one abstentions were developed countries, including upstream States, suggesting, at least, perhaps some perceived concern about extraterritorial implications stemming from the right to water in a transnational or international context. Recalling that lack of access to adequate water for personal and domestic uses is often an internal State governance matter, *Russell* and *McCaffrey*, *Darrow* and *Khalfan* seem to agree that in a non-occupational context, moving along the spectrum of duties, - from the obligation to respect, to protect, to fulfil, - the strength of any extraterritorial element decreases. Thus, while States likely have an obligation to respect the right to water of individuals living in other States and to do no harm or cause damage beyond areas of national jurisdiction, it is much less likely that an obligation to fulfil the right to water reaches so far, though disagreement peeks through the three chapters. (In the occupational context, *El Jazari* notes, however, that under international humanitarian law, an occupying power, such as Israel, is generally responsible for the welfare of civilians and thus must ensure that those living in occupied territory are able to access basic necessities, including water.)

If a violation of any extraterritorial duty is thought to exist, the chapters by *Russell* and *McCaffrey*, *Darrow* and *Khalfan* discuss the challenges of demonstrating causation resulting from such a harm, as well as challenges of attribution and apportionment of responsibility. Whilst it naturally depends on the

[178] See for example, F. Coomans and M. Kamminga, *Extraterritorial Application of Human Rights Treaties* (Antwerp: Intersentia 2004); S. Skogly, *Beyond National Borders: States' Human Rights Obligations in International Cooperation* (Antwerpen; Intersentia, 2006); Langford, Vandenhole, Scheinin and Genugten, *Global Justice, State Duties: The Extraterritorial Scope of Economic, Social, and Cultural Rights in International Law*; G. Nystuen, A. Føllesdal and O. Mestad (eds.), *Human Rights, Corporate Complicity and Disinvestment* (Cambridge: Cambridge University Press, 2011).

[179] General Comment No. 15, paras. 30–36.

extent and complexity of transnational catchment area, these causation and attribution challenges tend to be even more troublesome in the climate and development context. Given this litigious reality, both *Russell* and *McCaffrey*, and *Darrow*, focus on the space for complementarity and mutual reinforcement between the inter-State environmental regimes – be it water-courses or climate – and the right to water; which in turn may have more traction in influencing policy and practice.[180]

### 3.3 *The Politics of Practice*

In light of the above, it is arguable that the right to water possesses a significant degree of hermeneutic determinacy and economic and institutional feasibility – at least as compared to many other human rights. Yet, the greatest and ultimate challenge possibly lies elsewhere. The politics of practice surrounding the right to water is central in many of the chapters. These concerns cut across the key focus areas of water allocation, accessibility, and urban and rural water reform. Two questions are central. What are the factors necessary to overcome political barriers and does the invocation of the right to water help in this regard?

A central puzzle is the extent to which a mere change in discourse, whether in law, politics or organisational culture, is sufficient to trigger change. Some scholars claim that discursive turns, including to rights, can inflect or even transform social and institutional behaviour. At the social level, it may change the meanings of acceptable conduct or invalidate certain types of reasons or positions in deliberation.[181] This inter-personal shift may be reinforced at the individual level whereby a social norm is 'acculturated' and a person's 'background' opinion changes.[182] In the case of the human right to water, this discursive effect is an important form of politics. Some claim it has been significant in countering hegemonic narratives that only place value on water's economic value or excessively privilege efficiency concerns in policy

[180] For a related book see T.S. Bulto, *The Extraterritorial Application of the Human Right to Water in Africa* (Cambridge: Cambridge University Press, 2014).

[181] See, e.g., A. Lanni, 'The Expressive Effect of the Athenian Prostitution Laws', *Classcial Antiquity*, Vol. 29, No. 1, pp. 45–67; R. McAdams, 'An Attitudinal Theory of Expressive Law', *Oregon Law Review*, Vol. 79 (2000), pp. 339–390; V. Schmidt, 'Discursive Institutionalism: The Explanatory Power of Ideas and Discourse', *Annual Review of Political Science* Vol. 11 (2008), 303–326.

[182] See respectively, R. Goodman and D. Jinks, 'Incomplete Internalization and Compliance with Human Rights Law', *European Journal of International Law*, Vol. 19, No. 4 (2008), pp. 725–748 and Schmidt, 'Discursive Institutionalism', ibid. 'By acculturation, we mean the general process by which actors adopt the beliefs and behavioural patterns of the surrounding culture': Goodman and Jinks, ibid., p. 726.

trade-offs.[183] It reframes what constitutes acceptable behaviour, particularly on issues of access and affordability.[184] Nonetheless, it is acknowledged that the relevance and power of the right will vary according to the receptivity of rights and their potential utility in different national, sectoral, local and community contexts.[185]

Other scholars begin from a more cautious standpoint, arguing that human rights norms only become effective when backed by some material advantage or threat[186] or political action and alliance-building.[187] As the presence of these factors tends to be contingent, care should be taken about over-estimating the effects of singular rights strategies. In-depth studies on the impact of strategies on economic, social and cultural rights certainly gravitate towards such nuanced conclusions.[188] The book's chapters tend to support this latter perspective. The broader political economy of human rights cannot be ignored. Discursive shifts may be necessary rather than sufficient conditions for social change. What is needed is concrete avenues to claim the human right to water or the mobilisation of political, institutional or economic support for such claims. Thus, while the right to water provides both symbolic and institutional resources, the diverse constellations of actors and institutions with their varying interests and discourses condition outcomes.

### Global Level

At the global level, the language of the human right to water has been creatively mobilised by actors to support claims in the development context. It has been prominent in efforts by European trade unions and civil society

[183] See, e.g., J. Wills, *Contesting World Order* (Cambridge: Cambridge University Press, 2016), chapter 5.

[184] L. Harris, L. Rodina and C. Morinville, 'Revisiting the Human Right to Water from an Environmental Justice Lens', *Politics, Groups and Identities*, Vol. 3, No. 4, pp. 660–665.

[185] Compare, for example, S. Robins, *Revolution to Rights in South Africa: Social movements, NGOs and Popular Politics after Apartheid* (London: James Currey, 2008) and M. Mutua, *Human Rights NGOs in East Africa: Political and Normative Tensions* (Philadelphia: University of Pennsylvania Press, 2008).

[186] J. Goldsmith and E. Posner, *The Limits of International Law* (New York, Oxford University Press, 2005).

[187] B. Simmons, *Mobilizing for Human Rights: International Law in Domestic Politics* (New York, Cambridge University Press, 2009).

[188] See Gauri and Brinks (eds.) *Courting Social Justice*; M. Langford, B. Cousins, J. Dugard and T. Madlingozi (eds.), *Socio-Economic Rights in South Africa: Symbols or Substance?* (Cambridge, Cambridge University Press, 2014); P. Gready (2009). 'Reasons to Be Cautious about Evidence and Evaluation: Rights-based Approaches to Development and the Emerging Culture of Evaluation'. *Journal of Human Rights Practice*, Vol. 1, No. 3 (2009), pp. 380–401.

organisations to change European development policy.[189] Within the UN system, some experts have mobilised the human right to water in efforts to try to ensure that measurement of access to water properly captures elements of discrimination, quality and affordability.[190] (Such a strategy may have further value given that multi-donor approaches to development programming in the water sector are becoming increasingly common.) Inter-agency initiatives on water and sanitation have adopted rights language and a sub-set of them with a number of traditional development NGOs even joined human rights organisations to create the Global Campaign on the Right to Water and Sanitation in Palestine.[191] Efforts to integrate the right to water have also extended to international economic law and adjudication. *Peterson* notes how human rights considerations, including the right to water, have been raised by States, as well as civil society organisations, in defence of their treatment of foreign owned water utilities.

Yet, the penetration of a right to water discourse is limited. It was thought that mention of the right may have been avoided at times by other actors, including for example States, perhaps to avoid any potential claims of extraterritorial reach, or perceived political intrusion into the affairs of other States, particularly in relation to development assistance.[192] In regard to the SDGs, the language of human rights was somewhat whitewashed from the substantive sections and perhaps unsurprisingly Goal 6 only partly reflects the substance of the right to water.[193] Further, the more demanding aspects of the right for middle- and upper-income countries are not included despite the universality principle that is central to the SDGs and which envisages them as global goals.[194] Beyond achieving basic access to water and sanitation, the bulk of the targets are dedicated to water resource efficiency concerns.[195]

[189] See e.g. www.right2water.eu

[190] See WHO and UNICEF, *Joint Monitoring Programme Working Group on Equity and Non-Discrimination: Final Report*, 2012; WHO and UNICEF, *Joint Monitoring Programme: Consolidated Proposal on Post-2015 Drinking-Water, Sanitation and Hygiene Indicators, Targets and Definitions*, 2013.

[191] M. Langford, *The Right to Water and Sanitation in Development Cooperation: The State of Play and the European Union*, Briefing Paper, European Parliament, November 2012, EXPO/B/DROI/2011/26.

[192] See more generally, A. Russell, 'International Organizations and Human Rights: Realizing, Resisting or Repackaging the Human Right to Water', *Journal of Human Rights*, Vol. 9 (2010), pp. 1–23, at 11.

[193] This is despite the fact that in the 2030 Agenda for Sustainable Development itself, States reaffirmed 'commitments regarding the human right to safe drinking water and sanitation' (para. 7).

[194] See discussion of the various but unsuccessful proposals in M. Langford and I. Winkler, 'Muddying the Water?'.

[195] M. Karunananthen,'Is the UN Turning Its Back on the Human Right to Water?', *The Guardian*, 19 June 2014.

This challenge becomes even more apparent when examining policy programmes. *Khalfan* asserts that donors and multilateral agencies need to move beyond 'rights based approaches' simply tacked-on to existing approaches to development, towards a serious legal analyses of human rights, including the right to water, in relation to financial and technical cooperation.[196] Others note that attempts to make EU development programmes on water more policy coherent have only resulted in technical adjustments, rather than the use of democratic norms and the human right to water to develop more transformative approaches.[197] Moreover, there has only been a lukewarm response to repeated resolutions by the European Union Parliament, which has urged the need to prioritise the human right to water in development assistance and avoid idealogically driven approaches to the choice of public or private forms of water delivery. While many development agencies dropped privatisation conditionalities for water sector funding in the mid-2000s, little priority has been given to water in financial allocations by many European national development agencies and the European Commission itself.[198] Likewise, while the treaty obligations of States to protect the right to water have been acknowledged in international investment treaty adjudication, their substantive impact on decisions is constrained by a strong countervailing emphasis on the duty of States to accommodate the rights of foreign investors in regulation in the water sector.[199]

### Domestic Level

Turning to the domestic level, the chapters indicate how the right to water has been mobilised in discourse, litigated in court and embedded in policy. The intention behind many of these manoeuvres is not simply an attempt to affirm or implement the right. Rather it is to change the political context for

[196] See also Russell, 'International Organizations and Human Rights: Realizing, Resisting or Repackaging the Human Right to Water', pp. 15–17.

[197] H. Koff, and C. Maganda, 'The EU and the Human Right to Water and Sanitation: Normative Coherence as the Key to Transformative Development', *European Journal of Development Research*, Vol. 28, No. 1 (2016), pp. 91–110.

[198] M. Langford, *The Right to Water and Sanitation in Development Cooperation.*

[199] See *Suez, Sociedad General de Aguas de Barcelona S.A., and Vivendi Universal S.A. (Claimants) and The Argentine Republic (Respondent); AWG Group (Claimant) and The Argentine Republic (Respondent)*, ICSID Case No. ARB/03/19, Decision on Liability, 30 July 2010 and *Suez, Sociedad General de Aguas de Barcelona S.A., and InterAgua Servicios Integrales del Agua S.A. (Claimants) and The Argentine Republic (Respondent)*, ICSID Case No. ARB/03/17, Decision on Liability, 30 July 2010, para. 262.

water policy. As to discourse, the right to water has been particularly mobilised in attempts to stop privatisation, while the right to sanitation has often been invoked in attempts to increase financial resource allocation. In recent years, the rights have been invoked in more diverse settings. Amnesty International, for example has, foregrounded the rights to water and sanitation in their campaigns on the rights of slumdwellers.

However, it is the merging of these frames with concrete political and policy action that has tended to prove more successful. For example, activists and advocates have also sought to utilise the opportunities offered by courts and other monitoring institutions. There have been successful cases on access to communal water reserves (Botswana),[200] halting of privatisation (Germany),[201] protection of groundwater resources (India) and remedial access to water supplies (Argentina). Yet, success has been varied. Applicants have lost in challenges to pre-paid meters and restrictive free water policies (South Africa),[202] initial challenges to privatisation (Indonesia),[203] and attempts to ensure prior and informed consent over use of water resources in indigenous territories (Chile).[204] The reasons for such losses have been varied, but in many instances it cannot be attributed to a poorly framed or substantiated case. Some courts appear reluctant, perhaps for cultural or strategic reasons, to develop their doctrinal understanding or exercise a stronger standard of review.

Yet, success in court is not necessarily correlated with impact on policy and practice. Politics becomes particularly salient in determining what happens outside the courtroom. In Nepal, advocates scored a strong victory on water quality in a major river, but senior judges soon tired of trying to enforce the order in the face of a government unwilling to tackle large polluters.[205] In the above South African case, advocates secured most of their demand on account of their accompanying political and media campaign and the legitimacy and self-confidence they built up from the successful decisions in lower courts.[206] Thus, a successful decision is not necessarily a necessary or sufficient condition for achieving change on the ground. Although it may build the jurisprudential basis for future litigation and create symbolic effects of its own.[207]

[200] C. Morinville and L. Rodina, 'Rethinking the Human Right to Water: Water Access and Dispossession in Botswana's Central Kalahari Game Reserve' *Geoforum*, Vol. 49 (2013), pp. 150–159.

[201] See Chapter 13. [202] See Chapter 7. [203] See Chapter 14. [204] See Chapter 3.

[205] Interview with Director of Pro Public, 20 November 2013. [206] See Chapter 7.

[207] See, e.g., S. Halliday and P. Schmidt, *Human Rights Brought Home: Socio-Legal Perspectives on Human Rights in the National Context* (Oxford: Hart, 2004).

**Democratising Politics**

An important claim about the contribution of the human right to water right is its democratic quality. A strong emphasis in General Comment No. 15 is on participation in decisions affecting the water sector. Thus, many chapters highlight the utility of the right from a more participatory perspective. For example, from a gender perspective, *Hellum*, argues that the right to water, and other rights, can affirm the importance of female leadership in water management, noting this to be central theme in gender and development research. The chapter on sanitation highlights the way in which the right to sanitation has been mobilised to increase participation in decision-making on sanitation in India. It also cites the Porto Alegre case in Brazil where participatory budgeting approaches led rapidly to full coverage of households in access to water and sanitation. *Singh* also details the drastic consequences when participation is not incorporated in policy and programmes. Even if water may be provided to communities, the right is not realised as the form of access is not culturally appropriate.

However, there are clear limits in seeking to improve participation in decision-making processes. These might be reasons of political control (exclusion of ethnic minorities, women), rent extraction (corruption or profitmaking), ideological (fear of alternative policy options) or geography (remote communities). *Cullett* charts all of these factors in India from the national to the local level. He argues that national government has promoted a model of supply that is overly reliant on cost recovery while local power dynamics disenfranchise women and others from participation in these policy processes. From an indigenous peoples' perspective, *Lovera*, notes that this lack of participation or recognition of participatory rights in decisions over natural resources, constitutes one of the main challenges for indigenous peoples in Chile. *Derman* and *Manzungu* argue that this perspective should be placed within a political ecology perspective, which identifies the interplay between political power and natural resources.

## 4 CONCLUSION: PROSPECTS FOR THE RIGHT TO WATER

What prospects does the future hold for the human right to water? On one hand, they seem relatively bright. The right to water (together with sanitation) has attained rapidly international legal recognition and has been integrated in the discourse and practices of multiple actors, from local civil society organisations through to some international organisations. While the privatisation debate continues to divide various actors, the enhanced pragmatism by international donors and experts has provided some space for new thinking around policy. The appointment of a UN Independent Expert, now Special Rapporteur, in 2007 also provided an international institutionalised mechanism to bolster this diffusion effect. At the domestic level, there has been a significant increase in strategic litigation on the right to water – both at the individual and collective level. There is also some evidence in this book and elsewhere that suggests right to water-based mobilisation, advocacy and policy has achieved material impacts under certain conditions.

The growing influence of the right to water is implicit in Goal 6 of the SDGs. A number of the targets directly incorporate a rights perspective, notably:

> 6.1 By 2030, achieve *universal* and *equitable* access to safe and *affordable* drinking water for all
> 6.2 By 2030, achieve access to *adequate* and *equitable* sanitation and hygiene for *all*, and end open defecation, paying special attention to the needs of women and girls and those in vulnerable situations
> 6.3 By 2030, improve water *quality* by reducing pollution, eliminating dumping and minimising release of hazardous chemicals and materials, halving the proportion of untreated wastewater, and substantially increasing recycling and safe reuse globally
> 6.4 By 2030, substantially increase water-use efficiency across all sectors and ensure sustainable withdrawals and supply of freshwater to address water scarcity, and substantially *reduce the number of people suffering from water scarcity* [and]
> ...
> 6.b Support and strengthen the *participation* of local communities for improving water and sanitation management[208]

The rights-sensitivity of the Goal 6 targets arguably provides a basis for actors to mobilise politically for their realisation,[209] and the concerted engagement by members of the water community with the human rights community should certainly be encouraged. However, as noted above, at present, indicators narrow the quantitative thrust of the right with no allowance for affordability or regularity in the indicator, while it is unclear on which basis the targets will be disaggregated according to different grounds of discrimination. Furthermore, the accountability mechanisms for the new agenda overall are likely to be weak, although they may be bolstered by the inclusion of Goal 16,

[208] Emphasis added.
[209] V. Gauri, *MDGs that Nudge: the Millennium Development Goals, Popular Mobilisation and the Post-2015 Development Framework*, Working Paper, World Bank, 2012.

which amongst other endeavours, aims 'to provide access to justice for all and build effective, accountable and inclusive institutions at all levels'.[210] Moreover, in light of the success of the MDGs in generating new data, and the UN Secretary-General's call for a data revolution, the SDGs should generate improved capacity for monitoring of the right.

That said, the current situation is also rather sobering. First, the scale of the supply-side challenges is rising just as some of the demand-side institutional constraints are being overcome. We now face a perfect storm of declining water reserves, rising contamination and climate change challenges. The question is no longer one simply of distribution, but also availability. Realising the right to water in the future will need to be intimately connected to advances in environmental protection.

Second, and relatedly, the slow progress on realising the right to sanitation is somewhat alarming.[211] While it has been argued that progress would be even worse without the international recognition of sanitation as a global target and right in the 2000s,[212] the rate of investment in sanitation is remarkably low. As discussed, this has particular consequences for the right to water.

Third, an equally persistent challenge is discrimination in access to water in high-income and middle-income States. Certain groups are constantly marginalised. This *problematique* is unlikely to be resolved by the new SDGs, despite the requirement that they be universally applicable to all countries, as well as Goal 10 that aims to 'reduce inequality within and among countries'. The threshold for realisation remains low and exclusion from adequate access to water – whether in Russia, Hungary, the United States, Vietnam or Israel – will continue to fly under the radar of the international agenda. Paradoxically, the calmer waters in the privatisation debate have reduced the mobilising force of the right to water as a global discourse.

Despite these challenges, it is important to take stock of the progress that has been made, particularly over the last decade and half, in accelerating

[210] For a general discussion of accountability issues, see K. Donald and S-A. Way, 'Accountability for the Post-2015 Sustainable Development Goals: A Lost Opportunity?', *Ethics and International Affairs*, Summer 2016.
Target 16.3 aims to promote the rule of law at the national and international levels, and ensure equal access to justice for all. Target 16.6 aims to develop effective, accountable and transparent institutions at all levels. Target 16.7 aims to ensure responsive, inclusive, participatory and representative decision-making at all levels. Target 16.b aims promote and enforce non-discriminatory laws and policies for sustainable development.

[211] See Chapter by Langford, Bartram and Roaf.

[212] See M. Langford and I. Winkler, 'Muddying the Water?'.

international recognition, discussion and reflection on the subject of the right to water. While deep integration of right to water in policies and practice has still a long way to go,[213] it is hoped that the chapters in this book will contribute to shaping the growing body of critical research around this right.

[213] P. Gready and W. Vandenhole, 'Failures and Successes of Human Rights-Based Approaches to Development: Towards a Change Perspective', *Nordic Journal of Human Rights*, Vol. 32 No. 4 (2014), pp. 291–311.

# 1

# Water Allocation

2

# Water Allocation, Customary Practice and the Right to Water

## *Rethinking the Regulatory Model*

BARBARA VAN KOPPEN*

### 1 INTRODUCTION

There is a remarkable gap between the growing global consensus to recognise access to water for basic domestic uses as a human right (or 'the right to water') and 'water rights' in the sense of the plural legal frameworks that factually govern people's negotiated claims to water of a certain quantity and of a certain quality at a particular place and time. This gap is unfortunate because the progress made by governments in realising the right to water for basic domestic needs, as well as other rights, such as sanitation, food and livelihoods, risks being jeopardised by those same governments' legislative reforms.

Over the past two decades, many countries have adopted new water laws, which tend to strengthen one particular model of allocation, namely administrative permit systems (or license, water right or concession systems). These laws generally prescribe that all earlier water uses under different systems must be 'regularised' or 'converted' into the updated permit system within one or two years. Contemporary water law reform commenced with Chile (Water Code of 1981) and was followed elsewhere in Latin America (for example, Mexico's National Waters Law of 1992) and throughout Sub-Saharan Africa, e.g., in Mozambique, Uganda, Ghana, Tanzania, Zimbabwe, South Africa, Kenya, Burkina, and Swaziland.[1]

* PhD. Principal Researcher International Water Management Institute, Southern Africa Regional Program, Pretoria, South Africa.

[1] The laws are respectively National Waters Law of 1992 (Mozambique), Water Statute 1995 (Uganda), Water Resources Commission Act 1996 (Ghana), Water Resources Management Act of 2009 and 1997 and 2002 Amendments to Water Ordinance (Control and Regulation) Act No. 42 of 1974 (Tanzania), Water Act No 31/1998 (Zimbabwe), National Water Act 1998 (South Africa), Water Act 2002 and 2016 (Kenya), Loi d'oriéntation relative a la gestion de l'eau 2001 (Burkina Faso), Water Act 2002 (Swaziland).

Global institutes such as the World Bank, Food and Agricultural Organization (FAO) and Global Water Partnership (GWP) promoted permit systems as a component of the broader reform package of integrated water resource management (IWRM). At least until the mid-2000s, it was expected that permit systems would ensure 'more efficient and better allocation of water resources' and thus the 'most beneficial use of available water resources, satisfying the public interest in the best way'.[2] These proponents focused on the regulatory dimensions of permits, meaning that the State can enforce conditions tied to permits. On their face, these reforms appear consistent with the right to water. For instance, one international official, who has worked on many such schemes, has stated that 'contemporary water rights allocation legislation appears to facilitate more than constrain' an approach based on the right to water since the 'top priority' in the licensing of water abstractions is given to vital human needs.[3]

However, GWP, FAO and others have increasingly acknowledged that permit systems are more complex and do not always function as planned.[4] Even stronger, as argued in this chapter, the entitlement dimensions of permit systems imply that the imposition of one single formal law annuls customary law. Moreover, both the design and implementation of permit systems relegate small-scale users' claims to water to a secondary status. Permit systems may work for well-organised formal water economies of large-scale users, such as governmental and parastatal service providers, private water companies, hydropower agencies, industries, mines and large irrigation estates. However, in agrarian, low- and middle-income countries, this large-scale formal sector represents the numerical minority of total water users. The majority are informal and small scale, largely operating outside the ambit of the State.[5] Water supply for basic domestic and productive needs is typically governed by

[2] See Global Water Partnership (GWP), Toolbox 2006, available at www.gwpforum.org; World Bank, 'Staff Appraisal Report, Tanzania', in *River Basin Management and Smallholder Irrigation Improvement Project*, Report No. 15122-TA (Washington: Agriculture and Environment Operations, Eastern Africa Department 1996); H. Garduno, *Water Rights Administration: Experiences, Issues, and Guidelines*, FAO Legislative Study No. 70. (Rome: FAO, 2001).

[3] S. Burchi, 'A Human Right to Water Perspective of Contemporary Domestic Water Resources Allocation Legislation', Presentation at the International Conference on the Right to Water and Sanitation, Oslo, 26–27 November 2008.

[4] GWP Toolbox 2008; S. Burchi, personal communication, 26 November 2008.

[5] T. Shah, 'Issues in Reforming Informal Water Economies of Low-income Countries: Examples from India and Elsewhere', in B. van Koppen, J. Butterworth and M. Giordano (eds.), *Community-based Water Law and Water Resources Management Reform in Developing Countries* (Oxford: CABI Publishers, 2007), pp. 65–95.

self-supply under customary law, especially in rural and peri-urban settings, where low-income families often depend upon water, in multiple ways, for diversified agriculture-based livelihoods. Yet, under recent reforms, customary or 'informal' water laws have been superseded on paper by administrative permits. The entitlement dimensions of administrative permit systems typically favour wealthier users who are administratively proficient, rather than poorer users. In addition to ignoring the legal system of customary rights under which many water users realise their human rights to water and food, permit systems also often fail to foster transformatory and effective State regulation of water allocation and pollution.

This chapter sets out to explore the contradictions and potential synergies between different paradigms of allocative water use. It begins in Section 2 by exploring the substantive disconnect between global/national and local understandings of water priorities, also providing a critical perspective of a narrow definition of the right to water for domestic uses only, ignoring vital productive water uses. It partly does so by highlighting an emerging approach of 'multiple-use water services' (MUS) and seeks to demonstrate how such a re-conception of prioritised uses can better help realisation of rights to water and food.

Section 3 then turns to permit systems and the manner in which entitlements are conceived. Here a tension is exhibited between global water reform models that encouraged this device and the consequences for universal human rights and customary water practices.[6] Permit systems create formal legal claims to use water while maintaining the State as owner of the nation's water resources. In historical perspective, the underlying rationale of permit systems in Africa and Latin America was dispossession rather than distribution. Their origins lie in the Roman Empire and European colonisation. Today's reforms unwittingly risk finishing the unfinished business of colonial dispossession in rural areas where the colonial laws have not been enforced to any significant extent and where meeting the human right to water and food is most urgent. However, synergy might be found by strengthening customary water rights within the framework of permit systems, particularly micro-scale or *de minimus* uses, which are *exempted* from the obligation to convert or apply for a permit.[7] These uses usually include water for domestic purposes,

[6] As will be argued, a recognition, in theory and law, of customary water practices and law together with a re-conception of public water services could realise the human rights to water, food and also livelihoods.

[7] S. Hodgson, *Land and Water – The Rights Interface*, Food and Agricultural Organization of the United Nations (FAO) Legislative Study No. 84 (Rome: FAO, 2004). The right to water for livelihoods could be grounded in the rights to food, work and an adequate standard

such as for some livestock or manual irrigation for 'subsistence' and appear to match human rights to water and food.[8]

The regulatory aspects of permit systems are discussed in Section 4. Many proponents of permit systems, in particular public water managers, see permits primarily as a vehicle to implement a range of regulatory goals, such as registration, taxation, pollution prevention, typically by attaching conditions to the permits. Besides challenging the assumption that one needs to change a legal system in order to exert regulatory power, the evidence presented here shows that permits as a blanket regulatory tool create more new problems than they solve in low- and middle-income countries with large numbers of customary small-scale users. Within the framework of permit systems, regulation in the public interest may work if well targeted at the few large-scale users in the formal water economies of the minority. Thus, the expanded application of priority exemptions may not only strengthen the water rights of the marginalised micro-users, but also render permit systems more effective and realistic as a well-targeted regulatory tool. This would better achieve the contemporary aims of water reform and human rights demands.

## 2 CUSTOMARY MULTIPLE WATER USES AS BASIC HUMAN RIGHTS

Customary water law is often associated with traditional hierarchical relationships that fail to align with modern constitutions and notions of basic human rights to water and food, and indeed the generally accepted merits of non-discriminatory practices. Whereas these concerns are important, a sweeping rejection of customary practices overlooks the fact that the majority of the rural poor in low- and middle-income countries obtain access to most of their water (for basic or just-above-basic domestic and productive uses) through self-supply under customary arrangements.[9] These intricate and dynamic local water arrangements have evolved since time immemorial,[10]

of living. In many developing contexts, where water meets multiple needs and informality abounds, expressing a right to a livelihood is a more sensible articulation of a human rights claim.

8 Obviously, most basic domestic and productive water uses as referred to in General Comment No. 15 of the Committee on Economic, Social and Cultural Rights would fall under or just above this category of *de minimis* uses: *General Comment No. 15, The Right to Water* (Twenty-ninth session, 2002), UN Doc. E/C.12/2002/11 (2003).

9 Shah, 'Issues in Reforming Informal Water Economies of Low-Income Countries'.

10 M. Ramazzotti, *Readings in African Customary Water Law*, FAO Legislative Study No. 58 (Rome: FAO, 1996). See also B. van Koppen and I. Hussain, 'Irrigation, Gender, and Poverty: Overview of Issues and Options', *Journal of Irrigation and Drainage*, Vol. 56, Nos. 2–3 (2007), pp. 289–298.

and as others have argued, the notions of water as a human right may mesh well with customary norms.[11]

Another feature of customary practice that appears fruitful for reassessing ways to realise the human rights to water *and* food is the holistic and integrated nature of customary practices and governance. When communities themselves construct infrastructure, they do so for multiple uses, including drinking, cooking, sanitation, hygiene, but also livestock, gardening, irrigation of crops and trees, fisheries and aquaculture, brickmaking and crafts, small-scale enterprise and cultural functions. People simultaneously use multiple natural and human-made sources, such as surface water bodies, wetlands, soil moisture or rooftop water, and individual or communal storage facilities, canals, groundwater wells and boreholes with or without household connections or public taps. This contrasts with the water services provided by the public sector. Conforming to the administrative structuring of the public sector according to single water uses, public water schemes are formally also designed for one single use, such as supply systems for domestic water or irrigation for crops. Yet, in reality, schemes planned for one use are invariably used for other, non-planned uses as well. Water agencies may label other uses as 'illegal' and try to prevent them, though usually unsuccessfully. This bias towards single water uses is anchored in administrative sub-sectors, which are divided according to singular uses, such as domestic, irrigation, livestock, fisheries and other sub-sectors. Indeed, this administrative conceptualisation haunts human rights, with the division of rights to water and to food.

Increasingly, water professionals realise that sectoral divides within the water sector are not particularly helpful for service delivery. Building on holistic customary practices, a new approach to water services has emerged, the so-called multiple-use water services (MUS). It has been discussed in global forums, such as the World Water Forum in Mexico (2006), Istanbul (2009,[12]) and Marseille (2012), and has found institutional expression in the global MUS Group.[13] The MUS approach is focused on the rural and

[11] A. Hellum, 'Human Rights Encountering Gendered Land and Water Uses: Family Gardens and the Rights to Water in Mhondoro Communal Land', in A. Hellum, J. Steward, S. Ali and A. Tsanga (eds.), *Human Rights: Interfacing Women's Realities and Plural Legalities* (Harare: Weaver Press, 2006); B. Derman, A. Hellum, E. Manzungu, P. Sithole and R. Machiridza, 'Intersections of Law, Human Rights and Water Management in Zimbabwe: Implications for Rural Livelihoods', in B. van Koppen, J. Butterworth and M. Giordano (eds.), *Community-based Water Law and Water Resources Management Reform in Developing Countries* (Oxford: CABI publishers, 2007), pp. 248–270.

[12] T. C. Disisleri Bakanligi, *Global Water Framework: Outcomes of the Fifth World Water Forum*, Istanbul: World Water Council, 2009).

[13] See www.musgroup.net.

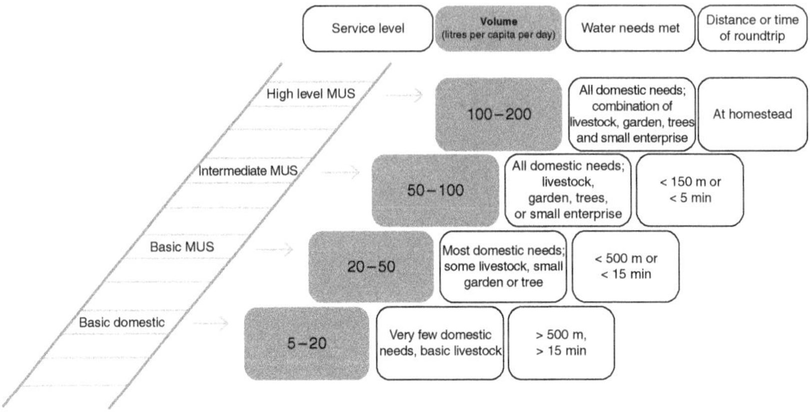


FIGURE 2.1 The multiple-use water ladder of service levels and water uses[14]

peri-urban poor and seeks to promote the meeting of multiple basic water needs for domestic uses, food and other livelihood and cultural needs in order to improve multiple interrelated dimensions of well-being.

The promotion of multiple uses of water at and around homesteads, or homestead-scale MUS, is particularly relevant from a human rights perspective. An international research project with 150 partners in 8 countries in 3 regions (Latin America, sub-Saharan Africa and Asia) found that wherever larger quantities of water are reliably available near the homestead, a significant proportion of the community, if not everybody, uses this water for productive activities, besides domestic uses.[15] As found in Ethiopia, the study country with the lowest levels of access to water, even at consumption levels of 8 to 17 litres per person per day, water is first used to realise food security before being used for 'luxury' domestic uses and sanitation.[16] By only promoting water for domestic needs and sanitation, such priorities of people themselves are ignored.

The multiple-use water ladder, depicted in Figure 2.1, reflects this reality. It thereby presents an implicit critique of the commonly used water ladder in

[14] Van Koppen *et al.*, Climbing the Water Ladder.

[15] B. Van Koppen, S. Smits, P. Moriarty, F. Penning de Vries, M. Mikhail and E. Boelee, *Climbing the Water Ladder: Multiple-use Water Services for Poverty Reduction*, Technical Paper Series 52 (The Hague: IRC International Water and Sanitation Centre and International Water Management Institute and Challenge Program on Water and Food, 2009).

[16] P. Scheelbeek, *Two Containers a Day: The Search for Proper Water Sources in Eastern Ethiopa. Water Quality and Sanitation in the Lege Dini Watershed Area, Ethiopia*, draft MSc thesis in irrigation and water engineering (Wageningen, The Netherlands: Wageningen University, 2006).

the domestic sector, which has also been transposed across to legal discourse on the human right to water. It assumes that water quantities at and around homesteads are exclusively used for domestic purposes, even up to 100 litres per person per day and more.

In setting strategic goals and establishing monitoring systems for public water service delivery to meet the human rights to water and food, the relationships between water quantities near homesteads and their multiple uses can be translated into 'service levels'. Thus, Figure 2.1 distinguishes between basic domestic services, basic multiple-use services, intermediate multiple-use services and high multiple-use services. Accordingly, it can be extrapolated that water services that provide, for example, 50 to 100 litres per person per day can effectively accelerate the realisation of the right to water and food. Generally, this available water improves many mutually reinforcing aspects of wellbeing: health, reduction of drudgery, food and income; and directly or indirectly, these improvements contribute to meeting the Sustainable Development Goals.

It should be ensured that 3 to 5 litres of water per person per day, but not necessarily more than this, are safe and available for drinking and cooking. This avoids wasting scarce public resources on providing high-quality water for uses that do not require such high standards. This is valid not only for most small-scale productive uses, like irrigation and crafts, but also for many domestic uses, such as sanitation or cleaning. Moreover, point-of-use treatment is increasingly being promoted by health experts in the domestic sector as it can be more effective.[17] This can be achieved through combining multiple water sources; for example, clean rooftop rainwater can be reserved for domestic uses, while unsafe piped supplies or run-off collected in tanks can be used for other purposes.

A range of additional arguments bolsters the importance of a shift towards MUS. First, it has been calculated that income generated from such productive activities is generally sufficient to repay the investment and operational costs for intermediate MUS within a period of six months to three years. Thus, the provision of water for domestic uses can be cross-subsidised from use for productive purposes.[18] This financial sustainability is especially important for the poorest of the poor.

[17] World Health Organization (WHO), *Combating Water-borne Disease at the Household Level: International Network to Promote Household Water Treatment and Safe Storage* (Geneva: WHO, 2007).

[18] M. Renwick, *Multiple Use Water Services for the Poor: Assessing the State of Knowledge* (Arlington, VA, USA: Winrock International, 2007).

Second, homestead-scale MUS often empowers women since they tend to have more say over the produce around homesteads compared to male-dominated distant plots.[19] In turn, women tend to allocate a greater share of household income and goods to their children and dependents. Moreover, homestead-scale MUS decreases women's burdens of fetching water, and can alleviate women's caring of the sick. Instead, it gives them more time to spend on income generation, leisure, family health care or community activities; and girls are also more likely to attend schools.

Third, improving access to water at and around homesteads also reaches the landless and sick: with no access to land or means to cultivate more distant land they are unable to take advantage of irrigation and other water schemes. For them, productive uses around the homesteads may well be the only way they can access water for productive purposes.

Fourth, universal implementation of homestead-scale MUS generally contributes to a fairer distribution of water resources. In most countries, there are more than sufficient water resources available for universal access to homestead-scale MUS. As domestic water supplies represent only a tiny fraction of water consumption, typically less than 5 per cent of total water resources, doubling or trebling service levels up to 50 to 100 litres per person per day generally maintains this relatively small proportion. For example, in a study on the water distribution in the rural areas of the Olifants Basin in South Africa, the Government of South Africa has calculated that 99.5 per cent of the rural population consume 5 per cent of the water resources (on the assumption that informal rural water users utilise 116 litres per capita per day as *de minimis* uses). The remaining 0.5 per cent of the rural population (the large-scale registered water users) accounted for 95 per cent of the water resources. If the water quantities for the rural majority were to more than double, up to 277 litres per person per day to allow for significant productive activities, large-scale users would have to share only 6 per cent of the resources that they currently use.[20] Given the huge current inequities in water use, promoting homestead-scale MUS can therefore contribute to a more equitable distribution of water.

[19] See also Chapter 9 in this volume: B. Van Koppen, *A Gender Performance Indicator for Irrigation. Concepts, Tools and Applications*. Research Report 59 (Colombo, Sri Lanka: International Water Management Institute, 2002); UNICEF, *Evaluation of Gender Policy Implementation* (New York: UNICEF, 2007).

[20] J. Cullis and B. van Koppen, *Applying the Gini Coefficient to Measure Inequality of Water Use in the Olifants River Management Area, South Africa*, Research Report No. 113 (Colombo, Sri Lanka: International Water Management Institute, 2007).

In sum, homestead-scale MUS recognises and strengthens often widespread customary water arrangements and are a cost-effective way to realise the human rights to water and food, as well as other human rights outlined in the Convention of the Elimination of all forms of Discrimination against Women of 1979.[21] Costs are considerably lower than if each right were realised through parallel implementation structures.[22] Hence, people's customary practices in self-supply or their employment of single-use designed 'domestic' systems for productive uses should not be discouraged and seen as illegal. Instead, access to at least 50 litres of water per person per day around homesteads for multiple uses should be recognised as a basic human right, with promotion of greater volumes.

## 3 PRIORITISING CUSTOMARY SMALL-SCALE WATER USES UNDER PERMIT SYSTEMS

The previous section highlighted the importance of customary practices relating to water service delivery in realising various human rights (or a re-conceptualised right to water). Achieving this will require a new approach to investments in infrastructure, whether public or private. But there is a second issue: allocation of the actual water. The water supply of poor people, typically governed by customary and informal arrangements, is seriously threatened under ongoing water rights reforms. This section specifically considers the entitlement dimensions of permit systems and how, in a context of legal pluralism, promulgation of one legal system cancels out or subordinates another. It also traces the discrimination and unfair treatment of small-scale users intrinsic within permit systems, both in obtaining permits and exemptions.

### 3.1 *Comparisons with Land Tenure*

As a prologue, it is revealing to take the case of sub-Saharan Africa and compare water permit systems with land tenure. In the case of land tenure, half a century of trial and error in introducing centralised land titling has revealed that one legal system (customary law) cannot simply be replaced by

[21] Convention on the Elimination of All Forms of Discrimination against Women (adopted 18 December 1979, entered into force 3 September 1981), 1249 UNTS 13.

[22] B. van Koppen, S. Smits and M. Mikhail, 'Homestead- and Community-scale Multiple-use Water Services: Unlocking New Investment Opportunities to Achieve the Millennium Development Goals', *Irrigation and Drainage*, Special Issue, World Water Forum, Vol. 58 (2009), pp. 73–86.

another system (statutory land titles). Moreover, the administrative burden of setting up cadastres appears immense. Maintaining and updating land registration systems typically exceed the capacity of under-resourced governments, leading to 'cadastre disasters' in sub-Saharan Africa.[23] It has been recognised gradually that land tenure reform in sub-Saharan Africa should begin from the bottom-up, starting from a complex yet well-understood reality of customary law to selected formalisation processes, such as to ensure gender equality.[24]

However, the water sector seems to have failed to take notice of lessons learned from land reforms, re-inventing the wheel instead by seeking to replace customary and collective water rights with administrative-based, individual and exclusive claims. On one level, 'water titling' is also more complicated than land titling. Water availability typically varies considerably over the seasons, and can never be fully predicted. Even just measuring natural streams and water bodies is costly. This further compounds the logistical burdens of any initial administration of water permits, as well as the updating of them. Even if permits are administered, they are often of little use in conflicts over water entitlements. Scarcity situations are seasonal, variable and erratic. Hence, an estimated average annual water volume allocated, as stipulated in most permits, is of little value for arbitration in changing contexts in which available water volumes are much lower than the average. Instead, prioritisation in sharing and conflict resolution mechanisms are needed, which are at the heart of other water rights regimes.

Lastly, unlike land frontiers, 'water frontiers' have not been reached in most of sub-Saharan Africa. Only 3.5 per cent of water resources have been 'developed' due to the lack of financial, technical and institutional resources to construct the storage and infrastructure to make more water available for regular human use.[25] Thus, the solution is not strictly one of regulating water but developing it. High-income countries followed this water development path, expanding infrastructure and storage in order to increase the amount of water

[23] R. Meinzen-Dick and L. Nkonya, 'Understanding Legal Pluralism in Water Rights: Lessons from Africa and Asia', in B. van Koppen, J. Butterworth and M. Giordano (eds.), *Community-based Water Law and Water Resources Management Reform in Developing Countries* (Oxford: CABI Publishers, 2007).

[24] P. McAuslan, 'Legal Pluralism as a Policy Option: Is It Desirable, Is It Doable?', Paper presented at the UNDP and International Land Coalition conference, 'Land Rights for African Development: From Knowledge to Action, Nairobi', 31 October–3 November 2005. Proceedings available at www.undp/drylands.

[25] A. Bahri, H. Sally, M. McCartney, R. E. Namara, S. Awulachew, B. van Koppen and D. van Rooijen, 'Integrated Watershed Management: Towards Sustainable Solutions in Africa', presented at Rosenberg International Forum on Water Policy, Water for Food: Quantity and Quality in a Changing World, June 2008, Zaragosa, Spain.

available for all. By portraying water scarcity as an inevitably limited 'pie' to be regulated via allocation, and sometimes even 'markets' of individual permits, attention is drawn away from this option. For the rare cases in sub-Saharan Africa, in which all physically available and environmentally sustainable water resources have been committed and basins are closing, the issue at stake is distributive water reform. Whereas distributive land reform is widely debated, there is even hardly any discourse that allocating water to realise people's human rights to water and food may imply that the 'haves' need to give up part of their water use.

### 3.2 *Permit Systems for Colonial Dispossession*

One reason for failing to learn lessons from the land sector is the strong colonial legacy of permit systems in Latin America and sub-Saharan Africa. The historical origins of these systems, which have hardly ever been challenged, are revealing.

The Romans invented permit systems around 500 BC. They spread widely and continue to do so, but their nature has little changed. The Romans classified water resources into public and private waters, and the authority to regulate public waters in the common interest was vested in 'the collective'.[26] Initially, this collective consisted of the few farmer tribes in Latinum around Rome; for them, water law primarily served the purpose of regulation in the common interest. However, with the expansion of the Roman Empire in the next millennium, the 'collective' morphed into the entity of the Roman emperor alone. More often than not, water resources of conquered tribes were declared to be 'public waters' and brought under his authority. This implied the cancellation of prior claims under customary regimes and the forced recognition of the Roman authority to vest any future claim. This system entered into a slow and gradual decline in western Europe. Between the fall of the Roman Empire and the 1800s, the authority of the aristocracy and their lower vassals over water gradually gave way to customary arrangements. Even when the emancipating bourgeoisie revived Roman water law in the 1800s, after the French Revolution, civil law countries maintained the distinction between public and private waters and tried to reduce any interference by rulers. Private waters were promoted and the appropriation of public waters was minimised. In common law countries with the riparian doctrine, there was no notion of ownership of water,

[26] D. A. Caponera, *Principles of Water Law and Administration (National and International)* (Rotterdam: Balkema, 1992), p. 260.

which because of its physical characteristics was recognised as an intrinsically common good (*res comunis omnium*).[27]

The use of permit systems was very different in the colonies of western European countries. Here, the colonialists deployed Roman water law as a means to dispossess conquered tribes from prior and future claims. Through the Papal Bull of 1493, the Catholic Pope encouraged Spanish colonisers to expropriate water resources in this way, granting the 'Catholic kings all newly discovered lands, including waters'. Water use became the subject of special royal permits granted by the Spanish authorities for particular purposes, such as domestic drinking needs and irrigation. The permits could be revoked and violations of requiring permits were punishable by a fine.[28]

In Mexico, permit systems were introduced in 1512, in the wake of the Spanish conquest. Ownership of water resources was vested in the Spanish king and a royal grant was required to use water. However, the factual 'granting' of concessions remained dormant until 1992. By then, only approximately 2,000 concessions had been granted.[29] It was the new Mexican water law of 1992 that reinvigorated the use of permits nation-wide.

In sub-Saharan Africa, 'lawful' colonial dispossession came later and was more diverse, as the different colonising nations introduced different legal regimes. Civil law colonisers introduced permit systems in the colonies: even though France, for example, had classified most of its waters as private, given that public waters were used predominantly for navigation. However, in their colonies, the French reasoned differently:

> [D]ue to climatic circumstances, i.e., of the fact that most African streams are seasonal and therefore non-navigable during certain periods of the year with the consequence that very little is left to the public domain, the distinction between navigable and non-navigable waters disappeared and, generally, all waters were placed in the public domain. Under this regime, every use of public water is subject to the obtention of an administrative authorization, permit or concession.[30]

Most British rulers exported complex forms of common law to Africa, often for specific water uses only. A patchwork developed: in some cases, legal arrangements were limited on pragmatic grounds to urbanising and industrialising areas, while elsewhere, they moved quickly to develop permit systems, as in Rhodesia and Tanzania (as well as Australia and the western United States for that matter). In South Africa, the Dutch colonisers introduced permit systems, but the

[27] Ibid. [28] Ibid. [29] See n.2.

[30] Caponera, *Principles of Water Law and Administration*, p. 99.

British brought common law with riparian rights. After decades of debate, the new Union of South Africa adopted riparian rights in 1912. By then, the British land title deed system was entrenching territorial segregation, as pronounced in the Land Act of 1913. Tying water rights to riparian land ownership therefore dispossessed Africans not only of 91 per cent of their land resources, but also their related water resources.[31]

At independence in both Latin America and sub-Saharan Africa, the new governments of the independent nations simply shifted custodianship of water resources to themselves, with little attention paid to the appropriateness of the colonial laws, which, anyhow remained largely dormant. However, the emergence of the neo-liberal and integrated water resource management discourse in the 1990s, taking either the example of Chile or Australia, revived and promoted the enforcement of permit systems, with even less interrogation into its colonial purposes.[32] Even Ghana, with its strong riparian tradition, adopted permit systems in 1996, formally superseding riparian and customary law. Thus, most countries strengthened the formal and practical elimination of customary water laws with a stroke of the pen. Only a few countries, like South Africa and Chile, maintained some formal protection of existing lawful uses.

### 3.3 *Recent Water Reform: Finalising the Unfinished Business of Colonial Dispossession?*

The often-cited earliest water reform, the Water Code of 1981 in Chile, exemplifies how administratively proficient (and largely wealthy) individuals and entities promote and benefit from permit systems as beneficiaries, at the expense of customary and other small-scale users. The Code was shaped in Pinochet's neo-liberal Chile, when the regulatory role of the State was strongly reduced in favour of free-market policies. Whereas permits had been earlier developed as 'use rights' of a public resource, the use conditions were removed, making these use rights almost as strong as private rights. The use rights could now be traded and even left unused. By merely submitting an administrative application, one could obtain an exclusive entitlement to the nation's water resources. This led to hoarding by a few large-scale water users. In 2006, the new government, to a

[31] B. van Koppen, 'Redressing Inequities from the Past from a Historical Perspective: The Case of the Olifant's Basin, South Africa', *Water SA*, HELP Special Edition, Vol. 34, No. 4 (2008).

[32] In addition to global neo-liberal influences, many proponents in Mexico and sub-Saharan Africa also expected that permits would be effective tools for redistributive-oriented regulation, as elaborated in Section 4.

certain extent, reduced this 'freedom' for permit holders, by stipulating that the water resources granted by the permit should at least be put to use.[33]

Interestingly, the formal legal status of customary rights is quite strong in Chile. The Water Code of 1981 recognises all existing water uses as being lawful, whether registered or not. However, the reality is different, as Lovera examines in depth in Chapter 3. The pressure to convert or regularise existing uses of water into permits, to gain official recognition, remained. Importantly, most indigenous peoples were not even aware of these procedures. The few communities who tried to convert their rights into permits encountered insurmountable administrative and conceptual obstacles, despite State support.[34] Conceptually, legal systems in which water is seen as common property are incompatible with permit systems that recognise absolute individual entitlements. In this way, administratively proficient individuals, both outside and within indigenous communities, who managed to obtain a permit, carved out their first-class entitlements, relegating claims under other normative frameworks to a secondary status. This *created* the tragedy of the 'commons'. As Boelens, Gentes, Guevara and Arteaga commented on the processes in Chile, 'the individualisation of formerly collective rights and management systems has created internal chaos'.[35]

In Bolivia, where indigenous people comprise the majority of the population, their resistance to appropriation by the powerful was more successful. Efforts to revive and implement the formal, but rather dormant, permit systems in rural and peri-urban areas led in part to the water wars in Cochabamba in 2002.[36] The proposed issuance of a permit to a foreign water company not only raised major concerns about people's access to affordable municipal water, but irrigators and water users in the areas surrounding Cochabamba also feared that this would challenge their prior customary rights, and joined the protest.[37]

[33] C. Bauer, *Siren Song: Chilean Water Law as a Model for International Reform* (Washington DC: Resources for the Future, 2004); Global Water Partnership Technical Committee, 'Water and Sustainable Development: Lessons from Chile', Policy Brief No. 2 (Stockholm: Global Water Partnership, 2006).

[34] Ibid. See also R. Boelens, I. Gentes, A. Guevara and P. Arteaga, 'Special Law: Recognition and Denial of Diversity in Andean Water Control', in D. Roth, R. Boelens and M. Zwarteveen (eds.), *Liquid Relations. Contested Water Rights and Legal Complexity* (New Brunswick: Rutgers University Press, 2005).

[35] Boelens, Gentes, Guevara and Arteaga, 'Special Law' (ibid.).

[36] See further Chapter 7, this volume.

[37] R. Boelens, R. Bustamante and H. de Vos, 'Legal Pluralism and the Politics of Inclusion', in B. van Koppen, J. Butterworth and M. Giordano (eds.), *Community-Based Water Law and*

In rural sub-Saharan Africa, where water use is principally governed by customary arrangements, the continuity of the colonial water laws into contemporary water reform is also strong. This is illustrated by the history of water law in Tanzania. Under German and, after the First World War, British colonisation, a system of water rights was established. However, in the 1923 water law, registration was restricted to foreign settlers. Water uses 'under native law and custom' were recognised, but Tanzanians could only participate in decision making through 'duly authorized representatives' or 'natives in addition to the District Commissioner'; customary law was tolerated, but only 'where it did not conflict with the interests of the colonial state'.[38] Chapter 257 of the subsequent Water Ordinance of 1948 stipulated that the 'entire property in water within the Territory is hereby vested in the Governor, in trust for His Majesty as Administering Authority for Tanganyika'. In the Water Ordinance of 1959, the option of registration was extended to native water users, but was not obligatory, while urban water supply and water use for mining operations were regulated separately. The main change after independence in 1961, as in other African countries, was that all water in Tanganyika became 'vested' in the United Republic under the Water Utilization (Control and Regulation) Act 1974 (section 8). For the sake of equality among citizens, this law rendered registration obligatory for all who 'divert, dam, store, abstract and use' water (section 14), thus making only registered water use lawful. However, this water law remained dormant and unenforced, particularly in rural areas.[39]

In step with the global shift in the 1990s, colonial permit systems were revived in Tanzania. Led by the World Bank, decades of support to infrastructure development gave way to implementation and enforcement of water legislation in rural areas. In addition, some small adjustments were made, such as grafting fees onto the colonial water rights system. In this way, enforcement of registration operationalised the new principles of 'user pays' and 'water as an economic good' for 'wiser water use'.[40]

In a similar fashion, the Water Act of 1998 in Zimbabwe adjusted colonial-era permit systems through superficial rather than substantial reform. Permits were made temporary, instead of providing perpetuity rights as the whites had claimed for themselves; and payment of fees was required for applications and

*Water Resources Management Reform in Developing Countries* (Oxford: CABI Publishers, 2007).

38 Water Ordinance 1923.

39 B. van Koppen, C. Sokile, N. Hatibu, B. Lankford, H. Mahoo and P. Yanda, *Formal Water Rights in Tanzania: Deepening a Dichotomy?*, IWMI Working Paper No. 71, (Colombo, Sri Lanka: International Water Management Institute, 2004).

40 Ibid.

renewals in order to finance the newly established catchment councils.[41] This move to enforce permit systems in remote communal rural areas ignored and superseded, again, customary water rights. In the other countries mentioned in the introduction to his chapter, including former Portuguese colonies, such as Mozambique, a similar pattern can be observed. In most cases, the drafting was dominated by development agencies and lawyers from these former colonies or donor countries.

In other words, recent water law reform in sub-Saharan Africa and Latin America could be viewed as a process of finishing the unfinished business of colonialism, expropriating and cancelling customary rights. However, unlike in Latin America, there was little protest by rural water users in sub-Saharan Africa. Water law reforms were driven centrally by a handful of legal experts without any of the public attention that was devoted to land reform. Nevertheless, the expropriation did not go entirely unnoticed, especially in Ghana, where the tribal authorities, or 'stools', remain politically and legally powerful. Moreover, the change from a legal pluralist patchwork of customary law and British common law, with permits in some places only, towards universal State ownership of water resources and permits, was more profound in Ghana than those States where permit systems had been the only colonial law. Referring to the Ghanaian Water Resources Commission Act of 1996, at least one water lawyer traced not only the radical nature of the law, but also its questionable constitutional status:

> By a stroke of the legislative pen and policy intervention, proprietary and managerial rights which had been held from time immemorial by families, stools, and communities have been taken away from a people some of who probably had no prior knowledge of the matter. Significantly, water in view of its appurtenance to land, has all along been regarded as part of land. The Constitution of 1992 recognizes customary land holdings and bars state intervention and/or appropriation of lands except under stringent conditions laid down under Article 20. Indeed, the 1992 constitution puts behind us the era of unbridled acquisition of land without payment of compensation. The issue is whether the Water Resources Commission Act can unilaterally hive off water from land and provide a separate institutional and legislative framework to address its use. If the constitution provides the regime of land tenure ought to be in conformity with customary law, then any attempt by the state to fashion out a separate regime for water that runs counter to this constitutional edict will offend the letter, if not the spirit, of the constitution. This is an issue that deserves to be examined having regard to the massive

[41] See further Chapter 19 in this volume.

> nature of the assault of the legislation on customary proprietary water rights... If the law on appropriation of land by the state is to be used as a guide on the matter, then it may be surmised that the Water Resources Commission, in spite of its far sweeping powers with regard to water appropriation, would have to yield to the constitutional requirement of providing, prompt, adequate, and effective compensation in accordance with Article 20 of the Constitution ...[42]

If governments and others seek to realise a human right to water and food in rural and peri-urban constituencies, they need to acknowledge the deep-rooted colonial legacy of imposing single water laws, which deny legal pluralism, in plural legal contexts. Instead, they need to fully recognise the informal and customary water arrangements that provide vital livelihoods to the poor. As permit systems have already been promulgated, the question at hand is whether legal pluralism can be accommodated within the existing framework of permit systems.

### 3.4 *Administrative Discrimination in Permit Systems and Prioritisation*

In order to find points of accommodation within the existing framework of permit systems, a flexible perspective is required: one cannot simply seek to replace one legal system with another. It is unlikely to succeed and is also politically unfeasible: the conversion of legal systems that recognise common property, such as under customary law, into individual titles challenges core notions of water as a shared resource.

Even if one assumes that these problems can somehow be solved, the 'solution' of conversion by application for a permit for new water uses has its own administrative obstacles. As argued below, the widespread assumption that 'everybody can equally apply for a permit' fails to hold, and discriminates against those who use the smallest quantities of water, often to meet their basic water needs for health and food. This applies to both those whose water uses just exceed *de minimis* uses and who are therefore formally obliged to obtain a permit, and those who are exempted, for different reasons.

For those who are obliged to apply for a permit, a considerable burden of proof for water uses that are already legitimate in customary regimes is added. Women, in particular, face the typical exclusion that they encounter in many administrative systems, which is that usually only one member of the

[42] G. Sarpong, *Customary Water Law and Practices* (Rome: FAO, 2005).

household can be registered for water rights permits. Men are often automatically seen as the household representative.[43]

Large-scale administratively proficient users may be intrinsically advantaged because conditions may be attached to permits that discriminate explicitly against small-scale informal users. A common condition is to have possession of some form of formalised land tenure, which is complex in customary land tenure. Also, metering devices are required.[44] Transaction costs are often disproportionately high for small-scale users, while their volumes of water use are low. The procedures and related transaction costs bear insufficient relation to the volumes under application.

Administrative proficiency grossly differs between users. Large-scale users are better informed, understand the formal language of the system, know how to fill in the forms, have bank accounts, can efficiently pay fees, are mobile and can draw on well-established connections with relevant officials. If needed, they can hire consultants and lawyers to carry out the job and hold bureaucracies to account. In South Africa, for example, large-scale users dominate complaints to the Water Tribunal over permit applications.

Governments lack the capacity and resources to process many permits. This limitation especially affects many small-scale users, who contribute to this administrative burden through the mere numbers of applications.

Last, but not least, the bureaucratic implementation of regulatory systems is often far from neat and orderly in practice, reality that especially affects the most marginalised. This was realised in time in Gujarat, India. Groundwater over-extraction was rampant and regulation was needed to address water scarcity. A groundwater bill, which included permits, was drafted by the National Ministry of Water Resources in 1970, but no federal state would adopt it. The Government of Gujarat rejected permits as potential regulatory tools, because of the new problems it would create, especially amongst the poor.[45] The Gujarati Chief Minister remarked, 'Can you imagine that as soon as this bill becomes a law, every

[43] S. Lastarria-Cornhiel, 'Impact of Privatization on Gender and Property Rights in Africa', *World Development*, Vol. 28, No. 8 (1997), pp. 1317–1334.

[44] In Zimbabwe in the 1950s, an obligation to install expensive measuring devices resulted in similar exclusions. E. Manzungu and R. Machiridza, 'Economic-legal Ideology and Water Management in Zimbabwe: Implications for Smallholder Agriculture', in B. van Koppen, J. A. Butterworth and I. Juma (eds.), *African Water Laws: Plural Legislative Frameworks for Rural Water Management in Africa: Proceedings of a Wworkshop hHeld in Johannesburg, South Africa, 26–28 January 2005* (Pretoria: International Water Management Institute, 2005).

[45] See UNDP, *Beyond Scarcity: Power, Poverty and the Global Water Crisis*, Human Development Report 2006 (New York: UNDP, 2006).

Village Level Revenue Official will have one more means at his disposal to extract bribes from farmers?'[46]

One way out of this Kafkaesque system is to exempt and prioritise *de minimis* uses, thus limiting the administrative burden for water uses that constitute a minute share of overall water resources. The South African National Water Act expands this notion and provides for so-called General Authorisations.[47] These are blanket authorisations for water uses in a certain area or for certain users, and the thresholds can in principle be set above the *de minimis* uses, classified as Schedule One uses under the Act. However, the question is whether exemptions are less discriminatory. Obviously, governments primarily introduce exemptions to reduce their administrative burdens. But exempted users also benefit. Exemptions remove the obligation to apply for a permit and the associated disproportionate transaction costs, either to prove the legitimacy of existing uses or to take up new uses. If the thresholds are sufficiently high to capture most rural customary water uses, the use of tools like the 'General Authorisations' could bypass the issue on how to convert customary rights into individual permits.

However, it is legitimately feared that exemptions relegate the majority of small-scale users to a second-class entitlement. Automatic entitlements for *de minimis* uses may create a 'curious type of residuary "right"':

> There is no great theoretical justification for exempting such uses from formal water rights regimes. Instead a value judgment is made by the legislature that takes account of the increased administrative and financial burden of including such uses within the formal framework, their relative value to individual users and their overall impact on the water resources balance... While they may be economically important to those who rely on them, it is hard to see how they provide much in the way of security... The problem is that a person who seeks to benefit from such an entitlement cannot lawfully prevent anyone else from also using the resource even if that use affects his own prior use/entitlement. Indeed the question arises as to whether or not they really amount to legal rights at all.[48]

Therefore, additional tools are needed to ensure equal legal status or, from the perspective of poverty alleviation and human rights, to sufficiently prioritise

[46] Shah, 'Issues in Reforming Informal Water Economies of Low-income Countries'.

[47] Department of Water Affairs and Forestry, *Assignment to Develop and Test Methodologies for Determining Resource-specific General Authorizations under the National Water Act*, prepared by Ninham Shand (Pty) Ltd and Umvoto Africa and Synergistics Environmental Services for Director, Water Allocation, Department of Water Affairs and Forestry, South Africa, November 2006, WFSP/WRM/CON6002.

[48] Hodgson, 'Land and Water – The Rights Interface'.

the exempted small-scale water uses. Such prioritisation could well be incorporated into existing priority schedules contained in most water legislation. Instead of referring to sectors, as these schedules typically do, the small scale of use would determine the priority. The National Water Resource Strategy (2004 and 2013) of South Africa stipulates such priority.[49] Such prioritisation has also been proposed by the Confederation of Indigenous Nationalities of Ecuador, with water for human and domestic use and subsistence agriculture having priority over water for commercial agriculture.[50] Thus, on paper and through enforcement, within the legal framework of permit systems, a 'shell' can be provided for small-scale users vis-à-vis large-scale users. For the many remaining water allocation issues, especially those among exempted small-scale users, living customary water law needs to be much better understood. Interventions to support the realisation of human rights to water and food will find strengths upon which they can build, while overcoming its weaknesses.

## 4 PERMIT SYSTEMS: OPPORTUNITIES OR OBSTACLES FOR REGULATION?

One reason why the problems of dispossession have received limited attention in sub-Saharan Africa, at least, is the overarching focus on permit systems as regulatory tools: the attachment of obligations and conditions to approved water use. Indeed, the question of equitable distribution for both the rights to food and water is raised four times in CESCR's General Comment No. 15.[51] Whereas cancellation of former claims to water may be drastic, it is perceived

[49] South Africa's National Water Resource Strategy stipulates the following order of priority: provision for the Reserve; international agreements and obligations; water for social needs, such as poverty eradication, primary domestic needs and uses that will contribute to maintaining social stability and achieving greater racial and gender equity; water for uses that are strategically important to the national economy; water for general economic use, which includes commercial irrigation and forestry. However, the author is not aware that the third priority has ever been applied. In: RSA Republic of South Africa. Department of Water Affairs and Forestry, *National Water Resource Strategy*, 1st edn (2004) and 2nd edn (2013) (Pretoria, South Africa: Department of Water Affairs and Forestry, 2004; 2013).

[50] Confederation of Indigenous Nationalities of Ecuador, *La Propuesta de Ley de Aguas* (Quito: CONAIE, 1996). Cited in R. Boelens and M. Zwarteveen, 'Anomalous Water Rights and the Politics of Normalization: Water Control and Privatization Policies in the Andean Region', in D. Roth, R. Boelens and M. Zwarteveen (eds.), *Liquid Relations. Contested Water Rights and Legal Complexity* (New Brunswick, New Jersey: Rutgers University Press, 2005), p. 116.

[51] General Comment No. 15, paras. 7, 37, 44(b), 44(c). In order to realise the right to food, 'Attention should be given to ensuring that disadvantaged and marginalized farmers, including women farmers, have equitable access to water and water management systems, including sustainable rain harvesting and irrigation technology.' In relation to the right to water, violations

as a legitimate measure by States as it allows them to better attach conditions and govern water in a public interest.

However, this regulatory vision was a departure from the legal substance and political discourse that has accompanied contemporary development of archetype permit systems. In Chile[52], Australia[53] and the western United States[54], the move to permit systems aimed at the opposite: to move away from State control towards self-regulation and the liberty of permit holders to trade to engage users in finding solutions for the growing problems of re-allocation of scarce water to new entrants and the environment. In arid Australia and the western United States, water resources had been fully developed and sophisticated permit systems have crystallised for over a century. In all three countries, the water rights of minority indigenous peoples were weakened or completely ignored.

In contrast, in Mexico and sub-Saharan Africa later, water reformers and managers moved in a different direction. They assumed that permit systems, with clear obligations attached to the permit, would strengthen State regulation and that the introduction of fees would finance newly established water resource management institutions. Water managers also invariably cite other regulatory goals such as using permit systems to improve water management, water allocation (in the case of scarcity) and, to a lesser extent, pollution prevention. Such general regulation can also be in the interest of the poor, who may be most affected by drought or pollution.

While the goals are salutary, the question is whether the measure is fit for purpose. Examples from Tanzania, Mexico, South Africa and other countries will be considered in order to assess whether permit systems meet that regulatory expectation, and for whom, and whether the system could be internally reformed. Remarkably, neither in Latin America nor in sub-Saharan Africa was there an *ex ante* impact analysis of the precise regulatory problem to be solved and possible alternatives. Nor were there quantitative estimates of the numbers of water users to be regulated or exempted from regulation

are said to include failure to prevent and remedy inequitable extraction and take steps facilitate equitable distribution of services and facilities (paras 44(b) and (c)).

52 See n. 34.

53 B. Haisman, 'Impacts of Water Rights Reform in Australia', in B. Bruns, C. Ringler, and R. Meinzen-Dick (eds.), *Water Rights Reform: Lessons for Institutional Design* (Washington, DC: International Food Policy Research Institute, 2005), pp. 113–152.

54 D.S. Kenney, 'Prior appropriation and water rights reform in the Western United States', in B. Bruns, C. Ringler, and R. Meinzen-Dick (eds.), *Water Rights Reform: Lessons for Institutional Design* (Washington, DC: International Food Policy Research Institute, 2005), pp. 167–182.

and the volume of water uses. Even the goal of better water allocation was premature in many countries: water resources were largely abundant and the primary problem was the lack of the financial, technical and institutional capacity to invest in water storage and other infrastructure.

The pilot implementation of the reformed Tanzanian water law illustrates the initial appeal of permits for water managers, but also the serious regulatory limitations. Tanzania is one of the few countries that has no exemptions for *de minimis* productive uses, because 'one cannot exclude the majority', as a senior water officer explained.[55] The Rufiji Basin in southwest Tanzania, an area with well-functioning customary arrangements, was one of the pilots in the early 2000s. Initially, the field water officer saw the permit systems that he was supposed to enforce as 'cakes and spears': granting formal first-class entitlements would be like showing a cake, while annual fee payment would be like holding a spear behind his back. At the start, water users appreciated the deal and applied for registration and paid the fee. After a few years, however, water users realised that the government had little means to ensure that their paper entitlement was concretised. In the absence of significant storage and infrastructure facilities, it was the climate that determined water availability, not the State. The water official shifted strategy and sensitised users about another part of the Tanzanian water law: the State is never accountable for making the waters stipulated in the entitlement available in reality. Similar provisions exist in virtually all permit-based systems. The Rufiji Basin office then continued enforcement of payment obligations, but increasingly separated this from the cumbersome entitlement applications. While users paid, application approvals were very slow and even kept on hold.[56] However, the transaction costs incurred in charging the multiple small users in remote areas, without post-offices or banks, were very high. Revenue collection was much more successful among large non-governmental and private formal users: the fees were minimal in comparison to the value of the resource.

In the official databases, only a minority of users were captured and the data became quickly outdated. In the Rufiji Basin, 47 per cent of the 990 water rights registered were 'not operated anymore';[57] in the Pangani Basin, the figure was 28 per cent of the 1638 (applied, provisional or granted) water rights.[58] Of interest is that, in both basins, water officers had initiated their own surveys

[55] W. Mwaruvanda, Basin officer Rufji Basin, personal communication 2006. [56] See n. 40.

[57] C. Sokile, Analysis of Institutional Frameworks for Local Water Governance in the Upper Ruaha Catchment, unpublished Ph.D. thesis, University of Dar-es-Salaam, 2006.

[58] H. Komakech, P. van der Zaag, A. Jonoski and B. van Koppen, 'Can Actor-Network Theory Help to Understand Water-sharing Practices in Makanya Catchment, Tanzania?' Paper for International Symposium WaterNet/GWP/WARFSA, Johannesburg, October 2008.

to establish the identity and patterns of water users: it was a more efficient and reliable procedure than the long road of processing permit applications.

In 1989 in Mexico, an effective fiscal measure for revenue collection was established: only formal large-scale water users were targeted. However, as mentioned, the colonial-era permit system was subsequently revived in 1992. Payment was tied with the issuance of new permits. As in Tanzania, the reform was initially endorsed by water managers. By 2000, 327,650 large-scale individual water users, companies and organisations had been registered, in a population of over 100 million Mexicans (which equates to slightly more than 25 million households).[59] However, logistically it was a huge investment of resources. The result has been over-registration and fraud in the trade of permits.[60]

Before the passing of the National Water Act of 1998, South Africa's water law was marked by plurality. It included riparian rights, government water control areas, some permit systems (for example in forestry, irrigation districts) and not-recognised living customary water rights in former homelands. The new Act recognised all 'existing lawful uses' (for which vested users had fiercely negotiated[61]) and only introduced permits for all new uses. Obviously, some existing uses needed to be regulated, and this was effectively done without first changing the entire legal system into permits.

Registration of existing uses, whether lawful or not, was made obligatory in 1999. This information was fed into a database primarily designed for information collection and billing purposes. The result was that over 63,000 individual and organised water users (out of a population of 47 million) were registered. Here, unlike in Tanzania, the government became very articulate about the difference between obligations, such as registration and payment, and a legal claim over water resources. Initially, some officials and some registered users assumed that registration and payment were the initial steps to convert their existing lawful use into the first-class entitlement of a permit. This motivated the Department of Water Affairs to clarify that there was no correlation between regulatory obligations, such as registration and payment, and any legal claims.

From the perspective of distributive historical justice, South Africa has been explicit in its policy goal of redressing the inequalities of the past, which

59 H. Garduno, 'Lessons from Implementing Water Rights in Mexico', in Bruns, Ringler, and Meinzen-Dick (eds.), *Water Rights Reform: Lessons for Institutional Design*, pp. 85–122.

60 H. Garduno, personal communication, 2006.

61 M. De Lange, 'Water Policy and Law Review Process in South Africa with a Focus on the Agricultural Sector', in P. Mollinga and A. Bolding (eds.), *The Politics of Irrigation Reform: Contested Policy Formulation and Implementation in Asia, Africa, and Latin America* (Aldershot: Ashgate, 2004), pp. 11–56.

includes, under certain conditions, re-allocating water from the 'haves' to the 'have-nots' (DWA 2013)[62]. Significantly, in the intra-government contest between the conservative and transformative powers, the myth surfaced that this regulatory goal must be preceded by a change in the legal system. Accordingly, the conversion of existing lawful uses into permit systems is portrayed as the only way to achieve this goal. However, costly pilot efforts of such area-specific conversion, called 'compulsory licensing' projects since 2003 have been stalled and not a single drop has been re-allocated in the name of historical justice. Even for new water uptake after 1998, the permit system favoured the vested powers. Out of the 1304 permits for new water uses that were allocated between 1998 and 2008, only 2.5 per cent were for Historically Disadvantaged Individuals (HDIs).[63] All other licenses were for white-controlled enterprises. Until today, the straightforward regulatory power that stems directly from the State's custodianship of water resources has received little attention. Simple options for distributive water reform that merely require political will and enforcement capacity, such as blanket prioritisation of both pre-1998 and post-1998 small-scale water uses by HDIs, and also medium-scale new water uses by HDIs and reducing the assurances of supply of vested users in physically stressed basins, remain untapped.

Another lesson from South Africa concerns the importance of quantification of the distribution of water use, not only for equity consideration, but also to highlight the futility of even just registering many small-scale users. As mentioned, the study in the Olifants Basin found that 0.5 per cent of the population (the large-scale registered water users) used 95 per cent of the water resources. Any regulation of the 99.5 per cent of the population who use 5 per cent of water volumes is meaningless.[64] Another study found strong inequities even among the minority of formally registered, relatively large-scale users. The largest 10 per cent of the registered users use a volume of water that varies by province, between 77 per cent (in Limpopo province) and 93 per cent (in Gauteng province).[65] The question is whether scarce

[62] RSA Republic of South Africa. Department of Water and Sanitation, *National Water Resource Strategy*, 2nd edn (2013) (Pretoria, South Africa: Department of Water Affairs, 2013).

[63] P. Dlamini and M. Msibi, *Compulsory Licensing*, Draft report (Pretoria: Water Research Commission South Africa, 2009).

[64] J. Cullis and B. van Koppen, *Applying the Gini Coefficient to Measure Inequality of Water Use in the Olifants River Management Area, South Africa*. Research Report 113, Colombo, Sri Lanka: International Water Management Institute.

[65] J. Cullis and B. van Koppen, 'Applying the Gini Coefficient to Measure the Distribution of Water Use and Benefits of Water Use in South Africa's Provinces', unpublished final draft,

public resources should be spent on further regulating 90 per cent of registered users who consume less than a quarter of total water resources.

Whereas middle-income countries such as Mexico and South Africa can maintain, to a certain extent, administrative systems, low-income countries such as Tanzania and Malawi have only been able to register and issue permits for a few thousand users nation-wide. In the case of Ghana, the country had issued permits to 154 large-scale users over 13 years (and no small-scale users), confirming that the Water Resources Commission could well have been funded under a simple fiscal measure among the few large-scale users.

In sum, these country experiences suggest that using permit systems for regulation in middle and low-income countries, where the majority of users are rural small-scale households using undeveloped water resources, is like killing a mosquito with a canon. Administrative regulatory measures, such as registration, payment and pollution prevention, appear to work for a tiny minority of formal large-scale users. However, fiscal measures or light surveys or even remote sensing can achieve the same objectives of either taxation or information collection. Permit systems create huge administrative and legal burdens, if not also gross arbitrariness and open space for fraud and corruption in regulation. In the implementation of permit systems in Tanzania and Ghana, and even in the formal stipulations of South Africa's National Water Act, governments started emphasising the clear distinction between an entitlement, which was downplayed, and an obligation, which was emphasised. Regulatory efforts concentrated, in practice, on a very small minority of water users.

Obviously, a legal system that only aims to reach, and effectively reaches, a small minority of its citizens cannot be seen as a legitimate way to define entitlements to water across a nation, including the water entitlements that are pivotal to meet people's human rights to water and food. Priority "General Authorisations" for the latter uses would formally avoid such arbitrariness, and, if clearly put at equal par with, or as priority to the entitlements of high-impact users, provided they fulfil certain obligations, strengthen the legitimacy of permit systems as pro-poor regulatory instruments.[66]

Water for Growth and Development Department of Water Affairs and Forestry (Pretoria: DWAF and IWMI, 2008).

66 Implicitly, this focus on a minority that realistically can and needs to be regulated, has also been proposed in Uganda. Here, the consultant unambiguously proposed to target the 200 largest users and the (partially overlapping) 200 largest polluters. It would cover the sixty to seventy major towns, and provide a more feasible and more credible regulatory tool. See n.2.

## 5 CONCLUSIONS

This chapter highlighted two ways in which the human rights to water, food (and arguably livelihood) for women and men can be realised more effectively, if customary water rights regimes occupy centre stage. This is not to deny that customary arrangements can be shaped by gender and age hierarchies and ethnicity-based exclusion: obviously, this need to be addressed. However, taking customary arrangements seriously allows the introduction of water services approaches like MUS, which are more effective in realising a broad range of socio-economic human rights: and the avoidance of the pitfalls of super-imposed legal systems.

A key feature of customary systems is their holistic approach to water development and management and the use of multiple sources for multiple domestic and productive uses. Overcoming counterproductive sectoral boundaries in both water services delivery and human rights definitions opens up new opportunities to realise the rights to water *and* food and improve gender equality. Providing at least 50 litres per person per day to homesteads, out of which 3 to 5 litres per person per day should be safe for drinking, improves health, food production and income and reduces the labour burdens of water fetching. The landless can also be reached by a universal increase of service levels. This requires both policymakers, the water community and the human rights community to be wary of over-categorisation and entrenching further legal, administrative and infrastructural divides. Instead, overcoming them will open up new concrete opportunities to realise human rights in a cost-effective manner.

Customary rights are also vital because they govern communities' own initiatives to ensure that water better contributes to meeting their basic health, food and income needs. The 'modern' water law of permit systems represents a 'paper assault' on these water entitlements of the poor. Imposing a single regime of permits ignores the reality of plural systems, certainly for those who cannot easily defend their claims. The legal incongruities of the newly promulgated permit systems are the result of a pervasive reproduction of the resource control that the Roman emperor and European colonisers, and then independent States pursued. Ill-advised by the international water and development community, governments still fail to use their power as custodians of their nations' water resources as the primary vehicle for reformulating their current permit systems.

With a stroke of the pen, governments can attach such priority to *de minimis* uses with thresholds that are sufficiently high to include quantities needed to meet human rights and that ensure fair administrative treatment. Although the water conflicts among the micro- and small-scale users cannot be solved by such measures alone, such prioritisation provides protection against larger-scale users and alleviates administrative burdens. As a result, governments can become more effective regulators. They can target and regulate the few large-scale users who can, and need to be, reached with feasible monitoring, administrative, water quality protection or fiscal measures. Such regulation also contributes to increased quantities of cleaner water to the poor, representing a much more effective way of ensuring water rights that advance human rights.

# 3

# Indigenous Peoples and the Sale of Water Rights

## *The Case of Chile*

DOMINGO A. LOVERA PARMO*

### 1 INTRODUCTION

The privatisation of water resources is a rare but emerging trend in a number of countries. In the international literature, Chile has represented the archetypal case.[1] In 1981, the Government of Chile reformed its property laws and provided that water, despite being legally qualified as a public good in terms of use, constituted a regular commodity in its natural state. Rights to the resource could be transferred and sold at will.

The ramifications of the imposition of such a full-scale property rights regime on water resources have been particularly significant for indigenous peoples. The water resources legislation has severely complicated attempts to redress historical injustices of indigenous peoples, which have often been mediated through the prism of law. After centuries of dispossession and policies of assimilation, indigenous peoples have struggled to recover their land, resources and culture.

In this struggle, human rights have emerged as an important means of drawing attention to indigenous demands. However, until recently, the impact of human rights on Chilean law and practice has remained marginal.[2] Chile remains one of the few Latin American countries that have not

* Assistant Professor, Universidad Diego Portales, Chile. The author would like to thank José Aylwin, Jorge Contesse, Matías Guiloff, Manual Prieto and Nancy Yañez for valuable information and references used in this research.

[1] See Chapter 2 by van Koppen.

[2] The cases described in Section 3.2 deal primarily with legal claims related to allocation and recognition of ancestral water resources. However, it is important to note that since the ILO Convention No. 169 (15 September 2009) came into force, several cases have come before Chilean courts. These cases are mainly, if not exclusively, related to the government violation of consultation and participatory rights. Detailed analysis in J. Contesse and D. Lovera, 'El Convenio 169 de la OIT en la Jurisprudencia Chilena: Prólogo del Incumplimiento', *Anuario de Derecho Público*, Vol. 2 (2011), pp. 127–51.

constitutionally recognised indigenous peoples while the Constitutional Court has considered that participatory rights contemplated in the International Labour Organisation (ILO) Convention No. 169 (Indigenous and Tribal Peoples Convention) were mere governmental guidelines rather than actual rights.[3] This politico-legal scenario may explain the long conflict that has been manifest in southern Chile, where water has been the subject of contestation between indigenous peoples and various commercial interests.

This chapter charts the clash between the legal commodification of water rights and the claims of indigenous peoples. Its aim is to assess whether governmental policies have taken indigenous peoples' rights and claims into consideration in policy design as well as highlight the use and reception of human rights discourse. Section 2 briefly chronicles the precarious situation of indigenous peoples in Chile while Section 3 is devoted to an analysis of Chile's water law, paying particular attention to the free trade innovations passed in 1981, which were designed to favour the hydroelectric industry. Section 4 examines the application of the Water Code of 1981 in indigenous areas, including an examination of conflicts provoked by the regulation, and demonstrates how indigenous groups and civil society organisations have sought to respond. In doing so, it identifies two particular phenomena that have undermined the bargaining power of indigenous peoples in maintaining control over traditional water resources: the existence of a weak governmental agency with responsibility for the free trade scheme (leaving conflicts to be resolved directly between indigenous peoples and private investors by private means, including buying off dissidence), and the lack of legalised and institutionalised participation.

An important caveat needs to be made. This chapter does not attempt to address the current state of water supply for indigenous peoples. The reason for this is that a human rights perspective diverges from a developmental one.[4] To put it simply, can human rights violations be pardoned if governmental policies were successful in improving development outcomes, including implementation of water-related policies? Nonetheless, some information on

3 International Labour Organisation, *Convention No 169, Indigenous and Tribal Peoples Convention* (Seventy-seventh session), Geneva, 27 June (1989). A detailed analysis of how the Constitutional Court of Chile understood participatory rights enshrined in the Convention is undertaken below in Section 3.3.

4 In fact, and as have been noted, a developmental approach has proven insufficient in addressing past injustices. Moreover, Chile might well be described as an example of the implementation of 'aggressive development policies' not considering indigenous peoples' viewpoints. L. Barrera-Hernández, 'Indigenous Peoples, Human Rights and Natural Resource Development: Chile's Mapuche Peoples and the Right to Water', *Annual Survey of International & Comparative Law*, Vol. 11, No. 1 (2005), pp. 2–3, 10.

these dimensions might be helpful and it demonstrates that Chile's good performance on water supply is an aggregative one and does not extend to all.

For a start, Chile has developed a water supply model that is focused on urbanised areas. According to governmental statistics this has been rather successful: in 2010, 99.8 per cent of national population living in urban areas has access to a safe water supply.[5] However, the same cannot be said for rural areas, where 35.2 per cent of indigenous peoples live.[6] Whereas the rate of indigenous peoples living in urban areas connected to public water services amounts to 98.3 per cent, it decreases to 20.7 per cent in rural areas.[7] The most recent governmental guidelines laid down to address indigenous demands have recognised this as one of the pending issues.[8] In the 'Región de la Araucanía', the province with the highest indigenous population living in rural areas, the government estimates that 77.7 per cent of dispersed rural population lacks access to safe water, 'becoming one of the most critical aspects in rural development'.[9] Indeed, some authors have denounced an 'environmental racism', noting that by 2005 this province shows a poor coverage of sewage treatment plants: 15 per cent compared to 81 per cent at national level.[10]

## 2 THE POOREST OF THE POOR: *CHILENOS* AND *INDÍGENAS*

### 2.1 *Cultural-Historic Context*

The relationship between indigenous peoples and the Chilean State has been, to put it finely, strained.[11] Chile's history shows a cultural backdrop of

5 Gobierno de Chile, *Informe de Gestión del Sector Sanitario* (Santiago: Superintendencia de Servicios Sanitarios, 2010) p. 12. However, it is worth noting water used for domestic uses, as well as industrial uses in urban areas, amount just to 6 per cent of total extractions – and 4 per cent of national consumptive uses (see this distinction in Section 4.1). World Bank, 'Chile: Diagnóstico de la gestión de recursos hídricos,' Documento 63392, available at: http://go.worldbank.org/GP5A4SJT80 (Washington D.C.: 2011), pp. 10,12.

6 Gobierno de Chile, *Estadísticas sociales de los pueblos indígenas en Chile. Censo 2002* (Santiago: Instituto Nacional de Estadísticas – Programa Orígenes, 2002), p. 18.

7 These rates get worse when noting that 46.9 per cent of non-indigenous people living in rural areas have an access to safe water. Ibid., p. 97.

8 Gobierno de Chile, *Plan Araucanía: Invirtiendo en Personas y Oportunidades* (Temuco: Gobierno Regional de la Araucanía, 2009), p. 4.

9 Gobierno de Chile, *Plan Araucanía*, p. 22.

10 Besides the aforementioned statistics, 85 per cent of sewage waters are directly thrown to lakes and rivers of the province. N. Yañez and R. Molina, *Las Aguas Indígenas en Chile* (Santiago: Lom Ediciones, 2011), p. 149.

11 Centro de Derechos Humanos, Universidad Diego Portales, *Informe Anual sobre Derechos Humanos 2003* (Santiago: Universidad Diego Portales, 2003), p. 295.

exclusion, forced integration and persecution against indigenous peoples (such as the Mapuche, Aimara, Rapa Nui, Atacameños, Coya), which the State has not shown much determination to reverse. Villalobos, a well-known conservative historian, has suggested indigenous peoples are themselves to blame for their current predicament. He argues that indigenous peoples were seduced by the temptations brought by Spanish conquerors to Latin America, mainly alcohol and trinkets. When they became involved in commercial negotiations,[12] 'natives did not always understand what buying entailed' due to a low 'cultural level'.[13] According to Villalobos, even if they regret the transactions, marginalisation was a result of their own doing.[14]

This marginalisation has persisted as official data shows. According to an official national survey, indigenous peoples in Chile are still the poorest of the poor.[15] In 2006, 6.6 per cent of Chile's population was declared to be a member of (an ethnic group of) indigenous peoples. Whereas average national poverty has diminished from 18.7 per cent of the population in 2003 to 13.7 per cent in 2006, the transition out of poverty has been much slower, and poverty rates much higher, for indigenous peoples. The proportion of indigenous individuals living in poverty was 19 per cent in 2006.

A deeper assessment of Chile's history suggests greater colonial and governmental responsibility. 'Land transactions' were accompanied by waves of ethnic cleansing and forced integration. Even today, indigenous-governmental relations occur in the shadow of broadly applied anti-terrorist legislation.[16] Forced integration was instigated as the Chilean State began to

[12] S. Villalobos, *Historia de los Chilenos, Tomo 2* (Santiago: Editorial Taurus, 2007), pp. 145–6 (author's translation).

[13] Ibid. Villalobos insists indigenous peoples preferred to exchange lands for alcohol and other goods, which once consumed seemed to them to result in an unfair trade. He rhetorically asks, who can stand in the way of a voluntary transaction, particularly when it involves unexploited lands that possess only symbolic and traditional value (author's translation).

[14] S. Villalobos, *Vida fronteriza en la Araucanía: El mito de la Guerra de Arauco* (Santiago: Editorial Andrés Bello, 1995), p. 121; 'En Chile, Indígenas Puros Propiamente No Existen', *El Mercurio*, 31 August 2008.

[15] CASEN (The National Characterization Socio-economic Survey) is an official survey carried out by the National Planning Ministry.

[16] It is worth noting that Chile has been questioned before the Inter-American Commission on Human Rights (IACHR) on discriminatory application of anti-terrorist legislation against indigenous peoples. IACHR, Case No 12.576, *Norín Catrimán y ot. con Chile*, 19 August 2011. On the application of antiterrorist legislation, including longer periods of incommunicado detention, the inclusions of 'faceless' witnesses, and higher sanctions, see UN Commission on Human Rights, *Report of the Special Rapporteur on the situation of human rights and fundamental freedoms of indigenous people, Mr. Rodolfo Stavenhagen, submitted in accordance with Commission resolution 2003/56, Mission to Chile* (Sixtieth session, 2004), UN Doc. E/CN.4/2004/80/Add.3 (2004), paras. 29–40.

take shape in the 1530s. The arriving Spaniards identified indigenous peoples as either savages to be subjugated or as pagans in need of evangelisation.[17] Yet, subjecting indigenous peoples to the new regime cost them half their population,[18] and even the process of Christianisation was accompanied by the use of violence and force.[19]

Eventually, in 1598, indigenous peoples responded with the launch of a war of resistance in southern Chile (*Guerra de Arauco*) that was largely sustained until the end of the nineteenth century. During these three centuries, several peace agreements were reached, known as '*parlamentos*' (literally parliaments, which represented each side in negotiations). These *parlamentos*, which helped create intermittent pacific relations on the southern frontier, represent one of the exceptional cases of the recognition of indigenous as independent peoples.[20] Nonetheless, whereas Spaniard conquerors were forced by resistance to recognise indigenous peoples as independent – by dialoguing with them through parliaments – they were unwilling to consider them as a people inside a nation, particularly once Chile's independence process started in 1810.[21]

This reluctance may be explained by both strategic and economic reasons, which is crucial for understanding the development of contemporary water law. As Chile was establishing its borders, its expansionist desire was comingled with the 'elite's commitment to a strong State', which meant that, 'regardless of social or economic costs, the State had to be protected from any external threat, real or imagined'.[22] This imperialist impulse included the

17 F. Campos, *Historia Constitucional de Chile*, 7th edition (Santiago: Editorial Jurídica de Chile, 2005), p. 23.

18 These deaths were not only caused by direct violence, but also by subhuman work conditions, the spread of diseases brought from Europe (e.g. typhus), and the scarcity of food provoked by the arrival of the new inhabitants: F. Portales, *Los Mitos de la Democracia Chilena: Desde la Conquista hasta 1925* (Santiago: Editorial Catalonia, 2004), pp. 21–3.

19 Ibid. Allegedly this was not the Spanish Crown's objective. Several studies have revealed the discrepancy between the orders of the Spanish Crown and the practice of evangelising colonists: Campos, *Historia Constitucional*, pp. 61-2; Portales, *Los Mitos de la Democracia* (ibid.), pp. 21, 27, 32–8.

20 The *parlamentos* not only constituted an implicit recognition of a frontier between the lands of the Crown and of indigenous peoples, but also facilitated commercial exchange and dialogue. These exchanges eventually impacted traditional forms of livelihoods in indigenous areas: Instituto de Estudios Indígenas-Universidad de la Frontera, *Los Derechos de los Pueblos Indígenas en Chile* (Santiago: Lom Ediciones, 2003), pp. 159–60.

21 J. Bengoa, *Historia de un Conflicto: Los mapuches y el Estado nacional durante el siglo XX* (Santiago: Editorial Planeta, 2007), pp. 33–4.

22 J. Faundez, *Democratization, Development, and Legality: Chile, 1831 to 1973* (New York: Palgrave Macmillan, 2007), p. 23. This may explain the strong top-down political order Chile has demonstrated during the last two centuries with little toleration for social participation.

northward extension of frontiers (with the war against the Perú-Bolivian Confederation) and internal colonialism, which was directed against indigenous peoples living south of the Bío-Bío frontier negotiated by the Spanish *parlamentos*.[23] Given the aridity of northern Chile, the southern regions provided potentially fertile agricultural lands.[24] According to Faundez, the initial idea was to allow commercial exchange of lands between Chileans and Mapuche, but this founded on different notions of property ownership and the latter's resistance triggered in 1850 a two-decade-long military campaign 'resulting in the death of hundreds of Mapuche people, the destruction of their way of life, and the expropriation, without compensation, of agricultural land'.[25]

The confiscation of natural resources, imposition of a new economic system, individualisation of property relations and introduction of western culture[26] were made possible through armed force, the primary objective of which was the removal of 'obstacles to the Nation's progress'.[27] This project of State building continued into the twentieth century with the final settlement (*radicación*) of the Mapuche in designated areas; a process that lasted fifty years and which became radicalised under Pinochet's dictatorship as attempts were made to remove all legal exceptions favouring indigenous peoples.[28] However, this pattern of counter-resistance and government

Attempts to question that order (Constitutional and legal) are quickly labelled as 'anarchy, subversion, or terrorism': G. Salazar, *Construcción de Estado en Chile (1800–1837): Democracia de los 'Pueblos', Militarismo Ciudadano, Golpismo Oligárquico* (Santiago: Editorial Sudamericana, 2005), pp. 18–19.

23 Faundez, *Democratization* (ibid.), p. 23.

24 Portales, *Los Mitos de la Democracia*, pp. 26–7.

25 Eventually, in 1866, the government passed a law dispossessing Mapuche people of their lands, making 'provisions for the sale of individual plots by the state to eligible buyers'. Faundez, *Democratization*, pp. 25–6. See also Portales, *Los Mitos de la Democracia*, pp. 82-3, 85-7; J. Contesse, 'The Rebel Democracy: A Look into the Relationship between the Mapuche People and the Chilean State', *Chicano-Latino Law Review*, Vol. 26 (2006), pp. 131–54, at 139 (insightfully addressing the close link existing between the expropriation of indigenous lands and current social protest movements headed by Mapuche).

26 Portales, *Los Mitos de la Democracia*, p. 95.

27 G. Salazar and J. Pinto, *Historia Contemporánea de Chile II: Actores, Identidad y Movimiento* (Santiago: Lom Ediciones, 1999), p. 140. As late as 1995, Villalobos wrote, 'Chile's economic development required an agricultural expansion where methodic and well-guided practices should either complement or improve that of the indigenous, always limited by their primitiveness, laziness and drunkenness'. Villalobos, *Historia de los Chilenos*, p. 148 (author's translation).

28 Portales, *Los Mitos de la Democracia*, pp. 264–9; Salazar and Pinto, *Historia Contemporánea*, pp. 150–2, 165–8; Bengoa, *Historia de un Conflicto*, pp. 74–5; Instituto de Estudios Indígenas-Universidad de la Frontera, *Los Derechos de los pueblos indígena*, pp. 162–5.

pushback has continued, with indigenous peoples showing renewed aggression in their attempts to defend and restore their rights over ancestral lands only to be met with a tough governmental response.

### 2.2 *Public Policies and Indigenous Peoples*

Within this cultural-historic context, laws and public policies addressing indigenous interests have unsurprisingly been viewed by indigenous peoples as forced regulations imposed on them, rather than expressions of their own beliefs and interests. As the political philosopher Waldron has argued, involving people in designing laws (and public policies regarding their own interests) recognises a people's own sense of justice.[29] On the contrary, when part of the political community is excluded from political processes, they have legitimate reasons to perceive laws not as their own decisions, but as 'external forces of whatever kind'.[30] These arguments are regularly overlooked when noting indigenous peoples' assessments of public policies passed ostensibly 'in their own favour'.[31]

In addition to the arc of laws and policies discussed above, there are a number of key developments regarding indigenous peoples' rights that occurred as early in the Chilean republic as 1819. As is common with the politics of assimilation, attaining citizenship status may pose more danger than benefit.[32] Under the O'Higgins regime (1817–1823), liberal ideals gained some momentum: indigenous peoples were not to be considered as second-class humans, but *upgraded* to the status of (full) Chilean citizens.[33] The negative effects of this policy were soon obvious. Whereas Villalobos praises the policy, which considered indigenous people as 'brothers',[34] the reality was that citizenship helped obscure and marginalise their specific demands. Furthermore, the decision of 'giving indigenous peoples the liberty to contract' was arguably made with the specific purpose of 'placing their lands within human commerce'.[35]

29 J. Waldron, *Law and Disagreement* (Oxford: Oxford University Press, 1999), p. 238.

30 Ibid. 31 Ibid.

32 Citizenship status will normally overshadow the specific demands of minorities to hide them behind a veil of impartiality, so that the State does not take sides with any disadvantaged minority: See W. Kymlicka, *Multicultural Citizenship: A Liberal Theory of Minority Rights* (Oxford: Clarendon University, 1995). On the close connection between nationality as prerequisite for citizenship, and subsequent homogeneity of population as one of the outstanding features of the nation-state, see H. Arendt, *The Origins of Totalitarianism* (San Diego: Harcourt, 1976), pp. 11–13.

33 Portales, *Los Mitos de la Democracia*, pp. 82–3.

34 Villalobos, *Historia de los Chilenos*, p. 71.

35 Bengoa, *Historia de un Conflicto*, p. 35 (author's translation). Villalobos, on the other hand, praises the liberty to contract this equal status recognised them: ibid., pp. 72–3. It is important

The discriminatory legacy of this policy was considered afresh after the return of democracy in 1990. Having agreed with indigenous peoples a new treaty, the *Acuerdos de Nueva Imperial*, in 1989,[36] then President Aylwin submitted to Congress a bill on indigenous rights. It principally included a constitutional amendment promoting the recognition of indigenous peoples. However, the amendment has remained dormant in Congress despite approval of fifty-eight other constitutional amendments in 2005 (including the total reconfiguration of the Constitutional Court).[37] The debate particularly turned on the specific form of recognition: a significant minority in Congress has opposed the use of 'peoples' ('Chile is but one and indivisible Nation'). The last bill submitted by President Bachelet timidly used the phrase 'different ethnicities'.[38]

One dimension of the original agreement succeeded, to a limited extent. In 1993, the Congress passed the Indigenous Law (*Ley Indigena*),[39] which addressed several demands included by the indigenous peoples in the *Acuerdos*. It recognised indigenous dominion over ancestral lands[40] and created the National Corporation for Indigenous Peoples Development

to note than even these early liberal egalitarians favoured assimilation. And one of them, Bilbao, argued commercial exchange was a perfect means to achieve that end: F. Bilbao, 'La Frontera', in J. Bravo (ed.), *Francisco Bilbao: El Autor y la Obra, 1823–1865* (Santiago: Editorial Cuarto Propio, 2007), pp. 417–20.

[36] The principal agreements in the 'Acuerdos' included the filing of a constitutional amendment for the recognition of indigenous peoples and the discussion of a new law on indigenous peoples' rights, which would be prepared by a committee open to indigenous participation and ratifying ILO Convention No. 169.

[37] D. Lovera, 'Implosive Courts, Law, and Social Transformation: The Chilean Case', *Cambridge Student Law Review*, Vol. 3 (2007), pp. 30–43. The only other excluded amendment was the reform of the electoral system.

[38] Phrases such as 'indigenous peoples', 'indigenous', 'indigenous peoples integrated in the Chilean Nation', as well as recently proposed amendments, including the language of 'indivisibility of the Chilean Nation', have also been rejected. M. Henríquez, 'Los pueblos indígenas y su reconocimiento constitucional pendiente', in F. Zúñiga (ed.), *Reforma Constitucional* (Santiago: LexisNexis, 2005), pp. 135–8. A detailed description of the bills discussed in Congress, and noting how all of them have failed in considering human rights standards, is available in J. Contesse, 'Indigenous Peoples in Chile: The Quest to Become a Constitutional Entity', *Studies in Law, Politics, and Society*, Vol. 55 (2011), pp. 25–30.

[39] Law 19.253 (1993).

[40] While recognised in the 'Ley Indígena', indigenous peoples' legal right to their ancestral lands has collided several times with the more traditional constitutional concept of property. The latter seems to be winning the confrontation, though certain developments have been witnessed too, particularly in the northern part of Chile. N. Yañez, 'Reconocimiento de Derechos de Agua Indígena en Chile: Impacto de la Gran Minería y la Política de Privatización de Derechos para los Pueblos Indígenas del Norte' in N. Yañez and J. Aylwin (eds.), *El Gobierno de Lagos, los Pueblos Indígenas y el 'Nuevo Trato'* (Santiago: Lom Ediciones, 2007), pp. 308–9.

(*Corporación Nacional de Desarrollo Indígena*), which administers the Land and Water Fund for Indigenous Peoples (*Fondo de Tierras y Aguas Indígenas*).[41] However, its original content was radically reshaped during its three years of debate in parliament. Despite the suggestions of the drafting commission, which included active indigenous participation, Congress eliminated provisions providing for mandatory consultation with indigenous peoples on public matters affecting them, as well as the recognition of their right not to be moved from their lands. It also authorised the exchange of indigenous lands for non-indigenous lands,[42] and eliminated a proposed preference right for indigenous peoples in allocation of water rights. Moreover, the Land and Water Fund has proved, at least from a monetary perspective, unsatisfactory.[43] Well-established inter-American jurisprudence suggests that the approach contravenes international human rights law, particularly regarding access to land and other natural resources.[44]

There has also been some shift in political discourse, at least on the subject of historical injustices.[45] In 2003, the presidentially appointed Commission on Historic Truth and a New Deal presented its report. Its principal purpose was to prepare the grounds for new era of public policy by investigating Chile's historical treatment of its indigenous peoples. Its conclusions were clear: the State's territorial occupation of indigenous territories with military support was coupled with systematic policies of exclusion, eradication and forced assimilation. Whereas the Commission recommended several initiatives, unsurprisingly, they were not significantly different from those made in the early 1990s and ignored by the State. The Commission insisted on the

[41] A fiscal fund destined, among other things, to grant indigenous peoples subsidies to buy new lands and to acquire and regularise water rights.

[42] See Article 13.3 of the 'Ley Indígena', which permitted the aforementioned exchange, though previous authorisation from the National Corporation for Indigenous Peoples Development was needed.

[43] UN Commission on Human Rights, *Report of the Special Rapporteur* para. 20; Instituto de Estudios Indígenas-Universidad de la Frontera, *Los Derechos de los Pueblos Indígena*, pp. 181–2.

[44] On the close connection established between land and access to natural resources by both the Inter-American Commission on Human Rights and the Inter-American Court of Human Rights (particularly noting the way the court has re-shaped the right to property), see C. Nash, 'Los Derechos Indígenas en el Sistema Interamericano de Derechos Humanos', *Inter-American and European Human Rights Journal*, Vol. 1 (2008), pp. 61–86. More generally, see A. García, *El Derecho Humano al Agua* (Madrid: Editorial Trotta, 2008), pp. 26–7, 36–8.

[45] For a critical examination, see J. Aylwin, 'La Política del "Nuevo Trato": Antecedentes, Alcances y Limitaciones', and P. Acevedo, 'El Discurso de Lagos, los Pueblos Indígenas y los Medios de Comunicación', in N. Yañez and J. Aylwin (eds.), *El Gobierno de Lagos*, pp. 29–58 and 467–91, respectively.

constitutional recognition of the collective existence of indigenous peoples', the implementation of new participatory rights, as well as the adoption and implementation of reparatory measures concerning their ancestral lands.[46]

In 2008, then President Bachelet announced a 'social covenant for multiculturalism'. Entitled *Re-Conocer* – Re-Cognition –,[47] and acknowledging a seemingly racist and insensitive Chilean culture, Bachelet declared a new policy aimed at improving the social position of indigenous peoples. Recognition and redistribution would form the policy's main pillars. Concerning land and water rights, the new social covenant concedes that the current state of affairs is unacceptable. Apparently, the policy would place particular attention on the recognition of indigenous claims over land, as well as natural resources, water, and water catchment areas.[48] These policies appeared promising and, without doubt, several improvements have been made. Still, the progress is halting and the authorities, which generally see themselves as belonging to a homogenous race, culture and nation, opted to adopt such policies without any consultation,[49] a fact that may explain the Chileno-Mapuche conflict in southern Chile.[50]

## 3 CHILE'S WATER CODE: PROPERTY RIGHTS AND FREE TRADE

In understanding Chile's water rights allocation system, Bauer has argued that three moments are decisive: it began with a somewhat balanced starting point, from which a pendulum radically moved to one side (characterised by a strong State) and then to the other (characterised by a *laissez faire* State or one with few and limited regulatory powers).[51] The first two phases occurred between

[46] Comisión Verdad Histórica y Nuevo Trato, *Informe de la Comisión Verdad Histórica y Nuevo Trato: Propuestas y Recomendaciones para un Nuevo Trato entre el Estado, los Pueblos Indígenas y la Sociedad Chilena* (Santiago: Gobierno de Chile, 2003), pp. 588, 645–8. Some voices within the commission opposed the idea. F. Larraín, 'Comisión de Verdad Histórica y Nuevo Trato: Opinión de Minoría', *Revista Estudios Públicos*, Vol. 92 (2003), pp. 5–18 (arguing that recognising specific territories for indigenous would be equivalent to creating of ghettos of poverty, and advocating for their 'integration to the national society enjoying of its developments, but keeping their identity'). In a similar sense, strongly opposing to the idea of recognising collective rights, L. Sierra, 'La Constitución y los Indígenas en Chile: Reconocimiento Individual y no Colectivo', *Revista Estudios Públicos*, Vol. 92 (2003), pp. 19–27.

[47] Gobierno de Chile, *Re-Conocer. Pacto Social por la Multiculturalidad* (Santiago: Ministerio de Planificación-Corporación Nacional de Desarrollo Indígena, 2008).

[48] Ibid., p. 14. [49] See further in Section 3. [50] Contesse, 'The Rebel Democracy', p. 148.

[51] C. Bauer, *Canto de Sirenas: El Derecho de Aguas Chileno como Modelo para Reformas Internacionales* (Bilbao: Bakeaz, 2004), pp. 64–5 (originally published in English as *Siren Song: Chilean Water Law as a Model for International Reform*, Resources for the Future, 2004).

1951 and 1973 and will be briefly analysed in the following subsection (3.1). More attention will be placed on the third: the democratic collapse precipitated by Pinochet's *coup d' etat* and the 'economic public order' (Section 3.2) that paved the way for the 1981 Water Code and the current regulation of water rights (Section 3.3).

### 3.1 *From the Centre to the Left (1951–1973)*

The starting point for water reforms may be located between 1951 and 1967. Chile's Water Code of 1951 was conceived as a mixture of property rights and a strong State.[52] Under this model, water rights were allocated through an administrative process. Once granted, water rights were protected under a scheme of regular property rights, instead of that of administrative permissions or concessions.[53]

However, the State maintained ample regulatory powers in the hands of the Ministry of Public Works, which can be attributed to earlier market failures.[54] Restrictions were imposed on the non-use of water: rights could be cancelled if water was not used within a five-year period. Concession applicants were asked to justify how they would use the water and describe the necessary infrastructure that would be employed for that purpose. Provisory rights were granted in the preliminary stages, and were transformed into definitive rights once the authority had verified the use requirements.[55] Once provided, rights holders were not permitted to alter the water use. If this occurred, the Code re-vested the rights in the State and a new application would be necessary.[56] Moreover, in any conflict over water uses, priority was to be given to domestic and potable uses; irrigation, hydroelectricity and other industrial purposes were granted a secondary status.[57]

As was the case with the subsequent phases, the Water Code of 1951 was a product of compromises between the then dominant political forces. Although adopted in 1951, it foreshadowed the period that followed Ibanez's authoritarian regime (1952–1958), which has been labelled a 'state of compromise'. Political stability was secured by an implicit agreement between the majoritarian centre-left coalition and the conservative right, its principal feature consisting of the acceptance by right-wing parties of an enhanced role

[52] Ibid., pp. 65–6.

[53] The issue is not an irrelevant one. Under the current scheme, a debate has emerged on the nature of the rights over waters. See Section 2.3.

[54] This market failure would be later crucial in the pendulum's next swing. Faundez, *Democratization*, pp. 90–1.

[55] Bauer, *Canto de Sirenas*, pp. 66–7. [56] Ibid., p. 67. [57] Ibid.

for the State in the management of the economy, in exchange for a commitment by the centre left not to undertake land reform.

This 'state of compromise' began to unravel in 1964. The Christian Democratic Party commenced a deep process of land reform, strongly resented by the right wing. The agrarian reform (*la reforma agraria*) – a comprehensive legal plan aimed at redistributing property rights over land and water[58] – marked the political background of the pendulum's first move in 1967. According to Frei's presidential campaign, the goal of the reform was to create 100,000 new property owners, particularly though the assignment of property rights to rural workers. Not only were several large landowners deprived of their land with little compensation, but the scheme also impacted water rights, as irrigation followed land distribution.[59] The constitutional amendment that was passed for the reform allowed the State to place all waters in the public domain and permitted the expropriation of privately owned water resources. With all waters in the public domain,[60] the new Water Code, passed in 1969, radicalised to a certain extent the centralised governmental administration.[61] The State water agency (*Dirección General de Aguas* or DGA) was created and endowed with a reasonable budget and broad authority,[62] including powers to resolve conflicts over water uses, thereby minimising the potential negative influence of the courts.[63]

Because the 'reform' sought the 'redistribution of water rights under the technical standards of rational and advantageous use',[64] certain lands – to which water rights were legally linked – were declared 'special zones for the rationalisation of water'.[65] Within those zones the DGA enjoyed the authority to reallocate water rights, according to certain criteria.[66] Water rights were also strictly limited, losing their property-like features in the new concession regime.[67] Moreover, separating water rights from the land to which they were attached was not permitted, while any form of commercial transaction concerning water was forbidden.[68]

58 See Law 16.640 (1967); and Faundez, *Democratization*, pp. 159–60.

59 Campos, *Historia Constitucional*, pp. 322–3. In preparing the reform, a constitutional amendment was passed in 1967 (Law 16.625) by which the right to property was adjusted to permit expropriation with compensation that took account of community interests. S. Carrasco, *Génesis y Vigencia de los Textos Constitucionales Chilenos*, 3rd edition (Santiago: Editorial Jurídica de Chile, 2002), pp. 159, 184–5.

60 See Chilean Civil Code, Article 589.

61 Bauer, *Canto de Sirenas*, pp. 67–8.

62 Ibid., p. 69.

63 Today, the current situation is precisely the opposite: a modest DGA without adjudicatory faculties. This is discussed further below.

64 Bauer, *Canto de Sirenas*, p. 69.

65 Ibid.

66 Ibid.

67 Being thus subjected to administrative regulations, instead of constitutional or legal ones.

68 Bauer, *Canto de Sirenas*, pp. 68–9.

In terms of indigenous lands and waters, a specific law was passed in 1972, under Allende's rule.[69] Its principal purpose was to further regulate the process for division of indigenous lands, requiring higher quorums of community members for any new demarcation.[70] It also established the Indigenous Development Institute (*Instituto de Desarrollo Indígena*) (which carried out several expropriations, transferring 710,816 acres in the Mapuche zone to indigenous communities as well as to non-indigenous rural workers.[71]

However, like many land reforms in the developing world, it enjoyed limited success due to landowner resistance and failure to maintain effective State control. According to Bauer, the scheme struggled with the social polarisation it helped produce (which culminated with Pinochet's *coup d' etat* in 1973) and the high amount of resources, staff and institutional capacity the model demanded.[72] It has also been suggested that the close link between the Mapuche and Allende helped lead to the counter-expropriation of these lands once Pinochet assumed power.[73]

### 3.2 *Constitutional Interregnum (1970–1980)*

The final swing of the pendulum occurred in 1981, when Chile radically moved from a regulatory State to an open free market model, under the auspices of the military dictatorship of Pinochet (however, in 2005, the pendulum was arguably pushed even further in this direction). This period was marked by the constitutional enshrinement of strong property rights, privatisation of former State-owned enterprises and the reduction of the authority of State agencies.[74] This was helped by the taming of democratic institutions: Congress was perceived as a populist and demagogical space and designated senators were subsequently 'incorporated' under a 'protected democracy', on the advice of the newly created National Security Council.[75]

[69] Law 17.729 (1972). Suggesting this law actually responded to indigenous demands, see Salazar and Pinto, *Historia Contemporánea*, pp. 158–9.

[70] Instituto de Estudios Indígenas-Universidad de la Frontera, *Los Derechos de los Pueblos Indígena*, p. 163.

[71] Ibid., pp. 164–5. [72] Ibid., pp. 69–70. [73] Ibid.

[74] E. Silva, 'Democracy, Market Economics, and Environmental Policy in Chile', *Journal of Interamerican Studies and World Affairs*, Vol. 38, No. 4 (1996), pp. 1–33, at 4.

[75] The National Security Council was a constitutional entity, composed of a majority of non-civilian actors, empowered to bring to the attention of the other branches of State any action that in its opinion threatened the institutions of the country. It was also entitled to choose four 'designated senators'. The Council still exists though with fewer attribution as amended in 2005. J. Couso, D. Lovera, M. Guiloff and A. Coddou, *International*

In order to understand this phase, it is important to chart the constitutional backdrop marked by the 1980 Constitution.[76] First, in one of his initial moves, the Pinochet regime overturned the 'agrarian reform' initiatives and paid monetary compensation to those whose property had been expropriated. It further strengthened property rights in both constitutional and legal schemes. Guzmán, who engineered much of the Pinochet reform, claimed that the former President Frei had 'massively violated the most basic of human rights, property'.[77] Land transferred to indigenous peoples was returned to the alleged previous owners under military pressure[78] and Salazar and Pinto have documented that more than 460,000 acres were lost after the decree laws passed in 1979.[79]

Second, fear of the recent past led the constitution's drafters to radicalise their defence of (what would be the hitherto unmovable basis for) free trade. This led to the constitutional establishment of the so-called 'economic public order'. Alarmed by the socialist government of Allende, Pinochet and his allies established the basis for a free-trade-oriented Constitution.[80] According to Cea, the Commission responsible for drafting the new Constitution 'understood that social rights are expectations or aspirations, of which materialization ... depends on the governmental resources set aside for those issues. Thus, the Commission pretended to avoid the demagogy, that so much pain caused to our country'.[81]

The 1980 Constitution thus fixed the basis for a free-trade-oriented economy. It was a 'complete constitution' which entrenched private property as the means of production was deeply entrenched. Only a subsidiary role was contemplated for the State, which had clearly demarcated and

*Encyclopaedia of Laws: Constitutional Law: Chile* (Alphen aan den Rijn: Wolters Kluwer, 2011), pp. 38–9.

76 As is well known, the radical implementation of neoliberal policies was strongly promoted in Chile by international financial institutions. J. Budds and G. McGranahan, 'Are the Debates on Water Privatization Missing the Point? Experiences from Africa, Asia and Latin America', *Environment and Urbanization*, Vol. 15 (2003), p. 108. The World Bank also strongly promoted the Chilean model.

77 Quoted in R. Cristi, *El Pensamiento Politico de Jamie Guzmán* (Santiago: Lom Ediciones, 2000), p. 156.

78 Bengoa, *Historia de un Conflicto*, pp. 228–9.

79 Salazar and Pinto, *Historia Contemporánea*, pp. 165–6.

80 R. Barros, *La Junta Militar. Pinochet y la Constitución de 1980* (Santiago: Editorial Sudamericana, 2005), pp. 270–3.

81 The 'pain caused to our country' that Cea refers to were the socially oriented policies that started to be implemented with the 'agrarian reform' and were later enhanced under Allende: J. Cea, *Derecho Constitucional Chileno* (Santiago: Universidad Católica de Chile 2003), p. 638.

limited regulatory powers.[82] Whereas some of its drafters viewed the constitution as agnostic on the choice of economic model (Guzmán, for instance, thought that charges of right-wing bias amounted to 'unfounded fears'[83]), Guzmán himself wrote 'there is no doubt about the libertarian compromise of this new democracy in economic matters'.[84] Not only were strong property rights recognised, but a constitutional injunction (*recurso de protección*) was created for individuals whose property rights were threatened, disturbed or deprived by the act or omission of either a government authority or another individual. A writ could be filed in a Court of Appeals and the matter would be given priority over all others.[85] With an allusion to natural law, the constitution also permitted the acquisition of any kind of property in all its dimensions, both material and immaterial.[86] Moreover, the Constitution mentioned water rights. The rights of private citizens over waters already constituted in conformity with the law were to be recognised as proprietorship.[87]

As Couso notes, the Constitution dedicates 'long paragraphs meticulously detailing the definition, nature, status of the right to private property . . . as well as a specific regulation of the limits imposed on Congress'.[88] Property's social function – highlighted during the period of agrarian reform – was drastically minimised. The State would assume only a subsidiary place, which meant a preference for private economic initiative in all spheres. Together with the constitutional recognition of the liberty to freely initiate any economic activity, these provisions were intended to help trigger a radical process of privatisation.[89]

82 Ibid., pp. 17–19.

83 J. Guzmán, 'La Definición Constitucional', in *Constitución Política de la República de Chile* (Santiago: Fundación Jaime Guzmán E., 1999), p. 32.

84 Ibid., p. 34.

85 C. Bauer, *Contra la Corriente: Privatización, Mercados de Agues y el Estado en Chile* (Santiago: Lom Ediciones, 2002), pp. 47–9.

86 Article 19, sections 23 and 24 of the Constitution.

87 Article 19 section 24, final paragraph of the Constitution. See also, Couso, Lovera, Guiloff and Coddou, *Constitutional Law: Chile*, pp. 233–4.

88 J. Couso, 'The politics of judicial review in Chile in the era of transition, 1990–2002', in S. Gloppen, R. Gargarella and E. Skaar (eds.), *Democratization and the Judiciary; The Accountability Function of Courts in New Democracies* (London: Routledge, 2004).

89 Under the proviso of not being against morality, public order and national security. Article 19(21) of the Constitution. However, it is important to highlight that this subsidiary role for the State is an interpretation imposed by scholars supportive of the Constitution of 1980, rather than what the text expressly notes. R. Vallejo and D. Pardow, 'Derribando Mitos sobre el Estado Empresario', *Revista Chilena de Derecho*, Vol. 35, No. 1 (2008), pp. 135–56.

### 3.3 *A Swing Back to the Right* (1981–2008)

Sustained by this fear of socialism (or a confidence in self-regulation and the market) water rights regulation underwent a radical transformation, which started as early in the military regime as 1979 with Decree Law 2.603.[90] The Decree was primarily constructed on the principles of free trade and the regularisation of rights previously allocated.[91] In support of free trade, it allowed property rights over water usage (although not the water itself, which remained under the public domain), the division of water rights from land ownership, and the commercialisation of water rights. As to the regularisation of previously allocated rights, it sought to reorganise the 'disorder' caused by the agrarian reforms and the regime's later counter-reform. Article 7 created a legal presumption of ownership of water rights in 'those owning lands currently using the water' and those 'currently and effectively using water'. It also created a tax on waters. The logic was paradoxical, but simple: taxing waters would enhance its image as a commodity, prompting owners to commercialise water rights apart from their (rights over their) lands. This would also give owners an economic incentive to build new irrigation infrastructure.[92]

In 1981, a more formal Water Code was passed. It maintained the aforementioned structure, except for the taxes.[93] In this new structure, the market would solely fix the price of water rights, with the DGA possessing limited powers of adjudication.[94] Even though water resources remained 'national goods of public use', Vergara argues that the 1981 reforms reveal that the State is not really the *de facto* owner. The phraseology is 'simply a legal technique to allow governmental regulation of economic activities', particularly to ensure the 'free transferability of rights'.[95] As Budds has suggested, this model rests on the following premises: 'that market pricing will force the highest value use of water in relation to its scarcity, that private property rights promote individual

[90] Although disputed by some, the constitutional basis for free trade was later replicated when enacting the new Water Code in 1981. See P. Ruiz-Tagle, 'Orden Público Económico, Subsidiariedad y Alternativa Democrática', in R. Cristi and P. Ruiz-Tagle (eds.), *La República en Chile. Teoría y Práctica del Constitucionalismo Republicano* (Santiago: Lom Ediciones, 2006), pp. 323–40.

[91] Bauer, *Canto de Sirenas*, pp. 74–5. As shown below, this latter aspect proved crucial in establishing the basis for indigenous peoples' legal recognition of their water rights.

[92] Bauer, *Canto de Sirenas*, p. 76. [93] Ibid., pp. 79–80.

[94] F. Segura, *Derecho de Aguas*, 3rd edition (Santiago: LexisNexis, 2006), pp. 197–8.

[95] A. Vergara, 'Estatuto Jurídico, Tipología y Problemas Actuales de los Derechos de Aprovechamiento de Aguas', *Revista Estudios Públicos*, Vol. 69 (1998), p. 192.

choice, and that the market is more politically neutral than the State in resource allocation'.[96]

In light of the previously mentioned guidelines, the Water Code of 1981 contained the following features: (a) the upgrading of property rights with full market value for expropriation;[97] (b) the removal of requirement to justify water use in DGA applications and allowance for uses to be changed;[98] (c) the separation of water rights from land rights, in order to encourage free transactions; (d) no prioritisation of water uses and if multiple requests for the same water resource,[99] allocation to be determined through a public auction for the highest price;[100] (e) applications for water rights not to be denied and discretion to granted them 'free of charge';[101] (f) water rights can 'be freely traded, mortgaged or transferred';[102] and (g) no obligation to use water rights despite the previous accumulation of water monopolies

As may be appreciated, the water rights market rests on the assumption that the rights will be optimally allocated when they are distributed to those most willing to pay.[103] Three observations are worth making about this model. First, it is not clear that there has been any significant increase in economic efficiency. Indeed, the scheme mostly benefited large companies, particularly those in the hydroelectric business, creating monopolies in the control of rights.[104]

96 J. Budds, 'Power, Nature, and Neoliberalism: the Political Ecology of Water in Chile', in *Singapore Journal of Tropical Geography*, Vol. 23, No. 3 (2004), pp. 322–42, at 323. The author has provided ample background on the technical discourse used to advance political objectives. J. Budds, 'Contested H2O: Science, Policy and Politics in Water Resources Management in Chile', *Geoforum*, No. 40, (2009), pp. 420–1.

97 In 1997, the Constitutional Court held that, according to the Constitution, water rights were administrative concessions in that they gave the holder no property right over the water itself. However, it also highlighted that the Constitution grants the holder a property right over that administrative concession, which constitutes the actual constitutional protection. Tribunal Constitucional de Chile, Rol No. 260, 16 September 1997.

98 This might change in light of 2005 water reforms. As Segura has argued, those asking for the allocation of water rights, needed only to state, 'the amount of water they *desire* to extract'. With 2005 reforms that expression was changed to 'the amount of water they *need* to extract'. This would give the DGA greater authority, but it is a debate still yet to come having in practice no significant impact. Segura, *Derecho de Aguas*, pp. 73–4.

99 Segura, *Derecho de Aguas* (ibid.), pp. 78–9.

100 This auction is thus open to anyone who wants to participate. Vergara has noted the importance of this procedure is that it leaves to the market the decision about adjudicating new rights: those (really) wanting water will pay (more) for it. Vergara, 'Estatuto Jurídico', p. 163.

101 Budds, 'Power, Nature, and Neoliberalism, p. 326. 102 Ibid.

103 M. Thobani, 'Tradable Property Rights to Water. How to Improve Water Use and Resolve Water Conflicts', in *Public Policy for the Private Sector*, No. 34 (Washington, DC: The World Bank, 1995), p. 4.

104 The formation of monopolies was one of the reasons behind a reform proposed by the Chilean government in 1992, a process that eventually failed. Bauer, *Canto de Sirenas*, p. 89.

Whereas the World Bank has argued that future allocations would lead to a more efficient equilibrium,[105] this endorsement has been criticised because of the lack of empirical evidence.[106] Second, environmental policies have been ignored. The initial and subsequent implementation of the Water Code of 1981 led to the exhaustion of water resources with little left for environmental protection.[107] Third, the model may value the highest monetary bidder, but it does not necessarily recognise who actually values the water the most – the supposed bedrock of neoclassical economics which is based on utility maximisation. The sale of indigenous water resources reveals especially this problematique.[108]

In a more recent assessment of the functioning of Chile's water rights model, the World Bank has recognised water's scarcity as legal, not factual. World Bank, 'Chile: Diagnóstico de la gestión de recursos hídricos,' p. 9.

105 M. Ríos and J. Quiroz, 'The Market for Water Rights in Chile: Major Issues', World Bank Technical Paper No. 285 (Washington, DC: The International Bank for Reconstruction and Development, 1995), pp. 28–9, suggesting radical reforms are not necessary, but '"fine tuning" of the current system' is required. R. Hearne and W. Easter, 'Water Allocation and Water Markets. An Analysis of Gains-from-Trade in Chile', World Bank Technical Paper No. 315 (Washington, DC: The International Bank for Reconstruction and Development, 1995), p. 38. ('The overall growth in the value of Chile's agricultural output during the last decade can be attributed to various reforms in both input and output markets'.)

106 Bauer, *Canto de Sirenas*, pp. 116–25. Confronted to evidence the World Bank itself has recently shown the market of water rights has been functioning in a very limited way – due not, of course, to legal provisions which as noted are all aimed at favouring it. World Bank, 'Chile: Diagnóstico de la gestión de recursos hídricos', pp. 30–3.

107 Silva has argued the impact of unregulated development – primarily promoted by Pinochet, and later maintained during democracy – has caused 'depletion of fisheries, destruction of natural forests, soil erosion and desertification, as well as pollution of water resources'. E. Silva, 'Democracy and Environmental Policy in Chile', p. 5.

108 In November 2016, the Chamber of Deputies passed relevant reforms to the Water Code. These reforms begin the strengthening of water qualification as a national public good. It includes specific provisions stating that the private exercise of water rights could be limited in light of 'public interest', defined as the protection of human consumption and sanitization, the protection and preservation of the ecosystem, availability, and sustainability. It also includes specific mention of indigenous lands: in indigenous territories – the bill goes on – the State shall protect existing waters for the benefit of indigenous communities, conforming to legal regulations and international treaty obligations (as it will be pointed out in the next section, this mention may prove crucial in leaving things as they are).

Besides these conceptual provisions, reforms also include (i) the limitation of water rights up to 30 years - and although these rights can be renewed, the DGA can prevent that renewal if it declares the non-effective use of water; (ii) expiration clauses for water rights in case of non-effective use; and (iii) a prohibition on allocation of rights over waters running in protected and glacial areas, amongst other regulations. As of December of 2016 these reforms await debate before the Senate, amid increasing claims against their constitutionality. In fact, some voices have claimed these new regulations affect property rights over waters. An excellent case arguing for these kinds of regulations' constitutionality can be found in F. Atria and

## 4 THE WATER CODE AND INDIGENOUS RIGHTS

According to Salazar, one of the main threats faced by indigenous peoples in Chile is the State's decision to exploit natural resources for energy generation.[109] Concerns expressed by environmentalist groups and indigenous peoples over the consequences have received little consideration.[110] The economic benefits, which are significant, were seemingly too difficult to dismiss. By November 2008, the National Environment Commission (Comisión Nacional de Medioambiente or CONAMA) – the State agency in charge of environmentally assessing projects – had received 1,366 applications, amounting to more than USD 33 billion.[111]

This section will trace some of the conflicts that have emerged between hydroelectric as well as mining companies and indigenous peoples in the shadow of the Water Code. It will begin by suggesting that the interests of indigenous peoples have been largely overlooked due to the institutional preference in the Water Code for hydroelectricity. It will then highlight the systemic failure to recognise participatory rights in these resource projects before moving on to discuss how resolution of conflicts is left largely in the hands of the market.

### 4.1 *Exclusion: Water as Solely an Economic Good*

As has been documented in Chile and elsewhere, environmental externalities disproportionately affect the most vulnerable groups of society. Rights to life, health, clean water, privacy, healthy environment, and property are amongst the rights often implicated. The most vulnerable groups who bear these costs are the poor and, within them, the poorest of the poor: indigenous peoples. In his report on Chile, the UN Special Rapporteur on Indigenous Peoples' Rights affirmed that several social conflicts can be understood in light of the perverse effects that recent development projects have had on

C. Salgado, *La propiedad, el dominio público y el régimen de aprovechamiento de las aguas en Chile* (Santiago: Legal Publishing, 2015).

109 'La urgencia de Chile para teñirse de verde', *El Mercurio*, 9 November 2008. What is striking is not the fact that the State has made the decision to focus its energy efforts on hydroelectricity, but that recourse to it is justified on environmental grounds.

110 Salazar and Pinto, *Historia Contemporánea*, pp. 169–70 (an argument notably similar to that made during the Chilean appropriation of indigenous lands by the 1880s).

111 'Grandes proyectos mineros y eléctricos apuntalan inversions en el país', *La Tercera*, 4 November 2008.

indigenous peoples' human rights.[112] Whereas development is usually not possible without some kind of environmental footprint, in this instance only a small portion of the population – both in number and political power – will bear its costs.[113]

Budds has suggested that this occurs because water is only considered as a material good. Privatisation of water rights assumes that nature (water) is fully appropriable and can be managed with various technical tools.[114] As the social aspect is marginalised, there is little room for the citizenry to have a say in its management. That is why political ecology 'focuses on the (unequal) power structures and politics that underline processes of environmental change and socio-political and environmental implications of changes in the way natural resources are allocated and managed, with particular emphasis on the interests of "weaker" social actors'.[115] In other words, a political ecology perspective opens space for considerations other than mere technical or economic views about nature, as often advanced by indigenous peoples. Consider for instance what Calderón suggests: 'In the Andean culture water is a living person, relative of the *ayllu*. Whilst for the modern West, water is a chemical-composed scientifically material resource'.[116]

These broader perspectives on nature are excluded from Chile's water model. Even though the model is meant to broadly promote the efficient allocation of water rights, the legal architecture and institutional incentives promote a narrower and sectoral goal: hydroelectric generation of energy. As Prieto has argued, the water rights market is not neutral:[117]

[112] UN Commission on Human Rights, *Report of the Special Rapporteur*, para. 24.

[113] Centro de Derechos Humanos, Universidad Diego Portales, *Informe Anual sobre Derechos Humanos en Chile 2008* (Santiago: Universidad Diego Portales, 2008), pp. 505–34 (showing actual cases of unfair distributions of environmental impact).

[114] Budds, 'Power, Nature, and Neoliberalism', p. 325.

[115] Ibid. See also, J. Budds, 'Contested H2O', pp. 425–6; M. Prieto, 'La Ecología (a)política del modelo de aguas chileno' in B. Bustos et al. (eds.), *Ecología política en Chile. Naturaleza, propiedad, conocimiento y poder* (Santiago: Editorial Universitaria, 2014), pp. 146-51.

[116] C. Calderón, 'Retos en la concepción del agua en el mundo', in J. Von Kessel and H. Larraín (eds.), *Manos Sabias para Cuidar la Vida* (Quito: Abeya-Yala, 1997), p. 331. The voice *ayllu* refers to the indigenous community. Some have suggested that certain core elements are collective property of the land anchored in a common prehispanic past. M. E. Choque, 'La Reconstitución del Ayllu y los Derechos de los Pueblos Indígenas', in F. García (ed.), *Las Sociedades Interculturales: Un Desafío para el Siglo XXI* (Quito: FLACSO, 2000), p. 13.

[117] Markets, as Bauer suggests, 'are built up on previous political decisions, formally expressed as legal norms and legal institutions [where] even a "free" market cannot be neutral, objective, or apolitical, as its defenders normally argue': *Canto de Sirenas*, p. 81. Or in the words of Budds: 'nature is not an objective entity, but is perceived differently according to

> [T]he current model in Chile is oriented towards assigning water resources exclusively to productive and extractive uses, while leaving other possible uses (e.g. ecological, cultural), and one in which hydroelectric power generation enjoys preferential and advantageous use in comparison with other possible sources of generation.[118]

The Water Code of 1981 distinguishes between two types of water rights: consumptive and non-consumptive. The former allows the right holder to consume the water (as occurs in irrigation). The latter makes it mandatory for the right holder to return the water to its source.[119] On its face, this does not represent a preference for 'non-consumptive' hydroelectricity. In theory, non-consumptive uses would also include those undertaken for ecological or recreational purposes. But in practice, Prieto notes that the track record of institutional choices reveals that non-consumptive water rights for non-hydroelectric objectives are 'practically non-existent'.[120] According to the Water Code, in requesting water rights, an applicant must indicate the specific place at which they will reintegrate water within the basin. Therefore, if the applicant does not indicate the place of return of waters, there is formally no 'extraction'. Thus it 'is not necessary to obtain water use rights', reasons the DGA, and they are not *formally* allocated.[121] Prieto notes that ENDESA (Empresa Nacional de Electricidad S.A.), the main electricity generating company, owns 55 per cent of all water rights granted in Chile. Of particular importance is the fact that in the 'Región de la Araucanía',

the actor, the time and the context, and, subsequently, *constructed* according to these positionalities and mobilized through discourses that support them'. 'Power, Nature, and Neoliberalism', p. 324.

[118] M. Prieto, 'Hydroelectric Power Generation in Chile: An Institutional Critique of the Neutrality of Markets Mechanism', unpublished Master thesis, Catholic University of Chile (2008), p. 1. This proves critical for indigenous peoples whose customs and local practices of water management (sometimes labeled as inefficient and anarchic) are ignored under the auspicies of cost-benefit analysis. M. Prieto, 'Privatizing Water in the Chilean Andes: The Case of Las Vegas de Chiu-Chiu', in *Mountain Research and Development*, Vol. 35, No. 3 (2011), pp. 223–28.

[119] Segura, *Derecho de Aguas*, p. 67.

[120] Prieto, 'Hydroelectric Power', p. 4.

[121] As Prieto has noted, if the applicant does not specify the specific place where water will be returned then it would be considered an *in situ* use of water (e.g. sailing on a lake), and allocation of water rights would be unnecessary (ibid). It is important to note the terminology used in a 2000 cadastre of water rights, conducted by a university with the support of the DGA. It refers to consumptive rights (e.g. irrigation), non-consumptive rights (e.g. hydroelectricity), and to a third category of non-consumptive and non-productive uses (not rights), specifically detailing recreational and environmental uses. Gobierno de Chile, Ministerio de Obras Públicas, Dirección General de Aguas – Universidad Austral de Chile, *Catastro y Localización de Usos Públicos No Extractivos o Usos* in situ *delaAgua*, SIT No. 65 (2000), pp. 9-13.

an administrative province in southern Chile and one with the highest indigenous population lives, it holds 98 per cent of allocated rights.[122]

With such a large percentage of water rights already allocated, any government attempt to redistribute them and land rights (although there has been no effort evinced thus far) would fall foul on the deeply entrenched property rights protections.[123] Moreover, institutional regulations are mainly, if not exclusively, directed to the extractive use of water, particularly hydroelectric power generation. When the Water Code of 1981 was finally amended in 2005, after more than thirteen years of discussion,[124] it confirmed Prieto's warning about the institutional promotion of a specific use of water. According to the recent amendments, a tax will be imposed on non-usage of water rights,[125] and applicants must now justify the amount of water they will use in light of the economic activity they will develop.[126] These reforms pose even stronger limits on the allocation of ancestral indigenous rights. Under the notion of 'non-economic' or non-productive usage, taxes will be imposed on all peoples not exploiting water as the authorities wish. The principle is now: use it or lose it.[127] Social, cultural and environmental considerations have been simply airbrushed out of water resources management in Chile.[128]

[122] Prieto, 'Hydroelectric Power', pp. 5–6. This might explain why only 2 per cent of water rights on indigenous territories are hold by indigenous peoples. L. Barrera-Hernández, 'Indigenous Peoples, Human Rights and Natural Resource Development', p. 25.

[123] As it has already been noted, several conflicts have arisen between 'formalised water rights' and those arguing an ancestral use of water – meaning, traditional rights acquired according to customary traditions. Segura, *Derecho de Aguas*, pp. 59–60, 70–1; Vergara, 'Estatuto Jurídico', pp. 166–7 (noting the impact of customary water rights recognised in the 'Ley Indígena'); Corte de Apelaciones de Iquique, Rol No. 817, 9 April 2008 (granting indigenous peoples in northern Chile property rights over ancestral water rights, in accordance with the 'Ley Indígena'); W. Alburquenque, 'Comunidad Indígena y Derechos sobre Recursos Naturales', *La Tercera*, 2 June 2008 (critiquing the previous decision for allegedly having given preference to indigenous rights over traditional and formalised rights).

[124] Law 20.017 (2005).

[125] According to some scholars, these taxes were thought of as a device to reduce water rights accumulation and future speculation. F. Segura, 'La Reforma del Código de Aguas', *Revista de Derecho, Universidad de Concepción*, Vols. 215–216 (2004), pp. 29–47, at 31.

[126] Yañez, 'Reconocimiento de Derechos de Agua Indígena en Chile', p. 305.

[127] Even the model's strongest supporters have argued against the imposition of this tax on the basis that it overlooks the interests of some who may not have used water under the reform's simplistic approach. A. Gómez-Lobo and R. Paredes, 'Mercado de Derechos de Agua: Reflexiones sobre el Proyecto de Modificación al Código de Aguas', *Revista Estudios Públicos*, Vol. 82 (2001), pp. 83–104, at 87–8.

[128] Ibid., pp. 306–7; Segura has suggested the only groups prejudiced by this reform would be large economic consortiums holding water rights. Segura, 'La Reforma del Código', p. 30.

## 4.2 *Contestation and State Abstention*

**The Case of Hydroelectricity**

In November 2008, the Regional Committee on Environment, which assesses projects (such as the hydroelectric ones) from an environmental standpoint, announced that one of the most contentious, hydroelectric initiatives – the 'HidroAysén', involving USD 3.2 billion of private investment in the Chilean Patagonia – received almost 3,000 questions from different public agencies. In May 2011, the Committee of Environmental Evaluation finally approved the project, dismissing many of the questions. The decision triggered massive demonstrations, with complaints about procedural irregularities and the role of the authorities in the approval of the project.[129]

Other projects have not even enjoyed such initial critical attention from the authorities. SN Power, a well-known energy multinational, was planning to expand its hydroelectricity projects in Chile. Through its subsidiary, Trayenko SA, it aimed to establish new hydroelectric power plants in southern Chile: Panguipulli, Lago Ranco, and Futrono.[130] Whereas indigenous peoples represent 30.8 per cent of the zone's population, nearly 80 per cent of them inhabit the territories to be used for hydroelectric projects.[131] Indigenous communities living around Lake Maihue claimed these projects would impair their way of life by constructing energy plants in ancestral territories and using large amounts of water.[132]

To articulate their opposition, indigenous peoples formed work committees in Liquiñe and Coñaripe.[133] The communities referred to ILO Convention No. 169 and argued that their economic, social, and cultural rights had

[129] 'Evaluador de EIA de HidroAysén: 'Creo que con los Errors Trataron de Coartar Su Revisión', *La Tercera*, 23 May 2011 (where an independent expert hired by the DGA to assess the project claims he received 'an illegible pdf file with several mistakes in figures and maps'); 'Los Conflictos de Interés que Contaminan la Evaluación Ambiental de HidroAysén', *Ciper Chile*, 13 July 2011 (on the conflict of interest several members of the committee); 'El Informe Crítico a Hidroaysén que Fue Eliminado por SERNAGEOMIN', *Ciper Chile*, 9 June 2011 (claiming some critical reports on the project were eliminated and not considered); 'HidroAysén: Funcionarias Ratificaron Denuncias de Irregularidades contra Seremi de Vivienda', *Radio Cooperativa*, 14 June 2011 (denouncing illegal changes on some of the evaluative reports of the project).

[130] S. Schönenberger and H. Silva, 'Los Proyectos Hidroeléctricos de SN Power en el Valle de Liquiñe Comuna de Panguipulli', Documento de Trabajo No. 8 (Temuco: Observatorio Ciudadano, 2009).

[131] Ibid., p. 10.

[132] 'Nuevo Escenario Territorial para Enfrentar Megaproyecto Hidroeléctrico Maqueo de Trayenko-SN Power', *Observatorio Ciudadano*, 5 December 2010.

[133] Schönenberger and Silva, 'Los Proyectos Hidroeléctricos', p. 12.

been violated.[134] They also took part in demonstrations to bring attention to possible violations of their rights.[135] Though no legal action was taken, SN Power eventually decided to withdraw, selling its 80 per cent stake in Trayenko SA. According to a financial newspaper, the corporation left the project, in part, because there were 'several problems [that] they faced with Mapuche and Huilliche indigenous communities in the region'.[136] A formal statement from SN Power stated that it was 'developing around the globe, and not only in Chile, [and decided to] concentrate on those projects that are further ahead'.[137] Indigenous communities expressed their happiness, highlighting the joint work several of the communities had undertaken and affirming they would be prepared for further resistance.[138]

It is worth highlighting the recourse communities made to international norms, accompanied with coordinated action, both in Chile and Norway. However, some caution must be taken about the utility of ILO Convention No. 169 in domestic courts. Several cases followed the coming into force of the Convention.[139] In the case of *Mini Central Cayucupil*, plaintiffs asked the Concepción Court of Appeal to void a decision authorising the construction of a hydroelectric power plant in the Cayucupil basin. The plaintiffs argued in the proceedings that the area where the power plant was to be built is a biodiversity sanctuary, and that no consultation was carried out with respect to those indigenous lands, thus violating the ILO Convention.[140]

The Court dismissed the claims, explaining that the environmental assessment – itself a market-oriented legal and policy model[141] – 'is a complex procedure, of a technical nature', and that arbitrariness or illegality was not present as several institutions justified the conclusion reached.[142] As numerous Chilean judicial decisions have held,[143] ILO Convention No. 169 norms must

134 'Nuevo Escenario Territorial'.

135 'Consejo Territorial Puel Huilli Mapu: Convocan a Marcha este Jueves en Futrono contra Proyecto Hidroeléctrico de SN Power', *Observatorio Ciudadano*, 18 January 2010.

136 'SN Power Evalúa Traspaso de Hidroeléctria Trayenko', *Diario Financiero*, 1 March 2011.

137 'SN Power Vende a Gustavo Pavez Activos de Proyectos hHdroeléctrico Trayenko', *La Tercera*, 22 April 2011.

138 'Comunidades Indígenas Valoran Retiro de SN Power de Proyecto Hidroeléctrico Ranco', *Biobiochile.cl*, 3 May 2011.

139 Of the cases, one refers to hydroelectricity. A review of these cases available in J. Contesse and D. Lovera, 'El Convenio 169 de la OIT'.

140 Corte de Apelaciones de Concepción, Rol No. 401-2010, 1 December 2010.

141 D. Tecklin et al., 'Making environmental law for the market: the emergence, character, and implications of Chile's environmental regime', in *Environmental Politics*, Vol. 20, No. 6 (2011).

142 Ibid., cons. 5° (author's translation).

143 See, J. Contesse and D. Lovera, 'El Convenio 169 de la OIT'.

be read within the scope of domestic legality,[144] in this case within the contours of Law 19.300.[145] The Court concluded that the environmental assessment of the hydroelectric power plant had been properly carried out, and that the presence of indigenous peoples does not preclude the government from developing the area in accordance with the law, as had occurred in this situation.[146]

### The Pascua Lama Mining Project

According to the UN Committee on Economic, Social and Cultural Rights, accessibility to water and water facilities also includes 'the right to seek, receive and impart information concerning water issues'.[147] However, access to information related to environmental projects in Chile was the first line of struggle, as was shown in the Pascua Lama mining project. News of the project first began to leak in email chains across Chile and Argentina, which accused governments of both countries of having authorised large-scale exploitation of one the of the world's largest gold, copper and silver reserves.[148]

Allegedly, the project would include the 'non-consumptive' use of water in basins in the upper region, and the open exploitation of the mountain's reserve, without affecting two large, ancient glaciers.[149] So conceived, the project would not only harm the environment in the region, but also farms in one of the world's most arid regions. However, little attention was given to the fact that the Huascoaltinos and other indigenous communities in the Huasco Valley (III Region) would be radically affected, particularly as their life and subsistence is principally based on agriculture and the consumptive use of waters descending form the Andes Mountains.[150]

[144] This is an interpretation anchored in Chile's Constitutional Court decision on the constitutionality of the Convention. See below in Section 4.3.

[145] See Section 3.3, where some of its participatory rights are briefly discussed.

[146] Corte de Apelaciones de Concepción, cons. 9° (author's translation).

[147] Committee on Economic, Social and Cultural Rights, *General Comment No. 15, The Right to Water* (Twenty-ninth session, 2002), UN Doc. E/C.12/2002/11 (2003), para. 12.

[148] The reserve is located in the Andes Mountains in northern Chile (III Region), occupying a large zone within the national frontier between Chile and Argentina.

[149] Some researchers have argued that preliminary explorations conducted between 1981 and 2000 have already affected the glaciers. (R. Torres and A. García, 'Conflictos por el Agua en Chile: El Gran Capital contra las Comunidades Locales – Análisis Comparativo de las Cuencas de los Ríos Huasco (Desierto de Atacama) y Baker (Patagonia Austral)', *Espacio Abierto: Cuaderno Venezolano de Sociología*, Vol. 18, No. 4 (2009), p. 700.) Little public attention has been paid to the fact that a smaller rocky glacier will be completely destroyed. (A. Brenning and G. Azócar, 'Minería y Glaciares Rocosos: Impactos Ambientales, Antecedentes Políticos y Legales, y Perspectivas Futuras', *Revista de Geografía Norte Grande*, No. 47 (2010), p. 153.)

[150] Budds has noted the usual conflicts mining projects pose on indigenous peoples' way of life. J. Budds, 'Derechos de Agua, Pobreza y Manejo Ambiental en Chile: Recursos Hídricos,

How should such conflicts be resolved? The DGA lacks the authority to resolve such disputes,[151] which in practice means that they are resolved according to the rules of the market. There is also the factor of political economy, since large investors typically have significant economic resources that enable them to buy off dissent. The *Pascua Lama* case is a clear example of this.[152] Worries about the impact the project would have on indigenous communities in the Huasco Valley and generally on water quality gained political and media attention with developing protests. Under the Water Code regulations, the so-called *Juntas de Vigilancia* (Security Committees) assemble right holders who are exploiting natural water flows in the same basin. These *Juntas* have the authority to self-regulate conflicts amongst different users.[153] However, individuals can only take part in these *Juntas* if they hold a water right. Consequently, as water rights are only granted for exploitation, several water users – whose uses have not been legally recognised – are left out, including indigenous peoples.

As soon as Barrick Gold, the mining company behind Pascua Lama, submitted its first public environmental assessment, critiques began to mount. The Huascoaltinos opposed the project, as it would be carried out on their ancestral lands, directly affecting their way of life, customs and social structure, and they noted that the project's direct impact on water was not fully assessed.[154] The *Junta* in the Río Huasco basin also opposed the project, and made several complaints to the administrative authorities. These critiques of the project were assembled in three environmental resolutions passed by the Regional Environmental Commission (Comisión Regional de Medioambiente or COREMA) – a regional state agency.[155] According to these resolutions, the mining company had to incorporate an anthropological component in its analysis of the project. As Yañez documented, this meant that the impact of the project on indigenous 'customs and way of life of the *diaguita*, their territory, natural resources, ancestral water resources, and archaeological patrimony' would need to be assessed.[156]

Minería y Pueblos Indígenas en el Norte Grande', unpublished dissertation, Congreso Internacional WALIR (2006), p. 165.

[151] Vergara, 'Estatuto Jurídico', p. 164; Bauer, *Canto de Sirenas*, p. 82.

[152] The same goes for conflicts surrounding hydroelectric projects. Prieto, 'Hydroelectric Power', pp. 10–11.

[153] Segura, *Derecho de Aguas*, pp. 189–96.

[154] Yañez, 'Reconocimiento de Derechos de Agua Indígena en Chile', pp. 326–7.

[155] These resolutions are named ICSARA I, II, and III.

[156] Yañez, 'Reconocimiento de Derechos de Agua ndígena en Chile', p. 327.

What was the response of the mining company? In 2005, it offered the *Junta* USD 60 million to compensate future adverse impacts. They accepted and in 2006 *Pascua Lama* was eventually approved. A project that affected ancestral lands for mining projects was left to be decided on the basis of a private agreement – one that did not consider indigenous claims. On May 2009, Barrick Gold started exploiting the lands.

**Traditional Water Rights Versus Ancestral Claims**

As noted above, the Water Code of 1981 established a water rights property register. An assessment found that not all water rights have been included in it[157] and highlighted how these rights have started to collide with ancestral usages recognised in the *Ley Indígena*.[158] The *Chusmiza-Usmagama* was one of these cases. The Aimara peoples in northern Chile sought to regularise their water rights in light of the *Ley Indígena* provisions.[159] In 2006, a local court recognised the water rights of the Aimara over the Chusmiza Slope.[160] The Court ruled that the *Chusmiza-Usmagama* community have the right to enjoy access to river water of a flow rate of 9 litres per second. The decision impacted the consumptive water rights of a mineral water company above the slope's basin, which was the respondent in the case. Appeals by the bottled water company to the Court of Appeal and then the Supreme Court were subsequently dismissed.[161]

This decision was perhaps surprising in light of others made by Chilean courts. It is worth noting that this final judgment came from a chamber of Supreme Court chamber other than the Constitutional Chamber. The case

[157] R. Yañez, 'El Mercado de las Aguas en Chile', Documento de Trabajo Informe Especial Vol. XIX, No. 200 (Santiago: Instituto Libertad, 2008), pp. 5–6.

[158] See Section 1.2. For a well-documented survey of different cases, see Yañez, 'Reconocimiento de Derechos de Agua Indígena en Chile'. See also, M. Cuadra, 'Teoría y Práctica de los Derechos Ancestrales de Agua de las Comunidades Atacameñas', *Estudios Atacameños*, No. 19 (2000), pp. 93–112; J. González, 'Los Pueblos Originarios en el Marco del Desarrollo de sus Derechos', *Estudios Atacameños*, No. 30 (2005), p. 88.

[159] The '*Ley Indígena*' contains specific provisions regarding the *aimara* peoples. See Article 64.

[160] It should be noted the *Chusmiza-Usmagama* community was seeking recognition, rather than attribution, of water rights. When an indigenous community seeks recognition, it is asking to have their ancestral rights acknowledged rather than conceded. The decision under review confirms a previous decision handed down by the Supreme Court, where it was held that the Constitution protects both recognised, as well as attributed, water rights. See, A. Fernández and C. de la Piedra, 'Implementación y Evolución de los Derechos Contenidos en el Convenio OIT 169: Aporte de la Jurisprudencia y Pronóstico de Desarrollo Futuro de Sus Implicancias Ambientales y Regulatorias', *Revista Estudios Públicos*, No. 121 (2011), pp. 100–2.

[161] Corte Suprema, Rol No. 2.840, 25 November 2009.

also represents one in which the ILO Convention No. 169 has been used to shed light on domestic legal provisions, particularly given the reluctance of the Constitutional Chamber to place much importance on the provisions of the Convention.[162] In reviewing the earlier decisions, the Supreme Court insisted that property rights, constitutionally protected, extended to those rights recognised, as well as those rights attributed, over waters. In light of this, constitutional protection must be granted not only to those rights granted by the authority, according to the provisions of the Water Code of 1981, but also to those rights that have been customarily exercised according to the Indigenous Law (*Ley Indígena*).[163] This interpretation, the Court went on to say, is consistent with the provisions of the ILO Convention No 169.[164]

### 4.3 *Participation – A Privilege rather than Right*

Recognition of participatory rights in decisions over natural resources, including water, constitutes one of the key challenges for indigenous peoples. Some years ago, *The Economist* termed the Chilean democracy 'flawed'.[165] According to the publication's standards, Chilean political participation scored only 5 points on a scale of 10, while its political culture was rated 6.25 out of 10.[166] The explanation for this evaluation was based on the predominance of a 'democracy of consensus'. The Chilean electoral system – and the particular historical conditions of Chilean democratic transition – forced the negotiation of big and ideologically broad agreements between two main political coalitions.[167] It is within these coalitions that political matters are often debated and agreed upon, rather than in public fora such as Parliament. In this context, dissidence is quickly eliminated, while critics of the politics of consensus are often labelled as 'anti-system' or part of an old-fashioned adversarial politics,[168] and excluded from future decision-making processes.[169]

Indigenous peoples are located in this category. Indigenous peoples' interests and rights have been underrepresented within Chile's political and legal system, particularly with regard to rights over their lands and natural resources.

[162] See J. Contesse and D. Lovera, 'El Convenio 169 de la OIT'. A remarkable, exceptional decision was handed down while the author was finishing this work: Corte Suprema, Rol No. 258, 13 July 2011 (a brief comment is included below in the following section).

[163] Corte Suprema, cons. 4°. [164] Ibid., cons. 7°.

[165] L. Kekic, 'A Pause in Democracy's March', *The Economist*, 16 November 2006. [166] Ibid.

[167] D. Lovera, 'El Futuro de la Democracia en Bobbio ¿En qué estamos?', in A. Squella (ed.), *El Pensamiento Jurídico y Político de Norberto Bobbio* (Valparaíso: Edeval, 2005) p. 247.

[168] C. Mouffe, *On the Political* (New York: Routledge, 2005), pp. 30 and 72–6. [169] Ibid., p. 30.

This contemporary lack of attention is perhaps most evident in the fact that Chile is one of the few Latin American countries that has not constitutionally recognised indigenous peoples.

Almost twenty years after the *Acuerdos de Nueva Imperial* were celebrated, Chile ratified ILO Convention No. 169 on Indigenous and Tribal Peoples.[170] However, it has emasculated much of its potential impact. Contesting the participatory rights enshrined in the Convention, a member of Congress from the right-wing coalition filed a writ before the Constitutional Court. The Court, which has the authority to assess the constitutionality of international treaties, handed down its decision in April 2008. It declared the Convention was constitutional, but there was a catch. Contrary to the trend across Latin America,[171] the Constitutional Court held that the participatory rights contemplated in ILO Convention No. 169 were mere governmental guidelines, rather than rights. The Convention was not unconstitutional, since the participatory rights in the Convention were to be read in light of the Chilean Constitution, meaning participatory rights were but a privilege granted by the government.[172] The dialogue between indigenous peoples and the government promoted by the Convention was thus to be understood as 'a means to gather information, but not as an obligatory decision-making process'.[173] It also found that consultations could not be an exercise of sovereignty, since sovereignty was entrusted in the nation as a whole, but not in collective actors.[174]

It was in this light that the Convention was found to be constitutional. Participatory rights enshrined in the ILO Convention are to be understood as governmental grants, not as mandatory processes. This is despite the fact that the same Court declared in 2000 that Articles 6 and 7 were self-executing

[170] It is worth emphasising that the Convention had been submitted to be considered by the Congress in 1991. This is not an irrelevant fact: the Chilean State proposed an interpretative declaration of the Convention aiming at limiting the scope of Article 35 to treaties ratified precisely at 1991 – leaving out the international treaties approved between 1991 and 2008. Centro de Derechos Humanos, Universidad Diego Portales, *Informe Anual sobre Derechos Humanos en Chile 2008*, pp. 368–71.

[171] See C. Courtis, 'Notes on the Implementation by Latin American Courts of the ILO Convention 169 on Indigenous Peoples', *SUR International Journal on Human Rights*, Vol. 10, No. 2 (2010), pp. 53–81.

[172] A detailed analysis of this decision is available in J. Contesse and D. Lovera, 'Pueblos Indígenas y Participación Política en la Óptica del Tribunal Constitucional', *Anuario de Derecho Público*, Vol. 1 (2010), pp. 21–37.

[173] Tribunal Constitucional de Chile, Rol No. 1.050, 3 April 2008, cons. 14° (author's translation).

[174] Ibid., cons. 13°. It is important to highlight that the government also argued the full implementation of the Convention would have to be carried out through new legislation. Gobierno de Chile, *Re-Conocer*, pp. 10, 14.

provisions.[175] If participatory rights are self-executing, but non-mandatory for the State, how are these instances 'of gathering information' to be carried out?[176] The invariable jurisprudence of Chilean courts has been that domestic laws regulating a specific issue are the appropriate means to promote indigenous (or other) peoples' intervention.[177] One of the few laws regulating participation is the environmental law.[178] This is the same law around which many of the judicial decisions discussed above regarding ILO Convention No. 169 have been focused.[179]

In light of this legal background, it is not difficult to understand the scarce attention indigenous peoples have received in Chile. It also partly explains why public policies towards indigenous peoples have been designed and implemented *for* them but *without* them. Indigenous peoples' participatory rights have been deficiently recognised and implemented,[180] particularly in relation to the assessment of environmental projects. According to Meunier, and in spite of participatory rights enshrined in the environmental law – one of the few exceptions in Chile's legal regime – citizen participation has been understood as the obligation to spread information and publicity for environmental projects, instead of implementing mechanisms to assure the public's involvement in assessment.[181]

175 Tribunal Constitucional de Chile, Rol No. 309, 4 August 2000, cons. 7°.

176 The State's first response to this was passing a by-law – without consulting indigenous peoples – which severely restricted the rights enshrined in the ILO Convention, even though the decree was claimed to be detailing Article 34 of 'Ley Indígena', a provision much more restricted when compared with those of the Convention. D.S. No. 124, 4 September 2009. The same governmental office that first published it, recently nullified the decree. Ministerio de Planificación, Res. Ex. No. 0755, 06 September 2011,

177 J. Contesse and D. Lovera, 'El Convenio 169 de la OIT'.

178 Law 19.300 (1994).

179 This same state of affairs explains why one of the most vivid debates on the implementation of ILO Convention No. 169 has turned around what should be done in those cases where no specific law on participation is available. Some have claimed no further detail is needed since the provisions of the Convention are enough, as they are self-executing. But it is important to note a distinction here. The fact that an international treaty contains self-executing norms says little about the specific ways rights contained within it are to be implemented. There is no doubt that self-executing treaty norms confer rights, but further details may be necessary in order to implement those rights. See S. Montt and M. Matta, 'Una Visión Panorámica al Convenio OIT 169 y Su Implementación en Chile', *Revista Estudios Públicos*, No. 121 (2011), pp. 190–1.

180 Yañez, 'Reconocimiento de Derechos de Agua Indígena en Chile', pp. 328–9.

181 P. Meunier, 'La Participación Ciudadana en el Sistema de Evaluación de Impacto Ambiental Chileno', in *Prevención y Solución de Conflictos Ambientales: Vías Administrativas, Jurisdiccionales y Alternativas* (Santiago: LexisNexis-Centro de Derecho Ambiental, Facultad de Derecho, Universidad de Chile, 2004), pp. 51–72, at 62–5.

Furthermore, several other aspects of legal regulation restrain participation. First, it is true that a period of public consultation is available, but it is limited to the preliminary stages of a process or project. In practice, only responding reports (*adenda*) submitted by the government are (partially) reviewed. Those of citizens and other public interest groups are not.[182] A public survey carried out by several civil society organisations showed participatory processes in environmental projects are regarded by the governmental authority (such as the CONAMA or the COREMA aforementioned) as a privilege, not a right. This discretionary understanding arguably means that once information is gathered it receives little weight in the final process – as *Pascua Lama* showed regarding the interests of the Huascoaltinos, and as this survey also demonstrated.[183]

Second, not all projects are subjected to public consultation. Some projects are assessed in light of public opinion, but others are not. Projects that trigger public participation are those that must be submitted for governmental assessment by means of an Environmental Impact Study ('Estudio de Impacto Ambiental' or EIA). Those that do not involve public participation, begin with an Environmental Impact Declaration ('Declaración de Impacto Ambiental' or DIA).[184] This was what occurred in the *Mini Central Cayucupil* case mentioned above.[185] Plaintiffs claimed the project was not publicly assessed and their opinions were not taken into account as *Mini Central Cayucupil* was classified as a project that does not trigger public participation.

## 4.4 *Participation – Opportunities Ahead?*

However, more recent decisions handed down by the Supreme Court reveals a more active judiciary. In the *Plan Regulador San Pedro de Atacama* case, for instance, the Supreme Court declared that urban regulations affecting indigenous communities are to be submitted for governmental assessment by means of an EIA thus triggering public participation and, most crucially, indigenous consultation as required by ILO Convention No. 169.[186] True, it can be claimed, that the Court was nothing but ordering the realisation of

[182] According to Meunier, the reason for justifying the public's exclusion in later stages is due to the fact that these later reports are technical assessments people would not be able to understand. P. Meunier, 'La Participación Ciudadana', ibid., pp. 69–70.

[183] Coalición Nacional para la Iniciativa de Acceso – Chile, 'Acceso a la Información, Participación y Justicia en Temas Ambientales en Chile: ¿Cuánto Hemos Avanzado?' (Santiago: Coalición Nacional para la Iniciativa de Acceso, 2005).

[184] This distinction is made in Articles 10, 11 and 12 of Law 19.300.

[185] See n. 149.

[186] Corte Suprema, Rol No. 258.

consultations. But it is also true that the Court switched to a more aggressive scrutiny of administrative decisions (*vis-à-vis Mini Central Cayucupil* case) as to what kind of environmental assessment was required. This is a trend that seems to have consolidated in recent years, sparking debate on whether the Court is abandoning its adjudicative role towards a more activist one.[187]

In fact, in *Parque Eólico*, the administration had authorised the building of a wind farm in the South of Chile following a previously filed DIA. Indigenous claimants argued the administrative decision authorising the project affected their consultation rights – as granted in the Convention – since the plant would impact the community's traditional way of life. The Puerto Montt Court of Appeals dismissed the claim reasoning in terms similar to those the Concepción Court of Appeals presented in *Mini Central Cayupil*: in its view the authorisation had been passed according to the norms of the 'Enviromental Law.[188] After quoting article 6(1)(a) of the ILO Convention No. 169, the Court concluded that these rights have been respected by the due intervention of the authorities that assessed all relevant facts that deserved consideration.[189]

The case reached the Supreme Court, which reversed the decision.[190] The Court – following *Parque Eólico* – reviewed the instances of participation the environmental authority had implemented, even though the project had been submitted to assessment by way of a DIA. The Court held that, 'voluntary meetings and instances of information provision to the community are far from satisfying the special characteristics of the process of consultation claimants argue were omitted'.[191] In fact – the Court went on – 'sharing information does not constitute an instance of consultation since those affected . . . have no actual possibilities of influencing the implementation, the place and development of the project . . .'.[192] As it has done before, the Supreme Court ordered the project to be assessed according to an EIA, again reading consultation rights through sectoral laws.[193]

In a very similar vein, the Supreme Court held in the *Paguanta* case that the duty to consult established in the Convention 'becomes a mechanism of

[187] L. Cordero, 'Corte Suprema y medio ambiente. ¿Por qué la Corte está revolucionando la regulación ambiental?' *Anuario de Derecho Público*, Vol. 3 (2012).

[188] Corte de Apelaciones de Puerto Montt, Rol No. 239, 11 October 2011.

[189] Ibid., cons 7°. The Court went even farther in affirming consultation rights established in ILO Convention No. 169 are to be reconciled (meaning to be read) with(in) the participatory processes detailed in the 'Enviromental Law', which in this case – according to the Court contended – was legally carried out (cons. 8°).

[190] Corte Suprema, Rol No. 10.090, 22 March 2012.

[191] Ibid., cons. 8° (author's translation).

[192] Ibid. (author's translation).

[193] Ibid., cons. 11° (author's translation).

participation that assures groups with their own cultural specificity, the essential right to participate and intervene in equal conditions' in decisions that may affect their spiritual and material life.[194] Therefore, any investment project that may affect their 'reality ... must be considered in light of their own particularities'.[195] After reviewing the instances of participation resorted to in the environmental assessment, the Court held 'information-sharing meetings do not amount to consultation processes since indigenous communities have no actual chance of influencing neither the design nor the development of the measure'.[196] Again, it unanimously ordered the project to be assessed according to an EIA.[197] However, here the Court went a little further by holding that the processes of participation triggered by an EIA 'ha[ve] also to be realised according to the terms in which ILO Convention No. 169 grants consultation rights'.[198]

As it can be seen, the Supreme Court has read consultation rights through sectoral laws – in these cases, through 'Environmental Law'. Although the Supreme Court has ordered that processes of citizen participation established in those laws are to be carried out in accordance with the ILO Convention No. 169, so far there is no case (perhaps because no one has asked it to do so) where it has challenged the very process of participation established in the 'Environmental Law'.[199] Thus by reading consultation rights through sectoral laws, the former are subjected to the limitations of the latter.[200]

It is true that in *El Morro I* case the Supreme Court reversed an authorisation granted after an EIA had been filed. However, it did so because developers had opened instances of participation to some community members while arbitrarily ignoring others. Although the Court resorted to the standards of

[194] Corte Suprema, Rol No. 11.040, 30 March 2012, cons. 5° (author's translation).

[195] Ibid. (author's translation). [196] Ibid., cons. 9° (author's translation).

[197] Ibid., cons. 11° (author's translation). [198] Ibid.

[199] As Nuñez has aptly indicated, the Supreme Court has rather understood there is an arominc relationship between consultation rights as established in the ILO Convention No. 169 and the participation process regulated in the 'Environmental Law'. M. Nuñez, 'La consulta indígena en el procedimiento de calificación ambiental: desarrollo reglamentario y configuración judicial', *Anuario de Derecho Público*, Vol. 5 (2014), p. 322. This, however, may have a political explanation. Because in 2013 a new by-law regulating the participation process of the 'Environmental Law' included, for the first time, explicit references to the participation of indigenous peoples. I thank Matías Guiloff for this illuminating comment.

[200] As explained before (in Section 4.3), it is not only that 'Environmental Law' itself offers a very weak instance of participation, but also that it is plainly inadequate to satisfy the standards (good faith, adequate procedures, etc.) the ILO Convention No. 169 establishes. C. Silva and G. Parot, 'Desempeño del sistema de Evaluación de Impacto Ambiental para canalizar la consulta indígena del Convenio No. 169 de la OIT', *Revista de Derecho Ambiental*, Año IV, No. 6 (2016).

ILO Convention No. 169 to explain what a proper consultation is, the decision was eventually grounded in arbitrary discrimination in the process.[201]

## 5 FINAL REMARKS: COMPLETING THE CIRCLE

President Bachelet herself, and in the name of the then governing coalition (the '*Concertación*'),[202] which was in power from 1990 through 2010, acknowledged Chile had (and has) a debt to its indigenous peoples, namely: the need to constitutionally recognise indigenous peoples, ratify ILO Convention No. 169, and end poverty.[203]

However, this acknowledgement has had modest results. ILO Convention No. 169 was ratified and later passed in Congress but with several restrictions and a contradictory and ambiguous reception by courts, while constitutional recognition seems improbable. And how is poverty to be addressed? A review of the conditions of the *Re-Conocer* (Re-Cognition) policy illustrates that land and water regulations are still conceived as a means of exploitation that may help indigenous peoples to produce wealth, and consequently, it is argued, to come out from poverty. The focus on free trade and enterprise still remains at the core after 400 years. Moreover, the reallocation of land and water rights, though implemented since 1993, has proved unsatisfactory. According to *Re-Conocer*, new funds will be injected in order to complete the reallocation of land and respective water rights. But far from conceiving water resources as part of ancestral property, it regards water as a means to exploit land, to produce, and to (in some sense, forcibly) take indigenous peoples into the

[201] Corte Suprema, Rol No. 2.211, 27 April 2012. In the *Pepiukelen* case, the Temuco Court of Appeals held that, even when development projects are filed for governmental evaluation by means of an EIA, consultation rights as established in the Convention must be respected. However, on later appeal, the Supreme Court dismissed this requirement. C. Sanhueza et al., *No nos toman en cuenta. Pueblos indígenas y consulta previa en las pisciculturas de La Araucanía* (Santiago: Universidad Diego Portales, 2013), pp. 44-5. The Supreme Court passed later in 2014 another decision on *El Morro II* (Corte Suprema, Rol No. 11.299, 7 October 2014). It again declared the illegality of an environmental assessment that had omitted the inclusion of an indigenous community.

[202] This coalition is well known as the '*Concertación de Partidos por la Democracia*', a conglomerate of center and left-wing political parties, which played a crucial role in restoring the democratic regime. They had formed by the mid 1980s, and directly negotiated the peaceful transition with Pinochet and his political allies, which today conform the '*Alianza por Chile*'. They also agreed with today's '*Alianza*', the constitutional amendments of 1989, deemed as the basis for a peaceful transition; and they still consent every other relevant amendment or political decision (i.e. 2005 constitutional amendments).

[203] Gobierno de Chile, *Re-Conocer*, pp. 6–7. There was no single word on constitutional recognition in the policies announced by the new governing coalition, the right-wing '*Alianza por Chile*'. Gobierno de Chile, *Plan Araucanía*.

capitalist cycle of exploiting-producing-trading.[204] *Re-Conocer*, no matter how broad the multicultural language used in it is, still pushes indigenous peoples to abandon their traditions. In light of Chile's history, this should not come as a surprise. The same is to be told of the policy laid down by the new governmental coalition, a policy completely focused in promoting use of land and natural resources for production.[205]

To put it another way, what the Chilean State wants from indigenous peoples is that they not only abandon their roots, but also start using water as any other Chilean would do: for production and for getting into the cycle of free trade. Trying to use water for purposes other than the cycle of acquisition-exploitation-sale-acquisition decreases indigenous peoples' chances of having their own way of life, their own conception of water, recognised.

[204] Gobierno de Chile, *Re-Conocer*, pp. 14–6, 18, 35–6, 48–9.
[205] Gobierno de Chile, *Plan Araucanía*, p. 3.

# 4

# Water for Food

## *A Human Rights Perspective*

INGA T. WINKLER*

### 1 INTRODUCTION

The human right to water has been criticised for being biased towards urban areas due to its focus on water for personal and domestic uses.[1] It has been pointed out correctly that people living in rural and peri-urban areas often require water not only to satisfy their personal and domestic needs, but also for other uses relating to livelihood security, such as food production and income generation.[2] A sustainable livelihoods approach to water management encompasses a broader scope comprising people's capabilities, assets and activities that are necessary for a means of living.[3] It aims to enhance 'the ability of poor people to use their assets and capabilities to make a living in conditions of

* Lecturer, Institute for the Study of Human Rights, Columbia University. An earlier version of this chapter was presented at the World Water Congress in Montpellier, France, in September 2008. The author would like to thank Mac Darrow, Björn Lüssem, Lena Partzsch and Anna Zimmer, as well as the editors, for their very helpful comments on earlier drafts of this chapter. All errors and omissions remain, of course, my own. The chapter draws on chapter 5 of Inga T. Winkler, *The Human Right to Water, Significance, Legal Status and Implications for Water Allocation* (Oxford: Hart, 2012).

1 See M. Langford, in M. Woodhouse and M. Langford, 'Crossfire: There is No Human Right to Water for Livelihoods', *Waterlines*, Vol. 28, No. 1 (2009), pp. 5–12, at 7.

2 Poverty-Environment Partnership (PEP), 'Linking Poverty Reduction and Water Management' (Stockholm/New York, 2006), pp. 31–32; A. Nicol, 'Adopting a Sustainable Livelihoods Approach to Water Projects: Implications for Policy and Practice', Working Paper 133 (London: Overseas Development Institute (ODI), 2000), pp. 7, 14; B. van Koppen, P. Moriarty and E. Boelee, 'Multiple-Use Water Services to Advance the Millennium Development Goals', Research Report No. 98 (Colombo: International Water Management Institute, 2006), p. 2.

3 Department for International Development (DFID): 'Sustainable livelihoods guidance sheets (London, 1999); see as well I. Scoones, 'Sustainable Rural Livelihoods - A Framework for Analysis', IDS Working Paper 72; D. Carney, 'Approaches to Sustainable Livelihoods for the Rural Poor', ODI Poverty Briefing (London: ODI, 1999).

greater security and sustainability'.[4] Many activities that enhance food and livelihood security, including small-scale farming, gardening, watering livestock and micro enterprises (e.g. laundry services, and small-scale manufacturing, such as brick-making and pottery) require access to water.[5] Water security is vital to the livelihoods of a large number of people living in poverty.[6] Some argue that the focus of the right to water on personal and domestic uses bypasses the reality of people living in rural areas in particular, who require water for multiple uses.[7] This raises the question as to whether such water uses are guaranteed by the human right to water or other human rights. This chapter addresses one aspect of this question through the framework of international human rights and focuses on water for food production for basic consumption, in particular, subsistence agriculture. Similar considerations are in place for other water uses, such as small-scale manufacturing or enterprises or the production of clothing.[8]

Looking at water for food production for basic consumption from the viewpoint of human rights, a number of human rights show close linkages, including the rights to food, water, health and life. The human right to food and the human right to water require more detailed consideration: water is one of the resources used in the production of food, and food is the outcome that is produced. When analysing the General Comments on food and water by the Committee on Economic, Social and Cultural Rights (CESCR), it becomes evident that the issue is not addressed in any significant depth. General Comment No. 12 on the right to food only includes broad references to natural resources, but does not mention water, although it is an essential input in the production of food.[9] However, the issue was a major topic of discussion in the drafting of General Comment No. 15 on the right to water,[10]

[4] PEP, 'Poverty Reduction', p. 29.

[5] Ibid., p. 31; Nicol, 'Sustainable Livelihoods Approach to Water Projects', p. 21; van Koppen, Moriarty and Boelee, 'Multiple-Use Water Services', pp. 14–15.

[6] United Nations Development Programme (UNDP), *Human Development Report 2006, Beyond Scarcity: Power, Poverty and the Global Water Crisis* (New York: Palgrave Macmillan, 2006), pp. 173 et seq.; World Water Assessment Programme (WWAP), *Water, a Shared Responsibility, United Nations World Water Development Report 2* (Paris/New York: Berghan Books, 2006), p. 268.

[7] Van Koppen, Moriarty and Boelee, 'Multiple-Use Water Services', pp. 4–9, 14–15; R. P. Hall, B. van Koppen and E. van Houweling, 'The Human Right to Water: The Importance of Domestic and Productive Water Rights', *Science and Engineering Ethics*, Vol. 20 2014, pp. 849–868.

[8] Winkler, *The Human Right to Water*, chapter 5.

[9] Committee on Economic, Social and Cultural Rights (CESCR), *General Comment No. 12, The Right to Adequate Food* (Twentieth session, 1999) UN Doc. E/C.12/1999/5 (1999), para. 12.

[10] CESCR, *General Comment No. 15, The Right to Water* (Twenty-ninth session, 2002), UN Doc. E/C.12/2002/11 (2003).

which highlights the essential nature of water for food production.[11] A draft of General Comment No. 15 issued in July 2002 explicitly considered water for food production under the right to food, in a section entitled, 'The Water Dimension of other Covenant Rights'. It stated that '[t]he right to adequate food entitles an individual or group to secure the water necessary for the production of food to ensure, at least, freedom from hunger, where there is no alternative to securing essential foodstuffs for the population concerned'.[12] This statement, which was not incorporated into the final version of General Comment No. 15, goes beyond water for personal and domestic uses to include other water uses necessary for the realisation of other human rights. However, no consensus could be reached on this statement, highlighting that the issue is complex and therefore difficult to treat as an add-on to a document focused on water for personal and domestic uses.[13]

The final version of General Comment No. 15, adopted in November 2002, acknowledges that water is also required for other purposes, such as producing food, and relates this use to the right to adequate food.[14]

> The [CESCR] notes the importance of ensuring sustainable access to water resources for agriculture to realize the right to adequate food (see General Comment No.12 (1999)). Attention should be given to ensuring that disadvantaged and marginalized farmers, including women farmers, have equitable access to water and water management systems, including sustainable rain harvesting and irrigation technology. Taking note of the duty in article 1, paragraph 2, of the Covenant, which provides that a people may not "be deprived of its means of subsistence", States parties should ensure that there is adequate access to water for subsistence farming and for securing the livelihoods of indigenous peoples.[15]

[11] CESCR, *Summary Record of the 46th Meeting, Preliminary Discussion of a Draft General Comment on the Right to Water* (Twenty-ninth session, 2002), UN Doc. E/C.12/2002/SR.46 (2002), paras. 13, 20, 42, 44; see also M. Langford, 'The United Nations Concept of Water as a Human Right: A New Paradigm for Old Problems?', *Journal of Water Resources Development*, Vol. 21, No. 2 (2005), pp. 273–282, at 276; O. Lohse, *Das Recht auf Wasser als Verpflichtung für Staaten und nichtstaatliche Akteure', Art. 11 Abs. 1, Art. 12 Internationaler Pakt über wirtschaftliche, soziale und kulturelle Rechte* (Hamburg: Dr. Kovač, 2005), pp. 25–26.

[12] CESCR, *Draft General Comment No. 15, The Right to Water* (Twenty-ninth session, 2002), 29 July 2002, para. 45.

[13] See CESCR, *Summary Record of the First Part (Public) of the 50th Meeting, Adoption of Draft General Comment No. 15 on the Right to Water* (Twenty-ninth session, 2002), UN Doc. E/C.12/2002/SR.50 (2002), para. 6.

[14] CESCR, *General Comment No. 15*, para. 6.

[15] Ibid., para. 7 (footnotes omitted). See also M. Langford, 'Ambition that Overleaps Itself? A Response to Stephen Tully's Critique of the General Comment on the Right to Water', *Netherlands Quarterly of Human Rights*, Vol. 24, No. 3 (2006), pp. 433–459, at 442.

The language used is somewhat vague and the General Comment does not explore the issue any further. The same holds true for various strands of research. While literature on the right to water focuses on water for personal and domestic uses, writings on the right to food do not adequately address the role of natural resources, such as water, in securing food rights.[16] This chapter investigates this issue in more detail and attempts to disentangle the rather complex questions involved. Accordingly, the chapter is narrower in scope than the sustainable livelihoods approach by being limited to water for food production for basic consumption. It starts from a broader perspective, though. While the focus is on the situation of people relying on subsistence agriculture, the chapter starts from the universal reach of international human rights and looks at the bigger picture of water used for agricultural production and its relationship to human rights.

A human rights entitlement to water for basic food production would result in a guarantee of significantly higher quantities of water than those required for personal and domestic needs. For an individual, the latter often can be assumed to be satisfied with about 100 litres per person per day (lpd)[17] but at least 2,000 to 3,000 lpd are required for producing sufficient food.[18] As these water quantities are much larger than those necessary to fulfil personal and domestic needs, a corresponding entitlement would require States to allocate a significant share of total withdrawals for agricultural purposes to produce sufficient food.

In practice, using global averages, currently around 70 per cent of overall water use is for agricultural purposes, around 20 per cent is used in the industrial sector, and households account for less than 10 per cent. The demand for water has increased over the few decades due to factors such as population growth, urbanisation, industrial development and changing diets.[19] Allocation has become even more difficult with new non-food uses of water in the agricultural

[16] But see L. Cotula, M. Djiré and R. W. Tenga, *The Right to Food and Access to Natural Resources, Using Human Rights Arguments and Mechanisms to Improve Resource Access for the Rural Poor*, Right to Food Studies (Rome: Food and Agriculture Organization of the United Nations, 2009) (focusing on land), as well as the references to water and natural resources in Food and Agriculture Organization of the United Nations (FAO), *Voluntary Guidelines to Support the Progressive Realization of the Right to Adequate Food in the Context of National Food Security* (Rome: FAO, 2005), pp. 16–19. High Level Panel of Experts on Food Security and Nutrition of the Committee on World Food Security, Water for Food security and Nutrition (Rome: 2015).

[17] See G. Howard and J. Bartram, *Domestic Water Quantity, Service Level and Health* (Geneva: World Health Organization, 2003), p. 22.

[18] WWAP, *World Water Development Report* 2, p. 247; D. Molden, *Water for Food, Water for Life, A Comprehensive Assessment of Water Management in Agriculture*, International Water Management Institute (London: Earthscan, 2007), p. 78. However, it must be noted that this amount does not necessarily have to come from irrigation, but also can include rainwater. For more detail, see section 3.2 of this chapter.

[19] UNDP, *Human Development Report* 2006, p. 173.

sector, such as bio-fuel production, putting increasing strain on resources.[20] At the same time, climate change models predict significant changes in regional and temporal water availability.[21] The oft resulting increased competition may give rise to conflicts between different users at the local level, for instance between industrial and agricultural users, rural areas and cities, or farmers and pastoralists.[22] When local water shortages increase and competition intensifies, people lacking voice – often smallholder farmers – frequently lose out and see their access to water diminished by more powerful constituencies.[23] In many instances, lack of access to water is not primarily a question of water availability, but rather a question of allocation, distribution and prioritisation that is shaped by power relationships.[24] The 2006 *Human Development Report* summarises this, stating that 'the scarcity at the heart of the global water crisis is rooted in power, poverty and inequality, not in physical availability'.[25]

It is therefore of timely importance to seek approaches to water allocation that allow for the realisation of every individual's human rights. It is acknowledged that various ways to augment the available supply of freshwater in a given region are currently discussed and already implemented, such as desalination and bulk water imports by tankers.[26] Yet, even in such cases, the question remains as to how the (increased) available resources should be allocated amongst different users. Therefore this chapter focuses on the question of allocation of total available water resources. In this regard, human rights can be a means to guide the prioritisation of different kinds of uses as the framework requires that water is allocated in a way that satisfies the basic human needs of all people.[27]

20 A. Eide, *The Right to Food and the Impact of Liquid Biofuels (Agrofuels)*, Right to Food Studies (Rome: Food and Agriculture Organization of the United Nations, 2008).

21 B. C. Bates, Z. W. Kundzewicz, S. Wu and J. P. Palutikof, *Climate Change and Water*, Technical Paper VI (Geneva: International Panel on Climate Change, 2008). On climate change and the right to water see Chapter 6, this volume.

22 See UNDP, *Human Development Report 2006*, pp. 177–178, 186 for examples from India, China, Yemen, Kenya and other countries.

23 Ibid., pp. 173, 177. 24 Ibid., p. 189. 25 Ibid., p. 2.

26 See in this regard A. Gowlland-Gualtieri, 'Legal Implications of Trade in "Real" and "Virtual" Water Resources', in P. Cullet, A. Gowlland-Gualtieri, R. Madhav and U. Ramanathan (eds.), *Water Law for the Twenty-First Century, National and International Aspects of Water Law Reform in India* (London: Routledge, 2009), pp. 59–80. See also E. Brown Weiss, 'Water Transfers and International Trade Law', in E. Brown Weiss L. Boisson de Chazournes and N. Bernasconi-Osterwalder (eds.), *Fresh Water and International Economic Law* (Oxford: Oxford University Press, 2005), pp. 61–89 for further discussion on bulk water transfers.

27 See I. Winkler, 'Das Menschenrecht auf Wasser – Priorität für die Erfüllung menschlicher Grundbedürfnisse', in C. Bastian, A. Gunkel, H. Leistert, T. Menniken, R. Rhodius and

In Section 2, this chapter examines whether access to water for food production for basic consumption is guaranteed by international human rights and whether it should be considered in the context of the right to water or the right to food. Section 3 continues by exploring the link between water use and food production, asking what water use relates to the right to adequate food and considering the situation of people relying on subsistence agriculture. In Section 4, the obligations borne by States regarding the right to food and the relevance of access to water resources for its realisation will be examined, again making specific reference to people who rely on subsistence farming.

## 2 POTENTIAL HUMAN RIGHTS GUARANTEES

Water for food production for basic consumption is linked to various human rights, as noted above, including the right to water, the right to food, the right to health and the right to life. Specifically, water use for food production could be covered by the right to water or the right to food, and these two rights will be considered as potential legal foundations.

### 2.1 *The Human Right to Water*

Water requirements for the production of food are often mentioned in the context of the human right to water.[28] Therefore the question of whether access to water for basic food production is encompassed in the normative content of the right to water is considered first. Consensus has developed in recent years over the existence of an international human right to water.[29] The 2010 resolutions by the UN General Assembly[30] and the UN Human Rights Council[31] affirmed the right to water as part of international law.

B. Schlipphak (eds.), *Wasser – Konfliktstoff des 21. Jahrhunderts? Von der Krisendiagnose zum Problemmanagement* (Heidelberg: Winter-Verlag, 2008), pp. 101–116.

[28] CESCR, *General Comment No. 15*, para. 6; A. Cahill, 'The Human Right to Water – A Right of Unique Status: The Legal Status and Normative Content of the Right to Water', *International Journal of Human Rights*, Vol. 9, No. 3 (2002), pp. 389–410, at 396.

[29] CESCR, *General Comment No. 15*, para. 3; E. Riedel, 'The Human Right to Water', in K. Dicke (ed.), *Weltinnenrecht – Liber amicorum Jost Delbrück* (Berlin: Duncker & Humblot, 2005), pp. 585–606, at 596; P. Gleick, 'The Human Right to Water', *Water Policy*, Vol. 1, No. 5 (1998), pp. 487–503, at 492.

[30] UN General Assembly, *The Human Right to Water and Sanitation*, UN Doc. A/RES/64/292 (2010).

[31] UN Human Rights Council, *Human Rights and Access to Safe Drinking Water and Sanitation*, UN Doc. A/HRC/RES/15/9 (2010).

The Human Rights Council resolution explicitly derived the right to water from the right to an adequate standard of living in Article 11(1) of the International Covenant on Economic, Social and Cultural Rights (ICESCR),[32] hence providing a firm legal basis for the right. However, there is still some discussion over the precise content of the human right to water. The most limited approach would be to see only access to water for survival needs covered, in particular, water for drinking purposes and basic health. However, Article 11 of the ICESCR articulates a right to an adequate standard of living, which extends beyond the standard of survival. In order to achieve an adequate standard of living, access to water for personal and domestic uses must be guaranteed, in particular personal hygiene and cleaning. General Comment No. 15 adopts this approach and, in fact, it is unquestionable that these water uses are covered by the right to water.[33]

Beyond personal and domestic uses, the question is whether water for food production for basic consumption is also included within the right to water.[34] In particular, water for kitchen gardens, small-scale subsistence agriculture and the raising of livestock are sometimes suggested as coming within the scope of the right to water. It is argued that these form part of 'domestic uses' in many rural settings.[35]

[32] International Covenant on Economic, Social and Cultural Rights (adopted 16 December 1966, entered into force 3 January 1976), 993 UNTS 3 (ICESCR).

[33] CESCR, *General Comment No.* 15, paras. 2, 12(a); Gleick, 'The Human Right to Water', p. 491; Cahill, 'The Human Right to Water', p. 392.

[34] Conversely, it has also been suggested to extend the right to food to all life-sustaining nourishment, including drinking water, see W. Kälin and J. Künzli, *Universeller Menschenrechtsschutz* (Basel: Helbing & Lichtenhahn, 2005), p. 305; A. Hildering, 'The Right to Access to Freshwater Resources', in N. Schrijver and F. Weiss (eds.), *International Law and Sustainable Development: Principles and Practice* (Leiden: Martinus Niijhoff, 2004), pp. 405–429, at 414; Commission on Human Rights, *The Right to Food, Report by the Special Rapporteur on the Right to Food, Mr. Jean Ziegler, Submitted in Accordance with Commission on Human Rights Resolution 2000/10*, 7 February 2001, UN Doc. E/CN.4/2001/53, para. 32. However, such a guarantee derived from the right to food would only cover water for drinking purposes, which seems too restrictive, as other non-consumptive water uses are also essential. Moreover, water is generally not regarded as part of food, but as a separate component of human sustenance. In everyday language, one speaks of eating and drinking, food and water, and hunger and thirst. Also, legal instruments such as the Geneva Conventions reflect this perception as two different components (also noted by Langford, 'Ambition that Overleaps itself?', p. 442). Finally, the same arguments put forward for the right to water not covering water for food production also apply vice versa. Therefore, it seems preferable to understand the right to water as distinct from the right to food.

[35] Langford, 'Crossfire', p. 7. See also Chapters 2 and 9 in this volume.

While the same sources of water are often used for a variety of purposes, in particular in rural settings, in other cases there are fundamental differences between access to water for personal and domestic needs and access to water for food cultivation. For example, the supply of water to households often requires infrastructure that is different from that required for water for agricultural purposes. Moreover, water quality standards for drinking water differ from those of water for agricultural use.[36] Even when the same water sources are used for multiple purposes and water uses cannot be separated in practical terms, this does not necessitate situating them under a single human right. It is perfectly conceivable that one activity relates to different human rights. This is the case in other areas of human rights law; for example, taking part in a demonstration may involve exercising one's freedom of assembly and freedom of expression at the same time. Hence, it seems preferable to distinguish water used for food production from water used for personal and domestic needs.

If water for producing food for basic consumption were guaranteed by the right to water, there would be no reason not to include water for food production more broadly. It would be difficult to draw a line between food from kitchen gardens or subsistence farming, and agriculture more broadly. Why should subsistence activities be covered, but not the production of food necessary to fulfil other people's human rights? The same question could be asked for water used in a range of livelihood activities, cultural and religious practices, energy production or other uses aimed at fulfilling basic human requirements. Water use necessary to realise any human right would come within the scope of the human right to water. As such, the right would risk being undermined by becoming unworkably broad and less tangible.

Most importantly, one must not lose sight of the purpose of the water use in question, which is determinative of linking it to the relevant human right. Water used for producing food is not aimed at fulfilling basic water requirements as such, but rather basic food requirements. From a human rights perspective, what is relevant is access to food, not access to water used for producing food.

Accordingly, the right to water does not cover water used for producing food for basic consumption. This does not mean that such water uses are ignored[37] or that they are not necessary for the realisation of an adequate standard of living or the realisation of other human rights. It only implies that they are not

[36] But see van Koppen, Moriarty and Boelee, 'Multiple-Use Water Services', pp. 13–14 for strategies of how to adapt to these different standards in practice by using the same source of water for multiple uses.

[37] Hall, van Koppen and van Houweling, 'The Human Right to Water', p. 850.

to be considered under an all-embracing right to water that covers all potential water uses linked to the realisation of other human rights. Some advocates might perceive linking productive water uses to the right to water as preferable as the right to water has received significant political attention since its explicit recognition in 2010. However, the recognition of the right to water is simply filling a gap in the human rights framework, whereas other human rights such as the right to food have been included in human rights instruments from their inception. Other water uses should be considered under the established relevant human rights guarantees.

This interpretation is in line with General Comment No. 15. As noted above, it recognises that water is required for a range of different purposes, including food production, and stresses the importance of sustainable access to water resources for agriculture.[38] However, the General Comment does not define the right to water as covering water for food production, but considers it in the context of the right to food. Even the draft General Comment that put more emphasis on water for food production, considered it under the heading of 'The Water Dimension of other Covenant Rights' and as an entitlement stemming from the right to food.[39] Accordingly, the human right to food is now examined as a potential legal basis for entitling individuals to water for producing food for basic needs.

### 2.2 *The Human Right to Food*

Article 11(1) of the ICESCR guarantees the right to food as part of the right to an adequate standard of living. Moreover, Article 11(2) recognises the fundamental right of everyone to be free from hunger. As examples, other relevant provisions can be found in Article 24(2)(c) and Article 27(3) of the Convention on the Rights of the Child[40] and Article 12 of the Convention on the Elimination of All Forms of Discrimination against Women.[41] According to the CESCR, the realisation of the right to food requires that everyone 'has physical and economic access at all times to adequate food or means for its procurement'.[42]

38 CESCR, *General Comment No. 15*, paras. 6, 7.

39 CESCR, *Draft General Comment No. 15, The Right to Water* (Twenty-ninth session, 2002), 29 July 2002, para. 45.

40 Convention on the Rights of the Child (adopted 20 November 1989, entered into force 2 September 1990) 1577 UNTS 3.

41 Convention on the Elimination of All Forms of Discrimination against Women (adopted 18 December 1979, entered into force 3 September 1981) 1249 UNTS 13 (CEDAW).

42 CESCR, *General Comment No. 12*, para. 6.

Article 11(2) of the ICESCR obliges States to prevent starvation and to guarantee access to essential food in sufficient quantity that is nutritionally adequate and safe to ensure freedom from hunger.[43] This can be regarded as the minimum level of realisation of the right to food.[44] In its full extent, the right to food reaches beyond this minimum level to include adequate food of a quantity and quality that is sufficient to satisfy the dietary needs of individuals.[45] It is also to be free from adverse substances and acceptable within a given culture.[46] This is specified further in General Comment No. 12.[47] For the purposes of this chapter, the most important features are availability and accessibility. It is not sufficient if food is generally available, but not accessible to individuals. Studies by Sen and others have shown that some of the worst famines have occurred in the midst of abundance.[48] Generally, the right to food can be realised in two ways: either by feeding oneself directly from productive land or other natural resources, or by having the means to procure food via distribution, transfer and market systems.[49]

Regardless of how the right to food is being realised, agricultural production is necessary to meet food requirements, which is impossible without water. The Voluntary Guidelines on the Right to Food stress the importance of access to water resources.[50] Therefore, it seems pertinent to consider access to

[43] Ibid., para. 14. It has been argued that there is strong evidence supporting the status of the right to be free from hunger as having evolved into customary international law, see S. Narula, 'The Right to Food: Holding Global Actors Accountable Under International Law', *Columbia Journal of Transnational Law*, Vol. 44, No. 3 (2006), pp. 691–800, at 791–796.

[44] C. Reimann, *Ernährungssicherung im Völkerrecht – Der Menschenrechtsansatz und seine Ergänzungsmöglichkeiten angesichts der Welthungerproblematik* (Stuttgart: Boorberg, 2000), pp. 170, 172; C. Breining-Kaufmann, Hunger als Rechtsproblem – völkerrechtliche Aspekte eines Rechtes auf Nahrung (Zürich: Schulthess, 1991), p. 163; P. Alston, 'International Law and the Human Right to Food', in P. Alston and K. Tomaševski (eds.), *The Right to Food* (Utrecht: Martinus Nijhoff, 1984), pp. 9–68, at 33.

[45] Alston, ibid., p. 32; R. Künnemann, 'The Right to Adequate Food: Violations related to its Minimum Core', in D. Brand and S. Russell (eds.), *Exploring the Core Content of Socio-economic Rights: South African and International Perspectives* (Pretoria: Protea, 2002), pp. 71–98, at 79.

[46] CESCR, *General Comment No. 12*, para. 8; A. Eide, 'The Right to an Adequate Standard of Living including the Right to Food', in A. Eide, C. Krause and A. Rosas (eds.), *Economic, Social and Cultural Rights, A Textbook*, 2nd edition (Dordrecht: Martinus Nijhoff, 2001), pp. 133–148, at 134; Alston, 'Human Right to Food', p. 33.

[47] CESCR, *General Comment No. 12*, paras. 8–13.

[48] See A. Sen, *Development as Freedom* (Oxford: Oxford University Press, 1999), pp. 165–166.

[49] CESCR, *General Comment No. 12*, para. 12; Eide, 'The Right to an Adequate Standard of Living', p. 135; Künnemann, 'The Right to Adequate Food', p. 79.

[50] FAO, *Voluntary Guidelines*, p. 18. The General Comment on the right to food does not mention the essential nature of water for agricultural production, see CESCR, *General Comment No. 12*, noted as well by Langford, 'Ambition that Overleaps Itself?', p. 442.

water for food cultivation under the human right to food. In Section 3, the extent to which water use is relevant for the realisation of the right to food is examined further.

## 3 WATER USE RELEVANT FOR THE REALISATION OF THE RIGHT TO FOOD

The agricultural sector uses the the largest amount of water. Yet, not all of the water used in agricultural production is necessary to fulfil the human right to food. The following sub-sections will examine what water use is relevant for the realisation of the right to food.

### 3.1 *Water Use Aimed at Food Production*

As discussed above, the agricultural sector accounts for about 70 per cent of global water use.[51] This percentage differs significantly between States in the Global South and the Global North. Whereas irrigated agriculture only accounts for 30 per cent of water use in Europe and 41 per cent in the United States,[52] up to 90 per cent of water withdrawals are used for agricultural purposes in many developing countries.[53]

Agriculture is a heterogeneous sector, ranging from large-scale industrial farming to subsistence agriculture. Moreover, the cultivation of a wide range of crops is not directed at fulfilling food requirements. One example is flower production. For instance, in 2001, Kenya exported 52 million tons of flowers to Europe, Japan and North America.[54] The same holds true for the increasing growth of crops for bio-fuel production, such as ethanol and biodiesel. As of 2007, Brazil accounted for 50 per cent of global ethanol exports,[55] but a number of other countries around the world are also employing or exploring the potential of bio-fuels.[56] In the European Union, about 10 per cent of crop

[51] WWAP, *World Water Development Report* 2, p. 245.

[52] M. Falkenmark and C. Widstrand, 'Population and Water Resources: A Delicate Balance', *Population Bulletin*, Vol. 47, No. 3 (1992), p. 14. Industrial use makes up a larger share.

[53] R. Engelmann, B. Dye and P. LeRoy, *Mensch, Wasser, Report über die Entwicklung der Weltbevölkerung und die Zukunft der Wasservorräte* (Hannover: Deutsche Stiftung Weltbevölkerung, 2000), p. 19.

[54] Wuppertal Institut für Klima, Umwelt, Energie, *Fair Future, Begrenzte Ressourcen und globale Gerechtigkeit* (Bonn: Bundeszentrale für politische Bildung, 2005), p. 111.

[55] S. Hughes, L. Partzsch and J. Gaskell, 'The Development of Biofuels within the Context of the Global Water Crisis', *Sustainable Development Law and Policy*, Vol. 7, No. 3 (2007), pp. 58–62, at 60.

[56] Ibid., p. 58.

cultivation is already used for the production of bio-fuels.[57] Evidently, these non-food water uses are not aimed at realising the right to food. However, as non-food uses of agricultural water become more prominent, they put greater strain on freshwater resources and the competition over water resources is intensified, thus reinforcing the need to set priorities in the allocation of resources in order to ensure that the basic needs of all people are met.[58] Accordingly, only agricultural production that is geared towards the production of food may fall under the guarantee of the right to food. However, this does not imply that all food production is guaranteed by the right to food. Human rights guarantee the right to adequate food, not to unlimited food, which will be discussed in the next section.

### 3.2 *Water Use Aimed at Securing an Adequate Standard of Living*

The first dimension of the human right to food is to be free from hunger and prevent starvation, as recognised in Article 11(2) of the ICESCR.[59] In order to estimate water requirements for this purpose, it seems pertinent to look at staple foods. Rice, wheat and other cereals are a major component of any diet; in terms of energy supply, they represent more than half of all food consumed.[60] Rice is probably the most common staple food.[61] For a suggested intake of 600 grams of rice per day,[62] approximately 1,600 litres of water are needed, on average, for its production.[63] This does not take into account water needed to produce the remaining necessary intake of food.

The right to adequate food goes beyond articulating minimum survival requirements to satisfying the dietary needs of individuals. In order to be adequate, a diet must be complete in terms of energy and balanced in terms of nutritional value. As for energy requirements, a value of 2,800 kcal per person per day can be taken as an approximate threshold for food security.[64] It is much more complex to determine the prerequisites for a varied and balanced diet. To ensure the necessary agricultural produce, water requirements are in the range of 2,000 to 5,000 lpd depending on diet, climatic conditions and efficiency of production systems.[65] Typically, a suitable

[57] F. Nuscheler, *Entwicklungspolitik* (Bonn: Bundeszentrale für Politische Bildung, 2006), p. 256.
[58] See Eide, 'The Right to Food and the Impact of Liquid Biofuels'.
[59] See CESCR, *General Comment No. 12*, para. 6.
[60] WWAP, *World Water Development Report 2*, p. 248.
[61] Howard and Bartram, 'Domestic Water Quantity', p. 9.
[62] Ibid.
[63] WWAP, *World Water Development Report 2*, p. 258.
[64] Ibid., pp. 245–246.
[65] Ibid., p. 247; Molden, *Water for Food*, p. 78.

vegetarian diet can be produced with 2,000 lpd, while a diet, which is largely based on meat and dairy products, requires 5,000 lpd.[66] As a rule of thumb, it can be assumed that on average one litre of water is necessary to produce one kcal of food.[67] These figures are rough estimates and simply provide an indication as to the amount of water needed for food production.

Importantly, these figures do not refer to the total amount of irrigation water necessary to produce food. On a global scale, most of the water used to produce crops – 80 to 90 per cent – is green water, i.e. rain water stored in the soil.[68] The remaining 10 to 20 per cent of water used is blue water, i.e. water withdrawn from rivers, aquifers, reservoirs or lakes for irrigation purposes.[69] The latter is referred to when speaking of the 70 per cent of total water withdrawals being used in the agricultural sector.[70] About 45 per cent of the gross value of crop production is grown on irrigated land, highlighting the significance of irrigation for efficient food production.[71] Generally, it cannot be determined what portion of irrigation water is necessary to produce crops in a given region, as the demand for supplemental irrigation varies greatly between countries and regions, due to climatic and geographic conditions.

From a human rights perspective, only water use for food production that is targeted at the realisation of the right to adequate food is covered. The aim is to achieve a complete, balanced and healthy diet. Food must also be culturally acceptable, which may result in preference for certain food stuffs and the exclusion of others. This can often be realised with about 2,000 to 3,000 lpd of water. According to FAO estimates, a 3,000 kcal per day diet, of which 20 per cent is animal protein, can be achieved with about 3,500 lpd.[72] Water use beyond these requirements is not relevant from a human rights perspective as the right to food does not guarantee the immoderate consumption of specific products. Apart from diets heavily relying on meat, this also may, for example, also relate to the consumption of citrus fruits, strawberries and grapes in the winter season by consumers in the Global North. Such products are

66 Falkenmark and Lannerstad quote 1800 cubic meters per person per year for a North American 'rich meat diet', which translates to about 5,000 lpd; see M. Falkenmark and M. Lannerstad, 'Consumptive Water Use to Feed Humanity – Curing a Blind Spot', *Hydrology and Earth System Sciences*, Vol. 9, Nos. 1/2 (2005), pp. 15–28, at 21.

67 Molden, *Water for Food*, p. 78.

68 WWAP, *World Water Development Report 2*, p. 247; Molden, *Water for Food*, p. 58.

69 Molden, *Water for Food*, p. 58. On alterations in green and blue water flows see Falkenmark and Lannerstad, 'Consumptive Water Use', pp. 18-21.

70 WWAP, *World Water Development Report 2*, p. 247.

71 Molden, *Water for Food*, p. 58.

72 Falkenmark and Lannerstad, 'Consumptive Water Use', p. 26.

produced as cash crops in many countries in the Global South in order to be exported to the North, where foodstuffs are already available in abundance. This sort of production does not relate to the right to adequate food, but rather increases competition for water resources in a similar fashion to non-food agricultural production.

### 3.3 *No Universal Reliance on Direct Access to Water for Food Production*

While water is of fundamental importance for agricultural production necessary to realise the human right to food, there are many variations in the type of reliance that is placed on water resources. Many people buy readily produced food stuffs, and the water resources used to produce these are often located at great distances away, including abroad.[73] Water for producing food is not necessarily used by the person consuming the food, or in the watershed or country where that person lives. Food can easily be transported from regions with high water availability to those with low water availability – noting, of course, that the feasibility and likeliness of distribution depends on a range of socio-economic and political factors, for instance in countries seeking to achieve food sovereignty. Still, people do not always depend on direct access to water resources and water used for food production does not necessarily need to be translated into a universal individual entitlement. There is no need for a specific human right to water for food production beyond the human right to food itself.

While this is not universal, a significant number of people do produce their own food and thus rely on water resources close to their home. In spite of continuing urbanisation, a large number of people depend, at least partially, on subsistence agriculture.[74] Apart from access to land in general and soil fertility in particular, access to water is a critical factor in determining the success of agricultural production in a given region.[75] Severe poverty often exists where access to water resources is uncertain due to unpredictable

[73] On the concept of virtual water see J. A. Allan, '"Virtual Water": A Long Term Solution for Water Short Middle Eastern Economies?', Paper presented at the 1997 British Association Festival of Science, University of Leeds, 9 September 1997; Gowlland-Gualtieri, 'Trade in "Real" and "Virtual" Water Resources'. This also raises the question of whether other States have an obligation to make water resources available for the production of food that is consumed by people in other countries. On extra-territorial obligations see Chapter 5, this volume.

[74] M. Brüntrup and F. Heidhues, 'Subsistence Agriculture in Development: Its Role in Processes of Structural Change', Discussion Paper No. 1/2002, University of Hohenheim, Center for Tropical Agriculture (Stuttgart, 2002), p. 7; Cotula, Djiré and Tenga, *Right to Food*, p. 21.

[75] PEP, 'Poverty Reduction', p. 22.

rainfall and flooding.[76] Therefore, reliable access to water for subsistence agriculture, home gardens and raising livestock is key to improving food security of those most vulnerable to hunger and malnutrition.[77]

The number of undernourished people has been declining over the past years, with 795 million people in 2015.[78] The food available to them is insufficient to meet their basic energy needs.[79] Every year about 20 million people die from undernourishment.[80] It is estimated that about a further 1 billion people are considered malnourished and lacking a balanced diet.[81] People experiencing food insecurity either do not have sufficient income to buy food stuffs or do not produce enough food for their own consumption. Their dependence on water resources differs according to where they live, including whether they live in rural or urban areas. About two-thirds of malnourished people live in rural areas and depend on agricultural production for employment, income and food.[82] This group includes smallholder farmers and landless rural people.[83] Hunger and malnourishment are thus to a large extent rural phenomena. It is estimated that 50 per cent of undernourished people are smallholder farmers, who directly depend on access to water resources for their own nutrition, as well as income generation.[84] For people in these types of situations, access to water is an essential factor in the realisation of the right to food.

However, to summarize, reliance on direct access to water is only one way of realising the right to food and cannot be generalised. As large parts of the world's population do not depend on direct access to water for producing food, but rely on other ways to realise their right to food, it is not necessary to consider a specific human right to water for food production from a universal and normative perspective. This does not mean that States have no human rights obligations relating to access to water for food production for basic consumption under the human right to food. The next section of this chapter addresses States' obligations regarding the right to food in more detail, determining the relevance of access to water for the realisation of the right to food, in particular for subsistence farmers.

[76] Molden, *Water for Food*, p. 71. In fact, research has shown that poverty is often significantly lower (about 20 to 30 per cent) in areas with irrigated systems than in areas that are not irrigated, see UNDP, *Human Development Report 2006*, p. 175.

[77] PEP, 'Poverty Reduction', p. 23.

[78] FAO, *The State of Food Insecurity in the World* (Rome: FAO, 2015), p. 4.

[79] PEP, 'Poverty Reduction', p. 13.

[80] Nuscheler, *Entwicklungspolitik*, p. 252.

[81] Nuscheler, ibid.; PEP, 'Poverty Reduction', p. 13.

[82] UNDP, *Human Development Report 2006*, pp. 173–174; Nuscheler, *Entwicklungspolitik*, p. 260.

[83] Molden, *Water for Food*, p. 65.

[84] Ibid.

## 4 OBLIGATIONS OF STATES TO REALISE THE RIGHT TO FOOD AND THE RELEVANCE OF ACCESS TO WATER

The ICESCR takes account of the fact that the realisation of socio-economic rights, such as the human right to food, is dependent on the availability of resources. States are not obliged to realise the right to food immediately, but progressively, as articulated in Article 2(1) of the ICESCR.[85] This does not imply that the realisation of the right to food is left entirely to the discretion of States. The CESCR has pointed out in its General Comment on the right to food that:

> The most appropriate ways and means of implementing the right to adequate food will inevitably vary significantly from one State party to another. Every State will have a margin of discretion in choosing its own approaches, but the Covenant clearly requires that each State party take whatever steps are necessary to ensure that everyone is free from hunger and as soon as possible can enjoy the right to adequate food.[86]

Moreover, States have to move 'as expeditiously and effectively as possible' towards the full realisation of the right to food.[87] This is to be achieved as quickly as possible and the speed by which States move towards this goal is not to be determined at their discretion, but by objective standards, such as the availability of resources.[88]

To further examine States' human rights obligations, the obligations to respect, protect and fulfil the right to food,[89] as well as obligations of non-discrimination and equality, are discussed. The focus of the discussion is on access to water resources, once again taking into account specific measures for people relying on subsistence agriculture.

[85] See generally on the concept of 'progressive realisation', M. Sepúlveda, *The Nature of the Obligations under the International Covenant on Economic, Social and Cultural Rights* (Antwerp: Intersentia, 2003), pp. 311–313.

[86] CESCR, *General Comment No. 12*, para. 21.

[87] CESCR, *General Comment No. 3, The Nature of States Parties' Obligations* (Fifth session, 1990), UN Doc. E/1991/23, Annex III at 86 (1991), para. 9.

[88] Riedel, 'The Human Right to Water', p. 595; M. Craven, *The International Covenant on Economic, Social and Cultural Rights, A Perspective on its Development* (Oxford: Oxford University Press, 1995), p. 131.

[89] See H. Shue, *Basic Rights: Subsistence, Affluence and U.S. Foreign Policy* (Princeton: Princeton University Press, 1980), p. 52; A. Eide, 'Economic, Social and Cultural Rights as Human Rights', in A. Eide, C. Krause and A. Rosas (eds.), *Economic, Social and Cultural Rights, A Textbook*, 2nd edition (Dordrecht: Martinus Nijhoff, 2001), pp. 9–28, at 23–24; Craven, ibid., at p. 109.

## 4.1 *Obligation to Respect*

The obligation to respect requires States to refrain from interfering with the enjoyment of human rights, and thus aims to prevent an infringement of rights that have been already realised.[90] States are required to respect existing access and not to take any measures that would interfere with it, at least not without providing alternative access.[91] Accordingly, people, who are able to produce or procure food by their own means, must not be deprived of the space and resources needed to do so.[92]

Access to water resources is one of the essential inputs for agricultural production. People who cultivate their own food must not be deprived of the water resources they need to produce sufficient food stuffs. Therefore, the State must not pollute these resources or divert and re-allocate them for different purposes, such as industrial uses, leaving people without the means to produce their own food.[93]

An example of a large-scale re-allocation aimed at satisfying the demand of the increasing population and urban development is the diversion of water resources from southern China and the provinces surrounding Beijing to northern China and Beijing.[94] The project was accelerated because of the Olympic Games held in Beijing in 2008. Farmers in regions from where water was diverted, such as the province of Hebei, experienced the negative impacts of the project as the availability of water for agriculture decreased significantly.[95] If it reaches a level where the water resources are insufficient to satisfy the food needs of the population and the State does not take measures to allow for alternative access to food, this would amount to a violation of the State's obligation to respect the right to adequate food.

## 4.2 *Obligation to Protect*

The obligation to protect refers to the duty of States to prevent third parties from interfering with the enjoyment of human rights.[96] It places a duty on

[90] Eide, ibid., at p. 23; Craven, ibid., at p. 109.

[91] CESCR, *General Comment No. 12*, para. 15; FAO, *Voluntary Guidelines*, p. 6; G. Kent, *Freedom from Want: The Human Right to Adequate Food* (Washington, DC: Georgetown University Press, 2005), p. 105.

[92] Eide, 'The Right to an Adequate Standard of Living', p. 142.

[93] Künnemann, 'The Right to Adequate Food', p. 95.

[94] China has been a State party to the ICESCR since 2001.

[95] J. Watts, 'Provinces Pay Price for Green Olympics, Millions of Gallons of Water are Being Diverted to Beijing from Areas Hit by Drought', *The Guardian*, 1 March 2008.

[96] Craven, *The ICESCR*, p. 109; Eide, 'Economic, Social and Cultural Rights', p. 24.

States to take the necessary measures to prevent private parties from undermining the rights of others. It means putting in place measures to ensure that third parties, such as companies or other individuals, do not deprive people of their access to adequate food.[97] The State must ensure that third parties do not hinder people's access to or pollute water resources on which others rely for producing food.[98]

An example is the case of Plachimada in India. A beverage company had set up a bottling plant in the village and was granted a license to extract groundwater. It resulted in the over-exploitation of groundwater. Almost 80 per cent of the population in the area depend on agriculture for their livelihood. The over-extraction of groundwater resulted in their wells running dry, and consequently constrained agricultural production.[99]

Another example relates to the operations of Shell in Nigeria, which resulted in contaminated water from oil spills and the disposal of toxic waste into the environment, which had disastrous effects on the Ogoni people. The Nigerian government was challenged in the case of *The Social and Economic Rights Action Centre and the Centre for Economic and Social Rights* v. *Nigeria*, brought before the African Commission on Human and Peoples' Rights.[100] The applicants argued that the exploitation of oil reserves resulted in the contamination of water, soil and air in Ogoniland. With respect to the right to food, the applicants argued that it is implicitly guaranteed in the African (Banjul) Charter on Human and Peoples' Rights in provisions on the right to life (Article 4), the right to health (Article 16) and the right to economic, social and cultural development (Article 22). The Commission found Nigeria in violation of Articles 4, 16 and 24 of the Banjul Charter. It held that '[t]he government has destroyed food sources through its security forces and State Oil Company; has allowed private oil companies to destroy food sources . . . and hence, is in violation of the right to food of the Ogonis'.[101]

97 CESCR, *General Comment No. 12*, para. 15; FAO, *Voluntary Guidelines*, p. 6.

98 Künnemann, 'The Right to Adequate Food', p. 95.

99 S. Koonan, 'Legal Implications of Plachimada - A Case Study', IELRC Working Paper 2007-05 (Geneva: International Environmental Law Research Centre, 2007), pp. 1–2; Wuppertal Institut, *Fair Future*, p. 114. The original decision of the single judge in the case is: High Court of Kerala, *Perumatty Grama Panchayat* v. *State of Kerala*, W.P.(C) No. 34292 of 2003, Judgement of 16 December 2003, available at: www.elaw.org/content/india-perumatty-grama-panchayat-vs-state-kerala-20031216-coca-cola-groundwater-exploitation-.

100 African Commission on Human and Peoples' Rights, *The Social and Economic Rights Action Center and the Center for Economic and Social Rights* v. *Nigeria*, Communication 155/96, decision taken at 30th Ordinary Session, Banjul, The Gambia, from 13th to 27th October 2001, ACHPR/COMM/A044/1659 ('*SERAC* v. *Nigeria*').

101 *SERAC v. Nigeria*, ibid., at para. 66.

The Commission appealed to the government to protect the environment and the health and livelihood of the Ognoni people by conducting an investigation, ensuring adequate compensation and undertaking a comprehensive cleanup of lands and rivers damaged by the oil operations.[102]

In cases where water resources on which people rely are no longer sufficient for food production due to depletion or unusable due to contamination and people have no other means to procure food, this constitutes a violation of a State's obligation to protect the human right to food.

### 4.3 *Obligation to Fulfil*

The obligation to fulfil requires States to adopt the necessary measures directed towards the full realisation of human rights.[103] States must facilitate access to food by enabling individuals to enjoy their rights. Only as a last resort, when individuals do not have the means to provide for themselves, does the obligation to fulfil turn into an obligation of direct provision.[104] The obligation to fulfil gives broad leeway to States in terms of the policy options they adopt to fulfil the right to food. The right does not prescribe particular measures to States as long as they comply with the standard of appropriateness as stipulated in Article 2(1) of the ICESCR.[105]

In examining State policies for realising the right to food, it must be kept in mind that it is primarily the individual who is responsible for the realisation of his or her right to food, taking all measures within his or her capacity.[106] The State's main role is to facilitate access by enabling people to provide for themselves and engaging in activities that are intended to strengthen access to and utilisation of resources.[107] General measures taken in this regard may include promoting economic development and employment opportunities in order to raise people's income.[108]

Only when people are unable to produce their own food or lack the means to procure it, does the role of the State as direct provider become relevant. This is particularly the case for people who are victims of natural or human-made disasters,[109] but also for people who are unable, for reasons beyond their

[102] *SERAC v. Nigeria*, paras. 71-2.

[103] Craven, *The ICESCR*, p. 109; Eide, 'Economic, Social and Cultural Rights', p. 24.

[104] Eide, ibid., p. 24. [105] Cotula, Djiré and Tenga, *Right to Food*, p. 16.

[106] Eide, 'The Right to an Adequate Standard of Living', p. 139; Cotula, Djiré and Tenga, *Right to Food*, p. 15.

[107] CESCR, *General Comment No. 12*, para. 15; FAO, *Voluntary Guidelines*, p. 6.

[108] FAO, ibid., p. 10, Reimann, *Ernährungssicherung im Völkerrecht*, p. 181.

[109] FAO, ibid., p. 29; CESCR, *General Comment No. 12*, para. 15.

control, to realise the right to food by the means at their own disposal.[110] In this respect, the State must establish food safety nets designed to protect those who are unable to provide for themselves.[111] The State can either provide direct food aid or social assistance or other social transfers that afford people the means to acquire food.

Overall, States must ensure that there is sufficient food available for procurement. States can either opt for self-sufficiency, by enabling sufficient food production domestically and ensuring that water resources are allocated appropriately, or else they can import food. Countries with limited water availability may decide to import agricultural products that contain a large amount of virtual water.[112] A number of countries, for example, Egypt and Jordan, do not have enough water to produce food for their populations.[113] There is no obligation for States to fulfil the right to food with domestically grown food, they are free to import it.[114] Moreover, there are significant variations in water availability within many countries, for example, in Brazil and China. In such cases, food can be produced in distant locations and transported to people in other areas, so that no local provision of water is required for this purpose.[115] What States are required to ensure is that sufficient food is available and that it is accessible to everyone. Thus, in general the State has an array of options on how to fulfil the right to food that do not necessarily require the local provision of water.

However, the situation of people who rely primarily or exclusively on subsistence agriculture, is a special case.[116] The situation of these people differs significantly from those who acquire readily produced food as far as reliance on water resources is concerned.

Agriculture is, and will continue to be, important for many people living in rural areas.[117] State options to fulfil the right to food must be examined in light of the fact that access to water resources is a critical factor in determining the success of agricultural activities. A subsistence farmer may rely on rain-fed cultivation if he or she does not have the means to connect to irrigation

[110] CESCR, ibid.; Kent, *Freedom from Want*, pp. 107–108.

[111] FAO, *Voluntary Guidelines*, p. 25, Reimann, *Ernährungssicherung im Völkerrecht*, p. 181; Cotula, Djiré and Tenga, *Right to Food*, p. 16.

[112] WWAP, *World Water Development Report 2*, p. 257; Allan, 'Virtual Water'.

[113] WWAP, ibid., p. 252.

[114] On food sovereignty as a political concept and its relation to human rights, see Cotula, Djiré and Tenga, *Right to Food*, pp. 20–21.

[115] Gleick, 'The Human Right to Water', p. 491.

[116] Cahill, 'The Human Right to Water', pp. 396–397.

[117] PEP, 'Poverty Reduction', p. 22; UNDP, *Human Development Report 2006*, p. 173.

systems. Yet, supplemental irrigation might be necessary to produce sufficient food for the family, especially during dry spells. Providing support, by facilitating access to water for subsistence farming (alongside other extension services), could be a suitable measure in this context. Depending on the circumstances, the provision of supplementary food aid or social transfers during dry spells could also be an appropriate measure. Whenever possible, the State must help people provide for themselves by engaging in activities that enable people to gain access to resources. This is in line with underlying principles of human rights, such as participation and empowerment.[118] This should be done in such a way that engages individuals as active subjects, whereas providing food aid may degrade people to passive objects of State policy. The latter may be necessary in certain circumstances, but ideally, and in the long term, people should be enabled to provide for themselves.

Other measures commonly discussed under the framework of rural development could be aimed at enabling people to earn an income from alternative sources. For instance, the Indian National Rural Employment Guarantee Act aims to boost the rural economy and enhance economic growth. It guarantees a minimum amount of paid employment on public works in rural areas.[119] In specific food-for-work programmes, food is provided in return for work aimed at rural development, such as the construction of streets or canals.[120] More generally, State policies could aim at the diversification of the rural economy in order to allow for alternative income opportunities.[121] In some contexts, measures may also include promoting the growth of cash crops for export in order to earn foreign exchange. However, States must not compromise the food requirements of their own population in the quest to earn foreign exchange. States may also choose to export high-value crops and to import staple foods at the same time. In any case, the overall aim is to enable people to obtain access to and use resources for their realisation of the right to food.

[118] CESCR, *General Comment No. 12*, para. 23; C. Moser and A. Norton, *To Claim our Rights: Livelihood Security, Human Rights and Sustainable Development* (London: Overseas Development Institute, 2001), p. 19; see generally on participation and empowerment as concepts that reach beyond mere economic empowerment B. Hamm, 'A Human Rights Approach to Development', *Human Rights Quarterly*, Vol. 23, No. 4 (2001), pp. 1005–1031, at 1018–1020; M. Darrow and A. Tomas, 'Power, Capture and Conflict: A Call for Human Rights Accountability in Development Cooperation', *Human Rights Quarterly*, Vol. 27, No. 2 (2005), pp. 471–538, at 506–510.

[119] For more details, see D. Sjoblom and J. Farrington, 'The Indian National Rural Employment Guarantee Act: Will It Reduce Poverty and Boost the Economy?', ODI Project Briefing No. 7 (London: Overseas Development Institute, 2008).

[120] Nuscheler, *Entwicklungspolitik*, p. 273.

[121] Cotula, Djiré and Tenga, *Right to Food*, p. 23.

It is beyond the scope of this chapter to discuss the advantages and disadvantages of all of these policy options in detail. Rather, the chapter simply acknowledges that States enjoy an array of options to fulfil the right to food, including for subsistence farmers, and are strictly not confined to any particular option from a human rights perspective. Ensuring access to water for food production is a key mechanism for realising the right to food, but there is no entitlement to have one's right to food realised in this way regardless of the circumstances. In general, States are not obliged to enable people to maintain a specific way of life, such as subsistence farming, as long as they do not violate cultural rights, for instance of indigenous peoples. Maintaining a particular way of life has to be considered as an element of their cultural rights.[122]

The most appropriate option to fulfil the right to food cannot be determined in the abstract, but requires a contextualised approach based on the participation of all those concerned. Specific conditions must be considered, such as socio-economic, climatic and geographic conditions, the availability of land, as well as the availability of water resources and existing infrastructure, in particular for irrigation.[123] Water cannot be considered in isolation as, for instance, land rights often affect access to water.

In arid regions, it might prove difficult to ensure access to sufficient water resources, and other options to fulfil the right to food might be more appropriate. On the other hand, facilitating access to water may be the most appropriate option, for example, when subsistence agriculture is the main source of securing food and other livelihood opportunities and access to markets are limited.[124] Access to an irrigation scheme can make a significant

[122] It is out of the scope of this paper to consider indigenous peoples' rights in detail. See in this regard J. Anaya, 'Indigenous Peoples' Participatory Rights in Relation to Decisions about Natural Resource Extraction: The More Fundamental Issue of What Rights Indigenous Peoples Have in Lands and Resources', *Arizona Journal of International and Comparative Law*, Vol. 22, No. 1 (2005), pp. 7–17; S. Damman, 'The Right to Food of Indigenous Peoples', in W. B. Eide and U. Kracht (eds.), *Food and Human Rights in Development, Vol. I, Legal and Institutional Dimensions and Selected Topics* (Antwerp: Intersentia, 2005), pp. 285–322; C. Groni, *Das Menschenrecht auf Teilhabe am kulturellen Leben, Inhalt, Grenzen und Justitiabilität von Art. 15 (1) lit. A) des Internationalen Paktes über wirtschaftliche, soziale und kulturelle Rechte* (Stuttgart: Boorberg, 2008), p. 242; L. Barrera-Hernández, 'Indigenous Peoples, Human Rights and Natural Resource Development: Chile's Mapuche Peoples and the Right to Water', *Annual Survey of International and Comparative Law*, Vol. 11 (2005), pp. 1–28; D. H. Getches, 'Indigenous Peoples' Rights to Water under International Norms', *Colorado Journal of International Environmental Law and Policy*, Vol. 16, No. 2 (2005), pp. 259–294; and generally A.-C. Bloch, 'Minorities and Indigenous Peoples', in A. Eide, C. Krause and A. Rosas (eds.), *Economic, Social and Cultural Rights - A Textbook*, 2nd edition (Dordrecht: Martinus Nijhoff, 2001), pp. 373–388.

[123] See Nuscheler, *Entwicklungspolitik*, p. 265; Cotula, Djiré and Tenga, *Right to Food*, p. 23.

[124] Cotula, Djiré and Tenga, ibid., at p. 23.

difference for many farmers. While modern irrigation techniques that allow for efficient water use, such as drip irrigation, have in the past been prohibitively expensive, more recently, low-cost models have been developed. For instance, small-scale bucket-and-drip kits can be used for vegetable cultivation and kitchen gardens.[125] Moreover, traditional techniques, such as rainwater harvesting, also have potential to enhance water security in rain-fed areas by increasing soil moisture, replenishing groundwater and providing reserves for supplemental irrigation during dry spells.[126] Water requirements of different crops vary significantly, so the choice of crops grown also has an impact of the amount of food that can be produced when water availability is low.[127] In many rural contexts, facilitating access to water by extending irrigation schemes or utilising traditional techniques, such as rainwater harvesting, is the most suitable policy option to realise the right to food, in particular when people have been relying on growing their own food, have the necessary skills and experience and consider subsistence farming as part of their way of live.

## 4.4 *Non-discrimination and Equality*

States have an obligation not to discriminate against certain individuals or groups, which cuts across other obligations. The CESCR understands discrimination as 'constitut[ing] any distinction, exclusion, restriction or preference or other differential treatment that is directly or indirectly based on the prohibited grounds of discrimination and which has the intention or effect of nullifying or impairing the recognition, enjoyment or exercise, on an equal footing, of Covenant rights'.[128] Article 2(2) of the ICESCR enumerates 'race, colour, sex, language, religion, political or other opinion, national or social origin, property, birth or other status' as prohibited grounds. The inclusion of 'other status' indicates this list is not meant to be exhaustive and the CESCR has identified a number of other grounds of discrimination, including disability, age, nationality, marital and family status, sexual orientation and gender identity, health status, place of residence, as well as economic and social

[125] UNDP, *Human Development Report* 2006, p. 197. [126] Ibid., p. 196.

[127] S. L. Postel, 'Securing water for people, crops, and ecosystems: New mindset and new priorities', *Natural Resources Forum*, Vol. 27, No. 2 (2003), pp. 89–98, at 96.

[128] CESCR, *General Comment No. 20, Non-Discrimination in Economic, Social and Cultural Rights* (Forty-second session, 2009), UN Doc. E/C.12/GC/20 (2009), para. 7. For a similar definition, see Article 1 CEDAW. The Human Rights Committee comes to a similar interpretation, see Human Rights Committee, *General Comment No. 18, Non-discrimination* (Thirty-seventh session, 1989), contained in UN Doc. HRI/GEN/1/Rev.1 at p. 26, paras. 6–7.

situation.[129] Some of these grounds are particularly relevant for the purposes of this chapter, for example, sex, ethnicity, property status, place of residence, as well as economic and social situation. When taking particular measures to facilitate the realisation of the right to food by enabling people to gain access to water resources for food cultivation, for instance, by expanding irrigation schemes or supporting rainwater harvesting, States must not exclude women or any of these groups.[130]

States not only are prohibited from discriminating with current and future measures, but also have to address existing de facto discrimination and inequalities and pay specific attention to disadvantaged, marginalised and vulnerable groups. This may require taking positive measures to remedy inequalities and conditions that perpetuate discrimination and improve the situation of targeted groups.[131] As mentioned above, undernourished and malnourished people live to a large extent in rural areas, often as smallholder farmers and landless rural people. Depending on the circumstances, targeted interventions to improve access to water for women, people lacking property rights and other groups that face disadvantages, may be needed.

## 5 CONCLUSION

The human right to food is of fundamental importance for human survival and an adequate standard of living. To produce sufficient food for the realisation of the right to food, a minimum of 2,000 to 3,000 lpd of water is necessary. It must be acknowledged that States can choose different policy options to fulfil the right. Food can be produced at distant locations and be transported to the location of consumption so that no local provision of water is necessary. States can also choose to import food from other States. Accordingly, there is no need to consider specifically access to water for producing food as a universal human right. However, for a significant number of people direct access to water resources is vital, in particular people relying on their own cultivation and/or livestock raising, often with limited access to food markets and little income to procure food.

[129] CESCR, ibid., paras. 15, 28.

[130] For an example of how discrimination may play out see Chapter 9, this volume, which discusses the biased allocation of assistance to large-scale farmers which indirectly discriminates against women farmers.

[131] Sepúlveda, *The Nature of the Obligations*, p. 385; Limburg Principles on the Implementation of the International Covenant on Economic, Social and Cultural Rights, UN doc. E/CN.4/1987/17, Annex (1987), para. 39; CESCR, ibid., para. 9.

A State's primary obligation to fulfil the right to food is to enable people to provide for themselves and to facilitate access to necessary resources. In order to do so, States can choose from a number of policy options, including the creation of alternative sources of income by strengthening rural development and providing access to markets. When States do not take any such measures and people depend on producing their own food and consequently on access to water, such water use must be accorded priority. Water allocation must not be influenced solely by the variable of power (whether based on income, socio-economic status or gender), but must be guided by human rights and carried out in such a way that the human rights of all individuals can be realised. Human rights do not prescribe particular measures, but they do require that certain principles, such as non-discrimination and equality, are complied with. They provide 'a subtle and principled framework for ensuring that the allocation of goods and services is not based simply on the distribution of power and wealth, but is made to respect human dignity'.[132]

In summary, rather than stipulating that there is a specific human right to water for food production, access to water for subsistence farming is an important means to achieve the realisation of the right to food. Direct access to water is a critically important factor for many people in securing livelihoods, achieving an adequate standard of living and realising their right to food.

[132] Langford, 'Crossfire', p. 12.

# 5

# Tapping Transboundary Waters

## *Implications of the Right to Water for States Sharing International Watercourses*

ANNA F.S. RUSSELL* AND STEPHEN MCCAFFREY**

### 1 INTRODUCTION

With population growth, and economic and agricultural development, placing greater strain on the world's limited supply of freshwater, reliable access to clean water is becoming increasingly difficult to secure. Watercourses on all continents are under threat of overuse, increased pollution and in certain cases, large-scale diversion. Not only has the sector faced historical neglect and poor governance, but climate change poses additional challenges for managing the sector and protecting the resource. The political geography of the planet is dominated by international drainage basins, yet the obligations of governments towards individuals in other countries relying on shared waters are unclear. Traditionally, the law of human rights has protected the individual against his or her government, not against actions of governments of other countries. Thus, for instance, the failure of an individual's government to take steps to progressively ensure access to adequate water would generally constitute a human rights violation. And, in fact, for most people who lack access to water, the problem lies internally within that country, and does not relate to use of a transboundary watercourse. However, if an individual's lack of access to water is due to a neighbouring State's use of an international watercourse, has that State violated the individual's right to water?

This chapter examines the implications of recognition of a human right to water for States sharing international watercourses. Section 2 provides some contextual background to transboundary water disputes and examples of uses of international watercourses that could infringe the human rights of individuals

* Visiting Fellow, Public International Law Group, Faculty of Law, University of Oxford.
** Distinguished Professor of Law, University of the Pacific, McGeorge School of Law, United States.

living in co-riparian States. Section 3 examines arguments relating to potential extraterritorial obligations of States to respect, protect and fulfil the right to water in the context of transboundary watercourses. Section 4 reviews accountability mechanisms for holding States responsible for any extraterritorial violations of the right to water. Section 5 discusses the influence of the right to water on existing international watercourse law along with suggestions as to how the right to water may inform the workings of international institutions (e.g. joint commissions) responsible for the management of such transboundary waters.

## 2 CONTEXTUAL SETTING: RISING TENSIONS OVER THE USE OF INTERNATIONAL WATERCOURSES

International river basins 'generate roughly 60 per cent of the global freshwater flow and are home to approximately 40 per cent of the world's population'. In 2002, it was found that 263 rivers 'either cross or demarcate international political boundaries', with 69 international basins in Europe, 57 in Asia, 40 in North America and 38 in South America.[1] Climate change threatens to alter significantly the hydrological regimes of these basins.[2] In mountain ranges in which some of the world's major river systems rise, for example, retreating glaciers and reductions in snow cover are forecast to have a negative effect on water availability, affecting more than one-sixth of the world's population.[3] And while the amount of water on earth does not change, the global population continues to increase. The United Nations predicts that it will reach 9.7 billion by 2050.[4] This portends greater competition for finite supplies of freshwater, much of which is internationally shared.

[1] UNEP, *Atlas of International Freshwater Agreements* (Nairobi: UNEP, 2002), pp. 1–2.

[2] For further information concerning climate change and alterations to the hydrological regime, see e.g., B. Nijssen, G. O'Donnell, A. Hamlet and D. Lettermaier, 'Hydrologic Sensitivity of Global Rivers to Climate Change', *Climatic Change*, Vol. 50, No. 1 (2001), pp. 143–175; V. Georgiyevsky and I. Shiklomanov, 'Climate Change and Water Resources', in I. Shiklomanov and J. Rodda (eds.), *World Water Resources at the Beginning of the Twenty-First Century* (Cambridge: Cambridge University Press, 2003), pp. 390–413; S. Eisenreich, 'Climate Change and the European Water Dimension: A Report to European Water Directors', European Commission – Joint Research Centre, (2005) EU Report No. 21553.

[3] Human Rights Council, 'Report of the Office of the United Nations High Commissioner for Human Rights on the Relationship between Climate Change and Human Rights', UN Doc. A/HRC/10/61 (15 January 2009), para. 29, citing IPCC, 'AR4 Synthesis Report', pp. 48–49. For further discussion of the impacts of climate change on the right to water, see Chapter 6 by Darrow in this volume.

[4] UN Department of Economic and Social Affairs, Population Division, 'World Population Projected to Reach 9.7 billion by 2050', 29 July 2015.

The utilisation and management of international watercourses has therefore come under increased scrutiny by co-riparian States, regional organisations and the international community.

The law of navigation on international waterways was the principal focus of treaties concerning shared freshwater until the late nineteenth century, though these were largely between European States. The law governing non-navigational uses of international watercourses was slower to develop. Indeed, while provisions on navigation may be found in multilateral treaties as early as the Peace of Westphalia in 1648, the first attempt to regulate non-navigational uses via such an agreement did not come until the early 1920s.[5] And it was not until 1997 that another universal agreement on the subject was concluded: the UN Convention on the Law of the Non-Navigational Uses of International Watercourses (UN Watercourses Convention).[6]

While pollution of shared waters has been a concern, a principal focus of States has been on water quantity and, in particular, the principles and rules for allocating water chiefly between upstream and downstream States.[7] Even today, most disputes over non-navigational uses of international watercourses involve surface waters, and relate primarily to quantity issues. It is not uncommon for lower riparian States to claim that the activities occurring within the territory of their upstream neighbours are resulting (or will result) in decreased river flows. The classic example is the Nile. Generally considered the longest river in the world, the Nile flows for some 4,000 miles from Lake Victoria to the Mediterranean Sea. Its basin encompasses ten countries and covers approximately one-tenth of the continent of Africa. The lowest riparian State, Egypt, contributes virtually no water to the river, and yet has been dependent on it for millennia, particularly for irrigated agriculture. With recent increased use and even further proposed uses of the waters by upper riparian States, and no treaty in force that includes all basin States, Egypt's access to the waters of the

5 This effort, under the auspices of the League of Nations, resulted in the Convention relating to the Development of Hydraulic Power Affecting More than One State (adopted 9 December 1923, entered into force 30 June 1925), 36 LNTS 76. While this may have been the first multilateral treaty of the kind in the modern era, there is evidence of bilateral treaties on water allocation of antiquity. The agreement of ca. 2450 BC ending one of the many wars between the Mesopotamian city-states Umma and Lagash is perhaps the best known example (A. Nussbaum, *A Concise History of the Law of Nations*, Revised edition (New York: Macmillan, 1954), pp. 1–2).

6 UN Convention on the Law of the Non-Navigational Uses of International Watercourses (adopted 21 May 1997, entered into force 17 August 2014), 36 ILM 700, UN Doc. A/Res/51/229.

7 P. Birnie, A. Boyle and C. Redgwell, *International Law and the Environment*, 3rd edition (Oxford: Oxford University Press, 2009), p. 536.

Nile remains vulnerable.[8] Another well-known example is the Ganges, which flows through India into Bangladesh. India constructed the Farraka Barrage just short of the Bangladesh border to divert Ganges water to the port of Calcutta. Bangladesh was concerned that the barrage would leave insufficient water to meet the existing needs of its population. Various water-sharing agreements have been negotiated, including provision for immediate consultation should the flow drop below a certain level.[9]

Although quantity disputes typically involve surface water flows, they may also arise in the context of transboundary groundwater or, since most groundwater is hydrologically related in some way to surface water, a combination of surface and groundwater. Excluding the water that is frozen in polar ice caps or glaciers, groundwater constitutes approximately 98 per cent of available freshwater, with approximately two-thirds of such water located in confined transboundary aquifers.[10] Confined transboundary aquifers, or fossil aquifers, are particularly contentious transboundary resources not only because they receive no recharge from surface waters, but also because of their relatively pure quality as they are generally situated at great depths away from any surface contaminants.[11] As technology improves, the palaeowaters in such aquifers are becoming more accessible, and increasingly risk over-exploitation and depletion, as well as pollution. One of the largest non-renewable transboundary aquifers is the Nubian Sandstone Aquifer, located under parts of Chad, Egypt, Libya and Sudan.[12] Being situated in a generally arid region, all four countries are reliant on the aquifer as a source of freshwater. Although a joint initiative is in place to optimise equitable use of the aquifer,[13] Libya's

8 For further discussion concerning the Nile, see S. McCaffrey, *The Law of International Watercourses*, 2nd edition (Oxford: Oxford University Press, 2007), pp. 258–272. A Nile Basin Cooperative Framework Agreement has been negotiated by nine of the ten basin States (all but Eritrea), but at the time of writing had garnered only three of the six ratifications needed for entry into force.

9 For further discussion concerning the Ganges, see McCaffrey, *The Law of International Watercourses*, pp. 292–296.

10 J. Barberis, 'International Groundwater Resources Law', FAO Legislative Study, No. 40 (1986), p. 1; A. Utton, 'The Development of International Groundwater Law', *Natural Resources Journal*, Vol. 22 (1982), pp. 95–118, at 97.

11 It is noted that the term 'fossil aquifers' is not entirely accurate. Confined transboundary aquifers often contain palaeowaters or fossil waters recharged during past wetter climates. Thus, when referring to fossil aquifers in this chapter, it is meant aquifers containing palaeowaters.

12 The Nubian Sandstone Aquifer does actually receive some recharge, but as it is negligible, it is considered a non-renewable aquifer.

13 For further information see International Atomic Energy Agency (IAEA), Technical Cooperation, 'Chad, Egypt, Libya and Sudan Agree on Framework for Joint Management of the Nubian Sandstone Aquifer System', 20 September 2013.

construction of the 'Great Man Made River' – a pipeline to carry water from the aquifer in the southern part of the country to coastal cities in the north – potentially threatens the water supply of the other States.[14]

Disputes primarily over the quality of international watercourses are also prominent with industrial waste, agricultural run-off and domestic sewage continuing to pollute international waters. For example, in Europe, the quality or pollution of international watercourses is more of a concern than quantity or variances in flow. Western Europe's longest river, the Rhine, is home to approximately 60 million people and provides drinking water to some 20 million of these. However, many of Europe's main industries are also situated along the river, and pollution, particularly chloride pollution, remains a continual concern.[15] Another example relates to the River Uruguay. Argentina brought a case before the International Court of Justice (ICJ) in part over concerns that the construction of pulp mills adjacent to the river in Uruguay would result in unacceptable levels of pollution in violation of the applicable treaty.[16]

Although the above examples have been discussed as primarily 'quantity' or 'quality' disputes, it is important to note that these categories to some extent over-simplify hydrological or hydrogeological reality. When a quantity issue or one regarding flow rates arises in relation to an international watercourse, it often gives rise to or exacerbates a quality issue, such as the water reaching the downstream State being more saline or containing more effluent, proportionally (i.e. on a parts-per-million basis). Similarly, it is often difficult to categorise many disputes as being primarily concerned with quantity or quality, or even with other issues. By way of illustration, the Colorado River, which flows through the south-western United States into north-western Mexico, is the subject of a multitude of disputes relating to both insufficient flow and transboundary aquifer recharge to Baja California, as well as unacceptable water quality, particularly related to elevated levels of salinity and pesticides.[17]

[14] Egypt is increasingly relying on the water for irrigation. For further information on Libya's 'Great Man-Made River', see McCaffrey, *The Law of International Watercourses*, p. 10; S. McCaffrey, *The Law of International Watercourses*, 3rd edition (Oxford: Oxford University Press, forthcoming), chapter 1; and www.water-technology.net/projects/gmr/.

[15] Note that pollution concerns are also present in the case of the Danube – the second longest river in Europe. For further information regarding both case studies, see McCaffrey, *The Law of International Watercourses*, pp. 298–305.

[16] ICJ, *Pulp Mills on the River Uruguay (Argentina* v. *Uruguay)*, (Judgment of 20 April 2010). Although the Court declared Uruguay had not breached its substantive obligations for the protection of the environment, it did find Uruguay had breached its procedural obligations to cooperate.

[17] For further discussion concerning the Colorado, see McCaffrey, *The Law of International Watercourses*, pp. 333–346.

When examining such disputes or potential disputes, it is useful to recall that there exists a general duty for States to cooperate with each other,[18] including in avoiding, identifying and investigating transboundary harm. Therefore if an activity is likely to have transboundary effects, specific duties may arise, such as notifying and consulting potentially affected States, carrying out environmental impact assessments, and the like. In relation to transboundary watercourses, many of these procedural obligations have now been codified in the 1997 UN Watercourses Convention.[19] Also reflected in the UN Watercourses Convention is the principle of customary international law that States have an obligation not to cause harm to other States or common spaces.[20] The UN Watercourses Convention contains other substantive obligations, including that States are to use an international watercourse in an equitable and reasonable manner, and 'with a view to attaining optimal and sustainable utilisation'.[21] Should there be a conflict between uses of an international watercourse special regard is to be given to the requirements of vital human needs.[22] According to a statement of understanding adopted by the committee that negotiated the UN Watercourses Convention, '[i]n determining "vital human needs", special attention is to be paid to providing

[18] Article 1(3) of the UN Charter explains that one of the purposes of the UN is '[t]o achieve international cooperation in solving international problems of an economic, social, cultural or humanitarian character'. Articles 55 and 56 pledge cooperation with a view to creating conditions of stability and well-being, and promoting higher standards of living, solutions of international problems and universal respect for human rights. This has been interpreted to imply an obligation not to carry out activities that may cause harm to the rights of those living in other States. See also article 74 relating to 'good neighbourliness'.

[19] UN Watercourses Convention. For example, the Convention articulates a general obligation to cooperate (article 8), an obligation of prior notification (article 12), an obligation to consult (articles 11, 17), and an obligation to exchange data and information on a regular basis (article 9). For further discussion of these obligations, see McCaffrey, *The Law of International Watercourses*, chapters 9 and 13. Note that within the Convention, there is also a due diligence provision concerning the prevention and mitigation of harmful conditions (whether resulting from natural causes or human conduct) (article 27), as well as extensive dispute settlement provisions, including mediation and impartial fact finding (article 33).

[20] UN Watercourses Convention, article 7 provides that watercourse States shall 'take all appropriate measures to prevent the causing of significant harm to other watercourse States'. Specific duties to prevent pollution, including the protection and preservation of ecosystems of international watercourses, are also outlined in part IV the Convention.

[21] UN Watercourses Convention, article 5. Factors relevant to equitable and reasonable utilisation include amongst other things the population dependent on the watercourse in each State, the effects of the use of the watercourse by one State on another, existing and potential uses, and the conservation and protection of the use of water resources (article 6(c), (d), (e), and (f)).

[22] UN Watercourses Convention, article 10(2).

sufficient water to sustain life, including both drinking water and water required for production of food in order to prevent starvation'.[23]

The UN Watercourses Convention, however, does not apply to fossil aquifers, such as the Nubian Sandstone Aquifer.[24] At its 2008 session, the International Law Commission adopted Draft Articles on the Law of Transboundary Aquifers.[25] The Draft Articles contain many similar substantive and procedural obligations to those reflected in the UN Watercourses Convention. However, substantively the Draft Articles also provide that each State has sovereignty over the portion of the aquifer located within its territory. Each State is to exercise its sovereignty in accordance with international law and the remainder of the provisions.[26] Remaining provisions include equitable and reasonable utilisation, an obligation not to cause significant harm, amongst others.

The sustainable management of many of the international watercourses and aquifers discussed above, as well as a number of others, is becoming increasingly challenging. Climate change is leading to increased changes in flows, including in extreme cases, droughts and floods, as well as altered chemical composition and aquatic diversity due to warming temperatures. Climate induced variability is increasing existing stress on international watercourses, and with greater demand for freshwater, it is likely that tensions over uses of international watercourses will continue to rise. Although uses of international watercourses are subject to regulation by the State, they may be by both State and non-State actors. Particularly in water scarce areas, actions by, or within, one co-riparian State may directly or indirectly affect individuals living in another co-riparian State, including potentially the realisation of their human rights, such as their right to an adequate standard of living or their cultural rights. Examples of such conduct could include

[23] 'Convention on the Law of the Non-Navigational Uses of International Watercourses - Report of the Sixth Committee Convening as the Working Group of the Whole', UN Doc. A/51/869 (11 April 1997).

[24] In article 2 of the UN Watercourses Convention, 'watercourse' is defined as 'a system of surface waters and groundwaters constituting by virtue of their physical relationship a unitary whole and normally flowing into a common terminus'.

[25] 'Report of the International Law Commission on the Work of its Sixtieth Session' (5 May-6 June 2008 and 7 July-8 August 2008), UN Doc. A/63/10, at pp. 19-27. The UN General Assembly took note of the Draft Articles later that year (UN Doc. A/Res/63/124 (15 January 2009)). See generally S. McCaffrey, 'The International Law Commission Adopts Draft Articles on Transboundary Aquifers', *American Journal of International Law*, Vol. 103, No. 2 (2009), pp. 272–293.

[26] UN Draft Articles on the Law of Transboundary Aquifers, article 3. There are other problems with the Draft Articles as well. For example, the Draft Articles are not restricted to confined transboundary aquifers.

pollution by a State facility, inequitable withdrawal of water from an international watercourse by local authorities, construction of a dam and withholding or diversion of water, and extraction of water from a confined transboundary aquifer. Other examples could involve similar conduct by non-State actors, such as corporations or other private entities, non-governmental enterprises or individuals.

Against this backdrop of rising tensions over the utilisation of international watercourses, the remainder of this chapter examines how recognition of an international human right to water may influence the utilisation of transboundary watercourses. As discussed in earlier chapters of this book, in 2002, the Committee on Economic, Social and Cultural Rights (CESCR) issued General Comment No. 15 interpreting existing obligations of the International Covenant on Economic, Social and Cultural Rights (ICESCR)[27] as including or being inextricably related to the right to water. This chapter does not engage in the debate as to the existence of an international right to water.[28] Rather, the analysis starts from the position that the right to water falls within the category of guarantees essential to secure an adequate standard of living as outlined in the ICESCR. Much of the following commentary therefore assumes that the States referred to are parties to the Covenant. While arguments exist that aspects of the right to water, as articulated in General Comment No. 15, find support in other sources of international law, a comprehensive discussion of such is beyond the scope of this chapter. By focusing on the right to water as derived from the ICESCR, an illustration of the implications of such a right for States sharing international watercourses is provided.

This chapter focuses primarily on the relationship between an individual's access to adequate water in relation to a co-riparian State's use of an international watercourse, rather than the relationship between the co-riparian States themselves, which is the subject of the UN Watercourses Convention. The following section therefore investigates whether individuals whose access to adequate water has been undermined as a result of actions in relation to an international watercourse by a co-riparian State might have a human rights claim in such circumstances and whether that State bears any responsibility

[27] International Covenant on Economic, Social and Cultural Rights (adopted 16 December 1966, entered into force 3 January 1976), 993 UNTS 3, UN Doc. A/6316.

[28] For related discussions, see, as examples, S. McCaffrey, 'The Human Right to Water', in E. Brown Weiss, L. Boisson de Chazournes and N. Bernasconi-Osterwalder (eds.), *Fresh Water and International Economic Law* (Oxford: Oxford University Press, 2005), pp. 93–115; T. Kiefer and C. Brölmann, 'Beyond State Sovereignty: The Human Right to Water', *Non-State Actors and International Law*, Vol. 5 (2005), pp. 183–208.

toward the individual under the ICESCR. An example of the controversy of this argument can be found in the 2008 Human Rights Council Resolution establishing an independent expert on the issue of human rights obligations related to access to safe drinking water and sanitation, which specifically leaves 'aside questions of international watercourse law and all transboundary water issues'.[29] However, before proceeding, it is worth re-iterating that for the majority of people without access to adequate water today, the problem lies with the State where the individual lives and does not relate directly to use of an international watercourse by another State.[30] It is also noted that questions arising under international humanitarian law are not included within the scope of this chapter.

## 3 APPLICABLE EXTRATERRITORIAL OBLIGATIONS OF THE RIGHT TO WATER IN RELATION TO INTERNATIONAL WATERCOURSES

Each State party to the International Covenant on Civil and Political Rights (ICCPR) 'undertakes to respect and to ensure to all individuals within its territory and subject to its jurisdiction the rights recognised in the present Covenant'.[31] Unlike the ICCPR, the rights in the ICESCR are not necessarily subject to respect only within a State's 'territory' or 'jurisdiction'. Rather, the ICESCR lacks an explicit jurisdiction clause limiting its application. Article 2(1) of the ICESCR states that each State party 'undertakes to take steps, individually and through international assistance and cooperation, especially economic and technical, to the maximum of its available resources' to achieve progressively the rights recognised in the Covenant. It is therefore

[29] UN Human Rights Council Resolution 7/22 (28 March 2008), preamble.

[30] P. Gleick, 'The Human Right to Water', *Water Policy*, Vol. 1, No. 5 (1999), pp. 487–503. It is worth re-iterating that the right to water involves an entitlement to access water for personal and domestic uses and thus in terms of quantity comprises approximately eight percent of available freshwater uses in developing countries and about fifteen percent in developed countries (UNDP, *Human Development Report 2006: Beyond Water Scarcity: Power, Poverty and the Global Water Crisis* (New York: Palgrave Macmillan, 2006), p. 138). For the majority of those without access to water, it is generally a result of institutional or governance issues, rather than a resource issue.

[31] International Covenant on Civil and Political Rights (adopted 16 December 1966, entered into force 23 March 1976), 999 UNTS 171, UN Doc. A/6316, article 2(1). Specific jurisdictional clauses are also present in the European Convention for the Protection of Human Rights and Fundamental Freedoms (adopted 4 November 1950, entered into force 3 September 1953), 213 UNTS 222, as amended by Protocols No. 3, 5, 8, 11 and 14, which entered into force on 21 September 1970, 20 December 1971, 1 January 1990, 1 November 1998 and 1 June 2010, respectively, article 1, and the American Convention on Human Rights (adopted 22 November 1969, entered into force 18 July 1978), 1144 UNTS 123, article 1.

debatable as to whether the drafters of the ICESCR intended it to have international scope.[32] What constitutes 'international cooperation' is also the subject of debate – despite reference to 'international assistance' in the same article, the term is often narrowly associated with aid.

Other articles of the ICESCR contain an international dimension. As examples, article 23 notes that international action for the achievement of rights 'includes such methods as the conclusion of conventions, the adoption of recommendations, the furnishing of technical assistance and the holding of regional meetings and technical meetings for the purpose of consultation and study'.[33] Furthermore, article 11, from which the right to water is derived in part, provides that State parties will take appropriate steps to ensure the realisation of the right to an adequate standard of living, 'recognising to this effect the essential importance of international cooperation based on free consent'.[34]

The debates concerning the extent of any extraterritorial obligations of State parties to the ICESCR remain in the development stages.[35] The CESCR has addressed the issue in a number of General Comments, ranging from international technical assistance measures,[36] to the nature of State parties'

32 F. Coomans, 'Some Remarks on the Extraterritorial Application of the International Covenant on Economic, Social and Cultural Rights', in F. Coomans and M. Kamminga (eds.), *Extraterritorial Application of Human Rights Treaties* (Antwerp: Intersentia, 2004), pp. 183–199, at 184–187. Note that article 29 of the Vienna Convention on the Law of Treaties (adopted 23 May 1969, entered into force 27 January 1980), 1155 UNTS 31 states that '[u]nless a different intention appears from the treaty or is otherwise established, a treaty is binding upon each party in respect of its entire territory'. However, this 'does not establish that the ICESCR, which is a treaty not explicitly restricted to be binding for each State party only in its territory, would automatically be binding outside and would need for its extraterritorial obligations a specific statement to this effect' (R. Künnemann, 'Extraterritorial Application of the International Covenant on Economic, Social and Cultural Rights', in Coomans and Kamminga (eds.), *Extraterritorial Application of Human Rights Treaties*, pp. 201–231, at 201).

33 The preamble to the ICESCR notes the obligation of States under the Charter 'to promote universal respect for, and observance of, human rights and freedoms'. Other articles of reference include article 11(2), which notes the importance of 'international cooperation' in relation to the right of everyone to be from hunger; and article 15(4), which notes that State parties 'recognise the benefits to be derived from the encouragement and development of international contacts and cooperation in the scientific and cultural fields'.

34 ICESCR, article 11(1).

35 The terminology used to classify such obligations of States is of some debate, including external, international, transnational, etc. The term 'extraterritorial' obligation is used in this chapter. For broader discussion, including and beyond the ICESCR, see M. Langford, W. Vandenhole, M. Scheinin and W. Van Genugten (eds.), *Global Justice, State Duties: The Extraterritorial Scope of Economic, Social and Cultural Rights in International Law* (Cambridge: Cambridge University Press, 2013).

36 CESCR, *General Comment No. 2, International Technical Assistance Measures (article 22)*, (Fourth session, 1990), UN Doc. E/1990/23 (2 February 1990).

obligations,[37] to the relationship between economic sanctions and respect for economic, social and cultural rights.[38] Such obligations have also been addressed in various 'right-specific' General Comments, including General Comment No. 15 on the right to water.[39] In terms of analysing the extraterritorial obligations of State parties to the ICESCR in relation to the right to water in the context of international watercourses, the tripartite obligations to respect, protect and fulfil,[40] provide a useful analytical framework and are discussed in more detail below. It is noted, however, that obvious critiques of such a categorisation exist, such as trying to isolate specific legal obligations (be they territorial or extraterritorial) into distinct components. Caution should therefore be taken in trying to place real life examples wholly within one of these obligations to the neglect of a more nuanced analysis.[41]

### 3.1 *Obligation to Respect*

Typically seen as a negative obligation, the obligation to respect requires that a State party to the ICESCR refrain from actions that would interfere with the enjoyment of the rights outlined in the Covenant. Various authors have stated that such an obligation includes refraining from conduct that would lead to a

[37] CESCR, *General Comment No. 3, The Nature of States Parties Obligations (article 2(1))*, (Fifth session, 1990), UN Doc. E/1991/23 (1 January 1991).

[38] CESCR, *General Comment No. 8, The Relationship between Economic Sanctions and Respect for Economic, Social and Cultural Rights*, (Seventeenth session, 1997), UN Doc. E/C.12/1997/8 (12 December 1997). Recently, the CESCR issued a *Statement on Public Debt, Austerity Measures and the International Covenant on Economic, Social and Cultural Rights*, UN Doc. E/C.12/2016/1 (22 July 2016).

[39] For example, see also CESCR, *General Comment No. 4, The Right to Adequate Housing (article 11(1))*, (Sixth session, 1991), UN Doc. E/1992/23 (1 January 1992); CESCR, *General Comment No. 12, The Right to Adequate Food (article 11)* (Twentieth session, 1999), UN Doc. E/C.12/1999/5 (12 May 1999); CESCR, *General Comment No. 14, The Right to the Highest Attainable Standard of Health (article 12)* (Twenty-second session, 2000), UN Doc. E/C.12/2000/4 (11 August 2000).

[40] Commonly, this tripartite typology has been adopted as a means of analysis by the CESCR, as well as various commentators. For a discussion of the evolution of the typology, see M. Sepúlveda, *The Nature of the Obligations under the International Covenant on Economic, Social and Cultural Rights* (Antwerpen: Intersentia, 2003), pp. 157–164.

[41] For further discussion of critiques of such an approach, see e.g., I. Koch, 'Dichotomies, Trichotomies, or Waves of Duties?', *Human Rights Law Review*, Vol. 5, No. 1 (2005), pp. 81–103; M. Craven, 'Assessment of the Progress on Adjudication of Economic, Social and Cultural Rights', in J. Squires, M. Langford and B. Thiele (eds.), *Road to Remedy: Current Issues in Litigation of Economic, Social and Cultural Rights* (Sydney: Australian Human Rights Centre and University of NSW Press, 2005), pp. 27–42; M. Langford, 'A Sort of Homecoming: The Right to Housing', in M. Gibney and S. Skogly (eds.), *Universal Human Rights and Extraterritorial Obligations* (Philadelphia: University of Pennsylvania Press, 2010), pp. 166–193.

violation of economic, social or cultural rights of individuals living outside of the offending State's territory and within the territory of another State.[42] Examples provided include refraining from food embargoes towards other States,[43] supporting a development project that threatens the livelihoods of vulnerable groups,[44] and imposing conditions on lending that would have an adverse effect on human rights.[45]

In the context of international watercourses, the actions of one co-riparian State can have a serious impact on individuals living in another co-riparian State who are reliant on the watercourse to maintain an adequate standard of living, including to meet their personal and domestic water needs.[46] As mentioned above, examples could include pollution of an international watercourse by a State facility,[47] excessive withdrawal of water by a local authority, construction of a dam and inequitably withholding water, diversion of a watercourse, and so on. Therefore, if India was to undertake a large-scale diversion project involving waters of the Ganges River, which threatened the livelihood of small-scale farmers in neighbouring Bangladesh dependent on the water, would the farmers have a human rights claim against India, assuming they would have a claim against their own government in similar circumstances?[48] If a dam constructed in Vietnam results in the depletion of fish stocks in north-eastern Cambodia preventing villagers from being free from

[42] Coomans, 'Some Remarks', pp. 192–193; Künnemann, 'Extraterritorial Application', pp. 216–217; M. Craven, *The International Covenant on Economic, Social and Cultural Rights* (Oxford: Clarendon, 1995), p. 147. The 'Maastricht Principles on Extraterritorial Obligations of States in the Area of Economic, Social and Cultural Rights' (2011), written by a group of human rights advocates, note that States are to refrain from conduct that would directly or indirectly interfere with the rights of persons outside their territories. This includes not impairing the ability of other States or international organisations to comply with their obligations, or aiding, assisting or coercing them into breaching them. According to the principles, States are also to refrain from adopting measures, such as sanctions or embargoes, that would impair the realisation of economic, social and cultural rights (principles 19–22).

[43] Coomans, 'Some Remarks', p. 193.

[44] Künnemann, 'Extraterritorial Application', p. 217.

[45] Craven, *International Covenant on Economic, Social and Cultural Rights*, p. 148, also referencing the comments of the CESCR, *General Comment No. 2*. See also the recent CESCR, *Statement on Public Debt, Austerity Measures and the International Covenant on Economic, Social and Cultural Rights.*

[46] At this point, it may also be worth noting that article 1(2) of the ICESCR provides that '... [i]n no case may a people be deprived of its own means of subsistence'.

[47] Note that 'few modern treaties endorse an absolute prohibition on detrimental alteration of water quality. Instead, the modern trend is to require States to regulate and control river pollution, prohibiting only certain forms of pollutant discharge, and distinguishing between new and existing sources' (Birnie, Boyle and Redgwell, *International Law and the Environment*, p. 547).

[48] The project also involves waters of the Brahmaputra River. For further information, see McCaffrey, *The Law of International Watercourses*, p. 296.

hunger, could a human rights claim be made by the villagers against Vietnam in such circumstances?[49] Could those indirectly reliant on drinking water from the Rhine (e.g. in the Netherlands) make a human rights claim against other States discharging waste salts into the river (e.g. France) if chloride concentrations exceeded drinking water standards, posing a threat to human health?[50]

If there is an obligation to respect the economic, social and cultural rights of individuals living outside of a State's territory, a party to the ICESCR would be under an obligation to refrain from using an international watercourse in such a way that would interfere directly or indirectly with the enjoyment of such rights, including the right to water, in other riparian States. Thus if a State was using an international watercourse in such a way that individuals' access to adequate water was being prevented in another State, there would likely be a case for arguing that the responsible State is violating the rights of these individuals and under an obligation to change its conduct. A similar position is taken in General Comment No. 15, which notes that State parties are to respect the enjoyment of the right to water in other countries, and are to refrain from actions that may interfere with this. It notes that '[a]ny activities undertaken within the State party's jurisdiction should not deprive another country of the ability to realise the right to water for persons in its jurisdiction'[51] and that 'State parties should refrain at all times from imposing embargoes or similar measures, that prevent the supply of water, . . . for securing the right to water'.[52]

### 3.2 *Obligation to Protect*

The obligation to protect is typically described as an obligation to prevent third parties, such as corporations or other entities, within the jurisdiction of the State, from interfering in any way with the enjoyment of rights. In the extraterritorial context, authors have suggested that, under the ICESCR, State parties have a duty to ensure that a corporation, or any other entity subject to its control, respects the enjoyment of the rights outlined in the

[49] See Harvard Law Bulletin-Summer 2008, 'Lawyers for the Damned', available at www.today.law.harvard.edu/lawyers-for-the-damned. There are also claims that surges from the dam led to drownings.

[50] For further information, see McCaffrey, *The Law of International Watercourses*, pp. 302–303.

[51] CESCR, *General Comment No. 15, The Right to Water* (Twenty-ninth session, 2002), UN Doc. E/C.12/2002/11 (20 January 2003), para. 31.

[52] CESCR, *General Comment No. 15*, para. 32, noting that CESCR, *General Comment No. 8* notes the disruptive effect of sanctions upon sanitation supplies and clean drinking water.

Covenant in other countries.[53] One author has suggested that the State may have an 'obligation to regulate, investigate and even bring before the courts' a corporation where '"a threshold of gravity" of human rights violations is at stake', and that States may be held responsible for violations of socio-economic rights that result from a failure to take steps to control the behaviour of corporations where there is a clear possibility to do so.[54] Examples provided include preventing corporations carrying out operations abroad from discriminating against workers on the basis of gender or interfering with their right to freedom of association,[55] stopping industries practicing dumping in international trade in another country against vulnerable groups such that their access to food is threatened as a consequence,[56] and not supporting the work of international financial or development agencies (or other organisations) if they do not respect the rights of individuals living in other countries.[57]

Many of the scenarios discussed earlier in relation to international watercourses, such as pollution or excessive withdrawals of water, could be carried out by non-State entities, such as private enterprises. The *Pulp Mills* case discussed above is an example involving a private entity. Interestingly in that case, an application was also brought to the Inter-American Commission on Human Rights by a group of Argentine residents against Uruguay in relation to

[53] Craven, *International Covenant on Economic, Social and Cultural Rights*, p. 148. See also P. Alston, 'International Law and the Human Right to Food', in P. Alston and K. Tomasevski (eds.), *The Right to Food* (Utrecht: Martinus Nijhoff, 1984), pp. 9–68, at 44. The 'Maastricht Principles on Extraterritorial Obligations of States in the Area of Economic, Social and Cultural Rights' (2011) note that States are to take action to protect economic, social and cultural rights extraterritorially. This includes taking necessary measures to ensure non-State actors, which they are in a position to regulate, do not impair their enjoyment, as well as adopting and enforcing other measures in specific circumstances (e.g. where harm originates on a State's territory). The principles go on to note that States in a position to influence the conduct of non-State actors to protect such rights should do so in accordance with international law and that all States have an obligation to cooperate (principles 23–27).

[54] Coomans, 'Some Remarks', p. 193 noting a due diligence standard. According to the 'Guiding Principles on Business and Human Rights', the State duty to protect human rights may require taking appropriate steps to prevent, investigate, punish and redress [human rights] abuse though effective policies, legislation, regulations and adjudication ('Report of the Special Representative of the Secretary-General on the Issue of Human Rights and Transnational Corporations and Other Business Enterprises, John Ruggie', UN Doc. A/HRC/17/31 (21 March 2011), para. 1).

[55] Coomans, 'Some Remarks', p. 193.

[56] Künnemann, 'Extraterritorial Application', pp. 219–220.

[57] Craven, *International Covenant on Economic, Social and Cultural Rights*, p. 148, making reference to CESCR, *General Comment No. 2*; See also Künnemann, 'Extraterritorial Application', pp. 221–222, in relation to other international organisations, as well as the 'Maastricht Guidelines on Violations of Economic, Social and Cultural Rights' para. 19 agreed upon by various human rights advocates.

the pollution risks from the pulp mills on the River Uruguay, which is shared by the two countries.[58] In the national context, arguments have been made alleging that a State has violated its obligation to protect rights related to the right to water in cases involving pollution of waters from oil companies,[59] as well as over-extraction of groundwater by bottling companies.[60] It is not unlikely that similar situations could occur in relation to watercourses that traverse State boundaries.[61] A company could easily be accused of discharging effluent into an international watercourse that has a detrimental effect on the quality of water relied upon by individuals living in downstream States to meet their basic needs. Similarly, a State could end up providing technical or financial support to an international organisation, such as a joint management institution, which actually impedes rather than fosters the realisation of the right to water of individuals living in co-riparian States. For example, if not all basin States are members of a joint commission or a treaty concerning the watercourse, it could be that decisions are made (e.g. regarding allocation of an international watercourse) that have a negative impact on the rights of individuals, including the right to water, in States which are not members of the joint commission or parties to the treaty. In such circumstances, would a State party to the ICESCR have an obligation to protect the rights of individuals, including their right to water, in other States who are dependent on the watercourse?

If there is an extraterritorial component of the obligation to protect, then State parties to the ICESCR would have to take appropriate steps to ensure that third parties within their jurisdiction respect the right to water of individuals living in other countries. This would include, for example, regulating extraction and pollution of waters that may cross State boundaries, as well as taking into account the basic needs of individuals reliant on the watercourse

58 A. Boyle, 'Human Rights or Environment Rights? A Reassessment', *Fordham Environmental Law Review*, Vol. 18 (2007), pp. 471–511, at 500–501.

59 For example, such arguments have been made in Argentina, where a case was brought on behalf of an indigenous community claiming that the State was failing to fulfil its obligation to protect the good health of the population due to water pollution by an oil company (COHRE, *Legal Resources for the Right to Water* (Geneva: COHRE, 2004, pp. 110–111).

60 For example, such arguments have been made in India in the Coca-Cola case, summarised at www.business-humanrights.org/en/coca-cola-lawsuit-re-india. (Note that the cases of the right to water being raised in response to the privatisation of water services are not directly relevant for the purposes of this chapter.)

61 For example, a watercourse case analogous to the ICJ air pollution case ICJ, *Aerial Herbicide Spraying (Ecuador* v. *Columbia)*, (filed 31 March 2008), could occur. (In this case, Ecuador claimed that aerial spraying of toxic herbicides by Colombia around the border violated international law. The case was removed from the Court's list on 13 September 2013.)

in co-riparian States when acting through or supporting the work of shared management schemes. If a State failed to take reasonable steps to control the behaviour of such non-State actors, and as a result, individuals' access to basic water was being hindered in another State, there would likely be a case for arguing that the State is responsible for the violation and under an obligation to take steps to regulate the conduct. General Comment No. 15 notes that State parties should take steps to prevent their citizens and companies from violating the right to water in other countries.[62] General Comment No. 15 explains that as members of international organisations, their actions should take due account of the right to water.[63] While not referenced explicitly in the General Comment, and likely aimed more at the international financial and development organisations, this would include international institutions responsible for the joint management of transboundary waters.

## 3.3 *Obligation to Fulfill*

The obligation to fulfil is often framed in the extraterritorial context as an obligation for wealthier States to provide aid to poorer States. During the drafting of the ICESCR there was a general consensus that States were entitled to ask for development assistance, but not claim it as a legal right. Members of the CESCR have since stated that States are to take positive measures to promote the realisation of rights in other countries.[64] In terms of subsidiary obligations to facilitate, promote and provide, the former will be the focus of the discussion in the context of international watercourses. The obligation to facilitate relates to States taking positive measures to assist individuals to enjoy the right.[65] In relation to the obligation to fulfil, General Comment No. 15 recognises the essential role of international cooperation

[62] CESCR, *General Comment No.* 15, para. 33.

[63] CESCR, *General Comment No.* 15, para. 36. See also paragraph 60 in relation to the international financial institutions. Under 'Obligations of Actors Other than States', CESCR, *General Comment No.* 15 also states that '[t]he incorporation of human rights law and principles in the programmes and policies by international organisations will greatly facilitate implementation of the right to water'. However, it seems to be referring to the specialised agencies and relevant UN programmes, rather than necessarily joint commissions.

[64] Craven, *International Covenant on Economic, Social and Cultural Rights*, pp. 148–149.

[65] The obligation to promote relates to improving public consciousness in relation to a right. In the case of the right to water, this would involve developing educational programmes on minimising water wastage amongst other things. The obligation to provide relates to the supply of goods or services. In the case of the right to water, this would involve providing water when individuals are unable to do so for reasons beyond their control with the means at their disposal.

and assistance, as well as the need to take joint and separate action to achieve full realisation of the right to water.[66] It also states that '[d]epending on the availability of resources, States should facilitate realisation of the right to water in other countries, for example through provision of water resources, financial and technical assistance, and provide necessary aid when required'.[67] It stresses the importance of international cooperation in assisting developing countries to fulfil their core obligations.[68]

In the context of transboundary waters, the question is whether under the ICESCR, a State might have a positive obligation to assist individuals living in co-riparian States to realise their right to water, for example, through a decrease in its use or a 'cleaner' use of international waters if such waters were necessary to meet the basic needs of individuals living in another State. In the debates that followed the issuance of General Comment No. 15, it was perhaps the concern that such assistance might be claimed as a legal right that underpinned, in part, various States' opposition to acknowledging the existence of an international right to water. For example, in 2003, the Canadian government stated that it did not accept the right to water particularly as between States.[69] However, any potential extraterritorial obligation to fulfil human rights relates to the realisation of rights of individuals living in other States, not to a State-to-State obligation, which as mentioned earlier is the

[66] CESCR. *General Comment No. 15*, para. 30.

[67] CESCR, *General Comment No. 15*, para. 34.

[68] CESCR, *General Comment No. 15*, para. 38. In relation to the obligation to fulfill, the 'Maastricht Principles on Extraterritorial Obligations of States in the Area of Economic, Social and Cultural Rights' (2011) note that States are to take action to fulfil economic, social and cultural rights extraterritorially. This includes creating an international enabling environment, coordinating with other States, contributing commensurate with capacity and resources to the fulfilment of rights extraterritorially, following certain principles and priorities in cooperation, providing international assistance where able to do so or seeking it where necessary, and responding to requests for international assistance or cooperation (principles 28–35).

[69] See the 2003 UN Commission on Human Rights statement by a Canadian representative stating that 'it did not agree that there was a "right" to drinking water and sanitation owed between States', UN Doc. E/CN.4/2003/SR.56 (19 May 2003), para. 49. (A number of years later, while Canada abstained from the 2010 General Assembly resolution recognising a human right to water (UN Doc. A/64/PV.108 (28 July 2010), p. 9), in a letter, dated 22 June 2012, from the Permanent Representative of Canada to the United Nations addressed to the Secretary-General of the United Nations Conference on Sustainable Development, he stated 'Canada recognises the human right of everyone to safe drinking water . . .'. He went on to add that the right 'does not encompass transboundary water issues, including bulk water trade, nor any mandatory allocation of international development assistance' (UN Doc. A/CONF.216/12 (17 July 2012), Annex).)

subject of the UN Watercourses Convention (or regional watercourses agreements) in the context of transboundary watercourses.

While not in the context of shared water resources, the CESCR has previously commented on the extent of States' international development cooperation, such as the percentage of their gross national product (GNP) given in aid, in reviewing their reports.[70] However, it has not gone so far as to prescribe the form of aid to be given or to whom it should go.[71] In discussing article 2(1) of the ICESCR, commentators have observed that 'on the basis of the preparatory work it is difficult, if not impossible, to sustain the argument that the commitment to international cooperation contained in the Covenant can accurately be characterised as a legally binding obligation upon any particular State to provide any particular form of assistance'. However, '[i]n the context of a given right it may, according to the circumstances, be possible to identify obligations to cooperate internationally. . .'.[72] Accordingly, under the ICESCR, it is unlikely that a claim to more water of acceptable quality from an international watercourse to meet the basic water needs of a State's citizens as a matter of their human rights would be successful.[73] In particular situations – for example, severe water shortages or contamination of water services within a downstream State – it might be arguable that there is an obligation on the upstream State to cooperate. However, this cooperation need not necessarily involve the upstream State using less water, but perhaps engaging in discussions regarding facilitating the provision of bulk freshwater (e.g. in supertankers) or bottled water (or funds to purchase bottled water) to assist individuals in the co-riparian State achieve access to adequate water.[74]

70 For reference to various concluding recommendations, see Künnemann, 'Extraterritorial Application', p. 211.

71 Craven, *International Covenant on Economic, Social and Cultural Rights*, p. 149. Accordingly, it seems unlikely that arguments related to the obligation to provide would ever be argued successfully in such a context.

72 P. Alston and G. Quinn, 'The Nature and Scope of States Parties' Obligations under the International Covenant on Economic, Social and Cultural Rights', *Human Rights Quarterly*, Vol. 9 (1987), pp. 156–229, at 191.

73 It is also worth re-iterating at this time, the provision in article 11 that recognises the importance of international cooperation based on free consent.

74 Similar arguments could be made in relation to other States. Such cooperation could even involve engaging in discussions regarding facilitating the provision of virtual water, for example, in the form of food. For further information, see e.g., J. Allan, 'Water Use and Development in Arid Regions: Environment, Economic Development and Water Resource Politics and Policy', *Review of European, Comparative and International Law*, Vol. 5, No. 2 (1996), pp. 107–115 and subsequent writings on virtual water; as well as D. Phillips, J. Allan, M. Claassen, J. Granit, A. Jägerskog, E. Kistin, M. Patrick and A. Turton, *The TWO Analysis: Introducing a Methodology for the Transboundary Waters Opportunity Analysis* (Stockholm: Stockholm International Water Institute, 2008).

## 4 ACCOUNTABILITY FOR EXTRATERRITORIAL VIOLATIONS OF THE RIGHT TO WATER

If it is argued that a State is in violation of obligations under the ICESCR owed to individuals in another country, the next question that arises is whether there are accountability mechanisms available to individuals making such claims. Broadly speaking, two formal systems of supervision exist to monitor implementation of the Covenant. The first, which is touched on above, involves the process of State reporting and the second involves possible complaints procedures.[75]

Although the following sub-sections focus on the formal accountability mechanisms under the ICESCR, it is important to bear in mind that other mechanisms can play an important role in situations where it is thought that one State's use of a watercourse is negatively impacting individuals' access to adequate water and human rights in another State. The change that can be brought about through political pressure or through the court of public opinion, may be as, if not more, effective than the utilisation of formal international human rights procedures.

### 4.1 *Review of State Reports*

Although the Covenant makes no provision for a monitoring committee, the CESCR was eventually established in the mid-1980s. Every five years States are expected to report on the steps they have taken to implement the rights outlined in the Covenant. The Committee's reporting guidelines explicitly provide that State reports should include information on various aspects of their international cooperation and assistance.[76] After examining a report and engaging in dialogue with representatives from the State, the Committee highlights areas of concern and makes non-binding recommendations called 'concluding observations'. Non-governmental organisations (NGOs) (but not

[75] Litigation in domestic courts may also be a possibility, where it would not be barred by sovereign immunity or other jurisdictional doctrines. There is an article on this possibility in the UN Watercourses Convention. Article 32 on 'non-discrimination' states that '... a watercourse State shall not discriminate on the basis of nationality or residence or place where the injury occurred, in granting to such persons, in accordance with its legal system, access to judicial or other procedures, or a right to claim compensation or other relief in respect of significant harm caused by such activities carried on in its territory'.

[76] See e.g. CESCR, *Guidelines on Treaty-Specific Documents to be Submitted by State Parties under Articles 16 and 17 of the International Covenant on Economic, Social and Cultural Rights*, UN Doc. E/C.12/2008/2 (24 March 2009), paras. 3(c) and 9.

individuals) are able to participate in this process by submitting relevant information regarding the State party's report, as well as making short oral presentations to the Committee on the first day of each reporting session.[77] As discussed earlier, in reviewing State reports, the Committee has commented on the extraterritorial obligations of various parties, both in the context of official development assistance and with respect to a State's role in an international organisation.[78] While these oft-short observations may focus attention on certain issues, the reporting process 'does not facilitate detailed consideration of particular cases and does not allow for timely consideration of alleged violations'.[79]

### 4.2 *Complaints Procedures*

Historically, partly because there was no individual complaints procedure under the ICESCR, economic, social and cultural rights were often seen as second-class rights and associated with being mere goals or aspirations.[80] However, on 10 December 2008, the General Assembly unanimously adopted the Optional Protocol to the ICESCR.[81] It opened for signature on 24 September 2009 and entered into force on 5 May 2013, though only a small number of States have ratified or acceded to it.[82]

#### Individual Complaints Mechanism

The Optional Protocol gives the CESCR competence to receive and consider communications regarding individual complaints of violations by a State party

77 Other briefings may also be accommodated.

78 See e.g. CESCR, *Concluding Observations on Sweden*, UN Doc. E/C.12/SWE/CO/5 (1 December 2008), para. 11; *France*, UN Doc. E/C.12/FRA/CO/3 (9 June 2008), para. 12; *Germany*, UN Doc. E/C.12/DEU/CO/5 (12 July 2011), para. 33; *Ireland*, UN Doc. E/C.12/IRL/CO/3 (7 July 2015), paras. 35–36.

79 A. Khalfan, 'Accountability Mechanisms', in Langford, Vandenhole, Scheinin and van Genugten (eds.), *Global Justice, State Duties*, pp. 391–416, at 395.

80 The ICESCR was one of only two major international human rights treaties to lack such a mechanism. The other was the Convention on the Rights of the Child. (The individual complaints mechanism under the International Convention on the Protection of the Rights of All Migrant Workers and Members of their Families (adopted 18 December 1990, entered into force 1 July 2003), 2220 UNTS 3, UN Doc. A/Res/45/158 has not yet entered into force.)

81 UN Doc. A/Res/63/117 (5 March 2009). It was adopted on the 60th anniversary of the Universal Declaration of Human Rights. For an overview of the drafting process, see C. Mahon, 'Progress at the Front: The Draft Optional Protocol to the International Covenant on Economic, Social and Cultural Rights', *Human Rights Law Review*, Vol. 8, No. 4 (2008), pp. 617–646.

82 For State status, see www.indicators.ohchr.org.

to the ICESCR.[83] In terms of who may submit communications to the CESCR, article 2 of the Optional Protocol states that '[c]ommunications may be submitted by or on behalf of individuals or groups of individuals, under the jurisdiction of the State party, claiming to be victims of a violation of any of the economic, social and cultural rights set forth in the Covenant by that State party.'[84]

What is immediately noticeable is that article 2 of the Optional Protocol uses the language of 'jurisdiction' as opposed to 'territory'. The question therefore becomes what dictates whether a State party to the Optional Protocol has jurisdiction over an individual or group of individuals. The issue does not seem to have been one of the main contentious issues in drafting the Optional Protocol.[85] Perhaps this is partly because where possible the chairperson of the various drafts of the protocol tried to use agreed language from other similar texts[86] and the term 'jurisdiction' is used in other international human rights agreements.[87] Accordingly, monitoring committees of other human rights treaties, as well as international and national courts, have been faced with determining whether a State party has jurisdiction in a range of extraterritorial contexts. A comprehensive review of such statements and decisions is beyond the scope of this chapter.[88] However, a brief discussion of various interpretations may provide some insight into the future direction of the Committee's understanding of article 2 of the Optional Protocol to the ICESCR in relation to events that occur beyond the territory of a State party. At the time of writing, four cases had been decided by the CESCR, none of which addressed this issue.

[83] Optional Protocol to the International Covenant on Economic, Social and Cultural Rights (adopted 10 December 2008, entered into force 5 May 2013), UN Doc. A/63/117, article 1.

[84] 'Where a communication is submitted on behalf of individuals or groups of individuals, this shall be with their consent unless the author can justify acting on their behalf without such consent.'

[85] Mahon, 'Progress at the Front'. See also C. Courtis and M. Sepúlveda, 'Are Extra-Territorial Obligations Reviewable under the Optional Protocol to the ICESCR?', *Nordisk Tidsskrift For Menneskerettigheter*, Vol. 27, No. 1 (2009), pp. 54–63, 58.

[86] Mahon, 'Progress at the Front', p. 620.

[87] For example, and as noted above and below, article 2(1) of the ICCPR.

[88] For further information, see e.g., M. Milanovic, *Extraterritorial Application of Human Rights Treaties: Law, Principles, and Policy* (Oxford: Oxford University Press, 2013) though the author's main focus is on treaties protecting civil and political rights; M. Gondek, *The Reach of Human Rights in a Globalising World: Extraterritorial Application of Human Rights Treaties* (Antwerp: Intersentia, 2009) covers treaties on civil and political rights and economic, social and cultural rights; chapters 5, 6 and 7 in Langford, Vandenhole, Scheinin and van Genugten (eds.), *Global Justice, State Duties* discuss jurisdiction in the context of international economic, social and cultural rights.

The Human Rights Committee, for example, which monitors implementation of the ICCPR, has addressed this issue of jurisdiction. As noted above, article 2(1) of the ICCPR provides that each State party 'undertakes to respect and to ensure to all individuals within its territory and subject to its jurisdiction the rights recognised in the present Covenant'. In General Comment No. 31, the Human Rights Committee explained that '[t]his means that a State party must respect and ensure the rights laid down in the Covenant to anyone within the power or effective control of that State party, even if not situated within the territory of the State party'.[89] Under the first Optional Protocol to the ICCPR, the Human Rights Committee can also receive and consider communications from individuals subject to a State party's jurisdiction. On a number of occasions it has examined the extraterritorial reach of the Covenant, including in the case of *López Burgos* v. *Uruguay*, which involved the abduction and arrest of a Uruguayan national by Uruguayan security forces in Argentina. The Human Rights Committee explained that an individual subject to a State party's jurisdiction under the Optional Protocol [to the ICCPR] does not refer to 'the place where the violation occurred, but rather to the relationship between the individual and the State in relation to a violation of any of the rights set forth in the Covenant, wherever they occurred'.[90]

The European Court of Human Rights (ECtHR) has the longest history of adjudicating cases involving alleged violations of human rights. Article 1 of the European Convention on Human Rights provides that State parties 'shall secure to everyone within their jurisdiction the rights and freedoms' defined in section I of the Convention.[91] In the 2011 case of *Al-Skeini* v. *United Kingdom*, concerning the death of five Iraqi nationals at liberty in the streets of Basrah, as well as one in custody of British troops in a detention centre in the city, the ECtHR attempted to clarify this issue of jurisdiction before determining there was such a link.[92] It wrote that a State's jurisdictional competence is primarily territorial, and that acts performed, or producing

[89] CCPR, *General Comment No. 31, The Nature of the General Legal Obligation Imposed on State Parties to the Covenant*, (Eightieth Session, 2004), UN Doc. CCPR/C/21/Rev.1/Add.13 (26 May 2004), para. 10. Note that in the ICJ, *Legal Consequences of the Construction of a Wall in the Occupied Palestinian Territory*, (Advisory Opinion of 9 July 2004), when referring to article 2(1) of the ICCPR, the ICJ explained that 'while the jurisdiction of States is primarily territorial, it may sometimes be exercised outside the national territory', para. 109.

[90] CCPR, *López Burgos* v. *Uruguay*, UN Doc. CCPR/C/13/D/52/1979 (29 July 1981), para. 12.2.

[91] European Convention for the Protection of Human Rights and Fundamental Freedoms, article 1.

[92] ECtHR, *Al-Skeini* v. *United Kingdom*, Application No. 55721/07 (7 July 2011), paras. 149–150. (The judgment of ECtHR, *Al-Jedda* v. *United Kingdom*, Application No. 27021/08 was handed down on the same day.)

effects, outside a State's territory can constitute an exercise of jurisdiction only in exceptional cases. The Court, in its case law, has recognised a number of exceptional circumstances, and each case is to be determined with reference to the particular facts.[93] The first of such exceptional circumstances, (often known as the personal model of jurisdiction[94]), is where a State, through its agents, exercises control and authority over an individual. This could include acts of diplomatic and consular agents, present on foreign territory in accordance with international law, who exert authority and control over others; situations when a State through the consent, invitation, or acquiescence of the government of the territory, exercises all or some of the public powers normally exercised by the government; and scenarios involving the use of force by State agents operating outside its territory where an individual is brought under the control of that State (e.g. taken into custody).[95] The second of such exceptional circumstances, (often known as the spatial model of jurisdiction[96]), is where as a consequence of lawful or unlawful military action, a State exercises effective control of an area outside its territory, whether that control is exercised by its own armed forces or through a subordinate local administration.[97]

Based on the above admittedly cursory survey, it seems unlikely that a communication submitted by individuals living in a State who are affected by another State's actions with respect to an international watercourse and who are claiming that their right to water has been violated[98] would be considered by the CESCR. Following the ECtHRs writings on 'jurisdiction', it would be difficult to argue that the affected individuals came within another State's agents' authority and control or that the offending State had effective

93 *Al-Skeini* v. *United Kingdom*, paras. 131–132.

94 See e.g. M. Milanovic, 'Al-Skeini and Al-Jedda in Strasbourg', *The European Journal of International Law*, Vol. 23, No. 1, pp. 121–139, at 128.

95 *Al-Skeini* v. *United Kingdom*, paras. 133–137. In regard to the last example, the ECtHR noted that jurisdiction did not arise solely from the control exercised by the State over buildings, aircrafts or ships in which individuals may be held, rather what is decisive is the 'exercise of physical power and control over the person in question'(para. 136).

96 Milanovic, '*Al-Skeini* and *Al-Jedda* in Strasbourg', p. 129.

97 *Al-Skeini* v. *United Kingdom*, paras. 138–140. In determining the existence of effective control, primary reference will be to the strength of the State's military presence, though indicators (e.g. military, economic and political support of the local subordinate administration) may also be relevant (para. 139). (A summary of the principles on the exercise of jurisdiction was repeated in ECtHR, *Jaloud* v. *Netherlands*, Application No. 47708/08 (20 November 2014), para. 139.)

98 Not only could individuals be claiming that they no longer have access to adequate water for personal and domestic uses, they could also be claiming they no longer have water needed to be free from hunger or to take part in cultural life, as examples.

control over the area where the affected individuals live. However, given the activism the CESCR has demonstrated in the past (e.g. through the issuance of General Comment No. 15), combined with the orientation of the ICESCR discussed earlier, it is possible that such arguments may be considered, and decisions by other adjudicative bodies, statements by commentators and writings by academics, certainly provide ample scope for doing so.[99]

A further issue worth noting at this stage relates to the difficulties in attribution of a human rights violation when more than one State is involved in action that violates the human rights of individuals living elsewhere.[100] In the above example regarding the decision of a joint institutional mechanism that affects access to water for individuals living in a co-riparian State not represented on the commission, the problem would arise as to whether the decision could be imputed to one or more of the represented States.[101]

**Inter-State Communications and the Inquiry Procedure**

The Optional Protocol also provides for inter-State communications and an inquiry procedure. In regard to inter-State complaints, a State party may claim that another State is not fulfilling its obligations under the Covenant, provided both States have recognised the competence of the CESCR to receive and consider communications.[102] While in theory individuals claiming an

[99] As examples, the 'Maastricht Principles on Extraterritorial Obligations of States in the Area of Economic, Social and Cultural Rights' (2011), state that jurisdiction includes situations over which a State's 'acts or omissions bring about foreseeable effects on the enjoyment of economic, social and cultural rights, whether within or outside its territory', as well as situations in which the State 'is in a position to exercise decisive influence to take measures to realise economic, social and cultural rights extraterritorially', principle 9(b) and (c); O. De Schutter, A. Eide, A. Khalfan, M. Orellana, M. Salomon and I. Seiderman, 'Commentary to the Maastricht Principles on Extraterritorial Obligations of States in the Area of Economic, Social and Cultural Rights', *Human Rights Quarterly*, Vol. 34, No. 4 (2012), pp. 1084–1169, at 1104–1109, containing references to various decisions; chapters 5, 6, 7 and 13 in Langford, Vandenhole, Scheinin and van Genugten (eds.), *Global Justice, State Duties*; Milanovic, *Extraterritorial Application of Human Rights Treaties* and his preference for a mixed model of jurisdiction whereby negative obligations (i.e. to refrain from specific acts) would be territorially unlimited and positive obligations (i.e. to ensure human rights) would require control of an area, pp. 209–228; Milanovic, '*Al-Skeini* and *Al-Jedda* in Strasbourg'.

[100] See e.g. M. Scheinin, 'Extraterritorial Effect of the International Covenant on Civil and Political Rights', in Coomans and Kamminga (eds.), *Extraterritorial Application of Human Rights Treaties*, pp. 73–81, at 78.

[101] For further discussion in relation to socio-economic rights, see A. Khalfan, 'Division of Responsibility amongst States', in Langford, Vandenhole, Scheinin and van Genugten (eds.), *Global Justice, State Duties*, pp. 299–331.

[102] Optional Protocol to the International Covenant on Economic, Social and Cultural Rights, article 10.

extraterritorial violation of their right to water could seek support from their own State to represent their interests, and there would be no jurisdictional hurdle to overcome, it is unlikely many States will opt-in to the mechanism. Rarely have similar inter-State communications been used by States in relation to other human rights instruments.[103]

In regard to the inquiry procedure, if the CESCR 'receives reliable information indicating grave or systematic violations by a State party' of any of the rights in the Covenant, it will invite the State to cooperate in examining the information and submitting observations in this regard.[104] The procedure could be employed to bring to the attention of the CESCR issues regarding alleged extraterritorial violations of a human right to water, provided the threshold could be met.[105] Again, although there is no jurisdictional hurdle to overcome with the inquiry procedure, it would also require a State to recognise the competence of the CESCR to conduct the inquiry.[106]

Given the limited number of parties to the Optional Protocol, as well as the hurdles that exist in relation to the various complaints procedures contained within it, engagement with NGOs to put forward information to the CESCR as part of the State reporting process, or utilisation of informal accountability mechanisms, may be more productive for individuals claiming their human right to water has been undermined by another State's use of an international watercourse.

## 5 MANAGING INTERNATIONAL WATERCOURSES IN THE SHADOW OF THE RIGHT TO WATER

States sharing international watercourses have a long history of establishing joint institutional mechanisms for their management.[107] During the last half

[103] Khalfan, 'Accountability Mechanisms', p. 399; Courtis and Sepúlveda, 'Are Extra-Territorial Obligations Reviewable', pp. 59-61.

[104] Optional Protocol to the International Covenant on Economic, Social and Cultural Rights, article 11(2).

[105] Courtis and Sepúlveda, 'Are Extra-Territorial Obligations Reviewable', pp. 61–62.

[106] Optional Protocol to the International Covenant on Economic, Social and Cultural Rights, article 11(1); Khalfan, 'Accountability Mechanisms', pp. 399–400; Courtis and Sepúlveda, 'Are Extra-Territorial Obligations Reviewable', pp. 61–62. For further information, see also M. Langford, B. Porter, R. Brown and J. Rossi (eds.), *The Optional Protocol to the International Covenant on Economic, Social and Cultural Rights: A Commentary* (Pretoria: Pretoria University Law Press, 2016).

[107] S. McCaffrey, 'International Watercourses', in R. Dupuy (ed.), *A Handbook on International Organisations*, 2nd edition (Dordrecht: Martinus Nijhoff and Hague Academy of International Law, 1998), pp. 725–751, at 733.

of the twentieth century, research showed that cooperative interactions between riparian States have 'outnumbered conflictive interactions by more than two-to-one'.[108] Therefore from a more proactive (rather than reactive) viewpoint, how should recognition of an international right to water influence the management of transboundary watercourses? If a State wishes to develop or further develop an international watercourse, how should potential extra-territorial obligations in relation to the right to water inform its activities?

First, article 23 of the ICESCR provides that international action for achieving the rights set out in the Covenant includes such methods as providing technical assistance and holding meetings for the purpose of consultation and study. Therefore in situations where States are heavily reliant on an international watercourse to meet the needs of their citizens, and demand on the watercourse is already intense, the human right to water could, in certain circumstances, necessitate meetings of basin States to facilitate international action (e.g. the exchange of information and cooperative management) for the achievement of the right.

Second, the UN Watercourses Convention states that no use of an international watercourse enjoys inherent priority over other uses.[109] As discussed above, in the event of a conflict between uses, special regard is to be given to the requirements of vital human needs. Recognition of access to water as a human right would therefore inform the determination of vital human needs.[110] In some respects, this would go farther that the statement of understanding mentioned earlier, which provides that the determination of vital human needs requires that special attention be paid to providing 'sufficient water to sustain human life, including both drinking water and water required for the production of food in order to prevent starvation'.[111] The importation of the right to water, and human rights law, into the equation raises the standard from the provision of sufficient water to sustain life to the provision of water necessary to live a life with dignity. Furthermore, if an individual were to have

[108] UNEP, *Atlas of International Freshwater Agreements*, pp. 2–3. The creation of joint commissions often plays a key role in efforts to mitigate conflict (p. 4).

[109] In the absence of agreement or custom to the contrary (UN Watercourses Convention, article 10(1)).

[110] McCaffrey, *The Law of International Watercourses*, pp. 369, 371.

[111] 'Convention on the Law of the Non-Navigational Uses of International Watercourses - Report of the Sixth Committee Convening as the Working Group of the Whole', as regards article 10. One author notes that general principles of transboundary water law protect the vital human needs of basin-dependent populations even without a hierarchy of the factors and criteria for determining equitable and reasonable use (C. Leb, 'The Right to Water in a Transboundary Context: Emergence of Seminal Trends', *Water International*, Vol. 37, No. 6, (2012), pp. 640–653, at 647).

access to adequate water but for the use of an international watercourse by another State, not only could human rights arguments be made, but this may also be a 'prima facie violation of the obligation of equitable and reasonable utilisation by the other State'.[112]

This discussion also illustrates one of various problems with the Draft Articles on the Law of Transboundary Aquifers. It is difficult to reconcile the notion of sovereignty over the portion of a transboundary aquifer or aquifer system located within a State's territory, with the obligation of equitable and reasonable utilisation. For example, how can Libya have unfettered discretion to use its portion of the waters of the Nubian Sandstone Aquifer and yet also not use the water in an inequitable and unreasonable way? Perhaps in similar scenarios where the water supply of aquifer States is at risk, extraterritorial human rights obligations may have effect.

Support for protecting the right to water in individual States within the context of shared watercourse agreements can also be seen at both the basin and regional levels. Interestingly, the human right to water has already been explicitly incorporated into international water agreements. The 2002 Senegal Water Charter between Mali, Mauritania, Senegal and now Guinea sets out various principles to guide the distribution of water. It then goes on to provide that these guiding principles 'will guarantee to the populations of the riparian States the full enjoyment of the resource, with respect for the safety of the people and the works, as well as the basic human right to clean water, in the perspective of sustainable development'.[113] Interestingly, the Charter also provides that the construction of two dams guarantee an artificial flood which occurred naturally before their construction in the 1980s so that indigenous peoples' flood recession agriculture may continue and water-borne diseases will decrease.[114] The 2008 Water Charter of the Niger Basin between Benin, Burkina Faso, Cameroon, Chad, Guinea, Ivory Coast, Mali, Niger and Nigeria also recognises the fundamental right of every individual to access water.[115] The right to water of the basin populations is

[112] McCaffrey, *The Law of International Watercourses*, p. 371. See similar conclusions in Birnie, Boyle and Redgwell, *International Law and the Environment*, p. 565.

[113] Charte des Eaux du Fleuve Sénégal (Water Charter of the Senegal River) (adopted 28 May 2002), OMVS Resolution 005, article 4. Information taken from McCaffrey, *The Law of International Watercourses*, pp. 274–275.

[114] McCaffrey, *The Law of International Watercourses*, pp. 274–275. For further information, see also M. Vick, 'The Senegal River Basin: A Retrospective and Prospective Look at the Legal Regime', *Natural Resources Journal*, Vol. 46, No. 1 (2006), pp. 211–243.

[115] Charte de l'Eau du Bassin du Niger (Water Charter of the Niger Basin) (adopted 30 April 2008), preamble; article 1(11) (definition).

to be a factor informing the determination of equitable and reasonable use.[116] Later, when discussing the principle of paying for water usage, it notes that the right to water must be guaranteed.[117]

While it does not contain explicit recognition of the right to water another example of its indirect incorporation into a freshwater treaty is, arguably, the 1992 United Nations Economic Commission for Europe (UNECE) Convention on the Protection and Use of Transboundary Watercourses and International Lakes through its 1999 Protocol on Water and Health. The 1992 UNECE Convention is the main multilateral freshwater treaty in Europe and aims to strengthen national measures for protecting and managing transboundary water in an ecologically-sound manner.[118] The more than 30 million cases of water-related diseases in Europe each year prompted States in the region to conclude the 1999 Protocol on Water and Health. The Protocol aims to protect human health and well-being through improved water management. It was the first international freshwater agreement adopted with the purpose of attaining an adequate supply of safe drinking water, and adequate sanitation, for everyone in the region.[119] State parties to the Protocol agree to take all appropriate steps for the purpose of ensuring 'adequate supplies of wholesome drinking water' and 'adequate sanitation', as well as 'effective protection of water resources used as sources of drinking water'.[120] The parties are to set targets for the achievement of the Protocol's objectives. The agreement was opened for signature prior to the issuance of General Comment No. 15 and other regional freshwater agreements could well also adopt protocols incorporating similar provisions. It will be interesting to see if future regional or basin treaties incorporate either explicit or implicit reference to the human right to water in order to ensure that the meeting of basic needs of populations of co-riparian States takes priority in the allocation of water resources.

[116] Water Charter of the Niger Basin, article 4.

[117] Water Charter of the Niger Basin, article 9. For a specific geographic focus on this broader issue, see T. Bulto, *The Extraterritorial Application of the Human Right to Water in Africa* (Cambridge: Cambridge University Press, 2014).

[118] UNECE, Convention on the Protection and Use of Transboundary Watercourses and International Lakes (adopted 17 March 1992, entered into force 6 October 1996), 1936 UNTS 269, preamble, article 2. (Since March 2016, States outside the ECE region can accede to the Convention.)

[119] UNECE and World Health Organisation (WHO)/Europe, Protocol on Water and Health to the 1992 Convention on the Protection and Use of Transboundary Watercourses and International Lakes, (adopted 17 June 1999, entered into force 4 August 2005), UN Doc. MP.WAT/2000/1 Eur/ICP/EHCO 020205/8Fin (18 October 1999). For further information, see www.unece.org/env/water.

[120] Protocol on Water and Health, article 4.

## 6 CONCLUSION

For most people who lack access to adequate water the problem stems from an intra- as opposed to inter- State governance issue. Yet with climate change, population growth and development posing increased challenges to managing watercourses, including transboundary watercourses, it is possible that cases alleging extraterritorial violation of the human right to water in relation to use of transboundary waters by another State become less unusual. This may be particularly the case given the reaffirmation of commitments regarding the human right to water in the 2030 Agenda for Sustainable Development,[121] as well as the renewed emphasis on ensuring water availability and sustainable management of the resource through the new, standalone development goal dedicated to freshwater – Sustainable Development Goal (SDG) 6.[122] While the obligations of States in relation to other States with respect to transboundary waters are set out in the UN Watercourses Convention, the obligations of States in relation to the rights of individuals living in other States are less clear. This is particularly the case for the rights recognised in the ICESCR, from which the human right to water is assumed to primarily derive for the purposes of this chapter. While there are obvious problems in trying to categorise the specific legal obligations of States in this regard, it seems likely that strong arguments could be made that States have both a duty to respect the right to water of individuals living in a co-riparian State, as well as a duty to take steps towards ensuring that third parties within their jurisdiction also respect the rights of these individuals. Under the ICESCR, it seems unlikely that States would have a specific obligation to fulfil the right to water of individuals living in co-riparian States – although arguments calling for cooperation in this regard could clearly be made if the lack of access was seen to relate to other States' use of the transboundary watercourse.

If it is thought that a State is violating the right to water of individuals living in a co-riparian State due to its use of an international watercourse, NGOs may submit information regarding such occurrences to the CESCR through the State report review process, which alongside less formal accountability mechanisms, such as the engagement of social movements, may be more productive than the various complaints procedures set out under the Optional Protocol to the ICESCR, to which a limited number of

[121] UN General Assembly Resolution (25 September 2015), 'Transforming Our World: The 2030 Agenda for Sustainable Development', UN Doc. A/Res/70/1 (21 October 2015), para. 7.

[122] For further information on 'Goal 6. Ensure availability and sustainable management of water and sanitation for all', see www.sustainabledevelopment.un.org/sdg6.

States are party. These may be particularly useful where individuals feel their government is not taking sufficient action on their behalf through inter-State legal or political means.

After reflecting on potential extraterritorial violations of the right to water, as well as both formal and informal accountability mechanisms, it is important to bear in mind that States have generally demonstrated a history of cooperation when it comes to sharing waters. Thus, while procedurally the ICESCR may act as another source for fostering cooperation between States, particularly in relation to economic, social and cultural rights, substantively, recognition of a right to water may start to influence how water is equitably allocated between States, having already worked its way into existing international freshwater agreements – both explicitly and implicitly.

# 6

# Climate Change and the Right to Water

MAC DARROW*

## 1 INTRODUCTION

It is difficult to think about climate change without thinking about water: rising sea levels, flooding and storm surges, damages to rain-fed agriculture, contamination of freshwater sources, increased aridity, and the disappearance of the Himalayan and Andean glaciers which supply clean water to hundreds of millions of people. To this extent, it may seem axiomatic or even tautological that climate change poses threats to the human right to water.

However, the relationship between climate change and the right to water is not as straightforward as it may first appear. Firstly, the right to water, as the term is understood in international law, only protects a limited set of 'personal and domestic' uses. The right to water is implicit in Article 11 the International Covenant on Economic, Social and Cultural Rights (ICESCR), as interpreted by the Committee on Economic, Social and Cultural Rights (CESCR, or the Committee).[1] The CESCR has defined the right to water as 'the right of

* PhD (Utrecht), Representative, Washington DC Liaison Office, Office of the United Nations High Commissioner for Human Rights (OHCHR). This chapter is written in a personal capacity, and does not necessarily represent the views of the United Nations or OHCHR.
The author is grateful to Inga Winkler for comments on an earlier draft.

[1] Article 11(1) of the ICESCR provides: 'The States Parties to the present Covenant recognize the right of everyone to an adequate standard of living for himself and his family, including adequate food, clothing and housing and to the continuous improvement of living conditions'. The right to water derives from the right to an adequate standard of living as well as the right to life: UN Doc. A/HRC/RES/15/9, Oct. 6, 2010. The General Assembly has acknowledged the rights to water and sanitation as human rights: UN Doc. A/RES/64/292, 3 August 2010. The Committee's interpretation is contained in CESCR, *General Comment No. 15, The Right to Water (arts. 11 and 12)* (Twenty-ninth session, 2003), UN Doc. E/C12/2002/11 (2002). See further discussion in Chapter 1.

everyone to sufficient, safe, acceptable, physically accessible and affordable water for personal and domestic uses'. By contrast, much of the climate change literature is on water for agricultural or related non-'personal' uses, which appear to fall outside the scope of the right to water as defined under international law.

Secondly, while the availability of water for personal or household uses may be limited by increased aridity, glacier melt and the other climate-related phenomena described above, there is not necessarily a direct correlation. Water scarcity is commonly defined as the condition in which the annual availability of renewable freshwater is 1,000 cubic metres or less per person.[2] Water for household use typically comprises a very small proportion of a given population's overall water requirements, less than 10 per cent in global average terms (compared with 70 per cent and 20 per cent for agriculture and industry, respectively).[3] If one assumes that an amount in the range of 100 litres per capita per day is required to realise the right to water, this amounts to 36,500 litres or 36.5 cubic metres per capita per year, representing a small fraction of the water available even in some of the more water scarce regions of the world. As the United Nations Development Program (UNDP) has observed, lack of sufficient access to water for household use is more a function of 'power, poverty and inequality', and a failure of governments to prioritise water allocation for basic needs and human dignity, than it is about scarcity *per se*.[4] Hence, even to the extent that climate change undermines water availability in a given country, it does not automatically follow that the right to water (for personal and domestic uses) will thereby be undermined.[5]

Climate-related threats to the right to water will of course vary significantly from country to country, depending – among other things – upon how flexibly one may interpret 'personal and domestic uses' in particular contexts. For example, analyses of water usage in certain poorer countries show that rural communities may prioritise water use for livestock and subsistence gardening, in addition to 'personal' uses of the kind typically seen in urban settings.[6] While there are inevitable limits on the extent to which any global conception and definition of a human right to water might be capable of embracing water

[2] See e.g. A. Sherbinin and V. Dompka (eds.), *Water and Population Dynamics: Case Studies and Policy Implications* (Washington D.C.: AAAS, 1998), glossary.

[3] United Nations Development Program, *Human Development Report 2006: Beyond Scarcity: Power, Poverty and the Global Water Crisis* (2006), p. 173.

[4] Ibid., at 2.

[5] The author is grateful to Inga Winkler for discussions on this theme.

[6] B. van Koppen, P. Moriarty and E. Boelee, 'Multiple-Use Water Services to Advance the Millennium Development Goals', Research Report No. 98 (Colombo, Sri Lanka: International Water Management Institute, 2006). See also Chapter 2.

uses related to food and livelihoods (indeed, the CESCR specifically rejected this possibility in the drafting process for General Comment No. 15, given the problem of indeterminacy),[7] this does not preclude more flexible interpretations of the right to water under domestic law to the extent that this would be contextually appropriate for 'personal and domestic uses'.[8] Neither does it impugn the proposition that climate-related threats to water availability may exacerbate water stress and conflicts over competing water uses, which – subject to the particular threats, vulnerabilities, water supply infrastructure and policy environment – may in turn undermine the realisation of the right to water in a given case.

Thirdly, not every threat or instance of damage from climate change necessarily constitutes a human rights violation. In order to demonstrate a human rights violation in a legal sense, it must be shown that a particular duty bearer (usually a State or public entity) owed a defined duty to a given claim holder that has been breached. A specific typology and framework of human rights obligations has evolved under international law, governing the scope of permissible legal claims for alleged breaches of the human right to water consequent upon climate change. There are a number of challenges to litigating human rights claims connected with climate change including the scientific complexity of climate change projections, and the difficulties in determining causation, attribution and liability for future harms, although as we will see these are not necessarily insurmountable. There are also manifold, but distinctive, challenges to mainstreaming human rights in climate change policy making at national and international levels.[9] International human

7 See Chapter 4, cautioning against too embracing a definition of the right to food under international law. For analogous arguments concerning the right to water, see M. Langford, 'Crossfire: There is no human right to water for livelihoods', *Waterlines*, Vol. 28, No. 1 (2009), pp. 5–12, at 5 and 10, asserting that the right to water should be interpreted and applied by national legislatures and tribunals in a manner that is sensitive to local priorities and contexts, but that there are inherent limits to the content and scope of this right under international law given the potential risks of indeterminacy.

8 Ibid., p. 10. Flexible and integrated approaches to water management may also be required, particularly in rural and peri-urban areas, to more appropriately reflect many communities' integrated need or uses of water beyond 'personal and domestic' uses envisaged in General Comment No. 15. See van Koppen et al., 'Multiple-Use Water Services to Advance the Millennium Development Goals', p. 2.

9 For overviews of these tensions, as well as possible synergies between the climate change and human rights legal regimes, see Office of the UN High Commissioner for Human Rights, *Report on the Relationship Between Climate Change and Human Rights* (2009), U.N. Doc. A/HRC/10/61 (15 January, 2009); S. McInerney-Lankford, M. Darrow and L. Rajamani, *Human Rights and Climate Change: A Review of the International Legal Dimensions* (Washington D.C.: World Bank, 2011); S. Humphreys, *The Human Rights Dimensions of Climate Change: A Rough Guide* (Geneva: International Council on Human Rights Policy,

rights law and the law relating to climate change have evolved in separate streams, as it were, and their inherent compatibility is not self-evident. 'Like oil and water', is how one commentator put it, albeit with specific reference to litigation rather than the broader relevance of human rights law to climate change policy making.[10]

Fourthly, as this chapter will show, the negative impacts (actual and prospective) of climate change upon the right to water cannot be understood within the framework of a water sector analysis, alone. Rather, the theoretical and functional interdependence and interrelatedness of human rights demands an inter-sectoral analysis of human rights impacts, looking at how the human right to water relates to possible climate-related abridgements of the right to adequate food, the right to health, rights relating to sanitation, political participation and so forth. It is only through a flexible, integrated and contextualised assessment of this kind that one may draw conceptually rigorous conclusions and operationally relevant policy recommendations concerning climate change and the right to water.

Finally, the role of international human rights law needs to be analysed in connection with its specific normative and functional interactions with the international climate change regime embodied in the UN Framework Convention on Climate Change (UNFCCC), Kyoto Protocol[11] and 2015 Paris Agreement (Paris Agreement).[12] Notwithstanding the distinctive histories and purposes of these regimes, and notwithstanding the evident normative tensions between them, as will be discussed, there is a presumption under international law that separate legal regimes should be interpreted in a manner that gives effect to a single set of compatible obligations.[13] Moreover,

2008); and S. Atapattu, *Human Rights Approaches to Climate Change: Challenges and Opportunities* (New York: Routledge, 2016).

[10] S. Tully, 'Like Oil and Water: A Sceptical Appraisal of Climate Change and Human Rights', *Australian International Law Journal*, Vol. 15 (2008), pp. 213–233, at 213.

[11] United Nations Framework Convention on Climate Change (adopted 9 May 1992, entered into force 21 March 1994), 1771 UNTS 107, 31 ILM 849 ('UNFCCC'); and Kyoto Protocol to the United Nations Framework Convention on Climate Change (adopted 11 December 1997, entered into force 16 February 2005), 2303 UNTS 148, 37 ILM 22.

[12] The Paris Agreement was concluded at the 21st Conference of the Parties (COP 21) of the UNFCCC and is intended to support the implementation of the UNFCCC through mitigation actions aimed at limiting global temperatures no more than two degrees Celcius above pre-industrial levels, and through adaptation and financing measures. The Paris Agreement entered into force on 4 November 2016 although at the time of writing its implementation modalities were still under negotiation.

[13] International Law Commission, *Fragmentation of International Law: Difficulties Arising from Diversification and Expansion of International Law: Report of the Study Group of the International Law Commission* (Fifty-eighth session, 2006), UN Doc. A/CN.4/L.682, at 1-25,

whatever the challenges in mounting a successful legal claim for the breach of the right to water in the context of climate change, the fact that identifiable individuals and communities are entitled to the enjoyment of a human right to water, and that this entitlement is being undermined or threatened by anthropogenic climate change, is beyond good faith scientific dispute.[14] The existing international human rights framework *does* enable the identification of duty bearers with ascertainable and enforceable duties to prevent, respond or remedy harms caused by Greenhouse Gas (GHG) emissions. A deeper appreciation of the normative and functional relationships between the human rights and climate change regimes would greatly strengthen climate change policy.

In section 2, this chapter provides a brief examination of the ways in which the right to water, within the understanding outlined above, may be undermined by climate change. The right to water is implicated within a range of fields of climate change policy making, including 'mitigation' (policies aimed at curbing carbon emissions) and 'adaptation' (policies and actions designed to respond to existing or foreseeable climate change harms). Following a short introduction to the right to water and climate change legal regimes in section 3, the chapter analyses the legal obligations at issue in the context of climate change harms and the right to water. Section 4 outlines the possibilities, as well as the constraints in identifying and vindicating legal claims under international law as presently understood, including the problems presented by the limited extraterritorial reach of international human rights law and how these may be addressed. Section 5 examines the right to water as part of the framework for climate change policy making, exploring the analytical contributions of the human rights framework, as well

para.154. For a discussion of the problem of fragmentation and the associated theory of systemic integration of international law, see C. McLachlan, 'The Principle of Systemic Integration and Article 31(3)(c) of the Vienna Convention', *International and Comparative Law Quaterly*, Vol. 54, No. 2 (2005), pp. 279–320; J. Pauwelyn, 'Bridging Fragmentation and Unity: International Law as a Universe of Inter-Connected Islands', *Michigan Journal of International* Law, Vol. 25, No. 4 (2004), pp. 903–916, at 904–905; compare with B. Simma, 'Universality of International Law from the Perspective of a Practitioner', *Fighting European Journal of International Law*, Vol. 20, No. 2 (2009), pp. 265–297, at 269–277.

[14] See International Energy Agency, *World Energy Outlook* (Paris: IEA, 2011); UN Water, *World Water Development Report 2015: Water for a Sustainable World* (Paris: UNESCO, 2015), pp. 65–67; IPCC, *Climate Change 2014: Synthesis Report, Contribution of Working Groups I, II and III to the Fifth Assessment Report of the Intergovernmental Panel on Climate Change* [Core Writing Team, R.K. Pachauri and L.A. Meyer (eds.)] (IPCC, Geneva, Switzerland, 2014) (IPCC Report 2014),pp. 67–71. The analysis and projections of the IPCC, an intergovernmental body including representatives from the major oil-producing and GHG-emitting States, while alarming, are generally considered to err on the side of conservatism.

as the importance of procedural rights, including the right to a remedy, strategic litigation, and how the right to water can inform substantive criteria for decision-making on financing and international cooperation. The chapter concludes in section 6 with recommendations as to how climate change policies based explicitly on the human right to water may strengthen the hand of individuals and communities most vulnerable to the adverse impacts of climate change, and strengthen the accountability of those with legal duties to respond. A number of key issues are identified for further research, as foundations for a more integrated and forward-looking vision of human rights and climate change law and policy.

## 2 IMPACTS OF CLIMATE CHANGE ON THE RIGHT TO WATER

Climate change has been characterised as a 'profound denier of freedom of action and a source of disempowerment'. By redrawing the maps of water availability, food security, disease prevalence, population distribution and coastal boundaries, climate change will likely exacerbate insecurity and violent conflict on a large scale.[15] Recent analyses by the Inter-governmental Panel on Climate Change (IPCC) and others show that adverse human impacts of climate change are already apparent in some regions of the world, and are likely to worsen. Climate change may have potentially profound implications for the realisation of internationally recognised human rights in many parts of the world, in industrialised as well as developing countries. The human right to water, as the Office of the UN High Commissioner for Human Rights (OHCHR) has argued, is among these.[16]

At present, 663 million people are estimated to lack access to an improved water source.[17] Climate change appears likely to further undermine the

[15] See e.g. O. Brown and E. Crawford, *Rising Temperatures, Rising Tensions: Climate Change and the Risk of Violent Conflict in the Middle East* (International Institute for Sustainable Development, 2009); N. Mabey, *Delivering Climate Security: International Security Responses to a Climate Changed World*, Whitehall Papers No. 69 (Royal United Services Institute, 2008); B. Chellaney, 'Climate Change and Security in Southern Asia: Understanding the National Security Implications', *Royal United Services Institute Journal*, Vol. 152, No. 2 (2007), pp. 62–69, at 63; and S. Atapattu (2016), pp. 242–265 (documenting armed conflicts relating to natural resource scarcity and forced population movements linked to climate change, forcing the issue of climate change onto the UN Security Council agenda for the first time in 2009).

[16] See OHCHR Report (2009).

[17] WHO and UNICEF, *Progress on Sanitation and Drinking Water: 2015 Update and MDG Assessment* (2015), p. 4. The number of people lacking 'safe' drinking water is likely much higher. The global monitoring indicator is the proportion of people using an 'improved' water source, however, not all improved sources provide drinking water that is safe.

availability and quality of water for many populations throughout the world, and result in a net increase in water stress.[18] Increased incidence and severity of droughts, increased aridity, and changes to the timing, magnitude and duration of precipitation events are among the main observed threats to water availability, along with diminution in freshwater supply through melting of land snow and ice.[19] Changing patterns of precipitation may relieve water scarcity to some extent in some areas, but at the same time, the increased frequency of heavy precipitation events may undermine the quality of surface and groundwater and contaminate water supplies.[20] The Stern Review[21] in 2006 estimated that even a 1 degree Celsius rise in temperature would threaten water supplies for 50 million people, and a 5 degrees Celsius rise in temperature would result in the disappearance of various Himalayan glaciers, foreshadowing water shortages for a quarter of China's population and hundreds of millions of people in India.[22] Declines in water quantity may also exert adverse impacts on water quality.[23] Beyond its direct impacts upon the global

[18] B. Bates et al. (eds.), *Climate Change and Water*, Intergovernmental Panel on Climate Change (IPCC) Technical Paper IV, June 2008, at 45 ('IPCC Technical Paper IV'). Water stress is assessed not only as a function of population and climate change, but also of changing water use, entailing the assessments and projections of per capita income, water use efficiency, water productivity and industrial production. Under the IPCC's modelling, water stress is calculated to decrease by the 2050s over 20 to 29 per cent of the global land area and to increase over 62 to 76 per cent of the global land area. See also IPCC, *Climate Change 2014: Synthesis Report, Contribution of Working Groups I, II and III to the Fifth Assessment Report of the Intergovernmental Panel on Climate Change* [Core Writing Team, R.K. Pachauri and L.A. Meyer (eds.)] (IPCC, Geneva, Switzerland, 2014) ('IPCC Report 2014'), pp. 67-71; United Nations Department of Economic and Social Affairs, *World Economic and Social Survey 2009: Promoting Development, Saving the Planet*, UN Doc. E/2009/50/Rev. 1, ST/ESA/319 (2009) (WESS 2009), p. xiv, noting the climate-related threats to water availability and quality; and United Nations Department of Economic and Social Affairs, World Economic and Social Survey 2016: Climate Change Resilience: An opportunity for reducing inequalities, UN Doc. E/2016/50/Rev., ST/ESA/363 (2016) (WESS 2016), pp. 6, 9 and 31.

[19] IPCC Technical Paper IV (ibid.), pp. 35–42; United Nations, *World Water Development Report* No. 3 (2009), p. 68. Increases in water availability through ice melt and increased glacial run-offs in the short term are predicted to be off-set by decreases in the longer term. However, for a cautionary note on the reliability of hydrologic projections see pp. 201–203.

[20] IPCC Technical Paper IV, at p. 41.

[21] N. Stern, *Stern Review on the Economics of Climate Change* (2006).

[22] Stern Review, ibid., part II, chapter 3 (How Climate Change will Affect People Around the World). On the technical complexities and competing projections on glacial melt see www.icimod.org/?page=737, and O. Schell, 'The Message from the Glaciers', *New York Review of Books*, Vol. 57, No. 9 (2010), pp. 46–50, and the studies referenced there.

[23] M. Falkenmark, 'Meeting Water Requirements of an Expanding World Population', *Philosophical Transactions of the Royal Society of London*, Vol. 352 (1997), pp. 929–936; M. Falkenmark and M. Lannerstad, 'Consumptive Water Use to Feed Humanity - Curing a Blind Spot', *Hydrology and Earth System Sciences*, Vol. 9 (2005), pp. 15–28; IPCC 2016, p. 44.

hydrologic cycle, climate change may exacerbate water stress indirectly through its effects on other external drivers, such as forced population movements, reduced economic growth and changing consumption patterns associated with rising living standards and growing middle classes in many developing countries.[24]

The right to water is intimately connected with a range of other human rights, in both theory and practice. Hence, climate-induced abridgements of the right to water need to be analysed together with impacts upon other relevant rights. Human rights relating to health,[25] housing,[26] food[27] and sanitation[28] are particularly noteworthy in this regard. Water plays an important role in many cultures and faiths and therefore reduced access to water could also violate certain cultural rights. The right to life, itself, is implicated: the UN has estimated that global warming has already contributed to an additional 150,000 deaths annually in low-income countries.[29]

While many human rights may be implicated, the rights to health and adequate food have attracted particularly close scrutiny. Climate change can affect health through multiple pathways, including greater frequency and intensity of heatwaves, increased floods and droughts, changes in the distribution of vector-borne diseases and its effects on the risk of disasters and malnutrition.[30] Two billion people already suffer disproportionately from diseases related to contaminated or insufficient water in dry regions of the world,[31] and it is estimated that up to 7 billion people may be at risk from increasing water stress by 2050.[32] Higher temperatures will likely increase the

[24] UNWDDR 2009 at 68–72.

[25] Art. 12, ICESCR. See nn. 39–41 and accompanying text.

[26] Art. 11, ICESCR; and see the references nn. 40–42 below and accompanying text.

[27] Art. 11(1), ICESCR. See also CESCR, *General Comment No. 12: The Right to Adequate Food*, UN Doc. E/C.12/1999/5 (1999); O. de Schutter, *Report of the Special Rapporteur on the Right to Food: Building Resilience: a Human Rights Framework on World Food and Nutrition Security*, UN Doc. A/HRC/9/23 (2008); O. de Schutter, *Contribution to the UN Commission on Sustainable Development at its 17th Session* (2009), at 3 and 6.

[28] The human right to sanitation has been recognised in UN Doc. A/HRC/RES/15/9, Oct. 6, 2010; and UN Doc. A/RES/64/292, 3 August 2010. The links with climate change are analysed in M. Darrow, J. Dugard, A-M. Karlsson and K. Lexén, *Climate Change and the Human Rights to Water and Sanitation*, Position Paper for the (former) Independent Expert on the issue of human rights obligations relating to access to safe drinking water and sanitation (2010).

[29] WESS 2009, at xiv.

[30] United Nations, World Water Development Report No. 3, p. 73; IPCC 2016, pp. 67–71.

[31] World Health Organisation, Ecosystems and Human Well-Being: Health Synthesis. A contribution to the Millennium Ecosystem Assessment (2005), cited in WESS 2009, at 79.

[32] J. Alcamo, M. Flörke and M. Märker, 'Future Long Term Changes in Global Water Resources Driven by Socioeconomic and Climatic Change', *Hydrological Sciences Journal*, Vol. 52, No. 2 (2007), pp. 247–275.

survival and replication rates of bacterial contaminants of food and water sources, exacerbating the impact on health, and increased water scarcity may worsen already inadequate sanitation and hygiene standards.[33] Strengthening public health prevention strategies, including improving water supply and sanitation services, is an essential component of an effective response to these threats.[34]

As for the right to food, irrigation water withdrawals presently account for almost 70 per cent of global water withdrawals.[35] Hence, increased water stress may have a significant impact on growing food insecurity. With rising global temperatures, water flows will become more variable and uncertain, and extreme events, such as droughts and floods, more commonplace. Productivity in agricultural production, especially by rain-fed production, is influenced as much by the timing of water flows as the volume.[36] According to recent estimates, climate change could increase global malnutrition by 15 to 26 per cent, increasing the absolute number of malnourished people by 75 to 125 million by 2080.[37]

The distribution of adverse climate impacts on water access will be uneven, with parts of Africa (because of low adaptive capacity and the extent of existing aridity and stresses on water systems), small island States (with high exposure of population and infrastructure to projected climate change impacts) and Asian and African mega deltas (due to the high density of human settlements and high exposure to sea level rise, storm surges and river flooding) among the most vulnerable areas.[38] Australia, Central Asia, the Mediterranean basin, the Sahel and the western United States, are among the regions already experiencing more frequent and more intense droughts, putting stresses on water systems.[39]

Inequalities within countries are a likely marker for vulnerability to climate shocks.[40] One recent quantitative assessment of the human impacts of

[33] *World Economic and Social Survey* 2009, at 79. [34] UNWWDR 2009, at 73.

[35] I. Shiklomanov and J. Rodda (eds.), *World Water Resources at the Beginning of the 21st Century* (Cambridge: Cambridge University Press and UNESCO, 2003), cited in WESS 2009, at 79.

[36] Human Development Report 2006, at 159. [37] Ibid., at 163.

[38] Human Development Report 2007/8; World Bank, *World Development Report 2010: Development and Climate Change* (2009), p. 6; WESS 2016, pp. 5–12.

[39] *World Development Report* 2010, ibid., at 4. At the same time, some parts of Africa are likely to benefit from increased rainfall even if there are floods and surges: L. F. Stige et al., *The Effect of Climate Variation on Agro-pastoral Production in Africa* (2006).

[40] Human Development Report 2007/8, p. 79; WESS 2016, pp.5–12. Compare with S. Eriksen and K. O'Brien, 'Vulnerability, Poverty and Sustainable Adaptation Measures', *Climate Policy*, Vol. 7, No. 4 (2007), pp. 337–352, arguing that being poor will not always make people vulnerable to climate change impacts.

disasters found that 'countries with high levels of income inequality experience the effects of climate disasters more profoundly than more equal societies'.[41] There is strong evidence that climate change impacts will be felt disproportionately by population groups who are already in vulnerable situations due to factors such as poverty, gender, age, race, ethnicity, minority status, and disability.[42] For example, given that women form a disproportionate share of the poor in developing countries and communities that are highly dependent on local natural resources, and given the traditional roles of women and girls in water collection in many of those communities, women will often be disproportionately vulnerable in terms of how climate change impacts upon the right to water.[43] In Myanmar, poor minority farmers suffered most from cyclone Nargis in 2008, due (in part) to discrimination and consequent lack of early warning systems.[44] African Americans living in poverty were among the most susceptible to the damage inflicted by Hurricane Katrina.[45] The United Nations Children's Fund (UNICEF) has suggested that climate change may disproportionately affect children by exacerbating existing health risks and disrupting the natural resource base sustaining nutrition and water security, among numerous other factors.[46] Extreme weather events and reduced quantity and quality of water already are leading causes of malnutrition and child death and illness. Climate change is likely to exacerbate these stresses.

Finally, it is important to recognise that climate change mitigation policies (such as reducing greenhouse gas emissions, applying clean technologies and protecting forests) and adaptation policies (such as expansion of rain-water storage and water conservation practices), as much as the direct impacts of climate change itself, may have significant implications for the

[41] Human Development Report 2007/8, at 80, citing IPCC Report 2007. See also WESS 2016, pp. 33-34; R. Warren et al., *Understanding the Regional Impacts of Climate Change*, Research Report Prepared for the *Stern Review* on the Economics of Climate Change. Research Working Paper No. 90, Tyndall Centre for Climate Change (2006); and T. Roberts and B. C. Parks, A *Climate of Injustice: Global Inequality, North-South Politics, and Climate Policy* (Cambridge, MA: Massachusetts Institute of Technology, 2007).

[42] OHCHR Report (2009), at para. 42; WESS 2016, pp. 33–38.

[43] Gender and Climate Change Network – Women for Climate Justice, 'There Will Be No Climate Justice without Gender Justice: Protecting Tropical Forests and Gender Justice', Position Paper presented at UNFCCC Conference of Parties 13 (Bali, Indonesia, 2007); and see Gender and Climate Change documents, available at www.gencc.interconnection.org/, and S. Atapattu (2016), chapter 8.

[44] WESS 2016, p. 36. [45] Ibid.

[46] United Nations Children's Fund, *Climate Change and Children: A Human Security Challenge* (2008); United Nations Children's Fund, *Our Climate, Our Children, Our Responsibility* (2008).

realisation of the right to water in particular circumstances. For example, it has been argued, controversially, that investment in biofuels research is needed as part of the international community's mitigation efforts. However, as noted by the World Development Report 2010, expanded production using the current generation of biofuels would displace large areas of natural forests and grasslands and compete with the production of food. Second-generation biofuels that rely on non-food crops may reduce competition with agriculture by using more marginal lands, but nevertheless may still lead to the loss of pasture land and grassland ecosystems and compete for water resources.[47]

## 3 LEGAL FRAMEWORKS GOVERNING THE RIGHT TO WATER AND CLIMATE CHANGE

The fact that climate change will undermine access to water does not necessarily mean that the human right to water will be infringed, even if the adverse impacts are discriminatory. A brief analysis is required of the human right to water under international law, set against the essential elements of the legal framework for climate change under the UNFCCC, Kyoto Protocol and Paris Agreement.

The right to water has been widely accepted as a self-standing human right,[48] and an essential condition for survival. The ICESCR has noted that the human right to water is 'inextricably related to the right to the highest attainable standard of health . . . and the rights to adequate housing and adequate food'.[49] The right to the 'highest attainable standard of health' includes underlying determinants of health, such as access to safe and potable water and adequate sanitation.[50] The core attributes of the right to adequate housing include availability of services, facilities, materials and infrastructure, including sustainable access to safe drinking water.[51] Moreover the supervisory body for the International Covenant on Civil and Political Rights (ICCPR), the Human Rights Committee, has stressed that the 'inherent right to life' should not be

[47] *World Development Report* 2010, Summary at p. 16. See also United Nations, World Water Development Report No. 3, p. 68, and Food and Agriculture Organisation (FAO), *The Right to Food and the Impact of Liquid Biofuels (Agrofuels)* (2008).

[48] See n. 1, and also CEDAW Article 14(2)(h), and CRC Article 24(2)(c).

[49] See generally CESCR, General Comment No. 15, para. 3.

[50] ICESCR, Article 12, and CESR, *General Comment No. 14: The right to the highest attainable standard of health*, UN Doc. E/C.12/2000/4 (2000), at para. 11.

[51] CESR, *General Comment No. 4: The right to adequate housing* (Sixth session, 1991), UN Doc. E/1999/23, annex III at 114, at para. 7 and 8(a).

understood in a restrictive manner, and that the protection of that right requires States to adopt positive measures to reduce infant mortality, to increase life expectancy and eliminate malnutrition and epidemics.[52] It is strongly arguable that life-threatening deprivation of access to water may, in many circumstances, constitute a violation of the right to life under Article 6 of the ICCPR.[53]

The UNFCCC, Kyoto Protocol and Paris Agreement are the legislative centrepieces of the international community's attempt to address the climate change problem. These instruments set in place a framework of common but differentiated responsibilities for GHG emissions reductions ('mitigation'), as well as support for national level measures to respond to extant or imminent climate change harms ('adaptation', which includes social protection, disaster risk reduction, natural resource management, and policy measures to strengthen resilience).[54] The UNFCCC is the umbrella agreement for the Kyoto Protocol, Paris Agreement, and related agreements and decisions. The UNFCCC Conference of the Parties serves as the meeting of the Parties to the Paris Agreement.[55] The Kyoto Protocol, which has been ratified by 187 States (the UNFCCC enjoys universal adherence), set binding emissions limits for certain industrialised countries (called 'Annex 1' countries) for two successive 'commitment periods', from 2008 to 2012 and 2013 to 2020. The Paris Agreement established a scheme of 'Nationally Determined Contributions' (NDCs), or self-defined mitigation goals, to the climate change response, applicable to all countries, with the aim of keeping the average global temperature 'well below 2 degrees Celcius above pre-industrial levels and pursuing efforts to limit the temperature increase to 1.5 degrees Celcius above pre-industrial levels'.

[52] Human Rights Committee, *General Comment No. 6: Article 6: The right to life* (Sixteenth session, 1982), UN Doc. A/37/40, pp. 93-94, at para. 5. In their concluding observations, the Human Rights Committee and the supervisory body for the Convention Against Torture and other Cruel, Inhuman or Degrading Treatment or Punishment (CAT), the Committee against Torture, have repeatedly stressed that poor sanitation conditions, which are intimately linked with the right to water, constitute a violation of the right of persons deprived of their liberty to be treated with humanity and with respect for their inherent dignity. *Report of the Independent Expert on the Issue of Human Rights Obligations Related to Access to Safe Drinking Water and Sanitation, Ms. Catarina de Albuquerque, Mission to Costa Rica*, UN Doc. A/HRC/12/24/Add.1 (2009), at para. 9.

[53] See, e.g., *Report of the Independent Expert on the Issue of Human Rights Obligations Related to Access to Safe Drinking Water and Sanitation, Ms. Catarina de Albuquerque*, UN Doc. A/HRC/12/24 (2009), at paras. 41–42.

[54] On the scope of adaptation policies *see* D. Nelson, W. Adger and K. Brown, 'Adaptation to Environmental Change: Contributions of a Resilience Framework', *Annual Review of Environment and Resources*, Vol. 32 (2007), pp. 395–419.

[55] Paris Agreement, article 16(1).

These agreements embody a distinctive scheme of differentiated obligations and reciprocity between States, as distinct from the international human rights framework, which essentially regulates relations between individual States and their own inhabitants. Article 4(1)(e) of the UNFCCC sets forth the commitment of States parties to '[c]ooperate in preparing for adaptation to the impacts of climate change; develop and elaborate appropriate and integrated plans for coastal zone management, water resources and agriculture, and for the protection and rehabilitation of areas, particularly in Africa, affected by drought and aridity, as well as floods'. The Paris Agreement contains one preambular paragraph which states that States Parties 'should, when taking action to address climate change, respect, promote and consider their respective obligations on human rights, the right to health', among others. However, there is no such reference in either the UNFCCC and Kyoto Protocol. The climate change agreements do not contemplate individual entitlements in a direct sense, and do not refer to the right to water specifically.

All countries have subscribed to at least one (and frequently several) of the core nine UN human rights treaties,[56] as well as the UNFCCC (and in almost all cases, the Paris Agreement and Kyoto Protocol). There is a growing literature on the relationship between climate change and human rights in the social and political sciences and international law.[57] Yet human rights arguments generally, and the right to water in particular, have yet to gain any appreciable traction within inter-governmental negotiations or national policy responses to climate change.[58] There are many possible reasons for this, including what some have called 'disciplinary path-dependency',[59] or the tendency for climate change policy making to be dominated by economic reasoning and 'hard' sciences. Political barriers are also clearly evident, with human rights perceived by some to overload what is already a politically charged and fragile climate change policy agenda. This can be seen in rich countries' objections to human rights arguments being marshalled in support of obligations of international assistance and cooperation in the context of adaptation financing and global burden-sharing for GHG emissions reductions. Correspondingly, certain developing countries have expressed concerns about human rights being imposed as 'conditionalities' on external assistance

56 For a list of the core conventions see www.ohchr.org.

57 See McInerney-Lankford, Darrow and Rajamani, Human Rights and Climate Change, and the bibliography at pp. 66–93.

58 See e.g. M. B. and J. Wentz, with J. Knox, *Climate Change and Human Rights* (Nairobi: United Nations Environment Program, 2015) at p. 31.

59 See Humphreys, *Rough Guide*.

for national adaptation programmes.[60] Institutional fragmentation – within national ministries as well as international institutions – is also widespread, presenting further barriers to policy coherence.[61] None of this diminishes the legal imperative to ensure harmonious interpretations and practical implementation of human rights and climate change agreements, in a manner that gives rise to an internally consistent set of overall obligations.[62] This is particularly important in view of the potential interactions of the intellectual property regime insofar as technology development and transfer in the context of adaptation needs in the water sector are concerned. But the legal, institutional and political barriers to policy coherence must be recognised. This problem is revisited in the concluding section of the chapter.

## 4 HUMAN RIGHTS OBLIGATIONS CONCERNING WATER AND CLIMATE CHANGE

What then are the specific obligations relating to the human right to water that are implicated in climate change policy making? The normative content of the right to water has been the subject of detailed study within this volume and elsewhere.[63] This section of the chapter seeks merely to summarise the essential framework and attributes of the legal obligations associated with this right, drawing upon socio-economic jurisprudence more generally. This framework will be reexamined in juxtaposition with the basic normative contours and policy making framework of the international climate change regime, as the basis for a short set of conclusions and recommendations to follow.

Article 2(1) of the ICESCR requires each of its parties 'to take steps, individually and through international assistance and co-operation, especially economic and technical, to the maximum of its available resources, with a view to achieving progressively the full realisation of the rights recognised in

[60] For a more detailed analysis of the politics of human rights and climate change negotiations, see M. Limon, 'Human Rights and Climate Change: Constructing a Case for Political Action', *Harvard Environmental Law Review*, Vol. 33 (2009), pp. 439–463.

[61] World Commission on the Social Dimension of Globalization, *A Fair Globalization: Creating Opportunities for All* (Geneva: ILO, 2004), at paras. 509, 605–606.

[62] See n. 11.

[63] See CESCR, General Comment No. 15, at paras. 10–12, discussing the substantive requirements of 'availability' (sufficient and continuous supply of water for personal and domestic uses), 'quality' (including safety and freedom from micro-organisms, chemical substances and other health hazards, and acceptable colour, odour and taste for each personal or domestic use) and 'accessibility' (including physical and economic accessibility, affordability for all, non-discrimination, and information accessibility).

the present Covenant by all appropriate means, including particularly the adoption of legislative measures'. This language gives States a reasonable degree of discretion as to how to meet its obligations, allowing for the progressive – rather than immediate – human rights realisation, within certain bounds. But this does not mean that socio-economic rights obligations cannot be defined with some precision, as international and national jurisprudence makes clear. First, States must take immediate, concrete and targeted steps towards the realisation of socio-economic rights. Second, States must dedicate the maximum extent of available resources towards the realisation of these rights. This is a critical prerequisite to claims for international assistance as will be discussed shortly. Third, there are certain obligations that are of immediate effect, whatever the resource constraints, including an obligation not to discriminate between different groups of people in terms of the legal, policy and budgetary measures taken to realise rights.[64] States must also ensure essential minimum levels of protection of socio-economic rights, implying that States should prioritise the basic survival needs of all.[65] Finally, the 'progressive realisation' requirement entails a presumption against retrogression in existing levels of human rights protection. Violations of the latter obligation might include, for example, arbitrary disconnections to existing water services or the formal repeal or suspension of legislation necessary for the continued enjoyment of the right to water.[66]

64 The non-discrimination requirement should not be read as prohibiting differential treatment between groups of people, however as long as any distinctions are objectively justifiable. Moreover, temporary special measures in favour of women, minorities, people with disabilities and disadvantaged groups are lawful under relevant international human rights instruments.

65 For illustrations of the 'minimum core content' of the right to water see General Comment No. 15, at para. 37. In terms of the Committee's jurisprudence, the obligation to guarantee 'essential minimum levels' and avoid retrogression in the realisation of socio-economic rights are qualified by resource availability: see CESCR, *General Comment No. 3: The Nature of State Parties Obligations*, (Fifth session, 1990), UN Doc. E/C.3/1991/3, annex III at 86 (1991). For more detailed critical discussion of the concept of minimum core content, see K. Young, 'The Minimum Core of Economic and Social Rights: A Concept in Search of Content', *Yale Journal of International Law*, Vol. 33, No. 1 (2008), pp. 113–175.

66 This obligation of non-retrogression operates as a legal presumption, rebuttable on demonstration by the State concerned that it has considered all alternative policy measures and that the retrogression in the achievement of a particular right is justifiable by reference to the totality of rights in the ICESCR in the context of the full use of available resources. CESCR, General Comment No. 3 (1990). For a fuller discussion of these obligations, see OHCHR, *Frequently Asked Questions on Economic, Social and Cultural Rights*, Fact Sheet No. 33 (2008). And for a more contextualised discussion on how these obligations may help to inform and frame economic policy making *see* Balakrishnan, D. E. Radhika and R. Patel, *Rethinking Macro Economic Strategies from a Human Rights Perspective (Why MES with Human Rights II)* (Carnegie Policy Innovations, 2009).

The CESCR and other international expert bodies have developed a reasonably consistent typology of obligations pertaining to socio-economic rights, reflecting the basic idea that all human rights entail duties involving positive action, as well as abstention or non-interference, contrary to the tenets of classical liberal theory, or in other words, to 'respect, protect and fulfil' human rights.[67] As applied to the right to water, the obligation to *respect* requires that State parties refrain from interfering directly or indirectly with the enjoyment of the right to water. The obligation to *protect* requires State parties to prevent third parties (including private actors) from interfering in any way with the enjoyment of the right to water. The duty to *fulfil* requires the State to adopt appropriate positive measures towards the full realisation of the right to water. National courts and certain regional tribunals have increasingly been enforcing these kinds of obligations.[68] Most findings of violations relate to a failure by government authorities to respect human rights, or implement existing policies or laws already on the statute books, and failures to protect human rights.[69] However, courts have also shown a cautious disposition to enforce obligations of a more positive kind, including failure to legislate, finance, plan, or otherwise take adequate and targeted steps to realise the right concerned.[70] Moreover, courts in certain jurisdictions have successfully dealt with claims connected with a failure by States to ensure the provision of essential minimum levels of basic social services.[71]

National and regional tribunals, and the human rights treaty bodies, are increasingly being asked to consider human rights claims arising from environmental harms, generating a rich comparative body of environmental

67 Inspiration for this categorisation can be traced to the work of the philosopher Henry Shue: H. Shue, *Basic Rights: Subsistence, Affluence, and US Foreign Policy* (Princeton, NJ: Princeton University Press, 1980), along with Asbjørn Eide's work in the 1980s on the right to food. This typology is best understood as a heuristic or explanatory device, however, rather than a straitjacket on the evolution of justiciable socio-economic rights obligations.

68 See M. Langford (ed.), *Social Rights Jurisprudence: Emerging Trends in International and Comparative Law* (Cambridge University Press, 2008). For analyses of the impacts and public policy implications of social rights claims see V. Gauri and D. Brinks, *Courting Social Justice: Judicial Enforcement of Social and Economic Rights in the Developing World* (Cambridge: Cambridge University Press, 2008); and A, E, Yamin and S. Gloppen, eds., *Litigating Health Rights: Can Courts Bring More Justice to Health?* (Cambridge, MA: Harvard University Press, 2011).

69 M. Langford, 'The Justiciability of Social Rights: From Practice to Theory', in Langford (ed.), ibid., pp. 3–45, at 14–20. This includes failing to regulate the activities of private companies and to ensure access to affordable services in the context of privatisation.

70 Ibid., at p. 22. This analysis of comparative jurisprudence shows, among other things, that so-called positive obligations need not necessarily be costly.

71 Ibid., at pp. 23–4.

human rights jurisprudence[72] including with respect to the right to water. [73] The complaints brought have been based most commonly upon rights to life, property, health, information, family and home life and the most common environmental harms have included air pollution, deforestation and water pollution.[74] Notwithstanding the diversity in jurisdictions and rights claimed, strikingly consistent jurisprudential trends are discernable. Courts have generally found that States have duties to regulate not only their own behaviour, but also that of private actors subject to their control (consistent with the duty to ' protect' human rights, outlined above). Courts have generally imposed quite strict procedural duties that States must follow before causing or allowing environmental harm – for example, relating to information disclosure, advance consultation and participatory decision making, *ex ante* impact assessment requirements and judicial redress in the event of violations – which are also specific normative attributes of the right to water.[75] Finally, courts have generally given States fairly wide discretion in connection with the policy choices associated with alleged environmental and human rights harms, subject to certain minimum substantive standards and the procedural requirements outlined above.[76] These minimum standards are not always clearly defined in the abstract, but the jurisprudence of courts and tribunals has helped to flesh out the core substantive content of human rights, within and beyond the context of claims arising from environmental harms, without undue prescriptiveness and without overstepping legitimate judicial bounds.[77]

[72] The literature is vast but see e.g. Report of the Independent Expert on the issue of human rights obligations relating to the enjoyment of a safe, clean, healthy and sustainable environment, John H. Knox, Mapping Report, UN Doc. A/HRC/25/23 (30 December2013) (Knox Mapping Report'); J. H. Knox, 'Climate Change and Human Rights Law', *Virginia Journal of International Law*, Vol. 50, No. 1 (2009), pp. 163–218; R. Picolotti and J. D. Taillant (eds.), *Linking Human Rights and the Environment* (Tuscon: University of Arizona Press, 2003); A. Boyle and M. Anderson (eds.), *Human Rights Approaches to Environmental Protection* (Oxford: Oxford University Press, 1996); J. G. Merrills, 'Environmental Rights', in D. Bodansky et al. (eds.), *The Oxford Handbook of International Environmental Law* (Oxford: Oxford University Press, 2007), pp. 663–680; D. Shelton, *Background Paper 2: Human Rights and the Environment: Jurisprudence of Human Rights Bodies*, UNEP-OHCHR Expert Seminar on Human Rights and the Environment (2002).

[73] Argentina, India and Nepal are examples.

[74] Shelton, ibid. Relevantly, in the *Gabcíkovo Nagymoros* case, Judge Weeramantry recognised the protection of the environment as a '*sine qua non* for numerous human rights such as right to health and the right to life itself'. Gabcíkovo-Nagymaros (*Hungary* v. *Slovakia*), 1997 ICJ Reports 7 (1997) (Separate Opinion of Judge Weeramantry).

[75] See CESCR, General Comment No. 15, at paras. 24, 37(f) and 48.

[76] Knox, 'Climate Change and Human Rights Law'.

[77] See e.g. Langford, Social Rights Jurisprudence.

Environmental human rights jurisprudence has a number of specific implications for climate change responses. Firstly, States clearly have obligations to respect, protect and fulfil the human rights of those within its own territory, jurisdiction or effective control, including with respect to the right to water, in respect of their national adaptation responses. States (particularly those with greatest responsibility for global emissions) may also be obligated under human rights law to mitigate their own carbon emissions in order to protect the human rights of those within their own territory, jurisdiction or effective control.[78] This argument may not seem self-evident on its face, given that most States individually produce only a fraction of 1 per cent of global emissions of GHGs. Hence for any one of these States to reduce its emissions, even to zero, would make little, if any, discernible contribution to the mitigation of global warming. However, while the climate regime is predicated upon the principle of inter-State reciprocity, human rights obligations are not qualified by the manner in which or extent to which others discharge their own duties. If a duty exists pertaining to an existing or foreseeable harm corresponding to a recognised human right, and if that duty is breached and can be attributed in whole or part to a specified duty bearer (usually a State), and if a sufficient causal connection between the breach and the harm can be established, a human rights claim can in principle be made out.[79] Therefore, in major emitting States where a reduction in carbon emissions might make a discernible (even if not decisive) contribution to the protection of human rights locally, and if other elements of a human rights claim can be made out, States may be required to reduce emissions for the benefit of their own populations irrespective of whether other States do likewise.[80]

Support for this interpretation can be found in a landmark decision of the district court in the Hague in June 2015,[81] wherein the Dutch government was

78 For full argument see Knox, 'Climate Change and Human Rights Law', at 196–198.

79 By analogy see International Law Commission, *Draft Articles on Responsibility of States for Internationally Wrongful Acts* (2001) (ILC draft Articles), particularly articles 1 and 2 (defining responsibility for internationally wrongful acts), 30–36 (on remedies) and 47 (on co-responsibility). The commentary to article 47 (para. 8) cites a specific example of joint and several responsibility of States for damages arising from environmental pollution. The requirement for 'cessation and guarantee of non-repetition' may include measures to prevent future environmental harm (article 30, commentary, para. 13, fn 447 and accompanying text, citing the *Trail Smelter* arbitration).

80 Ibid. To illustrate the point, Knox notes that China and the United States, the largest emitters, each produce close to 20 per cent of the total global emissions. If either were to reduce its emissions by half, it would thus reduce total global emissions by close to 10 per cent, bringing potentially tangible benefits for their populations.

81 Rechtbank Den Haag, 24-06-2015, C/09/456689 / HA ZA 13-1396. The English translation of the Court's decision is available at https://uitspraken.rechtspraak.nl/inziendocument?id=ECLI:NL:

ordered to limit its GHG emissions by at least twenty-five per cent by the end of the year 2020, compared with 1990 levels. The claim was brought under tort doctrine of 'social responsibility' for avoiding 'unacceptable danger creation' under the Dutch Civil Code. The Court, reviewing IPCC evidence, found climate change to be an 'unacceptable danger', and in considering whether the government's duty of care had been breached, took into account the obligations of the Netherlands under articles 2 and 8 of the European Convention on Human Rights (the rights to life and privacy) and environmental human rights jurisprudence. It also noted the human rights references in the Cancun Agreements (Decision 1/CP.16) including UN Human Rights Council Resolution 10/4. While the decision relates to a tort claim and is under appeal, the Court's reasoning is relevant to how a human rights tribunal might successfully address problems relating to the complexity of climate science, causation, State (co-)responsibility, attribution, and the challenges of dealing with future (foreseeable) harms.[82]

Determining the scope and content of extraterritorial obligations[83] associated with adverse impacts of climate change on the right to water is a more complicated matter, and there is comparatively little jurisprudence to draw from.[84] While the UNFCCC treaty regime is addressed to a quintessentially global problem based upon the principle of reciprocity between participating States, and establishes a relatively elaborate (even if poorly implemented) scheme of obligations regarding international assistance and cooperation for climate change mitigation and adaptation, international human rights law principally concerns the responsibilities of States towards individuals within

RBDHA:2015:7196. The author is grateful for discussions with Jan Hessebruege in relation to this case.

82 For a less successful nuisance action against a corporate defendant in the District Court of California in relation to alleged climate change harms, see *Kivalina v. ExxonMobil*, CP Cal 2008, no C08-01138 SBA. The claim was rejected, in part, because the Court was not persuaded that the damages complained of (the destruction of the village of Kivalina, Alaska, by floodwaters) were caused by the defendant's GHG emissions. For a discussion, see L. Westra, 'Climate change and the human right to water', *Journal of Human Rights and the Environment* Vol. 1, No. 2 (September 2010), pp. 161–188 at 75–80.

83 For the general purposes of this discussion, the term 'extraterritoriality' (or extraterritorial, in adjectival form) refers to the question of whether, and legal grounds upon which, a State's obligations under international human rights law can be said to extend to individuals *not* within that State's territory or effective control.

84 See Organization of American States, Inter-American Commission on Human Rights, *Petition Seeking Relief from Violations Resulting from Global Warming Caused by Acts and Omissions of the United States* (2005); Organization of American States, Inter-American Commission on Human Rights, *Petition Seeking Relief from Violations of the Rights of Arctic Athabaskan Peoples Resulting from Rapid Arctic Warming and Melting Caused by Emissions of Black Coal by Canada* (2013); and the discussion in Atapattu, *Human Rights Approaches to Climate Change* at pp. 89–91.

their own territory, jurisdiction or effective control.[85] This normative premise sets up a challenging paradox, inasmuch as the major emitting States would appear – on a strict understanding of this premise – to escape any responsibility for harms to human beings in third countries, including with respect to the right to water, associated with climate change. And to the extent that human rights law obliges States only to take care of their own, this would seem to place international financial and technical assistance and technology transfer on equally fragile legal foundations, insofar as human rights adaptation requirements and mitigation imperatives are concerned.[86]

However, while a State's human rights obligations are largely owed to individuals located within its own territory, jurisdiction or effective control, human rights treaty obligations do have extraterritorial dimensions in certain circumstances, for all kinds of rights.[87] In the case of the right to water, the CESCR has recognised a number of obligations with extraterritorial effect, springing from Articles 2(1), 11 and 23 of the Covenant.[88] According to the

85 See Articles 2(1) of the ICCPR and ICESCR. Under the ICCPR, States parties' obligations extend to both individuals within their national territory, and those outside their territory but within their effective control: Human Rights Committee, *General Comment No. 31: Nature of the General Legal Obligation on States Parties to the Covenant*, UN Doc. CCPR/C/21/Rev.1/Add.13 (2004). The CESCR has no equivalent statement, but seems to adopt the same position as the Human Rights Committee through its recognition in a number of General Comments that a State party could violate its Covenant obligations if it fails to protect persons 'within its jurisdiction' from infringements by third parties. Cf: M. Craven, 'The Violence of Dispossession: Extraterritoriality and Economic, Social and Cultural Rights', in M. A. Baderin and R. McCorquodale (eds.), *Economic, Social and Cultural Rights In Action* (Oxford: Oxford University Press, 2007), pp. 71–88, at 77 (citing statements by the United States and other developed countries that the ICESCR does not give rise to extraterritorial duties).

86 For a human rights analysis and recommendations concerning climate change technology policy see International Council on Human Rights Policy, *Beyond Technology Transfer: Protecting Human Rights in a Climate-Constrained World* (Versoix: ICHRP, 2011). Under the UNFCCC, until technology transfer is 'effective', poorer countries are not required to accept emission reduction targets.

87 The extraterritorial application of the ICCPR and ICESCR was upheld by the International Court of Justice, *Legal Consequences of the Construction of a Wall in the Occupied Palestinian Territory*, 9 July 2004, ICJ Reports 2004 p. 136 (Advisory Opinion).

88 Article 11 of the ICESCR. Article 2(1) provides, materially that: 'Each State Party to the present Covenant undertakes to take steps, individually and through international assistance and co-operation, especially economic and technical, to the maximum of its available resources, with a view to achieving progressively the full realization of the rights recognized in the present Covenant by all appropriate means...' Article 23 provides: 'The States parties to the present Covenant agree that international action for the achievement of the rights recognized in the present Covenant includes such methods as the conclusion of conventions, the adoption of recommendations, the furnishing of technical assistance' and other measures In 2011, a group of international lawyers and human rights experts adopted the 'Maastricht Principles on

Committee, States should respect the enjoyment of the right to water in other countries (e.g. avoid actions that may prevent another State party from discharging its own obligations under the Covenant, refrain from embargoes affecting the supply of water), protect that right (e.g. prevent their own citizens and companies from violating the right to water of individuals and communities in other countries, which may have implications for privatisation and user fees policies), facilitate access to water, provide the necessary aid when required and ensure that the right is given due attention in international aid agreements.[89] Various other international expert bodies have adopted similar interpretations of extraterritorial obligations relating to socio-economic rights.[90]

Taking into account the CESCR's jurisprudence and other sources of guidance, the legal foundations for extraterritorial obligations under general international law appear to be strongest when framed as duties of non-interference or avoidance of harm to individuals in other countries. This is also the case in international environmental law, wherein the obligation to avoid significant transboundary environmental harm (sometimes reduced to the shorthand: 'do no harm') is among the few obligations enjoying a strong claim to the status of customary international law.[91] This is generally

Extraterritorial Obligations of States in the Area of Economic, Social and Cultural Rights' [hereinafter 'Maastricht ETO Principles']. This document adopts a progressive interpretation of the scope and content of extraterritorial human rights obligations, drawing in particular upon the CESCR's jurisprudence. The Committee's approach to extraterritorial obligations has not always been consistent, but it has regularly questioned States about their fulfilment of their extraterritorial duties without undue objection, and has included its assessment of States' compliance with these duties in its concluding observations on the States' reports. See generally M. Craven, *The International Covenant on Economic, Social and Cultural Rights: A Perspective on its Development* (Oxford: Clarendon Press, 1995); W. Vandenhole, 'EU and Development: Extraterritorial Obligations under the International Covenant on Economic, Social and Cultural Rights', in M. E. Salomon, A. Tostensen and W. Vandenhole (eds.), *Casting the Net Wider: Human Rights, Development and New Duty-Bearers* (Antwerp: Intersentia, 2007), pp. 85–106, at 97. S. Skogly, *Beyond National Borders: States' Human Rights Obligations in International Cooperation* (Antwerp: Intersentia, 2006), at p. 152.

89 CESCR, General Comment No. 15, at paras. 30–36.

90 Examples include the Special Rapporteurs on the rights to education and health, and the Committee on the Rights of the Child. As to the latter, see the recommendations emerging from the Committee's General Day of Discussion on 'Resources for the Rights of the Child – Responsibilities of States' (2007).

91 *Trail Smelter Case (United States* v. *Canada)*, 3 RIAA 1905 (1938-1941). For further support for this principle, see International Court of Justice, *Legality of the Threat or Use of Nuclear Weapons*, 8 July 1996, ICJ Reports 1996 (Advisory Opinion), at 241-2. In the latter case the ICJ held (at 241, para. 29): 'The existence of the general obligation of States to ensure that activities within their jurisdiction and control respect the environment of other States or of areas beyond national control is now part of the corpus of international law relating to the

understood as an obligation of conduct – to exercise reasonable 'due diligence' – rather than an obligation of result (to avoid all harms *per se*).[92] International law also provides a qualified measure of support for extraterritorial duties to protect human rights by permitting States to regulate with extraterritorial effect, including with respect to the activities of transnational corporations.[93] States seeking to regulate with extraterritorial effect must establish one of the accepted bases of legal jurisdiction for doing so. The recognised bases for so-called 'prescriptive' extraterritorial jurisdiction (a case where regulating to protect third parties from violations in third countries by transnational corporations and business entities is concerned) include where the perpetrator or victim is a national (the so-called active or passive nationality principle); where the acts have substantial adverse effects on the State; or where specific international crimes are involved.[94] They must also meet an overriding requirement of reasonableness, which includes non-interference in

environment'. The 'do no harm' principle appears in the Stockholm Declaration on the Human Environment of the United Nations Conference on the Human Environment (adopted 16 June 1972), 11 ILM 1416 (1972), as well as the Rio Declaration, United Nations Conference on Environment and Development (adopted 3-14 June 1992), *Report Annex I: Rio Declaration on Environment and Development*, UN Doc. A/CONF.151/26/Rev.1 (1992), Principle 2. See also International Law Commission, Draft Articles on the Prevention of Transboundary Harm from Hazardous Activities (Fifty-third session, 2001), Supp. No. 10, ch. V.E.1, Articles III, IV, UN Doc. A/56/10, requiring States to *inter alia* 'take all appropriate measures to prevent, or to minimize the risk of, significant transboundary harm'. Similarly, a 'no significant harm' principle was codified specifically in the United Nations Convention on the Law of the Non-Navigable Uses of International Watercourses (adopted 21 May 1997, not yet in force), 36 I.L.M. 700, Article 7. For discussion see e.g. J. Wiener, 'Precaution', in D. Bodansky et al. (eds.), *Oxford Handbook of International Environmental Law*, pp. 597–612. at 604–607 (Oxford: Oxford University Press, 2007); cf: D. Bodansky, 'Customary (and Not So Customary) International Environmental Law', *Indiana Journal of Global Legal Studies*, Vol. 3, No. 1 (1995), pp. 105–119, at 110–119.

92 O. de Schutter, *International Human Rights Law* (New York: Cambridge University Press, 2010) at p. 415.

93 See e.g. Knox Mapping Report, paras. 62-68; Skogly, at 70; and UN Doc. A/HRC/17/31, 21 March, 2011, *Guiding Principles on Business and Human Rights: Implementing the 'Protect, Respect, Remedy' Framework* [hereinafter 'Guiding Principles on Business and Human Rights'], principles 1-10; and UN Doc. A/HRC/RES/17/4, June 16, 2011.

94 For more detailed discussion of these issues see e.g. United Nations High Commissioner for Human Rights, *State Responsibilities to Regulate and Adjudicate Corporate Activities under the United Nations' Core Human Rights Treaties*, Individual Report on the ICCPR (June 2007), at 48–52; and the corresponding report for the ICESCR, at 53-4; O. de Schutter, 'Extraterritorial Jurisdiction as a tool for improving the Human Rights Accountability of Transnational Corporations', Background Paper: Seminar of Legal Experts (3–4 November 2006); and principles 1–10 of the Guiding Principles on Business and Human Rights. *Cf.* principles 23–27 of the Maastricht ETO Principles, arguing (at principle 24) that States are obliged – rather than permitted – to regulate the extraterritorial activities of business enterprises where the grounds set out in principle 25 (which include but appear to transcend the more strongly established

other States' internal affairs, although this would not ordinarily pose difficulties where the concerned State is engaged in the extraterritorial protection of human rights.[95]

The Human Rights Committee has gone further and stipulated that States Parties to the ICCPR are obliged to take necessary measures to ensure that home State corporations to not violate human rights in third countries.[96] A typical example relating to the right to water would be a requirement that home States ensure that transnational corporations engaged in water provision do not violate the affordability attributes of the right to water in third countries. No international human rights body has yet stipulated that home States have

jurisdictional grounds referred to above) are established, and (at principle 27) that States have an open-textured obligation to cooperate for the protection of human rights 'of any persons'. See Ruggie and de Schutter, ibid.

95 Ibid. Many international human rights standards now enjoy the status of customary international law, and some even the status of higher order or 'peremptory' norms of international law from which no derogation is permitted. Moreover, it is generally agreed that certain categories of human rights obligation (those pertaining to norms of especially serious moral concern to the international community, and which are essentially prohibitive in nature, for example the prohibitions against torture, slavery and genocide) are owed by individual States to the international community at large (obligations '*erga omnes*'). International Court of Justice, *Barcelona Traction, Light and Power Company, Limited (Belgium* v. *Spain)*, Second Phase, Judgment of 5 February 1970, ICJ Reports 1970. For authoritative discussions on *jus cogens* (or peremptory) norms and obligations *erga omnes*, see M. Raggazzi, The Concept of International Obligations Erga Omnes 47 (1997); G. Gaja, 'Jus Cogens Beyond the Vienna Convention', *Hague Recueil*, Vol. 172, No. 3 (1981), pp. 290–301. Perhaps controversially, the UNHRC has argued that all internationally recognised human rights currently enjoy the status of obligations *erga omnes*. See Human Rights Committee, General Comment No. 31, para. 2, interpreting Article 2(1) of the ICCPR in light of the inter-State complaint mechanism under Article 41 of the Covenant and UN Charter based obligations of States to promote universal respect for and observance of human rights and fundamental freedoms. To similar effect, see Institut de Droit International, *Obligations Erga Omnes in International Law*, First and Second Report of the Special Rapporteur Giorgi Gaja, *Yearbook of the Institute of International Law*, Vol. 71 (2005), Part I, Session of Krakow, 2005 – First part, Preparatory Work, 119–151, 189–202. Cf. Raggazzi, ibid., at 145 and 163, and P. Weil, 'Towards Relative Normativity in International Law', *American Journal of International Law*, Vol. 77, No. 3 (1983), pp. 413–442, at 431–433. The latter (at 431–433) cautions against arbitrary expansion of *erga omnes* obligations, fearing that it could get out of hand, and any State could 'appoint itself avenger of the international community' and 'thus under the banner of law, chaos and violence would come to reign among States'.

96 See e.g. Human Rights Committee, Concluding observations on the sixth periodic report of Germany, 106th Sess., 15 October – 2 November, 2012, CCPR/C/DEU/CO/6, para 16 (12 November 2012). John Knox has argued that such a duty can be inferred from the requirement in the 1969 Vienna Convention on the Law of Treaties to implement treaty obligations in good faith. See Knox Mapping Report at para. 65, citing *Case concerning the Gabcikovo-Nagymaros project* (Hungary/Slovakia), 1997 ICJ Reports p. 7, para. 142.

an obligation to regulate to reduce carbon emissions of heavily emitting industries or corporations (such as major oil multinationals), but to the extent that water availability or other human rights in third countries may be undermined, there is no reason why they should not do so. Regardless of the extent to which international law presently obliges States to regulate with extra-territorial effect, States electing to regulate in the circumstances outlined above have solid legal grounds to do so.

Obligations of positive assistance and international cooperation are a more challenging matter. International cooperation is by definition indispensible in addressing the human rights impacts of a global problem like climate change, and is firmly grounded in international environmental law.[97] A normative framework constructed on the idea of international cooperation helps us transcend the traditional limitations of environmental human rights jurisprudence, which would encourage us to see climate change as a series of individual transboundary harms. International cooperation is also critical for managing the water security challenges posed by the combination of climate change and population pressures, even with improved water use efficiency. The World Bank has reported that one fifth of the world's freshwater renewable resources are shared between countries. This includes 261 transboundary river basins, which are home to forty per cent of the world's population. Water access is reportedly governed by over 150 international treaties that do not always include all riparian States. According to the World Bank, scaled-up cooperation and new regulatory arrangements are needed in order to manage these resources more successfully. Water allocation systems need to be revised due to the increased variability in water supply, in cooperation with all riparian countries involved.[98]

A duty to cooperate is well established under both human rights and environmental law, within certain parameters and limits. The UN Charter commits the international community to cooperate for the realisation of, *inter alia*, internationally recognised human rights.[99] Article 28 of the UDHR states that: 'Everyone is entitled to a social and international order in which the rights and freedoms set forth in this Declaration can be fully utilised'.

[97] See e.g. *Lax Lanoux Arbitration (France* v. *Spain)* (1957), 12 ILR 101, establishing a duty of transboundary cooperation in the control of transboundary environmental risks. This principle is supported in part by the law relating to the use of shared natural resources, and requires prior informed consultation. See also *Nuclear Tests (Australia* v. *France)*, ICJ Reports 1973, at 99; *Nuclear Tests (Australia* v. *France)*, ICJ Reports 1974, at 253; *Nuclear Tests (New Zealand* v. *France)*, ICJ Reports 1973, at 135; *Nuclear Tests (New Zealand* v. *France)*, ICJ Reports 1974, at 457, and the discussion in R. Lyster and A. Bradbrook, *Energy Law and the Environment* (Cambridge University Press, 2006), at 39, and the Knox Mapping Report, paras. 62–68.

[98] WDR 2010, Summary at 13–14.

[99] *See* United Nations Charter, Articles 1, 55 and 56.

Article 22 of the UDHR proclaims that economic, social and cultural rights should be realised 'through national effort and international cooperation'. Further specific duties to cooperate are found in the ICESCR, CRC, Convention on the Rights of Persons with Disabilities,[100] and a wide range of other international human rights instruments, including the 1986 Declaration on the Right to Development.[101]

The climate regime's commitments concerning international cooperation appear more detailed, differentiated and extensive than those reflected in the major international human rights instruments, with implications for the management of water resources generally. The Kyoto Protocol established a specific scheme of international cooperation for reduction of global GHG emissions, based upon the principle of 'common but differentiated responsibility' (CBDR).[102] The latter principle is reaffirmed in articles 2, 4(3) and 4(4) of the Paris Agreement.[103] The importance of cooperation is reflected in the requirements in Articles 7(6) of the Paris Agreement and UNFCCC Article 3

[100] A/RES/61/106 (13 December 2006), especially article 32 (international cooperation).

[101] A/RES/41/128 (4 December 1986).

[102] Developing countries do not have binding emissions reductions targets under the Kyoto Protocol. The three fundamental distinctions between wealthier and poorer countries reflected in the UNFCCC regime are: different historical responsibility and different relative contributions to climate change; differing likely impacts of climate change, with certain poorer countries including low-lying States being more vulnerable than many others; and different capacities to contribute to global mitigation and national adaptation efforts. These distinctions are brought out explicitly in Article 3 of the UNFCCC. The NDC scheme under the Paris Agreement is a universal one, guided by principles including CBDR. For a discussion, see Humphreys, *Rough Guide*, at 59; L. Rajamani, 'Ambition and Differentiation in the 2015 Paris Agreement: Interpretive Possibilities and Underlying Politics,' *International and Comparative Law Quarterly*, Vol. 65, No. 2 (2016), 493–514; L. Rajamani, *Differential Treatment In International Environmental Law* (Oxford: Oxford University Press, 2006); D. B. Magraw, 'Legal Treatment of Developing Countries: Differential, Contextual and Absolute Norms', *Colorado Journal of International Law and Policy*, Vol. 69, No. 1 (1990), pp. 69–99. There is no specific analogue to the common but differentiated responsibility concept in international human rights law, although human rights standards are framed and interpreted flexibly in order to take account of legitimate variation in contextual factors including resource constraints.

[103] Article 2 provides in part: 'This Agreement will be implemented to reflect equity and the principle of common but differentiated responsibilities and respective capabilities, in the light of different national circumstances.' Article 4(3): 'Each Party's successive nationally determined contribution will represent a progression beyond the Party's then current nationally determined contribution and reflect its highest possible ambition, reflecting its common but differentiated responsibilities and respective capabilities, in the light of different national circumstances.' Article 4(4): 'Developed country Parties should continue taking the lead by undertaking economy-wide absolute emission reduction targets. Developing country Parties should continue enhancing their mitigation efforts, and are encouraged to move over time towards economy-wide emission reduction or limitation targets in the light of different national circumstances.'

to give the specific needs of developing countries full consideration,[104] and in UNFCCC Article 4 to 'cooperate in preparing for adaptation to the impacts of climate change; develop and elaborate appropriate and integrated plans for coastal zone management, water resources and agriculture'.[105] Further parameters and focus areas for international cooperation are outlined in the Paris Agreement in Articles 7(7) and 7(13) (enhancing adaptation measures), 8 (in relation to loss and damages from climate change), 9 (finance), 10 (technology), 11 (capacity building) and 12 (knowledge, awareness and participation).

But these laudable principles conceal deep disagreement on the legal basis of obligations of positive assistance. The Paris Agreement, for example, notes the 'importance' but not a duty of cooperation. Its transparency and reporting provisions are legally binding but other commitments, including financing commitments and the achievement of NDCs, are not.[106] A duty of international cooperation was specifically rejected by the UN Human Rights Council in its initial deliberations on climate change, following objections by a number of developed countries.[107] On the limitations of international human rights law in this regard, Alston observes:

> No UN body, nor any group of governments, has accepted the proposition that any given country is obligated to provide specific assistance to any other country. Moreover, the persistent rejection of such a claim by developed countries, and the failure of even the most generous of donors to locate their assistance within the context of such an obligation, would present a major obstacle to any analysis seeking to demonstrate that such an obligation has already become part of customary law.[108]

[104] Paris Agreement, Article 7(6): 'Parties recognize the importance of support for and international cooperation on adaptation efforts and the importance of taking into account the needs of developing country Parties, especially those that are particularly vulnerable to the adverse effects of climate change'.

[105] UNFCCC, Article 4.

[106] Center for Climate and Energy Solutions, Paris Climate Agreement Q&A (October 2016), available at http://www.c2es.org/docUploads/paris-q-a-fact-sheet-10-16.pdf. The NDCs feature in an Annex, not the core text, of the Paris Agreement. The hybrid nature of the Paris Agreement – including binding and non-binding elements – was reportedly to enable US ratification by executive action rather than formal Congressional approval.

[107] M. Limon, 'Human Rights Obligations and Accountability in the Face of Climate Change', *Georgia Journal of International and Comparative Law*, Vol. 38, (2009–10), pp. 543, 565–66.

[108] P. Alston, 'Ships Passing in the Night: The Current State of the Human Rights and Development Debate as Seen Through the Lens of the Millennium Development Goals', *Human Rights Quarterly*, Vol. 27, No. 3 (2005), pp. 755–829, at 777. For a discussion of customary human rights law see B. Simma and P. Alston, 'The Sources of Human Rights Law: Custom, Jus Cogens and General Principles', *Australian Year Book of International Law*, Vol. 12 (1992), pp. 82–108; M. Akehurst, *A Modern Introduction to International Law*, 5th ed (New York: Routledge, 1984).

Nevertheless, international law may also be evolving to a point where it could support more concrete and meaningful, if not easily enforceable, obligations to cooperate internationally to address the human rights implications of global problems such as climate change, including in relation to the right to water, where (pursuant to the scheme of obligations outlined earlier) the claimant State has demonstrated that its inability to realise a particular right is due to lack of sufficient resources, and that maximum efforts had been undertaken (without success) to realise the right.[109] Recent global summit outcomes and political agreements on development and human rights issues, including on subjects such as aid, trade and debt relief,[110] may arguably be summoned as aids in interpretation of broadly textured obligations, such as those found in the UN Charter or the UDHR, or alternatively as evidence of relevant State practice for the purposes of emerging customary law rules.[111] International treaties, including the ICESCR and, in relation to the right to water, General Comment No. 15, draw extensively upon these sources.

[109] On the burden of proof of claimant countries *see* CESCR, General Comment No. 3 (1990); and CRC, General Day of Discussion on 'Resources for the Rights of the Child – Responsibilities of States' (2007), para. 51. As Alston argues: '[T]he emergence of a growing international consensus around the [Millennium Development Goals, or MDGs] provides a strong argument in favour of revisiting this debate [on the legally binding nature of obligations of international assistance] in the years ahead'. Alston argues that extraterritorial obligations of wealthier countries 'would, of course, be confined to situations in which a developing country had demonstrated its best efforts to achieve the [MDGs] and its inability to do so because of a lack of financial resources. At that point, it would have a plausible claim against wealthy countries as a group and the argument would be that each of the latter would at least have an obligation to ensure that the assistance required is forthcoming, whether from one country acting alone, from a group of like-minded countries, or from an institutional fund identified by those countries for that purpose'. Alston, 'Ships Passing in the Night', 777–778.

[110] The more pertinent political declarations include the UN Millennium Declaration, GA Res. 55/2, UN Doc. A/RES/55/2 (2000); the 2005 World Summit Outcome, A/RES/60/1 (Oct. 24, 2005); the United Nations, World Summit on Sustainable Development, *Report*, UN Doc. A/56/19 (2003); the Monterrey Consensus (adopted 22 March 2002), UN Doc. A/CONF.198/3, para. 3; the 2030 Agenda for Sustainable Development, A/RES/70/1 (Oct. 21, 2015) and in particular Sustainable Development Goal (SDG) 6 'Ensure availability and sustainable management of water and sanitation for all'; and the Addis Ababa Action Agenda, A/RES/69/313 (27 July 2015). SDG 13 ('take urgent action to address climate change and its impacts') contains only a few general commitments, in deference to the UNFCCC regime, however para 10 of A/RES/70/1 specifies that the 2030 Agenda is grounded in human rights and should be guided by existing international law.

[111] For a general discussion of the normative significance of the UDHR, see L. Sohn, 'The New International Law: Protection of the Rights of Individuals Rather than States', *American University Law Review*, Vol. 32, No. 1 (1982), pp. 1–64; H. Hannum, 'The Status of the Universal Declaration of Human Rights in National and International Law', *Georgia Journal of International and Comparative Law*, Vol. 25 (1995–1996), pp. 287–397.

There are numerous elements in the climate change regime that may be seen as fleshing out a cooperative scheme for the protection of certain dimensions of the right to water, with a particular focus on water availability and international financial and technical support for national adaptation needs. In 2001, the UNFCCC secretariat initiated a 'National Adaptation Programme of Action' (NAPA) process, under which Least Developed Countries (LDCs) may identify priority adaptation needs as a tool for international resource mobilisation.[112] A five-year programme of work (Nairobi Programme of Work, 2005–2010) was put in place by States parties, international organisations and others to help all countries, and, in particular, LDCs and low-lying countries, to improve their understanding and assessment of impacts, vulnerability and adaptation to climate change as a basis for informed decision making on climate change adaptation. [113]

In 2007, the 13th Conference of the Parties (COP) adopted the Bali Action Plan, the purpose of which was 'to launch a comprehensive process to enable the full, effective and sustained implementation of the [UNFCCC] through long-term cooperative action'.[114] The four pillars of the Bali Action Plan were mitigation, adaptation, financing, and technology transfer. At the 16th COP in Cancún, for the first time, the conference outcome document recognised the importance of 'fully respect[ing] human rights' in 'all climate change-related actions',[115] in relation to all four pillars of the Bali Action Plan, although the right to water was not specifically mentioned.

[112] Each least developed country is granted USD 200,000 to prepare its NAPA, which typically includes policy interventions regarding climate change vulnerability in coastal zones, marine systems management, insurance, early warning and disaster management, health and water resources, among others. Prioritised activities are identified in project proposals, which are then submitted to the Global Environment Facility (GEF). The UNFCCC's guidelines for NAPAs include water availability and accessibility and a focus on poor communities and ' vulnerable groups'; see UNFCCC, Step By Step Guide for Implementing National Adaptation Plans of Action (2009), at 17. Numerous NAPAs do prioritise water sector interventions, linked as appropriate to national development planning processes, but a human rights approach (in the sense embodied in General Comment No. 15) has made little if any impact upon these processes. For further details on NAPAs, see WESS 2009 at 82, and http://unfccc.int/cooperation_support/least_developed_countries_portal/frequently_asked_questions/items/4743txt.php.

[113] Decision 2/CP.11, UN Doc. FCCC/CP/2005/5/Add.1, at 5.

[114] See Decision 1/CP.13, *Bali Action Plan*, in United Nations Climate Change Conference, *Report of the Conference of the Parties on its Thirteenth Session*, UN Doc. FCCC/CP/2007/6/Add.1 (2008). There is no agreement as of yet on the legal form of this agreed outcome, but it is hoped to lead to a new climate agreement either to supplement or replace the Kyoto Protocol.

[115] Outcome of the work of the Ad Hoc Working Group on Long-term Cooperative Action (WG-LCA) under the Convention, advanced unedited version, adopted by the Conference of the parties to the UNFCCC, 16th Session, 4 December 2010, at para. 5. Moreover, perambular

A number of funds have been established under the auspices of the UNFCCC and cooperating institutions to support national adaptation efforts in developing countries. The 16th COP in Cancún introduced national mitigation pledges applicable to all countries, along with a range of measures to strengthen finance, transparency, technology transfer and other elements of the multilateral climate framework.[116] At COP 16 States also established a 'Green Climate Fund' as the centrepiece of international efforts to raise climate finance of USD 100 billion per year by the year 2020,[117] and agreed to establish an Adaptation Framework to enhance adaptation efforts by all countries and help LDCs to develop and implement national adaptation plans, as well as an Adaptation Committee to provide technical support.[118] At the 21st COP in Paris, States Parties extended the USD 100 billion financing goal through to the year 2025 and called for a new goal beyond that 'from a floor' of USD 100 billion per year. The Paris Agreement also stimulated a large volume of voluntary actions and initiatives by corporations, entrepreneurs and activists around the world.[119]

However, the failure of States Parties to agree upon legally binding emissions reductions targets and financing and technology development commitments has arguably undermined aspirations for clear and meaningful obligations of international cooperation. The Paris Agreement requires States to take into consideration the impacts of their own actions on other States Parties, especially developing countries,[120] but it falls well short of implying that a failure to do so could constitute an abridgement of human rights. The Paris Agreement included decisions in relation to an 'International Mechanism for Loss and Damage associated with Climate Change Impacts', however

para. 7 notes resolution 10/4 of the United Nations Human Rights Council on human rights and climate change, which recognises the adverse effects of climate change on human rights.

[116] The Cancún Agreements imported the essential elements of the Copenhagen Accord into the UNFCCC, including the voluntary mitigation targets and actions pledged under the Accord. The Agreements also took initial steps to implement the operational elements of the Accord, including a system of 'international consultations and analysis' to help verify countries' actions.

[117] UNFCCC, Report of the Conference of the Parties on its sixteenth session, held in Cancun from 29 November to 10 December 2010, FCCC/CP/2010/7/Add.1, March 15, 2011, at paras. 102–112.

[118] The Cancún decisions are available in full at http://unfccc.int/documentation/decisions/items/3597.php?such=j&volltext=%22cancun%20agreements%22#beg.

[119] M. Ivanova, 'Good COP, Bad COP: Climate Reality After Paris', *Global Policy* 7(3) (September 2016) 411–419 at 413.

[120] Article 4(15) provides : 'Parties shall take into consideration in the implementation of this Agreement the concerns of Parties with economies most affected by the impacts of response measures, particularly developing country Parties.'

States Parties specified that 'this does not involve or provide any basis for liability or compensation.'[121] An expert mechanism is being established to support the implementation of the Paris Agreement, but evidently not with the objective of accountability in mind.[122]

The scale of ambition and record of adherence to emissions reduction commitments are also highly problematic. On recent projections, in order to avoid dangerous levels of GHG emissions the total amount of global emissions needs to fall by at least 50 to 85 per cent from 2000 levels by 2050. This means that heavily polluting OECD countries will need to have cut their emissions by 80 to 90 per cent, and developing countries will probably need to cut their collective emissions by 30 to 60 per cent, having peaked by the year 2025.[123] According to one report, this would mean GHG emissions from the global South must begin to be reduced 'almost immediately, and must be dropping precipitously by 2025'.[124] This scenario would represent a radical departure from one of the fundamental premises of the climate regime, to the effect that poorer countries' development needs should not be sacrificed in the quest for global emissions reduction. The grim reality is that the cumulative impact of NCD's submitted to date, even in the unlikely event that they were adhered to, would likely be an average global temperature rise of around three degrees Celcius above pre-industrial levels, rather than the Paris commitment of two or (ideally) 1.5 degrees.[125]

Cooperative action has fallen well short on climate finance as well. The World Bank has projected that the financial requirements for mitigation

[121] The Paris Outcome on Loss and Damage, article 8 of the Paris Agreement and Decision 1/CP.21 Paragraphs 48–52 (FCCC/CP/2015/L.9/Rev.1).

[122] Paris Agreement, article 15. The mechanism is required to be 'facilitative' and 'non-adversarial and non-punitive' in nature. This is consistent with the soft approach to compliance under international environmental regimes generally. See M. Koskenniemi, 'Breach of Treaty or Non-Compliance? Reflections on the Enforcement of the Montreal Protocol', *Yearbook of International Environmental* Law, Vol. 3 (1992), pp. 123–62, at 125–134, 136, 147. For a deeper analysis of compliance theory design relating to the Kyoto compliance system specifically, see M. Doelle, *From Hot Air to Action? Climate Change, Compliance and the Future of International Environmental Law* (Toronto: Thomson/Carswell, 2005), at 69–108.

[123] S. Humphreys, 'Conceiving Justice: Articulating Common Causes in Distinct Regimes', in S. Humphreys (ed.), *Human Rights and Climate Change* (Cambridge: Cambridge University Press, 2010), pp. 299–319, at 305.

[124] P. Baer, T. Athanasiou and S. Karta, *The Right to Development in a Climate Constrained World* (Heinrich Böll Foundation, 2007), pp. 23–24.

[125] United Nations Environment Program, *Emissions Gap Report* (2016); Climate Action Tracker, 'Major challenges ahead for Paris Agreement to meet its 1.5 degree warming limit', 10 November 2016, at http://climateactiontracker.org/news/265/Major-challenges-ahead-for-Paris-Agreement-to-meet-its-1.5deg-warming-limit-.html. The author is grateful for conversations with Ben Schachter on these issues.

in developing countries could reach USD 140 to 175 billion a year by 2030 with associated financing needs of USD 265 to 565 billion, and that the additional investment and financing required for climate change adaptation purposes would be between USD 30 to 100 billion annually.[126] The 2014 report of the IPCC estimated that adaptation costs will be USD 100 billion annually by the year 2050 in developing countries alone.[127] These projections make a mockery of the USD 10.3 billion that had been committed to the Green Climate Fund as at June 2016.[128] As at 2014, developed countries had pledged only USD 3 billion cumulatively to multilateral climate funds, with reported deficiencies in targeted to countries and population groups of greatest need,[129] and only USD 62 billion in climate finance (a little over half the USD 100 billion target) had been mobilised for developing countries overall.[130]

When we look at mitigation and adaptation requirements for water and sanitation more specifically, there is further cause for concern. For example, an assessment in 2009 of donor organisations' policy frameworks on water resources and climate change showed that donors did not adequately address the climate change impacts at the macroeconomic level as a result of changing hydrological conditions, increasing vulnerability to rainfall variability and droughts and floods. This report recognised that several donors had shown concern for the impacts of climate change and linkages to water resources and energy, but had failed to identify and finance appropriate mitigation and adaptation strategies in the water and climate change sectors.[131]

Such findings should be interpreted in the context of the historic neglect of the water sector in bilateral and multilateral donors' aid policies. While donor commitments for water supply and sanitation increased between 2010 to 2012, actual disbursements remained constant and targeting problems continued.[132] This unflattering picture is compounded by shortcomings in official aid flows more widely[133] and persistent deficiencies in the quality and

[126] WDR 2010, pp. 22–23. [127] See FCCC/CP/2015/10/Add.1, decision 1/CP.21, para. 53.

[128] Center for Climate and Energy Solutions, p.3.

[129] Alice Carivani et al, 'Climate Finance Thematic Briefing: Adaptation Finance, Heinrich Boll Stiftung and Overseas Development Institute', *Climate Funds Update* (December 2014), p.1.

[130] WESS 2016, p.105, citing OECD estimates.

[131] A. Lindström and J. Granit, *Climate Change and Water Resource Policies among Major Donor Organization* (Stockholm International Water Institute, 2009). The assessed agencies were the Danish, British, Dutch, German, EU and US aid agencies.

[132] UN Water and WHO, *Investing in Water and Sanitation: Increasing Access, Reducing Inequalities;* UN Water Global Analysis and Assessment of Sanitation and Drinking Water, GLAAS 2014 Report (2014), pp. 41–54.

[133] Only five countries have so far reached the internationally agreed target for development aid of 0.7 per cent of Gross National Income (GNI). United Nations MDG Gap Task Force,

effectiveness of aid.[134] The gulf between the theory and practice of international cooperation does not bode well for the progressive development and practical utility of legal duties of international cooperation concerning climate change and the right to water specifically, although few would question the urgency of moving in this direction.

## 5 THE RIGHT TO WATER AS PART OF THE FRAMEWORK FOR CLIMATE CHANGE POLICY MAKING

It should be self-evident that climate-related threats to water availability, reliability and quality, and the disjuncture between climate change and human rights policymaking at global and national levels, cannot be remedied by international human rights law alone. Nevertheless, the scheme of human rights obligations outlined earlier offers a compass for policy orientation with a normative focus on human welfare, with procedural and minimal substantive safeguards to improve both processes and outcomes of climate change policy making. While it does not provide anything close to a blueprint for action, the normative framework of the right to water can at least help to frame and inform difficult policy choices and trade-offs that might otherwise proceed from cost-benefit or purely utilitarian calculations.[135]

*Millennium Development Goal 8: Taking Stokc of the Global Development Partnership* (New York: United Nations, 2015) at p.13.

[134] The OECD's 'aid effectiveness' survey in 2011 reported that only one out of thirteen internationally agreed aid effectiveness indicators had been met. OECD, *Aid Effectiveness 2005-10: Progress in Implementing the Paris Declaration* (Paris: OECD, 2011), at p. 20.

[135] On the comparative contributions of human rights and economics to policy making, see D. Seymour and J. Pincus, 'Human Rights and Economics: The Conceptual Basis for their Complementarity', *Development Policy Review*, Vol. 26, No. 4 (2008), pp. 387–405; cf. M. Langford, 'Social Security and Children: Testing the Boundaries of Human Rights and Economics', in S. Marks, B. A. Andrassen and A. Sengupta, *Freedom from Poverty as a Human Right: Economic Perspectives* (Paris: UNESCO Publishing, 2009), pp. 193–217. On the interaction between economic principles and human rights as moral claims in climate change decision making more specifically, see S. Caney, 'Human Rights, Climate Change and Discounting', *Environmental Policy*, Vol. 17, No. 4 (2008), pp. 536–555. The authors of WESS 2009 contend that: 'Economists are latecomers to the climate debate and, more generally, have entered the fray with a less-than-honourable record on environmental issues [citing P. Dasgupta, 'Creative Accounting', *Nature*, Vol. 44 (2008), pp. 456–468]. However, they have been quick to fashion policy options. Theirs is a language of risk assessment, measured trade-offs between costs and benefits, marginal price changes, discounting of future outcomes, etc. Their so-called integrated assessment models confer an aura of quantitative rigour and precision on their discussions, in which they typically endorse an overly cautious approach to policy, whether by demonstrating the advantages of going slow on climate action or by offering quick solutions to externalities, which allow the market to reassume its central role. In the context of climate change, practical policy advice has focused on the mechanics of carbon

Although water is an important component in most energy-generating processes, its role in climate change mitigation policy is comparatively minor. From an empirical standpoint, water and climate change are more strongly linked in adaptation policy, which functions in highly dynamic hydrologic, social, economic and demographic contexts.[136] A normative analysis leads to a similar suggested focus, in view of the dominant preoccupation of the international human rights framework in regulating intra-State relations. With these factors in mind, the practical contributions of the right to water framework are most clearly apparent in terms of informing and strengthening claims of vulnerable populations in connection with national adaptation measures (including National Adaptation Plans of Action), as well as responding to local human rights rights claims and impacts arising from mitigation measures or a failure to curb GHG emissions, exemplified in the 2015 District Court decision in the Hague discussed earlier.[137] But as we have seen, there are also numerous respects in which human rights standards and principles, reinforced by accepted principles of international environmental law, should guide decision making and strengthen accountability in relation to climate change and water sector issues at the global level.

The right to water framework, supported by environmental human rights jurisprudence and relevant principles of international environmental law, offers criteria for the process of negotiations and decision making on climate change issues affecting access to water for personal and domestic uses.[138]

taxes or trading schemes, and on the dangers of ambitious climate initiatives constraining future growth. Self-regulation has become the mantra, and when policy action is proposed the framework is predisposed to gradualism and delay [citing F. Ackerman, *Can We Afford the Future: The Economics of a Warming World* (New York: Zed Books, 2009)]. … Good climate policy requires the best possible understanding of how climatic change will impact on human lives and livelihoods, in industrialised countries and in developing countries. Unfortunately, many climate economics models suffer from a lack of transparency, in terms of both their policy relevance and their credibility. Building a model of the climate and the economy inevitably involves numerous judgement calls; debatable judgements and untestable hypotheses turn out to be of great importance in evaluating the policy recommendations of climate-economics models, and should be visible for purposes of debate'. WESS 2009, p. 13.

[136] United Nations, World Water Development Report No. 3, p. 74, while underscoring that for water adaptation measures to be effective there must be complementary climate change mitigation measures outside the water sector.

[137] Note 82, above, and accompanying text.

[138] Beyond the brief summary of environmental human rights jurisprudence provided earlier, see the Convention on Access to Information, Public Participation in Decision making and Access to Justice in Environmental Matters ('Aarhus Convention'), (adopted 25 June 1998, entered into force 30 October 2001), 38 ILM 517; and United Nations Conference on Environment and Development, June 3-14, 1992, *Report Annex I: Rio Declaration on Environment and Development*, UN Doc A/CONF.151/26/Rev.1 (1992). Principle 10 provides: 'Environmental issues are best handled with participation of all concerned citizens, at the relevant level. At the

The principle of active and informed participation is foremost among these, with human rights standards helping to ensure that participation is inclusive and empowering (rather than a technocratic or tokenistic exercise or, in the context of delivery of water services, a euphemism for cheap labour), particularly for the most disadvantaged and vulnerable groups.[139] The importance of participation has been recognised in the UNFCCC and Paris Agreement, but not as a matter of human right.[140] Access to information and freedom of expression and association are among the vital human rights prerequisites to any meaningful conception of participation. Participatory rights are important as a matter of principle, and from a purely instrumental perspective, participation may furnish critical inputs to decision-making processes, as well as enhance the legitimacy and sustainability of outcomes. This need is indispensible in the view of the complexity and dynamism of decision making on climate change issues, as the World Bank has recognised:

> Decision makers now have to contend with the changing climate compounding the uncertainties they already faced. More decisions have to be made in a context of changing trends and greater variability, not to mention possible carbon constraints.... Participatory design and implementation is critical, because it permits the use of local knowledge about existing vulnerability and fosters ownership of the strategy by its beneficiaries.[141]

national level, each individual shall have appropriate access to information concerning the environment that is held by public authorities, including information on hazardous materials and activities in their communities, and the opportunity to participate in decision-making processes. States shall facilitate and encourage public awareness and participation by making information widely available'.

[139] OHCHR, *Claiming the MDGs* (2008); Center on Housing Rights and Evictions (COHRE), *The Significance of Human Rights in MDG-based Policy Making on Water and Sanitation: An Application to Kenya, South Africa, Sri Lanka, Ghana and Laos* (2009), at 6; WESS 2016, pp.86-91; Knox Mapping Report, paras. 36–40.

[140] Article 12 of the Paris Agreement calls for cooperation to enhance participation and access to information. Paragraph 7 of the WG-LCA agreement, recognises 'the need to engage a broad range of stakeholders at global, regional, national and local levels, be they government, including sub-national and local government, private business or civil society, including youth and persons with disability, and that gender equality and the effective participation of women and indigenous peoples are important for effective action on all aspects of climate change'. See also paragraph 12 and Annex I of the WG-LCA agreement, calling for participation in connection with the Adaptation Framework and REDD. However, there is no reference to participation in the mitigation context. Article 6(8)(b) of the Paris Agreement refers to participation in the context of the private sector's contribution to the implementation of NDCs, although this bears no relation to human rights.

[141] WDR 2010, at 18. For a fuller discussion and recommendations concerning the integration of human rights procedural principles in climate change policy-making, with specific reference to the rights to water and sanitation, see Darrow *et al*, n.33 above, at 37–49.

The requirement for climate change impact assessments in the context of the right to water is specifically acknowledged in General Comment No. 15.[142] The 'do no harm' (or more specifically, 'do no significant transboundary harm') principle is among the few international obligations with widespread support under customary environmental law, as well as human rights law, as we have seen. Environmental impact assessments (EIAs) are viewed by many as compulsory under general principles of international law, regional customary law in Europe, as well as, arguably, emerging global administrative law.[143] *Ex ante* right to water impact assessments, integrated within environmental assessments,[144] can help decision makers and negotiators to identify in a more reliable, systematic and timely fashion the likely winners and losers of any proposed policy measure at the national or global level, as an operational expression of the do no harm principle. An integrated EIA and right to water assessment offers a potentially useful means to ensure that significant policy measures respect a given State's obligations under ratified human rights treaties, as well as the UNFCCC and (as appropriate) Kyoto, promoting policy coherence as well as generating compatible interpretations of the legal obligations under the respective treaty regimes.[145]

Neither General Comment No. 15, nor environmental human rights jurisprudence more generally, go to great lengths in spelling out the specific operational implications of an integrated right to water impact assessment in the context of climate change decision making. However, in general terms, such assessments should: (a) incorporate the right to water as outlined in General Comment No. 15, along with other applicable sources of law from national and regional levels, as informing the substantive focus and criteria for

[142] CESCR, General Comment No. 15, para. 28(e) provides: 'States parties should adopt comprehensive and integrated strategies and programmes to ensure that there is sufficient and safe water for present and future generations. Such strategies and programmes may include: . . . (*e*) assessing the impacts of actions that may impinge upon water availability and natural-ecosystems watersheds, such as climate changes, desertification and increased soil salinity, deforestation and loss of biodiversity. . .' International human rights bodies have consistently called for human rights impact assessments since the 1980s.

[143] See Aarhus Convention; O. W. Pedersen, 'European Environmental Human Rights and Environmental Rights: A Long Time Coming?', *Georgetown International Environmental Law Review*, Vol. 21, No. 1 (2008), pp. 73–111, at 104–109; and B. Kingsbury, et. al., 'The Emergence of Global Administrative Law', *Law and Contemporary Problems*, Vol. 68, Nos. 3–4 (2005), pp. 15–61.

[144] For an argument for integrating human rights and environmental impact assessments, see G. De Beco, 'Human Rights Impact Assessments', *Netherlands Quarterly of Human Rights*, Vol. 27, No. 2 (2009), pp. 139–166.

[145] See the discussion on systemic integration and policy coherence (nn. 12 and 61–62, and accompanying text), and WESS 2016, pp. 47–73 and 77–85; Knox Mapping Report, paras. 30–35.

the assessment; (b) identify indicators for the assessment that are consistent with relevant human rights standards; (c) focus upon people who are most excluded and marginalised along with responsible actors (not necessarily limited to organs of the State), drawing conclusions in terms of impact on the enjoyment of the right to water and fulfilment of corresponding obligations; (d) strive to ensure that the assessment, as far as possible, contributes to building the capacities of relevant national stakeholders (that is to say, identifiable rights holders and duty bearers); (e) ensure that the process of carrying out the assessment respects good process principles, such as those outlined earlier, both as a general matter of policy, and more particularly to the extent that those principles enjoy solid foundations in international human rights law binding upon the country(ies) concerned; and (f) seek to involve human rights mechanisms and actors as far as possible, for example national human rights institutions, subject to their mandated functions and capacities.[146]

Whatever the eventual outcomes of a particular negotiation or policy making process, the human rights legal framework requires that effective and accessible redress mechanisms, including but not limited to judicial mechanisms, be put in place to ensure that those whose human rights were overlooked or traded-off against other interests are adequately compensated.[147]

The requirement for effective remedies assumes particular importance in the context of climate change decision making, as a counterincentive and corrective to the accountability deficit in the climate change regime at the global level and the widespread impunity of States and corporations responsible for the greatest GHG emissions. The global and national dimensions of human rights accountability are equally important: 'International regimes influence national policies, but are themselves a product of domestic factors. Political norms, governance structures and vested interests drive the translation of international law into domestic policy, while shaping

[146] For an illustrative account of human rights impact assessment methodology in the context of trade policy assessments surveying the wider field of social and human rights impact assessments in the development field, see S. Walker, *The Future of Human Rights Impact Assessment of Trade Agreements* (Antwerp: Intersentia, 2009). More generally, see J. Harrison, 'Human Rights Measurement: Reflections on the Current Practice and Future Potential of Human Rights Impact Assessment', *Journal of Human Rights Practice*, Vol. 3, No. 2 (July 2011), pp. 162–187; WESS 2016, pp. 47–73 and 77–85; and Knox Mapping Report, paras. 30–35.

[147] The right to a remedy is a fundamental prerequisite of international human rights law, embodied in General Comment No. 15, at para. 55. See also CESCR, *General Comment No. 9: The Domestic Application of the Covenant* (Nineteenth session, 1998), UN Doc. E/C.12/1998/24 (1998), at para. 9; Aarhus Convention and Principle 10 of the Rio Declaration. The latter states: 'Effective access to judicial and administrative proceedings, including redress and remedy, shall be provided', in respect of environmental harms.

the international regime. And in the absence of a global enforcement mechanism, the incentives for meeting global commitments are domestic'.[148]

There are obvious limits to the impact that case-by-case adjudication can have on climate change globally, and the results to date from litigating climate change claims, particularly claims relating to transboundary harms, are mixed.[149] Nevertheless, in theory, there is a potentially wide range of courts and tribunals at global, regional and national levels to which suitable claims could be brought, including the International Court of Justice (under its contentious and advisory jurisdictions) and International Tribunal for the Law of the Sea.[150] Claims against third countries for climate-related harms have been brought to the Inter-American Commission on Human Rights, as discussed earlier, and the District Court in the Hague has shown how human rights treaty obligations can support a successful tort claim in response to climate-related harms at the national level. Moreover in the *Nigerian Gas*

[148] WDR 2010, at 19. See also Knox Mapping Report, paras. 41–43.

[149] For a discussion of the challenges and limitations of litigating human rights claims in the context of climate change, see S. Atapattu (2016), pp. 266–290; and Tully, 'Like Oil and Water'. *Cf* E. Posner, 'Climate Change and International Human Rights Litigation: A Critical Appraisal', *University of Pennsylvania Law Review*, Vol. 155, No. 6 (2007), pp. 1925–1945 (questioning the normative basis for claims that individuals have a human right that is violated by GHG emissions, and the prospects for vindicating such rights through litigation).

[150] See P. Sands, 'Climate Change and the Rule of Law: Adjudicating the Future in International Law', *Journal of Environmental Law* Vol. 28 (2016), pp. 19–35; S. Atapattu (2016), pp. 266–290; H. M. Osofsky, 'Climate Change Litigation as Pluralist Legal Dialogue', *Stanford Environmental Law Journal*, Vol. 26A (2007), pp. 181–237; W. C. G. Burns, 'Potential Causes of Action for Climate Change Impacts Under the United Nations Fish Stocks Agreement', *Journal of Sustainable Development Law and Policy*, Vol. 2, No. 1 (2007), pp. 34–41; H. M. Osofsky and W. C. G. Burns (eds.), *Adjudicating Climate Control: Sub-National, National And Supra-National Approaches* (Cambridge: Cambridge University Press, 2008); W. C. G. Burns, 'Potential Causes of Action for Climate Change Damages in International Fora: The Law of the Sea Convention', *Journal of Sustainable Development Law and Policy*, Vol. 1, No. 2 (2006), pp. 27–53, at 51; J. Smith and D. Shearman, *Climate Change Litigation: Analysing The Law, Scientific Evidence and Impacts On The Environment, Health and Property* (Presidian Legal Publications, 2006); A. Strauss, 'The Legal Option: Suing the United States in International Forums for Global Warming Emissions', *Environmental Law Reporter*, Vol. 33 (2003), pp. 10185–10191; and S. Kravchenko, 'Right to Carbon or Right to Life: Human Rights Approaches to Climate Change', *Vermont Journal of Environmental Law*, Vol. 9 (2008), pp. 513–547. While not dealing directly with the right to water, this body of scholarship critically explores the potential for litigating climate change claims in the International Court of Justice, the International Tribunal on the Law of the Sea, the European Court of Human Rights, the Inter-American Commission and Court of Human Rights, the African Commission of Human Rights and People's Rights, and national courts, encouraging the creative use of these international fora to address or, at least, highlight the issue of climate change, including the impact of climate change on the realisation of human rights.

*Flaring Case*[151] the High Court of Nigeria held that the practice of gas flaring by Nigeria in the Niger Delta, a practice which contributed more to climate change than all other sources in Sub-Saharan Africa, violated guaranteed constitutional rights to life and dignity.

In light of the foregoing, the practical importance of litigation as a defence mechanism for those most threatened by climate events, within broader strategies for advocacy and social mobilisation, should not be underestimated. Regardless of the outcome of a hypothetical right to water claim linked to climate change, a focus on specific injuries can help to build political support for action to address the impacts of climate change on the right to water, and the story-telling quality of legal cases can make climate change real and tangible in the public eye. Even unsuccessful legal claims may indirectly build pressure for policy and legislative action, as well as influence corporate behaviour.[152] The emerging experience from litigating socio-economic rights around the world affirms the important and potentially empowering role that litigation can play, subject to certain preconditions, within broader strategies and movements for social change.[153]

Experience to date suggests that human rights litigation is more likely to be effective at the intra-State level in the context of national adaptation imperatives, as a mechanism through which individuals and vulnerable communities might ensure that their continuing access to quality and affordable water is safeguarded and any unjust losses are compensated, and that national adaptation policy responses do not arbitrarily or unreasonably favour some groups over others. As far as mitigation actions are concerned, tort and administrative law claims in richer countries can strengthen incentives for regulatory action to promote clean energy investment and control emissions,[154] with positive potential impacts on the enjoyment of the human right to water whether or not this was an element of the claim. As the international system becomes

[151] *Jonah Gbemre* v. *Shell Petroleum Development Co. (Nigeria) Ltd. et. al.*, Unreported Suit No. FHC/B/CS/53/05 (14 November 2005) (Benin).

[152] Corporate responsibility is a critical element in the global accountability framework for human rights harms arising from climate change, raising tensions with the State-centric edifice of international human rights law. There is at least anecdotal evidence that, at the domestic level, liability claims pertaining to environmental harm have led to changes in behavior when such claims were directed against corporations. M. Faure and A. Nollekaemper, 'International Liability as an Instrument to Prevent and Compensate for Climate Change', *Stanford Environmental Law Journal*, Vol. 26A (2007), pp. 123–179, at 141.

[153] See Langford (ed.), Social Rights Jurisprudence; Gauri and Brinks (eds.), Courting Social Justice; and Yamin and Gloppen (eds.), Litigating Health Rights.

[154] See e.g. *Massachusetts* v. *EPA*, 549 U.S. 497 (2007); and Rechtbank Den Haag, 24-06-2015, C/09/456689 / HA ZA 13-1396, note 82 above.

more highly regulated in response to the demands of globalisation, and as the adverse impacts of climate change are felt more widely and acutely, the role of litigation may well be expected to evolve over time to deal as much with the concrete allocation of losses as with the raising of political consciousness.[155]

The scheme of socio-economic rights obligations reflected in the ICESCR adds other important qualitative dimensions to decision making in the climate change context. Under the ICESCR, State parties are obliged to move progressively forward in realising socio-economic rights, avoid arbitrary retrogression in the realisation of rights, undertake maximum efforts to realise rights within all available resources with priority given to the most excluded or vulnerable, ensure a core minimum level of rights for all, and – where best efforts are not sufficient – request international assistance.

The above process criteria have a clear scope of application in connection with planning decisions at the national or local levels on adaptation measures insofar as the right to water is concerned. They could also arguably play an important role as criteria for prioritising among competing national claims for international financial assistance, cooperation and technology transfer for climate change mitigation and adaptation. A minimally even-handed application of these process criteria may provide objective grounds for privileging the claims of those lower-income countries better able to demonstrate authentic efforts towards human rights realisation, while at the same time increasing the legal and moral impetus for the international community to provide support when it is both needed and requested. Human rights practitioners and economists have been working in closer collaboration in recent years to develop quantitative assessment tools and methodologies that, together with qualitative data and more traditional human rights monitoring methods, can help to call the bluff of States seeking international support for human rights realisation without having demonstrated 'maximum' effort at home.[156]

The right to water framework also informs the substance of decision making on climate change issues affecting access to water for personal and domestic uses. There are a number of substantive implications to consider in this regard. Firstly, having regard to the indivisibility and functional interdependence of human rights, climate change policy responses with implications for the right to water should be conceived and implemented in a manner that

[155] Strauss, 'The Legal Option' at 10 and 191.

[156] For overviews of relevant initiatives, see e.g. E. Anderson and M. Foresti, 'Assessing Compliance: the Challenge for Economic and Social Rights', *Journal of Human Rights Practice*, Vol. 1, No. 3 (2009), pp. 469–176; and E. Felner, 'Closing the "Escape Hatch": A Toolkit to Monitor the Progressive Realisation of Economic, Social and Cultural Rights', *Journal of Human Rights Practice*, Vol. 1, No. 3 (2009), pp. 402–435.

takes account of inter-relationships with other relevant rights, including rights relating to health, housing (including secure tenure), food and sanitation as outlined earlier. Correspondingly, mitigation and adaptation actions relating to agriculture, health, sanitation and so forth should take into account the right to water. Within this framework, great care is needed to ensure that planning to meet needs connected with the right to water does not unwittingly reinforce sectoral blinkers or a silo mentality. The challenge of policy coherence applies within the scope of applicable human rights standards, as much as across other relevant fields of international law. Water, sanitation, food, poverty and health issues should be seen as intimately connected, requiring holistic policy approaches integrating development and climate change issues and planning frameworks.[157] Human rights need to be seen as a central part of this package, noting that problems in the water sector are much more about correcting injustices and biases in distributions of power between individuals, institutions and groups, than they are about scarcity *per se*.[158]

General Comment No. 15 provides a potentially valuable framework for policy making in this regard, as recommended by the Millennium Project Task Force on Water and Sanitation.[159] General Comment No. 15 situates the right to water within a holistic understanding of its relationship with other sectors such as health, sanitation and housing, as well as with the development, political and economic policy contexts. This should begin with clear recognition of the right to water in national law, as part of the framework for national adaptation policy measures as well as mitigation, financial assistance and technology transfer. General Comment 15 provides a checklist (rather than a template) of key substantive considerations required to be factored into decision making, relating, for example,

[157] WESS 2009, at 78–79 and 88–90. There has been political resistance from some developing countries to proposals to 'mainstream' development into climate change policymaking, for fear of overloading an already fragile climate change policy agenda and perhaps distracting from very particular historical and social justice claims embodied in the UNFCCC and Kyoto framework (reflected in the explicit provision in the latter agreements for differential treatment between richer and poorer countries). However, both the WDR 2010 and WESS 2009 (see e.g. pp. 92–93 of the latter) make a compelling case for strengthened climate change and development linkages, linked in great part to aid effectiveness concerns, that is to say, the need to ensure coherence and coordination in national planning. Similarly the 2030 Agenda for Sustainable Development embodies an integrated vision and programme of action on the environment, development and human rights.

[158] Human Development Report 2006.

[159] Millennium Project Task Force on Water and Sanitation, *Health, dignity, and development: what will it take? UN Task Force Report* (Millennium Development Library, June 2005), at p. 178.

accessibility and affordability requirements of the right to water, the policy implications of the non-discrimination norm and criteria to be considered in the formulation, implementing and monitoring of a national plan (or NAPA, in the context of climate change adaptation) for the progressive realisation of this right. States should be setting longer-term targets for universal access, in addition to SDG-adjusted medium-term benchmarks,[160] disaggregated by reference to particularly vulnerable populations, as well as regional and local administrative units.

At a more fundamental level still, the framework of international human rights law buttresses economic and political economy arguments for more effective public action for the delivery of public goods. Greenhouse gases were described in the Stern Review as 'the greatest market failure that the world has ever seen'.[161] The right to water framework embodied in General Comment No. 15 does not purport to prescribe any particular division of responsibility for the public and private sectors in water provision, although the State is required, at a minimum, to set in place a regulatory framework to safeguard the right to water at the national level.[162] However, the role of public action will be particularly pertinent in the context of climate change and the right to water in many countries, given that it is primarily poor water management and lack of water entitlements, rather than physical water scarcity, that generate water-related tensions and poverty.[163] The variability in water availability, a direct threat to the legal requirement for sustainable access, will require increased resilience in water management systems. A number of countries have begun making inroads in this direction, however major public investments will be needed to achieve sustainable results.[164] Social policy is another critical focus for public action in the present context. Social policies 'reduce economic and social vulnerability' and help people to better cope with climate shocks and climate change.[165] General Comment No. 15 usefully signals the centrality of social policy responses to climate change, for example, in terms of the requirement for 'essential minimum levels',[166] or what others

[160] See note 111 and accompanying text. SDG 6 'Ensure availability and sustainable management of water and sanitation for all' sets out a range of targets relating to water and sanitation, which UN member States have committed to meet by the year 2030.

[161] Stern Review, cited in WESS 2009, at ix. [162] General Comment No. 15, at para. 24.

[163] G.E. Castillo, et al., 'Reversing the Flow: Agricultural Water Management Pathways for Poverty Reduction', in D. Molden (ed.), *Water for Food, Water for Life: A Comprehensive Assessment of Water Management in Agriculture* (London: Earthscan, 2007), pp. 149–91; cited in WESS 2009, at 90.

[164] WESS 2009, at 90. [165] WDR 2010, Summary at 13.

[166] General Comment No. 15, at para. 37(a).

call a 'minimum floor' of socio-economic rights, to be implemented as a matter of priority at the national level, and respected in international agreements and decisions on climate change globally.

## 6 CONCLUDING REMARKS AND DIRECTIONS FOR FURTHER RESEARCH

There is clearly considerable scope for mutual reinforcement between the principles underpinning the international legal regimes for human rights and climate change, notwithstanding certain normative tensions and their different historical origins and purposes. The human rights framework draws attention to the human face of climate change and bolsters accountability of governments towards their own populations, in particular, while also lending support for strengthened accountability for human rights impacts of transboundary environmental harms. The right to water and associated human rights principles – as elaborated through national, regional and international compliance mechanisms – may strengthen information, voice and participation in climate change policy, as well as provide redress for adverse human rights impacts of climate change. The framework of obligations in the ICESCR offers a potentially valuable metric for differentiating and prioritising between different States' claims for international assistance and technology transfer. All 164 States Parties to the ICESCR and all 196 States Parties to the CRC have undertaken to do their utmost to the maximum extent of available resources to fulfill the socio-economic rights of their own populations, with priority for the most vulnerable. Resource-constrained States that are able to demonstrate clear efforts in this regard should, arguably, be seen to have strengthened claims to international financial and technical assistance for national adaptation, and as appropriate, mitigation needs. This may also, at least indirectly, build pressure for strengthened international cooperation and aid commitments, by providing an objective basis for prioritisation and removing pretexts for inaction on the part of donors.

There are many issues with which a chapter of the present length and scope cannot possibly deal and a great many areas where further research and action are warranted, in order to protect the right to water from climate change harms, unleash the emancipatory potential of a human rights-based approach embodied in General Comment No. 15, and stimulate greater legal and policy coherence in public policy making on issues affecting climate change and water. The right to water has come a long way in a comparatively short time, in terms of legal recognition at national and international levels and enforcement in national tribunals. However, this right has achieved only rare and partial recognition in national development plans,[167] is virtually absent in NAPAs,[168] and (along with all other human rights) has had very little impact upon climate change negotiations at the global level. Nevertheless, the preceding discussion signals a number of avenues that may prove useful in addressing these gaps.

Firstly, if the counterincentives to effective mitigation and adaptation action on climate change are to be addressed, human rights accountability mechanisms must be more widely and strategically used, and strengthened. Public interest litigation is an important part of this equation. Courts and judges will of course not always prove to be responsive and independent agents for progressive social change in all settings. But whatever the relatively modest results from climate change litigation to date, it seems clear that the catalytic potential for strategic human rights claims in most jurisdictions is yet to be properly exploited. Whether seen as part of advocacy, campaigning, incentives for more effective regulation and responsible corporate behaviour, backup systems for regulatory failure, or safety nets for those whose access to water is most acutely threatened by climate change, this appears to be a topic in need of further research, together with further investigation into the various forums at global,[169] regional and national levels where legal action against emitting States and corporations might show promise, along with research into how litigated outcomes interact with and translate into regulatory and policy change in the climate change setting.

Secondly, in line with General Comment No. 15, administrative accountability mechanisms should be more widely tested and strengthened. Calls for human rights impact assessments have been commonplace for decades, and are core components of States' due diligence obligations in the present context.[170] The technical and methodological complexity of integrated

[167] See COHRE.

[168] As at 2016, only 4 per cent of NAPA's contained any reference to human rights. Forty-five per cent of national communications submitted under the UNFCCC between 2010 and 2015 noted actions to address climate harms related to health, food security and water and sanitation, however in the great majority of cases (66 out of 70) the corresponding human rights were not mentioned. Considerably more countries reported on human rights impacts of climate change under the Universal Periodic Review (UPR) process of the UN Human Rights Council, however only fourteen countries (16 per cent) included human rights impacts in both their UPR and UNFCCC reporting. See Mary Robinson Foundation, 'Incorporating Human Rights into Climate Action,' Version 2 (May 2016), pp. 5 and 11, available at http://www.mrfcj.org/wp-content/uploads/2016/05/Incorporating-Human-Rights-into-Climate-Action-Version-2-May-2016.pdf.

[169] On the roles of international human rights bodies, see J. Knox, 'Linking Human Rights and Climate Change at the United Nations', *Harvard Environmental Law Review*, Vol. 33 (2009), pp. 477–498, at 496–497.

[170] Rio Declaration on Environment and Development, Principle 17; Report of the UN Independent Expert on the issue of human rights obligations relating to the enjoyment of a

climate change and right to water assessments should not be overstated, in view of the significant recent progress towards human rights impact assessments more generally.[171] Generating demand, however, is surely a more challenging matter. Integrated climate change and right to water impact assessments should be promoted within the framework of wider public mobilisation efforts in order to strengthen incentives for policymakers and negotiators to examine and take responsibility for the human rights impacts of their actions. Data gaps are a closely associated problem, stemming both from capacity gaps, as well as deficits in political will. It is challenging in many contexts, particularly for the more data-intensive forms of socio-economic rights monitoring, to form definitive judgments about the extent to which human rights duty bearers (and particularly governments) are meeting their obligations to dedicate 'maximum available' domestic resources towards socio-economic rights, within the meaning of the ICESCR and CRC. Data problems are especially acute in respect of those living in informal settlements, internally displaced persons, certain ethnic minorities, migrants and other vulnerable groups who may not be properly reflected in national censuses or household surveys. Standard household surveys fail to disaggregate at these levels, and accordingly, so do the surveys of the WHO and UNICEF Joint Monitoring Programme for Water Supply and Sanitation (JMP).[172] The 2030 Agenda for Sustainable Development was intended to be undergirded by a 'data revolution'[173] for monitoring and accountability purposes, but at the time of writing there was no revolution in sight. Data and analytical gaps may increase dramatically in proportion to the scale of climate-induced forced displacement,[174] threatening the sustained water access for millions of people. Hence, in order to enable more meaningful human rights assessments, there

safe, clean, health and sustainable environment, John Knox, UN Doc. A/HRC/25/23 (30 December, 2013), paras. 47–57.

[171] See e.g. the human rights impact assessment tool developed by the International Finance Corporation together with the International Business Leaders Forum: International Finance Corporation, *Guide to Human Rights Impact Assessment and Management: Road-Testing Draft* (2007).

[172] See http://documents.wssinfo.org/resources/documents.html. The JMP is tasked with monitoring progress towards the MDG drinking water and sanitation target, within a longer term vision of encouraging universal access to safe drinking water and sanitation by the year 2025. It draws from standard household surveys, Living Standards Measurement Surveys, demographic and health surveys and others. Discrimination issues are not reflected, and neither are water safety, affordability or reliability issues.

[173] See http://www.undatarevolution.org.

[174] On recent predictions, as many as 200 million people may be displaced as a consequence of climate change by the year 2050, that is to say, approximately one person in every fourteen world-wide. This is likely to have potentially dramatic impacts upon the sustainability of access

is an important capacity-building agenda around the question of national statistical and analytical capacities, including in connection with water sector and climate vulnerability assessments.[175] Without this, the distributional impacts and severity of possible human rights harms associated with climate change may not adequately be anticipated and planned for, and those whose rights are violated may be precluded from seeking effective redress.

Thirdly, any comprehensive and effective approach to climate change policy must necessarily include a clear and effective framework of human rights accountability for the private sector. Collective action on climate change, as the United Nations has lamented, has been 'hampered by technocratic complacency, which privileged private means over public ends. A combination of deregulation, at both the national and international levels, and corporate leadership skills was deemed all that was needed to find the quickest and most efficient solutions to a wide range of contemporary policy challenges', including climate change. 'This mindset has been dominated by the rhetoric of targets, partnerships, synergies, etc., which, draining policy discussion of much of its substance, inevitably

to water. Entire nations, such as the Maldives and Tuvalu, are likely, if current GHG emission trends continue, to be lost to sea level rise, rendering their inhabitants stateless. Restrictive definitions in the 1951 Convention on the Status of Refugees, a regime already overburdened due to institutional and resource constraints, are likely to preclude claims under refugee law. In any event, the most vulnerable individuals and populations are often least able to migrate, and face serious protection concerns when they do. Hence, most population movements and consequent conflicts over water appear likely to take place within national borders. To the extent that forced displacement and associated threats to the right to water are caused by anthropogenic climate change, this appears to open up a large lacuna in the existing edifice of international law. For analyses of displacement in the context of climate change, see e.g. Intergovernmental Panel on Climate Change, *Climate Change 2007: Third Assessment Report* (2001); Stern Review, at 77; and B. Saul and J. McAdam, 'An Insecure Climate for Human Security? Climate-Induced Displacement and International Law', Legal Studies Research Paper 08/131 (2008). For proposed solutions, see e.g. B. Docherty and T. Giannini, 'Confronting a Rising Tide: A Proposal for a Convention on Climate Change Refugees', *Harvard Environmental Law Review*, Vol. 33, No. 2 (2009), pp. 349–403, at 372; and D. Hodgkinson, et al., 'Towards a Convention for Persons Displaced by Climate Change: Key Issues and Preliminary Responses', *The New Critic*, Issue 8 (2008). *Cf* Sumuda Atapattu (2016), pp.155-175 (arguing against a new convention or extention of the UN Refugee Convention on feasibility grounds, in favour of applying human rights law to climate-related displacement).

175 Top-down scenario-based model studies for assessment of national vulnerability to climate change are fairly well developed, relatively easily accessible and frequently used. However, grassroots-level tools to assess the vulnerability of particular communities are still under development and not widely available. The latter tools are vital to complement the 'top-down' assessments and for national/basin/regional planning and priority setting. See Cooperative Programme on Water and Climate, Recommendations: Towards a Water and Climate Alliance, at www.waterandclimate.org, and more generally WESS 2016, pp. 116–123.

tends to ignore or gloss over the conflicts and difficult trade-offs that accompany all big policy challenges'.[176]

Transnational corporations, including fossil fuel and agribusiness industries, have grown enormously in their economic and political influence in both richer and poorer countries. Corporations are often major users and providers of water services, and many of them bear a significant degree of direct responsibility for GHG emissions. Governments have the primary role in regulating for human rights protection and realisation and in creating incentives for climate action (through subsidies, taxes, caps, or regulations), providing information and education and correcting market failures. However, much of the needed finance will come from the private sector, particularly for adaptation, along with technological innovation.[177] Strategies to engage the private sector should take account of the Human Rights Council's Guiding Principles on Business and Human Rights,[178] as well as more specific research on the role of business in relation to the right to water.[179] The most important contribution that businesses can make to the Paris Agreement and SDGs is to respect human rights throughout their value chains:[180] 'naming and acclaiming' can be a powerful inducement for private sector engagement in this regard, but not at the expense of 'naming and shaming'.[181]

On technology policy more specifically, water can be used more efficiently through a combination of new and existing technologies, better information, and more sensible use. While low-cost local technologies should be prioritised, new technologies may be required for adaptation purposes in areas such as water storage and conservation, recycling, desalination, improved irrigation and nanotechnology for water purification, wastewater treatment and monitoring.[182] Analysis of technology needs in the water

176 WESS 2009, at 1. 177 WDR 2010, at 24. 178 See UN Doc. A/HRC/17/31, 21 March 2011.

179 For suggested priorities and orientations for research see Institute for Human Rights and Business, 'Business, Human Rights and the Right to Water: Challenges, Dilemmas and Opportunities', Consultation report (draft), January 2009.

180 See J. Ruggie, 'Making Globalisation Work for All: Achieving the Sustainable Development Goals through Business Respect for Human Rights', *SHIFT Viewpoint* (November 2016), at http://www.shiftproject.org/resources/viewpoints/globalization-sustainable-development-goals-business-respect-human-rights/. Ruggie notes the limitations of traditional Corporate Social Responsibility initiatives and the positive contributions of 'respecting' human rights throughout the value chain. He also exposes the false dichotomy between compliance and promotional activities, and notes that 'in human rights there is no equivalent to buying carbon offsets'.

181 *Contra*: Ivanova (2016) at p. 413.

182 WDR 2010, at 17–18; IPCC Technical Paper IV, at 46; and United Nations World Water Development Report No. 3, at 45. For technology-related needs relating to climate change adaptation in the water sector, see F. van Steenbergen and A. Tuinhof, *Managing the Water Buffer for Development and Climate Change Adaptation: Groundwater Recharge, Retention,*

sector should take full account of the root causes of lack of access, including barriers related to the structure of the relevant technology markets, the pricing and technology transfer models, as well as political or ideological barriers.[183] There is also an urgent research agenda around issues of technology transfer, climate change and human rights (including the right to water), mapping and analysing the international human rights, intellectual property, trade and investment legal regimes in order to identify areas of congruence as well as potential conflict. The latter endeavour is a critical prerequisite to ensuring that COP negotiating parties – richer and poorer countries alike – may be able to interpret these various regimes in good faith and in a manner that gives rise to a mutually compatible set of obligations, for the benefit of legal and policy coherence.[184]

Finally, it is difficult to imagine a more pressing research agenda than that relating to extraterritorial obligations connected with climate change and human rights. The theoretical and practical challenges relating to the realisation of the right to water in the context of climate change are as much global as local, requiring collective action in several important policy areas: mitigation, adaptation, financial assistance and technology transfer.

Extraterritorial obligations of non-interference and avoidance of harm are relatively well established in both international human rights and environmental law, along with obligations concerning human rights protection, within evolving parameters. But resistance to legally enforceable obligations of cooperation and positive assistance remains deeply entrenched among the more powerful and heavily emitting countries. The leadership of the USA and China, which together account for forty per cent of global GHG emissions, is critical to the success of the global climate regime. However the withdrawal by the United States from the Paris Agreement, announced on 1 June 2017, has

*Reuse and Rainwater Storage* (2009); and F. Ludwig, P. Kabat, H. van Schaik and M. van der Valk (eds.), *Climate Change Adaptation in the Water Sector* (London: Earthscan, 2009).

183 For fuller discussion of such factors in the health sector, by analogy, see S. F. Musungu, *Health: Human Rights, Climate Vulnerability and Access to Technology*, Background Paper (draft) (Geneva: International Council on Human Rights Policy, 2009).

184 See nn. 12 and 61–62 and accompanying text, and Center for International Environmental Law, *Technology Transfer in the UNFCCC and Other International Legal Regimes: The Challenge of Systemic Integration*, Background Paper, International Council on Human Rights Policy Review Meeting, at 9–10 (Geneva: International Council on Human Rights Policy, 2009). On the role of technology policy and intellectual property rights in the climate change context see WESS 2009, at 123–136; and International Council on Human Rights Policy, *Beyond Technology Transfer: Protecting Human Rights in a Climate-Constrained World* (ICHRP: Geneva, 2011).

struck a serious blow to global efforts to limit dangerous anthropogenic climate change. [185]

These developments should be seen in the light of larger threats to multilateralism linked to the resurgence of parochial and ethnonationalist political movements in many parts of the world, slow global growth and economic insecurity, growing inequalities within and between countries, environmental crises and increased competition and conflict over natural resources, regional security crises and large-scale forced population movements, and ongoing structural weaknesses and turbulence in the global financial system. The achievements at COP 21 were all the more notable in this context. But fear and insecurity breed parochialism, not solidarity, and the real test for Paris still lies ahead in the implementation phase.

It seems paradoxical that the moments of greatest need for international law are so often the moments when it is under greatest threat. The hostile global political environment may well constrain the wider acceptance of transboundary duties and positive impacts of legal claims for strengthened international cooperation in the short term. However the urgency of pursuing such claims, and understanding the prerequisities for their success, has never been greater, together with more broadly textured social justice claims and policy responses based upon enlightened self-interest.[186]

State responsibility and remedies are contingent upon the finding of a breach of an international obligation.[187] A focus on legal remedies is critical because, for an increasing number of people, it is already too late: untold damage has been done and further damage is unavoidable. The UNFCCC's scheme of financing and international cooperation may be likened to a global redress mechanism of the kind proposed by Alston,[188] subject to an objective assessment of individual countries' capacities and efforts. But if commitments are not backed by teeth and real accountability opposable against individual duty bearers, they are unlikely to offset the deeply entrenched counter-incentives to collaboration and more sustainable production and consumption patterns before the global tipping point is reached.

[185] See e.g. C. Mooney, 'Trump's Exit from Paris Climate Deal Makes an Already Tough Target Harder to Hit', The Washington Post (1 June 2017) (web version).

[186] For a brief discussion of the broader concept of environmental justice, see e.g. D. Shelton, 'Environmental Rights', in People's Rights (ibid.), pp. 185–258, at 257. On the case for international aid as a function of enlightened self-interest, see UNDP, *Human Development Report 2005: International Cooperation at a Crossroad: Aid, Trade and Security in an Unequal World* (New York: UNDP, 2005), pp. 77–79.

[187] ILC draft Articles, note 83 above, articles 1–2 and 30–36.

[188] Footnote 112 above and accompanying text.

This is an existential threat for millions of people across the globe. It may also prove to be an existential moment for international law, should the climate and human rights regimes prove unable to evolve in line with the most urgent needs and expectations of human rights claim holders, including the great many whose right to water is threatened by climate change through no fault of their own governments.

11

# Access to Water and Sanitation

# 7

# Determining Progress on Access to Water and Sanitation

## *The Case of South Africa*

JACKIE DUGARD*, MALCOLM LANGFORD**
AND EDWARD ANDERSON***

### 1 INTRODUCTION

During the past two decades, South Africa has been the poster child of the right to water. The right to access water was entrenched in the 1996 Bill of Rights, legislation was grounded in a rights-sensitive framework, and the policy menu embraced access targets, lifeline and steeped tariffs and equitable fiscal transfers. Rapid progress was soon reported: In 1994, an estimated twelve million South Africans (approximately a quarter of the total population) lacked access to piped water and twenty-one million to adequate sanitation.[1] By the mid-2000s, South Africa had already met the Millennium Development Goals and was soon setting universal access targets. The State soon emerged as a template, a best practice, in promoting the right to water. As UNDP concluded in 2006: 'South Africa has demonstrated how the human right to water can serve as a mechanism for empowerment and a guide to policy. Rights-based water reform has enabled it to expand access and overcome the legacy of racial inequality inherited from apartheid, partly through rights-based entitlements'.[2]

* Associate Professor at the University of the Witwatersrand, Johannesburg. This empirical analysis for this chapter is focused on the period 2001 to 2013 but has been updated in places.
** Professor, Faculty of Law, University of Oslo; Co-Director, Centre on Law and Social Transformation, University of Bergen and CMI.
*** Lecturer, School of International Development, University of East Anglia.

1 African National Congress (ANC), *Reconstruction and Development Programme (RDP)* (Johannesburg: Umanyo Publications), para. 2.6.1. Indeed, the ANC's first macroeconomic manifesto, the Reconstruction and Development Programme (RDP), explicitly prioritised the main goal of water management as 'meeting every person's health and functional requirements'. Ibid., para. 2.6.5.

2 Human Development Report, *Beyond Scarcity: Power, Power and the Global Water Crisis*, (New York: UNDP, 2006), p. 63.See in particular box 1.6, p. 64.

It is certainly to be acknowledged that the case of South Africa provides a compelling narrative for the right to water: helping to overcome arguments about vague content and its practicality in situations of scarce resources. However, the case also raises a series of deeper questions about how we determine progress and the desirability of certain policy options: what do we really mean by access to water and sanitation and how do we know if States are really complying with their obligations? Not only has the roll-out of sanitation been particularly slow, and this is generally acknowledged,[3] but since 2001, when water services was devolved to local government, poor households appear to have experienced high levels of water disconnections and restrictions with increasing frequency. Moreover, many urban and rural dwellers seem unable to move beyond the most basic level of access.[4] Water and sanitation is as much a field of contestation as it is celebration.

Acknowledging that the rights to water and sanitation involve more than physical and economic access alone, this mixed methods chapter sets out to understand the efforts to extend *access* to water and sanitation[5] in South Africa against the backdrop of the right to water and sanitation. In doing so, the right to water and sanitation forms both an *empirical* research object (i.e. to examine its role in various processes) and an *analytical* lens ( i.e. to use it to evaluate the level of progress and possible causes).

The chapter begins in Section 2 by *mapping* the legal, policy and jurisprudential framework, with its relatively sophisticated recognition of the right to water and sanitation, and its institutionalisation within a devolved and increasingly corporatised governance structure. Section 3 contrasts this framework with an examination of the realities of access to water and sanitation with a focus on both measures of statistical progress and experiences from daily life.

The next two sections seek to uncover *why* improvement has been slower than expected. Is it simply a case that authorities lack the necessary resources or require more time? Or are there fundamental policy and institutional choices that suggest that South Africa is not meeting its statutory, constitutional and international obligations to improve access to these rights? To answer this, Section 4 conducts a quantitative analysis designed to identify municipalities which are under-performing in terms of promoting physical

[3] Ibid.

[4] K. Tissington, A *Resource Guide to Housing in South Africa: Legislation, Policy, Programmes and Practice* (Johannesburg: SERI, 2011); B. Cousins and I. Scoones, 'Contested Paradigms of 'Viability' in Redistributive Land Reform: Perspectives from Southern Africa', *Journal of Peasant Studies*, Vol. 37, No. 1 (2010), pp. 31–66.

[5] While covering water and sanitation services (watsan), the chapter does focus more on water.

and economic access to water and sanitation services, given their available 'resources'. Section 5 adopts a more qualitative methodology and draws on interviews with seventeen municipalities in order to set out hypotheses for six different faultlines that shed light on some of the problems associated with policy and institutional design. These developments have, of course, not occurred in a political vacuum. South Africa has witnessed social and legal mobilisation around municipal services delivery. Section 6 then examines responses from below to these challenges with a particular focus on legal mobilisation on the right to water in the well-known *Mazibuko* litigation and its impacts in practice.[6] The conclusion draws together the threads to provide both a rights-based *picture* of actual progress in South Africa but also a sense to which a rights-based *approach* has made a difference.

## 2 LEGAL AND POLICY FRAMEWORK FOR WATER SERVICES IN SOUTH AFRICA

### 2.1 *The Constitution*

One of the notable aspects of the Constitution of the Republic of South Africa[7] is the insertion of socio-economic rights for all – including the 'right to have access to sufficient water'[8] – alongside more traditional civil and political rights. Whether civil and political or socio-economic, all rights in the Bill of Rights (chapter 2 of the Constitution) carry both negative and positive obligations and, according to section 7(2) of the Constitution, the 'State must respect, protect, promote and fulfil the rights in the Bill of Rights'. The highest court of appeal in constitutional matters, the Constitutional Court, has confirmed the justiciability of socio-economic rights in several judgments, and stated in the *Grootboom* case that: 'Socio-economic rights are expressly included in the Bill of Rights; they cannot be said to exist on paper only.... The question is therefore not whether socio-economic rights are justiciable under our Constitution, but how to enforce them in each case'.[9]

The right to water, as with almost all socio-economic rights in the Bill of Rights,[10] is formulated in two parts. The first part – section 27(1)(b) – establishes

[6] See also case studies in Chapter 10 in relation to the right to adequate sanitation.

[7] Act 108 of 1996 ('Constitution').

[8] Section 27(1)(b), Constitution. It should be noted that, unlike in other jurisdictions and international law, South African legislation uses the term section rather than article.

[9] *Government of the RSA* v. *Grootboom* 2001 (1) SA 46 (CC) (*Grootboom*), p. 20.

[10] The exception is Section 29(1)(a), The right to a basic education is set out as an unqualified right. Certain children's and prisoners' rights are also regarded as unqualified rights.

that 'everyone has the right of access to sufficient water'. The second part – section 27(2) – extols the State to 'take reasonable legislative and other measures, within its available resources, to achieve the progressive realisation' of the right. In this sense, the formulation echoes the provisions of the 1966 International Covenant on Economic, Social and Cultural Rights (ICESCR).[11] Nevertheless, although international law remains persuasive in constitutional interpretation,[12] the enforcement of socio-economic rights in South Africa occurs largely within the domestic framework. The South African Constitutional Court has been selective, for instance, in its emulation of the jurisprudence of the UN Committee on Economic Social and Cultural Rights (CESCR).[13]

Over and above the right to water, the Constitution more generally provides a progressive and integrated framework for all rights, anchoring them to its transformative vision and focus on substantive justice.[14] This is evident in the preamble[15] and the founding provisions, which include 'human dignity, the achievement of equality and the advancement of human rights and freedoms'. In relation to equality, section 9(3) prohibits the State from unfairly discriminating 'directly or indirectly against anyone' on a number of grounds, including race and gender while section 9(2) explicitly sanctions affirmative action.[16]

[11] (Adopted 16 December 1966, entered into force 3 January 1976) 993 UNTS 3. Yet, somewhat inexplicably, South Africa only ratified the ICESCR in 2015. The reasons for this remain unclear but the answer appears to lie in departmental uncertainty over authority for preparation of shadow reports.

[12] In S v. *Makwanyane and Another* (1995 (3) SA 391 (CC), para. 35, in the context of interpreting section 39(1)(b) of the Bill of Rights, the Constitutional Court found that courts were compelled to consider both binding and non-binding international law, which would thus include the ICESCR.

[13] The minimum core content argument was raised by the (different) *amici* in both *Grootboom* and *Minister of Health and Others* v. *Treatment Action Campaign and Others (No 2)* 2002 (5) SA 721 (CC). However, the Constitutional Court declined to pursue a minimum core content approach in these (and subsequent) socio-economic rights cases, instead favouring a weaker, 'reasonableness of government programmes', test. In *Mazibuko and Others* v. *City of Johannesburg and Others* in the Johannesburg High Court (unreported case no 06/13865) (*Mazibuko High Court judgment*), Justice Tsoka suggested that the matter had not been fully resolved in *Grootboom* but this was clearly rejected by the Constitutional Court in its final decision in this case: see discussion in Section 2.5 below.

[14] See K. Klare, 'Legal Culture and Transformative Constitutionalism', *South African Journal of Human Rights*, Vol. 14 (1998), pp. 146–188.

[15] 'We the people of South Africa, recognise the injustices of the past ... we therefore ... adopt this Constitution as the supreme law of the Republic so as to heal the divisions of the past and ... improve the quality of life of all citizens and free the potential of each person'.

[16] 'Equality includes the full and equal enjoyment of all rights and freedoms. To promote the achievement of equality, legislative and other measures designed to protect or advance persons or categories of persons disadvantaged by unfair discrimination may be taken'.

In the context of water services, this means not only that no water-related programme or policy may unfairly discriminate against any group of historically disadvantaged people (for example, any water credit control measure must not be imposed only on poor communities), but also that any discrimination in favour of historically disadvantaged people will not amount to unfair discrimination and is acceptable (meaning, for example, that water tariffs for the same level of consumption can be set lower in poor communities than in richer communities).

Protection of the right of access to sufficient water is significantly bolstered by section 33 of the Constitution, which establishes everyone's right to 'just administrative action that is lawful, reasonable and procedurally fair'. National legislation must be enacted to give effect to these rights, and the Promotion of Administrative Justice Act 3 of 2000 (PAJA) was adopted with this purpose. These protections are important because water services, whether publicly or privately undertaken, are *public* services, falling within the definition of administrative action. If anyone's rights are adversely affected by an administrative action (for example, a decision to disconnect water supply for non-payment), such action can be reviewed.[17]

Finally, the Constitution guarantees three other rights that directly intersect with the right to water in the sense that without adequate access to water, these rights are adversely impacted.[18] These are the right to inherent dignity (Section 10), right to health care (Section 27(1)(a)), and protection from eviction without an order of court, which effectively prohibits the practice of disconnecting water services to effect an otherwise unlawful constructive eviction (Section 26(3)).[19]

It should be noted that there is not an explicit right to adequate sanitation in the Constitution. However, it could be inferred from the right of access to housing in section 26 and the right to a healthy environment in section 24.

[17] There is some debate as to whether mechanised action, such as that effected by a prepayment water metre, can be considered to be administrative action, since it is initiated by a machine rather than by an administrator and hence it is difficult to review it as a decision: See Section 2.5. However, regardless of such debates, there are procedural protections in the Water Services Act 108 of 1997 (discussed below), which cover all disconnections, whether by an administrator or a prepayment metre.

[18] We do not include here the right to life (section 11), which we take as self-evidently related to the right to water. We also do not include other less directly related rights such as environmental rights (section 24) and cultural and religious rights (sections 30 and 31).

[19] Indeed, the Lands Claim Court has suggested that if the disconnection, denial or limitation of access to water services or supplies forces a resident to leave their home, then this amounts to a constructive eviction and is thereby regulated by constitutional provisions concerning forced eviction. See *Van der Walt & others* v. *Lang & others Case No. 102/98 (LCC); Dhladhla & others* v. *Erasmus* Case No. 11/98 (LCC).

In *Beja and Others* v. *Premier Western Cape and Others*,[20] the Western Cape High Court adopted such an approach and gave the right to sanitation genuinely meaningful content in terms of section 27 of the constitution and the rights to dignity and privacy. The Court also held that the Local Government: Municipal Systems Act 32 of 2000 echoes the constitutional precepts and obliges a municipality to provide all members of communities with 'the minimum level of basic municipal services', which includes the provision of sanitation and toilet services.[21] Whether this constitutional interpretation would pass muster in the Constitutional Court is unknown: In *Nokotyana and Others* v. *Ekurhuleni Metropolitan Municipality*,[22] the Court did not engage with the argument despite its airing by the applicants. In any case, section 2 of the Water Services Act, as well as the Strategic Framework for Water Services,[23] provides statutory recognition of the 'right to basic sanitation'.

### 2.2 *Additional Rights-Friendly Legislation and Regulations*

Bolstering the rights-based framework for water services are several pieces of legislation and regulations, which are aimed at protecting procedural and substantive aspects of water services. The National Water Act creates a comprehensive framework for the management of water resources, with a focus on water demand management. While recognising that water is a scarce resource, it emphasises the need for redistribution to ensure equal access to water for all[24] and gives priority to basic uses in allocative decisions.[25]

The main legal instrument governing accessibility and domestic water services is the Water Services Act. Section 3(1) sets out everyone's 'right of access to basic water supply and basic sanitation' and establishes that every water services institution must 'take reasonable measures to realise these rights'. In significant detail, the Act obliges every 'water institution' to take reasonable measures towards progressive realisation of the right to water, including developing plans and submitting to a system of monitoring; sets

[20] *Beja & Ors* v. *Premier Western Cape & Others* (Unreported), Western Cape High Court Case No. 21332/10, 29 April 2011.

[21] See further discussion of the case in Chapter 10 on sanitation in this book.

[22] *Nokotyana and Others* v. *Ekurhuleni Metropolitan Municipality* 2010 (4) BCLR 312 (CC).

[23] DWAF 'Strategic Framework for Water Services: Water is life, sanitation is dignity' (September 2003).

[24] National Water Act 36 of 1998, preamble.

[25] Ibid., Schedule 1. See discussion on this part of the Act by van Koppen in Chapter 2 in this volume.

the conditions for provision of water; requires that water services institutions give priority to ensuring basic access for all; and mandates that tariffs take into account the right to water as well as operational efficiency. The definition of basic water supply (although not sanitation), is set out in regulation 3 of the Compulsory National Standards. The standard is:

(b) a minimum quantity of potable quantity of water of 25 litres per person per day or 6 kilolitres per household per month –
   i. at a minimum flow rate of not less than 10 litres per minute;
   ii. within 200 metres of a household; and
   iii. with an effectiveness such that no consumer is without a supply for more than seven full days in any year.[26]

The Water Services Act also sets out procedures for the limitation or discontinuation of water services, which must be 'fair and equitable'; 'provide for reasonable notice of intention to limit or discontinue water services and for an opportunity to make representations'; and 'not result in a person being denied access to basic water services for non-payment, where that person proves, to the satisfaction of the relevant water services authority, that he or she is unable to pay for basic services'.[27] These protections are important because they not only establish a procedural protocol that must be followed prior to disconnection, but they stipulate that notwithstanding any procedural processes, basic water services cannot be denied to people who cannot afford to pay for such services.[28]

The Municipal Systems Act governs the provision of water services at the municipal level, reinforcing the emphasis on equitable access to water services. Section 4(2)(f) stipulates that municipalities must 'give members of the local community equitable access to the municipal services to which they are entitled' and, in relation to tariffs, section 74(2)(c) establishes that 'poor households must have access to at least basic services' through 'special' or 'life line' tariffs for 'low levels of use or consumption of services or for basic levels of service' and/or 'any other direct or indirect method of subsidisation", including cross-subsidisation by richer water users. Further legislation on tariffs is found in the Norms and Standards In section 2, water services are to be charged for according to a rising block tariff structure, forcing high quantity

[26] Regulations relating to Compulsory National Standards and Measures to Conserve Water, GN R509 in GG 22355 of 8 June 2001.

[27] Water Services Act 108 of 1997, Section 4(3).

[28] The procedural aspect of section 4(3) of the Water Services Act is echoed in section 3(2)(b) of PAJA, which requires that in order to be fair, administrative procedures for the disconnection or limitation of water supply need to, inter alia, provide adequate notice of the proposed action and reasonable opportunity to make representations regarding the action.

water luxury-end users to cross-subsidise low quantity users. The pricing structure is to include 'three or more tariff blocks with the tariff increasing for higher consumption blocks' and a 'first block or lowest block . . . set at the lowest amount, including, a zero amount'.[29]

### 2.3 *Water and Sanitation Policy*

Complementing the legislative schema are several official documents on water and sanitation, including four previous Department of Water Affairs and Forestry (DWAF)[30] White Papers.[31] They reinforce the social justice aspect of water services, albeit within a cost-recovery paradigm, which is discussed further below. For instance, the 1994 White Paper stipulated that 'where poor communities are not able to afford basic services, government may subsidise the cost of construction of basic minimum services *but not the operating, maintenance or replacement costs*'.[32]

Significantly advancing the concept of social justice, the water services framework has since 2001 included the national Free Basic Water (FBW) policy, which has been followed by a proposal for a national Free Basic Sanitation (FBS) policy as set out in the 2003 Strategic Framework for Water Services. The idea for both was first announced in the run-up to the December 2000 municipal government elections,[33] and in the wake of South Africa's worst recorded cholera outbreak, which has been attributed to the disconnection of water supply to thousands of poor people in rural KwaZulu/

[29] Section 2(e) also reiterates the principle that 'all households' must have access to 'basic water supply and basic sanitation'.

[30] Renamed the Department of Water and Environmental Affairs in 2009 and later Department of Water of Sanitation, but referred to as DWAF throughout this paper for the sake of convenience.

[31] *Water Supply and Sanitation White Paper* (1994), *White Paper on a National Water Policy for South Africa* (1997), *White Paper on Basic Household Sanitation* (2001) and *White Paper on Water Services* (2002).

[32] DWAF, *Water Supply and Sanitation White Paper*, 1994 (emphasis added), p. 19. The 1997 *White Paper on a National Water Policy for South Africa* stated: 'to promote the efficient use of water, the policy will be to charge users for the full financial costs of providing access to water, including infrastructure, development and catchment management activities', (p. 4). In effect, these early pronouncements on the cost-recovery paradigm for water services signaled that a retreat from the progressive water premise articulated in the RDP had begun almost at the same time the ANC took office. Nevertheless, legislation and policy continued to be formulated in social justice terms and it has only really been since the devolution of water services to the local government level that the cost-recovery emphasis has taken hold.

[33] Then South African President Thabo Mbeki first publicly committed the government to free basic services (both water and electricity) at the Congress of South African Trade Unions (Cosatu) in September 2000.

Natal following the commercialisation of water services in the area.[34] Translated into national policy via the Free Basic Water Implementation Strategy,[35] the policy extends to each household a free minimum quantity of potable water, benchmarked at six kilolitres (6 kL, which is 6,000 litres) per household per month. This translates into 25 litres per capita per person per day (25 lcd) working on an average of eight persons per household. However, it was intended that municipalities should move away from this minimal amount, to provide additional FBW, as soon as they are able to do so. This occurred in some municipalities.[36]

According to the FBW Implementation Strategy, municipalities were meant to implement the policy with immediate effect from 2002. In order to assist municipalities, the national government provides some funding to each municipality. This 'equitable share' is allocated according to the number of poor households per municipality. Although it is an unconditional grant, meaning that it is not ring-fenced and can be allocated at the municipalities' discretion.

Although introduced as a political salvo in the context of municipal elections, the FBW policy was in fact outlined in the ANC's 1994 RDP, which spoke of 'a lifeline tariff to ensure that all South Africans are able to afford water services' with 'a clean, safe water supply of 20–30 litres per capita per day (lcd) within 200 meters'.[37] Interestingly, it was only viewed as a short-term policy. It was complemented by a 'medium-term' aim of providing an 'on-site supply of 50–60 lcd of clean water'.[38]

Finally, the DWAF, *Strategic Framework for Water Services* (2003), with its slogan 'Water is life, sanitation is dignity', provided an over-arching policy umbrella for the water services sector, aligning legislation and policies with strategic goals. One of these goals was the transformation of DWAF into a

[34] See E. Cottle and H. Deedat, 'The Cholera Outbreak: A 2000–2002 Case Study of the Source of the Outbreak in the Madlebe Tribal areas, uThungulu Region, KwaZulu/Natal' (Rural Development Service Network and International Labour Resource and Information Group, ILRIG, 2002).

[35] In two versions of this policy document – the first in 2001 and the second in 2002.

[36] DWAF, 'Free Basic Water Implementation Strategy' (August 2002), p. 8; DWAF, 'Strategic Framework for Water Services: Water is Life, Sanitation is Dignity' (September 2003), p. 29.

[37] ANC, *Reconstruction and Development Programme (RDP)*, paras. 2.6.10.1 and 2.6.6.

[38] Ibid., para. 2.6.7. Progressive commentators understood the lifeline reference to be a reference to zero-rated, free water services; and the stipulated amounts to relate to the free allocation. This was also in line with section 2(c) of the Norms and Standards, which refers to a zero-rated first block within the water tariff structure. It is also consistent with Regulation 3(b) of the Compulsory National Standards and the interpretation in DWAFs 2002 FBW Implementation Strategy, para. 3.3.

national sector regulatory body. Yet, despite various strategy papers published by DWAF, no national water regulatory body has been established.

Indeed, the last five years have been typified by regulatory stasis. There have been no new major policy initiatives and draft documents (like the 2012 Draft National Sanitation Policy) have remained drafts.[39] Instead, there is only the technocratic adjustment of targets such as contained in the 2014 Medium-Term Strategic Framework – with targets to increase 'functional water service' coverage from 85 to 90 per cent between 2013 and 2019, and 'functional sanitation' from 84 to 90 per cent.[40] Most of the national policy action has instead centred around the use and allocation of national water resources – which has been welcomed warmly from some from a rights perspective and less so by others.[41]

### 2.4 *Devolution to Municipalities and the Corporatisation of Water Services*

In December 2000, South Africa's first full democratic local government elections were held, marking the final stage of the institutional transition from apartheid, which had begun with the historic national and provincial elections in April 1994.[42] Consequently, it was only from 2001 that local government began to function properly in a manner envisaged in the Constitution. The creation of autonomous spheres of government (national, provincial and local) was a product of political compromise – a concession by the ANC to the other main parties (notably the Inkatha Freedom Party, with its support base in KwaZulu/Natal, and the then Democratic Party, with its support base in Cape Town) to afford them some zone of political dominance.

Part of this devolution was a constitutionally-entrenched division of functions, in which water services became a local government mandate.[43] According to Section 152 of the Constitution, municipalities, within their 'financial and administrative capacity' are to 'provide democratic and accountable government for local communities', ensure service provision 'in a sustainable manner', promote 'social and economic development' and 'a safe and healthy

39 Statistics South Africa, *GHS Series VIII: Water and Sanitation: 2002-2016 report* (Government of South Africa, 2016), p. 19.

40 Ibid., p. 20.

41 See D. Takecs, 'South Africa and the Human Rights to Water: Equity, Ecology, and the Public Interest Doctrine', *Berkeley Journal of International Law*, Vol. 34, No. 2 (2016), pp. 55–108.

42 Elections were held between 1995 and 1996 for transitional local government structures but the Municipal Demarcation process took another four years.

43 Schedule 4B of the Constitution.

environment' and encourage community participation in local governance. In the event of conflict between these objectives, the Constitution appears to favour realising basic needs.[44]

The Water Services Act places similar obligations on municipalities when they act as water service authorities, which is common. Section 11(1) states that every water services authority 'has a duty to all consumers or potential consumers in its area of jurisdiction to progressively ensure efficient, affordable, economical and sustainable access to water services'. However, this duty is made subject to various conditions such as 'the availability of resources', the 'need for an equitable allocation of resources',[45] 'need to regulate access to water services in an equitable way', 'duty of consumers to pay reasonable charges', 'duty to conserve water resources', 'nature, topography, zoning and situation of the land in question' and right of the authority to 'limit or discontinue the provision' if there is a 'failure to comply with reasonable conditions'.

While this governance structure might be justified as means of matching spheres of governance and accountability with spheres of delivery, it has had serious implications for the way in which water services are framed. With the devolution of political power and functional autonomy to the local level, municipalities are under considerable pressure to become financially self-sufficient, and they are precluded from deficit budgeting. Indeed, payments for electricity and water services soon accounted for approximately fifty per cent of aggregated municipal revenue.[46] As is increasingly evident, the incorporation by most municipalities of vast areas of poverty-stricken, historically black residential and rural areas has meant that the majority of municipalities are struggling to break even. The pressure to become financially viable is strong and water officials and authorities often easily accommodated themselves to strong cost-recovery policies and a role of 'debt-collectors'.[47]

In South Africa, there was an experimentation with privatisation but it was sporadic and short-lived. Shortly after coming to office in 1994, the new

[44] Section 153(a) provides that a municipality must 'structure and manage its administration, and budgeting and planning processes to *give priority to the basic needs* of the community, and to promote the social and economic development of the community'. Emphasis added. However, it may be equally arguable that the section applies to both: that municipal processes must be geared towards prioritisation of basic needs and economic and social development as opposed to any other possible objectives.

[45] For both 'consumers and potential consumers'.

[46] N. Seidman, 'Local Government Budgets and Development', unpublished paper (March 2006), p. 8.

[47] This (regretted but realistic) title was expressed by several water services officials at a meeting in August 2011 in Cape Town of the Water Research Commission to discuss a research project on Water Demand Management Devices.

government signalled an intention to commercialise and privatise water services, stating 'the Department [of Water Affairs and Forestry] will consider proposals for the private sector to provide services where these may be in the public interest and where this approach is supported by the community concerned'.[48] Yet, in fact, at the height of the drive towards privatisation in the beginning of the 2000s, there were only two outright private water concessions in South Africa.[49] Nevertheless, between 1998 and 2004, a quasi-privatisation model was folllowed with corporatisation of water services and occasional awarding of management contracts. The multinational corporations Suez (ex-Lyonnaise des Eaux) was awarded a five-year contract to manage Johannesburg's water services in 2001, and several public-private partnerships were pursued in the Eastern Cape.

Most of these concessionary arrangements were terminated by municipalities relatively quickly or not renewed by municipalities, and indeed, the government has subsequently not pursued any further private water concessions. Part of the reason was significant popular resistance, such as a nationwide anti-privatisation strike in July 2002 organised by the main trade union confederation, the Congress of South African Trade Unions (COSATU), as well as the kind of localised resistance to outright privatisation by residents of Soweto as outlined later in this chapter, which was viewed as antithetical to attempts to distribute water services more equitably across the country.[50]

However, the causes of the abandonment of privatisation are likely to be diffuse. Comparative research generally finds that political resistance is only one factor; privatisation tends to be embraced by indebted municipalities (yet, municipal debt is not permitted in South Africa) and large municipalities on the grounds of economies of scale (yet, most municipalities in South Africa are of a medium-size).[51] Thus, these structural factors may equally lower rates

[48] Department of Water Affairs and Forestry (DWAF, 1994) 'Water Supply and Sanitation Policy White Paper', p. 12. For more analysis see D. McDonald and G. Ruiters, 'Theorizing Water Privatizations in Southern Africa', in D. McDonald and G. Ruiters (eds.), *The Age of Commodity: Water Privatization in Southern Africa* (London: Earthscan), pp. 13–42.

[49] These are: a 30-year private concession awarded in 1999 to Siza Water Company, majority owned by French multinational SAUR Services, to provide water services to Dolphin Coast (iLembe), and a 30-year private concession awarded in 1999 to a subsidiary of United Kingdom multinational Biwater to provide water services to Nelspruit (Mbombela).

[50] P. Bond and J. Dugard, 'The Case of Johannesburg Water: What Really Happened at the Prepayment 'Parish Pump', *Law, Democracy and Development*, Vol. 12, No. 1 (2008), pp. 1–28.

[51] For articulation of these factors generally, see G. Bel and X. Fageda, 'Factors Explaining Local Privatization: A Meta-Regression Analysis', *Public Choice*, Vol. 139, Nos. 1–2 (2009), pp. 105–119. See also discussion in Chapter 13 of this volume.

of privatisation in South Africa. Moreover, the period corresponds with a diminished appetite on the part of multinational companies for privatising the water supplies in emerging markets.[52] Additionally, in South Africa, the imposition by national government of the Free Basic Water (FBW) policy in 2001, which required all households to be provided with at least six kilolitres of free water per month, further undermined the prospect of profiteering from private water concessions.

Notwithstanding a retreat from outright privatisation, the corporate form was maintained in many cases after these experiments. For example, within this strategy, Johannesburg Water (Pty) Limited (Johannesburg Water) was established in 2001 as a ring-fenced corporation and the City's water services provider,[53] but operating as a wholly municipally-owned corporation. More generally, water services are pursued within an ideationally commercial paradigm.[54] In the South African context, this has entailed highlighting the role of water mainly as an economic good[55] and attempting to reduce price distortions, albeit while pursuing a limited form of obligatory means-tested subsidy in the form of the minimal FBW allocation, as well as the often ineffective rising block tariffs.[56] At the same time, poorer municipalities in particular are under considerable financial pressure as the municipal revenue model is still based on the much smaller apartheid boundaries and does not appropriately take into account the post-2000 incorporation of vast impoverished townships, peri-urban areas and rural settlements with hardly any ability to pay for water services.

## 2.5 *Jurisprudence*

The most significant judgment for the right to water, until recently, was the *Grootboom* judgment. Even though it concerned another right, it articulated

[52] See for example the analysis by C. Ogunbiyi, a project finance associate at international legal firm Cadwalader, Wickersham and Taft, who reported in 2004 that 'PPPs have not had much success in Africa's water sector' ('PPPs: Fad or good for SADC?' *SADC PPP Pathway*, SADC Banking Association PPP Capacity Building Programme Newsletter No. 1 (1 July 2004).

[53] City Power (Pty) Limited and Pikitup (Pty) Limited were established as the City's electricity and refuse service providers respectively.

[54] In many municipalities a genuinely commercial approach simply is not possible, yet the same cost-recovery model is applied to all municipalities regardless of their capacity and ability to extract revenue from non-poor households and industry, etc.

[55] The 1997 White Paper on a National Water Policy for South Africa explained: 'to promote the efficient use of water, the policy will be to charge users for the full financial costs of providing access to water, including infrastructure, development and catchment management activities'.

[56] See further discussion in Section 5.

State obligations for all socio-economic rights in the Constitution. In case of the right to housing, it opined that the authorities must take 'measures' to:

> [E]stablish a coherent public housing program directed towards the progressive realisation of the right of access to adequate housing within the State's available means. The program must be capable of facilitating the realisation of the right. The precise contours and content of the measures to be adopted are primarily a matter for the Legislature and the Executive. They must, however, ensure that the measures they adopt are reasonable.[57]

The Court went on to state that the measures must be 'comprehensive, coherent, coordinated', with appropriate allocation of 'financial and human resources', 'balanced and flexible' with provision for 'short, medium and long-term needs', 'reasonably conceived and implemented', 'transparent' and made 'known effectively to the public'.[58]

Senior officials in the DWAF acknowledged that this legal precedent affected policy calculations: if reasonable progress was not achieved fast enough, there was a concern that the DWAF could be subject to litigation.[59] In their research, Gilbert and Budlender found a similar *Grootboom* effect across a number of departments concluding that 'the government has begun factoring these issues into its budgetmaking processes and has become far more responsive to lawyers'.[60]

The Constitutional Court has also established some permissive principles that permit authorities to adopt equitable or pro-poor approaches in setting tariffs for local services. In *City Council of Pretoria* v. *Walker*,[61] the Court suggested that cross-subsidisation *per se* among consumers and that differentiation in tariffs for services is not unconstitutional.[62] The Court found that a policy of charging flat rates in a predominantly black community and

[57] *Government of the Republic of South Africa and Others* v. *Grootboom and Others* 2000 (11) BCLR 1169 (CC), para. 41.

[58] S. Liebenberg, 'South Africa: Adjudicating Rights under a Transformative Constitution', in M. Langford (ed.), *Social Rights Jurisprudence: Emerging Trends in International and Comparative Law* (Cambridge: Cambridge University Press, 2009), p. 85.

[59] C. Human, 'The Human Right to Water in Africa: The South African Example', in E. Riedel & P. Rothen (eds.), *The Human Right to Water* (Berlin: Berliner WissenschaftsVerlag, 2006), pp. 83–93.

[60] G. Marcus and S. Budlender, *A Strategic Evaluation of Public Interest Litigation in South Africa*, (Johannesburg, SA: The Atlantic Philanthropies, 2008).

[61] *City Council of Pretoria* v. *Walker*, 1998 (3) BCLR 257 (CC).

[62] The Court stated at para. 42 that 'There may be cases where it is not unfair to charge according to different rates for the same services; it seems to me to be inconsistent with the equality jurisprudence developed by this Court to hold that all cross-subsidisation is precluded by sect 8(2) of the 1993 Constitution'.

consumption-based rates in a neighbouring white community was necessary in order to ensure that disadvantaged communities enjoy access to basic services.[63] The flat rate was permissible 'while phasing in equality in terms of facilities and resources, during a difficult period of transition'.[64]

Many of the initial decisions concerning water itself concerned disconnection. In *Residents of Bon Vista Mansions* v. *Southern Metropolitan Local Council*,[65] the applicants of a housing complex had sought interim relief on an urgent basis for the reconnection of their water supply. The Court held that disconnection by a local authority is a *prima facie* breach of the Water Services Act provisions when read in light of its constitutional duty to respect the right of existing access to water. Similarly in *Highveldrige Residents Concerned Party* v. *Highveldridge Transitional Local Council and Others*,[66] the local authority was directed to reinstate water supply as a form of interim relief. While the judgment primarily deals with the *locus standi* of the applicant, the Court made an assessment of the balance of convenience. It reasoned that any potential pecuniary losses of the respondents could not outweigh the human need and suffering that would occur due to the lack of fresh water, referring to both sections 27 and 28 of the Constitution.

However, a High Court judgment in a prior case took a much more cautious approach to a situation where an individual could not pay on a regular basis. In *Manqele* v. *Durban Transitional Metropolitan Council*,[67] the applicant was an unemployed woman who resided in a flat owned by the municipality with her seven children. The water supply was disconnected due to non-payment and the applicant launched an application for reconnection on the basis of the Water Services Act. As the regulations defining the extent of the right in Section 3 had not yet been promulgated, Justice Duner held that this section was not justiciable.[68] The applicant also argued that she was entitled to continued access to water despite her inability to pay as per Section 4(3)(c). However, the judge responded that since the applicant had

[63] However, selective enforcement of payment for tariffs (not forming part of the special measures) was held to be a violation the non-discrimination clause.

[64] *City Council of Pretoria* v. *Walker*, para 27.

[65] *Residents of Bon Vista Mansions* v. *Southern Metropolitan Local Council*, 2002 (6) BCLR 625 (W).

[66] *Highveldrige Residents Concerned Party* v. *Highveldridge Transitional Local Council and Others*, High Court (Transvaal Provincial Division), Case No. 28521/2001, 17 May 2002, 705.

[67] *Manqele* v. *Durban Transitional Metropolitan Council* 2002, 2 All SA 39 (D).

[68] This holding was made despite the right to water being itself a justiciable right under the Constitution. It has been argued that the failure to promulgate the regulations itself should have been considered as a violation of the right to water under the Act as read with section 27(1)(b) of the Constitution.

used more water than that is available under the respondent's free water policy, she could not rely on the protection under this section.[69]

This conservative spirit was revived in the later judgment of the Constitutional Court in *Mazibuko and Others* v. *City of Johannesburg and Others* (*Mazibuko*).[70] The potential justiciable reach of the right to water was tempered in relation to the three areas discussed above: namely, progressive realisation, equitable access and disconnections. In this case, residents in Phiri, Soweto had argued that the City's FBW policy was insufficient to meet the basic needs (including waterborne sanitation) of poor, multi-dwelling households, where as many as twenty people had to share the single 6 kL FBW allocation. They also challenged the installation of prepayment meters on the grounds that they amount to an unlawful disconnection and breached the right to equality as they were only implemented in poor areas.[71] A broader attack was also made on the Compulsory National Standards where a 'minimum quantity of potable water of 25 litres per person per day or 6 kilolitres per household per month', in particular that it does not provide for 'sufficient' water as provided for in the Constitution and was irrationally determined.

The High Court ruled in favour of the applicants on the first two arguments declaring the prepayment meters unlawful and unconstitutional and the City's FBW policy unreasonable. The City was ordered to provide the applicants and all similarly positioned residents with 50 litres of FBW per person per day.[72] The judgment was appealed by the authorities to the Supreme Court of Appeal (SCA), which to a certain extent ruled in favour of the Phiri residents: finding PPMs unlawful (largely on the procedural ground that the City's bylaws only allowed installation in specific cases) and the City's FBW policy

69 'The applicant chose however not to limit herself to the water supply provided to her free of charge by the respondent, but to consume additional quantities of water in respect of which she has an obligation to pay. . . .This in my view, takes the applicant outside the ambit of being a person contemplated by section 4(3)(c)'. The respondent's policy later received national legislative imprint under the Regulations to the Water Services Act referred to above.

70 *Mazibuko and others* v. *City of Johannesburg and others* 2010 (4) SA 1 (CC) (*Mazibuko* Constitutional Court judgment).

71 The applicants' challenge to the meters was based on a number of legal arguments including the following: the decision to install them in Phiri without any prior consultation with residents violated section 4(1) PAJA; the rollout in only poor, black areas, despite the evidence of bad debt in all areas, amounted to unfair discrimination based on race; the automatic disconnection mechanism contravened procedural protections (reasonable notice and opportunity to make representation prior to disconnection) of section 4(3) of the Water Services Act; and the City's water bylaws do not allow for their installation except as a punitive measure for contravening the terms of a standpipe supply.

72 *Mazibuko* High Court judgment.

unreasonable.[73] It ordered the City to reformulate its policy with a view to providing 42 litres per person per day to indigent residents of Phiri.[74] The Phiri residents decided to appeal the judgment to the Constitutional Court because they felt there were serious problems with the SCA's order, particularly its suspension of the order of invalidity regarding the meters.[75]

On 8 October 2009, the Constitutional Court delivered its judgment, ruling against the Phiri residents on all grounds.[76] In relation to the claim for increased quantity under the FBW, the Court rejected the applicants' claims that the policy favoured the rich, unreasonably used the average-sized households as a basis for measurement, was insufficient for large households, and was inflexible or relied on a flawed system to help indigent resident obtain additional amounts of free water. They further affirmed that the City is under no obligation to provide a free minimum basic water supply even though it had done so.[77] The Court largely came to the positions on the basis that the FBW policy provided a reasonable way of addressing the challenges of designing an effective policy within financial and administrative constraints. The Court further established that the City had the power to introduce prepayment meters and that they did not amount to 'disconnection or limitation' of water supply. This was because the 'discontinuation … may be undone by the purchase of prepayment vouchers or the renewal of the basic water supply at the end of every month'.[78] While the Court reaffirmed the principle of substantive equality, they rejected the applicants' argument that the selective introduction of the meters discriminated in practice against poor or black neighbourhoods. It was justified by an effort to reduce water wastage and unaccounted-for water in Soweto. The judgment was not anticipated and its findings in constitutional and administrative law have been the subject of academic critique,[79] in particular its 'deferential and normatively thin concept

[73] *City of Johannesburg and Others* v. *Mazibuko and Others* 2009 (3) SA 592 (SCA) (*Mazibuko* SCA judgment).

[74] For a critique of the *Mazibuko* SCA judgment, see J. Dugard and S. Liebenberg, 'Muddying the Waters: The Supreme Court of Appeal's judgment in the *Mazibuko* case', *ESR Review*, Vol. 10, No. 2 (2009), pp. 11–17.

[75] The SCA suspended its order of invalidity regarding PPMs, giving the City two years in which to 'legalise the use of prepayment water metres in so far as it may be possible to do so'. *Mazibuko* SCA judgment, para. 62.

[76] *Mazibuko* Constitutional Court judgment. It is only the second judgment in the Court's history of socio-economic rights adjudication in which it did not grant *any* relief to the applicants (*Soobramoney* v. *Minister of Health, KwaZulu-Natal* 1998 (1) SA 765 (CC) was the other.

[77] *Mazibuko*, ibid., para 85. [78] Ibid., para. 124.

[79] See S. Liebenberg, *Socio-Economic Rights: Adjudication Under a Transformative Constitution* (Cape Town: Juta, 2010), pp. 466–480, and L. Williams, 'The Role of Courts in

of reasonableness review'[80] and its characterisation of prepayment meters as not violating entrenched procedural protections.[81] However, the legal mobilisation in the case has produced some unexpected and surprising results in water policy despite the decision of the Constitutional Court as we shall see in Section 6.

## 3 RHETORIC AND REALITIES

Taken collectively, South African legislation and policy suggests a dignified, equitable and just approach to water services, in which everyone has access to adequate, safe and affordable water and sanitation. Official statistics paint a somewhat rosy picture on the rollout of basic services. In the first decade, state efforts appear impressive: 13.4 million had been provided with a basic water supply through different government programmes.[82] Turning to the next decade, and if one uses the international MDG-based indicator, the change is equally dramatic: there is an increase in 'improved drinking water supply' from 60.9 per cent to 92 per cent in the period 2002 to 2016. Using South Africa's standard approach, which focuses more on degree of access rather than quality, the change is less dramatic.[83] In 2002, 85 per cent of 13.4 million households (average of 3.6 persons) had access to piped water *or* tap water in the dwelling, off-site or on-site; a figure that increased to 89.4 per cent in 2015.[84] With regard to sanitation, it is difficult to locate the necessary time series data. However, according to the government, access to a basic ('improved') level of sanitation increased from 62.3 per cent in 2002 to 80 per cent in 2015.[85] The improvement is greater in numerical terms than water. Indeed, a DWAF strategic overview of the water sector examining similar figures argues that there has been an improvement of 59 per cent in the period 1994–2010; the gap remains much more substantial that for water.

However, the reality on the ground (for both water and sanitation) is far more complex and, to varying degrees, problematic from a rights-based

the Quantitative Implementation of Social and Economic Rights: A Comparative Study', *Constitutional Court Review*, Vol. 3 (2010), pp. 141–199.

80 Liebenberg, *Socio-Economic Rights*, ibid., p. 480. For an extensive analysis of the decision see M. Langford, R. Stacey and D. Chirwa, 'The Right to Water', in S. Woolman, M. Bishop and J. Brickhall (eds.), *Constitutional Law of South Africa* (Cape Town: Juta/UCT Press, 2011).

81 G. Quinot, 'Substantive Reasoning in Administrative-Law Adjudication', *Constitutional Court Review*, Vol. 3 (2010), pp. 111–139.

82 H. Muller, 'The South African Experience on Legal, Institutional and Operational Aspects of the Right to Water and Sanitation', *Aquatic Procedia*, Vol. 2 (2014), pp. 35–41, at 38.

83 Statistics South Africa, *GHS Series VIII*, p. 26.

84 See Statistics South Africa, *GHS Series VIII*, p. 25.

85 Ibid., p. 70.

perspective. Millions of poor South Africans (and non-South African residents) still do not access adequate basic services. This reality belies the official statistics. There are five main reasons for this.[86] First, there are strong regional disparities. For example, in the Eastern Cape the level of access to improved drinking water source was 60.9 per cent in 2002, rising to 75.7 per cent by 2015.[87] Access to improved sanitation in Limpopo province was 54 per cent and in Mpumalanga it was 65.8 per cent. Second, national statistics on household connections to basic services derive from municipal data, which in many instances are not properly verified. Third, most data are aggregated, which means that entrenched inequalities in terms of which sectors/areas remain under-serviced are not readily highlighted. Some recent statistics reveal though these differences. For example, only 87 per cent of households in the lower two income quintiles were likely to have an improved water source compared to 93, 96 and 100 per cent in the upper three income quintiles.[88] Fourth, the data for infrastructural connections are quantitative and do not incorporate critical qualitative aspects of the services that impact their adequacy, particularly from a human rights perspective. These qualitative aspects include access by women and disabled people (physical access) and affordability (economic access). Fourth, in most municipalities there is a high rate of disconnection of water and electricity services for non-payment (particularly in poor residential areas), meaning that infrastructure connection does not translate to ongoing access to basic services i.e. statistics on household connection to basic services do not reflect how many households at any specific time are currently disconnected from electricity or water services (and sanitation as well where it is waterborne, by implication of water disconnection).

It is hard to quantify basic service disconnections, and the true scale of disconnections is simply not known. Most municipalities, as well as the national government, do not keep data on disconnections or are reluctant to share such information. Furthermore, in those municipalities that have installed prepayment meters in poorer residential areas, any disconnection is 'outsourced' as a private disconnection in the person's own home and not part of the municipality's administrative record (constituting 'silent disconnections'). Nevertheless, some authors have managed to track water disconnections for specific periods. A study of the Cape Town and Tygerberg administrations indicated 159,886 households had their water disconnected for reasons of non-payment

[86] See, e.g, K. Tissington, J. Dugard and P. Berkowitz, '*Submission on access to Water and Sanitation*' *for South African Human Rights Commission's Review of Millennium Development Goals and the Realisation of Economic and Social Rights in South Africa*, 9 February 2009.

[87] Statistics South Africa, *GHS Series VIII*.

[88] Ibid.

between 1999 and 2001. Most of these households were in poor areas where people struggle to pay water bills.[89] Using national household data and data collected in a 2001 national survey, McDonald estimated that between the years 2000 and 2001, 7.5 million people experienced both water and electricity disconnections.[90] These figures were fiercely contested by the Minister for Water Affairs and Forestry. He argued that 2 per cent of the population had their water disconnected in the relevant period but acknowledged in his 2003 budget speech that the monthly rate of disconnections in the three largest municipalities was 17,800 households.[91]

Undoubtedly, rural areas are objectively worst affected by non-delivery of basic services. For example, in Amathole District Municipality, a deep rural jurisdiction in the Eastern Cape Province, approximately thirty two per cent of the population in 2008 did not have access to the basic level of provision of water and approximately eighty two per cent do not have access to a basic level of sanitation – more than tripling the average national gaps at the time.[92] It is clear that many municipalities are buckling under the pressure to eradicate backlogs. In 2008, officials from Dr J. S. Moroka Municipality in Mpumalanga Province indicated that they anticipated that it would take the municipality ten more years to eradicate water supply backlogs and twenty years for sanitation backlogs.[93]

However, the problems of non- or under-delivery also affect poor urban areas, and many people in urban informal settlements, townships and inner-city areas suffer without adequate access to water, electricity and sanitation. Indeed, the odds of households living in rural areas, non-metro, traditional and informal dwellings not having access to improved water sources were estimated in 2016 at more than 1500 times the odds of households in formal urban areas, including townships.[94] The degree of physical and affordable access is determined by whether a poor household is located in an informal settlement, township or inner-city area. In informal settlements, typically there is neither in-house

[89] L. Smith, 'Neither Public Nor Private: Unpacking the Johannesburg Water Corporatisation Model', Social Policy and Development Programme Paper Number 27, United Nations Research Institute for Social Development, (2006).

[90] D. McDonald, 'The Bell Tolls for Thee: Cost Recovery, Cutoffs, and the Affordability of Municipal Services in South Africa', in D. McDonald and J. Pape (eds.), *Cost Recovery and the Crisis of Service Delivery in South Africa* (Pretoria: HSRC, 2002), p. 170.

[91] Kasrils: Water Affairs & Forestry Dept Budget Vote 2003/2004 (06/06/2003), available at www.polity.org.za/

[92] K. Tissington, M. Dettmann, M. Langford, J. Dugard and S. Conteh, 'Water Services Fault Lines: An Assessment of South Africa's Water and Sanitation Provision across 15 Municipalities', (Johannesburg: CALS, NCHR and COHRE, October 2008), p. 26.

[93] Ibid. [94] Statistics South Africa, *GHS Series VIII*, p. 39.

water nor in-house sanitation supply, so people must rely on water tankers or communal taps, and woefully inadequate toilets. In many informal settlements, people still have to use the 'bucket system' (or the bushes), while in others there are communal chemical toilets, which require residents to purchase relatively expensive chemicals, or Ventilated Pit Latrines (VIPs), which need to be manually emptied (either by the municipality or the residents).

Turning to formal township areas, these usually have in-house water as well as waterborne sanitation. However, in many townships, municipalities have installed technical mechanisms to attempt to minimise loss of revenue due to non-payment of basic services. These include water flow-restrictors (a metal disk with a tiny hole in the middle that is inserted snugly inside the diameter of the pipe and only allows a trickle of water through), and water and electricity prepayment meters.

In inner city areas, water and electricity supply is usually in-house (multi-storey apartment), with waterborne sanitation. However, poor tenants' access to basic services is typically mediated by landlords, which can compromise access in two critical ways. First, where landlords have abandoned buildings (absentee landlords), the occupiers generally are not able to contract directly with the municipality for services as most municipalities require a letter of permission from the landlord before they will enter contracts for services directly with tenants. As a consequence, there are many inner city buildings, particularly those housing unlawful occupiers but also those where tenure security has not been regularised or has been disrupted,[95] without any formal access to basic services.[96] Second, where landlords incorporate charges for basic services as part of rental, as is common practice, complications can arise especially when landlords do not pass on the water services payments to municipal authorities.

The realities of basic services as outlined are poignantly illustrated in a description of the living conditions in Harry Gwala informal settlement. Detailing the conditions for the applicants in Harry Gwala at the time of launching the *Nokotyana* litigation in the South Gauteng High Court in July 2008, Kristen Kornienko, an architect from Polvadera, New Mexico (USA),

[95] A similar problem occurs in collapsed sectional title schemes where there is no longer a formal mechanism (body corporate) to effect payments for municipal services, leading to massive debt and disconnection of basic services.

[96] For a Johannesburg-based study of such problems, see for example A. Wafer, J. Dugard, M. Ngwenya and S. Sibanda 'A Tale of Six Buildings: The Lived-Reality of Poor People's Access to Basic Services in Johannesburg's Inner City', Centre for Applied Legal Studies (CALS), Johannesburg, 2008, http://web.wits.ac.za/Academic/CLM/Law/CALS/BasicServices/ResearchReports.htm.

described an informal settlement of 1,500 households with six taps (less than half of what would be required to meet the regulated distance standard of 200 metres). The taps were poorly maintained, leaking and one did not meet the regulated flow-rate standard of ten litres per minute. The only toilets were pit latrines, which the residents of Harry Gwala had dug and furbished themselves, and for which the residents purchase chemicals to maintain some semblance of hygiene.[97]

The results of restricted water supply can also be tragic as the following example from Soweto demonstrates. In a fire at Phiri on 27 March 2005, residents tried to using the prepayment water meter supply that the Johannesburg Water company had recently installed. However, the water pressure was insufficient and, after a while, the pre-paid meter water supply automatically disconnected due to insufficient credit. After an hour of battling the fire, it was finally put out but not before the shack had burnt to the ground killing two small children who had been asleep within it.[98]

## 4 EXPLAINING AND ASSESSING THE GAP: A QUANTITATIVE ASSESSMENT

How can the uneven progress in realisation of water and sanitation across the country be explained? More importantly, are the reasons justifiable from a human rights perspective? Even in 2017, progress remains remarkably uneven. As discussed, the duty of progressive realisation does allow a municipality to argue that time is needed to roll-out new institutional infrastructure. Moreover, the lack of available resources is a legitimate defence. However, it may be possible that these 'capacity' defences do not explain progress at the municipal level and that other factors may be at play: policy design, lack of political will, discrimination or corruption, for example.

This section adopts a quantitative approach in trying to get at this puzzle of capacity versus politics. It provides an econometric analysis of municipalities according to their performance between 2001 and 2007 (the last date of the community survey with relevant information) in terms of promoting access to and affordability of water and sanitation, adjusted for indicators of their available resources or 'capacity'. This analysis is not provided in order

[97] Affidavit of Kristen Kornienko provided by *Nokotyana* applicants' lawyer, Moray Hathorn of Webber Wentzel Attorneys in Johannesburg.

[98] P. Bond and J. Dugard, 'The Case of Johannesburg Water: What Really Happened at the Prepayment "Parish Pump"?', *Law, Democracy and Development*, Vol. 12, No. 1 (2008), pp. 1–28, at 1.

to demonstrate a violation by a municipality of an obligation under the Constitution, but rather to identify 'outlier' municipalities which appear to be performing worse than would be expected, and which may require further more detailed examination. With regard to access, the analysis is done both for access to 'basic' as well as 'adequate' water and sanitation supply. Access to 'basic' water refers to the government's RDP minimum; 'adequate' water refers to piped water in the dwelling or yard; basic sanitation refers to toilets or VIP; and adequate sanitation refers to a flush toilet. Affordability is examined with reference to the cost of 12 kL of water per month for indigent households.

### 4.1 *Access to water and sanitation*

**Differences in Access to Water and Sanitation across Municipalities**

Using data from the 2001 Census and 2007 Community Survey, we are able to calculate the proportion of households with access to basic and/or adequate water and sanitation in 2001 and 2007, in 249 municipalities across South Africa. We also calculate the change in this proportion, and some summary statistics regarding this information are shown in Table 7.1.[99] In 2001, the average proportion of households with access to basic water (across all 249 municipalities) was 68 per cent, which had risen to 71 per cent by 2007. The average increase in access to basic water was 3 percentage points. For basic sanitation, the average proportion of households with access was lower in 2001 (52 per cent), but rose by more over the period to 63 per cent in 2007. The average increase in access to basic sanitation was 12 percentage points. Average levels of access to 'adequate' (as opposed to basic) water and sanitation are lower, but show broadly similar trends over the relevant period.

Clearly however, there is a great deal of variation across municipalities, both in the percentage of households with access in each year, and in the rate of increase in access over the period. In 2007 for example, 10 per cent of municipalities still had less than 30 per cent of households with access to basic water. Similarly, between 2001 and 2007, 10 per cent of municipalities saw reductions in the percentage of households with access to basic water by 8 percentage points or more. It is precisely this variation which we set out in the next sub-section to explain.

99 For a full list, see Appendix.

TABLE 7.1 *Access to water and sanitation in South Africa by municipality, 2001 and 2007*

| | Basic water | Basic sanitation | Adequate water | Adequate sanitation |
|---|---|---|---|---|
| **Percentage of households with access, 2001** | | | | |
| - mean | 68 | 52 | 58 | 45 |
| - median | 80 | 53 | 67 | 47 |
| - std.dev | 26 | 25 | 28 | 27 |
| - 10th percentile | 26 | 17 | 13 | 8 |
| - 90th percentile | 94 | 85 | 89 | 83 |
| **Percentage of households with access, 2007** | | | | |
| - mean | 71 | 63 | 64 | 54 |
| - median | 79 | 71 | 74 | 59 |
| - std.dev | 25 | 25 | 29 | 30 |
| - 10th percentile | 30 | 26 | 17 | 13 |
| - 90th percentile | 95 | 94 | 93 | 92 |
| **Increase in percentage of households with access, 2001–2007 (percentage points)** | | | | |
| - mean | 3 | 12 | 6 | 10 |
| - median | 2 | 10 | 6 | 8 |
| - std.dev | 10 | 14 | 11 | 14 |
| - 10th percentile | −8 | −4 | −4 | −4 |
| - 90th percentile | 14 | 30 | 18 | 26 |

*Source:* Authors' calculations using Census 2001 and Community Survey 2007 data.

## Explaining Differences across Municipalities Using Econometrics

Here we use econometric analysis to assess the extent to which the variation in performance across municipalities shown in Table 7.1 can be explained by readily observable indicators of the available resources or 'capacity' of each municipality.[100] Such indicators should meet three main criteria. First, they should affect the ability of the municipality to deliver water and sanitation services; second, they should be beyond the direct control of the municipality

[100] This type of analysis has been used increasingly at the national level, as a way of assessing State parties' compliance with obligations arising under the International Covenant for Economic and Social Rights; see for example S. Randolph, S. Fukuda-Parr and T. Lawson-Remer, 'Economic and Social Rights Fulfillment Index: Country Scores and Rankings', *Journal of Human Rights*, Vol. 9, No. 3 (2010), pp. 230–261.

itself; and third, they should be widely available. On these grounds, we identify five capacity indicators, namely:

- the average income of households in the municipality;
- the inequality of household incomes in the municipality, measured by the Gini coefficient;
- the population of the municipality;
- the dependency ratio in the municipality, measured by the number of people aged below 15 or above 65 as a ratio of those aged 15–65;
- the share of the working age population in the municipality with a higher education qualification.

Some comments on the justification for these capacity indicators are worth making. Higher average income can increase a municipality's ability to deliver water and sanitation services in various ways, for example, through its association with the local tax base. If incomes in a municipality are more equal, this may also make it easier for a municipality to raise revenue through local taxation and/or cost-recovery. By contrast, a larger population – particularly when combined with a higher dependency ratio – can raise pressures on a municipality to deliver other services, e.g. for the young and/or elderly, which could potentially lower a municipality's ability to deliver water and sanitation services. The share of the local population with a higher education qualification could raise ability to deliver services, by increasing the potential supply of trained personnel. And while a municipality might have some influence over each of these indicators, direct control is clearly very limited in comparison to provincial and national levels of government. Finally, each indicator can be calculated for each municipality using the same sources used to obtain the water and sanitation data (i.e. the 2001 Census and 2007 Community Survey).

The first aim therefore is to calculate the amount of variation in levels and changes in access to water and sanitation across municipalities, as shown in Table 7.1 and the extent to which it can be accounted for by the above five capacity indicators. Two sets of regressions were carried out. In the first, the dependent variable is the proportion of households in each municipality lacking access to a certain facility in a given year, and the explanatory variables are the level of each capacity indicator in the corresponding year. In this set, there are eight regressions in total. In the second set, the dependent variable is the reduction in the proportion of households in each municipality lacking access between 2001 and 2007, and the explanatory variables include the change in the level of each capacity indicator, as well as the initial level of average income and the initial level of access (to reflect the possibility that increases in access become harder to achieve as access gets closer to 100 per cent). In this set there are four regressions in total.

The results of the econometric analysis are shown in Table 7.2. The first thing to note is that each capacity indicator generally has the expected effect on access to water and sanitation. In particular, population, inequality and the dependency ratio generally have a negative effect, while average income and education generally have a positive effect. In addition, in the second set of regressions (panel C), initial income (in 2001) has a positive impact, while initial access (in 2001) has a negative impact, which again is as expected. In the majority of cases, the estimated effects are also statistically significant at conventional levels, and in no cases do we find an effect which is both contrary to expectation and statistically significant.

The second aspect to note from Table 7.2 is that the five capacity indicators are able to explain around 60–70 per cent of the variation in levels of access across municipalities (panels A and B), but a much lower proportion (around 25–30 per cent) of the variation in changes over time (panel C). The lower figure for changes over time is common in exercises of this sort, and is most likely a reflection of measurement error in the estimates of access to water and sanitation in each municipality, which is compounded – i.e. becomes much more serious – when considering changes over time. This needs to be born in mind. Nevertheless, even when considering levels of access it is clear that a substantial amount of variation in levels of performance across municipalities cannot be explained by differences in their capacity, at least when judged by readily available capacity indicators.

### Identifying Under-Performers

We now use the results of the econometric analysis in section 3.2 to ask whether there are any municipalities whose levels of access in 2001 or 2007, or whose rates of increase of access between 2001 and 2007, were much lower than would be expected given their levels of the capacity indicators. If there are, then these municipalities might be good candidates for an assessment of their compliance with obligations in relation to the rights to water and sanitation arising under the Constitution of South Africa. These municipalities we refer to as under-performers.

In order to proceed, we first we need to define what me mean by 'much' lower. Here there is no accepted cut-off point, so two alternative approaches are used. The first identifies municipalities in which levels of access can be classified in a statistical sense as (negative) 'outliers'. More specifically, where 'residual performance' – i.e. actual performance minus expected performance, on the basis of capacity – is more than 1.5 inter-quartile ranges below the

TABLE 7.2 *Regression analysis of water and sanitation access by municipality*

| | Basic water | Basic sanitation | Adequate water | Adequate sanitation |
|---|---|---|---|---|
| **A. Dependent variable: proportion of households with access, 2001 (log odds ratio)** | | | | |
| Explanatory variables (all relate to levels in 2001): | | | | |
| Population (log) | −0.22 (0.05) | −0.15 (0.0) | −0.20 (0.05) | −0.12 (0.04) |
| Income (log) | 0.90 (0.19) | 0.89 (0.16) | 1.12 (0.19) | 1.20 (0.19) |
| Inequality | 0.49 (0.86) | −3.39 (0.71) | 0.60 (0.85) | −2.09 (0.83) |
| Dependency ratio | −2.17 (0.72) | −1.17 (0.59) | −1.68 (0.71) | −1.28 (0.70) |
| Education | −1.07 (3.12) | 4.44 (2.56) | −2.69 (3.07) | 2.32 (3.02) |
| R-squared* | 0.72 | 0.74 | 0.75 | 0.75 |
| **B. Dependent variable: proportion of households with access, 2007 (log odds ratio)** | | | | |
| Explanatory variables (all relate to levels in 2007): | | | | |
| Population (log) | −0.21 (0.05) | −0.21 (0.05) | −0.24 (0.06) | −0.20 (0.06) |
| Income (log) | 1.04 (0.28) | 1.35 (0.28) | 1.01 (0.30) | 1.54 (0.29) |
| Inequality | −4.58 (1.08) | −5.30 (1.08) | −3.60 (1.18) | −5.46 (1.14) |
| Dependency ratio | −2.69 (0.86) | −0.93 (0.86) | −3.75 (0.94) | −1.57 (0.91) |
| Education | 1.84 (3.01) | 1.22 (3.02) | 1.73 (3.30) | 3.38 (3.18) |
| R-squared* | 0.63 | 0.58 | 0.65 | 0.65 |
| **C. Dependent variable: increase in proportion of households with access, 2001–2007** | | | | |
| Explanatory variables (all relate to increases between 2001 and 2007 # | | | | |
| Population (log) | 0.04 (0.07) | −0.14 (0.10) | −0.05 (0.08) | −0.20 (0.09) |
| Average income (log) | 0.41 (0.16) | 0.66 (0.22) | 0.27 (0.19) | 0.86 (0.21) |
| Inequality | −0.25 (0.08) | −0.44 (0.12) | −0.22 (0.10) | −0.52 (0.11) |
| Dependency ratio | −0.27 (0.08) | −0.39 (0.11) | −0.46 (0.09) | −0.42 (0.11) |
| Education | −0.11 (0.25) | −0.15 (0.36) | 0.20 (0.30) | −0.20 (0.34) |
| Initial income, 2001 | 0.03 (0.02) | 0.06 (0.02) | 0.03 (0.02) | 0.07 (0.02) |
| Initial access, 2001 | −0.15(0.04) | −0.20 (0.06) | −0.07 (0.04) | −0.09 (0.05) |
| R-squared* | 0.25 | 0.30 | 0.23 | 0.36 |

*Source:* Authors' calculations using Census 2001 and Community Survey 2007 data.
*Notes:* Standard errors are shown in parentheses. Data for 249 municipalities are included in the analysis. For a full list, see the Appendix to this chapter. *The R-squared figure shows the proportion of the variation in the dependent variable which can be explained by variation in all of the explanatory variables; # except initial access and initial income which relate to levels in 2001.

TABLE 7.3 *Identifying under-performers: 'negative outliers' approach*

| | Negative outliers |
|---|---|
| A. Levels of access, 2001 | Fetakgomo (4), Kruger Park South (1), Moretele (2), Pixley ka Seme (2), Umkhanyakude (5) |
| B. Levels of access, 2007 | Ezingoleni (5), Lephalale (3), Maphumulo (4), Moretele (6), Msinga (3), Umkhanyakude (3), West Rand (3) |
| C. Increases in access, 2007 | Frances Baard (3), Greater Letaba (3), Greater Marble Hall (1), Lephalale (4), Maphumulo (4), Mookgopong (5), Ndwedwe (2), Siyanda (4), Umkhanyakude (3), West Rand (1) |

*Source:* Authors' calculations using Census 2001 and Community Survey 2007 data.
*Notes:* A negative outlier is a municipality for which the difference between the actual and expected level of access (panels A and B) or increase in access (panel C) is more than 1.5 inter-quartile ranges below the inter-quartile range of those differences. The number after each municipality indicates for which access measure(s) this applies: 1=basic and adequate water; 2=basic and adequate sanitation; 3=basic water only; 4=basic sanitation only; 5=adequate water only; 6=adequate sanitation only.

25th percentile of the residual performance scores across all municipalities. Applying this yardstick, we identify five municipalities which were underperforming in terms of levels of access in 2001, seven which were underperforming in terms of levels of access in 2007, and ten which were underperforming in terms of change in access between 2001 and 2007. These are shown in Table 7.3.

The second approach is to choose a slightly lower cut-off point, namely a residual performance (which is more than one standard deviation below mean residual performance) but at the same time identify municipalities which under-perform in both water and sanitation. The results of applying this approach are shown in Table 7.4.[101]

There are of course many reasons why a municipality might be among the lists of under-performing shown in Tables 7.3 and 7.4. These include: (a) measurement error in the variables used (e.g. sampling error); (b) other unobservable capacity indicators (e.g. training and education of water staff); and (c) a lack of political will by local authorities to meet constitutional obligations related to water and sanitation. A more detailed assessment would be required to establish which of these potential explanations accounts for

[101] This was the approach used by Anderson and Morrissey in analysing performance at the national level: E. Anderson and O. Morrissey, 'A Statistical Approach to Identifying Poorly Performing Countries', *Journal of Development Studies*, Vol. 42, No. 3 (2006), pp. 469–489.

TABLE 7.4 *Identifying under-performers: the 'Across-the-board' approach*

| | **'Across-the-board' under-performers** |
|---|---|
| A. Levels of access, 2001 | Cacadu, Kruger Park South, Mafikeng, Midvaal, Nokeng tsa Taemane, Pixley ka Seme, Rustenburg, Siyanda, Thabazimbi, Umkhanyakude, West Rand |
| B. Levels of access, 2007 | Cacadu, eNdondakusuka, Frances Baard, Knysna, Lephalale, Mafikeng, Midvaal, Modimolle, Moses Kotane, Ndwedwe, Pixley ka Seme, Rustenburg Siyanda, Umkhanyakude, West Rand |
| C. Increases in access, 2001-2007 | Greater Marble Hall, Greater Letaba, Mafikeng, Mookgopong, Siyanda, Umkhanyakude |

*Source:* Authors' calculations using Census 2001 and Community Survey 2007 data.
*Notes:* An 'across the board' under-performer is a municipality for which the difference between the actual and expected level of access (panels A and B) or increase in access (panel C) is more than one standard deviation below the average difference, for all four access measures.

under-performance in any one municipality. For this reason, the analysis in this section is designed only to be the first stage of a more concerted and on-going assessment.

### 4.2 *Affordability of Water*

As discussed in section 1, figures for access to water and sanitation can sometimes shadow different obstacles in practice. One of these is the affordability of water. This is determined for each household by their income, the price of water and sanitation services, and the cost of other essential items for the household budget (particularly those necessary to meet other socio-economic rights).[102] However, DWAF did not collect data on affordability of water as they do for physical access and quality. They did not even keep a register of tariffs which are charged across the country by the different municipalities.

[102] For example, the CESCR states that 'Water, and water facilities and services, must be affordable for all. The direct and indirect costs and charges associated with securing water must be affordable, and must not compromise or threaten the realization of other Covenant rights'. *General Comment 15, The Right to Water* (Twenty-ninth session, 2002), U.N. Doc. E/C.12/2002/11 (2003), para. 12(c)(ii).

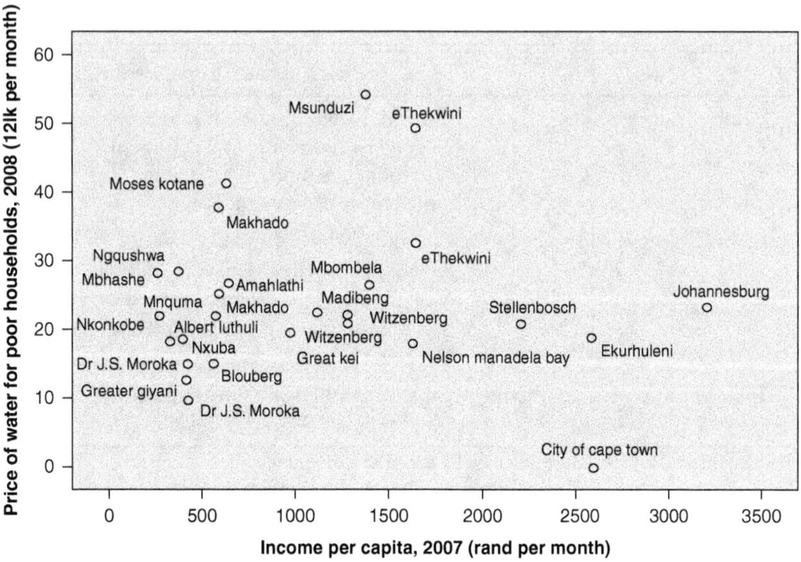


FIGURE 7.1 Affordability and municipal capacity
*Source:* Income data from Community Survey 2007; price data from Fault Lines Report.

In order to get a first look at affordability across South Africa, we focus on the financial cost of 12 kL of water per household for indigent persons per month in 2010 (see Figure 7.1). As already noted, the price of water is only one factor which affects its affordability. However, it is the factor that municipalities have most control over, and it is therefore appropriate to assess municipalities in terms of whether they are doing as much as possible to promote the economic accessibility of water, through the water tariffs that they set. Two kilolitres per month equates to what might be called a reasonable level of water for poor households: 50 litres per person per day on average for an eight-person household. This is higher than the minimum set out in the national regulations or that demanded by the Constitutional Court but accords with international standards which provide that 50 litres per person per day means an acceptable low as opposed to a high health risk. Moreover, there is a constitutional duty of progressive realisation to move beyond the minimum.

Therefore, we compare the cost of water to poor households (12 kL per month) by selected municipalities, correlated with average income of each municipality as the indicator of capacity. While we would expect the price for 12 kL to fall for higher levels of income per capita, there are quite a few outliers, such as Moses Kotane, Msunduzi, eThekwini and Johannesburg.

Unlike section 4.1, we do not use more formal econometric analysis, or a wider range of capacity indicators, mainly because our sample of municipalities is in this case substantially smaller, owing to the greater difficulties of obtaining information on the water tariffs set by each municipality in previous years. However, the graph is clear in suggesting significant variance between municipalities worth similar capacities – and some low income municipalities outperform high-capacity municipalities.

## 5 GAPS AND FAULT LINES

The discussion in the preceding sections suggests there are three principal access-related gaps in the South African water sector. The first is the *municipal capacity gap*, the strong disparity between municipalities, which appears to be only partly overcome by additional transfers from national government. The quantitative results showed that in 2001 and 2007, there is a very strong correlation between municipal capacity and overall access to water and sanitation at those points in time. This suggests increased attention needs to be given to this disconnect. In 2011, at a roundtable discussion in Johannesburg on 'Making Local Government Work', the Deputy Minister of Cooperative Governance and Traditional Affairs, Carrim, was asked: does local government have the capacity to meet its objectives as outlined by the Constitution? In answering this question, he touched on the issues at the core of this chapter's analysis, acknowledging that, not only is the one size fits all model not appropriate for most municipalities, but also, fundamentally, that:

> [T]he very premise of the current financial model is wrong. It's based on the presumption that municipalities can raise 95 per cent of their own revenue, but this was the case before 1994 when municipalities had much smaller boundaries, mostly excluded the African majority, and had a limited service delivery role! It cannot apply with the new municipalities, with their larger boundaries, significantly bigger number of residents, and expanded developmental role.[103]

In the same forum, Carrim also pointed to failures of national and provincial government to monitor and support municipalities adequately.[104] Indeed, lack of financial assistance has been frequently cited by water services authorities as a problem.[105] In this respect, it would seem that in particular for the poorer

[103] Y. Carrim cited in 'Making Local Government Work', Helen Suzman Foundation roundtable discussion, *Quarterly*, Vol. 19, May (2011), pp. 17–18.

[104] Ibid.

[105] See interviews with officials in Tissington et al., 'Water Services Fault Lines'.

municipalities, the main sources of inter-governmental financial assistance (Municipal Infrastructure Grant and the Equitable Share) are insufficient for achieving universal water coverage. This suggests that without a fundamental restructuring and redistribution of roles, functions and resources, the local government sphere will certainly collapse under the multiple political, developmental and financial pressures. As Gillian Hart argues,

> [L]ocal government has become not just *a* site of contradictions, but *the* site of contradictions in the post-apartheid era. Local government, in other words, has become the impossible terrain of official efforts to manage poverty and deprivation in a racially inflected capitalist society marked by vicious inequalities and increasingly precarious livelihoods for a large majority of the population.[106]

However, our analysis also suggests that this explanation is not absolute. The second gap is the *municipal effort gap*: there is only a partial correlation between a municipality's capacity or available resources and their performance in improving access, physical or economic, to water and sanitation. Some poor municipalities were able to move at a much faster rate than some richer and other poorer municipalities. This suggests that other local factors - whether politics, policy, administration, etc - or the structure of national policies may be highly important in explaining this gap. Indeed, the most senior water official, the Chief Director of the now Department of Water and Sanitation, recently acknowledged that the current framework – with the combination of the MIG and means-tested free basic water policy – was only a 'mixed success because it requires strong, technical, financial and managerial capacity, which were not available in all communities'.[107]

The third gap is the *reality gap*: the distance between the official rate of measured progress and the actual experiences of individuals and communities in practice. The qualitative evidence suggests that official data and measurement assumptions should be treated with caution. The responsibility for this gap potentially lies also with local and/or national policies or practices.

In relation to these latter two gaps, some of these explanatory factors have been identified in a study on 'fault lines' in the South African water sector.[108] In 2008, in-depth interviews were conducted with officials from fifteen

[106] G. Hart 'Local Government Contradictions', *South African Labour Bulletin*, Vol. 35, No. 3 (August/September 2011), pp. 32–34.

[107] H. Muller, 'The South African Experience', 39.

[108] Tissington et al., 'Water Services Fault Lines'. Two of the authors of this chapter were involved in authoring the report.

municipalities in seven different provinces[109] to gauge their attitudes and elicit factual information. This input was cross-checked against and supplemented with additional information (gleaned from Integrated Development Plans, WSDPs, publicised indigent registers and tariff and credit control policies). The information was tabled in a matrix, which plotted information about water services in each municipality across our survey questions. After efforts were made to verify data, a matrix was used to identify cross-cutting 'fault lines'. A number of these fault lines went beyond the access question (addressing quality issues for example) and there was no pretence that they represented all of the apparent problems at municipal level. Rather, they reflect what were perceived to be systemic obstacles to the provision of universal access to water services.[110]

Four findings are particularly relevant to the questions posed here: policy omissions, policy design, tariff structure and municipal governance. At its core, many of the water services-related problems experienced on the ground relate to the absence of national oversight and regulation of municipalities, as well as insufficient national funding especially to poor municipalities with limited potential to cross-subsidise from rich water users. The result is a vast range of approaches to water services, some of which do not comply with the legal and policy framework, and many of which are not appropriately pro-poor.

### 5.1 *Policy Omissions*

While some municipalities are still struggling to connect households to water and sanitation grids or systems, many more municipalities are making slow progress in ensuring adequate (as opposed to very basic) levels of water supply and sanitation – water on-site or in the yard and waterborne

[109] These were: *Western Cape Province* (City of Cape Town Metropolitan Municipality, Cape Winelands District Municipality, Stellenbosch Municipality and Witzenberg Local Municipality); *Mpumalanga* (Dr J.S. Moroka Municipality and Albert Luthuli Municipality); *Limpopo* (Lepelle-Nkumpi Local Municipality and Blouberg Municipality); *North West* (Moses Kotane Local Municipality and Local Municipality of Madibeng); *Kwazulu Natal* (eThekwini Metropolitan Municipality and Msunduzi Municipality); *Gauteng* (Ekurhuleni Metropolitan Municipality); and *Eastern Cape* (Nelson Mandela Metropolitan Municipality and Amathole District Municipality). In addition, a Vhembe District Municipality official (located in Limpopo) was also interviewed.

[110] Many of these issues were collaborated by secondary literature as well as interviews with national officials and civil society. For similar findings from a localised ethnographic study, see G. Hart, *Water is the Burning Issue: Fluid Politics and the Contradictions of Local Government*, available at www.history.ukzn.ac.za/node/1131.

sanitation. In the context of water provision, a common approach, which arguably violates the 'progressive realisation' principle is for some municipalities to focus only on providing everyone with a communal tap and not to improve any water access beyond that until all people in the municipality have communal tap access. Regarding sanitation, the majority of people who do have access to sanitation only have access to VIPs or other 'dry' forms of sanitation that do not require water. The appropriateness of VIPs and other dry systems has been questioned for humid environments where faecal matter dos not easily dry. In addition, once full, VIPs need to be emptied but in many municipalities this is not done in a timely way. Interviews revealed that some municipalities had not planned or budgeted for emptying because they thought VIPs would be a temporary measure. As noted by Eales, 'many VIPs are now full and unusable' and are now colloquially referred to as 'full-ups'.[111]

A structural difficulty in going beyond this very basic level of service, such as communal taps and VIPs, is the intrinsic relationship between water and sanitation supply and the provision of housing as part of attempts to formalise townships and informal settlements through the former National Department of Housing and/or provincial/local housing initiatives. Those living in informal settlements are often left at a very basic level of service for a long period of time while they wait to be upgraded *in situ* or to be allocated a new unit in a formal housing project. In cases of the latter approach, municipalities are reluctant to provide more water services than they absolutely have to, or improve infrastructure in informal settlements, if the aim is to move people away from the settlements in the future. The problem is that the waiting periods for both approaches are unacceptably long, with many people having been on waiting lists for better housing for more than ten years. The national 'Upgrading of Informal Settlements' housing programme,[112] has unfortunately been slow to get off the ground at all levels of government.[113] Another common problem is that many of those who are allocated new free or subsidised housing cannot afford to pay for water and electricity services, notwithstanding any FBW allocation.

[111] Cited in B. Amisi, P. Bond, D. Khumalo and S. Nojiyeza, 'The Neoliberal Loo', *Znet Commentaries* (18 February 2008).

[112] Chapter 13 of the National Housing Code (October 2004).

[113] According to M. Huchzermeyer the Government has failed to differentiate between the normative principle of the MDG slogan 'cities without slums', and the operational target of improving the levels of shackdwellers: 'Uplift slums, don't destroy them', *The Mercury* (12 July 2007).

The particularly slow progress on basic sanitation may also be explained by the absence of concrete and targeted policies. In 2001, DWAF's *White Paper on Basic Household Sanitation* specifically focused on the provision of a level of basic household sanitation to mainly rural communities and informal settlements, which it identified as the areas with the greatest need. In 2009, DWAF finalised its Free Basic Sanitation (FBSan) Implementation Strategy, however this is vague and has not been a properly implemented policy. There is very little national guidance on acceptable long-term methods and locally-appropriate forms of sanitation. The result has been a very uneven approach to sanitation provision across municipalities, and there is no common approach to the interpretation of free basic sanitation service policy by different municipalities.[114] In the absence of a coherent FBSan policy, people with waterborne sanitation often have to utilise some of their FBW allocation for sanitation, which consumes a relatively large amount of water, leaving less for drinking, bathing and washing food and clothes. In the faultlines survey, only a few municipalities appeared to take this fact into account, including Cape Town municipality, which provided 4.2 kL free sewerage (essentially a FBSan allocation) to those on the indigent register[115] with waterborne sanitation.

## 5.2 *Policy Design for Free Basic Water*

**Accessing FBW**

Contrasting with DWAF statistics, which suggest that almost everyone in South Africa receives FBW,[116] the research demonstrated that this was not the case. More than six years after DWAF's FBW policy dictated the immediate implementation of FBW, some municipalities were still not providing it. In the study of only 15, randomly selected, municipalities, one municipality – Dr J. S. Moroka – did not provide FBW. This suggested that, out of the total number of 283 municipalities, many more did not provide FBW. Moreover, it was clear that there are whole, sizeable, classes of vulnerable people who are not receiving FBW at all.

[114] N. Mjoli, G. Sykes and T. Jooste, *Towards the Realization of Free Basic Sanitation: Evaluation, Review and Recommendations*, Report to the Water Research Commission, November 2009, p. 17.

[115] The majority of municipalities use the indigent register as a mechanism for FBW allocation. The problems with this practice are discussed in part 4.4 below.

[116] See DWAF, Free Basic Water Project Implementation Status (November 2011), www.dwaf.gov.za/dir_ws/fbw/.

One particular class of people who struggle to access water or FBW are those who obtain water through third party intermediaries rather than the local authority. This generally occurs in two situations: in rural or farming areas where farm workers and dwellers living on privately-owned farms are reliant on the farmer for their water supply; and in urban centres and inner cities where tenants living in flats are reliant on their landlords as an intermediary for their water supply, or 'unlawful occupiers' who have no relationship with the WSA because they are living in collapsed sectional title units or in buildings with absentee landlords. In 2005, DWAF issued a document entitled *Ensuring Water Services To Residents On Privately Owned Land: A Guide for Municipalities* which deals with such issues.[117] Each municipality is meant to conduct a municipal survey of 'privately owned land', profile residents on such land, assess current levels of service and identify the 'water services intermediary'. Each municipality should also allocate funding for provision, including accessing Municipal Infrastructure Grants, set by-laws to regulate relationships, and monitor and regulate water services intermediaries.

However, these guidelines were generally not being implemented adequately, and worse still, municipalities interviewed were simply not aware of their existence. It is also notable that a report published by the Department of Land Affairs (DLA) considers these guidelines as only a partial solution in land reform situations.[118] In farming areas for example, the intermediary is often the farmer on whose land farm workers or dwellers reside, and who is largely responsible for water and sanitation provision. Msunduzi municipal officials stated that one of their biggest challenges has been the delivery of basic services to farm lands. If farmers refuse to allow the municipality to provide water and sanitation on the private property, the protocol is to provide a communal standpipe and a VIP toilet just outside of the property. In Cape Winelands District Municipality the strategy was to financially incentivise farm owners to improve the water and sanitation facilities available to farm workers resident on their farms via the Rural Subsidy Scheme. A farmer for example, would provide water and build a sanitation structure, which would subsequently be investigated by health inspectors. The municipality claimed

[117] These include commercial farms, game parks, mine-owned land, church-owned land, industrial-owned land (including privately owned enterprises) and sectional title/residential complexes and estates.

[118] Sustainable Development Consortium, 'Settlement and Implementation Support (SIS) Strategy for Land and Agrarian Reform in South Africa', Department of Land Affairs, Commission on Restitution of Land Rights, Belgian Development Cooperation and Belgian Technical Cooperation (2007), ch. 9.

that they had taken action against some farmers for not providing water and sanitation after an inspection, which has included writing letters and taking a few farmers to court, however the extent to which farmers are effectively monitored in their provision of adequate water services to those living on their property was unclear.

**The Sufficiency of FBW and FBSan in Cases of Waterborne Sanitation**

For people who do receive FBW, the sufficiency of the national policy allocation is questionable. The national FBW policy prescribes an allocation of 6 kL per household per month or 25 lcd (working on an average household of eight persons). It assumes that 25 lcd is sufficient to meet basic needs. However, international expertise suggests that 50 lcd is the minimum amount of water necessary to meet basic needs and to stay healthy (this 50 lcd amount excludes the amount necessary for waterborne sanitation, which can drive up the necessary daily allocation to around 100 lcd).[119] From the research, it was clear that some South African municipalities are taking the initiative to increase their FBW allocation to between 8-13 kL per month, but others remained stuck at the minimal 6 kL level. These are invariably the better-resourced metropolitan municipalities (e.g., Nelson Mandela Metropolitan, City of Cape Town[120] and eThekwini). Interestingly, until 2007, the richest municipality – City of Johannesburg – only provided the minimal 6 kL amount of FBW. It was only in response to the *Mazibuko* litigation, that the City increased its allocation of FBW to 10 kL per household per month to those on the indigent register.

Crucial to the sufficiency of the allocation, particularly in large households, is the formulation of FBW. The per household per month formulation automatically (and unfairly) discriminates against the kind of large, multi-dwelling, household commonly found in township areas, where one stand typically has a main house, as well as backyard shack dwellings, that must share the one FBW monthly allocation. In any such 'household' of

[119] Footnote 14 of General Comment No. 15 references two international experts on water sufficiency. The first source (J. Bartram and G. Howard, 'Domestic water quantity, service level and health: What should be the goal for water and health sectors', WHO (2002)), points to the fact that a water supply of around 20 lcd carries a high health risk. The second source (P. Gleick, 'Basic water requirements for human activities: Meeting basic needs', *Water International*, Vol. 21, pp. 83–92), is more specific, recommending 50 lcd to meet basic needs, excluding waterborne sanitation.

[120] In Cape Town, 6 kl of FBW is provided to those on the indigent register, who also receive a R30 grant, which purchases approximately 2.8 kl additional water supply. In addition, the city provides 4.2 kl of free sewerage. Thus, the net result is that indigent households are able to consume 13kl free water per month (8.8 kl of water and 4.2 kl of sewerage).

more than eight people, the standard FBW 6 kL amount does not ensure even the 25 lcd amount to each person each day. This fact was picked up by High Court Judge Tsoka in the *Mazibuko* judgment.[121] In very poor communities, which exist in many parts of the country and where the vast majority of people are unemployed and not able to pay for water at all without sacrificing other essentials such as basic food and energy, the FBW allocation makes all the difference between surviving and falling below the breadline. It is therefore essential to get the allocation right, ensuring that a sufficient amount reaches each person who needs it and a reformulation according to needs per person per day as opposed to per household per month.[122]

The FBSan Implementation Strategy recommends that for a household of eight people, 3 to 4 kL of water should be added to a municipality's FBW allocation to the household. This is based on its recommendation that 15 litres per person per day should be provided in terms of FBSan for waterborne sanitation systems.[123] It is unclear as yet how many municipalities pursue this policy. However, even for those municipalities that do adopt the FBSan policy, given that one flush of the toilet consumes approximately 13 litres of water, the suggested allocation for waterborne sanitation will in many cases be woefully insufficient to meet the basic needs, in particular of multi-dwelling or densely populated households.[124]

### Indigency Register

In most municipalities, FBW and FBSan are administered through an indigent policy which seeks to use means-tested targeting to restrict free basic services to qualifying households on the indigency register. Across the country there was no regulatory mechanism or oversight of indigency policies and they varied greatly from municipality to municipality, in terms of allocated benefits, conditions and qualifying income threshold. Indeed,

[121] *Mazibuko* High Court judgment, para. 168.

[122] There are obviously difficulties in accurately assessing the number of people living on each property, but census data could be supplemented through local surveys, and people could be encouraged to report any significant changes at local municipal offices. Such data verification processes could perhaps be supplemented in the course of monthly social grant collections.

[123] DWAF, 'Free Basic Water Implementation Strategy'.

[124] J. Dugard, 'Basic Services in Urban South Africa: Rights, Reality and Resistance', in M. Langford, B. Cousins, J. Dugard, and T. Madlingozi (eds.), *Symbols or Substance: The Role and Impact of Socio-Economic Rights Strategies in South Africa* (Cambridge: Cambridge University Press, 2014), pp. 275–309; K. Tissington, *Basic Sanitation in South Africa: A Guide to Legislation, Policy and Practice*, SERI Research Report, Johannesburg, July 2011.

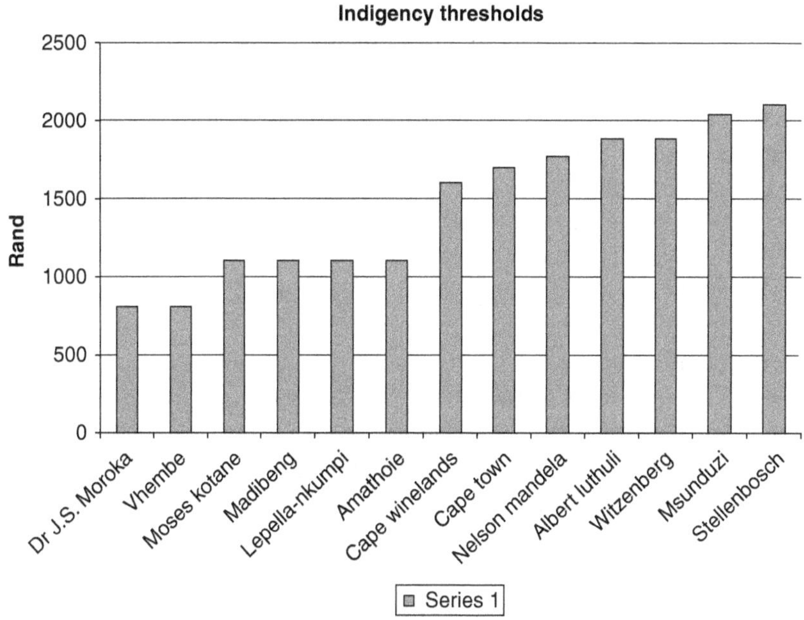


FIGURE 7.2 Indigency thresholds

there were four broad problems with the indigency register approach to allocating FBW/FBSan.

First, there are problems with defining the poor and the narrow definition of 'indigent'. Across municipalities different 'objective' criteria were used. As is apparent from the sample of 15 indigency thresholds represented in Figure 7.2, municipalities use different household income thresholds meaning that relatively poor households receive free basic services in some municipalities but do not in others. Some municipalities based their indigency threshold on twice the highest social grant, some based it on property or land value and some based it on ultimately arbitrary income thresholds.

Moreover, in the vast majority of municipalities, there was no policy for households that are still relatively poor but are just outside the qualifying threshold. This was despite the acknowledgement by many municipalities that 'those who suffer the most are just outside of the definition, but who still cannot afford the services'.[125]

The second problem is the ineffectiveness of such targeting to reach those in need, as evidenced by the chronic under-representation of formally qualifying households on the registers. As acknowledged by the former

[125] Tissington et al., 'Water Services Fault Lines'.

Department of Provincial and Local Government (DPLG),[126] there is a generalised under-capture of poor households on municipal indigency registers, which typically only capture a fifth of formally qualifying households.[127] In Johannesburg, for example, following an expansive process of revising the indigency policy, renaming in the Expanded Social Package or *Siyasizana* ('We help each other' in isiZulu), in June 2011 the City bemoaned the fact that only ten per cent of qualifying households had registered for the benefits.[128]

Obviously, where a targeted indigency policy is in place and households do not register, they are unable to receive the free basic benefits. While no direct research has been undertaken into the reasons why low-income households might be disinclined to register, it is likely that the generally onerous administrative process (outlined below), as well as the pernicious conditionalities (discussed in part 4.6) play a role. In addition, it is not far-fetched to assume that, particularly for very poor municipalities, there is a disincentive to actively publicise and promote the indigency policy.

The onerous administrative process to apply and register as an indigent is the third broad problem with municipal indigency policies. In most municipalities, beyond satisfying the particular income threshold criterion, a resident must be a municipal account holder (this excludes most poor tenants and certainly excludes informal occupiers) and have a South African identity document (this excludes many undocumented poor and vulnerable South Africans, along with all non-permanent residents). Beyond this, many municipalities required the completion of complex forms, and sometimes required letters from employers or social workers, proof of social grants or sworn affidavits. To add to this, it was common for municipalities to require re-registration every six or twelve months, failing which, benefits cease.

Finally, in many municipalities, successful registration is contingent on accepting problematic conditions such as the installation of a flow-restrictor or a prepayment metre (discussed in part 5.4 above).

### Punitive Credit Control

Notwithstanding increasing examples of municipalities unable to operate water services on a cost-recovery basis, this is often not for want of trying. The interviews revealed that, 'cost-recovery and financial sustainability

[126] Recently renamed the Department of Cooperative Governance and Traditional Affairs.

[127] (**Note to authors: insert reference: DPLG report?*).

[128] S. Huddelston, 'Poor Not Taking Up City Rebate Offer', *Business Day*, 20 June 2011.

pressures dominated local officials' attitudes and actions towards service delivery, especially in poorer and under-capacitated municipalities'.[129] For many municipalities, the easiest 'solution' to such pressures was to try to embark on damage control in the form of physically limiting the amount of water poor people can use through disconnections and/or water management devices such as flow restrictors and prepayment metres. Such devices, along with water services disconnection more generally, can have seriously adverse impacts on poor households ranging from diminished health, nutrition and hygiene, to lower economic productivity and compromised dignity, privacy and security.

## 5.3 *Tariff Structures*

In South Africa, local authorities have the mandate to determine their own water tariff structures, albeit within the national standards outlined above. Yet, in the absence of meaningful regulation, there is a startling variety of tariffs across the municipalities, many of which do not seem to have any rational or justifiable basis. One of the common problems with water tariffs is a high price for the second tariff block, meaning that any social equity gains from the first, zero-rated block are immediately wiped out if the household has to consume beyond the first block. This means that, despite FBW allocations, water remains relatively expensive for many low-income households. Yet very few, if any, municipalities, conducted affordability studies.[130] While there has not yet been a consolidated study, the tariffs for the fifteen municipalities (in Figure 7.3) suggested that many municipalities adopted inappropriate tariff structures.[131]

For example, Albert Luthuli Municipality had the same per kilolitre block tariff structure for residential households as it did for business, industry and government departments. This tariff policy unfairly discriminates against residential water users and runs counter to the philosophy of 'the more you use the more you pay'. The practice also violates section 4(1) of the Norms and Standards, which mandates the separation of different types of consumers, so that residential water users can attract a social justice aspect. Moreover, as

[129] Ibid., p. 50.

[130] Only two of the fifteen municipalities surveyed attempted to answer the question about what percentage of low-income household income is spent on water services. See Tissington et al., 'Water Services Fault Lines'.

[131] Ibid.

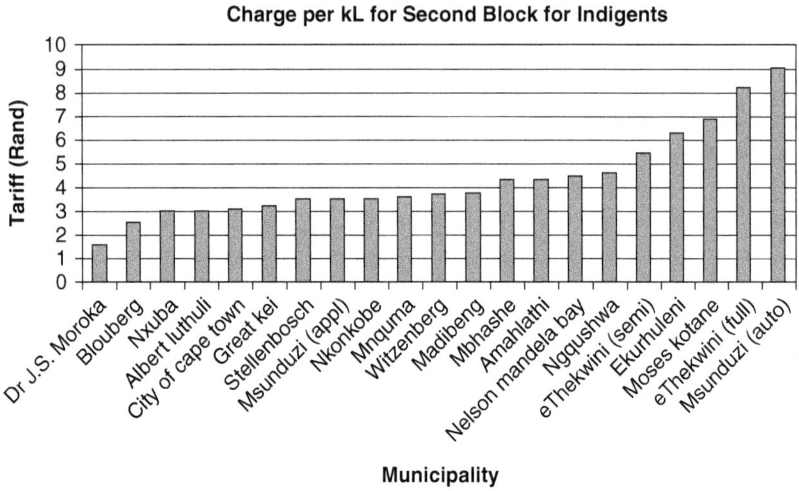


FIGURE 7.3 Tariffs for second block

discussed in section 4.2, these varying tariff structures reveal little correlation with the capacity of a municipality.

## 5.4 *Municipal Governance*

Across South Africa, local governance has been under threat. At the sharp end, there has been a ballooning of local protests over service delivery and governance since 2004,[132] with an average of over 19 such protests per month in 2009,[133] so that 40 per cent of local and metropolitan municipalities had been affected by protests by February 2011.[134] Underlying this relatively

[132] For an analysis of local protests, see for example Dugard, 'Basic Services in Urban South Africa'; P. Alexander, 'Rebellion of the Poor: South Africa's Service Delivery Protests – A Preliminary Analysis', *Review of African Political Economy* Vol. 37, No. 2 (2010), pp. 25–40; and L. Sinwell, J. Kirshner, K. Khumalo, O. Manda, P. Pfaffe, C. Phokela and C. Runciman, 'Service Delivery Protests: Findings from Quick Response Research on Four 'Hot-Spots' – Piet Retief, Balfour, Thokoza, Diepsloot, Centre for Sociological Research (CSR), University of Johannesburg, 2009.

[133] H. Jain, 'Community Protests in South Africa: Trends, Analysis and Explanations', Local Government Working Paper Series No. 1, Community Law Centre, University of the Western Cape, 2010.

[134] K. Heese and K. Allan, 'Are Fiery Street Protests Replacing the Vote?', *Business Day*, 18 February 2011.

upsurge of community dissatisfaction there are a number of factors linked to an escalating crisis of local democracy.

There is mounting evidence of maladministration and corruption in municipal government. For example, during 2010, collapses in municipal governance resulted in more than 20 municipalities being placed under national administration in terms of section 139 of the Constitution. Stories of municipal fraud and corruption abound: These include the exposé – following an official investigation precipitated by the killing of protestor Andries Tatane by police officers – that the Setsoto local municipality (Ficksberg) in the Free State is 'in total disarray, with no proper management and financial control with widespread theft, fraud and corruption at its core, which left it totally unstable'.[135] It is also clear that there is a high degree of incapacity, incompetence and unfilled positions at the municipal level, with many officials seeking opportunities in provincial or national government, which is viewed as more prestigious.[136] One official report found that in many municipalities, senior officials do not have the requisite skills and there is a widespread lack of skilled staff such as engineers, planners and electricians.[137]

Such malaise is aided by the list system of national and provincial political representation, which means that members of parliament and of provincial assemblies do not have constituencies and are largely absent from the direct political realm of municipal governance,[138] as well as the party-political dominance of formal vehicles for popular participation such as ward committees[139] – both which have the effect of constraining the spaces for residents to formally hold local government accountable. Added to this, is the practice of cadreship deployment – whereby political parties deploy loyal cadres to key municipal positions, where party loyalty rather than effectiveness are rewarded – and political patronage, in terms of which relatively junior members of a political party become councillors and find it hard to stand up to or exercise oversight over more senior party members within the council.

[135] Sapa, 'DA Wants the Full Ficksberg Report Released', *The Citizen*, 10 August 2011, http://citizen.cambrient.com/citizen/content/en/citizen/local-news?oid=216410&sn=Detail.

[136] A 2011 report by the Electoral Institute of South Africa (EISA) found that many municipal officials and particularly councillors lacked functional literacy, etc. See generally and specific articles in GGLN, *Community Voice and Dissatisfaction* (GGLN, 2011).

[137] Department of Cooperative Governance and Traditional Affairs, *State of Local Government in South Africa*' (2010), //www.polity.org.za/article/state-of-local-government-in-south-africa-october-2009-2009-10–22.

[138] Alexander, 'Rebellion of the Poor'.

[139] L. Piper and R. Deacon, 'Too Dependent to Participate: Ward Committees and Local Democratisation in South Africa', *Local Government Studies*, Vol. 35, No. 4 (2009), pp. 415–433.

In 2017, it is worth noting that this crisis of municipal governance has been somewhat overshadowed by the national government / ANC crisis of 'state capture' and declining support for an increasingly defensive and embattled ANC. It now means a crisis at both levels, which during the 2016 municipal elections saw the ANC losing their majorities in the main metropolitan municipalities of Johannesburg, Nelson Mandela Bay and Tshwane. It remains to be seen whether opposition parties will perform better. To be sure though part of the malaise at the local government level is rooted in the post-apartheid reality of having to do much with limited financial *and* human resources.

## 6 LEGAL MOBILISATION

These developments have, of course, not occurred in a political vacuum. South Africa has witnessing a rising political and legal mobilisation around municipal services delivery which has employed the right to water discursively and tactically. A direct consequence of the inadequate rollout of water services, as well as the limitation and disconnection of existing services, along with other associated grievances over local living conditions in South Africa's poverty-stricken urban areas, has been an explosion of local protests that have escalated since 2004, until in 2009 there was an average of over 19 protests each month.[140] The numbers have not lessened significantly with a conservative estimate of an average of 15 a month in the period January 2013 to December 2015.[141] Indeed, by February 2011, such protests 'had afflicted 40 per cent of local and metropolitan municipalities'.[142] According to a sample analysed by Jain, the lack of affordable and accessible housing was highest at 21.23 per cent followed by electricity at 10.81 per cent and water at 10.62 per cent, where 'protesters complained about inaccessibility to clean water, often alleging that little had changed since 1994'.[143]

Such struggles, which continue to mushroom across South Africa, have not yet been fully documented or analysed from a rights mobilisation perspective, nor are they purely about the right of access to water, but relate more generally to the collapse of local government.[144] For this reason, in this chapter we focus on a slightly older struggle, around prepayment water meters. Indeed, this is

[140] Jain, 'Community Protests in South Africa'.

[141] Vinayak Bhardwaj, 'Are There 30 Service Delivery Protests a Day in South Africa?', *Africa Check*, 8 June 2016.

[142] K. Heese and K. Allan, 'Are fiery street protests replacing the vote?', *Business Day*, 18 February 2011, p. 13. For a quantitative analysis of service delivery-related protest in South Africa see also Alexander, 'Rebellion of the Poor', pp. 25–40.

[143] Jain, 'Community Protests in South Africa', p. 32.

[144] See for example J. Dugard, 'Urban Basic Services in South Africa'.

the only concerted legal mobilisation struggle around the right to water to date in the post-apartheid period.

While there are clear financial constraints on poorer municipalities without the ability to cross-subsidise from wealthier residential or industrial users, in South Africa's richest municipality, the City of Johannesburg, the story is substantially different. Following the consolidation of its jurisdiction and powers in 2000, the City of Johannesburg embarked on a turnaround strategy for municipal financial management that included the corporatisation of municipal services. From the perspective of the newly established corporation, Johannesburg Water, it was essential to minimise inefficiencies and unpaid for revenue losses in water services.

One of the main areas identified for such losses was Johannesburg's biggest township, Soweto. However, while wanting to limit lost and unpaid-for water consumption in Soweto, the City was under a duty to implement the recently formulated national FBW policy of allocating 6 kilolitres of water per household per month to poor households. In mid-2001, the City devised a plan to physically restrict water consumption in Soweto to the obligatory FBW allocation unless the household could purchase additional water credit, by means of PPMs.[145] The plan was called Operation *Gcin'Amanzi* (which means to save water in isiZulu) or OGA. The high-density suburb of Phiri, one of the poorest in Soweto, with high unemployment and multi-dwelling properties (usually a 'matchbox' house[146] and several backyard shacks per small stand), was chosen as the OGA pilot project.

According to an undated Operation *Gcin'Amanzi* Report included in the minutes of Meeting of the Operations and Procurement Committee of Johannesburg Water (27 November 2002), Operation *Gcin'Amanzi* comprised an 'immediate, intensive and comprehensive intervention on a number of fronts' that sought to remedy the problems of 'over-supply', lack of 'ownership' of water consumption by residents and a 'non-payment paradigm amongst consumers' in Soweto.[147] Whereas other municipalities had remedied deemed consumption through conventional metering, Johannesburg was

[145] Notably this did not apply to households in the rich suburbs, which continued to access as much water as they liked – for their gardens, swimming pools and so on – without any direct pressure to conserve.

[146] Soweto's 'matchbox' houses typically comprise one bedroom, a kitchen and a living space. Commonly there is no bathroom and there is often an outside toilet, albeit linked to waterborne sanitation.

[147] Johannesburg Water, 'Operation GcinAmanzi Report', included in Minutes of Meeting of the Operations and Procurement Committee of Johannesburg Water (vol. B2, pp. 439–482, *Mazibuko* record, available from CALS., undated), p. 1.

determined that Soweto residents would not access more water than the FBW amount without first paying for it.

Seeking to 'reduce demand' for water among Phiri residents, as well as to improve the city's financial position, Johannesburg Water began the bulk infrastructure construction work for the installation of PPMs in Phiri on 11 August 2003. The first phase of individual house connections began in Phiri Block B in February 2004. In the first phase of rollout, where households indicated that they would not accept PPMs, the City disconnected the water supply completely, leaving many households without any water connection for up to six months.

Such was the case with Lindiwe Mazibuko,[148] who became the lead applicant in the subsequent *Mazibuko* case, the legal contours of which have been already discussed. Her water supply was abruptly disconnected without warning in March 2004 and remained disconnected until October 2004, when she capitulated and asked for a PPM so that she would have *some* water connection to her house. Many other Phiri residents experienced a similar process around the same time, although some households were given a choice between a PPM and a standpipe (a cold water yard tap, which is not connected to the household water and sanitation supply).

From the outset, PPMs compromised Phiri residents' access to water in very tangible ways. With an average number of 13 or more people living across multi-dwelling households,[149] the standard FBW allocation (6 kilolitres per property per month) was insufficient to meet the basic needs of Phiri residents. This meant that, in the context of high unemployment and endemic poverty, Phiri residents were forced to make undignified and unhealthy choices. As documented by Lindiwe Mazibuko,

> The free 6 kilolitres of water per month has never lasted the entire month, since it was installed on 11 October 2004. It usually finishes any time between the 12th and 15th of each month. We can often not afford to buy further water. This means that our household is without any water for more than half of every month.[150]

In August 2003, even before the first PPMs were installed, the initial digging of trenches for the bulk construction work met with widespread resistance.

148 Lindiwe Mazibuko died in May 2008, just weeks after the victorious High Court judgment was delivered in the *Mazibuko* case (discussed below). She was 37 years old and had suffered most of her life with diabetes that was never properly treated.

149 Because the backyard shacks on Phiri stands are not formally recognised by the city, they are not allocated separate FBW allocations. This means that all people on one property must share the one FBW allocation of 6 kilolitres per month.

150 Founding affidavit of Lindiwe Mazibuko, 3 July 2006 para. 101.

Residents such as Lindiwe Mazibuko had heard about PPM problems from residents of Orange Farm informal settlement, where such meters had recently been installed (many of which were subsequently destroyed by activists). Opposition mounted as it became clear that the City was determined to rollout PPMs throughout Phiri. Such opposition gained momentum through support from the Anti-Privatisation Forum (APF). Established in 2000, the APF is a left-wing social movement alliance comprising affiliated community-based organisations, activists and movements, the latter group including the Soweto Electricity Crisis Committee (SECC).[151]

Deeply rooted in community struggles against the commercialisation and corporatisation of public services such as water, the APF and the SECC were seemingly well placed to take up the struggle and become the vehicle for community resistance against PPMs in Phiri. In the early months of the resistance campaign, increasing numbers of residents joined the struggle, swelling the numbers at APF/SECC meetings in Phiri and at the APF's office in Johannesburg's inner city, and participating in mass marches to City and Johannesburg Water offices. In addition, direct resistance involved attempting to physically prevent Johannesburg Water employees from digging trenches. Under the auspices of the APF/SECC, spontaneous protests morphed into mass action, with residents refusing to allow Johannesburg Water to continue its work.

Such altercations held the potential to derail the entire project, and, in a drastic response to the rising number of incidents of direct action, the City and Johannesburg Water successfully applied to the Johannesburg High Court for an interdict, which was granted on 22 August 2003. In terms of the interdict, any interference with Operation *Gcin'Amanzi* was banned, and activists (as well as all members of the APF and SECC) were interdicted from coming within 50 metres of any physical work undertaken by the project. The interdict also authorised the sheriff of the court to engage the services of a private security company to assist with any violations of the terms of the interdict.

The APF responded in early September 2003 by establishing a Coalition Against Water Privatisation (CAWP), to re-focus activism against PPMs under a newly configured affiliation. However, the city followed up the interdict with a concerted effort to crush any opposition to PPMs, including arresting

[151] It was formed during the struggles against the City's commercialisation and corporatisation agenda, and brought together political activists and nascent community movements committed to the de-commodification of all basic needs. Among the APF's core objectives are: 'a halt to all privatisation of public sector entities and return of public control and ownership; the co-ordination and intensification of anti-privatisation struggles in communities'. D. McKinley, 'A New "Home of Struggle"', Unpublished draft in author's possession, undated.

and harassing activists. By the end of September 2003, 14 residents of Phiri and activists supporting them had been charged with 'public violence', 'malicious damage to property' and 'incitement' for handing out flyers. The APF and its affiliate organisations, especially the SECC and CAWP, had to divert much energy and funding to securing bail and defending those charged.

The ultimate failure to stop the installation of PPMs was perceived by the APF/SECC/CAWP alliance to mark a low point in the resistance campaign. Although many households continued to resist the installation of PPMs on their properties, without further disruption of the Operation *Gcin'Amanzi* operations, the structural work went forward and the first PPMs were installed in February 2004. For those households that refused to accept PPMs, the city deployed a new weapon: total water disconnection, which left households such as Lindiwe Mazibuko's without water for months until they capitulated.

Interviews with APF founder, Dale McKinley revealed that in July 2004, when the question of proactive use of the law was put to the APF by researchers from the Centre for Applied Legal Studies (CALS) at the University of the Witwatersrand,[152] several options emerged. First was an outright rejection of the legal route, accompanied by a proposal to escalate the resistance to 'all-out war'. The second option was to continue a low-intensity resistance campaign, which in discussion appeared to be compatible with the third option, litigation. The consensus position and one adopted at a mass meeting of Phiri residents was a strategic decision to pursue litigation, but not to suspend other forms of resistance. Clearly, the decision to take forward the litigation was not taken lightly. According to McKinley:

> For left/anti-capitalist activists, it is never an easy thing to adopt tactics that do not appear to fit into pre-configured, historically located understandings and approaches to such struggle... And so, it was in 2005–2006, with a great deal of trepidation and initial half-heartedness, that the APF and CAWP (with the assistance first, of the Freedom of Expression Institute and subsequently, the Centre for Applied Legal Studies) entered into the institutional-legal terrain of class struggle. . . The case was seen as a tactic, part of a larger, long-term strategy seeking to use all means available to ensure that water itself is seen and treated as a public resource, that water service providers remain publicly owned, managed and run and that water service delivery provides adequate, accessible and quality water to all.[153]

[152] One of the authors was one of the researchers, along with Mike Nefale.

[153] D. McKinley, *Water Struggles from Johannesburg and Beyond*, available at

Although five residents ultimately brought the litigation, it was explicitly framed as public interest litigation and was throughout supported by the APF and CAWP as part of the broader mobilisation against PPMs. The legal case was formulated around two aspects of the City's water services – PPMs and the City's FBW policy – as insufficient to meet the needs (including waterborne sanitation) of poor, multi-dwelling households.

As discussed, the applicants were successful before the Johannesburg High Court in having the PPMs declared unlawful and the FBW policy reviewed and set aside as unreasonable because it was insufficient to meet basic needs in the Phiri context.[154] But they were ultimately unsuccessful when on 8 October 2009, the Constitutional Court delivered a judgment that ruled against the Phiri residents on all grounds.

Yet, despite the judicial defeat – and notwithstanding the difficulties of attempting to ascertain a counter-factual, i.e. how the struggle against prepayment water meters might have fared without a court case – there have been significant impacts deriving from the litigation and particularly the legal mobilisation around it.[155] As documented,[156] the litigation has had a positive impact on reinvigorating water campaigns and public debates about the commercialisation of water services, which had died down following the abandonment of outright privatisation in the mid-2000s.[157] More specifically, in relation to the struggle against prepayment water meters, in the words of McKinley, *Mazibuko* 'provided something to organise around; hope and recognition after having been fucked over by the police – it became the centre of mobilisation and reinvigorated the struggle, as well as catalysing political discussions and refining strategy'.[158]

More than that, the litigation provided a platform, or stage, to voice the problems of poor Phiri residents in the media, which otherwise often does not focus on such issues. And, most surprisingly, the litigation resulted in material benefits despite the judicial defeat. This includes not only the delay

[154] See discussion of the legal aspects of the case in Section 2.5.

[155] For more detail on the impacts of the *Mazibuko* case, see Section 6 below.

[156] J. Dugard and M. Langford, 'Art or Science? Synthesising Lessons from Public Interest Litigation and the Dangers of Legal Determinism', *South African Journal on Human Rights*, vol. 27, No. 1 (2011), pp. 39–64.

[157] Further research is necessary to explore the causal links between the focused campaign against prepayment water meters in Phiri (2004 to 2009) and the upsurge in ongoing basic services related local protests across the country since 2004.

[158] Interview with Dale McKinley, cited in J. Dugard, 'Civic Action and Legal Mobilisation: The Phiri Water Meters Case', in J. Handmaker and R. Berkhout (eds.), *Mobilising Social Justice in South Africa: Perspectives from Researchers and Practitioners* (Pretoria: Pretoria University Law Press, 2010) pp. 71–99, at 94.

(for several years) of the roll-out of prepayment water meters in Phiri (and across South Africa) while the final judicial decision was pending, but also the material effects arising from the politicisation of the issue in the course of the litigation. Evidence of the impact includes the fact that, as a direct result of the politicisation surrounding the litigation (in the media, etc.), the City of Johannesburg raised the amount of FBW it provides to the poorest households in Johannesburg to 50 litres per person per day (the amount the applicants asked for).[159]

The City also indicated that the new generation of prepayment water meters it planned to install will have a 'trickler' device. This means that, following the exhaustion of the FBW amount, the water supply will not completely cease as it did previously but, rather, it will flow as a trickle until further FBW/credit is loaded. Moreover, as part of the new prepayment meter rollout, the City pledged not to prosecute residents for having destroyed their meters. In effect, this meant that the applicants and community have received the relief they litigated over, but through legal mobilisation rather than the judicial process.

## 7 CONCLUSION

This chapter not only aimed to understand to what extent progress on extending *access* to water and sanitation in South Africa conforms to the right to water and sanitation in policy and practice but also give a sense of the importance of rights in influencing that progress. In doing so, it sought to provide a grounded sense of the extent to which South Africa represents a template for the right to water. While South African authorities have made progress directly in laws and policies, the reality for many South Africans has not always accorded with this benign picture. Clearly, legal and policy recognition is only one part of the picture. In seeking to uncover reasons for this uneven progress, this chapter has demonstrated that part of the answer can be found in the lack of resources of poor municipalities, which would suggest that an increase in national support or re-distribution across municipalities is necessary. However, it also shows that variation in local capacity does not fully explain differences in progress. The quantitative results indicate that other factors may be critical, and we have suggested that the fault may lie in policy gaps, poorly designed policies, tariff structures, punitive credit controls and

[159] This is in terms of the City's Expanded Social Package, and applies up to a monthly household limit of 15 kilolitres. When the case was launched, the City provided a maximum of six kilolitres of FBW per household per month to poor households.

municipal governance. Addressing some of these factors requires reforms outside the water sector (particularly on municipal governance), but many of these elements remain within the control of national and local government. Finally, the chapter indicates that the constitutional recognition of the right to water has provided a limited but significant forum in which authorities can be made accountable. Even in the *Mazibuko* case where petitioners questionably failed on all grounds in the Supreme Court, court-centred mobilisation by social movements and civil society groups helped catalyse the desired policy reforms. However, the paucity of active legal mobilisation on right to water and its irregular presence in political discourse and mobilisation suggests clearly the limits of mere constitutional and legal recognition.

# 8

# Quantifying the Affordability Standard

## *A Comparative Approach*

HENRI SMETS[1]

### 1 INTRODUCTION

For many individuals in the world, access to water is essentially a question of money. Thus, it is no surprise that affordability of water for human consumption is an official policy target or legal requirement in many countries. It was also referred to in the Millennium Declaration and the Sustainable Development Goals (SDGs) and is a requirement under the right to water at both international and national levels. Whereas everyone agrees that drinking water prices should be reasonable, there is no universally agreed upon method of identifying what that would be despite past and current pressure for its measurement. Although water affordability is a requirement in many countries, it is often not enforced, possibly because of doubts over the precise requirement.

Through an inductive method, this chapter proposes that the economic affordability of drinking water, provided by supply networks and associated wastewater services, may be described by an index comparing the drinking water and wastewater bill of a household to its disposable income ('affordability index').

In industrialised countries, households with an income equal to the median disposable income generally spend around 1.1 per cent of their income on buying water and wastewater services. Poor households spend on average approximately 2.6 per cent. Higher indices are observed in some regions and for very poor people. In order to help vulnerable people, public authorities in Europe often take measures aiming to reduce water bills to less than 3 per cent. The similarity of indices in use in various countries and of approaches

[1] Member of the Water Academy, France. This chapter is drawn from the book, H. Smets, *De l'eau potable à un prix abordable* (Paris: Johanet, 2009).

could provide an objective basis for quantifying the concept of water affordability. By and large, State practice supports the choice of an affordability index of 3 to 4 per cent of disposable income of poor households in industrialised countries.[2]

In transitional and developing countries, the affordability index is generally higher depending on whether the country seeks to reduce subsidies for water. Median households often spend 2.5 per cent of their income on water, i.e., over twice what is common in industrialised countries. Consequently the affordability index of poor households is about three times larger (7.5 per cent) because of the low income of very poor households. State practice shows that such high levels of spending on water are generally tolerated. A number of developing States have adopted policies to promote an affordability index for poor households of 3 to 5 per cent, and to implement measures to reduce the burden of water expenses for people living in poverty.

This chapter proceeds by initially discussing the degree of recognition of the right to affordable water in international and national law and policy (section 2), and identifying various methodologies for measuring and assessing water affordability (section 3). An inductive method is then used to determine affordability patterns and targets in different countries (section 4), and to isolate the point at which social policies are triggered (section 5). Based on these findings, the chapter suggests some broad bands for in which affordability standards could be set, but emphasises the need for contextualised measures and adoption of social policies (section 6).

## 2 THE RIGHT TO AFFORDABLE WATER

It is difficult to contest the claim that, within the framework of economic and social rights, drinking water should be available to all at an affordable price, either as a political or moral objective or as a legal obligation. However, the meaning of an affordable price is generally undefined both at the international and national levels. In the context of this chapter, drinking water means water for personal or domestic uses of a quality suitable for drinking. It does not refer to water for agriculture, commercial or industrial uses or to water for domestic animals, professional use, leisure or gardening.

[2] The precise definition of the affordability index depends on the measures that will be carried out to guarantee that no one spends more than a certain amount. It is not enough to state that spending 3 per cent on water is too much; it must be said what measures will be actually taken.

Turning to legal sources, in General Comment No. 15, the United Nations (UN) Committee on Economic, Social and Cultural Rights (CESCR) stated that the human right to water entitles all individuals to 'sufficient, safe, acceptable, physically accessible and affordable water for personal and domestic uses'.[3] The obligation to fulfil that right is then said to require:

> States parties to adopt the necessary measures directed towards the full realization of the right to water. The obligation includes, inter alia, ... ensuring that water is affordable for everyone.... To ensure that water is affordable, States parties must adopt the necessary measures that may include, inter alia: (*a*) use of a range of appropriate low-cost techniques and technologies; (*b*) appropriate pricing policies such as free or low-cost water; and (*c*) income supplements.[4]

The General Comment does not provide us with any quantitative metric in determining what is affordable, although it does point strongly to the principle of equity in assessing it. For example, the Committee states that, 'Any payment for water services has to be based on the principle of equity', which means that the services are to be 'affordable for all, including socially disadvantaged groups', regardless of whether they are delivered publicly or privately.[5] Equity is further clarified as meaning that 'poorer households should not be disproportionately burdened with water expenses as compared to richer households'.[6] In this definition, the key word is 'disproportionately', but no indication is given to determine when it is excessive.

Almost as a rule, the total water expenses of poor people are lower than those of wealthy people as they consume less.[7] However, the burden of water expenses (water and wastewater) for poorer households is disproportionally higher if expressed as a proportion of household budget. This is demonstrated in Figure 8.1 for two countries. The affordability index of wealthy people can be ten times below the index of poor people.

In terms of international policy and human rights, affordable drinking water emerged in 1992 in the Dublin Statement on Water and Sustainable

[3] CESCR, *General Comment No. 15, The Right to Water* (Twenty-ninth session, 2002), UN Doc. E/C.12/2002/11 (2003), para. 2 (emphasis added). In para.12, the CESCR states, 'The direct and indirect costs and charges associated with securing water ... must not compromise or threaten the realization of other Covenant rights'.

[4] Ibid., paras. 26–27 (emphasis added). [5] Ibid., para. 27. [6] Ibid.

[7] However, water prices per litre in some informal settlements can be three to thirty times that of the price in the formal sector, meaning that poorer people may sometimes pay higher total amounts.

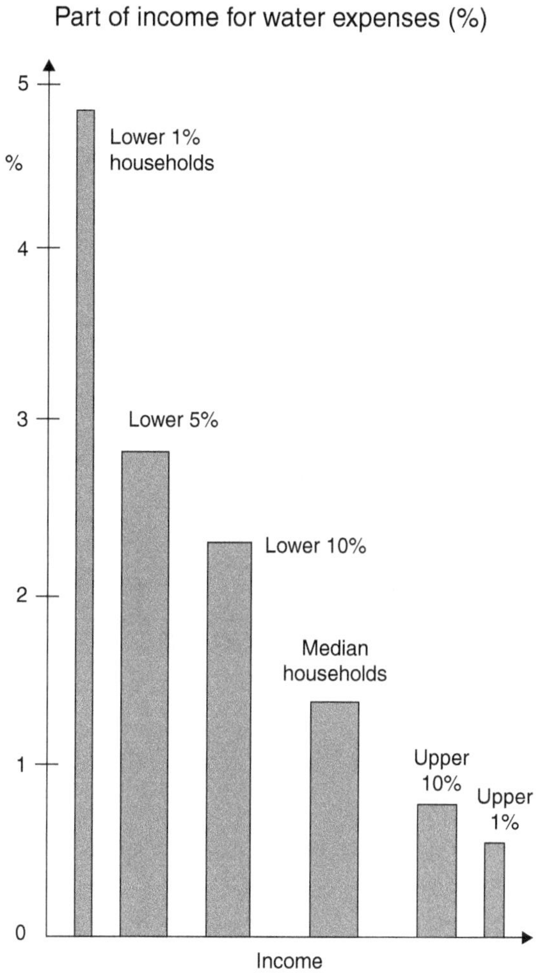


FIGURE 8.1 Water expenses as a proportion of income vs income level (decile): France and Mexico

*Data Source:* France: A. Reynaud, *Assessing the impact of public regulation and private participation on water affordability for poor households*, September 2006; Mexico: OECD, *Household Water Expenses*, 1999.

Development, which provided: 'it is vital to recognize first the basic right of all human beings to have access to clean water and sanitation at an affordable price'.[8] In March 2000, the Ministerial Declaration of The Hague on Water

8 Principle No. 4 states: 'Water has an economic value in all its competing uses and should be recognized as an economic good', and further that: 'Within this principle, it is vital to

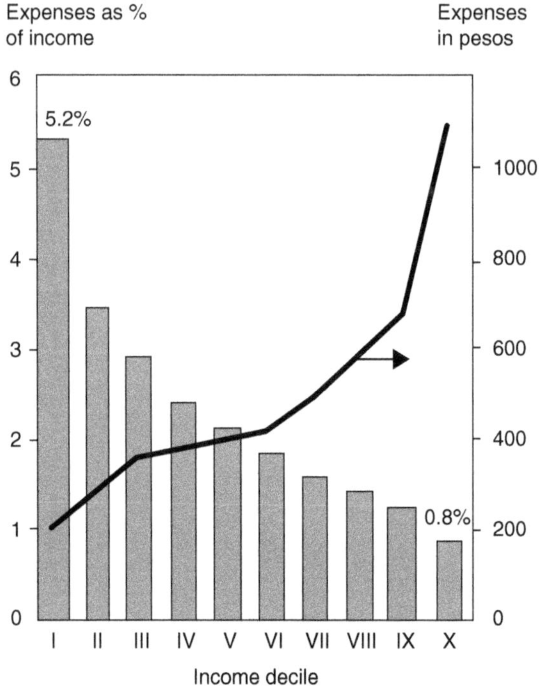


FIGURE 8.1 (*cont.*) - Mexico

Security in the 21st Century (Second World Water Forum) included the common goal that 'every person has access to enough safe water at an affordable cost to lead a healthy and productive life'.

The most notable recognition came in September 2000 when the UN General Assembly adopted the Millennium Declaration. In the first target, States committed themselves to halving by 2015 the proportion of people who 'are unable to reach or afford safe drinking water'.[9] However, affordability was quietly dropped

recognize first the basic right of all human beings to have access to clean water and sanitation at an affordable price. Past failure to recognize the economic value of water has led to wasteful and environmentally damaging uses of the resource. Managing water as an economic good is an important way of achieving efficient and equitable use, and of encouraging conservation and protection of water resources'.

9 The United Nations Millennium Declaration states that, 'We, heads of State and Government ... resolve further: To halve, by the year 2015, the proportion of the world's people whose income is less than one dollar a day and the proportion of people who suffer from hunger and, by the same date, to halve the proportion of people who are unable to reach

in 2001 when the Millennium Development Goals (MDGs) were published after a UN inter-agency process.[10] Target 7.C essentially replaced affordability with the vague and unmeasured concept of sustainability.[11] One of the architects of the MDGs, Vandemoortele, has justified the exclusion of affordability on the basis that it could not be measured:

> [I]n an age where numbers prevail, it was decided that only those targets with agreed indicators and with robust data were to be included - but not without making some exceptions. This is why the quality of education, the affordability of water, good governance and human rights (i.e. civil and political rights) and several other areas covered in the Millennium Declaration were not included in the MDGs.[12]

This omission is tragic, particularly because water deprivation as a result of high price is a very serious problem in poor areas where people have to sacrifice food or other basic necessities for water. The original emphasis on affordability in the Millennium Declaration should be stressed, but the exclusion from the MDGs has meant that it has received arguably less visibility in the international development context. Remarkably, the same has occurred with the SDGs. While affordability is now included as a target in SDG 6, no indicator has been selected for measurement.[13]

At the regional level, references to affordability for water or related issues are more diffuse. In Latin America, the Protocol of San Salvador (1988) states that, 'Everyone shall have the right to live in a healthy environment and to have access to basic public services'.[14] In Europe, the Protocol on Water and Health

or to afford safe drinking water'. UNGA, UN Doc. A/55/L.2, paras. 1, 19. Despite the adoption of this text by heads of State, it was subsequently modified by a group of international civil servants who decided without a specific mandate to remove any reference to affordability or similar concepts.

10 See discussion and critique in M. Langford, 'A Poverty of Rights: Six Ways to Fix the MDGs', *IDS Bulletin*, Vol. 41, No.1 (2010), pp. 83–91.

11 Target 7.C requires States to 'Halve, by 2015, the proportion of people without sustainable access to safe drinking water and basic sanitation'.

12 J. Vandemoortele, 'The MDG Story: Intention Denied', *Development and Change*, Vol. 42, No. 1 (2011), pp. 1–21, at 4.

13 Target 6.1 states 'By 2030, achieve universal and equitable access to safe and affordable drinking water for all' and indicator 6.1.1 is the 'Proportion of population using safely managed drinking water services'. Such exclusion could be explained by the lack of an internationally agreed definition of what is meant by 'affordable water'. For further discussion, see also M. Langford, 'Lost in Transformation? The Politics of the Sustainable Development Goals', *Ethics and International Affairs*, Vol. 30, No. 2 (2016), pp. 167–176, at 174.

14 Article 11, Additional Protocol to the American Convention on Human Rights in the Area of Economic, Social and Cultural Rights (adopted 17 November 1988, entered into force 16 November 1999), OAS Treaty Series No. 69 (Protocol of San Salvador).

ratified by member States of the UN Economic Commission for Europe and the Regional Office for Europe of the World Health Organization deals with State obligations concerning water supply and sanitation for all.[15] Article 5(l) provides that, 'Equitable access to water, adequate in terms both of quantity and of quality, should be provided for all members of the population, especially those who suffer a disadvantage or social exclusion'. While affordability is not explicitly mentioned, the reference to equitable access means that the price of water should be set at a level that the user can pay.

Of particular interest is Protocol No. 9 to the European Union (EU) Treaty of Lisbon (2007).[16] It introduces the concept of affordability in EU law for all essential services:

> The shared values of the Union in respect of services of general economic interest include in particular: … a high level of … affordability, equal treatment and the promotion of universal access and of user rights.[17]

Now in force, this Protocol would presumably require drinking water to be available to all persons in the EU (universal service) at an affordable price. EU directives already exist for the provision of affordable postal and telecommunication services,[18] and two new directives deal with affordable electricity and gas.[19] This supports the general principle that everyone should have access to essential services and that tariffs can be adapted to meet social objectives without causing a distortion to trade. Similarly, the Council of Europe in 2010 adopted a declaration on essential services, including affordable water supply and sanitation.[20] It notes that the 'prices paid for essential services are a major factor in ensuring their effective availability' and that prices 'should either be determined by the public authorities in respect of public services or be monitored, controlled or approved by them, so as to ensure their

[15] Article 4.2(a) and (b), UN Economic Commission for Europe and the Regional Office for Europe of the World Health Organization, Protocol on Water and Health to the 1992 Convention on the Protection and Use of Transboundary Watercourses and International Lakes (adopted 17 June 1999).

[16] Now renamed as Protocol N°26 on services of general interest. Consolidated version of the Treaty on European Union.

[17] Ibid., Article 1.

[18] See Directives 67/97/EC art.3.1, 98/10/EC and 2002/22/EC on universal service.

[19] Directive 2009/72/ EC of 13 July 2009 concerning common rules for the internal market in electricity. Directive 2009/73/EC of 13 July 2009 concerning common rules for the internal market in natural gas.

[20] Ministers responsible for spatial /regional planning of the Member States of the Council of Europe (CEMAT), Declaration on the contribution of essential services to the sustainable spatial development of the European Continent, July 2010. 15 CEMAT (2010) 6E Prov., paras. 4, 20, 22.

sustainability and strengthen social, economic and territorial cohesion'.[21] The Declaration goes on to note that subsidies and fiscal measures may be used where necessary and that the costs of essential services 'should be apportioned among all users so as to ensure that everyone has access to them under economic conditions acceptable to all'.[22]

In at least twenty countries, national laws provide that drinking water should not only be available to all, but also that the price of water must be 'equitable', 'fair', 'acceptable', 'accessible', 'affordable' or 'reasonable'. In Latin America, national water laws of many countries explicitly require the provision of basic services to the poor, or policies and systems to reach this goal (Bolivia, Chile, Ecuador, Colombia, Uruguay, Brazil, Argentina, Paraguay, Peru, Venezuela, Costa Rica, Honduras, Panama and Nicaragua). The same is true to a lesser extent in Africa (Algeria, Madagascar, Mali, Mauritania, South Africa and Zambia).[23]

However, national laws are generally silent and courts have probably not provided appropriate jurisprudence to assess disproportion when dealing with drinking water prices. For example, in France, the 2006 water law states that water for essential uses shall be available at economic conditions acceptable to all ('dans des conditions économiquement acceptables par tous'[24]) and that it is right of each physical person.[25] However the content of this right is still unclear in French law, as no affordability limit has yet been approved by Parliament.[26] Nevertheless, all actors in the water sector refer to a level of 3 per cent of income or household budget, which appears to stem from the support given to this figure by the Organization for Economic Co-operation and Development (OECD). In the last bill adopted by the National Assembly in June 2016, the 3 per cent limit is presented as a maximum a household should spend on water and sanitation for essential uses, as set out in the Report to National Assembly N° 758 (June 2016).

[21] Ibid., paras. 20–21, [22] Ibid., paras. 21–22.

[23] A survey of international agreements and national laws on affordability is given in Annex 1 of H. Smets, *De l'eau potable à un prix abordable* (Paris: V. Johanet, 2009).

[24] Loi n°2006-1772 du 30 décembre 2006 sur l'eau et les milieux aquatiques. Art. 1. Envir. Code, art 210–211.

[25] The text of the law refers to 'chaque personne physique, pour son alimentation et son hygiene', i.e. for essential uses. It does not deal with the price of water for any other use.

[26] A number of bills were presented to Parliament between 2011 and 2016 but are not yet approved; they aim to create a social fund for water financed by a 0.5–1 per cent tax on water bills. The National Committee on Water approved unanimously the 3 per cent affordability limit, which was also endorsed by the Minister of Ecology. The social mechanism could cost EUR 50 - 100 million per year, and would benefit approximately 500,000 households. So far no financing mechanism has been decided upon.

## 3 TOWARDS A YARDSTICK FOR AFFORDABILITY

As there is no generally accepted definition of affordability, there is a need to move towards consensus on an approach that is operational. Water affordability concepts were developed in the late 1990s in the United Kingdom and United States and by the OECD for use in developed and transition countries.[27] While various proposals have been made, neither the World Bank nor OECD have supported any indicator or benchmark in an officially approved document. The UNDP uses in its reports a target of 3 per cent for individual households,[28] the OECD 4 per cent, and BAD 5 per cent.[29] However, there was no explanation by the OECD for the choice of its target.

There are of course different ways to develop methods to measure affordability.[30] Water might be considered as unaffordable if it is more expensive than *elsewhere*: for instance, if the price exceeds what is paid by 90 per cent of other users. However, if water prices were uniform, this approach would be of little assistance. Another approach might be to examine excessive profit margins or corrupt payments that increase the price. But in the absence of such payments, which can exceed 30 per cent of the price, such an approach is also of little use.

A better approach would be to compare actual water expenses with household budget assuming that water expenses are paid directly by the household (and not through taxes). Water price means the price actually paid by a household for drinking water supply and wastewater services taking into account any subsidy and any rebate. The ratio of the water bill of a household to its disposable income describes what part of the household budget is used for water; it is called the 'affordability index' and varies with location and income. If the index is high, water is said to be too expensive, too costly or even unaffordable.

[27] OECD, *Social Issues in the Provision and Pricing of Water Services* (Paris: OECD, 2003); OECD, *Key Issues and Recommendations for Consumer Protection* (Paris: OECD, 2003). See also Annex 4 of Smets, *De l'eau potable à un prix abordable* for a full description of the position of international organisations.

[28] United Nations Development Programme (UNDP), *Beyond Scarcity: Power, Poverty and the Global Water Crisis*, Human Development Report 2006 (New York: UNDP, 2006). The 3 per cent target is unrealistic in many poor States.

[29] Contrary to a prominent statement suggesting otherwise, the OECD did not support a 3 per cent target, even if its Secretariat is in favour of such a level for developed countries. The level to be chosen in individual cases depends on a number of considerations which vary from case to case.

[30] See G. Hutton, 'Monitoring "Affordability" of Water and Sanitation Services after 2015: Review of Global Indicator Options', A paper submitted to the UN Office of the High Commissioner for Human Rights, (20 March 2012), and his engagements with my proposals.

This definition of affordability is in line with the UN CESCR's statement in General Comment No. 4 on the Right to Adequate Housing: 'Steps should be taken by States parties to ensure that the percentage of housing-related costs is, in general, commensurate with income levels'.[31] The same logic can be used for water expenses, which are considered to comprise a portion of housing expenses. The European Commission in both its Green and White books on services of general interest[32] expressed itself in favour of a definition of affordability based on the cost of services and the disposable income of the household.

Having defined an index of affordability, the issue is to determine under what conditions water can be said to be unaffordable, i.e., when is the right to water at an affordable price violated? The following analysis is limited to drinking water supplied by public networks under the control of public authorities and excludes water provided on the free market (i.e. water sold by vendors in buckets, by fountain keepers at a privately managed stand post or by a grocery shop in bottles).

To assess affordability, all expenses for water paid by a household when buying water should be taken into account, such as wastewater collection and treatment expenses and rates paid with water. To this, one should add water and wastewater expenses if identified and paid separately (through local rates and taxes). Water prices vary with consumption (when metered), technical and geographical conditions, quality of service, environmental standards, inclusion of rainwater expenses, and so on. To allow comparisons, consumption is standardised (e.g. 120 cubic metres or 200 cubic metres per year per household connected to a supply network). The water bill is generally below the cost of providing water because of generous subsidies of the water sector.

Water expenses are compared to disposable income of two types of households: a 'median' household where the disposable income is the median income and a 'poor' household, where the disposable income is much smaller. Identifying the latter is commonly done through a variety of methods: for instance, those with 50 or 40 per cent of the median income, those in the first income decile or quintile or the average income of the first decile. For present purposes, it will be defined as those having 40 per cent or less of the median income – clearly the poorest of the poor.

[31] CESCR, *General Comment No. 4, The Right to Adequate Housing,* (Sixth session, 1991), UN Doc. E/1992/23, annex III at 114 (1991), para. 8(c).

[32] Green Paper on Services of General Interest, COM (2003)270 Final, White Paper on Services of General Interest, COM(2004)374.

However, it is important to point out that water prices and disposable income vary considerably from one municipality to another. Regional or national averages can be calculated to derive aggregate affordability indices, but hide considerable differences. Moreover, when water prices increase, in principle poor people could reduce their water consumption, but this is difficult to achieve because actual water consumption is related to basic needs (e.g. food, beverage, health, hygiene, bathing, toilets) and thus is weakly dependant on income level. In other words, it is relatively price and income inelastic for poor people. Furthermore, water bills can be weakly dependant on water consumption levels when the annual fee exceeds 40 per cent of the water bill. Poor people could use unsafe water with the risk of becoming sick and spreading epidemics (such as typhoid or cholera). They could also partly forego other essentials, such as food or health expenses, to pay for their water.

In determining the appropriate affordability standard or benchmark for index, the next two sections set out observations of actual indices and policy measures in a large number of countries in order to determine whether a common approach exists. Over eighty countries from all parts of the world are covered, and use is made of environmental performance reports from the OECD and European Economic Community (EEC), as well as various studies by the European Bank for Reconstruction and Development (EBRD) and the World Bank. This large sample provides some comfort in making generalizable conclusions, such as the average behaviour that is assumed to be customary or usual.

## 4 THE WATER AFFORDABILITY INDEX IN VARIOUS COUNTRIES

The first step is to analyse the actual budgetary expenditures. Tariff data has been collected by a range of institutions.[33] However, one should exercise great caution because the data may not be fully comparable. Because of the large

[33] For example, the World Bank, ADERASA, EBRD, OECD, IWA, BIPE, GWI, NUS, and other organizations. See *De l'eau potable à un prix abordable* for detailed analysis and comparison. The index depends on the definition of the water consumption level, type of tariff, size of income, type of household, etc. To decrease the affordability index, it is convenient to consider the lowest quintile of income. To examine the more serious social problems, it is better to restrict oneself to the 5 per cent of individuals or households at the bottom of the income ladder. Disposable income can be defined very differently within a given country (based on national income, consumption studies, actual outlays). Reliable data on the very poor is rarely available, thus it is convenient to use 40 per cent of the median income in order to have less uncertainty. S. Fanhauser and S. Tepic, *Can Poor Consumers Pay for Energy and Water?*, BERD, Working Paper?, 2005; K. Komives, *Who Benefits from Utilities Subsidies*, World Bank, Working Paper, 2005.

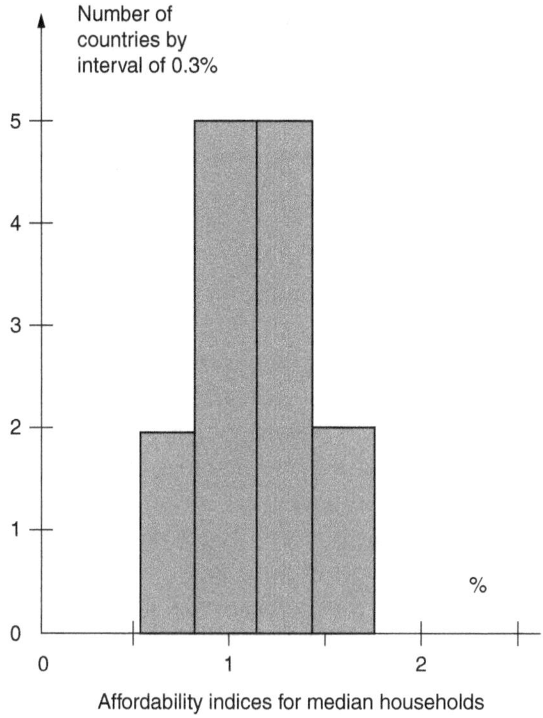


FIGURE 8.2 Distribution of affordability indices in fourteen European countries

number of parameters that influence the price of drinking water and sanitation and the level of household income, affordability indices vary by quite a wide range. It can be nil if water is freely available (e.g. public fountains or free stand posts), or very high when the user has to pay a water vendor in a slum. Consistent and reliable affordability indices are not easily available because water bills and disposable income are not assessed in the same way by statisticians or analysts. Caution should be exercised when comparing water affordability indices because water prices vary frequently in some countries. Affordability indices from reliable sources in reliable countries (e.g. International Water Association (IWA), National Utilities Services (NUS), Global Water Intelligence (GWI), BIPE (a French Economic Analysis Group), OECD, World Bank, etc.) are not always compatible. In order to keep consistency, this chapter uses the same water consumption data set for all countries in western Europe (IWA), the same income data (OECD), and the same definition of the income of poor people (40 per cent of median income).

In western Europe, the affordability index for median households is approximately 1.1 per cent. This can be seen in Figure 8.2, which is based on indices for Denmark, Portugal, France, Greece, UK, Germany, Austria, Sweden, Finland, Belgium, Switzerland, Netherlands, Spain, and Italy. The range of indices (from 0.6 to 1.3 per cent) is relatively limited, as if the rates were designed to correspond to each other in a fashion to keep water affordable. These values of the index represent the observed levels of the average index, not a policy target.

For households with 40 per cent of median income and identical water consumption (120 cubic metres per year),[34] the affordability index would be 2.75 per cent (i.e., 1.1 per cent divided by 0.4 per cent) when there is no social measure (social tariff, targeted aid for water, aid for water debts, etc.). The affordability index can be higher than the average 2.75 per cent if people are very poor (e.g. unemployed people living on State aid) or in municipalities where water is particularly expensive. Indices rarely exceed 5 per cent in western Europe. In some countries, social assistance alleviates problems created by high water prices, such as a reduction in food consumption, less medical and dental treatment, non-payment of other utilities, less attendance at schools and longer working hours.

An example of this can be seen in Figure 8.3. It shows the fraction of the population spending over x per cent of its income on water in the United Kingdom, and the effect that a 50 per cent rebate on the amount of water expenses in excess of 5 per cent of income would have if it were introduced. We can see that 10 percent of the population spends over 4 per cent of its income on water: this is the affordability index corresponding to the upper limit of the first decile of population. If only the part QP of the blackened curve is known, an extrapolated percentage is found by means of a straight line QP.

In developing countries with intermediate or low income at national level, the affordability index is generally higher than in western Europe. When income inequality is large and poverty is deep, the disposable income can be very low. Because of data constraints, affordability indices have been compared for only three groups of countries: transition countries, Latin America and Africa.

For eleven 'transition' countries in eastern Europe, the Caucasus and Central Asia (Russia, Ukraine, Slovakia, Hungary, Bulgaria, Rumania,

[34] Household figures are used because most users are households with at least two persons. The standard consumption of 120 cubic metres generally relates to a household of three or four persons. In a paper presented to Aqua Publica Europea in 2016, I pointed out that the calculation of the affordability index may be based on the minimal consumption for a decent living, which in France could mean 73 m$^3$ per year for a 4 person household. The 120 m$^3$ limit includes water that is wasted (not essential).

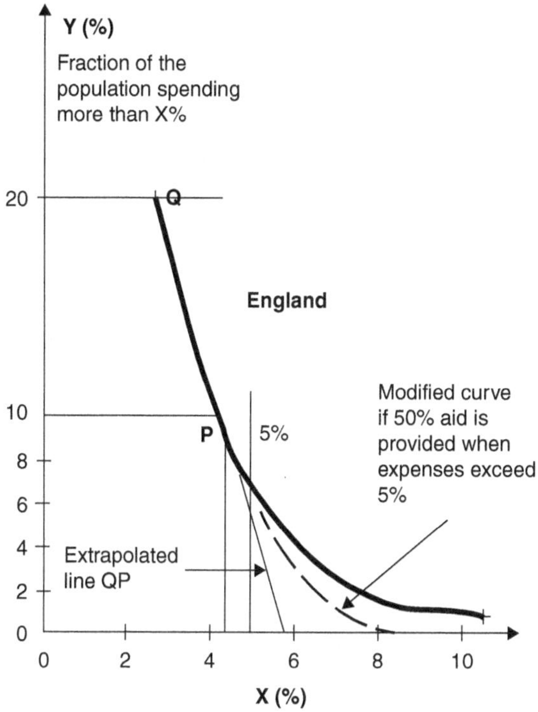


FIGURE 8.3 Distribution of population by spending on water: England

Estonia, Poland, the Czech Republic, Kyrgyzstan, Uzbekistan), the affordability index of median households is generally in the range 1.5 to 4.3 per cent with an average of 2.6 per cent. This is over twice the comparable index in western European countries. Closer examination of the data shows that there are probably two groups of countries: those with high water subsidies and low water prices (affordability index for median households near 1 per cent) and those with reduced subsidies and higher water prices (affordability index of median households nearing 3.5 per cent). Figure 8.4 shows the affordablility index over eleven transitional countries, with three of the eleven being seen as falling into this second group. While the former group of countries has no large-scale affordability problem, the latter group of transitional countries could have such problems because people in the lowest decile of income or below 40 per cent of median income would have an affordability index of 5 to 10 per cent. For instance, in Ukraine, 6.4 per cent of users have to spend over 6 per cent of their income on water. In Russia, people in the lowest decile spend more than 6 per cent on water.

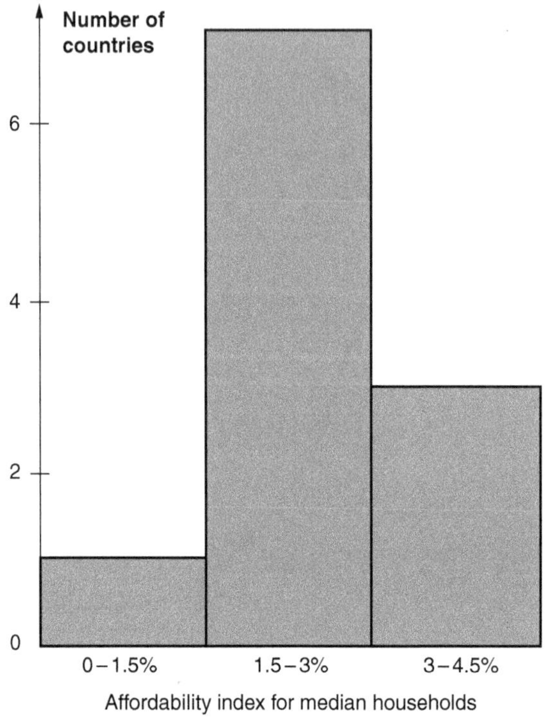


FIGURE 8.4 Distribution of affordability indices in eleven transitional countries

An affordability limit of 4 per cent, as proposed by the OECD for poor households in the transition countries, may not reflect State practice in all these States, and may even be difficult to achieve, as it could mean providing aid for drinking water to 20 per cent of the population. The 3 per cent affordability limit as proposed by the United Nations Development Programme (UNDP) would be even more difficult to implement and could be unrealistic in countries that already have high water prices.[35]

In Latin America, most countries have affordability indices above 4 per cent for median households (see Figure 8.5 based on the affordability index of a number of cities in Latin America). Because of social tariffs, the affordability index for poor households does not exceed 10 per cent and would generally be around 6 per cent for the first decile of income. This would show that many governments in that region consider that an affordability index for poor households of 6 per cent is acceptable. In Africa, the affordability index for

[35] UNDP, *Beyond Scarcity*.

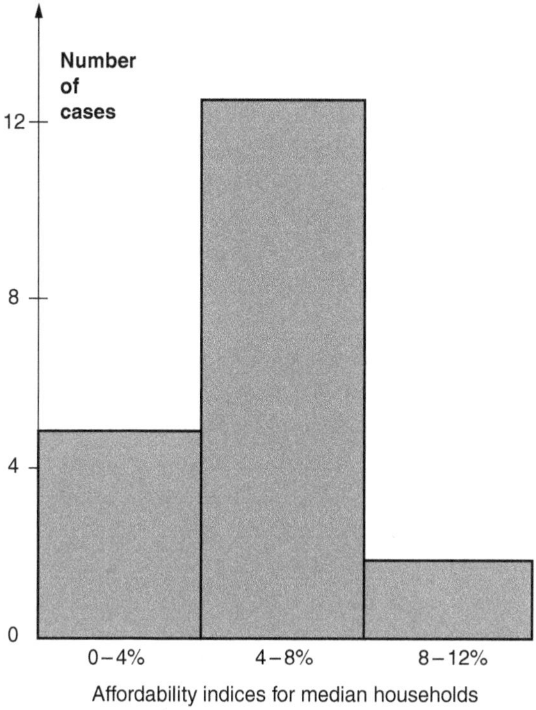


FIGURE 8.5 Distribution of affordability indices in Latin America[36]

median households is around 2.8 per cent, and for poor households connected to public water supply it can easily reach up to 7.5 per cent. Much higher values of the index have been observed in slums with water supplied by water vendors.

The limit of unaffordability – that is, the level of the affordability index above which developing or transition countries take special measures in favour of poor users – is likely to be around 7 per cent. Some developing countries have decided to make sure that water for poor households is not too expensive. For instance, in Morocco, the target of 3 per cent for water supply and sanitation of poor households is considered appropriate, and in slums the index is 5 per cent.

In some countries (see Table 8.2), national water laws or strategies prescribe a target of a maximum of 3 per cent for water expenses alone and a maximum of 6 per cent for water and sanitation expenses together. These are policy

[36] ADERASA, *Las tarifas de agua potable y alcantarillado en America Latina*, World Bank, Working Paper, 2005.

targets that would have to be implemented by various social measures and that would be likely to lead to higher affordability indices for the very poor. In Chile, a person having to pay more than the affordability limit is generally entitled to receive State aid in the form of a reduction of his bill. In Colombia, poor people pay less per cubic meter of water than rich people because water prices vary with housing characteristics. In Indonesia, a 2006 regulation prescribes that domestic expenses for the fulfilment of the standard of basic needs for drinking water should not exceed 4 per cent of the provincial minimum wage. In this case the objective is clear and social measures could be taken to meet the stated objective.[37]

However, an analysis of affordability indices for poor households in the world leads to the conclusion that many governments have accepted that water expenses of poor households exceed 7 per cent of their disposable income (see Table 8.1), i.e. much more than the target or benchmark of 5 per cent used by the Asian Development Bank.[38] This is not surprising, as water is essential for life and people die from thirst well before dying from hunger, and even if desperate will pay for it.

## 5 TARGETED AID AND SOCIAL TARIFFS

A second approach to identifying an affordability standard is to examine the policies for targeted aid and social tariffs. In a large number of countries with metered supply, water tariffs are progressive, with a first block of water consumption at a reduced price for all. Such measures are designed to help poor users, although the improvement in affordability will depend on the level of water consumption, the composition of households and the financing mechanism of the tariff reduction. Progressive tariffs may have a social function provided that they benefit mostly poor users. This requires a small first block and possibly the denial of the lower tariff to people who are not poor. Although, sometimes such tariffs are not progressive in effect since only wealthier groups are connected to the network. Cross subsidies with non-domestic users are frequent and help to reduce water expenses of households.

Targeted aid and social tariffs are implemented in over 34 developing countries and in over 20 OECD or EU countries to make water more

[37] Regulation No. 23/2006 on technical guidance and procedures for regulating tariff of drinking water in regional administration-owned drinking companies, stipulated on 3 July 2006.

[38] ADB, *Tariff, Subsidies and Development Funding*, 2001, chapter 11.

TABLE 8.1 *Examples of high affordability indices: population using above 5 per cent of disposable income - observed data*

| **Industrialised countries** | |
|---|---|
| France | 1% spend more than 4.8% |
| United Kingdom | 2% spend more than 8% |
| **Transition countries - Europe** | |
| Hungary | Lowest quintile spends more than 5.3% |
| Poland | Poor households[39] spend over 10.8% |
| Rumania | Lowest quintile spends more than 5.7%<br>Poor households spend over 8.1% |
| Latvia | Lowest quintile spends more than 5.1%<br>Poor householders spend over 6.3% |
| Russia | Lowest decile spends more than 6% |
| Ukraine | 6.4% spend more than 6% |
| Armenia | 12.3% spend more than 5% |
| **Latin America** | |
| El Salvador, Argentina and Jamaica | Lower quintile spends more than 11% |
| Uruguay | Lower quintile spends more than 10.4% |
| Surinam and Bolivia | Lower quintile spends more than 8% |
| Ecuador | Lower quintile spends more than 9% |
| Colombia | Lower decile spends more than 9% |
| Chile | Two lower quintiles in Valparaiso spend over 5% on average |
| **Africa** | |
| Burkina Faso | Lower quintile spends more than 29% |

*Source:* H. Smets, *De l'eau potable à un prix abordable* (Paris: Johanet, 2009), pp. 87–139.

affordable.[40] They provide a discount (or the equivalent in aid) ranging between 20 and 100 per cent on the price of water to people that can prove to be poor. The number of beneficiaries varies, from a few per thousand

39 Less than 50 per cent of median income.

40 Belgium, Argentina, Australia, Bulgaria, Bolivia, Cape Verde, France, Brazil, China, Greece, Chile, Gabon, Hungary, Colombia, India, Italy, Costa Rica, Indonesia, Lithuania, El Salvador, Japan, Luxembourg, Guatemala, Kenya, Malta, Mexico, Mongolia, Netherlands, Nicaragua, Morocco, Poland, Panama, Pakistan, Portugal, Paraguay, Singapore, Russia, Peru, South Africa, Spain, Saint Kitts, South Korea, Turkey, United States, Sri Lanka, Ukraine, Uruguay, Tunisia, United Kingdom, Venezuela, Mali, Mauritania, Niger, Zambia. This list does not refer to lifeline tariffs or to increasing block tariffs because such mechanisms are generally not sufficiently targeted (both poor and rich users receive an inexpensive water allocation). The list is based on a literature survey and cannot claim to be exhaustive.

TABLE 8.2 *Unaffordability limits for water or implementation of aid systems official policy objectives or legal requirements*[41]

| Country | Water | Sanitation | Benchmark | Type of disposable income |
|---|---|---|---|---|
| Lithuania | Y | Y | 2% | individual household |
| Northern Ireland | Y | Y | 3% | individual household |
| Argentina | Y | N | 3% | individual household |
| Venezuela | Y | Y | 3% | minimum salary |
| United States* | Y | N | 2.5% | median household |
| | Y | Y | 4% | median household |
| Indonesia | Y | N | 4% | minimum provincial salary |
| Chile | Y | Y | 5% | individual household |
| Kenya | Y | Y | 5% | individual household |
| Mongolia** | Y | N | 4% | individual household |
| | Y | Y | 6% | individual household |
| France | Y | Y | 3% | individual household |

* For the United States, the 2.5 per cent refers to the federal law for federal aid.
** The second Mongolian figure includes sanitation.

households to 20 per cent of the population, depending on the country and the means made available to fund the solidarity system.

Setting up targeted aid systems is not easy if there is no system in place able to identify poor users, and is not very useful if there is a high proportion of poor households. Rather than using an approach based on prices, countries have subsidised communal infrastructure that is specially designed for people with high affordability indices, such as water stand posts, public latrines or 'clever' water stand posts (with electronic cards).[42]

Targeted systems for water are difficult to implement when the social security system is not developed. Social tariffs are difficult to use when metering is unreliable or inexistent. However fixed aids can be provided to poor households in money or through a water stamp. In Johannesburg, indigent households receive an additional 4 kilolitres of free water per month and in some cases up to 9 kilolitres.[43]

[41] These benchmarks are either set at the national or sub-national levels.
[42] This card entitles the holder to a fixed amount of water, which he or she can take at the stand post when needed. It is used instead of coins or tickets and can be provided by municipalities with variable amounts of free water depending on individual circumstances. Additional water can be bought at the social tariff applicable to stand posts.
[43] See discussion in Chapter 7.

Some countries refuse to envisage special measures for water on the grounds that universal measures should be used for tackling poverty rather than targeted aid for various essential needs. Other countries do not separate water bills from housing bills, and provide aid for all housing-related expenses (this was a typical system in the former Soviet Union). There are also countries that do not provide social aid for water to poor people, and leave this issue to local communities or even to charitable organisations to manage.

By and large, it would seem that many targeted measures that are in force aim to bring down the affordability index to less than 5 per cent. In the absence of social measures to alleviate the burden of water expenses, the affordability index of very poor households is often above 7 per cent. Social measures, when they exist, sometimes introduce a discount on water expenses of 25 to 50 per cent that would bring down the index to approximately 5 per cent. In industrialised countries, few people have a high affordability index (i.e., over 7 per cent), because social assistance is being provided. In France, poor households with water debts are entitled by law to receive targeted aid, and a solidarity fund is being planned. In Colombia, water tariffs depend on the type and location of the user's dwelling and are smaller in poor areas.

In Chile, the State provides a water subsidy to poor users. This generous social measure was introduced when water prices were increased. Users belonging to the lowest income quintile may receive a discount on their water bills if they have to spend more than approximately 5 per cent of their income on water and sanitation. This aid is provided to 624,000 households in urban areas and to 87,000 households in rural areas identified by public authorities (16.6 per cent of the total population). The discount amounts to a reduction of 25 to 85 per cent of the bill (maximum 15 cubic metres); it is borne by the State budget (32.5 billion pesos or 5.9 per cent of water sales in 2006, USD 9 per household per year). The system was strengthened in 2004 to offer free water to 225,000 very poor households. Chile has recently approved a plan to implement an unaffordability limit of 3 per cent for water and sanitation.[44]

## 6 SELECTING LIMITS OF UNAFFORDABILITY

The average affordability index of poor households in a country gives an indication of what is generally or politically considered to be an acceptable

[44] Law No. 19–949 of 5 June 2004. Law No. 20–307 of 20 December 2008. In 2009, 15.9 per cent of the Chilean population received a subsidy for water amounting to 6.5 per cent of drinking water turnover.

price for water. Such an average is usually below the limit that triggers action by public authorities in favour of water for poor households.[45] The review of different measures in the preceding sections suggests that a limit for unaffordability could be based on the following considerations:

a) The water affordability index of poor households at the *upper limit* of the first quintile (or first decile) of income;
b) The unaffordability limits used in neighbouring or similarly situated countries (e.g., 3 to 6 per cent);
c) The unaffordability benchmarks proposed by international organisations (3 to 5 per cent);
d) The implicit unaffordability limit: i.e., that used in existing targeted aid systems at national levels;
e) A relative limit where the water affordability index of poor households should not be higher than three times the index for median households, or that poor households should not spend on water more than one tenth of what they spend on food; or
f) The affordability limit for access to electricity (when it exists), bearing in mind that water costs less than electricity.

However, the benchmarks used to measure progress or trigger responses may differ. For example, a *failure* to achieve affordability might be considered to have occurred if the affordability index of median households is exceeded in 10 (or 5) per cent of the municipalities; or the affordability index is exceeded within 10 (or 5) per cent of the households.

It is up to responsible authorities of each country to make the choice of an unaffordability limit for water using available statistics. On the basis of collected data, a reasonable limit might be that the index for poor people should be brought down to 3 per cent in industrialised countries or down to 5 per cent in developing countries.

However, the real issue is not to select such a figure as an overriding objective, but rather to develop and finance the corresponding social measures that favour people living in poverty. Improving access to affordable water requires paying attention to the affordability index and taking measures to reduce it, such as differentiated pricing, targeted aid programmes, cross-subsidy systems, or other initiatives. The right to affordable water can be implemented by managing water services in an efficient

[45] In many countries, there is a policy, but no concrete action. The real measure of concern for affordability is given by the number of people receiving aid for water or the total amount of aid given to poor people.

way, by providing sizable subsidies to the water sector, by adopting a social tariff for water or by providing targeted aid for water to poor households. Many countries have taken specific actions to promote access to water for the poor.[46] Social tariffs and targeted aid for water are used to a limited extent in developing countries, which often are satisfied with increasing block tariffs as a proxy for targeted social measures. In these countries, the lack of metering and of systems for identification of poor people makes it difficult to target aid.

Water stand posts should also be a supplemental policy. They were built during the Antiquity to provide free water to all as a symbol of solidarity. When they were introduced in western Europe, the operator had generally to support the expenses of the stand post in exchange for the right to lay pipes under the street and to sell water to private customers. Today, in wealthy countries with extensive water networks, new fountains are created as a social symbol and also for providing water at an affordable price to all, especially for homeless people. Water stand posts are also installed in transition countries and in developing countries, such as Ukraine, Morocco and Uganda (one stand post for 300 people). In some countries, users have to pay a small fee to the custodian of the equipment.

Some municipalities would prefer to close them down because they are costly, create a price inequality or attract the 'wrong' people. They consider that a valuable good, such as water, should not be provided without payment and object to what they describe as unfair competition for the water supply company. International financial institutions are said to suggest the closing down of stand posts in some developing countries where water prices have been increasing. Yet, stand posts are seen as the only available system to provide water at low cost when networks are not sufficiently developed. Stand posts with individual magnetic cards are being developed in Morocco to provide a free water allowance to poor households and to avoid water wastage.

## 7 CONCLUSIONS

In many countries, public authorities seek to maintain the water affordability index of poor households below 3 to 7 per cent of their disposable income. Lower values of this range are used in developed countries. In developing countries, higher values are often found. Affordability indices exceeding

[46] See the aforementioned list, although it is incomplete and does not include countries that use progressive tariffs, as this tariff is not targeted for the poor.

10 per cent are even observed for a small minority of poor people, but they should be viewed with some concern rather than as a possible representation of a reasonable outcome.

While affordability benchmarks of 3 to 5 per cent are promoted by international organisations, such limits will not be achieved unless targeted social measures are implemented and funded. In some cases, such benchmarks are not realistic because they would require providing aid for water to a large fraction of the population. Measures to make water more affordable for the most deprived people have been taken in many countries, but not in most. A few countries have well-designed social tariffs or targeted aids. Many developing countries have taken no action on affordability issues except by providing subsidies for water services that help affluent people to pay water they could have paid for themselves. While such subsidies can be useful, they should be redirected to people without access to water or sanitation rather than to those who have access to water.

In the future, public authorities should consider the following actions to support access to water and sanitation for all, while preserving their capacity to increase the price of water and sanitation, as needed, without creating social problems:

- Introduce the principle that drinking water should be affordable to all and enact within their legal systems the individual right to water at an affordable price;
- Adopt a definition of the water affordability index that can be used for assessment in different regions and population groups;
- Promote discussions on the choice of appropriate measures for water tariffs or targeted aid in line with user preferences, and on the financing of these measures in order for water to be affordable to all, bearing in mind other necessary household expenses;
- Examine whether bodies in charge of setting water tariffs are legally entitled to introduce differentiated tariffs, social tariffs or other systems of targeted aid to facilitate access to water for poor households;
- Develop the various elements of a social policy for water aimed to implement the principle of affordable water for all and to monitor and report on the implementation of this policy.

As to further research, it would be useful to seek to quantify affordability limits in relation to other social rights – in particular access to essential services such as housing, education, health, electricity, gas, heating oil, TV, internet and transportation. This could start from an analysis of existing measures that have been taken by States. In the United Kingdom, the affordability limit for water (3 per cent) was derived from the limit for energy (10 per cent). In Russia and Ukraine, the upper limit for all housing related expenses is 20 per cent. In France, the previously governing socialist referred to a maximum of all housing costs of 25 per cent, covering all house, energy, water related expenses. Examining the limits for these other social rights is important. There is an interrelation between expenses for all essential goods, which ultimately bear on the affordability of water.

# 9

# Engendering the Right to Water and Sanitation

## *Integrating the Experiences of Women and Girls*

ANNE HELLUM*

### 1 INTRODUCTION

'Where is the toilet?' During her time as a provincial health minister in Pakistan, this was the first question my colleague, Professor Shaheen Sardar Ali, would ask when she visited local health stations in the region.[1] It usually produced an embarrassing silence: there wasn't a women's toilet. Sardar Ali's seemingly innocent question provided a concrete means of demonstrating how the lack of a female toilet restrained the capability of women as both professionals and citizens in a public institution. The lack of female toilets barred women from seeking employment at local health stations, which in turn frustrated women's access to health services.

The question also constituted a conscious political strategy. It simultaneously addressed a number of interrelated human rights: water and sanitation, health, an adequate living standard and gender equality. These rights, as well as others, reflect the central place of water and sanitation in the livelihood struggles of women and affirm the importance of female leadership and participation in water services and management, a central theme in gender and development research.[2] The close relationship between women's marginalisation, social rights and inequality has been central to feminist thought, but less so in international human rights law.

* Professor, Department of Public and International Law and Director of the Institute of Women's Law, Child Law, Equality and Discrimination Law, Faculty of Law, University of Oslo.

[1] S. S. Ali, 'Where is the Toilet? Getting Down to the Basics in Accessing Women's Rights', in A. Hellum, J. Stewart, S. S. Ali and A. Tsanga (eds.), *Human Rights, Plural Legalities and Gendered Realities: Paths are Made by Walking* (Harare: Weaver Press, 2007), pp. 316–334.

[2] For a review of the gender and development discourses, see T. Wallace and A. Coles, 'Water, Gender and Development. An Introduction', in A. Coles and T. Wallace (eds.), *Gender, Water and Development* (Oxford: Berg, 2005), pp. 1–19.

Due in part to the schism between civil and political rights and economic, social and cultural rights, the capacity of international law to respond to the concerns of socially and economically marginalised women has been limited. As the principal forms of oppression against large groups of women operate in the socio-economic domain, feminist scholars have argued that international law, by according priority to civil and political rights, has little to offer women.[3] Some social rights scholars share the perspective.[4] Hunt puts it this way:

> The juridical marginalisation of social rights reflects the marginalisation of those who would most benefit from the legal protection of social and economic rights. Women are among the marginalised groups for whom social sights have a special relevance. Reflecting the public/private dichotomy, the juridical marginalisation of social rights is an example of the gendered nature of law.[5]

Nonetheless, there has been a gradual erosion of the effects of this rights schism in international law. If one focuses on water and sanitation, it is suggested that the UN General Assembly included these rights in the 1979 Convention on the Elimination of All Forms of Discrimination Against Women (CEDAW)[6] and, a decade later, in the Convention on the Rights of the Child (CRC).[7] This piecemeal legal development, along with water's centrality for basic needs and rights, such as the right to food, health and life, led the United Nations (UN) Committee on Economic, Social and Cultural Rights (CESCR) in 2002 to address the human right to water more directly under the right to an adequate standard of living and the right to health of the International Covenant on Economic, Social and Cultural Rights (ICESCR).[8] This development positively reflects the growing recognition of the significance of social and economic rights of women and girls in addressing marginalisation and the absence of substantive equality.[9]

[3] H. Charlesworth, C. Chinkin and S. Wright, 'Feminist Approaches to International Law', *American Journal of International Law*, Vol. 85, No. 4 (1991), pp. 613–645.

[4] P. Hunt, *Reclaiming Social Rights. International and Comparative Perspectives* (Aldershot: Dartmouth, 1996), pp. 71–106, at 106.

[5] Hunt, *Reclaiming Social Rights. International and Comparative Perspectives*, p. 106.

[6] Convention on the Elimination of All Forms of Discrimination Against Women (adopted 18 December 1979, entered into force 3 September 1981), 1249 UNTS 13, article 14.

[7] Convention on the Rights of the Child, (adopted 20 November 1989, entered into force 2 September 1990), 1577 UNTS 3, article 24.

[8] See, Committee on Economic, Social and Cultural Rights (CESCR), *General Comment No. 15, The Right to Water* (Twenty-ninth session, 2002), UN Doc. E/C.12/2002/11 (2003); and CESCR, *General Comment No. 14, The Right to the Highest Attainable Standard of Health* (Twenty-second session, 2000), UN Doc. E/C.12/2000/4 (2000); and International Covenant on Economic, Social and Cultural Rights (adopted 16 December 1966, entered into force 3 January 1976), 993 UNTS 3 (ICESCR).

[9] *Montreal Principles on Women's Economic, Social and Cultural Rights*, printed in *Human Rights Quarterly*, Vol. 26, No. 4 (1991).

More generally, the 1993 Vienna Declaration of Human Rights provided that, 'The equal status of women and the human rights of women should be integrated into the mainstream of United Nations system-wide activity'.[10] Endorsing the demand for a more holistic approach to human rights, States proclaimed that 'human rights are universal, indivisible and interdependent and interrelated'.[11] Feminist legal scholars, such as Otto, have emphasised the potential of this concept of indivisibility of human rights, a principle that can assist in protecting and promoting women's social and economic entitlements.[12] She sees the indivisibility principle, embedded in a number of declarations, as:

> [A] response to the gendered hierarchies and exclusions of human rights law itself. The appeal of the idea of indivisibility is that it suggests an organising principle that highlights interconnections, interdependencies, and holism in the increasingly fragmented paradigm of human rights.[13]

In international feminist and social rights jurisprudence, the question is thus no longer whether international law has anything to offer women and girls. Rather, it is a question of where in the UN system and beyond can the social and economic rights of women be best promoted and protected.[14] Farha has argued that the treaty with the greatest potential to influence the realisation of women's economic and social rights is the CEDAW, since:

> It is woman focused, it codifies a broad range of economic, social and cultural rights drawing on women's living conditions, it recognises the indivisibility of all rights, it has an expansive and progressive understanding of equality, it addresses women's inequality in both the private and public sphere, and it includes an individual complaints mechanism.[15]

[10] Vienna Declaration and Programme of Action (adopted 25 June 1993), World Conference on Human Rights, Vienna, 14–25 June 1993, para. 18.

[11] Vienna Declaration, Section I, para. 5

[12] D. Otto, 'Defending Women's Economic and Social Rights: Some Thoughts on Indivisibility and a New Standard of Equality', in I. Merali and V. Oosterveld (eds.), *Giving Meaning to Economic, Social and Cultural Rights* (Pennsylvania: University of Pennsylvania Press, 2001), pp. 52–62.

[13] Otto, 'Defending Women's Economic and Social Rights: Some Thoughts on Indivisibility and a New Standard of Equality', p. 66.

[14] L. Farha, 'Committee on the Elimination of Discrimination Against Women: Women Claiming Economic, Social and Cultural Rights – The CEDAW Potential', in M. Langford (ed.), *Social Rights Jurisprudence: Emerging Trends in International and Comparative Law* (Cambridge University Press, 2008), pp. 553–568, and M. Langford and J. A. King 'Committee on Economic, Social and Cultural Rights: Past, Present and Future', in Langford (ed.), *Social Rights Jurisprudence*, pp. 477–516.

[15] Farha, 'Committee on the Elimination of Discrimination against Women', p. 554.

Cutting across the rights to life, an adequate standard of living, health and food, as well as other human rights, the emerging recognition of the human right to water and sanitation is a good case for examining how the application of the principle of the indivisibility of human rights by human rights treaty bodies has brought, and could bring, poor rural women's concerns as providers of food and carers for families, the sick and elderly into, mainstream, international human rights discourse.

A closely related question is whether the current formulation of the human right to water and sanitation has 'engendered' social and economic rights. Fredman, in her approach to social and economic rights makes a distinction between spreading existing rights to women and engendering rights.[16] The concept of 'engendered social and economic rights', according to Fredman, entails the following:

> As a start it is necessary to recognise the distinctive nature of women's experience of poverty and disadvantage. This suggests that it is not sufficient simply to extend socio-economic rights to women. Instead, socio-economic rights need to be recast in light of the demands of substantive gender equality. Substantive gender equality goes beyond treating women in the same way as men and requires transformative measures. This in turn entails reconceptualising the rights themselves.[17]

The overall aim of this chapter is to explore whether and to what extent the human right to water and sanitation has helped re-interpret and re-shape human rights to accommodate the needs of rural women and girls. Towards this end, it examines international and national laws, policies and practices in light of how gendered perceptions, norms and practices inform rural women's and girls' day-to-day access and use of water and sanitation. It applies a grounded approach that marries a gendered understanding about the plurality of norms that have a bearing on local water and sanitation practices with evolving human rights principles.[18]

The chapter particularly focuses on the situation of the rural poor: 80 per cent of the world's 884 million without access to 20 litres of water per day live

[16] S. Fredman, 'Engendering Socio-economic Rights', *South African Journal of Human Rights*, Vol. 25, No. 3 (2009), pp. 410–441 at 410–411. These perspectives are further developed in S. Fredman, 'Engendering Socio-economic Rights' in A. Hellum and H. Sinding Aasen (eds.), *Women's Human Rights: CEDAW in International, Regional and National Law* (Cambridge: Cambridge University Press, 2013).

[17] Ibid.

[18] The grounded women's human rights approach is described in A. Hellum, J. Stewart, S. S. Ali and A. Tsanga, 'Paths Are Made by Walking: Introductory Thoughts', in Hellum, et al., *Human Rights, Plural Legalities and Gendered Realities*, pp. xx–xxi.

in rural areas.[19] Article 14 of the CEDAW highlights issues that impact disproportionately rural women, particularly discrimination in accessing land and water and by implication, the enjoyment of the right to food.[20] According to the CEDAW Committee:

> Globally, and with few exceptions, on every gender and development indicator for which data is available, rural women fare worse than rural men and urban women and men, and rural women disproportionately experience poverty and exclusion. They face systemic discrimination in accessing land and natural resources. They carry most of the unpaid work burden due to stereotyped gender roles, intra-household inequality, and lack of infrastructure and services, including with respect to food production and care work. [21]

As rural women and girls are often heavily marginalised, the realisation of their social and economic rights requires further and constant analysis of the plurality of international, national and local norms that have a bearing on their access to resources.

The chapter unfolds in three substantive sections. Section 2 sets out a 'grounded perspective', situating rural women's and girls' human rights at the interface of national and local norms and practices. Section 3 critically examines from this perspective the extent to which the human rights of rural women and girls' to water and sanitation have been mainstreamed into international law and policy, with a particular focus on three human rights treaty bodies. Section 4 addresses what should be the critical areas of focus for international legal practice and beyond in ensuring States respect, protect and fulfil the right to water and sanitation without discrimination. Case studies from different countries are used in the analysis.[22]

## 2 MAINSTREAMING GENDER: A GROUNDED PERSPECTIVE

The human right to water and sanitation is a social and economic right that arguably responds to poor women's basic concerns as providers of food and

[19] World Health Organization (WHO), *The Global Water Supply and Sanitation Assessment* (Geneva: WHO, 2000), p. 1.

[20] F. Banda, Article 14, p. 358 in M. Freeman, C. Chinkin and B. Rudolf (eds.), *CEDAW Commentary* (Oxford: OUP, 2012).

[21] CEDAW, *General Recommendation No. 34 on the Rights of Rural Women* (2016) UN Doc. CEDAW/C/GC/34, para. 5.

[22] Most of the examples are drawn from the socio-legal research compiled in A. Hellum, P. Kameri-Mbote and B. van Koppen (eds.), *Water is Life - Women's Human Rights in National and Local Water Governance in Southern and Eastern Africa* (Harare: Weaver Press, 2015).

carers of young, sick and elderly family members. Whether the human right to water in its present form recognises the struggles, hopes and aspirations of poor women and girls is an open question.[23] Without an approach that integrates the life experiences of women and girls, and how they may differ from those of men and boys, existing gender inequalities related to access to and control of water and sanitation may easily be perpetuated. The gender mainstreaming principle, implies that the gendered perceptions, uses and patterns of distribution of water and sanitation that exist 'on the ground' should be taken into consideration by lawmakers, policymakers and decision makers at the international, national and local levels.

Such mainstreaming has been formally called for by States at the international level. The 1993 Vienna Declaration and Programme of Action states that, 'The equal status of women and the human rights of women should be mainstreamed into United Nations system-wide activity. These issues should be regularly and systematically addressed throughout relevant United Nations bodies and mechanisms'.[24] This was affirmed in the 1995 Beijing Declaration,[25] and, in 1997, the UN Economic and Social Council formally adopted the principle of gender mainstreaming:

> Mainstreaming a gender perspective is the process of assessing the implications for women and men of any planned action, including legislation, policies and programmes, in all areas and at all levels. It is a strategy for making women's as well as men's concerns and experiences an integral dimension of the design, implementation, monitoring and evaluation of policies and programmes in all political, economic and societal spheres so that women and men benefit equally and inequality is not perpetuated. The ultimate goal is to achieve gender equality.[26]

This of course raises the issue of how the gendered norms and practices, which have a bearing on rural women's and girls' access to water and sanitation, have been taken into account by international and national lawmakers and policymakers. A major challenge in this regard is that women and girls often experience intersecting and overlapping marginalisations on the basis of

[23] P. Parmar, 'Revisiting the Human Right to Water', *The Australian Feminist Law Journal*, Vol. 28 (2008), pp. 77–96. Parmar argues that a shift from considering women merely as objects of human rights norms to recognition of women as sources of norm creation itself is needed.

[24] Vienna Declaration, para. 18.

[25] Beijing Declaration and Platform for Action (adopted 15 September 1995), Fourth World Conference on Women, UN Doc. A/CONF.177/20 (1995).

[26] UN Economic and Social Council Report (1997)A/52/3, p. 27. General Assembly Resolution of December 1997 (A/Res/52/100).

gender, race, ethnicity and social economic class.[27] In line with the demand of substantive equality embedded in different human rights instruments, attention must be given to how different groups of women experience water and sanitation related marginalisation and rights violations, which is linked not only to sex and gender, but also to other aspects of their identities.

A related challenge regarding the translation of international and national laws and policies into attainable entitlements is the reconciliation of universal principles with the plurality of norms and practices that exist on the ground. The harmful effects of water reforms that establish uniform statutory systems, without due consideration for the existence and effectiveness of local community-based norms, customs and practices, have been well documented.[28] Across the globe, the majority of poor rural women obtain access to water for food, productive and sanitary purposes by directly accessing water resources controlled by customary arrangements embedded in community-based water management systems.[29] In sub-Saharan Africa, land is largely regulated by customary arrangements for land tenure and related natural resources, such as water.[30]

Acknowledging that statutory law is not the sole regulatory mechanism in practice, socio-legal research has helped uncover the way in which women, in order to access, use and control land, water and common resources in Africa, Asia and Latin America rely on their rights as members of a family, social group or ethnic group.[31] Seeing the co-existence of statutory law, human rights law and principles and community-based norms

[27] K. Crenshaw, 'Demarginalising the Intersection of Race and Sex: A Black Feminist Critique of Antidiscrimination Doctrine, Feminist Theory and Antiracists Politics', *The University of Chicago Legal Forum*, Vol. 40 (1989), pp. 139–167.

[28] B. van Koppen, M. Giorano, J. Butterworth and E. Mapedza, 'Community-Based Water Law and Water Resource Management Reform in Developing Countries: Rationale, Contents and Key Messages', in B. van Koppen, M. Giordani, J. Butterworth (eds.), *Community-Based Water Law and Water Resource Management Reform in Developing Countries* (Oxford: CABI Publishers, 2007), pp. 248–270.

[29] Case studies from Asia, Africa and Latin America are compiled in B. R. Bruns and R. S. Meinzen-Dick (eds.), *Negotiating Water Rights* (New Delhi: Vistaar Publications, 2000) and B. van Koppen, M. Giordani, J. Butterworth (eds.), *Community-Based Water Law and Water Resource Management Reform in Developing Countries* (Oxford: CABI Publishers, 2007). On women's human right to water and customary law, see A. Hellum, 'The Indivisibility of Water, Land and Food in Local, National and International Human Rights Law: The Case of Women's Gardens in Mhondoro, Zimbabwe', in W. B. Eide and U. Kracht (eds.), *Food and Human Rights in Development*, Vol. 2 (Antwerpen-Oxford: Intersentia, 2007).

[30] S. Hodgson, *Land and Water – The Rights Interface*, Food and Agriculture Organization (FAO) Legislative Study No. 84 (Rome: FAO, 2004).

[31] See van Koppen, et al., *Community-Based Water Law and Water Resource Management Reform in Developing Countries*.

and practices helps draw attention to legal pluralism, where the same social space and the same activities are often subject to more than one body of law.[32] The legal pluralist perspective offers a set of tools that helps analyse how access to water and sanitation is or is not realised within a scenario of rights embedded in coexisting, overlapping and conflicting norms.[33]

From a women's rights perspective, the risk associated with overlapping norms and uses is related to the complex relationship between women's right to equality and the gendered character of local norms and practices.[34] While local customs and practices may facilitate women's access to water as part of a family and a local community, they are often moulded on hierarchical and asymmetrical constructions of gender relations. There is on the one hand, a need to ensure that customary norms recognising women's water needs as part of a group, and there is on the other hand, a need to consider how these customary norms are also placing a series of water-related duties on women and girls that are not shared by men and boys. The complex identities of women and girls as members of a group and as individual citizens call for careful analysis of the enabling and restricting dimensions of local customary law and its capacity to evolve and reflect the changing demands of sustainability and substantive gender equality by international and national law and policy makers.[35]

Substantive gender equality thus goes beyond treating women and girls in the same way as men and boys, as well as treating all women and girls similarly. It requires transformative measures that in turn entail reconceptualising the rights themselves.

[32] J. Griffiths, 'What is Legal Pluralism?', *Journal of Legal Pluralism*, Vol. 24 (1986), pp. 1–55; A. Hellum, *Women's Human Rights and Legal Pluralism in Africa* (Oslo/Harare: TANO/MHOND, 1999); F. von Benda-Beckmann, 'Who is Afraid of Legal Pluralism?', *Journal of Legal Pluralism*, No. 47 (2002), pp. 37–82; A. Griffiths, 'Legal Pluralism', in R. Banakar and M. Travers (eds.), *An Introduction to Law and Social Theory* (Oxford: Hart Publishing, 2002), pp. 289–310. R. N. Meinzen-Dick and L. Nkonya, 'Understanding Legal Pluralism in Water Rights: Lessons From Africa and Asia', van Koppen, et al., *Community-Based Water Law and Water Resource Management Reform in Developing Countries*.

[33] International Council on Human Rights Policy (ICHRP), *When Legal Orders Overlap: Human Rights, State and Non-State Law* (Geneva: ICHRP, 2009).

[34] Hellum, et al., 'Paths are Made by Walking'.

[35] Such an approach is developed in A. Hellum, P. Kameri-Mbote, B. van Koppen,'The Human Right to Water and Sanitation in a Legal Pluralist Landscape: Perspectives of Southern and Eastern African Women', in Hellum, Kameri-Mbote and van Koppen (eds.), *Water is Life*, pp. 1–30.

## 3 INTERNATIONAL LAW AND PRACTICE: A CRITICAL ANALYSIS

### 3.1 *UN Lawmakers and Policymakers*

To understand how the rights of different women and girls are mediated at the interface of international, national and local laws, policies and practices, attention is first turned to the international level, specifically the different UN actors that have influenced the development of the human right to water and sanitation. A key question is whether and to what extent laws and policies have been engendered or whether gender has simply been added to established understandings of rights.

In the early years of development cooperation, the focus in the water sector was on supporting publicly provided water services and supply. Whereas women were understood to bear the burden of the poorly functioning water sector, they did not discursively feature in water policy or implementation until the 1970s and 1980s.[36] This development is reflected in the CEDAW. In the preamble, the State parties declare themselves, 'Concerned that in situations of poverty women have the least access to food, health, education, training and opportunities for employment and other needs'. Article 14(1) of the CEDAW addresses the social and economic rights of rural women and obliges States to 'take into account the particular problems faced by rural women' as well as the 'significant roles that rural women play in the economic survival of their families'. Article 14(2)(h) goes on to provide that rural women have a right to 'enjoy adequate living conditions, particularly in relation to housing, sanitation, electricity and water supply, transport and communications' on an equal basis with men.

This recognition was further reflected in the CRC and the African Charter on the Rights and Welfare of the Child, which both provide or imply that a child has a right to clean drinking water.[37] In Africa, arguably the most recent manifestation of the human right to water is the 2000 Protocol to the African Charter on Human and Peoples' Rights on the Rights of Women in Africa (the Maputo Protocol). It obliges contracting States to take all appropriate measures to 'provide women with access to clean drinking water, sources of domestic fuel, land and the means of producing nutritious food'.[38]

[36] T. Wallace and A. Coles, 'Water, Gender and Development. An Introduction', in A. Coles and T. Wallace (eds.), *Gender, Water and Development* (Oxford: Berg, 2005), pp. 2–3.

[37] Article 28, CRC and article 14(2)(c), African Charter on the Rights and Welfare of the Child (adopted 11 July 1990, entered into force 29 November 1999), OAU Doc. CAB/LEG/24.9/49 (1990).

[38] Protocol to the African Charter on Human and Peoples' Rights on the Rights of Women (adopted 13 September 2000, entered into force 25 November 2005), OAU Doc. CAB/LEG/66.6 (2000).

However, the 1992 Dublin Statement on Water and Sustainable Development (often referred to as the Dublin Principles) more clearly represented the consensus in international water policy, as well as partly laid the discursive foundation for the subsequent wave of water reforms that took place in the late 1990s. It attempted to balance the prevailing neoliberal economic discourse, voiced by actors such as the International Monetary Fund (IMF) and the World Bank, with the growing movement for participatory natural resource management and sustainable development. Thus, Principle No. 4 states that 'water has an economic value in all its competing uses, and should be recognised as an economic good' but, to strike a balance, it continues, 'within this principle, it is vital to recognise the basic right of all human beings to have access to clean water and sanitation at an affordable price'.[39]

The Dublin Principles also took cognisance of the close relationship between water, gender and development. The gender dimension of sustainable water management was anchored in Principle No. 3: 'Women play a central part in the provision, management, and safeguarding of water'. Despite this recognition of women's role as local water managers, there was no explicit reference to article 14(2) of the CEDAW, which embodies a right to 'participate in and benefit equally from rural development' in paragraph (a), and to 'housing, sanitation, electricity and water supply' in paragraph (h).

When translated into national water laws and policies, these human rights dimensions were accorded little, if any, weight. Instead, the Dublin Principles, heralded a global policy shift that led many governments in the South to replace supply management systems with demand-based systems. Demand management, along with decentralisation, as well as privatisation, became the catchwords and modalities for water reform across the globe in the late 1990s. In the countries analysed below, the user-pays principle was adopted without reference to the human right to water or due consideration to the situation of poor urban and rural users. As providers of food and carers of children, sick people and the elderly poor, women and girls were, as will be discussed, particularly hard hit by this development.

[39] Dublin Statement on Water and Sustainable Development (adopted 31 January 1992), International Conference on Water and the Environment (ICWE), Dublin, Ireland 26–31 January 1992. The ICWE was attended by 500 participants, including government-designated experts. The Dublin Statement on Water and Sustainable Development was commended to the world leaders assembled at the UN Conference on Environment and Development in Rio de Janeiro in June 1992. See *Report of the United Nations Conference on Environment and Development* (Rio de Janeiro, 3-14 June 1992), UN Doc. A/CONF 151/26.

### General Comment No. 15 and Its Aftermath

The human right to water only gained real international traction a decade later. In November 2002, the Committee on Economic, Social and Cultural Rights adopted its General Comment No. 15 on the right to water. Although water is not specifically mentioned in the ICESCR, the Committee concluded that a human right to water is embedded in article 11 on the right to an adequate living standard, which it also interpreted in light of existing treaties, such as the CEDAW and the CRC, as well as the indivisibility of the rights to water, food and life.

The General Comment is generally sensitive to the needs of poor rural women in the articulation of the normative content of the right. Whereas the right to water applies to everyone, it states that:

> States Parties should give special attention to those individuals and groups who have traditionally faced difficulties in exercising this right, including women, children, minority groups, indigenous peoples, refugees, asylum seekers, internally displaced people, migrant workers, prisoners and detainees. In particular States parties should take steps to ensure that: Women are not excluded from decision-making processes concerning water resources and entitlements. The disproportionate burden women bear in the collection of water should be alleviated.[40]

Furthermore, in discussing access to water as an element of the right to food, it states that attention should be 'given to ensure that marginalised farmers, including women farmers, have equitable access to water and water management systems'.[41] More recently, in General Comment No. 20 on Non-Discrimination, the CESCR re-emphasised this point. The Committee observed that States have an immediate duty to adopt measures necessary to prevent, diminish and eliminate the conditions and attitudes that cause or perpetuate substantive or de facto discrimination, as well as to ensure that 'all individuals have equal access to adequate housing, water and sanitation', the achievement of which 'will help to overcome discrimination against women and girls and persons living in informal settlements and rural areas'.[42] In General Recommendation No. 27, the CEDAW Committee addresses the vulnerability of older women:

> In many countries, the majority of older women live in rural areas where access to services is even more difficult due to their age and poverty levels.

40 CESCR, General Comment No. 15, para. 16.

41 CESCR, General Comment No. 15, para. 7.

42 CESCR, *General Comment No. 20, Non-Discrimination in Economic, Social and Cultural Rights (art. 2, para. 2)* (Forty-second session, 2009), UN Doc. E/C.12/GC/20 (2009), para. 8.

> Many older women receive irregular, insufficient or no remittances from their migrant-worker children. Denial of their right to water, food and housing is part of the everyday life of poor, older women.[43]

Of great importance from a rights perspective was the Human Development Report of 2006. It concluded that the human right to water was one of the four foundations crucial for a solution to the global water and sanitation crisis.[44] The report addresses the gender division of labour assigning women's and girls' responsibilities to fetch water that men and boys do not share.[45] It shows how intra-household division of labour interacts with lack of water service provision to reinforce deep gender inequalities. The report concludes that empowering women may be one of the most successful mechanisms for stronger demand for water and sanitation at the level of local and national government.[46]

The right to sanitation has had less recognition, although this is changing. Sanitation is mentioned explicitly in CEDAW article 14(2)(h), alongside water supply, as an element of the right of rural women to equal enjoyment of adequate living conditions. Sanitation featured in Principle No. 3 of the Dublin Statement, but was not addressed as such in General Comment No. 15. In 2002, sanitation was however added as a target of the Millennium Development Goals (MDGs): Target 7.C was adjusted to say that States must halve by 2015 the proportion of people without sustainable access to safe drinking water and basic sanitation.[47] And, during the last decade, the movement for the right to sanitation gained pace.[48] In 2006, the right to sanitation was included in the Guidelines on the Realisation of the Right to Drinking Water and Sanitation by the former UN Sub-Commission on the Protection and Promotion of Human Rights.[49] In 2007, the UN Human Rights Council appointed an Independent Expert (now Special Rapporteur) on the issue of human rights

[43] CEDAW, General Recommendation No. 17 on Older Women and Protection of their Rights, UN Doc. CEDAW/C/GC/27, para. 24.

[44] United Nations Development Programme (UNDP), *Beyond Scarcity: Power, Poverty and the Global Water Crisis – Human Development Report 2006* (New York: UNDP, 2006). The four foundations crucial for success are: make water a human right, draw up national strategies for water and sanitation, support national plans with international aid, develop a global action plan, pp. 8–9.

[45] Ibid., pp. 47–48. [46] Ibid., p. 120.

[47] United Nations Millennium Declaration (adopted 8 September 2000), GA Res. 55/2, UN Doc. A/RES/55/2 (2000).

[48] See Chapter 10.

[49] UN Sub-Commission on the Promotion and Protection of Human Rights, Res. 2006/10, Promotion of the Realisation of the Right to Drinking Water and Sanitation, *Report of the Sub-Commission on the Promotion and Protection of Human Rights*, UN. Doc. A/HRC/Sub.1/58/L.11 (UN Sub-Commission Guidelines).

obligations related to access to safe drinking water and sanitation.[50] In line with the UN principle of mainstreaming gender, one of the tasks of the Independent Expert was 'to apply a gender perspective, including through the identification of gender-specific vulnerabilities'.[51] In her 2009 report, the Independent Expert draws on the concepts employed by the CESCR Committee in its analysis of the right to water.[52] She stresses that:

> States must ensure without discrimination that everyone has physical and economic access to sanitation, in all spheres of life, which is safe, hygienic, secure, socially and culturally acceptable, provides privacy and ensures dignity.[53]

These developments culminated in the 2010 General Assembly resolution which affirmed the human rights to water and sanitation, and in gender-neutral language.[54] In it, the General Assembly:

> 2. Calls upon States and international organisations to provide financial resources, capacity-building and technology transfer through international assistance and cooperation, in particular to developing countries, in order to scale up efforts to provide safe, clean, accessible and affordable drinking water and sanitation for all.

Subsequently, in a statement on the right to sanitation, the CESCR emphasised that 'girls do not go to school in many parts of the world for lack of toilets, or lack of separate toilets for them'.[55] In 2016, the CEDAW Committee in General Comment No. 34 addressed the lack of safe and culturally acceptable sanitation facilities for rural women and girls.

> In the absence of toilets or latrines, rural women and girls must also walk long distances in search of privacy. Lack of adequate sanitation also increases their risk of ill health. In order to remedy this situation, rural women and girls must have physical and economic access to sanitation, which is safe, hygienic and secure, as well as socially and culturally acceptable.[56]

50 Human Rights Council, Human Rights and Access to Safe Drinking Water and Sanitation, Res. 7/22, UN Doc. A/HRC/RES/7/22 (2008).

51 Human Rights Council, Res. 7/22 (ibid.), para. 2(d).

52 See section 4 above.

53 *Report of the Independent Expert on the Issue of Human Rights Obligations Related to Access to Safe Drinking Water and Sanitation, Catarina de Albuquerque* (2009), UN Doc. A/HRC/12/24, para. 63.

54 GA Res. 64/292, The Human Right to Water and Sanitation, UN Doc. A/res.64/292.

55 CESCR, Statement on the Right to Water and Sanitation (Forty-fifth session, 2010), UN Doc. E/C.12/45/CRP.1.

56 CEDAW General Recommendation No. 34, the Rights of Rural Women (2016), UN. Doc. CEDAW/C/GC/34, para. H 83.

Addressing the State obligation to ensure that rural women have access to essential services and public goods, including the CEDAW Committee in General Recommendation No. 34 provides that States should ensure: '[a]dequate sanitation and hygiene, enabling women and girls to practice menstrual hygiene and access sanitary pads'.[57]

The human right to water and sanitation clearly speaks to the needs of rural women and girls. The increasingly gender sensitive jurisprudence of different UN bodies regarding the right to sanitation, represents a jurisprudential breakthrough for the need for gender specific rights, and as such, a reconstruction of the right to sanitation in the light of the realities of women and girls.

**Between Productive and Domestic Uses of Water**

The question of recognition of the experiences of women and girls of water-related disadvantages raises a series of questions regarding the needs of different groups of women, and as such, the priority of different uses of water. In defining the content of the right to water in General Comment No. 15, the CESCR focused on personal and domestic uses. These were defined as water that is necessary for drinking, personal sanitation, washing of clothes, food preparation and personal and household hygiene.[58] Such an approach was also endorsed by the UN Sub-Commission in its guidelines on the right to water and sanitation.[59] While these uses form an integrated part of household chores, carried out overwhelmingly by women and girls in large parts of the world, a contested issue is whether, and to what extent, water that is necessary for livelihoods should be excluded. From a rural or semi-urban household perspective the drawing of a strict distinction between *domestic* and *productive* water use fails to capture the integrated way in which water is used for a multiplicity of livelihood purposes, ranging from drinking and washing to the watering of vegetables.[60]

Kitchen gardens, in particular, blur this boundary. Such gardens are of particular importance for rural and also peri-urban women since they represent a means by which they can provide basic food for their families. Kitchen gardens can be understood as different types of hand-irrigated home gardens – relying on water from nearby rivers, wells, boreholes or tap water – and are

57 Ibid., para. H 85. 58 CESCR, General Comment No. 15, para. 2.

59 UN Sub-Commission Guidelines, section 1.1.

60 B. Derman and A. Hellum, 'Neither Tragedy nor Enclosure: Are There Inherent Human Rights in Water Management in Zimabwe's Communal Lands', in T. A. Benjaminsen and C. Lund (eds.), *Securing Land Rights in Africa* (London: Frank Cass, 2003), pp. 31–50; B. van Koppen, S. Smits, and M. Mikhail, 'Homestead- and Community-Scale Multiple-Use Water Services: Unlocking New Investment Opportunities to Achieve the Millennium Development Goals', *Irrigation and Drainage*, Vol. 58, No. 3 (2009).

found throughout Africa, Asia and Latin America. The produce from these gardens, often sown, weeded and watered by women and girls, is used both for consumption and sale to meet the day-to-day needs of families.

The Food and Agricultural Organization (FAO) emphasises how gardens improve the viability of smallholders to meet interrelated concerns of food security, nutrition, health and economic security, particularly in the context of rising food prices.[61] Empirical research from South Africa shows that irrigation of kitchen gardens, through improved domestic water supply, offers an opportunity to lessen the burden of poverty experienced by marginalised groups and improve their food security and health.[62] Undertaken in the Limpopo Province, and encompassing female-headed households and male-headed households with home husbands and migrating husbands, the survey demonstrated that 70 per cent of households relied on kitchen gardens for food security. The magnitude of kitchen garden crops was significantly correlated with the amount of water access that was provided to the home. In Zimbabwe, studies of land and water management during its ongoing economic crisis reveal that it is single, divorced and widowed women with dependants, who are unemployed or do not receive cash-based assistance from family members, who rely most heavily on kitchen gardens for survival.[63]

This distinction between domestic and productive water use also does not sit well with the integrated way in which poor women use water for cooking, washing, sanitation and food production. Indeed, this integrated usage is reflected in part in the customary law of different groups of African peoples. Research from Zimbabwe documents how access to water resources vital for livelihoods is inherent in local norms and practices.[64] Water from rivers is considered a common pooled resource to be shared among villagers. Furthermore, those who need water for such uses are allocated land for gardens in

[61] FAO, *Livelihood Grow in Gardens: Diversifying Rural Incomes Through Home Gardens*, FAO Diversification booklet 2 (Rome: FAO, 2004).

[62] R. A. Hope, P. J. Dixon and G. von Malitz, 'The Role of Improved Domestic Water Supply in Livelihood and Poverty Reduction in Limpopo Province, South Africa', paper presented at WHRL symposium (2003).

[63] Derman and Hellum, 'Neither Tragedy nor Enclosure', pp. 31–50, A. Hellum, E. Sithole, W. Derman, L. Mangwanya, E.Rutsate, 'Zimbabwe's Urban Water Crisis and its Implications for Different Women: Emerging Norms and Practices in Harare's High Density Suburbs', in Hellum, Kameri-Mbote, van Koppen (eds.), *Water is Life*, pp. 347–383.

[64] N. Nemarundwe, 'Negotiating Resource Access: Institutional Arrangements for Woodlands and Water Use in Southern Zimbabwe', unpublished doctoral thesis (Uppsala: Swedish University of Agricultural Sciences, 2003); B. Sithole, *Use and Access to Dambos in Communal Lands in Zimbabwe: Institutional Considerations*, PhD thesis (Harare: University of Zimbabwe, 1999).

areas with available water sources. In local land and water allocation practices, these resources are made available because they constitute a key source of livelihood, food and self-reliance. To deny people access to these resources is associated with social and spiritual sanctions. These notions of a right to water are also embedded in the Zimbabwean Water Act of 1998, which defines primary water as water for household needs, animals and bricks to build houses.[65]

This empirical and contextual backdrop suggests that the Committee has understood domestic uses too narrowly or defined the contrast with productive uses too sharply.[66] If one of the criteria for establishing the existence and content of the right to water was health (as the Committee suggests), then water for kitchen gardens could or should be included in basic personal and domestic uses. In General Comment No. 14, the CESCR specifically included access to water as a condition necessary for living a healthy life.[67] In a similar vein, article 24 of the CRC links the right to health, clean water and nutritious food, describing a State duty 'To combat disease and malnutrition, including within the framework of primary health care, through *inter alia*, the application of readily available technology and through the provision of adequate nutritious foods and clean drinking-water, taking into consideration the dangers and risks of environmental pollution'.

An inclusive and progressive interpretation of domestic and personal use would therefore be in the best interests of one of the most vulnerable groups of children, typically those with single, divorced or widowed mothers. Moreover, in other General Comments, the CECSR has acknowledged the importance of cultural context in defining the content of rights.[68]

The CESCR has, however, sought to resolve the definitional dilemma by characterising kitchen gardening as a form of farming and analysing access to water resources in the context of the right to food.[69] The Committee states that beyond personal and domestic uses, priority in the allocation of water resources should be first given to uses that 'prevent starvation and disease'.[70] In this regard, it places particular emphasis on access by disadvantaged and marginalised farmers:

65 Government of Zimbabwe (1998a), Water Act, No. 31/1998.

66 See also similar arguments in M. Langford, 'Crossfire: There is No Human Right to Water for Livelihoods: A Debate with Melvin Woodhouse', *Waterlines*, Vol. 28, No. 1 (2009), pp. 5–12.

67 CESCR, General Comment No. 14, para. 4.

68 See for example, CESCR, *General Comment No. 4, The Right to Adequate Housing* (Sixth session, 1991), UN Doc. E/1992/23, annex III at 114 (1991).

69 See Chapter 4.

70 CESCR, General Comment No. 15, para. 6.

> Attention should be given to ensuring that disadvantaged and marginalised farmers, including women farmers, have equitable access to water and water management systems, including sustainable rain harvesting and irrigation technology.[71]

The Sub-Commission Guidelines take a similar approach by giving absolute priority to personal and domestic uses and then emphasising that 'marginalised or disadvantaged farmers and other vulnerable groups should be given priority to water resources for their basic needs' as part of their 'right to adequate nutrition and the right to earn a living through work'.[72]

This two-pronged approach, which maintains the distinction between water for domestic and productive purposes does not sit well with article 14 of the CEDAW. This article addresses the disadvantages experienced by rural women in accessing water, land and food. Article 14(1) obliges States to 'take into account the particular problems faced by rural women', as well as the 'significant roles that rural women play in the economic survival of their families'. Article 14(2) provide that rural women have a right to 'enjoy adequate living conditions, particularly in relation to housing, sanitation, electricity and water supply, transport and communications' on an equal basis with men. Furthermore, the CEDAW Committee, in its General Recommendation No. 21, states that women's domestic work should be put on an equal footing with productive work.[73] Applying this principle to the right to adequate water, the right should encompass rural and peri-urban women's integrated livelihood strategies and the way in which they use water for both domestic and productive purposes. The wording of article 14(2)(h), which links 'water supply' to 'the right to adequate living conditions', indicates a broad definition of the right to water, which includes water to produce food or other items that are necessary to prevent poverty, starvation and malnutrition. In General Recommendation No. 34, the Committee acknowledges that 'Rural women's and girls' rights to water and sanitation are not only essential rights in themselves, but also are key to the realisation of a wide range of other rights, including health, food, education and participation.'[74] In the light of this holistic approach, emphasising the indivisibility of the right to water, health and food, the Committee calls upon States to ensure that:

> rural women have access to essential services and public goods, including:

[71] CESCR, General Comment No. 15, para. 7.

[72] UN Sub-Commission Guidelines, section 4.3.

[73] CEDAW, General Recommendation No. 21, Equality in Marriage and Family Relations (1994), paras. 11–12, 32.

[74] CEDAW, General Recommendation No. 34, The Rights of Rural Women (2016), UN Doc. CEDAW/C/GC/34, para. H 81.

> Sufficient, safe, acceptable and physically accessible and affordable water for personal and domestic uses, as well as for agriculture/irrigation.[75]

All in all, the use of water to grow food that is necessary to prevent starvation and malnutrition has fallen between two stools of the domestic and productive sectors. As empirical studies of local water management practices demonstrate, the CESCR Committee's jurisprudence does not fully respond to the holistic way rural women manage and use water. Reinforcing the private/public dichotomy, it prevents international right to water discourse from expanding beyond the narrow confines of economic and legal paradigms, which can be biased both in terms of gender and class. The human right to water embedded in the ICESCR is still in part wedded to what Fredman terms an additive approach to socio-economic rights. The CEDAW Committee's interpretation of rural women's right to water under article 14, however, moves beyond this paradigmatic division of water use. Its holistic and indivisible approach, which includes water for agriculture, has the potential to be a fully engendered approach.[76]

### 3.2 *Human Rights Treaty Bodies and State Reporting*

The CESCR's dynamic and systematic interpretation of article 11 has been, nonetheless, a catalyst for a wide range of developments within the UN system. This can be seen particularly in the work of UN human rights treaty bodies in reviewing State reports, such as the CESCR, the CEDAW Committee and the CRC Committee. The remainder of this section takes a closer look at the practice of these bodies from 2005 until 2016 and the extent to which they have interpreted and shaped the human right to water and sanitation in light of the realities of women and girls.

**Committee on Economic, Social and Cultural Rights**

Following General Comment No. 15, the Committee's reporting guidelines ask States to provide information about the measures taken to ensure adequate and affordable access to water that is sufficient and safe for personal and domestic uses in the dwelling or within its immediate vicinity for everyone.[77] This is welcome, but the Committee's perspective is overwhelmingly group oriented and gender neutral.

[75] Ibid., para. H 85,a. [76] Fredman, 'Engendering Socio-economic Rights'.

[77] CESCR, *Guidelines on Treaty-Specific Documents to Be Submitted By States Parties under Articles 16 And 17 of the International Covenant on Economic, Social and Cultural Rights* (Forty-first session, 2008), UN Doc. E/C.12/2008/2 (2009).

In practice, the focus of CESCR's concluding observations on water and sanitation concern marginalised groups, such as slum dwellers, minorities, internally displaced persons, refugees and prisoners. There is no systematic consideration of the gendered uses of water and sanitation with a view to ensuring that women and girls within these groups benefit equally. For instance, commenting on Kenya's first report, the Committee paid particular attention to slum dwellers in Kibera, in Nairobi, urging the State to:

> Take immediate measures to ensure affordable access to adequate water and sanitation in informal settlements and arid or semi-arid rural areas, in line with the Committee's General Comment No. 15 (2002) on the right to water, by, inter alia, reducing waiting time for collecting water, adequately controlling prices charged by private water services and water kiosks, and connecting Kiberia to the Nairobi city sewage system.[78]

In the case of Australia, however, the Committee made reference to the situation of women and children in the context of a broader group. The Committee urged the State to:

> Take immediate steps to improve the health situation of indigenous people, in particular women and children, including by implementing a human rights framework that ensures access to the social determinants of health, such as housing, safe drinking water, electricity and effective sanitation systems.[79]

In a few instances, the vulnerabilities of specific groups of women, such as female prisoners in Yemen, or Bedouin women in Israel, are addressed.[80] In the former, it took notice of the '[l]iving conditions of prisoners and detainees, especially women, with regard to access to health-care facilities, adequate food and safe drinking water'.[81]

The Committee has in recent years paid regular attention to the huge disparities between rural and urban dwellers' access to water and sanitation. Commenting on Kenya's combined second to fifth period reports it expressed concern at:

> The insufficient access to safe drinking water and adequate sanitation with huge disparities between urban and rural areas, and formal and

[78] CESCR, *Concluding Observations: Kenya* (Forty-first session, 2008), UN Doc. E/C.12/KEN/CO/1 (2008), para. 30.

[79] CESCR, *Concluding Observations: Australia* (Forty-second session, 2009), UN Doc. E/C.12/AUS/CO/4 (2009).

[80] CESCR, *Concluding Observations: Yemen* (Thirty-first session, 2003), UN Doc. E/C.12/1/ADD.92 (2003), para. 18.

[81] Ibid., para. 18.

> informal settlements. It is also concerned at the lack of effective regulation of water prices.[82]

In a few instances the Committee has paid particular attention to rural women's access to water. In its concluding comments to Namibia the Committee noted with satisfaction its rights based water and sanitation policy, but was concerned that 'the responsibility for collecting water in rural areas falls mostly on women and girls, who have to walk long distances to the water points'.[83] In its comments to Nepal's third periodic report, the Committee was concerned about 'the high school dropout rate of girls, in particular during the transition between the primary and the secondary level, owing, inter alia to the unavailability of an adequate sanitary infrastructure'.[84] However, the Committee's comments are, for the most part, overwhelmingly gender neutral.

**Committee on the Elimination of Discrimination against Women**

In its advisory work, the CEDAW Committee has made passing reference to the right to water and sanitation. General Recommendation No. 27 on the Rights of Older Women makes mention of water and in General Recommendation No. 24 the CEDAW Committee noted that the rights contained in article 14(2)(h) are 'critical for the prevention of disease and the promotion of good health care'.[85] In General Recommendation No. 34, the Committee for the first time addresses the right to water and sanitation. It emphasises the gendered effects of water scarcity:

> Rural women and girls are among those who are the most affected by water scarcity; a situation which is aggravated by unequal access to natural resources and a lack of infrastructure and services. In order to access water, rural women and girls are frequently obliged to walk long distances to fetch it, sometimes exposing them to heightened risk of sexual violence and attacks. Due to poor rural infrastructure and services in many regions, rural women often spend four to five hours per day (or more) collecting water from sometimes poor quality sources, carrying heavy containers and suffering acute physical problems, as well as facing illnesses caused by the use of unsafe water.[86]

82 CESCR, *Concluding Observations: Kenya* (Fifty-seventh session, 2016) UN Doc.E/C.12/KEN/CO/2-5 (2016), paras. 49–50.
83 CESCR, *Concluding Observations Namibia* (Fifty-seventh session 2016) UN Doc. E/C.12/NAM/CO/1 /(2016), para. 61.
84 CESCR, *Concluding Observations Nepal* (Fifty-third session 2014), UN Doc.E/C.12/NPL/CO/3 /(2014), para. 28, b.
85 CEDAW, General Recommendation No. 24, para. 28.
86 CEDAW, General Recommendation No. 34, para. 82.

The Committee is also concerned about the lack of appropriate sanitation for rural women and girls:

> In the absence of toilets or latrines, rural women and girls must also walk long distances in search of privacy. Lack of adequate sanitation also increases their risk of ill health. To remedy this situation, rural women and girls must have physical and economic access to sanitation, which is safe, hygienic and secure, as well as socially and culturally acceptable. [87]

Surprisingly, the CEDAW Committee's reporting guidelines make no mention of the theme, but on the basis of article 14(2)(h) of the CEDAW, the Committee regularly refers in the periodic review process to the holistic relationship between women's right to participation and their right to development in terms of access to resources, such as land, water, credit and health services. Yet, this is pretty much as far it goes. The Committee's concluding observations are of a general character: most of the time, the Committee simply reiterates the formulation from the CEDAW.

For instance, in its consideration of the combined initial and second report of Mozambique the Committee, in general terms, recommended:

> That the State party take measures to increase and strengthen the participation of women in designing and implementing local development plans, and pay special attention to the needs of rural women, particularly women heads of household, ensuring that they participate in decision-making processes and have improved access to health, education, clean water and sanitation services, fertile land and income-generation projects.[88]

Considering the combined fourth and fifth periodic reports of India, the CEDAW Committee simply noted that it was concerned about the fact that 'rural women are particularly affected by poverty and food insecurity, lack of access to natural resources, safe water and credit facilities'.[89]

87 CEDAW, General Recommendation No. 34, para. 83.

88 Committee on the Elimination of Discrimination against Women (CEDAW Committee), *Concluding Comments: Mozambique* (Thirty-eighth session, 2007), UN Doc. CEDAW/C/MOZ/ CO/2 (2007), para. 41.

89 CEDAW Committee, *Concluding Comments: India* (Fifty eighth session 2014), UN Doc. CEDAW/C/IND/CO/4-5(2014), para. 32. For similar statements see CEDAW Committee *Concluding Comments: Pakistan* (fifty-fourth session 2013), UN Doc. CEDAW/C/PAK/CO/4 (2013), para. 33.c, *Concluding Comments: Mongolia (1381st and 1382nd meetings 2016), UN Doc. CEDAW/C/MNG/CO/8-9(2016), para. 32. Mozambique* (ibid.), para. 41; *Concluding Comments: Ghana* (Thirty-sixth session, 2006), UN Doc. CEDAW/C/GHA/CO/5 (2006), paras. 33–4; *Concluding Comments: Morocco* (Fourtieth session, 2008), UN Doc. CEDAW/CMAR/CO/4 (2008), para. 32; *Concluding Comments: Pakistan* (Thirty-eighth session, 2007), UN Doc. CEDAW/C/PAK/CO/ 3 (2007), para. 43.

Surprisingly, the Committee, in many of its most recent examinations of State reports, has not paid attention to the right to water and sanitation.[90] Even more surprising is the lack of attention to schoolgirls' right to appropriate sanitation facilities as a part of its consideration of the right to equal education. The Committee, in its comment to India's fourth and fifth periodic reports, however, urged the State party to 'ensure that schools are girl-friendly, within a reasonable distance of communities, and have supplies of potable water and separate hygienic toilets for girls'.[91] In its comment to Malawi's seventh period report, the Committee expressed concern at 'the persistence of structural and other barriers to girls. Access to quality education, in particular at the secondary level, owing, inter alia, to the lack of school infrastructure, including adequate sanitary facilities'.[92]

The Committee's approach to the right to water under article 14 involves taking into consideration the additional structural disadvantage experienced by rural women not only in relation to water, but also health, nutrition and education. Rural women are, as pointed out by Banda, mainly dealt with in the context of intersectionality – an analysis identifying additional structural disadvantages experienced by women as a result of an identity factor or situation in addition to their sex.[93] Due in part to this broad approach, and the general character of the information put before it by both States and nongovernmental organisations (NGOs), the Committee has in practice not been in a position to address the relationship between the gender neutral water laws and policies that in recent years have been adopted by most countries and the gendered uses of water and sanitation on the ground. General Recommendation 34 on the rights of rural women, however, speaks to the potential of CEDAW's holistic approach, which recognises the indivisibility of the right to an adequate living standard, particularly education, health, food, gender-sensitive sanitation and water to grow family food. While the CEDAW is arguably the treaty with the greatest potential to engender women's social and economic rights, the practice of the CEDAW Committee has been confined to add the concerns of women and girls to existing rights without making any significant contribution to *engendering* the human right to water and sanitation.

90 For example, Congo, Swaziland, Cameroon, Ghana, Malawi, Peru and Afghanistan.

91 CEDAW Committee, *Concluding Comments: India*, para. 27,b.

92 CEDAW Committee, *Concluding Comments: Malawi* (1351st and 1352nd meetings 2015), Un Doc. CEDAW/C/MWI/CO/7(2015), para. 30. A.

93 F. Banda, Article 14, p. 365 in Freeman, Chinkin and Rudolf (eds.), *CEDAW Commentary*.

**Committee on the Rights of the Child**

Despite reference to water in the CRC, the CRC Committee has not addressed the right to water per se in any of its concluding comments or in its reporting guidelines. Yet access to water is frequently addressed in the Committee's concluding observations regarding State reports. Often the number of children without water or sanitation is noted with concern or the State party is asked to collect data on water and sanitation.[94] Commenting on Pakistan's report the Committee noted the 'high number of children living in poverty, shortage of adequate housing, clean water, adequate sanitation and sewage, and problem of air pollution, all of which have serious negative impact on living conditions of children in the State, causing injuries, sickness and death'.[95]

Unlike the CEDAW Committee, the CRC Committee is more specific and concrete in reviewing progress on the right to water and sanitation. Yet, with its general focus on children within disadvantaged groups and families, it mirrors the CESCR in adopting an overwhelmingly group- oriented and gender-neutral approach. This general approach is evident on a topic that has gender implications: school sanitation facilities. In its concluding comments to Kenya's report, the CRC Committee remarked that: 'Rapid increase in school enrolment significantly challenges sufficient allocation of financial resources, commonly resulting in a poor physical school environment lacking adequate infrastructure, trained teachers and appropriate water and sanitation facilities'.[96] Similarly, in commenting on the Bangladesh periodic report, in 2003, it acknowledged the adoption of the National Policy for Safe Water Supply and Sanitation, but added concern that, 'Despite the measures taken by the State party about the extent of water contamination, specifically with arsenic, air pollution and low availability of sanitation facilities, have serious negative consequences for children's health and development.'[97]

[94] CRC Committee, *Concluding Observations: Kyrgyzstan* (Twenty-fourth session, 2000), UN Doc. CRC/15/ADD.127 (2000), para. 48; *Concluding Observations: Lebanon* (Twenty-ninth session, 2002), UN Doc. CRC/15/ADD.169 (2002), para. 47; *Concluding Observations: Armenia* (Twenty-third session, 2000), UN Doc. CRC/C/15/ADD.119 (2000), para. 40.

[95] CRC Committee, *Concluding Observations: Pakistan* (Thirty-fourth session, 2003), UN Doc. CRC/15/ADD.217 (2003), para. 58. In a similar vein the Committee in its comment to Mozambique's report noted that, 'Only very small portion of the population has access to electricity, sanitation and clean running water in their homes': *Concluding Observations: Mozambique* (Twenty-ninth session, 2002), UN Doc. CRC/C/15ADD.172 (2002), para. 54.

[96] CRC Committee, *Concluding Observations: Kenya* (Forty-fourth session, 2007), UN Doc. CRC/C/KEN/CO/2 (2007), para. 57.

[97] CRC Committee, *Concluding Observations: Bangladesh* (Thirty-fourth session, 2003), UN Doc. CRC/C/15/ADD.221 (2003), para. 53.

Nonetheless, in its analysis of access to water and sanitation in schools, the CRC Committee has in some instances emphasised the need for separate sanitation facilities of girls and boys in schools. In its 2009 observations on Bangladesh, it expressed concerns over 'reported mistreatment of children by their teachers and the frequent cases of bullying and sexual harassment, particularly of girls, at school and on the way to school; the lack of separate sanitation facilities of boys and girls'.[98] Overwhelmingly though, the CRC Committee is gender neutral. Given the vast documentation of how the lack of basic water and sanitation services translates into lost education opportunities for young girls, this is clearly an area that needs to be engendered.

**Gender Gaps in the Analysis**

While focusing on the right to water and sanitation from different angles, the work of the three committees clearly supplements and reinforces that of each other. However, none of the bodies pay systematic attention to the gendered uses of water and sanitation and how gender neutral laws and policies may reinforce existing inequalities. To engender the human right to water and sanitation, more attention clearly needs to be paid to the different uses of water by rural men and women and the different needs of girls and boys related to sanitation.

## 4 ENGENDERING THE DUTY TO RESPECT, PROTECT AND FULFIL - KEY ISSUES

The discussion now turns to the obligations of States to meet the human right to water under international human rights law, applying the general framework for the nature and level of State obligations.[99] The framework distinguishes between States' obligations to respect, protect and fulfil (the latter including facilitate, provide and promote) the human rights in question. With the objective of assessing how international legal sources respond and relate to the plurality of local laws, customs and practices that have a bearing on poor, rural women's and girls' access to water and sanitation, they are juxtaposed with empirical case studies describing the situation of women and girls on the ground in southern African countries. While the human right to water and

[98] CRC Committee, *Concluding Observations: Bangladesh* (Fifty-first session, 2009), UN Doc. CRC/BGD/CO/4 (2009), para. 74.

[99] Originally proposed by A. Eide in A. Eide, W.B. Eide, S. Goonatilake, J. Gussow and Omawale (eds.), *Food as a Human Right* (Tokyo: United Nations University, 1984).

sanitation clearly has made its mark on southern and eastern African States' constitutions, laws and policies. African States were off track from meeting the United Nations water-related MDGs with just 61 per cent water coverage.[100]

### 4.1 *Women's Customary Water Uses*

Turning to the obligation of States to respect and protect the right to water, it should be kept in mind that poor rural women rely heavily on common pool water resources embedded in local customs and practices. The existence and effectiveness of community-based arrangements in supporting members' right to water has been dealt with in recent studies on Africa, Asia and Latin America.[101] At the local level, the right to water and the right to livelihood are often seen as intimately interwoven and given high priority in land and water allocation.[102] In rural areas in Zimbabwe, for example, people's water management practices are underlain by a shared belief that they have a duty to share clean drinking water.[103] Denying people clean drinking water is seen as denying them life. Water, in rural, peri-urban and, under the circumstances, urban areas forms part of a broader right to livelihood, in terms of a right to access land with available water for vegetable gardens, close to rivers or wetlands, where women grow food for their families.[104]

According to the CESCR, the obligation to respect the human right to water includes a duty to refrain from interfering arbitrarily with customary or traditional arrangements for water allocation, unlawfully polluting water or destroying water services and infrastructure as a punitive measure.[105]

[100] www.un.org/waterforlifedecade/africa.shtml (last accessed 15 December 2013).

[101] F. von Benda-Beckman, et al., 'Local Law and Customary Practice in the Study of Water Rights', in R. Pradhan, et al. (eds.), *Water Rights, Conflict and Policy* (Colombo: International Irrigation Management Institute, 1997); R. S. Meinzen-Dick and B. R. Bruns, 'Negotiating Water Rights: Introduction', in R. S. Meinzen-Dick and B. R. Bruns (eds.) *Negotiating Water Rights* (New Delhi: Vistar Publications, 2000).

[102] B. Derman, A. Hellum, E. Manzungu, P. Sithole and R. Machiridza, 'Intersections of Law, Human Rights and Water Management in Zimbabwe: Implications for Rural Livelihoods', in van Koppen, et al. (eds.), *Community-Based Water Law and Water Resource Management Reform in Developing Countries*, pp. 248–270.

[103] B. Derman and A. Hellum, 'Neither Tragedy nor Enclosure: Are There Inherent Human Rights in Water Management in Zimbabwe's Communal Lands', in T. Benjaminsen and C. Lund (eds.), *Securing Land Rights in Africa* (London: Frank Cass, 2003), pp. 31–50.

[104] A. Hellum, E.Sithole, W.Derman, L. Mangwanya and E. Rutsate, 'Zimbabwe's Urban Water Crisis and its Implications for Different Women: Emerging Norms and Practices in Harare's High Density Suburbs', in Hellum, Kameri-Mbote and van Koppen (eds.), *Water is Life*, pp. 347–383.

[105] CESCR, General Comment No. 15, para. 21.

In articulating the content of the right to food, and taking note of the duty in article 1(2) of the ICESCR, which provides that people cannot 'be deprived of their means of subsistence', the CESCR has also opined that States parties should ensure that there is adequate access to water for subsistence farming and for securing the livelihoods of indigenous peoples.[106] This implies a duty to respect and protect traditional water use. The former UN Sub-Commission's Guidelines for the realisation of the right to drinking water and sanitation underscores this duty: 'States should enact and implement legislation to protect access by persons to traditional water sources in rural areas'.[107] Yet, tensions exist between, on the one hand, the State's duty to respect and protect local communities' customary water uses and, on the other hand, its duty to protect the environment and promote sustainable development. The CESCR Committee's Concluding Comments to Burkina Faso's initial report shows how the Committee seeks to protect traditional water uses:

> The Committee is alarmed by the harmful effect on the rights of rural communities, small farmers and agropastoralists of the activities of businesses that exploit the natural resources of their territories. It is extremely concerned at reports that these activities have a serious impact on the human rights of these communities, such as the right to health, environment, education, housing and water, particularly in the Essakane community, where by failing to build a school or to provide water for market gardens, the mining company concerned has not fully complied with its commitment to compensate displaced populations.[108]

**Customary Water Uses and Environmental Protection**

A question in former colonies in southern Africa is whether, and to what extent, the criminalisation of riverine and wetland cultivation can be reconciled with the State's duty to respect and protect access to traditional water sources in rural areas. Assuming that these practices disturbed the river flow and caused erosion, the colonial governments enacted legislation that prohibited wetland and stream bank farming.[109] Although newer hydrological

[106] Ibid., para. 7. [107] UN Sub-Commission Guidelines, section 3.4.

[108] CESCR Committee, *Concluding Observation: Burkina Faso*, 28th to 30th meetings (2016) E/C/12/BFA/CO/1, para. 31.

[109] The colonial government in Nyasaland (later Rhodesia and now Zimbabwe) enacted a series of laws prohibiting these forms of agriculture; the Water Act of 1927, the Natural Resources Act and the Stream bank Regulation of 1952. See W. Beinart, 'Soil Erosion, Conservationism and Ideas about Development: A Southern African Exploration, 1900–1960', *Journal of Southern African Studies*, Vol. 11, No. 2 (1984), pp. 52–83.

and agricultural research shows that sustainable wetland farming under proper management by communal farmers is possible and economically viable, these laws are still in force in Zimbabwe.[110] Since independence they have, however, been only randomly enforced. In some instances, the local authorities have used the regulations as a means of moving people away from riverbanks, and, as such, increased the work burden of women. This has to a large extent been the case in the Zambezi Valley were people were moved away from the rivers as large areas were designated for cotton production.[111] In other instances, these customary practices have been tolerated, because they provide a lifeline for poor communities.[112] This is the case under the present social and economic crisis in Zimbabwe.[113]

The duty to respect and protect customary land and water uses does not sit well with legislation that undermines poor women's access to common pool water sources, and, as such, their ability to support their families and ensure their children's right to nutritious food. Existing national regulation of riverbank and wetland cultivation in former colonies in Africa epitomises the tense relationship between, on the one hand, poor women's and families' right to a livelihood and, on the other, protection of the environment. How uses of riverbanks and wetlands under proper management by poor farmers can be made ecologically viable is an issue that calls for innovative, interdisciplinary and holistic approaches.

### *Customary Water Uses and Large-Scale Land Investment*

Transnational land deals reflect the process whereby agro-food-energy systems are becoming globalised under the influence of multinational companies. These deals can result in uncompensated loss of livelihood resources for poor and marginalised groups, so-called 'land grabbing'. These negative effects have given rise to a series of human rights initiatives seeking to strengthen the obligations of the host State to ensure protection of human rights under its jurisdiction, as well as addressing the extraterritorial human rights obligations

[110] T. Matiza, 'The Utilisation and Status of Dambos in Southern Africa: A Zimbabwe Case Study', in T. Matiza and H. N. Chabwela (eds.), Wetlands Conservation Conference for Southern Africa: Proceedings of the SADCC *Wetlands Conference held in Goborone,* Botswana, 3–5 June 1991 (Gland, Switzerland: IUCN, 1992), pp. 91–104.

[111] B. Derman, 'How Green Was My Valley! Land Use and Economic Development in the Zambezi Valley, Zimbabwe', in B. Isaac (ed.), *Research in Economic Anthropology* (Greenwich: Greenwood, 1997), pp. 331–380.

[112] B. Sithole, *Use and Access to Dambos in Communal Lands in Zimbabwe.*

[113] E. Rutsate, B. Derman and A. Hellum, 'A Hidden Presence: Women Farmworkes Right to Water and Sanitation inthe Aftermath of the Fast Track Land Reform', in Hellum, Kameri-Mbote and van Koppen (eds.), *Water is Life*, pp. 384–420.

of multinational companies. The former Special Rapporteur on the Right to Food addressed the negative effects associated with such land deals and underscored the obligation of States and private companies to ensure the affected local population's right to an adequate standard of living, and particularly respect and protect customary arrangements that ensure access to land to produce food.[114]

Water as both a target and a driver of this changing mode of agricultural production has so far been given less attention, despite the interconnectedness of the right to an adequate standard of living and the right to food (especially the need to access land and water to produce food for livelihood). The fluid nature of water and its hydrological complexity often obscures how water is appropriated as a result of transnational land deals and the associated impacts on local livelihoods and food security.[115] In practice, large-scale land and water deals between international companies and national governments can be framed by water laws that do not fully respect and protect local community based water rights. Local community-based water governance regimes, which have co-existed with the received western water laws since the colonial period, often lack formal legal recognition and are not integrated and protected by the laws and policies that frame national water governance systems.[116] Permits to use water for commercial agriculture are, as a result, often granted by national water governance institutions without sufficient consideration of the existing uses of small-scale users, who lack the resources to fulfill the formal requirements for obtaining a water permit. These micro-scale users, most of them women producing food and other items for livelihood, are easy victims of so-called water grabbing in a situation where governments may tend to side with large-scale users.

While calls for the recognition of a human right to water partially represented an attempt to protect the right to water against commercial agriculture, which is one of the largest users, this issue is poorly captured by the content of the right. As noted earlier, UN General Assembly Resolution 64/292 on the right to water and sanitation includes water for personal and domestic uses, but excludes water for broader livelihood needs. Other sources of international law, however, recognise the need to extend the human right to water for broader livelihood needs. Viewing the right to life, food, health and water as

[114] See A/HRC/13/33 and A/HRC/22/72.

[115] L. Mehta, G.J. Veldwisch and J. Franco, 'Introduction to the Special Issue: Water grabbing? Focus on the (Re)appropriation of Finite Water Resources', *Water Alternatives* Vol. 5, No. 2, 2012, pp. 193–207.

[116] Van Koppen Chapter 2 in this volume.

indivisible, section 8 of the right to food guidelines include access to water resources as one of its central obligations to ensure secure access to produce food for livelihood.[117] With a view to women's key role in food security at the family and local level, the Special Rapporteur on the Right to Food has emphasised the need to ensure that rural women's access to productive resources, particularly customary land and water uses, are respected and protected.[118]

This notion of 'water grabbing' as a human rights and gender issue thus underscores the need for mechanisms to hold States and international companies accountable in assuring that the basic human right to an adequate standard of living, particularly the right to food, involving water for personal, domestic and also livelihood uses, under article 11 of the ICESCR and article 14 of the CEDAW is respected and protected.

In striking a balance between conflicting water uses – particularly between large agricultural companies and poor small-scale farmers – the right to adequate food requires that both States and companies involved in transnational land deals that involve appropriation of water, consider the situation of vulnerable groups in order to ensure that they are secured access to productive resources, most importantly water, to grow food for livelihood needs.[119]

### 4.2 *Accessibility and Discrimination*

Water and sanitation services should be made accessible to everyone without discrimination. The human right to water and sanitation, to have a real effect on achieving substantive equality of women and girls, needs to be infused with protection against direct, indirect and structural discrimination. General Comment No. 15 states that, 'whereas the right to water applies to everyone, States parties should give special attention to those individuals and groups who have traditionally faced difficulties in exercising this right'.[120] The CESCR has addressed discrimination in relation to the right to water in light of article 2(2) of the ICESCR: discrimination on the grounds of sex, 'which has the

[117] The Voluntary Guidelines to Support the Progressive Realisation of the Right to Adequate Food in the the Context of National Food Security, adopted by the FAO in 2004.

[118] Report submitted to the UN Human Rights Council by the Special Rapporteur on the Right to Food, Olivier De Schutter, Women's Rights and the Right to Food, (24 December 2012). UN Doc. A/HRC/22/50.

[119] M. Windfuhr, Water for Food: a Human Rights Obligation. How States can Manage Conflicts between the Human Right to Water and the Human Rights to Adequate Food, German Institute for Human Rights, 2013.

[120] CESCR, General Comment No. 15, para. 16. See also, UN Sub-Commission Guidelines.

intention or effect of nullifying or impairing the equal enjoyment or exercise of the right to water' is said to contravene the Covenant.[121] The importance of eliminating substantive inequality was further articulated in General Comment No. 20 as discussed above.

Direct and indirect discrimination is often a result of systemic discrimination, understood as 'legal rules, policies and practices or predominant cultural attitudes in either the public or the private sector which create relative disadvantages for some groups and privileges for others'.[122] To come to grips with systemic discrimination, States must take proactive measures. Article 5(a) of the CEDAW and article 2(2) of the Maputo Protocol require that States parties commit themselves to take measures to modify the social and cultural patterns of the conduct of women and men which are based on the idea of the inferiority or the superiority of either of the sexes, or on stereotyped roles for women and men – so-called gender stereotypes. In light of this obligation, one would expect that national water and sanitation policies or water and sanitation programmes, carried out by international or national organisations, include measures addressing the widespread gender stereotype that women and girls are primarily responsible for obtaining water and ensuring that the water used for household purposes is clean and environmentally sound.

### Direct Discrimination - Fetching Water

Direct discrimination occurs when a difference in treatment relies directly and explicitly on distinctions exclusively on sex and characteristics of men or women, which cannot be justified objectively.[123] Direct discrimination is often related to gender stereotypes embedded in social, religious or cultural notions of how men and women are expected to behave. Gender stereotypes, according to Cook and Cusack, degrade women when they assign them subservient roles in society.[124] Prejudices about women's inferiority generate disrespect and devaluation of women. When societies fail to recognise and eliminate stereotypes they are, according to Cook and Cusack, 'exacerbating a climate of impunity with respect to women's rights'.[125]

[121] CESCR, General Comment No. 15, para. 13.

[122] CESCR, General Comment No. 20, para. 12.

[123] CESCR, *General Comment No. 16, The equal right of men and women to the enjoyment of all economic, social and cultural rights* (Thirty-fourth session, 2005), UN Doc. E/C.12/2005/3 (2005).

[124] R. Cook and S. Cusack, *Gender Stereotyping: Transnational Legal Perspectives* (Philadelphia: University of Pennsylvania Press, 2010), p. 1.

[125] Ibid.

Due to the gendered division of labour, women and girls, in large parts of the world, spend a far greater time fetching water than men and boys. The gendered division of labour between women and men, as well as between girls and boys, is underpinned by gender stereotypes embedded in customary or religious norms and beliefs. Article 5(a) of the CEDAW places an obligation on State parties to take all appropriate measures to eradicate or modify hierarchical gender norms, beliefs or practices.

According to UNICEF, about half of the girls in sub-Saharan Africa who drop out of primary school do so because of poor water and sanitation services.[126] The time burden of collecting and carrying water is seen as one explanation for the gender gaps in school attendance in many countries.[127] How the right to education is affected by the interplay between lack of accessible water and norms and practices that place a duty to fetch water on girls has been the object of both quantitative and qualitative research. A quantitative micro-data study carried out in eight developing countries suggests that better access to water, in countries where substantial gender gaps in schooling exist is associated with greater enrolment for both boys and girls.[128]

How girls are affected by lack of access to water is illustrated by a study of water management in four rural areas in Mozambique – Namaacha, Moamba, Mabote and Massinga.[129] In the six school areas, which were part of the study, two lacked pumps or boreholes, two had one borehole, and two had several boreholes and pumps. With some exceptions, group discussions with teachers revealed that the girls in the area had a familial duty to fetch water. Girls often came late to school because they were fetching water or they were occupied by the task (e.g. thinking of where to locate it next) and left school immediately to fetch water. According to a male teacher:

> I think that pregnancy and issues of early marriage are linked to water fetching activity. In a rural area, a girl who can fill up a 60 litre container with water is ready to get married. The parents can marry her off because she is sufficiently mature to provide water and food for the family. In our tradition, when a family escorts her daughter to the husband's family the greeting is as follows: 'Wuyane mate – welcome water'. This is to say that

[126] UNICEF, *State of the World's Children* (New York: UNICEF, 2005).

[127] UNDP, *Human Development Report 2006*, p. 47.

[128] G. Koolwal and D. van de Walle. 'Better Access to Water Raises Welfare, But Not Women's Off-Farm Work', *Economic Premise*, No. 67, World Bank, October 2011.

[129] I. Afonso, 'Access to Clean Water in the Southern Region of Mozambique and its Implications for Girls' Right to Education', Master Thesis in Women's Law, SEARCWL, University of Zimbabwe, 2004. The interviews with teachers and young girls below are quoted from the thesis.

> fetching water is a sign of adulthood and therefore girls are forced to drop out of school and marry because of our cultural practices.[130]

In the primary school of Tenga, in Momba Disctrict, the water points were about 14 kilometres from the residential areas, while the distance from the residential area to the school was 7 kilometres. An 11 year-old girl, who was interviewed at the school, explained:

> We are eight members in the family. I have three brothers and two sisters. We don't have water at home. We used to get water at a natural hole named Fussekan, a place that is very far from where I live. I go to school at 7 o'clock. Early in the morning, at about 4 o'clock, I go to fetch water and come back home at about 6 o'clock or half past. When I reach home I take my books and go to school. I am late for school and I do not have time to review my lessons. When I come back from school I go back to fetch water. I only read during the weekend when I am free. My brothers do not fetch water because they are boys. My sisters are very young and can't help me. My mother died. I live with my stepmother. She does not help me either. Only I fetch water for the family.[131]

Group discussions with women and men in the local communities brought out the stereotyped views that informed these practices. One woman in her forties, for example, stated:

> A girl can go to school, but after all, she has to be taught housework before she gets married. I will not be at her house when she gets married. She must know housework, including fetching water, so that she can become a good wife for her husband. She must provide water and food for him. What can she do with her education if she does not know housework? Her husband does not eat paper from school.[132]

The study indicated that some measures are being taken to eradicate stereotyped gender roles underlying discriminatory practices, at least by women's organisations. In a group discussion with youth in Kassimate, the girls and boys responded: 'We were taught by the Mozambican Women's Organisation that women and men are equal and both must do all the housework. There is no specific work for women and men'.[133]

Emphasising the indivisibility of rights, the CEDAW Committee members have described how they deliberately set out to make it 'difficult for States to sustain the argument of State sovereignty in preserving national cultures and traditions when the Committee demonstrates in its work that these customs

[130] Cited in ibid., pp. 20–30. [131] Ibid. [132] Ibid. [133] Ibid.

also deny basic rights in health, education and personal security'.[134] Yet the CEDAW Committee's concluding observations on State reports regarding rural women's and girls' rights have so far not engaged with the relationship between the right to water and gender stereotypes assuming that women and girls are primarily responsible for obtaining water. In the case of Mozambique, the Committee's concluding observations simply noted in gender neutral terms that only a 'very small portion of the population has access to electricity, sanitation and clean running water in their homes'.[135]

### Indirect Discrimination - Productive/Domestic Redux

Indirect discrimination occurs when a law, policy or programme does not appear to be discriminatory on its face, but has a discriminatory effect when implemented. It addresses the relationship between gender neutral laws and the gendered uses of land and water on the ground.

Inappropriate resource allocation can lead to discrimination that may not be overt. General Comment No. 15 indicates that investment should not disproportionately favour expensive water supply services and facilities that only are available to a small fraction of the population.[136] This can occur, for example, when women are disadvantaged compared to men with respect to the enjoyment of a particular opportunity or benefit due to pre-existing inequalities. With a view to the injustices deriving from the gendered division of labour and gendered uses of land and water, article 14(1) of the CEDAW states that: 'States Parties shall take into account the particular problems faced by rural women and the significant roles which rural women play in the economic survival of their families, including their work in the non-monetarised sectors of the economy'.

Policies, programmes and plans for improvements and investments in water, that overlook the gendered character of land and water uses, may leave existing gender inequalities in place or exacerbate them. A series of recent research projects on gender, water and development have documented systematic marginalisation of female water users as a result of gender insensitive approaches from technical water agencies assuming household unity that arguably constitute indirect discrimination.[137] An example is the Zimbabwean

[134] H. B. Schopp Schilling and C. Flintermann. *The Circle of Empowerment* (New York: Feminist Press, 2007).

[135] Mozambique para 54 CRC/C/15ADD.172(CRC 2002).

[136] CESCR, General Comment No. 15 The Right to Water, E/C.12/2002/11, para. 14

[137] F. Cleaver and D. Elson, *Women and Water Resources: Continued Marginalisation and New Policies*, Gatekeeper Series, No. 49 (International Institute for Environment and Development, 1995); F. Cleaver, 'Choice, Complexity and Change: Gendered Livelihoods and the

water reform from 2000, which put in place a uniform and gender neutral framework aimed at water for development.[138] Women's uses of land and water in the communal areas (for example, hand-irrigated vegetable gardens), which are crucial for family welfare and food security in Zimbabwe, and elsewhere in Africa, were not included in the new water policy. Instead the policy was underlain by a vision of development that favoured irrigated cash crops. The water policy thus had a clear class and gender bias. Female, small farmers' water uses were by conventional economic standards seen as domestic and, as such, unproductive.

The CESCR Committee and the CEDAW Committee, as we have seen, has so far not given any systematic attention to the relationship between gender-neutral laws and policies and the gendered water practices on the ground. A way forward, which should be considered, is the recommendation of gender experts that land and water polices be examined in light of gender mapping of agriculture in relation to both land and water policies and programmes. Gender mapping raises important distinctions between: (i) male farming systems, where most production sub-units are managed by men, but often with major contributions by women; (ii) female farming systems, where most production sub-units are managed by women; and (iii) separate male/female systems, where rather similar proportions of production sub-units are managed by men and women.[139]

### 4.3 *Affordability*

General Comment No. 15 signals that accessible water and sanitation implies that it is affordable: 'Water, and water facilities and services must be affordable for all. The direct and indirect costs and changes associated with securing water must be affordable and must not compromise or threaten the realisation of other Covenant rights'.[140] The Committee went on to opine that governments must adopt the necessary measures to ensure

Management of Water', *Agriculture and Human Values*, 15 (The Netherlands: Kluwer Academic Publishers, 1998), pp. 293–299; M. Zwarteveen, Water: From Basic Need to Commodity: A discussion on Gender and Water Rights in the Context of Irrigation, *World Development*, Vol. 25, No. 8 (1997), pp. 1335–1349.

[138] A.Hellum, 'Human Rights Encountering Gendered Land and Water Uses: Family Gardens and the Right to Water in Mhondoro Communal Lands', in Hellum, et al. (eds.), *Human Rights, Plural Legalities and Gendered Realities*, pp. 105–139.

[139] B. van Koppen, Paper Presented at the Conference Gender Human Rights and Water Governance, Lilongwe, 29 April 2011.

[140] CESCR, General Comment No. 15, para. 12 (c)(ii).

water is affordable, such as low-cost water,[141] and that water pricing policies should be based on the equity principle: this means that water and sanitation services are 'affordable for all, including socially disadvantaged groups' and that 'poorer households should not be disproportionately burdened with water expenses compared to richer households'.[142]

Similarly, the UN Sub-Commission Guidelines indicate that sanitation services, as well as water services, 'should be supplied at a price that everyone can afford without compromising their ability to acquire other basic goods and services'.[143] Establishing that a person's ability should be taken into account, the Guidelines state that 'No one should be deprived of the minimum essential amount of water or access to basic sanitation facilities.'[144]

These sources explicitly point towards an obligation for States to provide for water for personal and domestic uses in a situation where individuals for reasons beyond their control, such as poverty and discrimination, are unable to pay. However, most national laws, policies and practices have not been significantly transformed in this direction. In line with the integrated water resources management policy (IWRM), which was based on the Dublin Principles seeing water as both an economic and social good, most countries in Africa, Asia and Latin America shifted from supply to demand driven water management systems in the 1990s.[145] Recent research from African countries like Malawi, Kenya and Zimbabwe shows how the human right to water along with SADC initiatives have prompted constitutional protection of the right to water and new water policies which call for revision of existing water laws.[146] In the same vein, the best

[141] (General Comment 15 mentions appropriate pricing policies such as free or low-cost water) CESCR, General Comment No. 15, para. 27.b

[142] CESCR, General Comment No. 15, para. 26 [143] Section 1.3(d) [144] Section 6.4

[145] For a critical empirical analysis of the IWRM paradigm, particularly its effect on small-scale water users in Africa see *Water Alternatives*, Special issue. 'Flows and Practices: The Politics of Integrated Water Resources Management (IWRM) in Southern Africa', L. Mehta, B. Derman and E. Manzungu (guest eds.), Vol. 9, No. 3 (2016).

[146] The Southern African Development Community (SADC) water policy of 2005 went a long way toward recognising the need to prioritise water for sanitation, domestic, and livelihood needs in order to promote food security, better health, and poverty prevention, see SADC Regional Water Policy, August 2005. This policy was backed up by the Protocol to the African Charter on Human and Peoples' Rights on the Rights of Women in Africa (the Maputo Protocol), which obliges contracting States to take all appropriate measures to 'provide women with access to clean drinking water, sources of domestic fuel, land and the means of producing nutritious food' (adopted by the 2nd Ordinary Session of the Assembly of the Union, Maputo, CAB/LEG/66.6 (13 September 2000), entered into force 25 November 2005).

practices of State and non-State actors in these and other countries in Africa, Asia, America and Europe, collected by the UN Special Rapporteur on the Human Right to safe Drinking Water and Sanitation indicate that a number of initiatives that enhance the human right to water are emerging.[147] However, challenges remain in implementation as the following case studies reveal.

**Malawi**

In Malawi, democratic delegation of power to local level bodies has guided local government in general and land and water policies in particular. The Malawian water policy, which has been under revision since 2000 and was passed in 2005, embraces the creation of water catchment councils, based on stakeholder participation and demand management strategies.[148] According to the policy, water is to be managed as a social and economic good. The adoption of users pay principles implies that communities, NGOs and the private sector will bear the cost of maintenance and operation. The policy does not clearly provide for a right to water for the purpose of accessing water for livelihood purposes, but emphasises that the protection and use of water resources shall be accorded the highest priority over other uses.

Empirical research from Malawi conducted between 1999 and 2003 suggests that this process of political liberalisation and democratisation has not improved access to water for women from vulnerable groups. One large research project concluded that the reform was largely detrimental for the increasing number of impoverished rural female households, especially those composed of young widows with small children and grandmothers looking after grandchildren as a result of the HIV epidemic.[149] The research team observed the exclusion of poorer members of the community: contribution of labour or money was required to attain membership in the user associations

[147] C. De Albuquerque with V. Roa, *On the Right Track: Good Practices in Realising the Rights to Water and Sanitation* (Geneva/Madrid: UN Special Rapporteur on Right to Water and Sanitation/Entidade Reguladora does Servicos de Aguas e Residuos, 2012).

[148] Government of Malawi 2005, National Water Policy, Lilongwe, Ministry of Irrigation and Water Development.

[149] W. Mulwafu and A. Ferguson, 'Decentralisation, Participation and Access to Water Resources in Malawi', BASIS, Collaborative Research Support Programme, 2004.
A. Ferguson, 'Water Reform, Gender and HIV/AIDS: Perspectives from Malawi', in L. Whiteford and S. Whiteford (eds.), *Globalisation, Water and Health. Resource Management in Times of Scarcity* (School of American Research Press, James Curry, 2005).

that were established as part of the national water reform. Lists of approved users were posted and the borehole was locked to prevent non-contributors from using the facility. To meet household needs, poor women were turning instead to polluted or unprotected resources.

It is noteworthy that Malawi abstained when the UN General Assembly Resolution 64/292 on the human right to water and sanitation was adopted in 2010.[150] To be sure, the chapter on human rights in the Malawi Constitution does not explicitly address water.[151] It has, however, been argued that the right to water, in the light of international law and comparable law in other African countries, must be seen as part of article 11.2 on the right to life.[152] The Water Resources Act, which was passed by the Malawi Parliament in 2013, empowers the Minister to reserve water resources to meet domestic use.[153] The Act, in its definition of domestic use includes water to irrigate kitchen gardens.[154] The Act has not entered into force since it has not yet been gazetted by the Minister as required by the Act.[155] Malawi's Gender Equality Act of 2013 and the emphasis on gender equal participation in water governance forms part of the broad range of measures that have a bearing on the right to water.

Two recent studies of the operation of decentralised water governance institutions, however, indicate that lack of knowledge about international human rights, in combination with the unclear status of the right to water under Malawian law, weakens the ability to make the right to water at an affordable price real.[156] For example, the study of the Nkloto Water User Association (WUA) shows that in these decentralised water institutions, focus on notions of sustainability and water bills recovery is overshadowing other goals, including user participation, social equity and affordability. The rhetoric on women's participation in these institutions was more about

[150] Constitution of the Republic of Malawi 1994, as amended to 2010.

[151] Constitution of the Republic of Malawi 1994, as amended to 2010.

[152] N. Kanyangolo, T. Chirwa, A. Chiweza and M. Chasukwa, 'The Political Economy of the Human Right to Water and Women in Malawi', in Hellum, Kameri-Mbote and van Koppen (eds.), *Water is Life*, pp. 215–243.

[153] Water Resources Act No. 2 of 2013, section 37.

[154] According to section 2 of the Water Resources Act 'domestic use' includes 'use for the purpose of (a) human consumption, washing and cooking by persons ordinarily resident on the land where the use occurs; (b) watering not more than thirty livestock units; (c) irrigating a subsistence garden; and (d) watering a subsistence fish pond'.

[155] Ibid., p. 231.

[156] A. Chiweza, N. Kanyongolo, M. Chasukwa and T. Chirwa, 'Women's Right to Water and Participation in Practice: Insights from Urban Local Water Governance Systems' and M. Chasukwa , N.K anyongolo , A. Chiweza and T. Chirwa, 'Primary Actors on the Back Seat: Gender, Human Rights and Rural Water Governance in Malawi – Lessons from Mpenba and Chileka', in Hellum, Kameri-Mbote and van Koppen (eds.), *Water is Life* , pp. 244–300.

paying for water bills and selling water than influencing the actual decision making. Thus, the WUA, who oversees the pricing of water, made no effort to ensure a pricing system that catered for the needs of the very poor. The local community was treated as a homogeneous group that was equally able to afford the increasing cost of water. As a consequence, the most vulnerable groups, who could not afford to pay, had their needs met through an array of other sources, a majority of them classified as unsafe.

However, non-State actors are developing rights-based practices. For instance, the Churches Action in Relief and Development (CARD), are addressing both food security and water in rights based, solar-powered gravity and supply schemes.[157] In these schemes, communities write their own constitutions on how they will enable the elderly, orphans, chronically ill and people with disabilities to access free water, and utilise taps specifically designed for minority groups.

**Zimbabwe**

A wave of water reform took place in Zimbabwe shortly before the Fast-Track land reform and the following economic and political collapse in 2000.[158] It was partly informed by the Dublin Principles and IWRM and partly by a quest for greater racial justice in the water sector: to erase the colonial land and water legacy, where the bulk of agricultural water was owned by white commercial farmers.[159] However, the new national water management system, where water was nationalised, was to be managed on a commercial basis and funded through the sale of water. The planning, permitting and levying of water was decentralised and placed in the hands of self-funded catchment and sub-catchment councils without any consideration of gender equal participation.[160] In urban areas, the user pays principle was adopted with no consideration of the human right to water. With regard to rural water, the duty to respect the right to primary water, embedded in earlier water legislation, was upheld. As regards rural water, the Zimbabwean Water Act of 1998 defines primary water as water for household needs (including vegetable gardens), animals and bricks to build houses. In the context of an escalating economic and social crisis, the lack of conceptual clarity regarding the distinction between primary and commercial water provided

[157] De Alburquerque, *Good Practices*, p. 120. [158] See Chapter 19.

[159] Government of Zimbabwe, *Towards Integrated Water Resources Management* (Harare: Government of Zimbabwe Printers, 2000).

[160] Government of Zimbabwe, Zimbabwe National Water Authority Act, No. 11/1998, section 21; Government of Zimbabwe, Statutory Instrument 33, Water (Catchment Councils), Regulations, 2000; Government of Zimbabwe, Statutory Instrument 47 Water (Sub Catchment Councils) Regulations, 2000.

space for further commercialisation of rural water use.[161] Levies were often imposed in order to secure income for catchment councils, regardless of whether the uses were commercial or primary.

With the Zimbabwean Government of Unity (GNU) a new water policy was adopted. The GNU, who acknowledged the human rights to water, sought to integrate the human right to water in its new water policy.[162] In a situation where both the rural and urban water supply system has broken down, as a result of ten years of misrule and mismanagement, Zimbabwean NGOs have started to mobilise around the right to water. Civic organisations like the Zimbabwe Women's Lawyers Association (ZWLA), Women of Zimbabwe Arise (WOZA), Zimbabwe Lawyers for Human Rights (ZLHR) and Harare Citizen's Trust (HCT) were, in connection with the constitution-making process, demanding that social and economic rights like the human right to water are given constitutional protection. Section 77 of the new constitution, which was proposed by the Zimbabwean GNU[163] and adopted by Parliament in 2013, includes the right to water, but not the right to sanitation. The new Water Policy, which was adopted by the GNU, recognises the right to clean drinking water and primary water. In a 2014 decision, the High Court outlawed section 8 of the Harare by-laws, which empowers the City Council to cut off water from residents arbitrarily without a court order, with reference to the constitution. In defiance of this court order, the City of Harare cut off the water supplies of thousands of defaulters. Despite the high rate of water-borne diseases and the high number of people who are resorting to unsafe water because they cannot afford to pay, the State's duty to provide water for an affordable price is yet to be incorporated in the Water Act and the Urban Councils Act.

Rather than introducing enabling legislation and taking issue with illegal disconnections, the ZANU PF government, has taken steps to privatise the water sector and introduce water meters. Failure by the government to put in place legislation that ensures the right to water for people who are unable

[161] Chapter 19 in this volume.

[162] Zimbabwe voted in favour of UN General Assembly Resolution 64/292. In the *Ministry of Water Resources Development and Management Bulletin*, Issue No. 1 from 2011, the Minister of Water, S. Nkomo states that: 'The mandate of the Ministry of Water, acting in collaboration with agents such as local water authorities and ZINWA is to deliver clean water to all citizens. This is also in line with my Ministry's quest to ensure that water is available, accessible and affordable'.

[163] Agreement between the Zimbabwe African National Union Patriotic Front (ZANU PF) and the two Movement for Democratic Change (MDC) formations, on Resolving the Challenges Facing Zimbabwe (2008).

to pay is yet to be challenged in court as a violation of the State's obligation to take measures to achieve realisation of the right to water as required by section 77 of the constitution.

While the lack of affordable water is felt across society, Zimbabwean rural and urban women within vulnerable ethnic and socio-economic communities are disproportionately burdened as child bearers and family providers. Those who have suffered most from the breakdown of public water and sanitation services, illegal disconnections and lack of appropriate legislation are poor urban women nursing infants, caring for children, or looking after the disabled, the sick, and the chronically ill. In Harare's high density areas, these developments led to an increased use of alternative water sources, particularly shallow wells in backyards and wetlands. With water meters being introduced without legislation that caters for the increasing number of poor urban people who are unable to pay for water, poor people's reliance on open-access water sources and the subsequent depletion of the environment are increasing.

### 4.4 *Sanitation*

The right to sanitation was not addressed in General Comment No. 15 although it does mention various obligations to provide sanitation services to ensure the right to water. In a statement on the right to sanitation from 2010 the CESCR Committee emphasised that 'girls do not go to school in many parts of the world for lack of toilets, or lack of separate toilets for them'.[164] Article 1.2 of the UN Sub-Commission Guidelines state that, 'Everyone has the right to have access to adequate and safe sanitation that is conducive to the protection of public health and the environment'. With due consideration to the concerns of women and girls, the Guidelines emphasise that water and sanitation should be located within or in the immediate vicinity of the household, school, workplace or health institution and in a location where physical security can be guaranteed.[165]

As discussed above, young girls are less likely to attend school if suitable sanitation facilities are lacking. It has been estimated that about half of the girls in sub-Saharan Africa who drop out of primary school do so because of lack of adequate water and sanitation facilities.[166] To make sanitation facilities accessible, they must be constructed in response to the gendered perception of female and male physiology. Seemingly gender-neutral facilities often

[164] CESCR Statement The Right to Water and Sanitation, 19 November 2010E/C.12/45/CRP.1
[165] UN Sub-Commission Guidelines, section 3.1.
[166] UNICEF, State of the World's Children.

overlook these differences. For instance, a set of studies carried out in Zimbabwe, Kenya and Uganda explored how inadequate facilities for the management of adolescent girls' menstruation in schools significantly affected girls' access to education.[167] They show how inadequate management of sexual maturation and menstruation in schools, including lack of adequate sanitary facilities, which deprives girls of their private space, is one among several factors that may cause girls to drop out of school or lead to weak performance.[168] Two particular factors stood out: many parents could not afford sanitary pads and the school toilets did not provide disposal bins or a space to wash.

These and other studies demonstrate the need to take biological differences between girls and boys into account when implementing the right to sanitation. It also demonstrates the indivisibility of the right to water and sanitation and the right to education, physical integrity and human dignity. As recommended by these studies, guidelines for the implementation of the right to water and sanitation should explicitly ensure that planning for and provision of adequate facilities at all schools should address the needs of menstruating girls. Budgets should cover construction, upgrading or maintenance of school sanitary facilities, including disposal facilities for menstruating girls.

These insights have, as demonstrated above, had little impact on the general comments and the concluding observations of the CESCR, the CEDAW Committee and the CRC Committee. While the CRC Committee does address the right water and sanitation in schools, concluding observations are largely gender neutral. Yet the CRC Committee's concluding observations on Bangladesh illustrate the potential for an engendered approach as it focuses on the provision of separate sanitation facilities for boys and girls.[169]

## 5 ON THE WAY BUT NOT THERE YET

The human right to water and sanitation is, as we have seen, a social right that gradually is evolving in response to the basic needs of people living

[167] See P. Mutunga (ed.), *Life Skills, Sexual Maturation and Sanitation: What's (not) happening in our schools – An Exploratory Study from Kenya* (Harare: WLC and Weaver Press Harare, 2003), p. 198; E. Kirumira (ed.), *Life Skills, Sexual Maturation and Sanitation: What's (not) Happening in Our Schools – An Exploratory Study from Uganda* (Harare: WLC and Weaver Press, 2003), p. 178 and J.E. Stewart (ed.), *Life Skills, Sexual Maturation and Sanitation: What's (not) happening in our schools – An Exploratory Study from Zimbabwe* (Harare: WLC and Weaver Press Harare, 2004), p. 306.

[168] J. Stewart 'I Can't Go to School Today', in Hellum et al. (eds.), *Human Rights, Plural Legalities and Gendered Realities*, pp. 291–316.

[169] CRC Committee, *Concluding Observations on Bangladesh*, para. 74.

in poor urban and rural communities and women and girls within them. While lack of safe, adequate, available, acceptable and affordable water and sanitation affects all members of society, women and girls are in practice the ones that suffer most.

The interdependence between the right to water and sanitation and the right to health, food, education and gender equality is given increased attention by the different UN bodies. The CESCR Committee has through General Comment No. 15 on the Right to Water and General Comment No. 20 on non-discrimination laid a theoretical foundation for an approach that links the right to water to the right to substantive equality. In General Recommendation No. 34 on Rural Women, the CEDAW Committee reiterates that rural women's and girls' rights to water and sanitation are not only essential rights in themselves, but also are key to the realisation of a wide range of other rights, including health, food, education and participation. While providing different entry points for intervention, the treaty bodies supplement and reinforce each other.

Yet, poor women's and girls' concerns and experiences are not fully integrated in the human right to water as articulated by different UN bodies. A key concern in this regard is the relationship between gender neutral law and the gendered realities on the ground. The human right to water and sanitation, it is often assumed, constitutes an adequate response to the needs of poor women and girls. This assumption is challenged by qualitative research uncovering the gendered norms and practices that inform the uses of water and sanitation in different rural and urban localities. The human right to water and sanitation may, although it does not appear to be discriminatory on its face, have discriminatory effect when implemented. For the right to water and sanitation to be both non-discriminatory and engendered, a key concern is to ensure that the right itself is constructed, interpreted and monitored in such a way that it satisfies gender-differentiated needs. A grounded and gendered approach to human rights points to several themes requiring attention.

Firstly, the definition of the right to water itself calls for closer scrutiny. General Comment No. 15 includes water for personal and domestic uses. Other uses, such as water to grow food that is necessary for survival, is not seen as a right, but as a priority issue. This conceptual division between water for domestic and productive uses does not sit well with poor rural women's integrated and diversified livelihood strategies involving water from various sources for multiple uses.[170] By dividing water for livelihood into separate

[170] See Chapter 2.

domestic and productive sectors defined by narrow parameters, the needs of poor rural and peri-urban women as providers of food security in the family and local community are not sufficiently accommodated. Addressing the right to sufficient, safe and accessible water, the CEDAW Committee in General Recommendation No. 34 includes 'water for personal and domestic uses, as well as for agriculture/irrigation'.[171] Recognising the indivisibility of rights, having an expansive understanding of equality and addressing equality across the domestic-productive divide, CEDAW has the potential to engender the human right to water. Recognition of a broad notion of a right to water for livelihoods is important in that it overcomes the disjuncture between customary and statutory law and also the conceptual and administrative divides between productive and domestic spheres: these norms and spheres are in practice often indivisible for poor rural and peri-urban African women. Yet the CEDAW Committee's concluding observations on State reports are in most instances limited to a general reference to article 14 of the Convention. The Committee focuses on the additional structural disadvantage experienced by rural women not only in relation to water, but also health, nutrition and education. However, it does not pay any systematic attention to the relationship between gender-neutral water laws and policies and the gendered water uses on the ground. In its examination of State reports, the CESCR Committee does not pay systematic attention as to whether water for livelihood, in terms of kitchen gardens and other survival strategies, are given priority as required by the Sub-Committee's Guidelines. The Committee has, however, started to pay attention to conflicting water uses – particularly situations where small-scale farmers, customary water uses come into conflict with large agricultural companies, water rights.

Secondly, to promote substantive equality the provision of water and sanitation must include measures to relieve women and girls of the burden imposed on them by the water related duties they assume in the 'care' economy. Due to the gendered division of labour, women and girls, in large parts of Africa, spend far more time fetching water than do men and boys.[172] While there is, on the one hand, a need to ensure that customary norms recognising women's water needs as providers of care and food are respected and protected, there is, on the other hand, a need to consider how these customary norms are also placing a series of water-related duties on women and girls that are not shared by men and boys. The duty to address negative gender stereotypes is found in

[171] Ibid., para, 82.

[172] 'Women's Rights and the Right to Food'. Report submitted by the Special Rapporteur on the right to food, 24 December 2013, A/HRC/22/50, para. 39.

several conventions. Article 5(a) of the CEDAW places an obligation on States parties to 'take all appropriate measures to modify the social and cultural patterns of conduct of men and women, with a view to achieving the elimination of prejudices and customary and all other practices which are based on the idea of the inferiority or superiority of either of the sexes or on stereotyped roles for men and women'. While the ICESCR contains no similar regulation of gender stereotypes, the Committee has defined *systemic* discrimination as 'legal rules, policies and practices or predominant cultural attitudes in either the public or the private sector which create relative advantages for some groups and disadvantages for others'.[173] It is thus surprising that gender stereotyping neither is integrated in the CEDAW Committee nor the CESCR's general recommendations addressing the right to water and sanitation, nor in their examination of State reports. Clearly, the right to water (as a form of substantive equality) must entail measures that seek to transform the existing gender division of water related roles by redistributing tasks both within the household and in other spheres.

Thirdly, gender specific rights, to have effect, must be carefully monitored by the relevant human rights treaty bodies, as illustrated in particular with the right to sanitation. The right to sanitation was initially coined in gender neutral terms. Yet, empirical research documenting the high number of girls dropping out of school because of inadequate facilities prompted a gender specific approach.[174] Recognising that seemingly gender neutral facilities often overlook socially-constructed gender differences related to sanitation and hygiene, both the CESCR and the CEDAW Committee acknowledge the need for gender specific rights.[175] Yet both treaty bodies, in their examination of State reports, take an overwhelmingly gender-neutral approach to the right to sanitation. Similarly, the CRC Committee's focus on water and sanitation is overwhelmingly gender neutral. How girls' right to education is negatively affected through the combined effect of lack of accessible water and the gendered division of labour should be given systematic attention. In the same vein, the negative consequences of lack of adequate sanitation facilities for schoolgirls needs to be regularly addressed.

The right to water and sanitation is evolving in its meaning and content. An overall challenge for the treaty bodies is to infuse the right to water and

[173] CESCR, General Comment No. 20, para. 12.

[174] Report of the Independent Expert on the Issue of Human Rights Obligations Related to Access to Safe Drinking Water and Sanitation, Catarina de Albuquerque (2009), A/HRC/12/24, para. 63; CESCR Statement (2010), The Right to Sanitation, E/C.12/2010/1, para. 8.

[175] CESCR Statement (2010), Statement on the Right to Sanitation, 19 November 2010, E/C.12/2010/1, para. 5.

sanitation with the right to protection against direct, indirect and structural discrimination. To ensure protection against structural discrimination, a component that facilitates scrutiny of water-related gender stereotypes that put duties on women and girls that are not shared with men and boys should be included. Protection against indirect discrimination calls for scrutiny of water policies and practices that on their face are gender neutral so as to ensure that women's water uses, for example watering of kitchen gardens, are put on an equal footing with water for other forms of agriculture, often controlled by men. Most importantly, the gap between the increasingly gender sensitive jurisprudence of the human rights treaty bodies and the overwhelmingly gender neutral approach that is taken by the human rights treaty bodies in their examination of State reports must be bridged. To ensure that State parties are made accountable, a revision of the treaty bodies reporting guidelines must be considered with a view to ensuring that the necessary information concerning the relationship between the right to water and sanitation and the gendered realities on the ground is compiled by State parties and NGOs.

# 10

# The Human Right to Sanitation

MALCOLM LANGFORD*, JAMIE BARTRAM** AND VIRGINIA ROAF***

## 1 INTRODUCTION

Sanitation is not classically associated with the human rights lexicon. Removing and treating human excreta is generally associated with the discrete machinations of local service delivery, the technical concerns of health professionals or the occasional demands by environment advocates, not the somewhat lofty world of human rights. However, the scale and impact of the 'global sanitation crisis' gave impetus to demands for recognition of sanitation as a human right. The toll of poor sanitation in human development terms is monumental. The absence of sanitation facilities, together with the consequent pollution of water, is responsible for pervasive disease and death, chronic poverty and the creation of significant barriers to education and productive labour. Each day, approximately 1000 children are estimated to die from sanitation-related causes;[1] and the lack of sanitation accounts for 6 per cent of the global disease burden,[2] more than HIV/AIDS, malaria and tuberculosis combined.[3]

* Professor, Faculty of Law, University of Oslo and Co-Director, Centre on Law and Social Transformation, CMI and University of Bergen.

** Director of the Water Institute and the Don and Jennifer Holzworth Distinguished Professor at Gillings School of Global Public Health of the University of North Carolina at Chapel Hill.

*** Independent consultant working predominantly on the human rights to safe drinking water and sanitation.

1 JMP, *Progress on Sanitation and Drinking Water: 2015 Update and MDG Assessment – Key Facts*, UNICF and WHO, 2015.

2 J. Bartram and S. Cairncross, 'Hygiene, Sanitation, and Water: Forgotten Foundations of Health', *PLoS Med*, Vol. 7, No. 11 (2010), pp. 1–9 at 1.

3 Ibid.

By articulating access to sanitation as a human right, development practitioners, health workers, human rights activists and policymakers hope that the sanitation paradigm will be shifted away from one of charity to one of justice.[4] By framing sanitation as a matter of legal entitlement, access to sanitation is not simply understood as a policy option. Thus, whereas the inclusion of a sanitation target in the Millennium Development Goals (MDGs) in 2002, and strengthened in the Sustainable Development goals in 2015, represented an important global political commitment, there have been consistent calls to strengthen and reframe that pledge through the prism of human rights.[5] The slow progress on the sanitation target,[6] particularly for marginalised and low-income groups, has only emboldened these protagonists.[7]

This justice-oriented approach also seeks to challenge the myth of economic determinism: that the development of sanitation services would simply follow the path of rising economic growth. Despite rising national incomes across the developing world, the number of people without basic sanitation (approximately 2.6 billion) has been stubbornly persistent and has even risen in some countries.[8] This is despite the powerful economic arguments for sanitation. The benefits of having somewhere to defecate have been valued at nine times the cost of the investment in sanitation (in terms of improved health, savings in the household and health sector budgets and increased economic productivity).[9] Indeed, the consequences of failing to act can be immediate and dramatic: a cholera outbreak in Peru in 1991 killed 3000 people over a period of 15 months, costing the economy US $770 million – more than the investment in water and sanitation during the entire preceding decade.[10] This disconnect with the growth trajectory demonstrates that access to sanitation is not inevitable; its existence is fundamentally a result of political choices. Framing sanitation as a human right represents therefore an attempt

4 COHRE, UN-HABITAT, WaterAid and SDC, *Sanitation: A Human Rights Imperative* (Geneva: COHRE, 2008), p. 5.

5 See UN OHCHR, *Claiming the MDGs: A Human Rights Approach* (Geneva, OHCHR, 2008); M. Langford, 'A Poverty of Rights: Six Ways to Fix the MDGs', *IDS Bulletin*, Vol. 41, No. 1 (2010), pp. 83–91.

6 UN, *The Millennium Development Goals Report* (New York: United Nations, 2011).

7 UNICEF, *Progress for Children: Achieving the MDGs with Equity*, Report No. 9 (New York: UNICEF, 2010).

8 Bartram and Cairncross, 'Hygiene, Sanitation, and Water', p. 1.

9 G. Hutton, L. Haller and J. Bartram, *Economic and Health Effects of Increasing Coverage of Low-Cost Household Drinking-Water Supply and Sanitation Interventions in Countries Off-Track to Meet MDG Target 10*, Background report to the UNDP Human Development Report 2006, World Health Organization, Geneva, 2007, p. 53. Also published as Human Development Report Office Occasional Paper 2006/33. WHO/SDE/WSH/07/05, p. 20.

10 J. Bartram, 'Improving on Haves and Have-Nots', *Nature*, Vol. 452(2008), pp. 283–284, at 283.

to shift the calculus involved in those choices, by reshaping public attitudes and challenging decision-makers, the allocation of resources and the effectiveness of implementation.

The demand for sanitation to be treated as a human right has gained a considerable measure of success at the international level. In July 2010, the majority of the UN General Assembly recognised, along with water, 'sanitation as a human right that is essential for the full enjoyment of life and all human rights'.[11] Three months later, the UN Human Rights Council affirmed the right,[12] while UN experts and committees have outlined some of its potential content. And in 2015, sanitation was recognised in a consensus vote by the General Assembly as a distinct and separate right.[13]

This trend towards legal recognition has not been confined to the global sphere. In the last decade, the right to sanitation has been incorporated in a number of constitutions (e.g. Uruguay, Kenya, Maldives), national laws (e.g. Algeria, Brazil, France) and national policy instruments (e.g. Ghana, Nepal, Bangladesh). It has also been regularly included in regional political declarations such as those from the South Asian Conference on Sanitation (Sacosan) (2008, 2011 and 2014), African Conference on Sanitation and Hygiene (AfricaSan) (2015), and Latin American Sanitation Conference (Latinosan) (2013 and 2016).

Without doubt, the right to sanitation has gained significant legitimacy. But it retains its critics and doubters.[14] Does sanitation meet the criteria of human rights in moral theory or in international law? Is it simply another instance of human rights inflation? Does this right have any meaningful content? Will it enhance existing political and practical tools in addressing the root causes of the sanitation crisis? Or is it a rhetorical device that will fuel unrealistic demands and distract attention from the more urgent task of extending access?

[11] UN General Assembly, *The Human Right to Water and Sanitation* (Sixty-fourth session, 2010) UN Doc A/64/L.63/Rev.1, para. 1.

[12] UN Human Rights Council, *Human Rights and Access to Safe Drinking Water and Sanitation* (Fifteenth session, 2010) UN Doc. A/HRC/15/L.14.

[13] *The Human Rights to Safe Drinking Water and Sanitation*, UN GA Resolution 707169, UN doc. A/C.3/70/L.55/Rev.1, para. 1.

[14] Similar but not identical doubts were raised with the human right to water: see, e.g. S. Tully, 'A Human Right to Access Water? A Critique of General Comment No. 15', *Netherlands Quarterly of Human Rights*, Vol. 23, No. 1 (2005), pp. 35–63; P. Anand, 'Right to Water and Access to Water: An Assessment', *Journal of International Development*, Vol. 19 (2007), pp. 511–526; R. D'Souza, 'Liberal Theory, Human Rights and Water-Justice: Back to Square One?', *Law, Social Justice and Global Development*, Vol. 11 (2008), available at www2.warwick.ac.uk/fac/soc/law/elj/lgd/ (accessed 4 April 2012).

This chapter sets out to examine these challenges. Section 2 examines whether sanitation can be justifiably recognised as a human right given the initial opposition of a significant number of States and the standpoints of some human rights theorists. While this opposition may appear minimal, the weight of arguments for and against a right can significantly affect its reception in practice.[15] Sections 3 and 4 ask how the boundaries and content of the right should be delineated, particularly on the grounds of their feasibility. In doing so, it delves for the first time into the literature concerning the identity of the right to sanitation: asking whether it is an individual, collective or hybrid right and what are the consequences of this? Section 5 examines why, how and when a right to sanitation may constitute an ally in efforts to ensure access to sanitation. In an illustrative manner, it focuses on four selected areas where the right to sanitation has been used, or advocated for, in practice: the MDGs and SDGs, the demands for participation and democratisation, service delivery in situations of contested land tenure, and legal mobilisation and other forms of accountability.

Before proceeding, it is helpful to define what we mean by sanitation. Sanitation is an amalgam of different elements – being more a process than a good. In defining sanitation, one commonly distinguishes between the place and facilities for an *individual* to urinate, defecate and practice menstrual hygiene and the *system* for the disposal and treatment of that waste. For example, WHO states that sanitation 'generally refers to the provision of facilities and services for the safe disposal of human urine and faeces', as well as the 'maintenance of hygienic conditions, through services such as garbage collection and wastewater disposal'.[16]

However, this definition carries inbuilt normative expectations that should be made transparent. It assumes that the purpose of sanitation is primarily about personal, public and environmental health. As we shall see, this does not necessarily capture broader concerns in the human rights context about privacy and dignity or cultural acceptability. Thus, a sound definition from both a technical and human rights perspective, proposed here, might be that: *sanitation constitutes the ability to effectively access space and facilities (whenever and wherever needed), that afford privacy, dignity and safety, in which to urinate, defecate and practice related hygiene, including menstrual hygiene,*

[15] See M. Langford, 'Judging Resource Availability', in J. Squires, M. Langford, and B. Thiele (eds.), *Road to a Remedy: Current Issues in Litigation of Economic, Social and Cultural Rights* (Sydney: AHRC and University of NSW Press, 2005), pp. 89–108, at 107–8.

[16] WHO, *Health Topics: Sanitation*, available at www.who.int/topics/sanitation/en/ (accessed 3 October 2011).

*in a culturally acceptable manner, which by virtue of their design, management and accompanying services protect the user, the locality (e.g. households, school, workplace, hospital or community) and wider population from the adverse consequences of contamination from the process.*[17]

## 2 SANITATION AS A HUMAN RIGHT

### 2.1 *Moral Theory*

The claim that access to sanitation constitutes a 'human right' may be perplexing. Like other social and economic rights, sanitation seems to fit awkwardly with classic naturalistic rights theories that emerged at the end of the Enlightenment period and continue to enjoy some currency. Drawing on the thinking of Locke, Cranston has argued that:

> A human right, by definition, is something that no one, anywhere, may be deprived of without a grave affront to justice. There are certain actions that are never permissible, certain freedoms that should never be invaded, certain things that are sacred... Thus, the effect of a universal declaration that is overloaded with affirmations of economic and social rights is to push the political and civil rights out of the realm of the morally compelling into the twilight world of utopian aspirations.[18]

However, there may be different ways of viewing and justifying social rights in the naturalistic tradition. Indeed, Locke's own theory was premised on a state

[17] The UN Special Rapporteur has provided a definition of sanitation that is infused with rights dimensions. However, it mixes a rights-based definition with the corresponding duties and the content of the right. She states that 'sanitation can be defined as a system for the collection, transport, treatment and disposal or reuse of human excreta and associated hygiene. States must ensure without discrimination that everyone has physical and economic access to sanitation, in all spheres of life, which is safe, hygienic, secure, socially and culturally acceptable, provides privacy and ensures dignity'. See UN Human Rights Council, *Report of the Independent Expert on the Issue of Human Rights Obligations Related to Access to Safe Drinking Water and Sanitation, Catarina de Albuquerque* (Fifteenth session, 2010) UN Doc. A/HRC/12/24 (2009) para. 63. Our definition seeks to echo the articulation by the CESCR of the right to housing, with its emphasis on the basic underlying principles that shape the contours of the rights: 'In the Committee's view, the right to housing should not be interpreted in a narrow or restrictive sense which equates it with, for example, the shelter provided by merely having a roof over one's head or views shelter exclusively as a commodity. Rather it should be seen as the right to live somewhere in security, peace and dignity'. UN Committee on Economic, Social and Cultural Rights, *General Comment 4, The Right to Adequate Housing*, (Sixth session, 1991), UN Doc. E/1992/23, annex III at 114 (1991), para. 7.

[18] M. Cranston, 'Are There Any Human Rights?', *Daedalus*, Vol. 112, No. 4 (1983), pp. 1–12.

of nature in which all human beings have an equality of power[19] (which presumes some pre-existing level of social rights),[20] and it has been conveniently forgotten that he included health and subsistence amongst the more repeated rights to life, liberty and property.[21] Indeed, some scholars have questioned the selective historical interpretation of naturalistic thinking on human rights.[22]

The idea of freedom has also been interpreted in broader terms such as in Sen's idea of capabilities: it is not merely freedom from interference[23] but also the 'opportunity to pursue our objectives'.[24] Whereas Sen has been cautious as to precisely which capabilities are essential, Nussbaum has listed ten essential capabilities, some of which cover implicitly a number of social rights.[25] Capabilities are not human rights, which are primarily 'ethical affirmations' of what is important,[26] but social rights do mesh well with 'an understanding the importance of advancing human capabilities'.[27]

Other theories take a different departure point than freedom. As Heard puts it, 'Human rights are a product of a philosophical debate that has raged

[19] J. Locke, *Two Treatises of Government* (5th edn., London: Thomas Tegg, 1823). Locke describes a state of 'perfect equality' where 'all the power and jurisdiction is reciprocal, no one having more than another' (Part II, para. 4).

[20] Ibid., Part II. para. 7. Locke argues that everyone is 'born to all the same advantages of Nature'. But this assumption is difficult to sustain in a non-ideal world where individuals are born into households of different wealth, opportunity, geography and ethnicity and carry with them different markers of identity that can give rise to prejudice and discrimination.

[21] Ibid., Part II. para. 6. 'The state of Nature has a law of Nature to govern it, which obliges every one, and reason, which is that law, teaches all mankind who will but consult it, that being all equal and independent, no one ought to harm another in his life, health, liberty or possessions'. 'As justice gives every man a title to the product of his honest industry, and the fair acquisitions of his ancestors descended to him; so charity gives every man a title to so much out of another's plenty, as will keep him from extreme want, where he has no means to subsist otherwise: and a man can no more justly make use of another's necessity, to force him to become his vassal, by with-holding that relief, God requires him to afford to the wants of his brother'. Ibid., Part I, para. 42.

[22] 'Contrary to widespread belief, welfare rights are not a twentieth century innovation, but are among the first rights ever to be claimed. When in the twelfth and thirteenth centuries our modern conception of a right first appeared, one of the earliest examples offered was the right of those in dire need to receive aid from those in surplus'. J. Griffin, *On Human Rights* (Oxford: Oxford University Press, 2008), p. 177.

[23] A. Sen, *The Idea of Justice* (Cambridge M.A.: Harvard University Press, 2009) p. 228.

[24] Ibid.

[25] They are 'Life, Bodily Health, Bodily Integrity, Senses, Imagination, and Thought, Emotions. Practical Reason, Affiliation, Other Species and Play'. See M. Nussbaum, *Women and Human Development: The Capabilities Approach* (Cambridge: Cambridge University Press, 2000).

[26] Sen, *The Idea of Justice*, p. 358. [27] Ibid., p. 381.

for over two thousand years'.[28] Three other theories of human rights are worth mentioning here: agency, need and dignity. As to agency, Griffin's account draws on the notion of human rights that emerged at the end of the Enlightenment and argues that within it, we find an idea 'of a right we have simply in virtue of being human'[29] and that we often value 'human standing' and our 'personhood' more 'highly than even our happiness'.[30] He captures the idea of personhood as agency or, more precisely, *normative agency*:[31] the ability to deliberate, assess, choose and act. In order that agency is meaningful, a person must be 'capable' of choosing a path through life without control or domination by others (*autonomy*), with real choices (meaning a *minimum provision* of information, education, services and resources) and freedom to pursue what is worthwhile (*liberty*). Griffin does not discuss sanitation, but his discussion of the right to health (where he remains sceptical to maximalist demands for the highest attainable level) would provide room for such a basic element as sanitation.[32]

Needs-based approaches are often associated with social rights. In O'Manique's view, if X is necessary for survival, it is a right. However, while the 'belief that survival is good is virtually universal', it is not always immediately apparent what this entails.[33] Indeed, O'Manique develops his theory much beyond the notion of survival towards the full development of human potential making it difficult to use as an analytic frame. On first and literal glance, sanitation might be understood as a need but the key infrastructural and socially reflexive demands for sanitation fit awkwardly in a needs-based framework (e.g., toilets, privacy, environmental sanitation).

A more appealing approach may be to emphasise *dignity*. The notion of human dignity emerged separately from the idea of human rights, but since the end of the Second World War, human rights and human dignity 'have increasingly become fused'.[34] While the material dimension of both civil and

[28] A. Heard, 'Human Rights: Chimeras in Sheep's Clothing?', Simon Fraser University Online Working Paper, 1997, p. 2.

[29] Ibid., p. 13. [30] Ibid., pp. 32–33.

[31] This idea of agency could equally be an independent means of establishing human rights in a manner similar to capabilities. See A. Gewirth, *Reason and Morality* (Chicago: University of Chicago, 1978).

[32] 'On my account, we also have a right . . . to health care necessary for our functioning effectively as normative agents'. Griffin, *On Human Rights*, p. 208.

[33] J. O'Manique, 'Universal and Inalienable Human Rights: A Search for Foundations', *Human Rights Quarterly*, Vol. 12 (1990), pp. 465–485, at 437.

[34] J. Donnelly, *Human Dignity and Human Rights*, Working Paper, Swiss Initiative to Commemorate the 60th Anniversary of the UDHR, Protecting Dignity: An Agenda for Human Rights, June 2009.

social rights is important, it is not exclusive. It is the experience of humiliation, domination, powerlessness and debasement that makes us equally aggrieved. Dignity is a concept that can capture this sociological and psychological dimension. This idea of dignity and autonomy particularly resonates with the right to sanitation. The health implications of the lack of sanitation are of course profound, but issues of self-worth, privacy and equality are also prominent. After her appointment, the first UN Special Rapporteur on the human right to safe drinking water and sanitation stated that 'being forced to defecate in public is an affront to human dignity'.[35] She argued that, 'Dignity closely relates to self-respect, which is difficult to maintain when being forced to squat down in the open, with no respect for privacy, not having the opportunity to clean oneself after defecating and facing the constant threat of assault in such a vulnerable moment'.[36]

This link between sanitation and dignity is present in national political discourse. In South Africa, the bucket system for sanitation in many black townships has endured since the end of apartheid despite long-standing official targets for its eradication. Statements by politicians have emphasised the aspect of personal dignity: the previous President of South Africa stated that the government was on course to 'put an end to this *dehumanising* system'[37] and the former Minister for Water Affairs and Forestry acknowledged that the 'bucket system can only be described as *demeaning*'.[38] It has also been found in legal jurisprudence. In *Melnik v Ukraine*, the European Court of Human Rights found that the applicant's conditions of detention, which included 'unsatisfactory conditions of hygiene', amounted to cruel and degrading treatment since not only caused considerable mental and physical suffering but were aimed at 'diminishing his human dignity and arousing in him such feelings as to cause humiliation and debasement'.[39] Moreover, failure to address the personal dignity dimension of sanitation can multiply the negative effects on health. UNICEF has noted the problems women agricultural workers face as they wait

[35] 'Investing in sanitation is investing in human dignity, says UN expert', UN Press Release, 18 November 2008. Note that the UN Special Rapporteur was originally appointed as the Independent Expert on the issue of human rights obligations relating to access to safe drinking water and sanitation.

[36] *Report of the Special Rapporteur*, para. 57.

[37] 'State of the Nation Address of the President of South Africa, Thabo Mbeki: Joint Sitting of Parliament', 9 February 2007. Department for International Relations and Cooperation, Government of South Africa.

[38] L.B. Hendricks, Minister of Water Affairs and Forestry, Speech at Sundays River Valley Local Municipality, Eastern Cape, 13 December 2007 (emphasis added).

[39] Application no. 72286/01, judgment dated 28 March 2006, para. 110.

to defecate at night in privacy.[40] Children, and especially girl children, are also less likely to attend school if sanitation facilities are not available or are not separated by gender.[41]

### 2.2 *International Law*

An alternative approach is to look at developments in international law, that is, taking a legal positivist or politically deliberative approach. Bilder has gone as far as to say that a claim amounts to a human right if the General Assembly 'says it is'.[42] Philip Alston agreed but proposed a stricter set of procedures to ensure some quality control in pronouncements coming out of the General Assembly.[43] Whereas international law may not represent the definitive articulation of what human rights truly represent, the motivations of drafters being diverse and contradictory, it carries at least the imprimatur of the deliberation of all States in the world. Indeed, Beitz has discerned in contemporary international human rights law a relatively coherent moral theory.[44] According to him, human rights are 'requirements whose object is to protect *urgent* individual interests against certain predictable dangers' under 'typical circumstances of life in a *modern world* order composed of States' to which 'political institutions' must respond.[45] This formulation allows us to make sense of conditional, detailed and contemporary rights in international law, such as fair trial or trade union rights, or the right to sanitation.

Until very recently, it has been difficult to conclude with any degree of certainty that there is a freestanding right to sanitation in international law. However, there has been a range of international human rights as well as humanitarian law instruments[46] that explicitly protect and promote access

[40] See, e.g. Arlette Yepdujo and Christian Guerre, 'Introducing SanPlat latrines in Niger', *UNICEF WATERfront*, No. 13, December (1999), pp. 7–10, at 7.

[41] C. Jasper, T. Thi Le and J. Bartram, 'Water and Sanitation in Schools: A Systematic Review of Health and Educational Outcomes', *International Journal of Environmental Research and Public Health*, Vol. 9, No. 8 (2012), pp. 2772–2787.

[42] R. Bilder, 'Rethinking International Human Rights: Some Basic Questions', *Wisconsin Law Review*, No. 1 (1969), pp. 171–217, at 173. In 1984,

[43] P.- Alston, 'Conjuring Up New Human Rights: A Proposal for Quality Control' *American Journal of International Law* Vol. 78 (1984), pp. 607–621.

[44] C. Beitz, *The Idea of Human Rights* (Oxford: Oxford University Press, 2009). For the sake of brevity, we ignore in this discussion agreement-based theories of human rights.

[45] Ibid., p. 109. Emphasis added.

[46] While formally outside human rights law, international humanitarian law strengthens many of these conclusions. The Geneva Convention (III) relative to the Treatment of Prisoners of War, 1949, provides that occupying powers are 'bound to take all sanitary measures necessary to ensure the cleanliness and healthfulness of camps and to prevent epidemics' and that article continues to specify in some detail the type of measures. See Article 29, Geneva Convention IV

to sanitation. This *integrative* approach is evident in Article 14(2)(h) of the Convention on the Elimination of All Forms of Discrimination against Women which explicitly obliges State parties to ensure that women in rural areas have the right to 'enjoy adequate living conditions, particularly in relation to housing, *sanitation*, electricity and water supply, transport and communications'.[47] The Convention on the Rights of the Child provides a more expansive view. In implementing the right to health, States are required in Article 24(2) to take appropriate measures to combat the 'dangers and risks of environmental pollution' of water in combating disease and to ensure that everyone is 'supported in the use of basic knowledge' about hygiene and environmental sanitation.[48]

A number of social rights have also been interpreted by UN human rights treaty bodies to include access to sanitation. According to the Committee on Economic, Social and Cultural Rights (CESCR), the right to housing includes 'sanitation and washing facilities' and 'site drainage'.[49] With regard to the right to health, the same Committee listed sanitation as one of the underlying determinants of health, and thus part of the right to health, on the basis of the drafting history of the Covenant and wide wording of the provision.[50] It is also viewed as a constitutive element in defining the availability, quality and accessibility of health. The UN Special Rapporteur on water and sanitation also demonstrates how sanitation is relevant to a wide range of human rights including education, work, decent working

on the Protection of Civilian Persons in Times of War, prisoners of war are to 'shall have for their use, day and night, conveniences which conform to the rules of hygiene' with separate sanitary facilities for women prisoners of war. Prisoners of war are also to be provided with sufficient water and soap for their 'personal toilet'. The same treatment is required in relation to civilian internees (Article 89). Water resources and infrastructure, which would arguably include sewage treatment plants and potentially extended to include other sanitation facilities, must also be protected during armed conflict: See Protocol Additional to the Geneva Conventions of 12 August 1949, and relating to the Protection of Victims of International Armed Conflicts (Protocol I), 1977, Article 54; and Protocol Additional to the Geneva Conventions of 12 August 1949, and Relating to the Protection of Victims of Non-International Armed Conflicts (Protocol II), 1977, Article 14.

47 Convention on the Elimination of All Forms of Discrimination against Women (adopted 18 December 2979, entered into force 3 September 1981) 1249 UNTS 13, UN Doc A/34/46 (emphasis added).

48 Convention on the Rights of the Child (adopted 20 November 1989, entered into force 2 September 1990) 1577 UNTS 3 (emphasis added).

49 Committee on Economic, Social and Cultural Rights, *General Comment 4, The Right to Adequate Housing* (Sixth session, 1991), UN Doc. E/1992/23, annex III at 114 (1991), para. 8(b).

50 Committee on Economic, Social and Cultural Rights, *General Comment 14, The Right to the Highest Attainable Standard of Health* (Twenty-second session, 2000), UN Doc. E/C.12/2000/4 (2000), para 4.

conditions, life, physical security, prohibition of inhuman or degrading treatment and equality of men and women.[51]

Sanitation was given some attention in the CESCR's General Comment No. 15 on the Right to Water.[52] The content of the right to water is said to include water for personal hygiene and sanitation. The Committee further emphasised that access to sanitation was both 'fundamental for human dignity and privacy' and a 'principal mechanism for protecting the quality of drinking water supplies and resources'.[53] The effective provision of sanitation was also articulated as a clear State responsibility: 'States parties have an obligation to progressively extend safe sanitation services, particularly to rural and deprived urban areas, taking into account the needs of women and children'. However, the integration of sanitation into the General Comment was criticised as being insufficient by some experts at the Day of General Discussion that preceded the General Comment's adoption.[54]

This interplay between sanitation and various social rights is particularly visible in national jurisprudence. The first Indian public interest case on social rights concerned sanitation. In the 1980 judgment of *Municipal Council, Ratlam* v. *Shri Vardhichand & Others*, the Supreme Court of India found that the failure of a municipality to provide toilets for informal settlements and drainage not only violated the Municipality Act but threatened human health and implicated human rights due to the assault on decency and dignity.[55] Moreover, in the first reported case that invoked the 2002 General Comment No. 15 on the Right to Water, sanitation was at the forefront. Provincial and municipal authorities in Argentina were found to have violated the rights to health and right to water by failing to prevent pollution of communal water sources, with the culprit being an under-maintained and overstretched sewage-treatment plant.[56]

Until 2010, the international recognition of a *freestanding* or independent right to sanitation – including as a co-right with water – was thin. The first instance of such a recognition was in the so-called Dublin Principles: 'it is vital

[51] *Report of the Special Rapporteur*, paras. 13–54. This will not be discussed in this chapter in detail but the jurisprudence and experience from other rights will be returned to in delineating the content of the right and the correlative duties in the next section.

[52] See the final outcome: Committee on Economic, Social and Cultural Rights, *General Comment 15, The Right to Water* (Twenty-ninth session, 2002), UN Doc. E/C.12/2002/11.

[53] *CESCR General Comment* 15, ibid., para. 29.

[54] Committee on Economic, Social and Cultural Rights, *Preliminary Discussion of a Draft General Comment on the Rights to Water*, (Twenty-ninth Session), 27 November 2002 UN. Doc. E/C.12/2002/SR.46 (2002).

[55] *Municipal Council, Ratlam* v. *Shri Vardhichand & Ors* [1981] SCR (1) 97.

[56] *CEDHA* v. *Provincial State and Municipality of Córdoba* (AC).

to recognize first the basic right of all human beings to have access to clean water and *sanitation* at an affordable price'.[57] Two years later, 177 States at the 1994 Cairo Conference on Population and Development endorsed a Programme of Action that recognised that all individuals have the 'right to an adequate standard of living for themselves and their families, including adequate food, clothing, housing, water and *sanitation*'. The later UN-Habitat Global Plan of Action (1996) contains identical language,[58] but the Johannesburg Declaration (2002) is more circumspect and refers to dignity rather than rights.[59]

During the drafting of the General Comment No. 15 on the Right to Water, the CESCR was pressed by NGOs and international health experts to imply the right to sanitation along with water.[60] However, the Committee declined. It is difficult to speculate as to reasons why - they were not made public. Although, some Committee members have indicated that they did not believe there was sufficient international support in international law.[61] Nonetheless, the Committee's position gradually evolved. In its General Comment No. 19 of 2008, it appears to suggest that sanitation was a right on par with others in the Covenant.[62]

Ultimately, the Committee recognised a clear right to sanitation after political developments in the UN charter bodies. In 2001, a UN Sub-Commission on Human Rights Special Rapporteur drafted guidelines which began with the assertion that sanitation was 'unquestionably a human right' and go on to state that 'Everyone has the right to have access to adequate and safe sanitation that is conducive to the protection of public health and the environment'.[63] Little resulted from that but in 2006, a request from the

57 International Conference on Water and the Environment: Development Issues for the 21st Century, 'Dublin Statement on Water and Sustainable Development', UN Doc. A/CONF.151/PC/112 (1992). Emphasis added. It was not a formal government declaration, but the statement was endorsed by international experts from a hundred countries. It is also a formal UN document.

58 UN-Habitat, *The Habitat Agenda Goals and Principles, Commitments and the Global Plan of Action* (Nairobi: UN-Habitat, 1996), Istanbul, Turkey, para. 11.

59 Adopted at the 17th plenary meeting of the World Summit on Sustainable Development, Johannesburg, South Africa, 4 September 2002.

60 *Preliminary Discussion of a Draft General Comment.*

61 Private conversations with the first-named author of this chapter.

62 When discussing the coverage for certain social security benefits, it uses the language of rights in relation to sanitation: 'Family and child benefits, including cash benefits and social services, should be provided to families, without discrimination on prohibited grounds, and would ordinarily cover food, clothing, housing, water and sanitation, or other rights as appropriate'. Committee on Economic, Social and Cultural Rights, *General Comment No. 19, The Right to Social Security* (Thirty-ninth session, 2007), UN Doc. E/C.12/GC/19 (2008), para 6.

63 The Guidelines are available at: UN Commission on Human Rights, *Final report of the Special Rapporteur on the Relationship between the Enjoyment of Economic, Social and*

newly formed Human Rights Council[64] led to a study by the UN High Commissioner for Human Rights which acknowledged that it was an open debate on whether water and sanitation were human rights but forcefully concluded that it was time to consider sanitation as a human right.[65] In 2009, the then UN Special Rapporteur on the human right to safe drinking water and sanitation in her report to the General Assembly came to a similar conclusion, noting 'a trend towards recognition of such a distinct right'.[66]

The issue was finally resolved in 2010 when the UN General Assembly recognised 'the right to safe and clean drinking water and sanitation as a human right that is essential for the full enjoyment of life and all human rights'.[67] However, a high number of States abstained from voting for the resolution: 122 voted in favour to none against, with 41 abstentions. The majority of abstaining States noted that their vote was not premised on substantive opposition or agnosticism. Rather it was procedural: the matter was also being handled by the UN Human Rights Council, and they felt it was premature for the General Assembly to take a vote.

Some States, however, were substantively opposed. For the United Kingdom, the problem with the resolution was the very inclusion of the right to sanitation:

> The representative of the United Kingdom said her delegation had abstained for reasons of substance and procedure. Concerning substance, there was no sufficient legal basis for declaring or recognizing water or sanitation as freestanding human rights, nor was there evidence that they existed in customary law.[68]

This dissent was overcome in September 2010 when the UN Human Rights Council affirmed the recognition of the right to sanitation without the need to hold a vote.[69] The members of the Council included many States who had previously abstained in the General Assembly. This was followed in

*Cultural Rights and the Promotion of the Realization of the Right to Drinking Water Supply and Sanitation*, (Fifty-sixth session, 2004), UN Doc. E/CN.4/Sub.2/2004/20.

64 Decision 2/104, *Human Rights and Access to Water*, 31st Meeting, 27 November 2006.

65 UN Human Rights Council, *Report of the United Nations High Commissioner for Human Rights on the scope and content of the relevant human rights obligations related to equitable access to safe drinking water and sanitation under international human rights instruments* (Sixth session, 2007), UN Doc. A/HRC/6/3 (2007), para. 66.

66 Report of the Special Rapporteur , para. 59.

67 *The Human Right to Water and Sanitation*, para. 1.

68 *General Assembly Adopts Resolution Recognizing Access to Clean Water, Sanitation*, UN Information Release, 28 July 2010.

69 *Human Rights and Access to Safe Drinking Water and Sanitation*, Resolution.

2015 by a new General Assembly vote in which sanitation was recognised as a distinct right, which we discuss below.

The authoritative recognition by the General Assembly and the endorsement by the UN Human Rights Council appear to have settled the status of the right to sanitation in international law. Moreover, in the Human Rights Council (HRC) resolution, the legal foundations of the right were clearly established. Namely, that the right to sanitation was derived from the right to adequate standard of living and related to the right to health.[70] Simultaneously, the CESCR moved to declare that the right to sanitation could be derived from these rights in the ICESCR:

> The Committee reaffirms that, since sanitation is fundamental for human survival and for leading a life in dignity, the right to sanitation is an essential component of the right to an adequate standard of living, enshrined in Article 11 of the International Covenant on Economic, Social and Cultural Rights. The right to sanitation is also integrally related, among other Covenant rights, to the right to health, as laid down in Article 12 paragraphs 1 and 2 (a), (b) and (c), the right to housing, in Article 11, as well as the right to water, which the Committee recognized in its General Comment No. 15.[71]

Interestingly, it chose not to update General Comment No. 15 (following the practice of the Human Rights Committee in light of new developments or case-based jurisprudence) but issued a separate document on the right to sanitation.

## 3 IDENTIFYING THE NATURE OF THE RIGHT

Unlike other human rights, the recognition of the right to sanitation was not significantly preceded or followed by a scholarship that sought to tease out its essential nature and relationship to other rights. This section tries to understand the nature of the right to sanitation: how does it relate to the right to water and is it an individual, collective or hybrid right?

### 3.1 *A Co-Right with Water?*

One primary legal question until recently has been somewhat technical and linguistic. Is sanitation a stand-alone right or a co-right with water? What was

70 *Human Rights and Access to Safe Drinking Water and Sanitation*, Resolution, para. 3.
71 UN Committee on Economic, Social and Cultural Rights, *Statement on the Right to Sanitation*, (Forty-fifth sesión, 2010), UN Doc. E/C.12/2010/ 1, para. 7.

interesting (and concerning for some) about the recognition of the right to sanitation in international law was the use of a *singular* not a plural noun. Water and sanitation were referred to as a human right, not human rights, in all the legal instruments cited above. This suggested that sanitation is conceived as a co-right with water. Such a twinning seemed natural: water quality is largely dependent on the provision of sanitation (waterborne or dry), water and sanitation combine with good hygiene to provide a very effective health intervention, and the infrastructure and management for waterborne sanitation is usually twinned with water. It may have also made political sense: it is more feasible to recognise one rather than two 'new' rights.

Nonetheless, this approach was contested. The UN Special Rapporteur frequently referred to 'rights' to water and sanitation.[72] On account of its dignity dimensions, she emphasised that sanitation was a 'distinct right'.[73] The CESCR did not take a clear position but noted that: 'sanitation has distinct features which warrant its separate treatment from water in some respects. Although much of the world relies on waterborne sanitation, increasingly sanitation solutions which do not use water are being promoted and encouraged'.[74]

Objections went further. Environmentalists typically express the concern that the lumping of water and sanitation together in development (and now human rights) discourse promoted water-based solutions to sanitation. Some sanitation and human rights advocates worried that expressing sanitation as a co-right with water would also lead to the former being overshadowed in political commitments, funding or implementation.[75] Although the benefits from investing in sanitation are at least as considerable as investments in water, requirements for the water sector are easier to finance than requirements for the sanitation sector, which garners only 37 per cent of aid funding and an average of 20 per cent of government spending.[76] The CESCR has noted these extreme differences. In its concluding observations on Nepal's periodic report, it noted that '29 per cent of the population has no access to

[72] *Report of the Special Rapporteur.*

[73] Ibid., paras. 58–59: 'One might argue that, because dignity pervades the issue of sanitation and sanitation cannot be entirely subsumed into any other existing human right, it should be considered a distinct human right' (para. 58). For an extended argument on de-linking, see K. Ellis and L. Feris, 'The Right to Sanitation: Time to Delink from the Right to Water', *Human Rights Quarterly* Vol. 36 (2014), pp. 607–629.

[74] Ibid.

[75] In South Africa, local water services managers received directives from national government to meet the national water targets first and then concentrate on sanitation afterwards. Communication from local official to Malcolm Langford, 17 February 2009.

[76] UN-Water, *Global Annual Assessment of Sanitation and Drinking-Water (GLAAS)* (Geneva: WHO, 2010), pp. 28–29.

safe water, 90 per cent has no access to health services and 84 per cent has no access to sanitation'.[77] However, some recent evidence suggests that sanitation may not be so under-prioritised in comparison to water[78] and arguably both receive too little attention.

There are also a number of operational differences. Outside the domain of centralised sewerage systems, there is rarely a clearly assigned responsibility for direct provision of sanitation services. Similarly, governmental responsibilities towards sanitation are commonly distributed amongst different agencies, departments and ministries. Moreover, when water services fail, they tend to fail in a geographic area (e.g. a well with handpump or a centralised piped supply), thereby sparking public demand for improvement or replacement services. When sanitation services fail, they are more likely to fail by household (e.g. because of a full latrine pit or septic tank), so public demand for improvement may be more localised. Sanitation is also very much a process rather than a complete and actual good and possibly suffers from not playing the deep role that water does in many religions and societies in terms of water sharing and cultural practices.

These concerns eventually proved decisive. In November 2015, the General Assembly declared that 'human rights to safe drinking water and sanitation as components of the right to an adequate standard of living are essential for the full enjoyment of the right to life and all human rights'.[79] And, at the end of the day, it is not clear whether the linguistic construction of the right is decisive. The real challenge may be to articulate and emphasise sanitation as a right, and its constituent elements, rather than on dwelling on the semantic ontology. Analogies can perhaps be made with the civil right to 'freedom of thought, conscience and religion', as it is expressed in the International Covenant on Civil and Political Rights.[80] These three interests are sufficiently related so as to be placed naturally together even if they have clearly distinct characteristics.[81]

77 CESCR, *Concluding Observations of the Committee on Economic, Social and Cultural Rights: Nepal* (Twenty-sixth sesión, 2001), UN Doc. 24/09/2001. E/C.12/1/Add.66, para. X.

78 O. Cumming, M. Elliott, A. Overbo and J. Bartram, 'Does Global Progress on Sanitation Really Lag behind Water? An Analysis of Global Progress on Community- and Household-level Access to Safe Water and Sanitation', *PLoS ONE*, Vol. 9 no. 12 (2014): e114699.

79 *The Human Rights to Safe Drinking Water and Sanitation*, UN GA Resolution 707169, UN doc. A/C.3/70/L.55/Rev.1, para. 1.

80 International Covenant on Civil and Political Rights (adopted 19 December 1966, entered into force 3 March 1976) 999 UNTS 171, UN Doc. A/6316 (1966), Article 18.

81 The UN Human Rights Committee has thus described the right as 'far-reaching and profound' since 'it encompasses freedom of thought on all matters, personal conviction and the commitment to religion or belief'. *General Comment 22, Article 18* (Forty-eighth session, 1993). Compilation of General Comments and General Recommendations Adopted by Human Rights Treaty Bodies, UN Doc. HRI/GEN/1/Rev.1 at 35 (1994).

### 3.2 *Individual, Group or Hybrid Right?*

However, sanitation may diverge from water in a more important way, which raises different categorical questions. On closer inspection, the right to sanitation could be said to possess the features of a group right (like environmental health or peace) rather than an individual right. A group right has been defined as such:

> [A] group of individuals has a collective right if their shared interest is sufficient to ground a duty in others, and if the interest of any single member of the group is insufficient by itself to ground that duty.[82]

Raz argues that a collective right can be identified when the three following conditions hold:

> First, it exists because an aspect of the interest of human beings justifies holding some person(s) to be subject to a duty. Second, the interests in question are the interests of individuals as members of a group in a public good and the right is a right to that public good because it serves their interest as members of that group. Thirdly, the interest of no single member of that group in that public good is sufficient by itself to justify holding another person to be subject to a duty.[83]

Why might sanitation constitute this type of right? Sanitation is frequently promoted by health and development practitioners and policymakers on the basis of its *public health* benefits. As discussed, human faeces is the leading cause of water pollution and a major cause of preventable illnesses that can lead to death. Indeed, this collective dimension is clear when practitioners frequently express frustration with a lack of demand for it: 'people need to be educated', 'people need to be made aware' and so on.[84] If human rights are meant to spring from universal and basic demands, do we need to be educated to ask for them? Helped to demand them?

Thus, attention is not principally focused on *individual* access to a toilet or other modality; it is equally on the right of *all* people to *access* sanitation and the duty of all persons to *use* sanitation facilities so as to not infringe the rights

[82] P. Jones, 'Group Rights', in E.N. Zalta (ed.), *The Stanford Encyclopaedia of Philosophy (Winter 2008 Edition)*, section 4, p. 9.

[83] J. Raz, *The Morality of Freedom* (Oxford: Clarendon Press, 1986), p. 208.

[84] This includes advocates within the human rights community: see *Report of the Special Rapporteur*, para. 68. The participatory dimension of the right is important since 'achieving community ownership and dedication in order to bring about the required behavioural changes'. Whether individuals have a duty to practice safe sanitation is taken up by Inga Winkler, 'The Human Right to Sanitation', *University of Pennsylvania Journal of International Law*, Vol. 37, No. 4 (2016), pp. 1331–1406.

of others: this way, *everyone* will be protected from the *effects* of human excreta.[85] If we focus on the environmental and health benefits of sanitation, then our primary interest is public rather than personal. It is difficult to individualise in rights terms such a collective demand. Whereas almost all rights have a collective dimension (often in the means of implementation), they can be at least expressed in individual terms. In the case of sanitation, can one argue that a *single individual's* interest in sanitation services being universally provided would be sufficient to justify the creation of an entire sanitation system? This is different from water: one can clearly speak of a duty to ensure individuals have access to water on the basis of their individual interest.

Importantly, the idea of group rights has been challenged on many grounds. Some argue that it is impossible for groups to possess rights since groups are 'fictitious entities'[86] or that even if they are not, they cannot claim human rights since these are reserved for individuals.[87] Others require that rights claimants meet certain thresholds of normative agency (whether individual or institutional)[88] or that group rights may only be justifiable to the extent they are reducible to the rights of individuals.[89] To this are added the concerns that accepting group rights allows the translation of any public good into a human right, thus fuelling further human rights inflation.

One way of responding to this conceptual dilemma is to try and mount a case for sanitation on purely individual grounds. This could be done by turning to dignity: the denial or lack of individual access to sanitation is in and of itself an affront to individual human dignity. A lack of sanitation clearly raises issues of privacy, individual health, personal dignity as well as safety and equality. This impact at the personal level could be sufficient for arguing that sanitation is a human right. However, this only takes us so far. Dignity would

85 In this sense, it is not surprising to see a movement for environmental sanitation which focuses not just on human excreta but developing sanitation systems that deal with all types of waste and which demands not just a collection point of excreta but also safe transport, treatment and disposal. See WHO, *What Is Environmental Sanitation?* (Geneva: WHO, 2002).

86 J. Graff, 'Human Rights, Peoples, and the Right to Self-Determination', in J. Baker (ed.), *Group Rights* (Toronto: Toronto University Press, 1994), pp. 186–214, at 194.

87 J. Donnelly, *Universal Rights in Theory and Practice* (2nd edn., Ithaca: Cornell University Press, 2002).

88 C. Wellman, 'Liberalism, Communitarianism, and Group Rights', *Law and Philosophy*, Vol. 18, No. 1: 13–40 (1999). Although some would allow institutional, rather than collective entities, to possess rights on the grounds of their independent decision-making procedures. See *Stanford Encyclopaedia of Philosophy*, section 6, p. 17.

89 'Groups can have many concrete rights, as do individuals. But do they have a fundamental right to survive and flourish as do individuals? The answer depends on what view one takes on the sacredness of groups'. V. Haksar, 'Collective Rights and the Value of Groups', *Inquiry*, Vol. 41, No. 1, pp. 21–43, at 41.

ground a right to a private and safe place in which to urinate, defecate and manage menstruation; individual health concerns would also support the removal of that waste so as to avoid pollution. However, it would not support the treatment or transport of human waste in such a way as to avoid health effects for other individuals. In order to protect the dignity of an individual, different ways could be used to get rid of the waste that would not necessarily be in the interest of others. In the case of water, this puzzle does not arise: there is an individual interest in a system of supply and quality control as it will be consumed by the individual. Thus, the justification of a fully functioning system of sanitation and collective behavioural change cannot be fully grounded in individual interest in sanitation *per se*.[90]

Thus, we need to look for an alternative and complementary justification for the 'collective dimensions' of the right to sanitation. The best and the most pragmatic approach seems to transcend an individualist fixation with human rights. Group rights could be defended by recognition that some goods 'are fundamental to human life and human well-being' and that 'if we ignore that fact, our conception of human rights will not match the reality of the human condition'.[91] In international human rights treaty law and declarations, we find broader group-based rights such as self-determination,[92] the benefits of scientific progress and its applications,[93] development[94] and indigenous peoples' rights.[95] Moreover, behavioural change is often sought for the realisation of other rights: for example, we encourage or make compulsory voting to improve democracy; likewise primary education is made compulsory in human rights treaties. Thus, the right to sanitation appears more defensible if we downplay the theoretical difficulties of recognising a human right as solely an individual right and acknowledge that a right with strong

[90] Although it could be justified on an individual basis through other rights such as health or water – i.e. the *duty* to ensure access to sanitation in order that these rights are respected. But this starts from a right to water or health and *not* sanitation.

[91] *Stanford Encyclopaedia of Philosophy*, section 9, p. 21.

[92] International Covenant on Economic, Social and Cultural Rights (adopted 16 December 1966, entered into force 23 March 1976) 993 UNTS 3, UN Doc. A/6316(1966), Article 1 and ICCPR.

[93] ICESCR, Article 15.

[94] UN General Assembly, *Declaration on the Right to Development*, G.A. *res*. 41/128, UN Doc. A/41/53 (1986).

[95] Convention concerning Indigenous and Tribal Peoples in Independent Countries (ILO No. 169), 72 ILO Official Bull. 59, entered into force Sept. 5, 1991; UN General Assembly, Declaration on the Rights of Indigenous Peoples, G.A. Res. 61/295, UN Doc. A/RES/47/1 (2007).

collective or group dimensions is acceptable within the global human rights and international law framework.

Sanitation should be conceived therefore as a hybrid right, with individual and group components. It protects basic needs and dignity but also entails a focus on the broader right to a clean and health-supporting environment. While generally synergistic, there are both favourable and adverse interactions between these two categories. For example, extension of access to sanitation in households contributes to the realisation of the individual right, but it may support or infringe the collective dimension. This would depend on whether a population's exposure to hazardous faeces is reduced by the individual access to a toilet (e.g. by reduction in open defecation replaced with household latrines) or increased (e.g. when shared latrines are replaced by piped sewerage with no accompanying treatment of sewage produced). This rise in hazardous risks may be quite wide or very specific, for example, a move from open defecation to community-level sewerage may lead to a transportation of human waste from the environment of the sewered community into the environment of 'downstream' communities.

Interestingly, sanitation is framed as such a hybrid right in section 2 of the South African Water Services Act. The provision reads that everyone has 'the right of access to a basic water supply and the right to basic sanitation necessary to secure sufficient water and an environment not harmful to human health or well-being'. The purpose of the recognition of the right is not just individuals, but it extends also to the environmental protection that is important to the health and well-being of all people. Similar language is used in the UN Sub-Commission guidelines, which arguably go further since they aim to protect the environment generally and not just human health.[96] Thus, in our view, the conditions conducive to attaining both individual and collective/group benefits and for managing trade-offs between these two should be recognised.

## 4 CONTENT AND OBLIGATIONS

It has been claimed that social rights are indeterminate since there 'is no universal and non-arbitrary standard for distinguishing need from luxury' and thus it is equally difficult to adduce what a minimum or adequate level of the rights may be.[97] Added to this are worries that it is difficult to identify who is

96 Principle 1.2 states 'Everyone has the right to have access to adequate and safe sanitation that is conducive to the protection of public health and the environment'.

97 D. Kelley, *A Life of One's Own: Individual Rights and the Welfare State* (Washington, D.C.: Cato Institute, 1998), p. 16.

the relevant duty bearer, that social rights are highly resource dependent and lack justiciable qualities and that their implementation is enormously complex and will necessarily interfere with the fulfilment of other rights. These concerns may be projected onto the right to sanitation, particularly when it has received little political, jurisprudential and scholarly attention. This potentially makes these questions more difficult to answer. This section examines whether it is possible to discern meaningful and feasible obligations and entitlements that would meet basic human rights criteria.

### 4.1 *Obligations*

As discussed in Chapter 1, social rights have been critiqued on the basis that both the duty bearer and the duties pass unidentified: 'We normally regard claims or entitlements that nobody is obligated to respect and honour as null or void, indeed undefined' and that 'abstract rights to goods and services' fall squarely in this category.[98] The challenge of the indeterminateness of the responsible *actor* can be addressed in two ways. The first is to focus on those individuals or entities that are proximate or in a position to help, a long tradition in ethics and even natural rights thinking.[99] The second is to narrow the scope and confine duties to States for pragmatic and principled reasons, for example, the presumed social contract between a State and its citizens/residents.[100]

This latter approach is dominant in international human rights law, but the duties of other actors are increasingly receiving attention.[101] The human rights responsibilities of transnational corporations and intergovernmental organisations are subject to a rapidly growing body of international soft law,[102]

98 O. O'Neill, 'The Dark Side of Human Rights', *International Affairs*, Vol. 81 (2005), pp. 427–439, at 430, 428.

99 Griffin, *On Human Rights*; T. Pogge, *World Poverty and Human Rights: Cosmopolitan Responsibilities and Reforms* (2nd ed, Cambridge: Polity Press, 2008).

100 T. Paine, *The Rights of Man* (New York: Penguin Books, 1985).

101 For an overview of constitutional developments that place social rights obligations on private actors, see M. Langford, 'Justiciability of Social Rights: From Practice to Theory', in M. Langford (ed.), *Social Rights Jurisprudence: Emerging Trends in International and Comparative Law* (Cambridge: Cambridge University Press, 2008), pp. 1–45. In armed conflict, non-state actors are bound to respect various fundamental interests, including the provision of sanitary facilities to prisoners and protection of sewerage works from attack

102 See, for example, ILO Tripartite Declaration of Principles Concerning Multinational Enterprises and Social Policy in 1977 and the OECD Guidelines for Multinational Enterprises 1976 and revision in 2000 and 2011. See also UN Human Rights Council, *Report of the Special Representative of the Secretary-General on the issue of human rights and transnational corporations and other business enterprises, John Ruggie*, (Seventeenth session, 2011) UN Doc. A/HRC/17/31 (2011).

with claims that some have hardened in customary international law.[103] These obligations tend to be characterised negatively, but there is some recognition that there may be more positive duties of 'due diligence' to ensure that the particular institution is not contributing to the denial or frustration of the achievement of human rights.[104] For example, private actors should not only provide adequate sanitation for their employees, patients, pupils and so on but also consider how they could contribute to the realisation of the right more broadly.[105] For reasons of space and the fact that the duties of States have been more firmly established in international law, we will devote our attention to them.

Up to the time of writing, no authoritative determination of the obligations of States in relation to a freestanding right to sanitation has been made in international law. In its 2010 statement, the CESCR simply expresses the view that the right to sanitation requires 'full recognition by States parties in compliance with the human rights principles related to non-discrimination, gender equality, participation and accountability'.[106] However, the general scholarship and jurisprudence on economic, social and cultural rights is relatively developed and can be drawn upon.

The former UN Special Rapporteur attempted precisely that although there are a number of issues that remain unresolved. According to her, the duty of *respect* requires States to refrain from acts or measures that 'threaten or deny individuals or communities existing access to sanitation'.[107] It may be difficult to imagine States willingly interfering with sanitation, but the issue often arises

[103] M. Darrow, *Between Light and. Shadow: The World Bank, the International Monetary Fund and International Human Rights Law* (Oxford: Hart Publishing, 2003); O. De Schutter (ed.), *Transnational Corporations and Human Rights* (Oxford: Hart Publishing, 2006); S. Skogly, *The Human Rights Obligations of the World Bank and the IMF* (London: Cavendish Publishing, 2001).

[104] See generally O. De Schutter (ed.), *Transnational Corporations and Human Rights* (Oxford: Hart Publishing, 2006).

[105] For example, the UN Special Rapporteur on Right to Water and Sanitation has stated that, 'While it is the obligation of the State to put into place the necessary regulations, providers also have responsibilities in the operation of services. As outlined above, they must exercise due diligence to become aware of, prevent and address adverse impacts on human rights. To meet this responsibility, service providers should take certain measures, such as ensuring that the water they provide is of safe quality, ensuring the regularity of supply, not discriminating in their operations, adopting fair procedures in cases of disconnections due to non-payment and refraining from disconnections when people are unable to pay and the disconnection would leave them without access to minimum essential levels of water'. UN Human Rights Council, *Report of the independent expert on the issue of human rights obligations related to access to safe drinking water and sanitation, Catarina de Albuquerque*, (Fourteenth session, 2010) UN Doc. A/HRC/15/31, para. 49.

[106] CESCR, Statement, para. 8.

[107] *Report of the Special Rapporteur*, para. 64.

in the context of water disconnections – the denial of access to water renders waterborne sanitation impossible. In some cases, it is more direct. In many informal settlements and some rural areas, sanitation facilities are constructed separately, and there are often claims that forced evictions result in the destruction of sanitation facilities. It is possible to argue that demolition and denial of access would breach the right to sanitation unless there were exceptional circumstances,[108] due process[109] and the provision of alternatives.[110]

The duty to *protect* entails taking steps to ensure that non-State actors respect the right to sanitation. Where private actors have the opportunity to deliver sanitation services, the obligation to protect assumes particular relevance. If aspects of service provision are owned, managed or operated by the private sector, the State retains the duty to not only establish a regulatory framework but also maintain effective control in practice. Caution also needs to be exercised in the process of facilitating private sector involvement: in the development of frameworks for privatisation in the late 1990s, some governments/municipalities demonstrated a tendency to split the concessions, with the (fully or partly privatised) utility delivering (more profitable) water but not (more costly) sanitation. This raises the risk that sanitation will be deprioritised if the public sector is not expected to maintain an equivalent or improved service in the shadow of enhanced private sector participation.[111] Thus, if private sector service delivery can be justified and is desired, then States need

[108] See, for example, the articulation of this in Committee on Economic, Social and Cultural Rights, *General Comment 7, Forced evictions, and the right to adequate housing,* (Sixteenth session, 1997), UN Doc. E/1998/22, annex IV at 113 (1997).

[109] This has already been set out by the CESCR in General Comment No. 15 in relation to the Right to Water and would equally apply to a right to sanitation. Replacing water in paragraph 56 with sanitation, the duty would read as follows: 'Before any action that interferes with an individual's right to sanitation is carried out by the State party, or by any other third party, the relevant authorities must ensure that such actions are performed in a manner warranted by law, compatible with the Covenant, and that comprises: (a) opportunity for genuine consultation with those affected; (b) timely and full disclosure of information on the proposed measures; (c) reasonable notice of proposed actions; (d) legal recourse and remedies for those affected; and (e) legal assistance for obtaining legal remedies (see also General Comments No. 4 (1991) and No. 7 (1997)). Where such action is based on a person's failure to pay for sanitation their capacity to pay must be taken into account. Under no circumstances shall an individual be deprived of the minimum essential level of sanitation'. *CESCR General Comment* 15.

[110] In the report by COHRE et al., this qualification is explicitly added: 'Governments are obliged to refrain from preventing people from accessing sanitation, for example, by arbitrarily interfering with customary or traditional arrangements for sanitation, without providing adequate and culturally acceptable alternatives', p. 27.

[111] For a discussion on this dilemma, see the chapter by Langford in this volume that directly discusses corporatisation of urban water services.

to establish the enabling environment that encourages companies to engage/emerge and to manage their business in the public interest.[112] Moreover, in the case of right to sanitation, the duty to protect should also extend beyond legal and institutional regulation of private providers and treatment plants. It might target individuals and others that may cause physical harm: e.g., ensuring sufficient policing and street lighting where sanitation is not available within the home.

The *duty to fulfil* is often subject to the critique of excessive abstractness and lack of feasibility. The basic treaty obligation is to take steps using the maximum of available resources, towards the progressive realisation of the right to sanitation.[113] Drawing on the jurisprudence of the CESCR, the UN Special Rapporteur has stated that this means taking 'deliberate, concrete and targeted steps', thereby 'moving as expeditiously and effectively as possible' towards 'ensuring access to safe, affordable and acceptable sanitation for all, which provides privacy and dignity'.[114] It would also mean ensuring that there is no retrogression in the realisation of the right to sanitation, for example, through permitting a deterioration of facilities and services or lowering relevant entitlements. Deliberate retrogressive measures are said to require very strong justification.[115]

Sometimes, this may involve choices as different dimensions come into conflict with each other. A State may provide a sewerage connection to a settlement and remove shared latrines, but if there is poor waste treatment, the collective dimension of the right may regress and the individual dimension as well, if those in the wider population are also negatively affected. Such effects could possibly be justified in the short term as part of the 'growing pains' of progressive realisation but not in the long term. Indeed, the worst affected by sewage outfalls tend to be those who are already disadvantaged, while more privileged groups often have the benefit of toilets and environmentally healthier localities.

112 See also *Report of the Independent Expert*.

113 See ICESCR, Article 2(1) and CRC, Article 4.

114 *Report of the Special Rapporteur*, para. 64.

115 Note that the Special Rapporteur paraphrases this obligation, perhaps in an unintentionally conservative manner. She opines that States must, 'Carefully consider and justify any retrogressive measures'. The CESCR has stated though in relation to the right to water that: 'There is a strong presumption that retrogressive measures taken in relation to the right to water are prohibited under the Covenant. If any deliberately retrogressive measures are taken, the State party has the burden of proving that they have been introduced after the most careful consideration of all alternatives and that they are duly justified by reference to the totality of the rights provided for in the Covenant in the context of the full use of the State party's maximum available resources'. *CESCR General Comment* 15, para. 19.

In terms of the concrete steps to be taken, the Special Rapporteur has identified 'creating an enabling environment' for 'hygiene promotion and education', 'immediately developing and adopting a national sanitation strategy and plan of action' and ensuring 'full participation' of individuals and communities in the development and implementation of policy.[116] Developing such national plans may be a particularly effective way of mobilising resources and effort towards realising the right, but sufficient detail should be provided. For example, Kenya's Second National Health Sector Strategic Plan (2006) set out a target to be reached by 2010 for 50 per cent of the population to have access to 'good sanitation' but was criticised for failing to set out any substantial measures to achieve progress on 'basic sanitation'.[117]

States are responsible for also ensuring that 'effective judicial or other appropriate remedies' are available where there are 'violations of human rights obligations related to sanitation'.[118] This last requirement has traditionally been controversial. It was assumed by many that social rights were not justiciable.[119] While this debate continues in different forms, national and international jurisprudence has demonstrated that all aspects of social rights are justiciable.[120] As we shall see in Section 4.4, the right to sanitation is no exception. Moreover, the CESCR has increasingly asked States to justify why they haven't provided such remedies at the national level,[121] and the new Optional Protocol for the ICESCR would now presumably provide for claims concerning the right to sanitation.[122]

In addition to provision of remedies, there is the broader need for general monitoring and accountability: 'States and other relevant actors should

[116] *Report of the Special Rapporteur*, paras. 64 and 66. This participatory dimension is discussed in more detail below in section 4.1

[117] See M. Katui Katua, A. Khalfan, M. Langford and M. Lüke, *Kenya-German Development Cooperation in the Water Sector, Assessment from a Human Rights Perspective* (Eschborn: GTZ, 2007), p. 29.

[118] Ibid., para. 64.

[119] E. W. Vierdag, 'The Legal Nature of the Rights Granted by the International Covenant on Economic, Social and Cultural Rights', *Netherlands Yearbook of International Law*, Vol. IX (1978), pp. 69–105.

[120] See M. Langford (ed.), *Social Rights Jurisprudence: Emerging Trends in International and Comparative Law* (Cambridge: Cambridge University Press, 2008); R. Gargarella, D. Pilar, and T. Roux, *Courts and Social Transformation in New Democracies: An Institutional Voice for the Poor?* (Aldershot/Burlington: Ashgate, 2006).

[121] CESCR, *General Comment 9, The Domestic Application of the Covenant* (Nineteenth session, 1998), UN Doc. E/C.12/1998/24 (1998).

[122] Optional Protocol to the International Covenant on Economic, Social and Cultural Rights (adopted 10 December 2008, awaiting entry into force, UN General Assembly Resolution (Sixty third session, 2008), UN Doc A/RES/63/117 (2008).

monitor changes over time to gauge the effectiveness of interventions and the impact of policy reforms and investments' as well as 'establish effective, transparent and accessible monitoring and accountability mechanisms, with power to monitor and hold accountable all actors, both public and private'.[123] What is particularly worrying is that in many countries, not even the basic step of monitoring access to sanitation in a way that supports policy decisions has been achieved. For example, for a decade in Kenya, the Water Services Trust Fund (established in 2002) targeted those without adequate water and sanitation on the basis of the 1999 census. Civil society can of course be encouraged to complement this monitoring and include approaches such as report cards for sanitation service providers, as well as 'integrity pacts' to promote transparency and challenge corrupt practices.[124]

Moreover, and arguably, States have committed themselves to realise the right to sanitation universally, subject to their maximum available resources. Article 2(1) of the ICESCR provides that States are to realise the right through 'international assistance and cooperation'. The Special Rapporteur has emphasised that sanitation should be reflected in budgets for international assistance and cooperation' and that 'Development agencies should prioritize interventions in the sanitation sector and put the human rights obligations related to sanitation at the core of their projects'.[125]

Beyond this, and consistent with the Committee's jurisprudence, the Special Rapporteur demonstrates caution in articulating the obligations more specifically. In particular, she refrains from identifying the precise *speed* at which realisation must happen[126] likewise which dimensions of the right should be *prioritised* in sequence other than the demands of non-discrimination and equality. These requirements are to be politically decided upon at the national or international level as well as reviewed in national monitoring process, which can better take account of context.

Thus, the only named immediate and predetermined requirements in terms of result are those consistent with the Committee's jurisprudence.

[123] *Report of the Special Rapporteur*, p. 28.

[124] Integrity pacts are a method of corruption prevention in public tendering and contracting. The government agency and tendering companies make an agreement that that they will abstain from bribery, collusion and other corrupt practices.

[125] Ibid., paras. 81(d), (e).

[126] For a discussion of speed, see J. Luh, R. Cronk and J. Bartram, 'Assessing Progress towards Public Health, Human Rights and International Development Goals Using Frontier Analysis', *PLoS ONE*, Vol. 11, No. 1 doi: 10.1371/journal.pone.0147663; J. Luh, R. Baum, and J. Bartram, 'Equity in Water and Sanitation: Developing an Index to Measure Progressive Realization of the Human Right', *International Journal of Hygiene and Environmental Health*, No. 216 (2013), pp. 662–671.

States must 'ensure at least minimum essential levels of sanitation for all people' and that they 'are not discriminating against certain groups in providing access'.[127] In understanding what this may entail, we need to look further at the content of the right. This is potentially easier than some other rights (such as health care and social security) which are broader in scope, but the different demands for sanitation – particularly health and privacy/security – can make articulation more complicated and complicate resource allocation decisions under conditions of scarcity. For instance, it would be easy to reiterate the minimum necessary provisions for health – absence of disease transmission and the sufficiency to protect again such transmission – but this needs to be accompanied by commensurate provisions for the protection of broader dignity concerns.

### 4.2 *Content of the Right*

In determining the content of the right to sanitation, much thinking can be borrowed from the interpretive development of other social rights, particularly water and health. However, caution should be exercised in using such templates. Despite attempts by some to standardise interpretation (e.g. through frameworks such as the AAAQ model: availability, accessibility, affordability and quality),[128] each right arguably possesses qualities that demand specific attention.[129] Moreover, there is a tension between trying to specify a content that is universal and contextually relevant and distinguishing between that which should be realised immediately and progressively within maximum available resources.

Returning to our definition that takes account of human rights, we said that:

> Sanitation comprises the ability to effectively access space and facilities (whenever and wherever needed) that afford privacy, dignity and safety in which to urinate, defecate and practice related hygiene, including menstrual hygiene, in a culturally acceptable manner; and which by virtue of their design, management and/or accompany services protect the user, the locality (e.g., households, school, workplace or hospital) and wider population from the adverse consequences of contamination with the associated wastes.[130]

[127] Ibid., para. 67.

[128] See UN Commission on Human Rights, *Report of the Special Rapporteur Submitted in Accordance with Commission on Human Rights Resolution 1998/33, Katarina Tomasevski*, (Fifty-fifth session, 1999), UN DOC. E/CN.4/1999/49, paras. 51–56 (1999).

[129] See discussion on this point in M. Langford and J. A. King, 'Committee on Economic, Social and Cultural Rights: Past, Present and Future', in *Social Rights Jurisprudence* (n. 119), pp. 477–515.

[130] See Section 1 of this chapter.

The question, from the perspective of the right to sanitation, is how this translates into specific entitlements or at least a right imbued with some meaningful content?

The first question is what sort of sanitation system, services or facilities should be made *available*. In the emerging discussion on the right to sanitation, the focus is largely on the individual dimension of availability rather than the broader system of sanitation (including treatment) system.[131] For now we will concentrate on this dimension. The typical questions are what is the requisite level of technology? Or more precisely, what makes a 'toilet'? Does everyone have the right to a flush toilet or a dry toilet with equivalent effect? Are ventilated pit latrines or community toilets acceptable in any case or only when there are insufficient resources? Does the right apply differently in rural and urban areas? And what would be acceptable as an immediate minimum and what should be left for attainment over time?

The answers to these questions are diverse. Many development agencies have favoured the use of ventilated pit latrines (VIPs): it is associated with lower water demand and maintenance and no need for cost recovery and revenue collection. However, some question the appropriateness of 'dry systems' for humid environments where, in fact, faecal matter does not easily dry, or in urban areas, where there is no space for VIPs. While pits can be dug deeper – if the water table is not too high – VIPs need periodic and frequent emptying in larger settlements, which often does not happen.[132] This suggests, leaving aside the issue of personal dignity, that such systems may *not* be as cost effective as assumed.[133]

The Special Rapporteur in her report does not seek to solve this debate. Instead, she emphatically leaves the issue open for deliberation, with different priorities for the short, medium and long term. She concludes that States are

[131] Contrast this with the way in which the CESCR addresses the need for a system of social security in *General Comment 19, The Right to Social Security* (art. 9) (Thirty-ninth session, 2007), UN Doc. E/C.12/GC/19 (2008). Indeed, there is thus a certain overlap in the discussion of *availability* and *physical accessibility*.

[132] In South Africa, Eales notes that, 'VIPS are now called full-ups' and that the government 'under-estimated the scale of technical support required'. B. Amisi, P. Bond, D. Khumalo, and S. Nojiyeza, 'The Neoliberal Loo', 18 February 2008, available at www.greenleft.org.au/content/south-africa-neoliberal-loo (accessed 25 March 2017).

[133] The Special Rapporteur also recognises the practical problems of intermediate technologies: 'Ensuring safe sanitation requires adequate hygiene promotion and education to encourage individuals to use toilets in a hygienic manner that respects the safety of others. Manual emptying of pit latrines is considered to be unsafe (as well as culturally unacceptable in many places, leading to stigmatization of those burdened with this task), meaning that mechanized alternatives that effectively prevent direct contact with human excreta should be used'. *Report of the Special Rapporteur*, para. 74.

'not obliged to provide everyone with access to a sewerage system' since '[h]uman rights law does not aim to dictate specific technology options, but instead calls for context-specific solutions'.[134] She proceeds to provide a definition of what should be made 'available', although in essence it concerns accessibility at the individual or household level. In her view, there must be sanitation facilities 'within, or in the immediate vicinity, of each household, health or educational institution, public institutions and places, and the workplace'.[135] In addition, there must be a sufficient number of such facilities to avoid excessive waiting times.[136] The Special Rapporteur notes that 'it is tempting to determine a specific minimum number of toilets'[137] but concedes that such specifications can be 'counterproductive'. Instead, she emphasises context-based and participatory assessments at the community level, including attention to the needs of particular individuals with different needs.

In addressing the question of whether the full realisation of the right, an adequate level, would require a *toilet* in one's *dwelling*, the UN Special Rapporteur answers negatively.[138] But she indicates that this is the direction a State must move as a proximate and safe facility is only an intermediate or minimum realisation of the right.[139] Thus, the question of the level of technology seems very much an open issue. Whereas it should be further clarified in public debate and contextual assessment, there is a danger that the UN Special Rapporteur has conflated here the definitions of sanitation and water. In borrowing the terms 'proximity' and 'vicinity' from General Comment No. 15 on the Right to Water, the issue of privacy and safety has been overlooked. These concerns seem to suggest that access to sanitation services in the home or very close vicinity deserve a higher priority. One of the authors of this paper has argued that:

> The evidence base for the health gains from potential sanitation benchmarks remains appallingly weak. Public toilets may be considered a key intermediate step and a means to ensure at least some dignity and safety. But some speak of dangers, especially to women, of rape and assault; and poorly maintained facilities are themselves a danger to health.[140]

Personal dignity and freedom from harassment point in the direction of urgently making sanitation accessible within the home (and workplace, institution, etc.) unless a country's resources or natural environment do not permit.[141] Indeed, the

[134] Ibid., para. 67. [135] Ibid., para. 70. [136] Ibid., para. 69. [137] Ibid., para. 71.
[138] Ibid. [139] Ibid. [140] Bartram, 'Improving on Haves and Have-Nots', p. 284.
[141] In some situations, such as in slums or in peri-urban areas, where formal service provision is not yet possible, interim solutions, such as shared toilets or informal water vendors, may be a necessary standard of service until longer-term plans can be executed. These can also be the

Special Rapporteur seems to hint at this in her definition of cultural acceptability, as set out below. One practical solution to this problem in developing countries is the approach developed in the well-known Orangi Pilot Project (OPP). Households in informal settlements organised to provide low-cost, small-bore solutions for the local-/tertiary-level reticulation of sewage while simultaneously lobbying authorities to provide secondary and primary (trunk) sewerage.[142]

The UN Special Rapporteur is on steadier ground when she sets out various other substantive elements of the right: quality, physical accessibility, affordability and cultural acceptability. These echo articulations of the CESCR of other social rights and provide a useful and clear rights perspective on sanitation.

To meet the standard of *quality*, there is a focus both on the individual user and the affected collective. As to the first, 'Sanitation facilities must be hygienically safe to use' and also includes the facilities and water 'for hand washing as well as menstrual hygiene, and anal and genital cleansing' and 'the hygienic disposal of menstrual products'. While these standards appear reasonable, they certainly represent a challenge, particularly in relation to menstrual hygiene and cleansing where many toilets around the world would not meet these standards. As to the collective dimension, quality is said to include 'Regular cleaning, emptying of pits or other places that collect human excreta' as well as 'maintenance ... for ensuring the sustainability of sanitation facilities and continued access'.[143] Indeed, some studies indicate that open defecation can be less dangerous for children than using school latrines that are not well maintained.[144]

In relation to the *physical accessibility*, the choice of technology obviously plays a key role as to where it will be placed, as discussed above. However, it is important to note the underlying ambition behind the Special Rapporteur's definition of beyond home: it is to include 'health or educational institutions,

most realistic affordable options for sanitation provision for those who do not have land tenure or space to build a household latrine. However, shared or public toilets may be contrary to human rights if they do not ensure safety and good hygiene or if they are not affordable. Access to a toilet in the home is preferable for reasons of dignity and privacy.

142 A. Hassan, *Working with Communities* (Karachi: City Press, 2001), pp. 1–42, 159–166. The OPP model has been viewed as a model example of 'coproduction' that overcomes collective action problems as local communities and utilities focus on their comparative advantage: G. McGranahan, 'Realizing the Right to Sanitation in Deprived Urban Communities: Meeting the Challenges of Collective Action, Coproduction, Affordability, and Housing Tenure', *World Development*, Vol. 68 (2015), 242–253.

143 *Report of the Special Rapporteur*, para. 72.

144 See, e.g., J. Kwiringira, P. Atekyereza, C. Niwagaba, and I. Günther, 'Descending the Sanitation Ladder in Urban Uganda: evidence from Kampala Slums', *BMC Public Health*, Vol. 14 (2014), p. 624.

public institutions and places, and the workplace'.[145] Not all Western countries have attained this standard, and some high-income countries with poor public access to sanitation, such as France, have been recently working to address this, using the right to sanitation as justification for making access to public toilets in Paris free.[146]

Of equal importance is the nature of the physical accessibility. Here, a human rights perspective can be particularly useful. The Special Rapporteur states importantly that toilets 'must be reliable, including access at all times of day and night', and the 'location of sanitation facilities must ensure minimal risks to the physical security of users'.[147] She also mentions the needs of other groups such as persons with disabilities and older persons. This condition is particularly important given that development projects have often not taken account of the risk of violence against women and children in designing placement of sanitation facilities. The lack of integration of disability into governmental and development planning has long been criticised on this basis.[148] Estimates indicate that 5 to 10 per cent of the population in different countries had credible difficulty in use of sanitation facilities without universal access features.[149]

As to *affordability*, the Special Rapporteur states that States are also not obliged to provide 'sanitation free of charge' and this requirement only arises when people are genuinely unable to pay for the service.[150] Instead, 'access to sanitation facilities and services, including construction, emptying and maintenance of facilities, as well as treatment and disposal of faecal matter, must be available at a price that is affordable for all people without limiting their capacity to acquire other basic goods and services, including water, food, housing, health and education guaranteed by other human rights'. This is a classic formulation of economic accessibility in social rights jurisprudence, and as Smets shows elsewhere in his book, it may be possible to measure. However, ensuring that sanitation is affordable can mean paying attention to other factors than the general provision of 'water facilities' – such as particular charges for sewerage or the costs charged at separate sanitation facilities.

145 *Report of the Special Rapporteur*, para. 75.

146 UNECE-WHO, *No One Left Behind: Good Practices to Ensure Equitable Access to Water and Sanitation in the Pan-European Region*, February 2012.

147 Ibid.

148 M. Stein, C. McClain-Nhlapo and J. Lord, 'Disability Rights, the MDGs and Inclusive Development', in M. Langford, A. Sumner and A. Yamin (eds.), *Millennium Development Goals and Human Rights: Past, Present and Future* (Cambridge: Cambridge University Press, 2013), pp. 274–294.

149 WHO, *World Report on Disability* (Geneva: WHO, 2011).

150 *Report of the Special Rapporteur*, para. 67.

Lastly, it is said that sanitation facilities and services must be culturally acceptable. This may appear odd in a human rights document concerning universality but accessibility in practice requires attention to local conditions. As Singh has argued in this volume, sociocultural barriers can easily impede implementation. For example, latrines dug 'for' an indigenous community in Latin America were not used since in their cosmology; the closed underground is inhabited by one's revered ancestors.[151] The Special Rapporteur states 'Personal sanitation is still a highly sensitive issue across regions and cultures and differing perspectives about which sanitation solutions are acceptable must be taken into account regarding design, positioning and conditions for use of sanitation facilities. In many cultures, to be acceptable, construction of toilets will need to ensure privacy'.[152] For instance, the South African government has created a catalogue of sanitation technologies, which considers costs and appropriateness for a number of different contexts, including considering costs to the user.[153]

### 4.3 *Equality and Other Human Rights*

The second immediate duty is that of guaranteeing non-discrimination in the realisation of the right to sanitation: see, for example, Article 2(2) of the ICESCR. This duty extends beyond a formalistic duty to refrain from explicitly distinguishing between groups on prohibited grounds of discrimination but actively seek to address the needs of groups characterised by those markers of distinction.[154] The Special Rapporteur has interpreted this substantive equality requirement to mean that States must 'pay special attention to groups particularly vulnerable to exclusion and discrimination in relation to sanitation, including people living in poverty, sanitation workers, women, children, elderly persons, people with disabilities, people affected by health conditions, refugees and IDPs, and minority groups, among others'.[155]

[151] See WSP, *An Anthropological View of Sanitation Issues in Rural Bolivia. A Summary*, available at www.wsp.org/sites/wsp.org/files/publications/2272007102015_ruralboliviaanthroview.pdf (accessed 25 March 2017).

[152] Ibid., paras. 70–80. These elements are also mentioned but not elaborated on in UN Sub-Commission on the Promotion and Protection of Human Rights, *Res. 2006/10, Promotion of the Realization of the Right to Drinking Water and Sanitation*, UN Doc. A/HRC/Sub.1/58/L11, adopting the *Draft Guidelines for the Realization of the Right to Drinking Water and Sanitation*, UN Doc. E/CN.4/Sub.2/2005/25, section 1.3.

[153] *Sanitation for a Healthy Nation: Sanitation Technology Options*, South Africa Department of Water Affairs and Forestry, February 2002.

[154] See CESCR, *General Comment 20, Non-Discrimination in Economic, Social and Cultural Rights* (Forty-Second Session, 2009), UN Doc. E/C.12/GC/20 (2009).

[155] *Report of the Special Rapporteur*, para. 65.

In doing so, States will often need to look at the intersection of the right to sanitation and other rights. Without adequate sanitation, the rights to water, health, education and housing are not realisable. It has been argued that girls, particularly after they reach puberty, are less likely to attend school if there is inadequate sanitation provision, including separate toilets for girls and boys. Although the evidence is equivocal due to methodological constraints.[156] School and other public or shared latrines must also ensure that all pupils, teachers and others are able to use the facilities, for example, making provision for those with physical disabilities. Further, it is increasingly recognised that school and other public latrines must ensure adequate facilities and space to ensure that women and girls can take care of the particular needs of menstruation.[157] Elderly, sick and intellectually disabled individuals may also require particular consideration when accessing sanitation.

Finally, for those who are living or working away from their homes, such as at the workplace, in hospitals, prisons or other institutions, where they are not able to take care of their own sanitation needs, the right to sanitation requires that this is made available, to ensure health, privacy and dignity.[158] There are real grounds for concern here. One report cites half the schools in Tajikistan being without water.[159] As to prisons, the European Committee for the Prevention of Torture, after a visit to Portuguese prisons in 2008, found the practice of 'defecating in a bucket in a confined space used as a living area to be degrading'.[160] Following this, the Portuguese prison authorities reportedly worked towards eliminating the practice.[161] Similarly in Fiji, a court found that lack of access to adequate sanitation in

[156] I. Birdthistle, K. Dickson, M. Freeman and L. Javidi, *What Impact Does the Provision of Separate Toilets for Girls at Schools Have on their Primary and Secondary School Enrolment, Attendance and Completion? A Systematic Review of the Evidence* (London: EPPI-Centre, Social Science Research Unit, Institute of Education, University of London, 2011). See also E. Oster and R. Thornton, 'Menstruation, Sanitary Products and School Attendance: Evidence from a Randomized Evaluation', *American Economic Journal: Applied Economics*, Vol. 3, No. 1 (2011), pp. 91–100.

[157] *Claiming the MDGs*.

[158] J. Bartram, R. Cronk, M. Montgomery, B. Gordon, M. Neira, E. Kelley and Y. Velleman, 'Lack of Toilets and Safe Water in Health-Care Facilities', *Bull World Health Organ*, April 2015 (editorial).

[159] UNDP, 'World Water Day: Situation critical for water supply and sanitation in Europe and Central Asia', News Release, 22 March 2011, available at http://europeandcis.undp.org/home/show/707ADE83-F203-1EE9-BF3D08FC372EA619.

[160] Council of Europe, *Report to the Portuguese Government on the Visit to Portugal Carried Out by the European Committee for the Prevention of Torture and Inhuman or Degrading Treatment or Punishment (CPT) from 14 to 25 January 2008*, 19 March 2009.

[161] Ibid.

prisons constituted cruel, inhuman and degrading treatment under the Constitution as well as UN Standard Minimum Rules for the Treatment of Prisoners.[162]

### 4.4 *Tensions between Sanitation and Other Human Rights*

In addition to the limitations of resources, the realisation of the right to sanitation may sometimes pose a challenge to claiming or implementing other rights, or vice versa. An example of the former is the management of piped sewerage, which often poses pollution risks for water resources and drinking water supplies.[163] In right to water litigation in Argentina, a court found a violation of the right to water and health due to provincial and municipal authorities failing to prevent pollution of communal water sources, caused by an under-maintained and overstretched sewage-treatment plant.[164] Arguably though, the order was beneficial from the perspective of the right to sanitation. The Court ordered the municipality to 'adopt all of the measures necessary relative to the functioning of the [facility], in order to minimise the environmental impact caused', and also ordered the authorities to create a financing mechanism by which funds would be made available to maintain the quality of sewerage services.[165]

Indeed, attempts to build sewage-treatment facilities are often challenged on the ground of property, environmental and housing rights. Most local communities tend to oppose the development of such facilities in their neighbourhoods. The result is that the land of poorer or disadvantaged communities, often with poor security of tenure, are targeted for building such works, with the presumption that resistance will be less. However, this raises the risk of violations of the right to housing. The issue has come to the fore in cases brought by communities to the World Bank Inspection Panel (WBIP), who complained that the building of environmental sanitation works, financed through the Bank, was resulting in their forced evictions.

[162] *Sailasa Naba and Others* v. *the State*, High Court of Fiji, No. HAC0012 of 2000L, 4 July 2001.

[163] The Special Rapporteur flags this issues as a possible duty under respect for the right to sanitation but it is really a question of ensuring other rights are not impacted: she says that 'states must also ensure that the management of human excreta does not negatively impact on human rights'. *Report of the Special Rapporteur*, para. 64.

[164] *CEDHA* v. *Provincial State and Municipality of Córdoba* (AC), 233. See R. Picolotti, 'The Right to Safe Drinking Water as a Human Right', *Housing and ESC Rights Quarterly*, Vol. 1, No. 4 (2005), p. 1.

[165] Quoted in ibid. However, it is not clear if these services are available to the community.

In both instances, the WBIP found, to different degrees, that the World Bank management had not acted sufficiently to ensure compliance with the Bank's involuntary resettlement guidelines.[166]

Another tension concerns the rise of Community-Led Total Sanitation approaches and civil society monitoring of services, that put civil society empowerment at the centre of delivery mechanisms. These efforts have become essential aspects of ensuring that sanitation is understood not just as hardware but as a change in behaviour.

This is not to claim that Community-Led Total Sanitation methods are always in line with human rights standards. Their implementation, however, has been criticised from a human rights perspective – for example, shaming open defecation through extreme methods such as photographing people or throwing stones at them or singular instances of refusing to help prosecute cases of rape that occurred when women were defecating outside.[167] It can also be asked whether the focus of the development sector on Community-Led Total Sanitation is distracting attention from government responsibilities.

## 5 THE RIGHT TO SANITATION IN PRACTICE

The drive for recognition of the human right to sanitation has primarily come from development and health practitioners[168] and only partly from human rights organisations.[169] It has featured as part of a broader push for a general rights-based approach to sanitation. In doing so, practitioners have highlighted the instrumental benefits of a 'human rights approach to sanitation': 'holding to account those responsible' for facilitating access to sanitation, promoting 'information sharing and genuine participation in decision making', giving attention to 'vulnerable and marginalised groups', providing 'minimum' universal requirements and creating [a] rights-friendly framework for reforming

[166] See World Bank Inspection Panel, *GHANA: Second Urban Environmental Sanitation Project (UESP II) (IDA Credit No. 3889-GH)*, Report No. 47713 – GH, 13 March 2009; World Bank Inspection Panel, *Nigeria: Lagos Drainage and Sanitation Project (Credit No. 2517-UNI)*, Report and Recommendation on Request for Inspection.

[167] See J. Bartram, K. Charles, B. Evans, L. O'Hanlon, S. Pedley, 'Commentary on Community-Led Total Sanitation and Human Rights: Should the Right to Community-Wide Health Be Won at the Cost of Individual Rights?', *Journal of Water Health*, Vol. 10, No. 4 (2012), pp. 499–503.

[168] For example, WaterAid and Bread for the World, Freshwater Action Network, WSSCC, World Health Organisation and UN-HABITAT.

[169] For example, Centre on Housing Rights and Evictions and Amnesty International.

public policies and resource allocation.[170] Whereas these claims are often made in the context of development, they clearly have relevance in wealthier countries where sanitation is not universal, particularly amongst marginalised ethnic minorities, or where sewage contamination continues to impact the wider population.

Despite the increasing uptake of a rights-based approach to development amongst development practitioners and policymakers, it has been queried on various grounds. The practical critique is that the 'tools' offered by human rights do not add anything to the operational challenge of extending access[171] or that is premised on high levels of literacy amongst the general population and strong public institutions, such as courts and bureaucracies.[172] A more conservative critique is that it may increase conflict between users, delivery organisations and the governments,[173] inculcate a culture of dependency and unwillingness of users to participate in infrastructure development, management and payment[174] or add another layer of unwanted bureaucracy.

A different type of practical critique of human rights approaches is their alleged lack of transformative power.[175] They represent mere 'pleas for human rights to be conferred by the state' rather than an emancipatory and assertive politics of 'rights to be fought for' and defined in the struggle.[176] The result may be depoliticization of important political questions as strong moral claims

[170] *Sanitation: A Human Rights Imperative*, ibid., p. 5.

[171] See overview of these criticisms in E. Filmer Wilson, 'Human Rights-Based Approach to Development: The Right to Water', *Netherlands Quarterly of Human Rights*, Vol. 23, No.2 (June 2005), pp. 213–241; P. Uvin, *Human Rights and Development* (Sterling, VA: Kumarian Press, 2004).

[172] D. Banik, 'Support for Human Rights-Based Development: Reflections on the Malawian Experience', *The International Journal of Human Rights*, Vol. 14, No. 1 (2010), pp. 32–48.

[173] For example, the co-founder of Slum Dwellers International, Joel Bolnick, has resisted using rights-based approaches on the basis that 'Public declarations have a habit of compromising our capacity to negotiate with and on behalf of organised shack dwellers'. J. Bolnick, 'Slum-Friendly Approach: SDI Letter to the Witness in Response to Article by Ndivhuwo Wa Ha Mabaya' (2009).

[174] See M. Ramphele, cited in P. Green, '100 Days, 11 Issues', *Mail & Guardian*, 17 August 2009.

[175] See overview of the political conception of rights in M.-B. n. d. Dembour, 'What Are Human Rights? Four Schools of Thought', *Human Rights Quarterly*, Vol. 32, No. 1 (2010), pp. 1–20. See specific concerns on right to sanitation in McGranahan, 'Realizing the Right to Sanitation', section 6.

[176] M. Neocosmos, 'Civil Society, Citizenship and the Politics of the (Im)possible: Rethinking Militancy in Africa Today', *Interface: A Journal for and About Social Movements*, Vol. 1, No. 2, pp. 263–334, at 278.

are tempered in the process of legalisation, and these claims are further diluted as lawyers, bureaucrats or development elites fashion their meaning.[177]

Does the right to sanitation 'add value'? Can it provide linguistic, strategic and technical resources for communities, policymakers and practitioners? In 2011, the United Kingdom's Department for International Development (DFID) conducted a study on the impact of recognition of a right to sanitation in four countries.[178] It found that it was still too early to judge conclusively that the right to sanitation has made a difference but noted that 'Formal recognition' of the right 'can be an important accelerator if it is combined with a range of political drivers which build an enabling environment and support inclusive implementation towards rights fulfilment'.[179] Regional recognition has also created some effects. After the Third South Asian Conference on Sanitation, civil society organisations successfully lobbied governments to make more significant policy and fiscal commitments and prioritise vulnerable and marginalised groups. In Nepal, there is a Master Plan for Sanitation and Hygiene, and the budget dedicated to sanitation was doubled.[180] Bangladesh is carrying out a baseline study of access to sanitation, in order to better align their sanitation policy with need and excluded communities.[181]

This section seeks to take the analysis further by examining four particular areas of policy and practice: the MDGs, democratisation, challenging land tenure and legal mobilisation.

## 5.1 *Development Goals*

In the field of sanitation, the target-based Millennium Development Goals (MDGs) were ascendant in development thinking. The international target to 'halve the proportion of people living without access to basic sanitation by

[177] P. Bond, 'Macrodynamics of Globalisation, Uneven Urban Development and the Commodification of Water', *Law, Social Justice & Global Development Journa* , Vol. 1 (2008), pp. 1–14.

[178] S. Crawford and M. A Brocklesby, *Assessing the Impact of a Right to Sanitation on Improving Levels of Access and Quality of Services: Summary*, DFID Draft Working Paper, April 2011.

[179] Ibid., p. 3.

[180] 'South Asia/Nepal: Summary', WASHWatch, available at www.washwatch.org/en/countries/nepal/summary/?declaration=SWANepal (last accessed 4 April 2017). This website www.washwatch.org also tracks whether countries are fulfilling their commitments to SacoSan and AfricaSan and so on.

[181] Bangladesh National Hygiene Baseline Survey Preliminary Report, International Centre for Diarrheal Diseases Research, Bangladesh (icddr,b) WaterAid Bangladesh, Policy Support Unit (PSU) Local Government Division Ministry of Local Government, Rural Development and Cooperatives Dhaka, Bangladesh, June 2014.

2015' was inserted in the agenda in 2002. From an initial global population of 5.3 billion in the MDG baseline year (1990), the MDG's framework required 'basic sanitation' rising from 54 per cent to 77 per cent (while keeping up with population growth).[182]

The MDG target certainly heightened awareness on the issue. It has been argued that the MDGs have possibly made their greatest contribution in the area of sanitation and maternal mortality as they highlighted previously and deeply neglected topics in international development.[183] Interviews with EU officials illustrated the particular way the target worked in practice. Through its ACP-EU Water Facility, the EU has supported water infrastructure and supply projects, particularly in rural areas and with a focus on the poorest of the poor. Yet, while partner governments readily and regularly sought support for water, EU officials stated that they used the existence of the sanitation target to encourage these governments to also apply for support on sanitation.[184]

However, sanitation remained one of the most 'off-track' MDG targets.[185] In Indonesia's 2008 MDG Report, the government acknowledged that sanitation was a low priority, and the World Bank estimated in 2008 that less than 1 per cent of the investment in sanitation needed to reach the sanitation target in Indonesia had been made.[186]

Moreover, the level of ambition in the target was disturbingly low. In seeking only to halve the proportion of persons without access, there was arguably a temptation for States to 'cherry-pick' the relatively well-off amongst the poor and ignore long-suffering and excluded minorities, informal settlements or remote rural areas. While cost-effectiveness may be a consideration for decision-making when there are difficult trade-offs in meeting human rights,[187] the MDG approach could encourage normatively problematic choices and disguise prejudices against particular groups.[188] Thus, there

[182] Bartram, 'Improving on Haves and Have-Nots'.

[183] See discussion in M. Langford, A. Sumner and A. Yamin (eds.), 'Introduction: Situating the Debate', in M. Langford, A. Sumner and A. Yamin (eds.), *Millennium Development Goals and Human Rights: Past, Present and Future* (Cambridge: Cambridge University Press, 2013), pp. 1–34.

[184] Interview with André Liebaert, Water policy officer, EuropeAid Unit C2, Brussels, 2 October 2012.

[185] United Nations, *The Millennium Development Goals Report* (New York: UN, 2011).

[186] *Economic Impacts of Sanitation in Indonesia: A Five Country Study Conducted in Cambodia, Indonesia, Lao PDR, the Philippines and Vietnam under the Economics of Sanitation Initiative*, World Bank Research Report, August 2008, p. 16.

[187] See D. Seymour and J. Pincus, 'Human Rights and Economics: The Conceptual Basis for Their Complementarity', *Development Policy Review*, Vol. 26, No. 4 (2008), pp. 387–405.

[188] For example, one World Bank official informed one of the authors, Langford, that in one African country, they explicitly prioritised on the basis of cost effectiveness.

was a demand that measurement capture progress on equality.[189] Proposals were made that the MDG and future targets be disaggregated by income quartiles, quintiles or deciles and a target added to capture progress on equality.[190] For instance, a country could only said to be 'on-track' for the *sanitation equality* target if there is progress in all income brackets or the lowest-income bracket(s). Alternatively, a proportionate reduction in the Gini coefficient for sanitation, a single index of inequality, could be required. However, if we move to a multiple ladder for progress on sanitation (and it is not reducible to a single index), then overlaying the equality measurement may prove too complicated. In this case, one option would have been to require progress on the ladder for the lowest-income group.

Whereas poor progress on the MDG target spurred initiatives such as the UN International Year of Sanitation in 2008 and the Sustainable Sanitation: Five Year Drive to 2015,[191] it has also strengthened calls for increasing a rights focus in the strategies for realisation of the MDG targets.[192] A rights-based approach offered a more fair and effective way of understanding, interpreting and setting targets, which was a subject of growing interest in discussions over a post-2015 development agenda.[193] The debate on the post-2015 development agenda was equally driven by a rights consciousness (although with varied success).[194]

In the resulting SDGs, sanitation was articulated as a single target as part of a new goal on water and sanitation:

> By 2030, achieve access to adequate and equitable sanitation and hygiene for all and end open defecation, paying special attention to the needs of women and girls and those in vulnerable situations

[189] See, Luh, Cronk and Bartram, 'Assessing Progress'.

[190] See discussion of different options in M. Langford, 'Rethinking the Metrics of Progress: The Case of Water and Sanitation', in M. Langford, A. Sumner and A. Yamin (eds.), *Millennium Development Goals and Human Rights: Past, Present and Future* (Cambridge: Cambridge University Press, 2013), pp. 461–483.

[191] 'UN Secretary-General launches the "Sustainable Sanitation: Five-Year Drive to 2015"', UN News Release, 21 June 2011.

[192] See, for example, *Claiming the MDGS*; *Pathway to Gender Equality: CEDAW, Beijing and the MDGs* (New York: UNIFEM, 2004).

[193] See overview in M. Langford, 'Lost in Transformation? The Politics of the Sustainable Development Goals', *Ethics and International Affairs*, Vol. 30, No. 2 (2016), pp. 167–176.

[194] Already there have been numerous meetings in different countries and thematic sectors, the gradual development of international campaigns and processes and a growing academic literature. For the first publications on the topic, see A. Sumner and M. Tiwari, *After 2015: International Development Policy at a Crossroads* (London: Palgrave Macmillan) and *MDGS and Beyond* (2009), Special Issue of *IDS Bulletin*, Vol. 41, No. 1 (2010).

The ambition of reaching full coverage by 2030 with a gendered perspective and focused on vulnerable groups seems very appropriate. However, it is still possible to be critical from a human rights perspective. First, the current indicator still relies on a binary form of measurement: 'Proportion of population using safely managed sanitation services, including a hand-washing facility with soap and water.' The formula for measurement regards every human as either 'having' or 'not having' these key amenities, which is 'simple, robust and easy to present' but is plagued by significant weaknesses.[195] It provides no significant motivation for countries near the top or the bottom of the international spectrum to tackle their sanitation. For example, a traditional pit latrine with an earth floor does not score in global monitoring since it lacks a solid floor slab; but such a latrine is ranked as 'improved' by national authorities in Zimbabwe.[196]

The pass–fail criterion is a straightjacket that alienates worthwhile efforts and fails to recognise progressive realisation[197] and does not reward acceleration in efforts.[198] Monitoring standards need to recognise not only a latrine at home but also successful efforts to make shared or even public facilities work in fast-growing, peri-urban areas as part of progressive realisation. Overall, there should be a sequence of benchmarks reflecting individual steps and potentially different routes to improvement.[199] WHO and UNICEF showed in 2008 that moving beyond the simple haves and have-nots categorisation reveals progress at lower levels of the ladder.[200] For example, open defecation was declining in all regions (24 to 18 per cent) and rapidly in sub-Saharan Africa (36 to 28 per cent).[201] Half of decline captured was in the rise of shared facilities, although there are questions about degree of adequacy and of sustainability with overloaded pits.

Second, for wealthier and transition countries, the low ambition of the MDGs hid the lack of progress on fully meeting the right for all and penalises efforts by low-income countries.[202] The metric not only risked imposing a 'one-size-fits-all' standard across the world, it raised problems from a human

[195] Bartram, 'Improving on Haves and Have-Nots', p. 183. [196] Ibid.

[197] Bartram, 'Improving on Haves and Have-Nots'.

[198] See, for example, S. Fukuda-Parr and J. Greenstein, *How Should MDG Implementation Be Measured: Faster Progress or Meeting Targets?* (Brasilia: International Policy Centre for Inclusive Growth, 2010).

[199] Bartram, 'Improving on Haves and Have-Nots'.

[200] WHO and UNICEF, *Progress on Drinking Water and Sanitation: Special Focus on Sanitation* (Geneva: United Nations, 2008).

[201] Ibid.

[202] One of the authors of this chapter, Bartram, was challenged by a minister from one of the countries of the former Soviet Union, which needed to improve its drinking water and

rights perspective. States were only expected to *progressively realise* the rights within their *maximum available resources*. But setting one global standard for all lets middle- or high-income countries off the hook, while low-income countries may not be politically rewarded: Zambia, Cameroon and Mali increased improved sanitation by 27 to 29 per cent even though that doesn't meet target.[203] Research revealed that lower-income countries rate higher on MDG progress if outcomes were adjusted for a variety of capacity indicators.[204] While there were recommendations that the SDG targets should be adaptable to be relevant to all countries, this did not occur with the SDGs.[205] However, at least the final target requires all countries to meet a 100% target even if measured progress will not take account of starting points.

Third, the SDG indicators should have led to a better system that would have a firm grounding in health, well-being and livelihoods and evidence from public policy as well as human rights. This would include measuring access to a toilet in the home as a target and, more ambitiously, 'overlaying' evidence onto the sequence of benchmarks. The latter could be controversial and difficult to measure – for example, flush toilets would be marked down if they discharge untreated wastewater into a nearby river rather than to a treatment facility.[206] In fact, one study found that if we account for how much of the global population is lucky enough to have their sewage treated as a criteria for sanitation access, more than 3.5 billion people, or 52 per cent of the global population, live without basic sanitation 'security'.[207]

Fourth, additional indicators need to be considered. If sanitation protects health best when practised by all, one would need to not only record whether a household has sanitation but also the sanitation status of the surrounding community or 'sanitation catchment area'. Moreover, households are not the only place where people need to go to the toilet or wash their hands. An improved monitoring system will recognise that safe water and sanitation in schools, workplaces, hospitals, markets and other public places are also important.[208]

sanitation. It wanted to be part of the MDG effort but couldn't find a 'way in' because the definitions meant that it had little left to do.

203 *Progress on Drinking Water and Sanitation*.

204 E. Anderson and M. Langford (2013), A *Distorted Metric: The MDGs, Human Rights and Maximum Available Resources*, University of Oslo Faculty of Law Research Paper No. 2013-10, available at SSRN.

205 A. Sumner and C. Melamed (2010), 'Introduction – The MDGs and Beyond: Pro-Poor Policy in a Changing World', *IDS Bulletin*, Vol. 41, No. 1, pp. 1–6.

206 Bartram, 'Improving on Haves and Have-Nots'.

207 R. Baum and J. Bartram, *Sanitation: A Global Estimate of Sewerage Connections without Treatment and the Resultant Impact on MDG Progress* (forthcoming).

208 Ibid.

While the MDG targets for drinking water and sanitation represented a very limited ambition – seemingly leaving many millions without the most basic needs for health protection, dignity and development even if they are met – the SDGs are thus only a partial improvement in seeking to address these challenges. Improving targets through the prism of the right to sanitation would recognise progressive improvements relevant to a country's capacity and context, reflect the range of actions that contribute to health and well-being and better align with programming needed for stepwise improvements.

### 5.2 *Democratisation of Sanitation*

Inherent in the right to sanitation is a demand for participation and access to information. This not only calls for involvement in implementation but a role in macro, meso and micro policymaking and whether it be technical choices, priority setting, budgeting and tariff setting. The UN Special Rapporteur has stated that:

> States are also obliged to ensure that concerned individuals and communities are informed and have access to information about sanitation and hygiene and are enabled to participate in all processes related to the planning, construction, maintenance and monitoring of sanitation services. Full participation, including representatives of all concerned groups is key to ensuring that sanitation solutions answer the actual needs of communities and are affordable, technically feasible, and culturally acceptable.[209]

The consequences of poor participation are not hard to find. In Southern Portugal, the German Government funded and constructed a large sewage-treatment plant, but it was only briefly used. It was built without adequate consultation with the relevant municipalities and without the necessary institutional and financial framework to ensure sustainability.[210]

Moreover, there is always the risk that even when they exist, participation processes are minimalised in practice: the involvement of users and affected groups occurs at the bottom of the participation ladder (passive involvement, information giving, consultation) rather than towards the top (functional, interactive, self-control/ownership).[211] Women or disadvantaged groups may be also

[209] *Report of the Special Rapporteur*, para. 66.

[210] Communication from Jaime Baptista, CEO of ERSAR, to Virginia Roaf (8 June 2011).

[211] See, for example, R. Jackson, 'Community Participation: Tools and Examples', Paper presented at the Management Planning Workshop for the Trans-Himalayan Protected Areas, Leh, Ladakh, 25–29 August 2000. One should be aware that human rights approaches can easily fall into such a trap if they are overly technical: McGranahan, 'Realizing the Right to Sanitation'.

excluded: 'Male dominated NGOs, trade unions and professional associations are unlikely to prioritize the gender interests of poor women.'[212] Thus, a genuine and full-throttled human rights approach to participation emphasises the need to critically scrutinise the existing forms of participation[213] and ensure that processes help identify the underlying causes of the problem. A democratisation of development means creating the space to destabilise existing ideas and power relations and offer and cement alternatives. As Offenheiser and Holcombe argue:

> Instead of focusing on creating an inventory of public goods or services that must be provided and then seeking to fill the deficit via foreign aid, the rights-based approach focuses on trying to identify the critical exclusionary mechanisms. What are those systemic obstacles that are standing in the way of people's ability to access opportunity and improve their own lives?[214]

Indeed, it is notable that modern public sanitation systems emerged on the back of political engagement. In 1849, John Snow identified that a cholera outbreak in London was caused by the seepage from a sewerage pit into groundwater used for a local water pump and not from contagion.[215] He encountered denial from the medical community and resistance from the political class on account of the fiscal implications. Significant campaigning led however to a closure of the water pump, the Public Health Act in 1852 and, with growing political pressure, the establishment of household waterborne sanitation systems and the 1866 Sanitation Act, which compelled local authorities to improve local conditions and remove health hazards.[216]

It is too early to judge how the right to sanitation will play a role in democratising and politicising in contemporary times. Some utilities and policymakers have attempted more genuine forms of participation. Drawing partly on the right to water, but also principles of general equity and water

[212] Mwero, cited in UN-HABITAT, *Not about Us Without Us: Working with Grassroots Organisations in the Land Field* (Nairobi: GLTN, 2009), p. 11.

[213] See *Claiming the MDGs*.

[214] R. Offenheiser and S. Holcombe, 'Challenges and Opportunities of Implementing a Rights-Based Approach to Development, an Oxfam Perspective', Paper presented to the Northern Relief and Development Conference, 2–4 July 2001, Balliol College, Oxford UK.

[215] J. Snow, *On the Mode of Communication of Cholera* (London: John Churchill, 1855).

[216] The municipalities became responsible also for the provision of sewers, water and street cleaning. The Act enforced the connection of all houses to a new main sewer; it set definite limits for the use of cellars as living rooms and established the definition of 'overcrowding'. Every town was to appoint sanitary inspectors, and the home secretary was empowered to take action where local authorities failed to do so. See M. Bloy, 'Victorian Legislation: A Timeline', *The Victorian Web*, available at www.victorianweb.org/history/legistl.html (last accessed 4 April 2017).

conservation, the Tamil Nadu Water Supply and Drainage Board in India embarked on a 'democratisation' project in 2004. This involved first addressing attitudes amongst public engineers and other staff, which was followed by establishing genuine participatory forums in which the other 'public' would jointly decide on priorities but also take responsibility and the consequences of those choices, including safe sanitation methods and practice.[217] The project revealed that that participation and access was hampered by discriminatory attitudes amongst engineers, other professionals and local communities. In order to ensure 'full inclusion', the concept of citizenship was introduced, which has reportedly resulted in a threefold increase in the number of officials visiting, taking note of and acting on the needs of women and Dalit communities.[218] In addition to large cost and water savings through the process, 65 per cent of all projects are in 2005 in villages where more than 50 per cent of the population are living below the poverty line.[219]

Court cases from South Africa also reveal the surprising potential political impact of the right to sanitation. The 2011 local government elections were labelled the 'Open Toilet' election. The Youth League of the ANC party politicised and publicised a largely neglected issue to their political advantage by focusing on unenclosed toilets in an informal settlement, Khayelitsha, in the City of Cape Town, controlled by the national opposition party, the Democratic Alliance. 'Politicians, journalists and the electorate seemed stunned by the sight of these open toilets' as matters of 'dignity and privacy, so central to South Africa's constitution, seemed to be rendered meaningless by images of toilets without walls'.[220] The intervention sparked multiple protests and counter-accusations from both parties, and the matter was eventually taken by residents to court. The Democratic Alliance then responded by launching a similar case against the ANC concerning Moqhaka in the Free State. The results was not only a national dialogue during the election campaign but a strong judgment (which was not appealed) upholding almost all claims of the applicants and significantly pushing the government policy further than it

[217] See V. Suresh and P. Prabhu, 'Democratisation of Water Management as Way to Reclaiming PublicWater: The Tamil Nadu Experience', Transnational Institute (April 2007), available at www.tni.org/sites/www.tni.org/archives/books/watertamilnadusuresh.pdf (accessed 19 October).

[218] V. Nayar, *Democratisation of Water Management – Nurturing Democratic Change: The Tami Nadu Experience*, Symposium on Learning Alliances for Scaling Up Innovative approaches in the Water and Sanitation Sector, 7–9 June 2005, Delft, Netherlands. The term Dalit designates a group of people traditionally regarded as 'Untouchable', consisting of numerous 'lower' castes throughout South Asia.

[219] Ibid. [220] S. Robins, 'Toilets That Became Political Dynamite', *Cape Times*, 27 June 2011.

currently existed.[221] The Court decided that one toilet per five families during a slum upgrading process could not be justified under existing legislation and that unenclosed toilets provided on this basis violated constitutional safeguards which:

> [M]ust provide for the safety and privacy of the users and be compliant with the fundamental rights guaranteed in the Constitution. Any housing development which does not provide for toilets with adequate privacy and safety would be inconsistent with s 26 of the Constitution and would be in violation of the constitutional rights to privacy and dignity.[222]

Media reports shortly afterwards indicated that the community began to gain access to enclosed toilets with one resident commenting that 'This is what we fought for. It is our right to have these toilets covered'.[223] Robins notes though that the strategy was a double-edged sword: despite the important material and political impacts, the 'politics of the spectacle also obscured the more mundane indignities, health hazards and forms of structural violence that millions of poor people have to endure on a daily basis'.[224]

### 5.3 *Challenging Land Tenure Limitations*

Considering sanitation as a human right requires that governments ensure that safe sanitation is available regardless of where a person lives, and regardless of their tenure status. This was affirmed by the CESCR in relation to water services and would equally apply to sanitation: 'Deprived urban areas, including informal human settlements, and homeless persons, should have access to properly maintained water facilities. No household should be denied the right to water on the grounds of their housing or land status'.[225]

221 *Beja and Others* v. *Premier of the Western Cape and Others* [2011] 3 All SA 401 (WCC)) [2011] ZAWCHC 97, 21332/10 (29 April 2011).

222 Ibid., para. 143.

223 J. Kiewietz and B. Jooste, 'Residents Elated to Have Enclosed Toilets', *IOL News*, 29 August 2011.

224 Robins, 'Toilets That Became Political Dynamite'. It should be noted that Justice Erasmus also criticised the two parties for politicising the toilet issue at the expense of community members and questioned the propriety of the conduct of the Youth League, the judgment itself stated: 'What has become evident is that the [ANC Youth League] had a core function of promoting the interests of the City's contractor. . . Not only was the [ANC Youth League] in the pocket of the contractor but his role undermined the principle of community participation'. *Beja* v. *Premier of the Western Cape*, para. 104.

225 *CESCR General Comment* 15, para. 16(c).

However, the reality is that tenure status continues to strongly determine access to sanitation. UN-HABITAT estimated that there were 828 million urban slum dwellers in the world, which would grow to 889 million by 2020.[226] Service providers and relevant local authorities often use the ambiguous legal status of these households as an excuse to delay or even deny the provision of adequate sanitation services and, in some cases, are barred by law from servicing such areas. Likewise, in rural areas, communities may find their traditional right to live on their land is superseded by more formal ownership, or through policies that change the status of land by decree, such as by appointing a particular area as a game reserve, unsuitable for habitation by humans.[227]

In informal settlements, there are different ways to realise the right to sanitation. One obvious path gets at the root problem: upgrade settlements to some level of formal tenure. A few countries have dynamic and participatory slum upgrading programmes: Brazilian legislation allows slum dwellers themselves to initiate slum-upgrading processes themselves with the backing of administrative courts; Thailand has an independent housing agency that works with communities to upgrade their housing on the basis of a city-wide plan and matching funds. However, progress in slum upgrading is slow in most countries, and many projects are beset by public corruption and forced eviction of poorer residents.[228]

An alternative route is to claim rights to sanitation. Some countries, such as South Africa, have recognised in policy that all residents have a right to immediate basic sanitation including those living in informal settlements.[229] This customarily means establishing communal toilets as a first step although practice tends to vary considerably between communities.[230] In Bangladesh, the NGO Dushtha Shasthya Kendra (DSK) developed a dialogue between communities, the service providers and the local municipality in order to find a way of providing water and sanitation services to informal settlements in Dhaka. The tactic has been to avoid formal recognition of settlements as legal.[231] Although the risk of eviction remains, the

[226] UN-Habitat, *State of the World's Cities 2010/2011: Bridging the Urban Divide* (London: Earthscan, 2010), p. XII.

[227] See, for example, *Mosetlhanyane & Matsipane* v. *The Attorney General*, No. CACLB-074–10, Court of Appeal, Botswana, Judgment 27 January 2011.

[228] M. Langford, L. Quitzow and V. Roaf, *Human Rights and Slum-Upgrading: General Introduction and Compilation of Case Studies* (Geneva: Centre on Housing Rights and Evictions (COHRE), 2005).

[229] *Water and Sanitation Service Standard*, City of Cape Town (2008).

[230] See discussion of this in the Chapter 7 on South Africa in this volume.

[231] See S.I.A. Jinnah, *Case Study: Rights of Water Connections for Urban Slum Dwellers in Bangladesh*, WaterAid Bangladesh (March 2007).

dialogue has opened up a direct line of communication with service providers for residents and increasing basic access to water and sanitation services. In Kenya, the Nairobi Water Company has advised NGOs that it does not consider the lack of secure tenure an obstacle to provision as the settlements are situated on government lands: it aims to deliver kiosk-level services to all informal settlements within 10–15 years.[232]

## 5.4 *Legal Mobilisation*

Whereas the right to sanitation has only been recognised recently in domestic and international law, it is possible to point to some specific instances of judicialisation. Given the increasing trend to adjudicate socio-economic rights, judicial remedies could form an important means of making States and other actors accountable for violations of the right.[233]

Many of the initial cases occurred in South Asia. As discussed above, the first Indian case on socio-economic rights, *Ratlam* v. *Shri Vardhichand*, concerned sanitation.[234] In other cases in India, High Courts have, in essence, constitutionalised statutory obligations, allowing petitioners to avail themselves of constitutional procedures and remedies in order to enforce local government responsibilities. For example, in *Rampal*, residents of Mandal in Rajasthan complained that untreated water drainage from other houses was accumulating with a possibility of epidemics. Bolstered by support from health bureaucrats, the Court directed the Municipal Board 'to remove the water and fifth collected in the chowk in Mundara Mohalla, Mandal by the construction of proper sewers and drains, so as to remove the cause of possible nuisance in the locality, within a period of three months'.[235]

In *Koolwal*, the High Court similarly relied on constitutional rights procedures and 'a right to know about the activities of the State', to address a petition concerning 'insanitation' in Jaipur city.[236] The Rajasthan Municipalities Act 1959 required every Board to make 'reasonable provisions', which

[232] Personal communication by GIZ official to Malcolm Langford, March 2010.

[233] See, for example, R. Gargarella, P. Domingo and T. Roux (eds.), *Courts and Social Transformation in New Democracies: An Institutional Voice for the Poor?* (Aldershot/Burlington: Ashgate, 2006); V. Gauri and D. Brinks, *Courting Social Justice: Judicial Enforcement of Social and Economic Rights in the Developing World* (New York: Cambridge University Press, 2008).

[234] See discussion at footnote 49.

[235] *Rampal and Ors* v. *State of Rajasthan and Ors*, AIR1981Raj121 (4 September 1980), para. 6.

[236] *J.K. Koolwal* v. *State of Rajasthan and Ors*, AIR1988Raj2, 1987(1)WLN134 (19 September 1986), para. 2.

included 'cleaning public streets, places and sewers' and 'removing filth, rubbish, night-soil, odour, or any other noxious or offensive matter from privies, latrines, urinals, cesspools or other common receptacles'.[237] The Court recognised that the Board had 'taken some steps' but found that the obligations had not 'been implemented in full', noting that the 'problem of sanitation is very acute' and a life 'hazard' for the citizens.[238] The municipality was directed to take sufficient actions within a period of six months and clean the entire city. A team of 'five eminent advocates' was also appointed as commissioners to follow-up and inspect the progress of implementation.[239] The municipality responded that the order was too onerous since it lacked resources, but the Court responded that it does not carry a duty 'to see whether the funds are available or not' when the duty is established in statutory law.[240]

However, if the concern is with the actual implementation and impact of the right, it is important to move beyond a simple focus on judicial outcomes. A mere judgment may strengthen the rule of law and the legal shadow of a right, but its broader and actual influence in practice is likely to vary according to context. Positive judgments may be poorly implemented or have negative consequences, while lost cases may catalyse significant impact.[241] If a political understanding is taken of litigation, the focus should be shifted to the different impacts that judgments can generate (whether material, political or attitudinal) and the conditions under which impact is maximised.

Let us take two examples. The first illustrates the importance of a responsive court. In *Human Rights Case No. 9* in Pakistan, the Karachi Administration Women's Welfare Society (KAWWS) complained about deteriorating basic infrastructure: the use of open storm water drains for the disposal of sewage was hazardous and the breakdown of the sewer system was contaminating drinking water.[242] The Supreme Court regarded the matter as being of public importance under Article 184(3) of the Constitution and dispensed with the ordinary strict rules of procedure. A Commission was constituted by the Court to investigate the complaints, and it reported back that the petitioners' claims were correct. The water and sewerage board and a housing society were identified as responsible, and the

237 Ibid., para. 5. 238 Ibid., paras. 8–9. 239 Ibid., para. 10. 240 Ibid.

241 J. Dugard and M. Langford, 'Art or Science? Synthesising Lessons from Public Interest Litigation and the Dangers of Legal Determinism', *South African Journal on Human Rights*, Vol. 27, No. 2 (2011), pp. 39–64; M. Langford, C. Rodríguez-Garavito, and J. Rossi (eds.), *Making it Stick: The Enforcement of Economic and Social Rights Judgments* (Cambridge: Cambridge University Press, 2017).

242 *Human Rights Case No. 9 – K/1992*, Supreme Court of Pakistan, unreported judgment.

Court ordered them to start the necessary work to repair the water and sewerage pipes.[243] According to a report, the pipes were repaired in 1992/1993 and an underground reservoir for the area was built.[244] When the drinking water was contaminated again, the necessary repairs were also reportedly undertaken.

A recent case from South Africa illustrates how broader mobilisation can be more important than legal outcomes. The residents of Harry Gwala informal settlement, which lies to the east of Johannesburg, had spent two decades mobilising to have their settlement upgraded with no success and despite an agreement with the municipality.[245] In August 2006, the municipality eventually submitted a proposal to the provincial government for upgrading, but no decision had been taken. The residents turned to the High Court, which ordered the municipality to provide taps and refuse collection, after the parties had agreed on this during the proceedings. But it dismissed the claim for temporary sanitation and for high-mast lighting. The decision was appealed to the Constitutional Court on the grounds that the constitutional right of access to adequate housing included rights to basic sanitation and electricity.

It was this mere process that helped push the municipality to some action: in April 2009, the residents were offered one chemical toilet per ten families. In the court proceedings, the residents rejected this offer, arguing for one VIP per household (based on government standards). However, the Constitutional Court was not prepared to order this and instead directed the provincial government to take a final decision on slum upgrading application within 14 months.[246] The decision to upgrade Harry Gwala was again delayed although the delay is partly due to environmental impact

243 Karachi Administration Employees Co-operative Housing Society and the Karachi Water and Sewerage Board (KWSB). During a later stage in the proceeding, the KWSB took over full responsibility.

244 *Legal Resources for the Right to Water and Sanitation: International and National Standards* (2nd edn, Geneva: COHRE, 2008).

245 See discussion of case in J. Dugard, 'Basic Services in Urban South Africa: Rights, Reality and Resistance' in M. Langford, B. Cousins, J. Dugard and T. Madlingozi (eds.), *Symbols or Substance? The Role and Impact of Socio-Economic Rights Strategies in South Africa* (Cambridge: Cambridge University Press, 2013), pp. 275–309.

246 *Nokotyana & Ors.* v. *Ekurhuleni Municipality* 2010 (4) BCLR 312 (CC). Note that Court chose not to explicitly address whether there was a constitutional freestanding right to sanitation as it focused on the legislation. For critique of the decision, see S. Liebenberg, *Socio-Economic Rights: Adjudication Under a Transformative Constitution* (Claremont: Juta, 2010), pp. 455–456; S. Wilson and J. Dugard, 'Constitutional Jurisprudence: the First and Second Waves', in Langford et al. (eds.), *Socio-Economic Rights in South Africa*, ibid., pp. 33–62, at 50–52.

assessments that a decision is repeatedly promised. Moreover, despite not being ordered to do so, the municipality provided more than one in ten toilets they had offered in court along with some high-mast lighting was also provided.[247] Other communities in surrounding East Rand area also viewed the decision as covering their settlements and used it in negotiations with municipalities.[248]

## 6 CONCLUSION

More than 150 years ago, a 'sanitary revolution' occurred in Europe as municipalities were pushed to make unprecedented investments in public drinking water and sanitation. The effect in controlling outbreaks of cholera, typhoid and other infectious diseases led to the *British Medical Journal*, after a 2007 survey, to crown sanitation as the most important medical advancement since 1840.[249] However, the consequences of poor sanitation across the world remain devastating. The UNDP has noted that diarrhoea has 'killed more children than all the people lost to armed conflict since the Second World War',[250] while even in wealthier countries, access is not universal.

Articulating sanitation as a human right offers an opportunity to highlight, support and legalise the continuing demands of this sanitation revolution. However, a human right to sanitation arguably offers more than just strengthening common demands for improved treatment and extended physical access from the sanitation sector. Fundamentally, it places the issue of equality at the centre of sanitation-related efforts: the most marginalised need to also benefit from access to sanitation facilities and the broader social and health benefits. It also brings a greater focus on dignity, focusing on demands such as privacy and security. Additionally, the focus on genuine participation, affordability and cultural acceptability brings into the foreground the need to ensure that sanitation systems are contextually appropriate, can be accessed and will actually be used in practice. This is not to say that articulating or enforcing this 'new' human right will provide a panacea for addressing the sanitation crisis. But as the examples demonstrate, under particular conditions, rights-based strategies to sanitation can make an important contribution.

[247] Dugard, 'Basic Services in Urban South Africa'.

[248] Interview with G. Moyo, Makuase Settlement, March 2011, by Malcolm Langford.

[249] *British Medical Journal*, No. 334, (2007), p. 111.2

[250] Human Development Report 1993, *Millennium Development Goals: A Compact among Nations to End Human Poverty* (New York: Oxford University Press, 2003), p. 9.

Moreover, our understanding of sanitation as a right remains nascent. This can be seen in our discussion of the justification and interpretation of the right – including many issues that have yet to receive any other scholarly attention. It is possible to justify sanitation as a human right in both moral and legal terms (at least at the international level). The initial demands for recognition of a right to sanitation also occurred in the context of the movement for the right to water. But the discussion in this chapter suggests that there may be very good grounds, technically and politically, for de-linking the two rights. Separating sanitation from water provides the opportunity for further detailed explanation of the content, perhaps with a new General Comment from the CESCR or update of General Comment No. 15. Our conclusion on this question is strengthened by our view that the right to sanitation possesses some particular collective features that require a partly different way of conceiving and implementing the right.

## 11

# Development Cooperation and Extraterritorial Obligations

ASHFAQ KHALFAN*

### 1 INTRODUCTION

Development cooperation can play an important role in progressively realising the right to water in countries with limited financial and other resources. Some bilateral and United Nations (UN) development agencies have now included the promotion of human rights in their programming efforts.[1] These include, for example, providing training on human rights, supporting access to justice initiatives, building the capacity of human rights groups and 'mainstreaming' human rights into sector-specific policies.[2] However, a critical element often missing from such efforts is an analysis by development agencies of their legal human rights obligations when they are engaged in development cooperation outside their borders. This approach persists even though it is well known that actions taken by development agencies can have negative effects on human rights.[3] For example, they can perpetuate discrimination or promote water supply distribution and pricing systems that exclude the poorest.

* Law and Policy Programme Director, Amnesty International. I am grateful for useful comments on earlier drafts of this chapter by Vaughan Lowe, the editors of this book, Rolf Künnemann, Magdalena Sepúlveda, Margot Salomon, Inga Winkler and two anonymous reviewers. This chapter is based on my academic research and is not intended to set out Amnesty International's policy.

1 In this chapter, 'donor' refers to an economically developed or economically developing country that is providing financial and technical assistance to another country. 'Developing country' refers to the country receiving assistance. These terms are used here, in spite of their limitations, as they reflect United Nations terminology. The term 'development agency' is used to refer to bilateral development agencies, as well as relevant inter-governmental organisations involved in development.

2 OECD-DAC, *Action-Oriented Policy Paper on Human Rights and Development* (2007), OECD Doc DDC/DAC (2007) 5/FINAL, at pp. 10–11.

3 Ibid., p. 16; OECD, *Integrating Human Rights into Development: Donor Approaches, Experiences and Challenges* (Paris: OECD, 2006), at pp. 38–52.

Development agencies have generally treated the developing countries that receive aid as the sole duty-bearers of human rights obligations in their countries, with development agencies reserving the right to impose – at their discretion – incentives for compliance with human rights. In some cases, the extent to which a development agency integrates human rights into its work in practice often depends on whether its senior decision makers believe that human rights serve the instrumental purpose of advancing economic and social development.[4] The Special Rapporteur on the rights to water and sanitation recently issued a report on development cooperation and took the view that while many donors refer to human rights principles explicitly or implicity, they do not necessarily recognise them as obligations, observe them in project implementation and reporting or use them as a criterion in selecting projects.[5]

People whose human rights are affected by development agencies, directly or indirectly, rarely have access to legally binding mechanisms to hold such agencies accountable for their decisions.[6] The available mechanisms are limited to the possibility to complain about the failure of certain international financial institutions (such as the World Bank) to comply with their own operational policies in projects that they support, and the so-far untested possibility for people to take legal action in the courts of a State whose development agency is alleged to have violated their rights extraterritorially.[7] However, there is a possibility of independent review of the conduct of development agencies, which can result in politically influential, although not legally binding, decisions. As will be shown below, some UN treaty monitoring bodies have begun addressing development cooperation in their periodic reviews of States' implementation of human rights treaties to which they are party. However, such reviews have been limited and not rigorous. Other mechanisms that could be used to assess compliance with human

4 A. Russell, 'International Organizations and Human Rights: Realizing, Resisting or Repackaging the Right to Water', *Journal of Human Rights*, Vol. 9, No. 1 (2010), pp. 1–23, at 11.

5 Report of the Special Rapporteur on the human right to safe drinking water and sanitation to the UN General Assembly, 5 August 2016, UN Doc. A/71/302, paras. 36 and 41.

6 Such mechanisms are examined in detail in A. Khalfan 'Accountability of States', in M. Langford, M. Scheinin, W. Vandenhole and W. van Genugten (eds.), *Global Justice, State Duties: The Extra-Territorial Scope of Economic, Social and Cultural Rights in International Law* (Cambridge: Cambridge University Press, 2013).

7 This possibility arises in regard to countries that treat international human rights law as part of national law, or where legislation requires that international assistance is consistent with human rights standards, for example, the Canadian Official Development Assistance Accountability Act 2008, s. 4.

rights in development cooperation include peer review processes established by the UN Human Rights Council and the Development Assistance Committee of the Organization for Economic Co-operation and Development (OECD-DAC).

This chapter uses the term 'extraterritorial obligations' to refer to obligations borne by a State in regard to the economic, social and cultural rights (ESC rights) of people outside its borders.[8] It assesses the extraterritorial obligations binding States in regard to the right to water, seeking to determine how specific these obligations are and what matters are left to State discretion. The chapter analyses the obligations of the 165 States that are party to the International Covenant on Economic, Social and Cultural Rights (ICESCR).[9] Article 2(1) of the ICESCR requires that each State party 'take steps, individually and through international assistance and co-operation, especially economic and technical, to the maximum of its available resources, with a view to achieving progressively the full realization of the rights recognized in the present Covenant by all appropriate means, including particularly the adoption of legislative measures'. The treaty's monitoring body, the UN Committee on Economic, Social and Cultural Rights (CESCR), has stated that 'international cooperation for development and thus for the realization of economic, social and cultural rights is an obligation of all States' that are parties to the ICESCR.[10]

Section 2 of this chapter assesses the legal basis for extraterritorial obligations in the ICESCR. Section 3 examines the obligation of bilateral development agencies to refrain from interfering with the right to water in other countries. Section 4 examines State obligations to ensure compliance with the ICESCR by multilateral development agencies of which they are members. Section 5 examines State obligations to engage in financial and technical cooperation to help realise the right to water of people outside their borders. While limiting the analysis to the right to water, the legal and policy issues canvassed in this chapter apply to other economic, social and cultural rights,

[8] The term 'territorial obligations' is used to refer to a State's obligations to realise the economic, social and cultural rights of people within its territory.

[9] International Covenant on Economic, Social and Cultural Rights (adopted 16 December 1966, entered into force 3 January 1976), 993 UNTS 3. For reasons of space, this chapter does not assess extraterritorial obligations arising under other relevant human rights instruments. Nor does it address obligations relating to international watercourses, which are addressed in Chapter 5 of this volume by Russell and McCaffrey.

[10] CESCR, *General Comment No. 3: The Nature of States Parties' Obligations* (Sixth session, 1990), UN Doc. E/1991/23 (1991), at para. 14.

in particular the less fashionable right to sanitation and other rights that require the provision of services, such as the right to health.[11]

## 2 LEGAL BASIS FOR EXTRATERRITORIAL OBLIGATIONS

There have been differences between States and between authors as to whether the undertaking in Article 2(1) of the ICESCR 'to take steps, individually and through international assistance and cooperation, especially economic and technical' imposes extraterritorial obligations on States to realise ESC rights and in particular whether there is an obligation to provide assistance. For example, in the negotiations on the Optional Protocol to the ICESCR (OP-ICESCR),[12] economically developing countries, such as African countries (speaking as a group on this issue), China, India, Indonesia and Iran, stated that international cooperation and assistance is a legally binding obligation in the ICESCR. Economically developed countries, such as Canada, Czech Republic, France, Portugal and the United Kingdom, stated that international cooperation and assistance was an important moral obligation, but not a legal entitlement, and that they did not interpret the ICESCR to impose a legal obligation to provide development assistance or give a legal title to receive such aid.[13]

This section briefly assesses the legal basis for extraterritorial obligations in the ICESCR. While most authors who have addressed this issue in detail endorse the CESCR's elaboration of extraterritorial obligations,[14] Vandenhole

[11] The UN Guidelines for the Realization of the Right to Drinking Water Supply and Sanitation (Sub-Commission Guidelines) and the CESCR's General Comment on the right to health take a similar approach to General Comment No. 15 on the issue of extraterritorial obligations relating to these rights. See UNHRC (Sub-Commission), Res. 2006/10 (2006), adopting the Guidelines for the Realization of the Right to Drinking Water Supply and Sanitation in the Report of the Special Rapporteur (2005), UN Doc. E/CN.4/Sub.2/2005/25, at 10, and CESCR, *General Comment No. 14: The Right to the Highest Attainable Standard of Health* (Twenty-second session, 2000), UN Doc. E/C.12/2000/4, at paras. 38–41 and 45 (2000).

[12] Optional Protocol to the International Covenant on Economic, Social and Cultural Rights (adopted 10 December 2008), GA Res. 63/117 (2008). UN Doc. A/RES/63/117.

[13] *Report of the Open-ended Working Group to Consider Options Regarding the Elaboration of an Optional Protocol to the International Covenant on Economic, Social and Cultural Rights on its Second Session*, UN Doc. E/CN.4/2005/52, at para. 76; *Report of the Open-ended Working Group to Consider Options Regarding the Elaboration of an Optional Protocol to the International Covenant on Economic, Social and Cultural Rights on its Third Session*, UN Doc E/CN.4/2006/47, at paras. 78 and 82; *Report of the Open-ended Working Group on an Optional Protocol to the International Covenant on Economic, Social and Cultural Rights on its Fourth Session*, UN Doc. A/HRC/6/8, at para. 164.

[14] For example: R. Künnemann, 'Extraterritorial Application of the International Covenant on Economic, Social and Cultural Rights', in F. Coomans and M. Kamminga (eds.),

has suggested that only specific aspects of the extraterritorial obligation to fulfil may be legally binding, while other aspects, in particular the obligation to provide development aid, are disputed and only soft law but may gradually evolve into hard law.[15] Coomans had taken the view that only the extraterritorial obligation to respect is binding law.[16]

The rules of treaty interpretation require that the ICESCR be interpreted in accordance with the ordinary meaning to be given to its terms in their context and in the light of its object and purpose.[17] The plain reading of Article 2(1) of the ICESCR is that each State party is required to take individual steps to realise ESC rights within its borders and to engage in international assistance and cooperation directed at realising ESC rights of people both within and beyond its borders (referred to below as the 'dual obligations' interpretation). However, an alternative reading of Article 2(1) (referred to below as the 'territorialist' interpretation) might view the reference to 'international assistance and cooperation' as referring only to an obligation of each State party to request international assistance where needed and to participate in international cooperation for the instrumental purpose of realising its territorial obligations.

The territorialist interpretation does not fit with the plain meaning of Article 2(1) in two ways. First, Article 2(1) does not specify that the State obligations in question, in particular those related to international assistance and cooperation, are limited only to residents of that State. Second, the obligation to take steps in Article 2(1), including through international assistance, is borne by all States parties. Article 2 (1) does not specify that the

*Extraterritorial Application of Human Rights Treaties* (Antwerp: Intersentia, 2004); M. N. Wabwile, *Legal Protection of Social and Economic Rights of Children in Developing Countries* (Antwerp: Intersentia, 2010), at pp. 134–144; and M. Sepúlveda, 'Obligations of "International Assistance and Cooperation" in an Optional Protocol to the International Covenant on Economic, Social and Cultural Rights', *Netherlands Quarterly of Human Rights*, Vol. 24, No. 2 (2006), pp. 271–303, at 280–9.

15 W. Vandenhole, 'EU and Development, Extraterritorial Obligations under the International Covenant on Economic, Social and Cultural Rights', in M. Salomon, A. Tostensen and W. Vandenhole (eds.), *Casting the Net Wider: Human Rights, Development and New Duty-Bearers* (Antwerp: Intersentia, 2007), at p. 97. Vandenhole does not elaborate on which aspects of the obligation to fulfil he considers to be legally binding.

16 F. Coomans, 'Some Remarks on the Extraterritorial Application of the International Covenant on Economic, Social and Cultural Rights', in F. Coomans and M. Kamminga (eds.), *Extraterritorial Application of Human Rights Treaties* (Antwerp: Intersentia, 2004), at p. 199.

17 Vienna Convention on the Law of Treaties (adopted 27 January 1969, entered into force 27 January 1980), 1115 UNTS 331, Article 31(1). Articles 31 and 32 of the Convention, which relate to the interpretation of treaties, are treated as by the International Court of Justice and other international tribunals as codifying international customary law, A. Aust, *Modern Treaty Law and Practice* (Cambridge: Cambridge University Press, 2007), p. 232.

obligation exists only 'where necessary.' If the obligation in question were only to request but not to provide international assistance, then this obligation would seemingly oblige even the wealthiest States parties to request assistance from others

In addition, Article 2(1) has to be read in light of the object and purpose of the ICESCR, which is to establish clear obligations for States parties in regard to the full realisation of ESC rights,[18] to establish conditions where everyone may enjoy their ESC rights and to promote universal respect for, and the observance of, human rights and freedoms.[19] The territorialist interpretation of the undertaking in Article 2(1) would leave to the discretion of States any engagement in international assistance and cooperation to realise ESC rights extraterritorially, even if States requiring assistance and cooperation had requested it. Such an interpretation would therefore appear contrary to the purpose of the ICESCR, as it would make it more difficult to create conditions in which ESC rights can be realised for all. As unanimously and repeatedly recognised by UN member States, international cooperation, including development assistance, is necessary in order to reduce poverty and achieve economic development for all.[20]

Article 2(1) explicitly refers only to positive obligations to fulfil ESC rights. However, an obligation to 'take steps, individually and through international assistance and cooperation', necessarily includes an implicit obligation not to interfere with – and to ensure that actors under a State's jurisdiction do not interfere with – ESC rights in other countries.

In interpreting a treaty, it is necessary to take into account, together with the context, any subsequent practice in the application of the treaty which establishes the agreement of the parties regarding its interpretation.[21] As already noted, there is no agreement between State parties to the ICESCR as to whether the ICESCR contains legally binding obligations of international assistance and cooperation. However, it is of significant importance that those countries that rejected legal obligations of international cooperation in the ICESCR did not put forward a territorialist interpretation of Article 2(1) of the ICESCR. Rather they simply argued that there are no legal obligations of international assistance and cooperation. Such a view is only consistent with the ICESCR if one reads Article 2(1) as only encouraging international cooperation, but no more. Such a view is not supported by the text of Article 2(1), as it refers to an

[18] CESCR, *General Comment No.* 3, para. 9.

[19] ICESCR, preambular paras. 2–4.

[20] For example, *Doha Declaration on Financing for Development: Outcome document of the Follow-up International Conference on Financing for Development to Review Implementation of the Monterrey Consensus* annexed to UNGA Res. 63/57 (12 December 2008), at paras. 2, 30, 40–43, 63 and 70.

[21] Vienna Convention, Article 31(3)(b).

*obligation* to take steps, including through international assistance and cooperation. Furthermore, the principles of effectiveness of treaties and the presumption against redundancy, contained in Article 31 of the Vienna Convention on the Law of Treaties,[22] means that a treaty provision may not be interpreted in a way that deprives clauses or paragraphs of a treaty of any meaning.[23]

The opposition by some developed countries to obligations of international cooperation in the ICESCR was focused on the obligation to provide assistance. However, all developed countries have accepted commitments that appear to reflect recognition of the extraterritorial obligations to respect ESC rights and to ensure that international policies are consistent with the realisation of ESC rights in other countries. In recent resolutions on the right to food, the UN General Assembly has consistently welcomed CESCR General Comment No. 12[24] on the right to food and referred to the CESCR's affirmation that the right to adequate food requires 'the adoption of appropriate environmental and social policies, at both the national and international levels, oriented to the eradication of poverty and the fulfillment of human rights for all'.[25] It also:

> Stresses that all States should make all efforts to ensure that their international policies of a political and economic nature, including international trade agreements, do not have a negative impact on the right to food in other countries.[26]

The Accra Agenda for Action (AAA), agreed at a 2008 ministerial conference organised by the Organisation for Economic Cooperation and Development, comprising over 100 countries, including all developed countries, states:

> Developing countries and donors will ensure that their respective development policies and programmes are designed and implemented in ways consistent with their agreed international commitments on gender equality, human rights, disability and environmental sustainability.[27]

22 Vienna Convention.

23 A. Orakhelashvili, *The Interpretation of Acts and Rules in Public International Law* (Oxford: Oxford University Press, 2008), pp. 397 and 424–425.

24 CESCR, *General Comment No. 12, The Right to Adequate Food (art. 11)* (Twentieth session, 1999), UN Doc. E/C.12/1999/5 (1999).

25 For example: UNGA Res. 71/191 (19 December 2016) (adopted without a vote), at para. 41; UNGA Res. 64/159 (18 December 2009) (adopted without a vote), at para. 32. The rights to food and self-determination are the only ESC rights on which the General Assembly (and therefore all States parties to the ICESCR) has consistently adopted annual resolutions over the last eight years.

26 UNGA, Right to Food (2016), para. 28; UNGA, Right to Food (2009), para. 20.

27 Accra Agenda for Action, Third High Level Forum on Aid Effectiveness (2–4 September 2008), UN Doc. A/63/537 (Letter dated 6 November 2008 from the Secretary-General to the President of the General Assembly), Annex, at para. 13(c).

The AAA does not specify the agreed human rights commitments to which it refers, but in the context of development, the ICESCR would be one of the most relevant human rights commitments. If the AAA is interpreted in good faith to refer to both treaties and to non-legally binding commitments, the AAA suggests that, at least in the context of development cooperation, all developed countries have accepted that they have an obligation under international human rights law to refrain from interfering with human rights in other countries and to ensure that international aid is provided in a manner that complies with human rights. The AAA and the General Assembly right to food resolutions only suggest, rather than prove, agreement between States parties. It is not clear that the AAA and right to food resolutions refer to the obligations in the ICESCR. In addition, the conclusion that all countries have accepted extraterritorial obligations to respect ESC rights and to ensure that international policies are consistent with the realisation of ESC rights can only be tenuous, as it relies on reconciling contradictions between the position of certain developed countries in the OP-ICESCR negotiations and the text of declarations and resolutions that they have accepted.

A dual obligations interpretation of the ICESCR is strengthened by several other rules of international law that require international cooperation for the realisation of ESC rights.[28] The UN Charter requires that States 'take joint and separate action in cooperation with the [United Nations] Organization' to achieve purposes set out in Article 55 of the Charter, which include '... universal respect for, and observance of, human rights and fundamental freedoms for all without distinction as to race, sex, language, or religion'.[29] It therefore establishes a general obligation of international cooperation for the realisation of human rights. Article 22 of the Universal Declaration of Human Rights (UDHR) states that everyone is '... entitled to the realization, through national effort and international co-operation and in accordance with the organization and resources of each State, of the economic, social and cultural rights indispensable for his dignity...'.[30] Article 28 of the UDHR stipulates that 'Everyone is entitled to

[28] When interpreting a treaty, it is necessary to take into account relevant rules of international law applicable to parties to that treaty, Vienna Convention on the Law of Treaties, Article 31(3)(c).

[29] Charter of the United Nations (adopted 26 June 1945, entered into force 24 October 1945), 1 UNTS XVI.

[30] Universal Declaration of Human Rights (adopted 10 December 1948), GA Res. 217 A (III) (1948).

a social and international order in which the rights and freedoms in this Declaration can be fully realized'.[31]

Article 4 of Convention on the Rights of the Child (CRC) requires that States take measures to implement the economic, social and cultural rights in the CRC '... to the maximum extent of their available resources and, where needed, within the framework of international cooperation'.[32] While this Article could initially be read as supporting either a territorialist or dual obligations interpretation, Articles 24(4) and 28(3) require that States promote and encourage international cooperation in relation to health and education, thereby indicating that the treaty includes at least some extraterritorial obligations. The CRC's treaty monitoring body has stated: 'When States ratify the Convention, they take upon themselves obligations not only to implement it within their jurisdiction, but also to contribute, through international cooperation, to global implementation'.[33]

Thus far, this analysis has relied on the 'general rule of interpretation' set out in Article 31 of the Vienna Convention on the Law of Treaties. Article 32 of the Vienna Convention permits recourse to the preparatory work of a treaty in order to confirm the meaning reached when applying Article 31 or if interpretation under Article 31 leaves the meaning of a treaty ambiguous, obscure or leads to a manifestly absurd or unreasonable result.[34] During the negotiations of the ICESCR, there was agreement between the drafters that international cooperation and assistance were necessary in order to realise ESC rights but disagreement as to whether there were any obligations to provide international assistance.[35] There was no suggestion of a

[31] For the purposes of this chapter, I take as given the contentious view that the provisions in the UDHR, including Articles 22 and 28, are legally binding because they provide an authoritative interpretation of the UN Charter or constitute legally binding general principles of international law. See: T. Buergenthal, 'International Human Rights Law and Institutions: Accomplishments and Prospects', *Washington Law Review*, Vol. 63, No. 1 (1988), pp. 1–20, at 9; and B. Simma and P. Alston, 'The Sources of Human Rights Law: Custom, *Jus Cogens*, and General Principles', *Australian Yearbook of International Law*, Vol. 12 (1988–9), pp. 82–108, at 100–102.

[32] All States parties to the ICESCR with one exception (Somalia, which is a signatory) are also party to the Convention on the Rights of the Child (adopted 20 November 1989, entered into force 2 September 1990), 1577 UNTS 3.

[33] Committee on the Rights of the Child, *General Comment No. 5: General Measures of Implementation for the Convention on the Rights of the Child* (Thirty-fourth session, 2003), UN Doc. CRC/GC/2003/5 (2003), at para. 5.

[34] Vienna Convention, Article 31(2).

[35] See: UN Doc. A/C.3/SR.742 (1957), at para. 14; UN Doc. A/C.3/SR.743 (1957), at para. 16; P. Alston and G. Quinn, 'The Nature and Scope of States Parties' Obligations under the International Covenant on Economic, Social and Cultural Rights', *Human Rights Quarterly*, Vol. 9, No. 2 (1987), pp. 156–229, at 188–189 and 223–229.

territorialist interpretation of Article 2(1). The negotiators either adopted a dual obligations reading of this Article or considered that it encouraged but did not require international assistance and cooperation, contrary to the plain meaning of Article 2(1). No vote was conducted to decide between these competing views and to reflect one of the contending views in the text. For this reason, the choice between the competing views of the drafters as to the interpretation of Article 2(1) should be reached on the basis of the general rule of interpretation. Although it may be suggested that States cannot be bound to obligations to which they did not explicitly support in the drafting of the treaty, such a view would imply that the views articulated by some parties to the negotiations, but which are not reflected in the final text, should be given preference over others, which would not be a good faith interpretation of the treaty.

As already mentioned, the CESCR has interpreted the ICESCR as containing extraterritorial obligations. The CESCR has been accused by some of interpreting the ICESCR in such a manner as to effectively amend the treaty.[36] However, it would be more accurate to state that the CESCR has clarified the meaning of vaguely formulated treaty provisions in a manner that gives meaning to such provisions. This is an appropriate role for a body of independent experts that has been given a mandate to do so. The UN Economic and Social Council (ECOSOC) invited the CESCR to adopt General Comments, a decision endorsed by the General Assembly.[37] The ECOSOC subsequently encouraged the CESCR to continue developing General Comments in order to 'develop a fuller appreciation of the obligations of State parties under the ICESCR'.[38]

Although the CESCR's interpretations of the ICESCR are authoritative, they are not legally binding. Nevertheless, they are influential whenever disputes on the ICESCR come before a tribunal that has the power to issue legally binding judgements. In the course of analysing the implications of the ICESCR, the International Law Commission (ILC) and the International

[36] M. Dennis and D. Stewart, 'Justiciability of Economic, Social, and Cultural Rights: Should There be an International Complaints Mechanism to Adjudicate the Rights to Food, Water, Housing, and Health?', *American Journal of International Law*, Vol. 98, No. 3 (2004), pp. 462–515, at 493 and 499–500.

[37] Economic and Social Council, Res. 1987/5 (26 May 1987), at para. 9; UNGA Res. 42/102 (7 December 1987), at para. 5.

[38] Economic and Social Council, Res. 1990/45 (25 May 1990), at para. 10. The General Assembly has stated on several occasions that it 'welcomes the continuing efforts of the Human Rights Committee and the Committee on Economic, Social and Cultural Rights to strive for uniform standards in the implementation of the provisions of the International Covenants on Human Rights, and appeals to other bodies dealing with similar human rights questions to respect those uniform standards, as expressed in the general comments of the Committees'. See, for example, UNGA Res. 58/165 (4 March 2004), at para. 24.

Court of Justice (ICJ) have relied on the CESCR's General Comments and Concluding Observations.[39] The General Comments may influence how States interpret and apply the ICESCR. For example, General Comment No. 15 influenced many States' recognition of the right to water. The Non-Aligned Movement, composed of 118 States at the time, referred specifically to General Comment No. 15 when it recognised the right to water in 2006.[40] In 2010, the Human Rights Council affirmed the legal basis for the right to water in terms very similar to that stated in General Comment No. 15.[41]

The analysis thus far has focused on the obligation of international assistance and cooperation. However, it is important to briefly note that there is an additional and overlapping basis whereby States can be bound by extraterritorial obligations in regard to ESC rights. In interpreting human rights treaties that do not include obligations of international cooperation, international courts and treaty bodies have established that States are bound by their treaty obligations extraterritorially where they exercise authority or control over territory or persons outside their sovereign territory, for example, in situations such as military occupation, arrest and detention of persons and acts of diplomatic agents.[42]

There are differences as to whether a State that does not fully exercise control over a person (or the territory in which they are located), but is in a position to interfere with that person's human rights, is thereby bound by an obligation to refrain from such interferences. The European Court of Human Rights (ECHR) notoriously held that persons killed during NATO's bombardment

39 International Law Commission, 'Draft Articles on the Responsibility of States for Internationally Wrongful Acts, with Commentaries', *Report of the International Law Commission on the Work of its Fifty-third Session* (Fifty-third session, 2001), UN GAOR, Supp. No. 10, UN Doc. A/56/10, at 50(1)(b) (2001); ICJ, *Legal Consequences of the Construction of a Wall in the Occupied Palestinian Territory*, 9 July 2004 (Advisory Opinion), ICJ Reports 2004, p. 136, at para. 112.

40 Fourteenth Summit Conference of Heads of State or Government of the Non-Aligned Movement, Final Document, 16 September 2006, NAM 2006/doc.1/rev.3, at para. 226.

41 Human Rights Council, Res. 15/9 (30 September 2010), at para. 3. See CESCR, *General Comment No. 15: The Right to Water* (Twenty-ninth session, 2002), UN Doc. E/C.12/2002/11 (2002), at para. 3. For further discussion on the General Comment, including its legal status, see Chapter 1 by Langford and Russell in this volume.

42 Human Rights Committee, *General Comment No. 31: The Nature of the General Legal Obligation Imposed on States Parties to the Covenant* (Eighteenth session, 2004), UN Doc. CCPR/C/21/Rev.1/Add. 13, at para. 10, European Court of Human Rights, *Al-Skeini and Others* v. *The United Kingdom* [GC], no. 55721/07, 7 July 2011, at paras. 134–9; Inter-American Commission of Human Rights, *Armando Alejandre Jr et al.* v. *Republica de Cuba*, Case 11.559, Report No. 86/99, OEA/Ser.L/V/II.106 Doc. 3 rev. at 586 (1999), para. 23. See also M. Gondek, *The Reach of Human Rights in a Globalising World: Extraterritorial Application of Human Rights Treaties* (Antwerp: Intersentia, 2009), pp. 354 and 364.

of a broadcasting station in Belgrade were not within the jurisdiction of the States carrying out that bombardment and therefore unable to seek a remedy under the European Convention on Human Rights.[43] However, in analogous circumstances, the ICJ, the Human Rights Committee (HRC – the treaty body that interprets the International Covenant on Civil and Political Rights) and the Inter-American Commission on Human Rights have held States responsible for interferences with the human rights of people outside their territory, even aside from situations of occupation and arrest and detention.[44] The ICJ, in applying the International Convention on the Elimination of All Forms of Racial Discrimination (CERD),[45] and the treaty body responsible for the Convention on the Elimination of All Forms of Discrimination against Women (CEDAW)[46] have held that these two treaties apply to the actions of States parties when they act beyond their territory.[47] The HRC has also held States responsible for violations of the ICCPR due to their support to military factions abusing civil and political rights in another State.[48] There is limited jurisprudence on the extraterritorial obligation to protect human rights on the basis of control. The Committee on the Elimination of Racial Discrimination has indicated that the CERD (which does not include obligations of international cooperation) applies to the conduct of States in regulating the extraterritorial actions of third parties under their jurisdiction, for example, calling

[43] *Banković and Others* v. *Belgium and others* (dec.) [GC], no. 52207/99, ECHR 2001-XII, at paras. 74–82. In that judgement, the Court did not consider the 'state agent authority and control' test to determine whether jurisdiction applies, which was later confirmed in the *al-Skeini* judgement of 2011 (ibid.). In addition, a number of cases decided by the ECHR after 2001 implicitly contradict the central premise of *Banković*, see M. Milanovic, *Extraterritorial Application of Human Rights Treaties: Law, Principles and Policy* (Oxford: OUP, 2011), pp. 184–186.

[44] ICJ, *Armed Activities in the Territory of the Congo (Democratic Republic of Congo v. Uganda)*, Judgment, ICJ Reports 2005, p. 168, at para. 220; HRC, *Concluding Observations of the Human Rights Committee: Iran*, UN Doc. CCPR/C/79/Add.25 (1993), at para. 9; *Armando Alejandre Jr et al.* v. *Republica de Cuba*, at para. 25.

[45] International Convention on the Elimination of All Forms of Racial Discrimination (adopted 7 March 1966, entered into force 4 January 1969) 660 UNTS 195.

[46] Convention on the Elimination of All Forms of Discrimination against Women (adopted 18 December 1979, entered into force 3 September 1981), 1249 UNTS 13.

[47] ICJ, *Application of the International Convention on the Elimination of All Forms of Racial Discrimination (Georgia v. Russian Federation)*, Provisional Measures, Order of 15 October 2008, ICJ Reports 2008, p. 353, at para. 109; Committee on the Elimination of Discrimination against Women, *General Recommendation No. 28 on the Core Obligations of States Parties under Article 2 of the Convention on the Elimination of All Forms of Discrimination against Women* (Forty-seventh session, 2010), UN. Doc. CEDAW/C/GC/2, at para. 12 (2010).

[48] HRC, *Concluding Observations of the Human Rights Committee: Yugoslavia*, UN Doc. CCPR/C/79/Add.16 (1992), at paras. 5 and 7; HRC, *Concluding Observations of the Human Rights Committee: Croatia*, UN Doc. CCPR/C/79/Add.15 (1992), at para. 7.

on the United States to 'take appropriate legislative or administrative measures to prevent acts of transnational corporations registered in the State party which negatively impact on the enjoyment of rights of indigenous peoples in territories outside the United States'.[49]

On the basis of the analysis in this section, it is concluded that there is a strong argument for stating that the ICESCR comprises extraterritorial obligations. This conclusion relies primarily on the textual analysis of Article 2(1), its interpretation by the CESCR and other relevant rules of international law. It is recognised, however, that fully resolving the legal debate on this issue deserves more detailed consideration than is possible in this chapter.

## 3 THE 'DO NO HARM' PRINCIPLE – BILATERAL DEVELOPMENT AGENCIES AND OBLIGATIONS TO RESPECT THE RIGHT TO WATER

The CESCR's General Comment No. 15 on the Right to Water reflects a 'do no harm' principle:

> To comply with their international obligations in relation to the right to water, States parties have to respect the enjoyment of the right in other countries. International cooperation requires States parties to refrain from actions that interfere, directly or indirectly, with the enjoyment of the right to water in other countries.[50]

General Comment No. 15 also stipulates a process obligation for international assistance: 'International assistance should be provided in a manner that is consistent with the [ICESCR] and other human rights standards, and sustainable and culturally appropriate.'[51] General Comment No. 15 further explains that States should give 'due attention' to the right to water in international agreements.[52] The General Comment's approach to development assistance has some parallels with the guidelines on human rights and development adopted by the Development Assistance Committee of the Organization for Economic Co-operation and Development (OECD-DAC). These indicate that donors should 'do no harm' and respect human rights principles in their policies and programming.[53] States are required to report periodically to the CESCR on

[49] Committee on the Elimination of Racial Discrimination, *Concluding Observations of the Committee on the Elimination of Racial Discrimination: United States of America*, UN Doc. CERD/C/USA/CO/6 (2008), at para. 30.

[50] General Comment No. 15, para. 31. [51] Ibid., para. 34. [52] Ibid., para. 35.

[53] OECD-DAC, *Policy Paper on Human Rights and Development*, p. 16.

the steps they have taken to implement the ICESCR. The CESCR's Reporting Guidelines require that States:

> Indicate the impact of international economic and technical assistance and cooperation, whether received or provided by the State party, on the full realization of each of the Covenant rights in the State party or, as the case may be, in other countries, especially developing countries.[54]

Most donors collect and report information on the cost of providing assistance to each partner country. They less commonly report on the impact of such assistance. However, the CESCR's guidelines require donors to assess the extent to which the assistance provided actually contributes to the realisation of economic, social and cultural rights. This is a challenging requirement, as it requires donors to systematically assess the outcomes and impact of their assistance in terms of human rights (relying, where appropriate, on reports from partner countries).[55] The CESCR does not require independent evaluations of the impact of international assistance and cooperation. However, as a policy matter, independent evaluations of a sample of each donor's projects are important, since one of the contributory factors to many failed development efforts is the lack of such assessments of development effectiveness.[56]

The level of a donor's involvement in policy decisions affecting the right to water will affect the level of its responsibility for any violations. Therefore, this section considers separately a donor's obligations in situations where it is directly implementing a project, where it is jointly implementing a project with a developing country and where a donor is only providing funds to a developing country's central or sector budget.

### 3.1 *Direct Project Implementation*

Where a donor country is directly implementing projects in another country, it is responsible for any violations caused by its staff in the course of their duties.[57] Extraterritorial interferences with the right to water could be

[54] CESCR, *Guidelines on Treaty-Specific Documents to be Submitted by States Parties under Articles 16 and 17 of the International Covenant on Economic, Social and Cultural Rights* (Forty-first session, 2008), UN Doc. E/C.12/2008/2 (2008), at para. 9.

[55] For an example of such an assessment, see M. K. Katua, A. Khalfan, M. Langford and M. Lüke, *Kenyan-German Development Cooperation in the Water Sector: Assessment from a Human Rights Perspective* (Eschborn: GTZ, 2007).

[56] See, for example, W. Easterly, *The White Man's Burden: Why the West's Efforts to Aid the Rest Have Done So Much Ill and So Little Good* (New York: Penguin, 2006), pp. 193–195.

[57] ILC Articles on State Responsibility, Article 4. The ILC articles both codify and progressively develop customary international law; see 'General Commentary' of the articles.

caused by development projects that, for example, lead to forced evictions, cause pollution of drinking water sources or are carried out in a manner that infringes upon the right of people to participate in decision-making processes affecting their right to water.[58] The latter violation might occur where a donor country carries out a water supply project without consulting with the people whose rights will be affected by the project or carrying out consultations in a discriminatory manner, for example, by inviting only the 'heads of the household' to consultations – a system that would normally exclude women.

In some cases, a directly implemented donor project may be carried out on the request or advice of the government of the developing country in question. The issue of the donor's obligations when acting on decisions by a developing country government is considered under section 3.2 below on joint project implementation. However, even if the developing country government has provided for the participation of relevant stakeholders in a decision to establish a particular programme or project, a donor directly implementing the project would have to ensure that affected stakeholders have an opportunity to participate in decisions taken in the course of implementing the project. For example, a government may invite a development agency to drill boreholes in a certain area, but critical details, such as their precise location, their ownership and the system to fund and maintain them, would still need consultation with the intended users.[59]

Even if the developing country authorises the acts in question, a donor State remains responsible for a violation of the right to water as no State is entitled to waive its people's human rights.[60] In addition, as part of its obligations to realise the right to water,[61] the developing country is implicitly required to ensure that other States acting within its territory do not interfere with the right to water of its people. Where a donor State interferes with the right to water, the developing country would be responsible for any actions it takes to support such violations or for omissions to take steps within its ability to prevent such a violation.

### 3.2 *Joint Project Implementation*

Where donors jointly implement a specific project or programme with a developing country, conditions imposed by donors could cause or contribute

[58] For the right to participation in the context of the right to water, see General Comment No. 15, paras. 16(a) and 48, and Sub-Commission Guidelines, ss. 8.1–8.2.

[59] It may be the case that a host government does not permit such consultation. The issues that arise when a developing country puts the donor in a position where its assistance may contribute to a violation is dealt with in the paragraph following footnote 68.

[60] See the ILC Articles on State Responsibility, commentary to Article 20(9).

[61] See for example, General Comment No. 15, para. 25.

to interferences with the right to water. For example, certain donors in some situations have made provision of development assistance to the water sector conditional upon a developing country's agreement to contract private corporations to manage water service and sewerage utilities in urban areas. In Madagascar in 2004, the World Bank, the French Development Agency and the European Investment Bank focused conditionality demands on private sector management.[62] However, General Comment No. 15 stipulates that States must establish an effective regulatory system to prevent private operators of water services 'from compromising equal affordable, and physical access to sufficient, safe and acceptable water'.[63] Where no effective regulator is in place and a donor country or a group of donor countries requires private sector management of water services (without referring to ensuring effective regulation) as a condition for debt cancellation or continuance of development assistance, such conditions constitute an indirect interference with the right to water if the changes to the system result in the denial of the right to water to any person. A donor would only be responsible for the indirect interference if the donor country's representatives either oppose the establishment of an effective regulator or are actually aware that the developing country would not establish such a regulator. The developing country would also be responsible for any interference with the right to water if it fails to establish an effective regulatory system for the utilities. However, the donors and not the developing country would be solely responsible for the violation if the developing country lacks the capacity to establish a regulatory system and it was forced to accept the private management of water utilities due to serious economic pressure from its donors that deprives it of any possibility of conforming with its obligations under the ICESCR.[64]

Where a violation of the right to water is instigated by a developing country, a donor would be held responsible for aiding and abetting the violation if it knew about the circumstances of the likely violation and continued to provide aid that facilitated the violation.[65] According to the International Law Commission, 'a State providing financial or other aid to another State should

[62] Water Aid, *Getting to Boiling Point: Turning Up the Heat on Water and Sanitation* (London: Water Aid, 2005) p. 27.

[63] General Comment No. 15, para. 24.

[64] For an elaboration of the standards for determining when a State has been coerced to carry out an internationally wrongful act and is therefore not responsible for such an act, see the ILC Articles on State Responsibility, Article 18 and Commentary [2–3].

[65] For an elaboration of the standards for determining when a State is responsible for aiding and abetting an internationally wrongful act, see the ILC Articles on State Responsibility, ibid., Article 16 and commentary.

not be required to assume the risk that the latter will divert the aid for purposes which may be intentionally unlawful'.[66] Thus, where a donor is not aware of a violation, it is not held responsible for aiding the donor country in the violation. However, if it is wilfully blind or negligent to a serious risk of an interference with the right to water caused by a project or programme that it supports, and does not take mitigating measures, it could be held responsible for failing to take steps to ensure that its international assistance is provided in a manner consistent with the ICESCR.[67]

Lack of participation of persons affected by projects became an issue in Kenya's water sector reforms, which commenced in 2002, funded and partly designed through technical assistance provided by several donors. A study commissioned by the German Technical Cooperation Agency (GTZ) found that there was insufficient information reaching the poor about water sector reforms.[68] Representatives of low-income groups had not sufficiently participated in water sector reform processes, while at the local level, consultation with users had not been carried out in some urban areas, leading to situations where, for example, water kiosks had been constructed at sites selected by the utility at locations far from the intended users.[69]

Where a donor's aid is being used in a manner inconsistent with the ICESCR, a donor may have to consider withdrawing such aid to avoid being responsible for the provision of such assistance. However, such a withdrawal may have a negative effect on progressively realising the right to water. In such a circumstance, a donor would have to assess whether continued provision of assistance to the developing country government, while calling on it to ensure that such aid is provided in a manner consistent with human rights standards, is a better policy option than the alternatives, such as providing assistance through non-governmental organisations in the country. However, the latter option may not be a sustainable solution for some forms of services, such as networked water provision and sewerage. In a situation where it is not clear which of the possible policy choices is required by the ICESCR, a donor would likely be compliant with the ICESCR where its decision on the

66 Ibid., Commentary to chapter IV [8].

67 For an example of a distinction between actual knowledge that a violation was going to occur and failure to exercise due diligence, see the International Court of Justice case examining Serbia's responsibility for genocide in Bosnia: ICJ, *Application of the Convention on the Prevention and Punishment of the Crime of Genocide (Bosnia and Herzegovina v. Serbia and Montenegro)*, Judgement, ICJ Reports 2007, p. 43, paras. 423–438.

68 Katua et al., *Kenyan-German Development Cooperation in the Water Sector*, pp. 5 and 39.

69 Ibid., pp. 39–41.

provision of aid is based on a reasonable analysis in good faith of the consequences of its decision for the enjoyment of human rights.

### 3.3 *Central or Sector Budget Assistance*

When a donor country provides financial support to a developing country's water sector institutions or to its central budget, and has neither proposed nor encouraged a violation, it is difficult to draw a causal link between such assistance and any interferences with the right to water carried out by the developing country government using these funds. There may be exceptions, for example, where the aid is given specifically in order to support the violation in question.[70] However, as already indicated, a donor is required to ensure that its international assistance is provided in a manner that is consistent with the ICESCR and other human rights standards.[71] Donors must therefore at least request that the developing country government commit to use donor resources in a manner consistent with the right to water and other human rights.[72] As a donor State is responsible for reporting to the CESCR on the impact of aid provided,[73] it would need to request that the developing country provide it with information on such impact in order to facilitate the donor's own report to the CESCR. For such a request to be practical, the donor would probably have to respond positively to any request by that developing country for assistance in establishing and maintaining the capacity to collect such information.

Where a donor's financial assistance is likely to be making a significant contribution to a violation of the right to water by a developing country, and the donor is – or should be – aware of this fact, it may be required to withdraw assistance. For example, where significant loan financing is provided to a government that is using the bulk of these resources for the personal uses of the ruler and its political supporters, the lenders are effectively helping the borrower transfer the resources required for repayment from future national budgets for misuse at present. The consequence is to reduce the level of public resources available for the implementation of ESC rights in that country in the future.

70 See the ILC Articles on State Responsibility, Commentary to Article 16 [4].

71 General Comment No. 15, para. 34.

72 If the developing country government in question is not a party to the main international human rights treaties, compliance with human rights could be requested on the basis of the rights contained in the Universal Declaration of Human Rights. For its legal basis, see n. 30. The UDHR, like the ICESCR, recognises the right to an adequate standard of living, a right from which the Human Rights Council has stated that the right to safe drinking water and sanitation is derived; see HRC Res. 15/9, para. 3.

73 CESCR, Reporting Guidelines (2008), para. 9.

There is a legitimate concern that conditionality ostensibly based on human rights could be misused by donors to advance their own political interests. This has been one of the primary concerns voiced by some developing countries when resisting the integration of human rights standards into the development operations of the United Nations.[74] However, the ICESCR limits the range of conditions (e.g. in relation to privatisation) that a donor may impose to those consistent with human standards. In addition, as discussed in section 5 below, the ICESCR may in some circumstances limit a donor's ability to withdraw or reduce aid to a particular country or even to fail to increase its overall level of aid. Thus, it imposes obligations both on donors and developing countries.

There is a good case for donors and developing countries to establish rules and mechanisms to limit the possibilities of abuse of conditionality by donors. In the interim, as a policy matter, all States should call for adherence to the process-based steps established by international development declarations. These require donors and developing countries to work towards a limited number of donor conditions, publicly stated, and efforts to ensure participation of all donors in order to ensure that conditions are harmonised.[75] Harmonisation of conditions is possible by using Sector-Wide Approaches to Planning (SWAPs), agreed between a country and its main donors, which set out domestic State and donor commitments, including financial allocations, processes for aligning donor action with country goals and agreement on the type of assistance to be provided.[76]

An innovative step was taken by the Kenyan Ministry of Water and Irrigation (MWI) in 2007, with the support of Germany's development agencies, to include human rights explicitly in national water resource management and water supply and sanitation standards, to propose steps to increase affordability of access and levels of participation and to establish a complaints system overseen by the Water Services Regulatory Board.[77] On this basis, the MWI argued that its reforms reflected the right to water and stated that 'As human rights are universal principles, the MWI expects donors to align themselves to these by harmonising their actions and programmes to the

[74] M. Darrow and L. Arbour, 'The Pillar of Glass: Human Rights in the Development Operations of the United Nations', *American Journal of International Law*, Vol. 103, No. 2 (2009) pp. 446–501, at 482–483.

[75] Accra Agenda for Action, para. 25.

[76] See, for example, Government of Kenya and Development Partners, 'Water Sector in Kenya, Sector Wide Approach to Planning, Partnership Principles' (Nairobi 2006).

[77] Ministry of Water and Irrigation, Kenya, *Water Sector Reform in Kenya and the Human Right to Water* (Nairobi: MWI, 2007), pp. 9–12.

sector policies and strategies'.[78] This is an important approach as it shows that a developing country could point to its compliance with human rights standards as a reason why donors should provide support through government channels, rather than through donor-administered programmes or non-governmental organisations (NGOs).

This section has addressed direct project implementation and support given by donors to developing country governments. It is worth noting that a donor's obligation to ensure that aid is provided consistently with human rights standards also applies when donors provide aid through private actors, such as corporations and NGOs. In addition, donors have further obligations in two circumstances. First, a State is responsible for the conduct of private actors if they are acting under its instructions or under its direction and control.[79] A donor is therefore required to ensure that private actors that it has contracted to provide services under its direction and control respect human rights. Second, General Comment No. 15 specifies that States should 'prevent their own citizens and companies from violating the right to water in other countries'.[80] Thus, where the private actor in question has the nationality of the donor, the donor has an obligation to take steps within its jurisdiction to the extent they are necessary to ensure that such private actors do not interfere with the right to water extraterritorially. However, the scope of this obligation to protect is not assessed here, as it deserves detailed analysis.

## 4 STATE OBLIGATIONS TO ENSURE COMPLIANCE BY INTERNATIONAL ORGANISATIONS WITH THE RIGHT TO WATER

The previous section has addressed the obligations of bilateral development agencies. What about multilateral development agencies? Can the member States of these organisations be held accountable for abuses of the right to water carried out by such organisations? General Comment No. 15 observes that:

> States parties should ensure that their actions as members of international organizations take due account of the right to water. Accordingly, States parties that are members of international financial institutions, notably the International Monetary Fund, the World Bank, and regional development banks, should take steps to ensure that the right to water is taken into account in their lending policies, credit agreements and other international measures.[81]

[78] Ibid., p. 5. [79] ILC Articles on State Responsibility, Article 8.
[80] General Comment No. 15, para. 33. [81] Ibid., at para. 36.

In several concluding observations following the ICESCR periodic reporting process, the CESCR has called on developed countries to do all that they can to ensure that the actions of international organisations conform to the ICESCR.[82] By requiring that a State 'does all it can', this implicitly requires that States refrain from actions that will lead an international organisation to interfere with the right, and that States take positive measures to ensure that the international organisation respect the right and that its programmes and policy advice is consistent with the right to water and other ESC rights.

A State's request to its representatives on the Board of an international organisation to vote in favour of a policy or programme that would interfere with any person's right to water would violate that State's obligation to respect the right. A State's request to the staff of an international organisation to carry out an interference with any person's right to water would have the same effect. Such responsibility can only arise if there is a significant link between the conduct of the member State seeking to avoid compliance with one of its own obligations and that of the international organisation.[83] States may not provide funding for a particular project or programme managed by an international organisation that would foreseeably interfere with a person's right to water and that does not contain the necessary safeguards.[84]

States are required not only to refrain from supporting interferences with the right to water but also to take those steps within their ability to oppose policies and programmes that interfere with the right to water and to promote due diligence measures by the international organisation to prevent such interferences. An example of a due diligence measure is an instruction to staff of the international organisation that all policies recommended to governments must be consistent with international human rights standards. Another example is the development or revision of relevant performance standards to

[82] For example, CESCR, *Concluding Observations of the Committee on Economic, Social and Cultural Rights: Germany*, UN Doc. E/C.12/1/Add.68 (2001), at para. 31. In response to this recommendation, Germany's subsequent periodic report stated that Germany 'used its influence with the World Bank to ensure that its decisions and commitments were in tune with the undertakings entered into by the States parties'. See Implementation of the Covenant on Economic, Social and Cultural Rights, *Fifth Periodic Report: Germany*, UN Doc. E/C.12/DEU/5 (2010), at para. 16.

[83] International Law Commission, 'Draft Articles on Responsibility of International Organizations with Commentaries', *Report of the International Law Commission on the Work of its 63rd session* (2011) UN Doc A/66/10, Article 61 (including commentary). The ILC concluded its work on the topic with its adoption of these articles in 2011.

[84] According to the ILC, a State that aids or assists an international organisation in the commission of an internationally wrongful act is responsible for doing so, if it does so with knowledge of the circumstances of the internationally wrongful act and the act would be internationally wrongful if committed by that State; ibid., Article 58(1).

ensure that only projects designed and implemented consistently with international human rights law are supported by the international organisation. In the event of a foreseeable interference with the right to water, responsibility would be jointly attributed to the States that did not propose or support reasonable steps to prevent the interference in question.

With regard to the World Bank specifically, eight States have representatives on the Bank's Board of Directors, who are accountable only to their States. These States are therefore entirely responsible for the actions and omissions of their respective representatives. Other States in groups of between three and 21 States jointly elect a representative to the Bank's Board. These States can be held responsible for any failure to request their representative to act in accordance with the ICESCR, even if that representative is not their national. The legal obligation here is not restricted to creditor States. Debtor countries are required to take reasonable steps to use their representation, however limited, within the Bank to seek to ensure compliance with the ICESCR.

The Articles of Agreement of the two development lending arms of the World Bank, the International Bank for Reconstruction and Development (IBRD) and the International Development Association, require that the Bank and its officials are not influenced by the political character of any State and that only impartially weighed economic considerations shall be relevant to the Bank's decisions. Historically, these provisions have been cited as a reason why the World Bank may not address human rights in its decision making. However, in 2006, the Senior Vice President and General Counsel of the World Bank at the time defined the prohibition on political interference as applying to partisan politics, thus requiring that the Bank refrain from endorsing or mandating a particular form of government, political bloc or political ideology. He stated: 'taking into account, where appropriate, human rights issues and members' international human rights obligations does not contravene the Articles' prohibition of political interference'.[85] Furthermore, 'the Articles of Agreement permit, and in some cases, require, the Bank to recognize the human rights dimensions of its development policies and activities since it is now evident that human rights are an intrinsic part of the Bank's mission'.[86]

85 R. Daniño, 'Legal Opinion on Human Rights and the Work of the World Bank' 27 January 2006, at para. 14.

86 Ibid., at para. 25. Daniño's opinion was endorsed by his successor, A. Palacio, 'The Way Forward: Human Rights and the World Bank', *Development Outreach* (World Bank Institute, 2006), pp. 35–37, at 36. However, Daniño's legal opinion was not presented for approval to the Executive Board of the World Bank, which has the authority to interpret the Articles of Agreement, as the senior management felt that the Board would be unable to reach a

The primary obstacle to ensuring compliance with extraterritorial obligations by World Bank members is political rather than legal. Explicit attention to human rights by the Bank in lending decisions is controversial and often simply equated to making provision of financing conditional upon human rights performance of the State receiving aid. There is not a majority of votes in the World Bank in favour of linking loans and grants to human rights performance, and even countries promoting considerations of human rights in the Bank, such as Sweden, have stated they do not believe that the Bank should have the role of 'policing' State compliance with human rights obligations, but rather that it should assist States in implementation of human rights obligations at their request.[87] Such views are consistent with the ICESCR only in that States and international organisations are not required to put pressure on other States to implement the ICESCR. This is different from the State obligation to ensure that international organisations of which they are members do not interfere and are not complicit in interfering with the right to water, and that the aid and policy advice provided by international organisations is consistent with the right to water. In addition, integration of human rights into development work is resisted by many staff in the World Bank and in other UN organisations, who take the view that attention to human rights unnecessarily politicises development cooperation and that they do not have a mandate to work on human rights.[88] The World Bank's environmental and social safeguards state that '… the World Bank's activities support the realization of human rights expressed in the Universal Declaration of Human Rights. Through the projects it finances, and in a manner consistent with its Articles of Agreement, the World Bank seeks to avoid adverse impacts and will continue to support its member countries as they strive to progressively achieve their human rights commitments'.[89] These safeguards therefore artfully use human rights terms, but fail to commit the Bank to refrain from causing or contributing human rights abuses that result from its activities.

consensus on this issue; see G. Sarfaty, 'Why Culture Matters in International Institutions: The Marginality of Human Rights at the World Bank', *American Journal of International Law*, Vol. 103, No. 4 (2009), pp. 647–683, at 665–667.

[87] Government of Sweden, 'The World Bank Takes on the Human Rights Agenda', 10 October 2006. This document was previously available www.manskligarattigheter.gov.se/, accessed 31 July 2011, and is on file with the author.

[88] Russell, 'International Organizations and Human Rights', pp. 11–12.

[89] World Bank, Environment and Social Framework, 4 August 2016, Vision for Sustainable Development, para. 3.

## 5 OBLIGATIONS TO FULFIL THE RIGHT TO WATER BEYOND BORDERS

The extraterritorial obligation to fulfil the right to water raises many questions for development cooperation. What forms of aid should be provided? Is a donor obliged to provide a particular amount of aid? Does a donor have complete discretion as to whom such aid can be provided? The CESCR's guidance is framed in broad terms. General Comment No. 15 states:

> Depending on the availability of resources, States should facilitate realization of the right to water in other countries, for example through provision of water resources, financial and technical assistance, and provide the necessary aid when required.... International assistance should be provided in a manner that is consistent with the Covenant and other human rights standards, and sustainable and culturally appropriate. The economically developed States parties have a special responsibility and interest to assist the poorer developing States in this regard.[90]

The CESCR has indicated that States also have an obligation to facilitate the realisation of the right to water by ensuring that relevant international standards and policies are conducive to its realisation. General Comment No. 15 indicates that 'States parties should ensure that the right to water is given due attention in international agreements and, to that end, should consider the development of further legal instruments'.[91] The CESCR has also indicated that the realisation of ESC rights requires that measures are urgently taken to remove global structural obstacles facing developing countries, including 'the absence of an equitable multilateral trade, investment and financial system'.[92] It is increasingly clear that development cooperation alone will not secure economic development and poverty reduction for developing countries, and that other forms of international cooperation are required for this purpose.[93]

[90] General Comment No. 15, para. 34. [91] Ibid., para. 35.

[92] CESCR, *Poverty and the International Covenant on Economic, Social and Cultural Rights* (Twenty-fifth session, 2001), UN Doc. E/C.12/2001/10 (2001), at para. 21.

[93] See for example, P. Collier, *The Bottom Billion: Why the Poorest CountriesAre Failing and What Can Be Done About It* (Oxford: OUP, 2007), pp. 124–172. The Center for Global Development also assesses measures likely to assist development in addition to aid, such as trade, development research, contribution to internationally approved peacekeeping missions and protection of global sea lanes: D. Roodman, *The Commitment to Development Index: 2013 Edition (Technical Paper)*, (Washington, D.C.: Center for Global Development, 2013).

The CESCR has also made clear that States that are unable to ensure ESC rights for their own people are obliged to actively seek necessary assistance and to ensure its use in a manner that will lead to realisation of ESC rights.[94]

### 5.1 *Quality of Aid*

Article 2(1) of the ICESCR requires States to take steps to realise ESC rights 'to the maximum of available resources'. States are not required to allocate all their resources towards the realisation of ESC rights, but there are limits on a State's discretion to allocate resources, which are considered in section 5.2 below.

With respect to territorial obligations, the CESCR has stated that 'Where the available resources are demonstrably inadequate, the obligation remains for a State party to ensure the widest possible enjoyment of economic, social and cultural rights under the prevailing circumstances'.[95] The CESCR's practice in reviewing State reports demonstrates that once a State has allocated resources towards social expenditures related to ESC rights, such as health and education, it is required to use these in an effective manner towards the realisation of ESC rights.[96] This requirement could also be adapted and applied to development cooperation. Once a donor has allocated resources for purposes related to the realisation of these rights (such as poverty reduction), it can be held accountable for providing such assistance in a manner aimed at achieving the widest possible enjoyment of ESC rights.[97]

94 See, for example, CESCR, *Concluding Observations of the Committee on Economic, Social and Cultural Rights: Democratic Republic of the Congo*, UN Doc. E/C.12/COD/CO/4 (2009), at paras. 16–17; CESCR, *Concluding Observations of the Committee on Economic, Social and Cultural Rights: Chad*, UN Doc. E/C.12/TCD/CO/3 (2009), at paras. 16, 18, 26, 31, 32 and 37; CESCR, *Concluding Observations of the Committee on Economic, Social and Cultural Rights: Sri Lanka*, UN Doc. E/C.12/TCD/CO/3E/C.12/LKA/CO/2–4 (2010), at para 12. See also Sepúlveda, 'Obligations of International Assistance and Cooperation', pp. 290–291.

95 CESCR, *An Evaluation of the Obligation to Take Steps to the 'Maximum of Available Resources' under an Optional Protocol to the Covenant* (Thirty-eighth session, 2007), UN Doc. E/C.12/2007/1, at para. 4.

96 M. Sepúlveda, *The Nature of the Obligations under the International Covenant on Economic, Social and Cultural Rights* (Antwerp: Intersentia, 2003), p. 315.

97 The obligation to provide aid consistently with the ICESCR and other human rights standards implicates both the extraterritorial obligations to respect and to fulfill ESC rights.
The significant overlap between these two obligations is only problematic if one takes the position that there are legally binding extraterritorial obligations to respect but not to fulfil ESC rights. The classification of obligations into duties to respect, protect and fulfil rights should be seen only as a helpful guide to understanding the State's obligations in particular contexts, rather than entirely separate legal obligations; that is, as 'ladders to be climbed and left behind,

Any assessment of a donor's compliance with its obligations should take into account the fact that a donor may only take actions in another country with the consent of that country's government. A donor can therefore only be held responsible for its own conduct, including its decisions as to the purposes to which it provides aid, the terms on which such aid is provided and the policy advice it provides. Therefore the analysis in Sections 3.2 and 3.3 also applies to circumstances in which a donor is attempting to fulfil the right to water extraterritorially in partnership with a developing country government or through the provision of funds to that government.

States are explicitly required to prioritise the realisation of minimum essential levels of ESC rights in their international assistance policies. In several General Comments, the CESCR stated that it 'wishes to emphasize that it is particularly incumbent on States parties and other actors in a position to assist, to provide international assistance and cooperation, especially economic and technical, to enable developing countries to fulfil their core obligations'.[98] The CESCR has also stated that:

> [C]ore human rights obligations create national obligations for all States, and international responsibilities for developed States, as well as others that are 'in a position to assist'.... When grouped together, the core obligations establish an international minimum threshold that all developmental policies should be designed to respect. In accordance with General Comment No. 14, it is particularly incumbent on all those who can assist, to help developing countries respect this international minimum threshold. If a national or international anti-poverty strategy does not reflect this minimum threshold, it is inconsistent with the legally binding obligations of the State party.[99]

Thus, donors may not provide funding directed at the fulfilment of non-core obligations in preference to funding aimed at core obligations without reasonable justification. This rule can be significant where donor funding is provided only for high-standard and high-cost interventions with the result that the benefits are only accessible to wealthier groups of society.[100] For instance,

not monuments to be caressed and polished'. H. Shue, *Basic Rights: Subsistence, Affluence and U.S. Foreign Policy*, 2nd edition (Princeton: Princeton University Press, 1996), p. 160. See also I. E. Koch, 'Dichotomies, Trichotomies or Waves of Duties?', Vol. 5, No. 1 (2005), *Human Rights Law Review*, pp. 81–103, at 91.

98 For example, General Comment No. 15, para. 38, General Comment No. 14, para. 45.

99 CESCR, *Poverty Statement*, paras. 16, 20.

100 See also General Comment No. 15 at para. 14, which states that a policy to disproportionately favour expensive water supply services and facilities that are often accessible only to a small, privileged fraction of the population, rather than investing in services and facilities that benefit a far larger part of the population, can lead to discrimination that may not be overt.

where large numbers of people are without basic access to water, a focus only on construction of household piped water connections is often likely to benefit those who already have basic access. The Special Rapportuer on the rights to water and sanitation has recently raised concern that development aid for basic systems (used mainly for urban poor and rural populations) is consistently less than for large systems, for example 24 per cent verses 50 per cent respectively in 2013.[101] In many circumstances, low-cost measures, such as public water access points, would often reach those without basic access and allow the available resources to benefit a larger number of people than would otherwise be the case. For example, a World Bank project in Bangladesh to provide piped water supplies in rural areas required a per person counterpart contribution from prospective users that was equivalent to two and a half times the monthly income for the poorest one-third of people in rural areas. In effect, the poorest were excluded from this project.[102]

The distinction between core and non-core obligations is not often clear-cut. For example, funding for expensive water and sewage treatment systems is often likely to be required to realise minimum essential levels of the right to water as well as the needs of those who already have secure access to water through household connections. It will be difficult to assess whether funding in such contexts is consistent with the donor's legal obligations by looking at outcomes alone. It is important to also assess whether the donor is making a good-faith attempt to prioritise core obligations. For example, if a donor's policy or strategy for providing financial and technical aid for water supply services does not aim to target the needs of those without access to minimum essential levels of water, this would establish a presumption that the donor has not taken an essential first step in prioritising core obligations.

A related qualitative requirement is that States providing aid not only must refrain from engaging in or supporting discrimination[103] but also should ensure that the needs of disadvantaged groups are addressed in their international cooperation measures.[104] It would be impossible for a water supply project to prioritise a minimum essential level of water in an area, for example, without ensuring that the project takes into account the needs of

[101] Report of the Special Rapporteur on the rights to water and sanitation to the UN General Assembly (2016), para. 22.

[102] Water Aid, *Getting to Boiling Point*, p. 18.

[103] CESCR, *General Comment No. 20: Non-Discrimination in Economic, Social and Cultural Rights* (Forty-second session, 2009), UN Doc. E/C.12/GC/20 (2009), at para. 14.

[104] This point was made in relation to international assistance for the right to adequate housing. CESCR, *General Comment No. 4: The Right to Adequate Housing* (Sixth session, 1991), UN Doc E/1992/23 (1991), at para. 19.

children – and thereby ensure that water pumps or taps are set at an appropriate level – or, in regard to urban areas, without incorporating informal settlements into water supply projects.[105]

## 5.2 *Quantity of Aid*

The ICESCR does not specify the proportion of a State's resources that a State must allocate towards the realisation of ESC rights within a State's territory and beyond its borders. The extraterritorial obligation in the ICESCR is one of 'international cooperation and assistance' rather than an obligation to ensure equal realisation of ESC rights globally. A State therefore bears greater responsibilities to people within its borders than those outside. The extent of this priority is not defined in the ICESCR. However, references to international assistance in the ICESCR would be meaningless if a State had absolute discretion to prioritise territorial obligations over extraterritorial obligations. If a State had such discretion, it would be able to use all its available resources to realise ESC rights to the greatest possible extent territorially (e.g. dramatically increasing the proportion of teachers to students in publicly funded education) with the result that it had no resources remaining for international assistance. Thus, it would be helpful for the CESCR to develop objective criteria to determine whether a State has allocated a reasonable proportion of its available resources towards the extraterritorial fulfilment of ESC rights. In order to do so, it could rely on the approaches that it has used to assess the allocation of resources towards the territorial fulfilment of ESC rights, to the extent that they are appropriate to apply by analogy to an extraterritorial context.

The ICESCR does not provide guidance on what proportion of a State's resources must be allocated to ESC rights in general or to specific ESC rights. The CESCR has indicated that it will 'respect the margin of appreciation of the State party to determine the optimum use of its resources'.[106] However, it has developed criteria to assess in a contextual manner whether a country has allocated resources towards the territorial fulfilment of ESC rights to the full extent of its ability to do so.

[105] COHRE, AAAS, SDC and UN-HABITAT, *Manual on the Right to Water and Sanitation* (Geneva: COHRE, 2008), p. 67.

[106] CESCR, *Resources Statement*, para. 12. This statement was made with reference to complaints under the Optional Protocol, but the criteria contained in it could also apply to the periodic reporting process.

The CESCR will assess whether measures taken by a State are 'adequate' or 'reasonable' taking into account factors such as:

> the extent to which the measures taken were deliberate, concrete and targeted towards the fulfilment of economic, social and cultural rights; ... whether the State party exercised its discretion in a non-discriminatory and non-arbitrary manner; ... where several policy options are available, whether the State party adopts the option that least restricts Covenant rights; ... whether the steps had taken into account the precarious situation of disadvantaged and marginalized individuals and groups and, ... whether they prioritized grave situations or situations of risk.[107]

The CESCR has also indicated that it would use objective criteria to assess a State's claims that a retrogressive step is explained by resources constraints. The listed criteria include a country's level of development, its current economic situation and whether a country has attempted to use low-cost options to realise ESC rights.[108] In the periodic reporting process, the CESCR has on occasion used two relatively specific indicators to assess whether a State's allocation of resources is consistent with the ICESCR. First, it has compared the proportion of a country's budget spent on a particular sector, such as health care, against corresponding amounts spent by other States at the same level of development. Where the percentage of the national budget is considerably lower than that of another State at a similar level of development, this has been treated by the CESCR as indicative of the non-use of the maximum of available resources.[109] Second, it has noted with concern circumstances in which a State has allocated significantly more funds to areas unrelated to the ICESCR as compared to those related to the ICESCR (or other international human rights obligations), for example, military defence as compared to health or education and ornamental public works over housing projects.[110]

Building on the CESCR's practice assessing resource allocation for territorial obligations, this sub-section outlines four potential criteria that could be utilised in combination with each other to assess the quantity of a State's development aid for compliance with the ICESCR.

The first criterion could be whether a State has carried out a process to assess its ability to fulfil ESC rights extraterritorially, assessing its available resources against the resources required to meet ESC rights for its people, to

[107] Ibid., para. 8.

[108] Ibid., para. 10. The CESCR has elaborated further criteria to assess any retrogressive steps in *General Comment No. 19: The Right to Social Security* (Thirty-ninth session, 2007), UN Doc. E/C.12/GC/19 (2008), at para. 42.

[109] Sepúlveda, *Nature of ICESCR Obligations*, p. 317.

[110] Ibid., pp. 317–318.

meet other international law obligations (e.g. under international environmental law) and to achieve objectives set out in national law and policy. The CESCR has indicated that each State is required to develop a detailed plan of action for the progressive implementation of ESC rights and to establish clearly stated and carefully targeted policies to reflect its obligations under the ICESCR. One objective of the ICESCR's periodic reporting process is to demonstrate that such principled policy making has in fact been undertaken.[111] A failure by the State to demonstrate that it had carried out such a process in relation to extraterritorial obligations would lead to a presumption that the State has failed to comply with the ICESCR.

A second criterion could be whether a State has achieved internationally agreed targets and unilateral commitments for provision of development aid. The most important target is the 0.7 per cent Gross National Project (GNP) development aid target, set by the UN General Assembly in 1970, which states:

> Each economically advanced country will progressively increase its official development assistance to the developing countries and will exert its best efforts to reach a minimum net amount of 0.7 percent of its gross national product at market prices by the middle of the decade.[112]

This target was reaffirmed at successive UN Summits. In 2005, most developed countries committed for the first time to actually meet the 0.7 per cent target, as opposed to simply promising to make efforts to do so.[113]

The CESCR routinely recommends or urges developed States to increase international assistance and to set a timeframe to meet the 0.7 per cent target of GNP to be directed towards international aid.[114] It has not indicated the basis for calling on States to meet this target and whether it represents the full extent of the obligation to extraterritorially fulfil ESC rights through the provision of resources. However, it can be suggested that since the 0.7 per cent GNP target has been agreed to by all States parties to the ICESCR, it can be understood as an indication as to what would be a reasonable allocation of a developed country's resources towards development aid in order to meet its international assistance obligations.

The 0.7 per cent aid target is not legally binding, and therefore a State that fails to meet it would not necessarily be infringing its obligations under the

[111] CESCR, *General comment No. 1: Reporting by States parties* (Third session, 1989), UN Doc. E/1989/22 (1989), at para. 3.

[112] UNGA Res. 2626 (XXV) (19 November 1970), at para. 43.

[113] This commitment was noted in the 2008 *Doha Declaration on Financing for Development*, para. 42.

[114] Sepúlveda, 'Obligations of International Assistance and Cooperation', p. 287.

ICESCR if it can demonstrate that it does not have the ability to allocate 0.7 per cent of GNP to development aid in view of its financial circumstances. The CESCR has indicated that events such as recessions, and 'other serious claims on the State party's limited resources' resulting, for example, from recent natural disasters or armed conflict would be taken into account in explaining retrogressive steps by a State.[115] Such criteria might also explain why a State's obligations in particular circumstances are less than that set out in international benchmarks.[116]

A third criterion could be whether the level of aid provided is reasonable in comparison to peer States. The proportion of aid provided by a developed country can be compared to the average proportion of Gross National Income (GNI) provided by developed countries to aid, which was 0.3 per cent in 2015, and the highest level of aid provided, which in 2015 was 1.4 per cent by Sweden.[117] A State claiming that its inability to meet an international aid target discussed in the second criterion above is due to a recession could be compared to similarly affected States in order to determine the credibility of this defence. As with the second criterion, peer State comparisons may create a presumption that a State is not meeting its obligations, which a State would have to justify. It might be suggested that a peer State criterion could also be used to assess aid levels provided by developing countries. However, a developing country that is unable to fulfil minimum core obligations for its own people would be fully justified in prioritising its resources on meeting this obligation over providing international assistance, even if States at a similar level of development are providing significant amounts of international aid. Therefore a developing country facing such circumstances should not be obligated to provide resource-intensive levels of international aid.

A fourth criterion could be whether a State has progressively increased the extent of its assistance as its available resources increase and whether it has avoided retrogressive steps without cause. Thus, a State's current performance can be compared to its past performance. Craven has suggested that a State can be viewed as not complying with its ICESCR obligations if the amount of aid it provides to other countries has declined

[115] CESCR, *Resources Statement*, para. 10.

[116] For further analysis, see A. Khalfan 'Division of Responsibility', in M. Langford, M. Scheinin, W. Vandenhole and W. van Genugten (eds.), *Global Justice, State Duties: The Extra-Territorial Scope of Economic, Social and Cultural Rights in International Law* (Cambridge: Cambridge University Press, 2013), pp. 320–330.

[117] These figures are contained in OECD, *Development Co-operation Report 2016* (Paris: OECD, 2016), pp. 152 and 263.

over a number of years.[118] There is a presumption that any retrogressive step is contrary to the ICESCR, and the burden shifts to a State to show that it has fully used available resources.[119] A donor would also need to justify its actions when it cancels or suspends aid to a particular country or programme for reasons that are not based on a reasonable assessment of levels of priority or aid effectiveness, for example, if development aid to a developing country is cancelled because it is not supporting security-related initiatives proposed by the donor.

The analysis thus far has only addressed the total proportion of aid that should be provided to ESC rights in general. There do not appear to be any limits on a donor's discretion as to which ESC rights it chooses to focus its assistance as long as such aid aims to realise minimum essential levels of such rights.

The extraterritorial obligation to fulfil ESC rights is owed to individuals whose ESC rights are unfulfilled for any reason. Where fulfilment of an ESC right requires international cooperation in the form of new or revised international regulations – for example, a rule that international development organisations must prioritise realisation of core obligations in their programmes and policy advice – all States (including both developed and developing countries) represented in the relevant international institutions are required to support necessary reforms.[120] However, the legal obligation is different where fulfilment of ESC rights requires the provision of international assistance or other measures directed at particular States or groups of people. It is difficult to show that the ICESCR creates a legally binding obligation upon a State to provide any particular form of assistance to any specific other State.[121] No UN body or any group of governments has claimed that an obligation of this nature exists.[122] Thus, while States can be held to account under the ICESCR for the level of aid provided, and for ensuring that it is provided in a manner that is consistent with the ICESCR (e.g. by prioritising minimum core obligations), they normally have significant discretion to determine where to target the benefit of their international aid. As the need for

[118] M. Craven, *The International Covenant on Economic, Social and Cultural Rights: A Perspective on Its Development* (Oxford: Clarendon, 1995), p. 150.

[119] CESCR, *General Comment No.* 3, para. 9.

[120] This obligation is contingent on the availability of resources where the application of the regulations would require significant amounts of State resources.

[121] Alston and Quinn, 'The Nature and Scope of States Parties' Obligations', pp. 186–191.

[122] P. Alston, 'Ships Passing in the Night: The Current State of the Human Rights and Development Debate as Seen Through the Lens of the Millennium Development Goals', *Human Rights Quarterly*, Vol. 27, No. 3 (2005), pp. 755–829, at 777.

assistance globally outstrips the availability of resources of any one State, a State can discharge its extraterritorial obligations to provide aid under the ICESCR by helping to realise the ESC rights of some rights holders, but not all of them. Therefore, in most circumstances, an individual could not make a claim against a particular State other than their own.

## 6 CONCLUSIONS

The legal obligations set out by the CESCR relevant to development cooperation are defined in broad terms. There remain many questions that cannot be dealt with in a single chapter. Are there any limitations on tied aid? Should the target to provide at least 0.15 of GNI as development aid to the least developed countries be treated as a target for the fulfilment of ESC rights? Is there an obligation to coordinate aid efforts in order to ensure that the aid is provided to the worst-off? Further analysis of these and many other complex issues is required.[123]

This chapter has shown that by applying the ICESCR to policy making and practice in the field of development cooperation, it is possible to ascertain standards of conduct that allow for greater accountability of donors to rights holders and that are feasible to implement. Such accountability can only help achieve the stated objectives of development cooperation, and this is of significant importance at a time when difficult questions are being asked about the effectiveness of development aid. Donors can and should move beyond experimenting with ad hoc 'rights-based approaches' as good ideas to enhance aid effectiveness and should now be asking serious questions about their compliance with their human rights obligations, including with respect to the right to water. Attention by development agencies to their human rights obligations in their daily work, and external scrutiny of these actions, is critical to ensure that development assistance succeeds in making the greatest possible contribution to the rights of people living in poverty.

[123] The issues in this chapter will be analysed in greater depth in a book-length publication currently in preparation.

12

# The Occupied Palestinian Territory

## *Challenges to Progressive Realisation*

LARA EL-JAZAIRI[*]

### 1 INTRODUCTION

The State is the traditional human rights duty bearer and primarily responsible for respecting, protecting and fulfilling the human rights of those under its jurisdiction. Under the International Covenant on Economic, Social and Cultural Rights (ICESCR), the State has the obligation to take steps 'to the maximum of its available resources, with a view to achieving progressively the full realization of the rights recognised in the present Covenant by all appropriate means'.[1] Arguably, this includes the human right to water and sanitation.[2]

However, within the context of the occupied Palestinian territory (OPT), a number of challenges arise with regard to this conception. Palestine is not a recognised State, and the Palestinian National Authority (PNA) is not a party to the ICESCR. Yet, the PNA, as the actor mandated to regulate the water and sanitation sector in the occupied Palestinian territory, has expressed its commitment to realising the human right to water for the Palestinian people, notably through its explicit inclusion in Water Law No. 3 (2002) and the inclusion of a number of human rights principles in water sector policy and strategies.[3] However, the question remains as to what extent the PNA can realise this right within the context of the occupation.

* Lara El-Jazairi was formerly the Programme Policy and Communications Coordinator for Oxfam GB in the Occupied Palestinian Territory and Israel. The chapter was written in 2011.

1 International Covenant on Economic, Social and Cultural Rights (adopted 16 December 1966, entered into force 3 January 1976), 993 UNTS 3 (ICESCR), Article 2(1).

2 For a discussion on this argument, see Chapter 1 by Langford and Russell. In regard to a right to sanitation specifically, see Chapter 10 by Langford, Bartram and Roaf.

3 Palestinian Water Authority, Water Law No. 3, approved by the Legislative Council on 18 February 2002.

This chapter is divided into six sections. Section 2 sets out the Palestinian institutional and legislative framework for water and sanitation provision. Section 3 examines the obligations of an occupying power in relation to water and sanitation. Section 4 examines the impact of the occupation and Israeli policies and practices on the realisation of the right to water and sanitation in the occupied Palestinian territory. It argues that the ability of the Palestinian Authority to progressively realise the right has been considerably obstructed. In light of this reality, Section 5 of this chapter explores the extent of the obligations of both the occupying power and the international community to realise the human right to water and sanitation of the Palestinian people. Section 6 provides a conclusion.

## 2 THE PALESTINIAN NATIONAL AUTHORITY (PNA) AND LEGISLATIVE RECOGNITION OF THE RIGHT TO WATER

The PNA was created in 1994, following the Oslo Accords, to govern parts of the West Bank (excluding occupied East Jerusalem) and the Gaza Strip on an interim basis for five years, during which time a permanent settlement was to be negotiated leading to an independent Palestinian State.[4] Under the terms of The Israeli-Palestinian Interim Agreement on the West Bank and Gaza Strip (Oslo II: 1995), the West Bank was divided into three jurisdictional areas. Area A, mainly urban centres, was placed under the full control of the PNA; Area B was placed under PNA civil administration, but Israeli security control; and Area C, which covers the Jordan Valley region, settlements and their surrounding areas, remained under full Israeli control and constitutes approximately 61 per cent of West Bank territory. In the Gaza Strip, the PNA was granted administrative control over all areas except the settlement blocks and military bases, which were removed following Israel's unilateral disengagement from the Strip in 2005.

In 1995, the Palestinian Water Authority (PWA) was established, which acts under the direct supervision of the President of the PNA. The PWA is the administrative body responsible for water resources and their management and development in Palestine. While Palestine is not a recognised State and the PNA is not a party to the ICESCR, the PA Water Law No. 3 (2002)

[4] The Oslo Accords, or Declaration of Principles on Interim Self-Government Arrangements, were signed between the government of Israel and the Palestinian Liberation Organization in 1993 and set out the framework for future negotiations between the Israelis and Palestinians with a view to resolve the ongoing conflict. So far, negotiations between the parties have not reached a resolution.

explicitly recognises water as a human right. Article 3(3) provides that 'Every person shall have the right to obtain his needs of water of a suitable quality for his use, and every official or private institution that provides water services must take the necessary steps to ensure this right and to make the necessary plans for developing these services'.[5] The National Water Policy reaffirms that 'all citizens have a right to water of good quality for personal consumption at costs they can afford', ensures public participation in water management, and promotes the sustainable development of resources.[6] The PWA is also mandated to coordinate and supervise water service providers in the West Bank and Gaza Strip and takes charge of donor coordination in the water and sanitation sector. Therefore, it can be assumed that, as the PNA is the main actor for the water and sanitation sector in the occupied Palestinian territory, it holds primary responsibility for respecting, protecting and fulfilling the right to water for the Palestinian people, and by assumption the right to sanitation, even though it is not explicitly recognised in water legislation.[7] Yet, the ability of the PNA to progressively realise the right has been significantly eroded due to Israeli policy and practice in the occupied Palestine territory (OPT).

## 3 THE OBLIGATIONS OF AN OCCUPYING POWER IN RELATION TO WATER AND SANITATION

The laws governing belligerent occupation applicable to the OPT include The Hague Regulations of 1907, the Fourth Geneva Convention of 1949 and customary laws of belligerent occupation.[8] These laws are intended to provide some protection to the civilian population living under the control of a foreign military power. While under military occupation, the occupying power

5 Palestinian Water Law No. 3, Ramallah, 17 July 2002.

6 Palestinian Water Authority, *Coping with Water Scarcity* (Ramallah, 2007), p. 2.

7 While the PWA is the planner and regulator for the water and sanitation sector in the occupied Palestinian territory, a number of other actors play key roles, including the National Water Council, the Bulk Utilities, the Joint Service Councils and the municipalities. However, responsibilities are fragmented.

8 The Israeli Supreme Court of Justice in *Ayyoub* v. *Minister of Defence* ruled that The Hague Regulations are customary law and therefore automatically part of municipal law and justiciable in Israel. Many of the provisions of the Geneva Conventions are considered customary international law, and the International Court of Justice has advised that Israel is bound by both the Fourth Geneva Convention and The Hague Regulations in the OPT. See International Court of Justice (ICJ), *Legal Consequences of the Construction of a Wall in the Occupied Palestinian Territory*, 9 July 2004 (Advisory Opinion), ICJ Report 2004, para. 89. Customary laws are laws that have developed through State practice and the opinion of the international community and are binding on all States, regardless of whether they have ratified a treaty or not.

exercises control over the territory, and the powers of legitimate government are suspended; the temporary nature of occupation means that no change in sovereignty occurs. Therefore, while the occupying power may create laws deemed necessary to realise its military objectives and to maintain and restore public order and safety, it may not make changes to institutions, laws or administrative practices in place prior to the occupation that go beyond this scope. Article 43 of The Hague Regulations of 1907 provides that 'The authority of the legitimate power having in fact passed into the hands of the occupant, the latter shall take all the measures in his power to restore, and ensure, as far as possible, public order and safety, while respecting, unless absolutely prevented, the laws in force in the country'.[9] Moreover, while being the de facto administrator of the occupied territory, as opposed to the legitimate sovereign, under Article 55 of The Hague Regulations, an occupying power may not utilise the resources of the occupied territory for the benefit of its civilian population, and utilisation of the resources is strictly limited to military necessity and must not exceed normal use.[10] The Hague Regulations further prohibit the confiscation of private property (Article 46) and pillage (Article 47).

Under international humanitarian law, an occupying power is responsible for the welfare of the civilian population and must ensure that civilians are provided with or allowed to secure the basics for survival including food, water, medical supplies and shelter. Internees and/or protected persons are guaranteed access to drinking water, water for personal hygiene and sanitation under the Geneva Conventions.[11] Moreover, an occupying power is obliged to ensure public health, and hygiene is maintained in the occupied territory, which necessitates the provision of clean drinking water and basic sanitation.[12] The Fourth Geneva Convention states: 'If the whole or part of the population of an occupied territory is inadequately supplied, the Occupying Power shall agree to relied schemes on behalf of the said population, and shall facilitate them by all the means at its disposal'.[13] The Fourth Geneva Convention prohibits attacks on, and destruction of, civilian property, including drinking

[9] The Hague Convention (IV) Respecting the Laws and Customs of War on Land (adopted 18 October 1907, entered into force 26 January 1910), Article 43.

[10] The article states: 'The occupying State shall be regarded only as an administrator and usufructuary of public buildings, real estate, forests and agricultural estates belonging to the hostile State, and situated in the occupied country. It must safeguard the capital of these properties, and administer them in accordance with the rule of usufruct'.

[11] Convention (IV) Relative to the Protection of Civilian Persons in Time of War (Geneva, 12 August 1949), Article 85 (Fourth Geneva Convention).

[12] Ibid., Article 56. [13] Ibid., Article 59.

water installations, and prohibits the withholding of food or water that may lead to the forced movement of the population.[14]

As an occupying power, Israel also holds obligations towards the Palestinian population under international human rights law. This includes the right to water and sanitation, a component of the right to an adequate standard of living, guaranteed under Article 11(1) of the ICESCR and also inextricably related to the right to the highest attainable standard of health guaranteed in Article 12(1) of the ICESCR.[15] The right to water and sanitation is also explicitly recognised in the Convention on the Elimination of All Forms of Discrimination against Women[16] and the Convention on the Rights of the Child.[17] Israel has ratified these treaties and is therefore legally bound by their provisions in all territories under its effective control, including in the occupied Palestinian territory.[18] The right to water and sanitation is commonly understood to entail the rights of everyone to safe, clean, accessible and

[14] Ibid., Article 54.

[15] States that have ratified this treaty have repeatedly declared that the right to an adequate standard of living includes access to water and sanitation. For example, the Programme of Action of the 1994 Cairo Conference on Population and Development, endorsed by 177 States, and the Habitat Agenda, adopted in the framework of the Second United Nations Conference on Human Settlements (Habitat II), endorsed by 171 States. On 28 July 2010, the United Nations General Assembly adopted a resolution recognising access to water and sanitation as a human right.

[16] Convention on the Elimination of All Forms of Discrimination against Women (adopted 18 December 1979, entered into force 3 September 1981), 1249 UNTS 13 (CEDAW). Article 14(h) of CEDAW obliges States to ensure that rural women have access to water supply and sanitation.

[17] Convention on the Rights of the Child (adopted 20 November 1989, entered into force 2 September 1990), 1577 UNTS 3 (CRC). Article 24(2)(c) of the CRC guarantees children's right to the enjoyment of the highest attainable standard of health and requires States to combat disease and malnutrition 'through the provision of adequate nutritious foods and clean drinking water'.

[18] In its Concluding Observations on Israel, the UN Committee on Economic, Social and Cultural Rights (CESCR) stated that the ICESCR applies to 'all territories and populations under its effective control' and that 'the applicability of the rules of humanitarian law does not by itself impede the application of the Covenant or the accountability of the State under article 2(1) for the actions of its authorities'. See *Concluding Observations of the Committee on Economic, Social and Cultural Rights: Israel* (Thirtieth session 2003), UN Doc. E/C.12/1/Add.90, para. 31. The International Court of Justice has also ruled that the ICESCR is 'applicable in respect of acts done by a State in the exercise of its jurisdiction outside its own territory. In the case of the International Covenant on Economic, Social and Cultural Rights, Israel is also under an obligation not to raise any obstacle to the exercise of such rights in those fields where competence has been transferred to the Palestinian authorities'. ICJ, *Wall* opinion, para. 112.

affordable drinking water and sanitation.[19] The realisation of other human rights, such as the right to food, the right to adequate housing, the right to gain a living by work and the right to take part in cultural life, also depends on access to adequate water and sanitation.

A more in-depth look at Israel's obligations under international law (and the obligations of other actors) towards the Palestinian population living under occupation is provided in the following sections.

## 4 ISRAELI HINDRANCE OF IMPLEMENTATION OF THE HUMAN RIGHT TO WATER AND SANITATION UNDER OCCUPATION

### 4.1 *Inequitable Access to Water Resources: Occupation and Military Orders*

The primary challenge faced by the Palestinians regarding water is that they lack control over their water resources, which places significant constraints on the ability of the PNA to allocate and manage those resources.[20] As the occupied Palestinian territory shares the overwhelming majority of its water resources with Israel, the PNA is dependent on an adequate allocation of these resources in order to implement the right to water and sanitation in the territory. The law of international watercourses sets out principles as to how transboundary water resources should be used and allocated amongst co-riparian States.[21] The United Nations Convention on the Law of the Non-Navigational Uses of International Watercourses (1997) enshrines the principle of 'equitable and reasonable utilization'[22] as a key principle

[19] CESCR, *General Comment No. 15: The Right to Water* (Twenty-ninth session, 2002), UN Doc. E/C.12/2002/11 (2003); UN Sub-Commission on the Promotion and Protection of Human Rights, Draft Guidelines for the Realization of the Right to Drinking Water and Sanitation (Fifty-seventh session, 2005), UN Doc. E/CN.4/Sub.2/2005/25; and 'The Human Right to Water and Sanitation', GA Res. 64/292, UN Doc. A/64/L.63/Rev.1 and Add.1 (2010).

[20] In the case of transboundary water resources, it is recognised that this means equitable and reasonable utilisation and participation concerning the shared resource.

[21] The main principles of the UN Convention on the Law of the Non-Navigational Uses of International Watercourses (1997) are generally considered to constitute international customary law. In a dispute between Hungary and what is now Slovakia over the waters of the Danube River, the International Court of Justice based its ruling in part on the principles of the UN Convention on the Law of the Non-Navigational Uses of International Watercourses; see ICJ, *Case Concerning the Gabcikovo-Nagymaros Project* (Hungary/Slovakia), Judgment of 25 September 1997, ICJ Reports 1997. Also the International Law Association's Helsinki Rules 1996 (concerning the uses of international rivers) and the 1986 Seoul Rules (concerning groundwater resources) provide authoritative statements on customary international water law.

[22] UN Convention of the Law of the Non-Navigational Uses of International Watercourses (adopted 21 May 1997), UN Doc. A/Res/51/229, Article 5.

governing the use of transboundary water resources, and riparian States are under an obligation not to cause significant harm to another watercourse State.[23] Article 6 states that factors to be considered in determining what constitutes equitable and reasonable utilisation include the 'social and economic needs of the watercourse States' and the 'population dependent on the watercourse in each watercourse State'. While no use of an international watercourse is to enjoy inherent priority over other uses (in the absence of an agreement or custom to the contrary), Article 10 further establishes that 'in the event of a conflict between uses of an international watercourse ... special regard [shall be] given to the requirements of vital human needs'.[24] In defining what constitutes 'vital human needs', it is generally understood that this includes sufficient water to sustain life, including both drinking water and water required for the production of food in order to prevent starvation.[25] The emphasis on priority of allocation of water resources to satisfy vital human needs could be considered to be consistent with both the human right to water and sanitation and the human right to food.

The 1967 occupation by Israel of the West Bank and Gaza Strip brought all of the region's water resources under Israeli control. In the West Bank, this comprised the Mountain Aquifer, which consists of three sub-aquifers (Western, North Eastern and Eastern). These three aquifer basins, depicted in Figure 12.1, are shared transboundary water resources, with more than 90 per cent of the recharge occurring in the West Bank.[26] The water of the Coastal Aquifer, which runs along Israel's coastal plain and the Gaza Strip, was also secured. These aquifers constitute the Palestinians' only source of groundwater,[27] while Israel has access to additional aquifers located within Israeli territory.[28]

23 Ibid., Article 7. 24 Emphasis added.

25 UN Convention on the Law of the Non-Navigational Uses of International Watercourses, Article 10(2) and the accompanying 'Statement of Understanding' (Convention on the Law of the Non-Navigational Uses of International Watercourses – Report of the Sixth Committee Convening as the Working Group of the Whole, UN Doc. A/51/869). See also the International Law Association, Berlin Rules on Water Resources, Article 14 and commentary. The Rules were prepared by international legal experts in the field and are considered to be a persuasive articulation of international customary law.

26 Eastern Aquifer Basin 100 per cent, North Eastern Aquifer Basin 95 per cent and Western Aquifer Basin 80 per cent. Figures provided to the author by Hydrologist C. Messerschmid.

27 Besides minor local shallow aquifers in the West Bank, such as the Pleistocene and the Eocene aquifers.

28 These include the Mount Carmel Basin, Negev and Arayah Basins, Kinneret Basins and the Western Galilee Basins (according to Israeli nomenclature and division). However, most of these aquifers are in contact with the above aquifers and thus might also be considered to be shared resources.

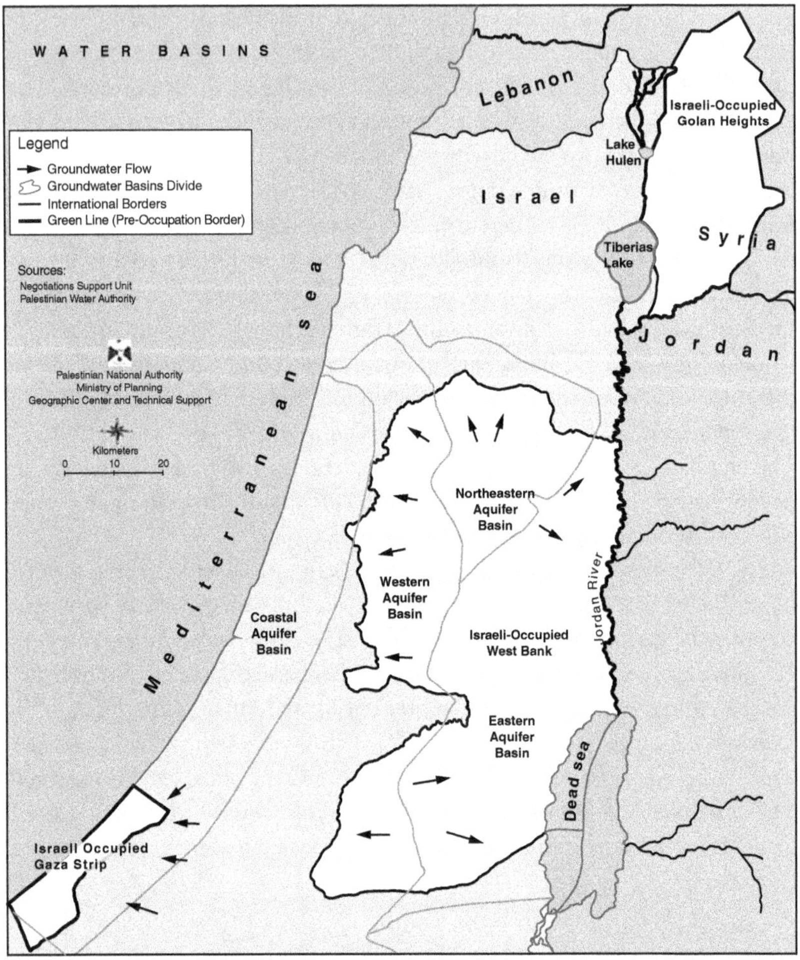


FIGURE 12.1 Groundwater resources in the West Bank and shared with Israel (*Source*: Palestinian National Authority)

Israel also secured control of the surface waters of the entire Jordan River Basin and most of Wadi (Valley) Gaza, a wetland south of Gaza City. Palestinians have had no access to the Jordan River, their main surface water resource, since 1967 when its lower part was declared a closed military zone. Further, as Israel unilaterally diverted the entire freshwater flow of the Jordan River at Lake Tiberias/the Sea of Galilee through its National Water Carrier beginning in 1962 and pumps saline and wastewater into the Lower Jordan, the river has been reduced to a foul trickle, the main cause of the shrinking of the Dead Sea.

Following the occupation of Palestine, Israel issued three military orders relating to water.[29] Military Order 98 (15 August 1967) transferred all authority over water resources to an Israeli official appointed by the Area Military Commander; Military Order 158 (19 November 1967) forbade the unlicensed construction of any new water installation; and Military Order 291 (19 December 1968) declared all prior settlements of disputes concerning water are invalid and any regulation in the law or any water transactions can be cancelled, even if confirmed by Israeli civil courts. The effect of these military orders was an absolute transfer of the power that local municipal authorities and village councils previously held over water resources and water management to the occupation authorities and the stifling of Palestinian groundwater development. The occupation authority's prevention of Palestinian water resource development is evidenced by the fact that not one permit has been issued for drilling new Palestinian wells in the largest and most productive of all the aquifer basins, the Western Aquifer, since 1967.[30] Therefore the PWA inherited a water sector that was underdeveloped, if not intentionally 'de-developed', and institutionally fragmented.

It is therefore suggested that Israeli legislation and military orders that were enacted subsequent to the 1967 occupation of Palestinian territory, which substantially changed or amended the civil laws in place relating to the allocation and utilisation of groundwater and surface waters, as well as changing the institutions responsible for administering water resources, violated the law of belligerent occupation, as the laws were not a military necessity nor required to ensure public order and safety.[31]

### 4.2 *Inequitable Access to Water Resources: Oslo II Accords and Institutionalising Discrimination*

The Oslo peace process served to formally institutionalise Israel's control over Palestinian water resources in the West Bank and to maintain inequitable allocation.[32] Under the terms of Article 40, Annex III of Appendix 1 of the

[29] A military order is a decree issued by Israeli military commanders that immediately becomes law for Palestinians living under occupation.

[30] C. Messerschmid, 'Water and the Politics of De-Development Part II - West Bank' (2008). Settler wells and West Bank Water Department wells, under Israeli control, have been drilled here.

[31] For previous discussion on this subject, see I. Scobbie, 'Natural Resources and Belligerent Occupation: Mutation through Permanent Sovereignty', in S. Bowen, *Human Rights, Self-Determination and Political Change in the Occupied Palestinian Territories* (The Hague: Martinus Nijhoff Publishers, 1997), pp. 221–290.

[32] Note that the Oslo II agreement only refers to groundwater resources in the West Bank and does not refer to the Coastal Aquifer, where Gaza lies downstream of Israel.

TABLE 12.1 *Oslo II Accords, Article 40, 1995 *allegedly 46% unused*

| Groundwater resource | Total annual recharge rate 'estimated potential' | Israel's annual allocation | Palestine's annual allocation |
|---|---|---|---|
| Western Aquifer | 362 million cubic metres (MCM) | 340 MCM (94%) | 22 MCM (6%) |
| North Eastern Aquifer | 145 MCM | 103 MCM (71%) | 42 MCM (29%) |
| Eastern Aquifer | 172 MCM | 40 MCM (23%)* | 54 MCM (31%)* |

1995 Oslo II Accords, an allocation of West Bank groundwater resources was agreed upon (see Table 12.1).

There are a number of problems associated with the figures given in the Oslo II Accords. Firstly, the negotiators relied exclusively on Israeli data. The recharge rates ('estimated potential') given under Article 40 are now refuted, particularly for the Eastern Aquifer Basin, where it is generally believed that the quantities given under the Oslo II agreement are not in fact available. Furthermore, the recharge rate of an aquifer is not static and varies from year to year depending on a number of factors, such as variations in rainfall. It is also important to note that the allocation of water given under the Oslo II agreement does not reflect the current situation. Figure 12.2 shows the amounts the Palestinian Water Authority and the Hydrological Service of Israel (HSI) provide for discharge from the Mountain Aquifer (wells and springs) between 1995 and 2007.[33]

As is clear from Figure 12.2, Israel abstracts more than the amount allocated to it under Article 40 of the Oslo II agreement. From the Western Aquifer, it can be seen that Israel abstracted on average 398 million cubic metres per year (MCM/year) during the stated period or 58 MCM over its Oslo allocations.[34] What is more, Israel abstracted in excess of the aquifer's annual sustainable yield (an excess of 36 MCM according to the Oslo II estimates) causing potentially irreversible damage to the long-term environmental sustainability of the aquifer. This is especially important, because in Oslo and since Oslo II,

[33] Cited in EWASH, *Fact Sheet: Water Resources in the West Bank* (2009).

[34] Figures provided by the World Bank (and quoted from the Hydrological Service of Israel) show that in 1999 the following amounts were abstracted by Israel: From the Western Aquifer 591.6 MCM; North Eastern 147.1 MCM; Eastern 132.9 MCM. The high quantities abstracted by Israel in 1999 could indicate Israel's overpumping of water resources in the run-up to the Camp David negotiations or complete disregard for Oslo commitments.

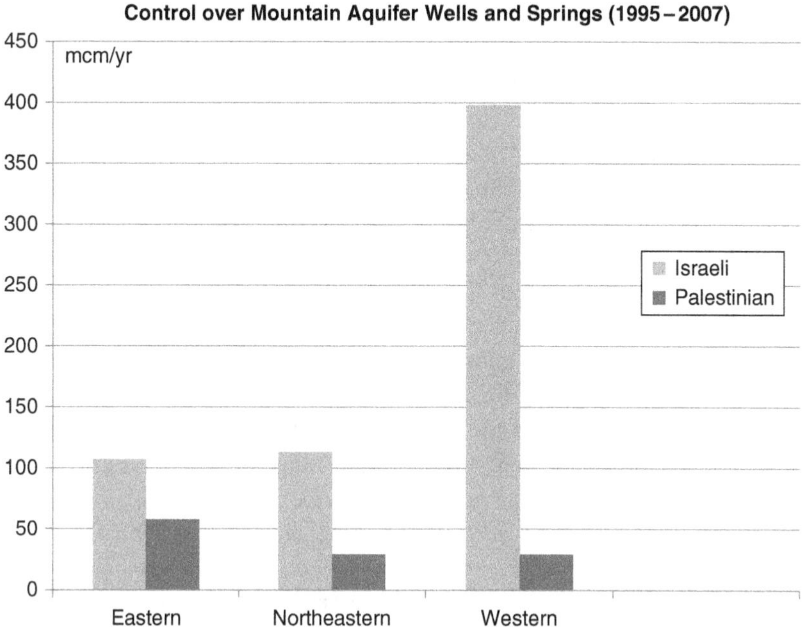


FIGURE 12.2 Total outflows (from wells and springs) in the three Mountain Aquifer basins, shared between the West Bank and Israel during the Oslo period
(*Source:* Palestinian Water Authority, Hydrological Service of Israel)

Israel argued that it could not allow any new Palestinian wells in the shared Western and North Eastern Basins because this would lead to over abstraction beyond the sustainable yield.

To deflect criticism, Israel has consistently argued that it supplies Palestinians more than the amount of water allocated to them in the Oslo II agreement. According to the Israeli Water Authority, 'Israel has responded to the needs of the Palestinians and has increased the quantity of water provided to them far beyond that specified in the Interim Agreement'.[35] Yet, allocation between Israel and the occupied Palestinian territory remains far from being equitable or reasonable. As the World Bank notes, 'Water withdrawals per capita for West Bank Palestinians are about one quarter of those for Israelis, and have declined over the past decade'.[36] The reduction in per capita

[35] Israel Water Authority, *The Issue of Water between Israel and the Palestinians* (March 2009), http://siteresources.worldbank.org/INTWESTBANKGAZA/Resources/IsraelWaterAuthorityresponse.pdf.

[36] World Bank, *Assessment of Restrictions on Palestinian Water Sector Development* (Washington, DC: World Bank, 2009), p. 13.

availability of water is largely due to the fact that the population of the West Bank has increased by approximately 50 per cent since 1995.

The expropriation and excessive utilisation of the water resources of the West Bank to the benefit of Israeli citizens and the settler population would appear to violate Article 55 of The Hague Regulations of 1907, as well as accepted principles of international water law. In relation to the transboundary water resources between Palestine and Israel (i.e. groundwater, the Jordan River and run-off), Israel abstracts and utilises around 89 per cent and the Palestinians about 11 per cent.[37]

The inequalities in allocation of water resources are reflected in per capita consumption. On average, a Palestinian in the West Bank consumes around 50 litres of water per day for domestic uses,[38] whereas an Israeli citizen's domestic consumption is around 280 litres of water per day[39] (5.6 times more than a Palestinian). According to the Israeli non-governmental organisation (NGO), B'Tselem, there is a gross inequality between consumption rates in Israeli settlements built in the West Bank in violation of international humanitarian law[40] and Palestinian communities. The 9,400 Israeli settlers in the Jordan Valley consume around 45 MCM/year from wells, the Jordan River, treated wastewater and manmade reservoirs.[41] This constitutes almost a third of the quantity of water allocated to the 2.5 million Palestinians living in the West Bank.[42] The diversion of water resources to Israeli settlements has facilitated settler development of water-intensive farming throughout the Jordan Valley and the production of a variety of crops, mainly for export. Meanwhile, Palestinian communities in the Jordan Valley have seen their springs and wells run dry, forcing people to abandon agriculture. Some communities rely on as little as 20 litres of water per person per day, well below the 100 litres the World Health Organization says is necessary to ensure all health concerns are met.[43]

The Israeli national water company, Mekorot supplies Palestinian communities in the West Bank with approximately 52 per cent of their domestic water supply.[44]

37 PLO Negotiations Affairs Department, 'Water for a Viable Palestinian State' (2009).

38 World Bank, Assessment of Restrictions, p. 14.

39 EWASH, *Fact Sheet 2: Water Resources in the West Bank* (July 2010).

40 Article 49 of the Fourth Geneva Convention states: 'The Occupying Power shall not deport or transfer parts of its own civilian population into the territory it occupies'.

41 B'Tselem, 'Dispossession and Exploitation: Israel's policy in the Jordan Valley and Northern Dead Sea' (May 2011).

42 Ibid. 43 EWASH, *Fact Sheet 2*.

44 Palestinian Central Bureau of Statistics, *Water Statistics in the Palestinian Territory Annual Report 2007* (August 2008).

According to Mekorot:

> The allocation of water to the Palestinian Authority is decided by the Israeli Water Authority in accordance with diplomatic agreements. Mekorot operates in accordance with the instructions of the water authority and transfers the amounts of water accordingly. [Mekorot] supplies the water to the Palestinian Water Authority, but is not responsible for the internal distribution in the communities of the West Bank; the body responsible for that is the Palestinian Water Authority.[45]

However, as the World Bank points out, the various water suppliers operating in the West Bank are often dependent on Mekorot and have interconnected supply systems.[46] The settlers receive an unlimited supply of water all year round, yet Mekorot often reduces or disconnects the supply to Palestinian villages in summer months when the demand is high in Israel.[47] Often the water supplied to Palestinian communities and the Israeli settlers is delivered through the same network, but the pipes leading to Palestinian communities are much narrower in diameter, only half an inch as opposed to two inches wide.[48] Israel also inserts 'unit roles' into Palestinian pipelines, which further reduce the flow of water and water pressure to Palestinian communities.[49] Moreover, the valves that supply water to Palestinian communities are often located within or adjacent to the settlements, and there are numerous cases where the valves have been turned off by settlers, preventing the supply of water from reaching Palestinian communities.[50] The preferential treatment afforded to the residents of the illegal settlements, on the basis of national identity, religion and ethnicity, violates international human rights law, as well as Article 24 of the Fourth Geneva Convention, which provides that all persons in the occupied territory should be treated equally.

45 Cited in Y. Feldman and Uri Blau, 'A Dry and Thirsty Land', *Haaretz*, 20 August 2009.

46 World Bank, *Assessment of Restrictions*, p. 15.

47 West Bank Water Department water bills from 2009, issued by Israeli Civil Administration, Bet El.

48 C. Messerschmid, 'What Price Cooperation? Hydro-hegemony in Shared Israeli/Palestinian Groundwater Resources', in A. Aliewi et al. (eds.), *Sustainable Development and Management of Water in Palestine* (Ramallah: House of Water and Environment/UNESCO, 2008), pp. 347–363.

49 Ibid.

50 Palestinian Hydrology Group (Water, Sanitation and Hygiene Monitoring Programme), *Water for Life: The Dilemma of Development under Occupation – The obstacles to achieving the Millennium Development Goals and water rights in the occupied Palestinian territory* (2006), p. 47.

### 4.3 *Prohibiting Infrastructure Development in the West Bank*

Progressively realising the right to water and sanitation for all entails the obligation to take deliberate, concrete and targeted steps within the limits of available resources to extend water and sanitation services to unserved communities.[51] In the West Bank, about a third of all communities are not connected to the water distribution network.[52] These communities are dependent on rainwater harvesting and cistern storage, at the household level, or purchasing water from tankers for domestic consumption.[53] Many turn to untreated water, taken from agricultural wells or springs, for domestic use. Only 31 per cent of the communities in the West Bank are connected to the sewerage network, and the remaining 69 per cent of the population are dependent on cesspits and septic tanks.[54] Much of the water and sewage infrastructure in the West Bank is old and in need of repair. Water losses through the network are high, and lack of rehabilitation of water cisterns and lack of adequate sewage facilities place the water supply at risk of contamination. While the PWA has had some success in extending water and sanitation networks to unserved communities, Israeli prohibitions on infrastructure development in the West Bank have hampered its ability to ensure physical access to water facilities that supply safe, sufficient and regular water, as well as basic sanitation.

Under the Oslo II agreement, a Joint Water Committee (JWC) was established to implement Article 40 in the West Bank. The JWC is comprised of an equal number of Israeli and Palestinian representatives, and 'all decisions of the JWC shall be reached by consensus'.[55] All infrastructure development works must be approved by the JWC, including drilling wells and building water and sewerage networks, and either side may veto proposals. While theoretically Israelis and Palestinians are given equal rights and responsibilities under the JWC, the JWC de facto veto discriminates against Palestinians.[56] This is primarily because the Palestinians are the party requiring major

[51] CESCR, General Comment No. 15, para. 29; Draft Guidelines for the Realization of the Right to Drinking Water and Sanitation, section 5.1.

[52] World Bank, *Assessment of Restrictions*, p. 14.

[53] Often, water from local springs has to be transported via footpaths, donkey trails or dirt roads, inaccessible for tankers, because both building access roads and even installing simple small pumps require Israeli permits from the Israeli Civil Administration.

[54] World Bank, *Assessment of Restrictions*, p. 32.

[55] Oslo II Interim Agreement, Appendix 1, Annex III, Articles 40(13) and 40(14).

[56] For an in-depth critique of the JWC, see J. Selby, 'Joint Mismanagement: Reappraising the Oslo Regime', in H. Shuval and H. Dweik (eds.), *Water for Life in the Middle East*, Vol. 1 (Jerusalem: Israel-Palestine Center for Research and Information, 2006), pp. 322–340.

infrastructure development in the water and sanitation sector, which has been badly neglected by the occupation authorities since 1967, and the party needing to develop additional supplies of water to support population growth and socio-economic development. The second reason is that the JWC only has jurisdiction over water resources and water and sanitation development inside the West Bank. (Abstractions by Israeli authorities or settlers from West Bank aquifers, but outside the actual West Bank, have not been subject to JWC approval.) Israel has consistently exercised its effective veto power through the JWC by refusing to grant Palestinian permits (or excessively delaying project applications), thereby stifling Palestinian water and sanitation development. Of 417 projects submitted by the Palestinians to the JWC between 1996 and 2008, including well drilling, rehabilitating old water networks, building new pipelines to connect unserved communities and building cisterns for rainwater harvesting, only 57 per cent were approved.[57] Since the Oslo II agreement, not one new permit has been issued for agricultural wells. About 120 old Palestinian agricultural wells cannot be operated, lacking JWC approval for repair and maintenance.[58] There is also a crisis in wastewater treatment in the West Bank, with only one wastewater treatment plant existing, and approval for construction of others often made conditional upon connection of Israeli settlements to the proposed plant. Consequently, West Bank wadis (seasonal streams) have been subjected to excessive contamination caused by Israeli restrictions on Palestinian development of wastewater collection and treatment and by unregulated dumping in the West Bank. According to B'Tselem, by far the largest single polluted wadi is Wadi Nar (Kidron), where 17.5 MCM/year of sewage emerges from Jerusalem.[59]

In Area C, a further layer of bureaucracy complicates the work of the PWA and constrains aid agencies from implementing water and sanitation infrastructure projects. Any project to build or rehabilitate any structure, even a cistern for rainwater harvesting or laying a steel pipe more than two inches in diameter, must first be approved by all thirteen departments of the Civil Administration of the Israeli Defense Forces. Gaining the required permit from the Israeli Civil Administration is a long and protracted process and often results in failure. A large number of projects that were approved by the JWC have been delayed or refused by the Israeli Civil Administration. The World Bank states that 'of the 236 projects overall approved by the JWC 1996–2008, 151 (64%) have

[57] World Bank, *Assessment of Restrictions*, p. 48. [58] EWASH, Fact Sheet 2.

[59] B'Tselem, 'Foul Play, Neglect of Wastewater Treatment in the West Bank', June 2009 information sheet.

been implemented'.[60] The last well, applied for in the framework of a large (German) donor project, Al Hizmah well for Ramallah, has been under application since 2001 and, at the time of writing, had yet to receive a permit. Thirteen different sets of coordinates were checked, only to be rejected by the JWC, Israeli Civil Administration or Israeli army.[61] A number of aid agencies have been waiting for years to implement projects, such as connecting communities to the water network in Area C, providing a community with a water filling point or rehabilitating cisterns. Others that have gone ahead with construction in the absence of permission have had their projects destroyed. Between 2009 and 2011, some forty-four cisterns and rainwater-harvesting structures in Area C were demolished by the Israeli government, twenty of them between January and July of 2011 alone.[62] According to the UN Humanitarian Coordinator for the OPT, Gaylard, 'The removal of such critical infrastructure places serious strains on the resilience and coping mechanisms of these communities, who will become increasingly dependent on economically unsustainable sources such as tankered water. Such deliberate demolitions in occupied territory are also in contravention of Israel's obligations under international law'.[63]

### 4.4 *Restricting Water Access in the West Bank*

Israel has implemented a number of movement and access restrictions inside the West Bank, citing security concerns. These include the Wall, roadblocks, checkpoints and 'settler only' bypass roads which have further restricted Palestinian access to water and sanitation and prevented the PNA from ensuring progressive realisation of the right to access sufficient quantities of water, as well as affordable water and sanitation services.

In many instances, Palestinian communities have been isolated from their water resources. The hundreds of obstacles to movement in the West Bank have resulted in Palestinians having to travel long distances to reach water points. Large detours have increased prices for tankered water and sewage sludge removal trucks, in some cases, rendering these services unaffordable. As a result, many households are forced to reduce water consumption and

[60] World Bank, *Assessment of Restrictions*, p. 48.

[61] See Hizmah case study in Amnesty International, *Troubled Waters: Palestinians Denied Fair Access to Water* (London: Amnesty International, 2009), p. 31.

[62] Diakonia IHL Resource Centre, *Israel's Administrative Destruction of Cisterns in Area C of the West Bank* (September 2011), p. 1.

[63] Statement by the UN Resident and Humanitarian Coordinator for the occupied Palestinian territories, M. Gaylard, on Continuing Demolition of Water Cisterns in the West Bank (1 February 2011).

compromise on hygiene. Another consequence of restricted access to water resources in the West Bank is the prevalence of the unlicensed drilling of shallow wells or, in some communities, water theft from pipelines. These are practices that the PWA has failed to regulate adequately in areas that come under its jurisdiction.

The construction of the Wall inside Palestinian territory has been seen as an attempt by Israel in part to assert control over hydrologically sensitive areas.[64] In the Northern West Bank, the land to the west of the Wall constitutes the only area of the Western Aquifer Basin that has any significant future potential for well development and increasing water abstraction in the future.[65] Furthermore, it is believed that the Wall's main purpose is to ensure the future annexation of the settlements into Israel, many of which lie over key portions of the Western Aquifer Basin. A large number of Palestinian wells and springs have also been expropriated by the Wall, and water and sewerage infrastructure in many places has been destroyed by the Wall's construction. According to the UN Economic and Social Council:

> The construction of the barrier has closed off the access of Palestinians to 95 per cent of their own water resources . . . by destroying 403 wells and 1,327 cisterns. It has cut off access of owners to 136 wells providing 44.1 million m$^3$ of water annually. The barrier has closed 45 springs (23 million m$^3$/year) and 906 dunums [1 dunum = 0.1 hectares] of underground water (99 per cent of underground West Bank water). Consequently, over 7,000 Palestinian agriculture-dependent families have lost their livelihood in a region where water resources are scarce and increasingly costly to develop. The latest barrier route will isolate another 62 springs and 134 wells in the 'seam zone' [land trapped between the Wall and the Green Line/1949 Armistice Line].[66]

Communities in the northern Jordan Valley are particularly restricted in terms of water access. Located in Area C, since 2005, the Jordan Valley has been

[64] The 2004 Advisory Opinion of the International Court of Justice regarding the legal consequences of the construction of a Wall in the occupied Palestinian territory noted that the Wall made it increasingly difficult for Palestinians to access their sources of water and highlighted its concern at the annexation of the Western Aquifer Basin. The Court ruled that Israel's construction of the Wall in the occupied Palestinian territory is contrary to international law and Israel is obliged to cease all construction, to dismantle the Wall and to make reparation for all damage caused by the construction of the Wall. ICJ, *Wall* opinion (paras. 133 and 163).

[65] C. Messerschmid, 'Israel's Mauer und die Wasserressourcen', *Inamo*, Vol. 34 (2003).

[66] UN Economic and Social Council (ECOSOC), Economic and social repercussions of the Israeli occupation on the living conditions of the Palestinian people in the occupied Palestinian territory, including Jerusalem, and the Arab population in the occupied Syrian Golan, UN Doc. A/62/75-E/2007/13, 3 May 2007, para. 40.

off-limits to all Palestinians who cannot prove they reside there; and for those that can prove their residence, a strict regime of closures and checkpoints makes movement difficult. A large number of small communities of Bedouin and fellaheen (farmers) live in this area. Lacking connection to the water network, and prohibited from opening water filling points or building cisterns, many communities are dependent on water trucking. Some communities travel up to 13 kilometres to access the nearest water point, a journey which, due to delays at Israeli checkpoints, can take three to four hours.[67] Large detours made by water tankers have pushed up fuel costs, and some households are paying up to 40 per cent of their monthly income on clean drinking water, forcing them to reduce expenditure on other basic needs.[68] The NGO Action Against Hunger (ACF) found that, for some vulnerable families in the Tubas District, water consumption had fallen to 20 litres per person per day.[69] Living from agriculture and livestock, the survival and basic subsistence of such communities is highly dependent on a sufficient and regular water supply, both to generate income and to ensure food security.

Kinarti, chief advisor to the Head of the Israeli Water Authority, dismissed the claims that Palestinians are surviving on minimal quantities of water inadequate to ensure health concerns are met:

> They have enough water to drink . . . There are water tankers in Amman and Damascus too. That's how they do things. In the interim agreement they were given at least 70–80 million cubic meters of water [a year] from the eastern aquifer. They did nothing. They want us to bring them water and to live at our expense. They want Lake Kinneret, the coastal plain, what don't they want? . . . We let them dig wells in the eastern aquifer: there is water there so let them dig. . . . Why aren't they digging? For no reason, because it is easier to cry. Do they care about their nation? They want to be miserable.[70]

## 4.5 *Military Attacks, Sanctions and the Blockade on the Gaza Strip*

The situation in Gaza is somewhat different to that in the West Bank in that theoretically the PWA has administrative control over water resources and water and sanitation infrastructure development in Gaza. However, since the Hamas takeover of the Gaza Strip in 2007, the PWA has been paralysed in Gaza, due partly to inter-factional Palestinian splits and conflicts. However, the current crisis in the water and sanitation sector is primarily due to financial

[67] Information gathered by the author during interviews and field research. [68] Ibid.

[69] ACF International Network, Assessment of the Drought Situation in the Northern West Bank (WASH Perspective) Tubas District, 20 August 2008.

[70] Cited in Feldman and Blau, 'A Dry and Thirsty Land'.

and economic sanctions placed on the Gaza administration, the Israeli-imposed blockade and repeated military incursions.

Financial and economic sanctions were placed on the Gaza administration by both Israel and western countries following the Hamas victory in the Palestinian legislative elections in 2006. These sanctions have prevented the authorities in Gaza from providing an adequate service to the population. The withdrawal of direct budgetary support to the PNA by key donors, such as the European Union (EU), United States and Canada, following the legislative elections in an attempt to marginalise Hamas, crippled the Palestinian institutions responsible for water and sanitation provision. In the first half of 2008, a large number of municipal employees, including those responsible for water and wastewater services, had not been paid for a number of months – leading to a series of strikes by municipal workers in Gaza City, Khan Younis and Jabaliya. The withdrawal of donor funding, particularly by the United States Agency for International Development (USAID), previously the major donor for the water and wastewater sector in the occupied Palestinian territory, led to the suspension of a number of projects, including projects to build a desalination plant for the Gaza Strip and to construct a regional water pipeline. While the fiscal situation of the PNA has recovered somewhat due to Israel's freeing up of taxes it collects on behalf of the PNA and an increase in donor aid, the water and sanitation sector continues to be underfunded. Of the USD 38.6 million requested under the Consolidated Appeals Process mechanism[71] for funding of the water and sanitation sector in 2010, only 38 per cent of projects were funded.[72] While sanctions have been removed from the PNA in Ramallah, they still apply to the Gaza administration. The restriction of funding to humanitarian and emergency assistance has hindered the long-term development of the water and sanitation sector, as well as the institutional capacity of the PWA.

The blockade imposed by Israel on the Gaza Strip has caused a further obstacle to the progressive realisation of the right to water and sanitation in the Gaza Strip. While Israel has increasingly restricted the movement of both people and goods in and out of the Gaza Strip since the 1990s, the border crossings have been almost constantly sealed since June 2007. (It was at this time that Hamas ousted the opposition party Fatah from the Strip, leading to the collapse of the unity government.) Another factor in the blockade was the reduction in quantities of fuel and electricity supplied by Israel to the Gaza

[71] The Consolidated Appeals Process is a tool used by aid agencies to secure funding, plan, implement and monitor their interventions together.

[72] OCHA, The Monthly Humanitarian Monitor, Tables of Indicators, January 2011, p. 18.

Strip since September 2007 in response to increasing rocket attacks on Israel by militant Palestinian factions. Whilst Israel has both the right and duty to defend its citizens from attacks by Palestinian armed groups operating within Gaza who have violated international humanitarian law by firing rockets on Israeli civilians, the Israeli response to such attacks has been widely condemned as disproportionate. The International Committee of the Red Cross stated that 'The whole of Gaza's civilian population is being punished for acts for which they bear no responsibility. The closure therefore constitutes a collective punishment imposed in clear violation of Israel's obligations under international humanitarian law'.[73]

As a result of the blockade, equipment and supplies needed for the construction and maintenance of water and sanitation facilities have been denied entry, hindering the commencement of projects to repair, rehabilitate and upgrade existing infrastructure. Much infrastructure is old and in a bad state of disrepair or has been damaged in the course of Israeli military incursions. The 'easing of the blockade' announced by the Israeli government in June 2010, which amongst other measures relaxed import restrictions and allowed the entry of construction materials for international projects in Gaza approved by the PNA, has done little to improve the water and sanitation situation in Gaza. The Water, Sanitation and Hygiene (WASH) Cluster reports that, in 2011, less than 20 per cent of WASH materials listed as acceptable under the new guidelines and submitted to enter have been allowed into Gaza.[74] Entry for materials for large-scale projects such as the KFW-funded Central Gaza Sewage Project and the PWA's North Gaza Emergency Sewage Treatment Project (NGEST) has improved, but following high-level political intervention to ensure they are implemented. Numerous other projects have been brought to a complete standstill. Less than 2 per cent of the investment plan for water and sanitation in Gaza has been implemented.[75] This has meant that sewage projects that have been stalled have left treatment plants working over capacity and is thus releasing effluent that has not been fully treated into the sea, and damaged water networks have not been repaired.

Restrictions on the amount of fuel and electricity supplied to the Gaza Strip have hindered the operation of water wells and wastewater pumping stations, in some cases rendering them dysfunctional. For example, in September 2008, as a result of Israeli sanctions, the Coastal Municipalities Water Utility

[73] International Comities of the Red Cross, 'Gaza Closure: Not Another Year!', News Release, 14 June 2010.

[74] WASH Cluster oPt Monthly Situation Report, 30 June 2011.

[75] World Bank, *Assessment of Restrictions*, p. 44.

(the water service provider in Gaza) reported that 50 per cent of wells were out of fuel and were dependent on irregular electricity supply. It was further reported that five wells in Middle Gaza were without any fuel or electricity, leaving 250,000 people with a severe lack of water.[76] Due to an intermittent water supply, in many cases, the water consumption in Gaza has fallen to well below World Health Organization recommended levels sometimes to as little as 14 litres per person per day.[77] Since January 2010, there has been a further deterioration in the supply of electricity to Gaza's power plant, due to a lack of funds to purchase the industrial fuel required to operate it.[78] Due to a lack of fuel for operation, the Gazan authorities have been releasing 50 to 80 million litres of raw and partially treated sewage into the Mediterranean Sea on a daily basis since January 2008 to stop sewage from flooding into residential areas, as has happened on a number of occasions in the past. This is causing environmental harm and constitutes a threat to the population's health in both Palestine and Israel. Electricity shortages also prevent water being pumped for both domestic use and irrigation leaving people with severe shortages. As a result the Gazan authorities implement rolling blackouts throughout the Gaza Strip. In 2011, 15 per cent of the Gaza Strip population received a water supply for 6 to 8 hours, once every four days; 40 per cent of the Gaza Strip population received a water supply for 6 to 8 hours once every three days; 30 per cent of the Gaza Strip population received a water supply for 6 to 8 hours once every two days; and 15 per cent of the Gaza Strip population received a water supply for 6 to 8 hours once every day.[79]

The Israeli Defense Forces (IDF) have also deliberately targeted water and sewerage infrastructure in the course of military incursions. Under the laws of war, water resources and water and sanitation infrastructure are considered civilian objects, which are protected from attack and destruction under the Fourth Geneva Convention.[80] The United Nations reported that, between 2000 and 2006, the IDF destroyed 224 wells in the Gaza Strip, including two drinking water sources.[81] Many water supply lines and sanitation networks have been dug up using specially designed 'backhoe' tanks and bulldozers. During the Israeli military offensive on the Gaza Strip known as 'Operation Cast Lead' between 27 December 2008 and 18 January 2009, water wells, water networks, wastewater facilities and water tanks were destroyed, causing an

[76] OCHA, *The Humanitarian Monitor*, September 2008, p. 8.

[77] OCHA, *The Humanitarian Monitor*, February 2008, p. 18.

[78] OCHA, *Gaza's Electricity Crisis: The Impact of Electricity Cuts on the Humanitarian Situation*, May 2010, p. 1.

[79] WASH Cluster oPt Monthly Situation Report, 30 June 2011.

[80] Fourth Geneva Convention, Article 54.

[81] ECOSOC report, para. 19.

estimated USD 6 million of damage.[82] The Report of the United Nations Fact Finding Mission on the Gaza Conflict (the Goldstone Report) documented several incidents involving the destruction of water installations, including wells and sewage treatment plants. The report highlighted the case of a direct strike on the raw sewage lagoons of the Gaza Wastewater Treatment Plant, which caused the outflow of more than 200,000 cubic metres of raw sewage into neighbouring farmland. The report concluded that 'The circumstances of the strike on the lagoon suggest that it was deliberate and premeditated'.[83] The report also highlighted the case of the Namar wells complex in Jabaliya where two water wells, pumping machines, a generator, fuel storage, a reservoir chlorination unit, buildings and related equipment were all destroyed in multiple air strikes on the first day of Israel's aerial bombardment of the Gaza Strip. The fact-finding mission concluded that it found 'no grounds to suggest that there was any military advantage to be had by hitting the wells and noted that there was no suggestion that Palestinian armed groups had used the wells'.[84] The mission also found that 'there was a deliberate and systematic policy on the part of the Israeli armed forces to target … water installations'.[85] It further concluded that 'in the destruction of private residential houses, water wells, water tanks, agricultural land and greenhouses there was a specific purpose of denying them for their sustenance to the population of the Gaza Strip'.[86] At the height of the Israeli military offensive, up to one third of the Gaza population was left without access to clean water, some for ten or more days.

The blockade imposed by Israel has hindered the ability of humanitarian agencies from sending in materials as well as technicians required to carry out the necessary reconstruction work to water and wastewater facilities damaged during 'Operation Cast Lead'. In November 2009, almost eleven months after the cessation of hostilities, some 10,000 people in Gaza remained without access to piped water, as the reconstruction of damaged networks could not commence without access to materials, such as cement and pipes, which are barred due to the blockade. The remainder of the population had access to water for between six to eight hours, only one to four days a week.[87]

[82] Coastal Municipalities Water Utility, *Damage Assessment Report: Water and Waste Water Infrastructure and Facilities* (January 2009), p. 5.

[83] Human Rights Council, *Human Rights in Palestine and Other Occupied Arab Territories: Report of the UN Fact Finding Mission on the Gaza Conflict*, UN Doc. A/HRC/12/48 (Twelfth session, 2009), para. 52.

[84] Ibid. [85] Ibid., para. 54. [86] Ibid., para. 73.

[87] OCHA, *Protection of Civilians, 26 August–1 September 2009*.

Water quality is an issue of serious concern in the Gaza Strip, with only 5 to 10 cent of the Coastal Aquifer (Gaza's sole source of fresh water) meeting World Health Organization standards.[88] The deterioration and contamination of the Gaza portion of the Coastal Aquifer is partly due to overexploitation of the aquifer, which has led to seawater intrusion and increased salinity. This has been caused by lack of effective regulation by the Palestinian authorities and unlicensed well drilling, a result of the fact that the resources of the Gaza portion of the Coastal Aquifer are insufficient to provide for the Gaza population's needs and restrictions have been placed on the Palestinians by the Israelis preventing them from developing non-conventional sources of water, such as desalination plants, wastewater treatment for reuse and bulk water importation. Such sustained over extraction has caused serious damage to the quality of the water supply for Palestinians. As the Israeli Ministry of Environmental Protection noted, 'Over exploitation may lead to a rapid rate of saline water infiltration from surrounding saline water sources'.[89] Indeed, the situation is so serious that an environmental assessment by the United Nations Environment Programme (UNEP) recommends, amongst other measures, the immediate halt of all abstraction from the Gaza Aquifer to avoid further deterioration that could take centuries to reverse.[90]

Yet, the vast majority of pollution of the Gaza portion of the Coastal Aquifer is caused through sewage infiltration due to Israeli policies and practices outlined above that have led to the near collapse of the wastewater treatment plants, which are stretched beyond capacity and in desperate need of rehabilitation. This sewage infiltration, coupled with run-off from agricultural products and fertilisers, is causing the nitrate levels in the groundwater to increase. High quantities of nitrates in drinking water can have significant health repercussions, particularly for infants. UNEP recommends that a comprehensive study be conducted on the prevalence of methaemoglobinaemia (blue baby syndrome) in the Gaza Strip, a disease caused by nitrate contamination, which causes symptoms such as breathing difficulties, fatigue and loss of consciousness (particularly for infants) and can seriously impact upon a child's development. UNEP further recommended that safe water should immediately be provided to all children less than 1 year old, in order to ensure their health is protected.[91]

[88] World Bank, *Assessment of Restrictions*, p. 27.

[89] UNEP, *Environmental Assessment of the Gaza Strip Following the Escalation of Hostilities in December 2008–January 2009*, September 2009, p. 56.

[90] Ibid., pp. 70–71. [91] Ibid.

## 5 REALISING PALESTINIANS' RIGHT TO WATER AND SANITATION

It must be recognised that the PNA holds obligations towards the Palestinian people in terms of realising their right to water and sanitation, and some failures of the Palestinian Water Authority in relation to water and sanitation provision have been highlighted in this chapter. The PNA has also been criticised for corruption, lack of transparency and mismanagement. A recent World Bank report highlights that the Palestinian Water Authority is 'not performing up to expectations, and has lost capacity' and notes specific problems as including an outdated water strategy and investment programme, weak structure and management, institutional fragmentation and a lack of institutional capacity.[92] Similarly, a recent audit of the Palestinian water sector found that 'total chaos reigns in the water sector' and 'political/personal infighting has created a plethora of water service providers and utilities at many levels, none of which is fully effective and all of which fail to adequately cover their costs'.[93] There is optimism that the change of management in the PWA and refocusing of the water sector strategy will seek to mitigate some of these concerns.[94] However, as this chapter has demonstrated, the ability of the PNA to progressively realise the right to water and sanitation for the Palestinian people has been significantly undermined by the policy and practice of the State of Israel, the occupying power, throughout the occupied Palestinian territory. In the case of Gaza, the key problems relate to the acts and omissions of the international community, particularly western States that participated in the financial and economic boycott of the PNA and Hamas and have failed to hold Israel meaningfully accountable for war crimes, including collective punishment due to the blockade and military attacks on water and sanitation infrastructure.

The obligations that Israel holds as an occupying power in the OPT in relation to water and sanitation provision under both international humanitarian law and international human rights law have been outlined above. In both the West Bank and the Gaza Strip, Israel has engaged in actions that have reduced the accessibility of water and sanitation services and facilities; reduced the quantity of water available for personal and domestic needs, as well as water needed to ensure food security and secure livelihoods; reduced

[92] World Bank, *Assessment of Restrictions*, pp. 57–59.
[93] PWA, *An Audit of the Operations and Projects in the Water Sector in Palestine: The Strategic Refocusing of Water Sector Infrastructure in Palestine* (Final Report, 18 November 2008), pp. 78–79.
[94] See, for example, World Bank, *Assessment of Restrictions* , pp. 57–58.

water quality; reduced water quantity in some cases to well below World Health Organization levels; and reduced the affordability of water and sanitation, thereby requiring households to reduce consumption or sacrifice other basic needs. Israeli policies and practices have also reduced the ability of the Palestinian Water Authority to effectively respond to the population's needs.

Israeli control over the water resources of the West Bank has been identified as a primary factor hindering the PNA from realising the right to water and sanitation. This point has been identified repeatedly by the United Nations human rights monitoring mechanisms. For example, the UN Committee on Economic, Social and Cultural Rights (the Committee) noted it was 'particularly concerned about limited access to and distribution and availability of water for Palestinians in the occupied territories, as a result of inequitable management, extraction and distribution of shared water resources, which are predominantly under Israeli control'.[95]

The extraterritorial obligations of a State party to the ICESCR in terms of the allocation of transboundary water resources are the subject of debate.[96] In General Comment No. 15: The Right to Water, the Committee observed that the obligation to respect the right to water 'requires that States parties refrain from interfering directly or indirectly with the enjoyment of the right to water'.[97] According to the Committee, this obligation includes,

> *inter alia*, refraining from engaging in any practice or activity that denies or limits equal access to adequate water; arbitrarily interfering with customary or traditional arrangements for water allocation; unlawfully diminishing or polluting water . . .; and limiting access to or destroying water services and infrastructure as a punitive measure, for example, during armed conflicts in violation of international humanitarian law.[98]

In an earlier chapter of this book, in examining the relationship between international water law and the human right to water, Russell and McCaffrey examine the issue of whether 'a party to the ICESCR would be under an obligation to refrain from using an international watercourse in such a way that would interfere directly or indirectly with the enjoyment of such rights, including the right to water, in other riparian states'. It is certainly the case that inequitable and unreasonable allocations of transboundary water resources shared between Israel and Palestine have limited the ability of Palestinians to access water resources and, coupled with other policies and practices, have impeded the ability of the PNA to ensure progressive realisation of the right to

[95] CESCR, Concluding Observations on Israel, para. 26.
[96] See Chapter 5 in this book.
[97] General Comment No. 15, para. 21.
[98] Ibid.

water and sanitation. The ICESCR itself recognises that progressive realisation is dependent on the availability of resources.[99]

Under international human rights law, a State or peoples have the right to permanent sovereignty over their natural wealth or resources, as a basic element of the right to self-determination.[100] Common Article 1 of the International Covenant on Economic, Social and Cultural Rights and the International Covenant on Civil and Political Rights declares that 'all peoples have the right to self-determination' and 'may, for their own ends, freely dispose of their natural wealth and resources'.[101] The right of the Palestinian people to permanent sovereignty over their natural wealth and resources was affirmed for the first time by the UN General Assembly in December 1972[102] and has been reaffirmed numerous times since, for example, in General Assembly resolution 62/181 on 31 January 2008. The resolution confirms that the right of sovereignty over natural resources includes both land and water and calls upon Israel not to exploit or damage natural resources in the occupied Palestinian territory.[103] A study by the South African Human Sciences Research Council argues that Israeli denial of the economic dimension of self-determination, expressed as the right of permanent sovereignty over natural resources, as well as the creation of water dependence in the occupied Palestinian territory and the integration of Palestinian's water supply system into the Israeli system, amounts to a rejection of the rationale of the laws of occupation and instead 'demonstrates that the implementation of a colonial policy by Israel has not been piecemeal but is systematic and comprehensive'.[104] If indeed a colonial policy is being implemented in the occupied Palestinian territory, the international community holds tripartite obligations to cooperate to end the violation, not to recognise the illegal situation arising from it, and not to render aid or assistance to the State committing it.[105]

99 ICESCR, Article 2(1).

100 See Declaration of Permanent Sovereignty over Natural Resources, GA Res. 1803, UN Doc. A/5217 (1962).

101 The right of the Palestinian people to self-determination has been recognised in numerous UN resolutions and is considered to be the basic requirement for a just and lasting peace in the Middle East and creation of a viable Palestinian State. See, for example, GA Res. 3236 UN Doc. A/RES/3236 (XXIX) (1974); GA Res. 62/146, UN Doc. A/RES/62/146 (2008); Human Rights Council Res. 7/17, UN Doc. A/HRC/RES/7/17 (2008).

102 GA Res. 3005 (XXVII), UN Doc. A/8730 (1972).

103 GA Res. 62/181, UN Doc. A/RES/62/181 (2008), paras. 1–2.

104 Human Sciences Research Council, Occupation, Colonialism, Apartheid? A Re-assessment of Israel's Practices in the Occupied Palestinian Territories under International Law (May 2009), p. 16.

105 Ibid., p. 14.

The prohibition on discrimination is one aspect of the right to water and sanitation that is not subject to the concept of progressive realisation; according to the Committee on Economic, Social and Cultural Rights, it is a core obligation, which is non-derogable and must be complied with at all times.[106] The gross inequalities in the quantities of water available to Palestinians and Israeli citizens living both in Israel and the settlements violate this provision. Indeed, the UN Committee on the Elimination of Racial Discrimination has called upon Israel to 'ensure equal access to water resources for all without any discrimination'.[107] In terms of the allocation of transboundary water resources, the prohibition on discrimination can also be seen to be consistent with equitable and reasonable use of shared water resources.[108] These principles must override the Israeli claim of 'prior use' or even 'maintaining existing utilisation', whereby Israel argues that it has used the water from the Mountain Aquifer since before 1967 and therefore may continue to do so[109] without taking into consideration that the allocation of water is inequitable and unreasonable and violates both international human rights law and international humanitarian law principles of non-discrimination. In the case of Gaza, economic and financial sanctions imposed by both Israel and western countries and the blockade imposed by Israel have caused the near collapse of the water and sanitation sector. Under the ICESCR, sanctions or embargoes may not be imposed and applied in such a manner that they cause undue suffering on a civilian population, including denial of the right to water and sanitation. The UN Committee on Economic, Social and Cultural Rights has made clear that 'the inhabitants of any given country do not forfeit their basic economic, social and cultural rights by virtue of any determination that their leaders have violated norms relating to international peace and security'.[110] General Comment No. 15 further observes: 'States parties should never impose embargos or similar measures that prevent the supply of water, as well as goods and services essential for securing the right to water. Water should never be used as an instrument of political and economic pressure'.[111]

[106] CESCR, General Comment No. 15, para. 17.

[107] UN Committee on the Elimination of Racial Discrimination, Concluding Observations of the Committee on the Elimination of Racial Discrimination: Israel, UN Doc. CERD/C/ISR/CO/13 (2007), para. 35.

[108] Human Sciences Research Council, Occupation, Colonialism, Apartheid?, p. 139.

[109] Israel Water Authority, The Issue of Water between Israel and the Palestinians, p. 29.

[110] CESCR, *General Comment No. 8, The Relationship between Economic Sanctions and Respect for Economic, Social and Cultural Rights* (Seventeenth session, 1997), UN Doc. E/C.12/1997 (1997), para. 16.

[111] CESCR, General Comment No. 15, para. 32. Footnote in quotation omitted.

Therefore, when sanctions, embargoes or similar measures are applied on a State, the external party must take into consideration the effect the measures will have on economic and social rights; identify a range of exempt goods and services; monitor the impact of the measures taken on the rights of the affected population; and assume responsibility to respond to and to rectify any disproportionate suffering experienced by vulnerable groups in the targeted country, including through seeking and facilitating international assistance and cooperation.[112] It could also be argued that the actions of western States violate the extraterritorial obligations they hold under the terms of the ICESCR, to take steps to realise progressively the rights recognised in the ICESCR through international assistance and cooperation.[113] More specifically, as noted above, State parties to the ICESCR are obliged to respect the enjoyment of the rights guaranteed in the Covenant in other countries and 'refrain from actions that interfere, directly or indirectly, with the enjoyment of the right to water in other countries'.[114]

Both the deliberate targeting of water and sanitation infrastructure in the course of military incursions and the blockade on the Gaza Strip, which has prevented the entry of humanitarian aid and materials necessary to respond to the water and sanitation crisis, violate international humanitarian law. The Fourth Geneva Convention states, 'If the whole or part of the population of an occupied territory is inadequately supplied, the Occupying Power shall agree to relief schemes on behalf of the said population, and shall facilitate them by all the means at its disposal'.[115] International law requires that those who commit gross violations of international human rights law and serious breaches of international humanitarian law be held to account for their actions. The international community holds the obligation to ensure that an impartial and independent investigation is carried out, and where necessary prosecutions occur against those responsible for serious violations of international law, where effective and credible domestic investigations have failed to take place. This fact was reiterated by the UN Fact Finding Mission on the Gaza Conflict, which, as highlighted above, specifically examined the widespread destruction of water and sanitation infrastructure.[116] High Contracting Parties to the Geneva Conventions are bound to ensure all parties to a conflict comply with the Geneva Conventions (Article 1) and hold perpetrators responsible for grave breaches to account (Article 146). Further, the European Union

[112] CESCR, General Comment No. 8, paras. 12–15. [113] ICESCR, Article 2(1).

[114] CESCR, General Comment No. 15, para. 31. [115] Fourth Geneva Convention, Article 59.

[116] Human Rights Council, *Report of the UN Fact Finding Mission on the Gaza Conflict*, para. 1760.

Guidelines on Promoting Compliance with International Humanitarian Law (2005) call for the imposition of sanctions and other restrictive measures to ensure compliance with international humanitarian law and bring perpetrators of violations to justice before domestic courts or an international criminal tribunal. In light of these guidelines and EU Member State's responsibilities under international law, the European Union should make continuation of the agreement conditional upon a respect for human rights and fundamental freedoms.[117]

International law further guarantees that victims of gross violations of international human rights law and serious breaches of international humanitarian law have the right to both remedy and reparation. The UN General Assembly has stated that reparation includes restitution, compensation, rehabilitation, satisfaction and guarantees of non-repetition.[118] The UN General Assembly 'recognizes the right of the Palestinian people to claim restitution as a result of any exploitation, damage, loss or depletion, or endangerment of their natural resources resulting from illegal measures taken by Israel'.[119] The United Nations could examine the possibility of a Compensation Commission, similar to the one established by the UN Security Council in 1991 to process claims and pay compensation for losses, including environmental damage and depletion of natural resources, as a result of Iraq's unlawful invasion and occupation of Kuwait.

## 6 CONCLUSION

In conclusion, impediments to the realisation of the human right to water and sanitation in the West Bank include the limited territorial jurisdiction of the PNA; the unequal and discriminatory allocation of water resources shared between Israel and Palestine to the detriment of Palestinians; Israel's effective veto of infrastructure development or rehabilitation proposals through the Joint Water Committee; Israel's punitive destruction of water and sanitation infrastructure; and measures implemented by Israel on security grounds, such as the Wall, roadblocks and checkpoints, which restrict access to water resources, services and facilities. In the Gaza Strip, the financial boycott of the PNA coupled with the sanctions and blockade on Gaza, following

[117] EU-Israel Association Agreement (2000), Article 2.

[118] UN General Assembly, Basic Principles and Guidelines on the Right to a Remedy and Reparation for Victims of Gross Violations of International Human Rights Law and Serious Violations of International Humanitarian Law, UN Doc. GA/RES/60/147 (2006), para. 4.

[119] UN GA Res. 62/181, UN Doc. A/RES/62/181 (2008), para. 3.

Hamas's victory in the Palestinian legislative elections in 2006, and repeated military assaults have significantly undermined the ability of the PNA to provide an adequate service to the Palestinian population and caused further retrogression in the realisation of the right to water and sanitation.

While the PNA remains the primary actor involved in water and sanitation service provision in the occupied Palestinian territories, it is not the only actor that holds obligations in relation to the fulfilment the right to water and sanitation of the Palestinian people. The PNA's ability to progressively realise the right has been undermined by the actions of the occupying power and the international community. These actors must also take the responsibility to respect, protect and fulfil the right to water and sanitation for the Palestinian people or be held accountable for their actions under international law. The international community must ensure that it also acts to hold Israel accountable for gross violations of international human rights law and serious breaches of international humanitarian law. While Israel has legitimate security concerns, it must ensure that measures it takes to protect its citizens do not negatively impact on the Palestinian population's economic, social and cultural rights, including the right to water and sanitation.

## POSTSCRIPT

In 2014, a new Palestinian Water Law came into being, recognising the right to water, establishing mandates and responsibilities for key water sector institutions and setting out reforms for water governance. Subsequently, the Water Sector Reform Plan 2016–2018 was developed.[120] However, despite the recognition of much needed institutional change, the PWA will remain constrained in its ability to deliver due to the ongoing impact of the occupation on water resources and their management and development.

A report prepared by the Palestinian Central Bureau of Statistics in 2015 stated that the Israeli daily share per capita of water consumption was seven times higher than a Palestinian's, due to the inequality between Israel and Palestine in sharing water resources, and Israel's near total control over ground and surface water.[121] Israel has continued to exercise control over the development of water and sanitation infrastructure in the West Bank. Only 1.5 per cent of Palestinian applications for building permits in Area C were approved

[120] Palestinian Water Authority, 'Water Sector Reform Plan 2016-2018', April 2016.
[121] Palestinian Central Bureau of Statistics, 'Press Release on the Occasion of World Water Day', 22 March 2015.

between 2010 and 2014.[122] During 2016, 1,093 Palestinian-owned structures were demolished or seized throughout the West Bank, including East Jerusalem; many of them due to lack of a building permit, a number of them WASH related.[123] In Areas A and B, around 445,000 people are either not connected to the water supply or receive water once a week or less, in addition to 150,000 Palestinians in Area C.[124] At the same time, illegal Israeli settlements continue to expand. In May 2017, the JWC resumed its meetings after a break of a number of years, in the hope of accelerating the implementation of internationally funded infrastructure projects. Yet, this will do little to address issues of inequality in access to resources or the continuing obstruction on infrastructure development by the Israeli Civil Administration.

In Gaza, reconstruction of water and sanitation infrastructure damaged by conflict and the implementation of long-term solutions to the WASH sector crisis remains hampered due to the continuing blockade and restrictions on the import of over 5,000 WASH items.[125] Continuing restrictions on electricity supply mean that 40 per cent of Gaza's population receive only 5 to 8 hours of water supply once every three days.[126] In November 2016, the World Bank referred to the water situation in Gaza as 'alarming': It reported that only 10 per cent of Palestinians in Gaza have access to safe drinking water, in large part due to the salinisation of the aquifer and pollution from untreated waste water.[127] The right to water and sanitation for Palestinians remains a long way from being realised.

[122] UNOCHA, 'Under Threat: Demolition Orders in Area C of the West Bank', September 2015.
[123] UNOCHA, 'Record Number of Demolitions and Displacements in the West Bank during 2016', 10 February 2017.
[124] UNOCHA, 'Humanitarian Needs Overview 2017', November 2016. [125] Ibid. [126] Ibid.
[127] World Bank, 'Water Situation Alarming in Gaza', 22 November 2016.

# III

# Urban Water Reform

# 13

# Privatisation and the Right to Water

MALCOLM LANGFORD*

## 1 INTRODUCTION

The last two decades have witnessed a global experiment with the privatisation of water utilities. Promoted by the World Bank and bilateral donors and backed by generous loans and aid conditionalities, it sparked a strong counter-reaction. As Kanbur notes, 'While trade liberalization was perhaps the archetype disagreement on development strategy in the 1980s and 1990s, in the 1990s and 2000s this role has been taken over by water privatization and the passions it arouses'.[1] At the forefront of this opposition were a range of civil society movements. They used various tactics and strategies to oppose privatisation and, pointedly, their resistance was often expressed in the language of the right to water.

The actual spread of privatisation (whether fully or partially through concessions, leases and shareholdings) has not been as significant as expected. The rate of new forms of private participation in the urban water sector dropped off in the 2000s. Moreover, there has been no significant shift in the proportion of the global population served by major private operators.[2] This retarded development has a number of potential causes, which includes backlash against privatisation, the gradual dropping of donor conditionalities and the model of

* Professor, Faculty of Law, University of Oslo; Co-Director, Centre on Law and Social Transformation, University of Bergen and CMI.

1 R. Kanbur, 'Development Disagreements and Water Privatization: Bridging the Divide', *Journal of Poverty Alleviation and International Development*, Vol. 1, No. 1 (2011), pp. 1–20, at 1. It is important to note that the resistance was not restricted to urban water reform. The global water justice movement has been equally concerned with rural water reform, particularly in relation to commodification of water supplies and environmental protection. See V. Shiva, *Water Wars: Privatisation, Pollution and Profit* (Cambridge: South End Press, 2002).

2 P. Marin, *Public-Private Partnerships for Urban Water Utilities: A Review of Experiences in Developing Countries* (Washington D.C.: World Bank, 2009).

transnational corporation-led privatisation, which was exposed as fragile in the face of financial crises or currency devaluations.

But the trend has not fully stalled. Multinationals continue to promote their role in the sector, particularly in middle-income countries. In developing countries, local private companies have emerged as the new face of privatisation while there has been a steady increase in privatisation in Asia, Europe and the Middle East. Moreover, the ideational dimension of privatisation has endured. Some argue that privatisation laid the groundwork for the commercialisation of services.[3] This is manifest in the trend towards corporatisation (public ownership of utilities runs on commercial principles) and the institutional embedding of the concept of water as economic good rather than a public health-related service.[4] Concurrently, water companies have increasingly appropriated the language of the right to water to argue that they are best placed to ensure its effective realisation.[5]

After charting the rise and part fall of privatisation in Section 2, the chapter takes up three questions that concern both right to water and the privatisation movement. The first is normative in orientation: how should the relationship between the right to water and privatisation be understood? Is it one marked by antagonism, compatibility or contingency? Section 3 tackles this dilemma through a discursive analysis of arguments by civil society organisations, human rights lawyers and transnational corporations. The privatisation debate and struggle witnessed a most active and energetic uptake of the idea of the right to water, and it is worth reflecting on how it has been understood, appropriated and reshaped.

The second question is empirical. Did the shift to privatisation in practice harm or facilitate the realisation of the right to water? The debate and literature are filled with wildly varying claims over the benefits and costs of privatisation. In Section 4, a closer examination of the evidence is therefore undertaken and the results reveal a nuanced and variable picture. It is observed that the empirical case for privatisation ultimately depends on the choice of methodology and the interpretations of the necessary conditions for effective water utilities.

The third question is sociolegal. How did the right to water feature in the local and global movements that resisted privatisation? What is striking about

3 K. Bakker, 'The "Commons" versus the "Commodity": After-globalisation, Anti-privatisation and the Right to Water in the Global South', *Antipode*, Vol. 39, No. 3 (2007), pp. 430–455.

4 D. Hemson, 'Water for All: From Firm Promises to "New Realism"' in D. Hemson, K. Kulindwa, H. Lein and A. Mascarenhas (eds.), *Poverty and Water: Explorations of the Reciprocal Relationship* (London: Zed Books, 2008), p. 30; J. Magdahl, *From Privatisation to Corporatisation: Exploring the Strategic Shift in Neoliberal Policy on Urban Water Services* (Oslo: Fivas, 2012).

5 See A. Russell, 'Incorporating Social Rights in Development: Transnational Corporations and the Right to Water', *International Journal of Law in Context*, Vol. 7, No. 1 (2011), pp. 1–30.

the reaction to privatisation was the turn, in varying degrees, to rights talk and legal tactics by civil society organisations. Such strategies are often viewed with scepticism by those that view rights and law as ally of capitalism or an ineffective or elite-driven mode of tackling social injustice. Section 5 begins by tracking the resistance to privatisation and briefly examines the turn to rights in six countries, which involved a range of strategies from legal and constitutional reforms to direct and indirect court-based challenges to privatisation.

## 2 PRIVATISATION: THE RISE, FALL AND REFORMATION

Up and until 1990, private sector involvement in the delivery of *formal* urban water services was minimal and episodic.[6] The only country to experience significant private sector involvement was France where 80 per cent of water operators were private, though the public sector retained significant responsibility for financing new investments.[7] In developing and emerging economies, the figure was less than one per cent.[8] However, the emphasis in the next decade shifted dramatically. In the seven years from 1990, there was an 8,400 per cent increase in private sector investment levels in comparison to the previous sixteen-year period.[9] Southern countries alone awarded a hundred water contracts for water and sewerage projects to private companies between 1990 and 1997, compared to only eight between 1984 and 1990.[10] The number of contracts peaked in 1999 with thirty partnerships awarded that year, tapering off to just above ten in 2002.[11] By 2009, close to forty countries had experimented with some form of private sector participation.[12]

6 For a history, see N. Prasad, 'Privatisation of Water: A Historical Perspective', *Law, Environment and Development Journal*, Vol. 3, No. 2 (2007), pp. 217–233. Note that small-scale, communal and ad hoc provision accounts for 50 per cent of urban coverage in developing countries, primarily in informal settlements: J. Baumert and L. Bloodgood, 'Private Sector Participation ithe Water and Wastewater Services Industry', Office of Industries, US International Trade Commission, Working Paper, April 2004, p. 7.

7 This figure is at 2001. See A. Blanc and S. Botton, 'Introduction générale', in A. Blanc and S. Botton (eds.), *Services d'eau privé dans les pays en développement* (Paris: Agence française de développement, 2011), pp. 9–25, at 12; C. Cezon and L. Breuil, 'Les PPP pour développer les services d'eau potable: quelques leçons de l'experience française pour les PED', in Blanc and Botton, *Services d'eau privé dans les pays en développement*, pp. 51–71, at 56. Cezon and Breuil note though that the private companies agreed to accept more risk under their concessional and operational contracts as the public sector took on more responsibility for investments.

8 Marin, *Public-Private Partnerships for Urban Water Utilities*, p. 13.

9 G. Silva, N. Tynan and Y. Yilmaz, 'Private Participation in the Water and Sewerage Sector-Recent Trends', *Public Policy for the Private Sector*, Vol. 147 (1998), pp. 1–8, at 1–2. (25 billion divided by 297 million USD in 1997 USD dollars and expressed in percentage terms).

10 Ibid., p. 1.

11 Marin, *Public-Private Partnerships for Urban Water Utilities*, p. x.

12 Ibid., p. 2.

This dramatic shift was a natural development of the neoliberal turn by international financial institutions in the 1980s. It was also facilitated by a number of other factors. In the late 1980s, the United Kingdom had privatised its water sector, providing a reform blueprint for other countries while French multinationals sensed the potential for new markets and international expansion.[13] Pessimism was also marked in the water sector after poor progress on improving access to water in the South, despite the proclamation of the International Drinking Water Supply and Sanitation Decade 1981–1990.[14] There was room for alternatives.

The campaign for privatisation was conducted on several fronts. First, there was an ideational battle: a range of international standards and strategies that sought to legitimate privatisation heralded the shift in policy. One of the most significant was the 1991 Dublin Principles that clearly recognised water as an economic good:[15]

> Water has an *economic value* in *all* its competing uses and should be recognized as an economic good. *Within this principle*, it is vital to recognize first the basic right of all human beings to have access to clean water and sanitation at an affordable price.[16]

Whereas the human right to water was acknowledged, and basic uses prioritised, an economic frame bound these social dimensions. The Dublin Principles were to prove influential. They were echoed in the annual water forum meetings of Ministers throughout the 1990s and formed the basis for almost all donor policies in the period.[17] The most significant policy was the

[13] M. Barlow, *Blue Covenant: The Global Water Crisis and the Coming Battle for the Right to Water* (New York: New Press, 2008).

[14] General Assembly Resolution 35/18, Second Committee (55th Plenary Meeting), 10 November 1980. In proclaiming the period 1981–1990 as the International Drinking Water Supply and Sanitation Decade, the Assembly did not set quantitative targets but did state that 'Member States will assume a commitment to bring about a *substantial* improvement in the standards and levels of services in drinking water services and sanitation by the year 1990' (para. 1; emphasis added). Different causes were identified for failure to reach the 1990 water targets – from high population growth through to promotion of expensive technologies in rural areas. B. Diamant, 'Assessment and Evaluation of the International Water Decade', *Journal of the Royal Society for the Promotion of Health*, No. 4 (1992), pp. 183–188, at 184, 186. However, great emphasis had been placed on the virtues of the public sector in outlining strategies during the decade.

[15] 'Dublin Statement on Water and Sustainable Development', International Conference on Water and the Environment: Development Issues for the 21st Century, UN Doc. A/CONF.151/PC/112 (1992). It was not a formal government declaration, but the statement was endorsed by international experts from a hundred countries. It is also a formal UN document.

[16] Principle 4, emphasis added.

[17] See overview in M. Langford, 'Ambition that Overleaps Itself? A Response to Stephen Tully's "Critique" of the General Comment on the Right to Water', *Netherlands Quarterly of Human Rights*, Vol. 26, No. 3 (2006), pp. 433–459.

World Bank's *Water Resources Sector Strategy* in 1993, which emphasised the importance of economic incentives and efficiency and laid the ideational framework for the subsequent push for privatisation across international development policy and practice.[18] Western countries also sought to further entrench the principle in international law and standards by placing pressure on developing countries to include the water sector in the list of areas to be covered by the General Agreement on Trade in Services[19] and seeking to develop new privatisation-friendly water service standards under the mantle of the International Standards Organisation.[20]

Second, it was strategic. Donors and others sought to reshape the balance of benefits and costs for policymakers in order to make privatisation attractive and thus inevitable. The most concrete weapon was the use of conditionalities: debt relief programmes and concessional finance and grants for the water sector from bilateral and multilateral donors were made conditional on privatisation. Part of the process leading to the privatisation of Tanzania's water supply system has been described as follows:

> [I]n 2000, World Bank and IMF officials decided to include the privatisation of DAWASA (Dar es Salaam Water and Sewerage Authority) - under a concession agreement that would assign its assets to a private management company - as a condition for the country receiving HIPC debt relief. Meeting this conditionality would reduce Tanzania's debt service burden by $3bn over time, or between one half and one third each year. Moreover, the 2000 Country Assistance Strategy also required Tanzania to meet all conditions for HIPC debt relief in order to qualify for the baseline lending scenario of $260m each year between 2000 and 2003. If Tanzania failed to meet the triggers on schedule, Bank lending would fall to only $100m per year.[21]

Third, it was sociological as promoters sought to shift underlying collective action frames. Privatisation as the pre-eminent form of provision was woven into standard development technical assistance programmes through

[18] 'Water Resources Management Strategy', World Bank (1993). Note that the language was partly opaque in this document due to an internal struggle within the Bank. See G. Pitman, *Bridging Troubled Waters: Assessing the World Bank Water Resource Strategy* (Washington D.C.: World Bank, 2002), p. 2. It emphasises the role of market mechanisms generally rather than privatisation per se.

[19] See Chapter 15 by Lang in this volume.

[20] International NGO Network on ISO, *International Standards*, Pacific Institute for Studies in Development, Environment, and Security (2000), available at www.pacinst.org (accessed 3 December 2012).

[21] ActionAid International, *Turning off the Taps: Donor Conditionality and water privatisation in Dar es Salaam, Tanzania* (2004), p. 6, available at www.actionaid.org.uk (accessed 3 December 2012).

policy advice, knowledge transfer and commissioned research and consultancies.[22] In wealthier and Northern countries, these 'soft' forms were extensively used. Beveridge argues that enormous efforts were invested in shifting political narratives so that privatisation was 'inevitable': it was 'presented and perceived in increasingly commonsensical terms' and as the only 'alternative' given the collapse of communism and the inescapable realities of globalisation.[23] These discursive efforts were accompanied by a phalanx of consultants, often drawn from a few multinational accountancy firms, who worked both for municipalities and multinational corporations in managing the processes of drafting new laws, tendering and regulatory processes and contract negotiations.[24]

The actual pattern of privatisation suggests that the calculus of strategic action was critical. Political science studies reveal that the ideological orientations of key actors were not decisive in explaining the advance of privatisation: rather it was the extent to which privatisation was beneficial or costly in raw economic and political terms. In a meta-regression of 32 studies on the causes of privatisation, Bel and Fageda found that the ideological position of the incumbent political parties in local governments (who usually decide on implementation of water policy) had little influence on the decision to privatise or not.[25] According to this study, other factors appear to be important. Economically, municipalities with higher debts and budget deficits were more likely to opt for privatisation in order to secure fresh funds. Politically, the balance of supportive and oppositional civil society forces, particularly the relative strengths of the economic middle class, trade unions and broader civil society coalitions, qualified the likelihood of choosing full or partial privatisation.[26] These findings have been partly confirmed in qualitative studies. The degree of water privatisation across selected French and German municipalities correlates highly with the level of municipal debt and the relative strength of civil society opposition.[27]

22 Ibid., pp. 6–9.

23 R. Beveridge, *A Politics of Inevitability* (Berlin: Springer VS, 2012), pp. 20, 22.

24 R. Beveridge, 'Consultants, Depoliticization and Arena-shifting in the Policy Process: Privatizing Water in Berlin', *Policy Sci*, Vol. 45 (2012), pp. 47–68.

25 G. Bel and X. Fageda, 'Factors Explaining Local Privatization: A Meta-regression Analysis', *Public Choice*, Vol. 139, Nos. 1–2 (2009), pp. 105–119.

26 The authors also point out that larger municipalities were more open to privatisation, possibly because of the *perceived* economies of scale. An alternative explanation might be that potential profit for the private sector with these municipalities was greatest, and thus they were subject to greater lobbying and pressure to privatise.

27 K. Fitch, 'Water Privatisation in France and Germany: The Importance of Local Interest Groups', *Local Government Studies*, Vol. 33, No. 4 (2007), pp. 589–605. This might also

The privatisation revolution was only short-lived. The rate of uptake of private forms of provision significantly slowed in the 2000s. The causes arguably included massive civil society resistance (see Section 5), the inability of transnational corporations to return dividends to the North in the face of currency devaluations and a growing unease in the development community (including the World Bank's own Independent Evaluation Office) that privatisation was not delivering on its promise of improving access. In the 2000s, the annual number of new public-private partnerships (PPPs) awarded decreased, and the global population served by major private operators has not changed significantly:[28] only about 7 per cent of urban population in developing countries was served by formal public-private partnerships (PPPs) by 2007.[29]

This statistical picture has contributed to an oft-heard observation that the water privatisation project is largely dead. It has been enhanced by the crumbling of some high prestige projects (such as in Bolivia, Argentina and the Philippines) and the more cautious stance articulated by the World Bank in the mid-2000s. However, this perception is part myth. Water privatisation may be off the high-profile policy agenda but the empirical picture is complicated. A close look reveals adaption and mutation rather than demise. In some cases, full privatisation was adopted (i.e. a transfer of state assets) but more common were concessional arrangements (management of water services) or partial private ownership of utilities. In addition, weaker forms such as leases or contracting out of certain functions such as billing were adopted, making it difficult at times to determine whether a service was private or not.[30] Many countries also turned to a corporate model that maintained public ownership but sought to ensure water utilities ran on purely economic principles, with water revenues used to subsidise other arms of government.

Equally important is the shift in the distribution and profile of water privatisation, which hides the increasingly predominant form of private sector participation. Initially, the bulk of privatisation occurred in Latin America, and multinational water companies were the predominant face of the water sector. In 2000, Latin American countries accounted for 44 of 94 million persons reportedly served by private sector operators,[31] and five multinational companies accounted for 80 per cent of the market.[32] By 2007, the pattern had shifted with

suggest that privatisation is more likely in strong centralised states since 'it implies weak municipalities (both politically and in financially) *and* weak civil societies' (p. 597).

[28] B. Morgan, 'Building Bridges Between Regulatory and Citizen Space: Civil Society Contributions to Water Service Delivery Frameworks in Cross-National Perspective', *LGD*, No. 1 (2008), pp. 24, 35.

[29] Ibid. [30] See generally Marin, *Public-Private Partnerships for Urban Water Utilities*.

[31] Ibid., p. 24. [32] Ibid., p. 29.

Asia accounting for the highest share of private sector participation in terms of consumers (50 million out of 160 million served).[33] There were also considerable rises in Africa, Central Europe and the Middle East. Moreover, by 2007, at least 40 per cent of this market was being served by private operators from developing countries.[34] Conditionalities still persist: Greece was forced to privatise its water sector in order to gain financial relief from the IMF and EU.[35] Marin also notes that 84 per cent of contracts that have been awarded over the last two decades were still in place by 2007.[36] This suggests that post-privatisation resistance has been less successful than pre-privatisation resistance.

Privatisation or private sector participation is not a spent force. In fact, it is likely to gradually increase given that its economic base is more secured: that is, new contracts are increasingly being awarded in middle-income countries, and local private operators are better placed to avoid currency fluctuation risks by accessing local finance or equity investment. However, the rate of expansion has clearly slowed and one of the strongest trends is remunicipalisation.[37] Between 2000 and 2014, the public sector took back control from the private sector, with 81 occurring in the period 2010 to 2014. In the slight majority of cases remunicipalisation occurred through cancellation of a concession contract and in a slight minority through expiry. [38]

## 3 A NORMATIVE CLASH

The relationship between the right to water and privatisation has been almost as contested as much privatisation itself. In this normative tussle, many social movements and activists deployed the right as a core reason for rejecting a significant role for the private sector in water services. Transnational corporations argued the opposite: private companies are best placed to work with governments to ensure its realisation.[39] In between these two positions, one finds a more classical and partly agnostic human rights law position: private action to realise a right is permissible if there is appropriate regulation with the intention to ensure that all aspects of the right (including affordability and access) are progressively realised.

33 Ibid., p. 24. 34 Ibid., p. 31.

35 D. Hall, *Water in Europe*, Presentation to Attac ENA, Freibourg, August 2011.

36 Ibid., p. 26.

37 PSIRU, 'Here to Stay: Water Remunicipalisation as a Global Trend', Multinationals Observatory, November 2014.

38 Ibid., 4.

39 See Russell, 'Incorporating Social Rights in Development: Transnational Corporations and the Right to Water'.

### 3.1 *Three Discourses: Public Good, Corporate Rescue and Legal Agnosticism*

Each set of actors can mount a reasoned argument. Activists offer both substantive and procedural reasons. According to the Blue Planet project, profit-making and the often necessary increase in prices are incompatible with the need for water to be 'safe, affordable, and accessible to everyone – not just those who can afford to pay'.[40] Putting aside the question of the evidence for this assertion, which is discussed in the next section, it at least theoretically accords with the economics of monopoly provision - high prices. Procedurally, the concern is that a delegation of responsibility to the private sector also loosens the degree of public control and direction over water resources and services.[41] Thus, the participatory dimension of the right counsels against privatisation.

However, in the proposed principles for an International Treaty on the Right to Water (driven by these advocates), outright prohibition of privatisation is not proposed. Instead, a strong regulatory framework that limits its possibility is articulated. This would involve strong public control (with heavy direct citizen participation) over decisions on issues like extension of access and tariffs and the elimination of recourse by transnational corporations to international investment tribunals.[42]

The corporate case for active privatisation for the right to water is also compelling on its face. The public sector controls most of the world's water supply and progress on the right to water has been slow. Segerfeldt argues that 'there is no rights-based argument that justifies government management of water', questioning why anti-privatisation activists expend so much energy on trying to stop commercialisation when governments are 'violating the rights of 1.1 billion people who do not have access to water'.[43] Similarly, in October 2001, the Chief Executive Officer of Suez wrote in *Le Monde*: 'I think we should be able to agree that the universal right of access to water must be recognized and that we should get down to work now to turn that right into a reality every day.'[44]

[40] Blue Planet Project, *Water Is a Human Right: An International Campaign to Enshrine Water as a Human Right at the United Nations*, www.blueplanetproject.net/RightToWater/human_right.html (last sccessed 20 March 2012).

[41] Ibid. [42] See *Key Principles for an International Treaty on the Right to Water.*

[43] F. Segerfeldt, *Water for Sale: How Businesses and the Market Can Resolve the World's Water Crisis* (Washington D.C: Cato Institute, 2005).

[44] G. Mestrallet, 'La vraie bataille de l'eau', *Le Monde*, 26 October 2001. Translation taken from Suez Environment, *Human Rights and Access to Drinking Water and Sanitation*, Contribution to OHCHR Consultation, April 2007.

The right to water is cast therefore in pragmatic and access-oriented terms. However, such motivations are unlikely to be exclusive. In interviews with transnational corporations (TNCs), Russell further found tactical reasons counted strongly:

> The extent of rights language amongst the TNCs was proportional to the size of the corporation and its engagement in developing countries. The 'right to water' seemed to be used primarily by the larger water transnational to try improve access to certain markets and to enhance the legitimacy of the companies in developing country operations. It was also being used to counter the attempted capture of the language by the anti-privatisation movement, which may have caused initial hesitation in the use of the terminology.[45]

Such endorsement by corporations of the right to water has reinforced the views of some sceptics that the right to water, like other rights, embodies a liberal, rather than a transformative, agenda.[46]

The third position is taken by many in the international-oriented human rights community. Human rights NGOs, academic lawyers and UN experts have been reticent to make the claim that water privatisation is ipso facto inconsistent with the right to water. The reasoning is partly legal. The script from earlier international jurisprudence, which was encapsulated by the UN Committee on Economic, Social and Cultural Rights in General Comment No. 3, has been powerful. The Committee has refused to endorse any economic model for the progressive realisation of these rights. Instead, it has emphasised the achievement of outcomes and respect of democratic principles. The Committee states:

> [I]in terms of political and economic systems the Covenant [on ESC rights] is neutral and its principles cannot accurately be described as being predicated exclusively upon the need for, or the desirability of a socialist or a capitalist system, or a mixed, centrally planned, or *laisser-faire* economy, or upon any other particular approach. In this regard, the Committee reaffirms that the rights recognized in the Covenant are susceptible of realization within the context of a wide variety of economic and political systems, provided only that the interdependence and indivisibility of the two sets of human rights, as affirmed *inter alia* in the preamble to the Covenant, is recognized and reflected in the system in question.[47]

45 Russell, 'Incorporating Social Rights in Development', pp. 23–24.

46 See K. Bakker, 'The Commons versus the Commodity: Alter-globalization, Anti-privatization and the Human Right to Water in the Global South', *Antipode – A Radical Journal of Geography*, Vol. 39 No. 3 (2007), pp. 430–455.

47 *Comment* 3, *The Nature of States Parties' Obligations* (Fifth session, 1990), UN Doc. E/1991/23, annex III at 86 (1991), para. 8.

The jurisprudence of the Committee has subsequently focused on articulating result standards (e.g. affordability, access, minimum levels, non-discrimination), process standards (e.g. participation, negotiations and remedies) and conduct standards (e.g. legislation and action plans, allocation of resources and accountability institutions).

The reasoning by human rights NGOS and lawyers is also partly empirical. On the one hand, they often expressed scepticism to privatisation. Indeed, the development of access to water in Europe and the USA over the last two centuries was facilitated by 'publicisation' not privatisation. On the other hand, many of these actors were simultaneously battling violations of the right to water by public authorities, from disconnections of services through to failure to take steps to extend access to informal settlements. They appeared uncomfortable with an agenda that reduced the right to water to a question of maintaining public control.

The drafting of General Comment No. 15 on the Right to Water brought this debate into sharp relief. In 2002, the CESCR received submissions drawn from all three perspectives. The first draft of the General Comment, which was made publicly available for feedback, was novel. It went beyond previous general comments and called for deferral of privatisation until sufficient regulatory systems were in place.[48] The Committee had taken cognisance of the growing critique over privatisation. It clearly wished to remind States that effective regulation of private solutions was a non-negotiable part of the process. But the interpretation seemed too much of a break with past jurisprudence. In the final version, the Committee returned to more standard text although provided more elaboration on the nature of regulation:

> 23. The obligation to *protect* requires State parties to prevent third parties from interfering in any way with the enjoyment of the right to water. Third parties include individuals, groups, corporations and other entities as well as agents acting under their authority. The obligation includes, inter alia, adopting the necessary and effective legislative and other measures to restrain, for example, third parties from denying equal access to adequate water; and polluting and inequitably extracting from water resources, including natural sources, wells and other water distribution systems.

[48] 'Privatization of water services should be deferred until an effective regulatory system is in place, that is in conformity with the Covenant and this General Comment and that includes independent monitoring, genuine public participation and imposition of penalties for non-compliance'. Committee on Economic, Social and Cultural Rights, *Draft General Comment 15, The Right to Water*, para. 18.

> 24. Where water services (such as piped water networks, water tankers, access to rivers and wells) are operated or controlled by third parties, States parties must prevent them from compromising equal, affordable, and physical access to sufficient, safe and acceptable water. To prevent such abuses an effective regulatory system must be established, in conformity with the Covenant and this General Comment, includes independent monitoring, genuine public participation and imposition of penalties for non-compliance.[49]

The Committee also made an important addition. During the public session that discussed the final draft, some members of the Committee continued to express concern about privatisation, noting that it was not only an individual right; it was also a public good. This position was reflected in a new opening sentence of the General Comment: 'Water is a limited natural resource and a public good fundamental for life and health.'[50] This statement has been interpreted by some as a clear disinclination to favour private water solutions, as the recognition of water as a public good has been a clarion call of the anti-privatisation movement.

### 3.2 *A Depoliticised Right or Critical Norm?*

However, some commentators have been critical of the Committee for its cautiousness. Craven argues that the Committee should not be 'legislating for its own absence – or excluding its own competence' in an area 'in which the Committee's voice is perhaps most needed'.[51] Tully suggests that the General Comment fails to address the key culprit in the 'water crisis', the multinational water corporations: 'The General Comment template is symptomatic of continued reliance upon an increasingly obsolete State-centric model.'[52] Sultana and Loftus argue that this enhances the risk that the right to water becomes a depoliticised, 'empty signifier used by both political progressives and conservatives that actually does little to effect real change in water governance'.[53]

[49] Committee on Economic, Social and Cultural Rights, *General Comment 15, The Right to Water* (Twenty-ninth session, 2002), UN Doc. E/C.12/2002/11 (2003). For an extensive discussion, see K. Moyo, 'Privatisation of the Commons: Water as a Right; Water as a Commodity', *Stellenbosch Law Review*, Vol. 22 (2011), pp. 804–822.

[50] General Comment No. 15, para. 1.

[51] M. Craven, 'Some Thoughts on the Emergent Right to Water' in E. Riedel and P. Rothen (eds.), *The Human Right to Water* (Berlin: Berliner WissenschaftsVerlag, 2006), pp. 35–47, at 45–46.

[52] S. Tully, 'A Human Right to Access Water? A Critique of General Comment No. 15', *Netherlands Quarterly of Human Rights*, Vol. 23, No. 1 (2005), pp. 35–63.

[53] F. Sultan and A. Loftus, *The Right to Water: Politics, Governance and Social Struggles* (London: Routledge, 2012), p. 2.

These critiques are certainly fair and the Committee could have been more robust. But it is not clear that the Committee's caution has been harmful to the debate or that the right has been stripped of its critical edge. It has set a standard for any privatisation effort which corporations have for the most part discursively accepted. It has also avoided endless interpretive debates about the relationship between the right to water and privatisation but instead recognised that the decision over privatisation should be taken in the political spheres.

Both of these dimensions can be seen in practice. For instance, a year later in 2003, the European Union parliament drew on General Comment No. 15 to express concern about the donor-driven privatisation. It passed a resolution reaffirming that 'access to drinking water in a sufficient quantity and of adequate quality is a basic human right' and affirming the CESCR's General Comment No. 15.[54] It describes how the efforts of the Northern-dominated development community had largely failed:

> [The] most disadvantaged inhabitants of developing countries continue to face a shortage of drinking water despite the efforts undertaken so far by the international community, that the solutions focusing on the privatisation of drinking water supplies put forward by donors have failed, and that consequently there has been no improvement in access to drinking water and no decline in illnesses related to lack of water.[55]

The resolution further slates structural adjustment programmes spearheaded by international financial institutions that crippled the ability of developing countries to provide services and criticises the practice of Northern donors and international financial institutions for making receipt of loans conditional on the liberalisation of basic public services and the European Commission for pushing liberalisation in least developed countries as part of the negotiations on the General Agreement on Trade in Services (GATS). The parliament requested a reversal of policy in all three areas and greater caution in recommending privatisation.

Likewise, efforts at the national and international level to entrench the right to water focused on explicitly clarifying this issue. For instance, a two-tracked approach was adopted in the question put in the Uruguayan referendum in October 2004. It not only covered the constitutional recognition of the right to

[54] *European Parliament Resolution on the Commission Communication on Water Management in Developing Countries and Priorities for EU Development Cooperation* (COM(2002) 132 – C5-0335/2002 – 2002/2179(COS)), 4 September 2003, paras. 1, D.

[55] Ibid., para. 4.

water but also a requirement that the water supply was to remain in public hands. Similarly, Nicaragua adopted a new water law in 2007 which provided that service of potable water shall not be the object of privatisation, be it direct or indirect, and shall always be considered of public character.[56] At the international level, transnational networks sought to develop a treaty that would decisively take a position on privatisation, which sought to both entrench and develop further the General Comment.[57] However, these efforts have been less successful within the United Nations. Notably, the General Assembly, and Human Rights Council resolutions are silent on this point.[58]

## 4 EMPIRICAL CONTESTATION

The debate on privatisation has not been simply conducted in normative terms. Significant focus has been placed on whether privatisation has achieved its objectives, including realising the right to water. However, the challenge in answering this innocuous question is that it raises all the classical methodological problems in assessing impact. Three will be discussed along with the available evidence.

### 4.1 *Legitimacy versus Instrumentalism*

The first challenge is the relationship between normative and empirical frameworks. The benchmarks for measuring impact partly differ according whether one adopts the *consequentialist* perspectives of public policy, economic efficiency and sectoral investment levels or the more *deontic* lens of social justice, global development targets or the right to water and sanitation. While each viewpoint possesses an empirical concern with improved access to clean water and sanitation, the approaches diverge normatively over the means involved.

While acknowledging the divide, it is important to ask whether consequentialist approaches can be fully insulated from deontic approaches. Does the fact that water is a public good, public trust or human right affect the calculation? In theory, consequentialist analysis has to be limited by some moral norms. It is generally acceptable that one cannot assess morally repugnant policies (e.g. the economic value of child labour) in improving

[56] Article 4, General National Water Law, 15 May 2007.

[57] See discussion at note 40.

[58] General Assembly resolution, *The Human Right to Water and Sanitation*, UN Doc A/64/L.63/Rev.1; Human Rights Council resolution, *Human Rights and Access to Safe Drinking Water and Sanitation*, UN Doc. A/HRC/15/L.14.

socio-economic outcomes.[59] Could one include water privatisation in this category? Perhaps. It is sometimes referred to as the most 'public of public goods'. However, it is a stretch and the fact that the anti-privatisation movement has devoted considerable energy to making instrumental arguments against privatisation, something that is less present in the child labour debate, suggests it may only play a limited role.

But moral perspectives are relevant to instrumental analysis in another way, if we begin with a sociological rather than normative understanding of legitimacy.[60] The breadth of the opposition to privatisation may suggest there are utilitarian and democratic reasons for empirically considering these views. Kaul argues, for instance, that the categorisation of utility-generating public goods is a matter of social construction which cannot be determined in advance.[61] Citizens in many countries have been distinctively sceptical to water privatisation. Barometer surveys in Latin America reveal a particularly curious disjuncture. Even when respondents affirm that a private sector operator is performing well, there is very little support for privatisation, contrasting sharply with other goods, such as energy and telecommunications.[62]

This perception paradox has generated a wave of follow-up studies. World Bank staff and colleagues point to a 'psychological bias' in which media reporting on a few controversial privatisations has predominantly shaped public opinion: 'Popular views are shaped by extreme cases that invite media attention, while widely diffused benefits are rarely noticed.'[63] These researchers have also sought to disaggregate the respondents and demonstrate that

59 D. Seymour and J. Pincus, 'Human Rights and Economics: The Conceptual Basis for Their Complementarit', *Development Policy Review*, Vol. 26, No. 4 (2008), pp. 387–405.

60 As Buchanan and Keohane put it, '[t]o say that an institution is legitimate in the normative sense is to assert that it has the right to rule', through 'promulgating rules and attempting to secure compliance'. A. Buchanan and R. Keohane, 'The Legitimacy of Global Governance Institutions', in R. Wolfrum and V. Röben (eds.), *Legitimacy in International Law* (Berlin: Springer, 2008), pp. 25–62, at 25. Sociological legitimacy is concerned with whether individuals believe in 'a system of authority' and 'by virtue of which persons exercising authority are lent prestige' such that obedience of the subjects may follow: M. Weber, *The Theory of Social and Economic Organization*, T. Parsons (ed.) (New York: Free Press, 1964), p. 382.

61 I. Kaul and R. Mendoza, 'Advancing the Concept of Global Public Goods', in I. Kaul, P. Conceição, K. Le Goulven and R. Mendoza (eds.), *Providing Global Public Goods: Managing Globalization* (Oxford University Press, New York, 2002).

62 D. McKenzie. and. D. Mookherjee, 'Paradox and Perception: Evidence from Four Latin American Countries', in J. Nellis and N. Birdsall (eds.), *Reality Check: The Distributional Impact of Privatization in Developing Countries* (Washington: Centre for Global Development, 2005), pp. 33–84.

63 Ibid., 75. They also suggest that negative attitudes to other market reforms may strengthen these opinions: ibid., p. 76.

views are not uniform. An analysis of surveys in seventeen Latin American countries from 1998 to 2008 found that women, older individuals, couples as well as public employees, unemployed people and home workers 'are more dissatisfied', but private sector employees, those with above an average level of education, and students 'appear positively correlated with satisfaction'.[64]

This research provides a more nuanced explanation of the reasons for negative perceptions of privatisation. But it doesn't overcome the basic observation. Perceptions about water privatisation appear to significantly differ from privatisation of other goods: there is a normative unease in public opinion about privatisation. This sui generis aspect of water services may need to be weighed in any analysis of the impact of water privatisation.

### 4.2 *Establishing a Fair Baseline*

A second question is the choice of baseline. Should one measure performance against a future promised baseline, that is, an idealist expectation method that focuses on assured impacts? Or does one adopt a past baseline, that is, a 'before-and-after' approach? If one adopts the former method, the answer is clearly no: the move to greater private sector participation did not achieve the promised impact. This is widely acknowledged. The World Bank and its Independent Evaluation Office conclude that the levels of expected investment in the water sector, extension of coverage and efficiency savings were far below what was expected.[65]

However, there are problems in using an idealist expectation method. Segerfeldt complains, with some reason, that:

> Anti-privatisation activists use separate standards when judging public and private water management. As soon as any fault occurs in the private distribution of water, their anti-corporate bias … persuades them to blame privatization in general. Similar conclusions are very seldom drawn in those cases where public water distribution does not work properly.[66]

This is a fair argument: future-oriented baselines usually obscure the relative performance of alternatives. Moreover, they rarely resolve the debate. The evaluation of water privatisation policies by the World Bank's Independent

[64] C. Bonnet, P. Dubois, D. Martimort and S. Straub, 'Empirical Evidence on Satisfaction with Privatization in Latin America', *The World Bank Economic Review*, Vol. 26, No. 1 (2011), pp. 1–33, at 27.

[65] World Bank, *Reforming Infrastructure Privatisation, Regulation and Competition* (New York: Oxford University Press); Pitman, *Bridging Troubled Waters*.

[66] Segerfeldt, *Water for Sale*, p. 115.

Evaluation Office found that they had been oversold but recommended that they remain in place and be improved.[67]

Thus, a better approach is generally to use before-and-after models for assessing impact. But this is said with two caveats. First, if specific achievement-oriented standards have been negotiated and accepted by a private or public authority, this should be factored into the analysis. Whereas consideration needs to be given to subsequent mitigating factors, dialogical forms of benchmarking are highly credible since they seek to take into account actual context. Second, and most importantly, the counterfactual alternative should not be obscured in before-and-after analysis. The question is not whether privatisation was an improvement on public sector provision. Rather it is whether it performed better than a public utility is likely to have done in the same time period. The most effective method for addressing this requires looking at comparable municipalities that opted not to privatise.

### 4.3 *Weighing the Evidence*

The third step is to identify which impacts are to be measured, calculate them and weigh them for the purposes of analysis. Here we find another methodological disjuncture between the two epistemic communities. Kanbur notes that civil society and rights activists generally tend to focus on the 'losers, especially the poorest losers', adopt a short-term time horizon with an emphasis on 'immediate negative impacts' and take account of the prevalence of non-competitive markets, meaning that 'benefits of policy reform are likely to be appropriated by a powerful elite'.[68] Contrariwise, technocrats and economists tend to focus on 'aggregate gainers and losers', 'emphasise the medium-term benefits' and assume markets are competitive and will fairly distribute efficiency gains.[69] It is thus a case of methodological incommensurability: there are 'no external or neutral standards that univocally determine the comparative evaluation of competing theories'.[70] One's respective market reflexes appear to condition and bias the evaluation.

[67] See Pitman, *Bridging Troubled Waters* and discussion in V. Roaf, *After Privatisation: What Next?* (Berlin: Heinrich Böll Stiftung, 2006). See also Marin, *Public-Private Partnerships for Urban Water Utilities*, pp. 123–148.

[68] Kanbur, 'Development Disagreements and Water Privatization', p. 10. [69] Ibid.

[70] E. Oberheim and P. Hoyningen-Huene, 'The Incommensurability of Scientific Theories', in E.N. Zalta (ed.), *Stanford Encyclopedia of Philosophy* (Spring 2013 Edition), available at http://plato.stanford.edu/archives/spr2013/entries/incommensurability/., p. 12. (Last accessed 22 March 2013).

The empirical evidence for either position is certainly not conclusive, even if one adopts a more aggregate-based medium-term perspective. Supporters of privatisation tend to point to increased access, occasional decreases in tariffs and fiscal savings.[71] One of the most quoted studies in the field concerns the concession to Suez in Buenos Aires, Argentina. Galiani, Gertler and Schargrodsky found that 'child mortality fell by approximately 8 per cent in the areas where water systems were privatized' and that this was partly due to the expansion of the network into the poorest areas (where mortality declined by even greater rates).[72] However, critics in Buenos Aires argue that the company constantly failed to meet commitments to extend access to poorer areas.[73] Moreover, there was a significant rise in disconnections and prices (27 per cent against the promised 20 per cent decline) and a failure to build a waste-water treatment plant[74] and participatory power was redistributed away from the 'poorest social sectors'.[75]

This is clearly a case of incommensurability. Some comparative studies have tried to address it by weighting the different factors against one another. McKenzie and Mookherjee's comparison of water, energy and telecommunications privatisations in Argentina, Bolivia, Mexico and Nicaragua finds that there are no signficant patterns in the tariff effects of privatisation, and where there are increases in prices, 'their effects were *outweighed* by the corresponding increase acccess that occurred in the bottom or lower half of the distribution'.[76]

Large-N studies that move beyond single utilities, countries and small comparative case studies may provide a more balanced and possibly

[71] See, for example, D. Southgate and E. Figueroa, 'Reforming Water Policies in Latin America: Some Lessons from Chile and Ecuador', in K. Okonski (ed.), *The Water Revolution: Practical Solutions to Water Scarcity* (London: International Policy Press, 2006), pp. 73–91.

[72] S. Galiani, P. J. Gertler and E. Schargrodsky, 'Water for Life: The Impact of the Privatization of Water Services on Child Mortality', *Journal of Political Economy*, Vol. 113 (2005), pp. 83–120, at XX.

[73] See discussion of Argentina in Section 5.

[74] See Public Citizen, *Water Privatisation Fiascos: Broken Promises and Social Turmoil*, Report for Water for all Campaign (2003), p. 2, available at http://citizen.org (accessed 3 April 2012).

[75] D. Azpiazu et al., *D22 Strategic Country Report: Argentina, Barriers to and Conditions for the Involvement of Private Capital and Enterprise in Water Supply and Sanitation in Latin America and Africa Project*, PRINWASS, INCO2 – Research for Development, European Commission Fifth Framework Programme 1998–2002, p. 25.

[76] D. McKenzie. and. D. Mookherjee, 'Paradox and Perception: Evidence from Four Latin American Countries', in J. Nellis and N. Birdsall (eds.), *Reality Check: The Distributional Impact of Privatization in Developing Countries* (Washington: Centre for Global Development, 2005), pp. 33–84, at 77.

commensurate analysis. One World Bank-coordinated study tested 18 cities in Argentina, Bolivia and Brazil that privatised against 28 control cities in those countries that maintained full public sector control. They found that access to water and sanitation improved in the former group but 'also improved in cities that did not introduce private sector participation'.[77] They concede that privatisation did not 'directly improve coverage' but note that the results are consistent with a qualitative observation and hypothesis: that privatisation creates a competitive atmosphere and pushes public utilities to perform better.[78] A review by the World Bank of existing studies across 260 contracts comes to similar conclusions concering four markers of impact: coverage, service quality, operational efficiency and tariff levels.[79] It finds that the impact varies and the only consistent finding is improvement in operational efficiency. In terms of populations served, the study finds that 24 per cent of privatisations were 'active' and 'clearly successful', while the remainder were terminated, expired, recent or no data was available.[80]

These studies tend to take a largely bivariate approach in comparing the relative performance of the public and private sectors. Krause instead introduces a range of other possible explanatory variables. In a large cross-country sample, he finds there was no significant correlation between access to water and sanitation and the presence of private-public partnerships.[81] But he finds a positive correlation between the level of broader democratic governance and water governance (user participation and presence of civil society groups). This suggests a different hypothesis to the competition benchmarking: that the degree of democratic and user participation is crucial.

On balance, there appear to be some recognisable gains from private delivery of water services across different indicators. But the headline finding is that these gains are no different from those achieved in comparable public-operated utilities. The core of the rub is how to interpret this evidence. One school of thought is to argue against 'bad privatisations' and move towards sustainable privatisation. The proposals have focused on improved regulation before privatisation, a greater focus on the quality and sensitivity of potential private operators and greater social use of proceeds from privatisation.[82]

77 G. Clarke, K. Kose and S. Wallsten, 'Has Private Participation in Water and Sewerage Improved Coverage? Empirical Evidence from Latin America', *Journal of International Development*, Vol. 21 (2009), pp. 327–361, at 347.

78 Ibid. 79 Marin, *Public-Private Partnerships for Urban Water Utilities*, pp. 116–119.

80 Ibid., p. 118.

81 M. Krause, *The Political Economy of Water and Sanitation* (London: Routledge, 2009).

82 J. Nellis and N. Birdsall (eds.), *Reality Check: The Distributional Impact of Privatization in Developing Countries* (Washington: Centre for Global Development, 2005), pp. 1–30.

One World Bank study goes further, arguing for greater attention to cross-subsidisation and more graduated tariff increases.[83] Others warn that any shift back to full public ownership *and* control will have little impact on improving access to water services for marginalised groups unless services are made more efficient or there is '[e]ffective institutional governance and regulation of water services'.[84]

However, a legitimate response is to ask whether continued privatisation is worth the cost and effort, particularly given legitimacy concerns. The strongest argument for it seems to be that public utilities perform best under threat of privatisation. Existential threats to the public sector have a catalytic effect. This notional competitive threat could be viewed as a form of accountability. But a natural question to ask might be whether equivalent forms of accountability for the public sector can be developed and enhanced to ensure both efficiency and equity gains. Can one create competitive threats without needing to create notional market competition? Moreover, can effective democratic participation be incorporated in a market model if it is also critical to outcomes on the right to water and sanitation? This may be possible but it would suggest very nuanced models with high levels of public control and participation.

## 5 RESISTANCE AND RIGHTS

### 5.1 *Resistance from Below*

As noted earlier, the response of civil society movements and organisations was one reason for the partial demise of privatisation. Privatisation catalysed enormous reactions in many but not all countries in which it was introduced, and the right to water was prominent in the accompanying discourse. This section provides a brief overview of various struggles before drilling down on forms of mobilisation that were more legalistic in nature.

One of the leading activists describes the general resistance to commodification, including privatisation of services, in the following terms:

> A mighty contest has grown between those (usually powerful) forces and institutions that see water as a commodity and, to be put on the market and sold to the highest bidder, and those who see water as a public trust, a common heritage of people and nature and a fundamental human right.

[83] Marin, *Public-Private Partnerships for Urban Water Utilities*, pp. 135–136.

[84] M. Rouse, *Institutional Governance and Regulation of Water Services: The Essential Elements* (London: IWA Publishing, 2007), p. xiii.

> The origins of this movement, generally referred to as the global water justice movement, lie in the hundreds of communities around the world where people are fighting to protect their local water supplies.[85]

The most well-known and iconic struggle occurred in Bolivia, which gave birth to the 'water wars'. In 1998, the US company Bechtel won a concessional contract for the city of Cochabamba's water services. A three-fold increase for some consumers in the price of water and charges on household collection of rainwater engendered rapid civil society opposition. Although Segerfeldt argues that the average tariff rise was 39 per cent on a low base, which predominantly affected existing middle class consumers with access.[86] The Coalition in Defence of Water and Life was formed to call for the end for privatisation.[87] After formal negotiations with the government broke down, street protests were organised across the city. When a protestor was shot by police, the government asked the company to leave the country. The company responded by instigating a complaint under a bilateral investment treaty, but it eventually withdrew the claim.[88] Perhaps the principal effect of the investment arbitration was to help generate a transnational civil society campaign against the company, which included a civil society petition to present an amicus intervention.[89] The pressure appears to have embarrassed Bechtel into withdrawing the proceeding.[90]

However, the intensity, character and outcomes of these struggles varied from country to country and city to city. Despite the global nature of the struggle, most of the civil society struggles were organic reactions rather than a coordinated transnational response.[91] Four vignettes provide a picture. In Bolivia itself, Cochabamba was not the only case of privatisation. A much longer conflict simmered over the earlier privatisation in La Paz/El Alto. The concession to Suez was contested on the basis that the company had failed to meet its key commitments: for example, connection targets (slightly less than

85 Barlow, *Blue Covenant*, p. 102.

86 Segerfeldt, *Water for Sale*, pp. 84–85.

87 Barlow, *Blue Covenant*, p. 104. See also B. Morgan, 'Building Bridges between Regulatory and Citizen Space: Civil Society Contributions to Water Service Delivery Frameworks in Cross-National Perspective', *LGD*, No. 1 (2008).

88 *Aguas del Tunari S.A.* v. *Republic of Bolivia*, ICSID Case No. ARB/02/3. For discussion of the international arbitration in this case, see Chapter 16 in this volume.

89 See *Petition of La Coordinadora para La Defensa del Agua y Vida, et.al.*, 29 August 2002 available at www.ciel.org/ and Letter of Response from President of ICSID Tribunal, David Carson, to Earth Justice, 29 January 2003, available at http://ita.law.uvic.ca

90 *Aguas del Tunari, S.A.* v. *Republic of Bolivia*, ICSID Case No. ARB/02/3, Decision on Jurisdiction, 21 October 2005, available at http://ita.law.uvic.ca

91 D. Hall, E. Lobin and R. De La Motte, 'Public Resistance to Privatisation in Water and Energy', *Development in Practice*, Vol. 15, Nos. 3&4 (2005), pp. 286–301.

45,000 in five years), investment targets and consumer responsiveness.[92] Moreover, consumers were forced to pay the full cost of a new connection and sewerage was affecting a UNESCO World Heritage site.[93] In 2005, a series of strikes in protest against the privatisation ground the city to a halt, prompting the resignation of the country's president and catalysing negotiations with the company that led to its departure two years later.[94] However, controversy continues as the utility operates under a commercial model with little participation by civil society members or cross-subsidisation, both key demands of the water movement.[95]

In Kenya, as in other African countries, privatisation efforts accelerated from 1994 as part of the broader process of donor-supported water sector reform.[96] The resulting 1999 National Policy on Water Resources Management and Development sought to firstly separate water management and provision and secondly shift the role of government from service provision to regulation.[97] This latter proposal soon received critical attention. Unions and civil society organisations feared that it would allow for the entrance of multinational water corporations. Privatisation in Kenya under the Moi regime, particularly during the 1980s, was associated with corruption, unclear frameworks, the sale of assets that favoured undervalue bids by government associates and the massive retrenchment of workers.[98] In May 2001, these rising concerns exploded when a French company (Seureca Space, a subsidiary of Vivendi) was awarded a ten-year contract to manage the City of Nairobi's billing and revenue collection.[99] Critics pointed out that Sereuca would not invest any money in infrastructure and would earn 14.9 per cent of the Ksh12.7 billion (US $169 million) to be collected, while the City was to cover the cost of the computer equipment and hardware. Even the World Bank criticised the project for being expensive and lacking a tendering

92 See P. Jones, 'Bolivia and the Right to Water', Powerpoint Slides (on file with the author).

93 Barlow, *Blue Covenant*, p. 104. 94 Jones, 'Bolivia'. 95 Ibid.

96 K. Bayliss, 'Utility Privatisation in Sub-Saharan Africa: A Case Study of Water', Presented at the Development Studies Association Annual Conference, University of Greenwich, 9 November 2002. See also the chapters in Part IV of this book on water sector reform. While Maalim states that the process commenced in 1997, Sammy states that the 1999 water policy was drafted in 1992. Cf. S. Wymann von Dach, 'Water Sector Reform in Kenya: First Experiences Are Positive – Interview with Engineer Mahboub Maalim, Permanent Secretary of the Kenyan Ministry of Water and Irrigation', *Inforesources*, p. 1 and W. Sammy, 'Water Privatization in Kenya', *Global Issue Papers*, No. 8 (March 2004), p. 2.

97 Sessional Paper No. 1 of 1999. and while the tribunal rejected a civil society petition to present an amicus intervention.

98 Sammy, 'Water Privatization in Kenya', pp. 5–6.

99 'Kenya Water Privatisation Bid Goes Controversial', *Panapress*, 21 May 2001 and Bayliss, 'Utility Privatisation in Sub-Saharan Africa'.

process.[100] In the end, the Government succumbed to the pressure and suspended the contract despite offers of new contributions by Vivendi (a further $150 million in expansion, repair and maintenance of the network).[101]

In Ghana, the Government and World Bank showed greater determination. Despite a high-profile, highly coordinated and partly transnational civil society campaign, privatisation proceeded, although on slightly amended terms. From 1994, the sector was gradually corporatised and in 2001 the first step was taken with a lease contract to Azurix (a subsidiary of Enron) for Accra's water supply, but it was quickly rescinded after allegations of corruption emerged.[102] A new model was subsequently adopted through which private companies could secure management contracts in urban areas and governments and foreign donors would provide investment. Remarkably, the price of water was to be linked to the exchange rate, in order to satisfy overseas investors, and not to the income levels of Ghanaians.[103] In 2005, a Dutch and South African consortium won the contract to manage Ghana's urban water, but debate erupted in early 2011 over contractual renewal and whether the company has sufficiently met its targets or not;[104] and later that year the Government made a decision not to renew the contract.

A similar pattern developed in Chile. Hall, Lobina and De la Motte categorise it as a country where strong civil society campaigns against water privatisation were not successful.[105] It was authorised in 1999 by the outgoing president despite opposition from all political parties.[106] However, Morgan notes that civil society organisations largely avoided confrontational or 'unruly' tactics such as street protests, civil disobedience and court battles.[107] Instead, the struggle was largely conducted through lobbying and legislative attempts

[100] Bayliss, 'Utility Privatisation in Sub-Saharan Africa'.

[101] 'Kenya Water Privatisation Bid Goes Controversial'.

[102] K. Agyeman, 'Privatisation of Water in Ghana: Stopped in Its Tracks or a Strategic Pause', *International Journal of Environmental Studies*, Vol. 64, No. 5 (2007), pp. 525–536, at 530.

[103] World Bank, 'Project Appraisal Document on a proposed credit in the amount of SDR71million (USD 103 million equivalent) to the Republic of Ghana for an Urbanwater Project', 1 July 2004.

[104] See G. Amexo, 'Ghana: Privatization not Solution to Urban Water Delivery- German MP', *Public Agenda (Accra)*, 9 May 2011, available online at http://allafrica.com (accessed 30 March 2012).

[105] D. Hall, E. Lobina and R. De la Motte, *Making Water Privatisation Illegal: New laws in Netherlands and Uruguay*, 31 November 2004, available at www.waterjustice.org (accessed on 26 March 2012), p. 288.

[106] Ibid., p. 294.

[107] Morgan, 'Building Bridges between Regulatory and Citizen Space', p. 3. She suggests that this strategy may be partly because households are granted subsidies to provide protection against unaffordable tariffs for basic services (p. 4).

to reverse or moderate privatisation. There was an informal plebiscite in Concepcion which revealed strong opposition amongst those that participated, but privatisation proceeded.

### 5.2 *A Turn to Legal Strategies*

These four cases provide an insight into the different forms of bottom-up resistance. Many of these struggles against privatisation were characterised by such direct forms of politics – protests, negotiations, policy proposals, civil disobedience – and the right to water has featured significantly in the surrounding discourse.

However, many movements also turned to legal strategies where direct political strategies had failed to stop the advance of privatisation. This included citizen-initiated referenda and legislative reform, as well as proactive and reactive litigation. In some cases, legal strategies have been used to directly challenge privatisation programmes, while in other cases it has been indirect – changing incentives and standards, accessing information or challenging corporatisation that followed privatisation attempts. Much of it could be characterised as 'legal mobilisation' since it was part and parcel of broader campaigns and provided a rallying point for organisational efforts. It is a point at which 'a desire or want is translated into a demand as an assertion of one's rights'[108] but also where the instigation of legal process helps energise and empower civil society movements.[109]

However, some consider that the legalisation of political struggles will be of little impact in halting ideologically driven programmes such as privatisation: it transfers power from social movements to lawyers, courts and the state apparatus. Others are more sceptical on realist or practical grounds, doubting whether law has much significance for development processes particularly present in the strategies adopted by civil society formations.

The following sub-section analyses the turn to legal mobilisation by firstly looking at four countries where referenda and legal reform dominated (Uruguay, Colombia, Italy and Germany) and four litigious challenges on access – disconnections, affordability, quantity of water (Sri Lanka, Argentina, South Africa and Indonesia – the latter two by cross-referencing in the volume) – with a primary focus on the period 1998 to 2013 and occasionally beyond. In discussing each case, particular attention is given to a range of contextual

[108] F. Zeemans, 'Legal Mobilization: The Neglected Role of the Law in the Political System', *American Political Science Review*, Vol. 77 (1983), pp. 690–703.

[109] M. McCann, *Rights at Work: Pay Equity Reform and the Politics of Legal Mobilisation* (Chicago: Chicago University Press, 1994).

variables emphasised in scholarship on social movements: in particular, the political opportunities and threats, the available action repertoire and the resonating collective action or discursive frames.[110]

The case studies are described in Table 13.1. Two of the countries are dealt with elsewhere in the book (Indonesia by Colbran in Chapter 14, and South Africa by Dugard, Langford and Anderson in Chapter 7) in this book. The table shows the formal success of the legal tactic and whether it resulted in the intended legal victory and if the political victory against an element of privatisation was achieved. As can be seen, there is no automatic correlation between the legal and political victories but the correlation is fairly strong. However, the final column lists what is most likely a sufficient condition: the strength of social mobilisation. It is arguably an important explanatory variable for understanding the political victories or failures.[111] Thus, the strong successes in court in Germany and Sri Lanka and the successful referenda in Uruguay, Italy and Germany were not only matched by halts in privatisation but also by the presence of strong social mobilisation. Moreover, even when there was a loss in court or a referendum, the presence of strong social mobilisation through the litigation appears to have halted the degree of privatisation – except in the case of Colombia. Moreover, in Indonesia, there was only a principled legal victory in 2005 – but twelve years the later the Supreme Court is now hearing a renewed challenge after a lower court moved to annul the privatisation contract in Jakarta.

Before proceeding with the individual case studies, two notes. First, a political victory does not necessarily imply an improvement in access to water and sanitation (the previous section was largely devoted to that question). Rather the focus here is on understanding the relationship between the turn to law to contest privatisation and the objectives of civil society organisations. Second, it is important to note that the cases here are representative rather than exhaustive. If we looked elsewhere we would find, for example, that in Nicaragua, the Constitutional Court ruled directly against privatisation of wastewater infrastructure.[112] In the United Kingdom, a more indirect litigious approach was adopted to challenge the use of prepaid

[110] T. Madlingozi, 'Post-Apartheid Social Movements and Legal Mobilisation', in M. Langford, B. Cousins, J. Dugard and T. Madlingozi (eds.), *Symbols of Substance: The Role and Impact of Socio-Economic Strategies in South Africa* (Cambridge: Cambridge University Press, 2012), chapter 4.

[111] Though it may not always be sufficient: see J. Dugard and M. Langford, 'Art or Science? Synthesising Lessons from Public Interest Litigation and the Dangers of Legal Determinism', *South African Journal on Human Rights*, Vol. 27, (2011), pp. 39–64.

[112] Barlow, *Blue Covenant*, p. 110.

TABLE 13.1 *Overview of legal mobilisation strategies and outcomes in different countries*

| | Referendum | Citizen-driven law reform | Direct litigation | Indirect litigation | Legal victory | Political victory | General social mobilisation |
|---|---|---|---|---|---|---|---|
| Uruguay | x | | | | Win | Win | Strong |
| Colombia | x | | | | Loss | Loss | Moderate |
| Italy | x | x | | | Win: referendum Pending: law reform | Moderate win | Strong |
| Germany | x | x | x | | Win: referendum Part win: litigation | Mostly wins | Strong |
| Sri Lanka | | | x | | Win | Win | Moderate |
| Argentina | | x | | x | Part win | Win | Strong |
| South Africa | | | | x | Loss | Win | Strong |
| Indonesia | | | x | | Loss* | Moderate loss | Moderate |

* Note however the recent district court victory in 2015 and the pending Supreme Court decision. See postscript to Chapter 14 of this volume.

metres – a common tool in privatised and corporatised utilities.[113] The High Court held that automatic cut-offs of the water supply upon the exhaustion of credit in a prepaid metre were inconsistent with statutory notice requirements and the opportunity for consumers to make representations to the relevant social service department.[114] In Greece, in 2014, the Council of State ruled that a partial privatisation of the public water company in Athens was a violation of the right to health – although recent events suggest that the EU and Greek government may be seeking to evade effectively the ruling.[115] Third, legal mobilisation against privatisation is not restricted to civil society formations. Authorities have also been embroiled in litigation and law reform. Sometimes, it is proactive. In *Nkonkobe Municipality v Water Services South Africa (PTY) Ltd and others*,[116] this South African municipality was successful in nullifying a six-year-old water privatisation contract.[117] In the case of Germany discussed below, it was opposition political parties that initiated legal action.

**Uruguay**

The Uruguayan referendum of 2004 was the first instance of a national referendum being used to render water privatisation illegal.[118] In 1993, the Maldonado region granted a private concession to the Uruguayan company Aguas de la Costa, over which a Suez subsidiary later took majority ownership. In 2000, a second Maldonado concession was granted to Spanish multinational Aguas de Bilbao, which operated it through a subsidiary URUGUA. Local residents began to mobilise against the negative impacts of the private concessions from the 1990s and the movement soon became national. The complaints were focused on rises in tariffs, deterioration of water quality,

[113] M. Drakeford, 'Water Regulation and Prepayment Meters', *Journal of Law and Society*, Vol. 5, No. 4 (1998), pp. 588–602.

[114] *R v. Director of Water Services, ex parte Lancashire County Council, Liverpool City Council, Manchester City Council, Oldham Metropolitan Borough Council, Tameside Metropolitan Borough Council and Birmingham City Council* [1999] Env LR 114; [1998] EWHC 213 (QB). In 1999, the use of prepaid water meters was prohibited by legislation. Section 63A, The Water Industry Act of 1991, as amended in 1999.

[115] 8 Cte 1906/2014 Olom EYDAP, Judgment of 4 June 2014.

[116] Case No. 1277/2001 (unreported).

[117] The municipality brought the application after they could no longer afford the high management fees of R.400 000 per month being charged by the private contractor. Although the Court actually nullified the contract on the basis that the municipality had not complied with the necessary consultation and public participation requirements.

[118] Barlow, *Blue Covenant*, pp. 173–174. Hall, Lobina and De la Motte, *Making Water Privatisation Illegal*.

contractual revisions, the failure of the company to pay fees and the over-exploitation of the Laguna Blanca.[119]

In 2002, in letter of intent for the IMF, the Uruguayan government committed to further privatisation throughout the country as part of debt relief conditions.[120] The response to this was the formation of the National Commission in Defence of Water and Life (CNDAV), partly inspired by the Bolivian anti-privatisation movement CDAV. A broad coalition, it included water and sewerage workers, environmental movements and the left-wing Frente Amplio political party coalition, headed by Tabaré Vázquez, and focused on achieving a decisive end to the debate through a constitutional amendment at the time of national elections. In October 2003, the CNDAV presented to parliament the 283,000 signatures required for a referendum, and a year later on 31 October 2004, over 64 per cent of Uruguayan voters approved the measure to recognise the right to water and end water privatisation.

The resultant Article 47 of the Constitution defined access to drinking water and sewerage systems as a 'fundamental human right'. This was to be concretised through policies that are sustainable, ensure user and civil society participation in 'every instance of planning, management and control of water resources' and prioritise social and economic objectives. However, the amendment went a step further. Article 47(3) stipulates that, 'The public service of sewerage system and the supply of water for human consumption will be provided exclusively and directly by legal state representatives.'[121]

While the amendment had been championed by Frente Amplio, when the party entered office, it came under intense pressure from the corporations not to cancel the private contract, which included threats of international investment arbitration. The government produced an executive decree providing that existing concessions could continue contracts until they expired. The decree was legally dubious and proved unpopular: the CNDAV issued the Maldonado Declaration in which it rejected the decree.[122] In order to save face, the government moved to cancel the contract with URUGUA although on grounds of contractual non-compliance. The company issued a complaint to the World Bank's International Centre for the Settlement of Investment Disputes (ICSID), and a 'friendly' accord was finally reached with a payment of USD$15 million in compensation. Soon afterwards, the second

[119] C. Santos and A. Villarreal, 'Uruguay: Victorious Social Struggle for Water', in B. Brennan, O. Hoedeman, P. Terhorst and S. Kisimoto (eds.), *Reclaiming Public Water: Achievements, Struggles and Visions from around the World* (Transnational Institute, 2005), pp. 173–179 at 173–174.

[120] Ibid., p. 173. [121] Translation by Santos and Villarreal, 'Uruguay', p. 6. [122] Ibid., p. 175.

multinational Suez (Aguas de la Costa) also exited the country (in September 2006).[123] This was facilitated by the government paying the company $3.4m for its shares in Aguas de la Costa, amounting to sixty per cent of the total and creating a mixed company (60 per cent public and 40 per cent private). This arguably contradicted the new provision in the Constitution, but the private owner, an engineering company, has a majority public shareholding and public directorship. The re-municipalisation also encountered many of the teething problems apparent in Bolivia as the government and civil society organisations try to find consensus on new models. But there appears to be a greater focus on extending access to water services in rural areas[124] and moves to ensure popular participation in water services as per the constitutional amendment.[125]

### Colombia

Uruguay's constitutional reform has had a 'ripple' effect on water campaigns throughout Central and Southern America, and beyond.[126] Many sought to enshrine the right to water as a constitutional or legislative right and forestall privatisation: for example, in Bolivia, Ecuador, El Salvador, Mexico, Germany, France, Spain and the USA. But the results varied. A similar Uruguayan-styled campaign in Colombia was less successful.

The referendum proposal evolved in response to growing privatisation of water utilities, which was authorised by a 1993 amendment to the Constitution. By 2007, 40 per cent of the country's 349 water companies were privatised while six per cent were mixed.[127] However, successive local adminstrations in the country's large capital Bogota resisted pressure from the World Bank and the national government to privatise. Instead, the local public water company EAAB was able to transform itself into a highly 'efficient and equitable' utility, achieving close to universal access to water by 2001, utilising

[123] E. Lobina and D. Hall, *Water Privatisation and Restructuring in Latin America*, 2007, PSIRU 2007.

[124] See www.iadb.org/mobile/news/detail.cfm?language=English&id=7591

[125] In December 2005, Law 17.903, Article 331, a Counselling Commission for Water and Sewerage Management (COASAS), was created within the executive unit of the environmental ministry (DINASA): see R. Prando and A. Gambogi, *Water Resources in Uruguay: Main Features and Challenges Towards their Sustainable Use* (Calgary: Uruguayan Academy of Engineering, 2009). This was followed in 2006 by a National Directorate for Water and the Sewage System.

[126] J. Dugard and K. Drage, 'Law and Privatisation: The Use of Legal Tools to Secure Public Service Water Provision', Paper on File with Author, p. 10.

[127] H. Martinez, 'Colombia Campaign Seeks to Make Water a Constitutional Right', 24 August 2007, available at http://ipsnews.net/ (accessed 3 December 2012).

heavy cross-subsidisation as well as an education campaign to reduce total water consumption.[128] Some private companies also performed relatively well: in Cartagena, a private operator, with large public investments, managed to increase access from 25 to close to 100 per cent between 1995 and 2010.[129]

This model of privatisation did not generate the same intensity of critique as in other countries. This was partly because the government retained responsibilities for investments and extension of access (as in France), private operators only possessed minority ownership stakes, price rises were not exorbitant, access to the poor and informal settlements increased, and Colombian companies dominated. However, the rise in prices, part deterioration in water quality, corruption allegations and lack of participation fostered a backlash which was also able to tap into the fact that little progress had been made on improvement of access in rural areas.[130] There was also alarm at the continual pressure for successful public entities, such as EAAB, to further commercialise and possibly privatise.[131] Moreover, there is little evidence to suggest that public-private partnerships have performed better than public utilities. Krause finds that the degree of democratic participation in utilities is the best explanation across Colombia.[132]

The referendum campaign emanated from Ecofundo – a network of 150 environment, human rights and indigenous groups. Like its Uruguayan counterpart, it sought a constitutional right to water and ban on water privatisation but also sought to reaffirm the State's duty for water management, stabilise tariffs and provide a free minimum basic water supply to assist poor communities.[133] But despite gathering more than the necessary number of signatures to hold a referendum, the campaign was undone by the Colombian Congress in May 2010. The draft referendum bill was dismissed on the basis that it was idealistic and unrealistic, particularly the provision of a free basic minimum of water by public or private utilities.[134]

The Congress rewrote the bill in a manner that activists claimed denied the effectiveness of water as a right and public management of water. It dealt an 'enormous blow' to the campaign and facilitated the dissolution of the network and loss of funding sources.[135] However, the amended policy

[128] H. Vélez, 'Public Services in Colombia: A Matter of Democracy', in B. Brennan, O. Hoedeman, P. Terhorst, S. Kisimoto (eds.), *Reclaiming Public Water: Achievements, Struggles and Visions from around the World* (Transnational Institute, 2005), pp. 103–109, at 106.

[129] 'Looming Water Crisis: Is the World Running out of Water', in *Global Issues: Selections from CQ Researcher* (Thousand Oaks C.A.: Pine Forge Press, 2010), p. 207; P. Constance, *The day that water ran uphill: How a public-private partnership brought water and sanitation services to Cartagena's poorest communities*, *IDB America: Magazine of the Inter-American Development Bank*, available at www.iadb.org/ (accessed 3 December 2012).

[130] H. Martinez, 'Colombia Campaign'. [131] H. Vélez, 'Public Services in Colombia', p. 107.

[132] M. Krause, *The Political Economy of Water and Sanitation* (London: Routledge, 2009).

[133] Dugard and Drage, 'Law and Privatisation'. [134] Ibid. [135] Ibid.

proposed and implemented by Congress proved difficult to implement, and Ecofundo launched discussion forums and organised peaceful street protests in support of a new policy. In mid-2011, the government acknowledged the failings of its water policy, and it was reported in the media that plans are in motion for a new strategy, although the details of this project have not been shared with social movements. Moreover, a municipal law in Bogota was passed at the end of 2011 that reflected one of the key elements of the referendum campaign: a subsidised basic water supply of 50 litres per person.[136] Since then, there have only been sporadic attempts at privatisation, with private involvement in watsewater plants being the major focus.

### Italy

Greater success was achieved by social movements in a referendum in Italy. For two decades, the Italian government has been pushing for a 'new deal' for the privatisation of water services. In 1994, the 'Galli Law' facilitated a fundamental reorganisation of the highly fragmented water sector, establishing single water service utilities, creating powerful water basin authorities and more closely aligning tariffs with investment and operational costs.[137] What was controversial was the creating of a bidding process for the new utilities that provided space for private sector involvement. The result was a growth in the number of private operators (91 by 2010) but local campaigns halted a number of planned privatisations.[138]

In 2006, the Galli Law was superseded by the Environmental Code,[139] which guaranteed an 'adequate return on invested capital' in the sector, declared to be 7 per cent. The Code was soon complemented by Article 23 of Law 133/2008, which provided a more active framework for privatisation. Finally, on 6 August 2009, the Berlusconi government enacted the so-called Ronchi decree No. 135/2009 that mandated the privatisation of water, transport and waste utilities under Law 133. The law set a target for implementation – 70 per cent of public water companies listed on the stock exchange had to be in the hands of private investors by 1 January 2012 – and private companies were to be granted 'equal treatment'.

[136] Ibid.

[137] Law 5 May 1994, n. 36 'Disposizioni in materia di risorse idriche', Gazzetta Ufficiale della Repubblica Italiana, 19 January 1994, n. 14. For a discussion, see G. Formica, 'Law and Economics of Bundling by Non-Dominant Firms', German Working Papers in Law and Economics, No. 16 (2008), Berkeley University Press.

[138] A. de Sanctis and A. Senta, 'Abruzzo, Italia: A Struggle in Defence of Water and for Citizen's Participation', in B. Brennan, O. Hoedeman, P. Terhorst, S. Kisimoto (eds.), *Reclaiming Public Water: Achievements, Struggles and Visions from around the World* (Transnational Institute, 2005), p. 2, available at http://www.tni.org/ (accessed 3 December 2012).

[139] Law 152/2006.

The growing trend of privatisation catalysed the formation of various alliances and initiatives, beginning with the Italian Committee for a World Water Contract in 2000. In 2003, the Declaration of Rome called for a campaign to ensure every national, provincial and local authority recognised the right to water.[140] The complaints over growing privatisation were diverse, although some scholars put the blame on the structure of the tendering system.[141] Investment in the sector declined,[142] some water tariffs jumped by 20 per cent and tariffs varied significantly according to terrain, the state of waterworks and maintenance costs and the type of contract in place.[143] Concern was also directed at the lack of public participation in setting service standards, the weaknesses of regulators and emerging oligarchic market structures.[144] In 2006, the Italian Forum of Water Movements was formed, an alliance of local committees, environmental associations, Catholic associations, trade unions, NGOs and individuals. Upon adoption of the Ronchi decree, the Forum launched a campaign for a citizen referendum. Within six months, and without official funding or political support, it had secured the necessary 1.5 million signatures (three times more than needed), which was subsequently validated by the Constitutional Court. Two of the referendum questions dealt water: the repeal of the Ronchi decree and associated legislation and of Article 154 of the Environmental Code that required mandatory water profits.[145] The other two questions concerned the repeal of regulations allowing for the production of nuclear power and procedural immunities for Prime Minister and Ministers under criminal law, both of which helped the campaign garner wider support.

The results were resounding. On 12 and 13 June 2011, over 57 per cent of all voting Italians participated in the referendum and by 96 per cent rejected compulsory water privatisation. Amongst the legal consequences is the ability of municipalities to freely choose the most appropriate form of organisation of water services: the referendum has not outlawed private water services per se as it did in Uruguay. The Berlusconi government tried to nullify the effect of the referendum by effectively reintroducing the Ronchi decree. But this was ruled unconstitutional by the Constitutional Court in 2012. These legal successes and public support provided the Forum and allies a platform for participatory

[140] See also First People World Water Forum, *Final Declaration – For a Different Water Policy: Proposal and Commitments*, Florence, March 2003, available at www.contrattoacqua.it (accessed 3 December 2012).

[141] See *Water Privatisation: Reasons and Consequences!*, available at http://noipensiamo.altervista.org (accessed 28 March 2012); A. Chiara, *The Right to Water in Italy*, International Environmental Law Research Centre Briefing Paper, January 2008; Sanctis and A. Senta, 'Abruzzo, Italia', p. 2.

[142] Ibid. [143] Ibid. [144] Ibid. [145] Formica, 'Law and Economics'.

reform of water governance, drawing on both the idea of a water commons and the right to water, but the subsequent results have been mixed.[146]

**Germany**

In Germany, both referendums and courts have been used to challenge privatisation at the local level. Privatisation proceeded relatively quickly in Germany: by 2005, 27 million or 32 per cent of the population were reportedly served by partially privatised operators or private concessions to multinational corporations.[147] The move encountered strong but variable resistance, particularly from trade unions, housing associations, churches, environmental and social groups as well as some politicians and political parties. Kruger records that citizen-initiated local referendums were initiated to stop twelve municipalities from privatising, all of them successful with overwhelming majorities (in Dusseldorf, 90 per cent voted against).[148] In some cases, the privatisation process was stopped, as in Hamburg, upon the threshold for signatures to force a referendum was reached.[149] The mobilisation also prompted some municipalities to take alternative approaches to reducing municipal or water utility debts that included issuing bonds to local residents.[150]

The most prominent struggle was in Berlin. In 1999, the Berlin Water Company was partially privatised when 49.9 per cent of its shares were sold to Veolia Water and RWE Aqua. The consistently articulated justification was addressing the City's alarming budget deficit,[151] but Beveridge argues that no alternatives were seriously considered and that a discourse of 'inevitability' was created.[152] The original plan was, however, a full privatisation. But this was abandoned in the face of resistance from opposition parties (the Greens and PDS) and trade unions and the threat of legal action by housing associations.[153] The final straw was growing criticism from members of the local governing alliance (Christian Democratic Union and the Social Democratic Party), which was increasingly alarmed at the secretive and closed nature of the negotiations being conducted by the Finance Senator and a consultant team with the

[146] C. Carrozza and E. Fantini, 'The Italian water movement and the politics of the commons' *Water Alternatives*, Vol. 9, No. 1 (2016), pp. 99–119.

[147] H-W. Kruger, 'Germany: Public Water Services in Continual Retreat?', in B. Brennan, O. Hoedeman, P. Terhorst, S. Kisimoto (eds.), *Reclaiming Public Water: Achievements, Struggles and Visions from around the World* (Transnational Institute, 2005), pp. 85–93 at 90.

[148] Ibid., p. 91–92. [149] Fitch, 'Water Privatisation in France and Germany', p. 602.

[150] Kruger, 'Germany', pp. 92–93.

[151] Fitch, 'Water Privatisation in France and Germany', pp. 599–600.

[152] Beveridge, *A Politics of Inevitability*.

[153] Beveridge, 'Consultants, Depoliticization and Arena-Shifting in the Policy Process', pp. 58–60.

prospective companies.[154] Moreover, the local government supported the unions by signing an agreement with unions that no jobs would be lost at the company for fifteen years.[155]

However, the partial privatisation remained controversial. The opposition parties launched a legal challenge in the Berlin Constitutional Court, contesting the profit formula for shareholders (R + 2 per cent, where R refers to the returns from 10-year standard bonds over the last 20 years) and the duty of the company to provide such profit returns. The Court responded by striking down the 2 per cent profit addition on the grounds that it was inappropriate for a public-private monopoly but found the general duty to return profits constitutional as it was common practice in Germany.[156]

The second scene of controversy was the withholding of details of the privatisation from the public. This was bolstered by revelations that in the lead-up to the court challenge, the government had secretly signed a deal with the companies that the R + 2 per cent formula would be maintained even if the Court struck it down.[157] Tensions were also increasing over pricing. Initially, the 'efficiency' savings saw water prices frozen for the first four years after the sale, but thereafter, prices rose by 15 and then 20 per cent, making Berlin's water amongst Europe's most expensive.[158] In addition, there was a decline in employment in the company and the broader sector approximately, and in investment in the infrastructure.[159]

In 2007, Berliner Wassertisch (Berlin Water Table) was formed under the banner of 'Water belongs to everybody – Access to water is a human right'.[160] A network of citizens, it focused on disclosure of the contracts as a first step towards remunicipalisation and public control.[161] A key tactic was to invoke the referendum clause under Article 62(1) of the Constitution of Berlin. The paragraph for adoption provided that all contracts, decisions and side agreements concerning the water privatisation were to be published and publicly investigated in the local parliament with the participation of independent experts within six months, and any contracts or supplementary agreement not made public within six months were to be declared invalid.[162] The Berlin Water Table collected more than the required signatures but there was limited support within the Berlin Senate. Even though it was now led by the Social Democratic Party and the Left Party (a successor to the PDS), they

[154] Ibid. [155] Ibid., p. 60. [156] Ibid., pp. 62–63. [157] Ibid.

[158] *Referendum on Privatisation of Berlin's Water Supply*, available at wsws.org (accessed 28 March 2012).

[159] Ibid. [160] Ibid. [161] Dugard and Drage, 'Law and Privatisation'.

[162] *Volksentscheid über die Offenlegung der Teilprivatisierungsverträge bei den Berliner Wasserbetrieben*, available at www.wahlen-berlin.de/ (accessed 3 December 2012).

saw re-municipalisation as a long-term objective. They declared the referendum inadmissible since it violated property rights in the federal constitution,[163] at the same time as they published some contract details.[164] The Berlin Constitutional Court ruled however that the Berlin Senate had no jurisdiction over the matter, but the government continued its attempts to frustrate the holding of the referendum through various media and informational tactics concerning polling booths.[165] Despite this, on 13 February 2011, 98.2 per cent voted to pass the draft bill. The gradual publication of the contracts created further controversy, and the European Commission began investigating whether the side agreements amount to an illegal public subsidy and if procurement rules were breached.[166] Activists remained divided on which road to take in hastening re-municipalisation, including cancellation of the contract without punitive compensation costs, preparing a second referendum on municipalisation or launching legal action.[167] In September 2011 elections, three of the four major parties included remunicipalisation in their platform, which prompted a new but expensive policy. In 2012 and 2013, the city government bought back the shares in the company at a cost of 1.3 billion euros – which was to be funded by an increase in the price of water over a 30-year period.[168]

### Sri Lanka

The move towards water privatisation of Sri Lanka dates back to its Water Resource Policy, drafted with the World Bank in 1993.[169] However, it was loan conditionalities from the World Bank, Asian Development Bank and the IMF that finally pushed the Government towards implementation,[170] which was captured in the 2001 National Policy on Private Sector Participation in Water Supply.[171] In October 2003, the Water Services Reform Bill was tabled in parliament, with the intention of facilitating privatised water provision throughout the country under the supervision of the Public Utilities Commission, but was immediately challenged in the Supreme Court. The move towards privatisation catalysed the Alliance for the Protection of Natural

[163] Dugard and Drage, 'Law and Privatisation'.

[164] *Referendum on Privatisation of Berlin's Water Supply.*

[165] Ibid.

[166] *Germany: Berlin's Water Privatisation under Investigation by EU*, Wash New International, available at http://washinternational (accessed 28 March 2012).

[167] Dugard and Drage, 'Law and Privatisation'.

[168] PSIRU, 'Here to stay', 8.

[169] D. Pathirana, 'Privatisation of Water Resources and Human Rights', *Sri Lanka Journal of International Law*, Vol. 16 (2004), p. 18.

[170] Ibid.

[171] D. Hall and C. Violeta, *Aid and Trade in Water and Electricity in Tsunami-Affected Countries: India, Indonesia, Sri Lanka, Thailand*, Discussion Paper (London: PSIRU, 2005), p. 8.

Resources and Human Rights, some trade unions and other groups. The bill was particularly controversial since it allowed unilateral termination of contracts with consumers, provided no protections for poorer users and promoted prepaid water systems.[172]

The Supreme Court struck down the proposed law but did so on procedural rather than substantive grounds.[173] The first argument of the petitioners was that the law amounted to an interference with the constitutional powers of Provincial Councils who were responsible for water supply. Article 154G(3) of the Constitution establishes a specific procedure for any such legislation. The bill must be gazetted for comment by Provincial Councils and, if any object, it can only be passed with a special majority of parliament.[174] However, the Supreme Court declined to address the two substantive issues raised by the complainants. First, that the law unfairly favoured companies over consumers, thereby violating the equality rights provision in Article 12 of the Constitution. Second, that since General Comment No. 15 had recognised water as a right and Sri Lanka was a party to the ICESCR, vesting water in the private sector would be 'tantamount to an alienation' of the sovereignty of the people, a principle recognised in the Article 3 of the Constitution. The Court had earlier ruled that the citizenry had rights of the citizenry and that State was guardian of those resources in the public interest,[175] but the Court did not address the potential connection with privatisation of water services.

With renewed pressure from the Asian Development Bank and threat of loan cancellation, the new government (of a leftist persuasion) reluctantly reintroduced the bill to Parliament in December 2004.[176] However, the bill attracted renewed resistance and the Asian Development Bank was criticised for using post-tsunami infrastructure loans as a cover for privatisation.[177] The Government eventually abandoned the process in mid-2005 and an attempt to

[172] Pathirana, 'Privatisation of Water Resources and Human Rights', pp. 13–14. For a sober analysis of the reforms and their inappropriateness of addressing the core problems around politicisation of water resources, see R. Ariyabandu, *Swings and Roundabouts: A Narrative on Water Policy Development in Sri Lanka*, Working Paper 296, Overseas Development Institute, November 2008.

[173] Challenge based on the Constitutionality of Water Services Reform Bill before the Supreme Court, SC Special Determinations Nos. 24–25/2003.

[174] Pathirana, 'Privatisation of Water Resources and Human Rights', pp. 15–16.

[175] *Bulankulama* v. *Secretary, Ministry of Industrial Development and Others*, 2000 (3) Sri L.R. 243.

[176] Ariyabandu, *Swings and Roundabouts*, pp. 9-10; Hall and Violeta, *Aid and Trade in Water and Electricity in Tsunami-Affected Countries*, p. 8.

[177] Ibid., pp. 8–9; *Dodging Another Disaster: Sri Lanka's Water Privatization Wars*, 4 April 2005, available at cupe.ca (accessed 2 April 2012).

revive it again in 2006 was equally abandoned.[178] Water provision remained in the hands of local government although the National Water Supply and Drainage Board (NWSDB) provided the majority of services despite decentralisation.[179] However, reform is urgently needed in both urban and rural areas, particularly for slum-dwellers and small farmers but energy in the sector has dissipated. As Ariyabandu concluded, 'More than ten years of a mismanaged policy process have left a legacy of doubt and suspicion, and any efforts to address the serious water management issues are now met with public and media opposition.'[180]

### Argentina

Privatisation was at its most ambitious in Argentina. By 1999, 22 private operators were supplying 71 per cent of the urban population.[181] But the policy proved controversial. In the Tucumán province, for instance, disputes arose within a year of the French water company Vivendi securing a concession contract.[182] By 1996, the provincial authorities and the company were locked in heated negotiations over tariff levels, water quality and disconnections. This was accompanied by massive consumer payment boycotts, individual and collective legal challenges and organised civil society demands for new policies. The concession was soon cancelled by the province, and Vivendi responded by initiating legal action under the bilateral investment treaty between France and Argentina.[183]

This pattern of protest played itself out across Argentina: in Santa Fe province, a quarter of the population participated in an informal plebiscite to rescind the concession contract with Suez, while in neighbouring Cordoba provincial assemblies and large coalitions were formed to return water services to full public control.[184] The tension was exacerbated by the economic crisis and currency devaluation of 2001 as multinational corporations sought to increase tariffs to service foreign debt and equity, while Argentinean authorities were under tremendous pressure to alleviate an upsurge in poverty. By the beginning

[178] Ariyabandu, *Swings and Roundabouts*, p. 10
[179] Dugard and Drage, 'Law and Privatisation'.
[180] Ariyabandu, *Swings and Roundabouts*, pp. 15–16.
[181] J. Ducci, *Salida de operadores privados internacionales de agua en América Latina* (Washington, DC: Inter-American Development Bank, 2007), pp. 64–65.
[182] For the entire history of the dispute, see B. Morgan, 'Turning off the Tap: Urban Water Services Delivery and the Social Construction of Global Administrative Law', *The European Journal of International Law*, Vol. 17, No. 1 (2006), pp. 215–246.
[183] See discussion of the investment arbitration by Peterson in this volume (Chapter 16).
[184] Barlow, *Blue Covenant*, p. 106.

of the new millennium, privatisation was in retreat and by 2007 the number of urban residents covered by the private sector had fallen to 12.1 per cent.[185]

In Argentina, legal mobilisation against privatisation played itself out in various ways but primarily focused on strengthening the rights of users rather than stopping privatisation. There were many legislative proposals, particularly in relation to 'tariff structures, disconnection and the recovery of unpaid bills, both before and after the return of water services into public hands'.[186] However, these demands were simultaneously transformed into litigious demands. In the Tucumán province, the Ombudsman initially advised boycotting consumers on how to lodge administrative complaints in response to the 'brown water' and rising tariffs.[187] This resulted in the regulator discounting bills for those who applied: approximately 10 per cent of those who boycotted. The water company complied with the revised bills but then pursued the outstanding debts of the boycotters. The concessions usually included the right of the companies to halt provision upon non-payment for a certain period and a provision that users carry all the costs relating to disconnection and reconnection.[188] In response, the Ombudsman filed a collective action case on behalf of the defaulters but lower courts consistently evaded making a decision.[189]

In Buenos Aires, a similar collective case was taken by a consumer association to challenge the pattern of disconnection and debt proceedings. However, the court declined to view the case as one of collective action and refused to hear the arguments on the merits.[190] The reason behind the conservatism of the courts in both provinces is difficult to discern. It may be the result of political interference,[191] concern over the broader policy consequences of such a decision[192] or simply a matter of unreformed legal culture: the constitutional action right ('Accion de Amparo') was only introduced in

185 Dugard and Drage, 'Law and Privatisation'.

186 Morgan, 'Building Bridges between Regulatory and Citizen Space', p. 5.

187 Morgan, 'Turning off the Tap', p. 230.

188 E. Crenzel et al. 'Argentina - Buenos Aires Case Study' in Castro, Esteban (ed.), *Barriers to and Conditions for the Involvement of Private Capital and Enterprise in Water Supply and Sanitation in Latin America and Africa: Seeking Economic, Social, and Environmental Sustainability* (Oxford: PRINWASS, 2004), p. 29 cited in C. Fairstein, 'Legal Strategies and the Right to Water in Argentina', in E. R. a. P. Rothen (ed.), *The Human Right to Water* (Berlin: Berliner WissenschaftsVerlag, 2006), pp. 93–112, at 108.

189 Ibid., p. 230.

190 *Usuarios y Consumidores en Defensa de sus Derechos, Asociación Civil c/Aguas del Gran Buenos Aires. Amparo*, Supreme Court of Justice in the Province of Buenos Aires, 22 September 2004. See discussion in Fairstein, 'Legal Strategies and the Right to Water in Argentina', pp. 109–110.

191 See discussion in Morgan, 'Turning off the Tap', p. 231.

192 Fairstein, 'Legal Strategies and the Right to Water in Argentina', p. 110.

1994, and many courts were not accustomed to this new form of litigation, which also permits collective action.

However, individual litigation against disconnections and debt repayments proved more successful. Argentina has witnessed a wave of cases concerning disconnections against private companies and increasingly publicly owned companies.[193] For instance, in *U.M.Y. c/Absa s/amparo*, the private provider ABSA terminated the water connection for a woman who had not paid her bills for some months.[194] The woman responded by utilising the amparo procedure on an individual basis. The Court agreed with her request for interim measures for reconnection by recognising that human rights took precedence over commercial contracts. As Argentina had ratified the ICESCR and water was essential for human life and a human rights, minimum provision must be guaranteed.

In some instances, NGOs began to prepare more complex forms of individualised litigation for securing the right to water in the face of privatisation. From the mid-1990s, the Conet community in Buenos Aires repeatedly experienced the postponement of plans by the Aguas Argentina corporation to extend access to the settlement. Thus, a campaign was prepared in 2003 to secure access to plans and mobilise for their implementation, while a legal case was prepared in the event no action was taken.[195] In 2004, the community was included on the list of projects to be undertaken but the funds were then spent on other projects, and in 2005, Suez sold its 40 per cent stake in the company after failing to reach agreement with the government over water tariffs.[196] After receiving a renewed set of petitions from the community, the newly constituted utility and regulatory agency agreed to prioritise the community and the legal case was finalised.

## 6 CONCLUSION

This chapter set out to analyse the normative, empirical and sociolegal relationships between privatisation and the human right to water. Normatively the relationship is characterised by contestation. Competing actors (from corporations to anti-privatisation activists) have sought to both promote the right and stamp on it a particular content. Yet, both the general discourse and the development of legal standards were not captured by either ends of the

193 See discussion in Chapter 1.

194 The case is described in Fairstein, 'Legal Strategies and the Right to Water in Argentina', pp. 110–111.

195 Ibid, pp. 106–107.

196 See discussion of case by Peterson in this volume (Chapter 16).

debate. For better or worse, the more cautious legalistic approach has largely won the day – affirming that private provision is possible but that it must meet certain standards. Yet, such standards are not mere figleafs as the various case studies demonstrate. The various substantive and procedural dimensions of the right to water provided important tools in attempts to restrain or stop privatisation.

Empirically, the debate over the effectiveness of privatisation is almost impossible to resolve. Proponents and opponents point to respective benefits and costs that are largely incommensurable. Two things are certain. The first is that privatisation has not delivered on its promise. The second is that the some privatisations have matched at least the public sector in terms of performance or have placed pressure on public sector services to perform better. The question though is whether the second conclusion is sufficient to justify the significant political mobilisation (with financial costs) that is needed for privatisation. Are there perhaps better ways to reform and improve public sector services? Alternative forms of accountability may be more effective and could be properly tested. With a slow global turn to re-municipalisation, the question is increasingly how public sector utilities can be held to account.

Finally, the chapter analysed the use of right to water in civil society mobilisation with a particularly focus on the utility of law-inflected strategies. Analysing eight case studies, the chapter found that the turn to law was rarely a hollow hope – the use of referenda and litigation produced surprisingly effective results from the perspective of activists. However, it was contingent as the presence of strong social mobilisation was a condition for such outcomes. Yet the studies show the possibilities for the right to water to form an important part of social struggle and transformation.

# 14

# Piped Water in Jakarta

## *A Political, Economic or Social Good?*

NICOLA COLBRAN*

## 1 INTRODUCTION

Piped water supply in Jakarta is characterised by poor levels of access and quality. Less than one-third of Jakarta's estimated 12 million residents have access to piped water supply in their homes. Those that are connected frequently complain about the low quality of water supplied, the quantity and continuity of the water, poor water pressure and high water tariffs. The inadequate levels of access and quality have been attributed to corruption or lack of finance, urban poverty, insufficient regulation of service providers and urban growth outpacing infrastructure development.[1] While these factors no doubt contribute to the problems, they overlook the way the supply of water has been treated by governments in the past and the impact this has had on levels of access and the quality of piped water.

This chapter discusses the treatment of water by various administrations and private operators and argues that this treatment has in fact impacted on levels of access and the quality of piped water and influenced consumer choices and preferences for water sources. It also outlines the differences between the treatment of water in practice and in law.

Section 2 begins by considering the historical treatment of water in Jakarta. For more than a century, water was treated primarily as a political good,[2]

* Nicola Colbran was formerly the legal advisor in the Indonesia Program at the Norwegian Centre for Human Rights. She now works in the legal sector in Australia.

[1] These various reasons are quoted in M. E. Kooy, *Relations of Power, Networks of Water: Governing Urban Waters, Spaces, and Populations in (Post)Colonial Jakarta*, unpublished PhD thesis (University of British Columbia, 2008), p. 3.

[2] Where water is referred to as a 'good' in this chapter, it is reference to water as a physical good. Examples of literature that discusses water as a political good or as an economic good or as a social good include K. Schwartz and M. Schouten 'Water as a political good: revisiting the relationship between politics and service provision', *Water Policy*, Vol. 9 No. 2 (2007),

meaning that access to water supply was restricted to certain types of users and specific areas through deliberate urban planning and water supply management that followed the politics of the particular administration in power. The section continues by tracing the shift towards water taking being viewed as an economic good in addition to a political good during the term of the New Order government (1966–1998). During this period, the government began emphasising cost recovery, self-financing by water suppliers and the contribution of water revenue to economic growth. The section goes on to outline preparations for private sector participation in Jakarta's water supply network towards the end of the New Order period, which continued and strengthened this trend of viewing water as an economic good.[3]

Section 3 discusses private sector participation in the operation and expansion of the piped water network in Jakarta and explores the effect of treating water as both an economic and political good on access levels and water quality, as well as on consumer choices and preference for water sources.

While, in practice, various administrations have treated water as a political and economic good, Indonesian law since independence has emphasised the social aspect of water. It highlights the responsibility of the State to control water for the benefit of the people and prioritises water for daily needs over other uses. Section 4 discusses these laws and examines the 2005 Constitutional Court decision, which confirms the social function of water. It examines the differences between the treatment of water in law and in practice and concludes that while this difference remains, the right to water will not be fully realised for all Indonesians.

## 2 THE HISTORICAL TREATMENT OF WATER: A SHIFT IN EMPHASIS FROM A POLITICAL TO AN ECONOMIC GOOD

Beginning with the concept of water as a political good, there are four main stages in the history of Jakarta's piped water network. During each stage, the

pp. 119-129; P. Van Der Zaag and H. Savenije, *Water as an Economic Good: The Value of Pricing and the Failure of Markets, Value of Water Research Report Series*, No. 19 (UNESCO-IHE Institute for Water Education, Delft, the Netherlands, 2006); L. Veiga da Cunha 'Water: A human right or an economic resource?' in M. Ramon Llamas, L. Martinez Cortina and Aditi Mukherji (eds.) *Water Ethics: Marcelino Botin Water Forum 2007* (CRC Press Book, March 2009).

[3] The contracts are described as modified because the concessionaires were directly appointed (no tendering process was held), and the Jakarta government guaranteed that the concessionaires would suffer no financial losses: N. Ardhianie, *The Controversial Sell Out of PT Thames Pam Jaya (TPJ)* (AMRTA Institute for Water Literacy and Public International Services, 2007).

politics of the particular administration in power played a dominant role in determining the users and areas of Jakarta that could access piped water, as well as consumer choices and preferences for water sources.

Prior to the Dutch colonial government's construction of the artesian water supply in the mid-1800s, Jakarta's population relied on different combinations of river water and shallow groundwater for its water supply.[4] The new artesian water network was meant for use by European residents living in the small 'developed' central area of the city and was intended to mark European cultural superiority upon which the legitimacy of the colonial government was premised.[5] As such, Jakarta's first water supply infrastructure supported the desired racial division between Europeans and the local population and the urban areas where they resided.

The artesian water supply was only made available to the local population at the turn of the century when it was extended minimally through artesian hydrants.[6] However, the distance between households and the hydrants meant that local residents had to expend large amounts of time and effort in collecting water or had to purchase it at an increased cost from an ambulatory vendor. Unsurprisingly, local households continued to rely on non-piped water sources that cost less and were more easily accessible.

In spite of its convenience for European residents, piped artesian water had a number of drawbacks. The water was warm and smelt of sulphur. It had to be cooled and aerated prior to use, which was costly and required physical space, storage containers and infrastructure. Consequently, following considerable debate, a spring water system was developed during the 1920s that increased water production and delivered spring water to Jakarta through 53 kilometres of iron pipe (the 'second phase'). The water was supplied to 90 per cent of all European households at a rate of 140 litres per capita per day.[7]

Access to the network was again differentiated between European and local residents, but the differentiation was on the basis of developmental, rather than racial, superiority. In the latter half of the nineteenth century, new scientific discoveries had made connections between drinking water consumption and health and had articulated a definition of a hygienic water

4 Artesian water is groundwater trapped between layers of impermeable rock that is tapped or otherwise put under pressure.

5 M. Kooy and K. Bakker, 'Technologies of Government: Constituting Subjectivities, Spaces, and Infrastructures in Colonial and Contemporary Jakarta', *International Journal of Urban and Regional Research*, Vol. 32, No. 2 (2008), pp. 375–391.

6 Between 1910 and 1920, four public hydrants were installed for over 116,740 local (non-European) residents. 'Water (Never) For All', *Jakarta Post*, 16 January 2009.

7 Kooy, *Relations of Power*, pp. 55, 142.

supply.[8] The local population on the other hand was seen as undeveloped, as they used traditional sensory assessments to determine water quality without reference to such new scientific discoveries.[9]

In contrast to European households, the local population was provided with less water, at lower pressure, and via communal standpipes rather than household connections. Water from public hydrants also cost twice as much as that obtained from household connections. Again, unsurprisingly, the local population continued to use the most convenient and cost-effective water source. The colonial government saw this continued use of non-piped water sources as a temporary solution for the undeveloped local population.[10] However, after almost 100 years, non-piped water sources continue to be an important source of water for many Jakartan households.

Indonesia's independence in 1945 signalled the third stage in the historical treatment of water as a political good in Jakarta. This stage was defined by the rehabilitation of the piped network and the construction of surface water treatment plants. During the four-year battle for independence with the Dutch, Jakarta's infrastructure had been damaged and could not meet the demand for water as Jakarta's population increased.[11] Soekarno, Indonesia's charismatic first President, had a vision for Jakarta as a modern, progressive, independent city to be demonstrated by grand public monuments and highly visible infrastructure projects. His government began rehabilitating existing water network pipes in elite residential areas and constructing water treatment plants. With superior modern water treatment technology, Jakarta could utilise surface water rather than rely on artesian or distant spring water.[12] The construction of a large-scale surface water treatment plant (Pejompongan I) began in 1952 and was completed by 1957. Functionally and aesthetically modern, Pejompongan I was one marker of Indonesia's fledgling nationhood.

[8] C. Hamlin, '"Waters" or "Water"? – Master Narratives in Water History and Their Implications for Contemporary Water Policy', *Water Policy*, Vol. 2, Nos. 4–5 (2000), pp. 313–325.

[9] Sensory assessment of water is still used today to determine water quality. For example, a taxi driver interviewed by the author on 28 October 2008 stated that to test the quality of water, he makes a cup of tea and examines the colour of the tea. If it is the colour tea should be, then the water is good quality.

[10] Kooy, *Relations of Power*, pp. 58, 83, 135.

[11] Jakarta's population increased dramatically during this time, rising from 800,000 in 1945 to 3.15 million in 1965: S. Soetrisno, 'Groundwater Management Problem: Comparative City Case Studies of Jakarta and Bandung, Indonesia', in J. Chilton (ed.), *Groundwater in the Urban Environment: Selected City Profiles* (Rotterdam: Balkema, 1999), pp. 63–68, at 63; and Demographia.com, 'World Metropolitan Areas Over 5,000,000: Population Change from 1965: Total, Core & Suburbs'.

[12] The city's new water treatment plants changed the bulk of the source of water supply from mountain spring water to treated surface water taken from the city's flood canals.

A second plant (Pejompongan II) was completed by 1966. These two impressive plants increased the volume of water available to Jakartan residents by almost ten times the amount circulating during the colonial era.[13] Although this created the potential for a more even distribution of water throughout the city, the previous patterns of provision continued to guide post-colonial access through the existing infrastructure. There was no increase in the number of residents who had access to the piped water but merely an increase in the volume of water that a minority of residents could access. There was also little thought of water as an economic good. Wealthy residents paid virtually nothing for piped water. Water use by elite households was not even metred until the 1970s, two decades later.

During this period, no money was invested in improving access for the rest of the population, not even through basic infrastructure, such as public hydrants. By the end of the 1950s, around 80 per cent of the population continued to rely on Jakarta's increasingly polluted rivers, canals and groundwater for their water needs. The decision to exclude such a large section of the population from improved water sources began to affect Jakarta's 'modern' water system. The raw water supply for Jakarta's piped network was drawn from the Banjir canal, which was used by thousands of unserved residents. It did not take long before the technical capacity of the water treatment plants was compromised. By the late 1960s, the first complaints over the quality of piped water supply were recorded.

A violent transition from Soekarno's Old Order government to Soeharto's New Order in 1965 marked the fourth and final stage in the historical treatment of water as a political good. The vision for Indonesia supported by the New Order government focused on economic development and social stability. This approach influenced the development of the piped water network, which was expanded to assist and sustain industrial economic growth and to supply upper-class residential areas that were politically supportive of the New Order (Menteng, Kuningan and Kebayoran Baru and later Pondok Indah).[14] From 1965 to the late 1980s, investment focused on the construction of water treatment plants and the expansion (not rehabilitation) of the network. Two additional large-scale water treatment plants were constructed, as were small-scale treatment plants. Water supply production capacity increased threefold; however, distribution of the water through the piped network was in

[13] Kooy, *Relations of Power*, p. 62.

[14] P. McCarthy, *Understanding Slums: Case Studies for the Global Report on Human Settlements 2003: The Case of Jakarta, Indonesia* (Washington, D.C.: World Bank, 2003), p. 16; Kooy, *Relations of Power*, pp. 68, 70 and 149.

reality extended to less than one-quarter of the city's population and covered less than half the urban area.[15] Little was done to service the urban poor in spite of unprecedented sustained economic growth rates that averaged nearly 6 per cent per year from 1975 to 1996.[16] Those without access to piped water (nearly 80 per cent of the population) either used their own shallow groundwater wells, connected to other households' wells, or paid up to 20 per cent of their monthly income for water from public hydrants.[17]

During this period, the New Order government also began to emphasise water as an economic good. Soeharto established the mandate of Jakarta's regional water supply company (PAM Jaya) to support regional economic growth and generate profits.[18] In contrast to the Soekarno era, clean water had to be paid for by consumers as beneficiaries of the water.[19] To facilitate this approach, during the 1970s metres were installed, customers registered and the tariff structure reformed based on full cost recovery principles.[20]

By the end of the 1980s, in addition to limited network coverage and distribution capacity, Jakarta's piped network was losing more than 50 per cent of water produced because of real losses (leakage), as well as corruption and illegal sales and connections.[21] The quality of piped water was also low. Local newspapers reported incidents of people finding worms, sand or even needles in the water, which sometimes left a brown stain or a thin layer of mud in washbasins.[22] Heavy metal pollution was also registered in the water.[23] In spite of its official mandate, PAM Jaya was contributing little to regional economic growth and was not generating profits. In the three years prior to private sector involvement in Jakarta's water supply (1995–1997), it contributed only Rp.5 billion (USD 1.25 million) per annum.[24]

15 Kooy, *Relations of Power*, p. 68. 16 McCarthy, *Understanding Slums*, p. 2.

17 K. Bakker, M. Kooy, Nur Endah Shofiani, and E. J. Martijn, *Disconnected: Poverty, Water Supply and Development in Jakarta*; Human Development Report 2006, Human Development Report Office Occasional Paper, Draft, 13 March 2006, p. 11.

18 Any profits were transferred from PAM Jaya to the budget of the Jakartan government.

19 Government Decree No. 3, 30 April 1977 set out PAM Jaya's 'dual function' mandate: PAM Jaya, *PAM DKI 1922–1992. 70 Tahun PAM Jaya* (Jakarta, PAM Jaya, 1992), p. 115.

20 Bakker et al., *Disconnected*, p. 9; Kooy, *Relations of Power*, pp. 150–151. However, it is questionable whether the tariffs actually applied were at full cost recovery levels.

21 World Bank, *Staff Appraisal Report: Indonesia*, Second Jabotabek Urban Development Project (JUDP II) (Jakarta: Infrastructure Division, Country Department V, Asia Region, 1990).

22 International Consortium of Investigative Journalists, *Water and Politics in the Fall of Suharto*, February 2003.

23 For example, the Indonesian Consumers Foundation found in a 1990 survey that Jakarta water contained 0.0024 ppm of mercury, 2.4 times higher than the Health Ministry standard of 0.001: 'Pollution and Clean Water Shortage', *Jakarta Post*, 10 June 2001.

24 The exchange rate averaged Rp.3,000 = USD 1 during these three years.

As both the piped and non-piped water quality in Jakarta continued to decline, the city's piped water supply system increasingly created serious problems for human health and the environment and hindered economic development and poverty alleviation. The question remained how best to reverse this decline.

Beginning in 1990, loans from the World Bank and the Overseas Economic Cooperation Fund (OECF)[25] allocated a total of USD 190 million to the Indonesian government to support improvements in Jakarta's water supply.[26] The loans were also to prepare Jakarta's water sector for private sector participation (PSP),[27] which was seen as the most effective way of reversing the decline of piped and non-piped water quality in Jakarta. The rationale behind this approach was that private management, impelled primarily by a profit motive, was more efficient than public management, especially where government corporations were subject to political interference, overstaffing, nepotism, bureaucratic delays and corruption as they were in Indonesia.[28] By treating water as an economic good, private operators would have a financial stake in meeting the needs of the poor, who could choose the level of services they were willing to pay for.[29] These operators would expand access to clean water and sanitation thereby reducing the burden on constrained public budgets.[30] The loan from the World Bank and the OECF therefore focused on reforms necessary to improve cost recovery and economic efficiency, which were seen

25 The OECF is the implementing agency for loan aid provided by the Japanese government.

26 The loans were combined within the PAM Jaya System Improvement Project (PJSIP).

27 International Consortium of Investigative Journalists, *Water and Politics*.

28 T. Argo and A. Laquian, 'Privatization of Water Utilities and Its Effects on the Urban Poor in Jakarta Raya and Metro Manila', Paper delivered at the *Forum on Urban Infrastructure and Public Service Delivery for the Urban Poor, Regional Focus: Asia*, sponsored by the Woodrow Wilson International Center for Scholars and the National Institute of Urban Affairs, India Habitat Centre, New Delhi, 24–25 June 2004.

29 This was in line with the changing approach of international financial institutions to water, where these institutions promoted water as having a value to users who were willing to pay for it and who would utilise water so long as the benefits exceeded the costs incurred: J. Briscoe, *Water as an Economic Good: The Idea and What It Means in Practice*, presented at the World Congress of the International Commission on Irrigation and Drainage, Cairo, September 1996, p. 1. See also the Dublin Statement on Water and Sustainable Development adopted in 1992, which states that: 'Water has an economic value in all its competing uses and should be recognized as an economic good… Past failure to recognize the economic value of water has led to wasteful and environmentally damaging uses of the resource. Managing water as an economic good is an important way of achieving efficient and equitable use, and of encouraging conservation and protection of water resources'.

30 Friends of the Earth International, 'Water, the World Bank and the Asian Development Bank'.

as key to attracting private sector investment.[31] The loan also emphasised institutional reform to enable the government to take up its new role as regulator, not service provider, although ultimately no regulatory framework was set in place prior to private sector participation in Jakarta's water supply network.

While PSP was seen as the best solution to addressing the decline in Jakarta's piped and non-piped water, it ignored over a century of the political treatment of water. It also ignored the reasons Jakartan households and businesses used the water sources and distribution methods they did. Their choices were economically and politically rational and were heavily influenced by the way various administrations had treated water for over 100 years. By disregarding such rational choices and ignoring the impact that the treatment of water had on consumer choices and preferences, the private sector participation was destined to encounter serious challenges in achieving its ambitious aims.

## 3 INVOLVING THE PRIVATE SECTOR (1998– ): WATER AS AN ECONOMIC GOOD?

At the same time as preparations for PSP were taking place, discussions with foreign firms over this participation were also under way. The water services market in Indonesia appealed to foreign operators as an attractive investment prospect. Indonesia was a large middle-income country with an expanding middle class and relatively low penetration of networked water supply services. The contracts for Jakarta were expected to be lucrative as millions of unconnected residents were seen as potential customers.[32]

In early 1998, during the final months of the Soeharto government, two 25-year modified concession contracts for the operation and expansion of Jakarta's water supply system were awarded to two of the world's largest water service companies, Thames Water International and Ondeo (Suez-Lyonnaise des Eaux). Jakarta was split in half using the Ciliwung River as the dividing line. Thames was awarded the western half of Jakarta and Ondeo the eastern half.[33]

[31] Down to Earth, 'Water Privatisation', Down to Earth IFIs Factsheet Series, No. 28 (March 2003).

[32] See generally Bakker et al., *Disconnected*, and O. Braadbaart, 'Privatizing Water: The Jakarta Concession and the Limits of Contract', in P. Boomgaard (ed.), *A World of Water: Rain, Rivers and Seas in Southeast Asian Histories* (Singapore and Leiden: National University of Singapore and KITLV Press, 2007), pp. 297–320.

[33] On 26 July 2006, Suez (Palyja) sold 49 per cent of its shares to local partners PT Astratel Nusantara and Citigroup Financial Products Inc. Neither has experience in the water industry.

There was no open and transparent bidding process in the awarding of the two contracts; rather, the international water companies put forward unsolicited proposals directly to the government, and both of the local partners of Ondeo and Thames had direct ties to the Soeharto family. Thames partnered with the Sigit Group, controlled by Soeharto's son, Sigit Harjojudanto, and Ondeo partnered with the Salim Group, at the time Indonesia's largest conglomerate with extensive connections to the President.[34] Such a process deviated from the World Bank's 'good governance' regime (particularly transparency) and negated one of the reasons for shifting to private sector management, namely, to avoid political interference, nepotism, graft and corruption.

The two contracts were signed with PAM Jaya (the regional water supply company), which retained ownership of the water supply assets.[35] Both companies promised to improve water production, reduce water losses, increase the number of connections, improve the service coverage ratio, increase the volume of water billed and improve service standards.

However, according to Ahmad Lanti, the former Chair of the Jakarta Water Supply Regulatory Body,[36] the only technical target met by either operator is improved water production. Requirements relating to levels of water losses, service coverage ratio and volume sold have not been achieved, nor have those for water quality, water pressure, routine disturbances and the installation of new distribution pipelines.[37] Connection rates have improved in wealthy areas, with comparatively little progress in relation to low-income households.

Then, on 3 August 2006, Thames Water (TPJ) sold 100 per cent of its shares to Acuatico, a Singaporean consortium (95 per cent) and Alberta (5 per cent): 'City Told to Review Water Contract', *Jakarta Post*, 26 August 2006. Since 15 April 2008, TPJ has been known as PT Aetra Air Jakarta (Aetra).

[34] The contracts were awarded despite national laws prohibiting foreign investment in drinking water delivery (Law No. 1/1967; Ministry of Home Affairs Decision No. 3/1990) and local regulations (No. 11/1992 and No. 11/1993) preventing private sector involvement in community drinking water supply: Bakker et al., *Disconnected*, p. 25.

[35] The contracts were amended in 2001.

[36] The Jakarta Water Supply Regulatory Body was established to independently monitor and regulate policies and tariffs at the macro level, supervise the concessionaires on behalf of the Governor of Jakarta and the Ministry of Public Works and mediate disputes between PAM Jaya and the two private companies. This was provided for in the revised contracts signed by the private companies in 2001 and subsequently in a regulation issued by the Governor of Jakarta; see Schedule 20 of the Contract for a draft of the Decree of the Provincial Governor of the Special Region of the Capital Jakarta regarding the Regulatory Body (Keputusan Gubernur Propinsi Daerah Khusus Ibukota Jakarta Pembentukan Badan Pengatur Pelayanan Air Minum). Ahmad Lanti is also a former employee of the Department of Public Works and was reportedly involved in negotiating the PSP contracts with TPJ and Palyja.

[37] These achievements and failures continued in 2008: 'Palyja, Aetra Given Red Marks for 2008 Works', *Jakarta Post*, 15 January 2009.

Water tariffs have also increased dramatically since the private sector became involved and, in 2007, reached an average of Rp.7,025 (USD 0.80) per cubic metre or the highest in Indonesia.[38]

The achievements and failures outlined by Ahmad Lanti appear to reflect the treatment of water primarily as an economic good and the focus on profitability and rates of return. It makes sense from a profitability perspective that the private operators would achieve the improved water production technical target. Under the contracts, each operator is paid a fee by PAM Jaya based on water supplied to the distribution network and billed (the 'water charge'). Payment is not based on the revenue collected from customers, and any shortfall between revenue collected and the water charge is borne by the government. As such, the profits of the companies are unaffected by the risks and problems of cost recovery but are affected by water production levels.

The 'water charge' payment structure also provides an incentive to prioritise connection to middle- and upper-income households. As the companies are paid based on the amount of water supplied and billed, rather than the amount of revenue collected from users, it makes more economic sense to concentrate on extending piped water to wealthier neighbourhoods, where there are fewer problems of access. Poor neighbourhoods and informal settlements are highly dense and unstructured, making the underground extension of the network and the installation of connections more time-consuming.[39]

In 2005, official estimates of the number of households connected to the central network ranged from 46 to 56 per cent.[40] However, figures that attempt to include the large number of Jakarta's informal (and therefore illegal) households estimate only 25 per cent of the population is actually connected.[41] From an economic perspective, it is logical to refuse to provide water to poor and informal settlements because forced evictions and the demolition of

[38] *Pressure to Amend Cooperation Agreement Mounting*, 30 November 2007, available at www.jakartawater.org. On the other hand, the private water operators have highlighted their achievements. Palyja, for example, points to the following figures: from 1998 to June 2009, total connections have increased in its area of operation by 104 per cent to 407,949 connections; it has replaced 343,047 metres; it has invested Rp.1.28 trillion in the network; and to December 2008 has expanded the network by 843 kilometres and rehabilitated 769 kilometres: *Lembar Fakta, Palyja, June* 2009. However, these figures do not cross-refer to the actual requirements in the concession contract.

[39] Bakker et al., *Disconnected*, p. 29.

[40] Some 63 per cent of Jakarta's population is connected to the piped network, according to the *Report on the Achievement of Millennium Development Goals: Indonesia*, 2007 (Jakarta: United Nations and National Development Planning Agency, Indonesia, 2007), p. 83.

[41] Bakker et al., *Disconnected*, p. 13.

structures regularly occur in such areas.[42] Such demolition often results in the destruction of piped water infrastructure and thus jeopardises cost recovery. In addition, piped water is considered vulnerable to theft in such areas,[43] and, as stolen water is not billed, it will affect payment to the private companies through the 'water charge'.

The water charge may also indirectly affect the tariff banding structure intended to benefit poor households. The structure lowers PAM Jaya's revenues, which are the source of funds from which the private operators are paid. The lowest tariff is below the costs of the private operators[44] and therefore decreases PAM Jaya's revenues, increasing the chance of debt, a longer repayment period, and default by PAM Jaya.[45] Therefore the water charge provides an incentive to push for higher tariff rates 'so as not to greatly burden PAM Jaya, which has to pay the difference between the water charge and the water tariff'.[46]

In addition to reflecting an emphasis on water as an economic good, connection rates and tariff levels also highlight the effect of government continuing to treat water as a political good. From a political perspective, the government has put in place legal obstacles that mean many of the city's lowest income residents do not qualify for household water supply services.[47]

42 Argo and Laquian, 'Privatization of Water Utilities and Its Effects on the Urban Poor in Jakarta Raya'.

43 'Clean Water Luxury for North Jakarta Slum Dwellers', *Jakarta Post*, 27 January 2007; 'North Jakarta Squatters Still Without Clean Water', *Jakarta Post*, 15 September 2007.

44 WSP-EAP, *Small Scale Water Providers Study*, p. 40.

45 This is not an unfounded concern. From 1997 to 2004, PAM Jaya became increasingly indebted to the private companies. Following the devastating 1998 Asian financial crisis, the revenues PAM Jaya collected decreased dramatically, as did cost recovery. The water charge paid to the private operators was 11 per cent below the average tariff in 1997 but rose to over 60 per cent above the average tariff in early 2001. Subsequent tariff increases did not raise the tariff above the water charge until early 2004. PAM Jaya's (and thus the local government's) cumulative deficit by the end of 2001 was Rp.469 billion (USD 46 million) and reached Rp.990 billion (USD 97 million) by September 2003: K. Bakker 'Trickle Down? Private Sector Participation and the Pro-Poor Water Supply Debate in Jakarta, Indonesia', *Geoforum*, Vol. 38, No. 5 (2007), pp. 855–868, at p. 860.

46 See Judicial Review of the Water Resources Law (No 7/2004), No 058–059-060–063/PUU-II/2004 and 008/PUU-III/2005, at pp. 141–142 ( 'Judicial Review of the Water Resources Law').

47 This is contrary to the requirement that no households should be denied the right to water on the grounds of their housing or land status: UN Committee on Economic, Social and Cultural Rights, *General Comment 15: The Right to Water* (Twenty-ninth session, 2002), UN Doc. E/C.12/2002/11 (2002), para. 16(c). In 2005, Indonesia ratified the International Covenant on Economic, Social and Cultural Rights (adopted 16 December 1966, entered into force 3 January 1976), 993 UNTS 3 (ICESCR). It is also contrary to the statement by Indonesia's Constitutional Court that 'a person's need for water does not depend on their residence': Judicial Review of the Water Resources Law, p. 488.

To connect to the network, residents must have State-recognised residency for Jakarta in the form of a Personal Identification Card. To get such a Card, residents must have government permission to live and work in Jakarta[48] and must legally occupy the land. To legally occupy land, residents must have a certificate for the land on which they live, indicating a State-sanctioned right to live on or use the land. Many poor households do not have such certificates, either because they forgo the formal registration process, are renters of poor-quality housing or are illegal ' squatters' of unoccupied public or privately owned land. In other cases, residents simply do not have certificates to prove legal occupation of the land.[49] Accordingly, they are considered to be illegal occupiers of the land, even though many have lived or worked on the land for years, have paid for the land and have electricity and in some cases telephone connections provided by State-owned corporations.

The political motivation behind these legal obstacles is to discourage migration to Jakarta from other areas in Indonesia and to encourage migrants to return to their places of origin. Informal settlements in Jakarta are often blamed for a range of social ills, including disturbing public order, crime, prostitution, creating pollution, increased levels of flooding and generally decreasing the beauty of the city. The former Governor of Jakarta, Sutiyoso, has publicly stated that he is embarrassed by the slum dwellings in the flood canal areas near the airport,[50] and ridding the city of such settlements is a high priority for the government.[51] The government deliberately restricts water supply to certain users in accordance with urban planning and a vision for Jakarta as a clean, orderly, calm, pleasant and beautiful city.[52]

As seen here, water and access to water is again part of the politics of the regime of the time, and it in turn affects consumer choices and preferences for

[48] See, for example, Jakarta Government Regulation No. 8/2007 on Public Order, Article 56, which states that every person intending to live and settle in Jakarta must have, among other things, 'd. skills and qualifications; … e. a guaranteed place of abode and guaranteed employment'.

[49] There are over 80 million land parcels in Indonesia, of which only 17 million are currently registered: World Bank, 'Land Policy, Management and Administration', World Bank Policy Brief (January 2005), quoted in Human Rights Watch, *Condemned Communities: Forced Evictions in Jakarta*, Vol. 18, No. 10 (C) (September 2006), p. 21.

[50] Statement of former Governor Sutiyoso to Commission II of the House of Representatives, 7 February 2002: Sri Palupi *Perda tentang Ketertiban Umum Hasil Revisi Perda 11/1988: Upaya Sistematis Mengusir Orang Miskin dengan Dalih Ketertiban Umum*, unpublished paper, 16 September 2007.

[51] See Jakarta Government Regulation No. 8/2007 on Public Order, which allows the forced eviction of dwellings built in areas such as under bridges or flyovers, in green areas, parks and public places, river canals and river banks and in lake and pond areas.

[52] Jakarta Government Regulation No. 8/2007 on Public Order, Considerations.

water sources. The unconnected urban poor seek water supply from alternative sources, such as groundwater (through existing or new wells or by connecting to wells belonging to neighbours), or decentralised small-scale providers charging higher per-unit cost prices. It can often make sense for low-income residents to pay higher costs for water supply if it allows them to remain invisible. However, in some cases the higher price can be an extreme burden, jeopardising residents' ability to secure water without reducing their capacity to acquire other essential goods and services.[53] A study by the WASPOLA Project[54] indicates that in North Jakarta (which represents a poorer, more water-deficient area in Jakarta),[55] the average monthly household expenditure for various water sources was Rp.182,000 (USD 18) per month. This is an extraordinary amount given the monthly minimum wage was less than Rp.1,000,000 (USD 100) per month at the time the study was done.[56] It is also well above government requirements, which state that a tariff is affordable if it is not more than 4 per cent of total monthly income.[57]

Since the participation of the private sector in 1998, water tariffs have risen dramatically, increasing by 15 per cent in 1998,[58] 35 per cent in 2001, 40 per cent in 2003, 30 per cent in 2004[59] and 10 per cent in 2007. In 2009, Palyja (the water service provider for the western half of Jakarta) submitted a proposal to the Jakarta administration to increase water tariffs by an average of 22.7 per cent.[60] From 2004 to 2007, tariffs increased automatically every six months without the need for approval by the Jakarta regional parliament.[61]

53 General Comment No. 15, para. 12(c).

54 WASPOLA is the Water Supply and Sanitation Policy Formulation and Action Planning Project led by the Government of Indonesia drawing on assistance from AusAID and the World Bank.

55 Groundwater is brackish and cannot be used for household purposes. For example, residents have reported that taking a bath in groundwater makes them itch and that the colour of their clothes changes when washed in the water: 'North Jakarta Squatters Still Without Clean Water', *Jakarta Post*, 15 September 2007.

56 Out of a population of over 245 million people, 52 per cent of Indonesians live on less than Rp.20,000 (AUD 2.45) a day or Rp.600,000 per month, with an estimated 35 million living on less than 80 cents a day (Rp.6,500).

57 WSP-EAP *Indonesian Small Scale Water Providers Study* (Jakarta: Water & Sanitation Program, East Asia and the Pacific, World Bank 2007), p. 47, available at www.waspola.org. See also Article 3.2 of Home Affairs Ministerial Regulation 23/2006.

58 Following the financial and political turmoil in May 1998, the government was unwilling to further raise public tariffs because of public unrest.

59 'City Administration Quietly Raises Water Rates by 30 Percent', *Jakarta Post*, 6 January 2004.

60 According to Palyja Commissioner Bernard Lafronge, this is in accordance with the 20 per cent inflation rate over the last two years: 'Palyja Seeks Rate Hike, Vows Investment', *Jakarta Post*, 8 January 2009.

61 Surat DPRD DKI Jakarta Nomor 550/-1.778.1 tanggal 23 Juli 2004.

This appears contrary to the requirement in the private operator contracts that 'the level of Tariffs shall be set in accordance with the ability to pay of the Jakartan community'.[62] In addition, in some cases the increase in the tariff for low-income households has been disproportionately high when compared to the increase for upper-income households, industry and business. For example, in 2005, fees for low-income households rose by 63 per cent, while fees for upper-income households and industrial and commercial enterprises rose by less than 11 per cent.[63] There have also been sudden changes in criteria for the grouping of tap water customers. Although low-cost residential dwellings do pay less than luxury dwellings, the criteria for lower tariffs is becoming harder to fulfil. For example, in late 2008, Palyja changed the criteria for Group 2 consumers from 36 square metre buildings to 28 square metre buildings without informing customers. This resulted in an increase in tariffs from Rp.1050 to Rp.3550 (USD 0.10 to USD 0.35) per cubic metre.[64]

One of the biggest complaints regarding tariff increases is that they are not accompanied by concurrent increases in water and service quality. In 2004, the Central Jakarta District Court ruled that the 40 per cent increase in water rates in 2003 must be suspended and that the companies could not raise their tariffs 'until they can provide better services and proper information to the customers about their operations'.[65] In spite of this ruling, tariffs have continued to rise and in 2007 became the highest in Indonesia.[66]

The treatment of water as an economic (and political) good has greatly influenced the current pattern of water use and preferences among consumers. It has yet to lead to significant improvement in the water network in Jakarta as was originally anticipated. There are other sources of water available in Jakarta, such as groundwater, and Jakartans have shown that they will choose the cheapest solution they believe best meets their basic needs. Not only are the majority of households in Jakarta not connected to the piped network, but many actually opt out of the piped water network in favour of

[62] Article 26.2 of the Contract.

[63] 'Sutiyoso Defends Water Charge Increase', *Jakarta Post*, 11 July 2005. The then Governor of Jakarta, Sutiyoso, justified the 63 per cent tariff increase by comparing the price paid for water by poor households in two other large cities on Java, Semarang and Surabaya: 'Tarif Air Keluarga Miskin Naik 63 Persen', *Media Indonesia*, 2 July 2005.

[64] Tariffs average Rp.7,000 per cubic metre: Irzal Z. Djamal, Chair of JWSRB, quoted in 'Water Quality Tops Complaints in Consumer Survey', *Jakarta Post*, 22 December 2008.

[65] U. Hudiono, 'Court Orders Suspension of 2003 Water Rate Hike', *Jakarta Post*, 30 January 2004.

[66] *Pressure to Amend Cooperation Agreement Mounting*, 30 November 2007, available at www.jakartawater.org.

other water sources, or are zero-consumption customers.[67] Such choices are economically and politically rational and have been heavily influenced by the treatment of water.

## 4 THE TREATMENT OF WATER IN POST-INDEPENDENCE LAW: WATER AS A SOCIAL GOOD

While the treatment of water as a political and economic good has impacted on levels of access and quality of piped water, and has influenced consumer choices and preferences for water sources, this treatment has not necessarily been reflected in Indonesian law. Since independence, the Indonesian Constitution as well as other Indonesian law has consistently highlighted water as a social good, to be controlled by the State for the greatest benefit of all people.

Under Soekarno's government, the politics of piped water tended to prioritise modernisation and investments in repairing and expanding water networks. In practice, this served the elite because it followed an already established colonial network. However, Indonesia's newly drafted 1945 Constitution stated that water was to be controlled by the State and used for the greatest benefit of the people.[68] This meant that, on the one hand, politics guided the distribution and expansion of the piped water network to the elite, but on the other hand, the highest law in the country emphasised water as a social good. Interestingly, this approach to water set out in the Constitution was not originally intended to guarantee the right to water as understood in current human rights discourse. In fact, human rights were seen as unnecessary when the Constitution was drafted, and the drafters set out the basis for an integralist State where the State and the people are one entity, with their interests assumed to be identical:[69] 'There will be no need for a guarantee of [basic rights] of individuals against the state, for individuals are nothing else than organic parts of the state, having specific positions and duties to realise the grandeur of the state'.[70]

The transition to the Soeharto government in 1966 did not affect this treatment of water in law. In fact, the government passed water laws that cemented and expanded on the basic principles set out in the Constitution.

67 Zero-consumption customers are customers who are connected to the piped network and pay monthly connections fees and other costs but do not use the piped water.

68 Indonesian Constitution 1945, Article 33(3).

69 T. Mulya Lubis, 'The *Rechtsstaat* and Human Rights', in T. Lindsey (ed.), *Indonesia: Law and Society* (Sydney: Federation Press, 1999), pp. 171–185, at pp. 171, 173.

70 Raden Soepomo, the chief author of the Constitution, in H. Muhammad Yamin, *Naskah Persiapan Undang-Undang Dasar 1945*, Vol. 1 (1959), p. 114.

Law No. 11/1974 on Waters[71] stated that the use of water from its source for household purposes was free of charge with no licence requirements. It continued that the management and development of waters must be directed towards the public interest. All planning in the field must be for the public good, by considering the priority of water use. The priority of water use was to be classified into three groups under the Law, namely, Group A, drinking water, household needs, defence and national security, religious purposes and urban needs such as firefighting; Group B, community and commercial farming, animal husbandry, plantations and fisheries; and Group C, man-power, industry, mining, water traffic and recreation.[72] The Law also briefly referred to the requirement to pay for management services where members of the community received a direct benefit from water infrastructure.[73]

In practice, the piped water network was developed and expanded to support industrial growth and to supply upper-class residential areas that were politically supportive of the New Order government. In addition, during this period, water took on an economic aspect, with an emphasis on cost recovery and contribution to regional economic growth.

Following the fall of the Soeharto government in 1998, the Constitution was amended four times, with the second amendment in 2000 inserting a chapter on human rights into the Constitution. This chapter reflects many of the rights contained in international human rights instruments, such as the International Covenant on Economic, Social and Cultural Rights (ICESCR).[74] In regard to water, the new government also began the long process of restructuring Indonesia's water resources management legislation. In 2004, the government passed its framework piece of legislation on water resources management, Law No. 7/2004 on Water Resources. Law No. 7/2004 states that water has a social, environmental and economic function, which must be applied harmoniously to protect the economically vulnerable.[75] Under the Law, 'social function' means that water for the public interest should be prioritised over water for individual interests, and 'economic function' means water can be commercialised to promote business activities.[76] The Law also emphasises public consultation, transparency and participation in water management.[77]

[71] Law No. 11/1974 replaced the Dutch General Water Regulations of 1936. Law No. 11/1974 only contains 17 articles and is a framework act, with further elaboration in implementing regulations. See also Government Regulation No. 22/1982 on Water Management as the main implementing regulation.

[72] See Law No. 11/1974, Article 8 and Elucidation of Article 8. [73] Law No. 11/1974, Article 14.

[74] ICESCR. [75] Law No. 7/2004, Elucidation, point 4 and 9.

[76] Law No. 7/2004, Elucidation of Article 4.

[77] Law No. 7/2004, Article 34(4) and Elucidation of Article 34(4).

Under Law No. 7/2004, the State guarantees the right of every person to obtain water for minimum daily basic needs. Water for basic daily needs and small-scale farming in an irrigation system is free of charge and does not require a usage permit.[78] However, this does not include piped water.[79] Where water is supplied through a distribution channel (such as a piped water network), the supply must prioritise the social function of water and the fulfilment of basic daily needs,[80] and a service fee can be charged.[81] The service fee charged must take into account the cost of the service for business users and the ability to pay for both business and nonbusiness users.[82]

The Law also opens the possibility for PSP in the distribution of drinking water. It clearly states that regional State-owned water companies are responsible for the supply of drinking water, but that other entities, such as private operators, may play a role[83] or, where there is no regional water company, private operators may supply the water.[84] However, the Law lacks a clear framework for the subsequent implementation and regulation of private sector involvement.[85] Apparently, the only requirements in this regard are that the development of the distribution of drinking water aims to provide a quality network at an affordable price, to achieve a balance between the interests of service providers and consumers and to increase the efficiency and coverage of the drinking water network.[86] There is no reference, for example, to the need for an adequate regulatory framework.

The Law also acknowledges water as a cultural good, outlining the need to recognise indigenous peoples' rights when the State is exercising control over water resources. However, this recognition is heavily qualified by the requirement that indigenous peoples' rights must not be contrary to the national

[78] One practical problem with this 'free' water is that excessive and unlicenced groundwater use is causing significant pollution and salinisation of aquifers, making groundwater increasingly unfit for consumption or other daily needs.

[79] Law No. 7/2004, Article 8(1).

[80] Law No. 7/2004, Articles 26(2) and 26(7).

[81] In theory, this prioritisation requirement is a positive development from a human rights perspective. However, PAM Jaya, which is the government party to the water supply contracts, has publicly acknowledged that 'it cannot provide surface water' adequately and is only capable of supplying 54 per cent of the water needs of the people of Jakarta. This was acknowledged by PAM Jaya as reported by TvOne in its news story 'Krisis Air Tanah' on Apa Kabar Indonesia, 31 October 2008. See also 'Berlebihan, Eksploitasi Air Tanah', *Suara Pembaruan*, 18 November 2008.

[82] Law No. 7/2004, Articles 7, 8 and 80.

[83] Law No. 7/2004, Articles 40(3) and (4).

[84] Law No. 7/2004, Article 45(3).

[85] Under Indonesian law, laws (undang-undang) establish the framework law upon which subsequent regulations are based.

[86] Law No. 7/2004, Article 40(5). As seen in the discussion above, there are many aspects of the Jakarta PSP that are not in accordance with these requirements.

interest and laws, must 'still exist'[87] and must have been confirmed by local government regulation.[88] The rights must also be in accordance with developments in society and with the principles of the Unitary State of Indonesia.[89] As such, protection of access to traditional water sources and protection from unlawful encroachment and pollution are limited.[90]

Although, from the above description, Law No. 7/2004 appears to be a positive step in the treatment of water by the Indonesian government, the Law created significant controversy when it was passed. The government passed Law No. 7/2004 in recognition of 'the right of all persons to obtain water for daily needs and to regulate the right to water', and the Law acknowledges the dangers of treating water more as an economic rather than a social good.[91] However, NGOs accused the government of implementing World Bank policy in exchange for a USD 300 million loan, which required the government to treat water as a tradable economic good and to open the door to private sector participation.[92] This controversy culminated in five applications for judicial review of Law No. 7/2004 being lodged with the Indonesian Constitutional Court in 2004 and 2005.[93] The applicants argued that the Law violated the Constitution, firstly because it does not acknowledge the right to water as guaranteed by the Constitution and treats water as a commodity without sufficiently recognising the social and cultural aspects of water. Second, the applicants argued that facilitating privatisation allows vital production sectors to be removed from State control, meaning that water is no longer controlled by the State for the greatest welfare

[87] Indigenous peoples rights 'still exist' if the following three elements are satisfied: (a) the element of an indigenous community, that is, there is a group of people that still feels bound by their customary law as members of a legal unit, which recognises and applies the regulations of that unit in daily life; (b) the element of territory, that is, there is customary land which has become the living environment for members of that legal unit and the place has significance to their daily life; and (c) the element of a relationship between the community and its region, that is, there are customary rules regarding the management, control and use of customary land, which are still applicable and adhered to by members of the legal unit: Law No. 7/2004, Elucidation of Article 6(3).

[88] Law No. 7/2004, Articles 6(2) and (3).

[89] Law No. 7/2004, Elucidation, point 1.

[90] General Comment No. 15, para. 16(d).

[91] Law No. 7/2004, Elucidation, paras. 1 and 4.

[92] This accusation was repeated several times in the application for judicial review of Law No. 7/2004: Judicial Review of the Water Resources Law, pp. 98, 99.

[93] Indonesia's Constitutional Court was established in 2003, allowing judicial review of legislation for its compliance with the Constitution (Law No. 24/2003 on the Constitutional Court). The applicants (NGOs and members of the public) requested the Court to annul the Law in its entirety or that certain articles of the Law be annulled (these were Articles 9, 10, 26, 45, 46, 80, 91, 92, 39(2), 6(3) and (2), 38(2), 48(1), 29(5) and 49(4)).

of the people.[94] The applicants also used the PSP in Jakarta as an example of how privatisation results in water being treated as an economic good and leads to declining standards of water supply.[95]

In regard to the first argument brought by the applicants, the right to water is not explicitly mentioned in the Constitution. However, Article 28H states that every person has the right to live in spiritual and physical welfare, the right to housing, the right to a good and healthy environment as well as the right to obtain health care. The Constitutional Court confirmed that Article 28H guarantees the right to water.[96] The Court found that Article 5 of Law No. 7/2004, which requires the State to 'guarantee everyone's right to obtain water for their minimum daily basic needs', fulfils the right to water as guaranteed by Article 28H of the Constitution.[97] The Court interpreted Article 5 to apply irrespective of the source of water (i.e. whether the water was from a natural source or from a piped network).[98] The majority quoted several international instruments that it felt 'describe access to clean water as a human right', namely, the Constitution of the World Health Organization (WHO), Article 25 of the Universal Declaration of Human Rights, Article 12 of the ICESCR and Article 24(1) of the Convention on the Rights of the Child.[99] It is unclear why the Court did not refer to, or rely on, Article 11 of the ICESCR or General Comment No. 15 on the Right to Water.[100] This may be because the Indonesian Constitution does not specifically refer to the right to water, but rather the right is guaranteed by reference to health. The Court also stated that water usage rights, as referred to in the Law, must be interpreted as a derivative of the right to life.[101]

The second argument made by the applicants was that the Law facilitates privatisation, which allows vital sectors to be taken out of State control, and therefore is contrary to the requirement in the Constitution that such sectors be controlled by the State for the greatest welfare of the people.[102]

94 The objection raised by the applicants referred to privatisation (*swastanisasi*), rather than private sector participation more generally. Privatisation is the most far-reaching way of transferring power from the government to the private sector.

95 The Court made no comment in relation to this last point.

96 Article 28H. See Judicial Review of the Water Resources Law, at pp. 488.

97 At the time the application for judicial review was lodged, Indonesia had not ratified the International Covenant on Economic, Social and Cultural Rights. However, by the time the Court announced its decision on 19 July 2005, Indonesia had ratified the Covenant. The Court also found that Articles 14, 15, 16, 29(3) and 26(7) of the Constitution reflected the right to water.

98 Judicial Review of the Water Resources Law, pp. 491–492.

99 Judicial Review of the Water Resources Law, p. 486.

100 General Comment No. 15.

101 Judicial Review of the Water Resources Law, p. 495.

102 Constitution, Article 33(3).

The Court rejected this argument and held that the Law does not take away government control over water resources.[103] Sectors like water that are 'controlled by the State' are not open to appropriation by private entities through privatisation.[104] However, private entities may have the right to obtain, use or exploit water in an amount and manner determined and controlled by the government in accordance with licence conditions.[105] The government must retain responsibility over water resources and formulate policies, regulate and manage water resources, grant permits for water exploitation and supervise permit implementation.[106] The Court found that the government maintains its control over water resources under the Law in accordance with this interpretation.

The Court also outlined requirements regarding the content of any further regulation of water resources. Law No. 7/2004 is a framework law, and so the detail and method of implementing it will be outlined in subsequent implementing regulations. According to the Court, such regulations must clearly state that regional State-owned water companies must prioritise the social function of water so that the service fee paid by consumers for the water is just.[107] The service fee must not be expensive or profit-oriented (as water is 'res commune'[108] (sic) or belonging to all). This means that, in realising the right to water as set out in Article 5(1) of Law No. 7/2004, regional State-owned water companies must not act as profit-oriented companies. The community must be involved in determining the service fee, and the process must be transparent.[109] In regard to competing priorities over water use, the Court explained that the government must prioritise its responsibility to provide a drinking water supply because the ability to obtain water within a reasonable time and distance better fulfils the right to water.[110] The government bears primary responsibility for this and may involve the private sector only if it cannot fulfil these obligations itself. This does not mean, however, that the government no longer has the obligation to regulate, implement and supervise the management of water resources as a whole.[111] The Court

[103] Judicial Review of the Water Resources Law, pp. 498–499.
[104] Indonesian law defines privatisation as the selling of government shares in a State-owned enterprise to another party or parties in order to boost the performance and value of the enterprise and to expand public share ownership: Law No. 19/2003 on State Owned Enterprises, Article 1(12).
[105] Judicial Review of the Water Resources Law, pp. 496–498.
[106] Judicial Review of the Water Resources Law, pp. 497–498 referring to Law No. 7/2004, Articles 14, 15 and 16 for the central, provincial and district level governments, respectively.
[107] Reflecting Article 26(7): Judicial Review of the Water Resources Law, p. 492.
[108] Judicial Review of the Water Resources Law, p. 493. [109] Ibid. [110] Ibid., p. 494.
[111] Ibid.

concluded that if its considerations, which form the basis of its decision, are not observed by the government in the implementing regulations, the Law could be reviewed again.[112]

The Constitutional Court's decision to comment on the content of further regulations is a controversial one and may overstep its mandate. The Court's mandate is limited to determining whether or not laws (framework laws only, not implementing regulations) breach the Constitution. It does not have the authority to propose the content of further legislation or regulations.[113] The Court may also be seen to be interfering in the law and policymaking functions of the government. The Indonesian government is particularly sensitive to any perceived interference from the courts, particularly in regard to allocation of budgets. This sensitivity may result in the government simply ignoring the Court's decision. The government has previously declined to implement less controversial decisions by the Constitutional Court, such as its decisions that the government must spend 20 per cent of the national budget on education as mandated by the Constitution.[114] For three years the government consistently refused to implement these decisions on the basis that it did not have the money to do so.[115] If the government again fails to comply with the Court's decision, it could negatively impact on the image of the Constitutional Court as an effective means of redress for Indonesians whose constitutional rights have been breached by law. This would be unfortunate as, to date, the Court has been seen as a positive development in a judicial system otherwise marred by corruption and lack of transparency and accountability.[116]

It is also unclear how Law No. 7/2004 could be reviewed again if the government fails to observe the Court's considerations in further regulations. Under Indonesian law, the Court's decision is final[117] and of 'permanent legal force' once announced.[118] An application for repeated judicial review of laws that have been considered by the Court cannot be refiled.[119]

[112] Ibid., p. 495. [113] Law No 24/2003 on the Constitutional Court, Article 10.

[114] Constitution, Article 31(4).

[115] Three times, the Constitutional Court has ruled that the allocation of 9.1 per cent of the total national budget in 2006 and 11.9 per cent in 2007 and 2008 were not in compliance with the Constitution (Article 31(4)), which requires that 20 per cent of the state budget be spent on education.

[116] *Report of the Special Rapporteur on the independence of judges and lawyers Dato' Param Cumaraswamy, submitted in accordance with Commission on Human Rights resolution 2002/43. Report on the mission to Indonesia, 15–24 July 2002*, UN Doc. E/CN.4/2003/65/Add.2 (2003).

[117] Constitution, Article 24C(1); Law No. 24/2003 on the Constitutional Court, Article 10.

[118] Law No. 24/2003 on the Constitutional Court, Article 47.

[119] Law No. 24/2003 on the Constitutional Court, Article 60.

In addition to this controversy over the Constitutional Court's mandate, there were two dissenting opinions in the case. The dissenting opinion by Justice Mukthie Fadjar asserted that Law No. 7/2004 will make it increasingly difficult for individuals and groups who rely on non-piped water to access water and will eventually force them to use (and pay for) piped water, including for daily use and subsistence farming. This in effect facilitates a hidden form of water commercialisation. Justice Mukthie also commented that the Law, and in particular the failure to strike out the articles relating to private sector participation, facilitated hidden privatisation.[120]

The need to involve the private sector in developing adequate drinking water and sanitation facilities is something the Indonesian government has clearly advocated in the international arena.[121] However, any effort to involve the private sector should be preceded by the identification of key systemic obstacles that keep people from accessing opportunity and improving their own lives. In other words, the government should consider why people are unable to access clean, safe, affordable water, and the key systemic obstacles in this regard. In the case of Jakarta, the government does not appear to have clearly asked (and answered) this question. There is no requirement in Law No. 7/2004 that the government identify key systematic obstacles before involving the private sector. While the Constitutional Court addressed many issues in its decision, it did not comment on these shortcomings in the Law.

Since Law No. 7/2004 was passed, the government has made two regulations that are particularly relevant to drinking water. The first is Government Regulation No. 16/2005 on the Development of a Drinking Water Supply System, which was passed five months before the Constitutional Court case handed down its decision. Therefore it cannot be challenged for its failure to take account of the Court's decision. The second is the draft regulation on water usage rights.

Although Government Regulation No. 16/2005 cannot be challenged as being contrary to the decision of the Constitutional Court, it is worth considering its consistency with the Court's decision and Law No. 7/2004, as inconsistencies make the regulation of drinking water supply difficult to apply in practice. The government may also consider revising the Regulation in the future as it is extremely brief and does not adequately regulate drinking water.

[120] Judicial Review of the Water Resources Law, for example at pp. 510, 512.

[121] See, for example, Indonesia's 2004 and 2007 Millennium Development Goals Progress Reports.

Government Regulation No. 16/2005 for the most part repeats many of the general principles set out in Law No. 7/2004[122] and requires parties that develop a drinking water network to provide sufficient data to monitor and evaluate their performance.[123] In practice, however, this requirement does not appear to be implemented. In regard to the piped water network in Jakarta, the applicants in the Constitutional Court case claimed that PAM Jaya does not even know how much money is in the Escrow Account it shares with the two private operators,[124] and the Jakarta Water Supply Regulatory Board has complained that it does not receive enough information from the private operators to adequately monitor their performance.[125] Customers in Jakarta also often complain of negative experiences when dealing with the private companies, in particular that they receive no response to complaints raised and are not informed of tariff adjustments, network interruptions and network repair.[126]

The Regulation states that the development of a drinking water network is the responsibility of the central and regional governments, and it is their respective responsibilities to guarantee every person obtains drinking water for their minimum daily requirements for a healthy, clean and productive life.[127] If the governments, through regional water companies, are unable to improve the quality and quantity of the drinking water network, then with the agreement of the directors of the regional water company, the government may involve third parties, including the private sector, in the provision of water in their respective regions.[128] There is no further regulation of the private sector. This is unfortunate because PSP requires clear guarantees that the government will continue to fulfil its obligations in order to guarantee every person obtains water to fulfil his or her minimum daily needs. Specifically, under the Indonesian Constitution, the State has a duty to control water resources for the greatest benefit of the people. Water supply is not open to appropriation by private entities as defined in the Indonesian context,[129]

[122] See, for example, Articles 4 and 24(4) of Regulation No. 16/2005.

[123] Regulation No. 16/2005, Article 36(3).

[124] Judicial Review of the Water Resources Law, at p. 144.

[125] International Consortium of Investigative Journalists, *Water and Politics*.

[126] For example, one business customer complained that his water supplier had stopped his service for three days in late 2008 without any announcement: '1,000 Firms Fined for Overusing Groundwater', *Jakarta Post*, 12 December 2008. The private companies refute such claims. For example, on its website Palyja outlines the results of its customer satisfaction survey, which claim that in 2009, 73 per cent of its customers were satisfied overall with the services they received; available at http://id.palyja.co.id/layanan-pelanggan/survey-kepuasan-pelanggan-/.

[127] Regulation No. 16/2005, Article 37(1).

[128] Regulation No. 16/2005, Article 37(3).

[129] In the Indonesian context, this means that appropriation through privatisation where privatisation is the selling of government shares in a State-owned enterprise to another party or

and the government retains responsibility for formulating policies, regulating, managing water resources, granting permits for water exploitation and for supervising permit implementation.[130] However, the regulation is silent on this prohibition and also on the responsibility of the State stemming from its obligation to control water for the greatest benefit of the people. This criticism was also raised by Justice Mukthie Fadjar in his dissenting opinion. He stated that Article 40(3) of the Law, when read in conjunction with Article 1(9) of Government Regulation No. 16/2005, could be interpreted as relieving the government of its responsibility to provide drinking water.[131]

The regulation also makes a brief statement on service fees and tariffs. Tariffs are defined as a service fee for drinking water and are calculated and determined on the basis of affordability and justice, service quality, cost recovery, efficiency of water use, transparency and accountability and the protection of raw water. Tariffs consist of operational and management costs, depreciation/amortisation costs, interest on loans, other costs and reasonable or appropriate profits (although it is unclear what this means and how much weight may be attributed to this element in determining tariffs). Tariff structures must include progressive tariffs in the context of cross subsidisation between consumers. Where private operators are responsible for water supply, tariffs are determined by the regional head on the basis of the water supply contract.[132]

There is no clear requirement in the regulation that regional water companies must not act as profit-oriented companies. In fact, cost recovery, costs and profit are all factors that may determine tariffs where drinking water is provided by a government-owned or government-controlled corporation. This is not consistent with the Constitutional Court's decision. The regulation is also silent as to what considerations must be taken into account in determining the tariff structure where a private operator is involved. There is no requirement that the tariff must be affordable and not based on profit. There is also no requirement in the regulation that the community be involved in determining the tariffs and that the process be transparent, which is clearly required by the Court.[133] It is also questionable whether the power given to the water provider to completely disconnect customers for not fulfilling their

parties in order to boost the performance and value of the enterprise and to expand public share ownership: Law No. 19/2003 on State Owned Enterprises, Article 1(12).

[130] Judicial Review of the Water Resources Law, pp. 497–498 referring to Law No. 7/2004, Articles 14, 15 and 16 for the central, provincial and district level governments, respectively.

[131] Judicial Review of the Water Resources Law, p. 512.

[132] Regulation No. 16/2005, Article 60.

[133] Note that Interior Minister Regulation No. 23/2006 requires full cost recovery plus an appropriate or reasonable profit in regard to tariffs for State Owned Drinking Water Companies: Article 2(c) and 5(2).

obligations (such as paying for the service provided)[134] is consistent with the Constitutional Court's decision if they do not have access to water for their basic needs.

The second regulation that is relevant in regard to drinking water is the draft government regulation on water usage rights.[135] Again the draft regulation prioritises water for daily needs and community farming, which is based on the Constitutional provision that water is a national asset that must be used for the greatest benefit of the people.[136] However the draft regulation does not state that the prioritisation includes water from a piped water network. In other legislation, this prioritisation and general protection has been limited to water from its source unless otherwise specifically extended to water supplied through a distribution network. The draft therefore should include a clear statement prioritising water usage so that drinking water provided through a distribution network has priority above other commercial uses of water. This is particularly important as the draft also states that there has been a paradigmatic shift in the way water is viewed. Originally it was seen as a social good without value, but now it has begun to shift towards an economic good with value.[137] This is attributed in part to economic globalisation and trade liberalisation. Apart from its function of fulfilling daily basic needs, because of its economic value, water can be exploited for commercial purposes.[138] To better realise the right to water in accordance with Law No. 7/2004 and the Constitutional Court's decision, the regulation should emphasise that this economic value of water is subsidiary to its social function.[139]

The draft regulation outlines the meaning of the right of the State to control water, namely, it gives the State the right and obligation: (a) to regulate, guide, supervise and provide a service as well as to provide, secure and protect water in order to fulfil the needs of the community in all aspects of life; (b) to determine and regulate legal relations between people or legal entities and water; and (c) to determine and regulate legal relations between people or legal entities and legal action in connection with water.[140] Point (a) means that that government is responsible for regulating, developing, monitoring, protecting and supervising the use of water.[141] To ensure consistency with the

[134] Regulation No. 16/2005, Article 68(1)(e).
[135] Comments are based on the draft dated 10 June 2008.
[136] Draft Regulation on Water Usage Rights, Elucidation, point 3.
[137] Draft Regulation on Water Usage Rights, Elucidation, General, point 1.
[138] Draft Regulation on Water Usage Rights, Article 4(1).
[139] See Law No. 7/2004, Article 26(7), and Judicial Review of the Water Resources Law, p. 492.
[140] Draft Regulation on Water Usage Rights, Article 2(2).
[141] Draft Regulation on Water Usage Rights, Article 2(4).

Constitutional Court's interpretation of control, it would be better if the Regulation utilised the language of the Court's decision. The inconsistency in language use makes it difficult to ascertain whether the government is fulfilling its requirement to control water.

The draft regulation on water usage rights also contains provisions on licencing. A licence is not required for basic daily needs unless the manner in which water is used changes the natural condition of water sources, is used in large amounts (it is unclear what this means) or is used for community farming outside the existing irrigation system.[142] Where no licence is required, water usage rights are realised through a water allocation certificate, published on the basis of an inventory of population numbers, estimated water needs to fulfil basic daily needs and estimates of water needs for community farming in pre-existing systems.[143] The certificate is intended to guarantee the right of the certificate holder to manage the water resource.[144] It is doubtful that households considered to be illegally occupying land will be issued with such a certificate, although the Constitutional Court has noted that a person's need for water does not depend on their residence.[145] It is also doubtful given the increasing pollution of water available at its source, particularly in Jakarta, that many people will continue to be able to access water at its source for daily basic needs.

As can be seen from the above discussion, the treatment of water under the Indonesian Constitution and under water resources legislation emphasises the treatment of water as a social good and recently has also acknowledged that water has an economic, cultural and environmental value. While this is positive from a human rights perspective, it does not appear to have had an impact on the treatment of water by the various administrations or on the supervision or regulation of the private operators by the State. Individuals and households are still experiencing severe difficulties in accessing sufficient, safe, acceptable, physically accessible and affordable water for personal and domestic uses[146] and will continue to do so until the positive developments in the water resources laws are realised in practice.

## 5 CONCLUSION

Jakarta has a water supply system that has been restricted to certain users and areas since its inception in the nineteenth century. Such restrictions have

142 Draft Regulation on Water Usage Rights, Article 8(1) and (2).
143 Draft Regulation on Water Usage Rights, Article 20(1) and (2).
144 Draft Regulation on Water Usage Rights, Article 20(6).
145 Judicial Review of the Water Resources Law, p. 488.
146 General Comment No. 15, para. 2.

followed the ruling government's political interests and vision for Jakarta and Indonesia, thus making water a political good. Historically, approaching water in this manner did little to promote a high-quality water service, and, by the late 1980s, Jakarta's centralised piped water network had numerous problems. These included a water supply distribution network that was not capable of distributing the available water, limited water coverage and poor water quality, high levels of unaccounted-for water and a municipal water company that was inefficient and underperforming.

The PSP contracts signed in 1998 promised to address many of these problems, in particular to improve water quality and expand the network. However, key performance targets have not been met, and the contracts support a structure that encourages water to be treated primarily as an economic good. New connections appear to have targeted middle-class (and above) customers, and tariff increases have been higher for poorer customers, without real concurrent attempts to address issues of ability to pay and cross-subsidy mechanisms.

While in practice water has been treated as a political and economic good, the Indonesian Constitution and subsequent water laws have demonstrated a more nuanced approach. The Constitution and subsequent laws recognise the complexity of water by acknowledging that it primarily has a social function, with an associated economic, cultural and environmental function. The right to water requires all functions to be recognised, and all functions are essential to the realisation of the right to water. However, to date, this more nuanced approach has not been applied in practice.

In the future, a reliable, accessible and effective piped water network will become more important in Jakarta. Water is becoming increasingly scarce and shallow groundwater more polluted. Jakartans make politically and economically rational choices regarding the water sources and distribution methods they use. These choices have been influenced by the politics of particular administrations and the profit-seeking behaviour of private corporations. Future efforts to improve service levels of the network must acknowledge the reasons behind the patterns of water use in Jakarta. Such efforts must also reconcile the differences in the approach to water in Indonesia's Constitution and water laws and the approach to water in practice. Unless this occurs, any future improvements and reform of Jakarta's piped water network are destined to fail.

## POSTSCRIPT

Since this chapter was written, there have been several significant developments that affect piped water in Jakarta, and, ultimately, whether it is viewed as a political, economic or social good.

As noted in Chapter 13, in 2005 the Constitutional Court declared Law No. 7/2004 to be 'conditionally constitutional', warning that if the content of any further regulation of water resources did not observe the considerations that formed the basis of its decision, the Law could be reviewed again. A further challenge to Law No. 7/2004 was filed in September 2013 by Muhammadiyah, a social Islamic NGO with over 29 million members. The Court accepted the arguments put forward by Muhammadiyah, and in February 2015 annulled Law No. 7/2004 and reinstated Law No. 11/1974 until a new law is passed. The Court's view was influenced by the further implementing regulations (seven in total between 2005 and September 2013) and found the Law to be contrary to the 1945 Constitution, in particular the requirement in Article 33(3) that the land, the waters and natural resources within be under the powers of the State and be used to the greatest benefit of the people. The Court stated water to be 'res commune' (sic) and emphasised its character as a social rather than an economic good.

At the same time, the Coalition of Jakarta Residents against Water Privatisation (KMMSAJ) filed a type of class action in the Central Jakarta District Court seeking to annul the piped water contracts with private operators, Palyja and Aetra. In March 2015, the District Court handed down its judgment annulling the contracts and returning the management of drinking water to the Jakarta Government. It found, amongst other things, that the private operators had been negligent in fulfilling the right to water of Jakartans, and that the contracts had been detrimental to the nation and to Jakartans. However, in January 2016 the Jakarta High Court overturned the decision and reinstated the two contracts. In March 2016, KMMSAJ appealed to the Indonesian Supreme Court. As at June 2017, no decision had been handed down.

# 15

# Privatisation and Regulatory Autonomy

## *The Right to Water in International Economic Law*

ANDREW LANG*

### 1 PRELUDE

The 1990s saw a large wave of private sector investment in water infrastructure across many parts of the developing world. It was a time of some optimism about the benefits that private operators and investors could bring to this troubled sector: large capital reserves which were not available through traditional public financing, management expertise based on international best practice and a welcome depoliticisation of a sector which in some countries had been poorly managed for political gain. As a result, almost forty countries had experimented with some form of private sector participation by the end of the decade, in respect of project servicing close to 100 million people.[1] At the same time, however, this restructuring of the industry generated a new set of problems and considerable political resistance. A number of high-profile projects encountered difficulties as a result of a variety of factors including changing economic conditions, unforeseen problems with existing infrastructure, consumer reaction to pricing policies and quality control issues and contractual breaches. Furthermore, in some contexts and for some groups, water privatisation became a metonym for neoliberal globalisation, so that mobilisation against privatisation projects in the water sector came to be established as an important part of anti-globalisation activism in the years around the turn of the millennium. When the GATS 2000 negotiations began, and

* Professor of Law, London School of Economics. This chapter is taken from A. Lang, 'The GATS and Regulatory Autonomy: A Case Study of Social Regulation of the Water Industry', *Journal of International Economic Law*, Vol. 7, No. 4 (2004), pp. 801–838, with a new prelude prepared in 2010.

[1] P. Marin, *Public-Private Partnerships for Urban Water Utilities: A Review of Experiences in Developing Countries* (Washington DC: World Bank, 2009), p. 2.

particularly when certain documents were leaked in 2002 which suggested to some that market access commitments in the water sector were being sought by some participants in these negotiations, this activism began to centre around the WTO. Claims were made that the WTO (and the GATS in particular) was being enlisted in a project to expand and entrench commercialisation of the water sector and to limit the ability of governments to regulate in ways which may negatively affect the commercial interests of those private operators.

The republished article below was written in 2004, at a high point in that debate, and the research on which it was based was conducted in the early 2000s. It represents an attempt to assess the legal claims of the critics of the GATS on their own terms. Putting to one side the arguments that the GATS may formally *require* privatisation of water services – which were always the less probable of the many claims being made at the time – the article focussed on the extent to which the non-discrimination norms contained in GATS Articles II and XVII may affect regulatory interventions affecting private operators in the water sector. It drew three primary conclusions. First, while it is true that there is an important difference between prohibition of discriminatory regulation on the one hand and deregulation on the other, it is also true that the non-discrimination norm can be interpreted and applied in ways which blur that boundary and which in practice impose constraints on the substantive content of regulation. The article noted some evidence of this tendency within parts of GATT/WTO jurisprudence, particularly in respect of the national treatment obligation. Second, the GATS contains considerable ambiguities, qualifications and exceptions, even in respect of its core norms. As a result, it is possible to interpret these norms in ways which permit considerable scope for regulatory autonomy in appropriate cases. If there was a risk of undue regulatory constraint, in other words, it was at the level of interpretation, not text. Third, one's opinion of the regulatory constraints imposed by the GATS in the water sector depended in large part on the way one assessed the likely resolution of these many ambiguities. By and large, commentators were split between those who were convinced that they would tend to be resolved in the interests of large commercial enterprises and those who thought that WTO Members would always jealously guard their regulatory space from diminution by panellists and the Appellate Body.

In the years since that research was conducted was written, neither the legal nor the commercial context has stood still. At least four developments are worth noting, all of which in my view somewhat reduce the risks I identified in my earlier research.

### 1.1 *Negotiations on New Commitments and New Rules in the WTO Continue to Be Largely Unproductive*

At the time of the initial concerns about the GATS and impact on the water sector, negotiations on services in the WTO were – comparatively speaking – relatively active, and there was some indication that the water and sanitation sector was of offensive interest to some parties. The prospect of GATS commitments in the water and sanitation sector in the relatively near future therefore seemed to many to be a real possibility. At the end of 2009, however, it is fair to say that the possibility seems significantly more remote, for at least two reasons. First, specifically in response to activism around this issue, the EU has, for example, made it plain in its public statements that it is not participating in any request addressing water for human use. It has noted, furthermore, that it is not seeking the dismantling of public services and that it recognises the importance of strong domestic regulatory frameworks to accompany liberalisation.[2] Second, as the Doha Round has developed, services negotiations have taken a back seat to higher-profile issues relating to market access to agricultural and industrial goods. The result has been a relatively low level of 'ambition' in the services negotiations and a sense that major concessions are unlikely. (Both the United States and the EU, it should be acknowledged, have publicly expressed their commitment to achieving substantial outcomes in the services negotiations, but it is still the case that the level of offers currently on the table is very low.) At the time of writing, few if any close observers are seriously suggesting that major new commitments in the water and sanitation sectors are likely.

The same is true of other negotiation venues within the WTO which have some relevance to the water and sanitation sector. Negotiations on environmental goods and services – the latter of which in some formulations includes sanitation services and water for human use – have been stalled by a fundamental lack of agreement on what should count as an environmental good or service. Negotiations under GATS Article VI for new rules on domestic regulation have also so far produced few results in terms of concrete agreement – though it should be acknowledged that at the Hong Kong Ministerial, negotiators committed themselves to agreeing rules on non-quantitative,

[2] See, e.g., EC Commission press releases available at http://trade.ec.europa.eu/doclib/docs/2005/january/tradoc_121201.pdf; http://trade.ec.europa.eu/doclib/docs/2006/february/tradoc_127631.pdf; as well as the press release of the UK Department for Business Innovation and Skills at www.berr.gov.uk/whatwedo/europeandtrade/key-trade-issues/services-gats/gats_doha_development_round/page28625.html.

non-discriminatory domestic regulation by the end of the Doha Round,[3] and negotiations continue in principle on a draft text prepared by the Chair of the Working Party on Domestic Regulation.[4]

In the absence of major new developments at the level of new rules or new commitments, then, the result is that the GATS is likely to continue to be of only marginal relevance on the water and sanitation sector, at least for the foreseeable future. It contains few if any liberalisation commitments directly relevant to the water and sanitation sector[5] and establishes a framework of norms which are frankly not particularly well suited for application in the water and sanitation sector – a sector which is characterised by natural monopoly, by a high degree of market concentration, and in which commercial operations are often carried out through the vehicle of concession contracts and similar arrangements.

Some have noted what they see as a shift in the locus of efforts to open global water services markets – from multilateral negotiations in the WTO to regional and bilateral FTA negotiations. Given that the bulk of material documenting FTA negotiations are not available to the public, it is hard to assess the reality of these claims. However, it should at least be noted that the EU has offered essentially the same assurances in this context as it has in the multilateral context (see above) and that a number of developing countries are highly sensitised to this issue and have in the past been successful in excluding the water sector from concluded free trade agreements.[6] If there is a strong push to open water services markets through FTAs, it seems yet to have borne much fruit.

### 1.2 *Investment Treaty Arbitration Has Clearly Become the Centre of Gravity of International Dispute Settlement in the Water Sector*

A second development has been a shift of attention from trade law to investment law, as it has become apparent that investment treaty arbitration provides

3 See WTO, *Hong Kong Ministerial Declaration* (22 Dec. 2005), Doc. WT/MIN(05)/DEC, Annex C, para. 5, www.wto.org/english/thewto_e/minist_e/min05_e/final_annex_e.htm#annexc.

4 See WTO Working Party on Domestic Regulation, 'Disciplines on domestic regulation pursuant to GATS article VI:4 consolidated working paper: note by the Chairman' (Jul. 2006), Doc. JOB(06)/225 www.tradeobservatory.org/library.cfm?refID=88479.

5 Though as I note in the article below, this says nothing about the indirect relevance of commitments in other sectors.

6 For example, both Peru and Panama excluded water services from their free trade agreements with the United States.

a far more attractive and suitable mode of dispute settlement for foreign private investors in the water sector than WTO dispute settlement. This at least has been the experience of the past decade. As mentioned above, a number of high-profile water projects in the developing world ran into difficulties from around 2001 and in some cases earlier. Many of these were concentrated in Latin America – five concessions were terminated early in Argentina following its economic crisis, and three others in Bolivia and Uruguay similarly ran into difficulties. A substantial number were located in sub-Saharan African countries such as Mali, Tanzania, Chad and others. A flagship privatisation project in West Manila was also subject to early termination in 2005 and re-awarded to a different private operator. Overall, Marin calculates that roughly 10 per cent of contracts awarded since 1991 have been terminated early.[7] The fallout from these early terminations did not take long to surface in the investment arbitration context. Between 1996 and 2007, nine distinct cases were brought against Argentina involving disputes relating to water concessions,[8] while two others emanated from Tanzania and Bolivia,[9] representing roughly half of the early terminations of water concessions which occurred during the period. These cases are the subject of another chapter in this book, as well as other analyses.[10] What is significant for present purposes is simply that investment treaty arbitration has been – and will in all likelihood continue to be – the centre of gravity for international dispute settlement in

[7] See, generally, P. Marin, *Public-Private Partnerships for Urban Water Utilities: A Review of Experiences in Developing Countries* (Washington DC: World Bank, 2009), p. 27.

[8] *Compania de Aguas del Aconquija SA and Vivendi Universal v The Argentine Republic* (ICSID Case No. ARB/97/3); *Azurix Corporation v The Argentine Republic* (ICSID Case No. ARB/01/12); *Suez Sociedad General de Aguas de Barcelona SA and Interagua Servicios Integrales de Agua SA v Argentine Republic* (ICSID Case No. ARB/03/17); *Aguas Cordobesas SA, Suez, and Sociedad General de Aguas de Barcelona SA v The Argentina Republic* (ICSID Case No ARB/03/18); *Suez Sociedad General de Aguas de Barcelona SA and Vivendi Universal SA v Argentine Republic* (ICSID Case No. ARB/03/19); *Azurix Corporation v The Argentine Republic* (ICSID Case No. ARB/03/30); *SAUR International v The Argentine Republic* (ICSID Case No. ARB/04/04); *Impregilo SpA v Argentine Republic* (ICSID Case No. ARB/07/17); *Urbaser SA and Consorcio de Aguas Bilbao Biskaia, Bilbao Biskaia Ur Partzuergoa v The Argentine Republic* (ICSID Case No ARB/07/26).

[9] *Aguas del Tunari SA v The Republic of Bolivia* (ICSID Case No ARB/02/3); *BiwaterGauff (Tanzania) Limited v United Republic of Tanzania* (ICSID Case No. ARB/05/22). The case of *Branimir Mensik v Slovak Republic* (ICSID Case No. ARB/06/90) concerned a mineral water spring project; the proceedings were discontinued in December 2008.

[10] See, for example, Chapter 16; M.H. Mourra, 'Privatization of Water Management in Latin America' in M.H. Mourra and T.M. Carbonneau (eds.), *Latin American Investment Treaty Arbitration – the Controversies and Conflicts* (The Netherlands: Kluwer, 2008), pp. 83–104; E. Brown Weiss et al., *Fresh Water and International Economic Law* (Oxford: Oxford University Press, 2005), especially Chapters 10–13.

respect of water services concessions which turn sour. Investment arbitration offers a number of advantages for private investors over the WTO as a forum for dispute settlement, including control over the initiation and conduct of cases, the possibility of damages awards and the existence of a set of normative obligations more clearly suited to application in the context of concession contracts.

### 1.3 *WTO Jurisprudence Has Continued to Evolve in the Direction of Greater Regulatory Deference*

To the extent that regulation of private operators in the water industry may nevertheless be subject to the application of GATS disciplines in the future, it is significant that over the last five or more years the WTO's Appellate Body has consistently taken a cautious, careful and relatively deferential approach to cases involving regulatory disputes. While it is unnecessary to chart this trend in its entirety here, two points are worth mentioning in the present context.

I noted in the article below that the impact of the WTO's non-discrimination norm varies considerably, depending on whether the notion of 'discrimination' is understood as discriminatory protectionism on the one hand or mere differential treatment on the other.[11] Interpreting the norm against discrimination to catch only discriminatory protectionism tends to leave a good deal of room for regulatory autonomy, while equating discrimination with mere differential treatment tends to significantly reduce regulatory freedom. The first point to note, then, is that the former interpretation has gained ground in recent years. In *EC – Asbestos*, the Appellate Body famously made this remark in the context of interpreting the term 'less favourable treatment' in GATT Article III:

> A Member may draw distinctions between products which have been found to be 'like', without, for this reason alone, according to the group of 'like' imported products 'less favourable treatment' that that accorded to the group of 'like' domestic products.[12]

I noted in the original article that this sentence at the very least suggested that the Appellate Body understood the norm of non-discrimination in GATT

[11] The classic article on this issue remains Lothar Ehring, 'De Facto Discrimination in World Trade Law: National Treatment and Most-Favoured-Nation Treatment – Or Equal Treatment?', *Journal of World Trade*, Vol. 36, No. 5 (2002), p. 92.

[12] WTO, *European Communities – Measuring Affecting Asbestos and Asbestos-Containing Products* (12 Mar. 2001), Doc. WT/DS135/AB/R, para. 100.

Article III to catch measures which were much closer to the 'protectionist' rather than 'mere differential treatment' end of the continuum. Since then, the Appellate Body has followed up this statement with a similar observation in *Dominican Republic – Cigarettes*:

> the existence of a detrimental effect on a given imported product resulting from a measure does not necessarily imply that this measure accords less favourable treatment to imports, if the detrimental effect is explained by factors or circumstances unrelated to the foreign origin of the product, such as the market share of the importer in this case.[13]

Similarly, in *EC – Biotech*, the Panel expressly referred to the above jurisprudence of the Appellate Body and rejecting the complainants' claims of discrimination primarily on the basis that the differential treatment in question had not been proven to be on the basis of the foreign origin of the products in question but rather on the basis of the EC's perceptions of their safety.[14] The result is that a reasonably persuasive body of evidence can be marshalled in support of the proposition that non-discrimination norms contained in the WTO agreements are likely to be interpreted so as to prohibit primarily or even exclusively those measures which discriminate against foreign products *based on their foreign origin*. This will be of significant comfort for those concerned about the maintenance of states' regulatory autonomy.

The second observation is that the last few years have seen a generally expansive interpretation of the general exceptions provisions in GATT Article XX and GATS Article XIV. As is well known, one of the key stages in the application of a number of the most important paragraphs of those articles is the 'necessity' test. The necessity test itself involves two stages: first, the weighing and balancing of factors including the importance of the values or interests at stake, the extent of the contribution to the achievement of the measure's objective and the measure's trade restrictiveness and, second, a comparison of the measure with possible alternatives, which may be less trade restrictive.[15] The decision of the Appellate Body in *Brazil – Tyres* apparently relaxed this test in a number of ways. For one thing, it made clear that when

[13] WTO, *Dominican Republic – measures affecting the importation and internal sale of cigarettes* (19 May 2005), Doc. WT/DS302/AB/R, para. 96.

[14] WTO, *European communities – measures affecting the approval and marketing of biotech products* (21 Nov. 2006), Doc. WT/DS291-3/R, paras. 7.2499–2517 (in relation to Article III:4), and paras. 7.2398–2419 (in relation to the non-discrimination norm contained in Annex C(1)(a) of the SPS Agreement); see also (in a different legal context), *EC – Trademarks/GIs* WT/DS174/R (20 Apr. 2005).

[15] See, e.g., *Brazil – Measures Affecting Imports of Retreaded Tyres* (17 Dec. 2007), Doc. WT/DS332/AB/R, para. 178.

considering the contribution of the measure at hand to the achievement of the respondent state's objectives, even a plausible claim back by relatively little evidence will sometimes suffice: there is no need to provide quantitative evidence, and evidence will often be difficult to obtain where the contribution is over the longer term and the measure is part of a larger package of measures, each of which makes some contribution.[16] In addition, the AB noted that measures which might appear to be less trade restrictive alternatives should not be considered such when they are in fact *complementary* measures which can in principle be implemented in tandem with the measures at issue.[17] Furthermore, although the public morals exception is unlikely to be of primary relevance in the water services context, it is probably also worth noting briefly that the Appellate Body has taken a relatively broad approach to the public morals exception in GATS Article XIV(a) in *US – Gambling*.[18] In that case, the United States argued that its restrictions on the cross-border provision of gambling services were 'necessary to protect public morals or to maintain public order'. Antigua questioned the plausibility of this argument, given the widespread consumption of gambling services throughout the United States. The Appellate Body disagreed with Antigua, affirming the Panel's view that Members ought to be given 'some scope to define and apply for themselves the concepts of 'public morals' . . .in their respective territories, according to their own systems and scales of values'.[19] The subsequent Panel decision in *China – Publications* closely followed this approach under GATT Article XX(a), signalling its intention not to scrutinise very closely the claim that a specific measure is designed to achieve objectives relating to public morals and choosing instead to focus on the question of whether that measure is the least trade restrictive means of doing so.[20]

Of course, it is also possible to draw out some points of concern from the same cases. The decision of the Appellate Body in *US – Gambling* to equate a 'total prohibition' of cross-border trade in services with a 'limitation on the number of service suppliers' under GATS Article XVI(2)(a) may open up the possibility that regulatory prohibitions may be newly vulnerable as market access restraints.[21]

16 Ibid., para. 151 and surrounding. 17 For example, ibid., para. 172.

18 WTO, *United States – Measures Affecting the Cross-Border Supply of Gambling and Betting Services* (20 Apr. 2005), Doc. WT/DS285/AB/R.

19 Ibid., para. 6.461.

20 WTO, *China – Measures Affecting Trading Rights and Distribution Services for Certain Publications and Audiovisual Entertainment Products* (19 Jan. 2010), Doc. WT/DS363/R, para. 7.759.

21 WTO, *US – Gambling*, paras. 223–239; see also J. Pauwelyn, 'Rien ne va plus? Distinguishing Domestic Regulation from Market Access in GATT and GATS', *World*

The possibility that the United States may have taken commitments on gambling services by mistake has also raised concerns for others about the vagueness of scheduling concerns and the Appellate Body's approach to their interpretation. In *Brazil – Tyres*, the lack of flexibility which the Appellate Body seemed to display in respect of the MERCOSUR issue may cause concern in light of the potential for similar structural issues (at the local rather than regional issues) in the water context.[22] Nevertheless, despite these general issues, it remains true in my view that the general trend in the 'regulatory jurisprudence' of the WTO is in the direction of greater deference and represents a far more cautious approach than that which prevailed in the late 1980s and 1990s.

### 1.4 *The Commercial and Policy Context Has to Some Extent Moved Away from Early Models of Private Sector Participation in the Water Sector, Which Were the Subject of the Original Controversies*

As noted above, the 1990s were a time of considerable optimism about the prospects of private sector participation in the water and sanitation services sector – both from the private side as a source of strong commercial returns and from the public side as a solution to decades of underinvestment in water infrastructure. But with the emergence of serious problems in a number of water concessions in the early part of this century, multinational commercial operators have become less bullish about the commercial opportunities in the sector and have adopted a much more cautious approach to new investments. The number of new public-private partnerships awarded decreased from almost 30 at its peak in 1999 to just above 10 in 2002. A brief resurgence of activity from 2004 to 2006 was concentrated solely in four countries, and since then levels of new activity have fallen.[23] The global population served by major private operators actually decreased in 2006, though has since recovered somewhat.[24] This was in part due to the complete disengagement by Suez from its projects in Latin America, after having been a dominant presence in that market for some time.

This new attitude of reticence and caution on the part of commercial operators has been reflected at the level of policy. We are currently in a period during which policy-makers are attempting to learn the appropriate lessons from the difficulties that have been experienced so far. There is now, for

*Trade Review*, Vol. 4, No. 2 (2005), pp. 131–70; R. Bates, 'The Trade In Water Services: How Does GATS Apply To The Water And Sanitation Services Sector?', *Sydney Law Review*, Vol. 31 (2009), pp. 121–142.

22 See Part I.A of the original article below.

23 Marin, *Public-Private Partnerships For Urban Water Utilities*, p. 24, figure 2.2.

24 Ibid., p. 35, figure 2.5.

example, significantly less emphasis on the private sector as a source of finance for water and sanitation projects. Instead, public financing – prominently including multilateral and bilateral development assistance – is seen as an essential element of the development of water infrastructure in the developing world, with private sector participation now seen as valuable primarily as a source of management expertise and operational efficiency.[25] Another change has been the growth of local private operators in the water sector. While during the 1990s, the vast bulk of private concessions were granted to foreign operators, some '90% of the growth in the number of people served by PPP projects since 2001 is due to private operators from developing countries'.[26] There is a sense that local operators may avoid some of the political difficulties which have beset concessions run by large foreign corporations. In any case, both of these changes are directly relevant in the present context, to the extent that the contemporary trend away from major new foreign private investment in the water sector may somewhat reduce the relevance of international economic law generally to the sector over the medium term.

The combined result of these four trends has been to reduce the level of public concern over the potential impact of the GATS on the water sector. This is probably entirely appropriate – the energies of NGOs and others with a special interest in the WTO are better directed elsewhere for the moment; and it is right to take some time to work out the appropriate lessons to be learnt from first period of major experimentation with water privatisation. Nevertheless, it would be surprising if the issue had permanently disappeared. The problems of lack of access to water in the developing world are only more urgent now than they were two decades ago. Private sector participation remains a key vector in most thinking about water sector policy, and to a great extent the unresolved questions, problems and potentials of privatisation continue to dominate the policy horizon in this area. The underlying constellation of commercial and political interests have not been fundamentally re-aligned, and management of water infrastructures remains a tremendously sensitive political issue. It is probably reasonable to expect, then, that debates over these issues will periodically erupt in and around various sites of international economic governance over the coming decade and beyond.

[25] Ibid., p. 8.

[26] Ibid., p. 9. For a sceptical view of the significance of local private operators in the water sector, see E. Lobina and D. Hall, 'The Private Sector in Water in 2009', PSI-PSIRU Research Paper, March 2009 www.acquabenecomune.org/IMG/pdf/The_private_sector_in_water_in_2009_-David_Hall_-Emanuele_Lobina-Greenwich_University.pdf.

### 1.5 *Introduction*

In June 2002, the UN High Commissioner for Human Rights released a report entitled 'Liberalization of trade in services and human rights', the third in its series of reports on interactions between the international trade regime and international human rights.[27] In this report, the High Commissioner noted that effective delivery of basic services such as water, health and education was a key factor in the protection of basic human rights. The impetus for the report came partly from the observation of an increasing trend towards the liberalisation of these service sectors and a concern that the human rights implications of this trend were as yet poorly understood.

The report identified, at a general level, a series of problems with the way in which liberalisation had so far been implemented.[28] One of these problems concerned the potential impact of international trade law on the degree of regulatory freedom enjoyed by states in respect of the water industry. The success or failure of water sector liberalisation, it argued, depends heavily on how effectively the state performs its function of monitoring, overseeing and directing private water operators through well-designed regulatory regimes:

> [i]n human rights terms, the need to regulate . . . is in fact a duty to regulate; the obligation on States to ' fulfil' human rights requires States to take appropriate legislative, administrative, budgetary, judicial and other measures towards the full realisation of such rights.[29]

There is a danger, it goes on, that international trade rules such as the General Agreement on Trade in Services (GATS) constrain the kinds of regulatory environment that governments can put in place and in this way undermines their ability to fulfil their international human rights obligations.

> Many government regulations are measures that can come within the scope of the GATS. While GATS acknowledges governments' right to regulate in its preamble, the question remains as to the extent to which GATS can affect

27 Economic and Social Council, *Liberalization of Trade in Services and Human Rights: Report of the High Commissioner* (Fifty-fourth session, 2002), U.N. Doc. E/CN.4/Sub.2/2002/9.

28 The High Commissioner refrained from commenting on the implication of liberalisation *per se* on human rights, noting that the key question from a human rights perspective is 'how to determine the right form and pace of liberalization to ensure the protection of human rights and how to reverse policies that are unsuccessful', ibid., para. 50.

29 Ibid., para. 50. In principle, the High Commissioner is referring here to all essential services traditionally supplied by governments. However, throughout the report, the High Commissioner consistently refers to water services, and it is that aspect that I have chosen to consider in this paper.

government regulations that might have an impact on trade – including government regulations relevant to the promotion and protection of human rights.[30]

While the report need not, and does not, attempt to set out exhaustively how such regulation 'might have an impact on trade', there is a clear concern that some useful forms of regulation may be viewed as discriminatory, or as unduly burdensome, or as effective barriers to market access for foreign service providers.[31] For example, the High Commissioner noted that subsidies have in the past been used to promote greater equality in service delivery but that the principle of non-discrimination may in some circumstances make subsidy regimes more difficult to sustain.[32] More generally:

> a measure calculated to promote the enjoyment of human rights - for example health or water safety standards - might have to consider its trade-restrictiveness as one of its decisive elements. The question arises whether this has the effect of subordinating human rights obligations to trade rules.[33]

These sentiments echo concerns which have been voiced by numerous non-governmental organisations concerned with human rights and development,[34] as well as an increasing body of scholarly research.[35]

The issue has drawn some attention from the Secretariat of the World Trade Organization. In a series of pamphlets,[36] press statements[37] as well as

[30] Ibid., p. 4 of the Executive Summary. [31] Ibid., para. 56. [32] Ibid., para. 60.

[33] Ibid., para. 58.

[34] There is now a large array of material of varying quality on the issue, published by NGOs, both in print and on the internet. See, for example, material from the Center for International Environmental Law (www.ciel.org), Canadian Centre for Policy Alternatives (www.policyalternatives.ca), Citizens' Network on Essential Services (www.servicesforall.org), Public Services International (www.psiru.org), The Center for Public Integrity (www.icij.org/water/), Public Citizen (www.publiccitizen.org), the World Development Movement (www.wdm.org) and The Pacific Institute (www.pacinst.org), among many others.

[35] See, for example, M. Krajewski, *National Regulation and Trade Liberalization in Services* (The Hague, London and New York: Kluwer Law International, 2003); E. Türk and M. Krajewski, 'The Right to Water and Trade in Services: Assessing the Impact of GATS Negotiations on Water Regulation', paper presented at CAT+E Conference, 'Moving Forward from Cancún', Berlin, 30–31 October 2003, copy on file with author.

[36] See WTO, ' GATS – Fact and Fiction', WTO Secretariat, www.wto.org/english/tratop_e/serv_e/gats_factfiction_e.htm; see also WTO, *Services: GATS*, Training Package, 15 December 1998, p. 58.

[37] D. Hartridge, ' WTO Secretariat Hits False Attacks against GATS', Speech delivered at the European Services Forum, Brussels, 27 November 2000; WTO, 'Director-General of WTO and Chairman of WTO Services Negotiations Reject Misguided Claims that Public Services Are under Threat', WTO Press Release of 28 June 2002, PRESS/299 www.wto.org/english/news_e/pres02_e/pr299_e.htm.

publicised personal communications,[38] the Secretariat has sought to discredit what it claims are fundamentally misguided concerns. It has pointed to the 'bottom-up' nature of the most important disciplines in the GATS, as well as the ability of WTO Members to impose limitations and qualifications on their commitments, as evidence of the regulatory flexibility which the GATS provides. Furthermore, it has argued, even unqualified GATS commitments in the water distribution sector 'would not affect the right of Governments to set levels of quality, safety, price or any other policy objectives as they see fit, and the same regulations would apply to foreign suppliers as to nationals'.[39] The Trade Committee of the OECD has also released a report on the issue, which aims to address the 'misconceptions' upon which the claims of GATS critics are based.[40] Like the WTO report, the OECD paper emphasises the wide variety of exceptions and safeguards contained within the GATS, not only as regards specific commitments and qualifications but also relating to the general exceptions contained in Article XIV. It also notes what it sees as a 'common mistake' in GATS critiques, to assimilate 'regulations to trade restrictions', and 'liberalisation [to] the process of regulatory reform'.[41] The trade regime, it argues, is not concerned with deregulation nor with the substance of regulatory standards – rather, it is concerned with altogether distinct matter of the transparency and efficiency of regulatory regimes.[42] Finally, the report appeals to a combination of common sense and rationality to make its point: '[i]t would be illogical for governments to negotiate away and surrender such an important governmental function [as regulation]'.[43]

To be fair, some of these points are counter-arguments to claims which none of the more sophisticated critics ever made. All understand that the GATS represents a complex and multi-faceted compromise between these twin goals of trade liberalisation and regulatory autonomy. The contours of this compromise are defined by a variety of rules and understandings (from the preambular 'right to regulate', to Article VI disciplines on domestic regulation, to the rules establishing the broad scope of the agreement, to rules concerning

38 D. Hartridge, ' GATS and Public Services' [letter by email to M. Waghorne, Public Services International] (31 May 2000), reference: 65-let 31 May 2000, cited in International Branch, Ministry of Employment and Investment Government of British Columbia, 'GATS and Public Service Systems: the GATS 'governmental authority' exclusion', Discussion Paper, 2 April 2001, http://members.iinet.net.au/~jenks/GATS_BC2001.html n. 35.

39 WTO, ' GATS – Fact and Fiction'.

40 OECD Working Party of the Trade Committee, *Open Service Markets Matter: Part 1 Stating the Case for Services Trade Liberalisation* (8 June 2001), Doc. TD/TC/WP(2001)24/Part1 www.uscsi.org/publications/GATS/7OpenSrvsMrktsMtt3.pdf.

41 Ibid., p. 6. 42 Ibid. 43 Ibid., p. 39.

the definition of *de facto* discrimination, to Article XIV general exceptions, to the Article I:3 carveout for public services and so on), as well as the informal understandings, practices and tacit agreements which make such rules workable. The debate is, of course, over the adequacy – in both practical and legal terms – of the protection provided by the exceptions, flexibilities and safeguards. Where proponents of the GATS view such safeguards as tolerably clear, and express confidence in the ability of the trade regime to interpret and apply its rules within the bounds of reasonableness, GATS critics tend to see them as inadequate and indeterminate and are suspicious of the tendency of ambiguity to be resolved in the interests of the powerful.

The debate about the GATS and regulation of the water sector is one instance of a now very large debate about the impact of the trade regime on domestic regulatory autonomy more generally. The standard explanation of this issue is easily set out. Regulations of all kinds, including food safety standards, consumer protection laws, competition law and so on, can be drafted and applied in ways which undermine international trade commitments. The trade regime would therefore seem to have a legitimate interest in disciplining the use of such regulation. At the same time, there is an equally clear interest in ensuring that governments have sufficient space to pursue such legitimate public policy objectives in the way that they see fit. Regulatory disciplines must therefore be crafted very carefully to ensure that they do not inadvertently catch regulation which affects international trade flows only as an incidental, accidental or necessary by-product of the pursuit of a legitimate policy. There is by now a small army of trade scholars and others working on this problem, devising legal tools to help strike the appropriate balance and reconciling such tools with the less than perfectly satisfactory wording of relevant GATT and GATS provisions.[44]

[44] The following represents an almost random selection of the voluminous literature: G. Verhoosel, *National Treatment and WTO Dispute Resolution* (Portland, Oregon: Oxford, 2002); T. Cottier and P. Mavroidis (eds.), *Regulatory Barriers and the Principle of Non-Discrimination in World Trade Law* (Michigan: University of Michigan Press, 2000); Krajewski, *National Regulation and Trade Liberalization in Services*; S. Cho, *Free Markets and Social Regulation: A Reform Agenda of the Global Trading System* (London, The Hague, New York: Kluwer Law International, 2003); F. Ortino, *Basic Legal Instruments for the Liberalisation of Trade: A Comparative Analysis of EC and WTO Law* (Oxford, Protland: Hart, 2004); R. Hudec, 'GATT/WTO Constraints on National Regulations: Requiem for an "Aims and Effect" Test' *The International Lawyer*, Vol. 32 (1998), p. 619; R. Howse and E. Türk, 'The WTO Impact on Internal Regulations – A Case Study of the Canada-EC Asbestos Dispute' in J. Scott and G. de Burca (eds.), *The EU and the WTO: Legal and Constitutional Issues* (Portland Oregon: Oxford, 2001), pp. 283–328; P. Eeckhout, 'Constitutional Concepts for Free Trade in Services' in Scott and de Burca (eds.), The EU and the WTO: Legal and Constitutional Issues; D.H. Regan 'Regulatory Purpose and 'Like Products' in Article III:4 of

This article concentrates on the debate about water sector regulation, as a way into, and a concrete instantiation of, the broader debate about regulatory autonomy. It deliberately approaches this debate on its own terms, as an argument about the degree of flexibility provided by GATS rules in relation to social regulation. It firstly sets out some examples of the ways in which water sector regulation could conceivably be challenged under the GATS as discriminatory. By subjecting them to detailed legal analysis, it aims to give some indication of the likelihood of success of such claims – or better, given the virtual impossibility of such a task, it gives at least a series of arguments which may be deployed to help the issue receive greater attention. More importantly, it isolates some of the key textual battlegrounds on which this debate will be enacted within trade disputes and identifies a series of argumentative strategies which may be used by those with an interest in preserving the regulatory autonomy of governments.

There are at least two limitations to the scope of this study, which should be noted at the outset. The first is that the paper does not deal with all GATS disciplines but only the two non-discrimination obligations in Articles II and XVII. It does not, for example, deal with rules on market access, nor does it speculate on the rules which may be generated by current negotiations in the areas of 'domestic regulation',[45] subsidies or safeguards, though once formulated these rules will certainly be important. Comprehensiveness is impossible in a study of this kind, and the choice to concentrate on non-discrimination obligations seems a natural one given that it has formed the focus of scholarly attention in the debate on regulatory autonomy in respect of the GATT. Nevertheless, this paper should therefore be seen as one slice of a much larger pie.

The second, and probably more important, limitation concerns the nature of the study. It was stated earlier that this article approaches the debate on its own terms. As a result, the focus of this piece is on the direct legal effects of the GATS on water sector regulation – that is to say, what the GATS does or does not legally oblige or require. But there are many other ways in which the

the GATT (With Additional Remarks on Article II:2)', *Journal of World Trade*, Vol. 36, No. 3 (2002), p. 443; J.P. Trachtman, 'Lessons for GATS Article VI from the SPS, TBT and GATT Treatment of Domestic Regulation', *Social Science Research Network*, 29 Jan. 2002, http://ssrn.com/abstract=298760; and J.P. Trachtman, 'The Domain of WTO Dispute Resolution', *Harvard International Law Journal*, Vol. 40 (1999), p. 333.

45 The term domestic regulation is used here in the particular sense given to it by GATS Article VI. It should not be taken to imply that, in the absence of rules negotiated in accordance with that section, GATS obligations do not apply to domestic regulation in any generic sense.

GATS may influence domestic regulation, many of which will be at least as important as the legal obligations it imposes, even if they are not as obvious. For example, GATS negotiations may have the effect of mobilising particular actors (such as corporate lobby groups), and thereby facilitating co-operative political action, and increasing the influence of such players at the domestic level. Or the increasing importance of the trade regime (including the proliferation of rules on services) may operate to concentrate governmental energy and resources on trade-related issues to the detriment of other issues and portfolios. Or the vocabulary and conceptual framework of trade law may operate implicitly to make certain kinds of regulations more or less 'thinkable', or legitimate. Many different kinds of effects can be imagined. By concentrating on technical questions of legal interpretation, this paper runs the risk of missing these alternative modes of influence. More importantly, it runs the risk of being complicit in a process by which such modes of influence are obscured, or portrayed as irrelevant or impossible to quantify, and thus made less contestable. Nevertheless, provided its limitations are understood and expressed, there is an important place for a technical legal analysis of this kind. By allowing human rights advocates (and other critics concerned with the social impact of the trade regime) to express their concerns in a language which the trade regime understands, it can in fact open up *new* forums for contestation and offers alternative strategies for resistance. It can enable the mobilisation of resources within trade texts and the trade regime more generally, which support alternative perspectives, and give a voice to those who might otherwise be unheard.

## 2 WATER INDUSTRY REGULATION AND THE POTENTIAL FOR DISCRIMINATION

The aims of this section are threefold. First, as a way of grounding the following discussion in concrete examples, it gives a short overview of relevant forms of regulation. Taking the arguments of international human rights institutions on their own terms, it concentrates solely on regulation which can be said to relate to the quality, availability, affordability and accessibility of drinking water.[46] (The term 'social regulation' is used loosely to describe these kinds of regulation taken together.) Second, it addresses the – surprisingly common – claim that such regulations are inherently unlikely to be the

[46] This terminology is taken from para. 12 of General Comment No. 15 of the Committee on Economic, Social and Cultural Rights on the Right to Water www.unhchr.ch/tbs/doc.nsf/0/a5458d1d1bbd713fc1256cc400389e94?OpenDocument&Highlight=0,CESCR.

subject of a trade dispute. And third, it sets out a series of examples of regulatory treatment which could, at least at first blush, be argued to be discriminatory and contrary to GATS rules on non-discrimination.

### 2.1 *Relevant Regulatory Measures*

Regulation of the quality, affordability and accessibility of water services can take a variety of forms. Quality control regulation is relatively straightforward. Minimum standards are typically set in relation to the microbiological, chemical, radiological and physical properties of drinking water and are accompanied by ancillary obligations concerning monitoring and testing.[47] Service quality is also regulated. Network operators will, for example, be subject to obligations concerning the output pressure and flow rate of the network, continuity of service, targets relating to the minimisation of 'unaccounted-for water' as well as customer service obligations.

The prices of water distribution services are also typically strictly controlled. There are broadly three types of price regulation.[48] The first is rate-of-return regulation, according to which an appropriate maximum level of return, on capital investments made by the private operator, is fixed. The second is cost-of-service regulation, which is where the operator is responsible for large capital investments. In this case, a maximum allowable profit margin is set on the legitimate costs, which the private operator incurs in the provision of the service. The third kind of price regulation is simply a price cap, usually defined according to an assessment of the potential for efficiency improvements by the regulated utility. In all cases, there will usually be detailed rules setting out the mechanisms by which tariffs can be altered to reflect ongoing or one-off fluctuations in an operator's costs.

It has in the past been common for the price of water to be kept artificially low through price regulation of this kind. A complementary approach to the problem of affordability is through the use of subsidies. Implicit and explicit subsidies have for a long time been a core feature of water industry regulation:

> The traditional response of governments around the world has been to retain water companies under public ownership, and to keep tariffs artificially low

47 See, for an interesting example, Australian Government NHMRC, 'National Water Quality Management Guidelines: Australian Drinking Water Guidelines' (1996) www.nhmrc.gov.au/_files_nhmrc/file/publications/synopses/eh20.pdf.

48 For an overview of these different kinds of regulation, see the World Bank, *Toolkit 1: Selecting and Option for Private Sector Participation* (Washington DC: World Bank, 1997), appendix 1.

> through a range of more or less explicit subsidy measures. These have tended to include operational and investment subsidies aimed at bolstering the typically precarious financial position of publicly owned water utilities, as well as the progressive accretion of complex and frequently contradictory cross-subsidy mechanisms aimed at redistributing income between different social groups.[49]

Such operational and investment subsidies typically take the form of soft budget constraints, government equity investments or cash injections. Cross-subsidy mechanisms can take a variety of different forms, including uniform pricing schemes, fixed charges based on property value as well as specific concessions to certain customer classes, funded from the water authority's revenue. More recently, traditional cross-subsidies of this sort have been criticised for being poorly targeted and economically inefficient, and something of a sea-change has occurred in thinking about appropriate pricing policies.[50]

Most new regulatory models prefer tariffs which reflect the full costs of service delivery and the phasing out of both operational subsidies and cross-subsidisation measures. This can lead to very large cost increases, particular in rural areas where the costs of service are high. In order to cushion the impact of this 'rate rebalancing', the process is often accompanied by the establishment of a regime of direct subsidy payments to consumers, financed from general government funds. Direct subsidy systems of this kind are commonly praised as transparent and minimally distorting. But this model is neither universally in use nor easily applicable everywhere. In South Africa, the government has experimented with a policy of a free subsistence level of water for the entire population.[51] Argentina, to take another example, has chosen to fund some aspects of direct subsidies not from general funds but through the imposition of a special levy on all other consumers.[52]

[49] Foster et al., 'Designing Direct Subsidies for Water and Sanitation Services: Panama – A Case Study' (30 May 2000), World Bank Policy Research Working Paper WP2344 http://econ.worldbank.org/docs/1098.pdf, p. 1.

[50] P. Serra, 'Subsidies in Chilean public utilities' (30 Sep. 2000), World Bank Policy Research Working Paper WP 2445 http://elibrary.worldbank.org/content/workingpaper/10.1596/1813–9450-2445, at p. 11.

[51] See D. Hall et al., 'Water Privatization in Africa', Research Paper, Public Services International Research Unit, University of Greenwich, June 2002 www.psiru.org/reports/2002-06-W-Africa.doc.

[52] This is Argentina's Universal Service and Environmental Improvement (SUMA) fee, introduced in order to fund much needed extensions of the network to the barrios of Buenos Aires. See the account of this tax in D. Hall, 'The Water Multinationals 2002: Financial and Other Problems' (August 2002) www.psiru.org/reports/2002-08-W-MNCs.doc.

Subsidies may also be given by governments to private operators investing in water infrastructure, to ensure that consumers are not required to pay the entire cost of investment.[53] Such subsidies include preferential tax treatment, government grants, equity or subordinated debt contributions for which governments do not expect commercial returns, government guarantees, informal agreements or asset discounting.[54]

The accessibility of drinking water is affected, for example, by regulation concerning the coverage of a distribution network. A concession contract will often contain minimum investment obligations, relating to the proportion of the population covered, the number of network connections, the types of connections that are to be made as well as the geographic coverage of the network.[55] But accessibility is also affected by regulation concerning the procedure according to which non-paying consumers can be disconnected. This is often a key area for many private operators, and a variety of solutions exist. They range from a complete prohibition on the disconnection of any customer, to the establishment of minimum grace periods, to the use of 'trickle-flow' meters, among other methods.

### 2.2 *Consensus or Contestation?*

It is necessary at this point saying something about the claim that the kinds of regulation just described are inherently unlikely to give rise to trade disputes. Recall the comment noted earlier in the report of the OECD that it 'would be illogical for governments to negotiate away and surrender such an important governmental function [as regulation]'.[56] The WTO Secretariat, for its part, has pointed out that it 'is of course inconceivable that any Government would agree to surrender the right to regulate water supplies, and WTO Members have not done so'.[57] The claim here is social regulation of the water sector is so clearly and universally accepted to be necessary and desirable, that a dispute which calls into question the ability of governments to pursue such objectives is frankly unimaginable. Were such a dispute to be brought, it is equally unimaginable that GATS rules would be interpreted and applied so as to limit such a function to any extent.

53 See generally M. Dailami and M. Klein, 'Government Support to Private Infrastructure Projects in Emerging Markets' (31 Jan. 1998), World Bank Policy Research Working Paper WPS1868 http://papers.ssrn.com/sol3/papers.cfm?abstract_id=614977.

54 Ibid.

55 For a quick overview of the types of targets contained in the Manila water concessions, see www.adb.org/Documents/Events/2003/3WWF/Cities_Santos.pdf.

56 OECD Working Party of the Trade Committee, p. 24.

57 See WTO, 'GATS – Fact and Fiction'.

One might be forgiven for thinking such suggestions naïve. It is not just that a decade of experience with water privatisation has demonstrated that disputes about the shape and content of water regulation are common and often heated. It is also more generally that the difficulties of balancing trade liberalisation with regulatory autonomy, far from being irrelevant in the water sector, are *particularly* acute in that context. The sector has been historically associated with a high degree of political patronage, and probably more than its fair share of corruption and political interference.[58] Such cultures are difficult to eradicate, and in a context in which regulatory decisions are often highly discretionary, regulatory systems still partially experimental and privatisation often subject to a great deal of political resistance, the risk of such regulation being used for 'political' ends remains one of the key concerns of investors looking to enter a foreign market. In this context, the need for the GATS to contribute to the creation of a transparent, predictable and non-discriminatory regulatory environment is particularly strong. But, as has been pointed out, it is at the same time equally important to ensure that governments have sufficient room to pursue obviously important social objectives. A more realistic view of the political dynamic of water sector regulation would therefore not see it as characterised by a kind of universal consensus but rather by radical contestation and division.

Once it is realised that regulation of the water sector is rather more about contestation than consensus, it becomes apparent that assertions of consensus actually serve to contain or exclude oppositional voices. That is to say, such claims have the effect of foreclosing discussion of the kinds of objectives which should and should not be pursued in a particular regulatory system and how best they should be balanced against one another. To the extent that the objectives of water regulation are said to be subject to a near-universal consensus, such political questions are obscured, and the voices of actors wishing to challenge prevailing perspectives are silenced. GATS critics, then, should not be consoled by claims concerning the inconceivability of GATS disputes over water regulation. From one perspective, such claims instantiate the very point that critics are trying to make, that the trade regime implicitly helps to shore up and legitimate the influence that certain actors have over water sector regulation, while at the same time silencing others.

[58] See T.W. Wälde, 'Treaties and regulatory risk in infrastructure investment: the effectiveness of international law disciplines versus sanctions by global markets in reducing the political and regulatory risk for private infrastructure investment', *Journal of World Trade* Vol. 34, No. 2 (2000), pp. 1–62.

### 2.3 Examples of Discriminatory Regulation

If the first claim of GATS critics is that water sector regulation is fundamentally contested, the second claim is that the GATS affects the outcomes of such contestation by giving foreign water operators[59] new strategies to resist certain kinds of regulatory burdens, new languages in which to articulate them and a new forum in which to make them. GATS Articles II and XVII, for example, enable operators to argue in an international forum that certain forms of regulation are discriminatory. In broad outline[60]: Article II gives foreign service suppliers the right to demand from governments the same treatment as that afforded to other foreign service suppliers in the same country, while Article XVII gives them the right to demand the same treatment as that afforded to domestic service suppliers.

When might claims of discrimination conceivably be advanced? In the examples which follow, the net has been cast relatively widely, and not all situations will be as equally likely as others. All, however, raise interesting questions, and all are based on real-life examples.

First, take the example of a country in which water quality standards are set by local or regional authorities. If an operator in one part of the country is made subject to stricter standards than an operator in another part, requiring perhaps a significant capital investment in order to comply, and if there is no clear public health reason for the discrepancy, can it be argued that such different standards constitute discrimination? Second, assume that a local government politician is elected on an anti-privatisation platform. After she is elected, she imposes new and more burdensome regulatory obligations on the local private water operator while relaxing the obligations imposed on municipal operators within her jurisdiction. Third, take the case of a regulator with responsibility for hearing petitions for tariff increases from a variety of different operators. One operator feels it is consistently and systematically treated more harshly in such petitions than others, and there are allegations of corruption. Fourth, a national government introduces a policy of a free minimum quantity of drinking water to its entire population. Private operators which were operating before this policy was introduced are not obliged to

[59] I am speaking loosely here: it is of course only the governments of their home state which can bring actions.

[60] My purpose here is to simply sketch the effect of the non-discrimination norms in broad brushstrokes. A detailed legal account of their meaning is the subject of this paper. I should not be taken to be suggesting in this sentence that, for example, service suppliers are granted individual rights under the GATS.

implement it, as their tariffs were contractually agreed at an earlier time. However, other operators are so obliged. Alternatively, what if one operator refuses to implement the policy, and no action is taken against it?

Fifth, suppose that two foreign operators are granted concessions over two distinct halves of a municipal water district. Both operators are hit hard by a financial crisis which devalues the local currency, and both seek to renegotiate their contractual commitments. Would it be discriminatory if one were granted generous renegotiated terms while the other was not? Sixth, take the case of two companies working in different areas under the terms of two separate concession contracts. One operates in a poor region, and is thus granted preferential tax treatment and heavy subsidies, and subject to mild capital investment requirements, in order to keep the cost of water to consumers as low as possible. The other operator is granted no subsidies and is subject to burdensome requirements regarding network extension and the reduction of UFW.[61] Seventh, assume that in one country prior to privatisation, the pricing policies of public water operators operated so that richer consumers were subsidising water services for poorer consumers in other areas. After privatisation, the government tries to reintroduce such a policy by levying a charge on water operators in some areas and using the proceeds to provide subsidies to operators in other areas. Eighth, and relatedly, take the case of a government which operates a system of direct subsidies to consumers. Would it be discriminatory if these subsidies were poorly targeted, and thereby operated to the benefit of some operators rather than others, without objective justification in terms of a difference in the capacity to pay of their consumers?

It should be noted that were such claims successful, then one result could be what may be loosely described as a form of 'deregulation'. This is because, in many cases, the removal of an offending regulation may be the best or only practical means of removing the source of discriminatory treatment. If all operators were entitled to best-in-country treatment, for example, then absent regulatory co-operation, all jurisdictions would effectively have to follow the least burdensome standards imposed in any jurisdiction. Similarly, in a sector such as water distribution in which governments are often contractually locked in to a number of regulatory standards, non-discrimination can conceivably allow private operators to benefit from the least demanding level of regulatory obligations, or most generous regulatory concessions, applying to any service provider in the country. Moreover, if certain forms of subsidies

[61] Unaccounted-for water.

were considered discriminatory, then withdrawal of such subsidies may be the only practical option, where providing the subsidy on an objective basis to all operators is financially impossible. Reduction of regulatory standards can also be the result of a kind of 'regulatory chill', whereby regulators become cautious about imposing new or especially burdensome requirements in the absence of a high level of available evidence to objectively justify the measure. It may be that certain kinds of measures are inherently discriminatory, no matter how they are applied – certain forms of cross-subsidisation may fall into that category and may be susceptible to arguments that they are always inherently more discriminatory than, say, direct consumer subsidies.

## 3 ARTICLE I: 'ANY SERVICE IN ANY SECTOR', AND THE RELATED ISSUE OF SPECIFIC COMMITMENTS

The following sections examine some of the legal questions which might arise should the claims described above (or others) be made before a trade panel. These sections have at least two aims. The first is to assess in some way the likelihood of success of such claims. Given the current state of development of GATS jurisprudence, and the speculative nature of the subject matter, suggestions are clearly all that can be offered in this respect. The second is to identify potential counter-arguments which may be advanced against such claims, using textual resources in the GATS itself.

The starting point is Article I, which defines the scope of the agreement: '[t]his Agreement applies to measures by Members affecting trade in services'. For present purposes, it is assumed that all of the above regulations are 'measures' for the purposes of the GATS,[62] and in the current section, I examine the meaning of 'services'.

In principle, the GATS applies to the universe of different services. 'Services' are defined to include '*any* service in *any* sector except services supplied in the exercise of governmental authority'.[63] Putting to one side for the moment the governmental authority exception, there would appear to be

[62] There is a serious issue whether or not all measures contained in a concession contract (or other contract governing a concession-type arrangement) are 'measures' for the purposes of the GATS, as many seem to sit uneasily somewhere between public and private law obligations and have a mixed regulatory/commercial character. For reasons of space, I have excised a detailed examination of this issue.

[63] GATS Article I:3(b) (emphasis added). For completeness it should be noted that there are two presently irrelevant *a priori* exclusions relating to certain aspects of air transport services and financial services.

no reason to exclude any of the multitude of services supplied in the water sector. This position is complicated somewhat by the distinction drawn in the agreement between general obligations and specific commitments. One of the two articles under discussion here – Article XVII on national treatment – is a specific commitment, and it thus becomes necessary in principle to turn to country schedules to determine the level of specific commitments on national treatment in the water sector.

All country schedules are, by and large, set out in a common format, incorporating a standard system of classification containing all the different services to which the agreement applies (in principle, *all* conceivable services). This standard system of classification is contained in the Services Sectoral Classification List (SSCL), which was created by the WTO in order to provide a degree of certainty and commonality to specific commitments.[64] The SSCL was based on the then-current version of the United Nations Central Product Classification, now referred to as the Provisional CPC.[65]

The Provisional CPC was devised in 1989 at a time when liberalisation of the water industry was at an early stage. It has since been updated twice, and now refers in some detail to services supplied by the water industry, but at the time it did not clearly reflect the kinds of services supplied by private water operators.[66]

[64] The Services Sectoral Classification List is WTO document MTN.GNS/W/120 and can be found on the internet at the WTO's Services Gateway www.wto.org. For the status of Schedules as integral parts of the Agreement, see GATS Article XX:3; see also generally, F. Weiss, 'The General Agreement on Trade in Services 1994', *Common Market Law Review*, Vol. 32, No. 5 (1995), pp. 1177–1225, at 1208.

[65] The SSCL does not follow the Provisional CPC slavishly by any means. As a general rule, the SSCL categorises services at a higher level of generality than the UNCPC and on occasion (such as it telecommunications services) uses its own ad hoc classification system. What it does do, however, is cross-reference categories in the SSCL to their equivalents in the UNCPC.

[66] The Provisional CPC classified collection, purification and distribution services of water under sub-class 18000. However, this was not clear from the wording of sub-class 18000 itself, which referred only to 'Natural Water' with no explanation as to whether it applied to goods or services. It was only from the footnote to 94010, entitled 'sewages services', that it was apparent. The next version of the CPC was version 1.0, developed in 1997. Sub-class 18000 is retained in its original form, but a new entry is added in Section 6 – sub-class 69210 'Water, except steam and hot water, distribution through mains'. That sub-class included reading and maintenance of meters. Separate categories were created, however, for installation services of meters (sub-class 54611), operation services of irrigation systems for agricultural purposes (sub-class 86111) and water distribution services through mains on a fee or contract basis (sub-class 86223). The most recent version (version 1.1) of the CPC was developed in 2002 and has been refined yet further. Sub-class 69210 has been retained, but 'reading of meters' has been excised from it and has been added to sub-class 85990 'Other support services'. (Sub-class 86223 has also been retained but renumbered 86330.) Note also that this short summary only refers to those services which are exclusively related to water supply. Other services, including management services,

As a consequence, the SSCL also fails to identify those services clearly. Nowhere, for example, does it refer unambiguously to water distribution services through mains or to water purification and treatment services as a separate category. This problem has already been noted by at least one member of the WTO. A reclassification proposal has been made and is currently under discussion.[67]

The result is that there are currently no specific commitments by any country in relation to, for example, the core service of water distribution through mains. This fact has been used by some commentators to suggest that the most important obligations contained in the GATS do not, therefore, apply to the water sector at all. But while the flexibility offered through specific commitments is important, these arguments surely significantly overstate the extent of such flexibility and underestimate the present and potential future coverage of the GATS.

First, even if it were the case that no specific commitments had been made affecting the water industry, there would seem to be no obvious reason to think that such commitments will not be made in the future. The reclassification negotiations referred to above suggest that the sector is of interest to some WTO Members. As is the case in all sectors, liberalisation commitments in the water sector are likely to become progressively greater and greater from initially modest levels.

Second, the level of specific commitments is not relevant to the application of Article II (most-favoured-nation treatment), as it is a general obligation. There has been no suggestion that the absence of water treatment and distribution services from the SSCL implicitly demonstrates an intention that such services do not fall within the scope of the GATS. Such a suggestion, were it made, would be misguided. The SSCL was from the beginning no more than a convenient guideline for countries when drafting their Schedules.[68] It is perfectly possible for countries to add commitments in sectors which are not contained in the SSCL. The SSCL is not legally binding,[69] and

construction services, repair and maintenance services and so on, have always been included in the SSCL and have undergone a similar development in the intervening years.

67 See, in particular, WTO, *Communication from the EC (and their Member States) – Classification Issues in the Environmental Sector to the Committee on Specific Commitments* (28 Sep. 1999) Doc. S/CSC/W/25.

68 See A.K. Abu-Akeel, 'The MFN as It Applies to Services Trade', *Journal of World Trade*, Vol. 33, No. 4 (1999), pp. 103–129, at 111.

69 See WTO documents S/C/W/46, para. 10; MTN.GNS/W/164, MTN.GNS/W/120, S/L/92, S/CSC/W/30, MTN.GNS/W/164/Add.1; and see also M. Footer, 'The General Agreement on Trade in Services: Taking Stock and Moving Forward', *Legal Issues of Economic Integration*, Vol. 29, No. 1 (2002), pp. 7–25, at 16.

while most have followed it, a few countries have departed from it in some respects.[70] The Committee on Special Commitments (a subordinate body to the Council on Trade in Services) has in fact been working on updating the SSCL to better reflect commercial realities, as well as to reflect improvements made to the UN CPC in the years since the GATS was created.[71] Furthermore, it is a consistent theme throughout commentaries on the GATS, as well as material emanating from the WTO itself and its members, that the scope of the GATS is universal in relation to the kinds of services covered.[72]

Third, it is in reality wrong to say that no specific commitments have been made in the water sector. In order to see why this is the case, it is necessary to analyse in more detail the kinds of services which are supplied in the water industry. Classifying the services supplied in the water industry is not a straightforward task, partly because the manner in which they are classified depends heavily on the contractual and institutional context in which they are supplied. Generally speaking, the core tasks in relation to the provision of drinking water are water treatment and purification, bulk water supply and water distribution.[73] A private operator engaged in the task of water treatment and purification, for example, under a 'design-build-operate' contract, may be supplying a range of different services depending on its contractual responsibilities. In the initial stages before the treatment plant is operational, it may supply design services, architectural services, engineering services, project management services and construction services to the relevant governmental authority. For a so-called turnkey project, the services supplied are probably best characterised as integrated engineering services. Once the treatment plant is operational, the private operator can be tasked with the day-to-day running of the plant. These tasks may be classified as operation and maintenance services, management services, bulk water supply services or simply water treatment and purification services. These in turn may involve a range of ancillary services, from water testing and analysis services, to repair and maintenance services, to security services and so on.

[70] See L Altinger and A Enders, 'The Scope and Depth of GATS Commitments', *The World Economy*, Vol. 19, No. 3 (1996) pp. 307–332, at 313; and Krajewski, *National Regulation and Trade Liberalization in Services*, p. 101, nn. 92–93.

[71] Footer, 'The General Agreement on Trade in Services', n. 34.

[72] See, for example, Weiss, 'The General Agreement on Trade in Services 1994', p. 1182; Sauvé, 'Assessing the General Agreement on Trade in Services: Half-Full or Half-Empty?', *Journal of World Trade*, Vol. 29, No. 4 (1995), pp. 125–145, at 133; Altinger and Enders, 'The Scope and Depth of GATS Commitments', p. 315.

[73] In relation to sewage treatment, the analogous tasks are the collection and treatment of wastewater.

A similar kind of breakdown can be made with respect to the task of water distribution. Take the example of private operators tasked with the everyday running of a water distribution network, under an arrangement such as a lease, concession or management contract. Again, the characterisation of the core services supplied will depend on the nature of the contract. They may be supplying management services or operation and maintenance services to the relevant governmental authority. They may be providing water distribution services directly to consumers. These core tasks can be broken into a variety of different ancillary services, ranging from meter reading and maintenance services, to meter installation services, billing and bill collection services, customer relations services, water testing and analysis services, among others.

The SSCL does not refer to water treatment or distribution services *per se*, nor does it collect all the different services provided by water operators in one convenient category. It does, however, refer to a number of the other services described above, which either overlap with water treatment and distribution services or are ancillary to them.[74] For example, it contains categories for sewage services, project management services, 'other' management services, integrated engineering services, design and construction services, repair and maintenance services as well as technical testing and analysis services. Between them, these categories cover at least a significant part of the activities of water companies and are the subject to significant levels of commitments in country schedules.[75] The ultimate result is roughly the same as for many sectors – a patchwork of substantial but still incomplete coverage, which is likely to increase with each round of negotiations.

## 4 ARTICLE I:3(B) AND (C), 'SERVICES SUPPLIED IN THE EXERCISE OF GOVERNMENTAL AUTHORITY'

Despite the near-universal scope of the GATS in respect of the services covered, there is one important exception which must be borne in mind. Recall from above that 'services' are defined to include 'any service in any sector *except services supplied in the exercise of governmental authority*'.[76] A service supplied in the exercise of governmental authority is defined in

74 To take an almost random set of examples, it has categories which refer specifically to CPC Prov classes: 865-66 (including project management and other management services), 8763 (on integrated engineering services), 8676 (on technical testing and analysis services) and 9401 (on sewage services).

75 Altinger and Enders, 'The Scope and Depth of GATS Commitments' for precise figures.

76 Article I:3(b), emphasis added.

Article I:3(c) to mean 'any service which is supplied neither on a commercial basis, nor in competition with one or more service suppliers'.[77]

The interpretation of the terms of this exception will be crucial to the degree of regulatory flexibility accorded governments in the water sector. Interpreted widely, it could exclude the water sector almost entirely from the scope of the agreement, thus preserving states' regulatory freedom intact. Interpreted narrowly, it could provide minimal protection. The text has not yet been at issue before a WTO panel, and there remains a great deal of uncertainty about its meaning within the WTO itself.[78] Nevertheless, the little that we do have suggests that strong claims, asserting that the exception provides a high degree of protection, are probably best approached with a certain level of scepticism.

Krajewski has recently looked in some detail at the interpretation of 'on a commercial basis' and 'in competition with'.[79] Applying the basic rules of interpretation set out in Articles 31–33 of the Vienna Convention, he conducts an analysis of the text and context of these phrases, including the Schedules and Annexes to the GATS, as well as its *travaux préparatoires*. He suggests that the phrase 'on a commercial basis' probably requires that a service is supplied with a view to making a profit, though perhaps any service which is bought and sold may qualify.[80] 'In competition with', he argues, probably refers to direct consumer competition and would to a large extent be determined by the degree of elasticity of substitution between two services.[81] He concludes that the governmental authority exception is a narrow one and that most services commonly understood as public services are not excluded from the scope of the GATS. Krajewski's general conclusion as to the exception's narrowness would seem to be supported by comments made by Members in

77 Article I:3(c).

78 See Working Party on GATS Rules, Report of the Meeting of 6 October 1998, Note by the Secretariat, S/WPGR/M/18, 13 November 1998, p. 4 (in the context of the clarity of the government procurement exception); see also Working Party on GATS Rules, Report of the Meeting of 19 February 1999, Note by the Secretariat, S/WPGR/M/20, 17 March 1999, p.7; Environmental Services, Background Note by the Secretariat, Council for Trade in Services, 6 July 1998, S/C/S/46, p. 14ff.

79 M. Krajewski, 'Public Services and Trade Liberalization: Mapping the Legal Framework', *Journal of International Economic Law*, Vol. 6, No. 2 (2003), pp. 341–367; see also Krajewski, *National Regulation and Trade Liberalization in Services*, p. 68ff.

80 Interestingly, the Article XVIII definition of ' commercial presence' (which phrase is used in Article I:2(c) to describe one of the four modes of service supply, when combined with the definition of 'juridical person' in the same article has the effect that commercial presence includes any type of business or professional establishment even those carried on through the maintenance of a not-for-profit body.

81 M. Krajewski, 'Public Services and Trade Liberalization', pp. 352–353.

the course of Committee discussions,[82] by internal research material produced by the WTO Secretariat,[83] as well as by some external public relations material from the same body.[84] While such documents are of limited legal value, they are of interest at least as indications of the approach to this provision currently prevailing within the WTO.

It is an instructive exercise to attempt to apply the governmental authority exception more specifically to services supplied in the water industry. For the purposes of analysis, such services can be divided into three types. The first type consists of services supplied by private water companies to network operators. It is common for a public water authority to purchase certain services from commercial providers as an input into its business. This may include services such as meter reading and installation services, billing services, repair and maintenance services, water testing and analysis services, management services, even vehicle rental and management services.[85] Such services must almost certainly be supplied 'on a commercial basis' for the purposes of Article I:3. They are services contracts like any other, subject to commercial rates of remuneration, and purchased in the context of a competitive market for such services. The mere fact that a public authority is the purchaser of such services cannot by itself signify that they are not supplied 'on a commercial basis'. It is also typical for private network operators to enter into upstream contracts for service inputs. It is yet harder to see how such service supplies could be supplied on anything but a commercial basis.

The second type consists in those services provided by private operators directly to consumers. This may occur, for example, in a full privatisation,

[82] See, for example, WTO documents S/C/M/30, p5 WT/REG39/1, WT/REG39/M/4, and European Communities, Joint Communication from the Parties, Committee on Regional Trade Agreements, WT/REG50/2/Add.3; WT/REG51/2/Add.3; WT/REG52/2/Add.3 19 May 1999, Item 3, para. 3.

[83] See, for example, Council for Trade in Services, *Background Note on Environmental Services* (6 Jul. 1998), Doc. S/C/W/46, p. 14ff.; Council for Trade in Services, *Background Note on Health and Social Services* (18 Sep. 1998), Doc. S/C.W/50, pp. 10–11, suggesting that perhaps only services provided free of charge fall outside the scope of the agreement; and Council for Trade in Services, *Background Note on Postal and Courier Services* (12 Jun. 1998), Doc. S/C/W/39, p. 2; Council for Trade in Services, *Background Note on Legal Services* (6 Jul. 1998), Doc. S/C/W/43, p. 4, No. 15.

[84] D. Hartridge, 'GATS and Public Services' [letter to M. Waghorne, Public Services International] (31 May 2000), circulated by email in June 2000.

[85] In India, Madras Metro Water has contracted services ranging from the provision of staff cars to the operation and maintenance of sewage pumping stations. The water utility in Santiago de Chile has contracted out services accounting for about half its operating budget, including computer services, engineering consulting services, and repair, maintenance, and rehabilitation of the network; see World Bank, *Toolkit 1*.

where public water utilities are sold to private operators.[86] It may also occur in the context of a concession-type arrangement, though it will depend on a careful analysis of the concession contract to determine whether the concessionaire is providing services directly to consumers, or to the public water authority, or both. It is true that comments made in the Working Party on GATS Rules indicate that at least two members of the WTO regard services supplied under concession-type arrangements to be supplied 'in the exercise of governmental authority'.[87] But it is not clear why this should be so. True, there is some superficial appeal to this interpretation, given that concessions are granted by government authority and that the private operator is in a sense often taking the place of a public authority.[88] But concessionaires are indisputably commercial operators. They are businesses like any other, and the services they supply are of course done so for profit. It is very difficult to see how their services could be supplied on anything but a commercial basis. This conclusion is supported by the probability that were a public water authority to supply services in the same manner as a private concessionaire, it would itself (as argued below) not benefit from the protection of the government authority exclusion.[89]

[86] Full divestiture of network infrastructure has taken place only in the United Kingdom.

[87] See WTO document S/WPGR/M/18, at 18: 'The representative of Argentina recalled his doubts about the interpretation of some delegations of what activities might fall under Article XIII of the GATS and the possibility that concessions would be covered under the Agreement. For instance, the case of a concession granted for operating a motorway, where the government was not buying something for itself, but rather granting the right to operate a public service to a private operator, was a clear case of a service provided in the exercise of governmental authority. It was necessary to continue studying how concessions would be considered within the GATS framework'; and S/WPGR/M/22 at 27 'The representative of Hong Kong, China, would prefer a working definition of government procurement which would minimize the exclusion of transactions from GATS disciplines; such a definition should include cases in which the government did not consume directly the service. Regarding the distinction between concessions and government procurement, he felt that the criterion of financial responsibility was appropriate; if the government did not pay, a transaction could not be considered government procurement per se. Thus, concessions in the form of licenses and franchises would not fall under any government procurement rules. According to the representative of Thailand, the discussion should focus on defining government procurement as referred to in Article XIII. In Thailand the legal situation was clear. Relevant laws distinguished between concessions and government procurement; concessions were services supplied in the exercise of governmental authority'.

[88] This view seems to be based on the fallacious assumption that services supplied by governments receive the benefit of the exemption. Therefore, anything that effectively stands in the place of the government, by government authority, should also receive it. This is simply not the case – only those government services supplied not on a commercial basis, nor in competition with one or more other service suppliers, receive the benefit of the exclusion.

[89] The Background Note to Environmental Services, above footnote 83, envisages an exceptional case, in which a concessionaire is paid by the government rather than consumers, but the

This leaves only services supplied to consumers by a public water authority, which represent the most difficult case. There would seem to be a strong argument that the issue of whether or not a public authority is supplying services 'on a commercial basis' must to some extent be related to the degree to which that authority has been 'commercialised'.[90] The process of commercialising or corporatising a public water authority is now a fairly common one, and it is possible to identify a number of its well-accepted features. The process, to take a typical definition,

> involves creating an institutional framework that separates non-commercial from commercial objectives (which are separately funded), establishes financial autonomy, provides clear management objectives, increases managerial authority, establishes mechanisms for holding managers accountable, and ensures competitive neutrality with respect to private operators.[91]

This definition suggests a number of factors which may fruitfully be used in the context of the water industry to determine whether or not particular services are supplied on a commercial basis. To be sure, the level of prices charged will be one. The closer these are to cost-recovery or profit-making levels, the more likely the service will be considered to be supplied on a commercial basis. But restructuring tariffs to ensure full cost recovery is thus only one part of establishing financial autonomy. Putting in place hard budget constraints, funding social programmes through independent financing and limiting (or at least formalising) governmental financial support are others. Furthermore, the degree of managerial autonomy enjoyed by a supplier is also relevant. The disengagement of political actors from management control and the removal of 'political' factors from management objectives can serve as other indicators of a commercialised supplier. Importantly, also, commercialisation is also commonly associated with sector-wide structural and regulatory reform. It is often part of a broader process of restructuring the relationship of the industry to the private sector and can be associated with increased private sector participation in the industry. The level and nature of commercial relationships between a public water authority and private operators would therefore probably also be an

service supply is considered to be to the consumers not to the government. Precisely how concession contracts will be treated under the GATS remains to be seen.

[90] In this regard, it may be worth noting the reference in GATT Article XVII to an enterprise acting in accordance with 'commercial considerations'. I would suggest that a service supplier acting in accordance with commercial considerations would in all probability be supplying services on a commercial basis. This must be so despite the fact that the phrase 'on a commercial basis' refers to the services supplied and not the service supplier itself.

[91] D. Haarmeyer and A. Mody, *Worldwide Water Privatization* (London: Pearson Education, 1997), p. 34.

indicator of commercialisation. There is therefore good reason to suspect that where a public water authority has undergone – to any significant degree – changes to its management structure, its fiscal structure and/or its relationship to the private sector of the sort described above, the services it supplies are probably more likely to fall within the scope of the GATS.[92]

One further comment is necessary regarding the scope of the protection provided by the governmental authority exception. There may be some circumstances in which measures affecting services supplied in the exercise of governmental authority may nevertheless still be indirectly subject to GATS obligations. This is where the same measure also affects services which are *not* supplied in the exercise of governmental authority. Where, for example, a water authority provides some but not all services on a commercial basis, many measures regulating that authority will necessarily affect both types of service. An alternative example might be where a public water authority provides services in partnership with a private operator. A single measure may, again, necessarily affect services provided by both operators. This may be of particular concern in relation to claims based on discriminatory treatment. Where a claim is made that a certain measure discriminates against some subset of a group of services or service suppliers, such a measure conceivably affects *all* services or service suppliers in the larger group. If this were the case, such a measure would be exempt from GATS disciplines only in the unlikely event that all services provided by all service suppliers were provided in the exercise of governmental authority.

## 5 ARTICLE XIII: THE GOVERNMENT PROCUREMENT EXCEPTION

In addition to the governmental authority exception, there is another qualified exception, which covers services procured by governments. GATS Article XIII:1 reads:

Articles II, XVI and XVII shall not apply to laws, regulations or requirements governing the procurement by governmental agencies of services purchased for governmental purposes and not with a view to commercial resale or with a view to use in the supply of services for commercial sale.

There may be some situations in which this exception could provide a means of arguing that certain regulatory measures in the water sector are exempt from GATS disciplines. But such situations are likely to be relatively

[92] I do not complete the analysis here and go on to determine when water operators may be 'in competition with' one another. This issue is considered in Section 7 below in the context of 'like services and service suppliers'.

rare. First, the exception applies only to 'laws, regulations or requirements', which is narrower than the term 'measures' used to define the scope of the agreement.[93] Second, it applies only to laws, regulations and requirements 'governing . . . procurement'. Arguably, this refers only to measures in respect of the procurement process itself, rather than *all* measures which affect services covered by the exception. It would not cover, for example, those measures contained in the services contract itself.

Third, it applies only where there is 'procurement' of services by governmental agencies. It does not apply where services are procured by private network operators nor where services are procured directly by consumers. There must be some doubt, therefore whether it applies to services supplied in accordance with a concession-type arrangements, at least where the concessionaire has a direct relationship with the individual service consumer. While the position is admittedly far from clear, this opinion has been expressed by a number of Members in the course of Committee discussions.[94] It also represents the position in the national law of many Member states, where concession agreements are often excluded from procurement policies and directives.[95] Fourth, the exception only covers services, which are procured 'not with a view to commercial resale or with a view to use in the supply of service for commercial sale'. The interpretation of this phrase, and in particular the second part, probably raises very similar issues as does the interpretation of 'on a commercial basis' considered above. If this is true, then the result is that where services supplied by a public authority receive the benefit of the Article I:3 exception, upstream services supplied to that authority may be protected by Article XIII. On the other hand, where a public water authority does *not* receive the benefit of the governmental authority exception, upstream services supplied to it on a contract basis are not covered by

[93] See, for example, Panel Report, *Japan – Measures Affecting Consumer Photographic Film and Paper ('Japan – Film')* (31 Mar. 1998), Doc. WT/DS44/R, paras. 10.45 and 10.376 (concerning GATT XXIII:1); Panel Report, *India – Measures Affecting the Automotive Sector ('India – Autos')* (21 Dec. 2001), Doc. W/DS146/R, as modified by the Appellate Body Report, W/DS146/AB/R, at para. 7.245ff (looking at the meaning of measures under GATT XI); GATT Panel Report, *Japan – Trade in Semi-conductors ('Japan – Semi-conductors')* (4 May 1988), Doc. 35S/116, para. 106; and Appellate Body Report, *Guatemala – Anti-dumping Investigation Regarding Portland Cement from Mexico ('Guatemala – Cement I')* (2 Nov. 1998), Doc. WT/DS60/AB/R, n. 47.

[94] There have been some unresolved discussions in the WTO on precisely how to treat concessions under the GATS.

[95] See the submission by Thailand, and with respect to the European Union Directive on Government Procurement, see Rillaerts, 'Concessions in the Water Sector', *Desalination*, Vol. 124 (1999), pp. 13–17.

Article XIII. This is particularly important if, as I argued above, the contracting out of upstream services may in some circumstances be an indication that downstream services are supplied on a commercial basis.[96]

## 6 ARTICLES II AND XVII: THE RELEVANCE OF A COMPETITIVE RELATIONSHIP

It is now time to turn to the substantive GATS non-discrimination provisions and attempt to apply them to the range of regulations under consideration. Article II:1 enshrines the most-favoured-nation obligation:

> With respect to any measure covered by this Agreement, each Member shall accord immediately and unconditionally to services and service suppliers of any other Member treatment no less favourable than that it accords to like services and service suppliers of any other country.[97]

Article XVII contains the national treatment obligation:

> 1. In the sectors inscribed in its Schedule, and subject to any conditions and qualifications set out therein, each Member shall accord to services and service suppliers of any other Member, in respect of all measures affecting the supply of services, treatment no less favourable than that it accords to its own like services and service suppliers.
> 2. A Member may meet the requirement of paragraph 1 by according to services and service suppliers of any other Member, either formally identical treatment or formally different treatment to that it accords to its own like services and service suppliers.
> 3. Formally identical or formally different treatment shall be considered to be less favourable if it modifies the conditions of competition in favour of services or service suppliers of the Member compared to like services or service suppliers of any other Member. [footnote in original omitted][98]

96 That is to say, where a public water authority subcontracts a good deal of its activities to commercial providers, this may be an indication that the public authority itself is providing commercial services.

97 There are two further paragraphs in Article II which are not relevant for this article: '2. A Member may maintain a measure inconsistent with paragraph 1 provided that such a measure is listed in, and meets the conditions of, the Annex on Article II Exemptions. . . . 3. The provisions of this Agreement shall not be so construed as to prevent any Member from conferring or according advantages to adjacent countries in order to facilitate exchanges limited to contiguous frontier zones of services that are both locally produced and consumed'.

98 There is a footnote to paragraph 1, which reads 'Specific commitments assumed under this Article shall not be construed to require any Member to compensate for any inherent

This section is concerned with only one very particular aspect of these provisions. Discrimination can only arise under these provisions, it appears, only if a competitive relationship exists between the services or service suppliers under consideration. The notion of competition arises at two points. First, services and service suppliers probably cannot be 'like' one another unless they are in competition with one another in some way.[99] Second, treatment is probably 'less favourable' only if it modifies the *conditions of competition* between the services or service suppliers under consideration.[100]

The need for competition would at first sight appear to be a formidable barrier to the application of the GATS non-discrimination provisions to the water industry. Water services to consumers are typically provided by regional monopolies. If the non-discrimination provisions require some form of competitive relationship, how can these provisions ever apply to water services? There is much that can be said about the concept of a competition and the precise role that it plays in a determination of discrimination in WTO law. For the purposes of this article, only two key points need to be made.

### 6.1 *There May Rarely Be a Competitive Relationship Between Foreign Private Operators and Traditional Public Water Authorities*

Some of the main concerns of critics of the GATS relate to the preferential treatment which has traditionally been granted to public water operators, in the form of government loans, cash injections, subsidies and so on. Such treatment, they argue, can be crucial to the continued operation of the water operator and is also an important method by which water prices can be kept low. Some commentators are concerned that, put simply, non-discrimination obligations may make such treatment impossible, by requiring that any preferential treatment is offered on an objective basis to all service providers, whether public or private.

competitive disadvantages which result from the foreign character of the relevant services or service suppliers'.

99 See, most relevantly, Appellate Body Report, *European Communities – Measures Affecting Asbestos and Asbestos-Containing Products ('EC – Asbestos')* (12 Mar. 2001), Doc. WT/DS135/AB/R, paras. 98–99: 'a determination of "likeness" under Article III:4 is, fundamentally, a determination about the nature and extent of a competitive relationship between and among products'; see also generally Appellate Body Report, *European Communities - Regime for the Importation, Sale and Distribution of Bananas ('EC – Bananas')* (9 Sep. 1997), Doc. WT/DS27/AB/R, paras. 231–233 for comments on the use of GATT jurisprudence in the interpretation of GATS articles.

100 This is explicitly suggested by the text of Article XVII. It is not so clear in the case of Article II, but it was more or less assumed by the Panel in *EC – Bananas*, ibid., para. 7.304.

Were public subsidies challenged as discriminatory in this way, a strong argument could be made in their defence that there is no discrimination, because traditional public operators and private enterprises are not in a competitive relationship. For one thing, the *services* supplied by the two different operators are not in competition, at least not in the sense that consumers can make a choice between them. And in most cases, no competitive relationship will exist between the two service *suppliers*. It is true, admittedly, that such competition is possible. In Chile, for example, public operators compete among themselves, and with private operators, for rural infrastructure projects funded by the national government.[101] This, however, is rare and generally only occurs once public operators have been commercialised. Alternatively, an argument might also be made that the two service providers are at least *potentially* competitive.[102] On the one hand, any of the ancillary services which the public authority currently provides in-house *could* be subcontracted to alternative, and competing, private suppliers. On the other, it is possible that the public authority could choose at any time to provide those ancillary services commercially, though much will depend in that case on the specific statutory mandate of the public authority. Further, it could be argued that public and private water authorities are competitive in the sense that the existence of public water authorities effectively reduces the market share available to private operators and compete for scarce government resources in the water sector. Such arguments are, however, based on a broad, and somewhat indirect, notion of competition, removed from the concept of direct consumer competition which has so far arisen in the context of WTO dispute settlement. It would arguably only be in rare cases that a competitive relationship could reasonably be said to exist between a traditional public water authority and a private company operating in a different region of the same country.

### 6.2 *A Competitive Relationship Very Often Will Exist between Commercial Service Suppliers*

On the other hand, where a claim is made that a measure discriminates between commercial water operators (whether foreign or domestic and whether public or private), the need for a competitive relationship is probably less likely to be of use in resisting such a claim.

[101] This occurs under Chile's National Rural Drinking Water Program; see Serra, at p.14ff, as well as in Australia (Australian Industry Commission, Water Resources and Wastewater Disposal Report No.26.

[102] See (n. 103 below).

Consider first the case of two operators in the business of supplying ancillary services to a network operator. Ancillary services supplied on a contract basis, such as metre reading and installation services or repair and maintenance services, are typically subject to competitive tender. The market for such services is much like any other, characterised by numerous suppliers competing for work. Precisely the same argument can apply to services such as operation and management services, which are supplied to a network operator in accordance with a management contract or concession-type arrangement. It would come as a great surprise to some of the large players in the global water industry to be told that they were not in competition with one another. The nature and extent of this competitive relationship in a particular context might depend on such matters as frequency of tendering and re-tendering, the stringency of prequalification criteria in tenders, the number of players in international water markets, the advantages accruing to incumbents in different contexts and so on. This is particularly important given various statements from the Appellate Body to the effect that it would be appropriate to consider *potential* service suppliers as service suppliers themselves, with the effect that an integrated water operator may be taken to be in competition with commercial suppliers of all the incidental services carried out in the course of its activities.[103]

Secondly, consider two water operators supplying services to consumers in different regions. In this case direct competition between services is rare, though still possible in some circumstances.[104] Competition between service

[103] See the comment of the Appellate Body in *US – Cotton Yarn from Pakistan ('US – Cotton Yarn')* (5 Nov. 2001), Doc. WT/DS192/AB/R, para. 96: 'It [the ordinary meaning of competitive] has a wider connotation than "actually competing" and includes also the notion of a potential to compete ... Indeed, products which are competitive may not be actually competing with each other in the marketplace at a given moment for a variety of reasons, such as regulatory restrictions or producers' decisions. Thus, a static view is incorrect, for it leads to the same products being regarded as competitive at one moment in time, and not so the next, depending upon whether or not they are in the marketplace.' Very similar remarks were made in the course of *EC – Bananas*, in the Panel Report at para. 7.320, and in the Appellate Body Report at paras. 227–228.

[104] Competition between suppliers for consumer patronage is possible in a number of different forms. Certain ancillary aspects of water supply services – such as plumbing, repair and installation services – are commonly supplied to consumers by competing providers. It is also sometimes possible for consumers at the geographical boundary of two water districts to choose between water suppliers (the twin Manila water concessions are a good example). In addition, in the United Kingdom, there are proposals to introduce a system under which water suppliers in adjacent regions would compete to supply water to nearby large-scale industrial users. Ways of increasing the level of direct competition in the water sector are currently under research and are a matter of some experimentation.

*suppliers*, on the other hand, is common.[105] Commentators typically distinguish between three forms of competition.[106] The first and most important kind is what is known as 'competition for the market', which occurs when potential suppliers competitively bid to supply services in a particular geographic area under a concession-type arrangement. This not only introduces direct competition during the bidding phase, it can also produce 'reputational' competitive pressure between bids, as a supplier's ability to win future bids depends in part on their present performance in respect of a different contract. The second kind of competition is 'comparative' or 'benchmark' competition. This operates where decisions of regulators in one region of a country are based on information about the performance of operators in other regions. This is a particularly common approach, and work is currently underway to provide comprehensive international benchmarks for regulators. Finally, the third kind of competition is 'capital market competition', a diffuse form of competition which operates simply through the possibility that an underperforming company can be taken over by new investors who think that they can improve efficiency.

None of these forms of competition are identical to traditional forms of direct competition between suppliers for consumer patronage, which is usually considered in trade disputes. Nevertheless, it would be only a relatively minor refinement of the concept for these three forms of competition to qualify as evidence of a 'competitive relationship'. There have been a number of indications from the Appellate Body that it may be sensitive to the existence of multiple forms of competition.[107] Furthermore, it is hard to see how

[105] I am assuming that a determination about the likeness of service suppliers can be made independently of a determination about the likeness of suppliers. This may seem to have been called into question by the statement by the Panel in *EC – Bananas*, para. 7.322: 'in our view, to the extent that entities provide these *like services*, they are *like service suppliers*' (see also the Panel Report in *Canada – Certain Measures Affecting the Automotive Industry ('Canada – Autos')* (19 Jun. 2000), Doc. WT/DS139/R, as modified by Appellate Body Report (19 Jun. 2000), Doc. WT/DS139/AB/R, para. 10.248). This comment has received some harsh criticism from commentators: see W. Zdouc, 'WTO Dispute Settlement Relating to the GATS', *Journal of International Economic Law*, Vol. 2 (1999), p. 295, at 331ff; Krajewski, *National Regulation and Trade Liberalization in Services*, p. 104; and Verhoosel, National Treatment and WTO Dispute Resolution, p. 61. It would be a mistake to read too much into such a comment at this stage: we await some comment by the Appellate Body.

[106] A good breakdown of the different types of competition is given in the World Bank Water and Sanitation Toolkit.

[107] Recall from footnote 99 above that the Appellate Body characterised a determination of likeness as an enquiry into the 'nature and extent of a competitive relationship' between services. The use of the term 'nature' suggests, perhaps, a sensitivity to multiple forms of competition. A similar reference to the 'structure of competition' in a later case may indicate something similar (see Panel Report in *Canada – Autos*, para 174).

discriminatory treatment in the water sector could ever be disciplined by the trade regime if this kind of competitive relationship were *not* recognised. WTO dispute settlement bodies are arguably unlikely to prefer an interpretation of GATS provisions which would rob them of a large part of their efficacy – even if only in relation to an individual service sector.[108] The object and purpose of Article II, as well as Article XVII, is 'to prohibit discrimination against foreign services and service suppliers'.[109] Such discriminatory treatment is no less possible in the water sector than in any other, and it is no less objectionable.

## 7 ARTICLES II AND XVII: THE RELEVANCE OF REGULATORY PURPOSE

This section takes up another specific aspect of the interpretation of GATS non-discrimination provisions, namely, the relevance of the *purpose* of a regulation to a finding of discrimination. A regulation which has a differential effect on foreign and domestic services or service suppliers could be the result of a range of different background political dynamics. It may be in some sense a deliberate effort on the part of regulators. It may be an unavoidable consequence of the pursuit of a particular policy objective. Or it may simply have been an inadvertent or unforeseen[110] consequence, even if in principle avoidable. The examples given in section II above cover all these different situations.

As a general principle, international trade obligations recognise that these different situations should in some measure be treated differently. In the GATS, the primary mechanism for doing so is, of course, the general exception provision contained in Article XIV, which effectively excuses discrimination which is the necessary result of the pursuit of certain listed policy objectives. But partly as a result of inadequacies in the scope and application of such general exception provisions, a question has arisen as to whether or not regulations should be treated differently under GATS Articles II and XVII

[108] The Appellate Body has on a number of occasions explicitly preferred an interpretation which avoids the problem of opening up the potential to undermine the agreement. See, for example, the argument of the Appellate Body in *EC – Bananas*, para. 233. Also see the Panel Report in the same case at para. 7.303 and the Report of the Appellate Body in *Canada – Autos*, para. 142.

[109] Report of the Panel in *EC – Bananas*, para. 7.302.

[110] For an argument on the potential role of foreseeability in determinations of discrimination, see Türk and Krajewski, 'The Right to Water and Trade', p. 10, and Krajewski, *National Regulation and Trade Liberalization in Services*.

(and their GATT equivalents), depending on the 'purpose' – broadly understood – of the regulation in question. It is a proposition which has a strong intuitive appeal.[111] It is hard to disagree with Hudec that:

> [c]ommon sense tells us that whenever a panel member is asked to decide whether a particular regulatory measure is or is not playing by the rules, that panel member will instinctively want to know whether the measure has a bona fide regulatory purpose and to what extent its market effects are protective.[112]

It is arguably one of the flaws of the GATS that neither Article II nor Article XVII (and, perhaps to a lesser extent, their GATT counterparts) contains a clear textual basis for a consideration of regulatory purpose. Indeed, the first explicit attempt to incorporate a consideration of regulatory purpose into GATT jurisprudence – the much-discussed 'aims and effects' test – was unequivocally rejected by the Appellate Body, primarily because it lacked a textual basis.[113] But some argue that this rejection, rather than ruling out any consideration of regulatory purpose, instead has meant that such consideration is now more implicit than explicit. This section examines two ways in which regulatory purpose may conceivably be considered under GATS Articles II and XVII and assesses to what extent this may allow greater flexibility to regulators in the water industry.

The first way in which regulatory purpose may be relevant is in a determination of whether or not two services or service suppliers are 'like' one another. Some hints of this approach can be seen in the Appellate Body's reasoning in *EC – Asbestos*.[114] That dispute concerned a French decree banning the manufacture, processing, import, exportation, domestic marketing, sale and transfer of asbestos fibre and products containing asbestos fibre. The ban did

[111] Many of the proposals made by scholars writing on the problem of regulatory autonomy have included regulatory purpose in some form; see, for example, A. Mattoo and A. Subramanian, 'Regulatory Autonomy and Multilateral Disciplines: The Dilemma and a Possible Resolution', *Journal of International Economic Law*, Vol. 2 (1998), p. 303; A. Mattoo, 'National Treatment in the GATS: Corner-Stone or Pandora's Box?', *Journal of World Trade*, Vol. 31 (1997), pp. 107–135, at 131–132; also Verhoosel.

[112] R. Hudec, 'GATT/WTO Constraints on National Regulations: Requiem for an "Aims and Effect" Test', *The International Lawyer*, Vol. 32 (1998), p. 619, at 16.

[113] See Appellate Body Report, *Japan – Taxes on Alcoholic Beverages ('Japan – Alcohol')* (4 Oct. 1996), Doc. WT/DS10/AB/R, and Appellate Body report, *EC – Bananas*, para. 241. There has been some suggestion that the real objection to the test (at least from WTO Members themselves) was not so much that there was no textual basis for the test but rather that the standard of test used ('inherency') was too loose.

[114] See Appellate Body Report, *European Communities – Measures Affecting Asbestos and Asbestos-Containing Products ('EC – Asbestos')* (12 Mar. 2001), Doc. WT/DS135/AB/R.

not apply to 'PCG' fibres, and one question was whether the decree therefore unfairly discriminated as between foreign asbestos products on the one hand and domestic PCG products on the other. The French decree was clearly designed to protect public health. The distinction it drew between the two products was based on the different risks they posed to human health. The Appellate Body determined that there was no violation of GATT Article III. The interesting point is that this result was not (at least not explicitly) because the discrimination was justified. Rather, it was on the basis that there could be no discrimination, because the two products were not 'like' one another. And they were not like one another, rather circuitously, because they posed different health risks. This reasoning resonates with a comment of the Appellate Body in the same case, to the effect that the text of the agreement did not 'indicate *from whose perspective* "likeness" should be judged'.[115] It must be arguable that distinctions which are relevant from a regulator's perspective are at least potentially relevant to the issue of likeness.[116]

This approach to the problem has the virtue of greater fidelity to the text of the WTO agreements. Such virtue has, however, been bought at a significant cost. For one thing, it effectively hides from view the process by which a panel comes to a view on what is the 'purpose' of a particular regulatory measure and puts in its place a rather artificial discussion of the meaning of 'likeness'. It becomes impossible to see and criticise the standard that the panel uses when comparing the regulation's means and ends. This is important because for many critics it is at this point that trade panels can be most insensitive to the realities of policy-making. Equally, a panel is able to draw only minimal guidance for this process from previous cases.

Another difficulty is that the concept of 'likeness' is not infinitely malleable. There will be many forms of regulatory distinction which will not be easily assimilated into the concept of likeness, without the kinds of creative textual interpretation that it is trying to avoid. Take, for example, the case of two service suppliers in the water industry, which are treated differently purely because they operate in different jurisdictions. To what extent is it possible to regard two services or service suppliers as not 'like', on the sole basis that they operate in different areas? The ordinary meaning of the term 'like' would probably not permit such an interpretation. Two identical services do not lose their similarity simply because of a geographical separation. Indeed, if distinguishing between services based on their geographic origin is *a fortiori* illegitimate, it is difficult to see why the same should not apply to other geographic

[115] *EC – Asbestos*, para. 92.

[116] See generally Regan, 'Regulatory Purpose and "Like Products" in Article III:4 of the GATT'.

distinctions. This seems to be borne out by the (admittedly sparse) case law on the issue – comparisons across sub-federal jurisdictions have been made in at least one case and used to ground a determination of discrimination.[117]

This problem was explicitly discussed by a number of WTO Members in the context of sub-federal tax treatment. The United States inscribed a wide variety of sub-federal taxes as limitations to Articles II and XVII in its GATS Schedule of Commitments, on the grounds that state tax authorities would otherwise be required to provide foreign service suppliers with the most favourable treatment to be found in any other state.[118] This decision led to a series of interesting informal discussions.[119] Some members objected to the United States' scheduling practice because they argued that it implied that different tax treatment across sub-federal jurisdictions was contrary to GATS non-discrimination provisions. They argued that it was never the intent of the agreement to have such an effect with respect to tax treatment, as it was perfectly common for tax measures to vary from region to region within a country.[120] Some suggested that the problem could be solved by indicating that suppliers in different jurisdictions were not like, 'for tax purposes'.[121] The United States suggested that an interpretative note to the agreement or a statement by the Chairman of the Council for Trade in Services would be needed. All agreed on the existence of legal uncertainty, but no interpretative note has yet been forthcoming. At this stage, it is effectively assumed that members will 'refrain from taking issues arising in this area to dispute settlement'.[122]

A second example, again of particular relevance to the water industry, concerns the relevance of *context* to the likeness of services or service suppliers. In the water sector, the context in which water services are supplied will often be a ground for differential regulatory treatment of some kind.

[117] See GATT Panel Report, *United States – Measures Affecting Alcoholic and Malt Beverages* (*'Malt Beverages'*) (19 Jun. 1992), Doc. 39S/206.

[118] See WTO document, PC/SCS/W/4, para. A.1.

[119] See the account of these discussions in WTO document, S/C/W/13. [120] Ibid.

[121] Ibid., para. A.1, referring to a statement of the Chairman of the Negotiating Group on Services, 11 December 1993, MTN.GNS/49. A close reading of that latter document reveals that it makes no claim as regards whether or not suppliers in different jurisdictions are 'like' (see, e.g. the third paragraph under Heading 1).

[122] See the statement of the Chairman, above footnote 121, under Heading 4: 'I wish to re-emphasise, perhaps more strongly than in my earlier statement, that pending further clarification of this and other questions relating to the scope of the Agreement, that it is assumed that participants would refrain from taking issues arising in this area to dispute settlement but would try to settle them through bilateral consultations. However, participants must assume their own responsibilities in deciding whether any measures of this sort which they maintain should be scheduled or made the subject of MFN exemptions - though in this respect also it is hoped that restraint will be shown.' This remains the position now.

Significant elements of context will include the socio-economic conditions of the consumers being supplied, the extent of coverage and state of repair of the existing network, the geographical terrain as well as other more controversial matters such as political opposition to liberalisation, the regulatory framework and the nature of the relationship between the service supplier and the government. Other than a presently irrelevant reference in the Annex on Telecommunications,[123] the GATS contains no explicit mention of the likeness of 'circumstances' or 'context' in which services are supplied. This is in contrast to analogous provisions in NAFTA,[124] as well as certain OECD documents.[125] One WTO Member has suggested that a consideration of the likeness of circumstances *should* be included in a determination of discrimination but admits that there is scant textual support for such an approach.[126] Indeed, it would be hard to argue that two identical services were not like simply because of the socio-economic status of the consumers of that service. Such a distinction would be unthinkable in the goods context. The admittedly sparse case law on the matter indicates that context will generally be irrelevant to the issue of likeness. In *US – Gasoline*, an argument that only products from supplies 'in similar situations' were like was rejected.[127]

The second stage at which regulatory purpose may become relevant is during a determination of the existence of 'less favourable' treatment. There has been some indication from the WTO Appellate Body that the concept of less favourable treatment may implicitly authorise a panel to consider the regulatory purpose of a measure, at least in the context of the national treatment provision in GATT Article III.[128] In *EC – Asbestos*, the Appellate Body stated:

> The term "less favourable treatment" expresses the general principle, in Article III:1, that internal regulations "should not be applied ... so as to afford protection to domestic production". If there is "less favourable treatment" of

[123] See the reference to 'like circumstances' in note 15 of the Annex on Telecommunications. See also the chapeau of GATS Article XIV, which refers to 'like conditions'.

[124] See, for example, NAFTA Article 1202 on National Treatment in services and Article 1203 on Most Favoured Nation in Services, both of which refer to 'like circumstances'.

[125] See OECD, *National Treatment for Foreign-Controlled Enterprises* (Paris: OECD, 1993), p. 22, discussing enterprises 'in like situations'.

[126] See Communication from Brazil, 'MFN, National Treatment and *like circumstances*' (30 Nov. 2001), WTO Doc. JOB(01)/165.

[127] See Panel Report, *United States – Standards for Reformulated and Conventional Gasoline ('US – Gasoline')* (29 Apr. 1996), Doc. WT/DS2/R, as modified by the Appellate Body Report (29 Apr. 1996), Doc. WT/DS2/AB/R, para. 6.11.

[128] Howse and Tuerk note this in 'The WTO Impact on Internal Regulations: a case study of the Canada-EC Asbestos Dispute' in J. Scott and G. de Burca (eds.) *The EU and the WTO: Legal and Constitutional Issues* (Portland Oregon: Oxford, 2001), 283–328, at 289.

> the group of "like" imported products, there is, conversely, "protection" of the group of "like" domestic products. *However, a Member may draw distinctions between products which have been found to be "like", without, for this reason alone, according to the group of "like" imported products "less favourable treatment" than that accorded to the group of "like" domestic products.* In this case, we do not examine further the interpretation of the term "treatment no less favourable" in Article III:4, as the Panel's findings on this issue have not been appealed or, indeed, argued before us. [emphasis added][129]

It is possible to read into this dictum a suggestion that where a distinction is drawn between two 'like' service suppliers, such distinction may be acceptable provided it is drawn for a legitimate regulatory purpose or equivalently has some form of objective basis. It is too early to say, of course, how this statement might be used by future panels, and how readily it might be transplanted into the services context, but there is at least the possibility that this phrase will be used in the future as a creative means of ensuring a greater degree of regulatory freedom for governments.

## 8 ARTICLE XIV(B): 'MEASURES NECESSARY TO PROTECT HUMAN ... LIFE OR HEALTH'

Finally, it is necessary to examine GATS Article XIV and assess the level of protection that it may provide for social regulation of the water industry. Article XIV reads, in relevant part:

> Subject to the requirement that such measures are not applied in a manner which would constitute a means of arbitrary or unjustifiable discrimination between countries where like conditions prevail, or a disguised restriction on trade in services, nothing in this Agreement shall be construed to prevent the adoption or enforcement by any Member of measures:
>
> ...
>
> (b) necessary to protect human, animal or plant life or health ...

The Appellate Body in *Reformulated Gasoline*, which concerned the identically worded[130] exception in GATT Article XX(b), observed that a government wishing to invoke this provision was required to demonstrate three elements. First, that the policy in respect of the measures for which the provision was

[129] Appellate Body Report in *EC – Asbestos*, para. 100.

[130] The only (presently irrelevant) differences in wording between GATS Article XIV and GATT Article XX are that Article XX refers to the 'same conditions' where Article XIV refers to 'like conditions', Article XX refers to 'international trade' where Article XIV refers to 'trade in services' and Article XX refers 'contracting party' where Article XIV refers to 'Member'.

invoked fell within the range of policies designed to protect human, animal or plant life or health. Second, that the inconsistent measures for which the exception was being invoked were necessary to fulfil the policy objective. And third, that the measures were applied in conformity with the requirements of the introductory clause of the Article.[131]

The jurisprudence on the first element is relatively underdeveloped. This is no doubt partly because over the course of cases on GATT Article XX, the purported objective of the dispute has rarely been in question.[132] It is clear at least that the regulatory measure must address a demonstrated health risk.[133] Furthermore, the practical effects of the regulation can be considered in determining whether or not it is designed to protect human health.[134] But provided a sufficient nexus with the appropriate regulatory objective is demonstrated, it is not permissible for the panel to examine the necessity of the policy goal itself.[135] Importantly, there is possibly inconsistent authority on the question of whether it is sufficient for the protection of human health to be only one among a number of objectives of the measure at issue.[136]

While it is true that effective management of the water sector makes an obvious and highly significant contribution to the protection of human health, it does not follow that all social regulation in that sector is designed 'to protect human life or health'. Different aspects of water regulation may have a variety

[131] Report of the Appellate Body in *US – Gasoline*, p. 22; see also the Panel report at para. 6.20.

[132] The issue was in dispute in *EC – Asbestos*, but in that case the question turned on whether asbestos fibres presented a demonstrable health risk rather than a detailed examination of the purpose of the legislation. In *US – Gasoline*, the matter was not controversial nor was it considered in detail in *United States – Import Prohibition of Shrimp and Certain Shrimp Products ('US – Shrimp')* (15 May 1998), Doc. WT/DS58/R, as modified by the Appellate Body Report (12 Oct. 1998), Doc. WT/DS58/R. It was a serious issue in *Korea – Measures Affecting Imports of Fresh, Chilled and Frozen Beef ('Korea – Beef')* (10 Jan. 2001), Doc. WT/DS161/R, but only at Panel stage, it was not argued at appeal.

[133] See Report of the Panel in *US – Gasoline*, para. 6.21, and Report of the Appellate Body in *EC – Asbestos*, para. 157ff., as well as the Panel in that case at para. 8.170.

[134] Report of the Panel in *Korea – Beef*, para. 658.

[135] See the Report of the Panel in *EC – Asbestos*, 8.171; Report of the Panel in *US – Gasoline*, para. 6.22. See also the GATT Panel Report, *United States – Section 337 of the Tariff Act of 1930 ('US – Section 337')* (7 Nov. 1989), Doc. 36S/345, para. 5.26; GATT Panel Report *Thailand – Restrictions on Importation of and Internal Taxes on Cigarettes ('Thai Cigarettes')* (7 Nov. 1990), Doc. BISD 37S/200, para. 74

[136] Compare Report of the Panel in *Korea – Beef*, para. 658, with the decision of the Appellate Body in *US – Gasoline*, which suggested that it was more difficult to show that a measure was 'necessary for a particular objective under sub-paragraph (b) than 'primarily aimed at' an objective for the purpose of sub-paragraph (g). This may imply that the necessity test requires at least that the regulation in question is *primarily* aimed at the achievement of a human health objective.

of different objectives, ranging from ensuring equality of access to water resources to improving management efficiency in the sector, limiting the abuse of monopoly power, improving service quality and customer satisfaction, reducing the government's fiscal burden and improving the state of the network infrastructure. Regulation in respect of each of these matters may, but need not, have a direct or indirect effect on general health conditions. Regulation of water quality, for example, would certainly fall within the scope of Article XIV(b). Price regulation of private operators, however, would in most cases probably not. Price regulation is typically designed primarily to create incentives for efficiency and to control the abuse of monopoly power or alternatively is regulated for narrower 'political' reasons. Operator subsidies would also probably not be caught, for similar reasons. Whether or not consumer subsidies fell within the scope of Article XIV(b) would depend on all the circumstances. Such subsidies are sometimes created for reasons of social equity, as a matter of political expediency or even social engineering, rather than as a direct means of protecting human health. Furthermore, as suggested above, given the history of political interference in the water sector, and the present highly politicised nature of the sector, it may often be the case that a measure will have a mixed or ambiguous purpose, not wholly attributable to declared social objectives. It is probably fair to say that at least a substantial proportion of total social regulation of the water industry would not be caught by Article XIV(b).

The second element to be demonstrated is that the inconsistent measure is 'necessary' to fulfil its claimed policy objective. A measure is necessary if no reasonably available alternative measure exists which is either consistent with the GATS or less inconsistent than the measure in issue.[137] In the early years of GATT jurisprudence on this article, the meaning of 'reasonably available alternative' was understood strictly, to the extent that some commentators suggested that it was almost impossible to satisfy the conditions imposed.[138] Trade panels have been accused of being insensitive to the realities of policy-making, where first-best alternatives are rarely if ever practically available. Concerns have been expressed that such panels fail to appreciate the difficulties which limited resources create for regulators and the ways in which alternative measures may in practice undermine regulatory objectives in less than obvious ways. Indeed, some early decisions led a significant number of critics to be alarmed that domestic regulations were scrutinised in trade

[137] See *Thai Cigarettes*, para. 75; *US – Section* 337, 5.26, Report of the Appellate Body in *Korea – Beef*, p. 166, and Report of the Appellate Body in *EC – Asbestos*, para. 171.
[138] See, for example, Hudec, ' GATT/WTO Constraints on National Regulations'.

disputes with an unwarranted attitude of suspicion[139] and without a full appreciation of the importance of the regulatory objective in question.

More recent decisions and statements of the Appellate Body have begun to address such concerns, and some commentators have noted something of a relaxation of approach.[140] It has been made clear, for example, that the word 'necessary' is not limited to that which is indispensable or of absolute necessity. The determination of whether a measure is necessary:

> involves in every case a process of weighing and balancing a series of factors which prominently include the contribution made by the compliance measure to the enforcement of the law or regulation at issue, the importance of the common interests or values protected by that law or regulation, and the accompanying impact of the law or regulation on imports or exports.[141]

Where there are common interests or values at stake which are particularly vital, a panel will more easily be convinced that the measure is necessary. In addition, it is clear at least in principle that Members are entirely free to choose the level of protection they desire and cannot be required to use an alternative measure which provides even a slightly lower level of protection.[142] As to the relevance of any administrative or technical difficulties associated with implementing alternative measures, while it is true that the existence of administrative difficulties is insufficient to justify the measure at issue, there is some indication that panels will be sensitive to the various regulatory capacities of different countries.[143]

Nevertheless, some legitimate concerns remain. It is possible to envisage some times in which it will be difficult to demonstrate that no reasonably available alternative measure exists. This may be particularly the case where discrimination arises because of differences of treatment across jurisdictional boundaries. In addition, in the context of continuing regulatory experiment

[139] See, for example, Cho, Free Markets and Social Regulation, p. 40 and surrounding.

[140] J.H. Knox believes that the moderate approach forged recently by the Appellate Body has all but solved the problem of regulatory autonomy in the trade and environment context: 'The Judicial Resolution of Conflicts between Trade and Environment', *Harvard Environmental Law Review*, Vol. 28 (2004), pp. 1–78.

[141] Report of the Appellate Body in *Korea – Beef*, para. 164.

[142] See, for example, *Korea – Beef*, para. 176.

[143] The Panel in *EC – Asbestos*, para. 8.207 stated: 'We consider that the existence of a reasonably available measure must be assessed in the light of the economic and administrative realities facing the Member concerned but also by taking into account the fact that the State must provide itself with the means of implementing its policies. Thus, the Panel considers that it is legitimate to expect a country such as France with advanced labour legislation and specialized administrative services to deploy administrative resources proportionate to its public health objectives and to be prepared to incur the necessary expenditure.'

and refinement, it may well be the case that a less restrictive and more efficient equivalent measure may be available at the time that the measure is considered in a dispute. Furthermore, while the Appellate Body may agree that no less trade restrictive alternative should undermine the regulatory objective pursued, it will not always be clear in advance how this might happen. Take the example of cross-subsidies in the water sector. It is now commonly argued that direct consumer subsidies funded out of general government revenue are both more efficient and less discriminatory as between different service suppliers and, thus, arguably a less trade restrictive alternative. At the same time, however, such a transformation makes subsidy programmes subject to the processes of negotiation and dispute which inevitably affect all budgetary allocations from general revenue. Although it is impossible to say in advance, it stands to reason that at least in some cases this will have the effect of gradually reducing the level of funding available for such a programme.

The third element is the satisfaction of the requirements of the *chapeau* of Article XIV. A measure which falls within Article XIV must be neither an 'arbitrary or unjustifiable discrimination between countries where like conditions prevail' nor a 'disguised restriction on trade in services'. These requirements are possibly less likely to be of concern in relation to social regulation of the water industry.[144] The object of these introductory clauses is generally to prevent the abuse of the general exceptions.[145] They are, broadly speaking, designed to catch claims based on Article XIV which are not advanced in good faith.[146] Furthermore, they are (like all provisions of the agreement) to be interpreted in light of the Preamble to the GATS, which explicitly recognises 'the right of Members to regulate, and to introduce new regulations, on the supply of services within their territories in order to meet national policy objectives'.[147]

## 9 CONCLUSION

This piece began by invoking a debate between human rights and trade advocates concerning the potential of the GATS to restrict the ability of governments to enact socially desirable regulation of the water sector. It has engaged with this debate along only one of a number of possible axes – that of

[144] But see Cho, Free Markets and Social Regulation, p. 45 and following.

[145] See Report of the Appellate Body in *US – Gasoline*, p. 22.

[146] See Report of the Appellate Body in *US – Shrimp*, paras. 158–159.

[147] See the discussion of the use of preambular material to interpret GATT Article XX in *US – Shrimp*, paras. 153–155.

examining, as essentially a doctrinal matter, the legal basis of the claims of various participants in the debate. What conclusions can be drawn from the discussion?

First, some ground clearing is unfortunately still necessary in the debate. One still hears claims that trade disputes over social regulation in the water sector are essentially inconceivable (because such regulation is so obviously legitimate and desirable) and that by implication GATS critics are either scare-mongering or fundamentally misguided. Such claims are misleading. It is of course true that a broad consensus exists that governments should take measures to promote the universal availability and affordability of water services, as well as to ensure their quality. This much is not in dispute. However, no such consensus exists as to the legitimate means which a government can use to achieve such ends – and crucially, how much incidental trade restriction is tolerable. And this, in the end, is what really matters. Is it legitimate, for example, for a government to subsidise a heavily inefficient public water authority, using funds derived from levies imposed on private operators in other parts of the country? Is it legitimate to require one operator's customers to subsidise another's, through the operation of cross-subsidies, when an alternative, less discriminatory option exists of a subsidy system funded from general revenue? Is it legitimate to set prices at levels below those required to achieve a reasonable return on investment? Is it legitimate to prohibit one operator from disconnecting non-paying customers while not doing the same for others? Is it legitimate to have different health standards applying in different areas of the same country? The characteristic contemporary political dynamic of water sector regulation is one of passionate disagreement and contestation on these matters, rather than universal consensus. Claims to the contrary are best understood as attempts[148] to contain and limit such contestation and shore up existing orthodoxies.

Second, as far as claims of discrimination are concerned, the relatively brief doctrinal analysis possible here is inevitably hampered by a significant degree of uncertainty. This uncertainty has implications in two directions. On the one hand, one can identify potential argumentative strategies for those wishing to maintain a high degree of domestic regulatory autonomy in the water sector. At least three important strategies emerge from the above analysis. One is to advocate for a broad interpretation of the governmental authority exception, to include not only services supplied by corporatised public operators but also services supplied under concession arrangements. Another is to argue

[148] To avoid misunderstanding, the term 'attempt' is not, of course, used here to imply any form of conscious intention.

for a narrow understanding of the concept of 'competitive relationship', to exclude some of the more diffuse forms of competition found in the context of the water sector. And a third is to advocate for broader margin of appreciation to be granted to governments under Article XIV, particularly as regards measures which have health protection as only one of a number of possible policy objectives. To some extent, this last is already being done.

On the other hand, one can attempt the difficult task of assessing the risk that claims against water sector regulation will be successful. There is no doubt that at times, this risk has been overstated by GATS critics. But this analysis suggests that one must approach with caution claims that the risk is nothing more than minimal. Such claims are often based on unjustifiably robust views of the protection provided by the bottom-up nature of the agreement, by the governmental authority exception and by the Article XIV exceptions. As a matter of principle, there appears to be every reason to think that a significant amount of water sector regulation could potentially violate GATS non-discrimination provisions – particularly Article II on MFN treatment. It is clear that discrimination, in the broad sense of differential treatment, occurs often within the water industry, for legitimate and perhaps not so legitimate reasons. Neither Article II nor Article XVII contains a satisfactory method of distinguishing with certainty and predictability those forms of discrimination which are justified and those which are not.

This should not be understood as suggesting that discrimination on the grounds of social policy *necessarily* violates the GATS, nor is it saying it is impossible for panels to pursue creative interpretations of GATS provisions which substantially eliminate the problems addressed in this article. It is a major point of this article that the text of the GATS represents a careful balance between the two goals of trade liberalisation and regulatory autonomy. It is wrong to understand the GATS, or indeed any WTO agreement, as simply the pursuit of trade liberalisation as a single goal. It is a compromise. And, in fact, the compromise it represents is a dynamic one which is re-contested and redrawn each time key provisions of the GATS are interpreted and applied. It may be true that discrimination on the grounds of social policy might only be subject to WTO dispute resolution in the most difficult of cases, where regulatory objectives are open to competing interpretations. But regulatory regimes are designed with the difficult cases in mind, partly with a view to what happens in the event of a serious dispute. Nor should we underestimate how often such ambiguous cases might arise, given the highly politicised nature of the water industry.

Thirdly, and finally, it is worth recalling what was said earlier in relation to the consequences to a regulatory regime of vulnerability to claims of discriminatory treatment. One foreseeable consequence might be an increasing trend towards centralisation of certain regulatory and administrative tasks to forestall the possibility of claims of discrimination across jurisdictions and to control the possibility of capricious local treatment. Such a trend would, importantly, run directly counter to most current thinking in respect of water regulation. A second consequence may in fact be a trend towards lower overall standards of regulation. The distinction, so central to the WTO regime, between non-discrimination and deregulation is a fine one and can be deceptive if insisted upon too strongly. This is particularly the case in the water sector, which is characterised by contractually agreed regulatory standards and a high degree of regulatory discretion.

Human rights advocates are right to be concerned with such possibilities. But their voices need not be – and to be fair, often are not – purely oppositional and external. There are resources within the trade texts themselves which can be mobilised in their interest. For all the defects and inadequacies of the technical, legal language of trade disputes, important results can be achieved through an engagement with its domain and an articulation of alternative claims within its language.

# 16

# Bilateral Investment Treaties and Investment Arbitration

LUKE ERIC PETERSON*

## 1 INTRODUCTION

Over the last half-century, a de facto international regime has emerged for the protection of foreign direct investment flows. Although governments have attempted and failed on various occasions to conclude a single multilateral agreement on investment (MAI), they have quietly concluded a staggering number of bilateral treaties for the promotion and protection of foreign investment. Today, there are some 3000 bilateral investment treaties (BITs), and similar BIT-like obligations can be found in an ever-growing number of free trade agreements. For instance, the North American Free Trade Agreement and the Central American Free Trade Agreement both contain detailed chapters covering foreign investment.

A major catalyst of these international investment treaties has been the desire to protect investments in developing countries from expropriation or other forms of harm.[1] Investment treaties were often viewed as a supplement to domestic law protections – particularly where concerns were raised about the reliability of local courts. However, in practice, these international agreements can offer a complete alternative to the law of the host country. Thus, investment treaties typically contain a series of international law protections that governments undertake to provide to foreign investors. These protections typically include a promise of financial compensation in cases of expropriation

* Editor, InvestmentArbitrationReporter.com; Research for this paper was conducted in 2010 and – apart from the inclusion of a few recent statistics – may not reflect subsequent scholarly or legal developments. See also Editors' Note after the conclusion.

[1] For background see United Nations Conference on Trade and Development (UNCTAD), *Bilateral Investment Treaties in the Mid-1990s* (New York: United Nations, 1998), pp. 1–5. See K. Vandevelde, 'The Political Economy of a Bilateral Investment Treaty', *American Journal of International Law*, Vol. 92 (1998), pp. 621–641.

or nationalisation, protection against discrimination or arbitrary treatment, the freedom to transfer and repatriate funds and guarantees of 'protection and security' and 'fair and equitable treatment'.

Lest these words be viewed as merely hortatory, it should be stressed that most investment treaties provide for a powerful dispute settlement mechanism. This mechanism provides for the same style of individual claims seen in some regional human rights systems (such as the European and Inter-American systems) but with the added benefit of not requiring that domestic legal remedies be exhausted prior to the initiation of an international claim. (In general, arbitration also holds out the prospect of much more generous compensation than human rights litigation, and with arbitral rulings being more enforceable than a human rights court judgment.) Thus, where a foreign investor (either an individual or a corporation) believes that its host country has failed to live up to the terms of an investment protection treaty, that investor can bring a claim against the host country before a specially created international arbitration panel. This process takes place outside of the domestic courts of the host State and serves as a clear alternative to litigation in the domestic courts. Arbitration tribunals typically consist of three members: one chosen by the investor, one chosen by the host country and a third chosen by consensus or by some outside authority.

These investor-State arbitration tribunals have jurisdiction to determine whether the investment treaty has been breached by the host government. Moreover, tribunals do not simply issue declaratory judgments; rather they generally award cash damages for any losses suffered as a result of the treaty breaches. It is not uncommon for investment treaty disputes to involve tens or hundreds of millions of dollars in potential damages; some cases run into the billions, where major assets, such as oil fields, are at stake.

For several decades, international investment treaties remained obscure. However, beginning in the 1990s, and carrying into the following decade, a steady volume of arbitration claims began to be initiated by foreign investors – many of them by large multinational companies, such as British Petroleum, General Electric, Alstom and Siemens. These investment treaties can prescribe various modes or forums of arbitration, including several commercial arbitration centres that operate under strict rules of confidentiality. However, one venue that sees a substantial volume of investment treaty arbitrations is the World Bank's International Centre for Settlement of Investment Disputes, the vast majority of which pertain to alleged treaty violations by governments.[2] The Centre maintains a public registry where it lists all arbitrations being conducted.

[2] A modest number of ICSID claims relate to pure contractual disputes, where an investor or government alleges that the counterparty to a contract has breached the terms of that

Arbitrators at the ICSID grapple with everything from nationalisation claims brought by Exxon-Mobil against the government of Venezuela to claims by a pair of individual businesspersons alleging that Egypt seized land that was slated to be developed into a resort complex.[3] While the existence of these ICSID cases is a matter of public record, the arbitration proceedings themselves are usually closed to the public and the media. When final ICSID rulings ('awards') are rendered, they typically enter the public domain – thanks to one or the other party releasing them - but there is no requirement that they do so.

Outside of ICSID, a substantial, but unclear, number of investment treaty arbitrations are also taking place.[4] Whereas ICSID awards generally find their way into the public domain, there is not a similar culture of disclosure of non-ICSID awards. Many non-ICSID awards do surface, but others remain under wraps – with an unknown number of non-ICSID cases proceeding without any public knowledge whatsoever.

Overall, the regime of international investment treaties has given rise to many hundreds of international law claims brought by foreign investors against sovereign States. At one extreme, these cases can involve egregious and arbitrary conduct by States, including confiscation or destruction of property or the physical mistreatment or abuse of foreign investors or their agents and employees. At the other extreme, investor-State disputes may touch upon highly contentious questions of public policy. For instance, governments may introduce new regulations, taxes or policies which are said to promote important public welfare objectives – yet encounter opposition from foreign investors who object to the financial burden that such policies impose upon them.

Thus, while international investment treaties sometimes operate as alternatives to human rights protections for investors who have suffered bodily harm or destruction of property, at other times investment treaties may be wielded by foreign investors in an effort to challenge government policies or regulations – including, it has been argued, human rights policies or initiatives.[5]

agreement. For instance, ICSID has handled several cases where investors in the energy sector allege that a host government has failed to live up to contractual undertakings, such as the freezing or stabilisation of taxes applicable to the investment.

3 *Mobil Corporation and others* v. *Bolivarian Republic of Venezuela*, ICSID Case No. ARB/07/27 and *Waguih Elie George Siag and Clorinda Vecci* v. *Arab Republic of Egypt*, ICSID Case No. ARB/05/15.

4 While there are resources such as the *Investment Arbitration Reporter* (www.iareporter.com) news service, it is unknown what *proportion* of investment treaty arbitrations are brought to light through such investigative reporting channels.

5 See discussion of water disputes below, as well as the ICSID arbitration between *Piero Foresti and others* v. *Republic of South Africa*, ICSID Case No. ARB/(AF)/07/1, where European investors challenged certain Black Economic Empowerment (BEE) policies of South Africa.

One area where there has been particular speculation as to the relationship of investment treaties and human rights law is the water utilities sector. This chapter profiles several leading investor-State arbitrations that were resolved in the decade spanning 2000–2010 and arising out of disputes over water utilities. In each of these cases, foreign investors accuse their host country of mistreating a foreign-owned water utility – thereby breaching the terms of a bilateral investment protection treaty. Human rights considerations have been increasingly raised by States in defence and by civil society organisations intervening as amicus curiae.

## 2 INVESTMENT TREATIES AND HUMAN RIGHTS LAW: BACKGROUND

The overwhelming majority of investment treaties do not contain any reference to human rights – either in the treaty preamble or in the substantive provisions of the agreement. Historically, these agreements tended to be narrowly conceived and were negotiated with little discussion or publicity by the government agencies with oversight over trade or economic matters. As such, the agreements did not discuss – much less expand upon – the human rights law obligations of States or the human rights law responsibilities of foreign investors. Rather, the agreements focused upon various protections to be accorded to foreign investors – without any consideration of the impact of foreign investment (or of these treaty protections) upon human rights conditions in the host country.

Despite the typical silence of these treaties on questions of human rights, it has long been speculated that investor-State disputes might raise certain human rights issues.[6] On the one hand, some investor claims might easily be couched as human rights complaints – if they were brought through human rights adjudicative mechanisms. This is not unusual insofar as the historical precursor of foreign investor claims were diplomatic claims for protection of aliens. Such claims were premised on everything from destruction of foreign-owned property, to false imprisonment or physical maltreatment of foreign nationals, to persecution of foreigners on religious grounds.

Not surprisingly then, investors or their shareholders will sometimes pursue claims simultaneously under investment treaties *and* before regional human rights courts. For instance, when the Russian Federation was

For background see 'South African Mining Dispute over Black Economic Empowerment Headed for Resolution?', *Investment Arbitration Reporter*, 2 April 2009, www.iareporter.com/articles/20090922_16.

6 See for example, L. Peterson and K. Gray, 'International Human Rights in Bilateral Investment Treaties and Investment Treaty Arbitration', Paper prepared for Swiss Ministry of Foreign Affairs, April 2003.

accused of bankrupting and expropriating the giant Yukos Oil Company in 2004, the company and its shareholders mounted claims before the European Court of Human Rights and under various investment treaties signed by Russia.

Apart from the possibility that certain actions taken by States against investors might breach investment treaty protections and human rights law, there is also the prospect of the human rights of *non-parties* (e.g. citizens of the host country) being affected by foreign investment activity. For instance, foreign investors might be complicit in grave human rights violations, such as the use of slavery or forced labour. However, investment treaties typically did not grant human rights victims any means of suing foreign investors or holding them accountable. Nor did such treaties tend to impose any substantive human rights obligations on foreign investors or reference any existing obligations (e.g. the United Nations (UN) Global Compact, the Organisation for Economic Co-operation and Development (OECD) commitments or other standards). There is growing debate as to the circumstances where arbitrators could consider the human rights record of a foreign investor in the context of investment treaty arbitrations and what impact such records may have upon a tribunal's jurisdiction or its handling of the merits of investment treaty disputes.[7]

Similarly, and of particular relevance to this chapter, disputes are arising where some action by a State is alleged to breach an investment treaty, yet the State insists that the impugned measure was inspired by (or perhaps demanded by) human rights law obligations. For example, an earlier arbitration against the Republic of South Africa appeared likely to raise sensitive human rights law considerations.[8] In the claim brought by European mining interests, the claimants alleged that elements of South Africa's Black Economic Empowerment programme imposed burdens on foreign investors in the South African mining sector, leading to breach of South

[7] For discussion see L. Peterson, *Human Rights and Bilateral Investment Treaties: Mapping the Role of Human Rights Law within Investor-State Arbitration*, Vol. 3 of Investing in Human Rights series (Montreal: International Centre for Human Rights and Democratic Development, 2009).

[8] *Piero Foresti, Laura de Carli and others* v. *Republic of South Africa* (ICSID Case No. ARB (AF)/07/1; for background on this case, see L. Peterson and A. Beattie, 'Italian mining groups challenge Pretoria over BEE', *Financial Times*, 9 March 2007; L. Peterson, *South Africa's Bilateral Investment Treaties: Implications for Development and Human Rights*, Friedrich Ebert Stiftung Occasional Papers Series, No. 26, November 2006; M. Coleman and K. Williams, 'South Africa's Bilateral Investment Treaties, Black Economic Empowerment and Mining: A Fragmented Meeting?', *Business Law International*, Vol. 9, No. 1 (2008), pp. 56–94.

Africa's investment treaty obligations. The claim was discontinued before arbitrators were obliged to deal with the contentious human rights dimensions of the case.[9]

While investment treaties are typically silent with respect to human rights considerations, it is widely acknowledged that some human rights law (domestic and/or international) may be part of the governing law of investment treaty arbitrations. For example, treaty or arbitration rules may expressly provide that disputes be resolved in accordance with the investment treaty *and relevant principles of international law.*[10] Likewise, the Vienna Convention on the Law of Treaties and the customary international legal rules of treaty interpretation also provide certain gateways through which human rights law may be deemed relevant or applicable in investment treaty arbitrations.[11]

What this means in practice is that arbitrators interpreting and applying a State's investment treaty obligations to foreign investors may take into account the State's parallel human rights law obligations to its own citizens. Of course, this may raise more questions than it answers, insofar as it paves the way for arbitrators to determine how these different legal obligations shall be reconciled. In extreme cases, this task may be easy. For instance, a foreign investor alleging mistreatment of an investment which is itself premised upon the use of slave labour could find that the host State's *jus cogens* human rights obligations oblige it to bring a halt to such business activities. However, in other cases where this very narrow group of *jus cogens* human rights is not implicated, much more complex problems may arise. One area where there has been particular speculation as to the relationship of investment treaties and human rights law is the water utilities sector.[12]

9 See 'South African Mining Arbitration Ends with a Whimper, as Terms of Discontinuance Are Set Down in a Award', *Investment Arbitration Reporter*, 5 August 2010, www.iareporter.com/articles/20100818_6.

10 For an early discussion of this point, see L. Peterson and K. Gray, 'International Human Rights in Bilateral Investment Treaties and in Investment Treaty Arbitration', International Institute for Sustainable Development, Briefing Paper 2003.

11 A. Aaken, 'Fragmentation of International Law: The Case of International Investment Protection', *Finnish Yearbook of International Law*, Vol. 22 (2008), pp. 91–130.

12 M. Solanes and A. Jouravlev, *Revisiting Privatisation, Foreign Investment, Arbitration and Water*, UN Economic Commission for Latin America and the Caribbean (CEPAL) briefing paper, November 2007. Note that investment disputes related to bulk freshwater are not included within the scope of this chapter. For further information on this topic see E. Brown Weiss, 'Water Transfers and International Trade Law', in E. Brown Weiss, L. Boisson de Chazournes and N. Bernasconi-Osterwalder (eds.), *Freshwater and International Economic Law* (Oxford: Oxford University Press, 2005), pp. 61–89.

## 3 WATER UTILITY ARBITRATIONS AND THE RIGHT TO WATER

A surprising number of arbitration claims lodged under investment treaties have arisen out of disputes over water services concessions. At least a dozen known claims have been documented, and other similar claims may have been filed without public disclosure.[13] Five of the most prominent cases are profiled below. As will be seen, there appears to be a growing trend, whereby States are adverting to their obligations under human rights law in the course of defending such claims. In particular, there have been efforts by respondent governments, as well as by certain outside actors (so-called amicus curiae), to articulate increasingly sophisticated arguments as to the relevance and applicability of human rights law to these investment treaty arbitrations. However, as we note below, the willingness of arbitrators to grapple at length with such arguments has been limited.

### 3.1 Aguas del Tunari *v.* Bolivia

While not the first investment treaty claim launched by a water services corporation against a government, the *Aguas del Tunari* v. *Bolivia* arbitration was notable for garnering international headlines.[14] The arbitration was launched in response to a well-publicised 'water war' in Cochabamba, Bolivia. Aguas del Tunari, a subsidiary of the US conglomerate Bechtel, inked a deal

[13] *Compañía de Aguas del Aconquija S.A. and Vivendi Universal* v. *Argentine Republic* (ICSID Case No. ARB/97/3); *Aguas Provinciales de Santa Fe, S.A., Suez, Sociedad General de Aguas de Barcelona, S.A. and Interagua Servicios Integrales de Agua, S.A.* v. *Argentine Republic* (ICSID Case No. ARB/03/17); *Aguas Cordobesas, S.A., Suez, and Sociedad General de Aguas de Barcelona, S.A.* v. *Argentine Republic* (ICSID Case No. ARB/03/18); *Aguas Argentinas, S.A., Suez, Sociedad General de Aguas de Barcelona, S.A. and Vivendi Universal, S.A.* v. *Argentine Republic* (ICSID Case No. ARB/03/19); *Azurix Corp.* v. *Argentine Republic* (ICSID Case No. ARB/01/12); *Aguas del Tunari S.A.* v. *Republic of Bolivia* (ICSID Case No. ARB/02/3); *Azurix Corp.* v. *Argentine Republic* (ICSID Case No. ARB/03/30); *SAUR International* v. *Argentine Republic* (ICSID Case No. ARB/04/4); *Anglian Water Group* v. *Argentine Republic*, UNCITRAL arbitration filed in 2003; *Biwater Gauff (Tanzania) Ltd.* v. *United Republic of Tanzania* (ICSID Case No. ARB/05/22); Impregilo S.p.A. v. Argentine Republic (ICSID Case No. ARB/07/17); *Urbaser S.A. and Consorcio de Aguas Bilbao Biskaia, Bilbao Biskaia Ur Partzuergoa* v. *Argentine Republic* (ICSID Case No. ARB/07/26. For further discussion of some of these cases, see L. Boisson de Chazournes, 'Water and Economics: Trends in Dispute Settlement Procedures and Practice', in E. Brown Weiss, L. Boisson de Chazournes and N. Bernasconi-Osterwalder (eds.), *Freshwater and International Economic Law* (Oxford: Oxford University Press, 2005), pp. 333–365.

[14] *Aguas del Tunari S.A.* v. *Republic of Bolivia* (ICSID Case No. ARB/02/3); For press coverage, see J. Forero, 'Who Will Bring Water to the Bolivian Poor?', *The New York Times*, 15 December 2005; and W. Finnegan, 'Letter from Bolivia: Leasing the Rain', *The New Yorker*, 8 April 2002.

with the municipality of Cochabamba in September 1999.[15] However, public anger soon erupted over price hikes imposed upon water customers. After public demonstrations led to the imposition of martial law, company officials fled the country due to security concerns.[16] Aguas del Tunari's contract was ultimately cancelled, leading to an arbitration claim pursuant to the Netherlands-Bolivia bilateral investment treaty.

Notably, a group of non-governmental organisations, representing various Bolivian citizens and other concerned parties, petitioned the tribunal in 2002 to open its hearings to the public and to release arbitral documents.[17] In an accompanying legal petition, the petitioners made clear their concerns about the impact of the case upon the 'right to affordable and equitable access to water'.[18] In a reply letter, the arbitrators informed the petitioners that they lacked the power to open the hearings or release documents related to the case, unless the parties to the arbitration consented to such requests.[19] Moreover, at that juncture, the unanimous support of the parties was not forthcoming.

The tribunal also noted that it did not consider there to be a need, at the present time, for it to 'call witnesses or seek supplementary non-party submissions' at the jurisdictional phase. More cryptically, the tribunal noted that it would not prejudge its authority to 'receive information from non-parties on its own initiative'. The tribunal ended its letter by remarking upon the seemingly more generous authority granted to arbitrators under another investment treaty, which explicitly contemplates *amicus curiae* submissions. The tribunal's letter was interpreted by the petitioners as indicating that the tribunal lacked the authority to accept *amicus curiae* briefs from outside parties.[20] (However, in other cases, including the *Biwater* v. *Tanzania* and the *Aguas Argentinas* cases discussed below, tribunals have held that they have jurisdiction to entertain *amicus curiae* briefs; see separate discussions below.)

Ultimately, the tribunal's ambiguity as to whether it had the authority to admit *amicus curiae* briefs was never clarified by the arbitrators; the *Aguas del*

[15] Ibid. [16] Ibid.

[17] See Petition of La Coordinadora para La Defensa Del Agua y Vida, et. al., in *Aguas del Tunari* v. *Republic of Bolivia*, ICSID Case No. ARB/02/3, 29 August 2002, www.italaw.com/documents/Aguaaboliviapetition.pdf.

[18] Ibid., at paras. 18–28.

[19] See Letter from the President of the Tribunal in *Aguas del Tunari* v. *Republic of Bolivia*, 29 January 2003, www.italaw.com/documents/Aguas-BoliviaResponse.pdf.

[20] See 'Secretive World Bank Tribunal bans Public and the Media', press release of the Centre for International Environmental Law, 12 February 2003.

*Tunari* claim was settled in early 2006, shortly after a decision on jurisdiction was rendered in the case.[21] The decision did not address the merits of the dispute and, as such, did not touch upon investor responsibilities or any obligations the government might have with respect to the right to water. Little is known about the reasons why the investor chose to withdraw the claim in return for a nominal payment (less than USD 1). However, the claim had brought a torrent of negative publicity for the investor. Moreover, it remained for arbitrators to assess to what extent the company may have been the author of its own misfortune (as discussed below, the corporate failings of the investor have loomed large in another arbitration, *Biwater* v. *Tanzania*).

### 3.2 Aguas del Aconquija *v.* Argentina

While the *Aguas del Tunari* arbitration involving Bolivia grabbed worldwide headlines, the first known case where a foreign water company filed a claim against a government for breach of an investment treaty was the *Aguas del Aconquija and Vivendi Universal* v. *Argentina* dispute. The claim arose out of a privatised water concession operated by the claimants in the Tucumán province of Argentina. After complaining of various forms of interference by regulatory authorities, the claimants turned to international arbitration.

A panel convened to hear allegations that Argentina had breached the France-Argentina bilateral investment treaty held that it had jurisdiction over the dispute but determined that the allegations of treaty breach were too closely intertwined with allegations of contract breach.[22] Given that the relevant contract provided for the exclusive jurisdiction of the Argentine courts, the arbitrators held that the dispute should be heard there.[23] The claimants challenged this arbitration ruling and succeeded in having the decision annulled. In essence, a so-called ad hoc annulment committee at the ICSID ruled that the first tribunal should have examined the treaty breaches in their own right, irrespective of the contract's specifying a forum for resolution of contract-based claims.[24]

Following this holding, the claimants filed a second arbitration claim. In August of 2007, a new arbitration panel ruled that Argentina was liable

[21] Decision on Jurisdiction, 21 October 2005.

[22] *Compañía de Aguas del Aconquija S.A. and Vivendi Universal* v. *Argentine Republic* (ICSID Case No. ARB/97/3), Award of 21 November 2000.

[23] Ibid.

[24] Decision on Annulment, 3 July 2002. For further discussion, see S. Pannatier and O. Ducrey, in E. Brown Weiss, L. Boisson de Chazournes and N. Bernasconi-Osterwalder (eds.), *Freshwater and International Economic Law* (Oxford: Oxford University Press, 2005), pp. 289–302.

for breaches of the investment treaty and ordered the government to pay some USD 105 million in compensation plus substantial interest.[25] In its award, the tribunal acknowledged that the thirty-year concession had proven controversial and that a new provincial government came to power with the goal of cancelling or renegotiating the contract. However, the arbitrators held that the new provincial administration had engaged in improper and abusive treatment of the concession owners.

In defence of the case, he Argentine Republic appears to have raised some limited arguments as to its obligations with respect to the right to water, in an effort to justify the actions of the provincial authorities.[26] These arguments drew upon General Comment No. 15 of the UN Committee on Economic, Social and Cultural Rights[27] and emphasised Argentina's obligations to regulate so as to ensure citizen access to safe and reliable water.

However, these arguments were not addressed at any length by the tribunal. Rather, the tribunal appeared convinced that the actions of the provincial authorities (for which the Argentine Republic bore international responsibility) had been undertaken improperly and were not legitimate, good faith measures. Indeed, the tribunal pointed to instances where provincial officials had fanned public concern about water quality, without any scientific basis for so doing. In light of the tribunal's dim view of the motives and behaviour of the provincial authorities, it appears that they did not seriously entertain the argument that government officials were acting with certain human rights obligations in mind. This serves as an important reminder – even if not an explicit one – that arbitrators will peer behind the purposes or pretexts advanced by governments in this context, in order to assess whether measures are, in fact, legitimate, *bona fide* human rights measures.

### 3.3 Azurix *v.* Argentina

In 2006, the Argentine government was held liable for breach of the US-Argentina bilateral investment treaty in a dispute with the US water services company Azurix.[28] The Azurix case arose out of a thirty-year concession to operate a water utility in the province of Buenos Aires.

[25] Award of 20 August 2007, www.italaw.com/documents/VivendiAwardEnglish.pdf.

[26] Author interview with knowledgeable source, 5 April 2009.

[27] Committee on Economic, Social and Cultural Rights, *General Comment No. 15, The Right to Water* (Twenty-ninth session, 2002), UN Doc. E/C.12/2002/11 (2003).

[28] *Azurix Corp.* v. *Argentine Republic* (ICSID Case No. ARB/01/12), Award of 14 July 2006; Note that a second unrelated (and still pending) claim was filed by Azurix against Argentina in 2003 at the ICSID: *Azurix Corp.* v. *Argentine Republic* (ICSID Case No. ARB/03/30).

Azurix obtained the concession in 1999 and was at loggerheads with provincial authorities over the setting of tariffs and other performance issues.[29] Ultimately, arbitrators found fault with the posture of local regulators towards the foreign concession operator.[30] A contemporaneous summary of the 2006 award by the present author summarised several of the tribunal's key findings:

> Controversy erupted in April of 2000 when an algae outbreak led provincial health authorities to warn customers that they should boil their tap water. Azurix alleged that provincial authorities bore responsibility for failing to complete work on equipment and systems which were critical to algae removal. The company further accused the government of inciting public panic and encouraging consumers to refuse to pay their water bills following the incident. Ultimately, the tribunal presiding over the BIT dispute held that the province had shown 'a total disregard for their own contribution to the algae crisis and a readiness to blame the Concessionaire for situations that were caused by years of disinvestment and to use the incident politically . . . .' The tribunal added that the provincial authorities bore a responsibility to protect the public health, but in this instance they had 'contributed to the crisis rather than assisted (sic) in solving it'.[31]

The arbitrators identified a series of instances where the local authorities had acted unreasonably or engaged in political meddling with respect to the concession. In turn, these episodes gave rise to a finding that the Argentine Republic had failed to provide 'fair and equitable treatment'[32] and 'full protection and security' to the investors.[33]

On the other hand, the arbitrators gave some credence to the arguments put forward by Argentina to the effect that the US investor had bid opportunistically for the concession – with the longer-term goal of renegotiating the contract terms. Indeed, the arbitrators held that no 'well-informed investor' would have bid as much as Azurix did for the concession, and the tribunal declined to compensate the investor for having wildly overbid at the outset of the project.[34] Thus, arbitrators awarded only a fraction (USD 60 million) of the USD 438 million bid by Azurix for the concession. Added to this was approximately USD 105 million in compensation for capital investments made by Azurix over the life of the project.

[29] Ibid. [30] Ibid.

[31] L. Peterson, 'Azurix Wins Claim against Argentina, Recoups a Portion of Its Sunk Costs', *Investment Treaty News*, 26 July 2006.

[32] *Azurix Corp* v. *Republic of Argentina*, Award, paras. 358–378, in particular para. 377.

[33] Ibid., paras. 406–408. [34] Ibid., para. 426.

The *Azurix* award did not touch upon the right to water, and it is unclear if Argentina made arguments based on human rights law in the context of this case. It is known that Argentina's written arguments in the case were filed in 2004 –some time before the arguments discussed above in the Aguas del Aconquija case (with Argentina's pleadings on the merits being filed in November 2005 and May 2006 in that latter case). While the latter case saw some limited human rights argumentation by Argentina, it is unclear if the Republic was making such arguments as early as 2004 when the Azurix case was being briefed. Although Argentina sought to have the Azurix award overturned, in 2009 an ICSID committee denied this request.[35]

## 3.4 Biwater *v.* Tanzania

Another water-related investment treaty arbitration following on the heels of the others discussed above is the *Biwater* v. *Tanzania case*. Biwater Gauff (Tanzania) (BGT) Ltd filed for arbitration in 2005, alleging that Tanzania had breached the terms of an investment protection treaty with the United Kingdom by terminating a water services concession contract and forcibly deporting key company officials.

In summarising the facts of the case, the arbitral tribunal observed that both sides experienced difficulties in performing their contractual obligations. The tribunal conceded that BGT's subsidiary, City Water, did make certain improvements to the dilapidated water and sewage infrastructure of Dar es Salaam. However, arbitrators also held that the local entity made a poorly structured bid, failed to meet its subsequent obligations (including the deployment of modern customer billing software) and found itself in financial troubles 'at a very early stage' of the concession life.[36] Indeed, the Biwater case is notable for the degree to which the behaviour of the investor and the conduct of the investments would determine the outcome of the arbitration. In this respect, the case follows in the line of the *Azurix* v. *Argentina* case, where the investor was not compensated for losses arising out of its own ill-advised business decisions (e.g. wildly overbidding for the concession and hoping to recoup investments through price renegotiations with the government).

Of particular note, Tanzania argued in its defence that the government should enjoy a certain measure of appreciation – i.e. deference – with respect

[35] *Azurix Corp* v. *Republic of Argentina*, 1 September 2009.

[36] This paragraph draws from reporting that originally appeared in *Investment Arbitration Reporter*, Vol. 1, No. 6, 28 July 2008.

to its handling of the concession.[37] The government argued during the ICSID arbitration that a threatened collapse of the local water services company could have jeopardised water and sewerage delivery, with obviously deleterious effects upon the health and welfare of local citizens.[38]

The detailed legal arguments of Tanzania have never been published. However, the arbitral tribunal summarised one key Tanzanian argument thus: 'water and sanitation services are vitally important, and the Republic has more than a right to protect such services in case of a crisis: it has a moral and *perhaps even a legal obligation* to do so' (emphasis added).[39] From this passage, it seems that Tanzania demurred with respect to whether it operated under an international human rights law obligation to ensure the sanctity of the local water and sewerage service. As such, the tribunal's own analysis does not delve into this question.

Despite an earlier acknowledgement in a February 2007 procedural order issued by the tribunal as to the potential impact of the case upon human rights, the tribunal's 2008 award adverts to human rights considerations only obliquely when it acknowledges that it weighed arguments raised by certain non-governmental organisations (and which included human right arguments). In this vein, the tribunal acknowledged – without elaboration – that, in applying the 'fair and equitable treatment' standard of the UK-Tanzania treaty, the tribunal

> has also taken into account the submissions of the [p]etitioners, as summarised earlier, which emphasise countervailing factors such as the responsibility of foreign investors, both in terms of prior due diligence as well as subsequent conduct; the limit to legitimate expectations in circumstances where an investor itself takes on risks in entering a particular investment environment; and the relevance of the parties' respective rights and obligations as set out in any relevant investment agreement (here the Lease Contract).[40]

In the *amicus curiae* petition, the interveners argued for the relevance of human rights considerations, arguing that the right to water is 'so fundamental to developing countries' that it 'should be understood to increase the standards of responsibilities of investors in the water sector'.[41]

[37] *Biwater Gauff (Tanzania) Ltd.* v. *United Republic of Tanzania* (ICSID Case No. ARB/05/22), Award of 24 July 2008, para. 434.

[38] Ibid., paras. 434–436. [39] Ibid., para 434. [40] Ibid., para. 601.

[41] *Biwater Gauff (Tanzania) Limited and United Republic of Tanzania*, Case No. ARB/05/22, *Amicus curiae* submission of LEAT, LHRC, TGNP, CIEL and IISD, 26 March 2007, para. 11; the present author was a consultant to the IISD in the relevant time period, working on other

Indeed more pivotal for the arbitrators than obligations under human rights law of the host State were the behaviour and conduct of the investor.[42] Indeed, arbitrators held that the mismanagement of the concession by BGT had led to a situation where the investment was on the verge of collapse by the time that Tanzania took certain measures that were held to have breached the treaty. In effect, the overstepping by Tanzania of its treaty obligations occurred at a juncture where the fate of the project had been sealed. As such, a majority of the tribunal ruled that no damages could be awarded for the treaty breaches in this case. Viewed in the context of other water utility arbitrations, the *Biwater* case follows the *Azurix* case in holding that investor missteps were material considerations. In the *Azurix* case, this meant that the investor could not claim for certain losses; whereas in the *Biwater* case, these missteps were viewed as having deprived the investment of all of its value.

Also of relevance to the right to water, the question of access to information related to the case was a matter of some contention in the *Biwater* case. In 2006, the tribunal issued a procedural order which introduced heightened confidentiality requirements upon the two parties, following complaints from Biwater that the Tanzanian side was disclosing information about the case, including certain documents.[43] In this procedural order, the arbitrators opined that 'the prosecution of a dispute in the media or in other public fora, or the uneven reporting and disclosure of documents or other parts of the record in parallel with a pending arbitration may aggravate or exacerbate the dispute and may impact upon the integrity of the procedure'.[44] (The speculation that release of arbitral materials would jeopardise the integrity of the proceedings is seemingly belied by the ever-growing number of cases where parties agree to release their legal pleadings; rather, it seems that the tribunal should have drawn a distinction between mere disclosure of legal materials, and unhelpful conduct by the parties themselves in making public comments on the case or engaging in other antagonistic behaviour.)

While the arbitrators acknowledged that there was no explicit presumption of confidentiality in the ICSID rules, they took the view that there was 'a sufficient risk of harm or prejudice, as well as aggravation',[45] if information about the case continued to leak out while it was pending. Consequently,

research projects, but was not a member of the team working on the amicus curiae intervention.

42 See 'In an Unusual Outcome, Tanzania Held to Have Violated Treaty Protections, but No Damages Flow to UK Water Company', Investment Arbitration Reporter, 28 July 2008, www.iareporter.com/articles/20091229_10.

43 Procedural Order No. 3, 29 Sept 29 2006. 44 Ibid., para 136. 45 Ibid., para 146.

the tribunal ordered restrictions on disclosure of certain categories of documents and information while the case was pending.

### 3.5 Suez, AgBar and Vivendi *v.* Argentine Republic

In 2003, Suez, AgBar and Vivendi turned to arbitration alleging that Argentina's treatment of a Buenos Aires water concession breached the terms of the French and Spanish bilateral investment treaties.[46] The claimants, along with local investors, had entered into a thirty-year concession to operate the municipal water and sewage services for the city of Buenos Aires.[47] However, various disputes arose as to contractual performance and water quality and supply.[48] Relations fractured permanently with the onset of a major financial crisis in the early part of the twenty-first century. In their ICSID arbitration claim, the claimants alleged that Argentina's freezing of utility prices was contrary to contracts and relevant bilateral investment treaties. Argentina, for its part, accused the consortium of mismanaging the concession and of failing to recognise the need for emergency measures to be taken to rein in the cost of public services during the financial crisis.

Although the legal arguments in such investor-State arbitrations are not made public as a matter of course, they have been seen by the author as part of a separate research exercise.[49] Of particular note, Argentina's legal arguments raised, for the first (known) time, extensive discussion of its own human rights law obligations. Several specific arguments were raised by Argentina. First, lawyers for the government contended that Argentina's human rights law obligations should form part of the applicable law of the arbitration and that arbitrators should not interpret BIT obligations in a vacuum divorced from other international law obligations. Second, Argentina argued that the allegedly expropriatory measures were, in fact, legitimate and bona fide measures taken in pursuit of its 'overriding responsibility to ensure the availability of water to all members of society'.[50] Third, Argentina argued that the

46 *Aguas Argentinas, S.A., Suez, Sociedad General de Aguas de Barcelona, S.A. and Vivendi Universal, S.A.* v. *Argentine Republic* (Case No. ARB/03/19); (Note that the local concessionaire, Aguas Argentinas, withdrew as a claimant at a later juncture in the case; however, the foreign investors have continued with their own claims).

47 Ibid.

48 This discussion of the Aguas Argentina case draws upon L. Peterson, *Human Rights and Bilateral Investment Treaties*.

49 See summary of them in ibid.

50 Rejoinder of the Argentine Republic in ICSID Case No. ARB/03/19, August 17, 2007, para. 1003–1005,

treaty obligation to provide fair and equitable treatment needs to be interpreted in a manner that contemplates the broader context, including the major financial crisis of 2002 which exacerbated relations between the foreign investors and the host government (and threatened the well-being of Argentine citizens), as well relevant international law obligations, such as the right to water.[51] Fourth, Argentina also contended that any breaches of the investment treaty could be justified given the conditions of 'necessity' occasioned by the dramatic financial crisis which buffeted the country earlier this decade. In this vein, Argentina argued that the emergency situation obliged Argentina to act so in furtherance of the rights to life, health and sanitation embodied in various legal treaties including the Covenant on Economic, Social and Cultural Rights and the Convention on the Elimination of All Forms of Discrimination Against Women.[52]

For their part, the claimants contested the relevance and persuasiveness of such arguments. In particular, they insisted that Argentina could have taken less intrusive measures which would have met the regulatory and policy goals articulated by the Argentine government. For example, a system of subsidies for poor consumers could have been introduced, rather than freezing utility prices for all consumers – even while the Argentine Peso collapsed relative to the US dollar and placed foreign investors (with foreign-denominated debts) in a perilous financial situation.

Given the extent to which Argentina articulated human rights law arguments in the case, it seemed likely that the arbitrators would engage with such issues – even if it remained unclear whether such arguments will suffice to absolve Argentina for any alleged breaches of the relevant investment treaties. Indeed, governments raising human rights law arguments clearly invite arbitrators to inquire into the nature of these human rights obligations, the concrete demands of these obligations upon governments and whether such demands lie behind the measures which are under the scrutiny of the arbitration tribunal. Therein lies the Catch-22 for governments: arbitrators might rule, in certain circumstances, that governments have failed to live up to their human rights obligations, as well as their obligations to foreign investors.

[51] For more on the human rights arguments raised by Argentina in a series of foreign investor disputes arising out that country's financial crisis, see UNCTAD, *Selected Recent Developments in IIA Arbitration and Human Rights*, IIA Monitor No. 2 (United Nations: New York and Geneva, 2009). (Note that this UN report was based on a draft prepared by the author of the present paper).

[52] Counter-Memorial of the Argentine Republic, ICSID Case No. ARB/03/19), paras 1011–1025 and 1059–1061.

In July of 2010, arbitrators issued a Decision on Liability, which held Argentina liable for breaching the protections of the France-Argentina and Spain-Argentina bilateral investment treaties.[53] In particular, arbitrators held that Argentina had failed to accord 'fair and equitable treatment' as demanded by the treaty. The tribunal concluded that Argentine authorities had acted as to thwart the legitimate expectations of the investors to periodic revision of water tariffs in line with earlier contractual and legal commitments.

Of most note, the tribunal gave short shrift to Argentina's efforts to justify its treatment of the foreign investors by reference to the country's human rights law obligations. The tribunal took the position that Argentina's obligations under the BIT and under human rights law were 'not inconsistent, contradictory, or mutually exclusive'.[54] Hence, Argentina was obliged to respect both the terms of the BIT and human rights law.

This analysis seems to be premised on a specific reading on the part of the tribunal of the right to water, the right to health and other human rights cited by Argentina in its pleadings. However, the tribunal does not offer any meaningful description or analysis of these human rights law obligations in its written decision. Rather, the tribunal skips straight to its conclusion that the human rights obligations – at least on the tribunal's undisclosed reading of them – do not clash with Argentina's investment treaty obligation.

As a practical matter, one can appreciate the tribunal's reluctance to engage in a potentially contentious analysis of the human right to water. At the same time, the tribunal seems to beg the question by concluding that there is no conflict between that unexamined right on the one hand and Argentina's BIT obligations on the other.

At a later juncture in its award, the tribunal expresses the view that Argentina could have ensured water and sewage service for the poor – by means of a carefully tailored social tariff – while respecting its legal obligations *vis-à-vis* the foreign investors in the concession. However, the tribunal again declined to engage in the elementary task of explaining what were Argentina's human rights law obligations and to clarify what concrete demands these obligations placed upon the Argentine State.

[53] This analysis of the arbitral ruling draws upon the earlier reporting of *Investment Arbitration Reporter*.

[54] *Suez, Sociedad General de Aguas de Barcelona S.A., and InterAgua Servicios Integrales del Agua S.A.* v. Argentine Republic (ICSID Case No. ARB/03/17), Decision on Liability of 30 July 2010, para. 240.

## 4 CONCLUSION

Apart from the water cases discussed above, there are a string of other investor-State arbitrations that arise out of water services investments. Moreover, there may be other such cases which are not a matter of public record.

What is clear is that parties to these arbitrations are raising increasingly sophisticated arguments about two issues: first, the responsibilities of foreign investors and, second, the relevance and applicability of human rights law considerations, including in relation to the right to water. As noted above, several cases have hinged, at least in part, upon the foreign investor's conduct and management of its investment. Meanwhile, with respect to the human rights law obligations of governments, there has been increasing attention devoted to this topic in current arbitration proceedings. Indeed, in a matter of several years – from the filings by Argentina in the Vivendi case to the Republic's filings in the Aguas Argentina case – some governments have become much more expansive in their treatment of such issues.

However, such legal arguments are not always a matter of public record. The very existence of some arbitrations is confidential. Moreover, even where cases are a matter of public record, the pleadings and proceedings may not be open to public scrutiny. On occasion, journalists or researchers have investigated certain cases and helped to reveal more details of the human rights law arguments being raised. However, in the absence of such efforts, much information may remain 'below the radar'. It should also be recalled that outside actors, such as advocacy groups, are seeking to present legal arguments through *amicus curiae* briefs, and in several cases, arbitrators have acknowledged that they have the power to admit such briefs and to consider their relevance. However, the capacity of outside actors to present relevant arguments that are not redundant or inapposite will be limited where the arbitration proceedings are conducted in-camera.

Nevertheless, given that governments (and outside actors) are raising human rights law arguments in a more sophisticated fashion, the scene is set for arbitrators to make holdings which address the relationship of foreign investment law and human rights law. In turn, this is likely to spur further scrutiny of the capacity of arbitral tribunals to engage with such issues and the legitimacy of their pronouncing upon such important questions.[55] In the Decision on Liability in the Aguas Argentinas dispute, the arbitrators appear to have harboured certain views as to the concrete demands of human rights law obligations, but they declined to elaborate on these views in their ruling. Instead, the arbitrators skipped forward to a conclusion that there was no clash

[55] On this point, see Aaken, 'Fragmentation of International Law'.

or inconsistency between those human rights law obligations and the parallel obligations owed to foreign investors.

In the future, arbitrators may show a similar reticence with respect to laying bare their reading of human rights law obligations. Where human rights arguments appear to the arbitrators as disingenuous or inapposite, one can appreciate the reluctance of arbitrators to engage in the thankless task of expressing views as to the precise reading to be given to the cited human rights law obligations. However, in cases where the human rights arguments appear more bona fide, arbitrators may need to grasp the nettle.

Of course, it is a fact that most investment treaties are disturbingly silent with respect to how the treaty terms should be squared and reconciled with other international law norms. Left to their own devices, arbitrators will surely develop tests – or draw upon ones used in other contexts – in an effort to grapple with these vexing challenges. More generally, there is some prospect of governments becoming more attentive to such issues during the drafting of future investment treaties.

**Editors' Note**

Despite the passage of a few years since the writing of this chapter, its main findings and key predictions on arbitrator reticence and treaty developments remain accurate. In the major subsequent case raising the human right to water, *SAUR International SA* v. *Argentine Republic*, ICSID Case No ARB/04/4 (2012), the tribunal arrived at a similar decision to that in *Suez* (2010). In the only other major case on the human right to water, *Urbaser v Argentina* ICSID Case No. ARB/07/26 (Award, 8 December 2016), the tribunal accepted jurisdiction for a novel counterclaim – that the investor carried human rights responsibilities. However, the tribunal ultimately dismissed the claim as such investor responsibilities did not extend to the positive human rights obligations to 'provide' water services, the issue at hand.[56] The tribunal recognised that it should not only take into consideration the human right to water, but that it also must equally take into account the rights granted to foreign investors – and found for the investor after this balancing exercise. Peterson's prediction of some inclusion of human rights in future treaties is partly correct. For example, the Canada–EU Comprehensive Economic and Trade Agreement (CETA) permits a State to deny benefits to an investor if it is seeking to protect human rights (Annex 8-E).[57]

[56] See Guntrip, '*Urbaser v Argentina*: The Origins of a Host State Human Rights Counterclaim in ICSID Arbitration?', *EJIL:Talk!* 10 February 2017; J. Hepburn, 'Analysis: Arbitrators in *Urbaser v Argentina* water dispute deviate from *Impregilo* Award on Necessity and Damage', *Investment Arbitration Reporter*, 12 January 2017.

[57] See discussion in T. Meshel, 'Human Rights in Investor-State Arbitration: The Human Right to Water and Beyond', *Journal of International Dispute Settlement*, Vol. 6 (2015), pp. 207–307, at 300–1.

# IV

# Rural Water Reform

17

# A Poor Choice? Public Policy, Social Choice and the Right to Water

ROBERT A. HOPE*

## 1 INTRODUCTION

The global drive to increase domestic water access recognises the central role water supply plays in human development. Water policy norms reflect and share this vision shaped by a rationale of high returns, positive externalities, improved equity and welfare gains from a sufficient and safe water supply, particularly for women and children.[1] Water supply in rural areas is of particular concern, as global figures indicate 79 per cent of people using unimproved sources and 93 per cent of people using surface water live in rural areas.[2] Over two fifths of rural Africans are without access to improved water services, a net increase of more than 25 million people between 1990 and 2015.[3] It is estimated a third of handpumps are not working at one time in rural Africa, contributing to over 40 billion hours per year spent collecting water, mainly by women and children, linked to 350 million missed school days and 1.5 million deaths of children under five years old due to

* School of Geography and the Environment, University of Oxford, United Kingdom.

[1] *Human Development Report 2006 – Beyond Scarcity: Power, Poverty and the Global Water Crisis* (New York: United Nations Development Programme (UNDP), 2006); J. S. Wright, S. Gundry and R. Conroy, 'Household Drinking Water in Developing Countries: A Systematic Review of Microbiological Contamination between Source and Point-of-use', *Tropical Medicine and International Health*, Vol. 9, No. 1 (2004), pp. 106–117; G. Hutton and L. Haller, *Evaluation of the Costs and Benefits of Water and Sanitation Improvements at the Global Level* (Geneva: WHO, 2004). A. Ahuja, M. Kremer, and A.P. Zwane, 'Providing Safe Water: Evidence from Randomized Evaluations', *Annual Review of Resource Economics* Vol. 2 (2010), pp. 237–256.

[2] Improved water services are defined by WHO as: (a) piped water into dwelling, plot or yard; (b) public tap/standpipe; (c) tubewell/borewell; (d) protected dug well; (e) protected spring; or (f) rainwater collection. See *Progress on Sanitation and Drinking Water: Focus on Sanitation* (Geneva: WHO and UNICEF, 2015), p. 9.

[3] Ibid., p. 7.

unsafe water and sanitation facilities.[4] Achieving sustained delivery of acceptable, safe, reliable, sufficient and affordable rural water supply services has been an enduring challenge in developing countries that has led to a policy shift from a largely technocratic supply-orientated approach to one in which user demand has become a guiding policy principle for shaping the design and delivery of water services.[5] The urgency to find more effective and sustainable water services policy is heightened by predictions of more frequent and intense climatic extremes and the global projected costs of achieving the Sustainable Development Goal of safely managed water and sanitation services in rural areas of USD 32.0 billion per year (range: USD 21.4 to USD 43.6 billion per year).[6]

Uneven progress in global water access coverage has generated significant policy debate and interest in the international human right to water, which entitles everyone to sufficient, safe, acceptable, physically accessible and affordable water for personal and domestic uses. In 2002, the United Nations (UN) Committee on Economic, Social and Cultural Rights (CESCR) adopted its General Comment No. 15, which explicitly recognises an international human right to water.[7] The international human right to water diverges from a demand-responsive approach, as a moral philosophy that promotes universal, individual and equal (at least, non-discriminatory) rights above the primacy of consumer choice. General Comment No. 15 departs from the economic principle of a demand-led approach by treating water as a social and cultural good (and not primarily as an economic good) while reaffirming the right of individuals and groups, particularly women,

[4] R. A. Hope, T. Foster, A. Money and M. Rouse, 'Harnessing Mobile Communications Innovations for Water Security', *Global Policy*, Vol. 3, No. 4 (2012), pp. 433–442, November 2012.

[5] S. Arlosoroff, D. Tschannerl, D. Grey, W. Journey, A. Karp, O. Langeneffer and R. Roche, *Community Water Supply – The Handpump Option* (Washington, DC: World Bank, 1987). See also, World Bank, 'The Demand for Water in Rural Areas: Determinants and Policy Implications', *The World Bank Research Observer*, Vol. 8, No. 1 (1993), pp. 47–70. D. Narayan, *The Contribution of People's Participation: Evidence from 121 Rural Water Supply Projects*, Environmentally Sustainable Development Occasional Paper Series No. 1 (Washington, DC: World Bank, 1995), and J. Sara and T. Katz, *Making Rural Water Supply Sustainable – Report on the Impact of Project Rules* (Washington DC: UNDP-World Bank Water and Sanitation Programme, 1998).

[6] See 1, and also G. Hutton and M. Varughese (2016), The Costs of Meeting the 2030 Sustainable Development Goal Targets on Drinking Water, Sanitation, and Hygiene. World Bank, Water and Sanitation Program, Technical Paper 103171, pp. 10.

[7] Committee on Economic, Social and Cultural Rights, *General Comment No. 15, The Right to Water* (Twenty-ninth session, 2002), UN Doc. E/C.12/2002/11 (2003).

to participate in decision making as 'an integral part of any policy, programme or strategy concerning water'.[8]

This chapter contributes to the debate within the global water community amongst the alternative visions to progressively realise universal water access. With sub-Saharan Africa lagging behind global progress on improving water services, the enduring question on how to effectively deliver sustainable water services to the poor is caught and fractured between the uneven but considerable gains from over a decade of demand-led initiatives and the rising tide of nations embracing the human right to water. In this context, this chapter examines the extent and nature of progress made under the demand-led era with a view to identifying the role of social choice theory as a conceptual space charting theoretical contestations on the rights and agency of individuals in securing water access. The discussion concludes by offering a conceptual map of individual rights and consumer choices to provide a canvas from which to critically explore the conditions under which water policy norms may work in the public interest. While it is feasible to tease out common theoretical space between individual rights and consumer choices, the extent to which productive policy engagement and improved water access coverage will follow is likely to pivot on the contextual interpretation of the 'progressive realisation' of the human right to water. It is argued that the degree of 'genuine participation' in this process deserves further attention, particularly in establishing a stronger evidential base of the performance of water policy across competing policy design alternatives.

## 2 IDEOLOGICAL SHIFTS IN RURAL WATER POLICY

### 2.1 *The Fall of the Water Planner and the Rise of the Rural Consumer*

Towards the end of the International Drinking Water Supply and Sanitation Decade in the late 1980s, there was growing concern about the failure to achieve sustained rural water supply in developing countries. The winds of change in sub-Saharan Africa saw many newly independent countries use improved water access as a unifying policy instrument to promote political imperatives of development, equality and change with bold promises of universal water access. Therkildsen documents Tanzania's experience with multiple donor efforts to achieve universal basic water access, where the means (technocracy) justified the ends (donor targets) without adequate

[8] Ibid., paras. 11, 16a and 48.

project coordination or meaningful public participation.[9] This approach resulted in a growing sense of frustration and anxiety with a heavy-handed and externally driven, supply-orientated approach to rural water service delivery. Commentators attributed the failure to achieve sustained water services to an overly prescriptive and centralised water planning and engineering approach that did not adequately respond to the priorities of primary water users.[10] For example, Briscoe and de Ferranti estimated that as many as one in four rural water supply points were not working in developing countries in the 1980s and that the construction of new water points was not even keeping pace with the failure of existing ones.[11] This was in the context of an estimated annual investment of USD 4.5 billion per year on improved water supplies in 1988.[12] The time was ripe for an ideological shift. A demand-responsive approach became the new mantra of policy choice in recognition of a wider shift to recognise that 'policy and planning should be built on a better understanding of what improvements in their water services people really want and are willing to pay for'.[13]

### 2.2 *Demanding Times*

A demand-responsive approach reflects microeconomic theory where price and willingness to pay reflect the utility of alternative types and levels of water services.[14] For example, Sara and Katz describe the concept of demand as 'an economic function ... influenced by an individual's budget, the price of the good, the price of other goods, and individual preferences'.[15] As such, an expression of demand is an expression of value. Though not necessarily representative of the broader church of perspectives amongst the group of researchers within the World Bank-led, multi-country rural water demand studies of the 1990s, such a positivist worldview ran into theoretical and methodological traffic. Commentators challenged an overtly deterministic

[9] O. Therkildsen, *Watering White Elephants? Lessons from Donor Funded Planning and Implementation in Tanzania* (Uppsala: Scandinavian Institute of African Studies, 1998).

[10] A. K. Biswas, *From Mar del Plata to Kyoto: An Analysis of Global Water Policy Dialogues* (Third World Centre for Water Management, Mexico, 2003).

[11] J. Briscoe and D. de Ferranti, *Water for Rural Communities: Helping People Help Themselves* (Washington, DC: World Bank, 1988).

[12] E. Kleemeier, 'The Impact of Participation on Sustainability: An Analysis of the Malawi Rural Piped Scheme Program', *World Development*, Vol. 28, No. 5 (2000), pp. 929–944.

[13] See World Bank, 'The Demand for Water in Rural Areas'.

[14] See Briscoe and De Ferranti, *Water for Rural Communities*, World Bank, *The Demand for Water in Rural Areas* (ibid.), and Narayan, *The Contribution of People's Participation*.

[15] Sara and Katz, *Making Rural Water Supply Sustainable*, p. 3.

and reductionist perspective, partly based on the methodological issues of objectively and rigorously collecting nuanced data in an unbiased and legitimate manner. In particular, the concept of 'participation' as a key factor in leading to sustainable water services has been questioned by evidence of perverse welfare outcomes due to 'invisible' power dynamics in socially heterogeneous communities[16] and how 'good' water projects may fail through a more qualified understanding of the nature of participation in decision making to explain variation in project performance.[17] In effect, general and often sweeping assumptions of community homogeneity and non-discriminatory, customary rule are implicated in the justification of devolving power to rural communities, including water supply decision making, notionally 'empowering' communities and distancing the 'State' from responsibility. As Mamdani notes, in post-colonial Africa there is a 'political failure to grasp the specificity of the mode of rule that needs to be democratized … an infatuation with the notion of civil society, a preoccupation that conceals the actual form of power through which rural populations are ruled'.[18] However, the politically neutral, demand-responsive approach prevails and continues to inform the thinking of governments, donors and nongovernmental organisations (NGOs) in many developing countries, including India (see Chapter 19 of this volume).

The concept of a demand-responsive approach promotes the ideology of consumer choice in water services provision. While the State may act as guarantor of water services, this does not restrict service delivery to a homogenous good but offers the opportunity for societal choices to determine variable levels of water service provision.[19] The concept of 'informed choice' is considered critical to a demand-responsive approach and described as the level of service people want with an associated understanding of the implications of their decisions.[20] In this interpretation, choices are informed by three factors: (a) investment and recurrent costs, (b) expected participation in

[16] B. Cooke and U. Kothari, *Participation: The New Tyranny* (London: Zed Books, 2001).

[17] A. I. Khwaja, *Can Good Projects Succeed in Bad Communities?* (Cambridge: Harvard University, MA thesis, 2007).

[18] M. Mamdani, *Citizen and Subject. Contemporary Africa and the Legacy of Late Colonialism* (London: James Currey, 1996), pp. 288–289.

[19] J. Thompson, I. T Porras, J. Tumwine, M. Mujwahuzi, M. Katui-Katua, N. Johnstone and L. Wood, *Drawers of Water II: 30 Years of Change in Domestic Water Use and Environmental Health in East Africa* (London: International Institute for Environment and Development, 2001).

[20] Sara and Katz, *Making Rural Water Supply Sustainable*.

planning and implementation, and (c) responsibility for operation and maintenance of the water system.

Water supply design attributes can shape policy alternatives, but who is best placed to shape user choices? If choices are meant to be informed, common sense would suggest the primary water collectors would be suitable candidates to make such decisions. If the aim is to assess willingness to pay, then it may be appropriate to jointly elicit information from both the primary water collector and the person responsible for paying for an improved service. This may be one in the same person, but where the payer and the collector differ, it may be anticipated that differences in choice preferences will occur. In such cases, which choice represents the policy-relevant information? Intra-household dynamics, as well as community politics, present methodological and practical issues in determining who decides collective (well, standpipe) or private (yard tap) water point priorities that are likely to be contested within and between households in any community and across alternative water supply choices. In effect, this challenge is central to the following discussion of social choice theory and the challenge of aggregating individual preferences to shape public policy.

### 2.3 *Choices Are Shaped by How They Are Framed*

Habits and tastes are formed over time by the specificities of social and cultural boundaries and relationships that define practices and behaviour that become ingrained as a 'way of life'.[21] In this sense, women collecting water is a 'habit', and understanding the boundaries within which acceptable changes can be made is important. Tastes influence choices for goods and services, often in counter-intuitive ways when the symbolic capital perceived to be embedded in a particular type of technology may influence choice more than rational processes of functionality in terms of ease of access, reliability or quality. Where decision makers are not primary users and therefore may not directly pay the penalty for poor choices, the opportunity for political expediency to trump people's priorities is likely to occur.[22] In participatory processes even where people have an equal opportunity to 'speak out', the ability to challenge sociopolitical hierarchies may stifle majority but weak voices as the

[21] P. Bourdieu, *Distinction: A Social Critique of the Judgement of Taste* (London: Routledge, 2007). First printed by Librairie Droz, 1972. First English Translation 1977. This version printed in 2007 by CUP.

[22] J. Isham and S. Kähkönen, 'How do participation and social capital affect community-based water projects? Evidence from Central Java, Indonesia', in C. Grootaert and T. van Bastelaear (eds.), *The Role of Social Capital in Development: An Empirical Assessment* (Cambridge: Cambridge University Press, 1998), pp. 155–187, at 166.

less powerful wait for clues or prompts as to the right way to vote in collective 'dialogue' meetings.[23]

Beyond the sociocultural dimensions of choice and voice, there are behavioural anomalies that challenge the economic axiom of revealed preferences as a rational choice mechanism to reveal utility (satisfaction) due to uncertainty over the stability, completeness and coherency of preferences.[24] Mainstream economic thinking largely assumes that individuals have stable and coherent preferences, which individuals maximise subject to various constraints, commonly income. In other words, given a choice, people select the option that gives them the greatest level of satisfaction. Individual preferences are ideally revealed through market transactions, such as the exchange of goods and services, and based on observed data from which reasonable approximations of future behaviour can be modelled with an acceptable degree of accuracy. However, in situations where there is uncertainty or no available information, stated preferences may be elicited to determine choice preferences.[25] In this way, estimates of likely behaviour in response to future uncertain events, such as demand for a new type of technology, may be determined before committing to large and costly investment decisions.[26] However, with the recognition that there may be systematic differences between the utility of making a decision at a point in time and the utility derived from the decision over time,[27] there are significant challenges to capture objectively and rigorously individual preferences, in order to chart policy at the national or supranational level. Such concerns are equally applicable to normative judgements by epistemic communities of experts, civil society representatives or elected officials who also face uncertainty in making decisions in the public interest.

In rural communities, formal education levels are generally low and the ability of people to effectively engage in unfamiliar cognitive tasks requires

[23] C. Leeuwis, 'Re-conceptualizing Participation for Sustainable Rural Development: Towards a Negotiation Approach', *Development and Change*, Vol. 31, No. 5 (2000), pp. 931–959.

[24] J. Kahneman, J. L. Knetsch and R. Thaler, 'Anomalies: The Endowment Effect, Loss Aversion and Status Quo Bias', *Journal of Economic Perspectives*, Vol. 5, No. 1 (1991), pp. 193–206.

[25] J. J. Louviere, D. A. Hensher and J. D. Swait, *Stated Choice Methods: Analysis and Application* (Cambridge: Cambridge University Press, 2000).

[26] D. Hilton, 'Theory and Method in Psychology and Economics', in A. Lewis (ed.), *The Cambridge Handbook of Psychology and Economic Behaviour* (Cambridge: Cambridge University Press, 2008), pp. 9–38.

[27] D. Kahneman, 'New Challenges to the Rationality Assumption', *Journal of Institutional and Theoretical Economics*, Vol. 150, No. 1 (1994), pp. 18–36.

careful thought, particularly if introducing new or hypothetical information beyond the respondent's existing knowledge base. One approach to reduce the cognitive challenges of effectively presenting complex information to respondents with low education levels is to use pictorial images. Participatory rural appraisal techniques have used pictures in the rural water and sanitation sector in a variety of innovative and effective ways to amplify the voices of the poor.[28] However, pictures are no panacea, and issues of comprehension and interpretation require care in the design, presentation and evaluation of pictorial exercises in order that credible and accurate information is elicited.

Choices may be considered to be more reliable when primary water users actively engage in discussing alternatives before a final decision is made. This process is not common, and the literature largely depends on discrete observations of the percentage of people who participated in meetings to determine the level of technology, say between yard taps or sealed wells.[29] One limitation of this approach is that technology is presented as an aggregate good. What this means is that users are notionally given a choice between, for instance, a public standpipe and a yard (private) tap. All well and good, if user perceptions of service levels do not vary in terms of distance to source, walking and waiting time, quantity of water, reliability of technology or water quality. In most cases, there are variations in design specifications that are not shared with rural water users, confining them to rather crude decisions on technological choice at an aggregate level. Lancaster illustrated that most services are composite goods with individual attributes shaping consumer preferences and behaviour.[30] Payment level or in-kind contribution (e.g. labour days) are common budgetary constraints to then model water users' preferences across a range of technological options. By presenting fixed technological choices to users, policymakers greatly reduce their understanding of what policy pathways may be appropriate, by not fully exploring attributes that may shape choices for rural water services (see Figure 17.1 below).

Of note is the level at which decision making is made, and rigorous exploration of choice alternatives, particularly across technological alternatives. Community or household decision making leaves the policymaker uncertain as to whether the water collector has had any active and effective engagement with the 'choice' being made. This is important as women and young girls remain

[28] R. Chambers, *Whose Development Counts? Putting the First Last* (London: ITDG Publishing, 1997).

[29] Sara and Katz, *Making Rural Water Supply Sustainable*.

[30] K. Lancaster, 'A New Approach to Consumer Theory', *Journal of Political Economy*, Vol. 74, No. 2 (1966), pp. 132–157.

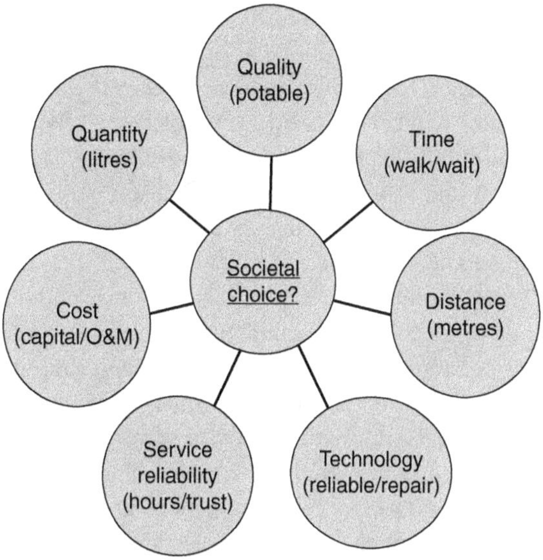


FIGURE 17.1 Attributes shaping user choices for rural water services

the 'drawers of water' throughout the rural world.[31] Community-level decision making inevitably encounters potential flaws and bias with evidence, illustrating how community leaders often unevenly reflect the interests and priorities of heterogeneous community members.[32] If people do really have a choice, then decision making may be argued most legitimately to take place at the lowest possible level, ideally with the people who face the direct costs of collecting water on a daily basis. Yet the purist form of this ideological position, embodied in concepts of decentralisation, empowerment and democracy, can shift management, financial and allocation decision making strongly towards local water consumers and away from the State as a guarantor of water service delivery, particularly where the reach and the purse of the State are limited.

## 3 CONTEXTUALISING CHOICE: ANALYSIS FROM GLOBAL RURAL WATER SUPPLY STUDIES

### 3.1 *Engaging with Community Water Choices*

Community selection for rural water projects may be shaped by objective measures of population served, water quality, distance to water point or health

[31] Thompson, et al., *Drawers of Water II*.
[32] Cooke and Kothari, *Participation: The New Tyranny*.

statistics. Narayan details how such criteria can drive selection of communities, only to learn that communities may prioritise other interventions when given a choice.[33] Overreliance on remote assessment of community demand for alternative water choices has the benefits of being relatively cheap and quick, but if 'community demand is not given primacy and if selection criteria are not transparent and supportive of decisionmaking at the local level, the scope for political selection of villages increases dramatically regardless of community demand, as experience bears out'.[34]

Alternatively, community self-selection may encourage communities to self-organise to undertake collective action for chosen water systems and be prepared to pay for repairs over time.[35] Self-selection presumes a level of community organisational skills and shared interests to be able and willing to effectively respond. Community capabilities are likely to vary; as such, the approach is prone to suffer from self-selection bias, which may prejudice those communities that lack political connections or social capital to access and complete self-assessment forms. Self-selection may thus result in the perverse outcome of excluding precisely those communities that most urgently need help.[36]

Water projects often claim participatory credentials but frequently run according to a project timeframe and budgetary plan that in effect define the outcome regardless of community engagement. Therkildsen documents how demand responsiveness was little more than a project mantra where strict project targets and disbursement patterns drove construction activities in Tanzania.[37] Path dependency, particularly from bilateral and multilateral donors, is common around the world where well-meaning projects confuse the 'means' with the 'ends', resulting in wasted resources and lost opportunities.[38] When projects match community water demand not only with water interventions but also with differing service levels, it is argued that formerly disinterested communities engage in establishing high levels of demand and contribute to high levels of service reliability.[39]

33 Breslin, 'Demand Responsive Approach in Practice'.

34 Narayan, *The Contribution of People's Participation*, p. 66.

35 See World Bank, 'The Demand for Water in Rural Areas', and Narayan, *The Contribution of People's Participation*.

36 Breslin, 'Demand Responsive Approach in Practice'.

37 Therkildsen, 'Watering White Elephants?'.

38 Narayan, *The Contribution of People's Participation*, and Breslin, 'Demand Responsive Approach in Practice'.

39 D. Dworkin and B. Pillsbury, *The Potable Water Project in Rural Thailand*, AID Project Impact Evaluation Report No.3 (Washington, DC: USAID, 1980), and Narayan, *The Contribution of People's Participation*.

### 3.2 *Who Chooses within a Community?*

Establishing the most effective level of decision making is considered to influence the sense of ownership and willingness to sustainably manage rural water systems. People's participation in decision making thus appears to be a desirable and constant factor, though their choices are likely to vary greatly.[40] It is therefore an important policy point to determine at what level and to what extent people should engage in decision making across community, household and individual levels and further to determine to what degree different levels of decision making affect project performance and effectiveness.

Sara and Katz provide a global synthesis from 125 rural community water systems from Benin, Bolivia, Honduras, Indonesia, Pakistan and Uganda to explore under what conditions sustainability is related to household and community demand responsiveness.[41] Of interest is the evaluation of 'informed choice', which measures the degree to which households felt they participated in water system design decisions and knew specific responsibilities for managing the chosen water system and to what degree their choices had been honoured. Results indicate most projects do not offer communities a substantial role in decision making, with 42 per cent of projects reporting someone from the community making the final decision about the type of water system to be built.[42] The assessment of informed choice includes sectoral priorities (water, energy, education, health, etc.), choice of water source, choice of technology, cost options, operation and maintenance responsibility, level of service and attribution of final decision (household, community, water committee, other). Findings further indicate limited and disappointing levels of choices made by households directly, with slightly improved results at the community level. Yet, with only 30 per cent of households reporting that they were offered differing levels of water supply services, the message seems clear that informed decision making is weakly achieved in practice even under the rubric of demand-led projects.

It is also important to note that cross-country analysis was conducted at the household and community level, but not at the level of water collector.[43] In the 121 rural water supply projects assessed by Narayan, although most projects identified women as the target beneficiary group, only 17 per cent of

[40] Narayan, ibid.

[41] Sara and Katz, *Making Rural Water Supply Sustainable*. 'Sustainability' is defined here as 'the maintenance of an acceptable level of services throughout the design life of the water supply system' (p. 30).

[42] Ibid., p. 22. [43] Sara and Katz, *Making Rural Water Supply Sustainable*.

projects achieved high levels of involvement of women. Unless women's participation was specifically targeted and resources invested, it simply did not occur.

Another World Bank study documents the degree of choice across three rural water supply projects in Java, Indonesia, that differed in institutional structures but were all 'designed based on what households wanted and were willing to pay for'.[44] The authors illustrate the limited decision-making role of primary water collectors, regardless of whether the State has provision in the project rules to be the final arbiter on the decision-making process or not. NGO projects appear as the only ones that reflect the user preferences at the household level, but not those of the primary water collectors. This may reflect the sociocultural politics of village life in a Muslim society and the wider rural reality that men are often the key decision makers in the household economy that involve economic or village-level decision making. The study makes this point in relation to the high proportion of low-cost, communal wells chosen in projects, which reflected more the preferences and interests of village leaders than those of the households.[45]

### 3.3 *What Conditions Influence People's Choices?*

Analysis of the determinants of rural water demand in selected sites in Brazil, Nigeria, Zimbabwe, Pakistan and India finds that user demand and choice for alternative water technology depends on the difference between the current levels of water supply compared with projected improved water supply scenarios.[46] Underpinning the demand-responsive message is a consistent finding that, where existing supplies incur high financial costs or time costs, demand for improved sources is high. So, while people might be willing to pay for improved services, the availability of substitute water sources and their associated quality, along with households' ability to pay, strongly influence people's choices.[47] Where existing water supply quality is poor, there was a tendency to be willing to pay more for an improvement, though the amount varies by location. Predictably, people were willing to pay more for private (yard) connections than public taps (100 per cent in Nigeria, 130 per cent in India); however, in Kenya, the perception of handpumps as an improvement on existing open public wells was low due to a concern that the technology

[44] Isham and Kähkönen, 'How do Participation and Social Capital Affect Community-Based Water Projects?', p. 162.

[45] Ibid., pp. 166–167. [46] World Bank, *The Demand for Water in Rural Areas*.

[47] Ibid., p. 54.

would fail.[48] A key finding of this multi-country study was that income alone was not a good predictor of willingness to pay for improved water services; more so, the existing level of service and, in particular, the reliability of the service were statistically more significant factors in decision making.

While many projects move beyond narrowly equating demand with willingness to pay, there is invariably a constraint on demand to moderate preferences across the feasible range of project alternatives.[49] However, Sara and Katz note that articulating demand through contributions is not always effective for the following reasons:

- Contributions were often perceived as a tax, rather than a stated preference of the type and level of service that users would receive;
- Different cost options were not presented to people when choices were being made;
- Contributions were so low or vague people did not feel they were making an economic trade-off for a higher level of service; and
- Contributions were often not voluntary, with many respondents feeling 'forced' to pay without a clear understanding of what they were paying for.[50]

Social cohesiveness was also found to be a key condition influencing the sustainability of water projects.[51] While water committees are often a criterion for community selection, Sara and Katz are less prescriptive in exactly what form community organisation should take place, noting that delegating water management to an existing community organisation resulted in no decline in management quality.[52] However, weak institutional links between the community and the district level can reduce water service performance where post-construction support, in terms of spare parts and technical support availability, is not adequately resourced. Alternatively, there is growing support for technology that is easier to repair with local materials, rather than externally sourced but reliable technology. Local sourcing makes communities independent from district government that may have weak capacity, limited resources or low motivation to work effectively with the choices made by communities.[53]

48 Ibid. 49 Narayan, *The Contribution of People's Participation.*

50 Sara and Katz, *Making Rural Water Supply Sustainable.*

51 Isham and Kähkönen, 'How do Participation and Social Capital Affect Community-Based Water Projects?'.

52 Sara and Katz, *Making Rural Water Supply Sustainable.*

53 P. Harvey and T. Drouin, 'The Case for the Rope-pump in Africa: A Comparative Performance Analysis', *Journal of Water and Health*, Vol. 4, No. 4 (2006), pp. 499–510.

### 3.4 A Sustainable Choice?

A key message from the rural water supply demand literature is that aligning rural water policy with societal choices is a necessary condition for increasing sustainability with metadata project analysis. For example, Narayan notes that 'without beneficiary participation rural water supply projects are unlikely to be sustainable'.[54] Sustainability is defined by Sara and Katz as the 'maintenance of an acceptable level of services through the design life of the water supply system'.[55] The determinants of sustainability include institutional, technical and social criteria, primarily at a decentralised or local scale.[56] The principle of sustainability here emphasises the agency and legitimacy of local choices to promote an enduring and appropriate level of water service. This does not exclude universal water access but influences the path to arrive at this goal. For example, where a community does not self-select or is unwilling to pay for basic services, there is an implicit argument that such a community will not manage its water system as effectively over time as a community with a higher level of social cohesion. With 663 million people worldwide without access to an improved water supply),[57] the consequentialist view favours expending effort on the lower hanging fruit, consistent with the notion of 'progressive realisation'. However, the demand rationale of self-selection is shaped more by the historical distribution of developmental capabilities by degree of political connections, human capital or wealth, rather than a random selection of the people without water access through a 'veil of ignorance'. Cross-country analysis of trends in water access between 1990 and 2000 indicates legacy (starting-point) effects matter in terms of predicting coverage performance over time though no clear pattern by economic growth, income inequality or legislative environment emerges as may be expected at this scale and due to the variability in the quality of data provided across countries.[58] In this context, the international right to water has gained momentum to contribute to global water access goals.

## 4 SOCIAL CHOICE AND THE RIGHT TO WATER

The CESCR's General Comment No. 15 outlines aspects of the normative basis of the international right to water, which 'entitles everyone to sufficient,

[54] Narayan, *The Contribution of People's Participation*, p. 75.
[55] Sara and Katz, *Making Rural Water Supply Sustainable*, p. 30.
[56] *Progress on Drinking Water and Sanitation.* [57] Ibid.
[58] P. B. Anand, *Millennium Development Goal 7: An Assessment of Progress with respect to Water and Sanitation – Legacy, Synergy, Complacency or Policy*, UNU Wider, Research Paper 2006/01.

safe, acceptable, physically accessible and affordable water for personal and domestic uses'.[59] The General Comment differs from a demand-led approach by treating water as a social and cultural good and not primarily as an economic good.[60] Water access is an entitlement and freedom that States are to progressively realise for human dignity, life and health. The basis for a water entitlement is derived from legal precedent rather than empirical evidence in a particular situation that a right is the appropriate policy instrument. The freedom to choose is bounded within the right as framed by the General Comment, though variability in people's preferences, water resources and institutional capacity is acknowledged, as 'the right to water may vary according to different conditions'.[61] Specific inclusion of women in decision making[62] and the right of individuals and groups to participate in decision making to shape water policy[63] coincide with principles of societal choice earlier discussed. The inferred flexibility in decomposing attributes of water services into discrete elements of physical access, affordability, quality, availability, non-discrimination and access to information departs from the technological determinism that has implicitly shaped water policy in rural areas for decades. The right to access water does not deny or exclude water users' opportunity to choose water service levels but rather prescribes societal choices by obligating governments to allocate maximum available resources to the progressive realisation of universal water access. For example, to accelerate the goal of universal water access, coverage rates will logically increase where lower levels of service provision are prioritised; however, users who are willing and able to fund a higher level of water service provision may not be restricted in their choices in the wider goal of accelerated provision to all. The example of productive uses of domestic water is an emerging but unproven model used to illustrate this potentially perverse outcome, where higher-level water services can be used to generate income and support the financial sustainability of the water system.[64] A rights-based approach does not, of course, preclude such opportunities, for instance, where water resources are adequately available, but it could foster a deterministic or suboptimal approach.

A rights-based approach to public policy has been debated long before Jeremy Bentham's quip in the eighteenth century that the rights of man were

[59] General Comment No. 15. [60] Ibid., para. 11. [61] Ibid., para. 12. [62] Ibid., para. 16.

[63] Ibid., para. 48.

[64] N. Stacey, H. T. Phuong, J. Sousan and J.C. Lovett, 'The Impact of Domestic Water on Household Enterprises: Evidence from Vietnam', *Water Policy*, Vol. 12, No. 2 (2010), pp. 237–247.

'nonsense on stilts'.[65] More recently, Amartya Sen has engaged with the question by recasting rights as freedoms and framed the debate in terms of 'threshold conditions' to determine an ethical importance and corresponding obligation of fulfilment.[66] Adopting the position that there are a plurality of competing social justice claims leads Sen to raise the issue of choice and trade-offs within the wider dilemma of how an individual right can be realised independently of a broader economic, legal and political system. This in turn opens up the question of absolute versus contingent social rights[67] in situations where an abuse of a right, such as discrimination in access to water services, may result in the right being upheld but an individual being made worse off due to temporary or permanent loss of water services. For example, almost no water quality testing is conducted on handpumps in rural Africa on a regular and effective basis, yet the water users are aggregately assumed to have safe and adequate water access with no intention of withdrawing access to existing pumps or providing additional pumps until adequate water safety plans can be implemented.

### 4.1 *Equality and Non-Discrimination*

Equality of water access is embedded in the principle of non-discrimination.[68] In contrast to a demand-responsive approach where water is primarily an economic good, the principle of non-discrimination inherent to the right to water implicitly recognises that water is also a social and cultural good. Vulnerable groups by income, housing, land status or age, for example, have an entitlement to an equal opportunity of access to domestic water. Non-discrimination ensures water access does not systematically exclude certain groups or communities by housing, land status, religion, age or any other proscribed or analogous grounds. Water services are not free, but tariffs cannot be set in such a way that they are unaffordable. In addition, specific provision is made for low-cost targeted programmes.[69]

On one reading, the principle of non-discrimination is time intransitive in the sense that it does not make it clear if over a period of time whether the

[65] J. Bentham, *The Works of Jeremy Bentham* (Vol. II, Edinburgh: William Tait, 1833), p. 501.
[66] A. Sen, *The Idea of Justice* (Cambridge, MA: Belknap Press, 2009), pp. 366–370.
[67] H. J. Steiner, 'Social Rights and Economic Development: Converging Discourses?', *Buffalo Human Rights Law Review*, Vol. 4 (1998), pp. 25–42.
[68] See, *Manual on the Right to Water and Sanitation* (Geneva: COHRE, AAAS, ADC and UN-HABITAT, 2007).
[69] General Comment No. 15, para. 27.

principle is being adhered to by achieving 100 per cent coverage of urban water users in the first ten years followed by 100 per cent coverage of rural users in the next ten years. Whether this would be more or less desirable than balancing coverage improvements in rural and urban sectors over a thirty-year period is unclear. Take the dilemma of how to decide whether to promote a more rapid but more uneven realisation of universal water coverage or a slower but non-discriminatory coverage. It is likely to be interpreted and answered differently by an economist and a rights advocate.

Non-discrimination and affordability principles recognise distributional inequalities that pervade many countries. As non-discrimination prohibits exclusion of vulnerable groups from a domestic water entitlement, affordability permits alternative tariff structures to be set across wealth groups. In this way, water access can be moderated on economic criteria, but not on social, political or cultural criteria.

### 4.2 *Participation*

Within the obligation to protect the right to water, 'genuine public participation' is advocated.[70] What is meant by 'genuine' is unclear, though by implication one senses that there is an implicit recognition of power processes that often can play out in sociopolitical engagement.[71] The Committee in General Comment No. 15 further elaborates on participation by stating:

> The right of individuals and groups to participate in decision-making processes that may affect their exercise of the right to water must be an integral part of any policy, programme or strategy concerning water.[72]

The CESCR's direct reference to inclusive participation in decision making as an integral part of planning is notable and is subsequently developed to stress the special importance of involving women in the decision-making process.[73] While the General Comment offers few textual clues, there are references to the process of social choice mechanisms that imply the importance of engaging with people in a meaningful manner to determine the scope and type of water service levels that may be appropriate within the framework of a right to water. Whether this interpretation is overly optimistic is open to question as the process of participation merits less ambiguous language to promote more rigorous and effective engagement with water users to ensure sustainable water systems.

[70] Ibid., para. 24. [71] Cooke and Kothari, 'Participation: The New Tyranny?'.
[72] General Comment No. 15, para. 48. [73] Ibid., para. 16(a).

### 4.3 *What Is Progressive Realisation?*

One of the most intriguing aspects of General Comment No. 15 is the language of engagement embodied by the notion of progressive realisation of the right to water. As mentioned, the temporal boundaries of realising the right to water are difficult to impose uniformly due to variation in the economic, institutional and political contexts across States. However, the malleable timeframe juxtaposes the quantitative nature of halving the number of people without access to improved water services in 1990 by 2015 as stipulated by Millennium Development Goal, Target 7C. Through the process of non-discriminatory planning with genuine public participation, more concrete timeframes will no doubt emerge. From a societal choice perspective, the imperative for a basic level of improved water access is likely to be constant and imperative. Where water cannot be accessed in sufficient quantities of acceptable quality, people are forced into undignified, costly and often tragic decision making. Water is neither a luxury nor a substitutable good; the demand for a minimum quantity of drinkable water is inelastic and is required by every person on a daily basis.

Of course, adopting a human right is far from realising it. The financial and institutional measures that need to be in place to convert lofty words into grounded action are significant in most developing regions. To this end, according to General Comment No. 15, States are obliged to draw upon financial, human and technical resources to realise the right to water,[74] and the international community is obliged to support the realisation of the right where States are justifiably unable to meet their obligations. For example, member states of the World Bank are obliged to ensure that it cooperates and promotes the right to water in its lending portfolio along with other UN institutions.

### 4.4 *Framing Individual Rights and Consumer Choice for Domestic Water Service Access*

Despite limited engagement exploring theoretical and conceptual aspects of economic consequentialism and normative legal principles,[75] the preceding discussion suggests that a common purpose unites artificially separate

[74] For differing perspectives on the extent of extraterritorial obligations, see Chapters 5 and 12 of this volume.

[75] D. Seymour and J. Pincus, 'Human Rights and Economics: The Conceptual Basis for their Complementarity', *Development Policy Review*, Vol. 26, No. 4 (2008), pp. 387–405.

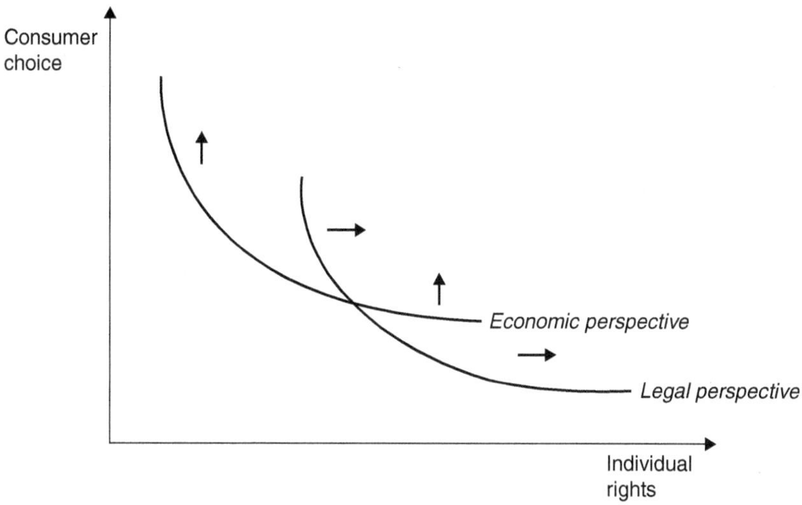


FIGURE 17.2 Mapping theoretical perspectives across individual rights and consumer choice

pathways. Conceptually, a rights-based approach to water policy may be anathema to some neoclassical economists, who wring their hands over the implicit equality-of-outcome argument that raises spectres of inefficient and unsustainable interventions, planning determinism and disenfranchisement of consumer choice. Alternatively, rights advocates may wince at the economic determinism of the 'invisible hand' of the market, which may benefit the aggregate good but sidesteps issues of distributional inequalities, the public interest and discrimination against vulnerable groups. As Seymour and Pincus note, such polarised positions often reflect a failure to engage in a theoretical or ideological exchange to explore the common ground of the autonomy of the individual.[76] As Figure 17.2 below attempts to illustrate, there is likely to be some theoretical common ground between axes of an 'individual right' and a 'consumer choice'.

A demand-led approach to improving rural water supply arguably shares the same scepticism of the effectiveness of government as rights-based norms, which explicitly limit politicians' ability to tinker with policy to suit circumstances. In this view, both approaches aim to strengthen agency by providing structures that are equitable, universal and inclusive. However, they depart in their theoretical interpretation of societal choice mechanisms, with human rights' primary interest in evaluating choices by rules and norms, in

[76] Ibid.

contradistinction to economic instrumentality's primary interest in evaluating choices by results. Whereas the application of a human right is not contingent on outcomes, economists must labour with establishing metrics to calibrate priorities for public policy action. In this way, economists are keenly interested in people's preferences and how those preferences modify behaviour and development outcomes. Alternatively, rights advocates champion all rights as equal to avoid a scalar politics of human rights' priorities. Yet trade-offs in public policy are inevitable, and normative principles may be weakly related to individual priorities and the financial trade-offs that constrain developing country policy implementation. Equally, policy design based solely on societal choices may lead to perverse outcomes that may poorly coincide with the 'public interest'. In effect, each theoretical domain is shaped by alternative visions of society, and while there may be an overlapping theoretical intersection, there are clear points of departure at the margin.

## 5 CONCLUSION

This chapter has examined the extent and nature of progress made under the demand-responsive era of drinking water supply provision in rural Africa with a view to identifying conceptual space and common ground between a social choice theory perspective and an individual's rights perspective of improved water access in theory and in practice. The individual is central to both perspectives, though the rules of engagement vary in terms of rights advocates' promotion of guarding a common set of inalienable rights from above, compared to economists' prioritisation of eliciting preferences to shape policy design from below. Of course, this characterisation obscures the fluidity across scales and hegemony of economic approaches in water policy design and delivery over the last thirty years in developing countries.

The urgency to find more effective and sustainable water services policy is heightened by predictions of more frequent and intense climatic extremes and the increased vulnerability of people living in countries hampered by stagnant economic growth or ineffective governance. In this context, reliance on any one approach is questionable. The demand-responsive approach has led to significant gains in improved water access globally, but these positives must be weighed against the uncertain distributional impacts of the approach and the often unqualified and obscure nature of participatory processes. Particularly the limited degree to which female water users meaningfully engage in decision making. The legacy of failed water projects across Africa illustrates the human costs of ineffective policies that have resulted in sub-optimal investment outcomes.

Within the contested space of global water policy, the human right to water has emerged to offer a normative framework to coherently promote universal access to sufficient, safe, acceptable, physically accessible and affordable water for personal and domestic uses. Progressive realisation of the human right to water offers a language of engagement for economists and rights advocates within an area of overlapping conceptual boundaries across differing political, economic, social and legal contexts. While it is feasible to tease out common theoretical space between individual rights and consumer choices, the extent to which productive policy engagement and improved water access coverage will follow is likely to pivot on the contextual interpretation of the progressive realisation of the human right to water. In this respect, the degree to which 'genuine participation' may play in this process deserves further attention, particularly in establishing a stronger evidential base of the performance of water sector delivery across competing policy design alternatives. Social choice mechanisms offer one route to examine the often fractured and opaque process of testing public policy goals against the myriad voices of the poor.

# 18

# Socio-Cultural Norms, Human Rights and Access to Water and Sanitation

NANDITA SINGH*

## 1 INTRODUCTION

Water is a natural resource indispensable for women, men and children to lead healthy lives with dignity. Access to water has found recognition as a human rights standard by being implied within various international treaties, declarations and other instruments. In 2002, it was acknowledged as an inextricable aspect of Articles 11 and 12 of the International Covenant on Economic, Social and Cultural Rights.[1] Access to adequate sanitation is likewise considered indispensable for leading a life with dignity. Subsequently, it has been treated as a right alongside water, potentially as a twinned right.[2]

Recognition of access to water and sanitation as a human right is often seen as important because it clarifies the role of States in improving access to basic services or supply, sets standards that can be monitored and prioritises those currently without access, particularly the vulnerable and marginalised, in a non-discriminatory manner. Consequently, significant focus has remained on the machinery and mechanisms for implementing the right. Perhaps an important assumption is that, once action for implementing the right is undertaken, access to water and sanitation and hence realisation of the right will be progressively achieved. However, do actions taken to implement the

* Docent, Royal Institute of Technology (KTH), Sweden.

1 The Committee on Economic, Social and Cultural Rights (CESCR) recognised the right to water as implicit in the Covenant as such in its *General Comment No. 15, The Right to Water* (Twenty-ninth session, 2002), UN Doc. E/C.12/2002/11 (2003). International Covenant on Economic, Social and Cultural Rights (adopted 16 December 1966, entered into force 3 January 1976), 993 UNTS 3.

2 COHRE, UN-HABITAT, Water Aid and SDC, *Sanitation: A Human Rights Imperative* (Geneva: Centre on Housing Rights and Evictions, 2008). See Chapter 10 by Langford, Bartram and Roaf in this volume and discussion of its recognition of the right by the UN General Assembly and UN Council of Human Rights.

right necessarily lead to its realisation? Can a duty bearer guarantee exercise of the right by rights holders solely because essential legal frameworks have been created and actions within their scope undertaken?

Similar questions have been raised elsewhere. For instance, some have argued that a human rights-based approach brings a focus to community power relations, a factor that can otherwise impinge on effective access to resources by more marginalised groups.[3] From an anthropological perspective, it has been argued that the practice of human rights takes place between different global and local understandings and meanings of humanness and rights.[4] One sociology of law perspective contends that law, including international legal and political agreements, often obtains content only when first implemented.[5] Therefore implementation should be investigated at the local level.[6]

It has also been argued that the human right to water is not enjoyed automatically by rights holders solely because relevant policies and laws have been created, institutional frameworks laid down, or appropriate programmes and interventions implemented. It is important to consider the 'context' in which these actions unfold, which primarily deal with water resources management and water governance questions.[7]

Drawing upon such arguments, and looking at the realities on the ground in regard to the realisation of the right to water and sanitation in India, in particular, this chapter seeks to explore the processes lying at the interface between the community where rights holders lead their lives and the State that implements actions in accordance with the legal formulation of the right. This chapter is therefore comprised of four main sections. Section 2 presents the conceptual framework underpinning this research. Section 3 reviews the case study that was used to build on this conceptual framework, including a discussion of recognition of the right to water in India, why the country was selected as a case study and the methodology employed. Section 4 describes

[3] For example, M. Langford, 'Ambition That Overleaps Itself? A Response to Stephen Tully's "Critique" of the General Comment on the Right to Water', *Netherlands Quarterly of Human Rights*, Vol. 26, No. 3 (2006), pp. 433–459.

[4] M. Goodale, 'Introduction: Locating Rights, Envisioning Law between the Global and the Local' in M. Goodale and S. E. Merry (eds.), *The Practice of Human Rights: Tracking Law between the Global and the Local* (Cambridge: Cambridge University Press, 2007), pp. 1–38.

[5] H. Hydén and P. Wickenberg (eds.), *Contributions in Sociology of Law: Remarks from a Swedish Horizon* (Lund: Lund University, 2008).

[6] H. Hydén, *Normvetenskap/Norm Science* (Lund: Lund University Press, 2002).

[7] N. Singh, 'Translating the Human Right to Water into Reality: Concluding Remarks' in N. Singh (ed.) *The Human Right to Water: From Concept to Reality* (Zurich: Springer International Publishing, 2016), pp. 223–234.

the factors at the interface between the rights holders and the State (or other agencies) as duty bearers when action for promoting the right to water and sanitation is implemented. Section 5 discusses the processes through which these factors influence realisation of the right and the final outcome at the level of individual exercise of the right despite common actions taken for all rights holders.[8]

## 2 CONCEPTUAL FRAMEWORK

The research presented in this chapter is rooted in the actor-oriented approach, which is based on the idea of social interfaces where people interact. Although the word 'interface' tends to convey the image of some kind of two-sided confrontation, social interface situations have been seen as more complex in nature, containing many different interests, relationships and modes of rationality and power.[9] Thus, every situation is conceived of as an arena in which various actors come face to face and interact with one another. Examples include departments within a government that have resources and wish to effect action, nongovernmental organisations (NGOs) sharing similar concerns, local groups within a community with different interests and individuals who have their own agenda vis-à-vis the intended action.

People are social actors who do not merely react mechanically to what happens around them but also have the capacity to process social experiences and respond accordingly. Because people and institutions, acting based on diverse histories and worlds, have different interpretations of situations and events, they develop different responses to similar conditions and processes, thereby changing the meaning of institutions and the course of events in unpredictable and multidirectional ways.[10] Using the concept of 'interface', this chapter attempts to identify actors and their contexts in order to understand the interlinkages with respect to implementation of the right to water and sanitation.

Actor-oriented studies on human rights practice contend that people live in a context of legal and cultural pluralism and strategically draw on cultural and religious norms, as well as formal rights regimes, in dealing with real-life

8 Ministry of Rural Development (Government of India), Annual Report 2001–2002 (MRD, 2002).

9 See N. Long, 'The Multiple Optic of Interface Analysis', UNESCO background paper on Interface Analysis (1999).

10 N. Long, 'From Paradigm Lost to Paradigm Regained? The Case for an Actor-Oriented Sociology of Development', in N. Long and A. Long (eds.), *Battlefields of Knowledge: The Interlocking of Theory and Practice in Social Research and Development* (London and New York: Routledge, 1992).

situations. Both cultural norms and formal rights regimes are argued to provide opportunities and challenges for rights holders in specific situations.[11] Thus there is a need to understand human rights violations within their socio-cultural context. With respect to women's rights, in particular, the role of private actors, and their embedment in culture, customs and practice, is often a source of such violations.[12]

Closely related to these actor-oriented studies are anthropological perspectives on 'rights as culture', which delineate the connections of rights to other aspects of social life, and 'culture as a heuristic analytical device', whereby culture is to be employed as a means of analysing and better understanding the particular ways that rights processes operate as situated social action. Thus, human rights can be approached as a cultural process that impinges on human subjects and subjectivities in multiple ways.[13] From the sociology of law perspective, it is necessary to understand legal norms not only as material norms formulating legal imperatives but also as a means of directing power and obligations to implement law.[14]

Drawing upon this theoretical background, this chapter proposes that if the primary concern lies with actual realisation of the right to water and sanitation, there is a need to move beyond international and national levels of implementation of human rights norms to an analysis at a level that is defined by the context of the society and the culture where local women, men and children are expected to realise their rights.

The analysis in this chapter derives from the concept of a 'norms triad', wherein norms are defined as action directives that guide human actions or behaviour and consist of three dimensions. The first dimension is that norms are an expression of a *will* – someone wanting to do something. However, this is not enough – he or she must also have the *knowledge* and competence to carry out what he or she proposes. Knowledge, together with cognition, is therefore the second dimension of the norms concept. The third dimension is related to *system conditions* characterising the context of the society in which

[11] C. Nyamu-Musembi, 'Towards an Actor-Oriented Perspective on Human Rights', IDS Working Paper No. 169, Institute of Development Studies (2002); C. Nyamu, 'How Should Human Rights and Development Respond to Cultural Legitimization of Gender Hierarchy in Developing Countries?', *Harvard International Law Journal*, Vol. 41, No. 2 (2000), pp. 381–418; R. T. Nhlapo, 'Cultural Diversity, Human Rights and the Family in Contemporary Africa: Lessons from the South African Constitutional Debate', *International Journal of Law and the Family*, Vol. 9, No. 2 (1995), pp. 208–225.

[12] D. O'Byrne, *Human Rights: An Introduction* (London: Pearson Education Limited, 2003).

[13] J. K. Cowan, M. Dembour and R. A. Wilson (eds.), *Culture and Rights: Anthropological Perspectives* (Cambridge: Cambridge University Press, 2001).

[14] Hydén, *Normvetenskap*.

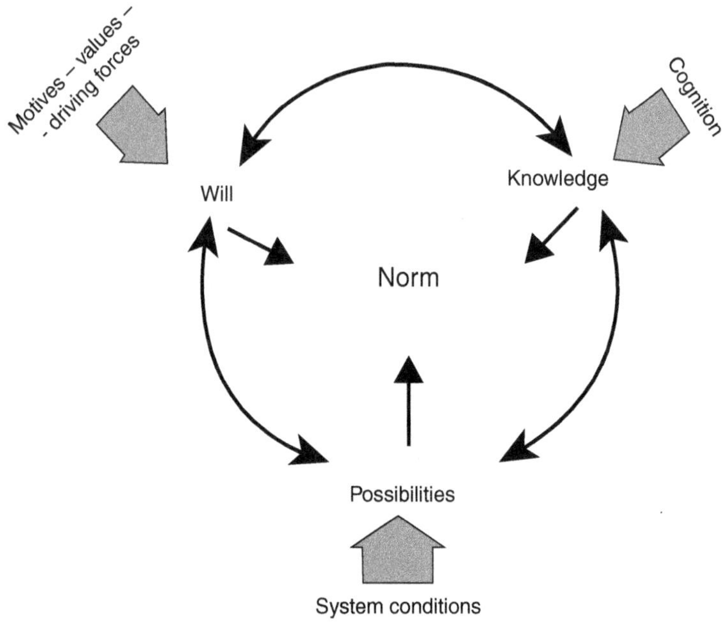


FIGURE 18.1 Norm triad[15]

the actions, and consequently the norms, occur.[16] The dimensions of the norms triad, as illustrated in Figure 18.1, are explored here in relation to the implementation of the right to water and sanitation. This chapter seeks to decipher the complexities of the context that influences the process of realisation of the right even when enabling factors are facilitated by the State as a part of its obligation to progressively realise the right.

## 3 CASE STUDY

### 3.1 *The Norm Triad and Rural India*

The right to water and sanitation is a basic human right, universal realisation of which is a goal towards which all nations should strive. This goal is all the more important for developing nations where problems with access to safe

[15] Ibid.

[16] H. Hydén, 'Putting Law in Context: Some Remarks for the Implementation of Law in China', in H. Hydén and P. Wickenberg (eds.), *Contributions in Sociology of Law: Remarks from a Swedish Horizon* (Lund: Lund University, 2008).

water and sanitation loom large. Also, many of these nations are known to be rooted strongly in traditions. India is a developing nation with a population of more than 1 billion people, which displays marked socio-cultural heterogeneity. Rights holders must realise their rights against the backdrop of diverse cultural norms. Rights realisation in India must also be assessed in the context of long-term efforts by governmental and nongovernmental agencies to enable people's access to water and sanitation. The government bureaucracy and NGOs have taken a leading role in the country in implementing programmes and projects, especially in rural parts where access to water and sanitation has been seen as an important problem.[17] Given this background, India is a useful case study to examine the nexus of cultural and legal norms relevant to the realisation of the right to water and sanitation.

### 3.2 *Right to Water and Sanitation in India's Legal and Policy Framework*

India is a signatory to numerous human rights instruments, and the government has made consistent efforts to improve universal access to water and sanitation. Those efforts include Constitutional safeguards, legal provisions, policies and targeted programmes. The Constitution of India recognises the essential tenet of equal access to water, as Article 15(2) states that no citizen shall 'on grounds only of religion, race, caste, sex, place of birth or any of them' be subject to any disability, liability, restriction or condition with regard to 'the use of wells, tanks, [or] bathing ghats'.[18] Article 21, which articulates the right to life, has been interpreted liberally by the Supreme Court of India to include all facets of life, including water.[19] Although nonjusticiable, the Directive Principles of State Policy recognise the principle of equal access to the material resources of the community.[20] Article 39(b) mandates that 'the State shall, in particular, direct its policy towards securing that the ownership and control of the material resources of the community are so distributed as best to serve the common good'.[21]

17 MRD, 2002.

18 Castes in the Indian social system are ranked, named, endogamous groups, membership in which is achieved by birth. S. Muralidhar, 'The Right to Water: An Overview of the Indian Legal Regime', in E. Riedeland and P. Rothen (eds.), *The Human Right to Water* (Berlin: Berliner Wissenschafts-Verlag, 2006), pp. 65–81.

19 Ibid.

20 Article 37 of the Constitution states that the directive principles of State policy 'shall not be enforceable by any court, but the principles therein laid down are nevertheless fundamental in the governance of the country and it shall be the duty of the State to apply these principles in making laws'.

21 For further analysis of the right to water in India, see Chapter 20 by Cullet in this volume.

The legislative powers are distributed between the Parliament of India and the Legislative Assemblies of the different states.[22] In accordance with the power under the Union List, Parliament has passed laws concerning 'regulation and development of inter-state rivers and river valleys'.[23] Parliament can also make laws on topics in respect of which it has no powers, provided the legislatures of two or more states resolve that Parliament should make such law. Laws pertaining to control of water pollution have been made under this power. The legislatures of the different states have sought to enact a large number of statutes that touch upon the various aspects of the control, regulation and distribution of water. Thus, there exists an elaborate network of laws relating to canals and irrigation, use of water sources, water sewerage and drainage and groundwater.[24]

At the policy level, there have been attempts to promote the needs and interests of all water users. The National Water Policy (1987, 2002, 2012) recognises the provision of adequate safe drinking water facilities as priority area for action.[25] Similarly, since women are recognised as primary domestic water managers, the National Policy on Empowerment of Women (2001) provides that special attention shall be given to their needs in the provision of safe drinking water within accessible reach of households.[26] Recently, access to sanitation and safe drinking water has been recognised as a basic right in the South Asian region, according to the national priority to sanitation.[27] In 2008, the government of India approved a new National Urban Sanitation Policy, which aims to make sanitation facilities universally available in urban areas.

To translate policy guidelines into action, a number of government interventions have been designed. Provision of water supply has been organised as a 'mission' activity and a number of target-oriented programmes implemented for more than five decades. The oldest and most widespread programme has been the Accelerated Rural Water Supply Programme (ARWSP), initiated in 1972–1973, and aimed at ensuring coverage of all rural habitations and

22 As at present, there are twenty-eight states and seven union territories in India.

23 Muralidhar, 'The Right to Water'. The Union List of the Constitution identifies the subjects concerning legislative jurisdiction of the Union government at the centre.

24 For details see, Muralidhar, 'The Right to Water'.

25 Ministry of Water Resources (MWR), National Water Policy (New Delhi: Government of India, 1987), Ministry of Water Resources (MWR), National Water Policy (New Delhi: Government of India, 2002), and Ministry of Water Resources, River Development and Ganga Rejuvenation, National Water Policy (New Delhi: Government of India, 2012).

26 Department of Women and Child Development (DWCD), National Policy on Empowerment of Women (New Delhi: Government of India, 2001).

27 The Third South Asian Conference on Sanitation (SACOSAN), 'Sanitation for Dignity and Health', New Delhi, 16–21 November 2008.

reaching particularly those without access to safe drinking water.[28] Special initiatives have been taken for tackling the problem of severe water shortage (in arid zones) and that of groundwater quality (in areas with high levels of fluoride and arsenic). Gender concerns in these interventions have also been expressed, with women identified as the target group to benefit in domestic water supply programmes. Improved, reliable and safe water sources close to home, most commonly the hand pump, were to be facilitated. For addressing problems of quality, suitable community-based water treatment plants have been installed.

Similarly, sanitation has been recognised as an important development goal and addressed through the Central Rural Sanitation Programme launched in 1986. The programme was restructured in 1999, with a new approach comprising a demand-driven, community-led and people-centred campaign. The Total Sanitation Campaign was focused on information, education and communication, as well as cost sharing in the construction of sanitation facilities. An interesting incentive has been the award given to *villages* and *panchayats* that achieve total sanitation coverage, primarily in terms of infrastructure construction.[29]

Statistics show that the overall coverage figures as a result of water and sanitation efforts in the country have risen dramatically over the decades. For example, more than 96 per cent of rural habitations (720 million people) are claimed to have access to water infrastructure to supply residents with at least 40 litres per capita per day (lpcd). Sanitation coverage, defined as access to toilets by households, has also improved from 14 per cent in 1990 to only 31 per cent in 2011. This means that less than one in five toilets reportedly constructed is in place.[30]

However, despite the long history of state-level action and initiatives to protect the right to water, with special attention being paid to traditionally marginalised groups, a recent study found that as many as one-fifth of the population in

[28] 'Access' to safe water is defined in the following terms: provision of 40 litres per capita per day (lpcd) of drinking water for human beings, with one hand pump or stand post for every 250 persons and availability of water source (either private or public) in the habitation or within 1.6 kilometres in the plains and 100 metres elevation in hilly areas. Potable water for humans is meant for meeting the following daily requirements: drinking, cooking, bathing, washing and ablution.

[29] A panchayat refers to the local government at village, block and district levels. The award is variously named as 'Nirmal Gram Puraskar' ('open defecation free village'), or other such titles.

[30] World Bank, *Rural Water Supply and Sanitation Brief* (World Bank, 2009), Census of India, 2011 (www.censusindia.gov.in/2011census/hlo/Data_sheet/India/Latrine.pdf).

rural India lacks sustainable access to water.[31] Also, though poorer habitations of the 'scheduled castes' and 'scheduled tribes' are to be prioritised while deciding upon the source location, an early study recorded that only 16 per cent of the water points that were in public locations were actually located in poor areas, which made up one-third of all localities in the ninety-nine villages studied.[32] This raises doubts regarding the access of the poor in these villages to the remaining 84 per cent of the water points. Similarly, other studies in the neighbouring region indicate that toilets constructed to promote safe sanitation are not used for sanitation purposes but instead are used for other domestic or productive purposes. Given such a scenario, an attempt was made to understand the micro-level processes at the 'interface' that lead to the gaps between action for implementing the right to water and sanitation and its results in terms of realisation of the right in local communities.

### 3.3 *Methodology*

The findings of this chapter are built upon a qualitative analysis of observations from a first-hand ethnographic study undertaken between 2005 and 2007 in select pockets of rural India, situated in the states of Madhya Pradesh, West Bengal, Bihar, Gujarat and Orissa. The focus of the study was twofold, to evaluate: (a) options for mitigation of water quality problems, especially high fluoride and arsenic in drinking water, and (b) sanitation facilities offered under relevant programmes.[33]

Primary data for the study was collected from rural communities and implementing agencies in the above states.[34] The latter included concerned government departments, local NGOs and international organisations, such

[31] See FIAN, *Investigating Some Alleged Violations of the Human Right to Water in India: Report of the International Fact Finding Mission to India* (D-Heidelberg, Germany: FIAN International Secretariat, 2004).

[32] The terms 'scheduled castes' and 'scheduled tribes' refer to categories mentioned in the Indian Constitution. These categories are considered to be weaker sections of society whose interests need to be safeguarded and promoted. Socially, these groups are seen as occupying the lower rungs of local hierarchies. Programme Evaluation Organization, Planning Commission, *Accessibility of the Poor to the Rural Water Supply* (Government of India, 1980).

[33] While arsenic contamination in groundwater has emerged as an enormous problem in West Bengal and recently in Bihar, high fluoride in groundwater sources is an important problem in Madhya Pradesh and Gujarat. A high level of iron in groundwater is a problem in some parts of Orissa. Access to sanitation was studied in Bihar, Madhya Pradesh and Orissa, where open defecation is known to be commonly practised.

[34] 'Implementing agencies' refer to all agencies – governmental and nongovernmental – that have been concerned with and engaged in implementing action for protecting and promoting the right to water and sanitation.

as the United Nations Children's Fund (UNICEF). The primary data was procured through a combination of two methods. First, key actors involved in the process of realisation of the right were identified, followed by in-depth fieldwork conducted in thirty-two villages, using techniques such as participant observation and interviews with key informants using open-ended questions and focus group discussions. Also, case studies of individuals, families and villages were collected to procure a detailed understanding of the underlying factors and processes in operation. In addition, a number of secondary sources were referred to for information on the policy context.[35]

In the villages sampled, the key informants primarily comprised traditional leaders – both women and men – from different castes and religious and ethnic groups, young persons interested in the issues of concern, modern democratically elected leaders of both genders, women of younger generations who generally work indoors and less-vocal members of underprivileged sections of society. The information collected from the key informants was generally crosschecked at focus group discussions. In total, twelve focus group discussions were held, of which four were held with only women. In the implementation agencies, two kinds of key informants were identified – those in managerial positions and the field staff working in the villages under study. Interviews were the main tool for data collection by the implementation agencies.

The data collected was used to construct community-based and group-based profiles with details on social norms, cultural beliefs and values; social dynamics, and knowledge with respect to water and sanitation; and agency profiles regarding the specific actions, attitudes, knowledge and will, resources and so on. Organisational profiles were developed to understand agencies' perspectives on their roles and capacities. In addition to the data collected for the purpose of this study, published findings from a previous study have also been used to draw support for the arguments presented here.[36] The analysis in this chapter is based on an interdisciplinary approach combining anthropological and sociology of law perspectives. While the anthropological approach was aimed at understanding the existing socio-cultural context related to water and sanitation within the communities under study, the sociology of law perspective focused on the interactions of the community with the legal and action frameworks that guided the agencies.

[35] For example, policy manuals, programme guidelines, progress reports, NGO plans.

[36] N. Singh, G. Jacks and P. Bhattacharya, 'Women and Water: Encountering the Challenges of Water Resource Management in Rural India from a Gender Perspective', Scientific Report 2003–2006, TRITA-LWR Report 3025 (KTH, Stockholm, 2009).

## 4 APPLYING NORM TRIADS AT THE 'INTERFACE'

For the purposes of this chapter, it is assumed that current water policy and water sector practice in India are directed at the realisation of the right to water. This is justified on the basis that constitutional safeguards, legal provisions, policies and target-oriented programmes have worked hand in hand to increasingly improve people's access to water. The study conducted between 2005 and 2007 indicates that at the interface where the stage for performing action to implement the right to water and sanitation is set, the duty-bearing agents come face to face with the rights holders in the community. State agents act within the context of implementation of their obligations, while rights holders interpret that action within the context of their existing socio-cultural norms.[37] This interface, as depicted in Figure 18.2, is the arena where micro-processes of interaction between the two sides lead to realisation or non-realisation of rights.

These micro-processes are guided by a set of norm triads rooted in a given context on each side, the interaction of which ultimately determines the outcomes of the actions for implementing the right.

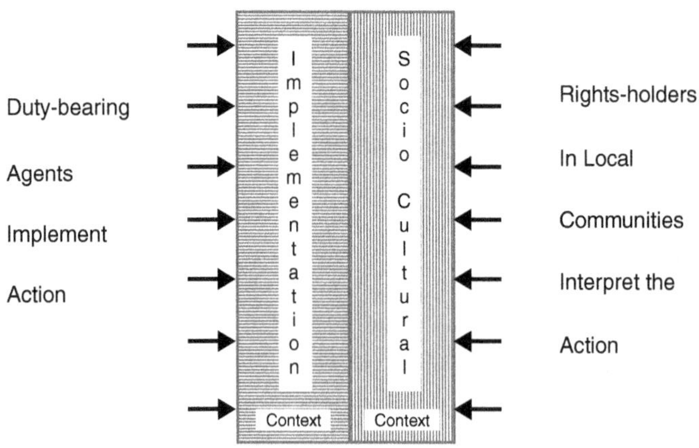


FIGURE 18.2 The 'interface' of action
*Source:* Singh, 2016.[38]

[37] Even when a 'participatory approach' is adopted this study assumes that the approach itself becomes a part of the implementation process and it is interpreted by the rights holders in accordance with the context of their socio-cultural norms.

[38] N. Singh, 'Realizing the Human Right to Water in Local Communities: An Actor-Oriented Analysis', In N. Singh (ed.) *The Human Right to Water: From Concept to Reality*, (Zurich: Springer International Publishing, 2016), pp. 17–31.

### 4.1 *Norm Triad within the Implementation Context*

Within the implementation context, the norm triad comprises knowledge about the action, will of the government and other organisations and the possibilities and constraints with respect to systemic conditions brought by the development process.

**Knowledge about Action**

Knowledge refers to the understanding and perceptions regarding the interventions that are implemented at the local level for facilitating implementation of the right. This largely reflects the global perspectives on development in general and programmes and projects on water and sanitation in particular. There is often little attempt to link this global knowledge with local realities. Consequently, on the part of the implementers, there is an attitude of deliberate ignorance or lack of sensitivity to the local socio-cultural context of the rights holders. Therefore water and sanitation projects fail to be intrinsically adopted on the part of local communities.

As an example, empirical data from this research shows that, for the implementers or duty bearers, safety of drinking water is scientifically explained as the absence of microbiological and chemical contamination. However, for rights holders, this conception makes less sense in comparison to the cultural understanding of good quality water, which is defined on the basis of more tangible parameters, such as taste, smell, colour, clarity and freshness. It was observed that this cultural understanding prevents rights holders from obtaining drinking water from arsenic and fluoride removal plants, as well as from piped water supplies. However, these alternate sources are being used widely for other purposes in affected areas.

Similarly, empirical data shows that the cultural concept of pollution resulting from a toilet situated inside the main part of the house deters construction of a toilet at a point where it is easily accessible to all. The scientific perspective of safe sanitation defined in terms of prevention of infections and other kinds of contamination makes little sense. Consequently, toilets have been found to be located outside the house or on the terrace, where the possibility of its regular use by all members of the household, especially women, is greatly diminished.

**Will of Duty-Bearing Agencies**

Duty-bearing agencies must express their will to ensure uninterrupted access of the rights holders to access basic water and sanitation services. However, more often the implementation context reflects that the will is based on the achievement of globally defined targets. Accordingly, the will of the agency is reflected as a mere interest in reaching statistical highs, such as the numerically achievable Millennium Development Goals (MDGs) and possibly Sustainable Development Goals (SDGs), through the construction of infrastructure, rather than paying attention to the extent of effective, equitable and sustainable use of that infrastructure. Thus, while India boasted that 96 per cent of its rural population had access to a safe water supply, which is statistically calculated as the availability of at least one safe water source for 250 people, many of the people residing in these covered localities continued to lack access to safe water.[39]

Similar is the fate of toilets in many areas where either communal toilet blocks have been constructed or people have been motivated to voluntarily build low-cost toilets in their houses. From the empirical evidence collected during the research, it emerges that a will to monitor the effective and equitable use of the infrastructure is at least as important as the will to install it, if the right to water and sanitation is to be realised.

## Possibilities and Constraints

The implementation context is governed by possibilities and constraints that range from the choice of policies and programmes to the availability of financial and physical resources. While, on one hand, policy guidelines in the sector are recent and revised and therefore offer new possibilities to improve access to basic water and sanitation, it is noteworthy that these are only a restatement of global aspirations. The policy frameworks are often divorced from local needs, and the programmes are designed without consideration of compatibility with local realities. Hence, these remain inadequate and, at times, inappropriate.

As an example, according to global guidelines, the notion of participation of local stakeholders, especially women and other disadvantaged groups, has been incorporated into the National Water Policy. However, the mechanisms adopted for eliciting local participation within water and sanitation programmes fail to incorporate provisions that encourage equitable and effective participation of these groups. There is a lack of clarity on several issues and problems at the local level with communities.

Similarly, new infrastructure designs with respect to toilets and drinking water sources offer new possibilities for people lacking adequate access to

[39] Rajeev Gandhi National Drinking Water Mission, *Guidelines for Implementation of Rural Water Supply Program* (New Delhi: Department of Drinking Water Supply, Ministry of Rural Development, 2000).

water and sanitation. However, the nature of the design itself may end up hindering expected access. For example, single pit latrines offer a new possibility for safe sanitation but pose practical limitations as users fear that the single pit will fill up. This, in turn, discourages optimum use. With respect to arsenic and fluoride removal plants, new technologies may bring new hopes to the people, but most of these plants are cumbersome and difficult to maintain locally, which in turn hinders sustainable use.

### 4.2 *Norm Triad within the Socio-Cultural Context*

Within the socio-cultural context, the norm triad contains: (i) traditional knowledge of the rights holders, (ii) the will of the local elite to promote the right of all to water and sanitation and the will of the people to adopt new interventions as well as (iii) possibilities and constraints within existing traditional social institutions.

#### Traditional and Cultural Knowledge

The traditional and cultural knowledge of rights holders refers to indigenous perceptions regarding water and sanitation needs, knowledge of local water resources and technologies for harnessing them and local beliefs and practices with respect to water and waste management. Different kinds of needs are rooted in the wider social, economic and religious systems, and the appropriateness of water for each of these uses is defined on the basis of certain attributes. For example, in rural India, good quality water for drinking and cooking is generally expected to be colourless, odourless, sweet and fresh. These qualities, in turn, are seen as closely related to local concepts of purity, health and hygiene. Salinity, for example, is undesirable as saline water is believed to be unsuitable for cooking, as well as posing taste problems and being ineffective in quenching thirst. Similarly, freshly drawn water is regarded as pure, as well as safe on health grounds. Any water filled on the previous day may be taken for washing or discarded, since stored water is regarded as stale and unhealthy.[40]

Similarly, sanitation needs are linked to social and economic networks. For instance, waste management has links to the economy, as animal and other organic waste is composted as manure and human waste is seen as a source of nutrients in fields. Also, the empirical data shows that open

[40] For details see, N. Singh, P. Bhattacharya, G. Jacks and J-E. Gustafsson, 'Modern Domestic Water Supply Systems: Need for a Holistic Perspective', *Water Resources Management*, Vol. 18, No. 3 (2006), pp. 237–248.

defecation serves an important social function of communication, especially amongst women of different households who are otherwise more restricted to their domestic spaces.

**Will of Local Elite and Rights Holders**

Traditionally, leaders in a community have been responsible for ensuring access to the basic amenities of life for all residents. However, in recent times, this responsibility has been eroded considerably and replaced by more opportunistic behaviour and inequitable practices in pocketing government resources for the benefit of the leaders and their own caste or social group. Evidence of such behaviour comes from a number of case studies where water points provided by various organisations have been installed within localities of the local elite or near their individual premises even when they have private water sources at home.

In one case study, Village L in Madhya Pradesh, a hand pump was intended to benefit women of scheduled castes. The sole hand pump was installed along the main road of the village next to the Brahmin neighbourhood. Although this is a public location, due to social pressures imposed by the caste system, the location of the pump has implications for its effective availability to the intended beneficiaries. The Brahmins are an upper caste and are also dominant in this village.[41] Due to the customary social norm for the scheduled castes to keep out of the Brahmin neighbourhood, these women are excluded from accessing the pump. In addition, most of the Brahmin households are well off and own private wells. The public hand pump represents merely an additional water source to them. However, for the scheduled caste women, the public hand pump is their only source of clean, safe water within a reasonable distance. Thus, despite the ARWSP installing a working hand pump, in reality, the scheduled caste women continue to draw water from their traditional source, which is a distant well. Depending on this well as their sole water source poses additional hardships during the summer months, when it usually dries up.

In another case study in the same state, Village S, the hand pump meant for the Jatav, a peripherally located scheduled caste group, was installed in a public location towards the middle of the settlement, between the Brahmin

[41] Dominant caste denotes one that preponderates numerically over other castes and may also wield greater economic and political power. Higher position in the local caste hierarchy, access to western education and external occupations are also factors that enhance social dominance. A dominant caste exercises control over the use and management of space and resources in its village and influences decisions affecting the lives of all community members. More details can be found in M. N. Srinivas, 'The Dominant Caste in Rampura', *American Anthropologist*, Vol. 61, No. 1 (1959), pp. 1–16.

and Yadav areas. These two castes belong to the upper- and middle-level orders, respectively, within the local caste hierarchy. Together they are socially dominant in the village and own a number of private hand pumps that are shared with neighbours of the same caste. However, the Jatav lack access to any source of safe water of their own. Again, due to social norms with regard to the separation of castes, the Jatav are denied access to the public hand pump installed by the ARWSP and continue to depend on a distant well for their domestic water needs.[42]

Also important is the will of rights holders themselves to adopt new interventions. In many instances, in relation to both water and sanitation facilities, research has shown that new water delivery technologies are rejected for drinking and cooking on grounds of either cultural mismatch between expected and delivered water qualities or on grounds of convenience or maintenance hardships.[43] During research in West Bengal, qualitative assessment of the utilisation pattern of nineteen working arsenic removal units installed by different agencies revealed that women from only about 38 per cent of the target households were actually using the water for drinking and cooking. The others rejected the units on cultural grounds.

An important observation made during the field work was that although the pipelines supplying treated surface water had been installed in the villages under study as an alternative for addressing the problem of arsenic contamination, women tended to treat the taps as an additional source that could be used for multiple purposes other than drinking or cooking. In the case of a deep tube well, which is culturally regarded as a good source of water for drinking and cooking, in as many as five instances, it was recorded that women preferred to fetch drinking water from deep tube wells that were located far away in adjoining villages, either by themselves or sending their children, even when a pipeline was available within the vicinity. The deep tube well water is regarded as sweet in taste, clean and safe from bacteriological contamination.

Similarly, in many villages sanitation facilities are not constructed for underprivileged families, as use of the funds is decided by the local elite. Further, even where facilities are constructed, use is not regular due to certain attitudinal barriers. Amongst the barriers identified were, first of all, doubts and fears about long-term adequacy of the new technology in case of regular

42 N. Singh, P. Bhattacharya and G. Jacks, 'Women and Community Water Supply Programmes: An Analysis from a Socio-Cultural Perspective', *Natural Resources Forum*, Vol. 29, No. 3 (2005), pp. 213–223.

43 See more examples in N. Singh, 'Women, Society and Water Technologies: Lessons for Bureaucracy', *Gender, Technology and Development*, Vol. 10, No. 3 (2006), pp. 341–360.

use by the entire family. For example, residents perceived the size of the pit to be very small. Second, there were reservations about fetching water from distant sources for the toilet, especially in the summer and in drier areas. Third, the content of the IEC messages[44] was often not convincing and sometimes even contradictory to cultural beliefs and practices.[45] Fourth, there may be a feeling of alienness about a toilet as an asset for daily use, which may have been the reason informants gave interesting explanations about absence of soap in the toilets supposedly used on a regular basis.[46] This aspect of the will of the rights holders to exercise the right as influenced by behavioural factors and attitudes is extremely important for effective realisation of the right to water and sanitation. Otherwise infrastructure will be constructed and yet remain unused.

## Possibilities and Constraints

Within the socio-cultural context, possibilities are offered by the traditional water management system, wherein lies a body of indigenous knowledge on water resources and culturally compatible harnessing technologies, as well as organisational frameworks for facilitating and regulating efficient and equitable use of water resources by everyone in the community.[47] However, the socio-cultural context also creates barriers through social institutions preventing equitable access. For example, as explained earlier, social spaces in the community are distributed amongst different caste groups, and access to a common resource is determined by membership in the group. Thus, individuals from lower castes cannot access water from a point located in an area belonging to upper castes. Similar social rules operate with respect to religious groups in the community. This implies that, if a safe water source has been installed within the boundaries of an upper caste locality, then it can be accessed only by members of that caste and other closely ranked groups, but not by those placed lower in the hierarchy.

[44] IEC refers to 'Information, Education and Communication' – a component often associated with many development programmes, including water and sanitation, which are aimed at enhancing awareness, promoting behavioural change and enhancing adoption of new interventions.

[45] For instance, the cultural notion that faeces bring pollution to home interiors contradicts with the IEC message that a toilet inside the house is essential for good health and hygiene.

[46] In Bihar and Orissa, a number of informants explained that soaps kept for hand washing outside the toilet were stolen by crows. Otherwise they claimed a regular use by all family members even when physically the toilets clearly appeared to be unused.

[47] N. Singh, 'Indigenous Water Management Systems: Interpreting Symbolic Dimensions in Common Property Resource Regimes', *Society and Natural Resources*, Vol. 19, No. 4 (2006), pp. 357–366.

Empirical evidence collected from Gujarat further indicated that community size, social homogeneity and high levels of social cohesion can play an important role in facilitating access to safe water and hence realisation of the right. A comparative study between two villages within a mega-water supply project showed that households in Village G, where the project was initiated, were able to get a one-hour supply of water for only four days in a month, while those in Village A were able to get a daily supply for half an hour. In-depth exploration revealed that while Village G was a large village, with more than 2,700 households distributed amongst different castes and religious groups, the community at Village A was less than one-third that size and largely homogenous in social constitution. Consequently, while Village G had no clear community leadership nor any working formal participatory institutions, Village A had local leadership that was well accepted, and the formal participatory institution worked efficiently, facilitating equitable enjoyment of the right even by underprivileged sections. In fact, lack of social cohesion in Village G had partly made it possible for a new local industry to take a large share of the daily water supply, causing water scarcity.

## 5 PROCESSES AT THE INTERFACE

At the interface, the two norm triads are continuously interacting in a complex way with the consequence that action to implement the right at the micro level does not necessarily lead to its realisation. In fact, in a given community, individual rights holders were observed to exhibit a continuum with respect to realisation of the right to water and sanitation (see Figure 18.3).

At one end of the continuum are the 'unaware' rights holders, while at the other end are the 'full realisers'. The unaware rights holders lack knowledge of their rights or of the actions undertaken by the implementers and the benefits. Consequently, they continue with the traditional way of life. The full

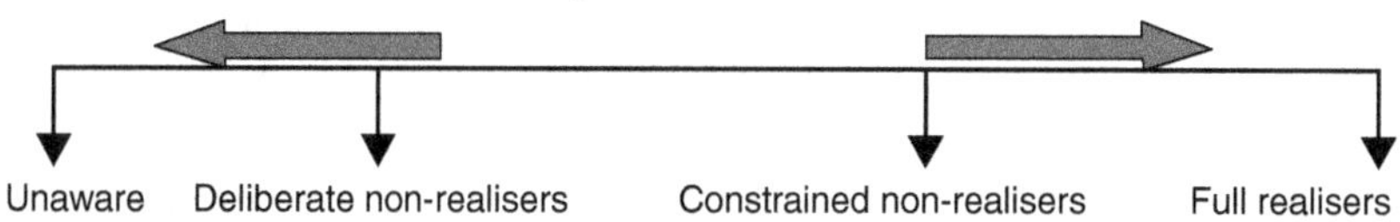


FIGURE 18.3 The rights realisation continuum
*Source:* Singh, 2016[48]

[48] Singh, *The Human Right to Water: From Concept to Reality*, pp. 17-31.

realisers are those rights holders who have knowledge of the interventions available, enjoy access to improved infrastructure, and continue to use these sustainably over time.

In between the two poles are a number of categories at different levels of non-realisation. Among the major categories of these are first the 'deliberate non-realisers', who have the requisite knowledge but lack the will to adopt change due to attitudinal barriers rooted in the traditional beliefs, practices and systems. Second are the 'constrained non-realisers', who are aware of the available interventions and possess the will to adopt change, but are denied access on grounds of socio-cultural constraints rooted in the social organisation, religious groupings or political factions.

The existence of this continuum was noted in a number of villages. For example, in fluoride-affected Village P, the fluoride removal plant in the middle of the village was not utilised for drawing drinking water by many women because they lacked clear knowledge of the fact that their well and hand pump water contained high fluoride, which affects their health adversely. There were others who were 'deliberate non-realisers' because, although they possessed knowledge, there was strong doubt over the quality of the treated water since they found the plant visibly dirty. Other lower down in the local caste hierarchy and residing on the periphery of the village were 'constrained non-realisers' because they had the knowledge and the intention to use the water from the treatment plant for drinking but were excluded by the upper caste people from approaching the plant. Very few users of the plant actually used the treated water for drinking and cooking, thus becoming the 'full realisers' of the right to water.

## 6 CONCLUSIONS

From the findings of the research, it clearly emerges that progressive realisation of the right to water and sanitation is a complex process. It is not necessarily affected by the drafting or redrafting of a legal framework or by the undertaking of development action in a community. The latter only serves as a starting point for the process, introducing the context for enabling realisation of the right. Whether or not the right will be realised depends on the interaction between the implementation context and the socio-cultural context of the rights holders. Norms exist within both of these contexts and each context is defined by a different norm triad. The underlying norms within these triads are created at different levels and result in a dynamic situation. The norms produce behaviour and hence determine action regarding realisation of the right, which can vary individually.

The importance of norms within a socio-cultural context is paramount and cannot be ignored if all rights holders are to be enabled to become 'full realisers'. In order to find a way forward, a number of suggestions are made. First, there is a need to sensitise implementing agencies about the role of socio-cultural norms at the interface in the process of progressively realising the right to water and sanitation. Second, since the constituents of the norm triads in the socio-cultural context ultimately relate to behavioural issues, there is a need to conceptualise adoption of safe water and sanitation as an issue of behavioural change. This behavioural change is as much required on the side of the duty bearers as the rights holders. The former need to change their attitude towards evaluating outputs, for example, by looking at final outputs qualitatively rather than keeping only numerical records of the interventions implemented. For the latter, the 'deliberate non-realisers' should undergo attitudinal change and be sensitised about the importance of changing their habits. For the 'constrained non-realisers', behavioural change is required for those who are responsible for constraining the intended rights holders. Finally, there is a need to develop suitable interventions to address those socio-cultural norms that act as barriers for full realisation of the right. An example would be target-specific, need-based information, education and communication packages for different kinds of 'non-realisers'.

The conclusions of this study are based upon the findings in some limited pockets of India. However, since there is great similarity in the socio-cultural characteristics across the length and breadth of the country, validity of the outcomes of this research can be expected to be high and tested accordingly. Further, these findings and the theoretical insights emerging from the study would also hold true in other developing country contexts, where traditional knowledge and socio-cultural frameworks retain significant meaning. Each of those contexts could be markedly different but could play an important role in the realisation of the right to water and sanitation by local populations.

# 19

# Reflections on the Right to Water from a Political Ecology Perspective

## *Tensions in Zimbabwe's Water Governance*

BILL DERMAN* AND EMMANUEL MANZUNGU**

### 1 INTRODUCTION

In the context of shifting legal frameworks, the cocktail of political, economic and environmental tensions surrounding water resources and services in Zimbabwe provides fertile ground for a political ecology analysis of the right to water. During the 1990s, Zimbabwe attempted a far-reaching water reform as part of the broader global strategy of Integrated Water Resources Management (IWRM).[1,2] The emphasis in the reforms was on commercial water use. There was an identified need to collect as much water revenue as possible to support the vision of a self-financing water sector. Continuing the colonial division of water, Zimbabwe's waters are effectively divided into three categories (primary, commercial and urban) and the latter was largely excluded from the reforms as well as industrial and mining waters. In law and in policy, these various reforms remain in place, although they

* Professor of International Environment and Development Studies, Norwegian University of the Life Sciences.

** Professor, Department of Soil Science and Agricultural Engineering, University of Zimbabwe.

1 IWRM is defined as 'A process that promotes the co-ordinated development and management of water, land and related resources, in order to maximise the resultant economic and social welfare in an equitable manner without compromising the sustainability of vital ecosystems'. Global Water Partnership ('GWP'), 'Integrated Water Resources Management', Global Water Partnership Technical Advisory Committee, Background Paper No. 4 (2000). GWP was established in 1996 as a donor initiative to take forward the Dublin Rio Principles for Water (1992). The Partnership was designed to act as an international 'network of networks' to encourage learning and sharing of global experience, in order to promote an integrated approach to water resources management.

2 In the Water Act, the term is Urban, Industrial and Mining (UIM).

have fallen into disuse in many parts of the country due to the broader political, economic and social crises that have characterised Zimbabwe since 2000.[3]

In these reforms, there is no explicit mention and much less recognition of a right to water.[4] Nonetheless, the continuation of the legal category 'primary water'[5] amounted to recognition of a rural right to water for drinking and homestead purposes, including small-scale irrigation. Moreover, the new Water Act 1998, in line with IWRM, sought to govern and manage all of Zimbabwe's waters in a holistic and coordinated fashion. While provision of water and sanitation in urban areas fell under the Urban Councils Act of 1985, cities and towns were expected to participate in the new institutions created by the Act. The Water Act emphasised water resources management rather than water supply. However, all waters were to be considered together and urban residents drinking needs had the highest priority of water use when there was scarcity.

The human rights terrain has shifted, however, with the adoption of a new constitution in 2013 and the acceptance of a new national water policy in 2013. Section 77 of the constitution provides that the government will provide clean, safe and potable water. However, there has been no supporting legislation to indicate how this constitutional provision would or could be implemented. The new water policy does state that Zimbabwe will follow international requirements. This would include the right to clean drinking water and sanitation. A right to sanitation can be found in Zimbabwe's Water Policy although also not supported by legislation.[6] It is also worth noting that Zimbabwe voted in favour of the United Nations General Assembly Resolution on the right to water and sanitation.[7]

A political ecology approach provides a means to examine how Zimbabwe's water reforms are inextricably linked to the broader political processes and processes that have led to a series of crises in the water sector. It also helps us frame how Zimbabwe's waters have been understood and used over time.

3 The dates can only be approximate since discussions and donor funding emerged between 1992 and 1995 while the formation of catchment and sub-catchment councils and the establishment of Zimbabwe National Water Authority (ZINWA) occurred in 1999–2000. While catchment and sub-catchment councils continue to exist (mostly on paper), ZINWA continues to function and has expanded its functions as discussed below.

4 This was despite the implications of Dublin Principle 4 of 1992, which included the phrase 'it is vital to recognise first the basic right of all human beings to have access to clean water and sanitation at an affordable price'.

5 Discussed in detail below in Section 2.

6 National Water Policy, para. 6.7.

7 General Assembly Resolution 64/292 'The Human Right to Water and Sanitation' (2010).

The best-known Zimbabwean water crisis involves Harare, the capital city, which has polluted its own drinking water sources and is driving its ground water deeper and deeper while being unable to provide sufficient water to its residents. By understanding the sources and exercise of power over water and land by the ruling party known as the Zimbabwe African National Union – Patriotic Front (ZANU PF)[8] we can obtain a clearer understanding of the relationship between water governance and management, and Zimbabwe's broader political, economic and environmental situation.[9]

Political ecology permits us to examine how political power is exercised over what appear to be the more technical issues of water supply, water infrastructure and sanitation. Linking water issues to questions of power can be accomplished through a political ecology framework which considers environmental decision-making (including all dimensions of water) as contestations often around competing narratives, as well as in whose interests these policies are being made or not being made. The environmental or ecological consequences of such discursive practices[10] are the second part of political ecology. These practices frame how water issues and conflicts are to be understood in a particular context. And, lastly, a political ecology framework enables us to examine the social nature of water. This implies a shift from regarding water as the object of social processes, to a form of nature that is both shaped by, and shapes, social relations structures and subjectivities.[11] Water in the political ecology literature provides a way to examine how the distribution of water shapes and has been shaped by, power.[12]

This approach leads to a number of arguments. The first is that the technical approach was doomed to fail because it occluded political ecology considerations. The underlying framework for Zimbabwe, at least at the national level, in the period leading up to the Water Acts of 1998 was

[8] There were two parties which merged in 1989 forming ZANU-PF but with ZANU holding the most important political offices.

[9] B. Derman and F. Gonese, 'Water Reform: Its Multiple Interfaces with Land Reform and Resettlement', in M. Roth and F. Gonese (eds.), *Delivering Land and Securing Livelihood: Post-Independence Land Reform and Resettlement in Zimbabwe* (Harare and Madison, WI: Centre for Applied Social Sciences, University of Zimbabwe and Land Tenure Centre, University of Wisconsin, 2003), pp. 287–307.

[10] Discursive practice addresses the processes by which cultural meanings are produced and understood.

[11] J. Linton and J. Budd, 'The Hydrosocial Cycle: Defining and Mobilizing a Relational Dialectical Approach to Water', *Geoforum*, Vol. 57 (2014), pp. 170–180.

[12] A. Loftus, 'Rethinking Political Ecologies of Water', *Third World Quarterly*, Vol. 30, No. 5 (2009), pp. 953–968.

integrated water resources management which did not take into account customary laws and practices, political organisation, or the right to water. Authorities and donors attempted to reconfigure water management on a technical non-political basis. From a political ecological standpoint, this is not possible as we shall show. The second is that by using IWRM as the master framework led authorities to either ignore or resist a human rights framework. The third is that the outbreak of cholera in 2008 and 2009, and now typhoid in 2016 and 2017, was caused by several factors all involving the intersection of human and ecological systems, which all become transparent in a political ecology approach.

The chapter is organised as follows: Section 2 examines the extent to which a political ecological framework can contribute to understanding the power dimensions underlying water governance, management and use. Section 3 considers the history of water management in Zimbabwe. Section 4 briefly discusses the period of 'water reform' including the Water and ZINWA Acts of 1998. Section 5 discusses agricultural water and we considers the new water policy and the constitutional provision of a right to drinking and sanitation. Section 6 considers the urban water crises and section 7 discusses how civil society organisations are responding to the water crises. The conclusion returns to how political ecology can be used to help explain why and how the current government cannot genuinely support a right to water and sanitation.

## 2 USING A POLITICAL ECOLOGY FRAMEWORK

Studies of fresh water use and management constitute an important arena for the application of a political ecology framework. From this perspective, water flows are a consequence of a humanised nature that has altered, diverted, blocked or changed how rivers flow. In turn, changes in water reshape human societies. Indeed, rivers can be altered so much that they no longer flow into the ocean or they flow in new directions.[13] Rivers, even in less developed countries, are interrupted by dams, lakes, canals, irrigated fields, factories, mines and ponds for fish. These interrupted rivers reflect human intentions, but affected to lesser and greater degrees by the environment through which the waters flow. Key environmental factors include forests, the slope of the land, the soil types, amounts of rainfall, the upstream uses of the water,

[13] M. Reissner describes how the waters of the Colorado River have been dramatically altered as various U.S. states have competed for its waters in his *Cadillac Desert: The American West and Its Disappearing Water* (NY: Penguin Books, 1993).

population density along the river, the chemicals put into water through mining, the economic value of fish, and so on..

Political ecology is just as relevant in urban settings. Water features in multiple ways through efforts to protect urban wetlands, to drain water out of cities, to urban gardening, to the sanitation system based upon toilets and a separate sewage system. In addition we can see how colonial powers provided drinking water to white segregated areas, of southern Africa through the construction of dams while black African populations often had to fight for themselves. The poor lacked access because of power that restricted the means to the funding and resources necessary to provide water to some and not to others. The provision of water for urban populations ripples in its effects to those living downstream of its dams for drinking water.

In adopting a political ecology framework for understanding water control and management, we examine how people, places and industries access and secure their supply of water, and how ecological processes shape and affect human intentions. In broad historical terms, the control of water has often been linked to the rise of States and empires. This includes the original research by Wittfogel on how irrigation systems shaped the political and economic systems of Asia differently than those in Europe.[14] China and other Asian civilisations were built in his view through bureaucratic control of human populations as a result of the demands of vast irrigation systems. He thought that these controls could provide an explanation for despotism in Asia and democracy in Europe and the United States. In contrast, the environmental historian Worster has used this approach to analyse how control and redirecting of rivers in the western United States shaped its politics and economy not that differently from what occurred in other empires.[15]

A political ecological framework can assist in comprehending ancient water systems and twenty-first-century ones alike. It can also include the socio-economic and political contexts, which shape practices of large dam construction, irrigation, flood control and other forms of contemporary water management. Contemporary processes to control water through large dams for hydropower, irrigation, drinking water and recreation, diversion of river systems and other purposes reflect the command and control of sufficient resources and political power to implement them. Water projects require large

[14] In his classic work *Oriental Despotism: A Comparative Study of Total Power* (New Haven: Yale University Press, 1957).

[15] D. Worster, *Rivers of Empire: Water, Aridity and the Growth of the American West* (New York: Pantheon, 1985). Worster does use the term empire for understanding American history.

economic commitments and the capacity to move populations, to construct power lines, to accurately measure and assess flood potential, to do formidable economic and social analyses of irrigations' success and to balance mining and agricultural interests. In sum, the control of water requires political power.[16] Those who hold power tend to reflect dominant economic interests, which in turn determine how waters will be managed and what principles of distribution and redistribution are enacted.

Integrated water resources management as a strategy was intended to remove political and economic interests from determining water policies. Water policies were to result from a balancing of environmental, economic and broad human needs. However, when efforts are made to reallocate water availability or to shift priorities of access, water management then becomes a site of contestation.[17] Political ecology points us toward asking questions about such political struggles, which can clearly be observed in Zimbabwe. For example, when commercial farmers resisted paying increased rates for water, or when the new parastatal Zimbabwe National Water Authority resisted accountability to what were to be new participatory institutions, namely catchment and sub-catchment councils.

In short, the political ecology of water reflects broader power contestations in society, although they are often masked by the use of economics, engineering sciences and other discourses to make it appear as though decisions are adopted only on technical and scientific grounds. In this perspective, rivers and streams are seen as part of a natural system, external to human experience and decisions. Decisions about what to do with water is primarily

[16] Other examples of using political ecology include the work of Tvedt, who has documented the enormous British effort to control the Nile in order to control Sudan and Egypt. He subtitled his book appropriately *Political Ecology and the Quest for Economic Power.* Despite the new dispensation in South Africa, the post-apartheid State has strong national interests to control the waters from Lesotho. The enormous dam-building agenda of China will arguably serve to maintain its hegemonic position over Southeast Asia. Also, in the subcontinent of India, incorporation and subjugation of tribal peoples has gone hand in hand with its dam-building programmes especially on the Narmada River and its tributaries.

[17] There is now a rich literature documenting the failures of IWRM in Africa. See: K. Conca, *Governing Water: Contentious Transnational Politics and Global Institutions Building* (Cambridge, Massachusetts: MIT Press, 2006); P. Van der Zaag, 'Integrated Water Resources Management: Relevant Concept or Irrelevant Buzzword? A Capacity Building and Research Agenda for Southern Africa', *Physics and Chemistry of the Earth*, Vol. 30, Nos. 11-16 (2005), pp. 867–871; F. Molle, 'Nirvana Concepts, Narratives and Policy Models: Insight from the 'water sector', *Water Alternatives*, Vol. 1, No. 1 (2008), pp. 131–156. Most recently, a special issue of Water Alternatives is devoted to an examination of IWRM in Africa: L. Mehta, S. Movik, A. Bolding, B. Derman and E. Manzungu 'Introduction to the Special Issue: Flows and practices – The politics of Integrated Water Resources Management (IWRM) in southern Africa', *Water Alternatives*, Vol. 9, No. 3, (2016). pp. 389–411.

informed by engineers and economists using technical and production-oriented solutions. These arrangements are also based on differential power and tend to overlook ecological considerations.[18] From a political ecological standpoint, there is always a political element to all decision-making about natural resource management and environmental issues. For example, the rising dominance of water as commodity is justified by the notion of water scarcity. In political ecology, one would ask who defines water scarcity, who decides where and when it exists and whose interests will they put first when there is, for example, reduced flow in rivers. In Zimbabwe it has been the state's inability to invest in infrastructure and water services and the decline in service provisions which has provided the rationale for cost-recovery and marketisation which conveniently has fitted with World Bank policy prescriptions for the water sector.[19]

In Zimbabwe, there were power contestations over who would control the Zimbabwe National Water Authority (ZINWA). This new institution created by the water reform, which was intended by donors (especially GTZ) to be independent from government, to generate its own revenues from the slogan 'user pay' and to be relatively independent of the State. With the creation of ZINWA, the Department of Water was shrunk and its personnel moved to the new agency.[20] The government moved quickly to control this new agency and block genuine participation by Catchment and Sub-catchment Councils, the new institutions of water management. In short, a new arena of contestation was created around the strategic resource of water. From a political ecology framework it also becomes easier to understand why the water problems of Zimbabwe's second largest city, Bulawayo, have been deliberately sidelined since independence. Residents of Bulawayo have opposed the ruling party and voted for the opposition since 2000. Prior to that Bulawayo residents supported the Zimbabwe African Peoples' Union

[18] There is much rethinking of decision-making around water. For example, 'Rethinking the Role of Humans in Water Management: Toward a New Model of Decision-Making', by M. Brugnach and H. Ingram in B.R. Johnston, L. Hiwasaki, I.J. Klaver, A. Ramos Catillo and V. Strang (eds.), *Water, Cultural Diversity, and Global Environmental Change: Emerging Trends, Sustainable Futures?* (Dordrecht, Heidelberg London, New York: Springer, 2012), pp. 49–64. The purpose of this volume is to incorporate cultural diversity in water management.

[19] Karen Bakker provides an excellent theoretical framework for recognising water crises while unpacking the conceptual frameworks that underlie privatization of water in her chapter 'Commons versus Commodities: Political Ecologies of Water Privatization' in R. Peet, P. Robbins and M. J. Watts (eds.), *Global Political Ecology* (London and New York: Routledge, 2011), pp. 347–370.

[20] This has been reversed post-2013.

(ZAPU) led by Joshua Nkomo rather than the Zimbabwe African National Union (ZANU) led by the current President Mugabe.[21]

For most of agrarian Africa, provision of clean water first by colonial governments and then by independent ones was given low priority. The dominant issue for the colonial powers was the provision of water for mines, large-scale commercial agriculture and the white portions of urban areas. This has been less true for what had been the white cities of southern Africa, where in the case of Zimbabwe a reasonable system had been put in place that included the segregated urban black areas by the 1960s. Independent African governments have tended to neglect water infrastructure and become overwhelmed by urban migration and the tremendous expansion of urban populations. In Zimbabwe, the urban water infrastructure has decayed over the years while private and government interests increased waters for irrigation. While most of Zimbabwe's water was and is used for irrigation, there has been a loss of state capacity to manage its waters for the last decade. We now turn to the specifics of Zimbabwe to understand its political ecology of water.

## 3 ZIMBABWE'S WATERS: HISTORICAL BACKGROUND

In both water law and usage, white commercial farmers gained control over Zimbabwe's rivers and many of its best soils through conquest and colonial policies. The land was divided into segregated zones, with almost half of the best land appropriated by Europeans in a system of private tenure and the rest for Africans under a system of communal tenure. Unlike South Africa, the economy of Zimbabwe focused heavily on agriculture.[22] While irrigation development was uneven in relation to race and geographical distribution, the control of rivers, dam construction and irrigation channels have become increasingly important over time. Ironically, and due to the political and economic dominance of white farmers, most of the irrigation was developed in the well-watered parts of the country instead of the dry areas where irrigation was more needed. The colonial State's water strategy, while not attracting the same attention as land, made it very difficult for small holders to improve

[21] M. Musemwa, 'Disciplining a "Dissident" City: Hydropolitics in the City of Bulawayo, Matabeleland, Zimbabwe, 1980-1994', *Journal of Southern African Studies*, Vol. 32, No. 2 (2006), pp. 239–254.

[22] E. Manzungu, A. Senzanje and P. van der Zaag, *Water for Agriculture in Zimbabwe: Policy and Management Options for the Smallholder Sector* (Harare: University of Zimbabwe Press, 1999); J. Makadho, P. Matondi, M. Munyuki-Hungwe, 'Irrigation Development and Water Resource Management', in M. Rukuni, P. Tawonezvi, C. Eicher (eds.), *Zimbabwe's Agricultural Revolution Revisited* (Harare: University of Zimbabwe Press, 2006), pp. 217–259.

their agricultural production and to compete with white agriculture since they were pushed out of the better-watered areas. The result was many protests by black Africans against their resettlement in water-scarce areas.

The development of large-scale irrigation was made possible by private actors with support of the colonial government, while small-scale irrigation in the communal areas was initiated by the colonial administrator Alvord in eastern Zimbabwe.[23] To block the growing support of independence it was expanded in the 1960s in a belated attempt to bring development to the tribal trust areas. Irrigation in the communal areas (the former tribal trust lands) greatly expanded after independence in 1980. In Rhodesian water law, rights to water were attached to land use. Those who applied and were granted water rights earlier had highest priority for water. These rights were granted in perpetuity. Over time, River Boards were formed by white farmers to deal with conflicts over water amounts, use and allocation. To be a member of a River Board, one had to have a water right and thus almost all black Zimbabweans were excluded. It's easy to see in this case how colonial power was exercised over the key resource of water. It becomes harder to see when that control is designed by primarily engineers, and couched in engineering and economistic terms. River Boards were terminated with the Water Act of 1998 and were to be replaced by Sub-catchment Councils.

Another dimension of the water practices by the settler state was to leave water supply and sanitation on the commercial farms to the farm's owners. Farm workers who comprised the largest number of formal sector employees relied upon farm owners' for their water. There was no independent system of regulations for the provision of dignified bathing or showering facilities, nor for testing for bacteria or general water quality. Farms were regarded as private and therefore under the control of owners.

In summary, it can be said that the system of water allocation in the colonial period was based on the matrix of ideas of large-scale and labour-dependent farming rooted overall in European power. According to Campbell, the process was held almost entirely in male hands with an extension of racial and patriarchal notions toward the great African majority who were denied both adequate land and water.[24] He further argued that the settler State's planning mechanism was organised around the concept of the scarcity of water, a narrative that continues to the present day. Politicians, agricultural

[23] E. Alvord designed the first peasant irrigation schemes in what was then Rhodesia. Most of his writings are unpublished in the Annual Report of the Chief Native Commissioner.

[24] H. Campbell, *Reclaiming Zimbabwe: The Exhaustion of the Patriarchal Model of Liberation* (Johannesburg: David Philip Publishers, 2003).

extension officers, water resource managers, hydrologists, engineers, planners and economists propagated the concept of water scarcity when, in reality, the problem of water availability for black Zimbabweans was primarily distribution, not scarcity. This was reinforced by the myth that only whites could have an efficient and productive agriculture. African farmers, despite their early successes, were excluded from access to water.[25] The division of Rhodesia's waters between primary and commercial waters began in the 1920s and continues through the present.[26]

## 4. WATER REFORM IN THE 1990S

It took fifteen years after independence for there to be a focus on water reform. This was due first to the growing recognition of profound inequalities in water access by the Zimbabwean government,[27] and second to the growing global concern around water management.[28] There was an originality and uniqueness to the water reform enterprise in the 1990s that manifested itself in significant and ongoing debates among government, a growing donor sector, and the World Bank and water researchers. There were significant differences between the donor-funded projects. For instance, the pro-poor perspective of the Dutch Wageningen researchers and their Zimbabwean counterparts stood in stark contrast to Deutsche Gesellschaft für Technische Zusammenarbeit's (known commonly as GTZ, the German Development Corporation, now renamed GIZ) approach, which fostered economic models based on the user pay principle for commercial water. Despite IWRM-based water reforms, water supply and sanitation continued to fall under the National Action Council, an inter-ministerial committee formerly headed by the Ministry of Local Government, with participants from all the relevant

[25] I. Phimister, *An Economic and Social History of Zimbabwe, 1898–1948* (London and New York: Longman, 1988); T. Ranger, *Peasant Consciousness and Guerrilla War* (London: James Currey, 1985).

[26] B. Derman, A. Hellum, E. Manzungu, P. Sithole and R. Machiridza, 'Intersections of Law, Human Rights and Water Management in Zimbabwe: Implications for Rural Livelihoods', in B. van Koppen, M. Giordano and J. Butterworth (eds.), *Community-Based Water Law and Water Resource Management Reform in Developing Countries* (Wallingford, UK: CABI, 2007).

[27] M. Rukuni, Report *of the Commission of Inquiry into Appropriate Agricultural Land Tenure Systems*, Vol. II: Technical Reports (Harare: Government Printers, 1996).

[28] B. Derman, 'The Incredible Heaviness of Water: Water Policy and Water Reform in the new Millennium in Southern Africa', in L. Whiteford and S. Whiteford (eds.), *Globalization, Water and Health: Resource Management in Times of Scarcity* (Santa Fe, New Mexico: School of American Research, 2005), pp. 209–230.

ministries and departments and dependent upon donor funding. Like so many other parts of the Zimbabwean government, it no longer functions nor has any resources.

The rationale for Zimbabwe's water reform was based upon increasing access to water by black Zimbabweans while ensuring the productive uses of water, and to manage all of Zimbabwe's waters in a holistic fashion.[29] New participatory structures called Catchment and Sub-catchment Councils were created to increase access to water management decision-making. Each one of newly defined seven hydrological zones had its own Catchment Council. There was very heavy donor involvement at all levels, including GTZ, the Dutch Embassy, UK Department for International Development (DfID), Swedish International Development Cooperation Agency (SIDA), Norwegian Agency for Development Cooperation (NORAD) and the World Bank. The donors all withdrew their support from all levels in the water sector due to human rights violations during the elections of 2000 and the farm occupations and seizures. However, due to the outbreak of cholera in 2008 and 2009 some donors returned on the basis of humanitarianism and not development. Since then, development activities have resumed. The most important donors now at the national scale are: The World Bank, the African Development Bank, the Australian government, UNICEF, the Development Bank of Southern Africa and increasingly, Chinese government State-run companies.

Water reform focused upon changing the laws that underlay water management. The new laws were the aforementioned Water Act and the Zimbabwe National Water Authority Act No. 11/1998 (ZINWA Act), which were to incorporate the new global principles and national priorities for water management. In 2002, the Environmental Management Act (EMA) was passed, which has provisions for protecting water resources through sound environmental practices. The three laws incorporate the Rio- and Dublin principles, such as decentralisation, participation and water as an economic and social good, and women as important water managers. There was no formal recognition of the right to water until the new constitution.

[29] See, among others: D. Dube and L. Swatuk, 'Stakeholder Participation in the New Water Management Approach: A Case Study of the Save Catchment, Zimbabwe', *Physics and Chemistry of the Earth*, Vol. 27 (2002), pp. 867–874; S. Mtisi and A. Nicol, *Caught in the Act: New Stakeholders, Decentralisation and Water Management Processes in Zimbabwe*, Sustainable Livelihoods in Southern Africa Research Paper No. 20 (2005); A. Hellum and B. Derman, 'Negotiating Water Rights in the Context of a New Political and Legal Landscape in Zimbabwe', in F. von Benda-Beckmann, K. von Benda-Beckmann and A. Griffiths (eds.), *Mobile People, Mobile Law: Expanding Legal Relations in a Contracting World* (Aldershot and Burlington, Vermont: Ashgate, 2005), pp. 177–198; Derman and Gonese, 'Water Reform'.

Under the Water Act, all water is vested in the President and no person can claim private ownership of any water. This is consistent with Zimbabwe's history as a centralised State even while appearing to incorporate new global water management policies.[30] The 1998 water legislation transferred most national planning functions from the Department of Water Development to the new parastatal ZINWA with oversight from the Ministry of Water Development and Rural Resources (now the Ministry of Environment, Water and Climate).[31] ZINWA is funded through the sale of water collected behind government dams, the provision of water to cities and the levying of water charges to large-scale users. Management of Zimbabwe's water is to be shared with the new stakeholder organisations of Catchment Councils and Sub-catchment Councils.[32] Since irrigation is the largest use of water, the large-scale commercial farms were to be the major source of funding for ZINWA, Catchment Councils and Sub-catchment Councils. This organisational model for how things were to work has, however, broken down since 2000. Cities were to purchase raw water from ZINWA and the treat it to provide drinking water to urban residents at a price. The pipes, pumps, treatment plants were all government owned.

The Water Act specifies that, subject to certain provisions, any person has a right to abstract water for primary purposes[33] and that this does not require a water permit. Thus, Sections 33, 35 and 49 protect access to primary water use by providing that:

> a) The catchment councils can limit the amount of water abstracted for primary water use to ensure equitable distribution, b) No permit is required to drill a borehole for primary water use, c) The appropriate minister should take steps to ensure that the primary water interests of communal or rural people are safeguarded.

The Act also calls upon the Minister of Water Resource Development and Management[34] to ensure availability of water to all citizens for primary purposes, equitable allocation of water to cater for all interests and the

[30] B. Derman, F. Gonese and A. Ferguson, *Decentralization, Devolution and Development: Reflections on the Water Reform Process in Zimbabwe* (Harare: Centre for Applied Social Sciences, University of Zimbabwe, 2001).

[31] Most recently, the Ministry has clawed back its role and importance from ZINWA.

[32] These are the Sanyati, Manyame, Mazowe, Save, Runde, Mzingwane and Gwayi.

[33] Primary use of water is defined as reasonable use of water for basic domestic needs in and about the residential premises, support of animal life other than fish in fish farms or animals in or poultry in feedlots, making bricks for private use of the owner or lessee or occupier of the land and dip tanks (section 2 of the Water Act).

[34] At that time it was the Minister of Water Development and Rural Resources.

provision of affordable water to consumers in underprivileged communities (Section 6). There is also a provision for stakeholders to be involved in the management of water resources within the framework of Catchment and Sub-Catchment Councils. The representatives are from different user groups, and are supposed to be popularly elected, although this was not achieved in practice. In sum, these provisions could have provided the basis for a right to water (drinking and livelihood) for most rural populations.

The ZINWA Act was established to provide for the formulation of national policies and standards on water resources planning, management and development. The National Water Authority is responsible for advising the Minister on the formulation of national policies and standards on water issues such as planning, development and management, quality and pollution control and pricing. ZINWA is also involved in water supply in small town and rural centres, and it became the owner of all of Zimbabwe's medium- and large-scale dams following fast track land reform (see below), a role that has been expanded to cover all urban areas in the country.

The Environmental Management Act (EMA) provides for sustainable management of natural resources. The Act also provides for the establishment of a National Environment Council, which advises on policy formulation and the implementation of the Act among other functions. Water issues are to be catered for under the Standards Enforcement Committee, which sets the criteria for measuring water quality. For example, it recommends minimum water quality standards for different uses of water. According to the EMA, individuals, corporate bodies and classes of people can enforce their environmental rights. Section 4(2) allows for a class action to be brought in terms of environmental protection. The Act therefore can be seen as protecting the human right to access water through ensuring the provision of clean water via the environmental rights route. However, the separation of water quality from other water management concerns has posed significant communication issues between the two ministries. We know of no class action suits that have entered the judicial system of Zimbabwe. However, since water and environment are part of the same ministry perhaps communication will improve.

With regards to water supply, it is important to note that there is no single piece of legislation that regulates the provision of water services. In rural areas, water services are administered by the Rural District Councils Act[35] and the District Development Fund (DDF) Act.[36] The DDF is responsible for drilling and repairing water points, while the Department of Agricultural, Technical

[35] Zimbabwe Government, Rural District Councils Act, 1998.
[36] Zimbabwe Government, District Development Fund Act, 1982.

and Extension (AREX) assists communities with their permit applications. AREX, whose name has been changed back to its name since the early 1980s, the Department of Agricultural, Technical and Extension Services (AGRITEX) - which suffered greatly after 2000 in terms of budget, personnel and support. In urban areas, it is the Urban Councils Act,[37] which, in relation to water, renders power to the municipalities to provide and maintain a supply of water within or outside the council area. The take-over of water and sanitation in urban areas was in violation of the legislation in place. And as discussed for Harare below, it has had devastating consequences.

Research investigating different Catchment Councils nationwide demonstrates that the intention of the new Water Act to 'ensure the availability of water to all citizens for primary purposes' was not realised.[38] Indeed, the emphasis was upon catchments and sub-catchments to raise revenue for them and for ZINWA. For example, as already noted in the Mzingwane catchment, which had limited commercial water to levy, there was a suggestion to levy a charge for every herd of cattle. In the Save Catchment Council levies were proposed for any water use where some income was realised.

This lack of conceptual and policy clarity also applies to the thousands of boreholes currently used in Zimbabwe. ZINWA's policy was to register all boreholes and then charge borehole owners for water, because like all water, it belongs to the government. On the other hand, the Presidential Land Review Committee under the Chairmanship of Dr. Charles Utete recommended that levying water from boreholes should be stopped because 'it discourages investment in water resource development and the enhancement of production on farms through irrigation'.[39] No attention was paid in this report to the scale and intensity of borehole water use or how to regulate it over time. The recommendations may have been coloured by the fact that a good number of the commissioners were beneficiaries of the land reform programme. Boreholes have become of increasing importance for irrigation and drinking water and unlike commercial water, there are no charges. A major exception has been in the city of Harare, where boreholes have been registered. The Upper Manyame Sub-Catchment Council, which includes the city, charges a high fee for borehole owners to register. The Council

[37] Zimbabwe Government, Urban Councils Act, 1998.

[38] E. Manzungu, *Water for All: Improving Water Resource Governance in Southern Africa*, International Institute for Environment and Development Gate Keeper Series No. 113, Paper 20 (Brighton: Sustainable Livelihoods in Southern Africa Research Paper Series, 2004); Mtisi and Nicol, *Caught in the Act* Dube and Swatuk, 'Stakeholder Participation'.

[39] C. Utete, *Report of the Presidential Land Review Committee*, Vol. 1 (Harare: Government of Zimbabwe, 2003), p. 177.

includes Harare's major reservoirs, as well. It is less than clear exactly what services it provides. Most recently, Harare's boreholes are said to be unsafe due to recent flooding in January and February 2017.[40]

In terms of a human rights framework, the Dublin Principles and IWRM were, as adopted by Zimbabwe, non-rights-based. The rights-based South African constitution and South Africa's Water Act were rejected or not known by the architects of Zimbabwe's water reforms. The notion of a human right to water as practiced in rural Zimbabwe was of no interest at that time to those focused on securing water payments. However, as noted above, primary water remained mainly untouched. There was some attention paid to how to assist poor urban residents in their water needs through cross-subsidisation but this never occurred.

According to Human Rights Watch and our own research[41] 'water revenue in Harare now represents the largest source of revenue for the Harare City Council. However, rather than being ploughed back into the system for service upgrades and infrastructure projects, much of that money is diverted from the water account into the general City Council. The money is poorly accounted for and may be unlawfully allocated towards paying the salaries and benefits of City Council members'. Even though the residents received no water they still had to pay their water bills and the City of Harare claims the right to disconnect water for non-payment of bills. This is done despite an earlier court ruling that the city had to get a court order to disconnect. The Department of Social Welfare has no money to assist and they have no policies to support poor people who cannot afford to pay for water.[42]

From a political ecological perspective, there were significant elements missed including: to consider water in a holistic fashion; to increase the power of water users over the governance and management of water; to incorporate pollution control as part of these new structures; to enable reallocation of waters to the majority of Zimbabweans (although never specified how it could and should be done). The democratisation of water governance, in turn,

[40] The headline from the *Sunday Mail* (a government newspaper) reads *No Water in Harare is Safe – EMA* (Environmental Management Agency), February 4, 2017.

[41] *Human Rights Watch Troubled Water: Burst Pipes, Contaminated Wells, And Open Defecation In Zimbabwe's Capital*, p. 5, www.hrw.org/report/2013/11/19/troubled-water/burst-pipes-contaminated-wells-and-open-defecation-zimbabwes.

[42] For a systematic consideration of the consequences of Zimbabwe's water crisis see A. Hellum, B. Derman, L. Mangwanya and E. Rutsate, 'Zimbabwe's Urban Water Crisis and Its Implications for Different Women: Emerging Norms and Practices in Harare's High Density Suburbs' in A. Hellum, P. Kameri-Mboti and B.V. Koppen (eds.), *Water is Life: Women's Human Rights in National and Local Water Governance in Southern and Eastern Africa* (Harare: Weaver Press, 2015), pp. 347–383.

could have led to a re-appropriation of some of Zimbabwe's waters that seemed to be an intention of the Water Act.

## 5 AGRICULTURAL WATERS

### 5.1 *A Right to Water in the Rural Communal Areas of Zimbabwe*

The right to water in rural and urban Zimbabwe needs to be differentiated conceptually, legally, and in practice. The category of primary water is a colonial one but maintained in the Water Act and current water policy. In rural areas, we are obliged to examine customary law and practices in addition to the legislative concept of primary water.

As we have noted, Zimbabwe's rural waters are still divided into two categories – commercial water and primary water. Primary water includes water used, domestic human needs in or about the area of residential premises'. What is meant by this phrase is, however, not clear. In sum, it is not restricted to drinking water, but seen as an integrated part of livelihood necessities, such as food and housing in communal areas. The State is obliged to respect and protect the right to primary water as embedded in the Act. Thus, the 1998 Water Act (section 51.1) asserts the importance of primary water:

> No permits granted by a catchment council, other than permits for the use of water granted to a local authority for primary purposes, shall have the effect of depriving persons of the use of water for primary purposes.

Thus the Water Act provides for primary water users not to lose their basic access, but to actualise this right. However, to actualise this right means knowing how further water abstractions would affect primary users, which water authorities are not required to do. The authors are unaware of any case where primary use took precedence over commercial water use. In addition, the amount of water used for primary water use has not been quantified. While a general national estimate has been made of rural primary water use, amounting to a very low 1 per cent,[43] there are no detailed empirical estimates of actual use. It has been assumed that the amount of use has not justified registration in comparison to commercial water use. It is also significant that no water standards for quality have been determined in the definition of primary water use even though most of this water is designated for human and animal consumption.

[43] Government of Zimbabwe, *Towards Integrated Water Resources Management* (Harare: Government of Zimbabwe Printers, 2000).

During the 1980s and early 1990s there was an emphasis upon communal areas in general and water and sanitation in particular. Boreholes were dug, hand pumps were supplied and assistance was provided to dig Blair toilets. In research done in the late 1990s, Derman and Hellum describe how even where boreholes were intended for private use, they became subject to communal use.[44] At least since 2000, the government has withdrawn from providing assistance to the water sector and it has been left to non-governmental organisations. According to the government, 75 percent of rural hand pumps are non-functional and 48 percent of Zimbabwe's rural population does not have toilets.[45]

In the context of the water reform process, it can be difficult to create simple boundaries between primary and commercial waters. New innovative forms of commercial cropping have emerged within the common property regimes in the communal lands, such as gardening for consumption and sale, as well as water provision for cattle intended for sale. These uses render problematic the division between commercial and primary water. Under the Water Act, it is only water used for commercial purposes that requires a permit in terms of section 34. The definition of commercial water depends upon use - water used for purposes including agriculture, mining, livestock, hydroelectric power, etc. It follows from the ZINWA Act, section 41 that only permitted water is subject to the user pays principle[46] in terms of the water levy.[47] Thus, rural primary water users do not have to pay this. However, this practice may be subject to contestation. We have found that most catchments focus on how to charge people for water use since sub-catchment councils and ZINWA are dependent upon revenues from commercial water. In the Mzingwane Catchment,[48] for example, there have been efforts by ZINWA to charge everyone who owns cattle to pay for the water their animals drink.

[44] B. Derman and A. Hellum, 'Neither Tragedy nor Enclosure: Are There Inherent Human Rights in Water Management in Zimbabwe's Communal Lands?', *The European Journal of Development Research*, Vol. 14 (2002), No. 2, (2002) pp. 31–50.

[45] Government of Zimbabwe 2013 National Water Policy.

[46] In its policies the Zimbabwe government shifted its pricing policies for water to include the actual costs of supplying water from behind government dams as well as from private ones. They were attempting to move away from the practice of a single blend price for only government water (despite the differences in costs between government dams) and to include a price of water stored behind private dams as according to the Act, the President of Zimbabwe is the owner of all the water. The implementation of pricing policies has been haphazard following fast track land reform.

[47] In accordance with Section 41 of the ZINWA Act, the Minister may, in consultation with the approval of the Minister responsible for finance, by statutory instrument, impose a water levy on any person holding a permit issued in terms of the Water Act (chapter 20:24).

[48] This constitutes the Limpopo river basin in Zimbabwe. It is a dry area where most of the water is in government dams, which by regulation, can only be sold by ZINWA. Sub-catchments,

The complexities and cost of such an undertaking has, for the time being, delayed any implementation of the idea beyond the catchment level. From a legal perspective, cattle-owners could have argued their right to primary water, but we have not found any cases where this argument has been made.

Derman, Hellum, Manzungu and others have found that throughout rural Zimbabwe there is recognition of a right to drinking water whatever the source, including privately dug wells.[49] Moreover, this right to use water includes livelihood purposes. While not framed in human rights terms, customary law and practices support this interpretation.[50] There is little political and legal precedent though on how to turn local practices into national law, especially in this context where commercial water has been emphasised. African States in general have given high priority to central State control rather than more decentralised ones which recognise diverse cultural practices and local norms. Primary water could be a starting point for national legislation and policies to include a 'right to water' and a 'right to livelihood'. The idea of a priority right to primary water for basic human needs, including domestic, animal and house-building functions, is found in Mozambique, South Africa and Tanzania.[51] It has meant that such water in principle has been protected from the growing demand for 'user pay' which, according to the Water Act, is restricted to commercial water. However, the pressure upon a more commercial-oriented water sector, led by ZINWA, to be self-financing in the context of a national economic crisis demonstrates the need for greater legal and political clarity for primary water. Indeed, the primary goal of water reform was to decrease the size of the civil service and to fully fund ZINWA

which rely on levying water in rivers (commercial use of groundwater is negligible), were keen to boost their revenue base. This was not the case in wetter parts of the country.

49 B. Derman, A. Hellum, E. Manzungu, P. Sithole and R. Machiridza, "Intersections of Law, Human Rights and Water Management in Zimbabwe", Zimbabwe: Implications for Rural Livelihoods', in B. van Koppen, M. Giordano and J. Butterworth (eds.), *Community-based Water Law and Water Resource Management Reform in Developing Countries* (Wallingford, UK: CABI, 2007), pp. 248–270.

50 See Chapter 9 by Hellum this volume.

51 In South Africa, there is a comparable division whereby Schedule One water use in the National Water Act describes permissible uses of water that do not require a licence and do not have to be registered. Water use activities that fall under Schedule One include those that, due to the small quantities used, have a very small impact on water resources and therefore pose minimal or no risk. These include: taking water directly from any water source for domestic use in households provided that water users have lawful access to that water; storing and using run-off water from a roof; small gardening that is not for commercial use; watering animals for subsistence use; using the water surface or surrounding land for recreational use; and using water for emergencies, such as fire fighting and drought relief. See B. Derman and P. Prabhakaran, 'Reflections on the Formulation and Implementation of IWRM in Southern Africa from a Gender Perspective', *Water Alternatives*, Vol. 9, No. 3 (2016), pp. 644–661.

through 'user pay'. The only way to do this was to increase the amount of water that could be labelled 'commercial' rather than 'primary' in order to increase revenues to the new parastatal, which would replace funding from the national government. The beneficiaries were intended to be new black Zimbabwean farmers who could take advantage of re-allocated waters. The idea of primary water runs, nonetheless, against the dominant narrative of user pay. Yet, the concept of primary water has been operationalised effectively by water users across Zimbabwe and not by water bureaucrats. But given the growing scarcity of resources, we have observed Catchment Councils attempting to obtain revenues by defining for example, small gardens or animal watering points as commercial ventures, in which case they will be said to be using commercial water, which requires a price.[52]

### 5.2 *Commercial Farming and Fast Track Land Reform*[53]

Because Zimbabwe is an agricultural based economy highly dependent upon irrigation, the reorganisation of the rural sector has had major consequences on the water sector. Following the 2000 defeat of a new constitution, proposed by ZANU-PF and President Mugabe, land occupations of white commercial farms were organised and carried out by liberation 'war veterans', ZANU-PF youth militia and ZANU-PF party members. While there are multiple debates about how this process was planned, organised and implemented, the outcome has been the violent and coercive removal of all but a few white commercial farmers from their lands.[54] In terms of the broader political context, it has been argued that land redistribution was the political tool used by ZANU-PF to reconstitute its political base, to block farmers and farm workers from supporting the opposition party, the Movement for Democratic Change (MDC), and to reward its own powerful followers without regard to what constituted a good and necessary land reform programme, including water.[55] In terms of the

[52] Derman's field notes from attendance at Manyame, Sanyati and Mazowe Catchment Councils in 1999 and 2000.

[53] Fast Track is the name given to the farm occupations and subsequent resettlement begun in 2000. It is termed 'fast track' to indicate that occupation came first and planned resettlement came after. There is now a large literature considering the process and its outcomes.

[54] There is a substantial literature on the human rights violations produced by this process and the land reform process itself. Almost every human rights organisation has issued reports on Zimbabwe. The single best Zimbabwe source for documentation is www.hrforumzim.com. Last accessed February 14, 2017.

[55] A. Hellum and B. Derman, 'Land Reform and Human Rights in Contemporary Zimbabwe: Balancing Individual and Social Justice through an Integrated Human Rights Framework', *World Development*, Vol. 32, No. 10 (2004), pp. 1785–1805.

present, however, and whatever the explanations for Fast Track, Zimbabwe's former commercial farm areas have been transformed into largely smaller-scale farms with a greatly reduced area for larger-scale farms.[56]

There has also been a long period of economic distress including agriculture, tourism and manufacturing, and an emigration of approximately 25 per cent of its population to the United Kingdom and surrounding countries.[57] Since most of Zimbabwe's waters in its agricultural economy are used for irrigation, and farm workers had constituted the largest percentage of formal workers, what happens on the land has profound consequences for water management. As of 2016 there were less than 400 remaining 'white farmers' out of what had been approximately 5,400. Thus, virtually all of Zimbabwe's large-scale commercial farmland has been appropriated by the government on behalf of two types of resettlement types – A1 and A2. The A1 villagised model has been used since the early 1980s. It replicates a village with planned residential, field and grazing areas. Analyses of A1 resettled farms find that irrigation systems were dismantled and dam storage systems unused.[58] A2s are intended for those with the means to run viable commercial farms. However, ownership of very profitable farms close to Zimbabwe's urban areas were disproportionately transferred to powerful officials including ministers, permanent secretaries, generals, police officers and governors.[59]

In analysing the interface of fast track land reform and water reform, it is significant that neither took the other into account. Land reform was based upon receiving land for free, while water reform was founded upon increasing the number of people paying for the cost of water. The major source for funding water was to have been commercial farmers who had the means to pay. Because of the resettlement program and broad economic difficulties

56 'The Fast Track Land Reform Programme, begun in 2000, allocated to new farmers over 4,500 farms making up 7.6m hectares, 20 per cent of the total land area of the country, according to (admittedly rough) official figures. In 2008-09, this represented over 145,000 farm households in A1 schemes and around 16500 further households occupying A2 plots' (I. Scoones, N. Marongwe, B. Mavedzenge, F. Murimbarimba, J. Mahenehene and C. Sukume, 'Zimbabwe's Land Reform: A Summary of Findings'). (http://zimbabweland.net/Zimbabwe's%20Land%20Reform%20Booklet%20Web.pdf. Last accessed December 20, 2016.)

57 Following the Government of National Unity in 2009 the economy was dollarised, the Zimbabwe dollar terminated which brought inflation under control and stabilised the economy.

58 Derman and Gonese, 'Water Reform'.

59 There is not space here to review the debates around who received the white farms. N. Marongwe in recent article documents how rich and powerful people received farms in a district near Harare. N. Marongwe, 'Who was allocated Fast Trackland, and what did they do with it? Selection of A2 farmers in Goromonzi District, Zimbabwe and Its Impacts on Agricultural Production', *Journal of Peasant Studies*, Vol. 38, No. 5 (2011), pp. 1069–1092.

collection of revenues for water use has been extremely low. It was also the white farm owners who supplied drinking water to the tens of thousands of full and part-time farm workers. In her research on four resettlement farms, Rutsate found that most resettled farmers lost their borehole pumped drinking water and drunk from unprotected sources of dams, shallow wells, and rivers.[60] Next to the resettled farms was one farm owner who was able to afford the electricity and kept supplying his workers with water.

The 1990s saw a rapid growth of large- and small-scale irrigation. Unfortunately, the fast track process did not plan for dams and water management systems in resettlement unless a farm was taken over in its totality. [61] In its casual disregard of water resources, water management and water infrastructure fast track undermined the irrigation infrastructure in place on the former commercial farms.[62] In terms of small-scale irrigation systems, little or no government resources remained for supporting this sector. In the communal areas, the most important irrigation component was and is gardens mainly worked by women. These are hand irrigated and have been almost completely ignored by water experts and government.[63] In more general terms, there has been a loss of focus on small-scale farmers' interests in communal areas. The emphasis in the resettlement areas is now upon command agriculture,[64] which has made new inputs available for larger-scale farmers who claim to be able to produce five tons of maize (or more) per hectare. This tension between whether to support large- or small-scale farmers will not disappear any time soon.

The future remains opaque and uncertain for rural agriculture-based livelihoods. Simplifying the picture for the period after 2002 with respect to water

[60] E. Rutsate, Women's Participation in Water Governance and Reform in Zimbabwe: A Case Study of Four A1 Resettlement Farms in Mazowe Catchment, Post the Fast Track Land Reform and Resettlement Programme. Doctoral Thesis, University of Zimbabwe (2016).

[61] C. Zawe, *Reforms in Turbulent Times: A Study on the Theory and Practice of Three Irrigation Management Policy Reform Models in Mashonaland, Zimbabwe*, PhD Thesis (Wageningen: Wageningen University, 2006); Derman and Gonese, 'Water Reform'.

[62] In the past several years, dammed waters have often gone unused because of the decline in irrigated agriculture.

[63] See B. Derman and A. Hellum, 'Livelihood Rights Perspective on Water Reform: Reflections on Rural Zimbabwe', *Land Use Policy*, Vol. 24, No. 4 (2007), pp. 664–673.

[64] Command Agriculture is the Zimbabwe government's newest program to increase food production. Zimbabwe recently launched the command agriculture programme, under which government is targeting the production of two million tonnes of maize on 400,000 hectares of land. Under the programme, 2,000 farmers will be given inputs, irrigation and mechanised equipment. They will, however, be required to give five tonnes per hectare to government as repayment. www.pindula.co.zw/Command_Agriculture_2016. Last accessed on February 10, 2017.

for agriculture, resettled farmers, like most communal areas, remain reliant upon wetlands cultivation for food and rainf for maize and cash-crops especially tobacco. The wetland areas have tended to be managed by women and over time have become critical for food security. Small-scale irrigation schemes have in general collapsed. Irrigation services according to the Irrigation Officer, Conrad Zawe, suffered a huge blow.[65] On the newly resettled areas, it was recognised by 2002 that most commercial farm irrigation systems were no longer functional.

Most systems were vandalised, taken or sold by the outgoing farmers, criminals, war veterans and sometimes resettled farmers. It was at this point the government attempted the Winter Wheat Irrigation Rehabilitation Programme to address dramatically falling wheat production. To fund this, the new smallholder irrigation projects were suspended and the money transferred. The wheat programme failed. Not surprisingly there was no programme for supplying drinking water to the newly resettled farmers.

From a human rights perspective, fast track land reform constituted a series of human rights violations in how the farms were occupied and how farm workers were treated in general. In addition, land reform and water reform did not take each other into account. Paying for water and other aspects of water management has been greeted with great suspicion by resettled farmers. From a political ecology perspective, ZINWA is seen by almost all farmers as interested overwhelmingly in revenue, not in managing the waters for rural peoples' benefit. Under these circumstances, participation in institutions in water management has meant little while in the communal areas there has been little incentive for poorer and small-scale farmers to participate. Given ZINWA's continuous search for funds there appears to be little reason for farmers to support Catchment and Sub-catchment councils.

## 6 URBAN WATER

Since 1980, significant strides have been made in the provision of safe water and improved sanitation in Zimbabwe's cities. By the mid-1990s, it was estimated that 99 per cent of the urban population had access to safe water compared to 64 per cent in the rural areas, while sanitation coverage was estimated at 99 per cent and 48 per cent, respectively.[66] However, Swatuk puts

65 Zawe, *Reforms in Turbulent Times*, p. 64.

66 M. Chenje and P. Johnson (eds.), *Water in Southern Africa* (Maseru/Harare: SADC/IUCN/SIRDC, 1996).

access to safe water at 81 per cent of the total population and access to adequate sanitation at 53 per cent as of 2004.[67] These figures are now much lower because of socio-political and economic factors that have gripped the country since 1999.[68] According to the government the access to urban water supply fell to 40 percent while the hours of supply dropped from 24 hours a day to between 6 and 12 and often less (See government of Zimbabwe Water Policy, 2013).

The broad national social, political and economic processes after 2000 have undermined the water and sanitation achievements of the previous twenty years. To examine the full effects of these processes, we detail what has happened in Zimbabwe's largest and capital city, Harare. Unlike in the earlier part of the paper, we are here concerned with water for domestic purposes (that includes drinking, cooking, laundry and sanitation uses). The suitability of the water is assessed in relation to the quantity and quality of water for household needs in line with international standards. Politics and power deeply influence or shape water issues. In 2000 the ruling party lost political control of the nation's capital to the then opposition party, Movement for Democratic Change (MDC) which in 2009 became a partner for four years (until 2013) in a Government of National Unity.[69] In the absence of access to ZANU-PF's documents, we can only guess that part of the explanation for the national government's indifference to critical issues in the city rests in the political sphere. The President and his party can no longer win elections in capital city while continuously interfering with the city's governance.[70]

The story of Harare's water and sanitation is inextricably linked to its surrounding urban areas, all of which lie within a 50 kilometre radius. These include Chitungwiza, (Zimbabwe's third largest city), Norton, Ruwa and Epworth. In practice these are Harare's dormitory towns, which do not have much by way of an economic base and consequently are labour

[67] L. Swatuk, 'A Political Economy of Water is Southern Africa', *Water Alternatives*, Vol. 1, No. 1 (2008), pp. 24–47.

[68] E. Manzungu, 'Running out of Options? The Status of Service Delivery in the Harare-Chitungwiza Metropolis', in E. Manzungu (ed.), *Towards a New Water Creed: Water Management, Governance and Livelihood in Southern Africa* (Bonn/Harare: Inwent/Weaver Press, 2008), pp. 11–24.

[69] The president was from ZANU-PF, the Prime Minister from MDC and the ministries are divided between them.

[70] For example, when MDC won the mayoral election, he was promptly removed by the Minister of Local Government, Rural and Urban Development Minister Ignatius Chombo. The same minister, currently in a divorce battle, has had his illegal assets made public. See The *Herald*, 5 November 2010.

reservoirs for Harare.[71] Between them, the urban settlements in the Greater Harare area are home to some 3 million people and account for at least 25 per cent of the country's population.[72]

Harare's water supply system was designed to provide water to all the urban settlements. Given the increased population and the lack of investment in Harare's water supply system, especially pumps and pipes, there has been a decreased availability of water for Harare's residents. The city pumped only 80 per cent of daily water needs by 1999.[73] Table 1 shows decreasing water availability at household level over the last two decades. By 2005 there were already some high-density suburbs that were not getting the basic water requirement of 50 litres per capita per day.[74]

Harare uses a planning figure of 70 litres a day to cater for losses which are very high due to collapsing infrastructure including pipes. The situation worsened in 2008 when the water available was below the basic water requirement threshold in both the low- and high-density areas, and in many areas no water was supplied at all. The pumping capacity of the city's water supplies of 450 megalitres per day can only satisfy 40 per cent of the city's population of over two million in 2012.[75]

At the same time the city was not able to pump adequate amounts of water, and there were growing issues of water quality. The major source of Harare's drinking water lies in Lake Chivero. Due to multiple systemic failures, raw sewage and untreated industrial and farm pollutants have been flowing into the lake.[76] Even during the best of times when the waters were properly treated, the water quality was declining. With the failure of the treatment plants, the power cuts which affected the pumps, water quality issues became a crisis. Since Harare is at the source of Zimbabwe's major rivers, significant water pollution issues will have significant, if as yet unknown, consequences downstream. They will also have broad consequences for Harare since it is

[71] After 2000 formal employment plummeted, poverty levels soared, and life in these areas grew increasingly difficult.

[72] E. Manzungu and R. Machiridza, 'An Analysis of Water Consumption and Prospects for Implementing Water Demand Management in the City of Harare, Zimbabwe', *Physics and Chemistry of the Earth*, Vol. 30, Nos. 11–16 (2005), pp. 925–934.

[73] Manzungu, 'Running Out of Options?'.

[74] P. Gleick, 'Implementing the Human Right to Water', in E. Riedel and P. Rothen (eds.), *The Human Right to Water* (Berlin: BWV Berliner Wissenschafts-Verlag, 2006), pp. 143–147.

[75] ZimStat (Zimbabwe National Statistics Agency), *Zimbabwe Population Census 2012: National Report*. Harare, Zimbabwe, 2012.

[76] N. Moyo, *Lake Chivero: A Polluted Lake* (Harare: University of Zimbabwe Publications, 1997); I. Nhapi, 'The Water Situation in Harare, Zimbabwe: A Policy and Management Problem', *Water Policy*, Vol. 11, pp. 221–235.

built on its own watershed.[77] Prior to dollarisation in 2009, the city was refused adequate foreign currency by the national government to purchase the chemicals required for water purification.[78]

The poor water quality has increased over time. Data from the City Health Department indicates that in the past five years (2004–2008) the diarrhoea cases have been increasing and are substantially higher in the high-density suburbs than the low-density suburbs. This has been attributed to the fact that relatively rich low-density residents were able to afford alternative water sources, ranging from boreholes to protected deep wells and purchased water in tanks, whereas in the high-density areas it was much more difficult to utilise these solutions.

Faced with a severe financial crisis, The Government permitted ZINWA to let it provide water for the city of Harare so it could increase its revenues. The Government did this without enabling legislation (only a cabinet directive), which was illegal.[79] It took the outbreak of cholera in 2008 to signal though the comprehensive crisis in the water supply and wastewater management systems. The cholera spread to 55 of Zimbabwe's 62 districts which demonstrated links between Harare and the rest of the country's waters.[80]

The World Health Organization (WHO) has estimated that cholera, which had usually been at a chronic, if low, level in Zimbabwe, had escalated to become an epidemic in 2009 despite denials by the government. As is the case with many environmental issues, even the spread of microbes can be linked to an understanding of political forces in affecting aquatic ecologies. Government funding for public health had declined and the capacity to provide intravenous drips for victims of diarrheal diseases was absent in public hospitals and clinics. By 28 January 2009, the cholera death

77 L. Zinyama, 'The evolution of the spatial structure of Greater Harare, 1890 to 1990', in L. Zinyama, D. S. Tevera and S. D. Cumming (eds.), *Harare, The Growth and Problems of the City* (Harare: University of Zimbabwe Publications, 1995).

78 While plans had been made to build a new dam known as Kunzvi, whose purpose was to increase the quantity of water available and to mix good water with the impure water from the older reservoirs to improve water quality, it was never begun. Construction of the dam, which was supposed to start in 2004–5, did not start. Costs estimated at USD 4 million were estimated to have increased sevenfold to USD 28.5 million in January 2004. It is anyone's guess as to what the current figure is. R. Machiridza, E. Manzungu and J. Matande, *Possibilities for Implementing Water Demand Management at the Household Level in the City of Harare, Zimbabwe*, Selected proceedings of the Water and Wastewater Management for Developing Countries Conference, 28–30 July 2004 (Victoria Falls, Zimbabwe, 2005), pp. 243–256.

79 The handover contravened the Urban Councils Act of 1985, which gave the mandate of providing water and sanitation services in urban areas to elected city councils.

80 WHO, *Cholera in Zimbabwe*, WHO Epidemiological Bulletin No. 27 (2009), p. 2.

toll in Zimbabwe was 3,028.[81] By the 30 May 2009, there were 98,424 suspected cases, including 4,276 deaths (which is a high case fatality rate of 4.3 per cent) reported by the Ministry of Health and Child Welfare (MoHCW) of Zimbabwe. Apparently acknowledging the failure of ZINWA, the national government returned the management of water supply back to the City of Harare in February 2009.

Demonstrating the links among health, disease, political corruption, and indifference to suffering, what might be viewed as the political ecology of health, Human Rights Watch wrote in 2013 that: 'In 2008, as the country's economy declined, the appalling water and sanitation situation gave way to the most devastating outbreak of cholera on the African continent in 15 years. Between 2008 and 2009, over 4,200 people died and at least 100,000 people became sick. In the high-density suburbs of Harare, the lack of water, sanitation facilities, information about the epidemic, and healthcare services, all contributed to the ferocious nature of the epidemic. Rather than muster resources to slow the epidemic, the government denied its severity and prematurely declared an end to the outbreak although thousands were still suffering'.[82]

While the cholera epidemic came to an end through the dry season of 2009, it remains a sustained threat since the major causes have not been addressed. Moreover, the true illness and death toll will never be known because so many victims died outside the health system. One needs to emphasise that the lack of clean water dramatically affects all health-care institutions, and there are an unknown number of premature AIDS-related deaths and other deaths.

The main local organisations attempting to redress the water situation in Harare have been the Combined Harare Residents Association (CHRA) and Harares Resident's Trust. They are very active civic associations trying to mobilise in a very difficult political environment. However, water and sanitation were only some of the crises that they had to deal with in terms of failing service delivery and corruption. Marking a shift in political discourses in the country, CHRA began to focus on the right to clean drinking water and the failure of ZINWA to provide it.

An off-shoot and new civic group, Harare Residents' Trust (HRT), began organising meetings to assess water delivery to the various areas of Harare and

[81] WHO, 'Cholera in Zimbabwe - update 4' (9 June 2009), last accessed 8 February 2010; available at www.who.int/csr/don/2009_06_09/en/index.html.

[82] Human Rights Watch, *Troubled Water: Burst Pipes, Contaminated Wells, and Open Defecation in Zimbabwe's Capital* (2013), 15.

then formulate strategies to resist payment if water was not being delivered. They also sought to prevent water cut-offs when residents fell behind in their payments.

In two high density suburbs of Harare, Mabvuku and Tafara, we found that during a three-year period almost no water was pumped into these two areas. Residents, who had piped water and toilets in their homes, now sought water in the neighbouring wetlands. Over a few months they tired of carrying water to flush them and used the wetlands for defecation, thus polluting their new water supply.[83] With the outbreak of cholera UNICEF constructed boreholes, bought large water containers, and contracted with individual truck owners to fill them with 'clean' water,[84] but not before cholera caused severe illness and deaths. As individuals dug their own wells, they could not protect them since the sewage system was leaking. The water department has been unable to close them because there is an inadequate water supply combined with limits on what residents can afford.

In other areas of Harare, the northern suburbs, residents have invested in deep boreholes or else tanks which are filled by private business tankers. There has been the informalisation of water services with new entrepreneurs entering at various scales (tankers to wheel barrows).

The situation in Bulawayo however has been different. Musemwa, an environmental historian, has demonstrated that political and economic power concentrated in the hands of the white settler State provided water to itself and not to, for example, the black township of Makokoba. As Bulawayo's population grew and water demand increased, the central government dominated by the ruling party systematically denied water projects to this city which had supported a different political party throughout the 1980s. Once again, it demonstrated how water distribution and water projects are subject not just to the semi-arid scarcity of Bulawayo, but also to the power of the central state.[85]

Primary water as discussed earlier includes water used for domestic purposes. Urban agriculture if carried out by households or families appears to be within the definition, but there have been no legal findings. Since independence, there have been significant policy changes regarding urban

[83] Some NGOs have introduced ecological sanitation, which makes use of human waste and turns it into something useful and valuable and poses a minimum risk of polluting the environment and no threat to human health. However, to date there has been great resistance to these.

[84] Field notes, November 2010.

[85] M. Musemwa, 'A Tale of Two Cities: The Evolution of the City of Bulawayo and Makokoba Township under Conditions of Water Scarcity 1894-1953', *South African Historical Journal*, Vol. 55 (2006), pp. 186–209; and M. Musemwa, 'Disciplining a "Dissident" City'.

agriculture. A decade after independence, urban agriculture was prohibited in 1990. There were only minor concessions in the case of land set aside for migrant labour and a few co-operatives. The major reason for this policy was anticipated environmental degradation. However, urban agriculture has been steadily gaining grudging acceptance because of the potential benefits it presents for food security of the urban poor households. A survey was carried out in selected residential areas in Harare to assess the practice of environmental governance on the basis of cultivators' perceptions, revealing some interesting results.[86] Access to land was mostly through 'open access', which means on the one hand that families are able to gain access, but on the other it bodes ill for environmental protection. The researchers found that there was limited knowledge of the impacts of urban agriculture on the environment and specifically on water in relation to land preparation, chemical usage and agronomic practices which will have longer-term consequences for Harare's water supply.

In recognition of recent economic realities, urban agriculture has become accepted by government officials and the control of wetlands cultivation has been relaxed. In sum, there are few or no regulations enforced with respect to accessing wetlands and practicing urban agriculture in Harare. In the current climate of impunity, many new luxury homes are being built in wetlands as well. The years of 2015 and 2016 were dry years and there was increased building and farming in Harare's wetlands. So far 2017 has been a very wet year and many homes and gardens in Harare have been flooded. Today the economic reality reflected in increasing poverty means that urban agriculture has become an important livelihood and income-generating strategy for many urban families. Wealthier individuals gain access to wetlands and hire labour to produce crops for market. Unfortunately the environmental considerations have received little interest until early 2017.

## 7 A NEW CONSTITUTION, MOBILISATION AND A RIGHT TO WATER?

The adoption of a new, Zimbabwean written, constitution, has not meant much change. Human rights and social and economic human rights have continued to take a back-seat for government's adherence to the policy of user pay. Despite mobilisation by several civil society and human rights

[86] R. Machiridza and E. Manzungu, 'The Food Security Environment Nexus in Urban Agriculture', in E. Manzungu (ed.), *Towards a New Water Creed: Water Management, Governance and Livelihood in Southern Africa* (Bonn/Harare: Inwent/Weaver Press, 2008), pp. 81–88.

organisations for greater socio-economic rights, especially given the increasing levels of poverty in Zimbabwe, little change has occurred. It seems that neither Zimbabwe signing the General Assembly Resolution on the right to water, nor the the new constitution including a right to water, has made any difference in terms of the operations of the Ministry of Environment, Water and Climate, the Zimbabwe National Water Authority or the City of Harare. The current Water Policy does acknowledge the international responsibilities held by the government and introduces new if somewhat perplexing language concerning the International Covenant on Economic, Social and Cultural Rights (ICESCR), General Comment No. 15 (2002) on the human right to water. The Public Health Act (chapter 15:09) clearly states that it is the duty of a local authority to furnish water supplies in line with health requirements. In addition, the Public Health Act requires the local authority to maintain existing water supplies in good working order. The Water Policy also requires any other agency providing water in an area, such as ZINWA, to comply with this requirement. The SADC regional water policy of 2005, of which Zimbabwe is a signatory, stipulates that states will prioritise the allocation, access and utilisation of water resources for basic human needs over any other allocation, access and utilisation. The policy does link primary water and the right to water, but with no discussion of how to do this or any further discussion to our knowledge: 'Water for primary needs is a right for all Zimbabweans. Access to WSS [water and sanitation] services in sufficient quantity and adequate quality to sustain life is a human right which is accompanied with the responsibility of all to meet their obligations to other users and water service providers. Equity in access to water by all Zimbabweans is a right. Specific attention to equity, that takes into account the different needs of different communities and inclusion of disadvantaged communities are integral to realising this right'.[87]

A number of civil society organisations, in addition to the CHRA and HRT, have mobilised around water issues. The Zimbabwe Coalition on Debt and Development (ZCDD)[88] has noted that there is a contradiction between the current emphasis on prepaid meters in Harare and other cities and towns and the right to water. Since water is indispensable and a human right, it needs to be enjoyed by every Zimbabwean regardless of social or economic status. In light of this, the installation of prepaid water meters has been resisted across Zimbabwe by civic organisations on the basis that it is unconstitutional, and a breach of Zimbabwe's obligations to respect, protect and fulfil the human

87 Ministry of Environment, Water and Climate, National Water Policy 2013.

88 The Zimbabwe Coalition on Debt and Development, ZIMCODD is a Social and Economic Justice coalition established in February 2000. It is registered as a trust.

right to water as it deprives those citizens who fail to pay from enjoying their constitutional right without hindrance. Prepaid water meters ensure that access to water is only guaranteed to those who have the ability to pay. According to the ZCDD, this is tantamount to privatisation and commodification of water.

## 8 CONCLUSIONS

The complex flows of water, its hydrosocial cycles due to human uses and interventions make water governance and management very challenging. IWRM when introduced into Zimbabwe sought a holistic management system including land and environment dimensions. However, as described above, land, water and environment remained separate and even within the water sector efforts to manage river systems proved to be very difficult. The loss of funding for the water sector, the devaluation of the Zimbabwe dollar from 2000-2009, the government's indifference to the people of Harare and the city's dependence upon water revenues for its operation (and not for the water sector) has produced an enormous crisis. The solution for that crisis has been turned over to the World Bank, the Chinese government and the African Development Bank to fund. None of these actors seem to be particularly keen on the human right to water.

In the meantime uncontrolled 'development' in Harare's wetlands, non-monitoring of the broader environment, pollution of its waters (ground and reservoirs), and a water ministry with few resources, which are mostly committed to a large agricultural dam for growing sugar cane (Tokwe-Mukorsi), are just some of the elements of a profound long-term crisis.

Sub-Saharan Africa has been characterised by legal pluralities. The colonial States and the independent States have often lacked the resources, moral authority and/or the coercive capacity to override local institutions. This has resulted in normative and institutional pluralism for multiple resource arenas, including water. In Zimbabwe, a national formal legal distinction has been made between primary and commercial water. This distinction, which makes sense to water managers, makes little sense to the women and men in rural Zimbabwe. Nonetheless this distinction between primary and commercial water could have been the legal basis for at least recognition of a rural right to water, which has included, as we have argued elsewhere, a right to livelihood.

The toxic socio-political situation has produced and continues to produce profound echoes in the water and sanitation sector as well as more broadly in water management. This has rendered the implementation of a right to water and sanitation a difficult goal in the present circumstances. The decline of

Zimbabwe's water management system reflects the broader multiple crises that transcend almost all areas. Events in Zimbabwe certainly demonstrate how the shaping and reshaping of power relations are reflected in the political ecology of water.

The failure of ZINWA to manage and supply water can be viewed as a political failure by the government that has neglected its urban populations in light of its other political priorities. Deteriorating services, the cholera epidemic, systemic corruption and now a typhoid epidemic can be directly attributed to the State. In the rural arena, there have been parallel failures. The process of resettling commercial farms paid little or no attention to existing irrigation systems. Blaming current hunger and agricultural declines upon drought, while disregarding existent water and irrigation systems during resettlement and permitting their dismantlement, is disturbingly consistent with ZANU-PF's long-term disregard for the rural poor and indifference to infrastructure, in this case, irrigation works and drinking water supply. In addition, there are the difficulties faced by civil society trying to engage in criticism of existing government practices.[89]

Water reform has died a premature death although some Catchment Councils struggle on. Even if much of the reforms did not meet the water needs of Zimbabwe's small-scale farmers, they provided the logic for addressing profound water inequalities and perhaps institutions that might have been more responsive. Since 1998, in our view, there has been a neglect of small-scale farmers, women and existing water management systems in the water reforms.[90] There have been highly competent scholar-practitioners like Bolding, Manzungu and van der Zaag who were presenting significant alternatives for how to make water reform address the needs of small-scale farmers and to stimulate greater water availability for them.[91] Despite the existence of policy alternatives, these ideas went unutilised and then discarded. In the midst of land invasions, catchment and sub-catchment councils attempted to

[89] For a complete documentation of the violence and torture that have characterised Zimbabwe since 2000, see the website for the Zimbabwe human rights forum at www.hrforumzim.com (accessed 20 June 2016). There is also extensive documentation by Human Rights Watch, Amnesty International among many international human rights organisations.

[90] Hellum and Derman, 'Negotiating Water Rights in the Context of a New Political and Legal Landscape in Zimbabwe'; Derman, Hellum, Manzungu, Sithole and Machiridza, 'Intersections of Law, Human Rights and Water Management in Zimbabwe'.

[91] A. Bolding, E. Manzungu and P. van der Zaag, 'A Realistic Approach to Water Reform in Zimbabwe', in E. Manzungu, A. Senzanje and P. van der Zaag (eds.), *Water for Agriculture in Zimbabwe: Policy and Management Options for the Smallholder Sector* (Harare: University of Zimbabwe Press, 1999).

avoid politics and continue focusing on water reform and debated water allocation, distribution and reform with a mix of water engineers, catchment managers, ZINWA officials, commercial farmers, representatives of small-scale commercial areas, chiefs, representatives of donor organisations and academics. The spirit of open debate and decision-making came to an end with the parliamentary elections of 2000 and the presidential election of 2002. In contrast to water, what kind of land reform, who should carry it out, who should benefit, and so on, could not be debated as the President declared that water was a 'political issue' and could not be discussed in any fora not approved by the president.[92]

The experimental use of 'natural' hydrological boundaries faltered on the basis of land reform. The efforts to manage Zimbabwe's waters holistically could not overcome the continued silo approach to sectors: agriculture, health, environment, irrigation, drinking water, etc. al. The focus on revenue collection impeded rather than facilitated the adaption of water management to large numbers of new users despite the political importance of land. In addition, little attention has been given to women for their water needs. Rutsate notes that men focused on irrigation water ignoring women's family needs for clean drinking water.[93]

Large-scale commercial farms will continue but occupying a much smaller percentage of the Zimbabwean landscape. Water reforms now will need to be linked to ongoing land reform and the new farmers on the land. However, without new revenues this is unlikely as ZINWA focuses on higher revenue sources. Due to the emphasis upon resettlement on the former large-scale commercial farms, the communal areas have tended to be neglected. A refocus on communal area needs is called for since it remains the case that the majority of Zimbabweans live in communal areas. And of course there will be a new and dramatic need to reconstruct water supply to cities. There remains a clear urgency to consider Zimbabwe's waters holistically. We could envision smaller-scale systems which would be more adaptable and more flexible than those relying on very large dams. Even though there is the intention to increase the capital budget for water infrastructure, most of it will be allocated to large dams like the Tokwe-Mukosi in Masvingo Province whose waters are dedicated for sugar production. Large regions of Zimbabwe have sufficient water resources to greatly increase water availability for

92 See B. Derman and E. Manzungu, 'The Complex Politics of Water and Power in Zimbabwe: IWRM in the Catchment Councils of Manyame, Mazowe and Sanyati (1993–2001)', *Water Alternatives*, Vol. 9, No. 3 (2016), pp. 513–530 for an analysis of this use of 'political'.

93 Rutsate, Women's Participation in Water Governance and Reform in Zimbabwe.

domestic and productive uses. More local strategies need to be adopted for coping with rain-short years rather than investing in huge dams.

There are very different and competing knowledge frameworks for and about water. These are expressed in co-existing systems of water management. How to take these into account when rethinking systems of water management will depend upon the reorganisation of power in the coming years. If, as we have argued, the control of water is indeed decisive to centralisation and increasing State power, then we suggest greater polycentrism and decentralisation.[94] In moving toward smaller-scale agriculture much of it with irrigation, smaller units of water management would be favoured but with the appropriate safeguards to protect downstream users from upstream monopolisation. In addition, as the recognition of an international human right to water grows in importance along with the right to livelihood,[95] Zimbabwe could begin with a far more gendered and people-centred approach to water and water management. We can look forward to a time when the linking of land, water, environment and health are debated and seriously addressed. Ironically, while land markets other than urban ones have been ended for the time being, water is now being bought and sold by new entrepreneurs with the collapse of the formal water supply system. Commodification of water from above and below has proceeded much further in the rest of southern Africa than in Zimbabwe, and so there remains the possibility of instituting and formalising a right to water as part of the incorporation of economic, social and cultural rights into the new constitution. Simultaneously, there is a health emergency stemming from drinking water supply and sanitation that demands a broad and effective governmental priority. The government's and ZINWA's inability to successfully respond to the crisis has further delegitimised the government. Whether a new government can rethink its water strategies based on social and economic rights hangs in the balance as the new constitution continues to be debated and as civil society tries to assert its political space.

94 B. Lankford and N. Hepworth, 'The Cathedral and the Bazaar: Monocentric and Polycentric River Basin Management', *Water Alternatives*, Vol. 3, No. 1 (2010), pp. 82–101.

95 See A. Hellum, 'Towards a Human Rights Based Development Approach: The Case of Women in the Water Reform Process in Zimbabwe', *Law, Social Justice and Global Development*, Vol. 1 (2001); B. Derman and A. Hellum, 'Livelihood Rights Perspective on Water Reform: Reflections on Rural Zimbabwe', *Land Use Policy*, Vol. 24, No. 4 (2007), Special Issue: *Exploring New Understandings of Resource Tenure and Reform in the Context of Globalisation*, edited by T.A. Benjaminsen, B. Derman and E. Sjaastad, pp. 664–673. For elaboration of what a human rights-based approach would mean for land reform, see also A. Hellum and B. Derman, 'Land Reform and Human Rights in Contemporary Zimbabwe: Balancing Individual and Social Justice through an Integrated Human Rights Framework', *World Development*, Vol. 32, No. 10 (2004), pp. 1785–1805.

## 20

# The Right to Water in Rural India and Drinking Water Policy Reforms

PHILIPPE CULLET*

### 1 INTRODUCTION

The human right to water is well established in India, having been recognised by the Supreme Court of India for a number of years.[1] However, there is little substance to the right beyond its formal recognition.[2] The case law is not particularly detailed with regard to the content of the right, nor has the Parliament of India ever adopted framework legislation that would provide specificity to this right.

In strict legal terms, India has little beyond formal recognition of the right to water. Yet, this does not reflect its importance in practice. Indeed, the crucial importance of water for survival has led the Government of India and state governments to undertake a number of policy initiatives over the past several decades that amount, at least in part, to attempts to foster the realisation of the right.[3] Since the mid-1990s, the law and policy framework concerning drinking water has evolved dramatically.[4] On the one hand, the seventy-third amendment to the Constitution has provided for a significant devolution of

* Professor of International and Environmental Law, SOAS University of London. This chapter was last revised in March 2011. Since then there has been no major change in rural water policy.

1 See, for example, *Subhash Kumar* v. *State of Bihar*, AIR 1991 SC 420 (Supreme Court of India, 1991).

2 See further, S. Muralidhar, 'The Right to Water: An Overview of the Indian Legal Regime', in E. Riedel and P. Rothen (eds.), *The Human Right to Water* (Berlin: Berliner Wissenschafts-Verlag, 2006), pp. 65–81.

3 In particular, the Accelerated Rural Water Supply Programme for rural areas.

4 In this chapter, drinking water includes not only water for personal use but also some livelihood-related uses, such as water for cattle, as specified in Government of India, Accelerated Rural Water Supply Programme Guidelines (1999–2000), s. 2(2)(2) ('ARWSP Guidelines').

competences to panchayats.[5] Accordingly, a number of states have amended their panchayat legislation.[6] On the other hand, the policy framework governing drinking water supply at the union level has evolved in ways that reflect in part the constitutional amendments, as well as a series of policy reforms known as water sector reforms.[7]

The fact that not all ongoing reforms derive from the same premise implies that they do not necessarily propose the same solutions to identified problems. This is not problematic in itself but requires close scrutiny. Indeed, the essence of the legal framework is to be organised in a certain way that puts, for instance, constitutional principles and fundamental rights above other rules and norms. Thus, any policy reform must be seen in light of its contribution to the realisation of constitutional principles. In the context of drinking water in rural areas, it is unclear that all ongoing reforms pull in a direction that directly contributes to the realisation of constitutional objectives.

## 2 THE HUMAN RIGHT TO WATER AND DRINKING WATER REGULATION IN INDIA

### 2.1 *The Human Right to Water*

The Constitution of India does not explicitly include a human right to water. Yet, a number of judicial pronouncements have made it clear that the right exists. First, the Supreme Court has repeatedly derived a human right to water from the right to life.[8] The Court has viewed the unavailability of drinking water to all citizens as constituting a violation of United Nations (UN) human rights instruments and the right to life under the Constitution.[9]

Second, courts have also derived the human right to water from Article 47 (duty of the State to raise the level of nutrition and the standard of living and to improve public health) of the Constitution. In the *Hamid Khan* case, the complaint focused on the health consequences of the supply of water with excessive fluoride content. The High Court found that, under Article 47

5 Constitution of India, Article 243(G) and Eleventh Schedule. Panchayats are defined at article 243(d) of the Constitution of India as institutions of self-government for the rural areas.

6 In the case of Uttar Pradesh, see Uttar Pradesh Panchayat Raj Act, 1947 (as amended).

7 On water sector reforms, see, for example, P. Cullet, *Water Law, Poverty and Development – Water Law Reforms in India* (Oxford: Oxford University Press, 2009), p. 63ff.

8 See, for example, *Subhash Kumar* v. *State of Bihar* and *Narmada Bachao Andolan* v. *Union of India* AIR 2000 SC 3751 (Supreme Court of India, 2000).

9 *Narmada Bachao Andolan* v. *Union of India*.

of the Constitution, the state has a duty 'towards every citizen of India to provide pure drinking water'.[10]

Third, courts have found on repeated occasions that the human right to water includes a duty on the part of the state to provide water. This was recognised in the *Hamid Khan* decision, and the same position has been restated in strong terms in the case of *Vishala Kochi Kudivella Samarkshana Samithi* v. *State of Kerala*, in which the High Court of Kerala held that:

> We have no hesitation to hold that failure of the State to provide safe drinking water to the citizens in adequate quantities would amount to a violation of the fundamental right to life enshrined in Article 21 of the Constitution of India and would be a violation of human rights. Therefore, every Government, which has it priorities right, should give foremost importance to providing safe drinking water even at the cost of other development programs. Nothing shall stand in its way whether it is lack of funds or other infrastructure. Ways and means have to be found out at all costs with utmost expediency instead of restricting action in that regard to mere lip service.[11]

The cases mentioned above confirm that the right is well established in law. Yet, the actual content of the right has not been elaborated on in judicial decisions. Further, there is no general drinking water legislation that would provide this missing content. As analysed in the next subsection, this is not to say that no initiative has been taken concerning rural drinking water supply, but these initiatives do not amount to a comprehensive binding legal framework covering the main attributes of the human right to water.

### 2.2 *Law and Policy Framework for Drinking Water Supply*

Drinking water is acknowledged as the primary concern in the water sector. In legal terms, this is mostly visible through the recognition of the human right to water. Indeed, there is no framework drinking water law to complement the recognition of the human right to water, and, as a result, there is not a general set of principles that apply to drinking water supply throughout the country nor specific rules giving content to the human right to water.[12]

[10] *Hamid Khan* v. *State of Madhya Pradesh*, AIR 1997 MP 191 (Madhya Pradesh High Court, 1996), para. 6.

[11] *Vishala Kochi Kudivella Samarkshana Samithi* v. *State of Kerala*, 2006 (1) KLT 919 (High Court of Kerala, 2006), para. 3.

[12] The only proposal for drinking-water-focused legislation at the union level is limited to certain issues linked to water quality and would not constitute comprehensive drinking water legislation if it were adopted. See Department of Drinking Water Supply, Draft Guidelines for Preparation of Legislation for Framing Drinking Water Regulations (2007).

The absence of broad-based drinking water legislation is a serious concern. Yet, the vital importance of drinking water supply in rural areas has ensured that the union and state governments have given it significant attention. Over time, a patchwork of general policy instruments, quality standards and panchayat laws has developed. This has constituted the framework within which the provision of drinking water has been organised in rural areas.

First, at the union level, several policy initiatives have been taken even though the main responsibility for drinking water supply rests in principle with states. The main instrument from 1972 to 2009 was the Accelerated Rural Water Supply Programme (ARWSP). The ARWSP Guidelines, first introduced in 1972, for a number of years provided the core framework used by the Rajiv Gandhi National Drinking Water Mission in ensuring the provision of drinking water to all habitations in the country.[13] They included a number of key elements:

- They first defined different levels of coverage in terms of quantity. 'Non-covered habitations' were defined as having access to less than 10 litres per capita per day (lpcd). 'Partially covered habitations' were those having access to 10 to 40 lpcd. 'Covered habitations' were defined as having access to 40 lpcd. The figure of 40 lpcd was used to determine the minimum level of coverage necessary to define a habitation as covered and was identified through an amalgamation of figures for different basic minimum water uses: 3 litres for drinking, 5 litres for cooking, 15 litres for bathing, 7 litres for washing utensils and the house and 10 litres for ablutions.
- The Guidelines further specified that the source of water had to be within 1.6 km, or within 100 metres of elevation in mountainous areas. The water was not to be affected by quality problems even though no specific standards for determining quality were included. Another criterion was that a given public source of water, such as a handpump, was not to be used to serve more than 250 people.
- The Guidelines also acknowledged the direct link between drinking water for human beings and water for cattle. Consequently, in a certain number of states particularly affected by drought, the Guidelines mandated that an additional 30 lpcd should be provided for cattle.[14]

[13] ARWSP Guidelines. Note that a 'habitation' in the ARWSP is a locality within a village where a cluster of around twenty families (or 100 people) resides.

[14] Ibid., ss. 2(2) and 2(3).

- The minimum level of 40 lpcd was acknowledged in the ARWSP Guidelines as a minimum level of coverage that should be increased over time. Thus, in states where all habitations had been covered at the level of 40 lpcd, the Government of India had already approved that the next level of service should be 55 lpcd within 500 metres of the house or within 50 metres of elevation in mountainous areas.[15]

Second, the union has attempted to introduce various quality standards for drinking water supply. These include the Bureau of Indian Standards Water Quality Standards IS:10500, 1991, and the Manual on Water Supply and Treatment issued by the Central Public Health and Environmental Engineering Organisation.[16] While these are in principle applicable country-wide, the absence of any legislation directly referring to these standards means that to date their legal status is partly inchoate.

Third, various states have adopted legislation that give panchayats control over water supply at the local level. Different formulations are used, and different acts give a different set of competencies to panchayats. There is nevertheless broad agreement among panchayat acts in giving control to panchayats over drinking water supply at the local level.[17] Some acts are more detailed than others. Some specify the kind of activities that panchayats can engage in, such as constructing, repairing and maintaining tanks or wells, streams and watercourses and specify their powers, such as the capacity to contract someone for water supply.[18] While panchayat acts are not detailed with regard to water supply rights and obligations of the panchayats, they provide a general binding framework within which all water supply at the local level must be organised.

## 3 POLICY REFORM FOR DRINKING WATER SUPPLY IN RURAL AREAS

The framework for water supply in rural areas has been evolving over time. The legal context got a significant boost following the seventy-third constitutional amendment and the adoption or amendment of a number of panchayat laws that now specifically refer to water supply. At the same time,

[15] Rajiv Gandhi National Drinking Water Mission – Department of Drinking Water Supply, Submission to the National Advisory Committee (2005).

[16] Bureau Indian Standards Specifications for Drinking Water (BIS Specification 10500), 1991 and Central Public Health and Environmental Engineering Organisation, *Manual on Water Supply and Treatment*, 3rd edition (New Delhi: Ministry of Urban Development, 1999).

[17] See, for example, Himachal Pradesh Panchayati Raj Act, 1994, s. 11(2).

[18] See, for example, Karnataka Panchayat Raj Act, 1993, s. 77.

drinking water supply in rural areas has never been framed within a general legal context giving it overall direction and specificity. In large part, it is this lack of legal context that has allowed for tremendous policy changes in the 2000s. These reforms have not directly impacted existing laws, nor introduced any new norms, but their impact has been immense, partly because the policy reforms adopted at the union level come with significant financial incentives for states to adopt them.

The first harbinger of the reforms was a pilot project sponsored by the World Bank, the principles of which were adopted in the Swajaldhara Guidelines, 2002.[19] The Guidelines were used as a template for reforms that eventually led to a complete rethinking of the existing policy framework, leading to the disbanding of the ARWSP and the adoption of an entirely new policy framework known as the National Rural Drinking Water Programme (NRDWP).[20]

### 3.1 *Progressive Development of a New Policy Framework*

The Uttar Pradesh Rural Water Supply and Environmental Sanitation Project (Swajal project) – a pilot project funded by the World Bank starting in 1996 – was one of the important drivers of change in the rural drinking water sector.[21] It was based around a string of important policy propositions, seeking to introduce a demand-driven approach to replace the supply-driven approach deemed to result in 'inefficient service delivery and poor quality of construction'.[22] The Swajal project thus sought to introduce participation, allowing users to determine their own contributions to the scheme and to manage operation and maintenance. This participation was not part of the decentralisation agenda introduced with the seventy-third constitutional amendment, but rather promoted people's control over schemes at the local level while introducing new obligations and responsibilities for villagers.

Another new principle under the Swajal project was cost recovery under which villagers were asked to shoulder 10 per cent of the capital costs of new projects and the full costs of the operation and the maintenance of those schemes. The idea was that all projects should be fully self-sufficient.

19 Ministry of Rural Development, Guidelines on Swajaldhara, 2002.

20 Department of Drinking Water Supply, National Rural Drinking Water Programme, *Movement Towards Ensuring People's Drinking Water Security in Rural India: Framework for Implementation* (2010) ('NRDWP 2010').

21 On the general framework for water policy reforms in rural areas, see Chapter 17 in this volume.

22 World Bank, Staff Appraisal Report – Uttar Pradesh Rural Water Supply and Environmental Sanitation Project (Report No. 15516-IN, 1996), p. 6.

However, it was decided that full cost recovery should only be imposed with regard to operation and maintenance in the first instance. This was linked to the perception that villagers would be willing to pay for this service, while poverty might preclude demand for new expensive schemes in favour of maintaining or repairing existing infrastructure.

The Swajal project and related initiatives taken in the late 1990s were generally assessed positively by policymakers.[23] This led to the formulation of the Swajaldhara Guidelines, 2002, which during the tenth Five-Year Plan (2002–2007) extended the key principles of the Swajal project to the whole country. Twenty per cent of funds allocated to the ARWSP were directed to reform projects under the Swajaldhara Guidelines during this period.

The Ministry of Rural Development spearheaded the introduction of Swajaldhara through the adoption of the Guidelines.[24] The Guidelines were premised on the fact that the understanding of water as a social right was misplaced and that it should rather be seen as a socio-economic good.[25] Further, the Guidelines were based on an understanding that the delivery of water by the government had not sufficiently taken into account the preferences of users and was ineffective in carrying out operation and maintenance activities. This thus called for a demand-led approach. The link between the demand-led approach and the new conception of water as an economic good is succinctly brought together in the Guidelines, where they assert a demand-driven system should take into account the preferences of users 'where users get the service they want and are willing to pay for'.[26] The imposition of full cost recovery of operation and maintenance and replacement costs on the communities was expected to generate a sense of ownership and ensure the financial viability of the schemes.

The Swajaldhara Guidelines were remarkably similar to the ones introduced under the Swajal project.[27] First, the Guidelines provided for the adoption of a demand-led approach that included participation of the community, from the choice of the drinking water scheme up to its actual implementation. Second, the Guidelines sought a form of decentralisation and requested that drinking water assets be owned by the relevant panchayat and that communities should have the power to plan, implement and operate all drinking water schemes. Third, the participation and decentralisation elements were brought together in the context of the financial principles that

[23] See, for example, Ministry of Rural Development, *All India Evaluation Study: Sector Reforms Projects in Rural Drinking Water Supply* (2005).

[24] Ministry of Rural Development, *Guidelines on Swajaldhara*.

[25] Ibid., s. 1(1).

[26] Ibid., s. 1(2).

[27] Ibid., s. 3(1).

were a compromised version of full cost recovery. Thus, while users were to bear the entire responsibility for the operation and maintenance of drinking water schemes, their contribution to capital costs was to be limited. In practice, this was first set at 10 per cent for a service level of 40 lpcd, but, in a number of situations, this percentage was exceeded. Under the Swajaldhara Guidelines, at least half of the 10 per cent contribution had to be in cash, which much more than under the Swajal project. Exceptions were, for instance, provided for scheduled tribe areas where the cash contribution was first reduced to one-quarter of the community contribution.[28] Subsequently, in 2006 an amendment to the Guidelines provided that the contribution in the case of villages where scheduled castes and scheduled tribes constituted more than half of all habitations could be in any form without any stipulation of a contribution in cash.[29] Fourth, from an institutional perspective, one of the consequences of a demand-led perspective was the rethinking of the role of the government. The Guidelines here specifically provided that the aim was to shift the government's role from 'direct service delivery' to only supporting a limited number of activities such as planning, policy formulation, monitoring and evaluation.

### 3.2 *A New Policy Framework: The National Rural Drinking Water Programme*

The experience gathered during the tenth Five-Year Plan led the government to suggest an entirely new framework for rural drinking water supply. The need for further changes after the introduction of the Swajaldhara Guidelines can be explained by a variety of factors. In general, the implementation of the reforms has been fraught with difficulties and setbacks. From the government side, the first difficulty was that government agencies engaged in the implementation of drinking water supply policy frameworks were not necessarily keen on the changes that saw them having to hand over some of the decision-making power they had enjoyed earlier. At the same time, some of the reform principles seem to have been found to be politically unappealing for state governments. For instance, in Madhya Pradesh's Barwani district, villages that were implementing Swajaldhara projects did not actually follow the Swajaldhara Guidelines. This is not

28 L. Sabha, 'Unstarred Question No 2451', Swajaldhara Yojana, Answered by Minister of State in the Ministry of Rural Development (Shri A. Narendra) on 18 March 2005.

29 Government of India Department of Drinking Water Supply, Office Memorandum – Amendment to Swajaldhara Guidelines, Doc. No. W-11021/2/2003-TM.IV (SW), 15 May 2006.

particularly surprising given the imposition of a portion of capital costs on villagers, something that was never likely to be politically appealing given the central place of drinking water in rural life. Thus, at best, the overall assessment of the Swajaldhara years was mixed, and this explains why significant policy uncertainty underlined the future of reforms in the eleventh Five-Year Plan (2007–2012).[30] From the point of view of external assessments, the limited independent work done concerning the implementation of the Swajaldhara scheme showed that there were serious concerns with the proposed reform principles.[31]

The above assessments seem to lead naturally to the conclusion that a new framework was necessary. This is indeed what the government decided to do for the eleventh Five-Year Plan. In fact, in a bid to demarcate the new policy principles from earlier reforms, the policy instrument was given a new name and is now known as the National Rural Drinking Water Programme (NRDWP).[32] Yet, even though the new framework seeks to demarcate itself both from the ARWSP and from the reforms initiated through the Swajaldhara Guidelines, the first version of the new Programme argued that 'In order not to lose any time, States/Union Territories shall initiate activities for universalization of the sector reforms/Swajaldhara principles'.[33]

The NRDWP has brought a number of key changes to the policy framework for drinking water supply in rural areas. At the broadest level, it emphasises the need to conceive of drinking water supply in a wider context. Thus, it makes a much more direct link with sanitation than was the case earlier. Further, it proposes links further afield with health policy and even with the Mahatma Gandhi National Rural Employment Guarantee Scheme.[34]

The NRDWP is a relatively comprehensive document, full analysis of which is not the object of this section. Instead, the following subsections focus

[30] On the evolving policy framework between 2007 and 2009, see, for example, Cullet, Water Law, Poverty and Development, pp. 168–170.

[31] See, e.g., P. Sampat, '"Swa"-jal-dhara or "Pay"-jal-dhara – Sector Reform and the Right to Drinking Water in Rajasthan and Maharashtra', *Law, Environment and Development Journal*, Vol. 3, No. 2 (2007), pp. 101–125.

[32] NRDWP 2010.

[33] Department of Drinking Water Supply, National Rural Drinking Water Programme, *Movement towards Ensuring People's Drinking Water Security in Rural India – Framework for Implementation 2009–2012* (2009), p. 45 ('NRDWP 2009'). This paragraph does not figure anymore in the 2010 version of this document.

[34] National Rural Employment Guarantee Act, 2005. This scheme seeks to provide at least 100 days of guaranteed wage employment in every financial year to every household in notified rural areas.

on certain aspects of the NRDWP that are specifically relevant in the context of this chapter.

**Water as a Basic Need and a Public Good**

The NRDWP sees water as a 'public good' that everyone can demand and as a 'basic need'.[35] At the broadest level, this does not seem controversial. From a legal point of view, however, this is revealing of the overall orientation of the NRDWP.

The recognition of water as a public good is interesting but does not fit within the existing legal framework. Indeed, the Supreme Court has repeatedly stated that water is a 'public trust'.[36] This specifically rests on the basis that water is of such importance to people that 'it would be wholly unjustified to make [it] a subject of private ownership'.[37] The Court further specified that the government is supposed to protect water for the enjoyment of the general public rather than allow its use for commercial purposes. Water being a public trust can thus not be a good, even in its characterisation as 'public'.

The second understanding of water under the NRDWP is that it is a basic need. In a general sense, the fulfilment of basic water needs contributes to the realisation of the human right to water or at least its core content. Yet, from a legal perspective, the notion of basic needs is different from that of a human right. In other words, legal instruments that choose to speak the language of basic needs do not speak the language of human rights.

In terms of basic principles, the striking aspect of the NRDWP is thus that it ignores both the basic principle of water law that water is a public trust and the existence of the human right to water. This could be simply an oversight and an inappropriate choice of language from a legal point of view. The fact that the NRDWP omits the language of human rights is, however, confirmed by a comparison of the two different versions put out respectively in 2009 and in 2010. Indeed, the 2009 version, using a formulation reminiscent of the Dublin Statement,[38] specified that water is a 'socio-economic good and demand for basic drinking water needs is a fundamental right'.[39] While arguably this formulation does not amount to a recognition of the human right to water since it frames a human right within an understanding of water as an economic good, it has at least the merit of including the language of human

[35] NRDWP 2010, s. 2.

[36] *MC Mehta* v. *Kamal Nath* (1997), 1 SCC 388 (Supreme Court, 1996). [37] Ibid., para. 25.

[38] Dublin Statement on Water and Sustainable Development, International Conference on Water and the Environment, Dublin, 31 January 1992, principle 4.

[39] NRDWP 2009, s. 12(1).

rights. Further, the 2009 version also recognised as one of its basic principles that the commodification of water was problematic because it shifts the focus away from 'human rights (sic) to water for livelihood'.[40] Both the reference to a 'fundamental right' and to a 'human right' were removed from a later version of the NRDWP, thus confirming a decision not to conceive of drinking water supply within the context of human rights.

**From an Individual Entitlement to Household Drinking Water Security**

The NRDWP goes further than simply omitting the language of human rights. In fact, it constitutes a complete reversal of the policy followed since the 1970s by suggesting that measuring the sufficiency of drinking water provision in terms of a quantity of water per capita per day is inappropriate.[41] The NRDWP suggests moving from a fixed minimum to the concept of drinking water security.

Drinking water security is not given a specific definition, but it is clearly opposed to the per capita norm followed earlier. Indeed, the NRDWP specifically states it is necessary to 'move *ahead* from the conventional norms of liters per capita per day (lpcd) norms to ensure drinking water security for all in the community'.[42] The basic unit now considered is the household. The NRDWP premises the shift from the individual to the household on the fact that 'Average per capita availability may not necessarily mean assured access to potable drinking water to all sections of the population in the habitation'.[43] It does not, however, explain how the shift ensures better coverage in a given habitation.

This framework is startling from a human rights perspective. The key concern is that the focus on the individual has been replaced by a focus on the household. In addition, the foreword to the NRDWP Guidelines specifically indicates that 'norms and guidelines need to be flexible' and further states that flexibility is preferable to the 'adoption of universal norms and standards'.[44] This makes sense in terms of giving panchayats the leeway to manage drinking water in the way most suited to local conditions. However, in terms of broad regulation, this does not fit within a human rights framework that is based on ensuring the same realisation of the right (at least its 'core' content) to everyone, even if specific additional needs of certain categories of people can also be taken into account.

[40] Ibid., s. 2.

[41] Note that at the same time the Guidelines indicate that the overall goal is to 'provide every rural person with adequate safe water for drinking, cooking and other domestic basic needs'. NRDWP 2010, s. 1.

[42] Ibid., s. 4 (emphasis added). [43] Ibid., s. 9(1). [44] Ibid., iv.

### Sustainability and Drinking Water Security

One of the key notions underlying drinking water security is the 'sustainability' of water supply. This is significant because sustainability is intrinsically linked to equity and has the potential to foster an understanding of drinking water security that contributes to the realisation of the human right to water.

The main text of the NRDWP does not define sustainability, but an annex on sustainability provides interesting insights. The starting point is the notion of sustainable development expounded in the report of the World Commission on Environment and Development (Brundtland Commission).[45] According to the Brundtland Commission, sustainable development is development that meets today's needs without compromising future generations' options. One of the key tenets of the definition is the need to give 'overriding priority' to the essential needs of the world's poor.[46]

The understanding of sustainability propounded under the NRDWP is fundamentally different from that of the Brundtland Commission. The NRDWP emphasises four dimensions of sustainability: source, system, financial and, finally, social and environmental sustainability.[47] The focus is on ensuring availability of water (source sustainability), on optimising the cost of production of water and capacity building (system sustainability), on cost recovery of 'at least' 50 per cent (financial sustainability) and on 'proper reject management and involvement of all key stakeholders' (social and environmental sustainability).[48]

The above definitions fall within a context where there is no generally agreed definition of sustainable development in either Indian law or international law. Yet, the NRDWP frames its understanding of sustainability in the context of the Brundtland Commission's report. In doing so, it acknowledges that sustainability first evolved from an environmental perspective and gave utmost priority to the poor.[49] It is thus surprising to find that 'social and environmental sustainability' is the fourth and last component of the definition. In addition, the NRDWP frames the environmental dimension of sustainability in a narrow framework focused on waste management. On the whole, the sustainability dimension of drinking water security as expounded in

[45] Report of the World Commission on Environment and Development, *Our Common Future*, Official Records of the General Assembly (Forty-second session), Supplement No. 25, UN Doc. A/42/25 (1987), Annex.

[46] Ibid., p. 54.

[47] NRDWP 2010, Annexure II: Guideline for Implementation of Sustainability – Swajaldhara Project.

[48] Ibid., Annexure II, s. 2.

[49] Report of the World Commission on Environment and Development, p. 54.

the NRDWP fails to provide a basis for fostering the realisation of the human right to water.

**Centralisation within Decentralisation**

The NRDWP puts a new emphasis on the need for infrastructure that provides water from outside a given village through a grid fed by pipelines or other means of connecting major water sources.[50] Alongside the focus on conjunctive use of surface and groundwater and reliance on multiple sources of water, a grid can make an important contribution to the provision of water. It can also lead to more equality among regions since, in principle, everyone could be provided the same amount of clean water regardless of geographical location. This would constitute a major step forward in ensuring that the minimum level of realisation of the human right to water is fulfilled in the same way for everyone.

At the same time, this is a momentous change from reliance on local sources of water and should be integrated in a much broader policy discussion. Indeed, from the point of the principles and the concepts being proposed, there is tension or perhaps even direct conflict between the move to foster decentralisation and participation and the move towards having a grid covering all villages. The latter will by definition imply a new level of centralisation that has never been present in rural drinking water supply schemes until now. This may be a positive factor to the extent that the whole framework is conceived with appropriate safeguards and accountability. It cannot, however, be introduced under the guise of participation and decentralisation, and the two streams thus need to be clearly distinguished. Further, in a context where other legal instruments, such as infrastructure acts, specifically call for private sector participation in water supply infrastructure,[51] it is imperative to have a full debate on the consequences of the establishment of a grid.

## 4 LOOKING AHEAD – ENSURING THE REALISATION OF THE RIGHT TO WATER IN THE CONTEXT OF POLICY REFORMS

The period 1997 to 2011 was momentous in terms of the evolution of the law and policy framework concerning drinking water. The existence of the human right to water in India has been confirmed on various occasions and in different contexts by the courts. While courts have not developed the content

[50] NRDWP 2010, s. 6.

[51] See, for example, Gujarat Infrastructure Development Act, 1999.

of the right in detail there is no doubt that the right is part of everyone's human rights in India. Beyond this recognition, there is little legislation that confirms and expands upon the right. However, the union government took a number of policy measures over the years that constituted steps towards its realisation. In particular, the ARWSP established a framework for providing water in rural areas that was both bold and significant. The decision to put the minimum quantity of water to be supplied at 40 lpcd in the 1970s reflected a good understanding of actual water needs in rural areas. This can be compared to the much lower assessments made at the international level in later decades.

As a result of these different law and policy measures, significant steps had been taken towards the realisation of the core content of the human right to water for a great number of people by the end of the century. This was far from adequate since millions of people still did not have access to sufficient water, but the approach had been broadly in the appropriate direction. In this sense, there was progress towards realisation of the right.

The reforms undertaken have in principle not affected the basic content of the human right to water because they have come in the form of policy documents that do not create legally binding rights and obligations. However, there has been a major shift in the policy framework concerning drinking water supply in rural areas that is not without impact on the realisation of the human right. The paradigm shift that has been implemented progressively has led, for instance, to a focus on demand-led rather than supply-led schemes, and an emphasis on efficiency rather than equality. The focus has also been on redefining water as a socio-economic good rather than a social right. The changes in the policy framework have further sought to move away from conceiving of water provision as an individual entitlement, which could be measured in terms of certain benchmarks, such as a minimum quantity per person per day, in favour of the vaguer concept of drinking water security, which only considers entities from the household level upwards.

In the context of the right to water, the reforms can be considered from two different perspectives. On the one hand, policy reforms sideline and ignore the human right to water though they cannot affect its status since policy instruments are not legally binding. It is thus possible to expect that ongoing reforms may constitute a different way to realise the right to water. On the other hand, reforms have specifically sought to move away from a social right and human right perspective and have introduced concepts that can be understood as regressive from a human rights point of view.

The perspective that sees no contradiction between the human right to water and ongoing policy reforms can be pursued up to a certain point. It is guided by the idea that law and policy do not necessarily evolve in a coordinated fashion. This is not inappropriate to the extent that policy instruments remain subordinated to law. In practice, the tendency in the water sector over the reform period to emphasise the primacy of policy instruments as providing the key lineaments of the framework governing the water sector has tended to eclipse the hierarchically superior position of law.

In general, the primacy of human rights is well established and undisputed. Yet, in a context where the content of the human right to water has not been clearly determined by the courts, the question of its specific content remains under discussion. Given the absence of specificity, the move from an understanding of the right that includes the provision of free infrastructure, such as handpumps, to a right that is restricted to a right to access water in a context that emphasises the need for participation by all individuals is not remarkable. In other words, from a theoretical perspective, a different understanding of the right has evolved over the past decade through policy instruments. Yet, the broad parameters guiding past and present policy can at a general level probably be justified under a human rights perspective.

The idea that different policy can support the realisation of a given human right is not problematic. Further considerations, however, need to be brought into the analysis. Indeed, the flexibility that governments have in the means they choose to realise human rights is limited, as indicated by the following two points.

First, it is now widely acknowledged that any measures to foster the realisation of a human right must prioritise the situation of the poorest, thereby contributing to the overall realisation of the right but starting from the people who are most disadvantaged in this regard.[52] In this context, the experience with reforms over the past decade does not indicate that the policy framework is geared towards a focus on the most disadvantaged or able to preferentially foster the realisation of the right for the most marginalised.[53] This is related to the emphasis on the need for individuals to pay either the costs of running the infrastructure providing access to water or part of the costs of any new infrastructure. The implementation of reforms seems to have the effect of

[52] This is in fact what the Brundtland Commission called for in its definition of sustainability (see section 'Sustainability and Drinking Water Security').

[53] See, for example, P. Cullet, 'New Policy Framework for Rural Drinking Water Supply – The Swajaldhara Guidelines', *Economic and Political Weekly*, Vol. 44, No. 50 (2009), pp. 47–54.

bypassing the poorest because of the emphasis on financial investment as the primary driver of better access. In effect, it is firstly the wealthier members of any given community who get additional water supply, and generally people who can afford it. In the case of piped supply, where community taps are part of the planning, they tend to be closed off early on by the locals running the scheme, usually because of non-payment of related charges.[54] This is problematic because even if the poor do not suffer from the new measures put in place, they do not benefit from them. Additionally, in the long term, the poor will be affected when the maintenance of their existing sources of water supply is sidelined in favour of maintenance of the newer infrastructure created under ongoing reforms.

Second, whereas the government has the choice of the policy measures it wants to implement to foster the realisation of human rights, this must be undertaken within the existing rights framework. This framework happens to focus mostly on individual entitlements. In this context, the move away from an individual entitlement that is measured in terms of a minimum quantity of water in favour of a non-quantified standard applying at no smaller a unit than the household is a step away from a human rights framework. Leaving aside the possibility to have a collective right to water, something that no country seems to have considered in-depth yet, the move away from an individual entitlement in favour of a collective notion has already been seen to lead to inappropriate results in South Africa in the context of the free water policy.[55] In this case, it is the poorer households that suffer because they are often the largest, in part because more people cohabit a smaller space than wealthier households. As a result, they lose out in the case of any household-based measure, which goes against the idea of preferentially alleviating the situation of the least well off, first.[56]

The overall outcome of the reforms is to foster better water supply to parts of rural communities. The focus of the reforms on availability of money as the yardstick that drives better access ends up making the new policies an instrument favouring the wealthier members of a given community over the poorer ones. This is problematic in the context of the realisation of human rights and the focus on poverty eradication where the situation of the poorest is the most important issue to address. In addition, the move away

54 Ibid., p. 50.

55 South Africa, Regulations Relating to Compulsory National Standards and Measures to Conserve Water 2001, s. 3.

56 See, for example, L. Smith, *Neither Public nor Private: Unpacking the Johannesburg Water Corporatization Model* (Geneva: UN Research Institute for Social Development, 2006), p. 21.

from an individual entitlement tends to dilute the content of the right without helping the poorest households.

The more general problem that emerges is that the policy framework for reforms effectively only pays lip service to human rights. The constructive interpretation suggested above that sees reforms as proposing a different way to realise the human right to water goes in fact further than what the reforms themselves seek to do. More precisely, policies have moved away from conceiving of water as a social right, instead viewing water as an economic good, in keeping with the 1992 Dublin Statement and international consensus. At the national level, there is no doubt that human rights are not subordinated to anything else. The Dublin Statement, which is not even a piece of soft law endorsed by the UN, has little legal bearing on what States must do at the national level. The only thing that matters in this context is respect for the constitutional framework. This happens to mandate that human rights prevail over other interests. There is thus a need to reconceive of ongoing reforms so that they fit within the human right to water framework rather than the other way round.

# List of Cases

## AFRICAN COMMISSION ON HUMAN AND PEOPLES' RIGHTS

*The Social and Economic Rights Action Center and the Center for Economic and Social Rights* v. *Nigeria*, Communication 155/96, 2001, **136, 137**

## ARGENTINA

*CEDHA* v. *Provincial State and Municipality of Córdoba* (AC), 2004, **355, 378**
*Quevedo Miguel Angel and Others* v. *Aguas Cordobesas S.A. and Others*, Civil and Commercial First Instance Court, 8 April 2002, **34**
*Usuarios y Consumidores en Defensa de sus Derechos, Asociación Civil* v. *Aguas del Gran Buenos Aires*, Supreme Court of Justice in the Province of Buenos Aires, 22 September 2004, **500**

## BELGIUM

Arrêt n_36/98 du 1 Avril 1998, Commune de Wemmel, Moniteur Belge, 24/4/98, **3**

## CHILE

*Chusmiza-Usmagama*, Corte Suprema, Rol No. 2.840, 25 November 2009, **110**
*El Morro I*, Corte Suprema, Rol No. 2.211, 27 April 2012, **116–117**
*El Morro II*, Corte Suprema, Rol No. 11.299, 7 October 2014, **117**
*Mini Central Cayucupil, Corte de Apelaciones de Concepción*, Rol No. 401-2010, 1 December 2010, **107**
*Plano Regulador San Pedro Atacama*, Corte Suprema, Rol No. 258, 13 July 2011, **111, 114**
*Paguanta*, Corte Suprema, Rol No. 11.040, 30 March 2012, **115–116**
*Parque Eólico*, Corte de Apelaciones de Puerto Montt, Rol No. 239, 11 October 2011, **115**
*Parque Eólico*, Corte Suprema, Rol No. 10.090, 22 March 2012, **115**
*Pepiukelen case*, the Temuco Court of Appeals, **117**
Tribunal Constitucional de Chile, Rol No. 309, 4 August 2000, **113**
Tribunal Constitucional de Chile, Rol No. 1.050, 3 April 2008, **112**

## EUROPEAN COURT OF HUMAN RIGHTS

*Al-Jedda* v. *United Kingdom*, Application no. 27021/08, **165–167**

*Al-Skeini* v. *United Kingdom*, Application no. 55721/07 (7 July 2011), **165–167, 406–407**
*Banković and Others* v. *Belgium and Others* (dec.) [GC], no. 52207/99, ECHR 2001-XII, **407**
*Jaloud* v. *Netherlands*, Application no. 47708/08 (20 November 2014), **166**
*Melnik* v. *Ukraine*, Application no. 72286/01, judgment dated 28 March 2006, **352**

## FIJI

*Sailasa Naba and Others* v. *the State*, High Court of Fiji, No. HAC0012 of 2000L, 4 July 2001, **378**

## INDIA

*Hamid Khan* v. *State of Madhya Pradesh*, AIR 1997 MP 191 (Madhya Pradesh High Court), **678–679**
*Hussain* v. *Union of India*, High Court of Kerala OP 2741/1988 (Judgment, 26 February 1990), **3**
*J.K. Koolwal* v. *State of Rajasthan and Others*, AIR1988Raj2, 1987(1) WLN134 (Supreme Court of India), **391**
*MC Mehta* v. *Kamal Nath* (1997), 1 SCC 388 (Supreme Court), **686**
*Municipal Council, Ratlam* v. *Shri Vardhichand and Others* [1981] SCR (1) 97 (Supreme Court of India), **355, 391**
*Narmada Bachao Andolan* v. *Union of India* AIR 2000 SC 3751 (Supreme Court of India), **678**
*Perumatty Grama Panchayat* v. *State of Kerala*, High Court of Kerala, W.P.(C) No. 34292 of 2003, Judgment of 16 December 2003, **136**
*Rampal and Ors* v. *State of Rajasthan and Others*, AIR 1981 Raj 121 (Supreme Court of India), **391**
*Subhash Kumar* v. *State of Bihar*, AIR 1991 SC 420 (Supreme Court of India), **677, 678**
*Vishala Kochi Kudivella Samarkshana Samithi* v. *State of Kerala*, 2006 (1) KLT 919 (High Court of Kerala), **679**

## INTERNATIONAL COURT OF JUSTICE

*Aerial Herbicide Spraying (Ecuador* v. *Columbia)*, Application instituting proceedings 31 March 2008, **158**
*Application of the Convention on the Prevention and Punishment of the Crime of Genocide (Bosnia and Herzegovina* v. *Serbia and Montenegro)*, Judgment, 2007 ICJ Reports, p. 43, **412**
*Application of the International Convention on the Elimination of All Forms of Racial Discrimination (Georgia* v. *Russian Federation)*, Provisional Measures, Order of 15 October 2008, ICJ Reports 2008, p. 353, **407**
*Armed Activities in the Territory of the Congo (Democratic Republic of Congo* v. *Uganda)*, Judgment, ICJ Reports 2005, p. 168, **407**
*Barcelona Traction, Light and Power Company, Limited (Belgium* v. *Spain), Second Phase*, Judgment of 5 February 1970, ICJ Reports 1970, p. 3, **196**
*Case Concerning the Gabcikovo-Nagymaros Project (Hungary/Slovakia)*, Judgment, ICJ Reports 1997, p. 7, **434**
*Legal Consequences of the Construction of a Wall in the Occupied Palestinian Territory*, 9 July 2004, ICJ Reports 2004 (Advisory Opinion), **193**
*Nuclear Tests (Australia* v. *France)*, ICJ Reports 1973, p. 99, **197**
*Nuclear Tests (Australia* v. *France)*, ICJ Reports 1974, p. 253, **197**
*Nuclear Tests (New Zealand* v. *France)*, ICJ Reports 1973, p. 135, **197**
*Nuclear Tests (New Zealand* v. *France)*, ICJ Reports 1974, p. 457, **197**
*Pulp Mills on the River Uruguay (Argentina* v. *Uruguay)*, Judgment, ICJ Reports 2010, p. 14, **148**

## INTER-AMERICAN COMMISSION OF HUMAN RIGHTS

*Armando Aleiandre jr and Others.* v. *Republica de Cuba*, Inter-American Commission on Human Rights (IACHR) (1999) Case 11.559, Report No. 86/99, p. 586, 406–407

## INTERNATIONAL ARBITRATION

*Aguas Argentinas, S.A., Suez, Sociedad General de Aguas de Barcelona, S.A. and Vivendi Universal, S.A.* v. *Argentine Republic* (ICSID Case No. ARB/03/19), 588, 596
*Aguas Cordobesas SA, Suez, and Sociedad General de Aguas de Barcelona SA* v. *The Argentina Republic* (ICSID Case No ARB/03/18), 535, 588
*Aguas del Tunari S.A.* v. *Republic of Bolivia*, ICSID Case No. ARB/02/3, 483, 535, 588–589
*Aguas del Tunari, S.A.* v. *Republic of Bolivia*, ICSID Case No. ARB/02/3, Decision on Jurisdiction, 21 October 2005, 483
*Aguas Provinciales de Santa Fe, S.A., Suez, Sociedad General de Aguas de Barcelona, S.A. and Interagua Servicios Integrales de Agua, S.A.* v. *Argentine Republic* (ICSID Case No. ARB/03/17), 588
*Anglian Water Group* v. *Argentine Republic*, UNCITRAL arbitration filed in 2003, 588
*Azurix Corporation* v. *The Argentine Republic* (ICSID Case No. ARB/01/12), 537, 588, 589
*Azurix Corporation* v. *The Argentine Republic* (ICSID Case No. ARB/03/30), 538, 588, 591
*Biwater Gauff (Tanzania) Limited* v. *United Republic of Tanzania* (ICSID Case No. ARB/05/22), 236, 535, 588–590, 593–595
  Amicus curiae submission of LEAT, LHRC, TGNP, CIEL and IISD, 26 March 2007, 591
  Award of 24 July 2008, 591
*Branimir Mensik* v. *Slovak Republic* (ICSID Case No. ARB/06/90), the proceedings were discontinued in December 2008, 535
*Compania de Aguas del Aconquija SA and Vivendi Universal* v. *The Argentine Republic* (ICSID Case No. ARB/97/3), 535, 588, 590
*Lac Lanoux Arbitration (France* v. *Spain)* (1957), 12 ILR 101, 197
*Impregilo SpA* v. *Argentine* Republic (ICSID Case No. ARB/07/17), 535, 588
*Mobil Corporation and Others* v. *Bolivarian Republic of Venezuela*, ICSID Case No. ARB/07/27, 584
*Piero Foresti and Others* v. *Republic of South Africa*, ICSID Case No. ARB/(AF)/07/1, 584, 586
*SAUR International* v. *The Argentine* Republic (ICSID Case No. ARB/04/04), 535, 588, 600
*Suez, Sociedad General de Aguas de Barcelona S.A., and InterAgua Servicios Integrales del Agua S.A. (Claimants) and The Argentine Republic (Respondent)*, ICSID Case No. ARB/03/17, Decision on Liability, 30 July 2010, 49, 535–588, 598
*Suez, Sociedad General de Aguas de Barcelona S.A., and Vivendi Universal S.A. (Claimants) and The Argentine Republic (Respondent); AWG Group (Claimant) and The Argentine Republic (Respondent)*, ICSID Case No. ARB/03/19, Decision on Liability, 30 July 2010, 49, 538
*Urbaser SA and Consorcio de Aguas Bilbao Biskaia, Bilbao Biskaia Ur Partzuergoa* v. *The Argentine Republic* (ICSID Case No ARB/07/26), 535, 588, 600
*Waguih Elie George Siag and Clorinda Vecci* v. *Arab Republic of Egypt*, ICSID Case No. ARB/05/15, 584

## IRELAND

*Ryan* v. AG [1965] IR 294, at 315 (High Court of Ireland) 3

## ISRAEL

*Ayyoub* v. *Minister of Defence*, Israeli Supreme Court of Justice, **431**

## NIGERIA

*Nigerian Gas Flaring Case, High Court of Nigeria, Jonah Gbemre* v. *Shell Petroleum Development Co. (Nigeria) Ltd. et. al.*, Unreported Suit No. FHC/B/CS/53/05 (14 November 2005) (Benin), **211**

## PAKISTAN

Human Rights Case No. 9 – K/1992, Supreme Court of Pakistan, unreported judgment, **392**

## SOUTH AFRICA

*Beja and Others* v. *Premier Western Cape and Others* 2011] 3 All SA 401 (WCC)) [2011] ZAWCHC 97, 21332/10 (29 April 2011) **230**, **388**
*Dhladhla and Others* v. *Erasmus* Case No. 11/98 (LCC) (Land Claims Court), **229**
*City Council of Pretoria* v. *Walker*, 1998 (3) BCLR 257 (CC) (Constitutional Court of South Africa), **238**, **239**
*City of Johannesburg and Others* v. *Mazibuko and Others* 2009 (3) SA 592 (SCA) (Supreme Court of Appeal), **241**
*Government of the RSA* v. *Grootboom* 2001 (1) SA 46 (CC) (Constitutional Court of South Africa), **227**, **228**, **237**, **238**
*Highveldrige Residents Concerned Party* v. *Highveldridge Transitional Local Council and Others*, High Court (Transvaal Provincial Division), Case No. 28521/2001, 17 May 2002, **705**, **239**
*Manqele* v. Durban Transitional Metropolitan Council 2002, 2 All SA 39 (D)( Durban High Court), **239**
*Mazibuko and Others* v. *City of Johannesburg and Others* High Court of South Africa (Witswatersrand Local Division) (30 April 2008) Case No 06/13885, **34**, **228**, **240**, **262**
*Mazibuko and Others* v. *City of Johannesburg and Others*, The Supreme Court of Appeal of South Africa Case No. 489/08 (25 March 2009), **34**
*Mazibuko and Others* v. *City of Johannesburg and Others* 2010 (4) SA 1 (CC); 2010 (3) BCLR 239 (CC) (Constitutional Court of South Africa), **34**, **38**, **240**, **241**
*Minister of Health and Others* v. *Treatment Action Campaign and Others* (No 2) 2002 (5) SA 721 (CC) (Constitutional Court of South Africa), **228**
*Nkonkobe Municipality* v. *Water Services South Africa (PTY) Ltd and Others*, (1277/2001) [2001] ZAECHC 3 (14 December 2001), **489**
*Nokotyana and Others* v. *Ekurhuleni Metropolitan Municipality* 2010 (4) BCLR 312 (CC) (Constitutional Court of South Africa), **230**, **245**, **246**, **393**
*Residents of Bon Vista Mansions* v. *Southern Metropolitan Local Council*, 2002 (6) BCLR 625 (W), **239**
S v. *Makwanyane and* Another (1995 (3) SA 391 (CC) (Constitutional Court of South Africa), **228**
*Soobramoney* v. *Minister of Health, KwaZulu-Natal* 1998 (1) SA 765 (CC) (Constitutional Court of South Africa), **241**
*Van der Walt and Others* v. *Lang and Others* Case No. 102/98 (LCC)(Land Claims Court), **229**

## THE NETHERLANDS

Rechtbank Den Haag, 24-06-2015, C/09/456689 / HA ZA 13-1396, **211**

## UNITED KINGDOM

R v. *Director of Water Services, ex parte Lancashire County Council, Liverpool City Council, Manchester City Council, Oldham Metropolitan Borough Council, Tameside Metropolitan Borough Council and Birmingham City Council* [1999] Env LR 114; [1998] EWHC 213 (QB), **38, 48**

## UN HUMAN RIGHTS COMMITTEE

*López Burgos* v. *Uruguay*, Communication No. R.12/52 (6 June 1979), UN Doc. Supp. No. 40 (A/36/40) at 176 (1981), **165**

## UNITED STATES

*Massachusetts* v. *EPA*, 549 U.S. 497 (2007) (US Supreme Court), **211**

# Index


Aarhus Convention on Access to Information, Public Participation in Decision-making and Access to Justice in Environmental Matters, 206, 208–209
abstraction, 32, 44, 71, 140, 190, 365, 439, 445, 451, 545, 549, 655
access to information, 108, 207, 386, 595, 617
accountability, 9–10, 15, 44, 52, 78, 145, 162, 172, 179, 203, 206, 209, 211, 215–216, 218, 221, 234, 267, 275, 328, 344, 348, 366, 369, 391, 397, 415, 417, 420, 428, 433, 452, 458, 473, 482, 502, 523, 526, 561, 586, 649, 689
  complaints procedure, 58, 78–79, 163, 166, 196, 391, 483, 490, 631, 638, 643, 656, 678
  human rights assessments, 217
  inquiry procedure, 1, 167
  inter-State complaints procedure, 15, 46, 167, 172–173, 191, 196
  reporting procedure, 7, 162, 168, 199, 216, 317, 320, 322, 344, 397, 413, 416, 423, 425, 477, 584, 593, 595, 598, 613
Accra Agenda for Action (AAA), 402, 414, 485
Additional Protocol to the American Convention on Human Rights in the Area of Economic, Social and Cultural Rights, 1999 (Protocol of San Salvador), 281
affordability, 3, 10, 16–17, 24, 31–32, 35–38, 40, 47–48, 52, 70, 175, 187, 189, 196, 211, 214, 217, 231–235, 242–244, 246, 253, 258, 263, 265, 268, 270, 276–278, 280–290, 292–298, 309, 312, 317, 333–334, 336, 338, 340–341, 348, 350, 356, 368, 371, 374–375, 386, 394, 411, 414, 431, 434, 444, 453, 466, 470–471, 473–474, 486, 489, 515, 519, 524, 526, 528, 546–547, 573, 579, 589, 604, 617, 619, 623, 656, 658, 664, 668, 670, 692
Africa, 16–17, 34, 46–47, 57, 59, 62, 64–68, 71–72, 74–77, 79–80, 97, 146, 171, 182, 186, 211, 225–227, 234, 236–238, 242, 244, 262, 266, 268, 274, 283, 288, 290, 293, 304, 306, 308, 313, 324–326, 330, 333–334, 339, 342, 352, 380, 384, 388, 391, 393, 470, 480, 484–485, 500, 548, 584, 586, 603, 605, 607, 615, 618, 622, 627, 648–649, 651, 653–654, 657–658, 661, 666, 671, 673, 676
African (Banjul) Charter on Human and Peoples' Rights, 136, 308, 334
African Charter on the Rights and Welfare of the Child, 308
agriculture, 14–15, 30–31, 58, 61, 76, 89, 95, 97–99, 101, 108, 120–122, 124–135, 138–142, 144, 146, 148, 170, 174–175, 182, 184, 186, 199, 213, 277, 314, 317, 325–328, 333, 337, 342, 344, 352, 432, 440, 442–443, 446, 450–451, 533, 554, 647, 649, 651, 653, 660, 662–664, 670, 673–676
alliances, 271–272, 494–495
Argentina, 50, 108, 148, 158, 165, 190, 283, 293–294, 355, 378, 469, 480, 486, 488, 499–501, 535, 548, 560, 590–593, 596–599
armed conflict, 26, 40, 88–89, 92, 96–97, 99, 166, 179, 272, 354, 365, 394, 406–407, 424, 426, 430–431, 436–437, 447–449, 452–453, 456, 458, 588, 662, 665
Asia, 62, 66, 79, 97, 145, 179, 182, 288, 306, 314, 324, 334, 377, 381, 388, 391, 464, 470, 508–509, 515, 648–649
Australia, 68, 77, 174, 182, 197, 293, 318, 503, 566

Bangladesh, 147, 155, 322, 340, 347, 381, 390, 422
bathing, showering, 259, 286, 629, 631, 652, 680
Bolivia, 4, 70, 283, 293, 376, 469, 480, 483–484, 491, 535, 588–590, 613
Botswana, 50, 326, 390
Brazil, 6, 129, 138, 283, 293, 347, 481, 537, 539, 573, 614
budgets and financial resources, 38, 43, 75, 95, 244, 284, 295, 381, 409, 413, 424, 468, 495, 508, 523, 548, 559, 561, 584, 606, 657, 675
  taxation, 60, 99, 105, 249, 283, 548, 552, 572, 615
bulk water, 35, 123, 160, 451, 556

Canada, 160, 192, 194, 399, 447, 568
capabilities approach, 22, 119, 198, 350–351, 612, 616
capacity
  assistance, 7, 17, 40, 48–49, 142, 152–153, 159–162, 169, 186–187, 192–193, 197, 199–200, 212–213, 215, 220, 233, 255, 271–272, 284, 302, 312, 314, 367, 370, 396–401, 404, 406, 408, 410–414, 418–423, 425–428, 447, 454, 456, 467, 492, 507, 515, 540, 648, 658, 660
  capacity to influence, 8, 15, 52, 95, 145, 151, 157, 167, 169, 173, 209, 211, 219, 249, 287, 302, 326, 392, 406, 416, 468, 546, 550, 608, 613–614, 626, 666
caste system, 629, 638, 640, 642
causation, 45, 96, 110, 167, 176, 192, 613
Chad, 147, 170, 420, 535
children, 2, 9, 17, 36, 39, 64, 183, 225, 227, 239, 246, 308–309, 311, 315, 318, 322–323, 326, 335, 339, 345, 353, 355–356, 374–376, 394, 423, 433, 451, 476, 480, 603, 624, 627, 639
Chile, 11, 15, 39, 50–51, 57, 69–70, 77, 84–89, 91–98, 100–115, 117–118, 140, 283, 292–294, 391, 480, 485, 559, 566
China, 123, 135, 138, 180, 191, 220, 293, 399, 538, 560, 628, 648–649
cholera, 232, 286, 346, 387, 394, 647, 654, 668–670, 674
citizenship, 27–30, 90, 388
civil and political rights, 2, 28, 164, 227, 281, 301, 407
coastal zone, 186, 199, 201
Colombia, 4, 10, 28, 158, 283, 292–293, 295, 486–488, 491–492
colonialism/colonial legacy, 18, 59, 67–69, 71–73, 87, 89, 325, 327, 337, 454, 505–507, 517, 644, 648, 651–652, 659, 673
commercialisation, 11, 76, 85, 87–89, 91, 95, 99, 233, 236–237, 260, 271, 273, 277, 327, 337, 464, 471, 484, 492, 501, 516, 518, 524, 527, 532, 534, 539–540, 549, 553, 556, 558–564, 566–567, 583, 644, 649, 651–653, 655, 657, 659–665, 673–675, 686
commodification, 11, 13, 84–85, 99, 349, 463, 482, 520, 650, 673, 687
community, communal water sources, 12, 26, 47, 50, 52, 61–62, 64, 72, 82, 90, 95–96, 103, 110, 115–116, 146, 158, 184, 196–197, 212, 231, 235–236, 238, 245–246, 258, 260, 267, 271, 274, 294, 307, 325, 327, 333, 335, 337, 342, 349, 355, 361, 364, 372–373, 376, 378, 385, 387, 389–390, 430–431, 444, 452, 454, 456, 458, 465, 469, 472, 475, 501, 506, 511, 516, 518, 520, 522, 526–528, 605, 607–608, 611–613, 615–616, 620, 625–626, 629, 633–634, 636, 638, 640–642, 651–652, 655, 659–660, 664–665, 675, 683, 687, 692
complicity, 418, 546, 586 *see also* causation
consent, 50, 117, 153, 161, 164, 166, 421
constitution, 4–6, 12, 28, 34, 72, 91, 93, 95–98, 100, 111–112, 117, 211, 226–230, 239, 241, 252, 254, 275, 334, 338, 365, 388–389, 391, 393, 465, 475, 490–492, 496–498, 500, 523, 634, 641, 645, 647, 654, 658, 662, 671, 673, 676, 678, 681–682, 693
consumers, 19, 231, 484, 499–500, 503–505, 510, 514, 517, 531, 544, 553, 558, 563, 566–568, 576, 578, 604–605, 607, 610, 621, 623
Convention against Torture and Other Cruel, Inhuman or Degrading Treatment or Punishment, 185, 542
Convention on the Elimination of All Forms of Discrimination Against Women (CEDAW), 2, 17, 24, 127, 141, 184, 301–304, 308–312, 316–317, 319–322, 328–333, 340, 342–343, 383, 407, 433
Convention on the Rights of Persons with Disabilities (CRPD), 198
Convention on the Rights of the Child (CRC), 3, 17, 24, 127, 163, 184, 198, 200, 215, 217, 301, 308, 310, 315, 317, 322, 332, 340, 343, 354, 368, 404, 433, 504, 521
cooking, 21, 61, 63, 314, 336, 631, 637, 639, 642, 666, 680, 687
corporate social responsibility, 266

corporations, 8, 12, 36, 44, 58–59, 70, 72, 79, 100, 102, 104, 109–110, 136, 151, 156, 158–159, 189, 194–196, 202, 207, 209, 211, 216, 219, 237, 246, 265, 271, 292, 297, 325–328, 342, 365, 368, 370, 408, 411, 415, 440, 464–465, 467, 469–474, 480, 483–485, 489–493, 496–501, 508–514, 516, 518–519, 522, 525–526, 529, 540, 547, 552, 557–560, 566–568, 583, 586–587, 589–593, 654, 670
subsidiary, 97–98, 106, 159, 236, 484, 489, 527, 588, 593
corruption, 9, 42, 51, 81, 246, 267, 284, 370, 390, 452, 484–485, 492, 503, 508–509, 511, 523, 550–551, 669, 674
cost recovery, 38, 51, 372, 504, 508–509, 512–513, 518, 526, 561, 682–683, 688
user fee, 194
Costa Rica, 6, 185, 283, 293
costing, 346
cruel and degrading treatment, 6, 352 *see also* torture
cultural acceptability, 35, 51, 348, 374, 394, 408, 419
culture, 25, 27, 46, 84, 89, 93, 103, 111, 128, 380, 500, 584, 627
socio-cultural, 20, 627, 629, 633–635, 637, 640, 642–643
customary international law, 128, 149, 194, 196, 366, 409, 431
customary law, 14, 25, 58, 65, 69, 71–73, 199–200, 208, 306–307, 314, 357, 400, 431, 434–435, 520, 647, 659, 661
customary norms, 61, 307, 342
customary practice, 60–61, 65, 326

dams, 170, 647–648, 655–656, 660, 664, 675
debt, 117, 200, 236, 240, 245, 288, 295, 411, 467–468, 490, 495, 499–500, 513, 549, 597
democracy, democratic, 49, 51, 91, 94, 96, 98, 101, 111, 117, 234, 267, 335, 363, 472, 477, 481–482, 492, 611, 648
Denmark, 288
deregulation, 218, 532, 543, 552, 581
desalination, 35, 123, 219, 447, 451
desertification, 647
developed countries, 8, 29, 31, 39, 42, 45, 66–69, 77, 86, 89, 124, 129, 131, 141, 145, 152, 179, 182, 185–186, 189, 193, 199, 201, 204, 206, 217–218, 238, 241, 257, 269, 276, 284, 287–289, 292–297, 303, 307, 327, 345, 366, 374, 390, 396, 399, 402–403, 416, 419, 421, 423, 425–428, 431, 435, 438–439, 447–448, 452, 455, 469, 475, 482, 485, 505, 510, 513, 515, 518, 533, 554, 582, 584, 619, 633, 638, 647–649, 651, 663, 668, 680, 689
developing countries, 3–4, 11–12, 16, 19, 25, 29–30, 34–38, 47, 50, 57, 60, 64, 66, 68–69, 74–77, 79–82, 93, 96, 107–109, 115, 128–129, 132, 145, 152, 159–160, 174, 179, 181, 183, 186, 199–200, 202–204, 206–207, 213, 225–228, 230, 232–237, 242–245, 247–248, 250, 252–253, 255–256, 259–262, 264–269, 273–274, 277, 283, 288, 291–292, 296–298, 303, 309, 312, 314, 330, 337, 346–347, 352, 356, 359, 362, 364, 369, 372, 374, 376, 381, 388, 390–394, 396–397, 399, 405, 409–415, 419, 421, 425–427, 431, 451, 454, 463–467, 469–470, 472, 475, 485, 487–489, 524, 527, 531, 534–535, 540, 548, 582, 584, 586, 594, 604–605, 607, 620, 622, 627–628, 630, 643, 646, 649, 651, 658, 661, 670, 692
least developed countries, 201–202, 212, 385
development
aid/assistance, 22, 40, 48–49, 138–139, 142, 152–153, 159–160, 162, 169, 186–187, 192–194, 197, 199–200, 204–205, 212–213, 215, 220–221, 255, 272, 284, 288, 290, 292, 294, 296, 298, 311–312, 314, 350, 357, 359, 367, 370, 387, 396–401, 403–404, 406, 408, 410–415, 418–428, 443, 447, 454, 456, 463, 467, 509, 515, 540, 660
commitment to spend 0.7 of GDP on, 204, 251, 425
development cooperation, 17, 20, 35, 45, 161, 308, 396–397, 403, 418–420, 428
donor conditionality, 49, 186, 264, 411, 414, 463, 467, 497
donors, 20, 49, 51, 199, 204, 215, 397, 402, 408, 410, 412, 414, 421, 428, 447, 463, 467, 475, 485, 607, 612, 647, 650, 654
lending, 155, 215, 415, 417–418, 467, 620
Official Development Assistance (ODA), 397
disability rights, 38, 141, 183, 188, 207, 243, 337, 339, 375–376, 402, 629
disconnections, 36, 38, 44, 229, 231–232, 239–241, 243, 245–246, 265, 268, 270, 272, 366, 489, 500, 549, 670

diseases
  infectious, 394
  water-borne, 170, 338
Dublin Statement on Water and Sustainable Development, 3, 278, 309, 311, 356, 466, 509, 686, 693
due diligence principle, 149, 157, 195, 216, 366, 412, 416, 594

Economic and Social Council (ECOSOC), 305, 405, 445, 449, 541
ecosystems, 101, 141, 149, 184, 644
education, 4, 6, 23–24, 42, 64, 194, 219, 227, 249–250, 252, 281, 288, 298, 308, 316, 320–321, 323, 325, 330–331, 340, 342–343, 345, 351, 354, 363, 369, 372, 375, 377, 385, 404, 420, 423–424, 478, 492, 523, 541, 609, 613, 631, 638, 643
Egypt, 138, 146–148, 584, 649
environment
  biodiversity, 107, 208
  climate change, 1, 9, 15, 17, 33, 40, 45–46, 53, 78, 123, 144–145, 172, 174–187, 191–193, 197–201, 203–220, 222, 329, 671
  common but differentiated responsibility, 185–186, 198, 296, 298, 505, 659
  pollution, 3, 9, 34, 44, 52–53, 59–60, 77, 81, 101, 136–137, 144, 146–149, 151, 155, 157–158, 161, 174, 190–191, 315, 322, 345, 349, 354–355, 361, 363, 371, 378, 380, 410, 442–443, 451, 508, 514, 519–520, 528, 630, 632, 635, 639–640, 656, 658, 667, 673
environmental impact assessment (EIA), 106, 114–116, 149, 208, 394
epidemic, 185, 286, 335, 353, 391, 668–669, 674
equality and non-discrimination, 2, 9, 17, 22, 27–28, 35, 38–39, 42, 48, 52–53, 65, 71, 82, 117, 134, 141–143, 183, 207, 228, 238, 240, 246, 300, 302–305, 307, 310, 312, 328–329, 332, 334, 341–344, 349–350, 352, 355–356, 362, 366, 370, 376, 383, 394, 396, 402, 421–422, 455, 498, 536–537, 542, 551, 565–566, 569, 571–574, 576, 579–581, 583, 605, 618, 621, 689–690
  disadvantaged group, 7, 15–16, 28–29, 31, 39, 42, 52–53, 60, 74, 76, 90, 102–103, 121, 133, 142, 147, 155, 157, 179, 182–183, 188, 198–199, 201, 206–207, 209, 211–212, 214–215, 217–218, 228, 239, 259, 264, 276, 278, 301, 304, 310, 314–316, 318, 322, 326, 328, 332, 334–335, 337, 339, 346, 352, 368, 376, 378–379, 381, 383–384, 386, 394, 422, 424, 446, 456, 475, 482, 513, 518, 538, 619, 621, 624, 631, 636, 672, 691
  substantive equality, 241, 301, 306, 328, 341–342, 376
equitable allocation, 235, 655
equity, 30–31, 76, 80, 198, 265, 278, 334, 336, 387, 470, 482, 499, 548–549, 576, 603, 672, 688
ethnic minority, 30, 51, 87, 217, 306, 339, 380, 633
European Convention on Human Rights, 165, 192, 406
European Court of Human Rights, 165–167, 210, 352, 406, 586
European Union (EU), 16, 49, 129, 145, 282, 285, 447, 457, 475, 480, 497, 563

families, 59, 64, 72, 139, 141, 174, 190, 303, 305–308, 313–314, 316, 321–322, 324, 326, 328, 330–333, 339, 342, 356, 389, 393, 445–446, 511, 633, 639–640, 670–671, 675, 680
financial crisis, 513, 552, 596–597, 668
financial resources, 15, 27, 33–34, 43, 79, 81, 83, 92, 225, 283, 381, 387, 447, 480, 562, 576
fisheries, 61, 101, 518
flower farming, 129
Food and Agricultural Organization (FAO) of the United Nations, 58–60, 73, 122, 128, 131, 133, 135–137, 147, 184, 306, 314, 328
food, nutrition, 3–4, 24, 58–59, 62, 66, 77, 119–120, 122–123, 125, 127–140, 142, 154, 157, 181–183, 185, 214, 265, 306, 314–316, 321, 323, 327–328, 342, 402, 405, 433, 678
  food security, 62, 130, 133, 179, 216, 314, 327–328, 333–334, 337, 342, 446, 452, 665, 671
foreseeability, 167, 178, 191–192, 417, 534, 581
France, 68, 119, 156, 163, 197, 276, 279, 283, 288, 293–294, 299, 347, 375, 399, 465, 468, 491–492, 495, 499, 577
free water, 35, 50, 233, 237, 240–241, 256, 261, 294–295, 297, 337, 692
freedom of expression, 126, 207

gender, 17, 27–28, 35, 51, 66, 76, 82, 141, 143, 157, 183, 207, 228, 300, 303–305, 307–309, 311–313, 317, 319, 321–323, 328–333, 336–337, 340–344, 353, 366, 387, 402, 661

General Agreement on Trade in Services (GATS), 18, 467, 475, 531–533, 536–538, 540–543, 545, 547, 549–551, 553, 555, 557–558, 560–565, 568–570, 572–574, 576, 578–580
General Comment No. 4 on the Right to Adequate Housing (UNCESCR), 24, 30, 154, 184, 285, 315, 349, 354, 422
General Comment No. 12 on the Right to Adequate Food (UNCESCR), 120, 127–128, 130, 134–137, 139, 154, 181, 402
General Comment No. 14 on the Right to Health (UNCESCR), 24, 31, 154, 184, 301, 315, 354, 399, 421
General Comment No. 15 on the Right to Water (UNCESCR), 3, 7, 17, 21, 24, 26, 29, 31–35, 39, 41–42, 44–45, 51, 60, 76, 108, 120–121, 124, 127, 151, 154, 156, 159–160, 167, 171, 174, 176, 184, 187–188, 190, 194, 200–201, 208–209, 213–214, 216, 253, 261, 278, 301, 310–311, 313, 315–317, 324, 328, 332–334, 339, 341, 347, 355–356, 358, 367–368, 373, 389, 395, 399, 406, 408, 410–411, 413, 415, 419, 421, 434, 442, 453, 455–456, 473–474, 498, 513, 515, 520–521, 528, 546, 591, 604, 616, 618–620, 624, 672
Geneva Conventions, 125, 353, 431–432, 440–441, 449, 456
Germany, 50, 163, 196, 288, 414, 416, 468, 486–489, 491, 495–497, 632
Ghana, 57, 69, 72, 81, 207, 320, 347, 485
Global Water Partnership (GWP), 58, 70, 644
globalisation, 212, 468, 527, 531 *see also* corporations, international financial institutions
  economic governance, 540
good
  cultural good, 519, 604, 617–618
  economic, 3, 18, 71, 237, 279, 309, 335, 466, 503–504, 507–509, 512–513, 517, 520, 527, 529, 604, 617–618, 683, 686, 693
  public good, 84, 101, 214, 313, 316, 361–362, 387, 474, 476–477, 518, 686
  social good, 3, 334, 503, 517, 520, 527–528, 654
governance, 10, 19–20, 45, 61, 144, 152, 172, 209, 226, 235, 257, 266–267, 275, 327, 481, 622, 629, 658, 666, 671
  good governance, 281, 511
  water governance, 10, 327, 336, 474, 481, 625, 646–647, 658, 673
groundwater, 50, 61, 74, 136, 141, 147, 158, 180, 387, 434–435, 437, 440, 451, 505, 507–508, 515–516, 519, 529, 630–632, 661, 689

hand pump, 631, 638, 642, 660
hand-washing, 384
hazardous, 52, 207, 364, 392
health, 2–4, 6–7, 22–24, 27, 29–31, 33–34, 36, 42, 63–64, 73, 82, 102, 120, 124–125, 136, 141, 156, 158, 171, 177, 181, 183–184, 186–187, 190, 194, 201, 213, 216–217, 220, 225, 229, 254, 260, 265, 286, 288, 298, 300–301, 303, 308, 312, 314–316, 318–322, 325, 327, 332, 334, 339, 341–342, 345–346, 348, 350–352, 354–356, 358–364, 371, 373–379, 385–387, 389, 391, 394, 399, 404, 420, 424, 432–433, 440, 446, 449, 451, 474, 505, 509, 521, 541–542, 551, 571, 574–575, 577, 579–580, 592, 594, 597–598, 612–613, 617, 637, 640, 642, 668–670, 672, 675–676, 678, 685
  HIV/AIDS, 335, 345
household budget, 37, 253, 278, 283–284
housing, 4, 6–7, 23–24, 35, 42, 174, 181, 184, 213, 229, 238–239, 245, 258, 261, 268–270, 285, 292, 295, 298, 308–311, 316, 318, 322, 325, 331, 349, 354, 356, 358, 367, 375, 377–378, 389–390, 392–393, 422, 424, 432, 434, 495, 513–514, 521, 618, 635, 640, 659, 680–681
  eviction, 229, 367, 390, 512, 514
  home, 35, 132, 145, 148, 190, 196–197, 212, 229, 243, 313–314, 331, 368, 373–374, 377, 384–385, 387, 478, 551, 631, 638, 640, 667
human dignity, 6–7, 23, 29, 31, 33, 143, 169, 175, 185, 211, 213, 228–230, 233, 265, 270, 312, 340, 348–349, 351–352, 355–356, 358–359, 362, 364, 368, 371–373, 377, 386, 388–389, 394, 403, 617, 620, 624
humanitarian assistance, 185, 201
humanitarian law, 45, 125, 152, 353, 431–433, 440–441, 448–449, 452–453, 455–458
hydration, 33
hydropower, 58, 94, 102, 104, 106–107, 648
hygiene, 29, 33, 52, 61, 125, 182, 246, 265, 283, 286, 313, 343, 348–349, 352, 354–355, 359, 369, 371–372, 374, 383, 386, 432, 445, 637, 640
  menstrual hygiene, 313, 340, 348, 363, 371, 374, 377

ILO Convention No. 169, Indigenous and Tribal Peoples Convention, 84, 91, 106–107, 111–114, 116–117, 322, 363, 484, 627
India, 3, 20, 35, 50–51, 58, 74, 123, 136, 147, 155, 158, 180, 190, 293, 320, 355, 388, 391, 399, 497, 509, 559, 563, 607, 614, 625–626, 628–633, 636–637, 643, 649, 677–679, 681–685, 689
indicators, 16, 37, 52, 163, 166, 179, 205, 209, 242, 246, 248–250, 252, 254, 281, 284, 304, 385, 424, 481, 561
  indexes, 276–278, 284–290, 295–298, 383, 669
indigenous peoples, 15, 26, 39, 51, 70, 77, 84–93, 97, 99, 102–106, 108–109, 111–113, 116–118, 121, 140, 170, 207, 325, 363, 408, 519
indivisibility, 91, 212, 302, 310, 316, 321, 331, 340, 342, 472
Indonesia, 18, 50, 183, 292–294, 382, 399, 487–488, 497, 503, 506–521, 523–524, 529, 608, 613–614
Industry, 14, 18, 85, 175, 237, 265, 350, 510, 516, 518, 531, 536, 541, 547, 554–556, 559, 561, 565, 567, 570–572, 574, 576, 578, 580, 641
informal accountability, 168, 173
informal settlement, 10, 37, 39, 217, 244–245, 258–259, 271, 278, 287, 310, 318–319, 355, 367, 374, 382, 388, 390, 393, 423, 465, 473, 492, 512, 514, 667
injury, 18, 22, 45, 108, 149–150, 157, 162, 176, 183, 190–191, 194, 208, 211, 220–221, 265, 272, 350, 352, 368, 435, 438, 445, 449–451, 454, 457, 464, 582, 584, 595
integrated water resources management (IWRM), 58, 334, 337, 644–645, 647, 649, 658–659, 661, 673, 675
intellectual property, 187, 220
Inter-American Commission on Human Rights, 87, 92, 157, 192, 210, 407
Inter-American Court of Human Rights, 92
Intergovernmental Panel on Climate Change (IPCC), 145, 178–181, 183, 192, 204, 218–219
International Centre for the Settlement of Investment Disputes (ICSID), 36, 49, 483, 490, 535, 583–584, 586, 588–591, 593–598
International Convention on the Elimination of All Forms of Racial Discrimination (ICERD), 407
international cooperation, 17, 27, 40, 49, 149, 152–153, 160–162, 172–173, 179, 186–187, 192–193, 197–199, 201–202, 205, 207, 212, 215, 220–221, 312, 370, 396, 398–401, 403–404, 406–409, 419, 421–423, 427–428, 456, 552 *see also* development
International Court of Justice (ICJ), 148, 158, 165, 190, 193–194, 196–197, 210, 400, 406–407, 412, 431, 433–434, 445
International Covenant on Civil and Political Rights (ICCPR), 2, 28, 152, 164–165, 167, 184, 193, 195–196, 360, 363, 407, 454
International Covenant on Economic, Social and Cultural Rights (ICESCR), 2, 6–7, 21, 24, 28, 30, 38, 40–41, 43, 125, 127, 130, 134–135, 137, 141–142, 151–158, 160–164, 167–169, 172, 174, 181, 184, 187–188, 193, 195, 198, 200, 212, 215, 217, 228, 301, 310, 317, 325, 328, 343, 358, 363, 368–370, 376, 398–399, 401–405, 408, 411–414, 416–420, 423–430, 433, 453, 455–456, 498, 501, 513, 518, 521, 624, 672
international financial institutions (IFIs), 11, 97, 159, 397, 415, 466, 475, 509–510
  Asian Development Bank, 292, 497–498, 509
  Inter-American Development Bank, 492, 499
  International Monetary Fund (IMF), 43, 309, 366, 415, 467, 470, 490, 497
  structural adjustment programme, 475
  World Bank, 9, 11, 25, 52, 58, 71, 86, 97, 100–101, 176, 182, 197, 203, 207, 284, 286–287, 291, 309, 330, 366, 378, 382, 397, 411, 415–418, 422, 438–443, 448, 451–452, 463, 467, 469, 477–478, 481–482, 484–485, 490–491, 497, 507–509, 511, 514–515, 520, 535, 547–549, 559, 568, 583, 589, 604, 606, 612, 614, 620, 631, 650, 653–654, 673, 682
International Labour Organization (ILO), 43, 84, 91, 106–107, 111–114, 116–117, 187, 363, 365
International Law Commission, Articles on State Responsibility, 409–411, 413, 415
International Law Commission (ILC), 150, 177, 191, 195, 221, 405, 409–411, 413, 415–416
international watercourses, 1, 15, 21, 144–173, 398, 434
investment, 19–20, 27, 36, 49, 53, 63, 79, 106, 116, 184, 204, 211, 220, 332, 346, 382, 419,

448, 452, 465, 470–471, 476, 478, 483–485, 490, 493, 496, 507, 510–511, 531, 534, 540, 548–552, 579, 582–591, 593–594, 596–600, 606–607, 609, 622, 657, 667, 692
investment treaties, 19, 49, 483, 499, 534, 582–591, 593, 596–598, 600
irrigation, 31, 58, 60–64, 68, 76, 79, 94, 99, 104, 121–122, 131, 139–140, 142, 148, 182, 219, 314, 316–317, 342, 449, 519, 528, 554, 630, 645, 648, 651–652, 655, 657, 662–665, 674–676
Israel, 17, 45, 53, 318, 429–431, 433–441, 443–444, 447, 449–450, 452–455, 457–458
Italy, 288, 293, 486–488, 493–494

Joint Monitoring Programme (JMP) for Water Supply and Sanitation, 217
judicial review, 98, 520–521, 523
jurisdiction, 22, 45, 152, 156, 158, 164–167, 172, 191, 193–195, 235, 244, 269, 326, 350, 401, 404, 407, 415, 429, 433, 443, 445, 457, 497, 551–552, 583, 586, 590, 630
justiciability, 32, 189, 227, 239–240, 365, 369, 431

Kenya, 4, 10, 57, 123, 129, 207, 293–294, 304, 318–319, 322, 334, 340, 347, 369–370, 391, 412, 414, 484, 614
kitchen gardening, 17, 26, 61, 120, 175, 277, 315, 648, 660–661

labour rights, 8, 10, 12, 22, 29, 33, 37, 58, 60, 65, 81–82, 88, 106, 111, 133, 137, 139, 157, 159, 161, 189, 201, 207, 270–272, 292, 300, 304, 308, 311, 316–317, 319, 323, 326, 330–332, 335, 342–343, 345, 354, 384, 393, 397, 404, 414, 416, 418, 428, 434, 443, 450, 470–471, 476, 478, 496, 514–515, 540, 567–568, 577, 586–587, 592, 605, 610, 615, 622, 633, 639, 648–649, 655, 667, 671, 685
lakes, 86, 104, 131, 514, 647, 667
land rights 4, 43, 64–67, 69, 72, 74, 84, 89, 92–93, 95–96, 99–100, 103, 105, 117, 122, 128, 131–132, 140, 180, 184, 235, 260, 263, 304, 306, 308, 314, 316, 320, 324, 326, 328, 332–334, 336–337, 348, 374, 378, 381, 389, 445, 450, 454, 513–514, 520, 528, 584, 618, 644, 646–647, 651–652, 655–657, 660–665, 671, 673–676 (see also housing and food)
land tenure, housing tenure, 65, 72, 74, 213, 245, 306, 348, 374, 378, 381, 389–391, 651
Latin America, 12, 57, 59, 62, 67, 69, 72, 77, 79, 84, 87, 97, 112, 281, 283, 288, 290, 293, 306, 314, 324, 334, 347, 376, 391, 469, 477–478, 480–481, 491, 500, 535, 539, 587
legal mobilisation, 227, 242, 268–269, 273–275, 348, 381, 486, 488, 500
legal pluralism, 65, 73, 307, 626, 673
liability, 176, 203, 211, 629
liberalisation, 1, 18, 335, 475, 533–534, 541, 543, 554–555, 573, 580
liberty, 22, 43, 77, 90, 98, 165, 185, 350–351
Libya, 147–148, 170
litigation, 5, 10, 38, 50, 52, 176, 179, 210–211, 216, 227, 238, 245, 261, 272–273, 378, 392, 486–488, 501–502, 583
livestock, 26, 60–61, 120, 125, 133, 142, 175, 336, 446, 660

Maastricht Guidelines on Violations of Economic, Social and Cultural Rights, 157
Maastricht Principles on Extraterritorial Obligations in the Field of Economic, Social and Cultural Rights, 155, 157, 160, 167, 193
maintenance, 232, 335, 340, 348, 372, 374–375, 386, 443, 448, 485, 494, 537, 554, 556–559, 567, 608, 613, 616, 639, 682–683, 692
Malawi, 81, 304, 321, 323, 334–336, 606
margin of discretion/appreciation, 100, 134, 170, 188, 190, 233, 397–398, 401, 419–420, 423–424, 427, 580–581
menstruation, 313, 340, 348, 363, 371, 374, 377
meters, 38, 131, 233, 240–241, 243, 245, 268, 271, 273–274, 338, 446, 489, 549, 554, 672 see also pre-paid
Mexico, 4, 57, 61, 68–69, 77, 79, 81, 148, 245, 279, 293, 480, 491, 563, 606, 653
middle-income countries, 43, 53, 58, 60, 81, 464, 470, 510
migrant workers, 310
Millennium Declaration, 36, 200, 276, 280–281, 311
Millennium Development Goals (MDGs), 24, 27–28, 36, 39–41, 43, 52, 200, 207, 281, 311, 324, 346, 348, 375, 377, 381–385, 387, 636
minimum essential level/subsistence, 15, 23, 26, 31, 42, 60, 76, 108, 120–122, 124–126, 129, 132–134, 138, 140, 143, 155, 175, 188, 228, 325, 336, 350, 366–367, 371, 421–422, 426–427, 446, 524, 548, 661

minimum recharge levels (water resource), 9
mining, 58, 71, 102, 108–110, 325, 518, 586, 644, 647, 649, 651, 660
minority groups, 310, 337, 376 *see also* ethnic minorities
mobilisation, 10, 47, 52, 201, 217, 227, 268, 273, 275, 393, 482, 487, 495, 502, 531, 546, 671
Monterrey Consensus on Financing for Development, 200, 401
moral duties and theories, 13, 21, 23–24, 27, 196, 205, 212, 277, 347, 353, 380, 395, 399, 476–477, 594, 604, 673
Morocco, 291, 293, 297, 320
Mozambique, 57, 72, 304, 320, 322–323, 330, 332, 391, 661
multiple-use water services, 59, 61–62

national human rights institution, 209
national plan, 213–214, 311, 369, 655
natural resources extraction, 51, 77, 104, 151, 158, 451, 453
needs, 2, 7, 15, 23, 26, 29, 33, 38, 44, 52, 57–58, 60, 62, 68, 73, 76, 81–82, 85, 119, 122–123, 125–128, 130, 133, 135, 147, 149, 155, 158, 160–161, 169, 171, 175, 177, 187–188, 199, 201, 203–204, 213, 215, 219, 222, 235, 238, 240, 250, 255, 261–262, 270–271, 273, 286, 292, 295, 301, 303, 307–308, 310, 313–316, 320, 323, 327–328, 334, 336–337, 340–342, 355, 364, 367, 371, 373, 375–377, 383, 386, 388, 422, 431, 435, 439, 446, 451–452, 479, 504, 507, 509, 516, 518–521, 525, 527–528, 597, 607, 630, 636–637, 639, 645, 649, 655, 658–659, 661, 666–667, 669, 672, 674–675, 686–687, 690
Nepal, 50, 190, 319, 347, 359, 381
Netherlands, 3, 24–25, 62, 121, 156, 166, 192, 208, 288, 293, 333, 347, 369, 380, 388, 400, 466, 474, 485, 504, 535, 625
no-harm principle, 45, 194–195, 408
non-governmental organisation (NGO), 162, 390, 440, 446, 467, 614, 633
non-nationals, 113, 116, 218, 267, 310, 440, 471, 480, 494, 514, 591, 629, 651, 671, 679
non-State actors, 4, 15, 17, 19, 23, 31, 44–45, 49, 58, 101, 134–135, 137–138, 145, 150, 154, 156, 158, 169, 171, 189–191, 193–195, 215, 227–228, 237, 272, 304, 323–327, 335, 337, 349, 353, 363–364, 366–367, 370–371, 390, 407, 415, 420, 431, 452, 458, 473, 483, 503, 518–519, 527, 538, 542, 565–566, 571, 574–575, 582, 592, 594, 619, 631, 648, 655, 659, 670, 672, 676, 686 *see also* corporations, international financial institutions
North American Free Trade Agreement (NAFTA), 573

obligations
complementary, 206, 363, 538, 547
concurrent, 516, 529
conduct, 46, 149–150, 154, 156–157, 159, 168, 195, 260, 265, 329, 343, 389, 397, 407, 415–416, 421, 428, 473, 536, 584, 593–595, 599
due diligence, 149, 157, 195, 216, 366, 412, 416, 594
erga omnes, 196
extraterritorial, 15–16, 44–45, 48, 145, 153, 156, 158–160, 163–165, 168–170, 172–173, 178, 192–195, 200, 220, 326, 398–399, 402–408, 418–420, 423, 425, 427, 453, 456, 620
minimum core, 15, 23, 26, 31, 42, 60, 76, 108, 120–122, 124–126, 129, 132–134, 138, 140, 143, 155, 175, 188, 228, 325, 336, 350, 366–367, 371, 421–422, 426–427, 446, 524, 548, 661
mutual, 46, 215
negative, 13, 15, 22, 43, 90, 95, 135, 145, 154, 158, 167, 177, 227, 250, 252, 322, 326, 342–343, 352, 392, 396, 402, 412, 477, 479, 489, 525, 590
obligation to fulfil, 7, 15, 33, 44–45, 81, 122, 126, 129, 132, 134, 137–138, 140, 142, 145, 154, 158–160, 172, 189, 191, 227, 278, 304, 323, 368, 400–401, 419–421, 424–427, 458, 516, 522, 525, 527–528, 541, 575–576, 672
obligation to protect, 4, 15, 17, 23, 31, 44–45, 49, 101, 134–135, 137–138, 145, 154, 156, 158, 169, 171, 189–191, 193–195, 215, 227–228, 304, 323–327, 349, 353, 363–364, 367, 371, 407, 415, 420, 458, 473, 483, 518, 527, 538, 571, 574–575, 582, 592, 594, 619, 631, 648, 655, 659, 670, 672, 676, 686
obligation to respect, 15, 19, 21, 25, 32, 44–45, 107, 134–136, 138, 143, 145, 149, 152–154, 156, 158, 162–163, 165–166, 169–170, 172, 185–186, 189–191, 193–196, 201, 206, 208–209, 217, 219, 227, 239–240, 255, 282, 304, 323–327, 329, 332, 337, 352, 359, 365–367, 372, 378, 400–403, 405, 408,

415–416, 420–421, 423, 428, 433, 453, 456–458, 472, 531–532, 536, 539, 541, 545, 553, 556–557, 561, 563–564, 568, 572, 574, 576, 581, 587, 590–594, 598–600, 616, 623, 626, 630, 633, 635–636, 640–641, 659, 664, 671–672, 693
parallel, 65, 587, 595, 600, 674
positive, 1, 22, 29, 43, 142, 159–160, 167, 185, 189, 197, 199, 211, 219–221, 227, 250, 273, 366, 401, 416, 481, 519–520, 523, 528, 603, 689
prevent, 21, 31, 44, 61, 75, 77, 101, 128, 130, 135, 149–150, 156, 159, 169, 178, 189, 191, 194–195, 271, 310, 315–316, 336, 353, 355, 366, 372, 378, 408, 410–411, 415–416, 435, 449, 455, 473–474, 564, 574, 578, 670
primary, 3–4, 20, 23, 28, 42, 76, 78, 82, 89, 143, 166, 219, 315, 319, 330–331, 337, 339, 358, 362–363, 374, 414, 418, 431, 434, 453, 458, 522, 532, 538, 569, 606, 608, 610, 614, 621, 627, 630, 633, 644, 653, 655, 657–661, 672–673, 679, 692
progressive realisation, 20, 24, 40, 134, 188, 214, 228, 230, 238, 240, 246, 254, 258, 368, 384, 444, 447, 453, 455, 472, 605, 616–617, 620, 623, 642
reasonableness test, 95, 149–150, 159, 169, 171, 188, 195, 228–231, 235, 238, 240–241, 254, 276, 283, 296, 298, 367, 374, 391, 413, 417, 421, 423–425, 427, 434, 439, 455, 522, 526, 540, 544, 579, 609, 638, 651, 655
reciprocal, 22, 26, 350
regulate, 18, 35, 67, 83, 96, 146, 155, 157, 159, 189–190, 195, 197, 235, 260, 429, 445, 511, 520, 522, 524, 527, 532, 541, 543, 549, 578, 591, 657
result, 8, 11, 15, 19, 33, 38, 40, 79, 82, 87, 122, 131, 146, 148, 151, 157, 159, 180, 195, 204, 231, 257, 259, 261, 274, 281, 321, 326, 329, 332, 335, 338, 346, 367, 370, 378, 380, 397, 404, 411, 418, 421, 423, 444, 448, 451, 453, 457, 473, 493, 500, 523, 531–534, 537, 540, 545, 552, 555, 557, 563, 565, 569, 571, 583, 612, 618, 631, 642, 648–649, 652, 679, 682, 690, 692
retrogression, 188, 212, 368, 458
secondary, 58, 70, 94, 257, 321, 374, 633
supplemental, 201, 341, 582
take steps, 39–41, 77, 144, 152, 157, 159, 172, 187, 193, 310, 368, 398–402, 410, 412, 415, 420, 429, 456, 473, 655
territorial, 69, 92, 154, 165, 283, 400, 420, 423–424, 457
occupation 17, 30, 45, 92, 406–407, 429, 431, 434–435, 437, 443, 445, 454, 457, 514, 662
*see also* armed conflict, jurisdiction
Occupied Palestinian Territory, 17, 35, 165, 193, 406, 429
Office of the High Commissioner for Human Rights (OHCHR), 8, 40, 174, 179, 183, 188, 207, 346, 471
opportunity cost, 32
Organisation for Economic Cooperation and Development (OECD), 37, 203–205, 279, 283, 286–287, 290, 292, 365, 396, 402, 426, 543, 549, 573, 586

Paris Agreement, 15, 177, 184–186, 198–199, 202–203, 207, 219
parliament, 92, 267, 475, 490, 496–498, 515
participation, 10–11, 17–20, 23, 44, 51–52, 71, 85, 88, 91–92, 100, 111, 113–116, 139–140, 163, 177, 199, 206, 215, 235, 267, 279, 300, 309, 316, 320, 335–337, 341, 348, 366–367, 369, 379–380, 386–387, 389, 394, 400, 410, 412, 414, 431, 434, 463, 465, 469–471, 473–474, 478, 481–482, 484, 489–492, 494, 496, 504, 509–510, 515, 518, 520–521, 524, 531, 539–540, 561, 604–608, 613–614, 616–617, 619–620, 623, 636, 645, 650, 654, 665, 682–683, 689, 691
permits, 14, 57–60, 65–77, 79–82, 207, 404, 442–443, 501, 522, 526, 619, 646, 659
piped water, 18, 34, 63, 225, 242, 247, 360, 364, 378, 422, 450, 474, 503–510, 512–513, 516–519, 521, 524–525, 527, 529, 603, 635, 670, 692
pipelines, 148, 441, 443, 445, 447, 511, 639, 689
political ecology, 20, 51, 103, 644–651, 665, 669, 674
political economy, 1, 47, 109, 214
political party, 117, 267, 468, 485, 489–490, 495, 670
political will, 80, 217, 246, 252
pollution, 3, 9, 34, 44, 52–53, 59–60, 77, 81, 101, 136–137, 144, 146–149, 151, 155, 157–158, 161, 174, 190–191, 315, 322, 345, 349, 354–355, 361, 363, 371, 378, 380, 410, 442–443, 451, 508, 514, 519–520, 528, 630, 632, 635, 639–640, 656, 658, 667, 673
Portugal, 288, 293, 377, 386, 399

poverty, 9, 15–16, 20, 36–37, 60, 62–63, 65, 73–75, 77, 82, 86–87, 93, 102, 117, 119, 123, 132, 144, 175, 182–183, 185, 201, 213–214, 226, 229, 231–233, 240–241, 243–245, 254, 256–257, 262–264, 269–270, 273–274, 276, 278, 281, 283–288, 290, 292–298, 303–304, 306, 308–310, 314, 316, 319–320, 322–324, 326, 328, 330, 334, 336–337, 339, 341, 345, 368, 375–376, 378, 382–383, 386, 388–389, 394, 401–402, 412, 419–420, 422, 428, 466, 492, 499, 503, 508–509, 512, 514–516, 529, 552, 597–598, 605, 608, 610, 614, 623, 632, 648, 658, 667–668, 671, 674, 682–683, 688, 692
  poverty reduction, 419–420
power relations, 22, 123, 387, 625, 674
pre-paid meters, 38, 50, 489, 498, 672
prioritisation, 21, 49, 66, 75, 80, 83, 100, 123, 175, 188, 201, 215, 235, 334, 381, 421–423, 427, 490, 501, 512, 517, 519, 522, 527, 612, 622, 672, 691
prisoners, 87, 165, 227, 310, 318, 352, 354, 365, 377, 406–407
privacy, 6, 35, 102, 192, 230, 265, 312, 320, 348–349, 351, 353, 355, 362, 368, 371, 373–374, 376–377, 388–389, 394
privatisation, 1, 9, 11–12, 18, 24, 36, 44, 49–51, 53, 84, 96, 98, 158, 189, 194, 235–237, 271, 273, 309, 338, 367, 414, 463–464, 466–487, 489–498, 500–501, 520–521, 524–525, 531–532, 535, 540, 550, 552, 560, 590, 673
profits, 284, 468, 496, 509, 526, 547, 558, 560
property, 14, 22, 38, 43, 70–71, 73, 84, 89, 91, 94–99, 101–103, 105, 110–111, 117, 141–142, 190, 260, 262–263, 270, 272, 350, 378, 432, 497, 548, 584–585, 660
property rights, 84, 92, 94–99, 101, 105, 111, 142, 497
proximity, 33, 51, 72, 78, 81, 246, 256, 321, 331, 373, 382, 505, 522, 533, 610–611, 638
public fountains, 285, 287, 297
public good, 84, 101, 214, 313, 316, 361–362, 387, 474, 476–477, 518, 686
public ownership, 464, 469, 482, 547
public trust, 482, 686

radiological, 34, 547
rain harvesting, 31, 76, 121, 316
rainwater, rainfall, 9, 63, 122, 133, 138, 141–142, 174, 182, 204, 285, 438, 442–443, 483, 603, 647
raw water, 507, 526, 655
reasonableness, 95, 149–150, 159, 169, 171, 188, 195, 228–231, 235, 238, 240–241, 254, 276, 283, 296, 298, 367, 374, 391, 413, 417, 421, 423–425, 427, 434, 439, 455, 522, 526, 540, 579, 609, 638, 651, 655
reciprocity, 22, 26, 46, 215, 350
redistribution, 14, 93, 95, 230, 256, 649, 662
referendum, 12, 475, 487–488, 490–496
regulatory chill, 553
religion, 28, 38, 141, 360, 403, 441, 618, 629
religious, 126, 229, 329–330, 518, 585, 626, 633, 637, 640, 642
remedies 77, 142, 178–179, 209, 269, 312, 320, 407, 457
  cessation, 191, 450
  compensation, 72, 77, 89, 95, 97, 110, 137, 142, 162, 174, 178–179, 191–192, 199, 203, 209, 269, 312, 320, 325, 407, 457, 490, 497, 536, 564, 582–583, 591–592, 595
  non-repetition, 191, 457
  rehabilitation, 186, 442, 451, 457, 506–507, 559
  reparation, 445, 457
  restitution, 457
  satisfaction, 42, 231, 319, 457, 478, 525, 576, 578, 609
right to a fair trial, 6, 353
right to an adequate standard of living, 7, 14, 24, 28–30, 60, 125–127, 142–143, 150–151, 153, 155, 174, 301, 303, 327–328, 356, 358, 360, 413, 433
right to development, 320
right to food, 4, 15, 26, 29, 31, 76, 120–121, 124–125, 127–128, 130–140, 142–143, 176–177, 182, 189, 301, 304, 310, 315, 325, 327–328, 342, 402–403, 434–435
riparian rights, 67, 69, 79, 146, 156, 169–170, 197, 435, 453
river, 9, 15, 50, 110, 145–146, 148, 155–156, 182, 197, 325, 385, 436, 505, 514, 630, 648, 660, 673
Roma and Travellers, 10, 39
Roman water law, 67

sanctions, 87, 154–156, 228, 315, 447–448, 450, 452, 455–457, 550
sanitation, 1–4, 6–8, 11–14, 16–18, 20, 27, 33, 35, 37, 40–43, 48, 50–53, 57, 61–63, 152, 156, 160, 171–172, 174, 177, 181–182, 184–185, 200, 204, 207, 213–214, 216–217, 225–227, 229–230,

232–233, 242, 244, 246–252, 255–260, 262, 270, 274, 279, 281–283, 287, 291, 294, 298, 300–301, 303–305, 307–314, 316–323, 325, 327–330, 332–334, 336, 338–349, 351–379, 381–395, 397, 399, 413–414, 422, 429, 431–434, 442–444, 446–449, 452–458, 466, 476, 481–482, 487, 492, 509, 524, 533, 539–540, 594, 597, 604, 610, 624–637, 639–643, 645–648, 652–653, 657, 660, 665–666, 668–669, 672–673, 676, 685
buckets, 245, 285, 352, 377
environmental sanitation, 351, 354, 362, 378
latrines, 246, 294, 312, 320, 353, 360, 364, 368, 372, 374, 376–377, 384, 392, 637
open defecation, 52, 364, 374, 379, 383–384, 631–632, 638
toilets, 230, 245–247, 260, 262, 269, 286, 300, 312, 320–321, 339–340, 351, 354–355, 361, 364, 368, 372–377, 385, 388–390, 393, 631–632, 635–636, 640, 648, 660, 670
waterborne, 240, 245, 258–259, 261–262, 269, 273, 359, 367, 387
self-determination, right to, 363, 402, 454
sewerage, 35, 86, 148, 259, 261, 318, 322, 354, 360, 364, 368, 373–375, 378–387, 380, 385, 392, 411–412, 422, 442–444, 448–451, 465, 484, 490, 556–557, 559, 593–594, 596, 598, 630, 648, 667, 670
sexual violence, 319, 373, 379
slum upgrading, 389–390, 393
small-scale users, 14, 58, 60–61, 63, 65, 69, 74–76, 80–81, 83, 120, 125, 141, 155, 327–328, 334, 342, 465, 507, 515, 519, 645, 652, 664–665, 674
social assistance, 138, 288, 295
social mobilisation, 211, 487–488, 502
social movement, 11, 172, 271, 275, 470, 486, 493
social security, 294, 356, 371–372, 644
solidarity, 26, 221, 294–295, 297
South Africa, 3–4, 16, 29–30, 34–38, 47, 50, 57, 64, 68–69, 74–77, 79–82, 128, 207, 225–228, 232–238, 242–244, 247–248, 250, 253, 255–256, 259–262, 264–269, 273–274, 283, 293, 303, 314, 352, 356, 359, 364, 372, 376, 388, 390, 392–394, 454, 485–489, 548, 584, 586, 627, 649, 651, 658, 661, 670, 692
sovereignty, 112, 132, 138, 150, 170, 331, 432, 454, 498
Spain, 66, 196–197, 288, 293, 491
State
domestic human rights obligations, 1, 4, 14, 16, 18, 20–21, 26–27, 29, 33–34, 36, 38, 42, 45, 49, 52, 57–65, 68, 76, 82, 86, 94, 107–108, 111, 113, 119, 121–122, 125, 148, 152, 155, 162, 166, 174–176, 187, 206, 209, 211–212, 217, 228, 230, 277–278, 292, 308, 313–317, 327–328, 333–334, 336, 341, 391, 414, 440, 442, 449, 452, 456, 528, 533, 536, 543–545, 551, 566, 569–570, 573, 576, 579, 582, 587, 603–604, 617–619, 623, 630–632, 638–639, 655, 659, 661, 666, 670, 676, 687
extraterritorial human rights obligations, 15–17, 24, 44–45, 48, 132, 145, 153, 156, 158–160, 163–165, 168–170, 172–173, 178, 192–195, 197, 200, 220, 326, 398–399, 402–408, 418–420, 423, 425, 427, 453, 456, 620
home State, 159, 171, 235, 237, 551, 649, 676
home State of corporations, 12, 157, 195, 219, 366, 464
member of international financial institutions, 510
State agent, 407
subsidies, 92, 219, 232, 237, 277, 283–285, 289, 292, 295, 297–298, 469, 485, 497, 542, 545, 547–549, 552–553, 565, 576, 578–579, 597
subsistence, 15, 23, 26, 60, 76, 108, 120–122, 124–126, 129, 132–134, 138, 140, 143, 155, 175, 325, 336, 350, 446, 524, 548, 661
Sudan, 147, 649
Sustainable Development Goals (SDGs), 16, 37, 40, 48, 52–53, 63, 219, 276, 281, 348, 383, 386

Tanzania, 28, 57, 68, 71, 77–79, 81, 467, 535, 588–589, 593–594, 605, 612, 661
target, 36, 40, 53, 81, 83, 204, 217, 258, 276, 280–281, 284, 288, 291, 297, 311, 327, 346, 368–369, 381–385, 422, 425–427, 450, 493, 511–512, 613, 631, 639
tariff, 1, 231, 233, 257, 265, 274, 286, 292, 297, 386, 480–483, 499–500, 508, 513, 515–516, 525–526, 529, 551, 619
social tariff, 288, 290, 292, 294, 297–298, 598
tort, 192, 210–211
torture, cruel and degrading treatment, 196, 674
trade, 11, 18, 47, 77, 79, 85, 87, 97, 99, 117–118, 157, 160, 200, 209, 220, 236, 282, 353, 387, 402, 419, 463, 468, 494–495, 498, 527, 533–534, 537–538, 541–543, 545–547, 549–550, 553, 568–569, 571, 574, 577–578, 580–582, 585
human rights clauses, 152, 239, 496, 575

trade liberalisation, 527, 543, 550, 580
trade unions, 47, 236, 353, 387, 468, 494–495, 498
trade-offs, 21, 36, 41, 47, 205, 219, 364, 382, 615, 618, 622
transnational corporations, 12, 19, 236, 468, 495, 499
 UN Global Compact, 586
 UN Guiding Principles on Business and Human Rights 157, 195, 219
 UN Secretary General Special Representative, 157, 196, 219, 365
transparency, 199, 202, 206, 370, 452, 511, 518, 523, 526, 543
*travaux préparatoires*, 558

UN Charter, 149, 196–197, 200, 403–404
UN Commission on Human Rights, 87, 92, 103, 125, 160, 192, 243, 356, 371, 523
UN Committee on Economic, Social and Cultural Rights (CESCR), 7, 12, 24, 26, 29–31, 33–35, 38, 41–42, 44, 60, 76, 108, 120–121, 124, 127–128, 130, 134–137, 139, 141–142, 151, 153–157, 159–164, 166–168, 172, 174, 176, 181, 184, 187–190, 193–194, 200, 208–209, 228, 253, 278, 285, 301–302, 310, 312–313, 315, 317–319, 322, 324–325, 328–329, 332–334, 339–340, 342–343, 349, 354–356, 358–360, 366–369, 371–372, 374, 376, 389, 395, 398–399, 401–402, 405–406, 408–409, 413, 416, 419–429, 433, 442, 453, 455–456, 472–475, 513, 518, 546, 591, 604, 616, 619, 624, 672
UN Committee on the Rights of the Child, 194, 317, 322, 340, 343, 404
UN Conference on Environment and Development (UNCED)
 Agenda 21, 3
 Rio Declaration on Environment and Development, 195, 206, 209, 216
UN Conference on Water, Mar del Plata Action Plan, 2–3, 606
UN Convention on the Law of the Non-Navigational Uses of International Watercourses, 146, 149–151, 161–162, 169, 172, 434
UN Declaration on the Rights of Indigenous Peoples, 363
UN General Assembly, 8, 25, 37, 45, 52, 124, 150, 160, 163, 172, 174, 280, 301, 305, 312, 327, 336, 338, 347, 353, 357, 360, 363, 369, 397, 401–403, 405, 422, 425, 433, 454, 457, 466, 476, 645, 672, 688
UN Human Rights Committee of the International Covenant on Civil and Political Rights (CCPR), 8, 124, 141, 145, 157, 165, 174, 176, 181, 184–185, 190, 193, 195–196, 217, 219, 311–312, 327–328, 342–343, 347, 349, 357–358, 360, 365–366, 376, 399, 405–407, 413, 450, 454, 476
UN Human Rights Council, 8, 25, 124, 145, 152, 192, 199, 202, 216, 219, 311, 328, 347, 349, 357–358, 365–366, 398, 406, 413, 450, 454, 456, 476 *see* also UN Commission on Human Rights
UN Human Rights Council, *see* also UN Human Rights Commission
 Universal Periodic Review (UPR), 216
UN Special Rapporteur on the Human Rights to Safe Drinking Water and Sanitaton (including earlier title of Independent Expert), 8, 36, 52, 181, 185, 190, 216, 311–312, 343, 349, 352, 357, 368, 397
United Kingdom (UK), 38, 165–166, 236, 284, 288, 293, 298, 357, 381, 399, 406, 466, 487, 560, 567, 593, 603, 663
United Nations (UN), 2–3, 7–9, 36–37, 39–40, 44, 48, 52–53, 60, 87, 92, 102, 108, 120–121, 124–125, 134, 141–142, 145–146, 149–154, 156–157, 159–160, 162–165, 169, 171–172, 174, 176–181, 184–186, 188, 190, 192–193, 195–197, 199–201, 204, 206, 209, 213–214, 216, 218–219, 228, 278, 280, 282, 284, 301–302, 304–305, 308–313, 315–320, 322, 325, 327, 329, 334–336, 338–339, 341, 346–347, 349, 352, 354–360, 363–369, 371–374, 376, 378, 382–383, 386, 396–399, 401–409, 416, 418–420, 422, 424–425, 427, 433–435, 444–445, 447, 450, 453–457, 466, 472, 474, 476, 513, 523, 541, 556, 586–587, 591, 597, 604, 620, 624, 678, 688, 692–693
United Nations Children's Fund (UNICEF), 9, 40, 48, 64, 179, 183, 217, 330, 339, 346, 352, 384, 603, 633, 654, 670
United Nations Development Programme (UNDP), 7–9, 13, 16, 29, 40, 66, 74, 120, 122, 133, 138, 141, 152, 175, 221, 225, 284, 290, 311, 330, 346, 377, 394, 603
United Nations Economic Commission for Europe (UNECE), 171, 282

United Nations Educational, Scientific and Cultural Organization (UNESCO), 178, 182, 205, 441, 484, 626
United Nations Environment Programme (UNEP), 145, 169, 451
United Nations Framework Convention on Climate Change (UNFCCC), 177, 183–186, 192–193, 198, 200–202, 207–208, 213, 216, 220–221
United Nations Human Settlements Programme (UN-Habitat), 346, 379, 387, 390, 423, 618, 624
United States of America (USA), 36, 53, 63, 68, 77, 129, 144, 148, 182, 191–194, 210, 220, 245, 284, 293–294, 408, 447, 473, 491, 533–534, 538–539, 572–573, 575, 648
Universal Declaration of Human Rights (UDHR), 2, 21, 163, 197, 200, 351, 403, 413, 418, 521
Uruguay, 4, 12, 148, 157, 165, 283, 293, 347, 485–491, 535
user fees, 20
utilitarianism, 27, 41, 205, 477

Vienna Convention on the Law of Treaties (VCLT), 153, 178, 196, 400–404, 558, 587
Vienna Declaration and Programme of Action, 302, 305
violation, 11, 17, 41, 45, 84, 135–137, 140, 144, 148, 155, 159, 162, 164–165, 167–168, 170, 172, 176, 181, 185, 193, 196, 239, 247, 339, 378, 389, 410–411, 413, 416, 440, 448, 453–456, 571, 580, 657, 678–679

washing facilities, 354
wastewater, 35, 52, 219, 276, 278, 284–285, 348, 385, 436, 440, 443, 447–451, 480, 487, 556, 668
water allocation, 14–17, 44, 46, 59, 76–77, 123, 146, 175, 293, 315, 324, 453, 528, 652, 675
water availability, 33, 78, 123, 132, 138, 141, 145, 172, 175–176, 179–180, 197, 201, 205, 208, 214, 649, 653, 667, 674–675
water catchment, 93, 335
water pumps, 387, 423
water resource management, 10, 58, 69, 77, 414
water scarcity, 2, 52, 67, 74, 180, 182, 214, 319, 641, 650, 653
water sector reform, 1, 412, 484, 678
water titling, 66
wells, 31, 61, 136, 313, 339, 437–440, 442, 445–446, 448–449, 473, 508, 515, 610, 614, 629, 638–639, 661, 664, 668, 670, 681
WHO Guidelines for Drinking-Water Quality, 34
women, 2, 17, 28, 31, 33, 39, 51–52, 64, 76, 82, 121, 142, 183, 188, 207, 243, 300–314, 316–321, 323–324, 326–336, 339, 341–342, 344, 352, 354–355, 373, 375–377, 379, 383, 387–388, 410, 433, 478, 603–604, 608, 610, 613, 617, 619, 624, 627, 630–631, 633, 635–636, 638–639, 642, 654, 664, 673–675
  girls, 17, 52, 64, 183, 301–305, 307–314, 316–319, 321, 323, 328–331, 339–344, 377, 383, 610
World Health Organization (WHO), 9, 33–35, 40, 48, 63, 122, 171, 179, 204, 217, 261, 282, 304, 346, 348, 359, 362, 375, 384, 440, 449, 451, 453, 521, 603, 668–669
World Summit on Sustainable Development (WSSD), 200, 356
World Trade Organization (WTO), 532–538, 540, 542–544, 549, 554–555, 558–560, 563, 565–566, 568–573, 576, 580–581
World Water Council (WWC), 61
World Water Forum (WWF), 13, 61, 65, 280, 494

Zimbabwe, 4, 20, 35, 57, 61, 71, 74, 304, 306, 314, 323–326, 330, 333–334, 337–338, 340, 384, 614, 644–647, 649–660, 662–669, 672–676

For EU product safety concerns, contact us at Calle de José Abascal, 56–1°, 28003 Madrid, Spain or eugpsr@cambridge.org.

www.ingramcontent.com/pod-product-compliance
Lightning Source LLC
LaVergne TN
LVHW052204200926
848481LV00001B/28
* 9 7 8 1 1 0 8 7 2 2 3 1 5 *